## ▪▪▪▪▪▪▪▪▪▪▪▪
## TO THE STUDENT

This text was created to provide you with a high-quality educational resource. As a publisher specializing in college texts for business and economics, our goal is to provide you with learning materials that will serve you well in your college studies and throughout your career.

The educational process involves learning, retention, and the application of concepts and principles. You can accelerate your learning efforts utilizing the Workbook accompanying this text:

- **Workbook for use with *Basic Business Communication*, Sixth Edition**

This learning aid is designed to improve your performance in the course by highlighting key points in the text and providing you with assistance in mastering basic concepts.

Get your copy at your local bookstore, or ask the manager to place an order for you today.

We at Irwin sincerely hope this text package will assist you in reaching your goals, both now and in the future.

# BASIC BUSINESS COMMUNICATION

### Sixth Edition

**RAYMOND V. LESIKAR**
University of North Texas

**JOHN D. PETTIT, JR.**
University of North Texas

**MARIE E. FLATLEY**
San Diego State University

**IRWIN**
Homewood, IL 60430
Boston, MA 02116

© RICHARD D. IRWIN, INC., 1979, 1982, 1985, 1988, 1991, and 1993

*All rights reserved.* No part of this publication may be reproduced, stored in a retrieval system, or transmitted, in any form or by any means, electronic, mechanical, photocopying, recording, or otherwise, without the prior written permission of the publisher.

Senior sponsoring editor: Craig Beytien
Developmental editor: Karen Perry
Marketing manager: Kurt Messersmith
Project editor: Karen Murphy
Production manager: Ann Cassady
Designer: Larry J. Cope
Art manager: Kim Meriwether
Photo research coordinator: Patricia A. Seefelt
Compositor: Better Graphics, Inc.
Typeface: 10/12 Times Roman
Printer: Von Hoffmann Press

**Library of Congress Cataloging-in-Publication Data**

Lesikar, Raymond Vincent.
    Basic business communication / Raymond V. Lesikar.—6th ed.
      p.   cm.
    Includes bibliographical references and index.
    ISBN 0-256-10936-2
      1. Commercial correspondence.   2. English language—Business
English.   3. Business communication.   I. Title.
HF5721.L37   1993
651.7'4—dc20                                    92-19974

*Printed in the United States of America*
1 2 3 4 5 6 7 8 9 0 VH 9 8 7 6 5 4 3 2

*To my dear departed parents
whose love, sacrifice, and encouragement
made this book possible.   R.V.L.*

*To my father, J. Douglas "Doug" Pettit
whose memory gives special meaning
to my work and my life.   J.D.P., Jr.*

*To my father and mother
who have instilled in me a love of learning
and an appreciation for quality.   M.E.F.*

# ABOUT THE AUTHORS

### RAYMOND V. LESIKAR

Dr. Raymond V. Lesikar has served on the faculties of the University of North Texas, Louisiana State University at Baton Rouge, The University of Texas at Austin, and Texas Christian University. He served also as a visiting professor at the University of International Business and Economics, Beijing, China.

Dr. Lesikar has been active in consulting, serving over 80 companies and organizations. His primary organization membership is with the Association for Business Communication, serving ABC in many capacities, including a term as president. He also holds membership in the Southwest Federation of Administrative Disciplines and the International Society for General Semantics.

### JOHN D. PETTIT, JR.

John D. Pettit, Jr., is Professor of Management in the Department of Management, College of Business, at the University of North Texas. He earned his Ph.D. degree from Louisiana State University and his M.B.A. and B.B.A. from the University of North Texas.

John's 30-year teaching experience includes courses in business communication, organizational communication, business research methods, and research for publication.

Presently, John is Executive Director of the Association for Business Communication and a former President and Fellow of ABC. He also holds membership in the Academy of Management and the Speech Communication Association.

### MARIE E. FLATLEY

Marie E. Flatley is a Professor of Information and Decision Systems at San Diego State University, where she teaches courses in communication and computing. She received her B.B.A., M.A., and Ph.D. from the University of Iowa. In addition, she has done post-graduate study in AACSB sponsored programs at the University of Minnesota and Indiana University. She is active in numerous professional organizations, including the Association for Business Communication, California Business Education Association, Delta Pi Epsilon, and the National Business Education Association. She is currently an Associate Editor for the *Journal of Business Communication*. Her current research interests involve using technology to assist with the communication process.

# PREFACE

This sixth edition of *Basic Business Communication* is the work of a new team of authors. We are modestly confident that our unique combination of expertise and talents has produced a book that is authoritative, thorough, and technologically current. We are also confident that more than ever before, we have achieved the two primary goals of the preceding editions: to present business communication in a way that is (1) more learnable for the student and (2) more teachable for the instructor.

## AUTHORITATIVE

Our efforts to present the subject matter authoritatively involved a thorough review of the field. The information presented and procedures recommended are not just our ideas and preferences, though we support them. They represent the mainstream of business communication thought developed by researchers, teachers, and practitioners over the years. We are confident they fully meet AACSB and ACBSP accreditation standards for communication.

## THOROUGH

We worked diligently to cover the subject thoroughly. The content of the earlier editions was based on the results of two extensive surveys of business communication teachers. In this edition we supplemented the results of those surveys with suggestions from the highly competent professionals who reviewed the book. The result is a book whose content has been developed and approved by experts in the field. As well as we can determine, this edition covers every topic that today's business communication leaders say it should have.

## TECHNOLOGICALLY CURRENT

Because the computer has affected business communication in so many ways, we worked this subject into the book wherever applicable. For example, when discussing form letters, we indicate how useful the merge function in word processing can be. In addition, we include a number of technical suggestions in boxes. Meant to give ideas and suggestions on how one can use computers in business communication, these boxes provide helpful hints on how to exploit the power of the computer in order to save time and improve quality.

## TEACHABLE AND LEARNABLE

As in the earlier editions, we worked hard to make the book serve both student and teacher in every practical way. For the student, we worked to make the learning experience easy and interesting. For the teacher, we did all in our power to lighten the teaching load.

**Successful Plan of the Past.** To implement these goals, we continued the following plan that proved to be highly successful in preceding editions:

**Readable writing.** The writing is in plain, everyday English—the kind the book instructs the students to use.

**Chapter objectives.** Placed at the beginning of all chapters, clearly worded objectives emphasize learning goals.

**Introductory situations.** A realistic description of a business scenario introduces the student to each topic, providing context for the discussion and examples.

**Preliminary outlines of letters.** To simplify and clarify the instructions for writing the basic letter types, outlines of letter plans precede the discussions.

**Margin notes.** Summaries of content appear in the margins to help students emphasize main points and to review text highlights.

**Challenging problems.** In-depth, realistic business cases are included for all letter and report types—more than any competing text.

**Discussion questions.** End-of-chapter questions emphasize text concepts and provide material for classroom discussion.

**Grading checklists.** Lists of likely errors keyed to marking symbols are available for letters, reports, and points of correctness. They help the teacher in the grading process and provide the students with explanations for their errors.

**Specialized report topics.** Lists of research topics by major business disciplines are available for teachers who prefer to assign reports in the student's area of specialization.

**Abundant illustrations.** Carefully selected examples with handwritten comments show how to apply the text instructions. Some contrasting bad examples clearly marked with the symbol shown in the margin also are included.

**Interest-gaining vignettes.** Boxes containing exciting, humorous, or classic material add interest and make points throughout the book.

**Cartoons.** Carefully selected cartoons emphasize key points and add interest.

**New Additions to the Plan.** In this edition we improved the original plan with these additions:

**Application exercises.** Although some application exercises appeared in earlier editions, we expanded them to all chapters for which they are appropriate.

**Photographs.** Carefully selected full-color photographs throughout the text emphasize key points and add interest to content.

**Chapter summaries by chapter objectives.** Ending summaries in fast-reading outline form and by chapter objectives enable students to recall text highlights.

**Computer applications.** Computer applications have been worked in throughout the book wherever appropriate—into topics such as readability analysis, graphics, research methods, and formatting.

**Computer use suggestions.** For students who want to know more about how useful computers can be in business communication, pertinent suggestions appear in boxes marked by the symbol shown in the margin.

**Realistic form illustrations.** The letter and report examples have been enhanced to appear realistic (letterhead paper, model computer formatting, etc.)

**New letter and report cases.** As in past editions, the realistic and thorough case problems are new.

**Teaching-Learning Helps.** Teaching-learning helps were available with all earlier editions, but we believe the greatly expanded package for this edition is the most useful and effective ever assembled for a business communication textbook. The support material for this edition consists of these elements:

**Workbook.** This optional supplement is designed to reinforce the text instructions in the students' minds by providing multiple choice, completion, and application exercises. For those instructors who use the workbook as an integral part of their course, it is also available combined with the text in paperback version. Contact your Irwin representative for more details.

**Instructor's resource box.** Arranged in file folders by chapter, the following support material is assembled for easy use with each lecture:
Sample syllabi and grading systems
Summary teaching notes
Teaching suggestions
Discussion guides for the transparencies
Answers to end-of-chapter discussion questions
Answers to end-of-chapter application exercises
Answers to workbook questions
Audio-visual list (annotated and with order information)

**Instructor's manual.** All the material found in the Instructor's Resource Box is available in this bound manual.

**Transparency package.** Fifty two-color acetates and 130 transparency masters provide additional examples to critique and summaries of key points for use in lectures and discussion.

**The IRWIN Business Communication Video Series.** This series consists of self-contained, informative segments covering such topics as writing correctly and the power of listening. Presented in a clear and engaging style, every segment holds students' interest while presenting the techniques for sharpening their communication skills. Contact your IRWIN representative for more information.

**Test bank.** This comprehensive collection of objective questions covers all chapters.

**Computerized Testing Software.** This advanced test generator enables the teacher to build and restructure tests to meet specific preferences.

**Tele-Test.** Customized exam preparation is furnished by the publisher.

## ORGANIZATION OF THE BOOK

We have retained the strong organization that has long characterized this book:

**PART I** begins with an introductory summary of the role of communication in the organization, including a description of the process of human communication in the organization.

**PART II** is a review of the basic techniques of writing. Here the emphasis is on clear writing and the effect of words.

**PART III** covers the basic patterns of business letters, beginning with the most common direct and indirect ones.

**PART IV** applies the contents of the preceding two parts to memorandums, collections, and job-search procedures.

**PART V** concentrates on report writing. Although the emphasis is on the shorter report forms, the long, analytical reports also receive complete coverage.

**PART VI** reviews the other forms of business communication. Included here are communication activities such as participating in meetings, interviewing, telephoning, dictating, and listening.

**PART VII** comprises a five-chapter group of special communication topics—technology-assisted communication, cross-cultural communication, physical presentation of letters and reports, correctness, and business research methods. Because teachers use them in different ways and in different sequences, these topics are placed in this final part so that they can be used in the sequence and way that best fit each teacher's needs.

## ADDITIONS TO CONTENT

As in the past, this edition was thoroughly updated throughout. We also added new topics wherever we and our reviewers thought it would improve content. Our most significant additions are the following:

**Ethics.** In support of both AACSB and ACBSP accreditation standards, the role of ethics in business communication is addressed wherever it applies throughout the book.

**The writing process.** A review of the process of writing prepares the student for the first writing assignment.

**Nonverbal communication.** A concise but comprehensive review of this topic is a part of Chapter 16.

**Informal speaking.** Also included in Chapter 16 are suggestions on how to improve day-to-day oral communication.

**New arrangement of oral communication chapters.** Expanded in content and rearranged on informal and formal lines, these chapters thoroughly and effectively cover the area.

**New framework for the technology chapter.** Thoroughly revised, this chapter focuses attention on the technology used in each step of the writing process—discussing both software and hardware as they assist the writer.

**Cross-cultural communication.** Coverage of this timely subject was revised and expanded to support AACSB and ACBSP standards.

**Interpretation of data.** A concise review of this topic appears in the instructions for planning the report.

**Memorandums.** Coverage of this part was expanded to include additional memorandum types and electronic memos.

**Job search, resumes, and application letters.** As in every past edition, this material was expanded and revised to reflect today's standards and practices.

**The law and business communication.** This appendix has been revised and expanded to further guide the students in their legal responsibilities in business communication.

## ACKNOWLEDGMENTS

Any comprehensive work such as this must owe credit to a multitude of people. Certainly, we should acknowledge the contributions of the pioneers in the business communication field, especially those whose teachings have become a part of our thinking. We should acknowledge also those colleagues in the field who served as reviewers for this edition. They are primarily responsible for the improvements that have been made. Although all identification was removed from the reviews given us, we were told that these people served as reviewers:

**Barbara Alpern, Walsh College**
**Stuart Brown, New Mexico State University**
**Joan Feague, Baker College**
**Robert Insley, University of North Texas**
**Charles Marsh, University of Kansas**
**Deborah Roebuck, Kennesaw State College**

Without exception, their work was good and helpful.

A very special acknowledgment is also due Mary Ellen Murray and Donald Evans, both of Stephen F. Austin State University, for their work in revising the material on the effects of the law on business communication. Their efforts give this book authoritative coverage of an area whose importance continues to grow. A special thanks also goes to Sandy Thomas, Kansas City Kansas Community College, for her many contributions to this edition.

Because this sixth edition has evolved from all the previous editions, we also acknowledge those who contributed to those editions. They include:

**Diane Reep, University of Akron**
**Carolyn Rainey, Southeast Missouri State University**
**Marilyn Price, Kirkwood Community College**
**Doris Phillips, University of Mississippi**
**George Walters, Emporia State University**
**Joan Beam, Ferris State University**
**Ben Crane, Temple University**
**Jerry Sullivan, University of Washington**
**Shelby Kipplen, Michael Owens Technical College**
**Jim Rucker, Fort Hays State University**
**Edwina Jordan, Illinois Central College**
**Cheryl Shearer, Oxnard College**

Dolores Osborn, Central Washington University
Ruth Walsh, University of South Florida
Michael Wunsch, Northern Arizona University
C. Douglas Spitler, University of Nebraska–Lincoln
Barbara Shaw, University of Mississippi
James Bell, Southwest Texas State University
Jon N. Loff, Allegany Community College
Lila B. Stair, Florida State University
Frank E. Nelson, Eastern Washington State College
Judy F. McCain, Indiana University
James J. Weston, California State University–Sacramento
Kathy Wessel, South Suburban College
Julia Newcomer, Texas Woman's University
Ethel A. Martin, Glendale Community College
David Ramsey, Southeastern Louisiana University
Peter Bracher, Wright State University
John J. Brugaletta, California State University–Fullerton
Carol L. Huber, Skagit Valley College
Gay Sibley, University of Hawaii at Manoa
Douglas H. Shepard, State University of New York
Dwight Bullard, Middle Tennessee State University
Andrea Corbett, University of Lowell
Phyllis Howren, University of North Carolina
Dan Armstrong, Oregon State University
Tim Sabin, Portland Community College
Evelyn Morris, Mesa Community College
Suzanne Lambert, Broward Community College

In addition, over the life of this book many of our professional colleagues have made a variety of inputs. Most of these were made orally at professional meetings. Our memories will not permit us to acknowledge these colleagues individually. Nevertheless, we are grateful to all of them.

Finally, on our respective home fronts, we acknowledge the support of our spouses—Lu Lesikar, Suzanne Pettit, and Len Deftos. Without their love, patience, and understanding, this project could not have been completed.

Raymond V. Lesikar<br>
John D. Pettit, Jr.<br>
Marie E. Flatley

# CONTENTS IN BRIEF

## PART ONE
### INTRODUCTION
1. SOME BASIC INTRODUCTORY WORDS — 2

## PART TWO
### FUNDAMENTALS OF BUSINESS WRITING
2. ADAPTATION AND THE SELECTION OF WORDS — 22
3. CONSTRUCTION OF CLEAR SENTENCES AND PARAGRAPHS — 48
4. WRITING FOR EFFECT — 72

## PART THREE
### BASIC PATTERNS OF BUSINESS LETTERS
5. DIRECTNESS IN INITIATING ROUTINE LETTERS — 97
6. DIRECTNESS IN ROUTINE RESPONSES — 142
7. INDIRECTNESS FOR BAD NEWS — 186
8. INDIRECTNESS IN PERSUASION AND SALES WRITING — 226

## PART FOUR
### APPLICATIONS TO SPECIFIC SITUATIONS
9. MEMORANDUMS — 268
10. PATTERN VARIATIONS IN COLLECTIONS — 296
11. STRATEGY IN JOB SEARCH AND APPLICATION — 328

## PART FIVE
### FUNDAMENTALS OF REPORT WRITING
12. BASICS OF REPORT WRITING — 378
13. REPORT STRUCTURE: THE SHORTER FORMS — 406
14. LONG, FORMAL REPORTS — 472
15. GRAPHICS — 536

## PART SIX

### OTHER FORMS OF BUSINESS COMMUNICATION

16. INFORMAL ORAL COMMUNICATION — 565
17. PUBLIC SPEAKING AND ORAL REPORTING — 594

## PART SEVEN

### SPECIAL TOPICS IN BUSINESS COMMUNICATION

18. TECHNOLOGY-ASSISTED COMMUNICATION — 618
19. TECHNIQUES OF CROSS-CULTURAL COMMUNICATION — 644
20. PHYSICAL PRESENTATION OF LETTERS, MEMOS, AND REPORTS — 664
21. CORRECTNESS OF COMMUNICATION — 700
22. BUSINESS RESEARCH METHODS — 728

APPENDIX A  CORRECTIONS FOR THE SELF-ADMINISTERED DIAGNOSTIC TEST OF PUNCTUATION AND GRAMMAR — 763

APPENDIX B  A GRADING CHECKLIST FOR LETTERS — 765

APPENDIX C  A GRADING CHECKLIST FOR REPORTS — 767

APPENDIX D  DOCUMENTATION AND THE BIBLIOGRAPHY — 771

APPENDIX E  UNITED STATES LAWS AFFECTING BUSINESS COMMUNICATION AT HOME AND ABROAD — 781

INDEX — 791

# CONTENTS

## PART ONE

### INTRODUCTION

1. **SOME BASIC INTRODUCTORY WORDS** — 2

The Role of Communication in Business — 3

    The Importance of Communication Skills to You — 3

    Why Business Needs to Communicate — 3

    Main Forms of Communication in Business — 4

    Communication Network of the Organization — 7

    Variation in Communication Activity by Business — 9

The Process of Human Communication — 9

    The Beginning: A Message Sent — 10

    Entry in the Sensory World — 10

    Detection by the Senses — 10

    The Filtering Process — 11

    Formulation and Sending of the Response — 11

    The Cycle Repeated — 12

    The Communication Process and Written Communication — 12

    Some Basic Truths about Communication — 12

    Resulting Stress on Adaptation — 14

The Goal, Plan, and Philosophy of This Book — 14

    The Plan: Situations, Solutions, Summaries — 14

    The Philosophy: Communicate to Communicate — 14

## PART TWO

### FUNDAMENTALS OF BUSINESS WRITING

2. **ADAPTATION AND THE SELECTION OF WORDS** — 22

The Basic Need for Adaptation — 23

    Visualizing the Reader — 23

    Technique of Adapting — 23

    Adaptation Illustrated — 24

    Adapting to Multiple Readers — 25

| | |
|---|---|
| Governing Role of Adaptation | 26 |
| Suggestions for Selecting Words | 26 |
|     Use Familiar Words | 26 |
|     Choose Short Words | 28 |
|     Use Technical Words and Acronyms with Caution | 29 |
|     Select Words with the Right Strength and Vigor | 31 |
|     Use Concrete Language | 31 |
|     Use the Active Voice | 33 |
|     Avoid Overuse of Camouflaged Verbs | 34 |
|     Select Words for Precise Meanings | 36 |
| Suggestions for Nondiscriminatory Writing | 38 |
|     Avoid Sexist Words | 38 |
|     Avoid Words That Stereotype by Race or Nationality | 41 |
|     Avoid Words That Stereotype by Age | 42 |
|     Avoid Words That Typecast Those with Disabilities | 42 |
|     In Conclusion about Words | 42 |
| **3. CONSTRUCTION OF CLEAR SENTENCES AND PARAGRAPHS** | **48** |
| Foundation of Adaptation | 49 |
| Emphasis on Short Sentences | 49 |
|     Limiting Sentence Content | 50 |
|     Economizing on Words | 51 |
|     Determining Emphasis in Sentence Design | 58 |
|     Giving the Sentences Unity | 60 |
|     Arranging Sentences for Clarity | 63 |
| Care in Paragraph Design | 63 |
|     Giving the Paragraphs Unity | 64 |
|     Keeping Paragraphs Short | 64 |
|     Making Good Use of Topic Sentences | 64 |
|     Leaving out Unnecessary Detail | 66 |
|     Giving the Paragraphs Movement | 67 |
| **4. WRITING FOR EFFECT** | **72** |
| Need for Effect | 73 |
| Conversational Style | 74 |
|     Resisting Tendency to Be Formal | 74 |
|     Avoiding the Old Language of Business | 75 |
|     Cutting Out "Rubber Stamps" | 76 |
|     Proof through Contrasting Examples | 78 |
| You-Viewpoint | 79 |
|     The You-Viewpoint Illustrated | 80 |
|     A Point of Controversy | 81 |
| Accent on Positive Language | 82 |
|     Effects of Words | 82 |
|     Examples of Word Choice | 82 |
| Courtesy | 84 |
|     Singling out Your Reader | 84 |
|     Refraining from Preaching | 85 |
|     Doing More than Is Expected | 85 |
|     Avoiding Anger | 86 |
|     Being Sincere | 87 |
| The Role of Emphasis | 88 |
|     Emphasis by Position | 89 |
|     Space and Emphasis | 89 |

| | |
|---|---|
| Sentence Structure and Emphasis | 90 |
| Mechanical Means of Emphasis | 90 |
| Coherence | 90 |
|     Tie-In Sentences | 90 |
|     Repetition of Key Words | 91 |
|     Use of Pronouns | 91 |
|     Transitional Words | 91 |
|     A Word of Caution | 92 |

## PART THREE

### BASIC PATTERNS OF BUSINESS LETTERS

### 5. DIRECTNESS IN INITIATING ROUTINE LETTERS    97

| | |
|---|---|
| The Process of Writing Letters | 99 |
|     Planning the Letter | 99 |
|     Gathering and Collecting the Facts | 99 |
|     Analyzing and Organizing Information | 99 |
|     Writing the Letter | 100 |
|     Rewriting Your Work | 100 |
|     Editing and Presenting the Final Document | 100 |
| Routine Inquiries | 102 |
|     Beginning with the Objective | 103 |
|     Informing and Explaining Adequately | 103 |
|     Structuring the Questions | 104 |
|     Ending with Goodwill | 105 |
|     Contrasting Inquiry Examples | 105 |
| Inquiries about People | 110 |
|     Respecting Human Rights | 111 |
|     Adapting Question Content | 111 |
|     Examples in Contrast | 112 |
| Claims | 115 |
|     Using Directness for Bad News | 116 |
|     Identifying the Situation | 116 |
|     Stating the Problem Directly | 117 |
|     Explaining the Facts | 117 |
|     Giving Choice in Correcting Error | 117 |
|     Overcoming Negativeness with a Friendly Close | 118 |
|     Contrasting Examples of Claim Letters | 118 |
| Orders | 121 |
|     Directly Authorizing the Order | 122 |
|     Specifically Covering the Sale | 122 |
|     Closing with a Friendly Comment | 122 |
|     Contrasting Orders | 123 |

### 6. DIRECTNESS IN ROUTINE RESPONSES    142

| | |
|---|---|
| Favorable Responses | 143 |
|     Beginning with the Answer | 143 |
|     Identifying the Correspondence Being Answered | 144 |
|     Logically Arranging the Answers | 144 |
|     Skillful Handling of Negatives | 145 |
|     Consideration of Extras | 145 |
|     Cordiality in the Close | 146 |
|     Contrasting Illustrations | 146 |
| Personnel Evaluations | 150 |
|     Directness in the Beginning | 150 |

| | |
|---|---|
| Reference to the Inquiry | 151 |
| Systematic Presentation of Information | 151 |
| The Problem of Fair Reporting | 152 |
| Natural Friendliness in the Close | 153 |
| Examples in Contrast | 153 |
| **Adjustment Grants** | **157** |
| Need to Overcome Negative Impressions | 158 |
| Direct Presentation of Decision | 159 |
| Avoidance of Negatives | 160 |
| Regaining Lost Confidence | 160 |
| Positiveness in the Close | 160 |
| Contrasting Adjustments | 160 |
| **Order Acknowledgments** | **164** |
| Acknowledgment in the Beginning | 164 |
| Goodwill Talk and Resale | 165 |
| Tact in Handling Delayed Shipments | 165 |
| A Friendly, Forward Look | 165 |
| Contrasting Acknowledgments | 166 |
| **Other Routine-Response Situations** | **169** |

## 7. INDIRECTNESS FOR BAD NEWS — 186

| | |
|---|---|
| **Situations Requiring Indirectness** | **187** |
| **Refused Request** | **188** |
| Developing the Strategy | 188 |
| Setting up the Strategy in the Opening | 189 |
| Presenting the Reasoning | 189 |

| | |
|---|---|
| Positively Handling the Refusal | 190 |
| Closing with Goodwill | 191 |
| Contrasting Refusals | 193 |
| **Adjustment Refusals** | **196** |
| Determining the Basic Strategy | 197 |
| Setting up the Explanation with an Indirect Opening | 197 |
| Presenting the Reasoning | 198 |
| Covering the Refusal Positively | 199 |
| Closing with Off-Subject, Friendly Comment | 199 |
| Contrasting Letters Refusing a Claim | 199 |
| **Credit Refusals** | **203** |
| Determining the Strategy | 203 |
| Setting up the Explanation | 204 |
| Justifying the Refusal | 205 |
| Refusing Tactfully | 205 |
| Closing with a Forward Look | 206 |
| Contrasting Credit-Refusal Illustrations | 207 |
| **Other Indirect-Order Letters** | **210** |

## 8. INDIRECTNESS IN PERSUASION AND SALES WRITING — 226

| | |
|---|---|
| **Need for Indirectness in Persuasion** | **227** |
| **Persuasive Requests** | **227** |
| Determining the Persuasion | 228 |
| Gaining Attention in the Opening | 228 |
| Presenting the Persuasion | 229 |

| | |
|---|---|
| Making the Request Clearly and Positively | 229 |
| Contrasting Persuasion Letters | 230 |
| Value of Sales Writing | 233 |
| Preliminary Efforts | 233 |
| Knowing the Product or Service and the Reader | 233 |
| Determining the Appeal | 235 |
| Structure of the Sales Letter | 236 |
| Determining Letter Mechanics | 236 |
| Gaining Attention in the Opening | 237 |
| Presenting the Sales Material | 239 |
| Stressing the You-Viewpoint | 240 |
| Choosing Words Carefully | 241 |
| Including All Necessary Information | 241 |
| Driving for the Sale | 242 |
| Urging the Action | 242 |
| Recalling the Appeal | 242 |
| Adding a Postscript | 243 |
| Evaluating Contrasting Examples | 243 |
| Using a Second Letter in the Mailing | 253 |

## PART FOUR

### APPLICATIONS TO SPECIFIC SITUATIONS

| | |
|---|---|
| **9. MEMORANDUMS** | **268** |
| The Nature of Memorandums | 269 |
| Variations in Form | 269 |
| Wide Range of Formality | 273 |
| Similarities and Differences in Memorandums and Letters | 273 |
| Memorandums Illustrated | 276 |
| Direct Memorandums—Routine Inquiries | 276 |
| Direct Memorandums—Routine Responses | 278 |
| Direct Memorandums—Policy Memorandums and Directives | 279 |
| Indirect (Bad-News) Memorandums | 282 |
| Indirect (Persuasive) Memorandums | 284 |
| The Memorandum to File | 284 |
| **10. PATTERN VARIATIONS IN COLLECTIONS** | **296** |
| The Collection Series | 297 |
| Collecting through a Series of Efforts | 297 |
| Determining the Collection Series | 299 |
| Using the Telephone to Collect | 299 |
| Using Computer-Generated Collections | 300 |
| Early-Stage Collections | 300 |
| Writing Reminder Letters | 301 |
| Contrasting Reminder Letters | 302 |
| Middle-Stage Collections | 305 |
| Analyzing the Strategy | 305 |
| Gaining Attention in the Opening | 306 |
| Persuasively Presenting the Appeal | 308 |
| Closing with a Request for Payment | 308 |

| | |
|---|---|
| Contrasting Form Collection Letters | 309 |
| Last-Resort Letters | 316 |
| Justifying Directness | 317 |
| Presenting the Action Directly | 317 |
| Interpreting the Action | 317 |
| Offering a Last Chance in the Close | 318 |
| Contrasting Last-Resort Letters | 318 |

### 11. STRATEGY IN JOB SEARCH AND APPLICATION — 328

| | |
|---|---|
| The Job Search | 329 |
| Building a Network of Contacts | 329 |
| Analyzing Yourself | 330 |
| Selecting Your Career Path | 332 |
| Finding Your Employer | 332 |
| Preparing the Application Documents | 334 |
| The Résumé | 334 |
| Selecting the Background Facts | 335 |
| Arranging the Facts into Groups | 335 |
| Constructing the Headings | 336 |
| Including Contact Information | 336 |
| Including a Statement of Objective | 337 |
| Presenting the Information | 337 |
| Handling the Special Groupings | 340 |
| Writing Impersonally and Consistently | 341 |
| Making the Form Attractive | 342 |
| Contrasting Bad and Good Examples | 343 |
| The Application Letter | 351 |
| Gaining Attention in the Opening | 351 |
| Selecting Content | 353 |
| Organizing for Conviction | 354 |
| Driving for Action in the Close | 355 |
| Contrasting Application Letters | 355 |
| The Interview | 357 |
| Following Up and Ending the Application | 364 |
| Other Job-Getting Letters | 364 |
| Writing a Thank-You Letter | 364 |
| Constructing a Follow-Up to an Application | 365 |
| Planning the Job Acceptance | 365 |
| Writing a Letter Refusing a Job | 365 |
| Writing a Letter of Resignation | 366 |

# PART FIVE

## FUNDAMENTALS OF REPORT WRITING

### 12. BASICS OF REPORT WRITING — 378

| | |
|---|---|
| Defining Reports | 380 |
| Determining the Report Purpose | 380 |
| The Preliminary Investigation | 380 |
| Need for a Clear Statement of the Problem | 381 |
| Determining the Factors | 381 |
| Use of Subtopics in Information Reports | 381 |

| | |
|---|---|
| Hypotheses for Problems Requiring Solution | 382 |
| Bases of Comparison in Evaluation Studies | 382 |
| Need for Subbreakdown | 383 |
| Gathering the Information Needed | 383 |
| Interpreting the Findings | 384 |
| Advice for Avoiding Human Error | 384 |
| Appropriate Attitudes and Practices | 385 |
| Statistical Tools in Interpretation | 386 |
| Organizing the Report Information | 386 |
| The Nature and Extent of Outlining | 387 |
| Introductory and Concluding Parts | 388 |
| Organization by Division | 388 |
| Division by Conventional Relationships | 389 |
| Combination and Multiple Division Possibilities | 391 |
| Wording of the Outline | 392 |
| Writing the Report | 395 |
| Requirement of Objectivity | 395 |
| Consistency in Time Viewpoint | 397 |
| Need for Transition | 398 |
| Maintaining Interest | 401 |
| **13. REPORT STRUCTURE: THE SHORTER FORMS** | **406** |
| An Overview of Report Structure | 407 |
| Characteristics of the Shorter Reports | 409 |
| Little Need for Introductory Information | 410 |
| Predominance of the Direct Order | 410 |
| More Personal Writing Style | 412 |
| Forms of Shorter Reports | 413 |
| The Short Report | 413 |
| Letter Reports | 414 |
| Memorandum Reports | 423 |
| Special Report Forms | 426 |
| The Staff Report | 426 |
| The Progress Report | 426 |
| The Audit Report | 428 |
| The Technical Report | 428 |
| The Proposal | 428 |
| **14. LONG, FORMAL REPORTS** | **472** |
| Organization and Content of the Longer Reports | 473 |
| The Prefatory Parts | 474 |
| Title Fly | 474 |
| Title Page | 475 |
| Letter of Authorization | 475 |
| Letter of Transmittal, Foreward, Preface | 476 |
| Table of Contents, List of Illustrations | 478 |
| Executive Summary | 478 |
| The Report Proper | 480 |
| Introduction | 480 |
| The Report Body | 482 |
| The Ending of the Report | 483 |
| Appended Parts | 484 |
| Structural Coherence Helpers | 485 |
| The Long Analytical Report Illustrated | 487 |
| **15. GRAPHICS** | **536** |
| Planning the Graphics | 537 |

| | |
|---|---|
| Placing the Graphics in the Report | 537 |
| Determining the General Mechanics of Construction | 538 |
|    Size Determination | 538 |
|    Layout Arrangement | 539 |
|    Rules and Borders | 539 |
|    Color and Cross-Hatching | 539 |
|    Numbering | 539 |
|    Construction of Titles | 540 |
|    Placement of Titles | 540 |
|    Footnotes and Acknowledgments | 541 |
| Constructing Textual Graphics | 541 |
|    Tables | 541 |
|    In-Text Displays | 543 |
|    Management Operations Charts | 543 |
| Constructing Visual Graphics | 544 |
|    Bar Charts | 544 |
|    Pie Charts | 546 |
|    Line Charts | 548 |
|    Statistical Maps | 552 |
|    Pictograms | 553 |
|    Combination Charts | 554 |
|    Other Graphics | 555 |
| Using Computer Graphics | 555 |

# PART SIX

## OTHER FORMS OF BUSINESS COMMUNICATION

| | |
|---|---|
| **16. INFORMAL ORAL COMMUNICATION** | **566** |
| Informal Talking | 568 |
|    Definition of Talking | 568 |
|    Elements of Good Talking | 569 |
| Listening | 570 |
|    The Nature of Listening | 570 |
|    Improving Your Listening Ability | 572 |
| The Reinforcing Role of Nonverbal Communication | 574 |
|    Nature of Nonverbal Communication | 574 |
|    Types of Nonverbal Communication | 575 |
| Interviewing People | 577 |
|    Guidelines for the Interviewer | 578 |
|    Guidelines for the Interviewee | 579 |
| Conducting and Participating in Meetings | 580 |
|    Techniques of Conducting Meetings | 580 |
|    Techniques for Participating in a Meeting | 581 |
| Using the Telephone | 583 |
|    Need for Favorable Voice Quality | 584 |
|    Techniques of Courtesy | 584 |
|    Effective Telephone Procedures | 585 |
|    Effective Voice Mail Techniques | 585 |
| Dictating Letters and Reports | 586 |
|    Techniques of Dictating | 587 |
|    Letter Dictation Illustrated | 588 |
| **17. PUBLIC SPEAKING AND ORAL REPORTING** | **594** |
| Making Formal Speeches | 595 |
|    Selection of the Topic | 595 |
|    Preparation of the Presentation | 596 |
|    Determination of the Presentation Method | 598 |

| | | | |
|---|---|---|---|
| Consideration of Personal Aspects | 599 | Tools for Collaborative Writing | 638 |
| Audience Analysis | 600 | Asynchronous Computer Tools | 638 |
| Appearance and Physical Actions | 601 | Synchronous Computer Tools | 639 |
| Use of Voice | 603 | A Look to the Future | 640 |
| Use of Visuals | 604 | **19. SPECIAL TOPIC: TECHNIQUES OF CROSS-CULTURAL COMMUNICATION** | **644** |
| A Summary List of Speaking Practices | 606 | | |
| Team (Collaborative) Presentations | 608 | Problems of Cultural Differences | 646 |
| Reporting Orally | 608 | Body Positions and Movements | 647 |
| A Definition of Oral Reports | 608 | Attitudes toward Factors of Human Relationships | 649 |
| Differences between Oral and Written Reports | 609 | Effects on Business Communication Techniques | 652 |
| Planning the Oral Report | 610 | Problems of Language | 654 |

## PART SEVEN

## SPECIAL TOPICS IN BUSINESS COMMUNICATION

| | | | |
|---|---|---|---|
| | | Lack of Language Equivalency | 654 |
| | | Difficulties in Using English | 656 |
| | | A General Suggestion | 660 |
| **18. SPECIAL TOPIC: TECHNOLOGY-ASSISTED COMMUNICATION** | **618** | **20. SPECIAL TOPIC: PHYSICAL PRESENTATION OF LETTERS, MEMOS, AND REPORTS** | **664** |
| Tools for Constructing Messages | 619 | Basics for All Document Preparation | 665 |
| Computer Tools for Planning | 619 | Layout | 665 |
| Computer Tools for Gathering and Collecting Information | 622 | Type | 669 |
| | | Media | 670 |
| Computer Tools for Analyzing and Organizing | 624 | Form of Business Letters | 671 |
| | | The Ideal Layout | 671 |
| Computer Tools for Writing | 624 | Fixed Margins | 671 |
| | | Format Preferences | 671 |
| Tools for Presenting Messages | 632 | Form of Memorandums | 683 |
| Software | 632 | Form of Letter and Memorandum Reports | 683 |
| Hardware | 636 | | |
| Tools for Transmitting Messages | 636 | Form of Formal Reports | 685 |

| | | | |
|---|---|---|---|
| General Information on Report Presentation | 685 | Standards for the Use of Numbers | 721 |
| Mechanics and Format of the Report Parts | 689 | Spelling | 723 |
| | | Rules for Word Plurals | 724 |

**21. SPECIAL TOPIC: CORRECTNESS OF COMMUNICATION** — 700

| | | | |
|---|---|---|---|
| The Nature of Correctness | 701 | Other Spelling Rules | 724 |
| Standards of Punctuation | 703 | Capitalization | 725 |

**22. SPECIAL TOPIC: BUSINESS RESEARCH METHODS** — 728

| | | | |
|---|---|---|---|
| Apostrophe | 703 | Secondary Research | 729 |
| Brackets | 704 | Finding Publication Collections | 730 |
| Colon | 704 | Taking the Direct Approach | 731 |
| Comma | 704 | | |
| Dash | 708 | Using Indirect Methods | 736 |
| Exclamation Mark | 708 | Primary Research | 742 |
| Hyphen | 708 | Searching through Company Records | 742 |
| Italics | 709 | | |
| Parentheses | 711 | Conducting the Experiment | 742 |
| Period | 711 | Using the Observation Technique | 745 |
| Question Mark | 711 | | |
| Quotation Marks | 712 | Collecting Information by Survey | 746 |
| Semicolon | 713 | | |
| Standards for Grammar | 714 | Analyzing and Interpreting Data | 755 |
| Adjective-Adverb Confusion | 714 | | |

**APPENDIX A   CORRECTIONS FOR THE SELF-ADMINISTERED DIAGNOSTIC TEST OF PUNCTUATION AND GRAMMAR** — 763

| | | | |
|---|---|---|---|
| Subjective-Verb Agreement | 715 | | |
| Adverbial Noun Clause | 715 | | |

**APPENDIX B   GRADING CHECKLIST FOR LETTERS** — 765

| | | | |
|---|---|---|---|
| Awkward | 716 | | |
| Dangling Modifiers | 716 | | |

**APPENDIX C   GRADING CHECKLIST FOR REPORTS** — 767

| | | | |
|---|---|---|---|
| Sentence Fragment | 717 | | |
| Pronouns | 717 | | |

**APPENDIX D   DOCUMENTATION AND THE BIBLIOGRAPHY** — 771

| | |
|---|---|
| Parallelism | 719 |
| Tense | 719 |

**APPENDIX E   UNITED STATES LAWS AFFECTING BUSINESSS COMMUNICATION AT HOME AND ABROAD** — 781

| | |
|---|---|
| Word Use | 720 |
| Wrong Word | 721 |

**INDEX** — 791

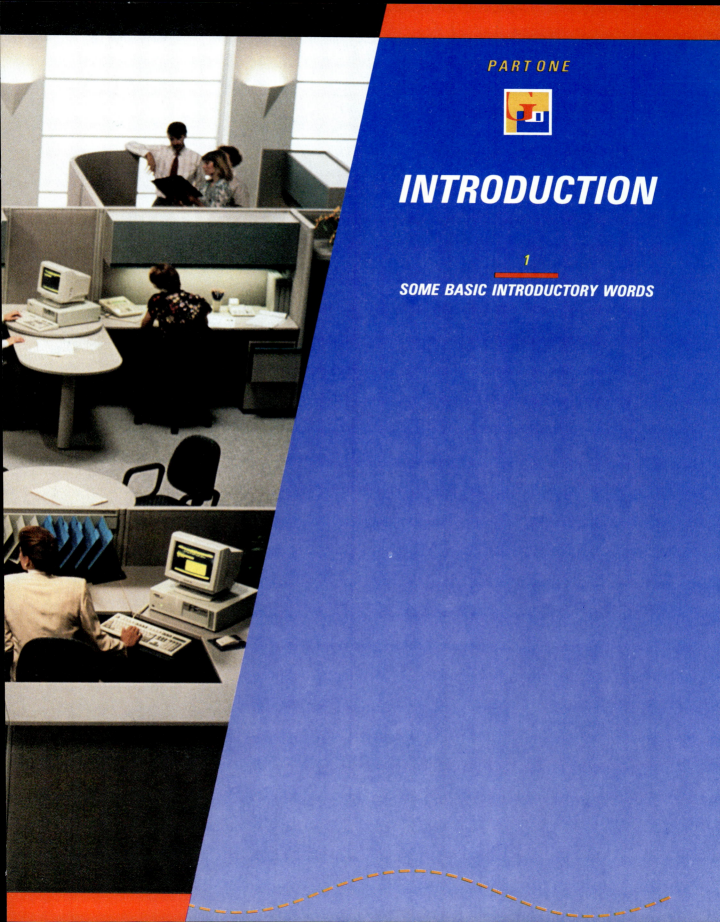

*PART ONE*

# INTRODUCTION

*1*

**SOME BASIC INTRODUCTORY WORDS**

# CHAPTER 1

# SOME BASIC INTRODUCTORY WORDS

## CHAPTER OBJECTIVES

*Upon completing this chapter, you will understand the role of communication in business. To achieve this goal, you should be able to*

**1**

Explain the importance of communication to you and to business.

**2**

Describe the three main forms of communication in the business organization.

**3**

Describe the formal and informal communication networks in the business organization.

**4**

Explain the process of communication among people.

**5**

Explain three basic truths about communication.

**6**

Describe the plan of this book.

# THE ROLE OF COMMUNICATION IN BUSINESS

Your work in business will involve communication—a lot of it—because communication is a major and essential part of the work of business.

*Communication is important to business.*

## The Importance of Communication Skills to You

Because communication is so important in business, businesses want and need people with good communication skills. All too often they do not get them, however, because most employees, even the college trained, do not communicate well. Among the recent studies that support this observation, perhaps the most notable[1] reports that one of the four major criticisms of today's college-trained people is their "poor communication and interpersonal skills." This study further reports that the shortcomings are in "both oral and, especially, written communication."

*Business needs good communicators, but most people do not communicate well.*

The communication shortcomings of employees and the importance of communication in business explain why you should work to improve your communication skills. The simple fact is that whatever position you have in business, your performance will be judged largely by your ability to communicate. If you perform (and communicate) well, you are likely to be rewarded with advancement. And the higher you advance, the more you will need your communication ability. One study reports that top-level administrators spend about 85 percent of their work time communicating.[2] The evidence is clear: Improving your communication skills improves your chances for success in business.

*By improving your communication ability, you improve your chances for success.*

## Why Business Needs to Communicate

To understand how important communication is to business, note how much communication business requires. Take, for example, a pharmaceutical manufacturer. Throughout the company workers send and receive information. They process information with computers, write messages, fill out forms, give and receive orders, and talk over the telephone. More specifically, salespeople receive instructions and information from the home office and send back orders and weekly summaries of their activities. Executives use letters and telephone calls to initiate business with customers and other companies and respond to incoming letters and calls. Production supervisors receive work orders, issue instructions, and submit production summaries. Research specialists receive problems to investigate and later communicate their findings to management. Similar activities occur in every niche of the company. Everywhere workers receive and send information as they conduct their work.

*Communication is vital to every part of business.*

Oral communication is a major part of this information flow. So, too, are various types of forms and records, as well as the storage and retrieval

*Communication takes many forms: oral, written, and computer.*

---

[1] Lyman W. Porter and Lawrence E. McKibbin, *Management Education and Development: Drift or Thrust into the 21st Century* (New York: McGraw-Hill Book Company, 1988), p. 99.
[2] Martha H. Rader and Alan P. Wunsch, "A Survey of Communication Practices of Business School Graduates by Job Category and Undergraduate Major," *Journal of Business Communication* 7, no. 4 (Summer 1980), pp. 37–38.

facilities provided by computers. Yet another major part consists of various forms of written communication—letters, memorandums, and reports.

All of this communicating goes on in business because communication is essential to the organized effort involved in business. Communication enables human beings to work together. In a business, it is the vehicle through which management performs its basic functions. Managers direct through communication, coordinate through communication, and staff, plan, and control through communication.

> All organized effort, including the work of business, requires communication.

### Main Forms of Communication in Business

The importance of communication in business becomes even more apparent when we consider the communication activities of an organization from an overall point of view. These activities fall into three broad categories: internal operational, external operational, and personal.

> There are three categories of communication in business:

**Internal-Operational Communication.** All the communication that occurs in conducting work within a business is classified as internal operational. This is the communication among the business's workers that is done to implement the business's operating plan. By *operating plan* we mean the procedure that the business has developed to do whatever it was formed to do—for example, to manufacture products, provide a service, or sell goods.

> (1) Internal operational—the communicating done in conducting work within a business,

Internal-operational communication takes many forms. It includes the orders and instructions that supervisors give workers, as well as oral exchanges among workers about work matters. It includes reports and records that workers prepare concerning sales, production, inventories, finance, maintenance, and so on. It includes the memorandums and reports that workers write in carrying out their assignments.

> such as giving orders, assembling reports, writing memorandums, and communicating by computers.

Nowadays much of this internal-operational communication is performed on computer networks. Workers send electronic mail through networks to others throughout the business, whether located down the hall, across the street, or around the world. As you will learn in Chapter 18, the computer also assists the business writer in many other aspects of communication.

"Our communications are excellent, but we're communicating the wrong things."

PART 1    Introduction

In the large business, much of the work done involves internal-operational communication.

**External-Operational Communication.** The work-related communicating that a business does with people and groups outside the business is external-operational communication. This is the business's communication with its publics—suppliers, service companies, customers, and the general public.

External-operational communication includes all of the business's efforts at direct selling—salespeople's "spiels," descriptive brochures, telephone callbacks, follow-up service calls, and the like. It also includes the advertis-

(2) External operational—work-related communication with people outside the business,

---

### Peter Drucker, on the Importance of Communication in Business

Peter Drucker, one of the most respected management consultants, educators, speakers, and writers of our time, made these observations about communication:

"Colleges teach the one thing that is perhaps most valuable for the future employee to know. But very few students bother to learn it. This one basic skill is the ability to organize and express ideas in writing and speaking.

"As soon as you move one step from the bottom, your effectiveness depends on your ability to reach others through the spoken or the written word. And the further away your job is from manual work, the larger the organization of which you are an employee, the more important it will be that you know how to convey your thoughts in writing or speaking. In the very large organization . . . this ability to express oneself is perhaps the most important of all the skills a person can possess."

---

**CHAPTER 1**  Some Basic Introductory Words

*such as personal selling, telephoning, advertising, and letter writing.*

ing the business does, for what is advertising but communication with potential customers? Radio and television messages, newspaper and magazine advertising, and point-of-purchase display material obviously play a role in the business's plan to achieve its work objective. Also in this category is all that a business does to improve its public relations, including its planned publicity, the civic-mindedness of its management, the courtesy of its employees, and the condition of its physical plant. And of very special importance to our study of communication, this category includes all of the letters that workers write in carrying out their assignments.

*Technology (computers, fax) assists in constructing and sending these communications.*

Technology assists workers with external-operational communication in both constructing and transmitting documents. For example, salespeople can keep database information on customers, check their company's computers for new product information and inventory information, and construct sales, order confirmation, and other letters for their customers. These letters can be transmitted by fax, electronic mail, or printed copy.

*Both internal and external communications are vital to business success.*

The importance of external-operational communication to a business hardly requires supporting comment. Certainly, any business is dependent on outside people and groups for its success. And because the success of a business depends on its ability to satisfy customers' needs, it must communicate effectively with them. In today's complex business society, businesses depend on each other in the production and distribution of goods and services. This interdependence requires communication. Like internal communication, external communication is vital to business success.

*(3) Personal communication— non-business-related exchanges of information and feelings among people.*

**Personal Communication.**   Not all the communication that takes place in business is operational. In fact, much of it is without purpose as far as the business is concerned. Such communication is called personal.

Personal communication is the exchange of information and feelings in which we human beings engage whenever we come together. We are social animals. We have a need to communicate, and we will communicate even when we have little or nothing to say.

*Personal communication affects worker attitudes.*

We spend much of our time with friends in communication. Even total strangers are likely to communicate when they are placed together, as on an airplane flight, in a waiting room, or at a ball game. Such personal communication also occurs at the workplace, and it is a part of the communication activity of any business. Although not a part of the business's plan of operation, personal communication can have a significant effect on the success of that plan. This effect is a result of the influence that personal communication can have on the attitudes of the workers.

*And attitudes affect worker performance.*

The workers' attitudes toward the business, each other, and their assignments directly affect their willingness to work. And the nature of conversation in a work situation affects attitudes. In a work situation where heated words and flaming tempers are often present, the workers are not likely to make their usual productive efforts. However, a rollicking, jovial work situation is likely to have an equally bad effect on productivity. Somewhere between these extremes lies the ideal productive attitude.

*The extent of personal communication permitted affects worker attitudes.*

Also affecting the workers' attitudes is the extent of personal communication permitted. Absolute denial of personal communication could lead to emotional upset, for most of us hold dear our right to communicate. On the other hand, excessive personal communication could interfere with the work done. Again, the middle ground is probably the best.

## Communication Network of the Organization

Looking over all of a business's communication (internal, external, and personal), we see an extremely complex network of information flow. We see an organization feeding on a continuous supply of information. More specifically, we see dozens, hundreds, or even thousands of individuals engaging in untold numbers of communication events throughout each workday.

*Information flow in a business forms a complex network.*

Most of the information flow of operational communication is downward and follows the formal lines of organization (from the top administrators down to the workers). This is so because most of the information, instructions, orders, and such needed to achieve the business's objectives originate at the top and must be communicated to the workers. However, most companies recognize the need for more upward communication. They have found that administrators need to be better informed of the status of things at the bottom. They have also found that information from the lower levels can be important in achieving company work goals.

*The flow is mainly downward, but upward communication is also important.*

**The Formal Network.** In simplified form, information flow in a modern business is much like the network of arteries and veins in the body. Just as the body has arteries, the business has major, well-established channels of information flow. These are the formal channels—the main lines of operational communication. Through these channels flows the bulk of the communication that the business needs to operate. Specifically, the flow includes the movements of information by reports, memorandums, records, and such within the organization; of orders, instructions, and messages down the authority structure; of working information through the organization's computer network; and of externally directed letters, sales presentations, advertising, and publicity. These main channels should not just happen; they should be carefully thought out and changed as the needs of the business change.

*The main (formal) lines of flow are like the network of arteries in the body.*

**The Informal Network.** Parallel to the formal network lies the informal network, a secondary network consisting primarily of personal communication (see Figure 1–1). Just as the formal network is like the arteries, the informal one is like the veins. It comprises the thousands upon thousands of personal communications that take place in a business. Such communications follow no set pattern; they form an ever-changing and infinitely complex structure linking all the members of the organization.

*The secondary (informal) network is like the veins.*

The complexity of this informal network, especially in larger organizations, cannot be overemphasized. Typically, it is really not a single network but a complex relationship of smaller networks consisting of groups of people. The relationship is made even more complex by the fact that these people may belong to more than one group and that group memberships and the links between and among groups are continually changing. Truly, the informal network in a large organization is so complex as to defy description.

*This secondary network is highly complex and continually changing.*

**FIGURE 1-1** Formal and Informal Communication Networks in a Division of a Small Manufacturing Company

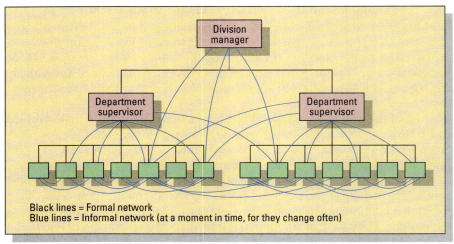

Black lines = Formal network
Blue lines = Informal network (at a moment in time, for they change often)

Managers can use this network (the grapevine) effectively.

Known as the *grapevine* in management literature, this communication network is far more effective than a first impression might indicate. Certainly, it carries much gossip and rumor, for this is the nature of human conversation. And it is as fickle and inaccurate as the human beings who are a part of it. Even so, the grapevine usually carries far more information than the formal communication system; and on many matters it is more effective

The informal communication network of a business consists of all the communicating of its employees whenever they get together.

**PART 1  Introduction**

in determining the course of an organization. Wise managers recognize the presence of the grapevine. They give the talk leaders the information that will do the most good for the organization. That is, they keep in touch with the grapevine and turn it into a constructive tool.

### Variation in Communication Activity by Business

Just how much communicating a business does depends on several factors. The nature of the business is one. For example, insurance companies have a great need to communicate with their customers, especially through letters and mailing pieces, whereas housecleaning service companies have little such need. The business's operating plan affects the amount of internal communication. Relatively simple businesses, such as repair services, require far less communication than complex businesses, such as automobile manufacturers. Also, the people who make up a business affect its volume of communication. Every human being is different. Each has different communication needs and abilities. Thus, varying combinations of people will produce varying needs for communication.

*The extent of a business's communication depends on the nature of the business, its operating plan, and the people involved.*

## ■■■■■■■■■■■■■■■■■■■■■■■■■■■
## THE PROCESS OF HUMAN COMMUNICATION

Although we may view the communication of a business as a network of information flow, we must keep in mind that a business organization consists of people and that the communication in the organization occurs among people. Thus, it is important to our basic understanding of business communication to know how communication among people occurs. The following review of the human communication process will give you that knowledge.

*The following review describes how communication among people works.*

In many small businesses, little need for operational communication exists. Much of the communicating done is with customers.

**CHAPTER 1** Some Basic Introductory Words   9

## The Beginning: A Message Sent

*The process begins when Marci sends a message to Kevin.*

To describe the communication process, we will use a situation involving two people—Marci and Kevin (see Figure 1–2). Our description begins with Marci communicating a message to Kevin. Her message could be in any of a number of forms—gestures, facial expressions, drawings, or, more likely, written or spoken words. Whatever the form, Marci sends the message to Kevin.

## Entry in the Sensory World

*The message enters Kevin's sensory world,*

Marci's message then enters Kevin's sensory world. By *sensory world* we mean all that surrounds a person that the senses (sight, hearing, smell, taste, touch) can detect. As we will see, Kevin's sensory world contains more than Marci's message.

## Detection by the Senses

*where his senses may detect it.*

From his sensory world Kevin picks up stimuli (messages) through his senses. We must note, however, that Kevin's senses cannot detect *all* that exists in the world around him. Just how much they can detect depends on a number of factors. One is the ability of his senses. As you know, not all eyes see equally well and not all ears hear equally well. And so it is with the other senses. Another factor is Kevin's mental alertness. There are times when he is keenly alert to all that his senses can detect, and there are times when he is

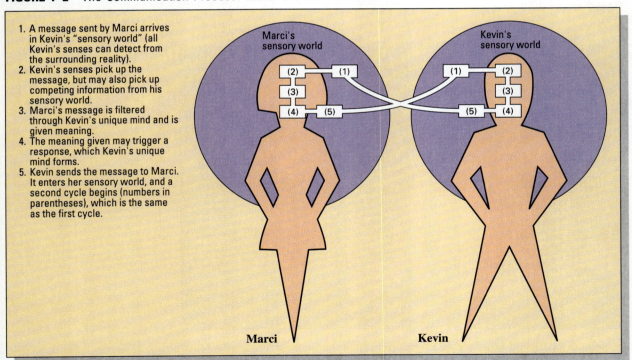

**FIGURE 1–2** The Communication Process: Marci and Kevin Communicate

1. A message sent by Marci arrives in Kevin's "sensory world" (all Kevin's senses can detect from the surrounding reality).
2. Kevin's senses pick up the message, but may also pick up competing information from his sensory world.
3. Marci's message is filtered through Kevin's unique mind and is given meaning.
4. The meaning given may trigger a response, which Kevin's unique mind forms.
5. Kevin sends the message to Marci. It enters her sensory world, and a second cycle begins (numbers in parentheses), which is the same as the first cycle.

PART 1  Introduction

dull—in a stupor, a daydream, or the like. Furthermore, Kevin's cultural background has sensitized him more to some stimuli than others. Yet another limiting factor is Kevin's will. In varying degrees, the mind is able to tune in or tune out events in the sensory world. In a noisy room full of people, for example, the conversation of a single person can be selected and the other voices ignored.

When Kevin's senses pick up Marci's message, they relay it to his brain—that is, as much or as little of the message as they detect. But Marci's message may not be all that Kevin's senses pick up. In addition to Marci's message, his sensory world may contain outside noises, movements of objects, facial expressions, and the like. In fact, his senses are continually picking up messages from the world around him. Marci's message is just the primary one at the moment. The others are there, and they might interfere with Marci's message.

*What Kevin's senses detect, they send to his brain,*

### The Filtering Process

When Marci's message gets to Kevin's brain, it goes through a sort of filtering process. Through that process Kevin's brain gives meaning to Marci's message. In other words, the message is filtered through the contents of Kevin's mind. Those contents include all his experience, knowledge, biases, emotions, cultural background—in fact, all Kevin is and has been. Obviously, no two people have precisely identical filters, for no two people have minds with precisely the same contents.

*where it goes through a filtering process.*

Because people's filters differ, the meanings they give to comparable messages may differ. Thus, the meaning Kevin gives Marci's message may not be precisely the same as the one that someone else would give it. And it may not be the meaning Marci intended. For example, assume that Marci used the word *liberal* in her message. Now assume that Marci and Kevin have had sharply differing experiences with the word. To Marci the word is negative, for her experience has made her dislike things liberal. To Kevin the word is positive. Thus, the message Kevin receives from the word would not be precisely the message Marci sent. And so it could be with other words in Marci's message.

*Because minds differ, message meanings differ.*

### Formation and Sending of the Response

After his mind has given meaning to Marci's message, Kevin may react to the message. If the meaning he received is sufficiently strong, he may react by communicating some form of response. This response may be through words, gestures, physical actions, or some other means.

*Kevin's mind reacts to the meaning, and he may respond.*

When Kevin elects to communicate a response, through his mind he determines the general meaning that the response will take. This process involves the most complex workings of the mind, and we know little about it. There is evidence, however, that ability, here and throughout this stage, is related to one's intelligence and the extent that one permits the mind to react. Kevin's ability to evaluate filtered information and formulate meaning is also related to his ability with language. Ability with language equips one with a variety of symbols (words and other ways of expressing meaning). And the greater the number of symbols one possesses, the better one can be at selecting and using them.

*Through his mind and its contents, Kevin determines the meaning of the response.*

Kevin ends this stage of the communication process by forming a message. That is, he converts meanings into symbols (mainly words), and then he sends these symbols to Marci. He may send them in a number of ways—as spoken words, written words, gestures, movements, facial expressions, diagrams on paper, and so on.

> *Kevin forms a message and sends it.*

### The Cycle Repeated

When Kevin sends his message to Marci, one cycle of the communication process ends. Now a second cycle begins. This one involves Marci rather than Kevin, but the process is the same. Kevin's message enters Marci's sensory world. Her senses pick it up and send it through her nervous system to her brain. There her unique mental filter influences the meaning she gives Kevin's message. This filtered meaning may also bring about a response. If it does, Marci, through her mind, selects the symbols for her response. Then she sends them to Kevin, and another cycle of communication begins. The process may continue, cycle after cycle, as long as Marci and Kevin want to communicate.

> *Then the cycle is repeated.*

### The Communication Process and Written Communication

Although our description of the communication process illustrates face-to-face, oral communication, it also fits written communication. But there are some differences. Perhaps the most significant difference is that written communication is more likely to involve creative effort. It is more likely to be thought out, and it may even begin in the mind rather than as a reaction to a message received.

A second difference is the time between cycles. In face-to-face communication, cycles occur fast, often in rapid succession. In written communication, some delay occurs. How long the delay will be varies. Fax messages may be read a few minutes after they are transmitted, letters in a few days, reports perhaps in days, weeks, or months. Because they provide a record, written communications may communicate over extremely long periods of time.

A third difference is that written communication usually involves a limited number of cycles and oral communication usually involves many. In fact, some written communication is one-cycle communication. That is, a message is sent and received, but none is returned.

> *Written communication differs from oral communication in that it (1) is more likely to involve creative effort,*
>
> *(2) has longer cycles, and*
>
> *(3) usually has fewer cycles.*

### Some Basic Truths about Communication

Analysis of the communication process brings out three underlying truths that will help us understand its complexity.

> *The communication process reveals some basic truths.*

**Meanings Sent Are Not Always Received.** The first underlying truth is that the meanings transmitted are not necessarily the meanings received. No two minds have identical filters. No two minds have identical storehouses of words, gestures, facial expressions, or any of the other symbol forms. And no two minds attach exactly the same meanings to all the symbols they have in common. Because of these differences in minds, errors in communication are bound to occur.

> *Because our mental filters differ, meanings sent may differ from meanings received.*

### *A Sure Way of Getting a Response*

In oral communication the cycles can go on indefinitely. In sharp contrast, written communication may end after a single cycle. How one imaginative mother used a written communication to assure a second cycle makes a classic story.

The mother was having difficulty in getting her college-student son to answer her letters. She wrote regularly but rarely received a reply. In desperation, she resorted to psychology. She wrote the usual letter filled with news from home. Then she ended with a reference to an enclosed check and instructions to "use it as you like." She mailed the letter, but she did not include the check.

In short order the son responded. His letter was filled with the kind of information mothers like to hear. At the end was a thank-you for the check, "which must have been forgotten, so please send it."

The son got the check, the mother got a letter, and, of course, a second communication cycle occurred.

---

**Meaning Is in the Mind.** A second underlying truth is that meaning is in the mind—not in the words or other symbols used. How accurately one conveys meaning in symbols depends on how skillful one is in choosing symbols and on how skillful the person receiving the symbols is in interpreting the meaning intended. Thus, you should look beyond the symbols used. You should consider the communication abilities of those with whom you want to communicate. When they receive your messages, they do not look at the symbols alone. They also look for the meanings they think you intended.

> Meanings are in the mind—not in symbols.

**The Symbols of Communication Are Imperfect.** The third underlying truth is that the symbols used in communication are imperfect. One reason for this is that the symbols we use, especially words, are at best crude substitutes for the real thing. For example, the word *man* can refer to billions of human beings of whom no two are precisely alike. The word *dog* stands for any one of countless animals that vary sharply in size, shape, color, and every other visible aspect. The word *house* can refer equally well to structures ranging from shanties to palatial mansions. The verb *run* conveys only the most general part of an action; it ignores countless variations in speed, grace, and style. These illustrations are not exceptions; they are the rule. Words simply cannot account for the infinite variations of reality.

> Because symbols are imperfect and people differ in their ability to communicate, communication is far from perfect.

Communication is also imperfect because communicators vary in their ability to convey thoughts. Some find it very difficult to select symbols that express their simplest thoughts. Variations in ability to communicate obviously lead to variations in the precision with which thoughts are expressed.

Communication across cultures is especially imperfect, for often there are no equivalent words in the cultures. For example, usually there is no precise translation for our jargon in other cultures. Words such as *condo, computer virus,* and *yuppie* are not likely to have equivalents in every other culture. Similarly, other cultures have specialized words unique and necessary to

> Communication across cultures is especially difficult.

them that we do not have. For instance, the Eskimos have many words for *snow*, each describing a unique type. Obviously, such distinctions are vital to their existence. We can get along very well with the one word. As you will see in Chapter 19, this subject is so vital to today's business communication that an entire chapter is devoted to it.

Although the foregoing comments bring to light the difficulties, complexities, and limitations of communication, on the whole we human beings do a fairly good job of communicating. Still, miscommunication often occurs. And people who attach precise meanings to every word, who believe that meanings intended are meanings received, and who are not able to select symbols well are likely to experience more than their share.

*Even so, we communicate reasonably well.*

### Resulting Stress on Adaptation

Understanding the communication process can help you become a better communicator. The process shows that communication is a unique event—that every mind is different from every other mind. No two of us know the same words; and no two of us know equal amounts about all subjects. Obviously, such differences make communication difficult. Unless the words (or other symbols) used in a message have the same meanings in the minds of both the sender and the recipient, communication suffers. Communication scholars have tried to solve this problem by stressing the adaptation of messages to the minds of their recipients. By *adaptation* we mean fitting the message to the recipients—using words and other symbols that they understand. As you will see, adaptation is the foundation for our review of communication principles in the pages ahead.

*The communication process shows the need for adaptation—an underlying principle in our study of communication.*

## THE GOAL, PLAN, AND PHILOSOPHY OF THIS BOOK

The preceding discussion shows that communication is important to business, that it is performed in various and complex ways, and that it is imprecise. These observations suggest that communicating in business is not to be taken lightly. If you want to excel at it, you must develop your communication skills. Helping you to do this is the goal of this book.

*The goal of this book is to help you improve your communication skills.*

### The Plan: Situations, Solutions, Summaries

To achieve this goal, the book introduces each major topic through a business communication situation that realistically places you in the business world. Each situation describes a possible communication problem. Then the following material instructs you on how to solve the problem. For your study convenience, summaries of the text material appear in the margins. A general summary by chapter objectives appears at the ends of the chapters.

*The book introduces topics by situations—then it shows solutions. Summaries help your study.*

### The Philosophy: Communicate to Communicate

In presenting this subject matter, the book takes a practical, realistic approach. That is, it views business communication as having one primary goal—to communicate.

*Successful communication is the purpose of communicating.*

**PART 1    Introduction**

Although this statement may appear elementary, it has significant meaning. All too often other goals creep in. For example, communicators sometimes seek to impress—perhaps by using big words and involved sentences. Or they seek to entertain with a clever choice of words. Good business communicators rarely have these goals. They primarily seek to communicate. They use words and sentences that communicate clearly and quickly. If the message has any difficulty, the reason is that the subject matter is difficult. In no way should the words and the sentence structures add to the difficulty.

*Some writers have other goals (to impress, to entertain). Business communicators should seek only to communicate.*

## ■■■■■■■■■■■■■■■■■■■■■
## SUMMARY (by Chapter Objectives)

1. Business needs and rewards people who can communicate, for communication is vital to business operations.
   - But good communicators are scarce.
   - So, if you can improve your communication skills, you increase your value to business and business will reward you.
2. The communicating in business falls into three categories:
   - The communicating a business does to implement its operating plan (its procedure for doing what it was formed to do) is called *internal-operational* communication.
   - The communicating a business does with outsiders (suppliers, other businesses, customers, and such) is *external-operational* communication.
   - Informal exchanges of information not related to operations are called *personal* communication.
3. The flow of communication in a business organization forms a complex and ever-changing network. Information continually flows from person to person—upward, downward, and laterally.
   - The communicating that follows the formal structure of the business forms the *formal* network. Primarily, operational information flows through this network.
   - The flow of informal (personal) communication forms the *informal* network.
4. The human communication process is as follows:
   - A message arrives in one's sensory world (all that one can detect with the senses).
   - The senses pick up the message and relay it to the brain.
   - The brain filters the message through all its contents (knowledge, emotions, biases, and such) and gives it a unique meaning.
   - This meaning may trigger a response, which the mind then forms.
   - The person then sends (by voice, marks on paper, gestures, or such) this message into the sensory world of another person.
   - Within this person the process described above is repeated (another cycle begins).
   - The process continues, cycle after cycle, as long as the people involved care to communicate.

1. Explain the importance of communication to you and to business.

2. Describe the three main forms of communication in the business organization.

3. Describe the formal and informal communication networks in the business organization.

4. Explain the process of communication among people.

| | |
|---|---|
| 5. Explain three basic truths about communication. | 5. The communication process reveals these truths:<br>• Meanings sent are not always received (our mental filters differ).<br>• Meaning is in the mind—not in the symbols (mainly words) used.<br>• The symbols we use are imperfect, primarily because the reality they describe is so complex. |
| 6. Describe the plan of this book. | 6. The plan of this book is to introduce you to the primary types of business communication problems through realistic situations.<br>• You are placed in a business communication situation.<br>• Then you are shown how to handle it. |

## QUESTIONS FOR DISCUSSION

1. Is the ability to communicate more important to the successful performance of a supervisor's job than to that of a company president's job? Defend your answer.
2. Make a list of types of companies requiring extensive communication. Then make a list of types of companies requiring little communication. What explains the difference in these two groups?
3. List the types of external-operational and internal-operational communication that take place in an organization with which you are familiar (school, fraternity, church, or such).
4. Identify the types of technology used primarily in internal- and external-operational communication to transmit messages. Explain what you think might account for the differences.
5. Discuss the question of how much personal communication should be permitted in a business organization. Defend your view.
6. Describe the network of communication in an organization with which you are familiar (preferably a simple one). Discuss and explain.
7. Describe what is in your sensory world at this moment. Contrast the parts that are usually in your awareness with the parts that are usually not in your awareness.
8. Using the model for the communication process as a base, explain how people reading or hearing the same message can disagree on its meaning.
9. Give an example of a simple statement that could be misunderstood. Explain why. Then revise the statement for more precise understanding.

## APPLICATION EXERCISES

1. Megan Cabot is one of 12 workers in Department X. She has strong leadership qualities, and all her co-workers look up to her. She dominates conversations with them and expresses strong viewpoints on most matters. Although she is a good worker, her dominating personality has caused problems for you, the new supervisor of Department X. Today you directed your subordinates to change a certain work procedure. The change is one that has proven superior wherever it has been tried. Soon after giving the directive, you noticed the workers talking in a group, with Megan the obvious leader. In a few minutes she appeared in your office. "We've thought it over," she said. "Your production change won't work." Explain what is happening. How will you handle the situation?
2. After noticing that some workers were starting work late and finishing early, a department head wrote this memorandum to subordinates:

   It is apparent that many of you are not giving the company a full day's work. Thus the following procedures are implemented immediately:

   a. After you clock in, you will proceed to your workstations and will be ready to begin work promptly at the start of the work period.
   b. You will not take a coffee break or consume coffee on the job at the beginning of the work period. You will wait until your designated break times.
   c. You will not participate in social gatherings at any time during the workday except during designated break periods.
   d. You will terminate work activities no earlier than 10 minutes prior to the end of the work period. You will use the 10 minutes to put up equipment, clean equipment, and police the work area.
   e. You will not queue up at the time clock prior to the end of the work period.

   The memorandum was not well received by the workers. In fact, it led to considerable anger, misunderstanding, and confusion. Using the model of communication as a base, analyze the memorandum and explain the probable causes of the difficulties.

3. After being introduced to a candidate for the presidency of their company, two workers had the following discussion. One worker is Scott, a young college-age man who is holding a full-time job while going to school part-time. The other is Will, an old-timer—a self-made man and master craftsman.

   **Scott:** I like the candidate. He appears young, energetic, and bright.
   **Will:** He's young all right. Too young! Too bright! That fancy Harvard degree won't help him here. Why, I'll bet he hasn't spent one day in a working-man's shoes.

**CHAPTER 1** Some Basic Introductory Words

**Scott:** Now that's not fair. He was trained to be an administrator, and he has had experience as an administrator—high-level experience. You don't need experience as a soldier to be a general.
**Will:** Don't tell me what this company needs. I've spent 40 years here. I know. I was here when old J.P. (the company founder) was president. He started as a machinist and worked to the top. Best president any company could have. We loved the man. He knew the business and he knew the work we do.
**Scott:** But that doesn't happen today. Administrators have to be trained for administration. They have to know administration, finance, marketing—the whole business field. You don't get that in the shop.
**Will:** All you kids think that knowledge only comes from books. You can't substitute book sense for experience and common sense. I've been here 40 years, son. I know.

The dialogue continued to accelerate and soon led to angry words. Neither Scott nor Will changed positions. Analyze the dialogue using the model of communication as the base.

**PART TWO**

# FUNDAMENTALS OF BUSINESS WRITING

**2**

**ADAPTATION AND THE SELECTION OF WORDS**

**3**

**CONSTRUCTION OF CLEAR SENTENCES AND PARAGRAPHS**

**4**

**WRITING FOR EFFECT**

# CHAPTER 2

# ADAPTATION AND THE SELECTION OF WORDS

## CHAPTER OBJECTIVES

*Upon completing this chapter, you will be able to adapt your language to specific readers and to select the most effective words for use in business communication. To reach this goal, you should be able to*

### 1
**Explain the role of adaptation in selecting words that communicate.**

### 2
**Simplify writing by selecting the short and familiar words.**

### 3
**Use technical words appropriately.**

### 4
**Discuss the differences in the strength of words and select the words that communicate your message best.**

### 5
**Write concretely and stress active voice.**

### 6
**Write with clarity and precision by avoiding camouflaged verbs, by selecting the right words, and by using idioms correctly.**

### 7
**Use words that do not discriminate.**

## INTRODUCTORY SITUATION

### to Choosing Words That Communicate

As a means of introducing yourself to business communication, place yourself in a hypothetical situation. You are the office manager of a manufacturing company. You have before you a memorandum from Mabel Schlitz, one of your assistants. Following your instructions, Mabel investigated your company's use of available space. She has summarized her findings in a memorandum report.

At first glance you are impressed with Mabel's report and with her ability. But after reading the report, you are not sure just what her investigation uncovered. Here is a typical paragraph:

> In the interest of ensuring maximum utilization of the subterranean components of the building currently not apportioned to operations departments, it is recommended that an evaluation of requisites for storage space be initiated. Subject review should be initiated at the earliest practicable opportunity and should be conducted by administrative personnel not affiliated with operative departments.

Mabel's problem is altogether too commonplace in business. Her words, though properly used, do not communicate quickly and easily. This and the following chapter show you what you can do about writing like this. ■

## THE BASIC NEED FOR ADAPTATION

The study of clear writing logically begins with adaptation. By *adaptation* we mean fitting the message to the specific reader. Obviously, readers do not all have the same ability to understand a message. They do not all have the same vocabulary, the same knowledge of the subject, or the same mentality. Thus, to communicate clearly you should first know the person with whom you communicate. You should form your message to fit that person's mind.

> For writing to be clear, it must be adapted to the reader.

### Visualizing the Reader

In adapting your message, you begin by visualizing your reader. That is, you form a mental picture of what he or she is like. You imagine what the reader knows about the subject, what his or her educational level is, and how he or she thinks. In general, you consider whatever you believe could have some effect on your reader's understanding of your message. With this in mind, you form the message.

> Adaptation begins with visualizing the reader—imagining what he or she knows, feels, thinks, and such.

### Technique of Adapting

In many business situations, adapting to your reader means writing on a level lower than the one you would normally use. For example, you will sometimes need to communicate with people whose educational level is below your own. Or you may need to communicate with people of your educational level who simply do not know much about the subject of your message.

> Often you will need to write at levels lower than your own.

**CHAPTER 2** Adaptation and the Selection of Words

### A Classic Case of Adaptation

There is a story told around Washington about a not-too-bright inventor who wrote the Bureau of Standards that he had made a great discovery: Hydrochloric acid is good for cleaning clogged drains.

He got this response: "The efficacy of hydrochloric acid is indisputable, but the corrosive residue is incompatible with metallic permanence."

Believing that these big words indicated agreement, this not-so-bright inventor wrote back telling how pleased he was that the bureau liked his discovery.

The bureaucrat tried again: "We cannot assume responsibility for the production of toxic residue with hydrochloric acid and suggest alternative procedure."

The inventor was even more gratified. He again expressed his appreciation to the bureau for agreeing with him.

This time the bureaucrat got the message. He replied in words any inventor would be certain to understand: "Don't use hydrochloric acid. It'll eat hell out of pipes."

---

*In writing to laborers, for example, you may need to simplify. You may write differently for highly educated people.*

To illustrate, assume that you need to write a memorandum to a group of laborers. You know that their vocabularies are limited. If you are to reach them, you will have to use simple words. If you do not, you will not communicate. On the other hand, if you had to write the same message to a group of highly educated people, you would have a wider choice of words. These people have larger vocabularies than the laborers. In either case, however, you would select words that the intended readers understand.

### Adaptation Illustrated

The following paragraphs from two company annual reports illustrate the basic principle of adaptation. The writer of the first report apparently viewed the readers as people who were not well informed in finance.

Last year your company's total sales were $117,400,000, which was slightly higher than the $109,800,000 total for the year before. After deducting for all expenses, we had $4,593,000 left over for profits, compared with $2,830,000 for 1992. Because of these increased profits, we were able to increase your annual dividend payments per share from the 50 cents paid over the last 10 years.

The writer of the second report saw the readers as being well informed in finance. Perhaps this writer believed that the typical reader would come from the ranks of stockbrokers, financial managers, financial analysts, and bankers. So this writer adapted the annual report to these readers with language like this:

The corporation's investments and advances in three unconsolidated subsidiaries (all in the development stage) and in 50 percent-owned companies was $42,200,000 on December 31, 1989, and the excess of the investments in certain companies over net asset value at dates of acquisition was $1,760,000. The cor-

In talking to a child, we naturally adapt the language to the child. Similarly, in business communication we need to adapt the language to the reader.

poration's equity in the net assets as of December 31, 1992, was $41,800,000 and in the results of operations for the years ended December 31, 1992 and 1991, was $1,350,000 and $887,500, respectively. Dividend income was $750,000 and $388,000 for the years 1992 and 1989, respectively.

Which writer was right? Perhaps both. Perhaps neither. The answer depends on what the stockholders of each company were really like. Both examples illustrate the technique of adaptation. They use different words for different audiences, which is what you should try to do.

### Adapting to Multiple Readers

Adapting your message to one reader is easy. But how do you adapt when you are communicating with two or more readers? What if your intended readers vary widely in education, knowledge of the subject, and so on? Writing to the level of the best-educated and best-informed persons would miss those at lower levels. Adapting your message to the lowest level runs the risk of insulting the intelligence of those at higher levels.

*If you write for one person in a group, you may miss the others.*

The answer is obvious. You have to adapt to the lowest level you need to reach. Not doing so would result in not communicating with that level. Of course, by writing for readers at the lowest level, you run the risk of offending those at higher levels. You can minimize this risk by taking care not to talk down. For example, you can carefully work in "as you know" and similar expressions to imply that you know the reader knows what you are writing about.

*To communicate with all of them, write for the lowest member of the group.*

**CHAPTER 2** Adaptation and the Selection of Words

## Governing Role of Adaptation

> Adaptation underlies all that will be said about writing. Apply it to the other writing instructions.

The preceding discussion shows that adaptation is basic to communication. In fact, it is so basic that you will need to apply it to all the writing and speaking instructions in the pages ahead. For example, much of what will be said about writing techniques will stress simplicity—using simple words, short sentences, and short paragraphs. You will need to think of simplicity in terms of adaptation. Specifically, you will need to keep in mind that what is simple for one person may not be simple for another. Only if you keep in mind the logical use of adaptation will you fully understand the intended meaning of the writing instructions.

## SUGGESTIONS FOR SELECTING WORDS

A major part of adaptation is selecting the right words. These are the words that communicate best—that have correct and clear meanings *in the reader's mind*.

> Selecting the right words is a part of adaptation. Following are some suggestions to help you select such words.

Selecting the right words depends on your ability to use language, your knowledge of the reader, and your good judgment. Few hard-and-fast rules apply. Still, you should keep in mind the suggestions presented in the following paragraphs. As you review them, remember that you must use them with good judgment. You must consider them in light of the need to adapt the message to your reader or readers.

> These suggestions stress simplicity for three reasons: (1) many people tend to write at a difficult level;

As you will see, most of the suggestions support simplicity in writing. This approach is justified by three good reasons. The first is that many of us tend to write at too difficult a level. Instead of being ourselves, we change character when we write. Rather than being friendly, normal people, we become cold and stiff. We work to use big words and complex structures. Winston Churchill referred to this tendency when he made his classic remark: "Little men use big words; big men use little words." We would do well to follow the example of this big man.

> (2) the writer usually knows the subject better than the reader; and

The second reason for simplicity is that the writer usually knows the subject of the message better than the reader. Thus, the two are not equally equipped to communicate on the matter. If the writer does not work at reducing the message to the reader's level, communication will be difficult.

> (3) the results of research support simplicity.

The third reason for simplicity is that convincing research supports it. According to such experts as Gunning, Dale, Chall, and Flesch, writing slightly below the reader's level of understanding communicates best.

### Use Familiar Words

> Familiar words communicate. Use them. Use your judgment in determining what words are familiar.

The foremost suggestion for word selection is to use familiar words. These are the everyday words—the words with sharp and clear meanings in the mind. Because words that are familiar to some people may be unfamiliar to others, you will need to select familiar words with care. You have no choice but to rely on your judgment.

Specifically, using familiar words means using the language that most of us use in everyday conversation. We should avoid the stiff, more difficult words that do not communicate so precisely or quickly. For example, instead of using the more unfamiliar word *endeavor*, use *try*. Instead of using

PART 2  Fundamentals of Business Writing

### A Case for Short, Familiar Words

In the Lord's Prayer, you will find 66 words—48 are of one syllable, a percentage of 72.

In "All the world's a stage" (Shakespeare's *As You Like It*), there are 212 words—150 are of one syllable, a percentage of 70.

In Abraham Lincoln's Gettysburg Address, there are 268 words—196 are of one syllable, a percentage of 73.

*terminate*, use *end*. Prefer *use* to *utilize*, *do* to *perform*, *begin* to *initiate*, *find out* to *ascertain*, *stop* to *discontinue*, and *show* to *demonstrate*.

The suggestion to use familiar words does not rule out some use of more difficult words. You should use them whenever their meanings fit your purpose best and your readers understand them clearly. The mistake that many of us make is to overwork the more difficult words. We use them so much that they interfere with our communication. A good suggestion is to use the simplest words that carry the meaning without offending the readers' intelligence. Perhaps the best suggestion is to write the words you would use in face-to-face communication with your readers.

The following contrasting examples illustrate the communication advantages of familiar words over less familiar ones.[1] As you read the examples, consider the effect on communication of an entire letter or report written in the styles illustrated.

> Difficult words are not all bad. Use them when they fit your needs and are understood.

| UNFAMILIAR WORDS | FAMILIAR WORDS |
| --- | --- |
| This machine has a tendency to develop excessive and unpleasant audio symptoms when operating at elevated temperatures. | This machine tends to get noisy when it runs hot. |
| Ms. Smith's idiosyncrasies supply adequate justification for terminating her employment status. | Ms. Smith's peculiar ways justify firing her. |
| This antiquated mechanism is ineffectual for an accelerated assembly-line operation. | This old robot will not work on a fast assembly line. |
| The most operative assembly-line configuration is an unidirectional flow. | The most efficient assembly-line design is a one-way flow. |
| The conclusion ascertained from a perusal of pertinent data is that a lucrative market exists for the product. | The data studied show that the product is in good demand. |
| Company operations for the preceding accounting period terminated with a substantial deficit. | The company lost much money last year. |

---

[1] For some of these examples, we are indebted to students and friends who gave them to us over the years.

**CHAPTER 2** Adaptation and the Selection of Words

An example supporting the use of familiar words came from Cape Kennedy while scientists were conducting research in preparation for long spaceflights. In one experiment, a monkey was placed in a simulated spaceship with enough food to last many days. With an unlimited supply of food available, the monkey simply ate too much and died. A scientist used these words to record the incident: "One monkey succumbed unexpectedly apparently as a result of an untoward response to a change in feeding regimen." Most readers of the report missed the message. Why didn't the scientist report in everyday language, "One monkey died because it ate too much"?

Another real-life example involved President Franklin D. Roosevelt. Across his desk came a memorandum advising federal workers to do the following in the event of an air raid:

Such preparations shall be made as will completely obscure all federal buildings and nonfederal buildings occupied by the federal government during an air raid for any period of time from visibility by reason of internal or external illumination. Such obscuration may be obtained either by blackout construction or by termination of the illumination.

Irked by the heavy wording, FDR sent this memorandum to the author:

Tell them that in buildings where they have to keep the work going to put something over the windows; and, in buildings where they can let the work stop for a while, turn out the lights.

In this and the preceding examples, the familiar words are clearly better. Readers understand them.

## Choose Short Words

*Generally, short words communicate better.*

According to studies of readability, short words generally communicate better than long words. Of course, part of the explanation is that short words tend to be familiar words. But there is another explanation: A heavy use of long words—even long words that are understood—leaves an impression of difficulty that hinders communication.

*Some exceptions exist.*

The suggestion that short words be chosen does not mean that all short words are easy and all long words are hard. Many exceptions exist. Few people know such one-syllable words as *gybe*, *verd*, and *id*. Even children know such long words as *hippopotamus*, *automobile*, and *bicycle*. On the whole, however, word length and word difficulty are related. Thus, you should concentrate on short words and use long words with caution. Use a long word only when you believe that your readers know it.

This point is illustrated by many of the examples presented to support the use of familiar words. But the following illustrations give it additional support. In some of them, the long word versions are likely to be understood by more highly educated readers. Even so, the heavy proportion of hard words clouds the message. Without question, the short-word versions communicate better. Note that the long words and their short replacements are in italics.

| LONG WORDS | SHORT WORDS |
|---|---|
| The decision was *predicated* on the *assumption* that an *abundance* of *monetary* funds was *forthcoming*. | The decision was *based* on the *belief* that there *would be more money*. |
| They *acceded* to the *proposition* to *terminate* business. | They *agreed to quit* business. |
| During the *preceding* year the company *operated* at a *financial deficit*. | *Last year* the company *lost money*. |
| Prior to *accelerating productive operation,* the supervisor inspected the machinery. | Before *speeding up* production, the supervisor inspected the machinery. |
| *Definitive* action was *effected subsequent* to the reporting date. | *Final* action was *taken after* the reporting date. |
| The *unanimity* of current forecasts is no *incontrovertible evidence* of an *impending* business *acceleration*. | *Agreement* of the forecasts is not *proof* that business *will get better*. |
| This *antiquated merchandising* strategy is *ineffectual* in *contemporary* business *operations*. | This *old sales* strategy *will not work* in *today's* business. |

Mark Twain understood the value of using short words when he made this often quoted statement: "I never use a word like *metropolis* when I can get the same price for *city*." One bureaucrat who did not understand the principle created a position to improve communication and gave it the title of Coordinator for the Obliteration of Proliferation of Obfuscation!

### Use Technical Words and Acronyms with Caution

Every field of business—accounting, computer science, engineering—has its technical language. This language can be so complex that in some cases specialized dictionaries are compiled. Such dictionaries exist for computers, law, finance, and other business specialties. There are even dictionaries for subareas such as databases, desktop publishing, and real estate.

*All fields have technical words.*

As you work in your chosen field, you will learn its technical words and acronyms. In time you will use these terms freely in communicating with people in your field. This is as it should be, for such terms are useful. Frequently, one such word will communicate a concept that would otherwise take dozens of words to describe.

*These words are useful when you communicate with people in your field. But they do not communicate with outsiders. Use them with caution.*

A problem comes about, however, when you use technical terms with people outside your field. Because these words are everyday words to you, you tend to forget that not everyone knows them. The result is miscommunication. You can avoid such miscommunication by using technical words with extreme caution. Use them only when your readers know them.

Examples of misuse of technical writing are easy to find. To a worker in the Social Security Administration, the words *covered employment* commonly mean employment covered by social security. To some outsiders, however, they would mean working under a roof. When a physician uses the words *cerebral vascular accident* with other physicians, they understand. Most people would get little meaning from these words, but they would understand a *little stroke*. *Annuity* has a clear meaning to someone in insurance. *A contract that guarantees an income for a specified period* would have more meaning to uninformed outsiders. Computer specialists know *C++* and *LISP* to be popular programming languages; but these words are meaningless to most others. To a trucker *bobtail* means a tractor cab without trailer. Nontruckers might get other meanings from that word—or perhaps no meaning at all.

> Some examples are *covered employment, cerebral vascular accident, annuity, bobtail.* These words are well known to people in special fields, but not to most outsiders.

Initials (including acronyms) should be used with caution, too. While some initials, such as IBM, are widely recognized, others, such as CIM (Computer Integrated Manufacturing), are not. Not only might the readers not know the initials, they might confuse it with others. For example, if you saw IRA, you might think of the Irish Republican Army and someone else might think of Individual Retirement Account. And your instructor might think of a committee named Instructionally Related Activities. If you have any question as to whether your reader is familiar with the initials, the best practice is to spell out the words the first time you use them and follow them with the initials. Also, if you are writing a long document with several pages between where you defined initials originally and where you use them again, it is courteous to your reader to spell out again.

> Use initials cautiously. Spell out and define as needed.

Probably the most troublesome technical language is that of the legal profession. Legal terms have too often worked their way into business communication. The result has been to add unnecessary words as well as words not understood by many business readers. Such words also produce a dull and formal effect.

> Legal language has worked its way into business writing.

Among the legal words that may add little real meaning are *thereto*, *therein*, *whereas*, *herewith*, and *herein*. For example, "the land adjacent thereto" can be written "the adjacent land" without loss in meaning. In addition, legal wordings such as *cease and desist* and *bequeath and devise* contain needless repetition.

> Words like *thereto, herewith,* and *ipso facto* are examples.

### Technical Language?

When an ordinary person wants to give someone an orange, he or she would merely say, "I give you this orange." But when a lawyer does it, the words are something like this: "Know all persons by these present that I hereby give, grant, bargain, sell, release, convey, transfer, and quitclaim all my right, title, interest, benefit, and use whatever in, of, and concerning this chattel, otherwise known as an orange, or *Citrus orantium,* together with all the appurtenances thereto of skin, pulp, pip, rind, seeds, and juice, to have and to hold the said orange together with its skin, pulp, pip, rind, seeds, and juice for his own use and behoof, to himself and his heirs, in fee simple forever, free from all liens, encumbrances, easements, limitations, restraints, or conditions whatsoever, any and all prior deeds, transfers, or other documents whatsoever, now or anywhere made, to the contrary notwithstanding, with full power to bite, cut, suck, or otherwise eat the said orange or to give away the same, with or without its skin, pulp, pip, rind, seeds, or juice."

Some legal words can be replaced with plain words. *Despite* can replace *notwithstanding. Ipso facto, sub judice,* and other such Latin phrases can be replaced by plain language with the same meaning.

Your technical language may not be any of the ones illustrated. But you will have one. You will need to be careful not to use it when you write to people who do not understand it.

> Replace legal language with plain words.

## Select Words with the Right Strength and Vigor

In a way, words are like people; they have personalities. Some words are strong and vigorous. Some are weak and dull. And some fall between these extremes. Good writers know these differences, and they consider them carefully. They use the words that do the best job of carrying the intended meaning. As a rule, they make the stronger words stand out.

> Words have personalities. Select the stronger ones.

Selecting words with just the right personalities requires that you learn language well—that you learn to distinguish shades of difference in the meanings of words. For example, you should recognize that *tycoon* is stronger than *eminently successful businessperson,* that *bear market* is stronger than *generally declining market,* that *boom* is stronger than *a period of business prosperity,* and that *mother* is stronger than *female parent.*

> To select words wisely, you should consider shades of difference in meanings.

You will not always want the strongest and most vigorous words. Sometimes, for good reason, you will choose weaker ones. The word *bill* is strong. Because it has a harsh meaning in some minds, you may prefer *statement* in some instances. The same goes for *debt* and *obligation, die* and *passed on, spit* and *saliva, labor boss* and *union official,* and *fired* and *dismissed.*

> Sometimes weaker words serve your purpose best.

In selecting the stronger words, you should keep in mind that the verb is the strongest part of speech. Second is the noun. Verbs are action words, and action carries interest. Nouns are the doers of action—the heroes of the sentence. Thus, they also attract attention.

> Verbs are the strongest words. Nouns are second.

Adjectives and adverbs are weak words. They add length and distract from the key words, the nouns and the verbs. As Voltaire wrote, "The adjective is the enemy of the noun." In addition, adjectives and adverbs are judgment words. As we will see, objectivity—which is opposed to judgment—is a requirement of much business communication. But you should know that adjectives and adverbs are among the weaker words, and you should use them sparingly.

> Adjectives and adverbs are weak words. They involve judgment. Use them sparingly.

## Use Concrete Language

Good business communication is marked by words that form sharp and clear meanings in the mind. These are the concrete words. You should prefer them in your writing.

> Use concrete words.

Concrete is the opposite of abstract. Abstract words are vague. In contrast, concrete words stand for things the reader can see, feel, taste, or smell. Concrete words hold interest, for they refer to the reader's experience.

> Concrete words are specific words.

Among the concrete words are those that stand for things that exist in the real world. Included are such nouns as *chair, desk, computer, road, automobile,* and *flowers.* Also included are words that stand for creatures and things: *John Jordan, Mary Stanley, Mickey Mouse, Spot,* the *Metropolitan Life Building,* and *Mulberry Street.*

> They stand for things that exist in the real world: *deck, chair, road.*

**CHAPTER 2** Adaptation and the Selection of Words

> Abstract nouns have general meanings: *administration, negotiation.*

Abstract nouns, on the other hand, cover broad meanings—concepts, ideas, and the like. Their meanings are general, as in these examples: *administration, negotiation, wealth, inconsistency, loyalty, compatibility, conservation, discrimination, incompetence,* and *communication.* Note how difficult it is to visualize what these words stand for.

> Concreteness also means exactness: *a 53 percent loss, the odor of decaying fish.*

Concreteness also involves how we put words together. Exact or specific wordings are concrete; vague and general wordings are abstract. For example, take the case of a researcher who must report the odor of a newly developed cleaning agent. The researcher could use such general words as "It has an offensive, nauseating odor." Now note how much more concrete language communicates: "It has the odor of decaying fish." The second example is concrete because it recalls an exact odor from memory. Notice the difference in communication effect in these contrasting pairs of wordings:

| ABSTRACT | CONCRETE |
|---|---|
| A significant loss | A 53 percent loss |
| Good attendance record | 100 percent attendance record |
| The leading company | First among 3,212 competitors |
| The majority | 62 percent |
| In the near future | By Thursday noon |
| A laborsaving robot | Does the work of seven workers |
| Light in weight | Featherlight |
| Substantial amount | $3,517,000 |

Now let us see the difference concreteness makes in the clarity of longer passages. Here is an example of abstract wording:

It is imperative that the firm practice extreme conservatism in operating expenditures during the coming biennium. The firm's past operating performance has been ineffectual for the reason that a preponderance of administrative assignments has been delegated to personnel who were ill-equipped to perform in these capacities. Recently instituted administrative changes stressing experience in operating economies have rectified this condition.

Written for concreteness, this message might read as follows:

We must cut operating expenses at least $2 million during 1992–93. Our $1,350,000 deficit for 1990–91 was caused by the inexperience of our two chief administrators, Mr. Sartan and Mr. Ross. We have replaced them with Ms. Pharr and Mr. Kunz, who have had 13 and 17 years, respectively, of successful experience in operations management.

Another illustration of concreteness is the story of the foreign nation that competed strenuously with the United States in an international automobile show. In one category, only automobiles from these two countries were entered. One would surely win first place, the other second. The U.S. automobile won. The government-controlled press of the losing country gave this report to its people: "In worldwide competition, our excellent entry was judged to be second. The entry from the United States was rated next to last." The words sound concrete—*second, next to last.* But they

**PART 2**  Fundamentals of Business Writing

omitted one fact needed for meaningful concreteness—that only two automobiles were entered.

### Use the Active Voice

You should prefer the active voice to the passive voice. Active voice produces stronger, livelier writing. It emphasizes the action, and it usually saves words.

> Prefer the active voice to the passive voice.

In active voice, as you will recall, the subject does the action. In passive voice, on the other hand, the subject receives the action. For example, the sentence "The auditor inspected the books" is in active voice. In passive voice, the sentence would read: "The books were inspected by the auditor."

> In active voice, the subject does the action. In passive voice, it receives the action.

These two sentences show the advantages of active voice. Clearly, the active-voice sentence is stronger. In it the doer of action acts, and the verb is short and clear. In the passive-voice sentence, the extra helping word *were* dulls the action. In addition, placing the doer of the action (*auditor*) in a prepositional phrase presents the information indirectly rather than directly. Note also that the active-voice sentence is shorter.

> Active voice is stronger and shorter.

For further proof of the advantages of active over passive voice, compare the following sentences:

| PASSIVE | ACTIVE |
| --- | --- |
| The results were reported in our July 9 letter. | We reported the results in our July 9 letter. |
| This policy has been supported by our union. | Our union supported this policy. |
| The new process is believed to be superior by the investigators. | The investigators believe that the new process is superior. |
| The policy was enforced by the committee. | The committee enforced the policy. |
| The office will be inspected by Mr. Hall. | Mr. Hall will inspect the office. |
| A gain of 30.1 percent was reported for hardware sales. | Hardware sales gained 30.1 percent. |
| It is desired by this office that this problem be brought before the board. | This office desires that the secretary bring this problem before the board. |
| A complete reorganization of the administration was effected by the president. | The president completely reorganized the administration. |

The suggestion that active voice be preferred does not mean that passive voice is incorrect or that you should never use it. Passive voice is correct, and it has a place. The problem is that many writers tend to overuse it, especially in report writing. Our writing would be more interesting and would communicate better if we used more active voice.

> Passive voice has a place. It is not incorrect.

Your decision on whether to use active or passive voice is not simply a matter of choice. Sometimes passive voice is preferable. For example, when

> Passive is better when the doer of the action is not important.

**CHAPTER 2** Adaptation and the Selection of Words

identifying the doer of the action is unimportant to the message, passive voice properly de-emphasizes the doer.

Advertising is often criticized for its effect on price.
Petroleum is refined in Texas.

Passive voice may enable you to avoid accusing your reader of an action:

The damage was caused by exposing the material to sunlight.
The color desired was not specified in your order.

Passive voice may also be preferable when the performer is unknown, as in these examples:

During the past year, the equipment has been sabotaged seven times.
Anonymous complaints have been received.

Yet another situation in which passive voice may be preferable is one in which the writer does not want to name the performer:

The interviews were conducted on weekdays between noon and 6 P.M.
Two complaints have been made about you.

In other instances, passive voice is preferable for reasons of style.

### Avoid Overuse of Camouflaged Verbs

An awkward construction that should be avoided is the camouflaged verb. When a verb is camouflaged, the verb describing the action in a sentence is changed into a noun. Then action words have to be added. For example, suppose you want to write a sentence in which *eliminate* is the action to be expressed. If you change *eliminate* into its noun form, *elimination*, you must add action words—perhaps *was effected*—to have a sentence. Your sentence might then be: "Elimination of the surplus was effected by the staff." The sentence is indirect and passive. You could have avoided the camouflaged construction with a sentence using the verb *eliminate*: "The staff eliminated the surplus."

Here are two more examples. If we take the good action word *cancel* and make it into a noun, *cancellation*, we would have to say something like "to effect a cancellation" to communicate the action. If we change *consider* to *consideration*, we would have to say "give consideration to." So it would be with these examples:

| ACTION VERB | NOUN FORM | WORDING OF CAMOUFLAGED VERB |
|---|---|---|
| acquire | acquisition | make an acquisition |
| appear | appearance | make an appearance |
| apply | application | make an application |
| appraise | appraisal | make an appraisal |
| assist | assistance | give assistance to |
| cancel | cancellation | make a cancellation |
| commit | commitment | make a commitment |

*Passive helps avoid accusing the reader.*

*Passive is better when the performer is not known.*

*It is also better when the writer prefers not to name the performer.*

*Avoid camouflaged verbs. You camouflage a verb by changing it to a noun form and then adding action words.*

*For example, if* cancel *becomes* cancellation, *you must add "to effect a" to have action.*

PART 2  Fundamentals of Business Writing

### Grammar and Style Checkers: Tools for Selection of Words

Grammar and style checking programs can assist in some writing tasks, but they are not yet perfect. However, two tasks grammar and style checkers do well are identifying jargon and passive voice.

As you have learned here, jargon refers to both special terms and special uses of terms unique to a particular kind of business. Nearly all businesses use jargon. You can probably readily recognize jargon in writing by others but it often creeps into your own undetected. As a student, you are probably familiar with the jargon unique to schools and academics, often referred to as *academicese*. Of course there is also computerese, legalese, etc. Notice how one grammar and style checker identified the legal examples given on page 30 in both its document analysis and its word review area.

whereas< <*_U7.LEGALESE: whereas *>>
therein< <*_U7.LEGALESE: therein *>>
herewith< <*_U7.LEGALESE: herewith *>>
herein< <*_U7.LEGALESE: herein *>>

<<WORDS TO REVIEW>>

Review this list for words that may confuse your message. These include words that are negative, frequently misused, colloquial, or jargon. As you review each word, think of its effect on the reader.

1 herein (Possible jargon)
1 herewith (Possible jargon)
1 therein (Possible jargon)
1 whereas (Possible jargon)

The following words from the text examples of computer and trucker terms were also identified in the *Words To Review* section but not in the document analysis.

1 C++ (Not widely understood)
1 annuity (Not widely understood)
1 bobtail (Not widely understood)
1 cerebral (Possible jargon)
1 LISP (Not widely understood)

Most grammar and style checkers do well in identifying passive voice. However, as you can see below, one checker simply points out the passive; you must determine whether and how to make it active.

The results were reported in our July 9 letter.
<<* S1.PASSIVE VOICE: were reported *>>
This policy has been supported by our union.
<<* S1. PASSIVE VOICE: been supported *>>
The new process is believed to be superior by the investigators.
<<* S1. PASSIVE VOICE: is believed *>>

Grammar and style checkers can be particularly useful in some aspects of adaptation and selection of words. However, once you've identified possible problems with your document, you must know how to improve them.

| ACTION VERB | NOUN FORM | WORDING OF CAMOUFLAGED VERB |
|---|---|---|
| discuss | discussion | have a discussion |
| investigate | investigation | make an investigation |
| judge | judgment | make a judgment |
| liquidate | liquidation | effect a liquidation |
| reconcile | reconciliation | make a reconciliation |
| record | recording | make a recording |

Note the differences in overall effect in these contrasting sentences:

| CAMOUFLAGED VERB | CLEAR VERB FORM |
|---|---|
| *Amortization* of the account *was effected* by the staff. | The staff *amortized* the account. |
| *Control* of the water *was not possible*. | They *could not control* the water. |
| The new policy *involved the standardization of* the procedures. | The new policy *standardized* the procedures. |
| *Application* of the mixture *was accomplished*. | They *applied* the mixture. |
| We must *bring about a reconciliation of* our differences. | We must *reconcile* our differences. |
| The *establishment* of a rehabilitation center *has been accomplished* by the company. | The company *has established* a rehabilitation center. |

> Avoid camouflaged verbs by (1) writing concretely and (2) preferring active voice. To comply with these suggestions, (1) make subjects persons or things and (2) write sentences in normal order.

From these illustrations you can see that our suggestion on camouflaged verbs overlaps our two preceding suggestions. First, camouflaged verbs are abstract nouns. We suggested that you prefer concrete words over abstract words. Second, camouflaged verbs frequently require passive voice. We suggested that you prefer active voice.

You can comply with these related suggestions by following two helpful writing hints. The first is to make the subjects of most sentences either persons or things. For example, rather than write "consideration was given to . . . ," you should write "we considered . . .". The second is to write most sentences in normal order (subject, verb, object), with the doer of the action as the subject. Involved, strained, passive structures often result from attempts at other orders.

## Select Words for Precise Meanings

> Writing requires a knowledge of language.

Obviously, writing requires some knowledge of language. In fact, the greater your knowledge of language, the better you are likely to write. Unfortunately, all too many of us treat language routinely. We use the first words that come to mind. We use words without thinking of the meanings they convey. We use words we are not sure of. The result is vague writing.

If you want to be a good writer, you will need to study words carefully. You will need to learn their precise meanings, especially the shades of

PART 2  Fundamentals of Business Writing

### Noah Webster on the Precision of Words

Illustrating precision in word usage is the following story about Noah Webster.

It happened that the great lexicographer's wife caught him in the act of embracing the chambermaid.

"Noah," she said, "I am surprised!"

Mr. Webster gazed upon her in mild reproof. "No, my dear," he replied, "you are amazed. It is we who are surprised."

---

difference in the meanings of similar words. For example, *weary*, *tired*, *pooped*, *fagged out*, and *exhausted* all refer to the same thing. Yet in most minds there are differences in the meaning of these words. In a rather formal message, *weary* would certainly be more acceptable than *pooped* or *fagged out*. Similarly, *fired*, *dismissed*, *canned*, *separated*, and *discharged* refer to the same action but have different shades of meaning. So it is with each of these groups of words:

> You should study language and learn the shades of difference in the meanings of similar words.

die, decease, pass on, croak, kick the bucket, check out, expire, go to one's reward
money, funds, cash, dough, bread, finances
boy, youth, young man, lad, shaver, stripling
fight, brawl, fracas, battle royal, donnybrook
thin, slender, skinny, slight, wispy, lean, willowy, rangy, spindly, lanky, wiry
ill, sick, poorly, weak, delicate, cachectic, unwell, peaked, indisposed, out of sorts

Knowledge of language also enables you to use words that carry the meanings you want to communicate. For example, *fewer* and *less* mean the same to some people. But careful users select *fewer* to mean "smaller numbers of items" and *less* to mean "reduced value, degree, or quantity." The verbs *affect* and *effect* are often used as synonyms. But those who know language select *affect* when they mean "to influence" and *effect* when they mean "to bring to pass." Similarly, careful writers use *continual* to mean "repeated but broken succession" and *continuous* to mean "unbroken succession." They write *farther* to express geographic distance and *further* to indicate "more, in addition." They know that *learn* means "to acquire knowledge" and *teach* means "to impart knowledge."

> You should learn the specific meanings of other words.

In your effort to be a precise writer, you should use correct idiom. By *idiom* we mean the way things are said in a language. Much of our idiom has little rhyme or reason, but if we want to be understood, we should follow it. For example, what is the logic in the word *up* in the sentence "Look up her name in the directory"? There really is none. This is just the wording we have developed to cover this meaning. "Independent of" is good idiomatic usage; "independent from" is not. What is the justification? Similarly, you "agree to" a proposal, but you "agree with" a person. You are "careful about" an affair, but you are "careful with" your money. Here are some additional illustrations:

> Use correct idiom. Idiom is the way ideas are expressed in a language.

**CHAPTER 2  Adaptation and the Selection of Words**

| FAULTY IDIOM | CORRECT IDIOM |
|---|---|
| authority about | authority on |
| comply to | comply with |
| different than | different from |
| enamored with | enamored of |
| equally as bad | equally bad |
| in accordance to | in accordance with |
| in search for | in search of |
| listen at | listen to |
| possessed with ability | possessed of ability |
| seldom or ever | seldom if ever |
| superior than | superior to |

*There is little reason to some idioms, but violations offend the reader.*

## SUGGESTIONS FOR NONDISCRIMINATORY WRITING

*Avoid words that discriminate against sex, race, nationality, age, or disability.*

Although discriminatory words are not directly related to writing clarity, our review of word selection would not be complete without some mention of them. By discriminatory words we mean words that do not treat all people equally and with respect. More specifically, they are words that refer negatively to groups of people, such as by sex, race, nationality, age, or disability. Such words run contrary to acceptable views of fair play and human decency. They have no place in business communication.

*We often use discriminatory words without bad intent.*

Many discriminatory words are a part of the vocabularies we have acquired from our environments. We often use them innocently, not realizing how they affect others. We can eliminate discriminatory words from our vocabularies by examining them carefully and placing ourselves in the shoes of those to whom they refer. The following review of the major forms of discriminatory words should help you achieve this goal.

### Avoid Sexist Words

All too prevalent in today's business communication are sexist words—words that discriminate against a person because of his or her sex. Although this form of discrimination can be against men, most instances involve discrimination against women. The reason is that many of our words suggest male superiority. This condition is easily explained: Our language developed in a male-dominated society. For reasons of fair play, you would do well to avoid sexist words. Suggestions for avoiding some of the more troublesome sexist words follow.

*Avoid using the masculine pronouns (he, him, his) for both sexes.*

**Masculine Pronouns for Both Sexes.** Perhaps the most troublesome sexist words are the masculine pronouns (*he, his, him*) when they are used to refer to both sexes, as in this example: "The typical State University student eats *his* lunch at the cafeteria." Assuming that State is coeducational, the use of *his* suggests male supremacy. Historically, of course, the word *his* has been classified as generic—that is, it can refer to both sexes. But many modern-day businesspeople do not agree and are offended by the use of the masculine pronoun in this way.

PART 2 Fundamentals of Business Writing

In business today, men and women, the young and the old, and people of all races work side by side in roles of mutual respect. It would be unfair to use words that discriminate against any of them.

You can avoid the use of masculine pronouns in such cases in three ways. First, you can reword the sentence to eliminate the offending word. Thus, the illustration above could be reworded as follows: "The typical State University student eats lunch at the cafeteria." Here are other examples:

You can do this (1) by rewording the sentence;

### SEXIST

If a customer pays promptly, *he* is placed on our preferred list.

When an unauthorized employee enters the security area, *he* is subject to dismissal.

A supervisor is not responsible for such losses if *he* is not negligent.

When a customer needs service, it is *his* right to ask for it.

### NONSEXIST

A customer who pays promptly is placed on our preferred list.

An employee who enters the security area is subject to dismissal.

A supervisor who is not negligent is not responsible for such losses.

A customer who needs service has the right to ask for it.

A second way to avoid sexist use of the masculine pronoun is to make the reference plural. Fortunately, the English language has plural pronouns (*their, them, they*) that refer to both sexes. Making the references plural in the examples given above, we have these nonsexist revisions:

(2) by making the reference plural,

If customers pay promptly, *they* are placed on our preferred list.
When unauthorized employees enter the security area, *they* are subject to dismissal.
Supervisors are not responsible for such losses if *they* are not negligent.
When customers need service, *they* have the right to ask for it.

as illustrated here;

**CHAPTER 2** Adaptation and the Selection of Words

| | |
|---|---|
| or (3) by substituting neutral expressions, | A third way to avoid sexist use of *he*, *his*, or *him* is to substitute any of a number of neutral expressions. The most common are *he or she*, *he/she*, *s/he*, *you*, *one*, and *person*. Using neutral expressions in the problem sentences, we have these revisions: |
| as in these examples. | If a customer pays promptly, *he or she* is placed on our preferred list.<br>When an unauthorized employee enters the security area, *he/she* is subject to dismissal.<br>A supervisor is not responsible for such losses if *s/he* is not negligent.<br>When service is needed, *one* has the right to ask for it. |
| Neutral expressions can be awkward; so use them with caution. | You should use such expressions with caution, however. They tend to be somewhat awkward, particularly if they are used often. For this reason, many skilled writers do not use some of them. If you use them, you should pay attention to their effect on the flow of your words. Certainly, you should avoid sentences like this one: "To make an employee feel he/she is doing well by complimenting her/him insincerely confuses her/him later when he/she sees his/her coworkers promoted ahead of him/her." |
| Avoid words suggesting male dominance, | **Words Derived from Masculine Words.** As we have noted, our culture was male dominated when our language developed. Because of this, many of our words are masculine even though they do not refer exclusively to men. Take *chairman*, for example. This word can refer to both sexes, yet it does not sound that way. More appropriate and less offensive substitutes are *chair*, *presiding officer*, *moderator*, and *chairperson*. Similarly, *salesman* suggests a man, but nowadays many women work in sales. *Salesperson*, *salesclerk*, or *sales representative* would be better. Other sexist words and nonsexist substitutes are as follows: |

| | |
|---|---|
| such as these examples. | **SEXIST**        **NONSEXIST** |

| SEXIST | NONSEXIST |
|---|---|
| man-made | manufactured, of human origin |
| manpower | personnel, workers |
| congressman | representative, member of Congress |
| businessman | business executive, businessperson |
| mailman | letter carrier, mail carrier |
| policeman | police officer |
| fireman | fire fighter |
| fisherman | fisher |
| cameraman | camera operator |

| | |
|---|---|
| But not all man-sounding words are sexist. | Many words with *man*, *his*, and the like in them have nonsexist origins. Among such words are *manufacture*, *management*, *history*, and *manipulate*. Also, some clearly sexist words are hard to avoid. *Freshperson*, for example, would not serve as a substitute for *freshman*. And *personhole* is an illogical substitute for *manhole*. |
| Do not use words that lower the status of women. | **Words That Lower Women's Status.** Thoughtless writers and speakers use expressions belittling the status of women. You should avoid such expressions. To illustrate, male executives sometimes refer to their female secretaries as *my girl*, as in this sentence: "I'll have my girl take care of this matter." Of course, *secretary* would be a better choice. Then there are the many female forms for words that refer to work roles. In this group are *lady* |

"How do you know they weren't done by cavewomen?"

From The Wall Street Journal, with permission of Cartoon Features Syndicate.

*lawyer, authoress, sculptress,* and *poetess.* You should refer to women in these work roles by the same words that you would use for men: *lawyer, author, sculptor, poet.*

Examples of sexist words could go on and on. But not all of them would be as clear as those given above, for the issue is somewhat complex and confusing. In deciding which words to avoid and which to use, you will have to rely on your best judgment. Remember that your goal should be to use words that are fair and that do not offend.

### Avoid Words That Stereotype by Race or Nationality

Words that stereotype all members of a group by race or nationality are especially unfair. Members of any minority vary widely in all characteristics. Thus, it is unfair to suggest that Jews are miserly, that Italians are Mafia members, that Hispanics are lazy, that blacks can do only menial jobs, and so on. Unfair references to minorities are sometimes subtle and not intended, as in this example: "We conducted the first marketing tests in the ghetto areas of the city. Using a sample of 200 black families, we . . . ." These words unfairly suggest that only blacks are ghetto dwellers.

> Words depicting minorities in a stereotyped way are unfair and untrue.

Also unfair are words suggesting that a minority member has struggled to achieve something that is taken for granted in the majority group. Usually well intended, words of this kind can carry subtle discriminatory messages. For example, a reference to a "neatly dressed Hispanic man" may suggest that he is an exception to the rule—that most Hispanics are not neatly dressed, but here is one who is. So can references to "a generous Jew," "an energetic Puerto Rican," "a hardworking black," and "a Chinese manager."

> Words that present members of minorities as exceptions to stereotypes are also unfair.

Eliminating unfair references to minority groups from your communication requires two basic steps. First, you must consciously treat all people equally, without regard to their minority status. You should refer to minority membership only in those rare cases in which it is a vital part of the message

> Eliminate such references to minorities by treating all people equally and by being sensitive to the effects of your words.

to be communicated. Second, you must be sensitive to the effects of your words. Specifically, you should ask yourself how those words would affect you if you were a member of the minorities to which they are addressed. You should evaluate your word choices from the viewpoints of others.

### Avoid Words That Stereotype by Age

*Words that label people as old or young can arouse negative reactions.*

Your sensitivity in not discriminating by sex should also be extended to include by age—both against the old and the young. While those over 55 might be retired from their first jobs, many lead lives that are far from the sedentary roles in which they are sometimes depicted. They also are not necessarily feeble, forgetful, or forsaken. While some do not mind being called *senior citizens,* others do. Be sensitive with terms such as *mature, elderly,* and *golden ager,* also. Some even abhor *oldster* as much as the young detest *youngster.* The young are often called *teenagers* or *adolescents* when *young person, young man,* and *young woman* are much fairer. Some slang terms show lack of sensitivity, too—words such as *brat, retard,* and *dummy.* Even harsher are *juvenile delinquent, truant,* and *runaway,* for these labels are often put on the young based on one behavior over a short period of time. Presenting both the old and young objectively is only fair.

As we have suggested, use labels only when relevant, and use positive terms when possible. In describing the old, be sensitive to terms such as *spry,* which on the surface might be well intended but can also imply a negative connotation. Present both groups fairly and objectively when you write about them.

### Avoid Words That Typecast Those with Disabilities

*Disabled people are sensitive to words that describe their disabilities.*

People with disabilities are likely to be sensitive to discriminatory words. While television shows those with disabilities competing in the Special Olympics, often exceeding the performance of an average person, common sense tells us not to stereotype these people. However, sometimes we do anyway. Just as with age, we need to avoid derogatory labels and apologetic or patronizing behavior. For example, instead of describing one as *deaf and dumb,* use *hearing and speech disabled.* Avoid slang terms such as *fits, spells, attacks;* use *seizures, epilepsy,* or other objective terms. Terms such as *crippled* and *retarded* should be avoided since they degrade in most cases. Work to develop a nonbiased attitude, and show it through carefully chosen words.

### In Conclusion about Words

*More about words appears in the following pages.*

The preceding review of suggestions for selecting words is not complete. You will find more—much more—in the pages ahead. But you now have in mind the basics of word selection. The remaining are refinements of these basics.

*The preceding suggestions are realistic ways to improve your writing. Use them.*

As you move along, you should view these basics as work tools. Unfortunately, the tendency is to view them as rules to memorize and give back to the instructor on an examination. Although a good examination grade is a commendable goal, the long-run value of these tools is their use in your writing. So do yourself a favor. Resolve to keep these basics in mind every time you write. Consciously use them. The results will make you glad you did.

## SUMMARY (by Chapter Objectives)

1. To communicate clearly, you must adapt to your reader.
    - Adapting means using words the reader understands.
    - It also involves following the suggestions below.
2. Select words that your reader understands.
    - These are the familiar words (words like *old* instead of *antiquated*).
    - They are also the short words (*agreed to quit* rather than *acceded to the proposition to terminate*).
3. Use technical words with caution.
    - For example, use *a little stroke* rather than *a cerebral vascular accident*.
    - However, technical words are appropriate among technical people.
4. Select words with adequate strength and vigor.
    - Develop a feeling for the personalities of words.
    - Understand that words like *bear market* are stronger than *generally declining market*.
5. Prefer the concrete words and active voice.
    - Concrete words are the specific ones. For example, *57 percent majority* is more concrete than *majority*.
    - In active voice, the subject acts; in passive voice, it receives the action. For example, use *we reported the results* rather than *the results were reported by us*.
    - Active voice is stronger, more vigorous, and more interesting. But passive voice is correct and has a place in writing.
6. Write more clearly and precisely by following these suggestions:
    - Avoid overuse of camouflaged verbs—making a noun of the logical verb and then having to add a verb (*appear* rather than *make an appearance*).
    - Select words for their precise meanings (involves studying words to detect shades of difference in meaning—for example, differences in *fight, brawl, fracas, donnybrook, battle royal*.)
    - Also, learn the specific ways that words are used in our culture (called *idiom*).
7. Avoid discriminatory words.
    - Do not use words that discriminate against women. (For example, using *he, him,* or *his,* to refer to both sexes and words such as *fireman, postman, lady lawyer,* and *authoress*.)
    - Do not use words that suggest stereotyped roles of race or nationality (blacks and menial jobs, Italians and the Mafia), for such words are unfair and untrue.
    - Do not use words that discriminate against age or disability.

---

1. Explain the role of adaptation in selecting words that communicate.

2. Simplify writing by selecting the short and familiar words.

3. Use technical words appropriately.

4. Discuss the differences in the strength of words and select the words that communicate your message best.

5. Write concretely and stress active voice.

6. Write with clarity and precision by avoiding camouflaged verbs, by selecting the right words, and by using idioms correctly.

7. Use words that do not discriminate.

## QUESTIONS FOR DISCUSSION

1. A fellow student says, "So I'm not a good writer. But I have other places to put my study time. I'm a management major. I'll have secretaries to handle my writing for me." Give this student your best advice, including the reasoning behind it.

2. Evaluate this comment: "Simplifying writing so that stupid readers can understand it is for the birds! Why not challenge readers? Why not give them new words to learn—expand their minds?"

3. Explain how you would apply the basic principle of adaptation to each of the following writing assignments:
    a. An editorial in a company newspaper.
    b. A memorandum to Joan Branch, a supervisor of an assembly department, concerning a change in assembly operations.
    c. A report to the chief engineer on a technical topic in the engineer's field.
    d. A letter to a laborer explaining pension benefits.
    e. A letter to company stockholders explaining a change in company manufacturing policy.

4. "Some short words are hard, and some long words are easy. Thus, the suggestion to prefer short words doesn't make sense." Discuss.

5. "As technical language typically consists of acronyms and long, hard words, it contributes to miscommunication. Thus, it should be avoided in all business communication." Discuss.

6. Using illustrations other than those in the book, discuss differences in word strength. Be sure to comment on strength differences in the parts of speech (nouns, verbs, adjectives, adverbs).

7. Define and illustrate active and passive voice. Explain when each should be used.

8. Discuss this statement: "When I use *he, him,* or *his* as a generic, I am not discriminating against women. For many years these words have been accepted as generic. They refer to both sexes, and that's the meaning I have in mind when I use them."

9. List synonyms (words with similar meanings) for each of the following words. Then explain the differences in shades of meaning as you see them.
    a. fat          f. understand
    b. skinny       g. dog
    c. old          h. misfortune
    d. tell         i. inquire
    e. happiness    j. stop

10. Discuss this statement: "The boss scolded Susan in a grandfatherly manner."

## APPLICATION EXERCISES

Instructions, Sentences 1–20: Assume that your readers are at about the 10th-grade level in education. Revise these sentences for easy communication to this audience.

1. We must terminate all deficit financing.
2. The most operative assembly-line configuration is a unidirectional flow.
3. A proportionate tax consumes a determinate apportionment of one's monetary flow.
4. Business has an inordinate influence on governmental operations.
5. It is imperative that consumers be unrestrained in determining their preferences.
6. Mr. Casey terminated John's employment as a consequence of his ineffectual performance.
7. Our expectations are that there will be increments in commodity value.
8. This antiquated mechanism is ineffectual for an accelerated assembly-line operation.
9. The preponderance of the businesspeople we consulted envision signs of improvement from the current siege of economic stagnation.
10. If liquidation becomes mandatory, we shall dispose of these assets first.
11. Recent stock acquisitions have accentuated the company's current financial crisis.
12. Mr. Coward will serve as intermediary in the pending labor-management parley.
13. Ms. Smith's idiosyncrasies supply adequate justification for terminating her employment.
14. Requisites for employment by this company have been enhanced.
15. The unanimity of current forecasts is not in-

controvertible evidence of an impending business acceleration.

16. People's propensity to consume is insatiable.
17. The company must desist from its deficit financing immediately.
18. This antiquated merchandising strategy is ineffectual in contemporary business operations.
19. Percentage return on common stockholders' equity averaged 23.1 for the year.
20. The company's retained earnings last year exceeded $2,500,000.

Instructions: Exercise 21 concerns adaptation and technical language. As you must find your own sentences for it, this exercise differs from the others.

21. From one of your textbooks, select a paragraph (at least 150 words long) that would be difficult for a student less advanced in the subject than you. Rewrite the paragraph so that this student can understand it easily.

Instructions, Sentences 22–58: Revise these sentences to make them conform to the writing suggestions discussed in the book. They are grouped by the suggestion they illustrate.

### USING STRONG, VIGOROUS WORDS
22. I have an idea in mind of how we can enhance our savings.
23. Ms. Jordan possesses qualities that are characteristic of an autocratic executive.
24. Many people came into the store during the period of the promotion.
25. We are obligated to protect the well-being of the hired employees.
26. Companies promoting their products in the medium of the newspaper are advised to produce verbal messages in accord with the audience level of the general consuming public.

### SELECTING CONCRETE WORDS
27. We have found that young men are best for this work.
28. She makes good grades.
29. John lost a fortune in Las Vegas.
30. If we don't receive the goods soon, we will cancel.
31. Profits last year were exorbitant.
32. Some years ago she made good money.
33. His grade on the aptitude test was not high.
34. Here is a product with very little markup.
35. The cost of the on-line database search was reasonable.
36. We will need some new equipment soon.

### LIMITING USE OF PASSIVE VOICE
37. Our action is based on the assumption that the competition will be taken by surprise.
38. It is believed by the typical union member that his or her welfare is not considered to be important by management.
39. We are serviced by the Bratton Company.
40. Our safety is the responsibility of management.
41. You were directed by your supervisor to complete this assignment by noon.
42. It is believed by the writer that this company policy is wrong.
43. The union was represented by Cecil Chambers.
44. These reports are prepared by the salespeople every Friday.
45. Success of this project is the responsibility of the research department.
46. Our decision is based on the belief that the national economy will be improved.

### AVOIDING CAMOUFLAGED VERBS
47. It was my duty to make a determination of the damages.
48. Harold made a recommendation that we fire Mr. Schultz.
49. We will make her give an accounting of her activities.
50. We will ask him to bring about a change in his work routine.
51. This new equipment will result in a saving in maintenance.
52. Will you please make an adjustment for this defect?
53. Implementation of the plan was effected by the crew.
54. Acceptance of all orders must be made by the chief.
55. A committee performs the function of determining the award.
56. Adaptation to the new conditions was performed easily by all new personnel.
57. Verification of the amount is made daily by the auditor.
58. The president tried to effect a reconciliation of the two groups.

Instructions, Sentences 59–70: Following is an exercise in word precision. Explain the differences in meaning for the word choices shown. Point out any words that are wrongly used.

59. Performance during the fourth quarter was (average) (mediocre).
60. This merchandise is (old) (antique) (secondhand) (used).
61. The machine ran (continually) (continuously).
62. The mechanic is a (woman) (lady) (female person).
63. His action (implies) (infers) that he accepts the criticism.
64. Her performance on the job was (good) (topnotch) (excellent) (superior).
65. On July 1 the company will (become bankrupt) (close its door) (go under) (fail).
66. The staff (think) (understand) (know) the results were satisfactory.
67. Before buying any material, we (compare) (contrast) it with competing products.
68. I cannot (resist) (oppose) her appointment.
69. Did you (verify) (confirm) these figures?
70. This is an (effective) (effectual) (efficient) plan.

Instructions, Sentences 71–80: These sentences use faulty and correct idioms. Make any changes you think are necessary.

71. The purchasing officer has gone in search for a substitute product.
72. Our office has become independent from the Dallas office.
73. The retooling period is over with.
74. This letter is equally as bad.
75. She is an authority about mutual funds.
76. When the sale is over with, we will restock.
77. Our truck collided against the wall.
78. We have been in search for a qualified supervisor since August.
79. Murphy was equal to the task.
80. Apparently, the clock fell off the shelf.

## AVOIDING DISCRIMINATORY LANGUAGE

Instructions, Sentences 81–90: Change these sentences to avoid discriminatory language.

81. Any worker who ignores this rule will have his salary reduced.
82. The typical postman rarely makes mistakes in delivering his mail.
83. A good executive plans his daily activities.
84. The committee consisted of a businessman, a lawyer, and a lady doctor.
85. A good secretary screens all telephone calls for her boss and arranges his schedule.
86. An efficient salesman organizes his calls and manages his time.
87. Our company was represented by two sales representatives, one Hispanic engineer, and one senior citizen.
88. Three people applied for the job, including two well-groomed black women.
89. Handicap parking spaces are strictly for use by the crippled.
90. He didn't act like a Mexican.

**CHAPTER 3**

# CONSTRUCTION OF CLEAR SENTENCES AND PARAGRAPHS

## CHAPTER OBJECTIVES

*Upon completing this chapter, you will be able to construct clear sentences and paragraphs by emphasizing adaptation, short sentences, and effective paragraph design. To reach this goal, you should be able to*

**1**

Explain the role of adaptation in writing clear sentences.

**2**

Write short, clear sentences by limiting sentence content and economizing words.

**3**

Design sentences that give the right emphasis to content.

**4**

Employ unity and clarity in writing effective sentences.

**5**

Compose paragraphs that are short and unified, use topic sentences effectively, show movement, and communicate clearly.

## INTRODUCTORY SITUATION

### to Writing Sentences and Paragraphs That Communicate

Continuing in your role as Mabel Schlitz's boss (preceding chapter), you conclude that not all of her writing problems involve word choice. True, her words detract from the readability of her writing. But something else is wrong. Her sentences just do not convey sharp, clear meanings. Although grammatically correct, they appear to be needlessly complex and heavy. Her long and involved paragraphs also cause you concern.

What you have seen in Mabel's writing are problems concerning two other determinants of readability—the sentence and the paragraph. As you will learn in the pages ahead, these two writing units play major roles in communicating. This chapter will show you (and Mabel) how to construct sentences and paragraphs that produce readable writing. ■

## FOUNDATION OF ADAPTATION

As you have seen, choosing the right words is basic to clear communication. Equally basic is the task of arranging those words into clear sentences. Just as with choosing words, constructing clear sentences involves adaptation to the minds of the intended readers.

Fitting sentences to the minds of readers requires the reader analysis we discussed in the preceding chapter. You should simply study your readers to find out what they are like—what they know, how they think, and such. Then construct sentences that will communicate with them.

In general, this procedure involves using the simpler sentence structures to reach people with lower communication abilities and people not knowledgeable about the subject. It involves using the more complex sentence structures only when they are appropriate, usually when communicating with knowledgeable people. As we will see, even with knowledgeable people, simplicity is sometimes needed for the best communication effect.

In adapting sentences, you should aim a little below the level of your reader. Readability research tells us that writing communicates best when it does not tax the mind. Thus, some simplification is best for all readers. Keep this point in mind as you read through the rest of this chapter.

*Sentences should be adapted to readers.*

*Use the simpler sentence structures for those less able to understand; use the more complex structures when appropriate.*

## EMPHASIS ON SHORT SENTENCES

Writing simpler sentences largely means writing shorter sentences. Readability research tells us that the more words and the more relationships there are in a sentence, the greater is the possibility for misunderstanding. Apparently, the mind can hold only so much information at one time. Thus, to give it too much information is to risk miscommunication.

*Short sentences communicate better because of mind limitations.*

*Short means about 16–18 words for middle-level readers.*

What constitutes a short, readable sentence is related to the reader's ability. Readability studies show that writing intended to communicate with the middle-level adult reader should average about 16 to 18 words per sentence. For more advanced readers, the average may be higher. For less advanced readers, it should be lower.

*Sometimes longer sentences are justified.*

This emphasis on short sentences does not mean that you should never use long sentences. You may use them occasionally, and you should—if you construct them clearly. Longer sentences are sometimes useful in subordinating information and in increasing interest by adding variety. The information needed to complete a thought sometimes requires a long sentence. What you should be concerned about is the average length of your sentences.

The following sentence from an employee handbook illustrates the effect of long sentences on communication:

> When an employee has changed from one job to another job, the new corresponding coverages will be effective as of the date the change occurs, provided, however, if due to a physical disability or infirmity as a result of advanced age, an employee is changed from one job to another job and such change results in the employee's new job rate coming within a lower hourly job-rate bracket in the table, the employee may, at the discretion of the company, continue the amount of group term life insurance and the amount of accidental death and dismemberment insurance that the employee had prior to such change.

The chances are that you did not get a clear message from this sentence when you first read it. The explanation is not in the words used; you probably know them all. Neither is it in the ideas presented; they are relatively simple. The obvious explanation is the length of the sentence. So many words and relationships are in the sentence that they cause confusion. The result is vague communication at best—complete miscommunication at worst.

*Short sentences are achieved in two ways.*

You can write short, simple sentences in two basic ways: (1) by limiting sentence content, (2) by using words economically. The following pages contain specific suggestions for doing this.

## *Limiting Sentence Content*

*Limiting content is one way to make short sentences.*

Limiting sentence content is largely a matter of mentally selecting thought units and making separate sentences of most of them. Sometimes, of course, you should combine thoughts into one sentence, but only when you have good reason. You have good reason, for example, when thoughts are closely related or when you want to de-emphasize content. The advantage of limiting sentence content is evident from the following contrasting examples:

**LONG AND HARD TO UNDERSTAND**

This memorandum is being distributed with the first-semester class cards, which are to serve as a final check on the correctness of the registration of students and are to be used later as the midsemester grade cards, which are to be submitted prior to November 16.

**SHORT AND CLEAR**

This memorandum is being distributed with the first-semester class cards. These cards will serve now as a final check on student registration. Later, they will be used for midsemester grades, which are due before November 16.

PART 2  Fundamentals of Business Writing

## LONG AND HARD TO UNDERSTAND

Some authorities in human resources object to expanding normal salary ranges to include a trainee rate because they fear that through oversight or prejudice probationers may be kept at the minimum rate longer than is warranted and because they fear that it would encourage the spread from the minimum to maximum rate range.

Regardless of their seniority or union affiliation, all employees who hope to be promoted are expected to continue their education either by enrolling in the special courses to be offered by the company, which are scheduled to be given after working hours beginning next Wednesday, or by taking approved correspondence courses selected from a list, which may be seen in the training office.

## SHORT AND CLEAR

Some authorities in human resources object to expanding the normal salary range to include a trainee rate for two reasons. First, they fear that through oversight or prejudice probationers may be kept at the minimum rate longer than is warranted. Second, they fear that this would increase the spread between the minimum and the maximum rate range.

Regardless of their seniority or union affiliation, all employees who hope to be promoted are expected to continue their education in either of two ways. (1) They may enroll in special courses to be given by the company. (2) They may take approved correspondence courses selected from the list in the training office.

Without question, the long sentences in the examples are hard to understand and the shorter versions are easy to understand. In each case, the difference is primarily in sentence length. Clearly, the shorter sentences communicate better. They give more emphasis to content and to organization of the subject matter.

However, you can overdo the writing of short sentences. A succession of short sentences can give the impression of elementary writing and draw attention from the content of the sentences to their choppiness. You should avoid these effects by varying the length and order of your sentences. But you should keep the length of your sentences within the grasp of your readers.

*Avoid overdoing this suggestion. Too many short sentences give a choppy effect.*

### *Economizing on Words*

A second basic technique of shortening sentences is to use words economically. Anything you write can be expressed in many ways, some shorter than others. In general, the shorter wordings save the reader time and are clearer and more interesting.

*Another way to shorten sentences is through word economy.*

Economizing on words generally means seeking shorter ways of saying things. Once you try to economize, you will probably find that your present writing is wasteful and that you use uneconomical wordings.

*Seek shorter ways of saying things.*

To help you recognize these uneconomical wordings, a brief review of them follows. This review does not cover all the possibilities for wasteful writing, but it does cover many troublesome problems.

*Following are some suggestions.*

**Cluttering Phrases.** An often used uneconomical wording is the cluttering phrase. This is a phrase that can be replaced by shorter wording without loss of meaning. The little savings achieved in this way add up.

*Avoid cluttering phrases. Substitute shorter expressions.*

## *Grammar and Style Checkers: Tools for Improving Clarity*

Grammar and style checkers can help you improve clarity by pointing out long sentences and counting words, sentences, and paragraphs. Furthermore, they can be useful in identifying roundabout construction and unnecessary repetition.

Depending on which program you use, you'll get various helps with recognizing problems with sentence length. Most programs will give you a report of the average number of words per sentence in your document. Others will tell you the number of syllables per word and the number of sentences per paragraph. In addition, some will identify the problem sentences where they occur. These problems are usually flagged by the software when the sentence exceeds some predetermined number of words. The number can be determined during the setup when you select the level and kind of writing you are analyzing, or you can tell the software how many words it should count before flagging a sentence as a long one.

Here is how one program reported on the long and hard to understand example shown in the text. Notice that it both identifies possible problems and gives some suggestions for correcting the problems. For sentence length, it reveals to the writer that this sentence has 47 words and recommends splitting it into two sentences.

> This memorandum is being distributed <<*_S1. **PASSIVE VOICE: being distributed** *>> with the first-semester class cards, which are to <<*_S14. **CONSIDER OMITTING: which are** *>> serve as a final check on the correctness of the registration of students and are to be used <<*_S1. **PASSIVE VOICE: be used** *>> later as the mid-semester grade cards, which are to <<*_S14. **CONSIDER OMITTING: which are** *>> be submitted <<*_S1. **PASSIVE VOICE: be submitted** *>> prior to <<*_U12. **WORDY. REPLACE prior to BY before** *>> November 16. <<*_G3. **SPLIT INTO 2 SENTENCES?** *>> <<*_S3. **LONG SENTENCE: 47 WORDS** *>>

Grammar and style checkers can also assist in identifying roundabout construction and unnecessary repetition. However, as you can see from the examples below, one program found some problems but missed others.

*Roundabout Construction*

> The president is of the opinion that the tax was paid.
>   <<* U12. **WORDY. REPLACE is of the opinion that BY believe** *>>
> It is essential that the income be used to retire the debt.
>   <<* U12. **WORDY. REPLACE BY you must or we must** *>>

*Unnecessary Repetition*

> Please endorse your name on the back of this check.
> We must assemble together at 10:30 a.m. in the morning.
>   <<* U13. **REDUNDANT. REPLACE assemble together BY assemble** *>>
>   <<* U13. **REDUNDANT. REPLACE a.m. in the morning BY a.m.** *>>
> Our new model is longer in length than the old one.

Grammar and style checkers are very useful in helping you diagnose problems with sentence length. In a limited way, the programs can also help improve clarity by pointing out some roundabout construction and unnecessary repetition. These programs clearly can help you improve the clarity of your documents.

### *A Marathon Sentence (308 Words) from U.S. Government Regulations*

That no person in the classified civil service of the United States shall be removed therefrom except for such cause as will promote the efficiency of said service and for reasons given in writing, and the person whose removal is sought shall have notice of the same and of any charges preferred against him, and be furnished with a copy thereof, and also be allowed a reasonable time for personally answering the same in writing; and affidavits in support thereof; but no examination of witnesses nor any trial or hearing shall be required except in the discretion of the officer making the removal; and copies of charges, notice of hearing, answer, reasons for removal, and of the order of removal shall be made a part of the records of the proper department or office, as shall also the reasons for reduction in rank or compensation; and the copies of the same shall be furnished to the person affected upon request, and the Civil Service Commission also shall, upon request, be furnished copies of the same: *Provided, however,* that membership in any society, association, club, or other form of organization of postal employees not affiliated with any outside organization imposing an obligation or duty upon them to engage in any strike, or proposing to assist them in any strike, against the United States, having for its objects, among other things, improvements in the condition of labor of its members, including hours of labor and compensation therefore and leave of absence, by any person or groups of persons in said postal service, or the presenting by any such person or groups of persons of any grievance or grievances to the Congress or any Member thereof shall not constitute or be cause for reduction in rank or compensation or removal of such person or groups of persons from said service.

Here is an example of a cluttering phrase:

*In the event that* payment is not made by January, operations will cease.

The phrase *in the event that* is uneconomical. The little word *if* can substitute for it without loss of meaning:

*If* payment is not made by January, operations will cease.

CALVIN AND HOBBES © 1981 Watterson. Dist. by UNIVERSAL PRESS SYNDICATE. Reprinted with permission. All rights reserved.

Similarly, the phrase that begins this sentence adds unnecessary length:

*In spite of the fact that* they received help, they failed to exceed the quota.

*Although* makes an economical substitute:

*Although* they received help, they failed to exceed the quota.

You probably use many cluttering phrases. The following partial list (with suggested substitutions) should help you cut down on them:

| **CLUTTERING PHRASE** | **SHORTER SUBSTITUTION** |
|---|---|
| Along the lines of | Like |
| At the present time | Now |
| For the purpose of | For |
| For the reason that | Because, since |
| In accordance with | By |
| In the amount of | For |
| In the meantime | Meanwhile |
| In the near future | Soon |
| In the neighborhood of | About |
| In very few cases | Seldom |

With the advent of computers, the way business messages are composed has changed, but the mental process involved remains unchanged. One still must select words and build sentences that form precise meanings in the minds of readers.

| CLUTTERING PHRASE | SHORTER SUBSTITUTION |
|---|---|
| In view of the fact that | Since, because |
| On the basis of | By |
| On the occasion of | On |
| With regard to, with reference to | About |
| With a view to | To |

**Surplus Words.** To write economically, eliminate words that add nothing to sentence meaning. As with cluttering phrases, we often use meaningless extra words as a matter of habit. Eliminating these surplus words sometimes requires recasting a sentence. But sometimes they can just be left out.

*Eliminate surplus words.*

This is an example of surplus wording from a business report:

*It will be noted that* the records for the past years show a steady increase in special appropriations.

The beginning words add nothing to the meaning of the sentence. Notice how dropping them makes the sentence stronger—and without loss of meaning:

The records for past years show a steady increase in special appropriations.

Here is a second example:

His performance was good enough *to enable* him to qualify for the promotion.

The words *to enable* add nothing and can be dropped:

His performance was good enough to qualify him for the promotion.

The following sentences further illustrate the use of surplus words. In each case, the surplus words can be eliminated without changing the meaning.

| CONTAINS SURPLUS WORDS | ELIMINATES SURPLUS WORDS |
|---|---|
| He ordered desks *that are of the executive type.* | He ordered executive-type desks. |
| *There are* four rules *that* should be observed. | Four rules should be observed. |
| *In addition to these defects,* numerous other defects mar the operating procedure. | Numerous other defects mar the operating procedure. |
| The machines *that were* damaged by the fire were repaired. | The machines damaged by the fire were repaired. |
| By *the* keeping of production records, they found the error. | By keeping production records, they found the error. |
| *In the period* between April and June, we detected the problem. | Between April and June we detected the problem. |
| I am prepared to report *to the effect that* sales increased. | I am prepared to report that sales increased. |

**Roundabout Constructions.** As we have noted, you can write anything in many ways. Some of the ways are direct and to the point. Some cover the same ground in a roundabout way. Usually the direct ways are shorter and communicate better.

*Avoid roundabout ways of saying things.*

CHAPTER 3 Construction of Clear Sentences and Paragraphs

This sentence illustrates roundabout construction:

The department budget *can be observed to be decreasing* each *new* year.

Do the words *can be observed to be decreasing* get to the point? Is the idea of *observing* essential? Is *new* needed? A more direct and better sentence is this one:

The department budget decreases each year.

Here is another roundabout sentence:

The union *is involved in the task of reviewing* the seniority provision of the contract.

Now if the union is *involved in the task of reviewing*, it is really *reviewing*. The sentence should be written in these direct words:

The union *is reviewing* the seniority provision of the contract.

The following sentence pairs further illustrate the advantages of short, direct wording over roundabout wording:

| ROUNDABOUT | DIRECT AND TO THE POINT |
|---|---|
| The president *is of the opinion that* the tax was paid. | The president *believes* the tax was paid. |
| *It is essential that* the income be used to retire the debt. | The income *must* be used to retire the debt. |
| *Reference is made to* your May 10 report *in which you concluded* that the warranty is worthless. | Your May 10 report *concluded* that the warranty is worthless. |
| The supervisors should *take appropriate action to determine* whether the time cards are being inspected. | The supervisors *should determine* whether the time cards are being inspected. |
| The price increase *will afford* the company *an opportunity* to retire the debt. | The price *will enable* the company to retire the debt. |
| *During the time she was* employed by this company, Ms. Carr was absent once. | *While* employed by this company, Ms. Carr was absent once. |
| He criticized everyone he *came in contact with*. | He criticized everyone he *met*. |

> Repeat words only for effect and emphasis.

**Unnecessary Repetition of Words or Ideas.** Repeating words obviously adds to sentence length. Such repetition sometimes serves a purpose, as when it is used for emphasis or special effect. But all too often it is without purpose, as this sentence illustrates:

We have not received your payment covering invoices covering June and July purchases.

It would be better to write the sentence like this:

We have not received your payment covering invoices for June and July purchases.

Another example is this one:

He stated that he believes that we are responsible.

**PART 2** Fundamentals of Business Writing

### *How My Business Is Doing, as Expressed by:*

An astronomer: "My business is looking up."
A cigarmaker: "Mine is going up in smoke."
An author: "Mine is all write."
A tailor: "Mine is just sew, sew."
A farmer: "Mine is growing."
An electric company worker: "Mine is light."
A ragpicker: "Mine is picking up."
An optician: "Mine is looking better."

---

This sentence eliminates one of the *thats*:

He stated that he believes we are responsible.

Repetitions of ideas through the use of different words that mean the same thing (*free gift, true fact, past history*) also add to sentence length. Known as redundancies, such repetitions are illogical and can rarely be defended. Note the redundancy in this sentence:

> Avoid repetitions of ideas (redundancies).

The provision of Section 5 provides for a union shop.

The duplication, of course, is in the meaning of *provides*. By definition, a *provision* provides. So the repetition serves no purpose. This sentence is better:

Section 5 provides for a union shop.

You often hear this expression:

*In my opinion, I think* the plan is sound.

Do not *in my opinion* and *I think* express the same thought? Could you possibly think in an opinion other than your own? This sentence makes better sense:

I think the plan is sound.

Here are other examples of redundancies and ways to eliminate them:

| **NEEDLESS REPETITION** | **REPETITION ELIMINATED** |
|---|---|
| Please *endorse* your name on the back of this check. | Please *endorse* this check. |
| We must *assemble together* at 10:30 A.M. *in the morning*. | We must *assemble* at 10:30 A.M. |
| Our new model is *longer in length* than the old one. | Our new model is *longer* than the old one. |
| If you are not satisfied, *return it back* to us. | If you are not satisfied, *return* it to us. |
| Tod Wilson is the *present incumbent*. | Tod Wilson is the *incumbent*. |
| One should know the *basic fundamentals* of clear writing. | One should know the *fundamentals* of clear writing. |

### The Malcolm Baldrige National Quality Award: An Award Named in Honor of a Word-Conscious Bureaucrat

The Malcolm Baldrige National Quality Award is an 18-K gold-plated medal inscribed with its name and "The Quest for Excellence" on one side and the Presidential seal on the other side. The highly coveted and sought-after national quality award is named in honor of a crusader for quality in writing. In fact, in his early years as Commerce Secretary he encouraged simple, clear writing. He criticized bureaucratese for taking 17 words when 7 would do. He pushed for eliminating unnecessary repetition such as *personally reviewed* or *new initiatives*. He told his staff he wanted lean sentences. In fact, in the early 1980s as computers were just beginning to make their way into government offices, his were programmed to flash "Don't Use This Word" for words or phrases such as *interface, bottom line, I would hope, at the present time, enclosed herewith, finalize*, and many others. He firmly believed that clear writing gets the meaning across most effectively. A man now remembered for his association with quality spent years advocating the virtues of clear writing.

---

**NEEDLESS REPETITION**

The *consensus of opinion* is that the tax is unfair.

By acting now, we can finish *sooner than if we wait until a later date*.

*At the present time*, we are conducting two clinics.

*As a matter of interest*, I am *interested* in learning your procedure.

We should plan *in advance for the future*.

**REPETITION ELIMINATED**

The *consensus* is that the tax is unfair.

By acting now, we can finish *sooner*.

We are conducting two clinics.

I am *interested* in learning your procedure.

We should *plan*.

### Determining Emphasis in Sentence Design

• You should give every item its due emphasis.

The sentences you write should give the right emphasis to content. Any written business communication contains a number of items of information, not all of which are equally important. Some are very important, such as a conclusion in a report or the objective in a letter. Others are relatively unimportant. Your task as writer is to form your sentences to communicate the importance of each item.

• Short sentences emphasize contents.

Sentence length affects emphasis. Short, simple sentences carry more emphasis than long, involved ones. They stand out and call attention to their contents. Thus they give the reader a single message without the interference of related or supporting information.

• Long sentences de-emphasize contents.

Longer sentences give less emphasis to their contents. When a sentence contains two or more ideas, the ideas share emphasis. How they share it depends on how the sentence is constructed. If two ideas are presented

**58**     PART 2   Fundamentals of Business Writing

equally (in independent clauses, for example), they get about equal emphasis. But if they are not presented equally (for example, in an independent and a dependent clause), one gets more emphasis than the other.

To illustrate the varying emphasis you can give information, consider this example. You have two items of information to write. One is that the company lost money last year. The other is that its sales volume reached a record high. You could present the information in at least three ways. First, you could give both items equal emphasis by placing them in separate short sentences:

The company lost money last year. The loss occurred in spite of record sales.

Second, you could present the two items in the same sentence with emphasis on the lost money.

Although the company enjoyed record sales last year, it lost money.

Third, you could present the two items in one sentence with emphasis on the sales increase:

The company enjoyed record sales last year, although it lost money.

Which way would you choose? The answer depends on how much emphasis each item deserves. You should think the matter through and follow your best judgment. But the point is clear: Your choice makes a difference.

*Determining emphasis is a matter of good judgment.*

The following paragraphs illustrate the importance of thinking logically to determine emphasis. In the first, each item of information gets the emphasis of a short sentence and none stands out. However, the items are not equally important and do not deserve equal emphasis. Notice, also, the choppy effect that the succession of short sentences produces.

The main building was inspected on October 1. Mr. George Wills inspected the building. Mr. Wills is a vice president of the company. He found that the building has 6,500 square feet of floor space. He also found that it has 2,400 square feet of storage space. The new store must have a minimum of 6,000 square feet of floor space. It must have 2,000 square feet of storage space. Thus, the main building exceeds the space requirements for the new store. Therefore, Mr. Wills concluded that the main building is adequate for the company's needs.

In the next paragraph, some of the items are subordinated, but not logically. The really important information does not receive the emphasis it deserves. Logically, these two points should stand out: (1) the building is large enough, and (2) storage space exceeds minimum requirements. But they do not stand out in this version:

Mr. George Wills, who inspected the main building on October 1, is a vice president of the company. His inspection, which supports the conclusion that the building is large enough for the proposed store, uncovered these facts. The building has 6,500 square feet of floor space and 2,400 square feet of storage space, which is more than the minimum requirement of 6,000 and 2,000 square feet, respectively, of floor and storage space.

The third paragraph shows good emphasis of the important points. The short beginning sentence emphasizes the conclusion. The supporting facts that the building exceeds the minimum floor and storage space requirements receive main-clause emphasis. The less important facts, such as the reference to George Wills, are treated subordinately. Also, the most important facts are placed at the points of emphasis—the beginning and ending.

**CHAPTER 3    Construction of Clear Sentences and Paragraphs**

The main building is large enough for the new store. This conclusion, reached by Vice President George Wills following his October 1 inspection of the building, is based on these facts: The building's 6,500 square feet of floor space exceed the minimum requirement by 500 square feet. The 2,400 square feet of storage space exceed the minimum requirement by 400 square feet.

The preceding illustrations show how sentence construction can determine emphasis. You can make items stand out, you can treat them equally, or you can de-emphasize them. The choices are yours. But what you do must be the result of good, sound thinking and not simply a matter of chance.

## Giving the Sentences Unity

*All parts of a sentence should concern one thought.*

Good sentences have unity. For a sentence to have unity, all of its parts must combine to form one clear thought. In other words, all the things put in a sentence should have a good reason for being together.

*There are three causes of unity error.*

Violations of unity in sentence construction fall into three categories: (1) unrelated ideas, (2) excessive detail, and (3) illogical constructions.

*First, placing unrelated ideas in a sentence violates unity.*

**Unrelated ideas.** Placing unrelated ideas in a sentence is the most obvious violation of unity. Putting two or more ideas in a sentence is not grammatically wrong, but the ideas must have a reason for being together. They must combine to complete the single goal of the sentence.

*You can avoid this error by (1) putting unrelated ideas in separate sentences, (2) subordinating an idea, or (3) adding words that show relationship.*

You can give unity to sentences that contain unrelated ideas in three basic ways: (1) You can put the ideas in separate sentences. (2) You can make one of the ideas subordinate to the other. (3) You can add words that show how

Modern executives often are extremely busy. They want and need their incoming messages to communicate easily and quickly.

60    PART 2    Fundamentals of Business Writing

the ideas are related. The first two of these techniques are illustrated by the revisions of this sentence:

Mr. Jordan is our sales manager, and he has a degree in law.

Perhaps the two ideas are related, but the words do not tell how. A better arrangement is to put each in a separate sentence:

Mr. Jordan is our sales manager. He has a law degree.

Or the two ideas could be kept in one sentence by subordinating one to the other. In this way, the main clause provides the unity of the sentence.

Mr. Jordan, our sales manager, has a law degree.

Adding words to show the relationship of ideas is illustrated in the revision of this example:

Our production increased in January, and our equipment is wearing out.

The sentence has two ideas that seem unrelated. One way of improving it is to make a separate sentence of each idea. A closer look reveals, however, that the two ideas really are related. The words just do not show how. Thus, the sentence could be revised to show how:

Even though our equipment is wearing out, our production increased in January.

The following contrasting pairs of sentences further illustrate the technique:

| UNRELATED | IMPROVED |
| --- | --- |
| Our territory is the southern half of the state, and our salespeople cannot cover it thoroughly. | Our territory is the southern half of the state. Our salespeople cannot cover it thoroughly. |
| Operation of the press is simple, but no machine will work well unless it is maintained. | Operation of the press is simple, but, like any machine, it will not work well unless it is maintained. |
| We concentrate on energy-saving products, and 70 percent of our business comes from them. | As a result of our concentration on energy-saving products, 70 percent of our business comes from them. |

**Excessive Detail.** Putting too much detail into one sentence tends to hide the central thought. If the detail is important, you should put it in a separate sentence.

This suggestion strengthens another given earlier in the chapter—the suggestion that you use short sentences. Obviously, short sentences cannot have much detail. Long sentences—full of detail—definitely lead to lack of unity, as illustrated in these contrasting examples:

> Excessive detail is another cause of lack of unity. If the detail is important, put it in a separate sentence. This means using short sentences.

| EXCESSIVE DETAIL | IMPROVED |
| --- | --- |
| Our New York offices, considered plush in the 1980s, but now badly in need of renovation, as is the case with most offices that have not been maintained, have been abandoned. | Considered plush in the 1980s, our New York offices have not been maintained properly. As they badly need repair, we have abandoned them. |

CHAPTER 3 Construction of Clear Sentences and Paragraphs

| EXCESSIVE DETAIL | IMPROVED |
|---|---|
| We have attempted to trace the Plytec insulation you ordered from us October 1, and about which you inquired in your October 10 letter, but we have not yet been able to locate it, although we are sending you a rush shipment immediately. | We are sending you a rush shipment of Plytec insulation immediately. Following your October 10 inquiry, we attempted to trace your October 1 order. We were unable to locate it. |
| In 1990, when I, a small-town girl from a middle-class family, began my studies at Darden University, which is widely recognized for its information systems program, I set my goal for a career with a major consulting firm. | A small-town girl from a middle-class family, I entered Darden University in 1990. I selected Darden because of its widely recognized information systems program. From the beginning, my goal was a career with a major consulting firm. |

*Illogical constructions can rob a sentence of unity.*

**Illogical Constructions.** Illogical constructions destroy sentence unity. These constructions result primarily from illogical thinking. Illogical thinking is too complex for meaningful study here, but a few typical examples should acquaint you with the possibilities. Then, by thinking logically, you should be able to reduce illogical constructions in your writing.

*Active and passive voice in the same sentence can violate unity.*

The first example contains two main thoughts in two correct clauses. But one clause is in active voice (*we cut*), and the other is in passive voice (*quality was reduced*).

First we cut prices, and then quality was reduced.

We achieve unity by making both clauses active, as in this example:

First we cut prices, and then we reduced quality.

*So can mixed constructions.*

The mixed constructions of the following sentence do not make a clear and logical thought. The technical explanation is that the beginning clause belongs with a complex sentence, while the last part is the predicate of a simple sentence.

Because our salespeople are inexperienced caused us to miss our quota.

Revised for good logic, the sentence might read:

The inexperience of our salespeople caused us to miss our quota.

These sentences further illustrate the point:

| ILLOGICAL CONSTRUCTION | IMPROVED |
|---|---|
| Job rotation is when you train people by moving them from job to job. | Job rotation is a training method in which people are moved from job to job. |
| Knowing that she objected to the price was the reason we permitted her to return the goods. | Because we knew she objected to the price, we permitted her to return the goods. |
| I never knew an executive who was interested in helping workers who had got into problems that caused them to worry. | I never knew an executive who was interested in helping worried workers with their problems. |
| My education was completed in 1992, and then I began work as a sales representative for Microsoft. | I completed my education in 1992, and then began work as a sales representative for Microsoft. |

**PART 2** Fundamentals of Business Writing

### Arranging Sentences for Clarity

As you know, various rules of grammar govern the structure of sentences. You know, for example, that modifying words must follow a definite sequence—that altering the sequence changes meaning. "A venetian blind" means one thing. "A blind Venetian" means quite another. Long-established rules of usage determine the meaning.

Many such rules exist. Established by centuries of use, these rules are not merely arbitrary requirements. Rather, they are based on custom and on logical relationships between words. In general, they are based on the need for clear communication.

Take the rule concerning dangling modifiers. Dangling modifiers confuse meaning by modifying the wrong words. On the surface, this sentence appears correct: "Believing that the price would drop, our purchasing agents were instructed not to buy." But the sentence is correct only if the purchasing agents did the believing—which is not the case. The modifying phrase dangles, and the intended meaning was probably this: "Believing that the price would drop, we instructed our purchasing agents not to buy."

Other rules of grammar also help to make writing clear. Unparallel constructions leave wrong impressions. Pronouns that do not clearly refer to a definite preceding word are vague and confusing. Subject-verb disagreements confuse the reader. The list goes on and on. The rules of grammar are useful in writing clear sentences. You should know them and follow them. You will want to study Chapter 21 for a review of these rules and complete the diagnostic exercise at the chapter end for feedback on your understanding of them.

*Clear writing requires that you follow the established rules of grammar.*

*These rules are based on custom and logical relationships.*

*For example, dangling modifiers confuse meaning.*

*So do unparallel constructions, pronouns without antecedents, and subject-verb disagreements.*

## CARE IN PARAGRAPH DESIGN

Paragraphing is also important to clear communication. Paragraphs show the reader where topics begin and end, thus helping organize information in the reader's mind. Paragraphs also help make ideas stand out.

How one should design paragraphs is hard to explain, for the procedure is largely mental. Designing paragraphs requires the ability to organize and relate information. It involves the use of logic and imagination. But we can say little that would help you in these activities. The best we can do is give the following points on paragraph structure.

*Paragraphing shows and emphasizes organization.*

*It involves logical thinking.*

### Giving the Paragraphs Unity

Like sentences, paragraphs should have unity. When applied to paragraph structure, unity means that a paragraph builds around a single topic or idea. Thus, everything you include in a paragraph should develop this topic or idea. When you have finished the paragraph, you should be able to say, "Everything in this paragraph belongs together because every part concerns every other part."

Unity is not always easy to determine. As all of a letter or a report may concern a single topic, one could say that the whole letter or report has unity. One could say the same about a major division of a report or a long paper. Obviously, paragraph unity concerns smaller units than these. Generally, it concerns the next largest unit of thought above a sentence.

*The contents of a paragraph should concern one topic or idea (unity).*

*But unity can vary in breadth. Paragraph unity concerns a narrow topic.*

A violation of unity is illustrated in the following paragraph from an application letter. As the goal of the paragraph is to summarize the applicant's coursework, all the sentences should pertain to coursework. By shifting to personal qualities, the third sentence violates paragraph unity. Taking this sentence out would correct the fault.

> At the university I studied all the basic accounting courses as well as specialized courses in petroleum, fiduciary, and systems. I also took specialized coursework in the behavioral areas, with emphasis on human relations. Realizing the value of human relations in business, I also actively participated in organizations, such as Sigma Nu (social fraternity), Delta Sigma Pi (professional fraternity), YMCA, and Men's Glee Club. I selected my elective coursework to round out my general business education. Among my electives were courses in investments, advanced business report writing, financial policy, and management information systems. A glance at my résumé will show you the additional courses that round out my training.

## Keeping Paragraphs Short

*Generally, paragraphs should be short.*

As a general rule, you should keep your paragraphs short. This suggestion overlaps the suggestion about unity, for if your paragraphs have unity, they will be short.

*Short paragraphs show organization better than long ones.*

As noted earlier, paragraphs help the reader follow the writer's organization plan. Writing marked by short paragraphs identifies more of the details of that plan. In addition, such writing is inviting to the eye. People simply prefer to read writing with frequent paragraph breaks.

*Most readers prefer to read short paragraphs.*

This last point is easily proved by illustration. Assume that you have a choice of reading either of two business reports on the same subject. One report has long paragraphs. Its pages appear solid with type. The second report has short paragraphs and thus provides frequent rest stops. You can see the rest stops at first glance. Now, which would you choose? No doubt, you would prefer the report with short paragraphs. It is more inviting, and it appears less difficult. Perhaps the difference is largely psychological, but it is a very real difference.

*About eight lines is a good average length.*

How long a paragraph should be depends on its contents—on what must be included to achieve unity. Readability research has suggested an average length of eight lines for longer papers such as reports. Shorter paragraphs are appropriate for letters.

*But length can and should vary with need.*

Keep in mind that these suggestions concern only an average. Some good paragraphs may be quite long—well over the average. Some paragraphs can be very short—as short as one line. One-line paragraphs are an especially appropriate means of emphasizing major points in business letters. A one-line paragraph may be all that is needed for a goodwill closing comment.

*A good practice is to question paragraphs over 12 lines.*

A good rule to follow is to question the unity of all long paragraphs—say, those longer than 12 lines. If after looking over such a paragraph you conclude that it has unity, leave it as it is. But you will sometimes find more than one topic. When you do, make each topic into a separate paragraph.

## Making Good Use of Topic Sentences

One good way of organizing paragraphs is to use topic sentences. The topic sentence expresses the main idea of a paragraph, and the remaining sentences build around and support it. In a sense, the topic sentence serves as a

PART 2  Fundamentals of Business Writing

headline for the paragraph, and all the other sentences supply the story. Not every paragraph must have a topic sentence. Some paragraphs, for example, introduce ideas, relate succeeding items, or present an assortment of facts that lead to no conclusion. The central thought of such paragraphs is difficult to put into a single sentence. Even so, you should use topic sentences whenever you can. You should use them especially in writing reports that discuss a number of topics and subtopics. Using topic sentences forces you to find the central idea of each paragraph and helps you check paragraph unity.

*Topic sentences can help make good paragraphs. But not every paragraph must have a topic sentence.*

How a topic sentence should fit into a paragraph depends primarily on the subject matter and the writer's plan. Some subject matter develops best if details are presented first and then followed by a conclusion or a summary statement (the topic sentence). Other subject matter develops best if it is introduced by the conclusion or the summary statement. Yet other arrangements are possible. You must make the decision, and you should base it on your best judgment. Your judgment should be helped, however, by a knowledge of the paragraph arrangements most commonly used.

*Placement of the topic sentence depends on the writer's plan.*

**Topic Sentence First.** The most common paragraph arrangement begins with the topic sentence and continues with the supporting material. As this arrangement fits most units of business information, you should find it useful. In fact, the arrangement is so appropriate for business information that one company's writing manual suggests that it be used for virtually all paragraphs.

*The topic sentence can come first.*

To illustrate the writing of a paragraph in which the topic sentence comes first, take a paragraph reporting on economists' replies to a survey question asking their view of business activity for the coming year. The facts to be presented are these: 13 percent of the economists expected an increase; 28 percent expected little or no change; 59 percent expected a downturn; 87 percent of those who expected a downturn thought it would come in the first quarter. The obvious conclusion—and the subject for the topic sentence—is that the majority expected a decline in the first quarter. Following this reasoning, we would develop a paragraph like this:

*A majority of the economists consulted think that business activity will drop during the first quarter of next year. Of the 185 economists interviewed, 13 percent looked for continued increases in business activity, and 28 percent anticipated little or no change from the present high level. The remaining 59 percent looked for a recession. Of this group, nearly all (87 percent) believed that the downturn would occur during the first quarter of the year.*

**Topic Sentence at End.** The second most common paragraph arrangement places the topic sentence at the end, usually as a conclusion. Paragraphs of this kind usually present the supporting details first, and from these details they lead readers to the conclusion. Such paragraphs often begin with what may appear to be a topic sentence. But the final sentence covers their real meat, as in this illustration:

*It can come last.*

The significant role of inventories in the economic picture should not be overlooked. At present, inventories represent 3.8 months' supply. Their dollar value is the highest in history. If considered in relation to increased sales, however, they are not excessive. In fact, they are well within the range generally believed to be safe. *Thus, inventories are not likely to cause a downward swing in the economy.*

CHAPTER 3 Construction of Clear Sentences and Paragraphs

*Or it can come in the middle.*

**Topic Sentence within the Paragraph.** A third arrangement places the topic sentence somewhere within the paragraph. This arrangement is rarely used, for good reason. It does not emphasize the topic sentence, although the topic sentence usually deserves emphasis. Still, you can sometimes justify using this arrangement for special effect, as in this example:

> Numerous materials have been used in manufacturing this part. And many have shown quite satisfactory results. *Material 329, however, is superior to them all.* When built with material 329, the part is almost twice as strong as when built with the next best material. It is also 3 ounces lighter. Most important, it is cheaper than any of the other products.

### Leaving out Unnecessary Detail

*In writing paragraphs, leave out unnecessary information.*

You should include in your paragraphs only the information needed. The chances are that you have more information than the reader needs. Thus, a part of your communication task is to select what you need and discard what you do not need.

*But deciding what to include is a matter of judgment.*

What you need, of course, is a matter of judgment. You can judge best by putting yourself in your reader's place. Ask yourself questions such as these: How will the information be used? What information will be used? What will not be used? Then make your decisions. If you follow this procedure, you will probably leave out much that you originally intended to use.

The following paragraph from a memorandum to maintenance workers presents excessive information.

> In reviewing the personnel history form you filled out last week, I found an error that needs to be corrected. The section titled "work history" has blank lines for three items of information. The first is for dates employed. The second is for company name. And the third is for type of work performed. On your form you wrote company name only, and it extended across all three blanks. You did not indicate years employed or your duties. This information is important. It is reviewed by your supervisors every time you are considered for promotion or for a pay increase. Therefore, it must be completed. I request that you come by my office and complete this form at your earliest convenience.

The message says much more than the reader needs to know. The goal is to have the reader come to the office, and everything else is of questionable

### Uniqueness and Clarity in a Definition

Written by a fifth grader, the following definition of a nut and bolt is a classic:

> A bolt is a thing like a stick of hard metal, such as iron, with a square bunch on one end and a lot of scratches going round and round the other end. A nut is similar to the bolt only just the opposite, being a hole in a little square sawed off short with rings also around the inside of the hole.

value. Even if some explanation is desirable, would it not be better to explain at the office? This revised memorandum is better:

Please come by my office at your earliest convenience to correct an error in the personnel form you filled out last week.

### Giving the Paragraphs Movement

Good writing has movement. Movement is the writing quality that takes the reader toward the goal in definite and logical steps, without side trips and backward shifts. The progress is steadily forward—step by step. The sentences move step by step to reach the paragraph goal, and the paragraphs move step by step to reach the overall goal.

Perhaps movement is best explained by example:

> Each paragraph should move an additional step toward the goal.

Three reasons justify moving from the Crowton site. First, the building rock in the Crowton area is questionable. The failure of recent geologic explorations in the area appears to confirm suspicions that the Crowton deposits are nearly exhausted. Second, the distances from the Crowton site to major consumption areas make transportation costs unusually high. Obviously, any savings in transportation costs will add to company profits. Third, the obsolescence of much of the equipment at the Crowton plant makes this an ideal time for relocation. The old equipment at the Crowton plant could be scrapped.

The flow of thought in this paragraph is orderly. The first sentence sets up the paragraph structure, and the parts of that structure follow.

### SUMMARY (by Chapter Objectives)

1. Writing that communicates uses words that the reader understands and sentence structures that organize the message clearly in the reader's mind. It is writing that is *adapted* to the reader.

   > 1. Explain the role of adaptation in writing clear sentences.

2. In general, you should use short sentences, especially when adapting to readers with low reading ability. Do this in two ways:
   - Limit sentence content by breaking up those that are too long.
   - Use words economically by following these specific suggestions:
     — Avoid cluttering phrases (*if* rather than *in the event that*).
     — Eliminate surplus words—words that contribute nothing (*It will be noted that*).
     — Avoid roundabout ways of saying things (*decreases* rather than *can be observed to be decreasing*.
     — Avoid unnecessary repetition (*In my opinion, I think*).

   > 2. Write short, clear sentences by limiting sentence content and economizing on words.

3. Give every item you communicate the emphasis it deserves by following these suggestions:
   - Use short sentences to emphasize points.
   - Combine points in longer sentences to de-emphasize them.
   - But how you combine points (by equal treatment, by subordination) determines the emphasis given.

   > 3. Design sentences that give the right emphasis to content.

**CHAPTER 3** Construction of Clear Sentences and Paragraphs

| | |
|---|---|
| **4. Employ unity and clarity in writing effective sentences.** | 4. Achieve unity and clarity in your sentences.<br>• Make certain all the information in a sentence belongs together—that it forms a unit. These suggestions help:<br>　—Eliminate excessive detail.<br>　—Combine only related thoughts.<br>　—Avoid illogical constructions.<br>• Ensure clarity by following the conventional rules of writing (standards of punctuation, grammar, and such). |
| **5. Compose paragraphs that are short, unified, use topic sentences effectively, show movement, and communicate clearly.** | 5. Design your paragraphs for clear communication by following these standards:<br>• Give the paragraphs unity.<br>• Keep the paragraphs short.<br>• Use topic sentences effectively, usually at the beginning but sometimes within and at end of the paragraph.<br>• Leave out unessential details.<br>• Give the paragraphs movement. |

## QUESTIONS FOR DISCUSSION

1. How are sentence length and sentence design related to adaptation?
2. Discuss this comment: "Long, involved sentences tend to be difficult to understand. Therefore, the shorter the sentence, the better."
3. What is the effect of sentence length on emphasis?
4. How can unity apply equally well to a sentence, to a paragraph, and to longer units of writing?
5. What are the principal causes of lack of unity in sentences?
6. Discuss this comment: "Words carry the message. They would carry the same meanings with or without paragraphing. Therefore, paragraphing has no effect on communication."
7. Defend the use of short paragraphs in report writing.
8. "Topic sentences merely repeat what the other sentences in the paragraph say. As they serve only to add length, they should be eliminated." Discuss.

## APPLICATION EXERCISES

Instructions, Sentences 1–8: Break up these sentences into shorter, more readable sentences.

1. Records were set by both the New York Stock Exchange Composite Index, which closed at 229.27, up 1.65 points, topping its previous high of 227.62, set Wednesday, and Standard & Poor's Industrial Average, which finished at 412.61, up 2.20, smashing its all-time record of 410.41, also set in the prior session.
2. Dealers attributed the rate decline to several factors, including expectations that the U.S. Treasury will choose to pay off rather than refinance some $4 billion of government obligations that fall due next month, an action that would absorb even further the available supplies of short-term government securities, leaving more funds chasing skimpier stocks of the securities.
3. If you report your income on a fiscal-year basis ending in 1993, you may not take credit for any tax withheld on your calendar-year 1993 earnings, inasmuch as your taxable year began in 1992, although you may include, as a part of your withholding tax credits against your fiscal 1994 tax liability, the amount of tax withheld during 1993.
4. The Consumer Education Committee is assigned the duties of keeping informed of the qualities of all consumer goods and services, especially of their strengths and shortcomings, of gathering all pertinent information on dealers' sales practices, with emphasis on practices involving honest and reasonable fairness, and of publicizing any of the information collected that may be helpful in educating the consumer.
5. The upswing in business activity that began in 1993 is expected to continue and possibly accelerate in 1994, and gross domestic product should rise by $65 billion, representing an 8 percent increase over 1993, which is significantly higher than the modest 0.05 percent increase of 1992.
6. As you will not get this part of medicare automatically, even if you are covered by social security, you must sign up for it and pay $7.75 per month, which the government will match, if you want your physician's bills to be covered.
7. Students with approved excused absences from any of the hour examinations have the option of taking a special makeup examination to be given during dead week or of using their average grade on their examinations in the course as their grade for the work missed.
8. Although we have not definitely determined the causes for the decline in sales volume for the month, we know that during this period construction on the street adjacent to the store severely limited traffic flow and that because of resignations in the advertising department promotion efforts dropped well below normal.

Instructions, Sentences 9–38: Revise the following sentences for more economical wording.

9. In view of the fact that we financed the experiment, we were entitled to some profit.
10. We will deliver the goods in the near future.
11. Mr. Watts outlined his development plans on the occasion of his acceptance of the presidency.
12. I will talk to him with regard to the new policy.
13. The candidates who had the most money won.

CHAPTER 3  Construction of Clear Sentences and Paragraphs

14. There are many obligations that we must meet.
15. We purchased coats that are lined with wolf fur.
16. Mary is of the conviction that service has improved.
17. Sales can be detected to have improved over last year.
18. It is essential that we take the actions that are necessary to correct the problem.
19. The chairperson is engaged in the activities of preparing the program.
20. Martin is engaged in the process of revising the application.
21. You should study all new innovations in your field.
22. In all probability, we are likely to suffer a loss this quarter.
23. The requirements for the job require a minimum of three years of experience.
24. In spite of the fact that the bill remains unpaid, they placed another order.
25. We expect to deliver the goods in the event that we receive the money.
26. In accordance with their plans, company officials sold the machinery.
27. This policy exists for the purpose of preventing dishonesty.
28. The salespeople who were most successful received the best rewards.
29. The reader will note that this area ranks in the top 5 percent in per capita income.
30. Our new coats are made of a fabric that is of the water-repellent variety.
31. Our office is charged with the task of counting supplies not used in production.
32. Their salespeople are of the conviction that service is obsolete.
33. Losses caused by the strike exceeded the amount of $14,000.
34. This condition can be assumed to be critical.
35. Our goal is to effect a change concerning the overtime pay rate.
36. Mr. Wilson replaced the old antiquated machinery with new machinery.
37. We must keep this information from transpiring to others.
38. The consensus of opinion of this group is that Wellington was wrong.

Instructions, Paragraphs 39–43: Rewrite the following paragraphs in two ways to show different placement of the topic sentence and variations in emphasis of contents. Point out the differences in meaning in each of your paragraphs.

39. Jennifer has a good knowledge of office procedure. She works hard. She has performed her job well. She is pleasant most of the time, but she has a bad temper, which has led to many personal problems with the work group. Although I cannot recommend her for promotion, I approve a 10 percent raise for her.
40. Last year our sales increased 7 percent in California and 9 percent in Arizona. Nevada had the highest increase, with 14 percent. Although all states in the western region enjoyed increases, Oregon recorded only a 2 percent gain. Sales in Washington increased 3 percent.
41. I majored in marketing at Darden University and received a B.S. degree in 1993. Among the marketing courses I took were marketing strategy, promotion, marketing research, marketing management, and consumer behavior. These and other courses prepared me specifically for a career in retailing. Included, also, was a one-semester internship in retailing with Olympic Department Stores.
42. Our records show that Penn motors cost more than Oslo motors. The Penns have less breakdown time. They cost more to repair. I recommend that we buy Penn motors the next time we replace worn-out motors. The longer working life offsets Penn's cost disadvantage. So does its better record for breakdown.
43. Recently China ordered a large quantity of wheat from the United States. Likewise, Germany ordered a large quantity. Other countries continued to order heavily, resulting in a dramatic improvement in the outlook for wheat farming. Increased demand by Eastern European countries also contributed to the improved outlook.

# CHAPTER 4

# WRITING FOR EFFECT

## CHAPTER OBJECTIVES

*Upon completing this chapter, you will be able to write business communications that emphasize key points and have a positive effect on human relations. To reach this goal, you should be able to*

**1**

Explain the need for effect in writing business letters.

**2**

Use a conversational style that eliminates the old language of business and "rubber stamps."

**3**

Use the you-viewpoint to foster goodwill in letters.

**4**

Employ positive language to achieve goodwill and other desired effects.

**5**

Explain the techniques of achieving courtesy in letters.

**6**

Use the four major techniques for emphasis in writing.

**7**

Write letters that flow smoothly through the use of a logical order helped by the four major transitional devices.

## INTRODUCTORY SITUATION

### Affecting Human Relations through Writing

To prepare yourself for this chapter, once again play the role of Mabel Schlitz's supervisor. As you review Mabel's work, you note that she writes more than reports. Like many people in office positions, she writes more letters than anything else.

The fact that she writes many letters causes you to think. What if she writes letters the way she writes reports? Letters go outside the company and are read by customers, fellow businesspeople, and others. Because poorly written letters would give bad impressions of the company, you decide to review Mabel's letters. Typical of what you find is this letter denying a request for an adjustment:

Dear Mr. Morley:

Your Dec. 3d complaint was received and contents noted. After reviewing the facts, I regret to report that I must refuse your claim. If you will read the warranty brochure, you will see that the shelving you bought is designed for light loads—a maximum of 800 pounds. You should have bought the heavy-duty product.

I regret the damage this mistake caused you and trust that you will see our position. Hoping to be of service to you in the future, I remain,

Sincerely yours,

In this letter, you detect more than just the readability problem you saw in Mabel's reports. You see problems of human relations. The words appear tactless, unfriendly, and lacking in warmth and understanding. Overall, they leave a bad impression in the reader's mind.

Clearly, Mabel needs to know more about letter writing. What specifically does she need to know? The answer is the subject of this chapter. ■

## NEED FOR EFFECT

As noted in the preceding chapters, clarity will be your major concern in much of the writing you will do in business. It will be your major concern in most of the writing you will do to communicate within the organization—reports, memorandums, procedures, proposals, and so on. In such writing, your primary concern will be to communicate information. Whatever you do to communicate information quickly and easily will be appropriate.

*Written communication within a business primarily requires clarity.*

When you write letters, however, you will be concerned about communicating more than information. The information in the letters will be important, of course. In fact, it will probably be the most important part. But you will also need to communicate certain effects.

*Letter writing requires clarity and planned effect. The goodwill effect is valuable to business.*

One effect that you will need to communicate is the goodwill effect. Building goodwill through letters is good business practice. Wise business leaders know that the success of their businesses is affected by what people think about the businesses. They know that what people think about businesses is influenced by their human contact with the businesses and that letters are a major form of human contact.

**CHAPTER 4** Writing for Effect   73

*Most people enjoy building goodwill.*

The goodwill effect in letters is not desirable for business reasons alone. It is, quite simply, the effect most of us want in our relations with people. The things we do and say to create goodwill are the things we enjoy doing and saying. They are friendly, courteous things that make relations between people enjoyable. Most of us would want to do and say them even if they were not profitable.

*For their success, letters often require other effects.*

As you read the following chapters, you will see that other effects sometimes ensure the success of letters. For example, in writing to persuade a reader to accept an unfavorable decision, you can use the techniques of persuasion. In applying for a job, you can use writing techniques that emphasize your qualifications. And in telling bad news, you can use techniques that play down the unhappy parts. These are but a few of the effects that you may find helpful in letter writing.

*Getting the desired effects is a matter of writing skill and of understanding people.*

Getting such effects in letters is largely a matter of skillful writing and of understanding how people respond to words. It involves keeping certain attitudes in mind and using certain writing techniques to work them into your letters. The following review of these attitudes and techniques should help you get the effects you need.

## CONVERSATIONAL STYLE

*Writing in conversational language has a favorable effect.*

One technique that helps build the goodwill effect in letters is to write in conversational language. By conversational language we mean language that resembles conversation. It is warm and natural. Such language leaves an impression that people like. It is also the language we use most and understand best.

### Resisting Tendency to Be Formal

*Writing in conversational language is not easy, for we tend to be stiff and formal.*

Writing conversationally is not so easy as you might think, because most of us tend to write formally. When faced with a writing task, we change character. Instead of writing in friendly, conversational language, we write in stiff and stilted words. We seek the big word, the difficult word. The result is a cold and unnatural style—one that doesn't produce the goodwill effect you want your letters to have. The following examples illustrate this problem and how to correct it.

**STIFF AND DULL**

Reference is made to your May 7 letter, in which you describe the approved procedure for initiating a claim.

Enclosed herewith is the brochure about which you make inquiry.

In reply to your July 11 letter, please be informed that your adherence to instructions outlined therein will greatly facilitate attainment of our objective.

**CONVERSATIONAL**

Please refer to your May 7 letter, in which you tell how to file a claim.

Enclosed is the brochure you asked about.

By following the procedures you listed in your July 11 letter, you will help us reach our goal.

**PART 2** Fundamentals of Business Writing

### STIFF AND DULL

This is in reply to your letter of December 1, expressing concern that you do not have a high school diploma and asking if a Certificate of Attainment would suffice as prerequisite for the TAA Training Program.

I shall be most pleased to avail myself of your kind suggestion when and if prices decline.

### CONVERSATIONAL

The Certificate of Attainment you mention in your December 1 letter qualifies you for the TAA Training Program.

I'll gladly follow your suggestion if the price falls.

## Avoiding the Old Language of Business

Adding to our natural difficulty in writing business letters conversationally are some deep-rooted historical influences. Unfortunately, the early English business writers borrowed heavily from the formal language of the law and from the flowery language of the nobility. From these two sources they developed a style of letter writing that became known as the "language of business." It was a cold, stiff, and unnatural style. But it was generally accepted throughout the English-speaking world. The following expressions typify this style:

*The early English business writers developed an unnatural style for letters. This "language of business" was influenced by legal language and the language of the nobility.*

### IN OPENINGS
Your letter of the 7th inst. received and contents duly noted

We beg to advise

### IN CONTENTS
Please be advised

Said matter

In due course

### IN CLOSINGS
Thanking you in advance

Trusting this will meet with your favor

---

### A Poem: The Old Language of Business

We beg to advise and wish to state

That yours has arrived of recent date.

We have it before us, its contents noted.

Herewith enclosed, the prices we quoted.

Regarding the matter, and due to the fact

That up until now your order we've lacked,

We hope you will not delay it unduly

And beg to remain yours very truly,

*Anonymous*

CHAPTER 4  Writing for Effect

| IN OPENINGS | IN CONTENTS | IN CLOSINGS |
|---|---|---|
| In compliance with yours of even date | Inst., prox., ult. | We beg to remain |
| Your esteemed favor at hand | Kind favor | Anticipating your favorable response |
| This is to inform you | Kind order | Assuring you of our cooperation |
| We have before us | Re: | Hoping to receive |
| Responding to yours of even date | In re | I am, Dear Sir, yours respectfully |
| Yours of the 10th ultimo to hand | Said matter | Trusting to be favored by your further orders, we are, Gentlemen, yours faithfully |
| Your favor received | Deem it advisable | |
| | Wherein you state as per our letter | |
| | In reply wish to state | |
| | Attached hereto | |

*This style reached a peak in the late 1800s. "Yours of the 7th inst. received and contents duly noted" typifies this manner of writing.*

This style of writing business letters reached a peak in the late 1800s, and it was still in much use in the early years of this century. A typical business letter of this period would begin something like this: "Yours of the 7th inst. received and contents duly noted. In reply wish to state. . . ." It would end something like this: "Hoping to hear from you at your earliest convenience, I remain, Yours Sincerely. . . ." The text between these parts would be equally stiff and unnatural. Further illustrating writing in the old language of business is this model letter from a leading letter book of the day:

Gentlemen,

    We have to thank you for yours of the 28th inst., enclosing cheque for $95.12 in payment of our invoice of the 17th inst. Formal receipt enclosed herewith. Trusting to be favored with your further orders,

                      We are, Gentlemen,
                      Yours faithfully,[1]

*The old language of business has faded away, but some of its expressions remain (please be advised, enclosed please find). Do not use them.*

Although the old language of business has faded away, some of its expressions remain with us. These include "enclosed please find," "please be advised," "this is to inform," "deem it advisable," and "take the liberty." You should not use them. Perhaps the most common remnants of the old language of business are the dangling closes (endings that trail off into the signature). Typical examples are "trusting to hear from you," "thanking you in advance, I remain," and "hoping to hear from you." These closes may express sincere feeling, but they belong to the past. You should leave them there.

## Cutting Out "Rubber Stamps"

*Rubber stamps are expressions used by habit every time a certain type of situation occurs.*

Rubber stamps (also called *clichés*) are expressions used by habit every time a certain type of situation occurs. They are used without thought and do not fit the present situation exclusively. As the term indicates, they are used much as you would use a rubber stamp.

---

[1] *Pitman's Mercantile Correspondence* (London: Sir Isaac Pitman & Sons, n.d.), p. 18.

PART 2   Fundamentals of Business Writing

### Grammar and Style Checkers: Tools for Identifying Rubber Stamps

Grammar and style checkers will catch some of those rubber stamps or clichés that creep into our writing. While they often seem appropriate for the context, rubber stamps usually cause readers to believe you are indifferent toward them. You will appear much more sincere to your readers by eliminating the clichés and replacing them with wording for the particular situation.

The phrases shown in the examples in this chapter were run through one popular grammar and style checking program. As you can see below, the grammar and style checker identified most of them as either clichés or colloquial expressions.

```
a blessing in disguise
as good as gold
    <<*S16.CLICHE: good as gold*>>
back against the wall
call the shots
    <<*U1.COLLOQUIAL: call the shots*>>
last but not least
    <<*S16.CLICHE: last but not least*>>
learning the ropes
    <<*S16.CLICHE: learning the ropes*>>
leave no stone unturned
    <<*S16.CLICHE: stone unturned*>>
to add insult to injury
    <<*S16.CLICHE: add insult to injury*>>
```

Although you can see that the programs can help, you still need to be able to identify the ones the software misses. Also, you will need to be able to recast the sentences to let your readers know you are sincere.

---

Because they are used routinely, rubber stamps communicate the effect of routine treatment, which is not likely to impress readers favorably. Such treatment tells readers that the writer has no special concern for them—that the present case is being handled in the same way as others. In contrast, words specially selected for this case are likely to impress. They show the writer's concern for and interest in the readers. Clearly, specially selected wording is the better choice for producing a goodwill effect. Some examples of rubber stamps you have no doubt heard before are listed below. These phrases, while once quite appropriate, have become stale with overuse.

*They give the effect of routine treatment. It is better to use words written for the present case.*

a blessing in disguise
as good as gold
back against the wall
call the shots
last but not least
learning the ropes
leave no stone unturned
to add insult to injury

Expressions from the old language of business account for many of the rubber stamps now in use. But modern business writers have developed

**Expressions from the old language of business are rubber stamps. Some new ones exist.**

many more. A widely used one is the "thank you for your letter" form of opening sentence. Its intent may be sincere, but its overuse makes it routine. Also overused is the "if I can be of any further assistance, do not hesitate to call on me" type of close. Other examples of modern business-letter rubber stamps are the following:

I am happy to be able to answer your letter.
I have received your letter.
This will acknowledge receipt of . . .
According to our records . . .
This is to inform you that . . .
In accordance with your instructions . . .

**You can avoid rubber stamps by writing in your conversational vocabulary.**

You do not need to know all the rubber stamps to stop using them. You do not even need to be able to recognize them. You only need to write in the language of good conversation, for these worn-out expressions are not a part of most conversational vocabularies. If you use rubber stamps at all, you learned them from reading other people's letters. You did not learn them from oral communication experiences.

### Proof through Contrasting Examples

The advantages of conversational writing over writing marked by old business language and rubber stamps are best proved by example. As you read the following contrasting sentences, note the overall effects of the words. The goodwill advantages of conversational writing are obvious.

In face-to-face oral communication, words, voice, facial expressions, gestures, and such combine to determine the effect of the message. In writing, the printed word alone must do the job.

| DULL AND STIFF | FRIENDLY AND CONVERSATIONAL |
|---|---|
| This is to advise that we deem it a great pleasure to approve subject of your request as per letter of the 12th inst. | Yes, you certainly may use the equipment you asked about in your letter of August 12. |
| Pursuant to this matter, I wish to state that the aforementioned provisions are unmistakably clear. | These contract provisions are clear on this point. |
| This will acknowledge receipt of your May 10th order for four dozen Hunt slacks. Please be advised that they will be shipped in accordance with your instructions by Green Arrow Motor Freight on May 16. | Four dozen Hunt slacks should reach your store by the 18th. As you instructed, they were shipped today by Green Arrow Motor Freight. |
| The undersigned wishes to advise that the aforementioned contract is at hand. | I have the contract. |
| Please be advised that you should sign the form before the 1st. | You should sign the form before the 1st. |
| Hoping this meets with your approval . . . | I hope you approve. |
| Submitted herewith is your notification of our compliance with subject standards. | Attached is notification of our compliance with the standards. |
| Assuring you of our continued cooperation, we remain . . . | We will continue to cooperate. |
| Thanking you in advance . . . | I'll sincerely appreciate . . . |
| Herewith enclosed please find . . . | Enclosed is . . . |
| I deem it advisable . . . | I suggest . . . |
| I herewith hand you . . . | Here is . . . |
| Kindly advise at an early date. | Please let me know soon. |

## YOU-VIEWPOINT

Writing from the you-viewpoint (also called *you-attitude*) is another technique for building goodwill in letters. As you will see in following chapters, it focuses interest on the reader. Thus, it is a technique for persuasion and for influencing people favorably.

In a broad sense, you-viewpoint writing emphasizes the reader's interests and concerns. It emphasizes *you* and *your* and de-emphasizes *we* and *our*. But it is more than a matter of just using second person pronouns. *You* and *your* can appear prominently in sentences that emphasize the we-viewpoint, as in this example: "If you do not pay by the 15th, you must pay a penalty." Likewise, *we* and *mine* can appear in sentences that emphasize the you-viewpoint, as in this example: "We will do whatever we can to protect your investment." The point is that the you-viewpoint is an attitude of mind. It is the attitude that places the reader in the center of things. Sometimes it just involves being friendly and treating people in the way they like to be treated.

*The you-viewpoint produces goodwill and influences people favorably.*

*The you-viewpoint emphasizes the reader's interests. It is an attitude of mind involving more than the use of you and yours.*

CHAPTER 4 Writing for Effect

Sometimes it involves skillfully handling people with carefully chosen words to make a desired impression. It involves all these things and more.

## The You-Viewpoint Illustrated

Although the you-viewpoint involves much more than word selection, examples of word selection help explain the technique. First, take the case of a person writing a letter to present good news. This person could write from a self-centered point of view, beginning with such words as "I am happy to report. . . ." Or he or she could begin with the you-viewpoint words "You will be happy to know. . . ." The messages are much the same, but the effects are different.

Next, take the case of a writer who must inform the reader that a request for credit has been approved. A we-viewpoint beginning could take this form: "We are pleased to have your new account." Some readers might view these words favorably. But some would sense a self-centered writer concerned primarily with making money. A you-viewpoint beginning would go something like this: "Your new charge account is now open for your convenience."

The third case is that of an advertising copywriter who must describe the merits of a razor. Now, advertising copywriters know the value of the you-viewpoint perhaps better than any other group. So no advertising copywriter would write anything like this: "We make Willett razors in three weights—light, medium, and heavy." An advertising copywriter would probably bring the reader into the center of things and write about the product in reader-satisfaction language: "So that you can choose the one razor that is just right for your beard, Willett makes razors for you in three weights—light, medium, and heavy."

*Even a bad-news situation can benefit from you-viewpoint wording.*

The you-viewpoint can even be used in bad-news messages. For example, take the case of an executive who must write a letter saying no to a professor's request for help on a research project. The bad news is made especially bad when it is presented in we-viewpoint words: "We cannot comply with your request to use our office personnel on your project, for it would cost us more than we can afford." A skilled writer using the you-viewpoint would look at the situation from this reader's point of view, find an explanation likely to satisfy this reader, and present the explanation in you-viewpoint language. The you-viewpoint response might take this form: "As a business professor well acquainted with the need for economizing in all phases of office operations, you will understand why we must limit our personnel to work in our office."

The following contrasting examples demonstrate the different effects that changes in viewpoint produce. With a bit of imagination, you should be able to supply information on the situations they cover.

| WE-VIEWPOINT | YOU-VIEWPOINT |
|---|---|
| We are happy to have your order for Kopper products, which we are sending today by Mercury Freight. | Your selection of Kopper products should reach you by Saturday, as they were shipped by Mercury Freight today. |
| We sell the Forever cutlery set for the low price of $4 each and suggest a retail price of $6.50. | You can reap a $2.50 profit on each Forever set you sell at $6.50, for your cost is only $4. |

**PART 2** Fundamentals of Business Writing

| WE-VIEWPOINT | YOU-VIEWPOINT |
|---|---|
| Our policy prohibits us from permitting outside groups to use our equipment except on a cash-rental basis. | As your tax dollar pays our office expense, you will appreciate our policy of cutting operating costs by renting our equipment. |
| We have been quite tolerant of your past-due account and must now demand payment. | If you are to continue to enjoy the benefits of credit buying, you must clear your account now. |
| We have received your report of May 1. | Thank you for your report of May 1. |
| So that we may complete our file records on you, we ask that you submit to us your January report. | So that your file records may be completed, please send us your January report. |
| We have shipped the two dozen Crown desk sets you ordered. | Your two dozen Crown desk sets should reach you with this letter. |
| We require that you sign the sales slip before we will charge to your account. | For your protection, you are charged only after you have signed the sales slip. |

## *A Point of Controversy*

The you-viewpoint has been a matter of some controversy. Its critics point out two major shortcomings: (1) it is insincere and (2) it is manipulative. In either event, they argue, the technique is dishonest. It is better, they say, to just "tell it as it is."

<aside>Some say that the you-viewpoint is insincere and manipulative. It can be insincere, but it need not be. Using the you-viewpoint is just being courteous. Research supports its use.</aside>

These arguments have some merit. Without question, the you-viewpoint can be used to the point of being insincere; and it can be obvious flattery. Those who favor the technique argue that insincerity and flattery need not—in fact, should not—be the result of you-viewpoint effort. The objective is to treat people courteously—the way they like to be treated. People like to be singled out for attention. They are naturally more interested in themselves than in the writer. Overuse of the technique, the defenders argue, does not justify not using it. Their argument is supported by research showing that a majority of personality types, especially the friendlier and more sensitive, react favorably to you-viewpoint treatment.[2] A minority, mainly the less sensitive and harsher personalities, are less susceptible.

On the matter of manipulative use of the you-viewpoint, we must again concede a point. It is a technique of persuasion, and persuasion may have bad as well as good goals. Supporters of the you-viewpoint argue that it is bad goals and not the techniques used to reach them that should be condemned. Persuasion techniques used to reach good goals are good.

<aside>The you-viewpoint can manipulate. But condemn the goal, not the technique.</aside>

The correct approach appears to lie somewhere between the extremes. You do not have to use the you-viewpoint exclusively or to eliminate it. You can take a middle ground. You can use the you-viewpoint when it is friendly and sincere and when your goals are good. In such cases, using the you-viewpoint is "telling it as it is"—or at least as it should be. With this position in mind, we apply the technique in the following chapters.

<aside>A middle-ground approach is best. Use the you-viewpoint when it is the right thing to do.</aside>

---

[2] Sam J. Bruno, "The Effects of Personality Traits on the Perception of Written Mass Communication," doctoral dissertation, Louisiana State University, Baton Rouge, 1971.

## ACCENT ON POSITIVE LANGUAGE

Of the many ways of saying anything, each has a unique meaning.

Whether your letter achieves its goal will often depend on the words you use. As you know, one can say anything in many ways, and each way conveys a different meaning. Much of the difference lies in the meanings of words.

### Effects of Words

Positive words are usually best for letter goals, especially when persuasion and goodwill are needed.

Positive words are usually best for achieving your letter goals. This is not to say that negative words have no place in business writing. Such words are strong and give emphasis, and you will sometimes want to use them. But your need will usually be for positive words, for such words are more likely to produce the effects you seek. When your goal is to change someone's position, for example, positive words are most likely to do the job. They tend to put the reader in the right frame of mind, and they emphasize the pleasant aspects of the goal. They also create the goodwill atmosphere we seek in most letters.

Negative words stir up resistance and hurt goodwill.

Negative words tend to produce the opposite effects. They may stir up your reader's resistance to your goals, and they are likely to be highly destructive of goodwill. Thus, to reach your letter-writing goals, you will need to study carefully the negativeness and positiveness of your words. You will need to select the words that are most appropriate in each case.

So beware of strongly negative words (*mistake, problem*), words that deny (*no, do not*), and ugly words (*itch, guts*).

In doing this you should generally be wary of strongly negative words. These words convey unhappy and unpleasant thoughts, and such thoughts usually detract from your goal. They include such words as *mistake, problem, error, damage, loss,* and *failure*. There are also words that deny— words such as *no, do not, refuse,* and *stop*. And there are words whose sounds or meanings have unpleasant effects. Examples would differ from person to person, but many would probably agree on these: *itch, guts, scratch, grime, sloppy, sticky, bloody,* and *nauseous*. Or how about *gummy, slimy, bilious,* and *soggy?* Run these negative words through your mind and think about the meanings they produce. You should find it easy to see that they tend to work against most of the goals you may have in your letters.

### Examples of Word Choice

To illustrate your positive-to-negative word choices in handling letters, take the case of a company executive who had to deny a local civic group's request to use the company's meeting facilities. To soften the refusal, the executive could let the group use a conference room, which might be somewhat small for its purpose. The executive came up with this totally negative response:

We *regret* to inform you that we *cannot* permit you to use our clubhouse for your meeting, as the Ladies Book Club asked for it first. We can, however, let you use our conference room, but it seats *only* 60.

The negative words are italicized. First, the positively intended message "We *regret* to inform you" is an unmistakable sign of coming bad news. "*Cannot* permit" contains an unnecessarily harsh meaning. And notice how the good-news part of the message is handicapped by the limiting word *only*.

PART 2 Fundamentals of Business Writing

Had the executive searched for more positive ways of covering the same situation, he or she might have written:

Although the Ladies Book Club has reserved the clubhouse for Saturday, we can instead offer you our conference room, which seats 60.

Not a single negative word appears in this version. Both approaches achieve the letter's primary objective of denying a request, but their effects on the reader differ sharply. There is no question as to which approach does the better job of building and holding goodwill.

For a second illustration, take the case of a correspondent who must write a letter granting the claim of a woman for cosmetics damaged in transit. Granting the claim, of course, is the most positive ending that such a situation can have. Even though this customer has had a somewhat unhappy experience, she is receiving what she wants. The negative language of an unskilled writer, however, can so vividly recall the unhappy aspects of the problem that the happy solution is moved to the background. As this negative version of the message illustrates, the effect is to damage the reader's goodwill:

We received your claim in which you contend that we were responsible for *damage* to three cases of Madame Dupree's lotion. We assure you that we sincerely *regret* the *problems* this has caused you. Even though we feel in all sincerity that your receiving clerks may have been *negligent,* we will assume the *blame* and replace the *damaged* merchandise.

Obviously, this version grants the claim grudgingly, and the company would profit from such an approach only if there were extenuating circumstances. The phrase "in which you contend" clearly implies some doubt about the legitimacy of the claim. Even the sincerely intended expression of regret only recalls to the reader's mind the event that caused all the trouble. And the negatives *blame* and *damage* only strengthen the recollection. Certainly, this approach is not conducive to goodwill.

In the following version of the same message, the writer refers only to positive aspects of the situation—what can be done to settle the problem. The job is done without using a negative word and without mentioning the situation being corrected or suspicions concerning the honesty of the claim. The goodwill effect of this approach is likely to maintain business relations with the reader:

Three cases of Madame Dupree's lotion are on their way to you by Mercury Freight and should be on your sales floor by Saturday.

For additional illustrations, compare the differing results obtained from these contrasting positive-negative versions of letter messages (italics mark the negative words):

| **NEGATIVE** | **POSITIVE** |
| --- | --- |
| You *failed* to give us the fabric specifications of the chair you ordered. | So that you may have the one chair you want, will you please check your choice of fabric on the enclosed card? |
| Smoking is *not* permitted anywhere except in the lobby. | Smoking is permitted in the lobby only. |

| NEGATIVE | POSITIVE |
|---|---|
| We *cannot* deliver until Friday. | We can deliver the goods on Friday. |
| Chock-O-Nuts do not have that *gummy, runny* coating that makes some candies *stick* together when they get hot. | The rich chocolate coating of Chock-O-Nuts stays crispy good throughout the summer months. |
| You were *wrong* in your conclusion, for paragraph 3 of our agreement clearly states . . . | You will agree after reading paragraph 3 of our agreement that . . . |
| We *regret* that we *overlooked* your coverage on this equipment and apologize for the *trouble* and *concern* it must have caused you. | You were quite right in believing that you have coverage on the equipment. We appreciate your calling the matter to our attention. |
| We *regret* to inform you that we must deny your request for credit. | For the time being, we can serve you only on a cash basis. |
| You should have known that the Peyton fryer *cannot* be submerged in water, for it is clearly explained in the instructions. | The instructions explain why the Peyton fryer should be cleaned only with a cloth. |
| Your May 7 *complaint* about our Pronto minidrier is *not* supported by the evidence. | Review of the situation described in your May 7 letter explains what happened when you used the Pronto minidrier. |

## ■ ■ ■ ■ ■ ■ ■
## COURTESY

<aside>Courtesy is a major contributor to goodwill in business letters.</aside>

A major contributor to goodwill in business letters is courtesy. By courtesy we mean treating people with respect and friendly human concern. Used in business letters, courtesy leads to friendly relations between people. The result is a better human climate for solving business problems and doing business.

<aside>Courtesy involves the preceding goodwill techniques.</aside>

Developing courtesy in a letter involves a variety of specific techniques. First, it involves the three discussed previously: writing in conversational language, employing the you-viewpoint, and choosing words for positive effect. It also involves other techniques.

### Singling out Your Reader

<aside>It also involves writing directly for the one reader.</aside>

One of the other techniques is to single out and write directly to your reader. Letters that appear routine have a cold, impersonal effect. On the other hand, letters that appear to be written for one reader tend to make the reader feel important and appreciated.

<aside>This means writing for the one situation.</aside>

To single out your reader in a letter, you should write for the one situation. What you say throughout the letter should make it clear that the reader is getting individual treatment. For example, a letter granting a professor permission to quote company material in the professor's book could end with "We wish you the best of success on the book." This specially adapted comment is better than one that fits any similar case: "If we can be of further assistance, please let us know." Using the reader's name in the letter text is another good way to show that the reader is being

### *A French General's Justification of Politeness*

Once, at a diplomatic function, the great World War I leader Marshal Foch was maneuvered into a position in which he had to defend French politeness.

"There is nothing in it but wind," Foch's critic sneered.

"There is nothing in a tire but wind," the marshal responded politely, "but it makes riding in a car very smooth and pleasant."

---

given special treatment. We can gain the reader's favor by occasionally making such references as "you are correct, Mr. Brock" or "as you know, Ms. Smith."

### Refraining from Preaching

You can help give your letters a courteous effect by not preaching—that is, by avoiding the tone of a lecture or a sermon. Except in the rare cases in which the reader looks up to the writer, a preaching tone hurts goodwill. We human beings like to be treated as equals. We do not want to be bossed or talked down to. Thus, writing that suggests unequal writer-reader relations is likely to make the reader unhappy.

Preaching in letters is usually not intended. It often occurs when the writer is trying to convince the reader of something, as in this example:

You must take advantage of savings like this if you are to be successful. The pennies you save pile up. In time you will have dollars.

It is insulting to tell the reader something quite elementary as if it were not known. Such obvious information should be omitted.

Likewise, flat statements of the obvious fall into the preachy category. Statements like "Rapid inventory turnover means greater profits" are obvious to the experienced retailer and would probably produce negative reactions. So would most statements including such phrases as "you need," "you want," "you should," and "you must," for they tend to talk down to the reader.

Another form of preachiness takes this obvious question-and-answer pattern: "Would you like to make a deal that would make you a 38 percent profit? Of course you would!" What intelligent and self-respecting retailer would not be offended by this approach?

### Doing More than Is Expected

One sure way to gain goodwill is to do a little bit more than you have to do for your reader. We are all aware of how helpful little extra acts are in other areas of our personal relationships. Too many of us, however, do not use them in our letters. Perhaps in the mistaken belief that we are being concise, we include only the barest essentials in our letters. The result is brusque, hurried treatment, which is inconsistent with our efforts to build goodwill.

The writer of a letter refusing a request for use of company equipment, for example, only needs to say no to accomplish the primary goal. This answer,

---

*The effect of courtesy is helped by not preaching (lecturing).*

*Usually preaching is not intended. It often results from efforts to persuade.*

*Elementary, flat, and obvious statements often sound preachy.*

*Doing more than necessary builds goodwill.*

of course, is blunt and totally without courtesy. A goodwill-conscious writer would explain and justify the refusal, perhaps suggesting alternative steps that the reader might take. A wholesaler's brief extra sentence to wish a retailer good luck on a coming promotion is worth the effort. So are an insurance agent's few words of congratulations in a letter to a policyholder who has earned some distinction.

Likewise, a salesperson uses good judgment in an acknowledgment letter that includes helpful suggestions about using the goods ordered. And in letters to customers a writer for a sales organization can justifiably include a few words about new merchandise received, new services provided, price reductions, and so on.

To those who say that these suggestions are inconsistent with the need for conciseness, we must answer that the information we speak of is needed to build goodwill. Conciseness concerns the number of words needed to say what you must say. It never involves leaving out information vital to any of your objectives. On the other hand, nothing we have said should be interpreted to mean that any kind or amount of extra information is justified. You must take care to use only the extra information you need to reach your goal.

*As the extras add length, they appear not to be concise. But conciseness means word economy—not leaving out essentials.*

### Avoiding Anger

*Rarely is anger justified in letters. It destroys goodwill.*

Expressing anger in letters—letting off steam—may sometimes help you emotionally. But anger helps achieve the goal of a letter only when that goal is to anger the reader. The effect of angry words is to make the reader angry. With both writer and reader angry, the two are not likely to get together on whatever the letter is about.

To illustrate the effect of anger, take the case of an insurance company correspondent who must write a letter telling a policyholder that the policyholder has made a mistake in interpreting the policy and is not covered on the matter in question. The correspondent, feeling that any fool should be able to read the policy, might respond in these angry words:

If you had read Section IV of your policy, you would know that you are not covered on accidents that occur on water.

One might argue that these words "tell it as it is"—that what they say is true. Even so, they show anger and lack tact. Their obvious effect is to make the reader angry. A more tactful writer would refer courteously to the point of misunderstanding:

As a review of Section IV of your policy indicates, you are covered on accidents that occur on the grounds of your residence only.

Most of the comments made in anger do not provide needed information but merely serve to let the writer blow off steam. Such comments take many forms—sarcasm, insults, exclamations. You can see from the following examples that you should not use them in your letters:

No doubt, you expect us to hold your hand.
I cannot understand your negligence.
This is the third time you have permitted your account to be delinquent.
We will not tolerate this condition.

The language used in a letter communicates more than the message. It communicates a picture of the writer. It tells how friendly, how formal, how careful the writer is—and more.

Your careless attitude has caused us a loss in sales.
We have had it!
We have no intention of permitting this condition to continue.

## Being Sincere

Courteous treatment is sincere treatment. If your letters are to be effective, people must believe you. You must convince them that you mean what you say and that your efforts to be courteous and friendly are well intended. That is, your letters must have the quality of sincerity.

The best way of getting sincerity into your letters is to believe in the techniques you use. If you honestly want to be courteous, if you honestly believe that you-viewpoint treatment leads to harmonious relations, and if you honestly think that tactful treatment spares your reader's sensitive feelings, you are likely to apply these techniques sincerely. Your sincerity will show in your writing.

**Overdoing the Goodwill Techniques.** There are, however, two major areas that you might alertly check. The first is the overdoing of your goodwill techniques. Perhaps through insincerity or as a result of overzealous effort, the goodwill techniques are frequently overdone. For example, you can easily refer too often to your reader by name in your efforts to write to the

Efforts to be courteous must be sincere.

Sincerity results from believing in the techniques of courtesy.

The goodwill effort can be overdone. Too much you-viewpoint sounds insincere.

one person. Also, as shown in the following example, you-viewpoint effort can go beyond the bounds of reason.

> So that you may be able to buy Kantrell equipment at an extremely low price and sell it at a tremendous profit, we now offer you the complete line at a 50 percent price reduction.

This example, included in a form letter from the company president to a new charge customer, has a touch of unbelievability:

> I was delighted today to see your name listed among Morgan's new charge customers.

Or how about this one, taken from an adjustment letter of a large department store?

> We are extremely pleased to be able to help you and want you to know that your satisfaction means more than anything to us.

*Exaggerated statements are obviously insincere.*

**Avoiding Exaggeration.** The second area that you should check is exaggerated statements. It is easy to see through most exaggerated statements; thus, they can give a mark of insincerity to your letter. Exaggerations are overstatements of facts. Although some exaggeration is conventional in sales writing, even here bounds of propriety exist. The following examples clearly overstep these bounds:

> Already thousands of new customers are beating paths to the doors of Martin dealers.
>
> Never has there been, nor will there be, a fan as smooth running and whispering quiet as the North Wind.
>
> Everywhere coffee drinkers meet, they are talking about the amazing whiteness Cafree gives their teeth.

*Superlatives (greatest, finest, strongest) often suggest exaggeration.*

Many exaggerated statements involve the use of superlatives. All of us use them, but only rarely do they fit the reality about which we communicate. Words like *greatest, most amazing, finest, healthiest,* and *strongest* are seldom appropriate. Other strong words may have similar effects—for example, *extraordinary, stupendous, delicious, more than happy, sensational, terrific, revolutionary, colossal,* and *perfection.* Such words cause us to question; we rarely believe them.

## THE ROLE OF EMPHASIS

*Emphasis also determines effect. Every item communicated should get the proper emphasis.*

Getting desired effects in writing often involves giving proper emphasis to the items in the message. Every message contains a number of facts, ideas, and so on that must be presented. Some of these items are more important than others. For example, the main goal of a letter is very important. Supporting explanations and incidental facts are less important. A part of your job as a writer is to determine the importance of each item and to give each item the emphasis it deserves.

*There are four basic emphasis techniques.*

To give each item in your message proper emphasis, you must use certain techniques. By far the most useful are these four: position, space, structure, and mechanical devices. The following paragraphs explain each.

PART 2 Fundamentals of Business Writing

## Emphasis by Position

The beginnings and endings of a writing unit carry more emphasis than the center parts. This rule of emphasis applies whether the unit is the letter, a paragraph of the letter, or a sentence within the paragraph. We do not know why this is so. Some authorities think that the reader's fresh mental energy explains beginning emphasis. Some say that the last parts stand out because they are the most recent in the reader's mind. Whatever the explanation, research has suggested that this emphasis technique works.

In the letter as a whole, the beginning and the closing are the major emphasis positions. Thus, you must be especially mindful of what you put in these places. The beginning and ending of the internal paragraphs are secondary emphasis positions. Your design of each paragraph should take this into account. To a lesser extent, the first and last words of each sentence carry more emphasis than the middle ones. Thus, even in your sentence design, you can help determine the emphasis that your reader will give the points in your message. In summary, your organizational plan should place the points you want to stand out in these beginning and ending positions. You should bury the points that you do not want to emphasize between these positions.

*Position determines emphasis. Beginnings and endings carry emphasis.*

*The first and last sentences of a letter, the first and last sentences of a paragraph, and the first and last words of a sentence all carry more emphasis than the middle parts.*

## Space and Emphasis

The more you say about something, the more emphasis you give it; and the less you say about something, the less emphasis you give it. If your letter devotes a full paragraph to one point and a scant sentence to another, the first point receives more emphasis. To give the desired effect in your letter, you will need to say just enough about each item of information you present.

*The more space a topic is given, the more emphasis the topic receives.*

"Has it ever occurred to you, Leland, that maybe you're too negative?"

*From* The Wall Street Journal, *with permission of Cartoon Features Syndicate.*

## Sentence Structure and Emphasis

> Sentence structure determines emphasis. Short, simple sentences emphasize content; long, involved ones do not.

As we noted in Chapter 3, short, simple sentences call attention to their content and long, involved ones do not. In applying this emphasis technique to your writing, carefully consider the possible sentence arrangements of your information. Place the more important information in short, simple sentences so that it will not have to compete with other information for the reader's attention. Combine the less important information, taking care that the relationships are logical. In your combination sentences, place the more important material in independent clauses and the less important information in subordinate structures.

## Mechanical Means of Emphasis

> Mechanical devices (underscore, color, diagrams, and the like) also give emphasis to content.

Perhaps the most obvious emphasis techniques are those that use mechanical devices. By *mechanical devices* we mean any of the things that we can do physically to give the printed word emphasis. The most common of these devices are the underscore, quotation marks, italics, boldface type, and solid capitals. Lines, arrows, and diagrams can also call attention to certain parts. So can color, special type, and drawings. These techniques are infrequently used in letters, with the possible exception of sales letters.

# COHERENCE

> Letters should be coherent. The relationships of parts should be clear.

Your letters are composed of independent bits of information. But these bits of information do not communicate the whole message. A part of the message is told in the relationships of the facts presented. Thus, to communicate your message successfully, you must do more than communicate facts. You must also make the relationships clear. Making these relationships clear is the task of giving coherence to your letter.

> Presenting information in logical order helps coherence.

The best thing you can do to give your letter coherence is to arrange its information in a logical order—an order appropriate for the strategy of the one case. So important is this matter to letter writing that it is the primary topic of discussion in following chapters. Thus, we will postpone discussion of this vital part of coherence. But logical organization is usually not enough. Various techniques are needed to bridge or tie together the information presented. These techniques are known as *transitional devices*. We will discuss the four major ones: tie-in sentences, repetition of key words, use of pronouns, and use of transitional words.

## Tie-In Sentences

> Sentences can be designed to tie together succeeding thoughts.

By structuring your letter so that one idea sets up the next, you can skillfully relate the ideas. That is, you can design the sentences to tie in two successive ideas. Notice in the following example how a job applicant tied together the first two sentences of the letter:

As a result of increasing demand for precision instruments in the Billsburg boom area, won't you soon need another experienced and trained salesperson to call on your technical accounts there?

With seven successful years of selling Morris instruments and a degree in civil engineering, I believe I have the qualifications to do this job.

PART 2  Fundamentals of Business Writing

Now substitute the following sentence for the second sentence above and note the abrupt shift it makes.

I am 32 years of age, married, and interested in exploring the possibilities of employment with you.

For another case, compare the contrasting examples of the sentence that follows the first sentence of a letter refusing an adjustment on a trenching machine. As you can see, the strategy of the initial sentence is to set up the introduction of additional information that will clear the company of responsibility.

**THE INITIAL SENTENCE**

Your objective review of the facts concerning the operation of your Atkins Model L trencher is evidence that you are one who wants to consider all the facts in a case.

**GOOD TIE-IN**

In this same spirit of friendly objectivity, we are confident that you will want to consider some additional information we have assembled.

**ABRUPT SHIFT**

We have found some additional information you will want to consider.

### Repetition of Key Words

By repeating key words from one sentence to the next, you can make smooth connections of successive ideas. The following successive sentences illustrate this transitional device (key words in italics). The sentences come from a letter refusing a request to present a lecture series for an advertising clinic.

Because your advertising clinic is so well planned, I am confident that it can provide a really *valuable* service to practitioners in the community. To be truly *valuable,* I think you will agree, the program must be given the *time* a thorough preparation requires. As my *time* for the coming weeks is heavily committed, you will need to find someone who is in a better position to do justice to your program.

> Repetition of key words connects thoughts.

### Use of Pronouns

Because pronouns refer to words previously used, they make good transitions between ideas. So use them from time to time in forming idea connections. Especially use the demonstrative pronouns (*this, that, these, those*) and their adjective forms, for these words clearly relate ideas. The following examples (demonstrative pronouns in italics) illustrate this technique:

Ever since the introduction of our Model V 10 years ago, consumers have suggested only one possible improvement—automatic controls. During all *this* time, making *this* improvement has been the objective of Atkins research personnel. Now we proudly report that *these* efforts have been successful.

> Pronouns connect with the words they relate to.

### Transitional Words

When you talk in everyday conversation, you connect many of your thoughts with transitional words. But when you write, more than likely you do not use them enough. So be alert for places that need to be connected or

> Use transitional words in your writing.

**CHAPTER 4** Writing for Effect

related. Whenever sharp shifts or breaks in thought flow occur, consider using transitional words.

> Transitional words tell the thought connection between following ideas.

Among the commonly used transitional words are *in addition, besides, in spite of, in contrast, however, likewise, thus, therefore, for example,* and *also.* A more extensive list appears in Chapter 12, where we review transition in report writing. That these words bridge thoughts is easy to see, for each gives a clue to the nature of the connection between what has been said and what will be said next. *In addition,* for example, tells the reader that what is to be discussed next builds on what has been discussed. *However* clearly shows a contrast in ideas. *Likewise* tells that what has been said resembles what will be said.

### A Word of Caution

> Do not use transitional words arbitrarily. Make them appear natural.

The preceding discussion does not suggest that you should use these transitional devices arbitrarily. Much of your subject matter will flow smoothly without them. When you use them, however, use them naturally so that they blend in with your writing.

### ■■■■■■■■■■■■■■■■■■■■■
### SUMMARY (by Chapter Objectives)

> 1. Explain the need for effect in writing business letters.

1. Although clarity is a major concern in all business writing, in letters you will also be concerned with effect.
   - Specifically, you will need to communicate the effect of goodwill, for it is profitable in business to do so.
   - Sometimes you will need to communicate effects that help you persuade, sell, or the like.
   - To achieve these effects, you will need to heed the following advice.

> 2. Use a conversational style that eliminates the old language of business and "rubber stamps."

2. Write letters in a conversational style (language that sounds like people talking).
   - Such a style requires that you resist the tendency to be formal.
   - It requires that you avoid words from the old language of business (*thanking you in advance, please be advised*).
   - It requires that you avoid the so-called rubber stamps—words used routinely and without thought (*this is to inform, in accordance with*).

> 3. Use the you-viewpoint to foster goodwill in letters.

3. In your letters, you will need to emphasize the you-viewpoint (*you will be happy to know . . . rather than I am happy to report . . .* ).
   - But be careful not to be or appear to be insincere.
   - And do not use the you-viewpoint to manipulate the reader.

> 4. Employ positive language to achieve goodwill and other desired effects.

4. You should understand the negative and positive meanings of words.
   - Negative words have unpleasant meanings (*We cannot deliver until Friday*).
   - Positive words have pleasant meanings (*We can deliver Friday*).
   - Select those negative and positive words that achieve the best effect for your goal.

> 5. Explain the techniques of achieving courtesy in letters.

5. You should strive for courtesy in your letters by doing the following:
   - Practice the goodwill techniques discussed above.
   - Single out your reader (write for the one person).
   - Avoid preaching or talking down.
   - Avoid displays of anger.

- Be sincere (avoiding exaggeration and overdoing the goodwill techniques).
6. Use the four major techniques for emphasis in writing.
   - Determine the items of information the message will contain.
   - Give each item the emphasis it deserves.
   - Show emphasis in these ways:
     —by position (beginnings and endings receive prime emphasis),
     —by space (the greater the space devoted to a topic, the greater is the emphasis.
     —by sentence structure (short sentences emphasize more than longer ones).
     —by mechanical means (color, underscore, boldface, and such).
7. You should write letters that flow smoothly.
   - Present the information in logical order—so that one thought sets up the next.
   - Help show the relationships of thoughts by using these transitional devices:
     —Tie-in sentences,
     —Word repetitions,
     —Pronouns, and
     —Transitional words.

6. Use the four major techniques for emphasis in writing.

7. Write letters that flow smoothly through the use of a logical order aided by the four major transitional devices.

## QUESTIONS FOR DISCUSSION

1. Discuss this comment: "Getting the goodwill effect in letters requires extra effort. It takes extra time, and time costs money."
2. "Our normal conversation is filled with error. Typically, it is crude and awkward. So why make our letters sound conversational?" Discuss.
3. "If a company really wants to impress the readers of its letters, the letters should be formal and should be written in dignified language that displays knowledge." Discuss.
4. After reading a letter filled with expressions from the old language of business, a young administrative trainee made this remark: "I'm keeping this one for reference. It sounds so businesslike!" Evaluate this comment.
5. "If you can find words, sentences, or phrases that cover a general situation, why not use them every time that general situation comes about? Using such rubber stamps would save time, and in business time is money." Discuss.
6. Discuss this comment: "The you-viewpoint is insincere and deceitful."
7. Evaluate this comment: "It's hard to argue against courtesy. But businesspeople don't have time to spend extra effort on it. Anyway, they want their letters to go straight to the point—without wasting words and without sugar coating."
8. "I use the words that communicate the message best. I don't care whether they are negative or positive." Discuss.
9. "I like letter writers who shoot straight. When they are happy, you know it. When they are angry, they let you know." Discuss.
10. A writer wants to include a certain negative point in a letter and to give it little emphasis. Discuss each of the four basic emphasis techniques as they relate to what can be done.
11. Using illustrations other than those in the text, discuss and illustrate the four major transitional devices.

## APPLICATION EXERCISES

Instructions: Rewrite Sentences 1–16 in conversational style.

1. I hereby acknowledge receipt of your July 7 favor.
2. Anticipating your reply by return mail, I remain . . .
3. Attached please find receipt requested in your May 1st inquiry.
4. We take pleasure in advising that subject contract is hereby canceled.
5. You are hereby advised to endorse subject proposal and return same to the undersigned.
6. I shall appreciate the pleasure of your reply.
7. Referring to yours of May 7, I wish to state that this office has no record of a sale.
8. This is to advise that henceforth all invoices will be submitted in duplicate.
9. Agreeable to yours of the 24th inst., we have consulted our actuarial department to ascertain the status of subject policy.
10. Kindly be advised that permission is hereby granted to delay remittance until the 12th.
11. In conclusion would state that, up to this writing, said account has not been profitable.
12. Replying to your letter of the 3rd would state that we deem it a great pleasure to accept your kind offer to serve on the committee.
13. I beg to advise that, with regard to above invoice, this office finds that partial payment of $312 was submitted on delivery date.
14. In replying to your esteemed favor of the 7th, I submit under separate cover the report you requested.
15. In reply to your letter of May 10, please be informed that this office heretofore has generously supported funding activities of your organization.
16. Kindly advise the undersigned as to your availability for participation in the program.

Instructions, Sentences 17–32: Write you-viewpoint sentences to cover each of the situations described.

17. Company policy requires that you must submit the warranty agreement within two weeks of sale.
18. We will be pleased to deliver your order by the 12th.
19. We have worked for 37 years to build the best lawn mowers for our customers.
20. Today we are shipping the goods you ordered February 3.

21. (From an application letter) I have seven years of successful experience selling office machinery.
22. (From a memorandum to employees) We take pleasure in announcing that, effective today, the Company will give a 20 percent discount on all purchases made by employees.
23. Kraff files are made in three widths—one for every standard size of record.
24. We are happy to report approval of your application for membership.
25. Items desired should be checked on the enclosed order form.
26. Our long experience in the book business has enabled us to provide the best customer service possible.
27. So that we can sell at discount prices, we cannot permit returns of merchandise.
28. We invite you to buy from the enclosed catalog.
29. Tony's Red Beans have an exciting spicy taste.
30. We give a 2 percent discount when payment is made within 10 days.
31. I am pleased to inform you that I can grant your request for payment of travel expenses.
32. We can permit you to attend classes on company time only when the course is related to your work assignment.

Instructions, Sentences 33–48: Underscore all negative words in these sentences. Then rewrite the sentences for positive effect. Use your imagination to supply situation information when necessary.

33. Your misunderstanding of our January 7 letter caused you to make this mistake.
34. We hope this delay has not inconvenienced you. If you will be patient, we will get the order to you as soon as our supply is replenished.
35. We regret that we must call your attention to our policy of prohibiting refunds for merchandise bought at discount.
36. Your negligence in this matter caused the damage to the equipment.
37. You cannot visit the plant except on Saturdays.
38. We are disappointed to learn from your July 7 letter that you are having trouble with our Model 7 motor.
39. Tuff-Boy work clothing is not made from cloth that shrinks or fades.
40. Our Stone-skin material won't do the job unless it is reinforced.
41. Even though you were late in paying the bill, we did not disallow the discount.
42. We were sorry to learn of the disappointing service you have had from our sales force, but we feel we have corrected all mistakes with recent personnel changes.
43. We have received your complaint of the 7th in which you claim that our product was defective, and have thoroughly investigated the matter.
44. I regret the necessity of calling your attention to our letter of May 1.
45. We have received your undated letter, which you sent to the wrong office.
46. Old New Orleans pralines are not the gummy kind that stick to your teeth.
47. I regret to have to say that I will be unable to speak at your conference, as I have a prior commitment.
48. Do not walk on the grass.

Instructions, Numbers 49 and 50: The answers to these questions should come from letter examples to be found in following chapters.

49. Find examples of each of the four major emphasis techniques discussed in this chapter.
50. Find examples of each of the four transitional devices discussed in this chapter.

# PART THREE

# BASIC PATTERNS OF BUSINESS LETTERS

**5**
**DIRECTNESS IN INITIATING ROUTINE LETTERS**

**6**
**DIRECTNESS IN ROUTINE RESPONSES**

**7**
**INDIRECTNESS FOR BAD NEWS**

**8**
**INDIRECTNESS IN PERSUASION AND SALES WRITING**

## CHAPTER 5

# DIRECTNESS IN INITIATING ROUTINE LETTERS

### CHAPTER OBJECTIVES

*Upon completing this chapter, you will be able to employ directness in initiating routine inquiries. To reach this goal, you should be able to*

**1**

Describe the planning stage of the process of writing business letters.

**2**

Describe the remaining stages of the process of writing business letters, explaining how following these procedures can improve your writing.

**3**

Write clear, well-structured routine requests for information.

**4**

Compose orderly and thorough inquiries about prospective employees that show a respect for human rights.

**5**

Write claim letters that explain the facts in a firm but courteous manner.

**6**

Write orders that begin with a clear authorization; contain an orderly arrangement of units, descriptions, and prices; cover all shipping information; and close with goodwill.

## THE PROCESS OF WRITING LETTERS

With this chapter you will begin writing business letters. As you write the letters, you should keep in mind what is involved in the process of writing. As you will see, following the process guidelines will enable you to get more from your writing efforts. The following brief review of this process should guide you in your efforts.

*Following is a review of the process of writing letters.*

### Planning the Letter

Your first step in writing a business letter should involve planning. This is the prewriting stage—the stage in which you think through your writing project and develop a plan for doing it.

*Begin by planning.*

First, you determine the objective of the letter—what the letter must do. Must it report information, acknowledge an order, ask for something, request payment of a bill, evaluate an applicant, or what?

*Determine the objective of the letter.*

Next you predict the reader's likely reaction to your objective. Will that reaction be positive, or negative, or somewhere in between? Of course, you cannot be certain of how the reader will react. You can only apply your knowledge of the reader to the situation and use your best judgment. Your prediction will determine the plan of the letter you write.

*Predict how the reader will react.*

### Gathering and Collecting the Facts

The next step in writing a business letter is to get all the information you will need. In a business situation, this means getting past correspondence; consulting with other employees; getting sales records, warranties, product descriptions, and inventory records—in fact, doing whatever is necessary to inform yourself fully of the situation. Without all the information you need, you may make costly mistakes. Moreover, if you do not have all the information you need, you will have to look for it in the midst of your writing. This breaks your train of thought and causes you to lose time.

*Get the information (facts) you need.*

In a classroom situation, the write-up of the problem is likely to contain the information you need. So you will need to study the problem carefully, making certain that you understand all the information.

### Analyzing and Organizing Information

If you predict the reader will react to your letter positively, or even neutrally, you will usually organize the letter in a direct plan. That is, you will get to your objective right away—at the beginning. In positive situations, you are likely to have no need for opening explanations or introductory remarks, for these would only delay achieving your objective. You simply start with the objective of the letter. This plan, commonly called the *direct order,* is easy to use. Fortunately, it is appropriate for most business letters.

*Select the letter plan. Use direct order for favorable reactions.*

If you predict that your letter will produce a negative reaction, you should usually write it in indirect order. *Indirect order* is the opposite of direct order. This plan gets to the objective after preparing the reader to receive it. As you will see, such a letter typically requires a more skillful use of strategy and word choice than does one written in direct order.

*Use indirect order for unfavorable reactions.*

This chapter and the next concern the routine, day-to-day correspondence that you will normally handle in direct order. In following chapters

**CHAPTER 5** Directness in Initiating Routine Letters

you will learn about indirect-order letters. And you will review some specialized letters that involve principles used in both direct and indirect order.

## Writing the Letter

*Then write the letter, striving for clarity and effect.*

After you have the plan in mind, you write the letter. You should write it in the clear and effective manner discussed in the preceding chapters—choosing words the reader understands, constructing sentences that present their contents clearly, using words that create just the right effect. In addition, you should follow carefully the text instructions for the letter you are writing. The end product of this effort is a first draft. As you will see, the process does not end here.

## Rewriting Your Work

*When time permits, review your work.*

In actual business practice, your first draft may well be the final draft, for often time does not permit additional work on the document. But now you are in a learning situation. You are preparing for the time when you will not have time. Your efforts now should be directed toward improving your writing skills—toward learning writing techniques that can become reflexive in the years ahead when you will write under time pressures. Even so, when you reach the stage of your career when you must write under time pressures, you would be wise to employ as many of the following suggestions as time will permit.

*Then revise it.*

After completing your first draft, you should review it carefully. Look at each word. Is it the right one? Would another one be more precise? Are there better, more concise ways of saying it? Did you say what you mean? Could someone read other meanings into your words? Is your organization the best for the situation? What we are suggesting is that you be your own critic. Challenge what you have done. Look for alternatives. Then, after you have conducted a thorough and critical review, make any changes that you think will improve your work.

*Get input from others,*

Input from others can also benefit your refinement of your writing. As you know, it is often difficult to find errors or weaknesses in your own work, yet others seem to find them easily. Thus, if your instructor permits or encourages any input from associates, use them. Receive these criticisms with an open mind, objectively evaluating them and using those that meet your review. Unfortunately, most of us are thin-skinned about such criticisms, and we tend to be defensive when they are made. You should resist this tendency.

*including your instructor.*

It goes without saying that the most valuable input may be the written comments your instructor makes about the work submitted. Perhaps this input comes too late to benefit you gradewise. But it does not come too late to benefit your learning. You would be wise to take these comments and revise a final time, ending with your best possible product.

## Editing and Presenting the Final Document

*Then process, edit, and proof the final draft.*

After you have made all the changes you think are needed, you should construct the final draft. Here you become a proofreader, looking for errors of spelling, punctuation, and grammar. You determine that the format is appropriate. In general, you make certain the final letter represents your very best standards—that it will reflect favorably on you and (in later years)

In most face-to-face business relations, people communicate with courteous directness. You should write most business letters this way.

your company. Then you present the letter. This final letter is the best you are capable of writing, and you have learned in the process of writing it.

### INTRODUCTORY SITUATION

## to Routine Inquiry Letters

Introduce yourself to your first letter (a routine inquiry) by assuming that you are assistant to the vice president for administration of Pinnacle Manufacturing Company. Pinnacle is a small manufacturer of an assortment of quality products. Because it is small, your duties involve helping your boss cover many company activities.

Today one of these activities requires that you write a letter for your boss. The letter is a request for information that Pinnacle management needs in making a decision. As a member of Pinnacle's executive team, your boss has been assigned the task of finding suitable sites for the company's expansion plant. In assisting your boss in this assignment, you have found a number of possible locations. One of them is described generally in an advertisement in today's *Wall Street Journal*.

The advertisement tells of a 120-acre tract on the Mississippi River 12 miles upstream from New Orleans. The location and price are right. But Pinnacle's executives want a number of specific questions answered before they proceed. Does the land have deep frontage on the river? What about the terrain? Is the land well drained? How accessible is it by public roads? Your task is to write the letter that will get the information Pinnacle needs. If the answers are favorable, the executives will want to inspect the tract. ■

**CHAPTER 5** Directness in Initiating Routine Letters

Answering inquiry letters that do not include adequate explanation can be frustrating.

## ROUTINE INQUIRIES

Letters asking for information are routine.

Letters that ask for information are among the most common in business. Businesses need information from each other. They consider requests for information routine, and they cooperate in exchanging information.

In such letters, there is usually no need to delay the request.

Because businesses usually cooperate in such situations, you can write most requests for information in the direct order. That order saves time for both the writer and the reader. It gets right down to business without delaying explanation or description.

An exception occurs if negative reader reaction is likely.

Directness is not preferred in some situations. As you will see in Chapter 7, directness may be inappropriate when there is doubt that the reader will respond favorably. In such cases, you may need to use the indirect order to explain or persuade.

Thus, the first step in planning the inquiry letter is to determine the reader's probable reaction.

From the preceding discussion, you can see that before writing a request for information you must determine how your reader will receive the letter. If you believe that the reader will not consider the request routine, you should use indirect order. But if you think that the reader will consider the request routine, you should use direct order. Specifically, you should use this direct-order plan:

Then follow this general plan.

- Begin directly with the objective—either a specific question that sets up the entire letter or a general request for information.
- Include necessary explanation—wherever it fits.
- If a number of questions are involved, give them structure.
- End with goodwill words adapted to the one case.

This plan is discussed and explained in the following pages.

## Beginning with the Objective

Because you normally have no reason to waste time in routine inquiries, you should begin them with the objective of the letter. As your objective is to ask for information, you can start with a question. A question beginning moves fast—the way most people want their work to go. Also, questions command attention and are, therefore, likely to communicate better than other sentence forms.

*When a favorable response is likely, you should begin with the request.*

The direct beginning of an inquiry letter can be either of two basic types. First, it can be a specific question that sets up the information wanted. If your objective is to ask a number of questions, it would be one that covers these questions. For example, if your objective is to get answers to specific questions about test results of a company's product, you might begin with these words:

*You may use either of two types of question beginnings: (1) a specific question that sets up the information wanted or*

Will you please send me test results showing how Duro-Press withstands high temperatures and long exposures to sunlight?

In the body of the letter you would include the precise questions concerning temperatures and exposures to sunlight. For example, you might ask questions such as these:

What is the effect when subjected to constant temperatures between 80 and 90 degrees?

What is the effect when subjected to long periods of below-freezing temperatures?

What are the effects of long exposure to direct sunlight?

The second type of beginning is a general request for information. This sentence meets the requirement:

*(2) a general request for information.*

Will you please answer the following questions about your new Duro-Press fabric?

The "will you" here and in a preceding example may appear unnecessary. The basic message would not change if the words were eliminated. In the minds of some authorities, however, including them softens the request and is worth the additional length.

Perhaps both of these direct approaches appear illogical to some. Our minds have been conditioned to the indirect approach that old-style writers have used over the years. Such writers typically begin with an explanation and follow the explanation with the questions. Clearly, this approach is slower and less businesslike. Contrasting examples on following pages illustrate the point.

*Either question beginning is better than the explanation-first plan.*

## Informing and Explaining Adequately

If your reader needs information or explanation to help in answering your questions, you will need to include explanation or information. If you do not explain enough or if you misjudge the reader's knowledge, you make the reader's task difficult. For example, answers to questions about a computer often depend on the specific needs or characteristics of the company that will use it. The best-informed computer expert cannot answer such questions without knowing the facts of the company concerned.

*Somewhere in the letter, explain enough to enable the reader to answer.*

Where and how you include the necessary explanatory information depend on the nature of your letter. Usually, a good place for general explana-

*Place the explanation anywhere it fits logically.*

**CHAPTER 5** Directness in Initiating Routine Letters

## How One Might Write a Routine Inquiry

Suppose one wants to write a routine inquiry—say, to find out about a merger. Here is how the letter might read when written by a

12-year-old public school student: "What gives on this merger?"

21-year-old college graduate: "Kindly inform me on current general economic and specific pertinent industrial factors relating to the scheduled amalgamated proposals."

40-year-old junior executive: "J.P.—Please contact me and put me in the picture regarding the mooted merger. I have nothing in my portfolio on it. Sincerely, W.J."

55-year-old member of the board, with private secretary: "Without prejudice to our position vis-à-vis future developments either planned or in the stage of actual activating, the undersigned would appreciate any generally informative matter together with any pertinent program-planning data specific to any merger plans that may or may not have been advanced in quarters not necessarily germane to the assigned field of the undersigned."

65-year-old executive, now boss of the company and very busy: "What gives on this merger?"

---

tory material that fits the entire letter is following the direct opening sentence. Here it helps reduce any startling effect that a direct opening question might have. It often fits logically into this place, serving as a qualifying or justifying sentence for the letter. In letters that ask more than one question, you will sometimes need to include explanatory material with the questions. If this is the case, the explanation fits best with the questions to which it pertains. Such letters may alternate questions and explanations.

### Structuring the Questions

*If the inquiry involves just one question, begin with it.*

If your inquiry involves just one question, you can achieve your primary objective with the first sentence. After any necessary explanation and a few words of friendly closing comment, your letter is done. If you must ask a number of questions, however, you will need to consider their organization.

*If it involves more than one, make each stand out. Do this by (1) placing each question in a separate sentence,*

Whatever you do, you will need to make your questions stand out. You can do this in a number of ways. First, you can make each question a separate sentence with a bullet, a symbol (●, ○, ■, and so on) used to call attention to a particular item. Combining two or more questions in a sentence de-emphasizes each and invites the reader's mind to overlook some.

*(2) structuring the questions in separate paragraphs,*

Second, you can give each question a separate paragraph, whenever this practice is logical. It is logical when your explanation and other comments about each question justify a paragraph.

*(3) ordering or ranking the questions, and*

Third, you can order or rank your questions with numbers. By using words (*first, second, third,* and so on), numerals (1, 2, 3, etc.), or letters (a, b, c, and so on), you make the questions stand out. Also, you provide the reader with a convenient check and reference guide to answering.

Fourth, you can structure your questions in question form. True questions stand out. Sentences that merely hint at a need for information do not attract much attention. The "It would be nice if you would tell me . . ." and "I would like to know . . ." types are really not questions. They do not ask—they merely suggest. The questions that stand out are those written in question form, those using direct requests: "Will you please tell me . . . ?," "How much would one be able to save . . . ?", "How many contract problems have you had . . . ?"

You may want to avoid questions that can be answered with a simple *yes* or *no*. An obvious exception, of course, would be when you really want a simple *yes* or *no* answer. For example, the question "Is the chair available in blue?" may not be what you really want to know. A better wording probably is "In what colors is the chair available?" Often you'll find that you can combine a yes/no question and its explanation to get a better, more concise question. To illustrate, the wording "Does the program run on an IBM? We have a PS/2, Model 57." could be improved with "What models does the program run on?" or "Does the program run on the IBM PS/2, Model 57?"

*(4) using the question form of sentence.*

*But take caution in asking questions that produce yes or no answers.*

### Ending with Goodwill

Because it is the natural thing for friendly people to do, you should end routine inquiry letters with some appropriate, friendly comment. This is how you would end a face-to-face communication with the reader, and there is no reason to do otherwise in writing. Ending your letter after the final question is like turning your back on someone after a conversation without saying good-bye. Such an abrupt ending would register negative meanings in your reader's mind and would defeat your goodwill efforts.

*End with a friendly comment.*

The facts of the case determine just what you should say in the close to make a goodwill impression. Your letter will receive a more positive reaction if you use words selected specifically for the one case. Such general closes as "A prompt reply will be appreciated" and "Thank you in advance for your answer" are positive, for they express a friendly "thank you." And there is nothing wrong with a "thank you" sincerely expressed here or elsewhere in business writing. The problem is in the routine, rubberstamp nature of many expressions including it. A more positive reaction results from an individually tailored expression such as "If you will get this refrigeration data to me by Friday, I will be very grateful."

*When possible, make the close fit the one case.*

### Contrasting Inquiry Examples

Illustrating bad and good techniques are the following two routine inquiry letters about land for a possible Pinnacle plant site. The first example follows the old-style indirect pattern. The second is direct. These examples include only the texts of the letters. But the examples that follow show complete letters (on letterhead paper and with inside address, salutation, complimentary close, signature, and such) along with handwritten comments pointing out highlights. These two illustration forms are used throughout the letter portion of this book.

*The following examples show bad and good inquiries.*

**The Old-Style Indirect Letter.** The less effective letter begins slowly and gives obvious information. Even if one thinks that this information needs to

CHAPTER 5  Directness in Initiating Routine Letters

### Bullets: Symbols that Draw Attention

Most high-end, full-featured word processing programs have a feature that will let you insert easily a variety of symbols in your documents. Of course, one of the most useful symbols in textual material is the bullet, used most often to draw the reader's attention to listed items. While the traditional bullet—●—is the symbol that most often comes to mind, you may be able to use others if your software and printer work together. Some you might want to use include:

| Symbol | Description |
|---|---|
| •, ○ | Solid and hollow bullet |
| ■, ❑ | Solid and hollow box |
| ■ | Small square bullet |
| • | Small bullet |
| ◘ | Inverse bullet |
| ◙ | Inverse hollow bullet |
| ♦ | Square lozenge |
| 〉 | Right angle bracket |
| → | Right arrow |
| ► | Solid triangle right |
| ◄ | Solid triangle left |
| → | Solid head right arrow |
| ✓ | Check mark |
| #, ♯ | Number or Pound, Sharp |

Try exploiting the power of your word processor and add some variety to the bullets you use when listing items.

---

be communicated, it does not deserve the emphasis of the opening sentence. The second sentence does refer to the objective of the letter, but it is not in the interest-gaining form of a question. The information wanted is covered hastily in the middle paragraph. There are no questions—just hints of needs for information. The items of information wanted do not stand out but are listed in rapid succession. They are not in separate sentences. The close is friendly, but old style. "By return mail" originated in the days when sailing ships shuttled mail across the seas.

### *Some Words of Advice on Letter Writing from the Old Masters*

A letter is a deliberate and written conversation.

*Gracian*

Remember this: write only as you would speak; then your letter will be good.

*Goethe*

There is one golden rule to bear in mind always: that we should try to put ourselves in the position of our correspondent, to imagine his feelings as he writes his letters, and to gauge his reaction as he receives ours. If we put ourselves in the other man's shoes we shall speedily detect how unconvincing our letters can seem, or how much we may be taking for granted.

*Sir Ernest Gowers*

Do not answer a letter in the midst of great anger.

*Chinese Proverb*

Seeing an epistle hath chieflie this definition hereof, in that it is termed the familiar and mutual task of one friend to another: it seemeth the character thereof should according thereunto be simple, plane and of the lowest and neatest stile utterly devoid of any shadow of lie and loftly speeches.

Angel Day, *The English Secretorie,* 1586
(early book on letter writing)

And to describe the true definition of an Epistle or letter, it is nothing but an Oration written, conteining the mynd of the Orator, or wryter, thereby to give to him or them absent, the same that should be declared if they were present.

William Fulwood, *The Enemie of Idlenesse,* 1568
(earliest known book on letter writing in English)

---

Dear Mr. Piper:

We have seen your advertisement for a 120-acre tract on the Mississippi River in the July 1 *Wall Street Journal.* In reply we are writing you for additional information concerning said property.

We would be pleased to know the depth of frontage on the river, quality of drainage, including high and low elevations, and the availability of public roads to the property.

If the information you supply us is favorable to our needs, we will be pleased to inspect the property. Hoping to hear from you by return mail, I am,

Sincerely,

First is the bad example. Its indirect beginning makes it slow.

**The Direct and Effective Letter.** The second example begins directly by asking for information. As the reader will welcome the inquiry, no need exists for delaying explanation. Because the direct opening may have a startling effect, explanatory information that justifies the inquiry follows.

This direct and orderly letter is better.

CHAPTER 5  Directness in Initiating Routine Letters

**CASE ILLUSTRATION**  Routine Inquiries. *(An Inquiry about Hotel Accommodations)*

This letter to a hotel inquires about convention accommodations for a professional association. In selecting a hotel, the organization's officers need answers to specific questions. The letter covers these questions.

---

# NATIONAL MANAGEMENT
## F · O · R · U · M

July 17, 1993

Ms. Connie Briggs, Manager
Lakefront Hotel
10017 Lakefront Boulevard
Chicago, IL 60613

Dear Ms. Briggs:

*Direct—a courteous general request that sets up the specific question*

Will you please help the National Management Forum decide whether it can meet at the Lakefront? The Forum has selected your city for its 1995 meeting, which will be held August 16, 17, and 18. In addition to the Lakefront, the convention committee is considering the De Lane and the White House. In making our decision, we need the information requested in the following questions.

*Explanation of situation provides background information*

*Specific questions—with explanations where needed*

Can you accommodate a group such as ours on these dates? Probably about 600 delegates will attend, and they will need about 400 rooms.

What are your convention rates? We need assurance of having available a minimum of 450 rooms, and we could guarantee 400. Would you be willing to reserve for us the rooms we would require?

What are your charges for conference rooms? We will need eight for each of the three days, and each should have a minimum capacity of 60. On the 18th, for the one-half-hour business meeting, we will need a large assembly room with a capacity of at least 500. Can you meet these requirements?

Also, will you please send me your menu selections and prices for group dinners? On the 17th we plan our presidential dinner. About 500 can be expected for this event.

*Questions stand out in separate paragraphs*

As convention plans must be announced in the next issue of our bulletin, may we have your response right away? We look forward to the possibility of being with you in 1995.

*Individually tailored goodwill close*

Sincerely,

*Patti Wolff*

Patti Wolff, Chair
Site Selection Committee

tr

17306 Milldale Avenue
St. Louis, MO 63118
314-878-4461

---

**PART 3**  Basic Patterns of Business Letters

**CASE ILLUSTRATION** Routine Inquiries. *(Getting Information about a Training Program)*

This letter is from a company training director to the director of a management-training program. The company training director has received literature on the program but needs additional information. The letter seeks this information.

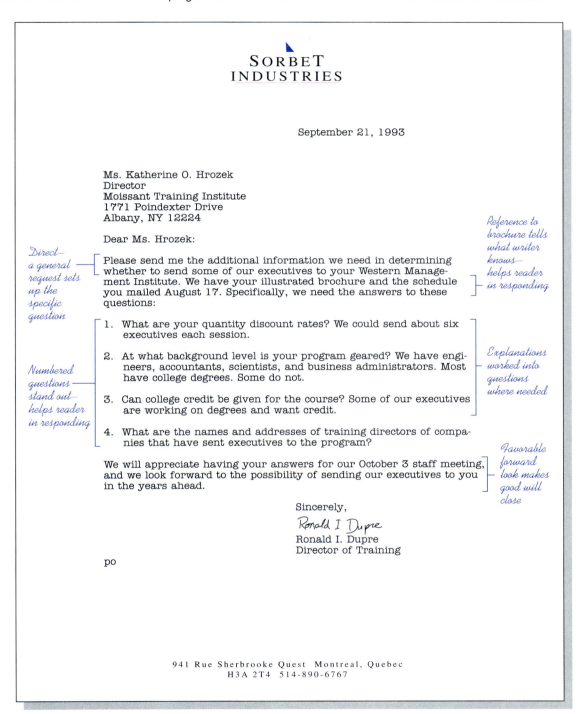

CHAPTER 5 Directness in Initiating Routine Letters

Next comes the remaining questions, with explanations worked in wherever they help the readers in answering. The letter closes with a courteous request for quick handling. In addition, the close suggests the good news of possible quick action on the property.

Dear Mr. Piper:

Will you please answer the following questions about the 120-acre tract you advertised in the July 1 *Wall Street Journal*? We are seeking such a site for a new plant, and it appears that your property could meet our needs.
- How deep is the frontage on the river at its shallowest and deepest points?
- What are drainage conditions on the land? A written description of the tract terrain should answer this question. In your description, please include a contour map showing minimum and maximum elevations.
- What is the composition and condition of the existing access road?

If your answers indicate that the site meets our needs, we will want to inspect the property. As we must move fast on the building project, may I have your answers soon?

Sincerely,

## INTRODUCTORY SITUATION

### to Inquiries about People

From time to time, your work at Pinnacle involves investigating applicants for employment. Of course, in your position you do no hiring. The Personnel Department conducts initial interviews, administers aptitude tests, and performs all the other screening tasks. Then it refers the best applicants to the executives in charge of the jobs to be filled. The executives, including your boss, make the final decisions.

This morning Personnel sent your boss a Mr. Rowe W. Hart, its selection for the vacant position of office manager. Mr. Hart appears to be well qualified—good test scores and employment record. After talking with him, your boss feels that he is bright and personable. Because your boss feels that he cannot judge ability from a single interview, he has asked you to follow your usual practice of writing the applicant's references for their evaluations. In Hart's case, the best possibility appears to be Ms. Alice Borders, who was his immediate supervisor for three years.

Your task now is to write Ms. Borders a letter that will get the information needed. The following discussion and illustrations show you how. ■

## INQUIRIES ABOUT PEOPLE

*Letters asking questions about people should follow this general plan.*

Letters asking for information about people are a special form of routine inquiry. Normally, they should follow this general plan:

- **Begin directly, with a general question seeking information or a specific question that sets up the entire letter.**
- **Explain the situation.**
- **Cover the questions systematically, with explanations as needed.**
- **End with adapted goodwill words.**

PART 3   Basic Patterns of Business Letters

As you can see from the following discussion, this plan is similar to the one for routine inquiries. But it involves a special requirement, which is why we review this letter type separately.

### Respecting Human Rights

Respecting the rights of the people involved is the special requirement. Letters about people are highly personal, and we do not always exchange personal information freely. Moral and legal rights are involved, and we should protect those rights. In fact, because legal rights are involved, on the advice of their attorneys some companies do not permit their personnel to write letters about people. The companies that do permit writing such letters should make every effort to protect the rights of the people involved.

*But such letters need to protect the rights of people. Some companies do not write them.*

To protect human rights in exchanging information about people is to seek truth and to act in good faith. Thus, you should distinguish carefully between fact and opinion. For the most part, you should report fact. You should ask only for information you need for business purposes. You should ask only when the person concerned has authorized the inquiry. You should hold all information about people in confidence. These points should guide you as you write letters asking for information about people. In fact, you would do well to include them in such letters, either in words or by implication.

*So in letters about people stress fact, write only for business use and when authorized, and treat information confidentially.*

### Adapting Question Content

Letters inquiring about job applicants vary, depending on the job to be done. For a sales job, for example, you would need to know about the applicant's personality. So you would ask questions about the applicant's ability to meet and get along with people, conversational skills, and aggressiveness. For an accounting job such information might be of little importance. Here you would probably seek information about knowledge of the field, experience, and work habits.

*The questions asked should fit the one person and the one job.*

From the preceding discussion, your procedure in determining the questions to ask is clear. First, you should analyze the job and the applicant. This analysis should lead you to the questions that will help you decide whether applicant and job match. In other words, you should ask for the specific information you need to consider the one applicant for the one job.

*Thus, you should select the questions after studying the job and the applicant.*

For legal (especially in the United States)[1] as well as ethical reasons, you should not ask questions that do not relate to the job. As a general rule, this means avoiding questions about the applicant's race, religion, sex, age, pregnancy, and marital status. Even questions about the applicant's citizenship status and arrest and conviction record are better not asked. So are questions about mental and physical handicaps and organization (especially union) memberships.

*Consider the legality and ethics of the questions.*

As in any routine inquiry, you should include with the questions any information or explanation that will help the reader answer. Usually the reader needs to know the nature, responsibilities, and requirements of the job.

*Explaining the job requirements helps the reader.*

---

[1] As required by the following acts and court cases relating to them: Wagner Act of 1935, Immigration and Nationality Act of 1952, Civil Rights Act of 1964, Vocational Rehabilitation Act of 1973, Age Discrimination Act of 1975, and Pregnancy Discrimination Act of 1978.

## Examples in Contrast

Following are good and bad examples of a personnel inquiry.

In applying the preceding instructions to Rowe Hart's application for the position of office manager at Pinnacle, assume that analysis of the applicant and the job tells you that you should ask four questions. First, is Hart capable of handling the responsibilities involved? Second, does he know the work? Third, how hard a worker is he? Fourth, is he morally responsible? Now, how would you arrange these questions and the necessary explanation in a letter?

**A Scant and Hurried Example.** The first letter example shows a not-so-good effort. The opening is indirect. The explanation in the opening is important, but does it deserve the emphasis that the beginning position gives it? Although the question part gives the appearance of conciseness, it is actually scant. It includes no explanation. It does not even mention what kind of position Hart is being considered for. The items of information wanted do not stand out. In fact, they are not even worded as questions but are run together in a single, declarative sentence. Though courteous, the closing words are old style.

This bad one is slow and scant.

Dear Ms. Borders:

    Mr. Rowe W. Hart has applied to us for employment and has given your name as a reference. He indicates that he worked under your supervision during the period 1986–89.
    We would be most appreciative if you would give us your evaluation of Mr. Hart. We are especially interested in his ability to handle responsibility, knowledge of office procedures, work habits, and morals.
    Thanking you in advance for your courtesy, I remain,

                  Sincerely yours,

**An Orderly and Thorough Example.** The next example gives evidence of good analysis of the job and the applicant. The letter begins directly with an opening question that serves as a topic sentence. The beginning also includes helpful explanation. But this part is not given unnecessary emphasis, as was done in the preceding example. Then the letter presents the specific

CATHY © 1982 Cathy Guisewite. Reprinted with permission of Universal Press Syndicate. All rights reserved.

**CASE ILLUSTRATION** Inquiries about People. *(An Inquiry about a Prospective Branch Manager)*

This is the case of a freight-line executive who is looking for a manager for one of the company's branches. The top applicant is a shipping clerk for a furniture company. With the applicant's permission, the executive has written this letter to the applicant's employer.

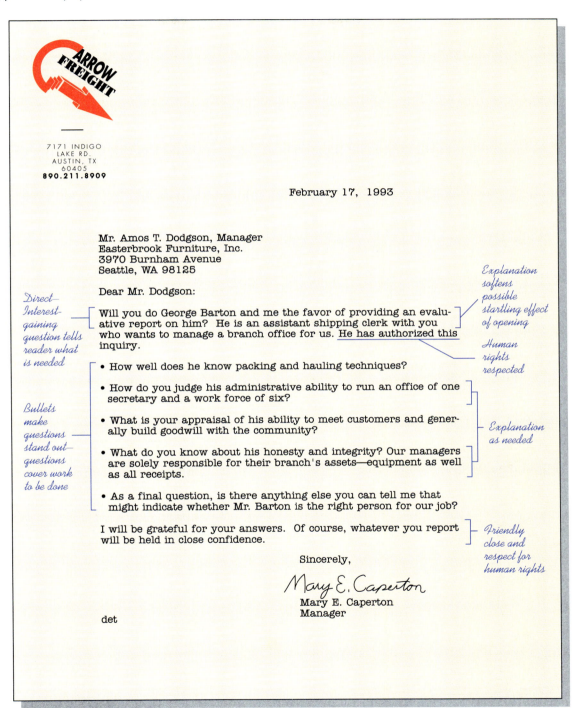

**CASE ILLUSTRATION**   Inquiries about People. *(Asking about a Prospective Accounting Supervisor)*

This letter was authorized by an applicant for an accounting position. It is commendable for its conciseness, its organization, and its concern for the applicant's rights.

---

**SWAIN-BAGWELL, INC.**
3711 N. Shelby Street, Milwaukee, WI 53202                                                                          414-890-7897

March 9, 1993

Ms. Fredonia Gomez, Controller
Bledsoe Milling Company
6901 Shingle Creek Drive
Minneapolis, MN 55430

Dear Ms. Gomez:

*Direct-general question sets up following specific questions* → May I have the benefit of your experience with Ms. Cleo Carpenter? She is a former employee of yours (1984–90) who is applying for the position of head of our accounting department. She has authorized this inquiry. In evaluating her, I need the answers to these questions: ← *Early explanation justifies inquiry* / *Shows concern for human rights*

*Orderly listing makes questions stand out* →
- What are Ms. Carpenter's administrative qualifications for heading an office of accountants?
- How well qualified is she as an accountant?
- What can you report on her record for honesty and reliability?
- How well does she get along with people?
- How conscientious is she in performing her work?

*Shows concern for applicant's rights* → I will be grateful for these answers and for any other information you think I should have. I assure you that this information will be held in strict confidence. ← *Goodwill close*

Sincerely,

*Rudolph O. Petri*

Rudolph O. Petri
Director of Personnel

ROP:LIS

questions. Worded separately and in question form, each stands out and is easy to answer. Worked in with each question is explanation that will help the reader understand the work for which Hart is being considered. The close is courteous and tailored for the one case. Note also, throughout the letter, the concern for the rights of the people involved. Clearly, the inquiry is authorized, is for business purposes only, and will be treated confidentially.

Dear Ms. Borders:

Will you help me evaluate Mr. Rowe W. Hart for the position of office manager? In authorizing this inquiry, Mr. Hart indicated that he worked for you from 1986 to 1989. Your candid answers to the following questions will help me determine whether Mr. Hart is the right person for this job.

What is your evaluation of Mr. Hart's leadership ability, including human-relations skills, to run an office of 11? How able is Mr. Hart to manage a rapidly expanding office system? Ours is a growing company. The person who manages our office will not only need to know good office procedures but will also need to know how to adapt them to changing conditions.

What is your evaluation of Mr. Hart's stamina and drive? The position he seeks often involves working under heavy pressure.

What is your evaluation of Mr. Hart's moral reliability? Our office manager is responsible for much of our company equipment as well as some company funds.

We will, of course, hold your answers in strict confidence. And we will appreciate whatever help you are able to give Mr. Hart and us.

Sincerely,

*This good example shows careful study of the job and the applicant.*

## INTRODUCTORY SITUATION

### to Claim Letters

Occasionally something goes wrong with the goods and services that Pinnacle buys. When this happens in your area of responsibility, your job is to look after Pinnacle's interests. Today it happened. You received by motor freight an order for two dozen fire extinguishers. All of them were damaged. Leaking acid had ruined their finish. As Pinnacle cannot accept them, you must write the seller, explaining what happened, and getting the seller to correct the situation. In other words, you have to write a claim letter. Because the local fire marshal has ordered Pinnacle to have the fire extinguishers in place by next Monday, you must act fast.

The facts of the case tell you that this is not a routine letter. The news in claim letters is bad—bad for the writer and bad for the reader. How best to handle claim situations certainly requires careful thought. The following discussion should guide your thinking when you must handle claims. ■

### CLAIMS

When something goes wrong between a business and its customers, usually someone begins an effort to correct the situation. Typically, the offended party calls the matter to the attention of those responsible. In other words, he or she makes a claim. The claim can be made in person, by telephone, or

*Claim letters are written to correct for damages. They should follow this plan.*

CHAPTER 5   Directness in Initiating Routine Letters      115

by letter. Our concern here is how to make it by letter. The following pages discuss a plan for handling claims by letter. In summary form, the plan is as follows:

- **Begin directly. Tell what is wrong.**
- **Identify the situation (invoice number, product information, etc.) in the text or in a subject line.**
- **Present enough of the facts to permit a decision.**
- **Seek corrective action.**
- **End positively—friendly but firm.**

## Using Directness for Bad News

*Claims carry bad news.*

Claim situations are bad-news situations. Goods have been damaged or lost, a product has failed to perform, or service has been bad. The situation is unhappy for both the writer and the reader.

*Even so, write them in the direct order for two reasons:*
*(1) the reader is likely to want to correct the error and*

When the news is bad, a letter in the indirect order is usually appropriate; but claim letters are exceptions. For two good reasons, they are most effective in the direct order.

First, most businesspeople want to please their customers. When they do not please, they want to know about it and to make the adjustment necessary. Thus, when you make a claim, you do not need to persuade the reader or to break the news gently. In other words, there is no good reason why you cannot begin with the claim.

*(2) the direct order is strong.*

Second, directness lends strength to the claim. Beginning with the claim emphasizes it and shows the writer's confidence in reporting it. In fact, some readers would interpret indirectness as weakness. Since your chances of getting a favorable adjustment depend in part on the strength of your claim, you should use the arrangement that strengthens it.

## Identifying the Situation

*Identify the transaction involved early in the letter.*

A claim letter concerns a particular transaction, item of merchandise, or service call. So that your reader will quickly know exactly what your claim is about, you will have to include the necessary identification information and place it somewhere near the beginning. What you include depends on what is needed in each case—invoice number, order number or date, serial number of product, and so on.

*You can do this incidentally or in a subject line.*

You can handle such identification incidentally or by subject line. Handling it incidentally simply means working it into the letter in a subordinate way. Handling it in a subject line means employing a mechanical device, usually after the salutation (see p. 119). Typically, the subject line contains some identifying term, such as *Subject:*, *About:*, or *Re:*, followed by appropriate descriptive words. The words, which may take various forms, identify the nature of the letter and the one situation.

*Strong wording is appropriate for the subject line, as in these examples.*

Because a direct beginning is appropriate in the claim letter, the subject line (which actually begins the message) may be direct. These examples illustrate good wording and content:

Subject: Damaged condition of fire extinguishers on arrival, your invoice No. 1314C

Subject: Breakage of Tira cologne shipped on invoice No. 31747, dated July 5, 1993

Subject: Failure of repairs on Damon L3 pump, Work Order 7133, to correct defect

### Stating the Problem Directly

A good claim letter is a combination of courtesy and firmness. You begin by stating the problem. This initial statement should move as far as possible into the facts of the situation. If the subject line does not cover some details of identification, you need to work these into your letter, preferably near the beginning.

> Begin the claim with a direct statement of the problem.

In some instances, you may choose to do more than just state the problem. You may also choose to explain the problem. A broken machine, for example, may have stopped an entire assembly line. Or damaged merchandise may have cost a loss in sales or even a loss of customers. Explaining such effects of the problem strengthens your claim. And you may sometimes need a stronger claim to get the relief you seek. The following two first sentences of claim letters illustrate this technique:

> For added strength, you may explain the damage caused by the problem (inconvenience, lost sales, and such).

The contents of 8 of the 11 cartons of Sea Mist cologne were broken on arrival and could not be used for our advertising promotion.

The Model H freezer (Serial No. 71312) that we purchased from you last September suddenly quit working, ruining $312 of frozen foods in the process.

### Explaining the Facts

After stating the problem, your next logical step is to present the supporting facts. You should do this in a straightforward manner, being as objective as you can. You will need to tell your reader just what went wrong, what evidence you have, what the damage is—in fact, everything you know that could affect the reader's decision.

> Give enough facts to justify the claim.

In presenting the facts of the case, you should choose your words carefully. Words that accuse or imply distrust may work against the claim. So may words of anger. Although anger works effectively in some cases, usually it does not, especially in cases that require persuasion. Angry and accusing words tend to put the reader on the defensive and to arouse resistance. This reduces your chances of getting a good settlement.

> Be careful to use words that do not show distrust or anger.

### Giving Choice in Correcting Error

The facts you present should prove your claim. So after presenting them, you logically move to the handling of your claim. How you handle your claim is a matter for you to decide, but the facts of the case often make one plan clearly superior.

> Next, handle the claim.

One possibility is to state what you want the reader to do. Perhaps you want your money returned, or new merchandise, or free repairs. Clearly stating what you want, as long as it is reasonable, strengthens your case, for it gives the reader a major hurdle to clear if he or she does not accept.

> You can state what you want done,

When you know that your reader has a favorable adjustment reputation, you may wish to let the reader decide what to do. Most companies try hard

> or you can leave the decision to the reader.

**CHAPTER 5**   Directness in Initiating Routine Letters

to make fair adjustments. In fact, they often do more than is necessary—and more than you would dare ask them to do.

## Overcoming Negativeness with a Friendly Close

*Your closing words should show your cordial attitude.*

Your final friendly words should remove all doubt about your cordial attitude. For added strength, when strength is needed to support a claim, you could express appreciation for what you seek. This suggestion does not support use of the timeworn "Thanking you in advance." Instead, say something like "I would be grateful if you could get the new merchandise to me in time for my Friday sale."

## Contrasting Examples of Claim Letters

*The following contrasting letters show good and bad handling of a claim.*

The following two letters show contrasting ways of handling Pinnacle's fire extinguisher problem. The first is slow and harsh. The second is courteous, yet to the point and firm.

**A Slow and Harsh Letter.** The first letter starts slowly with a long explanation of the situation. Some of the details in the beginning sentence are helpful, but they do not deserve the emphasis that this position gives them. The problem is not described until the second paragraph. The wording here is clear but much too strong. The words are angry and insulting, and they talk down to the reader. Such words are more likely to produce resistance than acceptance. The negative writing continues into the close, leaving a bad final impression.

*This bad one is slow and harsh.*

Dear Ms. Golby:

    As your records will show, on December 7 we ordered 24 Fireboy extinguishers (our Order No. 7135). The units were shipped to us by Red Arrow Freight (your Invoice No. 715C) and arrived at our loading docks December 15.
    At the time of delivery, our shipping and receiving supervisor noticed that all the boxes were soaked with fluid. Further inspection showed that your workers had been negligent in checking the cap screws. As a result of their negligence, acid leaked and destroyed the chrome finish on all the units.
    It is hard for me to understand a shipping system that permits such errors to take place. Pinnacle does not accept these fire extinguishers. Further, we want these damaged units taken off our hands and replaced with good ones. Because we will be inspected by the fire marshal Monday, we further insist that the replacements reach us by that date.

                Respectfully,

**A Firm yet Courteous Letter.** The second letter follows the plan suggested in preceding paragraphs. A subject line quickly identifies the situation. The letter begins with a clear statement of the problem. Next, in a tone that shows firmness without anger, it tells what went wrong. Then it requests a specific remedy and asks what to do with the damaged goods. The ending uses subtle persuasion by implying confidence in the reader. The words used here leave no doubt about continued friendship.

PART 3   Basic Patterns of Business Letters

**CASE ILLUSTRATION**  Claim Letters. *(A Consumer's Claim about a Damaged Air Conditioner)*
Written by a consumer, this letter presents a claim about a defective air conditioner purchased through mail order. The beginning words are direct, though somewhat general. They explain the difficulty clearly and with good moral persuasion.

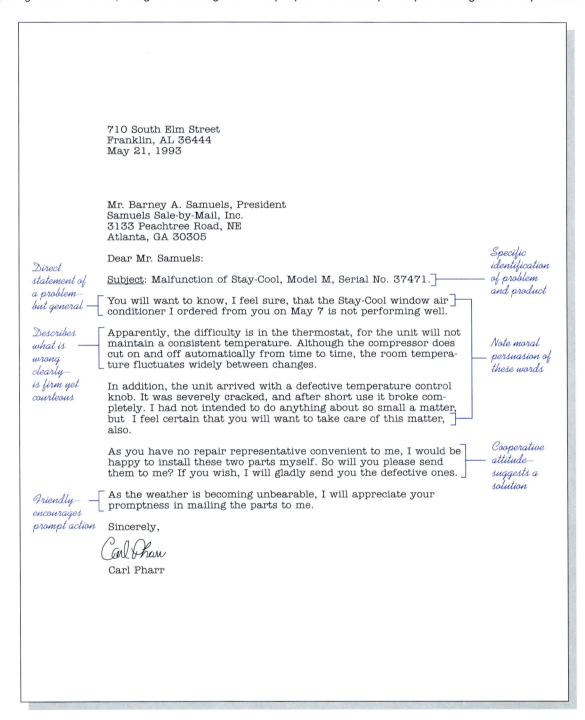

**CASE ILLUSTRATION**  Claim Letters. *(Polite Firmness in a Claim about Defective Carpeting)*

In this letter a hotel manager presents a claim about defective carpeting. She makes the claim directly and forcefully—yet politely. She explains the problem clearly and emphasizes the effect of the damage.

---

# CHARLES
# HOTEL

September 17, 1993

Mr. Luther R. Ferguson, President
Rich Carpet, Inc.
13171 Industrial Boulevard
Seattle, WA 98107

Dear Mr. Ferguson:

*Direct statement of problem* — Subject: Color fading of your Kota-Tuff carpeting, your invoice 3147 dated January 3, 1993. — *Clearly states problem and identifies transaction*

The Kota-Tuff carpeting you installed for us last January has faded badly and is an eyesore in our hotel pool area. As you can see in the enclosed photograph, the original forest green color now is spotted with rings of varying shades of white and green. The spotting is especially heavy in areas adjacent to the pool. Probably water has caused the damage. But your written warranty says that the color will "withstand the effects of sun and water."

*Emphasis on effect* — *Explains nature and extent of defect* — *Establishes case firmly*

*Suggests solution* — As the product clearly has not lived up to the warranty, we ask that you replace the Kota-Tuff with a more suitable carpeting. If you are unable to find a satisfactory carpeting, we request a refund of the full purchase price, including installation. — *Justifies claim*

I will appreciate your usual promptness in correcting this problem.

Sincerely,

*Luella E. Dabbs*

Luella E. Dabbs
Manager

tos

Enclosure (photograph)

2-201 East 15th Street
North Vancouver, BC V7M 1S2
604-678-9080

Dear Ms. Golby:

Subject: Acid leakage of Fireboy extinguishers, your Invoice No. 715C

    The condition of the 24 Fireboy extinguishers received today has affected their ability to function.

    At the time of delivery, the condition of your shipment was called to the attention of the Red Arrow Freight Company driver by our shipping and receiving supervisor. Upon inspection, we found all the boxes thoroughly soaked with fluid. Further investigation revealed that at least six of the extinguishers had leaked acid from the cap screws. As a result, the chrome finish of all the units had been badly damaged.

    As we are under orders from the fire marshal to have this equipment in our plant by Monday, please get the 24 replacement units to us by that date. Also, will you please instruct me what I should do with the defective units?

    I am aware, of course, that situations like this will occur in spite of all precautions. And I am confident that you will replace the extinguishers with your usual courtesy.

                       Sincerely,

*This better letter closely follows text suggestions.*

## INTRODUCTORY SITUATION

### to Order Letters

In your position at Pinnacle, you receive this month's *Business Administrator* in the morning mail. As usual, this professional journal is filled with articles useful to workers who want to advance into administration. One of the articles lists the 10 most valuable books for administrators. You are impressed. You want these books for your personal library.

    You might be able to get the books by looking for them at local bookstores, but this procedure would take more time than you can spare. You decide instead to order them from the publishers. As you do not have these publishers' order forms, you will have to order by letter. The article gives publisher names along with the prices and necessary descriptions of the books. A business directory in the company library contains the publishers' addresses.

    One of the order letters you write will be to Business Books, Inc., publisher of three of the books you want. You are ready to write the order. But how do you organize the letter? What information do you include? The answers to these questions appear in the following discussion. ■

## ORDERS

As most orders are now either placed orally with salespeople or made on order forms, order letters are not often written. When you must write an order letter, however, you would do well to follow the plan that the following pages discuss in detail:

- **Begin directly—with clear authorization.**
- **Systematically and consistently arrange items with identifying facts (number, units, catalog number, name, description points, unit price, total price).**
- **Cover shipping instructions and manner of payment.**
- **End with goodwill comment.**

*Rarely will you write an order letter.*

*But when you write one, follow this plan.*

CHAPTER 5   Directness in Initiating Routine Letters

## Directly Authorizing the Order

*Begin order letter directly, with a clear authorization.*

You should begin the order letter directly—with a clear authorization to ship goods. You have no reason to begin otherwise. The news is good, for the order means business and profits to the reader. So your first main words should say something like "Please send me . . ." Any less direct wording falls short of the ideal. For example, such beginnings as "I am in need of . . ." or "I would like to have . . ." are merely hints or suggestions. They are not clear authorization.

## Specifically Covering the Sale

*Identify the goods ordered clearly and in an orderly way.*

The remainder of your letter is an exercise in clear, orderly, and complete coverage of the details your reader needs. The letter is likely to contain many identifying facts. Unless these facts are in good order, they will probably confuse your reader. You should arrange them for quick and clear understanding.

*One good way is to begin with the number and units needed.*

There is no best arrangement for the items of information needed in an order except that the order be consistent from item to item. You would be wise, however, to begin with the number and units needed. One acceptable arrangement for the remaining items of information is the following:

*Then describe the items in this order.*

Catalog number.
Basic name (including trade names and brands when helpful).
Points of description (color, size, weight, and the like).
Unit price.
Total price.

In finished form, the information might read like this:

3 dozen   No. 712AC, Woolsey claw hammer, drop-forged head, hickory handle, 13 inches overall length, 16 ounces, at $44.74 per dozen .......................... $134.22

*For typing form, look at the illustrations in this chapter.*

For quick and easy communication, you will need to arrange this information in a neat and orderly form. As the following letter examples show, one such form places the quantities and units in a clear column to the left and sets off the remaining information to the right. (Notice that the carryover lines are aligned at the left with the first line of this information.) Prices are in a column, aligned at the right margin. Leaders help guide the reader's eye from the text to the amount.

*Cover all the information needed—shipping instructions, payment, and the like.*

In addition to describing the items ordered, you need to include other vital information. You need to give shipping instructions and information regarding payment (charge, cash, COD). You may work some of this information into the beginning of the letter, following the authorization statement. You may include the remainder with your closing remarks. The important point is that you should include all the information that the reader needs to fill your order.

## Closing with a Friendly Comment

*Close with friendly words. If possible, make them fit the one case.*

You should end the order letter with an appropriate and friendly comment. As we mentioned earlier, the close could include some of the shipping

## Tables: An Organizing Tool for Detail

Setting up tables within a document is now an easy task. Many word processors either have a tables feature or allow you to import spreadsheet files. In both cases, you arrange information in columns and rows, inserting detail in the cells. You can even format the column headings in addition to calculating with formulas. You can see these features illustrated in the example below. This table could be the detail you'd normally put in the body paragraphs of an order letter.

| Quantity | Item Number | Description | Color | Unit Price | Total |
|---|---|---|---|---|---|
| 3 Dozen | 2411 | Ball point pens, fine pt. | Black | 12.00 | 36.00 |
| 5 Reams | 12912 | Classic, 20 lb. laser paper | White | 5.70 | 28.50 |
| 1 | 12271 | Paper cutter, std. size | | 29.50 | 29.50 |
| | | Tax, Shipping & Handling | | | 9.99 |
| | | Total | | | 103.99 |

Organizing information with tables makes it easier for both you and your reader. You'll be sure to include all information since the headings prompt you for complete detail; your reader will be able to extract easily information needed to fill your order accurately.

---

instructions. But the main words should express a friendly comment. They should fit the one case as much as possible, as in this example:

As we have promised to make our first delivery on the 17th, would you please get the supplies to us by the 13th at the latest. We will sincerely appreciate your promptness.

### Contrasting Orders

The following contrasting letters for the case described earlier show good and bad ways of ordering books.

*The following two examples are of bad and good order letters.*

**A Slow and Disorderly Order.** The letter showing bad technique begins indirectly. The first sentence is useless and merely delays the main message. This message comes in the second sentence, but it is more a suggestion than an authorization. The information on the books is not orderly, and the format does not display it clearly. Neither the number of books wanted nor their prices stand out. One has to look for this information. The book titles are clear and will probably lead the reader to the right books. But edition numbers have been omitted, and this information could be important. Also, the items are ordered inconsistently. Payment details appear in the close, but they are vague and incomplete. The letter's abrupt ending will produce little goodwill.

**CHAPTER 5** Directness in Initiating Routine Letters

**CASE ILLUSTRATION** Order Letters. *(An Involved Order for Supplies)*
A business manager's small mail order for office supplies is illustrated in this letter. The items ordered require a detailed description, which the writer provided in an orderly way.

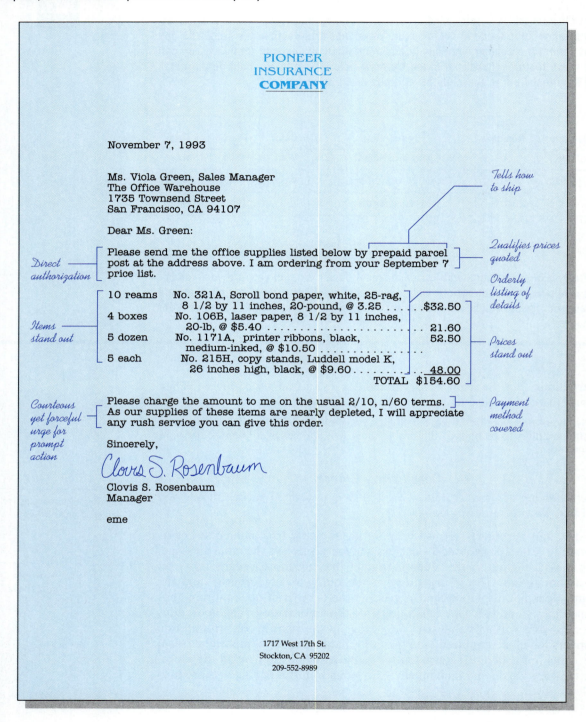

Dear Sales Manager:

Information I have indicates that your company is the publisher of three books I would like for my personal library. I would sincerely appreciate it if you would be so kind as to send them to me. They are as follows:

*Basic Management*, price $16.95, by Alonzo Bevins, 1 copy.

*Clear Writing for Business*, price $11.95, by Mildred Knauth, 1 copy.

*Managing Organizations*, 2 copies, by Hugo W. Bass, price $15.95.

I have enclosed a check in the amount of $60.80. I will pay any additional charges.

Sincerely,

This bad one is slow and disorderly.

**A Direct and Orderly Order.** The second letter avoids the faults of the first. It begins with a direct authorization to ship goods. Then it lists the books wanted in an orderly fashion. The numbers and units stand out. Clear identification information appears in the center position. Extensions in the right-hand column emphasize the price information, including the total cost. In the close, the remaining matter of additional charges is handled. Although the closing goodwill words are somewhat routine, they are appropriate for this routine situation.

Dear Sales Manager:

Please send me the following books:

1 copy Alonzo Bevins, *Basic Management*, 2nd ed., 1992,
@ $16.95 . . . . . . . . . . . . . . . . . . . . . . . . . . . . . $16.95

1 copy Mildred Knauth, *Clear Writing for Business*, 1993,
@ $11.95 . . . . . . . . . . . . . . . . . . . . . . . . . . . . . 11.95

2 copies Hugo W. Bass, *Managing Organizations*, 3rd ed., 1993,
@ $15.95 . . . . . . . . . . . . . . . . . . . . . . . . . . . . . 31.90

Total . . . . . . . . . . . . . . . . . . . . . . . . . . . . . . . . . $60.80

The enclosed check for $60.80 covers your 1993 list prices for the books. If prices have increased and/or if I owe shipping charges or sales taxes, please bill me for the additional amount. Or, if you prefer, I will pay on delivery.

I will appreciate your promptness in handling this order.

Sincerely,

This good order letter is fast and efficient.

## ■ ■ ■ ■ ■ ■ ■ ■ ■ ■ ■ ■ ■ ■ ■ ■ ■ ■ ■ ■
## SUMMARY (by Chapter Objectives)

1. The process of writing business letters begins with planning.
   - Begin by determining the objective of the letter (what it must do).
   - Next, predict the reader's probable reaction to the objective.
   - Then assemble all the information you will need.
   - Select the letter plan (direct order if positive or neutral reaction; indirect order if negative reaction).
2. Your remaining steps are as follows:
   - Write the letter, applying your knowledge of conciseness, readable writing, and effect of words.
   - Review your work critically, seeking ways of improving it.

1. Describe the planning stage of the process of writing business letters.

2. Describe the remaining stages of the process of writing business letters, explaining how following these procedures can improve your writing.

- Get input from others.
- Evaluate all inputs.
- Revise, using your best judgment. This end product is an improved letter, and you have had a profitable learning experience.

**3. Write clear, well-structured routine requests for information.**

3. The routine inquiry letter is the first type of letter discussed.
   - Begin it with a request—either (1) a request for specific information wanted or (2) a general request for information.
   - Somewhere in the letter explain enough to enable the reader to answer.
   - If the inquiry involves more than one question, make each stand out—perhaps as separate sentences or separate paragraphs.
   - Consider numbering the questions.
   - And word them as questions.
   - End with an appropriate friendly comment.

**4. Compose orderly and thorough inquiries about prospective employees that show a respect for human rights.**

4. Inquiries about people follow much the same order as described above.
   - But they require special care, as they concern the moral and legal rights of people.
   - So seek truth, and act in good faith.
   - Also, adapt your questions to the one applicant and the one situation rather than follow a routine.

**5. Write claim letters that explain the facts in a firm but courteous manner.**

5. Claim letters are a special case. Even though they carry bad news, they are best written in the direct order. The reason: the reader usually wants to correct the problem and requires only that the facts be presented; also, directness strengthens the claim. Follow this general plan:
   - Somewhere early in the letter (in a subject line or incidentally in the first sentence) identify the transaction.
   - Then state what went wrong, perhaps with some interpretation of the effects.
   - Follow with a clear review of the facts, without showing anger.
   - You may want to suggest a remedy.
   - End with cordial words.

**6. Write orders that begin with a clear authorization; contain an orderly arrangement of units, descriptions, and prices; cover all shipping information; and close with goodwill.**

6. Order letters are best written in the direct order, as follows:
   - Begin with a direct authorization to ship.
   - Carefully and systematically identify the items you want (catalog number, basic name, descriptive points, unit price, total price, and so on).
   - Include all other information vital to the sale (shipping instructions, method of payment, time requirements).
   - End with friendly, appropriate words that fit the one case.

## QUESTIONS FOR DISCUSSION

1. When is the direct order appropriate in inquiry letters? When would you use the indirect order? Give examples.
2. "Explanations in inquiry letters merely add length and should be eliminated." Discuss.
3. What should the letter writer do to respect the rights of people in inquiries about them?
4. "In writing inquiries about people, I do not ask specific questions. Instead, I ask for 'everything you think I should know' about the person." Discuss this viewpoint.
5. Usually bad-news letters are appropriately written in the indirect order. Why should claim letters be exceptions?
6. Justify the use of negative words in claim letters. Can they be overused? Discuss.
7. Explain what factors separate good questions from poor ones. Give supporting examples.
8. Discuss the relative directness of these beginnings of an order letter:
    a. "Please ship the following items . . ."
    b. "I would like to have the following . . ."
    c. "I need the following items . . ."
    d. "I would appreciate your sending me the following items . . ."
    e. "Can you send me the following items . . . ?"
9. Identify some word processing features that assist writers in inquiries, and orders.

## APPLICATION EXERCISES

1. List your criticisms of this letter inquiring about a convenience store advertised for sale:

   Dear Mr. Meeks:

   This is in response to your advertisement in the May 17 *Daily Bulletin* in which you describe a convenience store in Clark City that you want to sell. I am very much interested as I would like to relocate in that area. Before I drive down to see the property, I need some preliminary information. Most important is the question of financing. I am wondering whether you would be willing to finance up to $50,000 of the total if I could come up with the rest, and how much interest would you charge and for how long. I would also like to have the figures for your operations for the past two or three years, including gross sales, expenses, and profits. I need to know also the condition of the building, including such information as when built, improvements made, repairs needed, and so on.

   Hoping that you can get these answers to me soon so we can do business.

   Sincerely yours,

2. List your criticisms of this letter asking for information about an applicant for a job:

   Dear Ms. Bentley:

   Inez Becker has applied to us for a job as inventory clerk in our parts department. She listed you as a reference and claims that she worked for you as a records clerk in your parts department for the period May 1989 to August 1992. As I am impressed with Ms. Becker, I would like to have your evaluation of her.

   I am especially interested in her work ethic and how she gets along with other workers. I am curious about why she left the job with you. Also, please tell me whether you would hire her back if you had an opening. In addition, I would like to know about her honesty, character, and attitude.

   Thank you in advance for your prompt response.

   Sincerely yours,

## LETTER PROBLEMS

### ROUTINE INQUIRIES

1. Assume the position of assistant to the president of Goliath Industries and write a letter that will get information about a possible site for this year's executive retreat. Your boss, Cynthia Barrington, wants to go to Half Moon Lake Resort for this three-day work-and-play meeting. (She visited the place a few months ago and liked it.)

   The retreat is scheduled for the last Thursday,

Friday, and Saturday in August (arriving Wednesday afternoon and departing Sunday morning). Twenty-two of Goliath's top administrators will attend. The group will spend six hours each day in strategy and planning sessions. The remaining time they will spend at play—swimming, golfing, tennis, fishing, boating, and such. President Barrington has asked you to get all the information needed to plan the meeting.

You find most of the information you will need in a descriptive brochure that Barrington gave you. It tells much about the place—its two golf courses, 12 tennis courts, marina, fishing pier, boat rentals, and more. But you can't find all the information you need. Your needs are as follows.

First, you need to know about transportation facilities between the airport in Edburg City (where your people will arrive) and Half Moon Lake Resort. Your map indicates the distance to be about 65 miles. Perhaps the resort offers transportation service for its guests. Maybe your group will need to rent automobiles. Or maybe some form of private transportation is available.

Second, the brochure doesn't tell all about costs. It indicates a standard rate of $175 per person per day, single occupancy, including all meals. But the brochure probably was written for individual vacationers. You suspect groups such as yours get some form of discount. You'll find out.

Another question concerns the cost of the recreational facilities. As you understand the brochure, all such costs are included in the per-day charge. But the brochure is not specific on the point, so you'll clear up the matter in advance.

Also, the group will need a meeting room—one suitable for the 22 executives. It would be good if all could be seated around a single table, but other configurations would be acceptable. You will need a chalkboard, overhead projector, and screen. And it is important that the room be reasonably free from outside noises. Do they have such a room? And how much would it cost?

Yet another matter is that of the party boat President Barrington remembers. When she was at the resort, she had a delightful dinner cruise, and she would like to do the same with the executives on the last night (Saturday). The brochure gives none of the details, so you will have to get them (boat rental costs, boat availability, dinner costs).

Address the letter to Mr. Maxwell Worley, Director of Marketing (the name given on the brochure).

2. Play the role of vice president of sales for Norstar Chemical Company, Ltd. Today on the flight home from a regional sales meeting, you noticed an advertisement in the airline's magazine that just might solve one of your problems.

Your problem is that of finding a suitable gift to present to certain salespeople to be honored at your annual meeting. Every year Norstar honors those salespeople who have completed a multiple of five years of service (5, 10, 15, etc.) with the presentation of a suitable gift. And selecting the gift is your job. Over the seven years you have had the assignment, you have selected desk sets, art pieces, and sporting goods. You've had some difficulty coming up with something for this year—and then you saw the advertisement.

The advertisement is for a binder portfolio (three-ring), made of soft nappa leather by Varga Leather Crafts. As described in the ad, the portfolio features zip-around closure and has a retractable handle and two outside pockets. Inside are five divider pockets and an 18-month planner with tabs, letterpad, and pen. It is available in brown, black, and beige.

The picture in the ad shows the product with a company logo prominently displayed. You would want the same, but the ad mentions nothing about it. So you'll need to find out whether Varga could do one for you and at what cost. Also, you would like to have the salesperson's name printed below the logo.

The $199 price quoted in the ad is a little high, you think; you are hopeful that you can get a significant quantity discount. After all, you would be buying 66 of them.

You don't especially like the color choices. Perhaps for a large order Varga would make the portfolios in the color of your choice. You'd like a rich burgundy.

Then there is the question of time, for the annual meeting is only eight weeks away. Could Varga work up this special order in that time? You'll need a definite promise on this matter.

Now you will write the people at Varga for the answers to your questions. You have their address from the advertisement.

3. Assume the role of director of training for the Bay City Refinery of the Zenith Oil Company. Following a series of accidents in the plant, company management has been applying pressure for more emphasis on safety education. You started an in-plant program with several company executives as instructors, but the program has not been well received. And the accident rate has not declined. You will have to do more.

In this month's issue of *Training Journal* you found an advertisement that you think might hold the solution to the problem. It is for the services of

J. Jack Mueller, a nationally known safety expert. As the ad explains, Mueller's services include a thorough safety survey of a plant. He presents a list of all the safety problems he finds, and he suggests actions that should be taken to correct them. And most important of all, he presents to employees two hours of instruction guaranteed to make them more safety conscious. This instruction has received national acclaim (so says the ad).

You have heard about Mueller, for he is well known in training circles. In fact, you recall talking about him with Stephanie Jennings at last year's annual meeting of your professional organization, the International Association of Trainers. As you recall, Stephanie reported that her company, Zoro Motors, Inc., has been using Mueller for some time. You don't remember whether her experiences with Mueller were positive or negative.

Before you hire Mueller, you want some specific information concerning results, for your superiors will expect you to do your homework. So you will write Stephanie and find out what you need to know before taking action.

Specifically, you want information on three matters that concern you. First, you want to know how effective the program was—whether accidents decreased after Mueller had done his thing, and if they decreased, was the decrease permanent. You are hopeful that she collected before-and-after data on accident occurrence.

Second, you'd like to know how well Mueller was received by the workers (you already have a program that's not well received). Perhaps Stephanie used questionnaires to determine the participants' impressions of the instruction (a common practice in training work).

While results are important, what you pay for them must be considered. So you'll ask a concluding summary question about whether Stephanie and Zoro management feel that the services received were worth the money paid for them.

As you begin the letter, keep in mind that you know Stephanie primarily on a professional basis but well enough to address her by first name.

4. As marketing manager for Glasscraft, Inc., a new and struggling manufacturer of boats, you are considering an invitation from the manager of the Bigg City Boat Fair. The manager wants to sell you display space at a cost of $1,200 per stall. The fair may well be a good place to display your product line, but you don't know for sure.

The $1,200 cost of a stall appears reasonable, but you need to know more about what you would get for your money. Just how large are the stalls? You would want to display at least two of your boats and perhaps three. If the stalls are small, you may need more than one. You'd also like to know whether you have any choice of location. From experience you know that some locations are better than others. At one fair you recall being assigned a place away from the major traffic flow.

Although you have heard of this fair, you really don't know how well attended it is or how many companies display their products. So you will ask. Also, there is the matter of security. At some of the fairs costly equipment has been stolen during the night. You haven't been victimized yet, but you want to be sure that your property is reasonably protected.

Now write the letter that will get the information you need.

5. Your travel company, Globe Trotter Travel, will be moving into new offices soon. You've been asked to help select some of the decorations for these offices. Your president, Rosemary Lenaghan, has made it clear that the image the new offices should project is one of competence and quality. In addition, the president wants the environment to be pleasing for the employees but not lavish.

You have been reading lately that Eastern European pottery is still very reasonably priced. Czech pottery brought here by immigrants in the 1940s sells for $5–500 and can be found in flea markets, second-hand stores, and small antique stores. At these prices, the pottery is within your decorating budget.

You have also seen a few pictures of pieces you think would help set a cheerful environment. Most pieces are hand-painted in eye-popping colors, creating a stunning exuberance. They come in various patterns and designs from polka dot, checked, and striped to graphic florals.

Write a form letter to send to the managers/owners of nearby flea markets, second-hand stores, and small antique stores, inquiring about the availability of these Czechoslovakian wares as well as full descriptions and prices. Request that they send you pictures of any pieces as well as hours when you could come by to see them. Also, since these are becoming collectibles, you may want to ask about their authenticity.

*Optional*: Turn in the basic letter (primary document) with merge variables named and bracketed such as {First_Name}, {Last_Name}, {Title}, etc. Also, using the merge feature, combine the primary with the secondary document (variable data) to print three letters to different readers.

6. As the owner of several convenience stores, you are considering adding books on tape to your read-

ing section. While until now you have stocked only magazines, newspapers, and a limited supply of videotapes, you have had several requests recently for books on tape.

In the past you have stuck with the marketing reports which relate that people who purchase videos do so near home and those who purchase audiotapes do so near the office. However, new sales figures indicate that sales are picking up in a variety of settings from truckstops to airports. Because most of your stores are located in the suburbs, you think that those commuters who stop by regularly for coffee and a newspaper are excellent prospects for books on tape. Many of them are between the ages of 25 and 40, the age of most buyers of audiotapes.

Write a letter of inquiry to Robert Edwards, president of the Audio Publishers Association, asking for the latest data on sales figures for best-sellers on tapes as well as the demographics of those buyers. Be sure your letter asks for a breakdown between fiction, classics, and self-help books. Also, ask for a list of recommended distributors as well as any other information you may find useful in your decision as to whether to stock audiotapes.

7. As the buyer and manager for a beachwear boutique, you remember that a few years ago, hypercolor T-shirts were a popular summer item. When you touched these shirts with your hand, the temperature of your hand changed the color of the shirt. These shirts added a bit of fun to wearing a T-shirt. A new item you are considering adds practicality to wearing a T-shirt.

This shirt is made from a new fabric called Solarweave. While the typical T-shirt blocks out less than 50 percent of all UV rays, the new fabric blocks out more than 99 percent of the UVB rays that produce sunburns. The fabric also blocks 93 percent of the UVA rays that lead to premature aging of the skin.

While most people are aware of the thinning of the ozone layer and the need to protect oneself against damaging sun rays, you wonder whether the $40 price tag is prohibitive. Inquire of the Chicago-based Solar Protection Factory, Inc. as to other features of the shirt. Ask about its durability, its laundering instructions, and the availability of colors and styles. You may add any other questions you think your buyers would want to know. Be sure the questions are clear and will generate the answers you seek. Watch out for yes/no questions as well as two-pronged questions. Be sure you get the answers you need to decide whether or not your customers would be interested in buying these shirts.

8. You operate a sporting goods store, stocking a wide variety of items for campers and outdoorsy men and women. The majority of your customers are upscale, health-conscious 25–40-year-olds.

Recently you've read that Kanebo, a leading textile company in Japan, has been selling a unique pantyhose—one soaked in insect repellent. They've reported that the stockings are being snapped up at prices between $2.60 and $4.80 a pair by outdoorsy women. The textile maker also offers hose saturated with vitamin C or aloe as well as others soaked with fragrances such as Tea Rose, Fresh Lime, and Night Lavender.

Would these stockings appeal to your customers? Could they be saturated with chemicals that repel ticks as well as insects? How strong are the odors? Do the Japanese buyers' demographics and life-styles have any similarity to those of your customers? These are just some of the questions that have been occurring to you. Others include distributors and distributorships, availability, government approvals, etc.

Organize these questions along with any others you have. Gather as much information from the Japanese textile maker as you can. Be sure your organization is tight and your questions are clear.

9. Today, you are Maria Stutzman, sales manager at Longhorn Steel Company. You have just received your monthly expense report from the accounting department and one figure—year-to-date variance—catches your eye. It's $5,000 over the budgeted amount for the first six months of the fiscal year.

As you attempt to determine precisely what cost items have caused the variance, you zero in more specifically on the figures before you. Airfare, per diem ($40.00 per day), transportation costs (limos), and such seem to be in line. But one budget line—hotel expense—catches your eye. It's $5,000 over budget. As you backtrack on the problem, the accounting department tells you that most high expense vouchers contained high hotel costs—from big city locations!

It's your job to sell company products to industrial users in the United States and Canada. When your salespeople travel, they usually fly to locations to make customer contacts and presentations. Some, however, drive—especially when locations are remote. But the travel cost to remote locations is not the problem. The travel cost to central city locations is.

And this is where you must now apply your best thinking. If you could get lower rates from hotels at which your salespeople stay in big city locations, you could bring your cost items back in line. But as you think through the situation, you develop an alternate idea: Is it possible to get better accommodation rates at different locations, perhaps those that lie outside inner city limits in "off-the-beaten path" locations?

The idea stays with you most of the day; but as you peruse *The Wall Street Journal* late in the afternoon, this ad catches your eye:

> Tired of paying exorbitant hotel rates? Try our excellent facilities at moderate prices. We're located outside the inner hub of most large cities. Transportation to other locations complimentary. An all-purpose facility.
> *Brian Hotels, Inc.*

As you ponder the words, your thoughts focus on getting more information about these facilities. What are their prices? Do they give corporate discounts? How far removed from central business districts are they? And what does "all-purpose facility" mean? No doubt there are other questions you will need answered as well.

You decide to write an inquiry letter to the hotel. It will need to be complete, and it will need to explain the uniquenesses of your situation so that the hotel management can respond specifically with its answers. If the letter gets you the information, you'll use it as a model to send to similar hotel chains in other big cities.

10. As executive director of the Association of Marketing Managers, you have a special problem that's been troubling you for some time. The commercial printer that produces all your regular publications has obvious quality-control problems. On the last issue of one publication, you had numerous calls from subscribers/members complaining about blurred pages, missing pages, and pages out of sequence. And this is not the first time you have had complaints. It has happened periodically before, but the same mistakes are being made with more frequency. You think that now is the time to change printers; so you decide to write to several companies to get competitive bids.

Your budget for printing last year was $50,000. For that amount, you publish two quarterly journals for the 3,000 members you serve. In addition to these major publications, you also produce a membership directory each year, a program booklet for your annual meeting, and special publication volumes as they may arise. Along with these publications are mailing envelopes, stationery, and office printing supplies. Indeed, your account would be a profitable one for the right company. But you will have to have someone who can do quality work.

As you think more specifically about the type of questions to ask, you'll need information about lead time for production, turnaround time, and delivery. And who will pay for corrections that will need to be made? Also, will the printer provide a delivery person to pick up and return material for proofreading? And you'll need a price estimate on all orders. You can assume you print 3,700 of each quarterly publication. No doubt there are other items of inquiry you will need to cover in the letter.

Think through the situation. Then write an inquiry letter to the first printer on your list, Group Graphics, Inc. If the first letter gets you the information you need, you will send similar letters to other printers in the area.

11. Sit down at your personal computer today and assume the role of Bill Carter, tennis pro at Greenwood Country Club. The 75 members who play in organized leagues at your club have asked you to investigate the possibility of covering two of the six courts on which members play. They believe that covered courts would permit players to play in all types of weather conditions—extreme heat, rain, and cold. Covered courts would provide a luxury that competing public courts and other tennis facilities in your area do not have. Hence, you decide to explore the matter further for more details.

A casual conversation with one of the club members who is an engineer reveals that soil samples of the area to be covered are critical to the job. If there are sandstone substructures and water pockets, then different support piers would have to be constructed. Indeed, you have had trouble with cracks and shifting of the court surfaces over the years. And you remember that samples taken before the courts were constructed showed there were problems. But you can't remember specifics. Likely, new samples would have to be taken.

With these preliminary ideas in mind, you now try to focus on other specific points with the overall purpose of writing a routine inquiry letter that will serve as a request for bids from contractors in your area for the job. The letter will begin directly with the request for the submittal of a proposal. In addition, it will attempt to get you the information you want. If things progress, you will make a formal presentation to the club's board of directors for funding. More immediately, you want information to determine the type of facility that could be constructed and at what price.

The PTA (Professional Tennis Association) regulations state that beginning eave heights should start at 18 feet from the ground around the edge of the courts and ascend to 34 feet at the center of the net. Of course, you would want to have these dimensions in the covered facility. In addition, you wonder about summer heat in such a domed enclosure. Would it be too hot under the summer sun due to a dutch oven effect? Would open sides be enough to allow sufficient airflow? You're not considering a totally enclosed area—only a covering of the existing two courts. And could the existing lights be used in the covered facility?

Of course, you're also interested in color, guarantee, and the length of time it would take to construct such an enclosure. Perhaps there are other points that need to be included as well. Think through the questions you need to ask, organize your letter, and then write it to be sent to the top five contractors you have identified in your locale. You want to present a preliminary report to the members next month. So write your letter in a way that "serves" your purpose and the club you represent in a professional and courteous manner.

12. Your job as employee benefits manager for Bosco Corporation brings you into an interesting situation today—one requiring you to write a model inquiry letter. Each year, the company conducts an attitude survey of its 500 employees. Included in the survey is a statement about the adequacy of fringe benefits. Based on the results of the survey, most employees feel that the fringe benefit package you offer is adequate. Eleven people, however, suggested that dental insurance be added to the benefits you offer.

Bosco Corporation is a relatively young company. Begun 10 years ago as a family business, it grew to 100 employees in two years. Throughout its existence, the company has shown consistent, stable growth, reaching its present 500 employees in an undramatic but uniform manner. Employee benefits offered to the workers have also grown and changed over the years. Presently, you offer such fringes as a retirement program, hospitalization, and life and disability insurance. But with the write-in comments, you think you must now consider adding to the package.

At a recent Society for Human Resources Management meeting, you heard an update on fringe benefit offerings from a professor who teaches at a local university. National trends show that if dental insurance is added to the fringe benefit package companies often require a 50–50 split of the costs with employees. In addition, the coverage is generally optional.

With these ideas in your mind, you sit down at your PC to rough out a letter you will send to several insurance companies requesting information you need to consider adding dental coverage to your present package. First, you want to know exactly what is covered in dental plans. And are there deductibles?

Because most plans are optional, would there be a minimum number of employees needed before you could offer coverage? And you wonder too about what advantages might accrue to the company—particularly tax advantages. Moreover, what assistance will a company provide to your employees in filing claims? Will they send people on site to help employees? Or do they have an 800 number?

No doubt there are other questions you will need answered before you can make a good decision. Think through the situation completely, then write the letter to the first company you find in your benefits directory that offers such insurance—the Continental Life Company.

## INQUIRIES, PROSPECTIVE EMPLOYEES

13. As regional sales manager for Dura-Bilt Tools, Inc., you have just completed a recruiting visit to Kemper University where you interviewed nine prospects for the two openings you have on your sales force. One of the prospects is the highly personable and vivacious Joan Coco. From what you have seen of her, Joan is an outstanding prospect. Before you pursue the matter further, however, you will contact the references she listed on her application form. First you will write to Professor Thomas O. Pennington, who she reports was her employer (part-time work as a research assistant) as well as her teacher for two courses.

As you prepare to write the letter, you consider the work Joan would do for you. It is sales work primarily, calling on retailers, taking orders, assisting with displays, maintaining good customer relations, and generally promoting Dura-Bilt products. The ideal person for such work is self-motivated, for the work is done with little supervision. He or she should be a diligent and hard worker—one who is aggressive, has high goals, and is willing to do what is necessary to reach these goals.

Although the position involves no managerial duties now, you are always looking for people who have what it takes to move up in the organization. So you will want to check on her leadership potential, including her mentality for such a role.

Like all sales jobs, this job requires good interpersonal skills. More specifically, the person selected should like people and should be able to communicate with people easily. You believe you saw these qualities in Joan, but you want to verify your observations since you have been wrong in the past.

With the foregoing information in mind, you'll now determine the questions that you should ask the professor. Then write the letter.

14. For this problem you are the district manager for Cap'n Sam's Galley, a chain of seafood restaurants. Last week your manager at the Chanelview unit left you, so you have been searching for a replacement. After interviewing several applicants, you favor Rafer M. Quigley, who currently manages the snack bar at the Western Hills Country Club. Quigley told you that his boss, Alice Prather, is aware of his interest in your job. He has authorized you to write her.

Before you write the letter, you will get in mind a clear picture of the job to be filled. Then you will ask the questions that will get what you need in deciding whether Quigley is the right person for the job.

As you view the job, it involves every phase of restaurant operation—cooking, serving, record-keeping, buying, managing people, and so on. More specifically, the person selected must be able to manage a wide range of people types, varying from part-time college students to non-native English-speaking help. He or she must be able to do the detailed record-keeping required by the chain's central office—and to do it on time. He or she must know how to order food and supplies wisely. Also, the manager should know how to prepare food and how to organize the kitchen and the serving operations for most effective results. Perhaps most important of all, the manager must be willing to work long and hard, for your compensation plan is heavily based on the restaurant's profits.

With the foregoing analysis of the job of a manager in mind, you are ready to write. Make sure that the questions you ask will get the information you need.

15. Take over as the personnel director of O'Keefe and DeLoche, a major chain of department stores. You are in the process of recruiting six management trainees from the year's crop of graduates. One of the prospects you interviewed on the Asbury University campus is Diane Dionne. You liked what you saw in this marketing major, especially her outgoing personality and academic record. Now you must contact her references to verify your impressions. The first one on her list is Mr. Edmund E. Caldwell, a real estate broker for whom she worked part-time as a secretary for the past two years.

In determining what questions to ask Caldwell, you review the requirements for management trainees. Certainly those selected must be dependable. And they must be hard workers—people who have goals in life and aggressively work for them. Although management trainees aren't expected to know much about retailing at the beginning, they must be willing, eager, and able to learn.

Because trainees are expected to move up in the organization in time, they should have some potential for management from the beginning. Thus, signs of leadership ability should be present, as should a general knowledge of management. Personal qualities also are important, especially those that involve relating to and working with people. Good basic intelligence also is important. This quality may be reflected in grades to some extent, but there are observable measures as well.

You think Ms. Dionne will pass on all these requirements, but you must find out whether Mr. Caldwell agrees with you. After all, he knows her much better than you. He is expecting inquiries, for Ms. Dionne told you she has informed him that she is seeking a career job.

16. Running five dry cleaning stores keeps you busy. Linda Wingler, one of your most valued employees, recently moved out of state, and you need to find a replacement. You understand the importance of getting just the right person for this work. In addition to needing good interpersonal skills in order to work with customers, the person you hire needs to be honest and dependable. Because you cannot be at all five stores at the same time, the person you'll hire will need to be a self-starter and have basic math skills in order to balance the books on the days when you are not there.

Marina Munson responded to your ad in the Sunday newspaper. She and her husband will be moving to the area soon. While her resume and application letter make her look like an excellent candidate, you want to know more about those skills that can't be listed, such as interpersonal skills, dependability, and honesty. Since Marina's references are all out of town, you decide to write rather than call.

Marina's first reference is Michael Laing, a director of the Boys and Girls Club. While you can tell from the resume that Marina has worked there for the last two years, you want to know about her reliability. Did she work on the days scheduled? What was her absenteeism rate? Was she flexible on hours worked? Did she work well with colleagues and the parents of the children she worked with? Did she ever handle money or do any accounting? Did she ever have responsibility over others?

In your letter, ask those questions that are most important to you in deciding whether or not to interview Marina. Encourage disclosure by assuring Mr. Laing that his response will be confidential.

17. The Army recently moved a large division from one of its installations in your area to another state. Since only about one-third of the employees decided to move to the new location, your area has experienced a small surge in people looking for jobs. These people are hard workers and loyal to the area. However, as a private business owner, you wonder how these government civilian workers will do in the private sector. Therefore, before you interview Jane Adami, a well-qualified secretarial applicant, you decide to inquire about her.

Jane graduated from a local rural high school seven years ago. She obtained excellent training in business courses there and passed with ease the entry-level keyboarding test the Army required. Her first three years she worked in a secretarial pool, working for several bosses. However, her good attitude and excellent skills were quickly noticed. She was promoted to an administrative assistant to Lee Vault, the commanding officer, and worked for him the last four years.

Write Colonel Vault about Jane. Ask questions that concern you about her adaptability, her organization skills, and her decision-making ability. You know these are important characteristics for someone working for you, and you want to know what kinds of experience she has had in these areas. Be sure to ask about her willingness to learn new skills and procedures as well as any other questions you think appropriate.

18. You are regional manager for a large textbook publisher. You need to hire a marketing representative for the Los Angeles area again. You have had high turnover in this territory and are determined to hire someone right for the job this time.

You are experienced at hiring reps, but the Los Angeles territory presents some unique challenges.

In addition to having to drive the congested Los Angeles freeways, the accounts the representative will call on are extremely different. Both the private and public institutions are highly diversified. The representative will work with accounts ranging from private and generously endowed programs at the University of Southern California to accounts at the small private vocational and technical schools with cash-flow problems. Also, the rep will see a diverse population while dealing with large public schools such as California State University at Long Beach and small community colleges. In addition, both the faculty and students the representative will be working with are culturally diverse. In fact, in Los Angeles, voting ballots are printed in six languages. These special needs are in addition to those special qualities needed in a textbook marketing representative.

A marketing representative needs several other qualities. Being a well-organized self-starter is important. Also, since the products represented are changing constantly, the person you hire needs to be dedicated to keeping up on the new textbooks. Additionally, this job involves a lot of paperwork—the person cannot be a procrastinator. Furthermore, the person you hire must be willing to learn and use the portable computers now being assigned to the marketing staff.

You have received an excellent resume from Dana Robbins. She's had some sales experience, lives in the Los Angeles area, and loves reading books. While normally you would schedule an interview with her, this time you want to check her references first. Write Jennifer Stevens, the regional manager at the *Princeton Review,* where she last worked. While Jennifer now lives in Dallas, she worked closely with Dana for many years and should be able to give a good assessment of her work and personal skills.

19. As manager of the information systems department at Tubo, Inc., manufacturers and distributors of commercial ice-making machines, you receive continual requests for computer advice from employees throughout the plant. It seems that whenever anyone has a problem with hardware or software systems they call you and ask for assistance. You've tried to oblige them either by sending one of your 10 staff members to help them or by going to their workstations yourself. But such informal assistance is interfering with the productivity of your own department. Thus, your

president, Lara Wisyanski, has authorized a technical support liaison position to handle all technical computer support requests within the company.

The job of technical support liaison will involve a variety of duties. First, the person will respond to all calls for assistance with hardware or software systems. He or she will help with computer graphics, word processing, and statistical packages. In addition, the technical support person will also have to develop and conduct formal training programs to keep employees current in all phases of computer usage necessitated by the company's operations. Whenever there is a question about computer use or a computer problem, this person will be responsible for handling it. To be sure, the person whom you select for the job will have to have good technical and people skills.

To begin the recruiting process, you advertised in area newspapers in the classified section. From these ads, you received eleven resumes. After evaluating the resumes, you selected the top candidates and you interviewed each one personally. The top candidate is Jerry Walden, and you think he will be ideal for the job.

Jerry received a bachelor's degree in music education from State University six years ago. After graduation, he taught band at Dubose Junior High School for four years. He left his teaching job to become a retail software salesperson with RPC (Retailers of Personal Computers) because he needed more money to support his wife and two children. In college, Jerry had a minor in computer and electronic music, and RPC has sent him to many software training classes to keep him current in computer software programs.

He appears to have the teaching, technical, and personal attributes to do the job well. But you will not know for sure until you get information from his present employer. Write a personnel inquiry to Marvin Reese at RPC. Mr. Reese knows Jerry has applied for the job.

20. "She certainly appears to be a winner!" you think to yourself as Nelda Gonzalez leaves her interview with you. As manager of the public relations department at Alpha Packaging, you advertised for an editor/word processing operator/desktop publishing technician to add to your staff of five. You interviewed four of the nine people who applied for the job, but Nelda appears to be the leading candidate. Now you must write to her present employer to corroborate your evaluation of her qualifications for the job.

The job you advertised for is a new one for your department. It was authorized by President Lynne Schaffer after a Board of Directors meeting in which it was determined that a company newsletter could be used to improve worker morale as well as to "soft sell" the company and its products to present and potential customers. One of the directors reported that a recent *Wall Street Journal* article indicated that many companies are using newsletters this way and that they were a good investment. The article also noted that because more and more companies were preparing them, newsletters as morale boosters and selling tools would have to be more distinctive. Employees and customers were becoming quickly oversaturated.

To do the job correctly, a successful employee in your public relations department would need the right training, experience, and personal qualifications. The work would involve preparing good copy and designing the appearance of the newsletter. It would involve a myriad of activities from collecting information, to writing effective copy, to physically designing the newsletter itself. And the work would need to be done with desktop publishing equipment. Along with these technical aspects of the job, a person would need to be personally adaptive because of the various personalities on whom the newsletter and its contents depend. You plan to publish the newsletter four times per year.

Ms. Gonzalez appears to have the technical and interpersonal qualifications for the job. She earned a B.S. degree in information systems, so she should be well versed in word processing and desktop publishing. She also completed an M.A. degree in journalism at night while working full time in the information systems department of an electronics firm. To use her skills in journalism, she took her present job with Guardian Insurance Company where for three years she has been responsible for preparing company brochures and all internal policy and procedure manuals. For the last year, she has taught a night course in copyediting at the local community college. In her interview, she told you she wanted the job because "she wanted to specialize even more in employee communications."

Write your personnel inquiry letter about Ms. Gonzalez to Martina Polack, manager of the public relations department at Guardian. Ask the specific questions you need answers to so that you can evaluate Ms. Gonzalez's qualifications for the job.

21. As chair of the Tennis Selection Committee at Horseshoe Country Club, you are trying to hire a full-time tennis pro to replace the part-time pro you have employed for the last two years. Because

the part-time pro serves as the tennis coach at a local university, you now need to select a full-time tennis professional to develop and lead your tennis program.

You advertised for the job and received numerous applications. After rating the applications, you interviewed the top three persons. From this screening process, Betsy Zigmann has emerged as the top candidate. Now you are ready to ask her employer of the last three years what he thinks about her qualifications.

Zigmann noted in her interview that she wants to advance in her profession. At her current job as assistant tennis pro at Fossill Hill Country Club, located in a metropolitan area 50 miles away, she gives at least 45 hours of private instructions each week. So you believe her teaching skills are well honed. Zigmann earned a bachelor's degree in health education from Bossburg University, where she lettered in tennis for four years. After four years of college, she played professional tennis on the women's tour for four years, at one time being ranked 61 in the world. A knee injury forced her to retire and she returned to her university to finish the last 15 hours of her degree. During that year, she worked for the parks and recreation department of the local city, conducting tennis clinics and sponsoring city tennis leagues. After that, she joined the staff at the Fossill Hill Club.

The tennis professional's job at Horseshoe Country Club would be demanding. It would take long hours and hard work. First, the pro would have to sponsor two men's leagues (one singles and one doubles), a women's league (doubles), and two mixed doubles leagues. If there were more interest, the pro would have to sponsor other league play. Three of these leagues play at night and would require the pro to be on site during playing times. In addition, there would be developmental work—especially in the junior programs during the summer months.

Moreover, the pro would need to be available for private lessons and free clinics to sustain the interest in the ongoing league play. Presently, 75 of 525 club members are involved in tennis activity; so there is much potential for more tennis activity if a pro could "sell" the program. And, of course, the pro would have to manage the club's tennis shop with all of the equipment and services associated with such an operation.

Prepare a personnel inquiry letter about Ms. Betsy Zigmann to Richard Swatz, head tennis pro at Fossill Hill Country Club. He is aware that Zigmann has applied for the job. Ask the questions that will get you the information you need to verify Zigmann's qualifications.

## CLAIMS

22. Play the role of the executive secretary of the Alliance of Electronics Manufacturers. You have just returned from a 17-day trade mission to industrial centers in Europe with 31 industry representatives (group total of 32, counting yourself). As leader and organizer of the group, you made all the arrangements and served in the general role of tour leader. You worked up the tour through Travel Unlimited, a New York City agency with which AEM has worked for eleven years. The trip was highly successful from both a business and a pleasure point of view—except for a problem in Manchester, England.

    For the three nights in Manchester, the group was scheduled to stay at the Clifton Hotel, the best hotel in the city. Upon arriving at the hotel, however, you were told that because of unforeseen circumstances, the Clifton was overbooked. They had made arrangements for you to stay at the Ashley.

    The Ashley was adequate, but not nearly the quality that the Clifton was. Making matters worse, the Ashley charged extra for dinners each evening. According to your agreement with the agency, dinners were included in Manchester. You complained to the Ashley management but were told that the Ashley never includes meals in its contracts with tour groups.

    You can't determine precisely how much money is involved, but by comparing information obtained from the Clifton and Ashley desk clerks, you concluded that rooms are about $27 a day less at the Ashley. The prices of dinner varied somewhat, but you figured that they averaged about $14.50 per person per meal. Applying your best arithmetic, you conclude that Travel Unlimited owes the group $3,984, or $124.40 to each member ($27 per day for three days for 32 travelers and $14.50 each for three dinners for 32 people).

    Now you will write the Travel Unlimited people insisting that they correct the matter. You want them to give money back to each group member (they should have a list of names and addresses). And you'll ask that the agency write you an explanation of what they have done.

23. For the past few months, you have been busy

refurbishing your Wayside Motel—new paint, carpeting, curtains, and such. The last step was to be replacing all mattresses. As you have done for years, you ordered the mattresses from the factory showroom of the Sweet Dreams Mattress Company. Over the years you have had excellent service from this company and its products.

Today the mattresses arrived. To your disappointment, 11 of the 64 are damaged. The paperboard covers of the 11 are scorched, as are portions of the cloth coverings. In addition, all 11 mattresses have a heavy odor of smoke. Your obvious conclusion is that these mattresses have been in a fire. You don't want them, and you are concerned that this company would send them to you. You will have to take corrective action.

Specifically, you will write the Sweet Dreams people telling them what you have found and asking that they correct the matter. You want them to get 11 good mattresses to you right away. And you want them either to pick up the damaged goods, or tell you what to do with them. In writing the letter, you may supply whatever details you may need— invoice number, prices, models, delivery details, and such.

24. Assume the role of owner-manager of The Athlete's Closet, a sporting goods store in your favorite city. Today you received your order of three dozen jogging suits in assorted sizes and colors from Taylor Imports. When you unpacked the cartons you were very disappointed.

Unfortunately, these suits are not of the quality of the samples you inspected when the Taylor salesperson visited you. The material is of a lighter weight and coarser weave. The colors are similar to what you recall, but the designs are not the same. You recall solid color pants with a broad white stripe down the side and solid color jackets with a white stripe down the sleeves. These suits are also of solid colors with stripes, but they have three small white stripes running down the pants legs and jacket sleeves.

You haven't done business with Taylor before, so you aren't really sure about what happened. You want to think they made a mistake, but you can't be sure. So you will write them a forthright claim. You want them to replace the suits, if they sent the wrong ones, or to take them back. You do not intend to pay for them, for you could not sell these inferior products to your discriminating customers.

Now write the letter. You may supply any missing details about the transaction you need (invoice number, prices, dates, delivery details, and such).

25. Providing training for your employees is one of your major responsibilities as a member of your company's human resource department. Recently you sent three employees to an all-day seminar offered by Productivity Consultants to learn how to use the new version of a software program you rely on heavily. You paid and signed up these employees the first day you received the advertising brochure from the training company, nearly two months ago.

Last Friday, your employees were released from work with pay to attend the class. They drove 30 miles and paid downtown parking lot fees, only to discover they were more prepared to teach the class than the instructor. Additionally, because of overbooking, they had to share computers and watch others work rather than getting the hands-on practice the brochure promised. Furthermore, because of the overbooking, not enough handouts and practice exercises were available.

While you are upset at seemingly not getting your money's worth of training, you are more upset that your employees are still not efficient users of the program. Write a claim letter stating the problem, the facts, and your desire for immediate private training by a competent trainer.

26. Walking fever has really hit your city. Everyone is doing it. Walkers can be seen at any time of the day on city streets, on park trails, and in the shopping malls. Also, the trend is multigenerational. You see groups of retired folks, teenagers, and families out walking.

To capitalize on this trend and the interest in the environment, you've decided to stock an environmental walking shoe at the shoe store you manage. The DejaShoe is made from recycled polypropylene, paper bags, coffee filters, scrap tires, foam rubber and recycled metals. The brochure you ordered it from reports the shoe is comfortable, durable, and attractive.

For your tenth anniversary sale, you've promoted this shoe widely. Also, you've been telling your regular customers about it since your order was confirmed. You planned to sell it during this special sale for only $60.

However, when the order arrived today all the shoes were the same size and color. While delighted with the shoe, you are worried that only having it available in one size will hurt the goodwill of your regular customers as well as new customers your advertising will attract. Write a claim stating the problem, the facts, and your desire for an immediate express shipment of the sizes and colors you need for your anniversary sale. You'll fax the letter to the director of customer relations at (503) 636-1187. Be sure to ask how you should handle returning the shoes you do not want.

27. Winters is your favorite restaurant. It's near your home, has a cheery, upbeat atmosphere, and good food at reasonable prices. You've been a regular customer ever since you moved to the area two years ago. In fact, you probably average at least two meals a week there.

Recently, the waiter that has been assigned to your table has been irritating you. Although he is personable and knows the menu well, when he serves you his fingers are always in the food. This annoys you and is getting more annoying each time it happens.

You don't think the waiter should be fired for this, so you have not done anything about it other than hoping it would go away. However, it hasn't after three weeks, so you've decided to write a letter to the manager. All you want is to be served the food without the fingers. Your letter should stress the facts and what you want done. The tone should maintain the goodwill you feel toward the restaurant in general.

28. "I can't believe they fouled the job up so badly!"

Those are the words you think as you, executive director of the Society for Business Advancement, reflect upon your recent national convention held in New Orleans. You ordered 500 convention program booklets from Group Graphics for the 450 attendees at the convention. Prior to that, you printed and mailed 3,500 tentative programs to potential conventioneers in a pre-convention mailing. Most everyone was complimentary of the pre-convention booklet and commented favorably on its content and its production quality. But the final convention program booklet distributed on site was another matter.

At the convention, you distributed a convention packet to each of the attendees who registered. In that packet, you included a number of items, the most notable of which was the convention program booklet that featured 200 speakers, the titles of their papers, and the times and the locations of their presentation. During the first morning of the convention, registrants returned to the registration booth complaining that the program booklets contained numerous errors. After inspecting several of the programs, you agreed. You noticed that there were blurred pages, pages out of sequence, blank pages, and even some pages that did not relate to your program at all (they must have been from some other job the printer was doing). You estimate that approximately one-half of the programs were defective.

Indeed, you were professionally embarrassed because you assume total responsibility for the yearly convention. Group Graphics does all your printing—from stationery to the two quarterly journals you distribute to members. Usually, they are very reliable. On this job, however, they really goofed! And you now must write a claim letter to them explaining the problem you experienced.

In the letter, you'll begin directly with your dilemma. You will spell out specifically what went wrong, citing examples and including samples from the defective program booklets. In addition, you will ask for the printer to completely absorb the cost of the job—$2,470.00.

Write the letter that will make your claim. Be confident and forceful, but not obnoxious. Remember that Group Graphics does other work for you and they have done it well over the years. But you still need reassurance that such defective work will not happen again.

29. "He promised water! And he did it before 13 people," you say to yourself after you finish talking with the general manager of Meadows Country Club.

As president of the Board of Directors of the club, you thought it would be good insurance for the $500,000 golf course improvement project you just completed to drill a second water well to keep the course green and alive during the scorching summer months. You have one well but it sometimes reaches its pumping capacity in early July; and you need continuous watering through September. Thus you asked three drilling contractors to submit bids for drilling a second well at the club.

The lowest bidder, Madewell Company, proposed to drill a well for $31,684.00. Before you awarded the company the contract, you thought it would be prudent to have the owner, Billy Joe Madewell, present his proposal to your 13-member Board of Directors. This he did; and during the discussion one member asked Billy Joe if he anticipated additional expenses if he did not get water at the proposed well depth. He replied, "At the proposed price, I'll guarantee you get water." Accordingly, you awarded him the contract, agreeing to pay one-half the bid price at the beginning of the contract and the final half at the completion of the well. You also agreed that the time for the project would not exceed 30 days.

Today, the general manager of the club tells you that the well no longer pumps water. While Billy

Joe did complete the well on time and water did pump for a time (about a month), the flow has apparently stopped for one reason or another. Perhaps he hit a small pocket of water rather than a main artery. Or maybe the casings in the water shaft are clogged. Whatever the reason, you know that you do not have water for your golf course as you intended. You feel his guarantee must extend beyond 30 days.

So you decide you'll write Mr. Madewell a firm, specific, and complete claim letter. You'll spell out what has happened in detail. You'll ask that he fix the job right away. You need the well for the hot months that are coming soon.

30. As manager of Clarence Copies, you have a special problem today. You provide a full-service copying and duplicating facility to clientele in the campus area of Middle State University. You have been in business 10 years.

Six months ago, you received a letter from the president of Middle State University, which is immediately across the street from your business. In it, President James Marcy stated that the university had contracted with HGA, Inc. to film a movie, *Fast Break,* on the campus of MSU immediately after the spring semester. The movie is a comedy about a college basketball team as it goes through a "typical" season. For authenticity, HGA wanted to film most of the scenes in a university atmosphere. Thus, they offered MSU a lucrative contract. For the university, the timing, public relations benefit, and the direct monetary rewards were too good to turn down.

President Marcy, however, assured you and other businesses that there would be no interruption to your business and that the "traffic flow would not be more congested" during the filming. The letter was endorsed by the city council and the chamber of commerce of the community.

Today, however, you have before you the latest sales volume figures and they are alarmingly low compared to the volume for the same month one year ago. Whereas you typically have one of your best months in May because of term papers and the like, business for the month was $10,241, compared to $17,543 last year. The difference, you believe, had to be all the interruptions you experienced because of the filming of the movie.

Although the president promised that HGA, Inc. would not interfere with any local businesses, you found the opposite to be true. One week before the scheduled filming, large vans with sound equipment, props, and such lined the streets to begin setting up for the filming—scheduled to start after the semester was completed. Their trucks blocked customers from accessing your business at a high-volume time for you.

You believe you have a legitimate complaint and a tangible claim. You lost much business because of the early arrival of the film crews and their equipment. And you have the sales figures to document your actual loss. So write a direct claim letter to HGA, Inc. Ask for payment of the money you lost in sales as your claim.

## ORDERS

31. For this assignment you are the owner of The Gifte Shoppe. In your never-ending search for distinctive and unusual items, an advertisement of the Tyson Manufacturing Company in this month's issue of *Novelty Journal* caught your eye. The ad urges that you order the items described from your supplier; but "if they do not carry our products, order directly from us." You checked your suppliers, and they do not carry Tyson products. You will have to order from the manufacturer. The descriptions of the items you want are as follows:

*Tyson Ice Shaver.* Creates mounds of fluffy snow from ice cubes. Adjustable blades for different textures. Sturdy plastic body with non-skid bottom. Size: 3 1/2 in. high, 67 in. wide, 8 in. deep. Choice of white, black, or beige. Recommended retail price, $44. Your price, $24. No. DZX 331-770.

*Tyson Mini Air Compressor/Flashlight.* For tires, pool floats, sports balls. Compact compressor with handy flashlight for safe roadside use. Works off auto cigarette lighter. 12-foot cord, plug, sports needle, red lens. Protective cover. 0-145 psi. 12 volt DC power. Recommended retail price, $43; your price $23.50. No. DAH 453-651.

*Tyson 5-Band Shower Radio.* AM/FM radio with digital clock that displays day, date, and time. Water resistant. Mylar speaker. Internal antenna. Rust resistant. Attaches to wall or showerhead. Uses 4AA (radio) and 1 lithium battery (not included). Recommended retail price, $47. Your price, $26.50. No. DZW 389-991.

As stated in the advertisement, shipping and handling costs are $2 additional per item. You want 24 ice shavers (12 white, 12 beige); 12 air compressor/flashlights; and 30 shower radios (10 each in black, brown, and red). Now write the order.

32. Assume the role of the training director for Earhart-Downs Associates, one of the leading management consulting firms. In addition to coordinating the training of newly hired consultants, you have the duty of keeping the company library current. Periodically you send memos to the senior consultants and executives asking for suggestions for books for the trainees as well as for the library. From these suggestions you select the books to order.

   About two weeks ago you sent your periodic request for book suggestions, and you got a good number. Then you reviewed the suggestions and made your choices. Now you are ready to order. Three of the books you will order are published by the Hudson Publishing Company. These books are described in their sales literature as follows:

   *Too Many Chiefs* by Wendy A. Tatum, sale price $28.50 for hardcover and $15.95 for paperback. (You want 2 hardcover books for the library and 12 paperbacks for the trainees.)

   *The Art of Communication* by Frank W. Bartlett, sale price $27.95 for hardcover, $14.50 paperback. (You want 1 hardcover book for the library and 12 paperbacks for the trainees.)

   *Managing through Understanding*, 2d edition, by Boris B. Boedeker, $37.95 for hardcover, $19.95 paperback. (You want 1 hardcover book for the library and 12 paperbacks for the trainees.)

   Because you have ordered from Hudson in the past, they will bill you for the total cost plus shipping charges. As your training class will begin in 17 days, you will request rush delivery.

33. You work for the Price Club Co., a warehouse discount retailer. The company is always looking to expand into new markets. However, its directors are cautious decision-makers, demanding carefully planned expansion into good markets. They could be described as risk-averse when it comes to opening new stores in untested markets. However, management has compiled detailed profiles of its customers in its most successful markets. You've recently found that this kind of detailed information is collected from 5,000 sample households by the U. S. Bureau of Labor Statistic's Consumer Expenditure Survey.

   The survey is an ongoing project, collecting information in quarterly interviews and weekly diaries. Among the information collected is household income, socioeconomic characteristics, and average annual and weekly consumption patterns. This kind of data could help you identify quickly good markets for new Price Clubs.

   The data is available on CD-ROM to the public from Hopkins Technology in Hopkins, Minnesota. It costs $199 and is called Consu/Stats. Order the CD-ROM today. Be sure your letter asks for the most recent version available. State how you expect to pay and how it will be shipped.

34. As purchasing manager for Otasio Chemicals Inc., you receive a memo from Jane Sandowski, human resources manager, requesting new furniture for the human resources department. Last year, you bought new computers and software packages for her. This year, she wants to upgrade the physical appearance and comfort of her department. You agree that the request is a reasonable one and decide to approve the request.

   As you go through catalogs and price lists in your files, you determine that Stirco Company can give you the best deal. Accordingly, you will place an order with them for the following items:

   1. Model W40L7120 Credenza; in Walnut or Karpothian Elm; 71" × 20" top size.
      (You want 4 in Karopothian Elm)

   2. Recessed back panel, double pedestal desk, Model W 4026636R; in Walnut or Light Oak finish.
      (You want 3 in Walnut)

   3. Executive chair; Model 4421 with armrests; five-star tubular bore with contoured seat and back; waterfall front edge; in Brown Heather (B-7), Beaver (B-5), or Grey (G-3).
      (You want 5 in Brown Heather)

   Write an order letter that will get the furniture from Stirco. You will ask that the order be sent to you COD.

CHAPTER 6

# DIRECTNESS IN ROUTINE RESPONSES

## CHAPTER OBJECTIVES

*Upon completing this chapter, you will be able to answer routine business letters effectively. To reach this goal, you should be able to*

**1**

Use the direct approach, orderly arrangement, and goodwill in favorably answering business inquiries.

**2**

Compose responses that present both good and bad news yet maintain a friendly tone to foster goodwill.

**3**

Phrase personnel evaluations so that they systematically present the essential information and are fair to all concerned.

**4**

Compose letters involving adjustment grants that will regain the customer's confidence in your company or its products.

**5**

Write letters that acknowledge orders, cover order problems positively, and build goodwill.

> **INTRODUCTORY SITUATION**
>
> ## to Routine Response Letters
>
> To introduce yourself to this chapter, assume again your role as assistant to the vice president for administration of Pinnacle Manufacturing Company. Your correspondence work consists not only of initiating routine letters but also of answering some of the routine letters that Pinnacle receives.
>
> Some of this correspondence consists of inquiries from customers and potential customers who are seeking information about your products and services. Specifically, they ask questions about your products, credit terms, prices, discounts, and such. Some of the correspondence consists of orders to be acknowledged and requests for credit to be approved. Some of it is correspondence from other businesses that are seeking information freely exchanged by businesses—information on former employees, credit customers, and business operations.
>
> The first of these routine letters that you take from your in-basket is from a prospective customer for Pinnacle's Chem-Treat paint. In response to an advertisement, the prospective customer asks a number of specific questions about Chem-Treat. Foremost, she wants to know whether the paint is really mildewproof. Do you have evidence of results? Do you guarantee results? Is the paint safe? How much does a gallon cost? Will one coat do the job? You can answer all the questions positively except the last. Two coats are needed to do most jobs. You will, of course, answer the letter. Because the reader is a good prospect, you will write for the best goodwill effect. ■

## FAVORABLE RESPONSES

When you write letters that answer inquiries favorably, your primary goal is to tell your readers what they want to know. As their reactions to this goal will be favorable, you should use the direct order. Of course, you could write such letters, as well as the other letters covered in this chapter, in the indirect order and still get the job done. But, as the indirect letter is slow and takes more time, it is inconsistent with the needs of business in such situations. As noted in Chapter 5, you should use directness except when there is good reason not to use it. The direct plan recommended below generally follows these steps:

*Favorable reader reaction justifies this direct plan for the letter.*

- **Begin with the answer, or state that you are complying with the request.**
- **Identify the correspondence being answered either incidentally or in a subject line.**
- **Continue to give what is wanted in orderly arrangement.**
- **If negative information is involved, give it proper emphasis.**
- **Consider including extras.**
- **End with a friendly, adapted comment.**

### Beginning with the Answer

Using the direct order means giving readers what they want at the beginning. What they want are the answers to their questions. Thus, you should begin by answering. When a response involves answering a single question, you

*Begin by answering. If there is one question, answer it; if there is more than one, answer the most important.*

begin by answering that question. When it involves answering two or more questions, you begin by answering one of them—preferably the most important. In the Chem-Treat case. this opening would get the response off to a fast start:

Yes, Chem-Treat will prevent mildew if used according to instructions.

*Or begin by saying that you are complying with the request.*

An alternative possibility is to begin by stating that you are giving the readers what they want—that you are complying with their request. Actually, this approach is really not direct, for it delays giving the information requested. But it is a favorable beginning, and it does not run the risk of sounding abrupt, which is a criticism of direct beginnings. These examples illustrate this type of beginning:

The following information should tell you what you need to know about Chem-Treat.

Here are the answers to your questions about Chem-Treat.

*The traditional information beginnings are slow and obvious.*

Either of these beginnings is an improvement over the indirect beginnings that are used all too often in business. Overworked indirect beginnings such as "Your April 3 inquiry has been received" and "I am writing in response to your letter" do little to accomplish the goal of the letter. They also give obvious information. Although acceptable because of its courtesy, even the "Thank you for your April 7 inquiry" delays getting to the objective of answering.

## Identifying the Correspondence Being Answered

*You should identify the letter being answered.*

Even though the indirect examples in the preceding paragraph have shortcomings, they do something desirable. They identify the letter being answered. This identification information is useful for filing purposes. It also helps the reader recall or find the letter being answered.

*The subject line is one good way of identifying that letter. Include subject identification and the date of the letter being answered.*

One good way of identifying the letter being answered is the use of a subject line, a mechanical device discussed in Chapter 5. A useful subject line in routine-request letters would state the nature of the letter being answered and give a by-date reference to it. For the inquiry about Chem-Treat, these subject lines would be appropriate:

Subject: Your April 3 inquiry about Chem-Treat
About your April 3 inquiry concerning Chem-Treat

*Identification can also be made incidentally early in the response.*

Another way of identifying the letter being answered is to refer to it in the text of your letter. You should make such references incidentally, for they usually do not deserve strong emphasis. Illustrating this technique is the phrase "as requested in your April 3 letter."

## Logically Arranging the Answers

*If one answer is involved, give it directly and completely.*

If you are answering just one question, you have little to do after handling that question in the opening. You answer it as completely as the situation requires, and you bring whatever explanation or other information you need to do so. Then you are ready to close the letter.

*If more than one answer is involved, arrange the answers so that each stands out.*

If, on the other hand, you are answering two or more questions, the body of your letter becomes a series of answers. As in all clear writing, you should work for a logical order, perhaps answering the questions in the order your reader used in asking them. You may even number your answers, especially

PART 3   Basic Patterns of Business Letters

### *How Routine Responses Were Written in the Late 1800s*

The following model letter for answering routine inquiries appears on page 75 of O. R. Palmer's *Type-Writing and Business Correspondence.* Published in 1896, the book was a leader in its field.

Dear Sirs:

　Your favor of Dec. 18th, enclosing blue prints for tank received. In reply thereto we beg to submit the following:
　[*Here was a listing of materials for the tank.*]
　Trusting that our price may be satisfactory to you, and that we shall be favored with your order, we beg to remain,

　　　　　　　　　　　　　　　Very truly yours,

---

if your reader numbered the questions. Or you may decide to arrange your answers by paragraphs so that each stands out clearly.

### Skillful Handling of Negatives

When your response concerns some bad news along with the good news, you may need to handle the bad news with care. Bad news stands out. Unless you are careful, it is likely to receive more emphasis than it deserves. Sometimes you will need to subordinate the bad news and emphasize the good news.

　In giving proper emphasis to the good- and bad-news parts, you should use the techniques discussed in Chapter 4, especially position. That is, you should place the good news in positions of high emphasis—at paragraph beginnings and endings and at the beginning and ending of the letter as a whole. You should place the bad news in secondary positions. In addition, you should use space emphasis to your advantage. This means giving less space to bad-news parts and more space to good-news parts. You should also select words and build sentences that communicate the effect you want. Generally, this means using happy and pleasant words and avoiding unpleasant and sad words. Your overall goal should be to present the information in your response so that your readers get just the right effect.

*Emphasize favorable responses; subordinate unfavorable responses.*

*Place favorable responses at beginnings and ends. Give them more space. Use words skillfully to emphasize them.*

### Consideration of Extras

For the best in goodwill effect, you should consider including extras with your answers. These are the things you say and do that are not actually required. Examples are a comment or question showing an interest in the reader's problem, some additional information that may prove valuable, and a suggestion for use of the information supplied. In fact, extras can be anything that does more than skim the surface with hurried, routine answers. Such extras frequently make the difference between success and failure in the goodwill effort.

　Illustrations of how extras can be used to strengthen the goodwill effects of a letter are as broad as the imagination. A business executive answering a

*The little extra things you do for the reader will build goodwill.*

college professor's request for information on company operations could supplement the requested information with suggestions of other sources. A technical writer could amplify highly technical answers with simpler explanations. In the Chem-Treat problem, additional information (say, how much a gallon covers) would be helpful. Such extras genuinely serve readers and promote goodwill.

### Cordiality in the Close

**End with friendly words adapted to the one case.**

As in most routine business letter situations, you should end routine responses with friendly, cordial words that make clear your willing attitude. As much as is practical, your words should be adapted to the one case. For example, you might close the Chem-Treat letter with these words:

If I can help you further in deciding whether Chem-Treat will meet your needs, please write me again.

Or an executive answering a graduate student's questions concerning a thesis project could use this paragraph:

If I can give you any more of the information you need for your study of executive behavior, please write me. I wish you the best of luck on the project.

Notice that both of the examples above close with an offer of further help. Not only does this increase cordiality in the close, but it also signals the readers that all of their concerns have already been addressed. Using terms such as "further," "additional," and "any more" tells the reader the writer is willing to go a little extra if needed.

### Contrasting Illustrations

**Following are bad and good examples of response letters.**

Contrasting letters in answer to the Chem-Treat inquiry illustrate the techniques of answering routine inquiries. The first letter violates many of the standards set in this and earlier chapters. The second meets the requirements of a good business letter.

**An Indirect and Hurried Response.** The not-so-good letter begins indirectly with an obvious statement referring to receipt of the inquiry. Though well intended, the second sentence continues to delay the answers. The second paragraph begins to give the information sought, but it emphasizes the most negative answer by position and by wording. This answer is followed by hurried and routine answers to the other questions asked. Only the barest information is presented. The close belongs to the language of business in great-grandfather's day.

**The poor one is indirect and ineffective.**

Dear Ms. Motley:

I have received your April 3 letter, in which you inquire about our Chem-Treat paint. I want you to know that we appreciate your interest and will welcome your business.
In response to your question about how many coats are needed to cover new surfaces, I regret to report that two are usually required. The paint is mildewproof. We do guarantee it. It has been well tested in our laboratories. It is safe to use as directed.
Hoping to hear from you again, I remain

Yours sincerely,

146  PART 3  Basic Patterns of Business Letters

**CASE ILLUSTRATION** Routine Response Letters. *(Favorable Response to a Professor's Request)*

This letter responds to a professor's request for production records that will be used in a research project. The writer is giving the information wanted but must restrict its use.

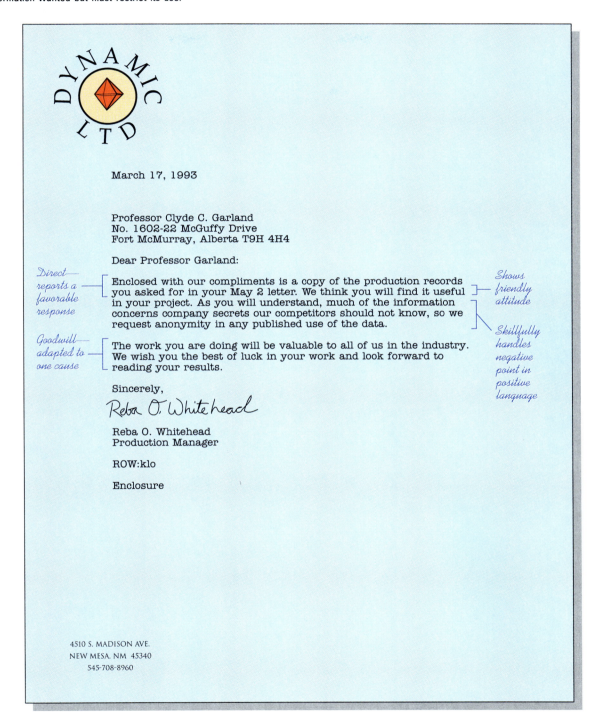

**CASE ILLUSTRATION**  Routine Response Letters. *(A Request for Detailed Information)*
Answering an inquiry about a company's experience with a word processing center, this letter numbers the answers as the questions were numbered in the inquiry. The opening appropriately sets up the numbered answers with a statement that indicates a favorable response.

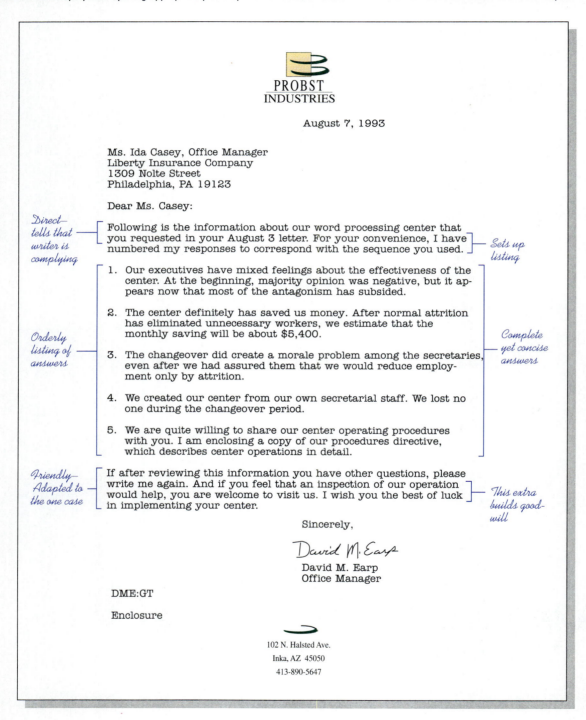

### Skillful (?) Handling of a Complaint

A traveling man once spent a sleepless night in a hotel room, tormented by the sight of cockroaches walking over the ceiling, walls, and floor. Upon returning home, he indignantly protested the condition in a letter to the hotel management. Some days later, to his delight, he received a masterfully written response. It complimented him for reporting the condition, and it assured him that the matter would be corrected—that such a thing would never happen again. The man was satisfied, and his confidence in the hotel was restored. His satisfaction vanished, however, when he discovered an interoffice memo that had been accidentally inserted into the envelope. The memo said, "Send this nut the cockroach letter."

**Effectiveness in Direct Response.** The better letter uses a subject line to identify the inquiry. Thus, it frees the text from the need to cover this detail. The letter begins directly, with the most favorable answer. Then it presents the other answers, giving each the emphasis and positive language it deserves. It subordinates the one negative answer, by position, volume of treatment, and structure. More pleasant information follows the negative answer. The close is goodwill talk, with some subtle selling strategy thrown in. "We know that you'll enjoy the long-lasting beauty of this mildewproof paint" points positively to purchase and successful use of the product.

Dear Ms. Motley:

Subject: Your April 3 inquiry about Chem-Treat.

    Yes, Chem-Treat paint will prevent mildew or we will give you back your money. We know it works, because we have tested it under all common conditions. In every case, it proved successful.
    When you carefully follow the directions on each can, Chem-Treat paint is guaranteed safe. As the directions state, you should use Chem-Treat only in a well-ventilated room—never in a closed, unvented area.
    One gallon of Chem-Treat is usually enough for one-coat coverage of 500 square feet of previously painted surface. For the best results on new surfaces, you will want to apply two coats. For such surfaces, you should figure about 200 square feet per gallon for a good heavy coating that will give you five years or more of beautiful protection.
    We sincerely appreciate your interest in Chem-Treat, Ms. Motley. We know that you'll enjoy the long-lasting beauty of this mildewproof paint.

                  Sincerely,

*This direct letter does the better job.*

---

### INTRODUCTORY SITUATION

## to Personnel Evaluations

A request for an evaluation of a Pinnacle employee is the next letter you take from the in-basket. The writer, Ms. Mary Brooking, president, Red Arrow Transport, Inc., wants information about George Adams, Pinnacle's assistant shipping clerk. Ms. Brooking is considering Adams for the position of manager of a Red Arrow branch office. In her letter she asks some specific questions about him and about his ability to do the job. As Adams works under the supervision of your office, he listed you as a reference.

You are well acquainted with Adams and his work. Just last week he came by your office to tell you that he was looking at an employment opportunity that offered advancement—something that Pinnacle, unfortunately, could not offer soon. Everything you have observed in his work supports your opinion that he is industrious and capable. He knows the shipping business, and he is an able supervisor. He tends to stick to his own ideas too strongly, and this has caused some friction with his superiors—you included. But you feel that this tendency reflects his independence and self-reliance, qualities that may be desirable in a branch manager with no immediate supervisors on the grounds.

Because you believe that Adams has earned the position he seeks, you want to write a letter that will help him. But because you are an honest person, you will report truthfully. Thus, you will write a letter that will be fair to all concerned—to Adams, to Ms. Brooking, and to you. ∎

## PERSONNEL EVALUATIONS

*Personnel evaluations satisfy the reader. Thus, they justify the direct order, as outlined in this general plan.*

When you receive a request to evaluate a former employee, company policy may prohibit you from answering. For legal reasons, as was discussed in Chapter 5, many companies do not permit such letters. But if you do write such a letter, you should organize it in the direct order. The justification for the direct order is that the message is favorable, since you are doing what the reader requested. It is favorable regardless of whether it contains positive or negative information about the employee because the reader is getting the information requested. As described in the following paragraphs, this procedure will produce a good direct-order letter.

- **Begin by (1) answering a question or (2) saying that you are complying with the request.**
- **Refer to the inquiry letter incidentally or in a subject line.**
- **Report systematically, giving each item proper emphasis, taking care to be fair, and stressing fact rather than opinion.**
- **End with adapted, goodwill comment.**

### Directness in the Beginning

*Begin by reporting a significant fact—one deserving the emphasis that the beginning position gives it.*

You have two good choices for beginning personnel evaluation letters. You can begin by reporting a significant fact—that is, by giving requested information. If you choose this approach, you should select information that deserves the emphasis that the beginning position gives it, perhaps information that serves as a qualifying fact for the remainder of your report. For example, this statement gives a significant fact and qualifies the remaining facts presented:

Mr. Chester Bazzar, the subject of your May 11 inquiry, worked under my supervision for four months in 1987.

Here is another example:

Ms. Mary Capone, about whom you inquired in your January 17 letter, has proved to be a well-qualified, competent, and conscientious office administrator in the three years she has worked for me.

Notice that this statement sets up the remainder of the letter. It leads the reader to expect that the body will include detail on the qualifications, the competence, and the conscientiousness of the applicant.

Your second choice of beginning is a statement that simply says you are complying with the request. Although not so direct as a beginning that reports specific information, this type appears less abrupt and more logical to some people. If skillfully worded, such a beginning can explain the situation and retain the effect of directness. This one does the job well:

> Another way of beginning is to say you are complying with the request.

As you requested in your May 8 letter, here is my evaluation of Mr. Carlton I. Bowes.

Here is another example, this one following a subject line that refers by date to the letter being answered:

I am pleased to present the following report on Ms. Carla A. Patan.

### Reference to the Inquiry

Because you write a personnel reference in response to a request, you should identify that request, preferably early in the letter. As illustrated in the examples given previously, you could acknowledge the inquiry letter incidentally in the opening sentence. But note that incidental acknowledgment means that this part is not the main message of the sentence. The main message is significant information about the person being evaluated. In other words, the date reference does not deserve main-clause emphasis, as in sentences beginning with "We have received your January 12 letter requesting information about . . ."

> Identify the request being answered incidentally and near the beginning.

An excellent device for identifying the letter being answered is a subject line. As described in Chapter 5, this device identifies the subject and the date of the letter. It places this information above and outside the text of the letter. Thus, it frees the text of the need to cover these details.

> Consider using a subject line.

### Systematic Presentation of Information

After an opening in which you begin reporting, you should continue reporting the information the reader needs. What you report is a matter you will have to decide. If the inquiry you are answering asks specific questions (as it should), you should answer those questions. But if the inquiry is a general one, you must decide what information is needed. Your decision should be guided by your analysis of the work for which the applicant is being considered. You should select the information you think is important in connection with doing that work.

> Report what the reader needs to know.

As with any situation in which a variety of information is reported, your major concern in this part of the letter is organization. You should present your information in an orderly manner.

> Organize the content logically.

Answering inquiries about people requires the most careful thought, for the lives and rights of human beings are affected.

---

**If specific questions were asked, organize around them. If not, organize by subject matter.**

If the letter you are answering asks specific questions, you can organize your information around those questions. You could even number the responses, especially if the questions are numbered in the inquiry. But if the inquiry is general, leaving the content for you to determine, you will need to work out a logical arrangement of the information. In such cases, you should seek an organization that keeps related information together and a sequence that makes the information flow logically and smoothly. In addition, you should try to organize so that there is no overlap or repetition of information (see case illustrations).

## The Problem of Fair Reporting

**Personnel evaluations should be fair to all.**

As a fair-minded writer, you will want your employee evaluation letters to convey an accurate picture. Presenting your information too positively would be unfair to your reader. Presenting your information too negatively would be unfair to the applicant. Your task is to convey just the right picture through your words.

**Selecting the words and facts for a true report is difficult.**

Conveying an accurate picture is no simple undertaking. Words have imprecise and inconsistent meanings in our minds. But words are not the only difficulty in our efforts to make a truthful report. Perhaps even more important are the information you include and the emphasis you give it.

**Stress facts, and use facts to back up opinions.**

In deciding what information to include, you should carefully distinguish between facts and opinions. For the most part, your report should contain facts. But the reader sometimes wants opinions. If you present opinions, you should clearly label them as such. You should support all opinions with facts.

**Because negative points stand out, the use of facts without explanation may make a report unfair.**

Even if every item in your report is verifiable fact, the report could be unfair. The reason is that negative points stand out. They overshadow positive points. For example, no matter how much you write about the

152   PART 3  Basic Patterns of Business Letters

merits of a person, if you end with the statement that the person once spent a night in jail, this one negative point would stand out. In some minds it might erase everything else.

The fact that negative points stand out means that in your personnel evaluation letters you must be careful in handling them. You must give them only enough emphasis to convey an accurate picture. Fair treatment often requires that you subordinate them. Not to do so would be to give them more emphasis than they deserve.

> Give the facts appropriate emphasis. Positive wording may be necessary for some negative points.

To illustrate, take a report on an employee who, in spite of a personality problem, has a good work record. If you place the personality problem in a position of emphasis or write too much about it, you make this one negative point stand out. To give this information the minor emphasis it deserves, you have to subordinate it.

Nothing we have said means that you should hide shortcomings or communicate wrong information. Quite the contrary. If your subject has a bad work record, you should report this. Purely and simply, your task is to communicate an accurate picture. You can communicate such a picture only by giving every fact the emphasis it deserves.

> The goal is to report precisely and truthfully.

In the United States, laws and court decisions have affected the information on job applicants that may be reported.[1] As was noted in Chapter 5, reports about an applicant's age, race, religion, sex, marital status, and pregnancy are generally prohibited. So are reports about an applicant's criminal record, citizenship, organization memberships, and mental and physical handicaps. Exceptions may be made in the rare cases in which such information is clearly related to the job. Because of these laws and court decisions and because the person evaluated can gain access to his or her file, many businesses have policies that limit reporting to verifiable facts. Some businesses do not evaluate former employees.

> Abide by legal requirements regarding the information that may be reported.

### Natural Friendliness in the Close

You should close employee evaluation reports with some appropriate goodwill comment. A sentence or two is usually enough. As in similar situations, you should make your words fit the one case, avoiding the rubber stamps that so often find their way into this type of letter.

> Close with adapted, goodwill talk.

### Examples in Contrast

Illustrating good and bad technique in personnel evaluations are the following contrasting letters about George Adams.

**A Slow, Disorganized, and Unfair Report.** The weaker letter begins indirectly—and with some obvious information. The first words are wasted. The letter shows little concern for proper emphasis. Note that the main negative point (the personality problem) receives a major position of emphasis (at a paragraph beginning). Even the information about the applicant's future at Pinnacle (which does not reflect on his abilities) gets negative treatment. The

---

[1] Based on the following acts and court cases relating to them: Wagner Act of 1935, Immigration and Nationality Act of 1952, Civil Rights Act of 1964, Vocational Rehabilitation Act of 1973, Age Discrimination Act of 1975, Pregnancy Discrimination Act of 1978.

### Truthful (?) Reporting in Recommendation Letters

Some choice double-entendres (two-meaning sentences) to be used in letters of recommendation when you don't want to lie or to hurt the person involved:

To describe a lazy person: "In my opinion, you will be very fortunate to get this person to work for you."

To describe an inept person: "I most enthusiastically recommend this candidate with no qualifications whatsoever."

To describe an ex-employee who had problems getting along with fellow workers: "I am pleased to say that this candidate is a former colleague of mine."

To describe a job applicant who is not worth further consideration: "I would urge you to waste no time in making this candidate an offer of employment."

To describe a person with lackluster credentials: "All in all, I cannot say enough good things about this candidate or recommend him too highly."

Robert Thornton

organization is jumbled. Information about personal qualities and about job performance, for example, appears in two different paragraphs. The close is an attempt at goodwill, but the words are timeworn rubber stamps.

This bad example violates the techniques emphasized.

Dear Ms. Brooking:

I have received your May 10 letter, in which you ask for my evaluation of Mr. George Adams. In reply I wish to say that I am pleased to be able to help you in this instance.
Probably Mr. Adams' greatest weakness is his inability to get along with his superiors. He has his own ideas, and he sticks to them tenaciously. Even so, he has a good work record with us. He has been with us since 1983.
Mr. Adams is a first assistant in our shipping department. He is thoroughly familiar with rate scales and general routing procedure. He gets along well with his coworkers and is a very personable young man. In his work he has some supervisory responsibilities, which he has performed well. He is probably seeking other work because there is little likelihood that we will promote him.
Mr. Adams' main assignment with us has placed him in charge of our car and truck loadings. He has done a good job here, resulting in significant savings in shipping damages. We have found him a very honest, straightforward, and dependable person.
Trusting that you will hold this report in confidence, I remain

Sincerely,

**Good Organization and Fairness in Direct Report.** The better letter begins directly, reporting a significant point in the first sentence. Use of the subject line frees the text of the need to identify the inquiry, which makes for a faster-moving beginning. The text presents the information in logical order, with like things being placed together. The words present the information fairly. The major negative point is presented almost positively, which is how

**CASE ILLUSTRATION** Personnel Evaluation Letters. *(Evaluating a Competent Person with Shortcomings)*

This letter reports on a person who is seeking work as a university instructor. Although the applicant is highly competent, he has two minor shortcomings. The letter gives proper emphasis to the positive and negative points and presents a fair appraisal.

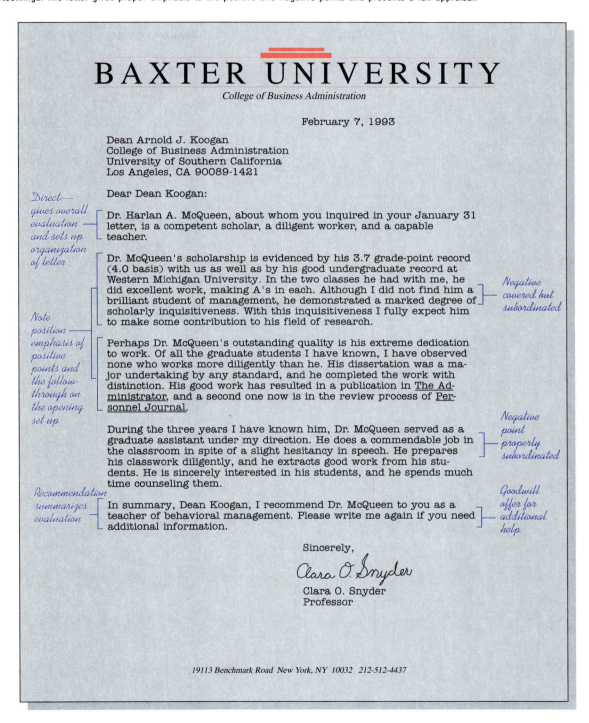

# BAXTER UNIVERSITY
College of Business Administration

February 7, 1993

Dean Arnold J. Koogan
College of Business Administration
University of Southern California
Los Angeles, CA 90089-1421

Dear Dean Koogan:

*Direct— gives overall evaluation and sets up organization of letter*

Dr. Harlan A. McQueen, about whom you inquired in your January 31 letter, is a competent scholar, a diligent worker, and a capable teacher.

*Note position emphasis of positive points and the follow-through on the opening set up*

Dr. McQueen's scholarship is evidenced by his 3.7 grade-point record (4.0 basis) with us as well as by his good undergraduate record at Western Michigan University. In the two classes he had with me, he did excellent work, making A's in each. Although I did not find him a brilliant student of management, he demonstrated a marked degree of scholarly inquisitiveness. With this inquisitiveness I fully expect him to make some contribution to his field of research.

*Negative covered but subordinated*

Perhaps Dr. McQueen's outstanding quality is his extreme dedication to work. Of all the graduate students I have known, I have observed none who works more diligently than he. His dissertation was a major undertaking by any standard, and he completed the work with distinction. His good work has resulted in a publication in The Administrator, and a second one now is in the review process of Personnel Journal.

During the three years I have known him, Dr. McQueen served as a graduate assistant under my direction. He does a commendable job in the classroom in spite of a slight hesitancy in speech. He prepares his classwork diligently, and he extracts good work from his students. He is sincerely interested in his students, and he spends much time counseling them.

*Negative point properly subordinated*

*Recommendation summarizes evaluation*

In summary, Dean Koogan, I recommend Dr. McQueen to you as a teacher of behavioral management. Please write me again if you need additional information.

*Goodwill offer for additional help*

Sincerely,

*Clara O. Snyder*

Clara O. Snyder
Professor

19113 Benchmark Road  New York, NY 10032  212-512-4437

**CASE ILLUSTRATION**  Personnel Evaluation Letters. *(Evaluation of a Good Worker)*

Evaluating a well-qualified office worker with no significant deficiencies, this letter presents its information systematically. The opening comment is general, but by informing the reader of a favorable response, it has the effect of directness.

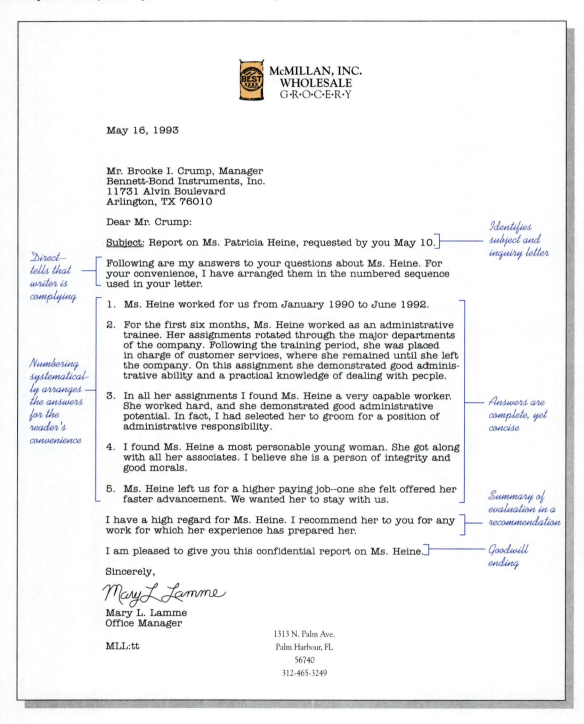

it should be viewed in regard to the job concerned. The letter closes with an appropriate goodwill comment.

Dear Ms. Brooking:

Subject: Your May 10 inquiry about George Adams.

    Mr. Adams has been our assistant shipping clerk since March 1985 and has steadily improved in usefulness to our company. We want to keep him with us as long as he wants to stay. But with things as they are, it will apparently be some time before we can offer him a promotion that would match the branch managership for which you are considering him.

    Of course I am glad to give you in confidence a report on his service with us. As first assistant, he has substituted at the head clerk's desk and is thus familiar with problems of rate scales and routing. His main assignment, however, is to supervise the car and truck loadings. By making a careful study of this work, he has reduced our shipping damages noticeably within the last year. This job also places him in direct charge of the labor force, which varies from six to ten workers. He has proved to be a good boss.

    We have always found Mr. Adams honest, straightforward, and dependable. He is a man of strong convictions. He has his own ideas and backs them up. He is resourceful and works well without direction.

    I recommend Mr. Adams to you highly. If you need additional information about him, please write me again.

    Sincerely,

*Directness, good organization, and correct emphasis mark this good letter.*

## INTRODUCTORY SITUATION

## to Adjustment Grant Letters

This time you pull an unhappy customer's letter from your in-basket. It seems that Ms. Bernice Watson, owner of Tri-City Hardware, is upset because the fire extinguishers Pinnacle sent her arrived badly damaged. She had ordered them for a special sale. In fact, she had even featured them in her newspaper advertising. The sale begins a week from next Saturday, and she has no fire extinguishers to sell. She wants a fast adjustment—either the merchandise by sale time or her money back.

You want to keep this unhappy customer's business. So you check out the situation immediately and plan to fax your response as soon as possible. You find that you can get more fire extinguishers to her in time for her sale. You also find that you can explain what happened. Now you will write Ms. Watson, handling her claim in the best way possible. You will tell her that the goods are on the way. You will try to regain any lost confidence in your company or its products with convincing explanation. Your goal is to hold onto this good customer. ■

### ADJUSTMENT GRANTS

When you can grant an adjustment, the situation is a happy one for your customer. You are correcting an error. You are doing what you were asked to do. As in other positive situations, a letter written in the direct order is

*Good news in adjustment grants justifies directness, as in this general plan.*

CHAPTER 6    Directness in Routine Responses      157

Writing letters the old-fashioned way can be wasteful and inefficient. Today's progressive business correspondents enjoy the advantages of electronic word processing.

appropriate. The direct-order plan recommended below follows these general steps:

- **Begin directly—with the good news.**
- **Incidentally identify the correspondence that you are answering.**
- **Avoid negatives that recall the problem.**
- **Regain lost confidence through explanation or corrective action.**
- **End with a friendly, positive comment.**

## Need to Overcome Negative Impressions

*Correcting the error does not overcome the reader's negative impressions.*

Even though your basic objective is a good-news one, the adjustment-grant situation is not entirely positive. If you place yourself in your reader's situation, you will understand why. As the reader sees it, something bad has happened—goods have been damaged, equipment has failed to work, or sales have been lost. The reader has suffered an unpleasant experience, and its ugly pictures remain in mind. The reader may even have ill feelings toward your company and toward your products or services.

*Overcoming negative impressions takes a special effort.*

Granting the claim is likely to take care of any ill feelings that your reader may have toward you or your company. Certainly, doing what the reader wants you to do improves relations. But just correcting the error may not regain the reader's lost confidence in your products or services. At this stage, the reader may conclude that you are good but that your products or services are bad.

### *Macros: Shortcuts for Improved Productivity and Quality*

Shortcuts can save time and improve quality. Macros are shortcuts for the business writer. A macro is a command you give your word processing software to tell it to execute a series of commands. It saves you time because you don't have to enter all the commands each time you need them (the computer can do it faster), and it improves quality by issuing the correct commands (no missed commands or incorrect keystrokes).

The heading and closing of letters are perfect candidates for macros. Since you use these each time you create a letter, a macro that sets them up is clearly a time-saving shortcut. The heading with the date and your letterhead logo and information or your return address would be a good, basic macro. Once you learn the macro language of your software, you can enhance this macro by having it prompt you for each line of the inside address, the salutation, and the subject line. And while closings aren't complicated, a macro which closed the letter, left room for your signature, typed your name and title will save you many keystrokes each time you use it.

Macros with fully spelled-out names of the companies or people you write to frequently are also useful. If you are not using Windows® software, you can create macros that act like buttons in Windows programs for such things as printing, spellchecking, justifying, and any other commands you use frequently. You can also use macros to insert bullets, graphics, or other special effects that you use occasionally. Creating a macro for these kinds of applications can save you time in having to look up information each time you need it.

You can also create macros for paragraphs you use repeatedly. If your customers need the same information, write a good, clear response and build it into a macro you can call up with just a few keystrokes. You might want to build a new macro each month on new products or promotions you are offering. Or you might want to build macros for special order acknowledgments. You could design the macro to stop at certain points for you to individualize portions of the message.

Take advantage of macro power for many time-saving, document-enhancing shortcuts.

## Direct Presentation of Decision

The adjustment grant is good news, so you logically begin your letter with a direct statement of this good news. Since the letter is a response to one that the reader wrote, you will need to identify the preceding correspondence—preferably near the beginning. You can do this by incidental reference or a subject line.

The news you have to present is certain to create a favorable response. For best effect, however, you should select words that add to the positiveness of your answer. You may, for example, present your decision in terms of customer satisfaction, as in this beginning sentence:

The enclosed check for $87.99 is our way of proving to you that we value your satisfaction highly.

*The adjustment grant appropriately begins with a direct statement of the answer. Select words for positive effect.*

## Avoidance of Negatives

*Avoid negative references to the problem. Emphasize correcting the wrong, not the wrong itself.*

In your opening as well as throughout your letter, you should avoid using words that recall unnecessarily the bad situation you are correcting. Your goal is to change your reader's mental picture of your company and your product from negative to positive. You do not help your case by recalling what went wrong. Your emphasis is better placed on positive things, such as what you are doing to correct the wrong.

Illustrating the point are the negative words that could be used to describe the situation—such words as *mistake, trouble, damage, broken,* and *loss.* Equally negative are such general references as *problem, difficulty,* and *misunderstanding.* If you need to talk about the problem somewhere in the letter, you should use a minimum of negative words in doing so.

Also negative are the apologies that are often included in such letters. Even though well intended, the somewhat conventional "We sincerely regret the inconvenience caused you . . ." type of comment is of questionable value. It emphasizes the negative happenings for which the apology is made. If you sincerely feel that you owe an apology, or that one is expected, you can choose to apologize and risk the negative effect of an apology. In most instances, however, your efforts to correct the problem show adequate concern for your reader's interests.

## Regaining Lost Confidence

A good-news beginning should put the reader in a happy frame of mind. You are doing what the reader asked. You are correcting the wrong. Now the situation is ideal for you to work on your secondary goal of regaining lost confidence.

*Work to regain lost confidence by explaining or telling of corrective action.*

Except in cases in which the cause of the difficulty is routine or incidental, you will need to regain lost confidence. Just what you must do and how you must do it depend on the facts of the situation. You will need to survey the situation to see what they are. If something can be done to correct a bad procedure or a product defect, you should do it. Then you should tell your reader what has been done as convincingly and positively as you can. If what went wrong was a rare, unavoidable event, you should explain this. Sometimes you will need to explain how a product should be used or cared for. Sometimes you will need to resell the product.

## Positiveness in the Close

*End the letter with a pleasant and positive comment.*

Regardless of how positively you handle the preceding parts of your letter, the problem is still filled with negative elements. Thus, for the best in goodwill effect, you should end your letter on a positive note. Your final words should move your reader's mind away from the unpleasant situation that caused the problem.

*Adapt the close to the one case. Avoid negative references.*

Your choice of subject matter for the close again depends on what is right for the case. It could be a forward look to happy relations, a comment about a product improvement, or talk about a coming promotion. You should not say anything that recalls the negative situation.

## Contrasting Adjustments

*Following are good and bad adjustment grants.*

The techniques previously discussed are illustrated by the following adjustment letters. The first, with its indirect order and grudging tone, is ineffec-

**PART 3** Basic Patterns of Business Letters

tive. The directness and positiveness of the second clearly make it the better letter.

**A Slow and Negative Treatment.** The ineffective letter begins with an obvious comment about receiving the claim. It recalls vividly what went wrong and then painfully explains what happened. As a result, the good news is delayed for an additional paragraph. Finally, after two delaying paragraphs, the letter gets to the good news. Though well intended, the close leaves the reader with a reminder of the trouble.

Dear Ms. Watson:

    We have received your May 1 claim reporting that our shipment of Fireboy extinguishers arrived in badly damaged condition. We regret the inconvenience caused you and can understand your unhappiness.
    Following our standard practice, we investigated the situation thoroughly. Apparently, the fault was in our failure to check the seals carefully. As a result, the fluid escaped in transit, damaging the exteriors of the fire extinguishers. We have taken corrective measures to assure that future shipments will be more carefully checked.
    I am pleased to report that we are sending a replacement order. It will be shipped today by Red Line Motor Freight and should reach you by Saturday.
    Again, we regret all the trouble caused you.

                    Sincerely,

This bad letter is needlessly slow.

**The Direct and Positive Technique.** The better letter uses a subject line to identify the transaction. The opening words tell the reader what she most wants to hear in a positive way that adds to the goodwill tone of the message. With reader-viewpoint explanation, the letter then reviews what happened. Without a single negative word, it makes clear what caused the problem and what has been done to prevent its recurrence. After handling the essential matter of disposing of the damaged merchandise, the letter closes with positive resale talk far removed from the problem.

Dear Ms. Watson:

Subject: Your May 1 report on invoice 1348.

    Two dozen new and thoroughly tested Fireboy extinguishers should reach your sales floor in time for your Saturday promotion. They were shipped early today by Red Line Motor Freight.
    As your satisfaction with our service is important to us, we have thoroughly checked all the Fireboys in stock. In the past, we have assumed that all of them were checked for tight seals at the factory. We learned, thanks to you, that we must now systematically check each one. We have set up a system of checks as part of our normal handling procedure.
    When you receive the new Fireboys, will you please return the original group by motor freight? We will pay all transportation charges.
    As you may know, the new Fireboys have practically revolutionized the extinguisher field. Their compact size and efficiency have made them the top seller in only three months. We are confident they will play their part in the success of your sale.

                    Sincerely,

This better letter is direct and positive.

**CASE ILLUSTRATION** Adjustment Grant Letters. *(Explaining a Human Error)*

This letter grants the action requested in the claim of a customer who received sterling flatware that was monogrammed incorrectly. The writer has no excuse, for human error was to blame. His explanation is positive and convincing.

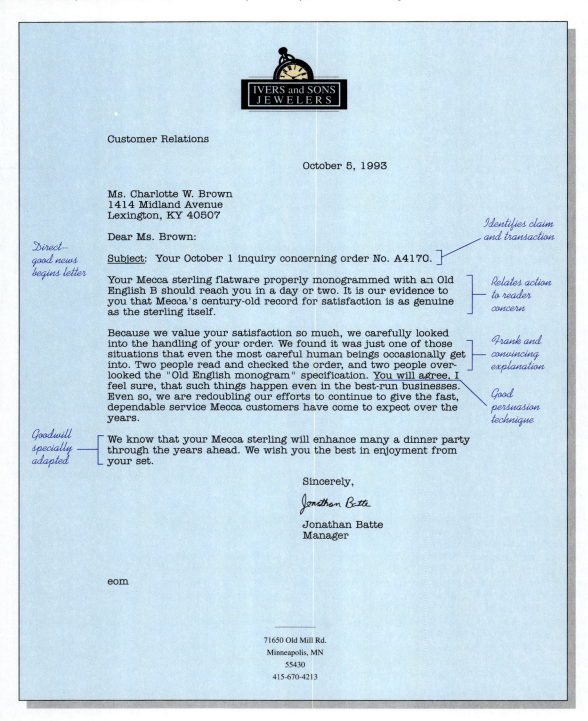

**CASE ILLUSTRATION** Adjustment Grant Letters. *(A Claim for Money Back)*

This letter grants a customer's claim regarding a suit that reached him with faded spots on the coat front. The angry customer returned the suit, demanding his money back. The letter grants the claim and then builds an explanation that will lead a fair-minded customer to give the product a second chance.

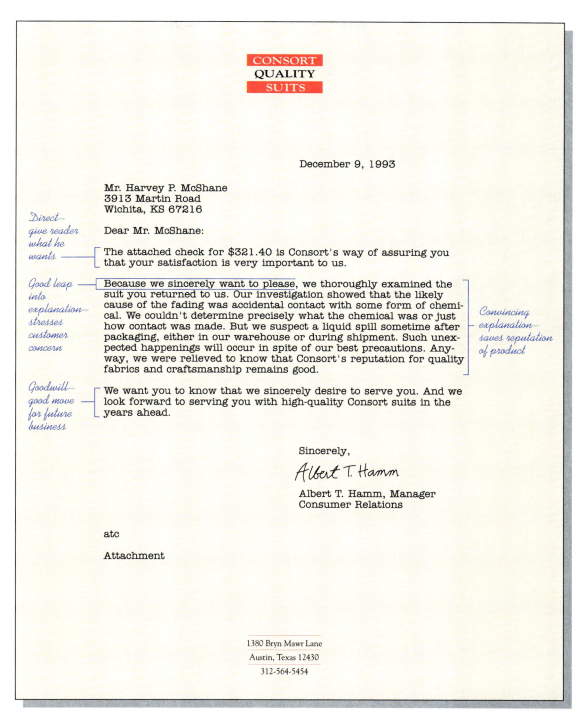

CHAPTER 6 Directness in Routine Responses

## INTRODUCTORY SITUATION

### to Order Acknowledgment Letters

The next work you take from your in-basket is an order for paints and painting supplies. It is from Mr. Orville Chapman of the Central City Paint Company, a new customer whom Pinnacle has been trying to attract for months. You usually acknowledge orders with individually typed letters, but this case is different. You feel the need to welcome this new customer and to cultivate him for future sales.

After checking your warehouse and making certain that the goods will be on the way to Chapman today, you are ready to write him a special letter of acknowledgment. ■

## ORDER ACKNOWLEDGMENTS

*Businesses usually acknowledge orders with form notes, but they sometimes use letters.*

As the description of the preceding situation implies, acknowledgments are sent to let people who order goods know the status of their orders. Most acknowledgments are routine. They simply tell when the goods are being shipped. Many companies use form letters for such situations. Some use printed, standard notes with checkoff or write-in blanks. But individually written acknowledgment letters are sometimes justified, especially with new accounts or large orders.

*Acknowledgment letters build goodwill, as shown in this general plan.*

Skillfully composed acknowledgment letters can do more than acknowledge orders, though this task remains their primary goal. These letters can also build goodwill. Through a warm, personal, human tone, they can reach out and give a hearty handshake. They can make the reader feel good about doing business with a company that cares. They can make the reader want to continue doing business with that company. To maintain this goodwill for repeat customers, you will want to revise your form acknowledgments on a regular basis. If your company offers goods or services that are consumed often, you'll need to revise these letters more frequently than a business offering durable goods or services.

The sequence below illustrates how you should approach such letters.

- **Acknowledge the order, giving its status.**
- **Include some goodwill—sales talk, reselling, or such.**
- **Include a thank-you.**
- **Report frankly or handle tactfully problems with vague or back orders.**
- **Close with adapted, friendly comment.**

### Acknowledgment in the Beginning

*Begin directly, reporting positive handling of the order.*

As with other routine response letters, you should begin a routine acknowledgment directly, getting to the point right away. Because this letter has a special goodwill need, you should try to make a positive impression with your opening words. You could, for example, report the news directly with such words as these:

Your April 4 order for Protect-O paints and supplies will be shipped Monday by Blue Darter Motor Freight.

PART 3  Basic Patterns of Business Letters

These words are positive, for they tell the reader good news. But an even more positive beginning is one that emphasizes receiving rather than sending the goods:

The Protect-O paints and supplies that you ordered April 4 should reach you by Wednesday. They are leaving our Walden warehouse today by Blue Darter Motor Freight.

Many businesspeople begin acknowledgment letters with some version of "Thank you for your order." Because thank-yous are positive, such beginnings are defensible. As courteous as they are, however, they tend to delay the good news. They do not tell what the reader most wants to know.

### Goodwill Talk and Resale

The individually written acknowledgment letter concentrates on the goodwill function and does some selling and reselling. It may tell about new products or new services, and it may tell about the goods being ordered or any other appropriate matters.

*The goodwill talk should be adapted to the situation.*

Somewhere in the letter, as a matter of courtesy, you will need to express your appreciation for the order. You are making a sale after all, and some form of thank-you is appropriate. If you are acknowledging a first order, your new customer deserves a warm welcome.

*An expression of appreciation is appropriate.*

### Tact in Handling Delayed Shipments

Sometimes you will not be able to send every item ordered. The order may not have included all the information needed, or you may be out of some items. In such cases, businesspeople often report the status of all items with routine frankness. They reason that their customers expect and understand such delays. But when they feel that customers will be upset by a delay, they may use a more tactful approach.

*When you can't send an item (vague or back order), you may elect to report frankly or explain tactfully.*

In such cases, you should handle the delay so as to minimize the negative effect of the message. In the case of a vague order, for example, you should ask for the information you need without appearing to accuse the reader of giving insufficient information. To illustrate, you gain nothing by writing "You failed to specify the color of umbrellas you want." But you gain goodwill by writing "So that we can send you precisely the umbrellas you want, please check your choice of colors on the enclosed card." This sentence handles the matter positively and makes the action easy to take.

*In vague orders, request the needed information positively.*

Similarly, you can handle back-order information diplomatically by emphasizing the positive part of the message. Instead of writing "We can't ship the Crescent City pralines until the 9th," you can write "We will rush the Crescent City pralines to you as soon as our stock is replenished by a shipment due May 9." If the back-order period is longer than the customer expects or longer than the 30 days allowed by law, you may choose to give your customer an alternative. You could offer a substitute product or service. Giving the customer a choice among alternatives builds goodwill. A more complete discussion of how to handle such negative news is provided in the following chapter.

*Emphasize receipt of the items in back orders.*

### A Friendly, Forward Look

An appropriate ending to your acknowledgment letter is a friendly, forward look. The subject matter you use here depends on your goodwill and selling

*A friendly, forward-looking comment makes a good ending.*

efforts earlier in the letter. If you stressed resale of the merchandise ordered, your close might well comment about enjoyable and profitable use of the product. If you stressed sales promotion, you might urge your reader to order again. If you used a customer-welcome theme, you might look ahead to additional opportunities to serve. In any event, you would do well to make your close tie in with the material that preceded it and fit the one case.

## Contrasting Acknowledgments

Following are contrasting examples.

The following two letters show bad and good technique in acknowledging Mr. Chapman's order. As you would expect, the good version follows the plan described in the preceding paragraphs.

**Slow Route to a Favorable Message.** The bad example begins indirectly, placing emphasis on receipt of the order. Although intended to produce goodwill, the second sentence further delays telling what the reader wants most to hear. Moreover, the letter is written from the writer's point of view (note the *we*-emphasis).

This one is bad.

Dear Mr. Chapman:

Your April 4 order for $1,743.30 worth of Protect-O paints and supplies has been received. We are pleased to have this nice order and hope that it marks the beginning of a long relationship.

As you instructed, we will bill you for this amount. We are shipping the goods today by Blue Darter Motor Freight.

We look forward to your future orders.

Sincerely,

**Fast-Moving Presentation of the Good News.** The better letter begins directly, telling Mr. Chapman that he is getting what he wants. The remainder of the letter is customer welcome and subtle selling. Notice the good use of reader emphasis and positive language. The letter closes with a note of appreciation and a friendly, forward look.

"First the good news—if I cure you, I'll become world famous."

From The Wall Street Journal, with permission of Cartoon Features Syndicate.

166   PART 3   Basic Patterns of Business Letters

## CASE ILLUSTRATION  Order Acknowledgment Letters. *(A Routine Acknowledgment)*
This letter to a long-time customer routinely reports that all the items ordered will be sent. Appropriately, the letter is short and direct.

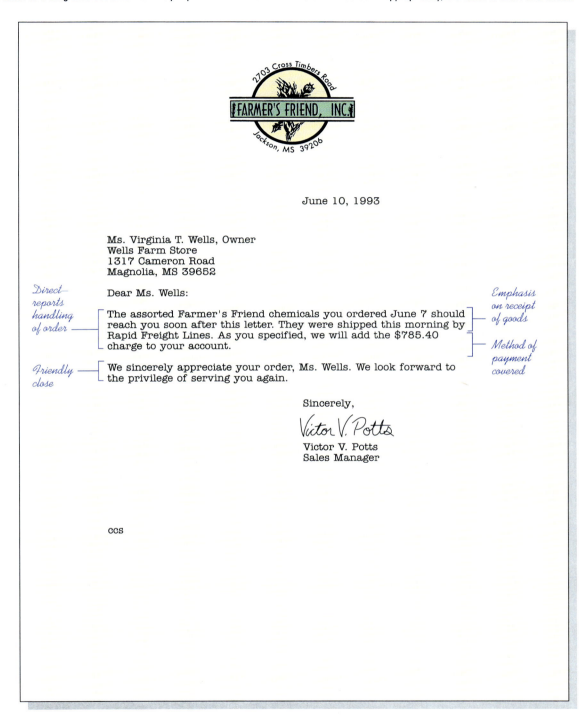

CHAPTER 6  Directness in Routine Responses

**CASE ILLUSTRATION**  Order Acknowledgment Letters. *(Acknowledgment with a Problem)*
This letter concerns an order that cannot be handled exactly as the customer would like. Some items are being sent, but one must be placed on back order and one cannot be shipped because the customer did not give the information needed. The letter skillfully handles the negative points.

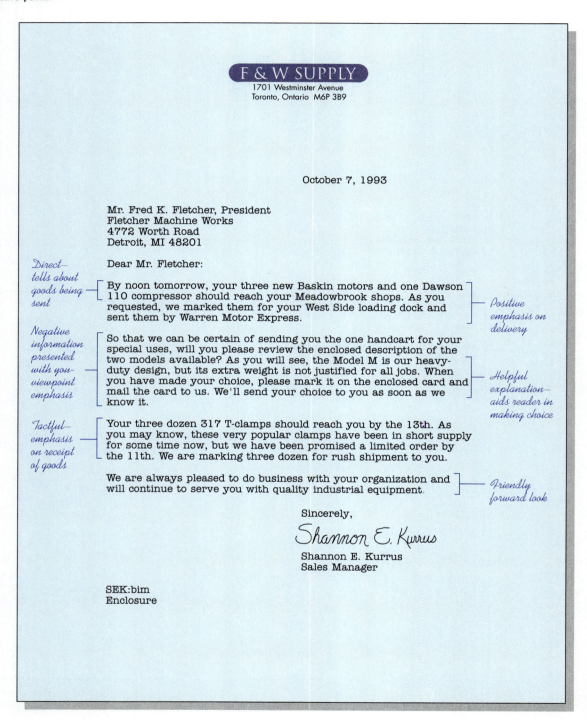

Dear Mr. Chapman:

Your selection of Protect-O paints and supplies should reach you by Wednesday, for the shipment left today by Blue Darter Motor Freight. As you requested, we are sending you an invoice for $1,743.30, including sales tax.

As this is your first order from us, I welcome you to the Protect-O circle of dealers. Our representative, Ms. Cindy Wooley, will call from time to time to offer whatever assistance she can. She is a highly competent technical adviser on paint and painting.

Here in the home plant we will also do what we can to help you profit from Protect-O products. We'll do our best to give you the most efficient service. And we'll continue to develop the best possible paints—like our new Chem-Treat line. As you will see from the enclosed brochure, Chem-Treat is a real breakthrough in mildew protection.

We genuinely appreciate your order, Mr. Chapman. We are determined to serve you well in the years ahead.

Sincerely,

*This letter is better.*

## OTHER ROUTINE-RESPONSE SITUATIONS

In the preceding pages, we have covered the most common routine-response situations. Others occur, of course. You should be able to handle them with the techniques that have been explained and illustrated.

In handling such situations, you need to keep in mind that whenever possible, you should get to the goal of the letter right away. You should cover any other information needed in good logical order. You should carefully choose words that convey just the right meaning. More specifically, you should consider the value of using the you-viewpoint, and you should weigh carefully the differences in meaning conveyed by the positiveness or negativeness of your words. As in all cordial human contacts, you should end your letter with appropriate and friendly goodwill words.

*Other routine-response situations occur.*

*You should be able to handle them by applying the techniques covered in this chapter.*

## SUMMARY (by Chapter Objectives)

1. When responding to inquiry letters favorably, you should begin directly.
   - If the response contains only one answer, begin with it.
   - If it contains more than one answer, begin with a major one or a general statement indicating you are answering.
   - Identify the letter being answered early, perhaps in a subject line.
   - Arrange your answers (if more than one) logically.
   - And make them stand out.
2. If both good- and bad-news answers are involved, be tactful.
   - Give each answer the emphasis it deserves, perhaps by subordinating the negative.
   - For extra goodwill effect, consider doing more than was asked.
   - End with appropriate cordiality.
3. Handle personnel evaluations directly.
   - Do so even if they contain negative information, for you are doing what the reader asked.

*1. Use the direct approach, orderly arrangement, and goodwill in favorably answering business inquiries.*

*2. Compose responses that present both good and bad news yet maintain a friendly tone to foster goodwill.*

*3. Phrase personnel evaluations so that they systematically present the essential information and are fair to all concerned.*

CHAPTER 6 Directness in Routine Responses

- You have two logical choices for beginning the letter.
  - —You can begin by answering a question asked, preferably one deserving the emphasis of the opening position.
    - —You can begin with a statement indicating you are complying with the request.
- Refer to the letter you are answering early in the letter (perhaps in the subject line).
- Present the information in a logical order, making each answer stand out.
  - —Numbering the responses is one way of doing this.
  - —Arranging answers by paragraphs also helps.
- Report fairly and truthfully.
  - —Stress facts and avoid opinions.
  - —Give each item the emphasis it deserves.
- End with appropriate friendly comment.

**4. Compose letters involving adjustment grants that will regain the customer's confidence in your company or its products.**

4. As letters granting adjustments are positive responses, write them in the direct order.
   - But they differ from other direct-order letters in that they involve a negative situation.
     - —Something has gone wrong.
     - —You are correcting that wrong.
     - —But you should also overcome the negative image in the reader's mind.
   - You do this by first telling the good news—what you are doing to correct the wrong.
   - In the opening and throughout, emphasize the positive.
   - Avoid the negative—words like *trouble, damage,* and *broken.*
   - Try to regain the reader's lost confidence, maybe with explanation or with assurance of corrective measures taken.
   - End with a goodwill comment, avoiding words that recall what went wrong.

**5. Write letters that acknowledge orders, cover order problems positively, and build goodwill.**

5. Write order acknowledgments in the form of a favorable response.
   - Handle most by form letters or notes.
   - But in special cases, use letters.
   - Begin such letters directly, telling the status of the goods ordered.
   - In the remainder of the letter, build goodwill, perhaps including some selling or reselling.
   - Include an expression of appreciation somewhere in the letter.
   - End with an appropriate, friendly comment.

## QUESTIONS FOR DISCUSSION

1. Discuss why just reporting truthfully may not be enough in handling negative information in letters answering inquiries.
2. Defend a policy of doing more than asked in answering routine inquiries. Can the policy be carried too far?
3. What can acknowledgment letters do to build goodwill?
4. Discuss situations where each of the following forms of an order acknowledgment would be preferred: form letter, merged letter, and a special letter.
5. Discuss how problems (vague orders, back orders) should be handled in letters acknowledging orders.
6. Discuss the relationship of positive and negative words to fair treatment in employee evaluation letters.
7. Why is it usually advisable to do more than just grant the claim in an adjustment-grant letter?

## APPLICATION EXERCISES

1. Point out the shortcomings in this response letter. The letter is a reply to an inquiry about a short course in business communication taught by a professor for the company's employees. The inquiry included five questions: (1) How did the professor perform? (2) What was the course format (length, meeting structure)? (3) What was the employee evaluation of the instruction? (4) Was the course adapted to the company and its technical employees? (5) Was homework assigned?

Dear Mr. Braden:

Your January 17 inquiry addressed to the Training Director has been referred to me for attention as we have no one with that title. I do have some training responsibilities and was the one who organized the in-house course in clear writing. You asked five questions about our course.

Concerning your question about the instructor, Professor Alonzo Britt, I can report that he did an acceptable job in the classroom. Some of the students, including this writer, felt that the emphasis was too much on grammar and punctuation, however. He did assign homework, but it was not excessive.

We had class two hours a day from 3:00 to 5:00 p.m. every Thursday for eight weeks. Usually the professor lectured the first hour. He is a good lecturer but sometimes talks over the heads of the students. This was the main complaint in the evaluations the students made at the end of the course, but they had many good comments to make also. Some did not like the contents, which they said was not adapted to the needs of a technical worker. Overall, the professor got a rating of B− on a scale of A to F.

We think the course was good for our technical people, but it could have been better adapted to our needs and our people. I also think it was too long—about ten hours (five meetings) would have been enough. Also, we think the professor spent too much time lecturing and not enough on application work in class.

Please be informed that the information about Professor Brett must be held in confidence.

Sincerely,

2. Point out the shortcomings in this letter granting a claim for a fax machine received in damaged condition. Inspection of the package revealed that the damage did not occur in transit.

Dear Ms. Orsag:

Your May 3 letter in which you claim that the Rigo FAX391 was received in damaged condition has been carefully considered. We inspect all our machines carefully before packing them, and we pack them carefully in strong boxes with Styrofoam supports that hold them snugly. Thus we cannot understand how the damage could have occurred.

Even so, we stand behind our product and will replace any that are damaged. However, we must ask that first you send us the defective one so we can inspect it. After your claim of damage has been verified, we will send you a new one.

We regret any inconvenience this situation may have caused you and assure you that problems like this rarely occur in our shipping department.

Sincerely,

■ ■ ■ ■ ■ ■ ■ ■ ■ ■
## LETTER PROBLEMS

### FAVORABLE RESPONSES

1. For this problem you are Maxwell Worley, director of marketing for Half Moon Lake Resort. You are beginning the task of answering the inquiry from the assistant to the president of Goliath Industries (see Problem 1, Chapter 5, for background information).

    In answering the question about transportation, you can suggest two possible means. One is to rent automobiles, which is what most convention groups do. The other is to use one of two shuttle services that provide transportation to and from resorts in the area. They charge $25 per person, round trip, from the airport. You would be pleased to make the arrangements.

    Yes, you do grant discounts to groups—15 percent off the standard $175 per person per day for meals and lodging. And, yes, the golf course, swimming pool, tennis courts, and boat docks are available to guests without extra charge. However, golfers do pay $10 per person for use of a cart (mandatory for your course).

    As the dinner boat cruise is one of the resort's most popular attractions, it would need to be booked well in advance. At the moment, the last Saturday in August is open. The boat charge is $360 for a three-hour cruise. Dinner, which would replace one at the resort, would cost only $3 per person extra for service. If desired, a bar could be set up at a cost of $3.50 for mixed drinks, $2 for beer and wine, and $1.50 for soft drinks.

    You have a conference room that you think is ideal for Goliath's needs. This soundproof room is beautifully paneled in walnut and elegantly furnished. It will easily accommodate 22 people around its massive long table. (Groups of 30 have used it.) An overhead projector, screen, and chalkboard are permanent fixtures in the room. The room rents for $240 a day (8 hours).

    Now write the letter that will answer the questions and bring the Goliath executives to your resort.

2. As manager of sales for Varga Leather Crafts, manufacturers of fine leather products, you receive a letter today from an executive of Norstar Chemical Company, Ltd. (see Problem 2, Chapter 5, for background information). The letter asks questions about your binder portfolio, and it offers the possibility of a very nice sale. You'll work extra hard to answer it completely and positively.

    In answering the question about the logo, you can give a clear yes. Varga does emboss company logos in a 5-inch-by-5-inch area on the side of the portfolio. This service is included in the cost of the portfolio, and the ad should have said so. The company will need to supply a clear picture of the logo when ordering. You also can answer yes about putting individual names on the portfolios, above or below the logo. But this service costs an extra $3 per name. The names should be submitted with the order.

    Yes, Varga does give quantity discounts. For orders between 50 and 100 units, the discount is 12 percent off the list price. And yes, Varga can make the portfolios in burgundy leather; but this will require at least six weeks of work time. Thus you could meet Norstar's eight-week deadline, but only if the order is placed right away. You are enclosing a small sample of your burgundy leather to make sure the color is right.

    Now you will write the letter that will give the Norstar executive the information requested. And you'll do it in a way that will enhance the possibility of a sale.

3. In the role of Stephanie Jennings, training director for Zoro Motors, you will respond to an inquiry from your counterpart at the Bay City Refinery of the Zenith Oil Company (see Problem 3, Chapter 5, for background information).

    You are very willing to report your experiences with safety expert J. Jack Mueller. In fact, you wish you had made similar inquiries before hiring the man. He is highly competent and he did good work for your company. Even so, you have reservations about whether Zoro got its money's worth.

    Concerning the question about whether accidents declined after Mueller worked with your people, the answer is yes. In the first six months the overall rate dropped 34 percent, and the rate of accidents with injury, 42 percent. However, over the next six months the rates increased. Now, a little over a year later, it appears that the rate is virtually the same as it was before Mueller began his work. You and your associates have concluded that safety education and awareness must be an ongoing effort—that the effects of a single program, however good, are temporary.

You will give a favorable report on Mueller's ability as a teacher and his knowledge of safety. Evaluations by your employees participating in the instruction were extremely high. Mueller generates excitement in the classroom, and he impresses the students with his mastery of the subject. His inspection of the plant and his pinpointing of problem areas clearly helped to reduce accident sources.

Answering the question about the overall worth of Mueller's services is not easy, in light of the professional job he did for you. It is hard to put a value on the prevention of accidents, injuries, and such. Even so, you and your management feel that Mueller's services were expensive and were made so primarily by his requirement that classes be limited to 20 students. In other words, you got good results; but you think you paid too much for what you got. In the future, you plan to conduct safety training through your own safety officer and other company personnel.

With the preceding information in mind you'll answer the letter from the Zenith training director. You will be careful not to be unfair to Mueller, who really is a highly competent professional.

4. To your office at the Bigg City Boat Fair, today's mail brings an inquiry from the marketing manager of Glasscraft, Inc. (see Problem 4, Chapter 5, for background information). The marketing manager has received your letter in which you attempted to induce Glasscraft to buy display space. But before buying, the marketing manager wants answers to some specific questions. Now you will answer these questions.

Concerning the question about size of a display stall, you must be general, for not all stalls are precisely the same. Generally, they run about 30 feet by 20 feet—quite adequate for one boat in the 20-foot range or two smaller ones. Some companies rent more than one. As to location, you handle this on a first-come, first-serve basis. You will enclose a diagram of the display area in Bigg City's convention and exhibition center with available stalls and stall sizes indicated.

You can report very positively about the success of the fair, now in its fourth year. Last year 81 companies bought display space. Seventeen were boat manufacturers and the others were manufacturers of other marine products. Current indications are that the total will approach 100 this year. Last year over 17,000 people attended over the two-day period. You are expecting more this year.

The fair's governing committee is well aware of the need for security. After some embarrassing incidents two years ago, the committee authorized hiring two off-duty policemen to patrol the area throughout the time when the fair is not open to the public. Last year not one incident was reported.

In writing the letter, you will have the underlying goal of getting Glasscraft to buy space at the fair.

5. As owner of Miss Kitty's Antiques, you are delighted that someone is finally interested in the Czechoslovakian pottery you've been acquiring the last five years (see Problem 5, Chapter 5, for background information). You've always thought it was beautiful, with brilliant colors and exquisite shapes.

Your inventory on these pieces includes six large pieces, varying from approximately 3 feet by 3 feet by 4 feet to 4 feet by 3 feet by 6 feet. You also have at least a dozen medium pieces and nearly two dozen small pieces. The large pieces are all painted with graphic designs; of the medium and small pieces, 80 percent are graphics and 20 percent florals. Since you've acquired many of these pieces from estate sales or individuals rather than from other dealers, your cost has been very low. Therefore, you are willing to offer Sally Peterson of Globe Trotter Travel a volume discount.

The authenticity of most pieces is easily verified since the pieces are signed and dated by the artists. Also, some of the pieces appear in the latest edition of *Kovel's Dictionary of Pottery,* a widely respected antiques reference book. The few pieces you have that are not signed are nearly identical to the other pieces in colors used, designs, and material age.

Write Sally Peterson a letter describing your inventory of these Czech pottery pieces. Send her pictures and prices for the six large pieces and price ranges for the medium and small pieces. Also, remember to include your regular store hours, but you'll want to also offer to arrange for a special showing at her convenience. Of course, you'll include your phone number so she can call you.

6. Audio book sales are soaring! As Robert Edwards, President of the Audio Publishers Association, you couldn't be more pleased with the latest sales data.

You'll be happy to send these figures to Terrence Patrick, the owner of five convenience stores in Homewood, Illinois (see Problem 6, Chapter 5, for background information).

The data on best-sellers are currently showing audiotape sales representing about 5 percent of total printed sales for nonfiction books. Nonfiction audiotape sales, on the other hand, are currently doing double this rate at 10 percent of printed copy sales. By category, self-help tapes account for nearly 50 percent of all sales, classics and fiction account for 15 percent, business tapes account for 25 percent, and all others account for the remaining 10 percent. The buyers of these tapes are split almost evenly by gender, with men purchasing 51 percent and women 49 percent. The largest number of sales is by people 25 to 40 years old, similar to tape buyers at most types of outlets nationwide.

Be sure to give Mr. Patrick the names and addresses of distributors you identify from your database as being near him, using his zip code and those adjacent to his area.

In responding to Mr. Patrick, you realize that organizing data in its most useful form is a good idea. You also recognize that tape sales data broken down by type could easily be presented in a pie chart. You may want to consider including a graphic in your letter.

7. As the director of public relations for the Chicago-based Solar Protection Factory, Inc., you are responsible for responding to inquiries about your company's products. You are always delighted to answer questions about your new Solarweave fabric, especially the type of questions raised by Kathleen M. Meersman, a buyer for a St. Petersburg, Florida, boutique (see Problem 7, Chapter 5, for background information).

Ms. Meersman wants to know more about Solarweave durability, laundering, and colors and styles. You can respond favorably on all these aspects. Both your own tests and those by Consumers Union reveal it is more durable than the average T-shirt. In fact, tests show that it wears nearly 50 percent longer in a variety of conditions. Its laundering is the same as most other T-shirts—machine wash with like colors and tumble dry on low heat. You can also report that after repeated laundering, your tests have found that Solarweave holds its color 100 percent longer than regular cotton T-shirts and 50 percent longer than polyester/cotton blend T-shirts. Your shirts can be specially produced in most popular cuts, sleeve types, and colors.

In your response, be sure to address any other questions Ms. Meersman asked. Also, send her a copy of your most recent pricing study, showing the $40 price is reasonable to customers in view of all the benefits of the fabric. Today's beachgoers are aware of the need to protect themselves from the damaging sun rays. These Solarweave shirts are an easy way to do this.

8. Assume the role of Milton Chen, Vice President for International Sales of a leading textile company in Japan. One of your products, an insect repellent pantyhose, has been generating attention in the United States and Canada. An astute businessman in Connecticut, Jeff Horen, has inquired about your product (see Problem 8, Chapter 5, for background information). His clearly worded and well-thought out questions have captured your attention, and you will write a favorable response.

The question that most intrigues you is whether the pantyhose could be saturated with chemicals that repel ticks as well as insects. You believe he has identified a new market niche—protective stockings for those who live, work, or play near tick-infested areas. Your research shows products are already on the U.S. market claiming to protect against the deadly tick. Therefore, you are willing to produce a prototype for testing.

In your response to Mr. Horen, you'll answer all his questions on demographics and life-styles and send several samples of the pantyhose to address the question on strength of odors. Let him know that you are currently distributing directly from Japan but would like to set up a distributorship in the United States. Ask him if he is interested in either establishing a distributorship or in helping you test the tick-repellent stockings. Thank him graciously for his interest in your product.

9. As sales manager of Brian Hotels, Inc., a chain with 120 hotels in all major cities in the United States and Canada, you will gladly supply information about your hotel as requested in the inquiry letter written to you by Maria Stutzman of Longhorn Steel Company (see Problem 9, Chapter 5, for background information). You think your rates are most reasonable because you do not pay for prime land locations that downtown hotels do and you have better control of labor costs because of your locations.

Brian Hotels are usually located close to transportation hubs but away from the noise of large airports. You provide free transportation to depots and airports but people need to make their reservations 12 hours in advance. In addition, you can transport people to any location as long as they meet the 12-hour reservation requirement.

Your rates average $70 for singles and $90 for doubles, U.S. dollars. Local rates will vary depending on local economic conditions and tax structures. And, yes, you can give a corporate discount of 15 percent. But people will need to ask for it and present a valid ID.

Your hotels are neat, clean, and new, as all hotels have been developed within the last five years. Each hotel has a restaurant, bar, workout room (weights, bicycles, and such), sauna, swimming pool, and tennis courts. This is what you mean by a "complete" facility. You offer all the services that a downtown hotel does but not at downtown prices.

You are quite happy with the competitive niche you have established. Give Ms. Stutzman the answers to her questions in an organized way so that she will give you the nod for scheduling her salespeople at your locations. Make it a distinctively Brian Hotels response.

10. As you read over the inquiry letter you received today from Eugene Carruthers, executive director of the Association of Marketing Managers (see Problem 10, Chapter 5, for background information), you think you can answer all of the questions he asks. Your business, Group Graphics, Inc., already publishes similar types of journals for three other organizations; so you know you can handle the job. Yours is a family-owned, medium-size publishing company that specializes in personal service to its customers. You will respond favorably and specifically to the inquiry letter from Mr. Carruthers.

On the issue of price, your bid for the *Journal of Technology and Communication* is $3,500 and for the *Communication Update* is $4,000, based on 3,200 produced and the number of pages in each of the sample issues you received. Prices could vary from this bid depending on the page length of each issue. In addition, you would have to have details of length, format, paper selection, and such before you could give a specific bid price on any special publication (the directory, the program booklet, and unique volumes indicated in the letter). You believe, however, that you would be competitive. And you would be glad to offer advice in the design and format of any publication. Service is a key feature of your business.

Yes, your quality control is excellent. The system you use is relatively simple but it works. The account representative for each customer personally oversees all production runs for his or her accounts; that is, the representative goes to the presses and physically observes each major press run, inspecting on site the publications as they are produced. You believe this system is good because it is personalized, it establishes identity with the customers, and it creates internal accountability.

For the turnaround on the major press runs, you can get a batch completed in 10 working days from the time you receive the camera-ready copy. You assume that Mr. Carruthers will furnish copy in this manner. If not, you charge $15.00 per hour for typesetting. Of course, you would have to get customer approval on all copy before it is set for production. Moreover, you have service personnel to deliver items and orders to customers in your service area (the office of the Association of Marketing Managers is 20 miles away). You'll be glad to deliver his orders free of charge as you have other customers in the area. And you can offer credit terms of 30 days; but you would have to have references and a credit check first.

Write your reply to Eugene Carruthers. You have a number of things to cover, so you'll need to organize the points in a logical sequence before you actually write the letter.

11. As Vice President of Marketing of W.A. Gordon Construction Co., respond to the information requested by Bill Carter of Greenwood Country Club (see Problem 11, Chapter 5, for background information). You have built many metal frame buildings; so you definitely believe you can construct the covered tennis courts he asks for.

You will submit a formal proposal with your letter that will detail many of the specifications of the construction. The proposal will include the building description, pier drilling specifications, wind load factors, steel framing, roof system, trim/flashing, and lighting standards. You will also include a blueprint of the proposed structure, color selections, and a product catalog explaining all phases of the metal framing building process. Your letter will tell Mr. Carter that you are responding with the actual proposal and will refer to the contents of it.

The price you will quote for the covered courts is $68,640.00. But this figure assumes that the soil sample you will take is solid enough to support the structure. If the engineering reports show different soil compositions, then you will have to add more pier supports. And more pier supports could increase the price significantly—probably $8,000–$10,000 more. Also, the proposal does include the PTA (Professional Tennis Association) regulations.

Although you have not covered tennis courts before, you did call several clubs within 100 miles of Greenwood Country Club and they report there is no problem with excessive heat from covered courts. The only real problem is with strong, blowing rain (it blows onto the courts). The winters are not severe at Greenwood Country Club, so the covered courts should permit many extended playing days in both winter and summer.

You will guarantee the structure for 10 years from any type of building defect. And you estimate that you could finish the project in 75 days. Also, you can furnish references who will attest to the quality of your work. If you get the job, you would expect full payment 30 days after completion.

Sit down to your computer now and prepare the favorable response to Bill Carter's inquiry. Make it complete and distinctively original.

12. You nod your head and smile as you, marketing manager for Continental Life, read the inquiry letter from Antonio D'Silva of Bosco Corporation (see Problem 12, Chapter 5, for background information). You believe that your answers to his questions can win his account, but you will need to present them directly and cheerfully to distinguish your letter from others he will no doubt receive.

You will include with the letter a table that will show the total benefits you can offer and a sample contract. (You may assume these two items accompany your answer). The actual dental plan includes three types of coverage: preventive, restorative, and major restorative procedures. The contract will detail what each of these procedures involves. There are no deductibles for preventive procedures but restorative procedures have a $50 deductible per calendar year. Major restoratives do not apply until the second year of contract coverage and have a $50 per calendar year deductible. Eligible charges are covered at 100 percent and 80 percent for preventive and restorative coverages during the first year and 50 percent for major restorative in the second year. All of these percentages apply after the deductible.

Orthodontic benefits are available after 12 months of coverage for dependent children less than 19 years old. There is a $50 deductible and 50 percent coverage limit. In addition, there is a $1,500 maximum benefit per year limit for all coverages.

The monthly charges for these coverages are as follows:

Employee only—$16.70
Employee and spouse—$32.40
Employee and dependent children—$36.40
Employee and family—$49.60

An industry standard is to have the dental costs split equally between the company and the employee (the 50–50 ratio that Mr. D'Silva mentions in his letter). If companies elect to pay for more of the costs, their expenses will increase for fringe benefits. The company expenses are deductible before gross profits; so there is a tax feature for the company. You will suggest that the company check with its accountant for specifics, though. Also, you will need to have 20 employees enrolled before you can extend the coverage.

To service the account, you will provide an account representative for four hours two times each month. This representative will be on site to answer questions about coverages, to help with claim forms, and such. In addition, you have a toll-free customer service line that will be available.

With these details in mind, organize your ideas and write the reply to Antonio D'Silva's inquiry. Make it specific and service-oriented so that it will win you this account.

## PERSONNEL EVALUATIONS

13. Move into the office of Professor Thomas O. Pennington, Kemper University, and prepare to answer the inquiry of the Dura-Bilt executive concerning Joan Coco (see Problem 13, Chapter 5, for background information). You know Joan very well. She has been a student in two of your courses and your research assistant for the past 15 months.

In responding to the question about Joan's potential for management, you will be positive. She appears to have good leadership qualities. She is outgoing and personable. She has good communication skills and gets along well with people. During the past year she has served as president of the Marketing Club, and as faculty adviser for this group, you observed firsthand what you consider to be outstanding leadership ability. In addition, her good record in her study of management and the other business courses should equip her well for future management responsibilities.

In the classes she had with you, Joan was adequate but not outstanding, making grades of C (Marketing Principles) and B (Marketing Research). Even so, you think she has a good mind and could have done better with more study time. Her work as your research assistant was very well done. Part of it involved visiting local businesses and getting cooperation on a survey you are conducting. She worked aggressively at the task and succeeded in every attempt. You feel her good oral communication skills and her outgoing personality contributed to her success.

Without question, Joan is a hard worker and would work well without supervision. In fact, much of her work for you was done without direct supervision. And she always got the work done in short time—and on time. You judge her to be highly dependable.

Over the past few months you have discussed Joan's future with her. From these conversations, you conclude that she has high career goals and will reach them. You think the company that hires her will be fortunate.

Now write the letter.

14. For this problem you are Alice Prather, manager of the Western Hills Country Club. You will write an evaluation of Rafer M. Quigley, manager of your snack bar (see Problem 14, Chapter 5, for background information).

Rafer has managed the snack bar for twenty-six months, and his performance has been good. During this time the bar's sales have increased 7 percent and profits have increased 12 percent. You give Rafer full credit for the increases. He has run a highly efficient operation. Also, his work has been appreciated by club members. In a recent survey of the membership, the snack bar got high ratings, especially for its food quality and service.

You feel Rafer has good management potential. Although his staff is small (a full-time cook and four part-time employees), he has demonstrated good leadership ability. He is intelligent and considerate. He gets good effort from his workers. You have been impressed with his ability to relate to people at all levels—kitchen help, administrators, and club members.

Rafer does not do the buying for his operation, but he does keep inventory records and makes purchase requests to the dining room manager (who does the actual buying). You believe Rafer could handle the entire buying operation, however, for he has worked closely with the dining room manager.

Whether Rafer is ready to manage a restaurant you can't say, for running a snack bar is not quite the same. Even so, this particular snack bar is a bigger operation than most. As the dining room is open only Monday through Friday evenings, the snack bar caters to the noontime needs of club members. Thus it serves more than just snacks—usually soups, salads, and a plate lunch. As Rafer is actively involved in the food preparation, he has good experience in this area.

You know Rafer to be a diligent and hard worker. On numerous occasions he worked long hours when the situation required it. He is aggressive. Although the record-keeping on his job is minimal, he has done everything required of him—and on time.

You would like to keep Rafer, but you want what is best for him. So you will write an evaluation that will fairly describe his performance and qualifications.

15. In the role of Edmund E. Caldwell, write an evaluation of Diane Dionne, your part-time secretary (see Problem 15, Chapter 5, for background information).

Diane has been a good secretary; in fact, she has been more than just a secretary. You were especially pleased when she came to you two years ago and quickly reorganized your files and generally gave order to the office operations of your small real estate business (which consists of you, three realtors, and a part-time secretary). She is bright, and she has a good knowledge of business. It is apparent to you that she is getting a good business education at the local college and is applying her knowledge to her work.

Yes, she is a hard worker—and highly efficient. As for her dependability, you can report positively, although you have one reservation. During school examination times and vacations she often asked for time off. You always granted her requests, but there were times when you really needed her.

Diane's friendly, warm, and outgoing personality most certainly is a major asset for her. All of your associates like her, and you feel she made many friends for the company. She appears to like people, and people like her. She has excellent oral and written communication skills.

Although she had no opportunity to use her management skills in your company, you think she has potential for management. She is aggressive. In her job with you she took over assignments and responsibilities beyond that expected of a part-time secretary (writing advertisements, answering mail, ordering supplies, and such). But always she did it with your approval. You think she has the necessary skills with people. You are impressed with her ability to apply her business training to her work.

As Diane still works as your secretary, you will process the letter yourself.

16. Directing the Boys and Girls Club in Solana Beach, California, for the past six years has kept you extremely busy. However, one person who always helped make your job easier was Marina Munson. Her husband will soon graduate from law school, taking a new position out of town. While you are sorry to see her go, you can easily give her an excellent recommendation. So when you received a letter today from a potential employer inquiring about Marina, you were delighted to answer questions about her (see Problem 16, Chapter 5, for background information).

Not only could you count on Marina to be extremely reliable, she also was flexible in her work schedule. The two years you worked with Marina, she never missed a single day of scheduled work. When she did need time off for special occasions, she requested it in advance and away from especially busy days. She has excellent interpersonal skills, working well with her colleagues, supervisors, and the boys and girls. She exhibited excellent listening skills, which allowed her to excel in all aspects of her work. In fact, in the last six months she worked for you, you gave her more responsibilities. One of these responsibilities included completely arranging for special bus trips for the club; this task involved both collecting fees and paying bills. She did this capably. While there was no opportunity for her to supervise others, you feel her excellent rapport with others as well as her leadership ability indicate she would be an effective supervisor.

Be sure to make it clear in your letter that you highly recommend Marina, especially for a position that requires the kinds of skills you've described.

17. Jane Adami, your excellent administrative assistant for the last four years, has recently applied for an executive secretarial position at a Davenport, Iowa, law firm. As her boss, Colonel Lee Vault, you've been asked about her adaptability, organization skills, and decision-making ability as well as her ability to learn new skills and procedures (see Problem 17, Chapter 5, for background information).

You recognize this employer is not asking about her qualifications per se but about her ability to fit with the firm. You solidly believe Jane would be an excellent assistant in nearly any setting, but you also recognize that you need to address the precise questions this employer has posed. You can speak highly of Jane on all aspects. In your response, address each of these areas, giving examples where Jane has clearly demonstrated competence. For example, you may want to tell how she quickly learned the EDI (Electronic Data Interchange) system when it was first installed. Also, you may want to enclose the instructions she wrote to assist the rest of the staff in following the new procedures for vacation time requests. In giving examples of her decision-making ability, be sure to include good examples without revealing the nature of any confidential projects.

18. As Jennifer Stevens, Regional Manager for the *Princeton Review,* you have been asked about Dana Robbins, a former marketing representative for you (see Problem 18, Chapter 5, for background information). Dana is being considered for a sales representative position in the Los Angeles area for a major college textbook publisher. Not only was Dana one of the best marketing representatives you have ever worked with, her energy and enthusiasm were highly contagious. You can highly recommend her.

Be sure your letter addresses the basics needed in most sales positions—being a self-starter, organized, and efficient with paperwork. You'll cite her experience with this kind of work as well as give specific supporting examples whenever possible. You might also want to stress her excellent interpersonal skills, using examples from her college sorority days to her present work with the local chapter of the Arthritis Foundation.

You'll also want to discuss why Dana is an excellent candidate for this position in other special ways. Not only is she experienced with the travel sales representatives do, but she is also familiar with the Los Angeles area since her grandparents lived there. She is mentally prepared for dealing with the congested freeways. You also think that her experience with selling the *Princeton Review* is very similar to selling textbooks. The review courses are constantly being updated to prepare students for the changing tests.

19. You are the owner of RPC, a retail distributor of computer software. In today's mail, you received a letter about Jerry Walden, one of your top floor

salespersons. In it, the information systems manager of Tubo, Inc. (see Problem 19, Chapter 5, for background information) wants you to evaluate Walden, who is applying for work in the IS department. Your task now is to organize the response you will write to the inquiry.

Jerry Walden began working for you two years ago, and he has developed into a good, solid performer. But he did not start that way. In fact, you considered letting him go during the first six months of his employment with you. During that time, he simply did not sell; and this is the primary criterion you use to evaluate floor salespeople. After counseling him, you determined that he was approaching his selling work in the same way that he had approached teaching (his job for four years before joining your firm). You suggested that he take more initiative in his work without being "pushy." In addition, you indicated that he might benefit by taking a Dale Carnegie course, and this he did. Since that time, his sales performance has increased steadily. Currently, he is a top performer for you.

You have found Jerry to be especially good at translating technical information into the needs of store customers. Perhaps his best attribute is his "keeping customers sold after the sale." Many times, customers will call him or drop by to ask his advice about a new application of a software program they have purchased. He always takes time to answer their questions, even though he might have to return their calls or ask them to wait while he is busy with a customer.

You know also that Jerry has a second job selling musical instruments at night and on weekends to youngsters who are beginning their musical training. But this second job has never interfered with his sales work for you. And he sings in the local community chorus as well.

With these points in mind, write the letter that will evaluate Jerry Walden's qualifications accurately and fairly for the work at Tubo, Inc.

20. As Martina Polack, manager of public relations at Guardian Insurance Company, respond to the inquiry you received today from the manager of public relations of Alpha Packaging (see Problem 20, Chapter 5, for background information). In her last performance appraisal, Nelda Gonzalez indicated she wanted to do more human interest work that would combine her information systems and journalism background. She appears to have found an opportunity to do it.

Neldo joined your staff at Guardian three years ago from Tri-Star Electronics, where she worked in systems analysis and design. She took the job because it gave her an opportunity to use her recently earned journalism degree. You assigned her to a variety of jobs in your department so that she could get a feel for public relations work. She adapted well to each one in your rotation patterns—from training and development support to graphic design for annual reports. But she seemed best suited for company brochure work and this is where you placed her. Before she joined the company, you had contracted with an advertising agency for brochure work. But Nelda convinced you she could do the work in-house. In addition, she also prepares and updates policy and procedure manuals for the company. She has met deadlines, written and proofed copy, and followed through on all of the work that she has done.

In addition to her good performance record, Nelda exhibits good work habits on the job. Frequently, she will arrive at work early so that she can get her work out on time. You remember one occasion when she found that the department had overcharged the sales department for its services. She immediately told you about it, and you contacted the accounting department to adjust the cost control budget. Indeed, she is hardworking and highly principled.

You know also that Nelda teaches a night course at Ferris Community College. She mentioned casually that she received good ratings from her students because of her "real world" approach to the class. And last year she won an essay contest in the local paper for her article on "Effects of Recent Legislation on the Insurance Consumer." If she has a fault it would be that she appears so driven that she has little time for social pleasantries on the job.

All told, you believe Nelda Gonzalez will be ideal for the job at Alpha Packaging. You wish you could keep her at Guardian, but you don't have a job similar to the one she has applied for at Alpha Packaging. Write the letter that will evaluate positively the work record of Nelda Gonzalez.

21. You are Richard Swartz, head tennis pro at Fossill Hill Country Club, and you must answer the inquiry from the chair of the Tennis Selection Committee at Horseshoe Country Club about your assistant pro, Betsy Zigmann (see Problem 21, Chapter 5, for background information). Betsy has worked for you for two years and you want to give her an equitable evaluation.

When she applied for the job of assistant pro at Fossill Hill two years ago, she had just graduated from college. But she easily adapted to the work that you outlined for her. Her experience on the pro tour and her love for the game made her a "natural teacher"—perhaps the best you have seen. She relates well to all types and ages of players. And she is in demand for tennis instruction. Many of your members will "wait for Betsy" rather than schedule a lesson with the other two pros that serve on your staff.

Many times you have seen her taking notes during organized league play at the club and discussing her notes with players after their matches. When you asked her about her discussions, she noted that she just wanted to help improve the quality of play in the leagues. In several cases, you wondered whether some members might resent her critiques since they primarily play for fun. Her personality, however, made her critiques appear to be suggestions. And many members have requested private instructions as the result of her comments. You do not feel that Betsy was trying to generate business for herself but only attempting to help players with their techniques.

As one of three assistants, she is responsible for selling merchandise and services in your pro shop; and she does this well. You, however, are responsible for all ordering, inventorying, and bookkeeping. Betsy was raised in a family-owned hardware store. So you believe she has the experience to administer a fully functioning pro shop operation.

Betsy has done all of the things you have asked her to do—and more! You believe that she has the experience, drive, and personality that the job will require. You do not want to lose her, but she deserves the job of pro at Horseshoe Country Club. Write the letter that will recommend her favorably for the job.

## ADJUSTMENT GRANTS

22. You, manager of Travel Unlimited, have a claim to handle from one of your better clients. The executive secretary of the Alliance of Electronics Manufacturers has asked for some money back on a group tour the organization sponsored (see Problem 22, Chapter 5, for background information).

    A quick review of the facts and a call to the Clifton Hotel in Manchester confirms the executive secretary's story. The Clifton Hotel representative explained that a convention group had stayed beyond the dates they had booked rooms; and he blamed the Ashley for the meal problem. You don't accept the explanation; and you'll not deal with the Clifton in the future. Even so, the fact remains that the group did get cheaper rooms at the Ashley, and they had to pay for meals that they had bought in the tour price. You will reimburse the travelers, but not precisely the amount the executive secretary stated in the letter.

    The actual difference in the room price was $24 per day (not $27, as the executive secretary had estimated). As for the out-of-pocket cost of the meals, you'll pay the amount ($14.50) requested. Actually, the meals at the Clifton would have cost you only $11 each, but you'll pay the amount the travelers paid. You'll try to get the Clifton to cover the difference, but that's another problem.

    Now you must write the executive secretary of the Alliance of Electronics Manufacturers telling what you are doing to satisfy the claim. You'll explain what happened, and you'll make it clear that you are taking steps to prevent such situations in the future. You will do what you can to regain any lost confidence in your service, for you want the organization's continued business.

23. You, the manager of the factory showroom of the Sweet Dreams Mattress Company, are embarrassed after reading a claim letter from the owner of the Wayside Motel (see Problem 23, Chapter 5, for background information). The owner received 11 fire-damaged mattresses. It shouldn't have happened, but it did. You think you know the cause of the problem.

    Last month there was a fire in the north wing of your warehouse, and your losses were extensive. Your warehouse personnel spent days going through the mattresses in the fire area and marking all that had sustained any visible damage. All the bad ones were destroyed, you thought; but apparently the workers missed a few.

    You will most certainly replace the 11 damaged mattresses, and you'll do it right away. In fact, you'll send your local delivery truck with them, even though the distance is almost 200 miles. The driver will pick up the damaged goods.

    Now write the motel manager telling what you will do. And do what you can to regain any lost confidence. You want to continue this business relationship.

24. How embarrassing! Your shipping clerks goofed. They sent the wrong jogging suits to The Athlete's Closet (see Problem 24, Chapter 5, for background information). Instead of your top-of-the-line Hyde Park Joggers they sent your economy suits, the Pace Setters. To the casual observer, the two may apear similar—same colors and similar stripes. But close inspection such as The Athlete's Closet owner gave them reveals great differences.

    After reviewing the claim letter from The Athlete's Closet owner, you tried to find out what happened. But you can't be certain, for it is impossible to pinpoint the cause. Your shipping manager explained that probably one of his new workers made the mistake. "They haven't learned our system yet," he explained. "I have decided to check personally every outgoing order until the new people learn what they're doing."

You will send the right suits to The Athlete's Closet immediately. In fact, the shipment is being assembled as you begin writing the letter that will tell The Athlete's Closet owner that you are granting the claim. In the letter you will tell that the goods are being sent by Red Comet Motor Freight, and you will ask that the reader send back the suits received in error. Of course, you will pay the shipping charges. Also, you will attempt to regain the confidence of this new customer; and generally you will work to build good future relations.

25. As the owner of Productivity Consultants, write Janet Murray in the Human Resource Department of McLaughlin Body Company, granting her claim (see Problem 25, Chapter 5, for background information). Offer to provide private, on-site training for three to six employees as soon as possible. Offer her a choice of day and of trainer.

While you were on vacation, your assistant decided to overbook your seminars, thinking it would improve business. Although the intent was innocent, it is something you would never do. In fact, you've prided yourself on your reputation for providing good training seminars without cutting corners. Not only do you never book more than one student per computer, you always leave at least 10 percent of the computers free. This helps assure that you'll have working computers for all who signed up in advance and leaves room for any walk-ins that might show up. You had no idea of the overbooking until the day of the seminar. Also, you recognize Janet's concern that her employees need to become productive users of the software as soon as possible.

As a goodwill gesture, offer Janet a 25 percent discount on all the seminars your company offers for the next year.

26. As the Director of Customer Relations of a small business, DejaShoe, Inc., you were delighted when your company received an order for your new walking shoe from a well-established sporting goods store in your area. You are both angry and embarrassed that the order was fouled up in shipping (see Problem 26, Chapter 5, for background information). You also realize the importance both to your customer and to you for having the shoes available for the anniversary sale. Write a letter to fax to your customer stating that you will make a special delivery of the correct order at 8:00 A.M. tomorrow morning. Be sure to let them know you'll pick up the wrong shoes at that time.

You may want to thank them again for the order and do some resale on the quality of the shoes.

27. Ever since you started managing Winters restaurant three years ago, everything has gone smoothly. However, today you received a claim letter from a good customer that looked humorous at first; you realized, though, that this problem of improper serving could have long-term implications on your repeat business (see Problem 27, Chapter 5, for background information).

In addition to taking care of the problem, you will write to the customer, Mel Short, to assure him the problem is corrected. Tell Mel that you have spoken to the dinner waiters, giving them all instructions on how to serve properly and without touching the food. You've also decided to add a special module on serving to the training all new waiters will get.

Thank him for bringing this to your attention. As a goodwill gesture, enclose coupons for a free dinner.

28. Assume the role of Cheryl Hearst, owner of Group Graphics. You were shocked when you read the claim from the Executive Director of the Society for Business Advancement (see Problem 28, Chapter 5, for background information). But the returned program booklets justify the company's right to be upset, and you will find out the reasons for the faulty work. The Society for Business Advancement is indeed a good, stable account for you.

You first check with the account representative. She tells you that 500 program booklets were mailed on October 1 by four-day delivery to the convention hotel in New Orleans to ensure that they would be available for the meeting beginning on October 25. Next, both of you visit with the shop foreman.

As you trace through the production scheduling for the job, you determine that the batch was run on September 24–25. The week prior to that time, the press operator who was assigned to the job took a week's vacation. During his vacation, however, he developed chicken pox and missed an extra week with sick leave. It was during the extended week of sick leave that the booklets were printed with the errors. Somehow, the substitute press operator missed the printing errors and the binder assembled them into final booklet form. Because of shorthandedness during the week, your quality control inspectors didn't catch the mistake. And the booklets were mailed to the hotel.

It is your normal procedure to schedule major press runs only with experienced press operators. When an experienced operator is on vacation, you schedule only minor jobs for the backup personnel (stationery, business cards, notepads, and such). But in this case, you were forced to use the inexperienced personnel to meet the production deadline because of the illness that occurred. The result was faulty work in a very important job for a very important customer.

Of course, you will grant the claim by crediting the Society for Business Advancement account for $2,470.00. In addition, you will work hard to explain what happened in a specific but concise way. You will also include resale to make sure that the Society for Business Advancement identifies with the good qualities of your printing products and services.

Write the adjustment grant letter that will keep this good, reliable account. Remember, you'll need to be direct, specific, and positive throughout the letter to keep the customer under your company umbrella.

29. Yes, you will keep your word to Meadows Country Club. You remember the statement you made to their Board of Directors during your proposal, and you will get them water (see Problem 29, Chapter 5, for background information).

As you review their letter and recall the facts of the case, you remember that the geologist's report that you used to guide your drilling work for the job showed good possibilities for water at 1,300 feet. You used the depth to estimate the cost of drilling the well and added your normal percentage for profit. That's the final quote you gave to the Board.

A remote possibility exists that there could be side-wall casing problems or a pump malfunction. You suspect, however, that these are not significant factors in losing the water in the well. A more plausible reason is that there was not sufficient water at 1,300 feet to support the pumping capacity for the well. Of course, you won't know for sure until you inspect the well.

What you think you will have to do is to reenter the well and drill several hundred more feet to tap into the next water ridge. The geologist's report indicated that the next possibility was at 1,530 feet. You will have to transport your drilling equipment to the site of the well again, set it up, and have your crew begin new drilling operations. While this reentry procedure might appear unusual to the Board, it is an infrequent—but expected—part of your drilling experience. It will likely take all the profit margin you loaded for the job. But you will do it just the same because you want to assure the Board and the 750 club members that your word is as good as the work you perform.

Sit down now at your computer and prepare the adjustment grant to the Board. Begin directly with granting the claim. After that, explain what you think is likely wrong with the well—but do it positively. Then you will want to reassure the Board that you are good to the last letter of your word. Sell them on your competence and integrity. Most probably, your letter will be duplicated for the Board and posted on a bulletin board for other club members to read.

30. As production manager of HGA, Inc., deal with the claim presented in the letter from Clarence Copies that has been forwarded to you from the company president (see Problem 30, Chapter 5, for the background information). You will grant the claim for $7,302, but you will also need to explain what happened and to reassure that you did not deliberately interrupt the traffic flow to Clarence Copies. The letter states that there is long-term damage to the business. You believe just the opposite: that the exposure from *Fast Break* will work to Clarence's and the community's benefit.

A review of the contract with Middle State University confirms that May 16–30 were the days you agreed to film on site. These dates were ideal for the university because there were no scheduled classes between the spring and summer semesters. A call to President Marcy's office also verifies that he did release an information memo that stated traffic flow would not be congested during the filming dates. His assumption, however, was that there would be little traffic on the campus anyway during that time. Thus, the traffic would likely not be congested because no classes were being held.

A check with your production scheduling foreman indicates that your crews did start setting up one week prior to May 16—during final exam week at the university. You had to set up at this time to begin filming on the contracted date. The tight two-week schedule and the extensive budget for the film ($1.6 million) dictated that you begin and end on time; otherwise you would have lost significant money.

How to present the explanation is a matter of using your best business thinking. Granting the claim will show your good intentions. But you will have to do more than that. You will have to explain what happened in a positive way. It was never your purpose to interrupt the business but only to begin your film on time. During the two-week period, you pumped money into the local community and that should have benefitted many. Plus, the exposure from *Fast Break* should benefit the university and local community in the long run.

In fact, one of the shots of the campus has Clarence Copies in the background. You will enlarge this frame and send an 8″ × 10″ photo of it along with your letter as a goodwill gesture. The actual film will be released in about a year.

Write the letter that will grant the claim and reassure Clarence Copies of your good intentions.

## ACKNOWLEDGMENTS (OF VAGUE ORDERS AND BACK ORDERS)

31. In the position of manager of mail-order sales for the Tyson Manufacturing Company, today you received a nice order from the owner of The Gifte Shoppe (see Problem 31, Chapter 5, for background information). The order specifies "24 Tyson Ice Shavers, 12 black, 12 white, 12 beige." You are confused! Do they want 36 ice shavers? Or did they make an error in specifying colors? You would rather not guess; so you will delay shipping the ice shavers until you get the correct information. You can send the remainder of the order (12 air compressors and 30 shower radios).

    You are not pleased with the complication in this first order from The Gifte Shoppe. You would much prefer to show them your usual prompt and efficient service. So you will write an order acknowledgment letter that will explain the handling of their order, get the information you need, welcome a new customer, and generally make the reader feel good about doing business with Tyson.

32. Play the part of the manager of mail-order sales for the Hudson Publishing Company. You have a problem with an order received from the training director of Earhart-Downs Associates (see Problem 32, Chapter 5, for background information). They ordered multiple copies of three of your books. Unfortunately, you cannot send all of them right now.

    One of the books, *Too Many Chiefs*, by Wendy A. Tatum, has been selling faster than you can print them. At the moment, you are completely sold out of copies in paperback. In less than a year, the paperback version has gone through five printings, and now it is in a sixth. The printer promises delivery in two weeks. If you send the books by overnight courier just as soon as you get them, they would arrive only a day or two after the Earhart-Downs trainees begin their training. You will absorb the extra cost of courier delivery.

    All the other books ordered are in stock and will be sent today by Ace Trucking Company. They should arrive soon after the acknowledgment letter you will write. This letter will explain the handling of the order, especially the back order part. It will attempt to maintain good relations with this major consulting firm. Now write the letter.

33. Take over as shipping manager for Woodcrafters, Inc., a small manufacturer of fine office furniture. For years your sales representative in the central region has been trying to sell to the prestigious House of Dunaway, a retailer of office furniture, and finally she succeeded. You have their first order, but there are problems.

    Dunaway wants six of your best desks, the Squire, with matching executive chair at $2,780 the set. These beautiful walnut, hand-carved, oversized (7 ft. by 5 ft.) desks are truly works of art. Usually you have a half dozen or so in stock, but today you have none. Your craftsmen will have to make the six desks ordered, beginning today. You can send the first two in two weeks, two more a week later, and the remaining two another week later.

    You will send the 12 Commodore desks ($780 each), 6 Lancer executive chairs ($280 each), and 12 Monarch computer workstations ($375 each) right away. They will go out on the Blue Darter Freight truck and should arrive in a day or two.

    Now you will write the Dunaway purchasing agent and report the status of the order. You will explain the delay on the Squire desks in a way that will make waiting appear worthwhile. You may supply any factual details that will help you explain the situation as long as they are consistent with the information given.

34. As Charles Hopkins, president of Hopkins Technology, you've been both delighted and overwhelmed with the orders you've received for your Consu/Stats CD-ROM (see Problem 33, Chapter 5, for background information).

    In determining how many CDs to press, you based your initial order on the number of businesses your research revealed that used CD technology and the size of your past sales for this kind of data from your last survey. However, it seems as though both the market and the number of businesses using CDs is increasing, and you've received more orders than you can fill from the initial pressing. While it's a nice problem, you still need to acknowledge the orders you've received that you cannot fill immediately.

    Write a letter to Robert Price of the Price Club

Co. acknowledging the order while letting him know it is not immediately available. You'll want to let Mr. Price know when he'll receive the CD and remind him how useful the technology will be for him. For goodwill, tell him you will hold his payment until his order is shipped. Also, when the CDs are ready, you'll send his priority mail at no extra charge.

35. Your company, Taliq Corporation, developed a smart window. The window turns from frosted to clear when voltage is switched on, causing liquid crystals to align and become transparent. These Vision Panels sell for about $80 per square foot and replace the conventional use of curtains, shutters, shades, etc. After the window was shown in *Fortune* magazine, you received several orders.

    The order you received from Mike McLaughlin at BeeLine Corporation was vague. While the order called for three panels each 80 square feet, the dimensions of the panels were missing. Also, trim colors for the windows were missing. Ask Mike whether he wants silver, goldtone, brown, or black. Also, you offer both interior- and exterior-use Vision Panels. The article in *Fortune* illustrated the interior window but also mentioned the exterior window. Mr. McLaughlin's order implied that the panels would be used to separate interior spaces, but you want to be sure before you ship the order.

    Your letter should acknowledge the order, but you need more precise information to deliver the correct panels. To help assure that you retain the order, make the response as easy as possible.

36. As Director of Sales for the Steamboat Development Corporation, a riverboat casino company in Bettendorf, Iowa, you recently received an order for 50 tickets on the Diamond Lady from Kate Matthews, a travel agent in Ruston, Louisiana. The order specified the day the tickets were needed, but it didn't specify which cruise.

    Acknowledge Ms. Matthews' ticket order but ask her to clarify which cruise she would like. This boat has daytime cruises both down- and upriver. The morning cruise goes downriver from Bettendorf, Iowa, to Muscatine, Iowa. The afternoon cruise goes upriver from Muscatine to Bettendorf. In both cases, buses can pick up visitors at either end and drive back to the original site. However, this service needs to be arranged in advance. The Diamond Lady also offers a spectacular sunset cruise. It consists of a buffet dinner, a variety of entertainment in the lounges, and the usual array of slot machines, card tables, crap tables, etc. It departs and returns to Bettendorf. The evening cruise begins at 10:00 P.M. and offers gaming, light snacks, and entertainment until midnight. It, too, departs and returns to Bettendorf. The prices for these cruises are $37.50 for the sunset cruise and $25.00 for the others.

    Because your tickets sell out well in advance for the weekends, the facts you need to fill Ms. Matthews' order should be asked for clearly. Be sure to provide your fax number so she can respond quickly in order to get the tickets she wants. You want to build goodwill in order to encourage Ms. Matthews to continue to book on your boats in the future. You may want to enclose some of your color brochures.

37. As business manager for the Metro Symphony Orchestra Association, you are quite proud of the increased interest and attendance at your performances over the last several years. You attribute much of this growth to the quality of the performances in general as well as to the addition of a Masterpiece Series, which features accomplished instrumentalists from throughout the world, and to a New Dimensions Series, which features new and unusual music. The total effect has resulted in increased ticket sales for all performances. To reserve tickets, patrons may telephone orders that can be billed to credit cards or mail them using the form you publish in your yearly brochure that publicizes the collective performances. As performances fill up, you must deal with the problems that full houses create. And that's the situation you must handle today.

    Mr. Robert DuPont sent a check for $745 along with his ticket preferences for the year's performances. On the order form, he indicated he wanted the following tickets: six for Brahm's Requiem, performed by the Orchestra and Oratorio Chorus, April 26; four tickets for the Masterpiece Series featuring Andre Watts, pianist, October 13; and eight tickets for the New Dimensions Series featuring the 100-voice Vocal Majority in "A Salute to the Red, White, and Blue," March 13. Usually, your staff fills orders that are routine; so you wonder why they passed along Mr. DuPont's order to you. As you look over it, however, you see the reasons. One of the requested performances is already sold out and for another you need more information to fill the order. So you will write a letter that will acknowledge the order from Mr. DuPont.

    In it, you will send the tickets for the Requiem as requested. The performance of the Vocal Majority, however, is full. You can schedule him for the March 14 performance; but you only have seats on the Main Floor, not the Mezzanine that he requested; and there is a difference of $8 more for each ticket. You've put a tentative hold on Main Floor tickes for the 14th for him. But he will have to confirm the order and pay you in 10 days or you will release them. Lastly, Mr. DuPont did not specify which date he wanted for the Masterpiece Series. Right now, both the October 13 and 14 dates are open. You have tentatively reserved tickets for him on the 13th; but he will need to confirm this or change the order within 10 days.

Write the acknowledgment letter to Mr. DuPont. You want it to be sales-oriented because you are in the entertainment business. You remember, also, when times were much leaner and you had to cut ticket prices for them to sell. You want to maintain your positive public relations to keep people happy and satisfied.

38. Assume that you are manager of mail-order sales for Video Illustrations. You have been advertising for two weeks in *The Wall Street Journal* and the ads have certainly pulled in sales. In fact, orders are so good that you are presently out of inventory for two of the videos you advertised. And some people are sending in the wrong amounts for their orders.

The ads you have been running feature five of your best training videos. WordPerfect for Windows Intermediate ($69.95 + $4.00 shipping—two hours); Introduction to WordPerfect ($49.95 + $4.00 shipping—34 minutes); Windows 3.1 ($69.95 + $4.00 shipping—60 minutes); DOS Intermediate ($69.95 + $4.00 shipping—60 minutes); and Lotus 1-2-3 for Windows Intermediate ($69.95 + $4.00 shipping—two hours). Your training videos permit people to see computer functions performed first and then to carry them out themselves on their computers. Of course, the videos can be viewed as many times as needed.

Also, you stated in the ad that rush orders (3-day delivery) would cost $5.00 more for each video. But people are substituting the $5.00 charge for the $4.00 shipping fee. The $5.00 charge is for labor and postage whereas the $4.00 fee is for packaging and postage. If people want 3-day delivery, they should add $9.00 to the base price of each video.

What you must do now is develop a letter that will accomplish three things: acknowledge the order, back-order the two out-of-stock videos, and clear up the money details. You will do this for the Roberts Village order that sits on your desk. But your letter will also serve as a form letter to be used for other orders you have to handle.

Mr. Edwin Roberts, owner of Roberts Village, sends a check for $544.65. He wants two each of the Lotus 1-2-3 for Windows Intermediate and WordPerfect for Windows Intermediate videos and one each of the others. And he wants 3-day delivery on all of them. You can send the DOS Intermediate, Windows 3.1, and Introduction to WordPerfect for Windows videos. But it will be two weeks before you can have another supply of WordPerfect for Windows Intermediate and Lotus 1-2-3 for Windows Intermediate. You will need full payment before you can send them, though.

As you prepare the letter, remember that it should not sound like a form letter. You want it to be personal, adaptive, and reflect goodwill in tone. Prepare the acknowledgment letter for Mr. Roberts.

# CHAPTER 7

# INDIRECTNESS FOR BAD NEWS

## CHAPTER OBJECTIVES

*Upon completing this chapter, you will be able to write indirect responses to convey bad news. To reach this goal, you should be able to:*

### 1
**Determine which situations require using the indirect order for the most effective response.**

### 2
**Use tact and courtesy in refusals of requests.**

### 3
**Write adjustment refusals that cover the refusal positively.**

### 4
**Compose personal or form credit refusals that are tactful but clear and close with a positive forward look.**

## INTRODUCTORY SITUATION

### to Refused Request Letters

To introduce yourself to the refused request letter, assume again the role of assistant to the Pinnacle vice president. Today your boss assigned you the task of responding to a request letter from the local chapter of the National Association of Peace Officers. This worthy organization has asked Pinnacle to contribute to a scholarship fund for certain needy children.

The request letter is very persuasive. It points out that the scholarship fund is terribly short. As a result, the association is not able to take care of all the needy children. Many of them are the children of officers who were killed in the line of duty. You have been moved by the letter, and you would like to comply. But you cannot.

You cannot contribute now because Pinnacle policy does not permit it. Even though you do not like the effects of the policy in this case, you think the policy is good. Each year Pinnacle earmarks a fixed amount—all it can stand—for contributions. Then it doles out this amount to the causes that a committee of its executives considers the most worthy. Unfortunately, all the money earmarked for this year has been given away. You will have to say no to the request, at least for now. You can offer to consider the association's cause next year.

Your letter must now report the bad news, though it can hold out hope for the future. Because you like the association and because you want it to like Pinnacle, you will try to handle the situation delicately. The task will require your best strategy and your best writing skills. ■

## SITUATIONS REQUIRING INDIRECTNESS

As explained in Chapter 5, when the main message of a letter is bad news, you should usually write in the indirect order. The indirect order is especially effective when you must say no or convey other disappointing news. The main reason for this approach is that negative messages are received more positively when an explanation precedes them. An explanation may even convince the reader that the writer's position is correct. In addition, an explanation cushions the shock of bad news. Not cushioning the shock makes the letter unnecessarily harsh, and harshness destroys goodwill.

*Usually bad-news letters should be in the indirect order.*

You may want to use directness in some bad-news situations. If, for example, you think that your negative answer will be accepted routinely, you might choose directness. You also might choose directness if you know your reader well and feel that he or she will appreciate frankness. And you might choose directness anytime you are not concerned about goodwill. But such instances are not the rule. Usually you would be wise to use indirectness in refusals.

*There are exceptions, as when the bad news is routine or when the reader prefers frankness.*

The following pages analyze some common letter situations that are usually best handled in the indirect order. As in preceding chapters, the situations reviewed include only the major possibilities. However, if you learn the techniques recommended for these situations, you should be able to apply your knowledge to the others.

*Following are typical letter situations calling for the indirect order.*

CHAPTER 7  Indirectness for Bad News     187

## REFUSED REQUEST

*Refusing a request calls for the indirect order.*

Refusal of a request is definitely a bad-news message. Your reader has asked you for something, and you must say no. How bad the news is varies from case to case. Even so, it is hard to imagine a refusal that is good news. Because the news is bad, you should usually write the request refusal in the indirect order.

*In refusals you have two goals: (1) to refuse, and (2) to maintain goodwill. The first goal alone would be easy, but the second goal makes both goals hard.*

Your reason for refusing indirectly has been mentioned, but its importance warrants repeating it. In the refusal letter you have two goals. The main one is to say no. The other is to maintain goodwill. You could achieve the first goal by simply saying no—plainly and directly. Maintaining goodwill, however, requires more. It requires that you convince your reader that the no answer is fair and reasonable. If you began with the no answer, you would put your reader in an unhappy frame of mind. Then the reader would not be in the mood to read your explanation. Your best strategy is to explain or justify first. From your explanation or justification, you can move logically to your refusal.

### Developing the Strategy

*Begin the letter by thinking through the situation. Look for the best explanation.*

In deciding on what explanation to use, you should think through the facts of the case. First, you should consider why you are refusing. Then, assuming that your reasons are just, you should try to find the best way of convincing your reader. In doing this, you might well place yourself in your reader's shoes. Try to imagine how the explanation will be received. What comes out of this thinking is the strategy you should use in your letter.

*Do not hide behind company policy. Justify it.*

Sometimes you must refuse because of company policy. When this is the case, you should be careful how you explain the refusal. Do not just say that you are refusing because it is company policy to do so. Instead, justify the policy. Explain its fairness to all concerned. For example, take a retailer's policy of refusing to return goods bought on sale. This policy clearly protects the retailer. But close inspection shows that it also benefits the customer. Only by cutting the costs of returns can the retailer give the customer the low sale price. Thus, the policy works to the benefit of both the customer and the retailer. Refusals based on that policy should say so.

*When the reader is clearly wrong, appeal to a sense of fair play.*

Sometimes you must refuse simply because the facts of the case justify a refusal. When those facts show that you are right and the reader is wrong, your goodwill goal is hard to reach. In such cases, you can use little you-viewpoint reasoning. Probably the best course is to review the facts of the case, taking care not to accuse or insult, and to appeal to the reader's sense of fair play.

There are other refusal problems—too many to cover in this brief review. Your procedure for each of these problems should be the same. You should study the facts of the one case and develop the strategy that best fits those facts. Then you should present that strategy in a letter following this general pattern:

*This is the letter plan you should follow.*

- **Begin with words that indicate response to the request, are neutral as to the answer, and set up the strategy.**
- **Present your justification or explanation, using positive language and you-viewpoint.**

188        PART 3    Basic Patterns of Business Letters

- **Refuse clearly and positively, including a counterproposal or compromise when appropriate.**
- **End with an adapted goodwill comment.**

### Setting Up the Strategy in the Opening

Having developed your strategy, you should put it into letter form. In general, your plan should be to explain before refusing. But you must be careful. You cannot just blurt out the explanation. Such directness would be just as awkward as beginning with the refusal.

*Do not begin explaining abruptly.*

Instead, you should begin indirectly with words that meet three requirements. First, they should clearly indicate that you are responding to the request. Second, they should be neutral. By *neutral* we mean that they imply neither no nor yes—that they should not give away the answer. Third, they should set up the strategy of your letter.

*The opening should (1) be on subject, (2) be neutral, and (3) set up the explanation.*

How these requirements should be met is best explained through illustration. First, take the case described at the beginning of this chapter—refusing an association's request for a donation. The following opening meets this case's requirements well:

> Your organization is doing a commendable job of educating its needy children. It deserves the help of those who are in a position to give it.

The beginning, on-subject comment clearly marks the letter as a response to the inquiry. It implies neither a yes nor a no answer. The statement "It deserves the help of those who are in a position to give it" sets up the explanation, which will point out that the company cannot help. Also, it puts the reader in an agreeable or open frame of mind—ready to accept the explanations that follow.

Or take another example—the beginning of a letter refusing a professor's request for information on personnel. The request must be denied because too much work would be required to assemble the information. The best the company can do is permit the professor or her staff to go through company records and get the information. The following words set up the strategy:

> Your interesting study of executive characteristics, described in your July 3 letter, should be a helpful contribution to management literature. It is certainly a project deserving as much help as businesses are able to give it.

Note that these words begin on subject, so that the reader recognizes them as a response to the inquiry. Also note that the words are neutral, giving no indication of the answer. Finally, note that the strategy of the letter is set up by saying that the project is one "deserving as much help as businesses are able to give it." The plan of the following explanation is to show that in this case the company is unable to help to the extent of the request.

### Presenting the Reasoning

The reasoning that justifies your refusal should flow logically from your opening. After all, your opening was designed to set up that reasoning. Of course, you should present the reasoning convincingly.

*The reasoning that supports the refusal comes next.*

To do this, you should use the writing techniques that help in persuasion. You should choose your words carefully, taking care to avoid the negative

*Handle this part skillfully. Use emphasis, you-viewpoint, positive wording.*

**CHAPTER 7   Indirectness for Bad News**

Bad-news letters should show the same friendly concern for others that caring people display in their face-to-face relations.

ones. You should use the you-viewpoint. In particular, you should use emphasis techniques. Play up the brighter parts of your message, and play down the gloomy parts. In general, you should use all your writing skills in your effort to sell the reader on your reasoning.

### Positively Handling the Refusal

*The refusal should flow logically from the reasoning. Do not emphasize it.*

Your handling of the refusal follows logically from your reasoning. If you have built the groundwork of explanation and fact convincingly, the refusal comes as a logical conclusion and as no surprise. If you have done your job well, your reader may even support the refusal. Even so, because the refusal is the most negative part of your message, you should not give it too much emphasis. You should state it quickly, clearly, and positively. You should keep it away from positions of emphasis, such as paragraph endings.

*State the refusal quickly,*

To state the refusal quickly, you should use as few words as possible. Laboring the refusal for three or four sentences when a single clause would do gives it too much emphasis.

*clearly, and*

To state the refusal clearly, you should make certain that the reader has no doubt about your answer. In the effort to be positive, writers sometimes become evasive and unclear. Take, for example, a writer who attempts to show that the facts of the case justify the company policy on which a refusal is based. Such words as "these facts clearly support our policy of . . ." would not communicate a clear refusal to some people. Another example is that of a writer who follows justifying explanation with a compromise offer.

PART 3 Basic Patterns of Business Letters

### On Controlling Anger in Letters: Some Words of Advice from Abraham Lincoln

An officer in the field had blundered badly, and Secretary of War Stanton was furious. "I feel that I must give this man a piece of my mind," he said to President Lincoln. "By all means, do so," said Lincoln. "Write him now while it's fresh on your mind. Make the words sting. Cut him up." Thus encouraged, Stanton wrote the letter, a masterpiece of angry words. He then pridefully took his letter to Lincoln.

After reading the letter, the president responded. "This is a good one," he said. "Now tear it up. You have freed your mind on the subject, and that is all that's necessary. You never want to send such letters. I never do."

---

In this case, such words as "it would be better if . . ." would make for a vague refusal.

To state the refusal positively, you should study carefully the effects of your words. Such harsh words as *I refuse, will not,* and *cannot* stand out. So do such timeworn apologies as "I deeply regret to inform you . . ." and "I am sorry to say . . ." You can usually phrase your refusal in terms of a positive statement of policy. For example, instead of writing "your insurance does not cover damage to buildings not connected to the house," write "your insurance covers damage to the house only." Or instead of writing "We must refuse," a wholesaler could deny a discount by writing "We can grant discounts only when . . ." In some cases, your job may be to educate the reader. Not only will this be your explanation for the refusal, it will also build goodwill.

*positively.*

If you can make a compromise, you can use it to include your refusal. That is, by saying what you can do, you can imply clearly what you cannot do. For example, if you write "The best we can do is . . ." you make it clear that you cannot do what the reader has requested. Yet you do this in the most positive way that the situation will permit.

If you can compromise, let what you can do imply what you cannot do.

### Closing with Goodwill

Even a skillfully handled refusal is the most negative part of your message. As the news is disappointing, it is likely to put your reader in an unhappy frame of mind. That frame of mind works against your goodwill goal. To reach your goodwill goal, you must shift your reader's thoughts to pleasanter matters.

End with a pleasant off-subject comment.

The best closing subject matter depends on the facts of the case, but it should be positive talk that fits the one situation. For example, if your refusal involves a counterproposal, you could say more about the counterproposal. Or you could make some friendly remark about the subject of the request as long as it does not remind the reader of the bad news. In fact,

Adapt the close to the one case.

### Grammar and Style Checkers: Style and Usage Features Identify Negatives

One feature of grammar and style checkers is their ability to identify negatives—both direct and implied. In addition to directly pointing out negativeness in sentence construction, these checkers can also identify the specific negative words and the number of times used. Here is the report from the bluntness example on page 200. You can use this information to recast your sentences and eliminate the negative words when possible.

<<**SUMMARY**>>

The document NEGLTR. was analyzed using the rules for general business writing at the college education level.

<<PARTIAL SAMPLE OF SENTENCE ANALYSIS>>

We must refuse <<*_U21.NEGATIVE: must refuse*>>
We regret very much the damage <<*_U21.NEGATIVE: regret very much the damage*>> and inconvenience our product has caused you. <<*_S11. IS SENTENCE TOO NEGATIVE?*>>

<<WORDS TO REVIEW>>

**Review this list for words that may confuse your message. These include words that are negative, frequently misused, colloquial, or jargon. As you review each word, think of its effect on the reader.**

1 cannot   (Negative)
1 damage   Negative)
1 damages   (Negative)
1 faded   (Negative)
1 inconvenience   (Negative)
1 limitation   (Negative)
1 not   (Negative)
2 regret   (Negative)
1 sanderson   (Not widely understood)

<<END OF WORDS TO REVIEW LIST>>
<<**END OF SUMMARY**>>

---

*Avoid ending with the old, negative apologies.*

your closing subject matter could be almost any friendly remark that would be appropriate if you were handling the case face-to-face. The major requirement is that your ending words have a goodwill effect.

Ruled out are the timeworn, negative apologies. "Again, may I say that I regret that we must refuse" is typical of these. Also ruled out are the equally timeworn appeals for understanding, such as "I sincerely hope that you understand why we must make this decision." Such words emphasize the bad news.

## Contrasting Refusals

The advantage of the indirect order in refusal letters is evident from the following contrasting examples. Both refuse clearly. But only the letter that uses the indirect order gains reader goodwill.

**Harshness in the Direct Refusal.** The first example states the bad news right away. This blunt treatment puts the reader in a bad frame of mind. The result is that the reader is less likely to accept the explanation that follows. The explanation is clear, but note the unnecessary use of negative words (*exhausted, regret, cannot consider*). Note also how the closing words leave the reader with a strong reminder of the bad news.

Dear Ms. Cangelosi:

We regret to inform you that we cannot grant your request for a donation to the association's scholarship fund.

So many requests for contributions are made of us that we have found it necessary to budget a definite amount each year for this purpose. Our budgeted funds for this year have been exhausted, so we simply cannot consider additional requests. However, we will be able to consider your request next year.

We deeply regret our inability to help you now and trust that you understand our position.

                      Sincerely,

This bad letter is harsh because of its directness.

**Tact and Courtesy in an Indirect Refusal.** The second example skillfully handles the negative message. Its opening words are on subject and neutral. They set up the explanation that follows. The clear and logical explanation ties in with the opening. Using no negative words, the explanation leads smoothly to the refusal. Note that the refusal is also handled without negative words, and yet is clear. Saying "the best we can do is . . ." also says what cannot be done. The friendly close fits the one case.

Dear Ms. Cangelosi:

Your efforts to build the scholarship fund for the association's needy children are most commendable. We wish you good success in your efforts to further this worthy cause.

We at Pinnacle are always willing to assist worthy causes whenever we can. That is why every January we budget for the year the maximum amount we believe we are able to contribute to worthy causes. Then we distribute that amount among the various deserving groups as far as it will go. As our budgeted contributions for this year have already been made, we are placing your organization on our list for consideration next year.

We wish you the best of luck in your efforts to help educate the deserving children of the association's members.

                      Sincerely,

This letter using the indirect approach is better.

## CASE ILLUSTRATION  Refused Request Letters. *(Refusing a Request for Letter Examples)*

Tact and strategy mark this refusal, in which an office manager turns down a textbook author's request. The author has asked for model letters that can be used as examples in a correspondence guidebook. The office manager reasons that complying with this request would take more time than should be expected.

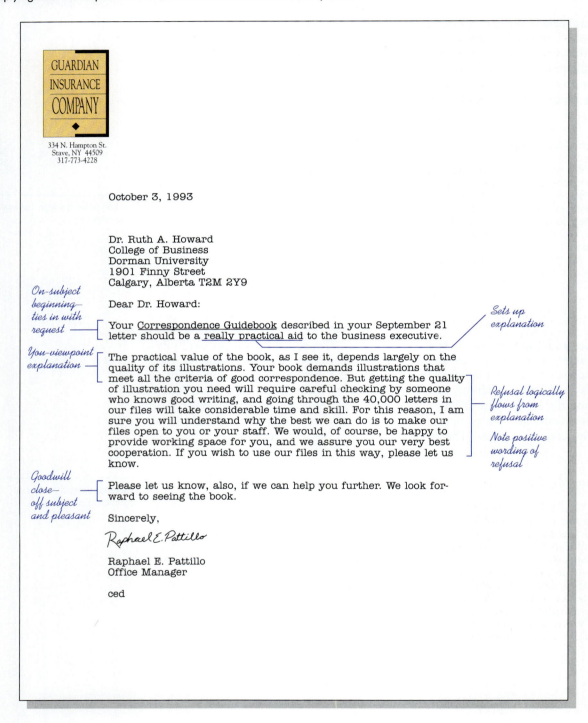

PART 3  Basic Patterns of Business Letters

**CASE ILLUSTRATION**  Refused Request Letters. *(Turning Down a Speaking Invitation)*
This example shows good strategy in turning down a request to speak at a convention.

---

**WILKERSON ASSOCIATES**
Consultants to Management

January 20, 1993

Mr. Thelbert H. Gooch
Executive Director
National Association of Administrators
7112 Avondale Road
Phoenix, AZ 85017

Dear Mr. Gooch:

*On-subject beginning— compliment gains reader's favor*

Your January 13 invitation to address the National Association of Administrators is a most distinct honor to me personally. I am well aware of the high quality of NAA's membership. — *Sets up explanation*

*Offer of alternative shows concern— builds goodwill*

Presenting a major paper to this quality group deserves a thorough and competent effort. Obviously, such an effort requires time. Because my time is fully committed to a writing project for the months ahead, I must suggest that you get someone who has the time to do the job right. May I recommend Ms. Paula Perkins of my staff? Paula is an outstanding speaker and an expert on the subject of women's progress in management. — *Reasonable, convincing explanation*

*Goodwill close— adapted to this one case*

If I can help you further in your efforts to get speakers, please write me again. I wish you good luck with the program.

Sincerely,

*Forrest Y. Wilkerson*

Forrest Y. Wilkerson
President

FYW:et

67890 W. Ninevh St.  Neenah, WI  56757  890-989-7865

---

CHAPTER 7  Indirectness for Bad News   195

## INTRODUCTORY SITUATION

### to Adjustment Refusal Letters

Sometimes your job at Pinnacle involves handling an unhappy person. Today you have to do that, for the morning mail has brought a strong claim for adjustment on an order for Pinnacle's Do-Craft fabrics. The claim writer, Ms. Arlene Sanderson, explains a Do-Craft fabric that her upholstering company used on some outdoor furniture has faded badly in less than 10 months. She even includes sample cuts of the fabric to prove her point. She contends that the product is defective, and she wants her money back—all $2,517 of it.

Inspection of the fabric reveals that it has been subjected to strong sunlight for long periods. Do-Craft fabrics are for inside use only. Both the Pinnacle brochures on the product and the catalog description stress this point. In fact, you have difficulty understanding how Ms. Sanderson missed it when she ordered from the catalog. Anyway, as you see it, Pinnacle is not responsible and does not intend to refund the money. At the same time, it wants to keep Ms. Sanderson as a customer and friend. Now you must write the letter that will do just that. The following discussion tells you how. ■

## ADJUSTMENT REFUSALS

> Letters refusing claims for adjustment are bad news.

Letters that refuse claims carry bad news. As with other bad-news situations, you should usually handle them indirectly. The indirect approach is especially necessary when there is reason to be concerned about your reader's sensitive feelings. Of course, not all claims are refused. Most are legitimate, and most companies try hard to correct for legitimate damages. But some claims are not well founded. They may be based on wrong information, or they may be dishonest. In such cases a company is likely to say no.

> Because the reader may be upset, tactful treatment is important.

Saying no clearly and tactfully in such cases requires your best communications skills. You may be dealing with people who honestly feel that they are right and you are wrong. Some of the people you deal with will know that their claims are weak, perhaps even dishonest. But even these people are likely to expect you to grant their claims. All of the people you deal with are likely to resist your efforts to justify the refusal.

### Determining the Basic Strategy

> Your first step is to find the best explanation.

Your first step in writing a letter refusing a claim is to decide how to explain your decision. Probably your best course is to base your explanation on the facts of the case. This approach implies that right is on your side. If it is not, you have no grounds for refusing.

> So you should review the case, putting yourself in the reader's place.

You should begin your search for an explanation by reviewing the facts of the case. Your review should help you determine precisely why a refusal is justified. It should help you assemble the facts that support your position. Then, with these facts in mind, you should search for ways of presenting your position convincingly. This mental effort requires that you place yourself in the reader's position. Limiting yourself to the reader's knowledge, you should work out in your mind what you must say to convince the reader

Happenings such as this are bitter disappointments to those involved. Letters correcting the wrong should not recall this scene unnecessarily.

that your answer is fair. Then you should arrange this thinking into an order that produces the results you want. Although variations may be justified, they should follow this general plan of organization:

- **Begin with words that are on subject, are neutral as to the decision, and set up your strategy.**
- **Present the strategy that explains or justifies, being factual and positive.**
- **Refuse clearly and positively, perhaps including a counterproposal.**
- **End with off-subject, friendly words.**

Then determine your strategy and write the letter in this order.

### Setting up the Explanation with an Indirect Opening

As in other refusal letters, your opening for the adjustment refusal should be both on subject and neutral. Additionally, and most importantly, it should set up the explanation. Because you are answering the reader's letter, you should also identify this letter. An incidental reference to it in the opening would do the job. For example, you could write "as mentioned in your May 3 letter." A subject-line reference would also be adequate. But if you use a subject line, make certain that its wording is neutral. "Your July 22 letter about Order No. 3175A" would meet this requirement, but "Refusal of your July 22 claim" would not.

Use an on-subject, neutral opening. Set up the explanation. Refer to the letter being answered—incidentally or in a subject line.

## A Not-So-Successful Refusal

Crusty old Mr. Whiffle bought an umbrella from a mail-order company. As the umbrella did not function to his requirements, Mr. Whiffle wrote the company a claim letter asking for his money back.

The mail-order company answered with a well-written letter of refusal.

Again Mr. Whiffle wrote, and again the company replied with a nicely written refusal.

Mr. Whiffle wrote a third time. The mail-order company refused a third time.

So angry was Mr. Whiffle that he boarded a bus, traveled to the home office of the mail-order company, and paid a visit to the company's adjustment correspondent. After a quick explanation of his purpose, Mr. Whiffle broke the umbrella over the adjustment correspondent's head. The correspondent then gave Mr. Whiffle his money.

"Now why didn't you do this before?" Mr. Whiffle asked. "You had all the evidence."

Replied the correspondent, "But you never explained it so clearly before."

---

*The opening subject matter can be anything appropriate.*

The subject matter of the opening could be almost anything that fits the situation. It could be some point on which you and the reader can agree, perhaps a point mentioned in the claim letter. For example, in regard to a claim about an air-conditioning unit that was not cooling an apartment satisfactorily, this would be a good opening sentence:

*For example, it could be a point of agreement,*

You are correct in believing that a 2-ton Deep Kold window unit should cool the ordinary three-room apartment.

The sentence makes contact on a point of common agreement. At the same time, it sets up the reasoning that will justify the refusal: the apartment in question is not an ordinary apartment.

*concern for the reader's well-being,*

An opening showing concern for the reader's well-being might be effective in some cases. Thus an interior decorator might begin a refusal with these words:

Assisting young couples to enjoy beautifully decorated homes at budget prices is one of our most satisfying goals. We do all we reasonably can to reach it.

From this goodwill opening, the writer could shift smoothly to proving that making the adjustment goes beyond what can reasonably be expected of the company.

In some cases, a statement showing mutual respect for honest intentions could form the basis for opening contact:

*or respect for honest intentions.*

Your straightforward report of the 13th shows that you are one who wants to get all the facts and to base a fair decision on them. So I am confident that you will want to consider the following information.

This statement sets up the new information that follows, which, of course, will justify the refusal.

### Presenting the Reasoning

The explanation that supports the refusal logically follows the opening. Your goal in this part of the letter is to convince. To be convincing, the explanation must be believable; to be believable, it must be factual. Unsupported claims are out.

In addition to using only convincing evidence, you should use your best writing skills in the explanation. Negative words irritate the reader and work against conviction, so positive language is especially desirable. For similar reasons, you should write nothing that questions the reader's honesty, and you should not belittle or insult the reader. Such comments as "If you had read the contract, you would have known . . ." or "Surely you know that . . ." do little to convince. Instead, they antagonize the reader and work against your goal.

*Make the explanation believable—factual.*

*Be persuasive. Write positively and honestly.*

### Covering the Refusal Positively

Your reasoning should take your reader logically and systematically to the refusal. If you have done your job well, the refusal will appear to be the logical outcome of what preceded it. It should not startle the reader. In fact, your decision should appear to be the one that the facts of the case support.

As with similar refusal problems, you should word your adjustment refusal clearly and positively. To be clear, your refusal should leave no doubt in anyone's mind. To be positive, its words must be carefully selected for effect. You may find it possible to refuse without using a single negative word. Perhaps you can clearly imply what you cannot do. For best effect, you will need to keep your refusal words away from emphasis positions.

Although it is hard to judge refusal sentences without the explanations that precede them, the following three, which are both clear and positive, seem to do a good job:

For these reasons, you will understand why we can pay only when our employees pack the goods.

Although the contract clearly ended our responsibility on May 1, we will do whatever we can to help repair the equipment.

In view of these facts, the best we can do is repair the equipment at cost.

*The refusal should flow logically from the explanation.*

*Refuse clearly. Use positive wording.*

### Closing with Off-Subject, Friendly Comment

Because your refusal is negative, you should follow it with some appropriate comment away from the subject of the refusal. Neither negative apologies nor words that recall the problem are in order. A good general topic is some more agreeable aspect of customer relations—new products, services, uses of products, industry news, and the like. Any friendly comment that appears logical in the one case will suffice.

*End with off-subject, friendly comment.*

### Contrasting Letters Refusing a Claim

Bad and good treatment of Pinnacle's refusal to give money back for the faded fabric are illustrated by the following two letters. The bad one, which is blunt and insulting, destroys goodwill. The good one, which uses the techniques described in the preceding paragraphs, stands a good chance of keeping goodwill.

*The following examples show the value of the preceding plan.*

CHAPTER 7 Indirectness for Bad News 199

**Bluntness in a Direct Refusal.** The bad letter begins bluntly with a direct statement of the refusal. The language is negative (*regret, must reject claim, refuse, damage, inconvenience*). The explanation is equally blunt. In addition, it is insulting ("It is difficult to understand how you failed . . ."). It uses little tact—little you-viewpoint. Even the close is negative, for it recalls the bad news.

The bad letter shows little concern for the reader's feelings.

Dear Ms. Sanderson:

Subject: Your May 3 claim for damages.

    I regret to report that we must reject your claim for money back on the faded Do-Craft fabric.

    We must refuse because Do-Craft fabrics are not made for outside use. It is difficult for me to understand how you failed to notice this limitation. It was clearly stated in the catalog from which you ordered. It was even stamped on the back of every yard of fabric. As we have been more than reasonable in trying to inform you, we cannot possibly be responsible.

    We trust that you will understand our position. We regret very much the damage and inconvenience our product has caused you.

                               Sincerely,

**Tact and Indirect Order in a Courteous Refusal.** The good letter begins with friendly talk on a point of agreement that also sets up the explanation. Without accusations, anger, or negative words, it reviews the facts of the case, which free the company of blame. The refusal is clear, even though it is made by implication rather than by direct words. It is skillfully handled. It uses no negatives, and it does not receive undue emphasis. The close shifts to helpful suggestions that fit the one case. Friendliness and resale are evident throughout the letter but especially in the close.

This better letter is indirect and tactful.

Dear Ms. Sanderson:

Subject: Your May 3 letter about Do-Craft fabric.

    Certainly, you have a right to expect the best possible service from Do-Craft fabrics. Every Do-Craft product is the result of years of experimentation. And we manufacture each yard under the most careful controls. We are determined that our products will do for you what we say they will do.

    Because we do want our fabrics to please, we carefully ran the samples of Do-Craft Fabric 103 you sent us through our laboratory. Exhaustive tests show that each sample has been subjected to long periods in extreme sunlight. As we have known from the beginning that Do-Craft fabrics cannot withstand exposure to sunlight, we have clearly noted this in all our advertising, in the catalog from which you ordered, and in a stamped reminder on the back of every yard of the fabric. Under the circumstances, all we can do concerning your request is suggest that you change to one of our outdoor fabrics. As you can see from our catalog, all of the fabrics in the 200 series are recommended for outdoor use.

    You will probably also be interested in the new Duck Back cotton fabrics listed in our 500 series. These plastic-coated cotton fabrics are most economical, and they resist sun and rain remarkably well. If we can help you further in your selection, please call on us.

                               Sincerely,

**CASE ILLUSTRATION**  Adjustment Refusal Letters. *(Refusing a Late Claim for Dead Plants)*

This letter from a mail-order nursery refuses an unjustified claim concerning plants that died 10 months after sale. As the nursery's guarantee is for 90 days, there is no reasonable basis for granting the claim.

# GREEN THUMB
## NURSERIES

September 4, 1993

Mr. Clarence S. Huddleston
R.R. 2, Box 171
Stockbridge, GA 30281

Dear Mr. Huddleston:

*Begins with point made in claim letter—on subject and neutral*

You were right in assuming in your August 30 letter that we would want to know about the plants you bought from us. We are always interested in doing whatever we can to make our sales satisfactory.

*Sets up explanation*

That is why we inspect every outgoing shipment. Of course, after the plants leave us, we no longer can give them our personal attention. As you know, the first weeks after planting are critical for plant survival. Proper planting is essential. And so is regular watering, especially during the hot summer months. Even though this vital care is out of our hands, we guarantee survival for the first 90 days, which is more than enough time to make certain that all plants delivered were healthy. In view of this explanation, we feel sure you will understand why we must stand by our guarantee policy in this case. It is a fair policy--for you and for us.

*Clear and honest review of policy—justifies decision*

*Clear yet positive refusal*

*Appeals to sense of fair play*

*Goodwill—Note the you viewpoint*

Thank you for this opportunity to explain. We shall continue to work hard to provide you with the healthy plants and good service you have a right to expect.

Sincerely,

*Suzanne T. Mervine*

Suzanne T. Mervine
Manager

cch

11703 MELLVILLE ROAD
AUGUSTA, GA 30906
312-789-9090

**CASE ILLUSTRATION** Adjustment Refusal Letters. *(Refusing a Refund for a Woman's Dress)*

An out-of-town customer bought an expensive dress from the writer and mailed it back three weeks later, asking for a refund. The customer explained that the dress was not a good fit and that she really did not like it anymore. But perspiration stains on the dress proved that she had worn it. This letter skillfully presents the refusal.

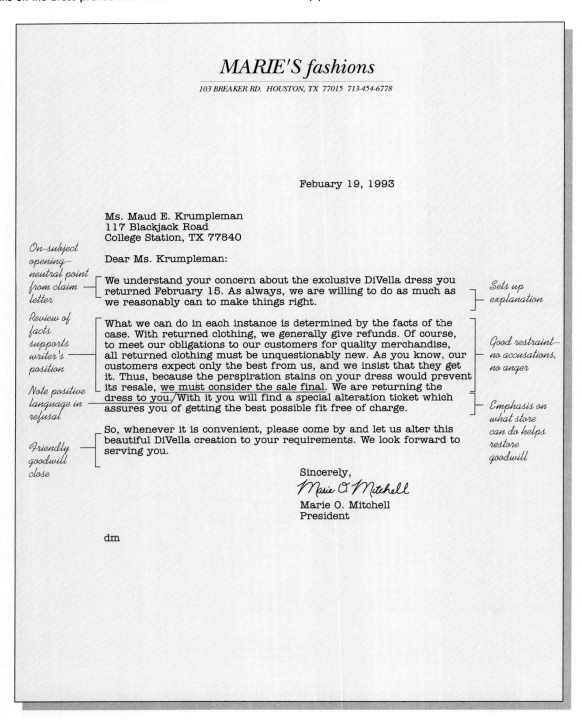

202   PART 3   Basic Patterns of Business Letters

## INTRODUCTORY SITUATION

## to Credit Refusal Letters

Although Chester Carter, your boss at Pinnacle, is in charge of the credit department, you do not normally get involved in credit work. But exceptions occur. Today, for example, the credit manager consulted with Chester about a request for credit from Bell Builders Supply Company, one of Pinnacle's longtime cash customers. The financial information Bell submitted with the request does not justify credit. Bell has more debt than it can afford, and still more debt would only make matters worse.

Because a refusal appears to be best for all concerned, Pinnacle will turn down Bell's request. The decision is fair, but it will not be good news to Bell. In fact, it might even end this firm's cash business with Pinnacle. Handling the situation is obviously a delicate task.

The importance of the case prompts Chester to ask you to write the refusal letter for his signature. A refusal letter from a top executive, Chester thinks, just might be effective. Now you are faced with the task of writing the letter that will refuse as well as keep the reader a cash customer. ■

## CREDIT REFUSALS

Letters that refuse credit are more negative than most refusals. The very nature of credit makes them so. Credit is tied to personal things, such as morals, acceptance in society, character, and integrity. So, unless skillfully handled, a credit refusal can be viewed as a personal insult. For the most positive results, such a refusal requires the indirect order and a tactful strategy.

*Because credit is personal, use tact in refusing it.*

Some will argue that you need not be concerned about the reader's feelings in this situation. As you are turning down the reader's business, why spend time trying to be tactful? Why not just say no quickly and let it go at that? If you will study the situation, the answer becomes obvious.

*Some think tact is not necessary.*

In the first place, being kind to people is personally pleasing to all of us. At least, it should be. The rewards in business are not all measured in dollars and cents. Other rewards exist, such as the good feelings that come from treating people with courtesy.

*But treating people tactfully pleases us personally.*

In the second place, being kind to people is profitable in the long run. People who are refused credit still have needs. They are likely to satisfy those needs somewhere. They may have to buy for cash. If you are friendly to them, they just might buy from you. In addition, the fact that people are bad credit risks now does not mean that they will never be good credit risks. Many people who are good credit accounts today were bad risks at some time in the past. By not offending bad risks now, you may keep them as friends of your company until they become good risks.

*It also gains future customers for your business.*

### Determining the Strategy

Your first step in writing a credit refusal letter is to work out your explanation. That explanation will depend on the reason for the refusal. If you are refusing because the applicant is a bad moral risk, you have a very difficult

*Begin by working out the refusal strategy. You can imply the reason with bad moral risks.*

**CHAPTER 7** Indirectness for Bad News

assignment. You cannot just say bluntly that you are refusing because of bad character. Even people with low morals would bristle at this approach. In such cases, you might choose a roundabout approach. For example, you might imply the reason. As the applicant knows his or her credit reputation, a mere hint is often enough to indicate that you also know it.

*But some authorities favor offering an explanation.*

Some credit authorities in the United States prefer a more direct approach for bad moral risks, citing the Equal Credit Opportunity Act of 1975 as support. This act states that applicants refused credit are entitled to written explanation of the reasons for the refusal. One way of implementing this approach is to follow the refusal with an invitation to come in (or telephone) to discuss the reasons. This discussion could be followed by a written explanation, if the applicant wants it. Opponents of this approach argue that the applicants already know the facts—that very few of them would pursue the matter further.

*Frank discussion is effective with weak financial risks.*

If you are refusing because your applicant's financial condition is weak, your task is easier. Weak finances are not a reflection on character, for they are related not to personal qualities, but to such factors as illness, unemployment, and bad luck. Thus, with applicants whose finances are weak, you can talk about the subject more directly. You also can talk more hopefully about granting credit in the future. In actual practice, cases do not fit neatly into these two groups. But you should be able to adapt the suggestions that follow to the facts of each case.

If you are refusing because the economy is bad—either in general or for that particular customer's business sector—your job is even easier. Oftentimes just educating your reader on what economic statistics are necessary to extend credit will convey the refusal without insulting the customer. Your honesty and genuine concern may even enable you to keep the customer on a cash basis.

In any case, as described below, your letter should follow this general plan of organization:

*Follow this organization plan.*

- **Begin with words that set up the strategy (explanation), are neutral as to the decision, and tie in with the application.**
- **Present the explanation.**
- **Refuse tactfully—to a bad moral risk, by implication; to a person with weak finances or in a weak economic environment, positively and with a look to the future.**
- **End with adapted goodwill words.**

## Setting Up the Explanation

As with the preceding refusal patterns, the beginning of a credit refusal should meet these requirements: (1) it should set up the strategy; (2) it should be neutral; and (3) it should be on subject.

*The opening has three requirements.*

*Your opening subject matter can be anything appropriate for the case—for example, a comment about the significance of the order.*

Your specific choice of subject is again a matter for you to think out. Almost anything that sounds sincere will do if it also meets the three requirements listed above. For example, if an order was included with the request for credit, you might say something about the order. This might be a compliment, a statement about the significance of the order, some words about the goods ordered, or the like. The following opening illustrates such possibilities:

Your January 22 order for Rock-Ware roofing shows good planning for the rush months ahead. As you will agree, it is good planning that marks the path of business success.

This opening ties in with the inquiry being answered. It is neutral, it sets up the refusal strategy with the reference to planning, and it puts the reader in an agreeable frame of mind. The following discussion shows that the best-planned businesses hold down their debts—something the reader also needs to do.

If no order accompanies the request for credit, any appropriate comment that fits the situation can make a good opening. An expression of appreciation for the request is one such possibility. But this approach has been used so often that it has probably lost some effectiveness. Even so, it is almost always appropriate. If you use it, try to vary the wording from the timeworn "Thank you for your application" variety. Something like this would be better:

*It could be a thank-you for the request.*

We are sincerely grateful for your credit application, Ms. Spangler, and will do all that we reasonably can to help you in getting your business started.

As they should be, these words are on subject and neutral. In addition, they set up the explanation that giving credit is beyond what the company can reasonably do.

### Justifying the Refusal

Your explanation logically follows the opening that sets it up. How you explain depends on why you are refusing. If you are refusing on moral grounds, you need to say little. As bad moral risks know their records, you need only imply that you also know. You do not need to say anything like "Your credit record is bad." A tactful sentence like this will do the job:

*Explanation to a bad moral risk can be vague.*

Our review of your credit record requires that we serve you only on a cash basis at this time.

Refusing an applicant with good credit morals but weak finances justifies a more open approach. You can discuss the reasons for refusing with as much frankness as your relationship with the applicant permits.

*Explanation to a weak financial risk can be more open.*

In your explanation, you can justify your credit policy and say that the reader does not qualify for credit. Of course, your words here should be carefully chosen. They should neither talk down nor imply moral wrongdoing. They might well show concern for the reader's credit problem. They might even educate the reader on ways to get out of his or her current financial bind. Whatever your explanation, it should be sound, believable, and convincing. It should lead logically to the refusal that follows.

### Refusing Tactfully

As we have noted, the refusal should be a logical follow-up to the explanation. You should take care to word it tactfully. Exactly how you word it will depend on your explanation. If your refusal is for moral reasons, you can

*The refusal flows logically from the explanation.*

"No."

*From* The Wall Street Journal, *with permission of Cartoon Features Syndicate.*

probably explain and say no by implication rather than in direct words. For example, you could write something like this:

**For a bad moral risk, it could be implied.**

As our credit check gives us insufficient evidence to grant you credit at this time, we invite you to join the tens of thousands of cash customers who save on Deal's discount prices.

**For a person with weak finances, a positively worded refusal is best.**

If you are refusing because of weak finances, you would also be wise to refuse positively. But you can look hopefully to the future in such cases. For good and bad examples of refusals to good people with bad finances, study the following sentences. This one is tactless:

For these reasons, we must refuse all applicants whose current assets-to-liabilities ratio falls below 2 to 1.

This one does the job well:

Thus, for the best interest of both of us, we must postpone credit buying until your current assets-to-liabilities ratio reaches 2 to 1.

### Closing with a Forward Look

**The close should be pleasant and friendly. It should fit the one case.**

Because the refusal is bad news, you should keep it away from an emphasis position. You would do well to follow it with more pleasant information—any goodwill information that fits the case. One possibility would be to suggest cash buying. You could support this suggestion with a comment about prices, merchandise, or service. But whatever closing subject you choose, it should leave a clear impression of courteous treatment in the reader's mind. One often-used but effective close is a courteous forward look to whatever future relations appear appropriate. Here are two such closes:

For your buying convenience, we are sending you our new spring catalog. We look forward to serving you with quality products and service.

As one of Meyers' cash customers, you will continue to receive the same courtesy, quality merchandise, and low prices we give to all our customers. We look forward to serving you soon.

### That College Touch in a Refusal

A merchant was finding it difficult to write a letter refusing a claim when in walked his college-student son.

"You're going to college," the merchant said to the boy. "Why don't you write this letter for me? This claim borders on fraud, but the guy spends good money with me. So use that college touch in turning him down."

The young man worked feverishly at his assignment. A short time later, he proudly handed his masterpiece to his dad.

"It has that college touch, all right," the merchant commented. "But since when do you spell *dirty* with a *u*; and why capitalize *rat*?"

### Contrasting Credit-Refusal Illustrations

The following two contrasting letters refusing Bell's credit application clearly show the advantages of tactful indirect treatment. The bad letter does little other than refuse. The good one says no clearly, yet it works to build goodwill and cultivate cash sales.

*The following letters contrast credit-refusal techniques.*

**Harshness as a Result of Tactless Treatment.** The weaker letter does begin indirectly, but the opening subject matter does little to soften the bad news. This obvious subject matter hardly deserves the emphasis that the opening gives it. Next comes the refusal—without any preceding explanation. It uses negative words (*regret, do not meet, weak, deny*). Explanation follows, but it is scant. The appeal for a cash sale is weak. The closing words leave a bad picture in the reader's mind.

Dear Mr. Bell:

    We have received your May 3 order and accompanying request for credit.
    After carefully reviewing the financial information you submitted, we regret to report that you do not meet our requirements for credit. It is our considered judgment that firms with your weak assets-to-liabilities ratio would be better off buying with cash. Thus, we encourage you to do so.
    We would, of course, be pleased to serve you on a cash basis. In closing, let me assure you that we sincerely regret that we must deny you credit at this time.

                Sincerely,

*This one is tactless.*

**Courtesy and Tact in a Clear Refusal.** The better letter generally follows the plan outlined in preceding pages. Its on-subject, neutral opening sets up the explanation. The explanation is thorough and tactful. Throughout, the impression of genuine concern for the reader is clear. Perhaps the explanation of the values of cash buying would be out of place in some cases. In this case, however, the past relationship between reader and writer justifies it. The letter ends with pleasant words that look to the future.

**CASE ILLUSTRATION** Credit Refusal letters. *(A Form Refusal for Bad Moral Risks)*

As the merge information in the address area indicates, this is a department store's form letter refusing credit to bad moral risks. Such stores ordinarily use form letters because they must handle credit on a mass basis. Because form letters must fit a variety of people and cases, they tend to be general.

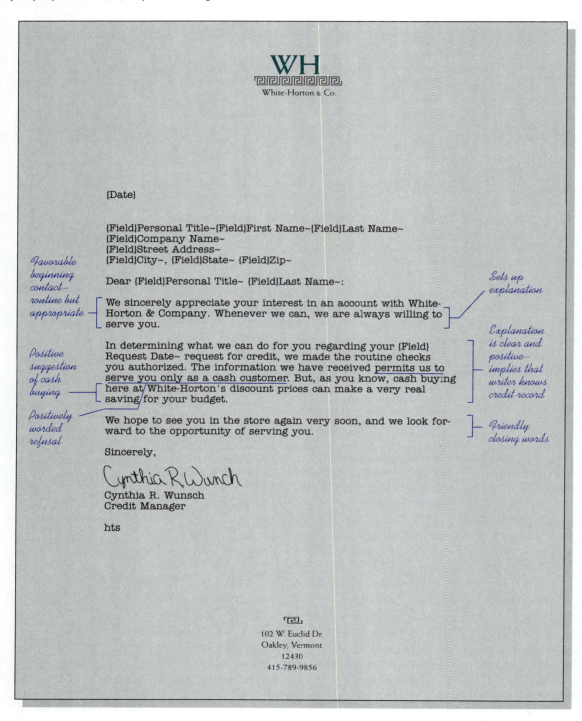

**CASE ILLUSTRATION**  Credit Refusal Letters. *(Courtesy and Frankness in a Form Refusal)*

As the merge information in the address area indicates, this credit refusal is also a form letter. Sent by a mail-order company to applicants who have overused their credit, the letter explains that these people would be better off if they reduced their credit buying.

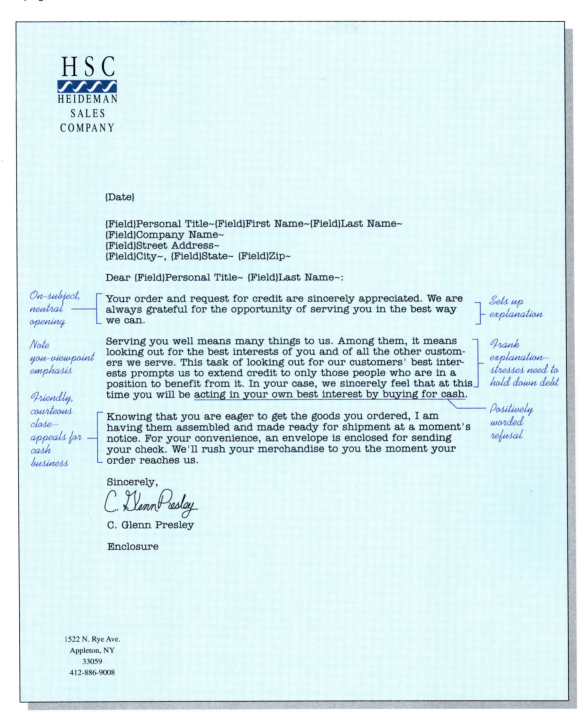

*This good letter refuses tactfully.*

Dear Mr. Bell:

Your May 3 order for Pinnacle paints and supplies suggests that your company is continuing to make good progress.

To assure yourself of continued progress, we feel certain that you will want to follow the soundest business procedures possible. As you may know, most financial experts say that maintaining a reasonable indebtedness is a must for sound growth. About a 2-to-1 ratio of current assets to liabilities is a good minimum, they say. In the belief that this minimum ratio is best for all concerned, we extend credit only when it is met. As soon as you reach this ratio, we would like to review your application again.

We appreciate your interest in Pinnacle paints and look forward to serving you.

Sincerely,

## OTHER INDIRECT-ORDER LETTERS

*Adapt the techniques of this chapter.*

The types of indirect-order letters covered in preceding pages are the most common ones. There are others. Some of these (sales, collections, and job applications) are rather special types. They are covered in the following chapters. You should be able to handle all the other indirect-order types that you encounter by adapting the techniques explained and illustrated in this chapter.

## SUMMARY (by Chapter Objectives)

*1. Determine which situations require using the indirect order for the most effective response.*

1. When the main message of the letter is bad news, use the indirect order.
   - But exceptions exist, as when you believe that the news will be received routinely.
   - Make an exception also when you think the reader will appreciate directness.

*2. Use tact and courtesy in refusals of requests.*

2. The refusal of a request is one bad-news situation that you will probably choose to treat indirectly.
   - In such situations, strive to achieve two main goals:
     —to refuse, and
     —to maintain goodwill.
   - Begin by thinking through the problem, looking for a logical explanation (or reasoning).
   - Write an opening that sets up this explanation.
   - Then present your explanation (reasoning), taking care to use convincing and positive language.
   - Refuse clearly yet positively.
   - Close with appropriate, friendly talk that does not recall the bad news.

*3. Write adjustment refusals that cover the refusal positively.*

3. Refusals of adjustments follow a similar pattern.
   - First, determine your explanation (reasoning) for refusing.
   - Begin with neutral words that set up your reasoning and do not give away the refusal.

PART 3 Basic Patterns of Business Letters

- Then present your reasoning, building your case convincingly.
- Refuse clearly and positively.
- Close with appropriate friendly talk that does not recall the refusal.

4. Letters refusing credit are more negative than most other types of refusal letters, for the refusal is tied to personal things.
   - As with other types of refusals, begin by thinking through a strategy.
   - If you are refusing because of the applicant's bad credit character, use a roundabout approach.
   - If you are refusing because of the applicant's weak finances, be more direct.
   - In either case, choose opening words that set up your strategy, are neutral, and tie in with the request being answered.
   - To the bad moral risk, imply the facts rather than state them bluntly.
   - In refusals because of weak finances, look hopefully to credit in the future.
   - End all credit refusals with appropriate positive words, perhaps suggesting cash buying, customer services, or other appropriate topics.

4. Compose personal or form credit refusals that are tactful but clear and close with a positive forward look.

## QUESTIONS FOR DISCUSSION

1. Give examples of when directness is appropriate for responses giving negative (bad-news) information.
2. Writing in the indirect order usually requires more words than does writing in the direct order. Since conciseness is a virtue in writing, how can the indirect order be justified?
3. What strategy is best in a letter refusing a request when the reasons for the refusal are strictly in the writer's best interests?
4. Apologies in refusal letters are negative, for they call attention to what you are refusing. Thus, you should avoid using them. Discuss.
5. An adjustment correspondent explained the refusal of a claim by saying that company policy did not permit granting claims in such cases. Was this explanation adequate? Discuss.
6. Is there justification for positive writing in a letter refusing credit? You are not going to sell to the reader, so why try to maintain goodwill?
7. Discuss the difference between refusing credit to a good moral risk with bad finances or in a poor economic environment and refusing credit to a bad moral risk.

## APPLICATION EXERCISES

1. Point out shortcomings in the following letter from a sports celebrity declining an invitation to speak at the kickoff meeting for workers in a fund-raising campaign for a charity.

   Dear Ms. Chung:

   As much as I would like to, I must decline your request that I give your membership a free lecture next month. I receive many requests to give free lectures. I grant some of them, but I simply cannot do them all. Unfortunately, yours is one that I must decline.

   I regret that I cannot serve you this time. If I can be of further service in the future, please call on me.

   Sincerely yours,

2. Criticize the following letter refusing the claim for a defective riding lawn mower. The mower was purchased 15 months earlier. The purchaser has had difficulties with it for some time and submitted with the claim a statement from a local repair service verifying the difficulties. The writer's reason for refusing is evident from the letter.

   Dear Mr. Skinner:

   Your May 12 claim of defective workmanship in your Model 227 Dandy Klipper riding mower has been reviewed. After considering the information received, I regret to report that we cannot refund the purchase price.

   You have had the mower for 15 months, which is well beyond our one-year guarantee. Even though your repair person says that you had problems earlier, he is not one of our authorized repair people. If you will read the warranty you refer to in your letter, you will see that we honor the warranty only when our authorized repair people find defects. I think you will understand why we must follow this procedure.

   If you will take the machine to the authorized service center in your area (La Rue Lawn and Garden Center), I am confident they can correct the defect at a reasonable charge.

   If I can be of additional service, please contact me.

   Sincerely,

## LETTER PROBLEMS

### REFUSED REQUESTS

1. As director of public relations at the corporate headquarters of Burleson Electronics, manufacturers of a wide assortment of electronic products, you must write a special letter for your company president. The letter will inform the manager of the Wellstown Chamber of Commerce (and the townspeople) that efforts to keep the Burleson plant in Wellstown have failed. The plant must shut down in six months.

   Following the initial announcement of the planned closing two months ago, the citizens of Wellstown responded vigorously. Newspaper editorials appealed to Burleson to reconsider. Letters from the townspeople flooded the corporate offices. Perhaps most significant was a letter from Charles T. Krause, manager of the Wellstown Chamber of Commerce. Signed by Krause, the mayor, the city council members, and 13,752 citizens, the letter made an impassioned plea to keep the plant open. It told of the 812 loyal workers who would lose their jobs and the suffering of their families. It told of the effect the plant closing would have on other businesses in the area. The case presented was most persuasive, but it did nothing to change the reason for the decision.

The reason for the decision is one of simple economics. The plant is old (built 32 years ago) and badly in need of renovation. The manufacturing machinery at the plant is obsolete and no longer can be used competitively. The costs of renovating the building and buying new machinery are not justified in light of current declining market demand for Burleson products. The products now made at the Wellstown plant can be made at Burleson's other plants (all more modern) with lower production costs and without additional investment.

Of course, Burleson management is concerned about its loyal workers at Wellstown. For this reason it will transfer as many as possible to its other plants. Preliminary information obtained from the workers indicates that about 12 percent are willing to relocate. Management is confident it can take care of all of them with five or more years of service. Also, Burleson will actively assist all remaining employees by setting up an employment assistance service. Through it, Burleson plans to help all laid-off workers find suitable employment.

Your job at the moment is to write a letter to the Chamber manager. Using gentle language you will present the decision clearly and finally. Also, you will explain the decision, showing that it is reasonable and, in fact, the only one Burleson management could make under the circumstances.

2. Your company, Greenhouse Fog Systems, has been making good progress in recent months. Using your patented swivel nozzles, your systems produce superfine, 10-micron droplets that form a natural, controlled humidity. The result is greatly increased production from greenhouse plants. So effective is your system that greenhouse operators have flooded you with orders. In fact, you are selling systems faster than your factory can make them.

Today's mail brings a letter from Thomas Y. Boudreaux, owner of TB's Greenhouse Builders in Meadowville. It seems Mr. Boudreaux saw one of your systems in operation, and he liked what he saw. He liked it so much that he wants the exclusive dealership for it in his region. In his rather persuasive letter, Boudreaux presented information that indicates he has a thriving business and could give your product exceptional exposure.

You will have to say no to the request—at least for the present. You have decided that you will market your product through your own sales operation. Your sales representative in Boudreaux's area is Shannon Wilder, who you will ask to call on Boudreaux at the earliest opportunity.

As you view the situation, Boudreaux may be useful in spreading the word about your product to potential customers. And even though you cannot use him as a distributor, perhaps he and his company could play a role in installing your systems. You'll ask Shannon to discuss this possibility with Boudreaux.

Now you must write Boudreaux giving him your decision. You will use tact, of course, for he may be influential with your potential customers in the area. Your goal is to explain so that he understands your policy and continues to feel good about your product.

3. Play the role of sales manager for the Admiral Bleu Hotel and refuse an unreasonable request made by the representative of the International Order of Tigers.

The Tigers are a fraternal order, and they are scheduled to have a regional convention in your city next month. For the past five months you have been dealing with their Mr. C. Wellington Hornsby, who is in charge of local arrangements. Mr. Hornsby has reserved 150 rooms for his group, and in doing so has bargained hard. You gave him exceptionally low convention rates and more complimentary rooms than a convention of this size warrants.

Today you received a letter from Hornsby asking for yet another concession. He wrote his request (*demand* may be a better word) in these words: "We will have an unexpected dignitary in attendance. He is our Supreme Tiger, Gaylord O. Huggins, who will be coming all the way from London. Thus we must have an additional complimentary suite suitable for him." You already have assigned the Tigers one complimentary suite and three complimentary rooms, and that is more than enough. You will refuse.

Even though you don't like Hornsby's pushy bargaining, you will handle the refusal diplomatically. You will write him a letter explaining that you have been generous already—that the agreement reached prior to the request is fair to all concerned. If they want a suite for their dignitary, you will reserve a suite for them and charge the convention rate ($200 per day rather than the normal $250).

4. Move into the future a number of years. You have been successful in your business career, so much so that your services on various boards and commissions have been in great demand. One such service involves participation on the advisory board of the College of Business Administration of Pennington University. You have served on this board for the past six years (two three-year terms) and have been an active member. You missed only one meeting in six years (the board meets quarterly), and you contributed heavily. In fact, as chair of the committee to develop a scholarship fund, you engineered a highly successful campaign, raising almost $2,000,000.

   You have enjoyed your work for Pennington and are proud of it. Even so, a few days ago you decided that you would have to decline an appointment to another term, if it is offered. During the coming two years you must devote more time to your business, which is entering a critical stage of development. You will not have the time to do justice to an assignment on the board. You know that the board will be launching a campaign to raise funds for two endowed chairs for the college, and this will require time. You would not be able to give that time.

   You had planned to inform Dean Ida R. Nathans of your decision before she sent you an invitation to serve another term. Now it is too late, for in today's mail arrived a letter from her, asking you to serve a third term. Dean Nathan's letter is most persuasive, citing your outstanding record of service and noting the critical needs of the college. But you must hold to your decision. You will say no.

   You want to help the dean as much as you can, so you decide to suggest some people who would be good members in your place. One is Sharon S. Sisson, owner-president of the Sisson Advertising Agency. You have worked with this dynamic woman on other committees and know that she is a producer. Another is Kevin T. Leeds, president of Leeds-Seymour Construction Company, a major commercial builder in the area. You have not worked with Leeds, but you know he has a good record of community service.

   In your letter to Dean Nathans, you will refuse positively, making certain that she understands why you must say no. Of course, some time in the future when your business has stabilized, you would be pleased to serve again. (You may supply any information you may need about your business and your need to refuse.)

5. You have recently received a request for a donation from Janet Baker, the director of your local high school's business education department. You realize the importance of these programs since you regularly hire several of this department's graduates. But your company decides what programs it will support only at the time its annual budget is determined. While you must refuse Mrs. Baker's request, you want to encourage her to apply for funds from next year's annual budget. Give her hints on the types of programs the directors like to fund, advising her to ask the company to support a specific project, such as buying equipment or supporting a particular program, rather than make a general donation.

   Also, you've recently read the Conference Board report, "Innovation and Change in Voc-Tech Education." The report focuses on the increasing future demand for technically skilled workers. You recognize the importance of maintaining a good relationship with your local source of skilled technical workers. Therefore, for the current year you offer the services of your employees as speakers on special topics. Be sure the letter conveys goodwill while clearly refusing the donation request.

6. In the guidelines drafted for compliance with the Americans with Disabilities Act of 1990, the blind are favored in sign rules to the detriment of others. In fact, you have just received a letter from Stephen Boro, president of the Society of Environmental Graphic Designers, calling for the revision of these guidelines.

   One guideline calls for all signs to be in all uppercase. Blind people read words by feeling them, and uppercase letters are more easily understood.

   But Mr. Boro reminds you that sighted people read word groups in upper and lower case better. The society believes that the guidelines sacrifice legibility and comprehension for the majority of the disabled and nondisabled populations. Also, he tells you that using all caps will reduce the amount of text on signs by as much as two-thirds.

   As government general counsel, write a letter to Mr. Boro refusing to withdraw the guidelines but indicating your willingness to be flexible. Suggest that revisions, changes, and clarifications will be made before the guidelines are final.

7. Julie Jahn, one of your most promising sales representatives, has proposed that all the sales staff be

given cellular phones for their business use. She cites her recent experience using a cellular phone provided in a rental car in the Los Angeles area. Not only was she able to conduct business while driving in her territory, but she actually saved time and money by checking with clients before calling on them. She firmly believes that the cellular phone would enhance the productivity of all sales staff.

You like getting ideas from people in the field since they are most in touch with the customers. However, you realize that not only would this be a large one-time expense, it would also generate ongoing expenses. Therefore, while you must refuse Julie's request, you decide to test the theory in the field. As a counterproposal, ask Julie and one person in each region to test the use of the phones for six months. The sales staff involved in the test must be willing to keep detailed records of their calls. Be sure your letter clearly refuses while continuing to encourage Ms. Jahn to submit ideas for improving business.

8. It's happening again—your company, Crayola, has decided to retire eight more crayon shades. In 1990 several traditional colors—blue gray, green blue, lemon yellow, raw umber, and violet blue—were replaced with cerulean, dandelion, fushsia, jungle green, royal purple, teal blue, vivid tangerine, and wild strawberry. At that time, Richard S. Gurin, President of Binney & Smith, which manufactures the Crayola brand, explained the new shades were brighter and more colorfully named. The initial announcement generated much more interest than anyone expected. When sales of the old colors climbed initially, Mr. Gurin promised to bring back the old colors if enough people demanded them. But the interest in the old colors waned.

As director of public relations, you must write Mary Adami refusing her request to bring back the eight colors you are now retiring. In addition to explaining your experience, you'll want to sell her on the new colors. In addition to keeping the cost of crayons down by limiting manufacturing and inventory to a fixed number of colors, the new colors are more in touch with today's youth. Your research on hundreds of preschool and school-age children showed the retired colors were the least used and the new ones were among the 10 percent most frequently used. Refuse Ms. Adami's request but maintain her goodwill.

9. As head of the frequent flyer program for International Airlines, you receive an interesting letter from Mr. Joshua Rosenthal today. Last month, Mr. Rosenthal traveled to Tokyo, Japan, on IA and then to Fukuoka, Japan, by Japan Airways to attend a production managers convention.

When he received his frequent flyer points for the trip, he noticed that he was credited with mileage only for the trip from Chicago to Tokyo and back but not the trip on Japan Airways. A message on the back of his JA tickets to and from Fukuoka, however, states that "mileage attained on Japan Airways qualifies for frequent flyer programs with other airlines, with certain restrictions applying." Mr. Rosenthal called the 800 number for IA and a service representative told him his mileage would apply to the IA program.

The letter he writes you asks that you credit his account for the round-trip mileage on Japan Airways. He says that he believes the mistake was simply an oversight and includes a copy of his tickets on Japan Airlines.

As you look at the tickets, you note that Mr. Rosenthal traveled economy class throughout his trip; however, your policy is to allow mileage points attained with cooperating airlines only for coach and first-class fares. Your reasons for this policy are simply economic. Travel agents and reservationists who book continuation flights on JA receive discounts on coach and first-class fares but not on economy fares. Probably, JA feels that discounting already low fares would make them lose money. For whatever reason, you exclude economy fares because of the discount structure between your airline and theirs.

Thus, you must write a letter that will refuse Mr. Rosenthal's request. Most likely, he will not be interested in your reasons for excluding the economy class because they are "writer oriented." But think through the strategy for reader-oriented ones—those that can be used for goodwill.

Mr. Rosenthal received mileage on your airline, didn't he? And he is interested in getting the most for his travel dollar. Are you trying to do the same? Perhaps there are other similarities and positive points that can be derived from the situation. Construct a smooth-flowing indirect letter for Mr. Rosenthal.

10. As head of communication services at Telecon Inc., you must deal with a request from Anita Furtado, a member of the Society for Communication Development (SCD). Ms. Furtado has written you a very persuasive letter requesting that you videotape a teleconference between selected members of her SCD group and businesspeople in Germany and Japan, respectively, in two different

taping sessions. You are going to have to refuse the request, but you will do so with good reasons and with tact.

SCD is a national organization of primarily university professors who study and research human communication. Ms. Furtado, who is head of SCD's Teaching Methodology Committee, believes that taping the sessions on international communication with the use of teleconferencing would do two things: (1) it would show different cultural orientations to communication; and (2) it would illustrate a technological development that relates to human interactions. What Ms. Furtado proposes is that she would have four speakers from her SCD group illustrate certain techniques of business communication from a U.S. point of view and then four speakers from Germany who would illustrate "how things are done" in that country. The same format would be repeated in a different session with Japanese representatives.

As Ms. Furtado explains, "My organization would provide the expertise and format; yours would provide the facilities and technology." After the taping, Ms. Furtado wants to make the tape available to SCD members (approximately 2,000) at cost, which she estimates to be about $7. "You would be helping the teaching and research of human communication," she reasons. Of course, Ms. Furtado wants you to offer your facilities free of charge as a professional service to SCD.

As you see it, the request is not as simple as Ms. Furtado makes it out to be. First, your teleconferencing facilities and filming crews are booked up for the next six months for "paying" customers. What Ms. Furtado asks for free you charge good money for in the real business world. With the global business environment expanding, organizations are using teleconferencing as a means of connecting offices and personnel for executive conferences, training sessions, sales meetings, and such. You just could not afford financially to do what she asks—and you won't commit to anything after six months either. Your first obligation is to make money for the company.

In addition, you sell training films of your own in the uses and techniques of teleconferencing—at good prices! If you cooperated with Ms. Furtado's request and the tapes were offered at cost, you would be competing against yourself. You see this duplication of effort as lowering your profit and being ultimately self-defeating.

For both of these reasons, and perhaps others you can think of, you will deny Ms. Furtado's request. But you want her to still have a favorable image of your company. Write an indirect letter that will retain her goodwill while refusing her request.

11. As Executive Director for Communication Strategists and Information Researchers (CSIR), you are responsible for the yearly convention for members. Each year, about 600 of your 4,500 members attend the convention, which includes exhibit booths of publishers and computer companies specializing in communication hardware and software. You generally have about 20 exhibitors whom you charge $350 per space to display their latest books and computer products. Most of your members are academics, although you have some training and development executives and consultants who belong.

For the last two years, Northeastern Publishers, a major textbook publisher, has given a welcoming cocktail reception for all members on the first evening of your three-day convention. They have typically offered heavy hors d'oeuvres and bar drinks for one and one-half hours. Because you work with catering departments of hotels to plan food and beverage functions, you know that the company spends $4,000–5,000 on the welcoming reception.

This year, however, Northeastern plans to host a mid-morning coffee break during the first day of the convention. A quick check of the hotel's catering prices indicates the company will likely spend about $600 for this function. And they have given up their hosting of the evening reception. You are disappointed, of course, because you want the most and best for your members who attend the annual convention. From the company's standpoint, you understand that competition and a dip in projected enrollments have forced many publishers to cut expenses drastically.

The big problem, however, comes as you look at the exhibitors' space contracts for the convention. The contract returned by Northeastern contains this note: "Space fee ($350) waived for sponsoring social function as per last two years." As you read these words, you remember that it has always been your policy to give a free booth space to any exhibitor who sponsors a major social event at the convention. You reason that certainly it is worth the trade-off for your members if they receive a major activity for $350 of revenue. Certainly, you could not provide a social activity for the members at that price. The price concession is, in essence, a goodwill gesture to the companies who spend the most for your members.

You interpret "major social event" to mean in the $4,000–5,000 price range, however. And you have two publishers for this year's convention who will spend that—not the estimated $600 Northeastern will spend. For this reason, you are going to have to write the company and tell them they will have to pay the $350 space fee. You'll need to remember that Northeastern advertises in your convention program book and in the two quarterly publications you distribute to members. And they do publish the books of several of your most respected members. So don't alienate them. Write them a fair-minded refusal that will keep their goodwill. You do want their business and you want them to reconsider the welcoming party next year.

12. Just last week, American Carriers, the airline for which you are director of the frequent flier program, filed for Chapter 11 bankruptcy protection. This action will permit you to continue operations without the threat of creditors. All of the news sources have provided coverage of your company's actions and interests. Along with that coverage, however, has come a number of letters from worried customers about the status of the frequent flier mileage program.

In fact, a stack of such letters now sits in the middle of your desk. The one on the top of the pile reads thus:

Dear Director:

Please transfer all of my mileage points to TransAtlantic Airlines. I read in *Business Week* about your agreement with them. I'd appreciate you doing this right away!

Sincerely,

John Krnek
Frequent Flier #8204

The agreement to which Mr. Krnek refers is part of a marketing agreement the company put together with two other carriers—TransAtlantic Airlines and Occidental Airways. It was the company's way of trying to assure passengers who were worried about the future of the company that they had some options. But your agreement is only for trips booked on current trips. Whenever a passenger purchases a ticket on your airline, he or she has the option to transfer the mileage to one of the two cooperating airlines' frequent flier programs. But transfer cannot be done retroactively after departure. And they certainly cannot be done for all accumulated miles in your program. It would not make any economic sense to transfer all your mileage liabilities this way.

Thus, you are going to have to deny Mr. Krnek's request. But you want to do so in a tactful way. So point out some of the advantages of your agreement to him. He has some options on current flights, correct? And you still have all of your routes from which he can choose to use his accumulated frequent flier mileage. No doubt, there are other reasons and benefits you can use to cushion the effect of the refusal.

Write a refusal letter to Mr. Krnek that can be adapted to other similar situations you expect to encounter with other members in the frequent flier program.

13. As owner of Friday's Office Supply, you have a challenging situation to consider today. You have expanded your business recently to include vending machines that you locate and service in schools, public libraries, and other places where people might need pencils, pens, scissors, rulers, and such. The expansion has provided a steady source of profit to the sales of office supplies you offer at two locations.

Mrs. Emily Wright, president of the Florence Elementary School PTA, writes you with this request: "Will you please donate half of your profits from the vending machine sales of supplies at Florence to our yearly fundraising project?" She goes on to say how worthy such a contribution would be because the PTA is trying to raise money for library books and office machines, which they would certainly purchase from you. In addition, Mrs. Wright indicates she would prefer not to compete with you but that the PTA could offer the same supplies for a lower cost at the school by setting up a booth and having volunteers sell supplies to students. To be sure, this situation will require delicate treatment and your best "be reasonable" response. But you are going to have to refuse her request.

You question Mrs. Wright's logic on several fronts as you begin to develop the strategy for your refusal. First, you wonder why volunteers would want to sit in a booth all day (8 A.M.–4 P.M.) and wait for students to purchase supplies. No doubt, such volunteers would better serve the school by acting as teacher's aides or doing office work for the overworked administrators. Second, you think about Mrs. Wright's business logic. The prices you charge for vending sales are not out of line, and the profit from them is not excessive. In fact, the return on your investment in the vending machines is the minimum you can take for the costs involved and the risks of the venture. If you contributed half the profits to the PTA, you would lose money and you would have to increase prices to the students.

For both of these reasons and perhaps others, you will have to say "no" to Mrs. Wright. But there is much at stake here; so write a smooth, winning letter that will build goodwill and refuse at the same time. You have contributed to the PTA fundraising in the past. This year, you have budgeted $500 for them. But this is not the basis for your refusal.

Write the letter to the PTA president.

## ADJUSTMENT REFUSALS

14. For this assignment you are manager of the Victorian Theater, an elegant former movie theater now catering primarily to traveling musical and stage shows. Last week The Trail Blazers, a musical group, came to the Victorian for a three-night stand. They expected to fill the theater's 700 seats every night, but it didn't work out that way. The theater was less than half filled the first night, and advance ticket sales for the following two nights were very low. The group canceled the remaining shows. Of course, refunds were made to those who had purchased tickets.

    Today you received a letter from Viola Smiley, the Trail Blazers' business manager, asking for an adjustment of the rental fee. "We used your facility only one of the three nights," she wrote. "So please refund the amount we paid in advance for the remaining two nights. As I calculate it, we are due $4,200 ($2,100 per night for two nights), less your charge for refunding tickets, which you indicated is $240."

    You can't do it. The group bargained for three nights, and they must pay for three nights. You could have rented the place to other groups. In fact, rarely is the theater not rented on weekend dates, and the dates in question were over a weekend.

    Your letter to Ms. Smiley will give your answer clearly and will justify the decision so convincingly that she will understand. Remember that the Trail Blazers still owe you $240 for the work involved in refunding tickets.

15. Your automobile rental company got a nice order last month when executives of the Mulkey-Bordelon Advertising Agency were in town for a conference. They ordered 10 medium-size automobiles for their people for the five days of the conference. You quoted them a price of $160 per week for each automobile, including up to a tank of gasoline. Then you promptly reserved the 10 automobiles.

    On the first day of the conference, Mulkey-Bordelon executives picked up five of the automobiles. On the second day they picked up a sixth. They returned all six automobiles at the end of the fifth day. The remaining four automobiles you had reserved remained on the lot unused. You kept them on reserved status even though there were times you could have used them, for you had made a commitment to Mulkey-Bordelon. You considered them to be rented. Apparently Mr. Timmothy B. Doggett, sales manager for Mulkey-Bordelon, viewed the matter as you did when, on the fifth day, he paid the bill for $1,600.

    Today you received in the mail a letter from the Mulkey-Bordelon business manager requesting an adjustment on the payment. "According to our records," he wrote, "we used only six automobiles. Therefore, please refund the overcharge of $640." You will refuse the request.

    Write the letter that will inform Mr. Doggett of your decision. And explain your decision in words that will convince him that your view is fair and logical.

16. Your little mail-order company does good business during the Christmas season selling businesses gifts for their employees, customers, friends, and such. The businesses buy the gifts from you and give you the addresses of the recipients. Then you mail the gifts. With few exceptions you have highly satisfied customers.

    One of the exceptions surfaced today. You received a letter from Tonya Treece, general manager for the Four D Company. Ms. Treece explained her problem this way: "We ordered 560 of your EZ Glide ballpoint pens with our logo imprinted thereon at a price of $9.60 each, including shipping. They were specified as Christmas gifts for some of our good customers. Unfortunately, the pens were not mailed until after New Year's Day. We were embarrassed. Frankly, we would like our money back; but we will split the difference and agree to a 50 percent refund ($2,688)."

You remember this order well. On December 18 you received it with a note in the margin signed by Frank D. Davenport, Four D's purchasing manager. The note read, "I know your advertisement specifies to allow 30 days for imprinting logos and mailing, but this is an emergency. Please rush!" You did just what Davenport asked. You handled the order in 16 days.

Perhaps Mr. Davenport was tardy in ordering the pens and Ms. Treece doesn't know it. You don't want to get the man in trouble with his superior, but you are not going to take the blame either. Neither are you going to give back money.

Now write the letter that will give Ms. Treece your answer and explain your reasoning. You will handle the situation delicately, but you will make it clear that you have provided only your usual good, efficient service.

17. You own a small beach house near San Diego that you have been renting out for years. One family from Kansas, the Stan Millers, have been good renters for at least five years. They take good care of the property and pay promptly. Usually they rent the house for the month of August, but this year they requested June. Everything seemed fine when you talked to the Millers when they left on June 30.

However, this morning's mail brought a claim letter from them requesting a rental rebate. Apparently, the Millers thought the rent included sunshine, but Southern California had its usual June gloom; only a few days even had sun in the afternoon. From Lisa Miller's letter, you'd think that the sunshine accounted for nearly 40 percent of the rental cost. She was asking for a $600 rebate on the $1,500 rent they paid.

You clearly will refuse her request. However, since you know the Millers are reasonable people, you realize you need to educate them so they'll understand your refusal yet continue to be good renters. Basically, June is known for its gloomy weather in Southern California—any good travel guide will tell you that. The weather they've been used to in August is the best. In fact, that's the reason the August rental is $2,000 rather than the June price of $1,500. To maintain the Millers's goodwill, you decide to offer to reserve next year's August for them at this year's price. Write a letter of refusal that maintains goodwill.

18. As assistant store manager, your boss, Leonard Deftos, gave you the following letter to handle. He told you to refuse the adjustment in a way you believe is appropriate. He believes that having the dishwasher for over a month makes it impossible for you to put it back in stock and resell as new. You may offer to service it, replacing parts free. You can guarantee it will work properly under the right conditions. Work to maintain this customer's satisfaction.

[Current Date]
Store Manager
Sears, Roebuck and Co.
La Jolla University Town Center
San Diego, CA 92014

Dear Manager:

I am very unhappy with both the dishwasher I ordered from Sears and the service from Sears.

As a single person, I use the dishwasher about once every five to seven days. In the six weeks I have had it, I have used it only about six or eight times. It then started to fill up with water and would not operate. I had to bail water from it twice.

When I called the repair service, the earliest they could service it was about eight days. Since I had business on the day they suggested, I called and rescheduled the service call for two days later. Apparently, your scheduler scheduled it earlier and I was not at home because of the error. When I called on the day you were scheduled to come, I was told the schedule was full. Then when I told the scheduler that I had stayed home from work just for the repairperson to come, the scheduler said they would be there that day. However, the repairperson did not show up after I waited over eight hours.

As you will agree, it is a very irritating situation not to mention the pile of dishes I have had to look at for days. At this point, the only thing you could do to make me a satisfied customer of Sears again would be to remove the dishwasher and credit my account for the charge. Please let me know when you will be here to remove it.

Sincerely,

Eleanor Braaten

19. An irate student from your school, Gabrielle Jerome, wrote your company, the local telephone company, a letter demanding that her bill be adjusted for calls she didn't make. Apparently, her former roommate made the calls and is responsible for paying them. She wants the charges and associated late payments removed from her bill and charged to the roommate. You must refuse this adjustment.

This refusal needs to educate Ms. Jerome on the responsibility honoring the contract she signed when she arranged for the service. Additionally, she is not denying the calls were made from her phone, only that she made them. You will refuse her request and ask her to pay you in full, settling the payment with her former roommate. You may suggest that if she has trouble collecting, she can take the roommate to small claims court. You may want to give her some other hints for dealing with this situation in the future. Refuse the request but maintain the goodwill of your customer.

20. Mr. James Jameson of Arlington, Virginia, wants his money back for a missed flight connection on a recent business trip from New York to Athens, Greece, to Paris, France. He writes you, Director of Marketing, Worldwide Airlines, the following:

Dear Customer Relations Manager:

Last week, I was traveling on business from New York to Athens with a connecting flight to Paris. I made these reservations because I could not get a direct flight to Paris on the days of my travel.

We experienced fog and couldn't land on time in Athens; so I missed my connection and had to take the next available flight—15 hours late. I got a hotel room but I was very inconvenienced.

When I returned home, my travel agent told me about your guarantee against missing connecting flights. Please send me a check for $2,638 (American) for my plane fare and expenses for the delay (room and food). My ticket and receipts are enclosed.

Sincerely,

James Jameson

As you reread the letter, you agree that you have a guarantee against missing connecting flights. It is printed on the back of each passenger ticket. But that's only part of the statement. You also state that "excluded are situations beyond Worldwide's control." Two of the most common exclusions are weather delays and air traffic control problems. Because Mr. Jameson was weather delayed, you cannot give him back his money.

How to present this information to your good-paying passenger will require your best thinking because you want to keep his business. When you developed the guarantee, you had in mind minor problems, such as baggage delays and routing problems. But you certainly did not want to include situations that were uncontrollable by the company. You'd lose too much money that way. The ticket agent in Athens, however, should have been more responsive. Whenever there are missed international connections—for whatever reason—you pay for hotel and food expenses until you can get passengers on another flight. So you will pick up $138 of Mr. Jameson's claim.

But do not let this gesture cloud the refusal you must give. Your message should not sound like a modified *no*! Develop reasons for denying his request and present them before the actual refusal and before you mention the payment you will give. You'll do everything you can to be tactful and fair to keep this customer "on time" for his next business trip.

21. "This can't happen!" you say to yourself as you look at the returned mink coat that arrived in the mail this morning. As you inspect the coat more closely, you note that the hair has fallen out of the coat in places and gives a "patchy" appearance. The letter that accompanies the coat explains more from its owner, Mrs. Valerie Adelstein, a socially prominent woman in Tulsa, Oklahoma.

In the letter, Mrs. Adelstein indicates that she purchased the mink several years ago from your store, Fashion Outlet, a retailer of exclusive and elegant attire in Chicago. She was in the city to attend a national meeting of the League of Women Voters and she purchased the coat so that she would look presentable at all the gala events she attends on behalf of the League. But she goes on to say that the coat should certainly last more than three years, especially since she paid $5,500 for it. She wants her money back because all of the hair is falling out.

As the person in charge of mail-order claims for Fashion Outlet, you must now deal with the situation. A careful examination of the coat shows that the mink hair is indeed falling out. But it is doing so in fairly even fashion—except for one large area on the right front side. As you look at the lining, you note that there is a tag from a Tulsa dry cleaning establishment. You conclude that the dry cleaner must have tried to remove a stain from the coat with chemicals. Certainly, among fine fur dealers, using chemicals on mink fur is a "no no." In fact, you note these words on the label: "Special Handling Required. Do Not Dry Clean."

In addition, the hair is falling out in other places. Your 20 years of experience in the industry tells you that this almost always occurs when people store their furs in a place that is too humid. With the purchase of each of your furs, you give special printed materials instructing customers to store their furs in facilities that prevent excessive moisture to accumulate. Most reputable cleaning businesses have fur storage vaults for this purpose. Furs should be stored in the off-season in them.

For both of these reasons, you are going to refuse to give Mrs. Adelstein her money back. It's obvious that she abused your product. But you don't want her "badmouthing" you in the social circles she frequents. So put on your "kid gloves" and write a polite but firm refusal to her claim. Remember, the facts are on your side, but don't be blunt and tactless.

22. As general manager for the Metro Lions, a major National Football League franchise, you must respond to a claim you received today from Willie Bandit. He is the agent for Rock Nudson, a 10-year star for the Lions who retired after last year's season. Mr. Bandit claims that you owe $10,000 as an incentive bonus to Rock because he gained 1,105 yards rushing in his final year with the Lions. He says he has been reviewing his players' contracts and ran across this unpaid contract obligation.

But your contract file and memos to file offer a different interpretation. Mr. Bandit helped Rock two years ago to renegotiate his contract for a higher base salary based on NFL statistics for fullbacks. Along with the contract were various incentive clauses based on actual performance. One of these related to yards rushing per season and indeed you offered $10,000 if he gained more than 1,000 yards.

The difference though is in how you interpret "season." The contract in your file contains a clause initialed by Rock stating that season means the 11-game schedule of regular games by the Lions—not including preseason and playoff games. As you calculate Rock's performance for regular season games, he gained 958 yards during the season, rather than 1,105.

You wonder whether Mr. Bandit is referring to the most current contract. The previous contract with Rock—before he renegotiated—did interpret season to mean all games played. But when you agreed to a higher base salary, you defined the performance incentives in higher numbers on a more restricted number of games. There are several other players Mr. Bandit represents who have contracts with a more liberal definition of season.

At first thought, you want to tell Mr. Bandit—in direct, forceful language—to read the most current contract. But as you think about the matter, you believe there are broader issues involved. Thus you will prepare an indirect message that will soften the bad news you have to convey. In the first place, Mr. Bandit represents several players on the team. So you want him to know you are reasonable and logical. In the second place, Rock does public relations work for the team and you don't want to belittle his career.

So write a refused adjustment letter to Mr. Bandit. Develop your reasons first so that he can see the logic of your decision.

## CREDIT REFUSALS

23. You don't want to refuse credit to Todd A. Porter, but you must. You know Todd from past years when you called on the major sporting goods store in the area and he was an employee there. You remember him as being a very nice young man—courteous, personable, hard working. You hope he makes a success of his new sporting goods store, but you aren't able to help him with credit right now, for your own small wholesale operation also is struggling.

From Todd's credit check you learned that his creditors think he has promise. But, unfortunately, he started his business on a shoestring. He has made some progress but still has a long way to go. He owes for every part of his business operation—the lease, the fixtures, the inventory. In fact, his financial situation is precarious. He is delinquent in payments to at least five of his suppliers as well as to his bank. To make matters worse, his sales in recent months have been slow.

So you will turn down Todd's request for credit which accompanied his $1,753 order for exercise equipment (your company's specialty). Because you like this young man and hope that the future will permit him to do business with you, you will treat him with respect and courtesy. (You may assume any specific facts you may need as long as they are consistent with the information given.)

24. Move the calendar ahead to vacation time. You are visiting your Aunt B (Beatrice Blocker), owner of B's Flower and Gift Shop. As you talk with her at her store, the conversation turns to her business problems.

"Seems I gross quite a lot," she explains, "but I have a hard time collecting what is owed me. I decided just last week that I have to be harder on granting credit. From here on, I'll make people apply. Then I'll run credit checks on them. I'll grant credit only to those who have earned it.

"My biggest problem right now," Aunt B continues, "is working up a letter telling people I must turn them down. I'm not very good at letter writing, but I'll show you what I have done. Since you studied business communication in college, maybe you can show me how to improve it." Then she pulls a letter out of her desk drawer and shows it to you. "Read this," she commands:

Dear _____:

I deeply regret to inform you that B's Flower and Gift Shop cannot grant your request for credit as your credit record does not justify it.

Thank you for your application. Have a nice day!

Sincerely yours,

After more conversation with Aunt B, you agree to rewrite the letter for her. It will be a form letter that will fit the predominantly middle-income people with whom she does business, but you'll try to make it not appear to be a form letter. Of course, the letter will refuse diplomatically, using words that make the refusal clear yet are friendly.

25. For this assignment you are the credit manager for The Manor House, a furniture store selling only very expensive lines. Most of your customers are rich, although some are people who mistakenly think they belong in this group. In the past you granted credit liberally on the assumption that people who buy expensive goods can and will pay. Your assumption has proved to be wrong. In fact, your bad debt losses have grown steadily in recent years.

As a result of these losses, you have decided to tighten credit. From now on you will require that all requests for credit be made formally. Then you will run credit checks on the applicants, and you will grant credit only to those whose records show they have earned it. Conversely, you will deny credit to those who have not earned it.

How to turn down credit to those who have not earned it is your problem at this moment. You will write a form letter, and you will take great care in writing it. You will use your very best diplomacy, for The Manor House wants no negative messages appearing under its letterhead. Also, although the letter will be a form letter, you do not want it to appear to be one or to read like one. You want readers to feel that it is individually written, for The Manor House takes pride in the personal attention it gives to all its customers.

Address the letter to Mr. Claude O. Kennedy, one of the people you must turn down for credit.

26. You work in the accounting department for Dow Jones & Company, Inc. You've recently received a letter from Mrs. Nancy Bailey, a teacher in Champaign, Illinois. She wants to order the student edition of *The Wall Street Journal* for her high school economics class beginning next term. She wants the paper available on the first day of the class and states she'll collect the $90 fee from the students during the first week. She's requesting you extend her credit until the class meets. Since she teaches classes in consumer economics, emphasizing economic and business literacy, you are certain that you can appeal to her economic sense when refusing the request.

You know she's excited about the paper. Remind her that in addition to providing articles from the real newspaper, the classroom edition program provides a monthly teacher's guide, video supplements, and other educational resources. These supplements are provided at no additional cost to teachers; you are expending this effort on behalf of the nation's drive to improve the economic literacy of its students. However, your experience since the inception of the program in 1991 shows that too many schools have been delinquent in their promised payments, causing your company to operate this nonprofit program on a cash-only basis.

Let Mrs. Bailey know that she made a good decision in choosing the program to supplement her economics class. Her careful planning is admirable. You are willing to take her order as a credit card purchase. You'll send the paper on the day she wants, charging it to her card at that time. By the time her credit card bill is due, she will have collected the money from her students. Write the refusal in a way that encourages Mrs. Bailey to participate in the program.

27. As Credit Manager for the local Montgomery Ward, you must refuse credit for a local college student. The student, Carol Weissmann, has written a highly persuasive letter, asking for a $5,000 credit line to buy a computer to use in her classes. However, she has no credit history and her job record shows she's only held short-term jobs.

While you recognize the importance of computers to today's student, you cannot justify extending credit based on the facts you have. In your refusal letter, you want to maintain Ms. Weissmann's goodwill as well as a potential sale of a computer system. You'll need to educate Ms.

Weissmann on what she can do to establish a credit history. Perhaps she could get a telephone in her name, paying the bill in a timely fashion. Perhaps she could buy smaller items on credit, paying promptly. Or she could put down a larger amount, paying the balance on a shorter term. Also, if she continues in her present job beyond six months, her job history record will improve.

Make the letter as helpful as you can while still refusing the credit. Strive to maintain goodwill. You may want to include some resale on the computer system she's indicated an interest in owning.

28. Being a loan officer at your local bank brings with it the responsibility of denying loans even to creditworthy customers. Sometimes, as in your area now, the conditions of particular industries or local economies force you to deny credit to good people with good intentions. One of these people is Perry Hansen. Perry has been an important person in your community. He's raised money for many charitable causes, donating both his time and energy to the community in numerous ways over the years. He's helped the community grow, improving the lives of many of its citizens.

Mr. Hansen has applied for a loan for a commercial real estate investment. He wants to buy some downtown property and convert it into an upscale senior citizen home. He thinks the long-term prospects are good with the demographics showing an aging population. He also firmly believes the community needs such a place.

While you are not denying his reasoning, the conditions in your area for commercial real estate are extremely poor. In this uncertain market, making the 90 percent loan he needs now would be a bad business decision. You'll refuse him the credit but encourage him to continue with the worthwhile project. You might even suggest some alternative ways he can get financing.

29. Banner Signs was purchased six months ago by Bob Fitzhugh. Bob earned an M.B.A. in Finance six years ago. Since then, he has worked in the trust department of a large bank and for a real estate developer for three years and two years, respectively. Because he had always wanted his own business, he used his personal savings and an inheritance from his father to make the down payment on the business.

To conduct business, Bob has numerous operating expenses. Thus, he has requested credit for the $985.14 of brochures, business cards, and computer supplies purchased from your business, Ransey's Copiers. You run your usual credit check on Bob and receive a not-so-good report. It appears that in the few short months Bob has operated the business he's been a "slow pay" account at best. On two of his six bank mortgage payments, he has been 10 days late. And he has not taken the cash discount available to him of 2/10 net 30 on his account for office furniture. Moreover, he factors his accounts receivable each month at a discount to get immediate cash. All of these indicators make you decide to refuse him credit.

Banner Signs was begun 30 years ago by Frank Millikin. Over the years, he developed the business into a stable, solid small business specializing in outdoor advertising. But failing health forced Frank to sell the business to Bob, and it now appears that Bob has problems generating enough revenue to meet his existing credit obligations. Perhaps he could cut back his spending or expand his revenue for more cash flow. But regardless of his short-term operating strategy, he does not need another credit obligation.

So write him a tactful credit refusal that will keep his cash business with you. Your experience shows that his type of account can be profitable in the long run. But he will have to manage things differently to qualify for credit.

30. As head of the credit department at Haffleman's, a bookstore/campus supply outlet near your campus, you must deny credit to Juanita Munroe, a second-year student at your school.

Juanita filled out a credit application when she was in your store yesterday. On the application, she estimates that she would purchase about $50 of items (art supplies, gifts, etc) each month, and she wants a 30-day pay account. As you look over the application further, however, you note that she has other obligations of indebtedness. She pays $350 each month on her car (a 1987 Buick), $100 on her stereo, and $250 for her apartment. Although she says she gets $650 each month from home and works 15 hours at a local restaurant as a cocktail waitress, you believe that another debt might very well be the "straw that broke the camel's back."

Juanita is an art major and carries 18 hours of course work this semester. With her schedule of classes and work, you feel that she would be stretching things too thin to take on another obligation. Actually, this situation is a typical one for you—the hardworking student who takes on too many financial responsibilities and ends up overburdened with indebtedness. Usually, the student does not pay the account.

In the best interest of the student and for your best interest, you will write Juanita a letter refusing her credit. But be tactful because she will be spending money for books, supplies, and gifts somewhere. It might as well be with you—but for cash. Also, you don't want her saying bad things about you to her friends and customers at the restaurant. Write a tactful letter that will deny credit to Juanita Munroe.

31. Monotel, Inc. wants 50 of the watches you advertised in *The Wall Street Journal* at $49.95 each. Monotel's sales manager, Gayle Ventrimo, plans to present the watches to their top salespeople at the company's annual sales meeting in Florida next month. Ms. Ventrimo writes in her order letter that she wants the Monotel logo imprinted on the face of the watch and she wants the awardee's name engraved on the back. (She includes a list of 50 names for this purpose.)

    Filling the order to her product specifications should be no problem. But granting the company credit for the order is, as Ms. Ventrimo asks you to bill her for credit terms of 2/10 net 45. You run a report check through the credit bureau in Nashville, the corporate headquarters for Monotel, and the news you receive is not good.

    It appears that the company might have good intentions, but they are a bit delinquent in their credit habits. Last year, they averaged 35-day payments on their 30-day credit accounts. Also, they were overdrawn on two occasions on their checking accounts. And their assets-to-liability ratio averaged 1:3 for the past fiscal year. Thus, while sales volume appears to be promising for the company, their cash flow and payment record do not appear to justify your granting credit to them. For these reasons, you are going to have to write a credit refusal letter to Ms. Ventrimo.

    While you certainly have good reason to deny credit to Monotel, you will keep the letter positive in tone and approach. The company still needs the watches and you're in business to sell them—for cash as well as credit. So write a letter that will refuse credit but will keep Monotel as a cash customer.

# CHAPTER 8

# INDIRECTNESS IN PERSUASION AND SALES WRITING

## CHAPTER OBJECTIVES

*Upon completing this chapter, you will be able to use persuasion effectively in making requests and composing sales letters.* To reach this goal, you should be able to

**1**

Use imagination in writing skillful persuasive requests that begin indirectly, use convincing reasoning, and close with goodwill and action.

**2**

Describe the choices available in determining the structure of a sales mailing.

**3**

Describe the preliminary steps of studying the product or service and selecting the appeals to use in a sales letter.

**4**

Discuss the choices of letter mechanics available to the sales writer.

**5**

Compose sales letters that gain attention, persuasively present appeals, and effectively drive for action.

## NEED FOR INDIRECTNESS IN PERSUASION

Although letters in which you ask for something that your reader may be reluctant to give need not involve bad news, they are also handled in the indirect order. For example, with a letter requesting a favor that will require some personal sacrifice, your chances for success will be greater if you justify the request before making it. This approach, of course, follows the indirect order. Or, for another example, when you write a letter selling a product or service, your readers will usually resist your efforts. To succeed, therefore, you have to begin by convincing them that they need the product or service. This approach also follows the indirect order. Such indirect letters involving persuasion are the subject of this chapter.

* Certain requests and sales letters are best written in the indirect order.

### INTRODUCTORY SITUATION

## to Persuasive Requests

Introduce yourself to the next business letter situation by returning to your hypothetical position at Pinnacle. As a potential executive, you spend some time working for the community. Pinnacle wants you to do this for the sake of good public relations. You want to do it because it is personally rewarding.

Currently, as chair of the fund-raising committee of the city's Junior Achievement program, you head all efforts to get financial support for the program from local businesspeople. You have a group of workers who will call on businesspeople. But personal calls take time, and there are many people to call on.

At its meeting today, the Junior Achievement board of directors discussed the problem of contacting businesspeople. One director suggested using a letter to sell them on giving money. The board accepted the idea with enthusiasm. With just as much enthusiasm, it gave you the assignment of writing the letter (for the president's signature).

As you view the assignment, it is not a routine letter-writing problem. Although the local businesspeople are probably generous, they are not likely to part with money without good reason. In fact, their first reaction to a request for money is likely to be negative. So you will need to overcome their resistance in order to persuade them. Your task is indeed challenging. ∎

## PERSUASIVE REQUESTS

Letters making requests that are likely to be resisted require a slow, deliberate approach. The direct order suggested for routine requests (Chapter 5) just will not do the job. Persuasion is necessary. By persuasion, we mean reasoning with the reader—presenting facts and logic that support your case. In this approach, which is discussed in detail below, you should generally follow this indirect plan.

* Requests that are likely to be resisted require persuasion.

- **Open with words that (1) set up the strategy and (2) gain attention.**
- **Present the strategy (the persuasion), using persuasive language and you-viewpoint.**
- **Make the request clearly and without negatives (1) either as the end of the letter or (2) followed by words that recall the persuasive appeal.**

* Generally follow this indirect plan.

**CHAPTER 8** Indirectness in Persuasion and Sales Writing

Persuasive requests and sales letters arrive uninvited. They have goals that are likely to encounter reader resistance. Unless they gain the reader's attention at the beginning, they are likely to end up in a wastebasket.

## Determining the Persuasion

*The persuasion is planned to overcome reader objections.*

Planning the persuasive request letter requires imagination. You begin by thinking of a strategy that will convince your reader. To do this, put yourself in your reader's shoes. Look at the request as the reader sees it, and determine the reader's objections. Think about what you can say to overcome those objections. From this thinking, you should develop your plan.

*Many persuasive appeals may be used—money rewards, personal benefits, and so on.*

The specific plan you develop will depend on the facts of the case. You may be able to show that your reader stands to gain in time, money, or the like. Or you may be able to show that your reader will benefit in goodwill or prestige.

In some cases, you may persuade by appealing to the reader's love of beauty, excitement, serenity, or the like. In other cases, you may be able to persuade by appealing to the pleasant feeling that comes from doing a good turn. Many other possibilities exist. You select the one that best fits your case.

## Gaining Attention in the Opening

*The opening sets the strategy and gains attention.*

In the indirect letters previously discussed, the goal of the opening is to set up the explanation. The same goal exists in persuasion letters, but persuasion letters have an additional goal. It is the goal of gaining attention.

*Attention is needed to get the reader in a mood to receive the persuasion.*

The need to gain attention in the opening of persuasion letters is obvious. You are writing to a person who has not invited your letter and probably does not agree with your goal. So you need to get that person in a receptive mood. An interesting beginning is a good step in this direction.

PART 3   Basic Patterns of Business Letters

Determining what will gain attention also requires imagination. It might be some statement that arouses mental activity, or it might be a statement offering or implying a reader benefit. Because questions arouse mental activity, they are often effective openings. The following examples indicate the possibilities.

From the cover letter of a questionnaire seeking the opinions of medical doctors:

What, in your opinion as a medical doctor, is the future of the private practice of medicine?

From a letter requesting contributions for handicapped children:

While you and I dined heartily last night, 31 orphans at San Pablo Mission had only dried beans to eat.

From a letter seeking the cooperation of business leaders in promoting a fair:

What would your profits be if 300,000 free-spending visitors came to our town during a single week?

*What you write to gain attention is limited only by your imagination.*

### Presenting the Persuasion

Following the opening, you should proceed with your goal of persuading. Your task here is a logical and orderly presentation of the reasoning you have selected.

As with any argument intended to convince, you should do more than merely list points. You should help convey the points with convincing words. Since you are trying to penetrate a neutral or resistant mind, you need to make good use of you-viewpoint. You need to pay careful attention to the meanings of your words and the clarity of your expression. Because your reader may become impatient if you delay your objective, you need to make your words travel fast.

*Your persuasion follows.*

*Present the points convincingly (selecting words for effect, using you-viewpoint, and the like).*

### Making the Request Clearly and Positively

After you have done your persuading, you move to the action you seek. You have prepared the reader for what you want. If you have done that well, the reader should be ready to accept your proposal.

Like other negative points, your request requires care in word choice. You should avoid words that detract from the request. You should also avoid words that bring to mind pictures and things that might work against you. Words that bring to mind reasons for refusing are especially harmful, as in this example:

I am aware that businesspeople in your position have little free time to give, but will you please consider accepting an assignment to the board of directors of the Children's Fund?

The following positive tie-in with a major point in the persuasion strategy does a much better job:

Because your organizing skills are so desperately needed, will you please serve on the board of directors of the Children's Fund?

Whether your request should end your letter will depend on the needs of the case. In some cases, you will profit by following the request with words of explanation. This procedure is especially effective when a long persuasion

*Follow the persuasion with the request.*

*Word the request for best effect.*

*Do not use a negative tone.*

*Be positive.*

*The request can end the letter or be followed by more persuasion.*

Ending with a reminder of the appeal is also good.

effort is needed. In such cases, you simply cannot present all your reasoning before stating your goal. On the other hand, you may end less involved presentations with the request. Even in this case, however, you may want to follow the request with a reminder of the appeal. As illustrated in the second example letter (p. 232), this procedure associates the request with the advantage that saying yes will give the reader.

### Contrasting Persuasion Letters

The following letters illustrate good and bad persuasion efforts.

The persuasive request is illustrated by contrasting letters that asked businesspeople to donate to Junior Achievement. The first letter is direct and weak in persuasion; the second letter is indirect and persuasive. The second letter, which follows the approach described above, produced better results.

**Obvious Failure in Directness.** The weaker letter begins with the request. Because the request is opposed to the reader's wishes, the direct beginning is likely to get a negative reaction. In addition, the comments about how much to give tend to lecture rather than suggest. Some explanation follows, but it is weak and scant. In general, the letter is poorly written. It has little of the you-viewpoint writing that is effective in persuasion. Perhaps its greatest fault is that the persuasion comes too late. The old-style close is a weak reminder of the action requested.

This bad letter has no persuasion strategy.

Dear Mr. Williams:

    Will you please donate to the local Junior Achievement program? We have set $50 as a fair minimum for businesses to give. But larger amounts would be appreciated.
    The organization badly needs your support. Currently, about 900 young people will not get to participate in Junior Achievement activities unless more money is raised. Junior Achievement is a most worthwhile organization. As a business leader, you should be willing to support it.
    If you do not already know about Junior Achievement, let me explain. Junior Achievement is an organization for high school youngsters. They work with local business executives to form small businesses. They operate the businesses. In the process, they learn about our economic system. This is a good thing, and it deserves our help.
    Hoping to receive your generous donation by return mail, I am,

                                Sincerely,

Calvin and Hobbes © 1985 Watterson. Dist. by Universal Press Syndicate. Reprinted with permission. All rights reserved.

**CASE ILLUSTRATION** Persuasive Request Letters. *(A Request for Information about Employment Applicants)*
In this letter a trade publication editor seeks information from an executive for an article on desirable job application procedures. The request involves time and effort for the executive. Thus, persuasion is necessary.

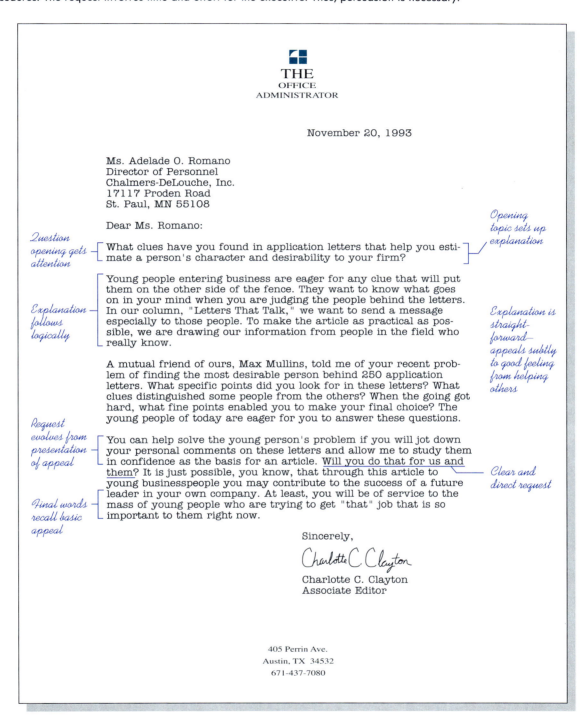

**Skillful Persuasion in an Indirect Order.** The next letter shows good imagination. It follows the indirect pattern described above. Its opening has strong interest appeal and sets up the persuasion strategy. Notice the effective use of you-viewpoint throughout. Not until the reader has been sold on the merits of the request does the letter ask the question. It does this clearly and directly. The final words leave the reader thinking about a major benefit that a yes answer will give.

Dear Mr. Williams:

*This better letter uses good persuasion strategy.*

Right now—right here in our city—620 teenage youngsters are running 37 corporations. The kids run the whole show, their only adult help being advice from some of your business associates who work with them. Last September they applied for a charter and elected officers. They selected products for manufacture—antifreeze, candles, and chairs, to name a few. They issued stock—and they sold it, too. With the proceeds from stock sales, they set up a production operation. Now they are producing and marketing their products. This May they will liquidate their companies and account to their stockholders for their profits or losses.

You, as a public-spirited citizen, will quickly see the merits of the Junior Achievement program. You know the value of such realistic experience to the kids—how it teaches them the operations of business and how it sells them on the merits of our American system of free enterprise. You can see, also, that it's an exciting and wholesome program, the kind we need more of to combat delinquency. After you have considered these points and others you will find in the enclosed brochure, I know you will see that Junior Achievement is a good thing.

Like all good things, Junior Achievement needs all of us behind it. During the 13 years the program has been in our city, it has had enthusiastic support from local business leaders. But with over 900 students on the waiting list, our plans for next year call for expansion. That's why I ask that you help make the program available to more youngsters by contributing $50 (it's deductible). Please make your check payable to Junior Achievement, and send it right away. You will be doing a good service for the kids in our town.

Sincerely,

## INTRODUCTORY SITUATION

## to Sales Letters

Introduce yourself to the next letter type by assuming the role of Anthony A. Killshaw, a successful restaurant consultant. Over the past 28 years, you have acquired an expert knowledge of restaurant operations. You have made a science of virtually every area of restaurant activity—menu design, food control, purchasing, kitchen organization, service. You have also perfected a simple system for data gathering and analysis that quickly gets to the heart of most operations' problems. Testimonials from a number of satisfied clients prove that the system works.

Knowing that your system works is one thing. Getting this knowledge to enough prospective clients is another. So you have decided to publicize your work by writing restaurant managers and telling them about what you have to offer.

At the moment, your plan for selling your services by mail is hazy. But your direct-mail package will probably consist of a basic letter, a printed brochure, and a form to be checked by prospective customers. The letter will carry the major message, and the brochure will cover the details. The recipients will be the major restaurant operations that are on the roster of the American Restaurant Association.

Because sales writing requires special skills, you have decided to use the help of a local advertising agency—one with good direct-mail experience. However, you have a pretty good idea of what you want, so you will not leave the work entirely up to the agency's personnel. You will tell them what you want included, and you will have the final word on what is acceptable. ■

## VALUE OF SALES WRITING

You will probably never write a sales letter—a real one, that is. Except in some small business operations, sales letters are written by professional writers. They achieve this status by having a talent for writing and by engaging in long, hard practice. Why, then, you might ask, should you study sales letters?

The answer is that even an amateurish effort to write sales letters gives you knowledge of selling techniques that will help you in many of your other activities. For one thing, it will help you in writing other types of letters, for in a sense every letter is a sales letter. In every letter you are selling something—an idea, a line of reasoning, your company, yourself.

Even in your daily life you will find good use for selling techniques. From time to time, all of us are called on to sell something. If we are employed in selling goods and services, our sales efforts will, of course, be frequent. In other areas of business, our sales efforts may consist only of selling such intangibles as an idea, our own competence, or the goodwill of the firm. In all such cases, we use selling techniques. Thus, sales writing and selling techniques are more valuable to you than you might think. After you have studied the remainder of this chapter, you should see why.

*Professionals usually write sales letters, so why study the subject?*

*The answer: Knowing selling techniques helps you in writing other types of letters.*

*It also helps in your daily life, for much of what you do involves selling.*

## PRELIMINARY EFFORTS

As you probably know from experience, most direct-mail efforts consist of more than just a letter. Typically, such efforts include a coordinated group of pieces—brochures, leaflets, booklets, foldouts, and so on. But a letter is usually the main piece. It carries the main message, and the other pieces carry the supporting details.

The following discussion emphasizes the letter, for it would be beyond the scope of this book to cover more. But much of what is said about the letter applies to other forms of sales literature. After you have studied the following material, you should have a general idea of how to sell by mail.

*Usually brochures, leaflets, and the like accompany sales letters.*

*But the emphasis in the following pages is on the letter.*

### Knowing the Product or Service and the Reader

Before you can begin writing, you must know about the product or service you are selling. You simply cannot sell most goods and services unless you know them and can tell the prospects what they need to know. Before prospects buy a product, they may want to know how it is made, how it

*Begin work on a sales letter by studying the product or service to be sold.*

**CHAPTER 8** Indirectness in Persuasion and Sales Writing

As in this excellent National Geographic example, most sales mailings consist of a letter and a coordinated group of support pieces.

works, what it will do, and what it will not do. Clearly, a first step in sales writing is careful study of your product or service.

In addition, you should know your readers. In particular, you should know about their needs for the product or service. Anything else you know about them can help—their economic status, age, nationality, education, and culture. The more you know about your readers, the better you will be able to adapt your sales message.

*Also, study your readers.*

In large businesses, a marketing research department or agency typically gathers information about prospective customers. If you do not have such help, you will need to gather this information on your own. If time does not permit you to do the necessary research, you may have to follow your best logic. For example, the nature of a product can tell you something about its likely buyers. Industrial equipment would probably be bought by people with technical backgrounds. Expensive French perfumes and cosmetics would probably be bought by people in high-income brackets. Burial insurance would appeal to older members of the lower economic strata. If you are purchasing a mailing list, you usually receive basic demographics such as age, sex, race, education, income, and marital status of those on the list. Sometimes you know more—interests, spending range, consumption patterns, and such.

*Research can help you learn about prospective customers. If research is not possible, use your best logic.*

### Determining the Appeal

With your product or service and your prospects in mind, you are ready to create the sales letter. This involves selecting and presenting basic appeals. By *appeals*, we mean the strategies you use to present a product or service to the reader. You could, for example, present a product's beauty or its taste qualities. You could stress that a product will provide hours of fun or that it will make one more attractive to the opposite sex. Or you could present a product through an appeal to profits, savings, or durability.

*Next, decide on what appeals and strategies to use.*

For convenience in studying appeals, we can divide them into two broad groups. In one group are emotional efforts to persuade. Such efforts affect how we feel, taste, smell, hear, and see. They also include strategies that arouse us through love, anger, pride, fear, and enjoyment. In the other group are rational appeals. These are appeals to the reason—to the thinking mind. Such appeals include strategies based on saving money, making money, doing a job better, and getting better use from a product.

*Appeals may be emotional (to the feelings) or rational (to the reason).*

In any given case, many appeals are available to you. You should consider those that fit your product or service and those that fit your readers best. Such products as perfume, style merchandise, candy, and fine food lend themselves to emotional appeals. On the other hand, such products as automobile tires, tools, and industrial equipment are best sold through rational appeals. Automobile tires, for example, are not bought because they are pretty but because they are durable, because they grip the road, and because they are safe.

*Select the appeals that fit the product and the prospects.*

How the buyer will use the product may be a major basis for selecting a sales strategy. Cosmetics might well be sold to the final user through emotional appeals. Selling cosmetics to a retailer (who is primarily interested in reselling them) would require rational appeals. A retailer would be interested

*The prospects' uses of the product often determine which appeal is best.*

**CHAPTER 8**   Indirectness in Persuasion and Sales Writing

### A Basic Lesson for Sales Writing

The neophyte sales writer's first sales letter had failed miserably. In discussing the matter with the advertising manager, the neophyte offered this explanation: "I think I have demonstrated that 'you can lead a horse to water, but you cannot make it drink.'"

"That's not an appropriate explanation," the advertising manager replied. "Your primary goal is not to make your readers drink. It is to make them thirsty."

---

in their emotional qualities only to the extent that these make customers buy. A retailer's main questions about the product are: Will it sell? What turnover can I expect? How much money will it make for me?

## STRUCTURE OF THE SALES LETTER

*Writing sales letters involves imagination.*

After selecting the appeal, you should write the sales letter. At this point, your imagination comes into the picture. Writing sales letters is as creative as writing short stories, plays, and novels. In addition to imagination, it involves applied psychology and skillful word use. There are as many different ways of handling a sales letter as there are ideas. The only sure way of judging each way is by the sales that the letter brings in.

*Sales-letter plans vary in practice, but this plan is used most often.*

Because sales letters can vary greatly, it is hard to describe their order. But you should usually follow this conventional pattern:

- **Gain favorable attention in the opening.**
- **Create desire by presenting the appeal, emphasizing supporting facts, and emphasizing reader viewpoint.**
- **Include all necessary information—using a coordinated sales package (brochures, leaflets, and such).**
- **Drive for the sale by urging action now and recalling the main appeal.**
- **Possibly add a postscript.**

This pattern is similar to the classic AIDA model (attention, interest, desire, action) developed almost a century ago. The techniques used in developing this pattern are discussed below. As you study them, bear in mind that in actual practice only your imagination will limit the possibilities open to you.

### Determining Letter Mechanics

*The makeup of sales letters differs somewhat from that of ordinary letters. For example, sales letters may use impersonal salutations, headlines for inside addresses, and attention-gaining devices.*

A part of your effort in planning a sales letter is to determine its makeup. The physical arrangements of sales letters may differ in many ways from those of ordinary business letters. With few exceptions, sales letters are mass-produced rather than individually processed. They may use individually processed inside addresses. This effective technique is often replaced by impersonal salutations, such as "Dear Students," "Dear Mr. Homeowner,"

**PART 3** Basic Patterns of Business Letters

or "Dear Sir." One technique eliminates the salutation and inside address and places the beginning words of the letter in the form of these parts. As shown below, this arrangement gives the letter what appears at first glance to be a normal layout.

IT'S GREAT FOR PENICILLIN,
BUT YOU CAN DO WITHOUT IT
ON YOUR ROOF . . . .

We're referring to roof fungus, which, like penicillin, is a moldlike growth. However, the similarity ends there. Unlike penicillin, roof fungus serves . . . .

Sales letters may use a variety of mechanical techniques to gain attention. Pictures, lines, diagrams, and cartoons are common. So is the use of different ink colors. Such devices as coins, stamps, sandpaper, rubber bands, pencils, and paper clips have been affixed to sales letters to gain interest and help put over the appeal. One letter, for example, was mailed on scorched pages to emphasize the theme of "some hot news about fire insurance." A letter with a small pencil glued to the page used the theme that "the point of the pencil is to make it easy to order" a certain magazine. As you can see, the imaginative possibilities in sales writing are boundless.

### Gaining Attention in the Opening

The opening of the sales letter has one basic requirement. It must gain attention. If it does not, it fails. The reason is apparent. As sales letters are sent without invitation, they are not likely to be received favorably. In fact, they may even be unwanted. Unless the first words of a sales letter overcome the barrier and gain attention, the letter goes into the wastebasket.

*The basic requirement of the opening is to gain attention.*

Your plan for gaining attention is a part of your creative effort. But the method you use should assist in presenting the sales message. That is, it should help set up your strategy. It should not just gain attention for attention's sake. Attention is easy to gain if nothing else is needed. A small explosion set off when the reader opens the envelope would gain attention. So would an electric shock or a miniature stink bomb. But these methods would not be likely to assist the selling.

*The opening should also set up the strategy.*

One of the most effective attention-gaining techniques is a statement or question that introduces a need that the product will satisfy. For example, a rational-appeal letter to a retailer would clearly tap his or her strong needs with these opening words:

Here is a proven best-seller—and with a 12 percent greater profit.

Another rational-appeal beginning is the first sentence of a letter seeking to place metered personal computers in hotel lobbies:

Can you use an employee who not only works free of charge but also pays you for the privilege of serving your clientele 24 hours a day?

Yet another rational-appeal beginning is this opening device from a letter selling a trade publication to business executives:

How to move more products,
Win more customers,
And make more money
. . . for less than $1 a week

**CHAPTER 8** Indirectness in Persuasion and Sales Writing

### Computer Graphics: Artwork Made Easy for the Business Writer

Sales letters and their supplements often include artwork to increase visual appeal as well as attract attention. Today's business writers need not be graphic artists to use artwork in their documents. Today's word processing and desktop publishing software easily incorporate graphics. Some readily available sources of prepared graphics include:

- graphics bundled with standard graphics, word processing, and spreadsheet software;
- clip art from both commercial and shareware sources; and
- scanned artwork from printed sources.

In addition, today's draw-and-paint software provide excellent, easy-to-use tools for both creating or modifying artwork and adding special effects. Here is a sampling of the variety of artwork easily combined with text either in word processing or desktop publishing programs.

---

This paragraph of a letter selling a fishing vacation at a lake resort illustrates a need-fulfilling beginning of an emotional-appeal approach:

Your line hums as it whirs through the air. Your lure splashes and dances across the smooth surface of the clear water as you reel. From the depth you see the silver streak of a striking bass. You feel a sharp tug. And the battle is on!

As you can see, the paragraph casts an emotional spell, which is what emotional selling should do. It puts a rod in the reader's hand, and it takes the reader through the thrills of the sport. To a reader addicted to fishing, the need is clearly established. Now the reader will listen to see how the need can be fulfilled.

As was mentioned previously, gimmicks are sometimes used to gain attention. But a gimmick is effective only if it supports the theme of the letter. One company made effective use of a penny affixed to the top of a letter with these words:

Most pennies won't buy much today, but this penny can save you untold worry and money—and bring you new *peace of mind*.

A paper manufacturer fastened small samples of sandpaper, corrugated aluminum, and smooth glossy paper to the top of a letter that began with these words:

You've seen the ads—
you've heard the talk—
now feel for yourself what we mean by *level-smooth*.

The use of a story is another opening approach. Most people like to read stories, and if you can start one interestingly, your reader should want to read the rest of it. Here is the attention-catching beginning of a masterpiece used by Boys Town to sell sponsor memberships:

A knock at the door, a swirl of snow over the threshold—and standing in the warm glow of the hall light was little Joe. His thin jacket was drawn tightly around his small body. "I'm here, Father. I'm here for an education," he blurted out.

Thus far, the attention-gaining techniques illustrated have been short. But longer ones have been used—and used effectively. In fact, a technique currently popular in direct-mail selling is to place a digest of the sales message at the beginning—usually before the salutation. The strategy is to quickly communicate the full impact of the sales message before the reader loses interest. If any of the points presented arouse interest, the reader is likely to continue reading.

*Summary messages are also effective.*

Illustrating this technique is the beginning of a letter selling subscriptions to *Change*. These lines appeared before the salutation, which was followed by four pages of text.

*A quick way to determine whether you should read this letter:*

If you are involved in or influenced by higher education—and you simply don't have the time to read copiously in order to "keep up"—this letter is important. Because it offers you a money-shortcut (plus a *free gift* and a money-back guarantee).

As a subscriber to CHANGE, the leading magazine of higher learning, you'll have facts and feelings at your fingertips—to help *you* form opinions. On today's topics: tenure, professors' unions, open admissions, the outlook for new PhDs . . . On just about any subject that concerns academe and you.

CHANGE has the largest readership of any journal among academic people. To find out why 100,000 people now read CHANGE every month, take three minutes to read the following letter.

## Presenting the Sales Material

After your attention-gaining opening has set up your sales strategy, you develop that strategy. What you do in this part of the letter is the product of the thinking and planning that you did at the beginning. In general, however, you should show a need and present your product or service as fulfilling that need.

> Plans vary for presenting appeals. Emotional appeals usually involve creating an emotional need.

The plan of your sales message will vary with your imagination. But it is likely to follow certain general patterns determined by your choice of appeals. If you select an emotional appeal, for example, your opening has probably established an emotional atmosphere that you will continue to develop. Thus, you will sell your product based on its effects on your reader's senses. You will describe the appearance, texture, aroma, and taste of your product so vividly that your reader will mentally see it, feel it—and want it. In general, you will seek to create an emotional need for your product.

> Rational appeals stress fact and logic.

If you select a rational appeal, your sales description is likely to be based on factual material. You should describe your product based on what it can do for your reader rather than how it appeals to the senses. You should write matter-of-factly about such qualities as durability, savings, profits, and ease of operation. Differences in these two sharply contrasting types of appeals are shown in the illustrations near the end of the chapter.

> Sales writing is not ordinary writing.

The writing that carries your sales message can be quite different from your normal business writing. Sales writing usually is highly conversational, fast moving, and aggressive. It even uses techniques that are incorrect or inappropriate in other forms of business writing—sentence fragments, one-sentence paragraphs, folksy language, and such. It uses mechanical emphasis devices (underscore, capitalization, bolding, italics, exclamation marks, color) to a high degree. It uses all kinds of graphics and graphic devices as well as a variety of type sizes and fonts. Its paragraphing often appears choppy. Apparently, the direct-mail professionals believe that whatever will help sell is appropriate.

## Stressing the You-Viewpoint

> You-viewpoint is important in sales writing. Use it.

In no area of business communication is you-viewpoint writing more important than in sales writing. We human beings are selfish creatures. We are persuaded best through self-interest. Thus, in sales writing you should base your sales points on reader interest. You should liberally use and imply the pronoun *you* throughout the sales letter.

The techniques of you-viewpoint writing in sales letters are best described through illustration. For example, assume that you are writing a sales letter to a retailer. One point you want to make is that the manufacturer will help sell the product with an advertising campaign. You could write this information in a matter-of-fact way: "Star mixers will be advertised in *Ladies' Home Journal* for the next three issues." Or you could write it based on what the advertising means to the reader: "Your customers will read about the new Star mixer in the next three issues of *Ladies' Home Journal*." For another example, you could quote prices in routine words such as "a four-ounce bottle costs $2.25, and you can sell it for $3.50." But you would emphasize the readers' interest with words like these: "You can sell the four-ounce size for $3.50 and make a 55 percent profit on your $2.25 cost." Using the you-viewpoint along with an explicit interpretation of how the facts benefit the reader will strengthen the persuasiveness. The following examples further illustrate the value of this technique:

| MATTER-OF-FACT STATEMENTS | YOU-VIEWPOINT STATEMENTS |
|---|---|
| We make Aristocrat hosiery in three colors. | You may choose from three lovely shades . . . . |
| The Regal has a touch as light as a feather. | You'll like Regal's featherlight touch. |
| Lime-Fizz tastes fresh and exciting. | You'll like the fresh, exciting taste of Lime-Fizz. |
| Baker's Dozen is packaged in a rectangular box with a bright bull's-eye design. | Baker's Dozen's new rectangular package fits compactly on your shelf, and its bright bull's-eye design is sure to catch the eyes of your customers. |

## Choosing Words Carefully

In persuasive messages, your attention to word choice is extremely important, for it can influence whether the reader acts on your request. Try putting yourself clearly in your reader's place as you select words for your message. Some words, while closely related in meaning, have clearly different effects on one's behavior. For example, the word *selection* implies a choice while the word *preference* implies a first choice. Here are some examples where a single adjective affects how one reacts to a sentence.

*Consider the effect of your words.*

You'll enjoy the sensation our hot salsa gives you.
You'll enjoy the sensation our fiery salsa gives you.
You'll enjoy the sensation our burning salsa gives you.

Framing your requests in the positive is also a proven persuasive technique. Readers will clearly opt for solutions to problems that avoid negatives. Here are some examples.

| ORIGINAL WORDING | POSITIVE WORDING |
|---|---|
| Reorganization Plan A will cause 10 percent of the staff to lose their jobs. | Reorganization Plan A will retain 90 percent of the work force. |
| Our new laser paper keeps the wasted paper from smudged copies to less than 5 percent. | Our new laser paper provides smudge-free copies more than 95 percent of the time. |

## Including All Necessary Information

Of course, the information you present and how you present it are matters for your best judgment. But you must make sure that you present enough information to complete the sale. You should leave none of your reader's questions unanswered. Nor should you fail to overcome any likely objections. You must work to include all such basic information in your letter, and you should make it clear and convincing.

*Give enough information to sell. Answer all questions; overcome all objections.*

In your effort to include all necessary information, you can choose from a variety of enclosures—booklets, brochures, leaflets, and the like. When you use such enclosures, you should take care to coordinate all the parts. In other words, all the parts in the mailing should form a unified sales message. As a general rule, you should use the letter to carry your basic sales message. This means that your letter should not shift a major portion of your sales effort to an enclosure. Instead, you should use enclosures mainly to supplement the letter. The enclosures might cover descriptions, price lists,

*Coordinate the sales letter with the accompanying booklets, brochures, and leaflets. But make the letter carry the main sales message. The enclosures should serve as supplements.*

### Successful Sales Letter

"Friend," the sales letter began, "let me show you how you can make an extra $25,000 a year. I am doing it this year—and you can do it, too. For detailed information, just send me $25."

One of the letters went to George Dimwitty. George was excited about the possibility of making money. So he mailed his $25. In a few days he got the following instructions:

"To make extra money just as I did, you first get a mailing list of suckers who want to make extra money. Then you write them 'Friend, let me show you how you can make an extra $25,000 a year. I am doing it this year—and you can do it, too. For detailed information, just send me $25.'"

---

diagrams, and pictures—in fact, all helpful information that does not fit easily into the letter. To ensure that all the parts in the mailing fit into a unified effort, you would be wise to direct your reader's attention to each of them. You can do this best through incidental references at appropriate places in the letter (for example, by saying "as shown on page 3 of the enclosed booklet" or "see page 7 of the enclosed brochure").

### Driving for the Sale

*End with a drive for the sale.*

After you have sold your reader on your product or service, the next logical step is to drive for the sale. After all, this is what you have been working for all along. It is a natural conclusion to the sales effort you have made.

*In strong selling efforts, a command is effective. For milder efforts, a request is appropriate. Take the reader through the motions.*

How you should word your drive for the sale depends on your strategy. If your selling effort is strong, your drive for action may also be strong. It may even be worded as a command. ("Order your copy today—while it's on your mind.") If you use a milder selling effort, you could use a direct question. ("Won't you please send us your order today?") In any event, the drive for action should be specific and clear. In no way should it resemble a hint. For best effect, it should take the reader through the motions of whatever he or she must do. Here are some examples:

Just check your preferences on the enclosed stamped and addressed order form. Then drop it in the mail today!

Won't you please permit us to deliver your Tabor recorder on approval? The number is 1-800-348-8821. Order it now, while you're thinking about it.

Mail the enclosed card today—and see how right the *Atlantic* is for you!

### Urging the Action

*Urge action now.*

Because readers who have been persuaded sometimes put things off, you should urge immediate action. "Do it now" and "Act today" are versions of this technique. You can make the technique especially effective if you tie it in with a practical reason for doing it now. Here are some examples:

. . . to take advantage of this three-day offer.

. . . so that you can be ready for the Christmas rush.

. . . so that you will be the first in your community.

### Recalling the Appeal

Yet another effective technique for the close of a sales letter is to use a few words that recall the basic appeal. Associating the action with the benefits that the reader will gain by taking it adds strength to your sales effort. Illustrating this technique is a letter selling Maxell videotapes to retailers. After building its sales effort, the letter asks for action and then follows the action request with these words:

> . . . and start taking your profits from the fast-selling Maxell videotape.

Another illustration is a letter selling a fishing resort vacation that follows its action words with a reminder of the joys described earlier.

> It's your reservation for a week of battle with the fightingest bass in the Southland.

*Recalling the appeal in the final words is good technique.*

### Adding a Postscript

Unlike other business letters where a postscript (P.S.) appears like an afterthought, a sales letter can use a postscript as a part of its design. It can be used effectively in a number of ways—to urge the reader to act, to emphasize the major appeal, to invite attention to other enclosures, to suggest that the reader pass along the sales message, and so on. Postscripts effectively used by professionals include the following:

> PS: Don't forget! If ever you think that *Action* is not for you, we'll give you every cent of your money back. We are that confident that *Action* will become one of your favorite magazines.
>
> PS: Hurry! Save while this special money-saving offer lasts.
>
> PS: Our little magazine makes a distinctive and appreciated gift. Know someone who's having a birthday soon?

*Postscripts are acceptable and effective.*

### Evaluating Contrasting Examples

The following two letters show good and bad efforts to sell Killshaw's restaurant consulting services. Clearly the bad letter is the work of an amateur and the better one was written by a professional.

*Following are bad and good letters.*

**Weakness in an Illogical Plan.** The amateur's letter begins with a dull statement about the consultant's services that is little more than an announcement of what the consultant does. Then, as a continuation of the opening, it offers the services to the reader. Such openings do little to gain attention or build desire. Next comes a routine, I-viewpoint review of the consultant's services. The explanation of the specific services offered is little better. Although the message tells what the consultant can do, it is dull. The drive for action is more a hint than a request. The closing words do suggest a benefit for the reader, but the effort is too little too late.

Dear Ms. Collins:

You have probably heard in the trade about the services I provide to restaurant management. I am now pleased to be able to offer these services to you.

From 28 years of experience, I have learned the details of restaurant management. I know what food costs should be. I know how to find other cost problems, be they the buying end or the selling end. I know how to design

*The bad letter is amateurish. It does little more than announce that services are available.*

menu offerings for the most profitability. I have studied kitchen operations and organization. And I know how the service must be conducted for best results.

From all this knowledge, I have perfected a simple system for analyzing a restaurant and finding its weaknesses. This I do primarily from guest checks, invoices, and a few other records. As explained in the enclosed brochure, my system finds the trouble spots. It shows exactly where to correct all problems.

I can provide you with the benefits of my system for only $500—$200 now and $300 when you receive my final report on your operations. If you will fill out and mail in the enclosed form, I will show you how to make more money.

Sincerely,

**Skillful Presentation of a Rational Appeal.** The better letter follows the conventional sales pattern described in the preceding pages. Its appeal is rational, which is justified in this case. The opening quotation attracts attention. It holds interest for a restaurant manager. Thus, the chances of getting the prospect to read further are good. The following sentences explain the service quickly—and interestingly. Then, in good you-viewpoint writing, the reader learns what he or she will get from the service. This part is loaded with reader benefit (profits, efficiency, cost cutting). Next, after the selling has been done, the letter drives for action. The final words tie in the action with its main benefit—making money.

Dear Ms. Collins:

"Killshaw is adding $15,000 a year to my restaurant's profits!"

With these words, Bill Summers, owner of Boston's famed Pirate's Cove, joined the hundreds of restaurant owners who will point to proof in dollars in assuring you that I have a plan that can add to your profits.

My time-proven plan to help you add to your profits is a product of 28 years of intensive research, study, and consulting work with restaurants all over the nation. I found that where food costs exceed 40 percent, staggering amounts slip through restaurant managers' fingers. Then I tracked down the causes of these losses. I can find these trouble spots in your business—and I'll prove this to you in extra income dollars!

To make these extra profits, all you do is send me, for a 30-day period, your guest checks, bills, and a few other items I'll tell you about later. After these items have undergone my proven method of analysis, I will write you an eye-opening report that will tell you how much money your restaurant should make and how to make it.

From the report, you will learn in detail just what items are causing your higher food costs. And you will learn how to correct them. Even your menu will receive thorough treatment. You will know what "bestsellers" are paying their way—what "poor movers" are eating into your profits. All in all, you'll get practical suggestions that will show you how to cut costs, build volume, and pocket a net 10 to 20 percent of sales.

For a more detailed explanation of this service, you'll want to read the enclosed information sheet. Then won't you let me prove to you, as I have in so many others, that I can add money to your income this year? This added profit can be yours for the modest investment of $800 ($300 now and the other $500 when our profit plan report is submitted). Just fill out the enclosed form, and place it along with your check in the addressed and stamped envelope that is provided for your convenience.

That extra $15,000 or more will make you glad you did!

Sincerely,

---

*Following the conventional pattern, the better letter uses good strategy and technique.*

**CASE ILLUSTRATION** Sales Letters. *(Using Emotional Appeal to Sell New Orleans)*

Sent to a select group of young business and professional people, this letter takes the readers through the experiences that they will enjoy if they accept the offer.

SUN
◄N►
FUN
TOURS

September 9, 1993

Ms. Kathy Pettit
71721 Boyce Street
Atlanta, GA 30329

Dear Ms. Pettit:

*Casts emotional spell—whets interest*

You slide back in the deep, plush chair, champagne tickles your nose, the hills of Georgia float swiftly away 30,000 feet below--and the cares of the week are left far behind in the steady whine of the jets.

Three more glasses, a mouth-watering selection of hors d'oeuvres, and suddenly you're deplaning and swept up in the never-ending excitement of America's fun capital--New Orleans. As the uniformed doorman of the world-famous Royal Orleans welcomes you to the understated elegance of the hotel's crystal chandeliered and marbled lobby, you understand why this "city that time forgot" is the perfect place for a completely carefree adventure--and that's what you're on--a fabulous Delta Jet-Set Weekend. Every detail is considered to give you the ultimate in enjoyment. You'll savor New Orleans as it's meant to be experienced--gracious living, unsurpassed cuisine, jazz-tempo excitement.

*Note you-viewpoint throughout*

*Good emotional description—vivid and exciting*

After settling in your magnificent Royal Orleans "home," you're off to dinner at Antoine's--spicy, bubbling Oysters Bienville, an exotic salad, trout almondine, selected fromages, all mellowed with a wine from one of the world's most famous cellars, and topped off with spectacular cherries flambe. A memorable meal sets you up for the night-spot tour of many-splendored delights--the spots where jazz was born, the undulating strippers, Pete Fountain's chic club, and the rollicking sing-along of Pat O'Brien's, where a tall, frosty Hurricane signals the close of a perfect evening. Then, just before returning to the hotel, time for a steaming cup of dark, rich French Market cafe au lait and some extra-special doughnuts.

*Reviews highlights of trip quickly yet thoroughly*

Saturday morning dawns bright and crisp--perfect for casual browsing through the "treasure" shops of the Quarter--the world of artists, antiques, and astonishing sights awaits you. From noon, you are escorted through some of the famous areas of the city--the Garden District (where the elegance of the past lives on), the lake area, and the most famous historical sights of the Quarter. Late afternoon finds you approaching famed Commander's Palace for an exclusive cocktail party and dinner. You'll practically hear the moan of ol' river steamers on the mighty Mississippi as you dine.

110 South Barkay
Bay, FL 45450
412-444-6758

CHAPTER 8 Indirectness in Persuasion and Sales Writing 245

Ms. Kathy Pettit
September 9, 1993
Page 2

Night ends back in the Quarter--with the particular pleasure of your choice. But don't sleep too late Sunday! Unforgettable "breakfast at Brennan's" begins at 11 a.m., and two hours later you'll know why it is the most famous breakfast in the world! Wrap up your relaxed visit with shopping in the afternoon; then the mighty Delta jet whisks you--back to Atlanta by 7 p.m. This perfect weekend can be yours for the very special price of only $375, which includes transportation, lodging, and noted meals. For double occupancy, the price per person is only $335. Such a special vacation will be more fun with friends, so get them in on this bargain--you owe yourself the pleasures of a Jet-Set Weekend in America's fun capital.

*Tells how need can be satisfied—gives details*

*Perhaps the action would be more effective if it were more direct, but it is persuasive*

This Jet-Set Weekend to dream about becomes a reality starting right now--a free call to the Delta Hostell at 800-491-6700 confirms your reservation to escape to the fun, the food, and the fantasy of New Orleans, city of excitement. The city is swinging--waiting for you!

*The final words link the action with the main appeal*

Sincerely,

Mary Massey

Mary Massey
Travel Consultant

**CASE ILLUSTRATION**  Sales Letters. *(Selling a Special Book on the Vatican.)*

Sent to subscribers of *National Geographic*, this four-page letter uses good emotional persuasion. Its appeal is to people who yearn to travel to exotic places. The words of the letter move the readers to the Vatican and through the experiences of being there. Then they tell how the readers can enjoy these experiences by buying the book.

---

NATIONAL GEOGRAPHIC SOCIETY
17th and M Streets N.W., Washington, D.C. 20036 U.S.A.

Office of the Senior Vice President

The year is 1991. But just for a moment, you feel the centuries roll back.

*[These preliminary sentences create an emotional need]*

Close your eyes and you can almost see Charlemagne kneeling to receive his crown as Holy Roman Emperor. Or an aging Michelangelo standing amid rubble, contemplating the still unbuilt, sky-size dome above.

You are in St. Peter's Basilica, heart of one of the most intriguing nations in the world . . .
Vatican City.

Dear Member,

Every now and then, you visit a place that leaves a lasting impression – and memories that linger long after you've returned home. The Vatican is one of those unforgettable places.

*[The letter opening continues discussion of the need, introducing the product that will satisfy it]*

As a devoted traveler, I have always believed that there is no substitute for being there — that is, before I saw the proofs of National Geographic's revealing new volume . . .

INSIDE THE VATICAN.

In some ways it's better than being there. Two veteran Geographic staff members — award-winning photographer James Stanfield and writer Bart McDowell — show you a side of the Vatican that you could never see if you were to visit as an ordinary tourist.

*[Then the words take the reader on a personal tour]*

You'll view sights and treasures that only a privileged few are ever allowed to behold. And have unprecedented access to the Vatican's museums and ceremonies, and to the people who live and work there.

Spend rare, behind-the-scenes moments with Pope John Paul II. Peer over the shoulders of restorers as they put life and color back into the Vatican's wealth of tapestries, mosaics, and paintings. Meet men and women you would never encounter on a public tour — cooks, gardeners, custodians, city officials — and get a taste of everyday life in this city-state.

Photographer James Stanfield spent nearly a year inside the Vatican, slowly

---

**CHAPTER 8**  Indirectness in Persuasion and Sales Writing

## CASE ILLUSTRATION (Continued)

gaining access to a realm that fiercely guards its privacy. His collection of pictures is as glorious as the Vatican itself.

The narrative draws you along in easy fashion as it reveals a fascinating story of a place that has been cloaked in mystery since the days of the Roman Empire. Author Bart McDowell goes beyond the tour guides and art books to show you the human side of the Vatican.

*Note the effect of headings to break up the long copy*

<u>Tour the most unusual country in the world</u>!

This will be no ordinary journey . . . because the Vatican is, without a doubt, an extraordinary nation.

Like an ancient fortress, the Vatican is walled in stone, except for the open expanse overlooking St. Peter's Square on the west. Although you could spend days touring museums, libraries, gardens, St. Peter's, and more, you can walk all the way around Vatican City in an hour or less!

Smallest state in the world, the Vatican counts no more than a thousand residents. Yet its leader – Pope John Paul II – reigns over a congregation of 906 million Roman Catholics around the world.

*Short paragraphs make the message appear to move fast*

Unlike other countries, citizenship in the Vatican is not an automatic right of birth. This special status is currently held by only about 400 people – the Holy Father, the Curial Cardinals, Vatican diplomats, the Swiss Guards, and permanent residents and employees.

You don't need a passport to cross the Vatican borders. However, no one enters through the gates of the Vatican without special permission. Private passes for specific destinations are dispatched to those who warrant them. Ordinary tourists are directed by the Swiss Guards to guided tours.

*The indented lines here and elsewhere break up the message and add interest*

    Personal protectors of the Pope, the Swiss Guards are a spectacle of Vatican pageantry. But don't be misled by their fanciful uniforms. You'll learn what it takes to join this elite force, and explore the Guards' heroic history.

INSIDE THE VATICAN even takes you to a department that evaluates candidates for sainthood: the Sacred Congregation for the Causes of Saints. In a fascinating interview with a monsignor in this office, you'll learn about the three "tests" a candidate must pass before canonization.

<u>Travel through centuries of war, intrigue, and discovery</u>.

Descend through twisting stone passages below St. Peter's to the ancient

## CASE ILLUSTRATION (Continued)

Roman necropolis, a site of archaeological treasure uncovered in the middle of this country purely by accident.

Tour elaborately frescoed funeral chambers from the days of Rome's greatest splendor — around A.D. 150. It's here also that you'll see what some scholars believe to be the bones of the first Pope, St. Peter. You'll read the story of this remarkable discovery.

Relive the Vatican's Renaissance days of glory and intrigue under the reign of the infamous Borgia popes. Discover how the Vatican was rebuilt after its brutal pillaging and destruction by Holy Roman Emperor Charles V in 1527.

Learn about the black market that operated within the walls during World War II. And hear — firsthand — the story of a German refugee who spent nine months within the Vatican hiding from the Nazis.

*Here and throughout, the writing is predominantly you-viewpoint, often with implied you's*

<u>Your personal pass to a treasury of cultural riches!</u>

Despite all you've heard, nothing prepares you for the abundance of riches found INSIDE THE VATICAN. This gorgeous volume takes you to . . .

Museum after museum of priceless paintings and sculpture. Exquisite architecture. Rooms full of breathtaking frescoes glittering with gold. An archive of rare documents that include the abdication letter of Queen Christina of Sweden, a treaty between Pope Pius VII and Napoleon, and a love letter from King Henry VIII to Anne Boleyn.

There will be no tour guide moving you along at a rapid pace. You'll stroll at your leisure through this unparalleled collection.

*The sales message is long, but interested readers get as much of the message as they need for making a decision to buy*

You'll talk with the man who may know Michelangelo's art best — the chief restorer of the Sistine Chapel ceiling. This expert spent more time on Sistine scaffolds than Michelangelo himself. As he cleaned away five centuries of candle soot and glue, the restorer came to understand Michelangelo the man and the artist.

<u>Meet John Paul II</u>

Indulge your curiosity about life behind the scenes and discover still another side of the Vatican that few are privileged to see.

Follow John Paul II through the year as he governs the affairs of the church, wields his influence as international diplomat, and bestows blessings upon his followers. By special invitation, you'll join him for Mass in his private chapel and at special Easter and Christmas celebrations. And accompany him to his summer retreat outside Rome.

## CASE ILLUSTRATION (Concluded)

You'll be hard-pressed to keep pace with this energetic and charismatic leader!

You'll discover why it's considered a special privilege to shop at the Vatican's one supermarket! Then tour the offices of L'Osservatore Romano, the quasi-official newspaper published in seven languages. Visit the Vatican Post Office, renowned among philatelists for its issues of beautiful stamps.

Tag along — at work and at play — with the boys who have been selected to attend the Vatican's prestigious altar boy school. And find out how their lives differ from those of other boys their age.

<u>Examine this magnificent volume — free in your home</u>!

Anyone with a traveler's wanderlust, a love of beauty, and a natural curiosity will find INSIDE THE VATICAN irresistible. It takes you to virtually every corner of the nation, revealing its wonders and even some of its secrets.

James Stanfield's unforgettable pictures capture the people, grandeur, and timelessness of the Vatican in spectacular color. The narrative penetrates the formality of an ages-old institution to reveal a dynamic nation.

You're invited to reserve this intriguing new volume now. Simply return the enclosed Reservation Card and your edition will be shipped for your free examination.

*This statement shows writer confidence, and writer confidence gains reader confidence*

<u>Send no money</u>. I'm confident that once you see this stunning book, you won't be able to put it down! INSIDE THE VATICAN offers you and your family many hours of delight and fascination.

*The action is direct and is followed by words that recall the appeal*

With no risk, and no obligation to buy, why not take a moment now — while you're thinking of it — and mail the enclosed card?

We look forward to having you join us on this remarkable journey.

Sincerely,

*Michela English*

Michela English

ME/ab

*A planned postscript suggests another reason to buy*

P.S. Remember, too, that this beautiful volume is a perfect gift for anyone who loves travel, history, or art. But it's available only by direct order through the Society.

**CASE ILLUSTRATION** Sales Letters. *(A Rational Message Selling Computer Software.)*

This sales letter is noteworthy for its fast-moving, hard-hitting copy. It quickly focuses on its intended prospects (users of Windows) and then highlights what the product will do for the readers. The presentation is rational and in words that clearly communicate the benefits. It closes with an appropriate drive for action, giving it extra strength with a deadline.

---

**WRITING TOOLS GROUP**

P.O. BOX 2030, CAMERON PARK, CA 95682 • 1-800-843-2204 • FAX: 1-916-677-3919

### SPECIAL UPGRADE OFFER — SAVE 70%

Introducing . . . Correct Grammar for Windows,
the only sentence checker that works
within <u>all</u> Windows applications.

Only $39 for current customers if you
order before September 30, 1991.

*The heart of the sales message is here for extra attention*

Dear Correct Grammar User:

If you're starting to use Windows, you'll want <u>Correct Grammar for Windows</u> — the only sentence checker that works within ALL Windows applications.

<u>Correct Grammar for Windows</u> has all the features you've come to depend on . . . plus all the features that make Windows applications so easy to use . . . PLUS new features to help you work faster and smarter.

Now you can:

- Check only the parts of your document you want to check (this is a real time saver).

- Create your own customized grammar rules with the new rule compiler.

- Sharpen your writing skills with an expanded help system, complete with a glossary of terms.

<u>Correct Grammar for Windows</u> installs automatically and creates its own icon on your Windows desktop. And like a desk accessory, it is always available from any Windows application.

<u>PC Computing</u> magazine has already named <u>Correct Grammar for Windows</u> the best Windows grammar checker available today. (The enclosed review tells you more.)

(please turn the page)

*Although these words are matter-of-fact, they gain the attention of Windows users*

*Good use of you-viewpoint in the rational presentation of the product's features*

**CASE ILLUSTRATION** (Concluded)

*Notice the explanation of savings*

*The drive for action is enhanced by the preceding guarantee . . .*

*. . . and by the deadline in the postscript*

**Only $39 for <u>Correct Grammar for Windows</u>**

*The special low price gets major emphasis*

Because you are already a Correct Grammar user, you can purchase <u>Correct Grammar for Windows</u> at the special, limited-time price of just $39, a savings of almost 70% off the regular list price of $199.

That's one good reason to order now.

Another reason: our 60-day money-back guarantee. If you aren't happy with the Windows version, simply return it within 60 days for a full refund.

Order your copy of <u>Correct Grammar for Windows</u> today, and put even more power, precision — and professionalism — into your writing.

Cordially,

*Camilo Wilson*

Camilo Wilson
Vice President

CW:wxj

P.S. This special offer expires September 30, 1991, so fax or mail the enclosed response form promptly. For faster service, call toll-free 1-800-843-2204 and ask for Operator 16.

## Using a Second Letter in the Mailing

A currently popular way of adding strength to the sales effort is to use a second letter (or note or memorandum) as a part of the mailing. This second letter is usually headed with a boldly displayed message saying something like "Don't read this unless you've decided not to buy." Apparently, the technique is effective. At least, direct-mail professionals seem to think it is, for they use it widely. An example of such a message follows.

Accompanying a letter selling subscriptions to a magazine, *The Texas Fisherman*, this second message reviews the main sales message of the letter. As you can see, it is really another sales letter. It even ends with a drive for action, and it has a postscript that intensifies the drive. This mailing was highly successful. Perhaps the second message contributed to its success.

*A second letter is often a part of the mailing.*

DON'T READ THIS UNLESS YOU HAVE DECIDED NOT TO CLAIM YOUR FREE TEXAS SALTWATER BIG 3 BOOK.

    Frankly, I'm puzzled.

    I just don't understand why every fisherman and boat owner in Texas doesn't run—not walk—to the nearest mailbox and return the enclosed FREE BOOK CERTIFICATE.

    Here's a guidebook that will bring you better times and better catches each and every time you head for that big beautiful Gulf. PLUS, you get a money-saving bargain on a subscription to THE TEXAS FISHERMAN—the news monthly that Texas outdoorsmen swear by. Month after month you'll be in on all the latest tips about where the big ones are biting. Each issue sports super-big photographs of fishermen grinning their heads off, holding up the catch for the day.

    And Dave Ellison is there each month telling you the latest there is about boating. Plus many other boating articles every month. Over 34,000 Texas boaters and fishermen are subscribing now. And the yearly renewal rate is just fantastic!

    But those 34,000 aren't important this morning. The important person to me today is YOU. I want YOU as a new subscriber—because I know you'll find more helpful advice here than in any other publication in the state today.

    Do yourself a favor. Send off your FREE BOOK CERTIFICATE now, today, while you're thinking about it. Have more fun and catch more fish!

                Sincerely for better fishing and boating,

                 Bob Gray, Publisher

P.S. Please hurry! We have only a limited supply of this FREE BOOK. Get yours now!

*Here is an example of a second letter.*

## SUMMARY

1. Requests that are likely to be resisted require an indirect, persuasive approach.
   - Such an approach involves developing a strategy—a plan for persuading.
   - Your opening words should set up this strategy and gain attention.
   - Follow with convincing persuasion.
   - Then make the request—clearly yet positively.

1. Use imagination in writing skillful persuasive requests that begin indirectly, use convincing reasoning, and close with goodwill and action.

CHAPTER 8 Indirectness in Persuasion and Sales Writing

2. Describe the choices available in determining the structure of a sales mailing.

3. Describe the preliminary steps of studying the product or service and selecting the appeals to use in a sales letter.

4. Discuss the choices of letter mechanics available to the sales writer.

5. Compose sales letters that gain attention, persuasively present appeals, and effectively drive for action.

- The request can end the letter, or more persuasion can follow (whichever you think is appropriate).
2. Sales letters are a special type of persuasive request.
   - Typically, a sales mailing contains a number of pieces—brochures, reply forms, and such.
   - But our emphasis is on the sales letter, which usually is the main item in the mailing.
3. Begin work on the sales letter by studying the product or service to be sold. Also, study your prospects, using marketing research information if available.
   - Then select an appropriate appeal (or appeals).
   - Appeals fall into two broad groups: emotional and rational.
     —Emotional appeals play on our senses (taste, hearing, and so on) and our feelings (love, anger, fear, and the like).
     —Rational appeals address the rational mind (thrift, durability, efficiency, and such).
   - Select the appeals that fit the product and prospects.
4. Before beginning to write, you determine the mechanics of the mailing.
   - Sales letters may use impersonal salutations (Dear Student), headlines rather than inside addresses, pictures, lines, and such to gain attention.
   - Your imagination is the major limitation on what you can choose to do.
5. Although innovations are frequently used, most sales letters follow this traditional plan:
   - The opening seeks to gain attention and set up the sales presentation.
   - The sales message follows.
   - In emotional selling, the words establish an emotional atmosphere and build an emotional need for the product or service.
   - In rational selling, the appeal is to the thinking mind, using facts and logical reasoning.
   - Throughout the letter, emphasis is on good sales language and the you-viewpoint.
   - All the information necessary for a sale (prices, terms, choices, and the like) are included in the letter, though references are made to details in the enclosures (brochures, leaflets, and so on).
   - Next comes a drive for a sale.
     —It may be a strong drive, even a command, if a strong sales effort is used.
     —It may be a direct question if a milder effort is desired.
     —In either case, the action words are specific and clear, frequently urging action *now*.
     —Taking the action may be associated with the benefits to be gained.
   - Postscripts often are included to convey a final sales message.

## QUESTIONS FOR DISCUSSION

1. Explain why a persuasive request letter is usually written in the indirect order. Could the direct order ever be used for such letters? Discuss.
2. What is the role of the you-viewpoint in persuasive request letters?
3. Discuss the relationship between a persuasive request letter and a sales letter.
4. What appeals would be appropriate for the following products when they are being sold to consumers?
    a. Shaving cream.
    b. Carpenter's tools.
    c. Fresh vegetables.
    d. Software.
    e. Lubricating oil.
    f. Ladies' dresses.
    g. Perfume.
    h. Fancy candy.
    i. CD players.
    j. Hand soap.
5. With what products would you use strong negative appeals? Positive appeals?
6. When could you justify addressing sales letters to "occupant"? When to each reader by name?
7. Rarely should a sales letter exceed a page in length. Discuss this statement.
8. Should the traditional sales-letter organization discussed in the text ever be altered? Discuss.
9. Discuss the relationship between the sales letter and its accompanying printed brochures, leaflets, and the like.
10. When do you think a strong drive for action is appropriate in a sales letter? When do you think a weak drive is appropriate?

## APPLICATION EXERCISES

1. Criticize the persuasive request letter below. It was written by the membership chairperson of a chapter of the Small Business Advisory Service, a service organization consisting of retired executives who donate their managerial talents to small businesses in the area. The recipients of the letter are recently retired executives.

    Dear Ms. Petersen:

    As membership chair it is my privilege to invite you to join the Bay City chapter of the Small Business Advisory Service. We need you, and you need us.

    We are a volunteer, not-for-profit organization. We are retired business executives who give free advice and assistance to struggling small businesses. There is a great demand for our services in Bay City, which is why we are conducting this special membership drive. As I said before, we need you. The work is hard and the hours can be long, but it is satisfying.

    Please find enclosed a self-addressed envelope and a membership card. Fill out the card and return it to me in the envelope. We meet the first Monday of every month (8:30 at the Chamber of Commerce office). This is the fun part—strictly social. A lot of nice people belong.

    I'll see you there Monday!

    Sincerely yours,

2. Criticize the sales letter below. It was written to people on a mailing list of fishing enthusiasts. The writer, a professional game fisher, is selling his book by direct mail. The nature of the book is evident from the letter.

    Have you ever thought
    why the pros catch
    fish and you can't?

    They have secrets. I am a pro, and I know these secrets. I have written them and published them in my book, *The Bible of Fishing*.

    This 240-page book sells for only $29.95, including shipping costs, and it is worth every penny of the price. It tells where to fish in all kinds of weather and how the seasons affect fishing. It tells about which lures to use under every condition. I describe how to improve casting and how to set the hook and reel them in. There is even a chapter on night fishing.

    I have personally fished just about every lake and stream in this area for over forty years and I tell the secrets of each. I have one chapter on how to find fish without expensive fish-finding equipment. In the book I also explain how to determine how deep to fish and how water temperature affects where the fish are. I also have a chapter on selecting the contents of your tackle box.

    The book also has an extensive appendix. Included in it is a description of all the game fish in the area—with color photographs. Also in the appendix is a glossary which covers the most common lures, rods, reels, and other fishing equipment.

    The book lives up to its name. It is a bible for fishing. You must have it! Fill out the enclosed card and send it to me in the enclosed stamped and addressed envelope. Include your check for $29.95 (no cash or credit cards, please). Do it today!

    Sincerely yours,

3. Criticize each of the following parts of sales letters. The product or service being sold and the part identification are indicated in the headings.

*Letter Openings*

**Product or service: a color fax machine**
a. Now you can fax in color!
b. Here is a full-color fax that will revolutionize the industry.
c. If you are a manufacturer, ad agency, architect, designer, engineer, or anyone who works with color images, the Statz Color Fax can improve the way you do business.

**Product or service: a financial consulting service**
d. Would you hire yourself to manage your portfolio?
e. Are you satisfied with the income your portfolio earned last year?
f. Dimmitt-Hawes Financial Services has helped its clients make money for over a half century.

*Parts of Sales Presentations*

**Product or service: a paging service**
a. Span-Comm Messaging is the only paging service that provides service coast to coast.
b. Span-Comm Messaging is the only paging service that gives you the freedom to go coast to coast and still receive text messages.
c. Span-Comm Messaging gives you coast-to-coast service.

**Product or service: a color fax machine**
d. The Statz Color Fax is extraordinary. It produces copies that are indistinguishable from the originals.
e. The extraordinary Statz Color Fax produces copies identical to the originals.
f. Every image the Statz Color Fax produces is so extraordinary you may not be able to tell a fax from an original.

**Product or service: Vermont smoked hams**
g. You won't find a better-tasting ham than the old-fashioned Corncob Smoked Ham we make up here on the farm in Vermont.
h. Our Corncob Smoked Ham is tender and delicious.
i. You'll love this smoky-delicious Corncob Smoked Ham.

**Product or service: a unique mattress**
j. Control Comfort's unique air support system lets you control the feel and firmness of your bed simply by pushing a button.
k. The button control adjusts the feel and firmness of Control Comfort's air support system.
l. Just by pushing a button you can get your choice of feel and firmness in Control Comfort's air support system.

*Action Endings*

**Product or service: an innovative writing instrument**
a. To receive your personal Airflo pen you have but to sign the enclosed card and return it to us.
b. You can experience the writing satisfaction of this remarkable writing instrument by just filling out and returning the enclosed card.
c. Don't put it off! Now, while it's on your mind, sign and return the enclosed card.

**Product or service: a news magazine**
d. To begin receiving your copies of *Today's World*, simply fill out and return the enclosed card.
e. For your convenience, a subscription card is enclosed. It is your ticket to receiving *Today's World*.
f. If you agree that *Today's World* is the best of the news magazines, just sign and return the enclosed card.

■ ■ ■ ■ ■ ■ ■ ■ ■ ■
## *LETTER PROBLEMS*
### *PERSUASIVE REQUESTS*

1. As a successful business leader in your city, you are a member of your Chamber of Commerce. At the Chamber's annual organizational meeting today, you were appointed chairperson of a committee formed to solve a problem relating to the area's homeless people. Specifically, your committee's goal is to find work for some of these unfortunate people.

    Labeled "Operation Bootstrap," the project will be conducted in cooperation with all the local shelters (Salvation Army, Helping Hand, and such). The shelter personnel will identify those among the homeless who are capable of helping themselves. In other words, they will screen the homeless and weed out those who cannot help themselves (the alcoholics, drug addicts, and mentally incompetent). Then your committee will help these people find work.

At the moment, the shelter personnel are screening the homeless in their care. So it is time for you to do your part of the operation—that is, to find the jobs. You hope to find the jobs through a letter you will write to local business leaders who are likely to have work needs that could be satisfied by the homeless. In the letter you will present your project clearly, and you will use the persuasion strategy that you feel is most likely to succeed in this case. You may use your imagination to supply any additional information you may need as long as it does not contradict the information given.

You will include in the mailing an addressed, stamped card on which the reader may respond. Spaces will be provided on the card for the number and types of jobs that can be offered. Also, you will give your telephone number with an invitation to call if there are any questions. Address the letter to the chief executive officer of one of the businesses on your mailing list.

2. Move the calendar ahead 15 years. You have been successful in your business career and as a result have been widely sought to serve on the boards of community service groups, charities, educational institutions, and such. Your latest such appointment is to the Advisory Board, College of Business Administration, Atlas University. This is one of the more prestigious appointments you have had, and you are proud of it.

At your first board meeting at Atlas University, you quickly demonstrated that you belonged by participating actively in the discussions. And when Dean Michelle Skinner asked for volunteers for the committee to plan the Career Day program for the College of Business Administration, you volunteered. Perhaps you really didn't know how much work was involved in this assignment, but you are finding out now.

As the words suggest, Career Day is a special event on campus designed to help business students find the career that is right for them. The day begins in the school auditorium where a well-known and successful executive presents the keynote address. Following a few words by the dean, the students then go to various rooms about the college for question-and-answer sessions with successful businesspeople in each of the career fields in business (accounting, retailing, banking, etc.).

Your assignment is to recruit the businesspeople who will perform on Career Day. First, you will secure the keynote speaker. For this assignment you will try to get Mr. Trey A. Selig, a highly successful entrepreneur and a graduate of Atlas's College of Business Administration. Soon after graduating 18 years ago, Mr. Selig went to work for an emerging computer software company. After a few years he founded his own company, Cutting Edge Data Systems. The company is now one of the industry leaders.

You will write a letter to Mr. Selig in which you will try to persuade him to give the keynote address. You haven't decided what appeal you will use, but you will consider all the possibilities and select the one you consider most likely to succeed. You will ask Mr. Selig to talk about "selecting the right career," suggesting that he illustrate with his real-life experiences. You can pay no honorarium, for the program operates on almost a zero budget; but you don't think Mr. Selig would want or expect one.

Supplying any other information you may need (as long as it is consistent with the information given), write the letter that will bring Mr. Selig back to his alma mater. Sign it as Chair, Career Day Program Committee.

3. A few days ago you were appointed membership chairperson for the Downtown Executives Club. As President Chad Berry explained, the club badly needs new members. "We have done all right after just one year in operation," he commented, "but we need more members if we are to function effectively. We have 87 members now. Our goal is to have 200 by the end of the year."

Your first step involved calling a meeting of your committee. After a two-hour discussion, the group decided to begin with a persuasive direct-mail campaign. A letter extolling the benefits of the club will be sent to every potential member that the current membership can find. (You will ask current members to submit names of qualified prospects.) You were elected to write the letter.

As you prepare to write the letter, you jot down these notes on things to include:

- Opportunity to meet and work with other executives. Good business contacts.
- Weekly luncheons at Benbow Hotel with educational programs planned to enhance professional development. Recent speakers include Dan C. Dodge, an internationally known authority on investment, and Monica Reimer, author of several business books, including the current best-seller *The Anatomy of Leadership*.
- Opportunity to participate in solving community problems (DEC's current activities involve

combatting gang-related problems through sponsorship of youth clubs and neighborhood recreation centers. Other projects are being considered.
- Prestige of membership (an elite organization open only to high-level administrators).
- Bronze membership plaque—a beautiful desktop ornament inscribed with the member's name and useful as a paperweight.
- Membership costs $50 per year plus cost of weekly luncheon ($8.50) at hotel.

You may think of other things to include before you finish the letter. Address it to any of the people on your mailing list. You will enclose a return mailing form, but you or one of your committee members will follow up with a telephone call to answer questions (and to apply subtle pressure, if necessary).

4. As the manager of a local restaurant owned by Ralston Purina, write John Regennitter, Vice President of Marketing, at the company headquarters and persuade him to add more vegetarian items to the menu. Suggest at least three items that complement your current menu.

Tell Mr. Regennitter that the image of the vegetarian is no longer that of a hippie but of a health-conscious individual. This trend toward vegetarianism is also being fueled by concern for animal welfare and the environment. Also, cite several big companies that you know have added vegetarian items to their menus and that have credibility with those at Purina's corporate headquarters. Among the better known ones you might cite are McDonald's, Walt Disney World, and American Airlines.

To support your request, use current data on the falling consumption per capita of red meat and the growing consumption per capita of fresh fruits and vegetables. Let Mr. Regennitter know that being sensitive to those interested in healthier eating will likely translate into more sales and, thus, higher profits. Be sure to call for specific action.

5. A recent article in *The Wall Street Journal* entitled "Fitness Center Gets Couch Potatoes Moving" caught your attention. Basically, it reported that fitness saves companies money. In fact, General Electric Co. estimated it saves up to $1 million a year in health insurance costs for employees who joined a fitness center. GE executives believe its fitness program had a bigger impact on those who were out of shape rather than on the healthy, superfit employees. Since GE is self-insured, every dollar not claimed in medical benefits is a dollar saved. Furthermore, the wellness programs also saved more than 700 workdays.

You think your company could benefit from a fitness program, too. You would like to see the company pay for health club memberships as well as provide some on-site facilities. You think hiring a reputable recreational therapist, such as Joan Marion, would increase employees' morale.

Write your persuasive letter with as much supporting data as you can gather. Address it to either your supervisor or to someone in the employee's union responsible for negotiating benefits. Choose the person you feel has the most influence on the decision makers.

6. Write a persuasive letter to In Focus Systems requesting that they sell their electronic projector to your school at cost. Their projector, called PC Viewer, is a computer-like display the size of a half-dozen notebooks. It rests on top of standard overhead projectors. Depending on the features, the selling price ranges from $1,000 to $6,000, far too costly for your school.

However, these projectors would be perfect in an educational environment. With cuts in school budgets and larger class sizes, projection equipment is becoming a needed but costly tool. The use of color and animation possible with this technology helps teachers deliver the material more effectively. It allows instructors to revise lectures easily, without the trouble of creating slides or overhead transparencies.

In persuading the company to sell you the projectors at cost rather than selling them to someone else for a profit, you'll need to give them as many benefits as you can think of. Some ideas you might incorporate in your letter include the name recognition the products will get in the classroom, inspiring today's students to buy them when they are in management positions in the future. You can also use the altruistic appeal of contributing to the improved quality of education for today's students. You could even offer your school as a live showroom for businesses wanting to see them in use.

7. As a member of the Greater North Texas Historical Society, you face a challenging situation today. Knob Hill, the highest point for 100 miles in all directions in the North Texas area, is currently being donated to the new Alliance Airport Authority by the Martin Foundation. Because of its historic and scenic significance to the area, you

believe that the site should be preserved and dedicated for better use.

Alliance Airport is to be constructed on 200 acres of land owned by the Martin Foundation just north of Fort Worth. The airport will be a major transportation hub for commercial air traffic in the area. Major airline service facilities and many manufacturing organizations are already planning to locate close to the airport. To be sure, the airport will provide many economic benefits to the region and the state. To assist with the economic development of the facility, the Martin Foundation donated the land for the airport facility. On the northern periphery of the land is historic Knob Hill.

A scenic point for all of the North Texas area, Knob Hill was the hideout in the mid-1800s for the notorious Sam Bass and his gang of outlaws. In fact, many of the trees on "The Hill" still bear carvings and initials made by the desperadoes as they sought a respite from their escapades. Moreover, the site provides a scenic and panoramic view of the landscape. And you believe this feature should be preserved and expanded upon.

As a member of GNTHS's long-range planning committee, you are going to prepare a persuasive request letter to the Martin Foundation that will ask them to donate Knob Hill to your organization. You will propose that Knob Hill be turned into an amphitheater for productions by regional musical and theater groups. If the foundation can donate land for the economic benefit of the area, you believe they can donate land and provide financial support for the cultural climate as well. You believe that an outdoor theater would certainly capture the scenic aspects of the area; and it would provide a place for spring, summer, and fall productions. Indeed, the cultural and aesthetic contributions would be many.

Think through the reasoning for the request; then develop a persuasive message that will move the reader to take the action you request. Address the letter to Mr. Jim Martin, President of the Martin Foundation.

8. Assume you are head of the accounting department at Petro Oil Company. You have been reading about the Adopt-a-High-School programs that various businesses have undertaken and you are quite interested in them. In fact, you think that an Adopt-a-High-School program would provide benefits for your department and the adopted school alike. Thus, you decide to try to get your 50 accounting employees to volunteer for such a program. Because there are certain negative aspects associated with their participation, you believe that a well-thought-out, persuasive request letter will do the best job of getting their cooperation.

The Adopt-a-High-School program you envision would send volunteers to a sponsored high school for two hours each week on company time. The volunteers would not be doing clerical work or bookkeeping activities for the school. Nor would they be in a teacher or curriculum evaluation role either. Rather, the accountants would serve in a support capacity to the school and, in turn, to classroom teachers.

In talking with a local high school principal, you determine that your people could counsel students, tutor, assist with classroom activities, serve as teachers' aides in any number of ways, and in general help with teaching activities in whatever ways that were needed. Operationally, you would permit participating employees two and one-half hours each week to work in the Adopt-a-High-School program. There would be one-half hour for travel to and from the high school and two hours for the actual conducting of activities. Right now, you believe that 9:30 A.M. to 12:00 noon on Fridays will be the designated time for the program. In addition, you will allow drivers a 25¢ per mile reimbursement if they drive their cars (you will encourage people to carpool).

For Petro, you believe that the publicity in the community will be a definite plus for the program. In the long run, you believe also that the program might attract good, young talent to the accounting profession. Indeed, if students can be shown how English, history, and other courses are important to accounting as a career, they might develop a keen interest in an area that could be developed throughout their college careers. And, of course, the high schools would benefit by having "free assistance" from your team of dedicated and college-trained staff.

All of these advantages and perhaps others can provide the basis for a smooth selling letter to be directed to your accounting department. You will ask for their participation in the program, but only after you sell them the benefits. Write the persuasive letter that will get you the requested action you want.

(Note: This situation could be adapted to other fields such as marketing, information systems, finance, personnel, etc. In addition, the situation could also be adopted to a program at a different

9. As Assistant Dean of Student Affairs at your college, you have an interesting assignment to complete. When students enter your school, either as freshmen or as transfer students, they must pay a $10 building use fee. This fee is generally used to establish a contingency fund for building maintenance, utilities, and such, to be used in the event that state or private sources fall short of the amount normally needed to maintain physical facilities. Whenever students graduate or drop out of school, the building use fee is refunded to them, provided it has not been used. To date, the school has had adequate funding to support the facilities without tapping the resource fund from student fees. Throughout their careers, most students forget about the fee until they graduate.

Because most students forget the money, you believe that they might be willing to donate the $10 to your college's Development Fund upon graduation—provided they can see the advantages of doing so. You've checked with authorities at your school, and they have OK'd your proposal to make the request. But now you must develop the persuasive reasoning to sell the students on taking the action. You feel that a direct approach asking outright for the money will not work. Thus, you will develop an indirect strategy, one that has reader benefits that precede your request.

As you start to develop this indirect strategy, you begin to think about why the students might want to contribute their money to your college. First, you believe that most of them would want good things to happen to their alma mater. And contributing money to the Development Fund would be a good investment in the college's future. The Fund provides student scholarships, research assistance to faculty, travel supplements, and such that enhance the college's goals. Second, you feel that contributing to the Fund would preserve the bonding process that began when the students first enrolled. The contribution would continue the ongoing relationship with the school that you want to preserve. Thus, pride in the school will be the central focus of your persuasive strategy.

With these ideas in mind, prepare a persuasive request letter that will convince graduating students they should donate their $10 fee to your college's Development Fund. (You may assume that a form for getting the student's permission accompanies your letter.) While each student's contribution may seem small, collectively the amount is significant. Address the letter to a person at your school who is graduating this semester. The letter would be sent to all graduating students.

## SALES

10. As the owner of your own advertising agency, today you were given the opportunity to write a sales letter for the school that trained you to write. The opportunity was given by Dr. Babs T. Stedman, who came to you presenting her need to publicize a program sponsored by the International Trade Institute, an operation at your alma mater.

Through the Institute, Dr. Stedman proposes to conduct a special program titled "How to Do Business in China." It will be conducted in Beijing, China, on the campus of the University of International Business and Economics (UIBE). Jointly sponsored by your school and UIBE, the program will be designed to do just what its title suggests: educate foreign businesspeople on how to conduct business in (and with) China.

Instructors for the program will be faculty members from UIBE, specialists from China's Ministry of Foreign Economic Relations and Trade, and Professor Stedman. All Chinese faculty members are fluent in the English language, and Dr. Stedman is an expert on international trade, especially with China.

The instruction will cover all facets of doing business with China. Major topics to be covered are the history and culture of China, nature of business in China (including operations of trading corporations, joint ventures, role of government, and current trends), areas of opportunity, making contracts and negotiating, handling the bureaucracy, and finance (banking, credit, pricing, insurance). In addition, those who desire will be introduced to experts in the Ministry of Foreign Economic Relations and Trade who will assist them in making contacts with the appropriate people for conducting business.

The program will begin on a Monday and end on the following Friday (you may select precise dates) and will include a total of 30 hours of instruction. Participants will arrive Sunday and will enjoy a traditional Chinese welcome banquet Sunday evening (complete with Beijing duck). They will enjoy a farewell banquet on Friday evening. During the week, time will be provided for short visits to the attractions in and near Beijing (Tiananmen Square, Great Hall of the People, Forbidden City, Summer Palace, Temple of Heaven). For those who choose to stay an additional day or two, trips to the Ming Tombs and the Great Wall may be taken at a moderate additional cost.

The participants will be housed in private rooms at the Great Wall Hotel, Beijing's finest. All breakfasts and dinners will be served here with choices of Chinese or Western food. Traditional Chinese lunches will be served on the UIBE campus. Transportation to and from the hotel will be by taxi; and local taxi service will be available to all participants at no extra charge throughout the week.

Total cost of the program is $6,200 from the West Coast (participants will choose the appropriate international airport). Included are all instruction, printed materials, lodging (private room), meals, and transportation (business class air). Of course, travel to the international airport, personal expenses, passport and visa expenses, and individual purchases are not included. The cost of the optional side trips to the Ming Tombs and the Great Wall are given in the brochure which you are enclosing. The brochure also describes other travel options that are available at the end of the course. The class will be limited to 24 participants.

Now you must write a letter selling the program to people on a list of executives Professor Stedman considers to be prime prospects. The letter will carry the primary message, but the details will be in the accompanying brochure (you don't need to write it, but you'll refer to it in the letter). You will develop the appeal (or appeals) you consider most effective in this case, and you'll describe the program clearly. Include a form for the reader to fill out and return along with a deposit of $500. If you need additional details, you may supply them as long as they are consistent with the information given. Address the letter to one of the executives on the list.

11. The Pierpoint Hotel, located in _____ (a major city near you), has a high occupancy rate on weekdays. On weekends, however, most of its rooms are empty. Pierpoint management has decided to try to attract weekend tourists as a means of correcting the problem. You, a free-lance copywriter, have been given the assignment of preparing a sales letter, with enclosures, that will do the job.

The main attraction of the weekend package Pierpoint will offer is price. All rooms will be discounted 50 percent. Rooms normally renting from $88 to $120 per night, double occupancy, will rent for $44 to $50; and suites normally renting for $150 to $240 will rent for $75 to $120. Included in the price are free newspaper and breakfast, delivered to the room. These low prices will be good for Friday, Saturday, and Sunday nights, although you suspect that most people will be interested in the first two nights only. In addition to the price savings, the hotel will offer its usual quality service, promising to pamper its guests at every opportunity.

For those traveling by air, the weekend package includes a 25 percent price reduction on flights with _____ (you determine the airlines). The hotel limousine will pick up all guests at the airport and will return them at the end of their stay at no charge. For those wanting a rental car, the package includes a similar price reduction with _____ (you select the rental company). All of these features are explained in a brochure that you will enclose.

What you can say to attract the weekend tourists to the city will depend on the location you have selected. But you will describe the best of what one can enjoy in that city—the theaters, sports attractions, restaurants, historic places, night spots, and such. You'll also emphasize the Pierpoint's own attractions. Foremost is the Top of the Point, the gourmet restaurant on the top floor. Here one can dine on the best _____ (French, Italian, German—you select) food while enjoying a panoramic view of the city and the relaxing music of Alfredo and his piano. Also at the hotel one can enjoy the heated pool just off the lobby, the gymnasium (with 1/8-mile track) in the basement, and the two tennis courts on the roof of the north wing.

In addition to the brochure noted earlier, the mailing will include a return form (to be checked and returned in the envelope enclosed). If the reader prefers, he or she can make all arrangements by telephone, so you'll note the hotel's 800 number in the letter. Prepare the letter for the signature of the Pierpoint's manager of marketing, Amanda Kessler. Address it to any person on the mailing list the hotel has assembled for this purpose.

12. As you sit at your desk beginning to write a sales letter for *Travel Adventure*, a new monthly travel magazine, you recall the words of the magazine's editor when you talked with him this morning. "*Travel Adventure* is not just another travel magazine. We have enough of them. It is a magazine for travelers who seek the unique, both when they travel and when they read about travel.

"*Travel Adventure* is not for those who choose the guided tours, frequent the tourist traps, and read the ordinary travel magazines. Its readers seek the extraordinary. They seek the travel secrets of the experts. They want to know about uniquely different places. They enjoy reading about these places in a uniquely different and lively style.

"In the magazine's pages will be articles about romantic, exciting places not yet discovered by tourists. And the magazine will report on the unique and great restaurants at these places. Yes, the magazine will appeal to those who look on travel as adventures in the really exciting things in life."

With the foregoing words in mind, you will write the letter that will attract the types of readers this magazine seeks. For class purposes, you may use your imagination to supply any specific facts you may need, but make them consistent with the information given. Assume that the letter will include a return envelope and an order card. The introductory subscription is $20 for 13 issues—$10 under the newsstand price. If the reader doesn't like the magazine, he or she may keep the first issue and you will refund the full subscription price. Address the letter to any person on the mailing list and sign it "Dustin O. Youngblood, Marketing Manager."

13. Your experience in the travel industry gave you the impetus you needed to venture out on your own. You've opened your own firm, specializing in the niche market of adventure travel. Now you need to write a sales letter to travel agents promoting your business.

You specialize in walking tours. Since you realize people have different levels of adventuresomeness, the tours will range from walking the beaches, mountains, and parks in this country to elephant trekking in Africa. One of the quality features of your business is its attention to detail. You plan for everything, including knowledgeable guides, medical matters, sleeping arrangements, visas, weather timing (the best you can), and such. This is particularly valuable on trips to countries like Zimbabwe, Botswana, and Kenya.

In your sales letter to the agents, describe at least three of your tours. Include tours varying in length, location, and cost. Also, include the incentives available to agents for bookings; you'll want them to be reasonable, but generous enough to get your business started fast so that it will be on sound financial footing as soon as possible.

14. As Butch Trevor, the owner of Trevor's True-Value Hardware Store, in Moline, Illinois, you've decided to stock PhoneMate's new answering machine in your housewares section. With the Christmas season approaching, you think it would make a perfect gift. Send a sales letter for PhoneMate's ADAM (ADvanced Answering Machine) to customers you've targeted as potential buyers.

Let your customers know this machine is state of the art. It uses digital signal processing to store signals in memory. It lets the user choose which message to listen to and how fast to listen. One can skip, repeat, or save specific messages. Also, because ADAM uses a computer chip, it has fewer moving parts to break. Of course, it has all the features of traditional machines such as call screening, remote playback, and such. During the Christmas season, you've decided to reduce ADAM from $249 to $199.

In your sales letter to customers present as many benefits as you can. Stress the reader viewpoint, putting the customer in the action whenever possible.

15. As a busy student who works part-time and goes to school full-time you are not very interested in spending time cleaning the house you live in. Actually, you like having a clean, orderly environment, and you don't mind cleaning up after yourself, but you don't think you should have to pick up after your roommates. So you and roommates agreed to hire a cleaning service that will clean every two weeks on a regular basis.

After searching the local papers for many days, you finally saw an ad for cleaners that appealed to you. The ad offered hard-working, Asian cleaners available on a regular basis. You arranged for them to clean your house; you've been delighted with the work they do. After getting to know them a little better, you learned that they are new immigrants to the United States. They clean both homes and businesses by day and by night. However, they would like to expand their business and aren't sure how to do this. While they are learning to speak English, their command of it isn't strong yet. So you volunteered to write a sales letter for them, one that would introduce their services.

Through carefully questioning them, you've determined they want to start expanding the residential side of their business since this work is done in the daytime. They recently named their business Chung's Cleaning Concepts. Write a letter targeted at residential customers that describes the work they will do. Stress the tasks you think are important to most residential customers. Be sure to include the idea that they have work references as well as how they can be reached.

16. Select a nearby city in your locale, region, or state.

Then assume that you are the director of economic development for it. One of the many aspects of your job is to promote and attract convention business to your city. Thus, you are going to prepare a sales letter that will persuade leaders of professional organizations, trade associations, and such to locate their annual conventions in your city.

To plan your letter for its greatest impact, you will need to select the appeals upon which you will base your sales strategy. On the one hand, you believe there are certain emotional appeals that you could use—enjoyment and excitement of the city for example. On the other hand, you feel that there are certain rational appeals, too—reasonable hotel rates, good convention facilities, and such. The idea, of course, is to choose the best appeals from both categories and to weave a unique package of appeals to sell the benefits of the city. You may assume that a brochure/booklet accompanies your letter. In the brochure/booklet are details about the city—cultural activities, sporting events, hotel availability, transportation, scenic attractions, etc.

Write the letter that will sell the city you choose. Address it to the first person on your mailing list: Ms. Cynthia Kopeki, Executive Director of the Society for Communication and Technology.

17. As business manager for the Metro City Symphony, you are quite concerned about ticket sales for the forthcoming year. Last year's sales dipped below those for the preceding year, but you thought that they would rebound for the coming year. Early ticket sales for forthcoming performances indicate that this will not be the case. So you decide to write a sales letter to potential season ticket purchasers. You have a list of season ticket holders for the past five years. You'll mail the letter to those who have not renewed their tickets for this season. And you'll mail to those on a list of "civic minded" newcomers to Metro City that you have purchased.

The performance series you've put together should whet any person's musical appetite. The Masterpiece Series, consisting of seven Saturday evening and seven Sunday afternoon performances, features the Metro Symphony and world-renowned instrumentalists in classical performances. The season finale will be Verdi's *Requiem*, performed by the Metro Grand Chorus and the Metro City Symphony.

In addition, the Virtuoso Series presents the Metro City Chamber Orchestra in eleven performances on Tuesday evenings with distinguished instrumentalists at each performance. And the Pops Series will be offered on seven consecutive Friday and Saturday evenings throughout the symphony season.

All performances are in the Metro City Symphony Hall, a showcase of beauty and acoustical elegance. Musical Notes, a pre-concert discussion with the symphony conductor, begins 60 minutes before the start of each Masterpiece and Virtuoso performance and is free to all ticket holders.

(You may use actual names of instrumentalists, vocalists, other performers, and conductors for various performances. Also, you may assume that four levels of prices exist for all series and all performances: Main Floor One—$100; Main Floor Two—$75; Mezzanine—$50; Balcony—$35.)

To begin work on the letter, you will need to identify the reasons that people might have for not purchasing tickets. Is it the quality of the performances? Lack of musical appreciation? Prices of tickets? Other activities that compete with scheduled performance dates? You'll explore these objections and others that you can think of. Next, you will need to develop appeals that will overcome the objections you have identified. These appeals will form the basis for the sales letter you will write.

Remember that you are trying to sell two things in the letter: (1) season tickets, and (2) a long-term musical interest in the Metro City Symphony. Orchestrate your letter with the quality that patrons will experience at the performances. You will include a descriptive brochure with your letter that will give dates, performances, and procedures to use to order tickets. Address the letter to Dr. Patricia Kozak, a new physician in Metro City. She is typical of the others who will receive the letter.

18. You are the owner of Financial Success Unlimited. Yesterday, you contracted with a nearby school district to provide 10½ hours of financial "seminars" for its teachers. But your contract is only for the right to offer the seminars. You will have to provide your own promotion to get the employees to sign up. Because the seminars will be conducted at night and because employees will have to pay for the package themselves ($39.95 for four sessions), you decide to write a winning letter that will sell the program to the 1,500 employees in the district.

Your overall objective for the sessions is to provide participants with a broad knowledge of the fundamentals of financial planning. You want persons who attend to be able to make informed choices about all types of investments concerning their financial futures. Your purpose will not be to use the seminars to increase the commissions you and your representatives receive.

Thus, you have designed three sessions for 2½ hours each and a fourth one that is optional to offer to the school employees. You also designed two series to run concurrently on consecutive Tuesday and Thursday evenings. In them, participants will learn how to minimize taxes, maximize investment returns, and provide secure futures for themselves and their families. They will learn which investments are safe and how to get the highest rate of return. And they will learn the various types of investments and how they work.

Specifically, you've designed the following format for the four sessions:

*Session 1*
Foundations for Financial Success
Putting Dollars to Work: The Basics

*Session 2*
Putting Dollars to Work: Advanced Concepts
Limited Partnerships
College Funding

*Session 3*
Tangible Assets
Retirement Planning
Risk Management

*Session 4* (Optional)
Personal Financial Planning Consultation

Each participant will receive a personal data form and audiotape, a seminar workbook (120 pages of exercises and illustrations), 10½ hours of instruction, and an optional planning consultation.

The $39.95 price is quite reasonable for the benefits received, you feel. But now you must convince the school district employees that it's worth their time, money, and effort to sign up for the seminar series. First, you need to develop appeals that will overcome objections the potential participants might have. Second, you will need to weave the appeals together to form a unified strategy for the letter you prepare. Write the letter and send it to the first person on your mailing list, Mr. Howard Shelton. You will include a brochure with your letter that will have a return card for signing up for the seminars.

## PART FOUR

# APPLICATIONS TO SPECIFIC SITUATIONS

**9**
*MEMORANDUMS*

**10**
*PATTERN VARIATIONS IN COLLECTIONS*

**11**
*STRATEGY IN JOB SEARCH AND APPLICATION*

# CHAPTER 9

# MEMORANDUMS

## CHAPTER OBJECTIVES

*Upon completing this chapter, you will be able to compose all the memorandum forms that are used within the organization. To reach this goal, you should be able to*

### 1
**Explain the variations in the form of memorandum stationery.**

### 2
**Discuss the wide range of formality used in memorandums.**

### 3
**Describe the primary differences between memorandums and letters written for similar situations.**

### 4
**Describe the primary differences between printed and electronic memos.**

### 5
**Write clear and effective memorandums for routine inquiries, routine responses, policies and directives, bad-news messages, and persuasive messages.**

### 6
**Explain the need for and compose memorandums to file.**

## INTRODUCTORY SITUATION

### to Memorandums

To introduce yourself to memorandums, go back to your hypothetical position with Pinnacle. Much of your work involves communicating with fellow employees. Of course, oral communication serves your needs most of the time, for the bulk of your communicating is with people near you or easily reached by telephone. But sometimes you must communicate within the organization in writing, especially if the person you want to reach is unavailable or in another location or if you want a permanent record of your communication. Writing the formal letters discussed in preceding chapters hardly seems appropriate in intercompany communication, for such communication tends to be informal. In intercompany communication, instead of writing a letter, you would probably write a memorandum, which is really an in-house letter. As you will see, the messages of memorandums are much like those of letters except that memorandum messages have a different physical arrangement and tend to be more informal. How to write memorandums is the subject of this chapter. ■

## THE NATURE OF MEMORANDUMS

The letter-writing instructions presented in the preceding chapters also apply to both printed and electronic memorandums (commonly called memos). Memorandums, of course, are letters written inside the organization, though a few companies use them in outside communication. Memorandums are primarily the written messages exchanged by employees in the daily conduct of their work. As you will see in Chapter 13, some memorandums communicate factual, problem-related information and are classified as reports. Those not classified as reports are the memorandums that concern us at this time. Nevertheless, much of the following discussion applies to both types.

> Memorandums are letters sent within the company.

### Variations in Form

Most large companies have stationery printed especially for memorandums. Sometimes, the word *Memorandum* appears at the top in large, heavy type. But some companies prefer other titles, such as *Interoffice Correspondence*, *Office Memo*, or *Interoffice Communication*. Below this main heading come the specific headings common to all memorandums: *Date, To, From, Subject* (though not necessarily in this order). This simple arrangement is displayed in Figure 9–1. Because memorandums are often short, many companies use 5 × 8½-inch stationery for them as well as the conventional 8½ × 11-inch size. As Figure 9–2 shows, memorandums are usually initialed by the writer rather than signed.

> Most large companies use printed memorandum stationery with *Date, To, From,* and *Subject* headings.

Large organizations, especially those with a number of locations and departments, often include additional information on their memorandum stationery. *Department, Plant, Location, Territory, Store Number*, and *Copies to* are examples (see Figure 9–3). Since in some companies memo-

> Some larger companies have additional headings (*Department, Plant, Territory, Store Number*, and such).

**FIGURE 9-1** A Popular Arrangement of Headings for Printed Memorandum Stationery

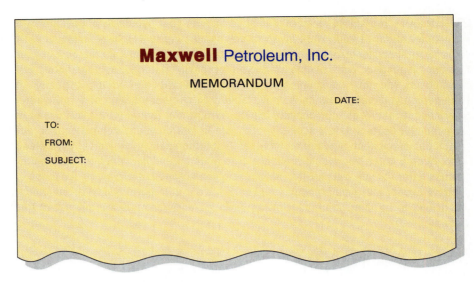

randums are often addressed to more than one reader, the heading *To* may be followed by enough space to list a number of names.

Not all companies have printed memorandum stationery. When employees in such companies write memorandums, they must type the headings along with the message. Individually typed arrangements of this kind vary as much as the printed ones. One of the most popular and easy to set up forms is displayed in Figure 9-2.

Today many companies use macros for memo headings in place of preprinted stationery and individually typed headings. A macro is a word processing feature that allows one to call up a string of commands with just a few keystrokes. Companies prepare macros both to improve productivity and to ensure consistency and quality.

Another variation in the memo form is the electronic memo. This memo is usually found on electronic mail (E-mail) systems. Most systems will prompt you for the variable components of the memo heading. Some will supply the date and sender's name automatically. Many systems allow the sender to create distribution lists for memos. Similar to macros, distribution lists identify a group of receivers whose names and E-mail addresses are entered automatically when the list command is invoked. For example, a regional sales manager might use this feature effectively to reach all the sales representatives with product updates, pricing information, new promotions, new policies, and such. Some systems allow businesses to design and arrange headings customized for the organization. You can see one in Figure 9-4. E-mail's timeliness and ease of use are helping the electronic memo grow rapidly in popularity and use.

---

Memorandum headings can be typed.

Macros for memo headings ensure consistency and quality.

Electronic memos are found on most E-mail systems.

---

PART 4 Applications to Specific Situations

**FIGURE 9–2** Illustration of Good Form for the Memorandum Not on Printed Stationery

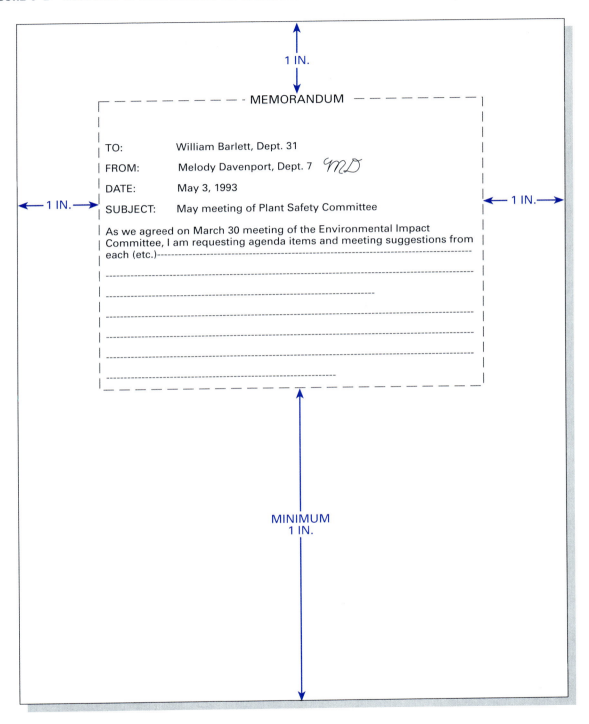

**FIGURE 9–3** Memorandum Stationery with Special Headings Adapted to the Needs of an Organization with Multiple Locations

## PENNY-WISE STORES, INC.

### MEMORANDUM

To:                                             Date:

                                                From:

Store:                                          Store:

At:                                             At:

Territory:                                      Territory:

Copies to:


**Subject:**   Form for in-house letters (memos)

This is an illustration of our memorandum stationery. It should be used for all written communications within the organization.

Notice that the memorandum uses no form of salutation. Neither does it have any form of complimentary close. The writer does not need to sign the message. He or she needs only to initial after the typed name in the heading.

Notice also that the message is single-spaced with double spacing between paragraphs.

**FIGURE 9–4** Illustration of cc:Mail, a Popular Electronic Mail System

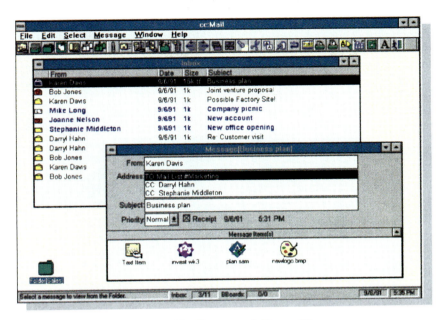

### Wide Range of Formality

Because memorandums are usually messages among people who work with and know one another, they tend to be informal. Even so, the degree of their informality varies somewhat. At one extreme are the highly informal, handwritten messages that workers write to one another. Such memorandums are typically one- or two-line messages—simple requests and responses that require little or no formality. For example, one worker might send another worker this simple, handwritten memorandum asking for certain file information: "Please send me copies of all invoices from the E. Y. Potts Company for the past 12 months." The second worker's response is also likely to be a brief, informal message, such as "Here are the invoices you requested."

*Memorandums can be informal notes.*

At the opposite end of the formality scale are memorandums written for high-level administrators by their subordinates. For example, a department supervisor who sends a memorandum to the board of directors, the company president, or such would obviously give the message more than the minimal degree of formality. Perhaps he or she would write in the third person rather than the first person used in most memorandums. (As we will see in our study of report writing, third person writing gives an impression of formality.) The typical memorandum falls somewhere between these extremes. It is written in a personal style (with *I* and *you* emphasis) and in conversational language.

*Memorandums can also be formal messages to top administrators.*

### Similarities and Differences in Memorandums and Letters

As we have noted, the principles for writing memorandums are much the same as those for writing letters. The reason is that the situations for both are very similar. Some memorandums ask for or give routine information;

*Memorandum writing principles are the same as those for comparable letters because the situations are similar.*

**CHAPTER 9 Memorandums** 273

*But memorandums differ from letters in two ways. First, most are direct, because they pertain to the company rather than to personal matters.*

*Second, in memorandums, unlike letters, the effect of words is of little concern.*

*Even so, memorandums should be courteous.*

*Electronic memos differ from printed memos in that they*

*(1) need to be more tightly organized,*

*(2) require greater care in constructing their subject lines,*

*(3) need to communicate their major contents early,*

thus, the direct order is appropriate. Others require the communication of negative messages; thus, the indirect order is appropriate. Still others require persuasion; in these cases, the indirect order is also appropriate.

Although memorandums and letters are much alike, they differ in two major ways. First, memorandums are more likely to be written in the direct order. Most letters also are direct, but an even greater percentage of memorandums are direct. As we have noted, indirect order in letters is appropriate when the reader will not receive the message favorably. Such occasions are relatively rare in memorandum writing.

Memorandums are usually direct because there is usually no reason for them to be otherwise. Most memorandums are mainly exchanges of information among people who are interested in the information only for work purposes. The information pertains to the organization's operation and is of little or no personal interest to the participants. For these reasons, there is rarely a need for preliminary explanation, justification, or preparation. The writer can best achieve the goal by getting right down to business.

The second major difference is that the writers of most memorandums have little need to worry about the effect of their words. By this we mean that they need not be heavily concerned about negative and positive language or about displaying the you-viewpoint. Instead of emphasizing the effect of words on readers, the memorandum writer's primary concern is for clear, straightforward communication—getting the message across quickly and easily. As you will see in the following pages, exceptions exist. Some memorandum situations require a delicate choice of words.

You should in no way interpret the preceding comments to mean that you should deliberately make memorandums rude, harsh, or cold. You should use the same courtesy in memorandums that all friendly people use when working together. The point of the preceding comments is that friendly people working together usually want and expect straightforward communication.

**Differences between Printed and Electronic Memos.** In addition to the preceding differences between letters and memos, electronic memos differ in six major ways from printed memos.

1. Electronic memos have a greater need to be tightly organized so that all related contents are in "chunks"—that is, within one screen size or less. The reason for this is that screens are limited to 24 or fewer lines. Readers like to see related information together rather than have to scroll through the message to find it.

2. Electronic memos require greater care in determining the contents of their subject lines. The reason is that readers of electronic memos must use the subject line's contents alone in deciding whether to read the message. For example, a descriptive or talking subject line such as "Assignments for the Company Picnic" would be more likely to attract the target readers than just "Company Picnic."

3. Electronic memos have a greater need to let the reader know the exact contents early in the message. While readers of printed memos can glance over a page or two of printed material easily and quickly, readers of

## Abbreviations and Symbols: Communication Tools of the Power E-Mail User[1]

While a written form of communication, E-mail's informality and speed make it seem closer to verbal communication. Power users of E-mail have adopted some conventions to give it more characteristics of verbal communication. For example, if the writer wants to lightly emphasize a point, the point will begin and end with the _underline_character. But if the writer wants to scream, the point will be made in ALL CAPS.

Power users will often try to speed up the written message by shortening commonly used phrases with abbreviations. Here is a sampling:

| | |
|---|---|
| btw | by the way |
| fwiw | for what it is worth |
| imo | in my opinion |

To add emotion to message, E-mail users often employ the following nonverbal symbols. Here are some that are read sideways.

| | |
|---|---|
| :-) or :) | = grin or smile |
| ;-) or ;) | = wink |
| :-( or :( | = frown |
| :D | = laugh |
| :* | = kiss |
| :X | = sealed lips |
| :'( | = sad or crying |

Before using this E-mail jargon, be sure your reader understands it or can interpret it easily. To the right reader, these abbreviations and symbols can communicate efficiently and effectively.

[1] "Electronic Punctuation and Hieroglyphics," *PC Publishing and Presentations,* August–September 1991, p. 40.

---

electronic messages require more time and experience greater difficulty looking at multiple screens.

4. Electronic memos have a greater need for subheads, which can be quite helpful to the readers as they scroll through the document.

5. Electronic memos should be organized with the most important chunks placed early in the document. Like newspaper readers, E-mail readers often read only the beginning part of the message.

6. If they are being composed on line rather than through uploading from another file, electronic memos should include a signal to the reader when additional pages are included. Symbols such as >> or !more! are used for this purpose. In fact, some E-mail systems automatically insert these symbols or page numbers. Some writers also let the reader know when they have reached the last screen with symbols such as ### or !END!.

> (4) have a greater need for subheads,
> 
> (5) should present the most important information early, and
> 
> (6) use signals to indicate additional pages.

Memos form a significant part of the communications used to coordinate the work in production units such as this.

## MEMORANDUMS ILLUSTRATED

**Look for the preceding points in these examples.**

Probably the best way to explain these points about memorandums is through examples. In the following pages, we review the basic types. First, we look at the direct-order forms, specifically at three variations: (1) the direct inquiry, (2) the direct response, and (3) the conveying of orders or work guidelines from administrators to subordinates. Called *policy memorandums* and *directives*, this third form has much in common with other direct-order memorandums, but it also has some unique characteristics. Next we review the indirect-order memorandum. Finally, we review a unique form of memorandum—the memorandum written to file. There are other forms of memorandums, but they are rare.

### Direct Memorandums—Routine Inquiries

**The problem chosen concerns a request for information about a meeting site.**

The direct-inquiry memorandum that we will review was written by Becky Pharr, an executive in a sales organization. The organization has an annual meeting for its sales force, and Becky's job is to plan it. This year she has tentatively decided to hold the meeting at Timber Creek Lodge, a recreational facility in the Rockies. Before making the final decision, however, she needs cost data. So she asks Remigo Ruiz, one of her subordinates, to get

"Before you write another memo, ask yourself: Does the environment really need another memo?"

*Victor's Funny Business*

the information for her. Actually, she made the initial request orally, but to avoid any misunderstanding, she decided to put it in writing.

Becky's memorandum typifies routine memorandums that seek information. Like an inquiry letter, it proceeds directly to the overall request and then systematically covers all the vital points. It displays logical arrangement and clear expression. Although the words are courteous, there is no need for delicacy to avoid offending the reader.

*The direct-inquiry memorandum generally follows the pattern of the direct-inquiry letter.*

DATE: April 1, 1993
TO: Remigo Ruiz
FROM: Becky Pharr
SUBJECT: Request for cost information concerning meeting at Timber Creek Lodge

As we discussed in my office today, will you please get the necessary cost information for conducting our annual sales meeting at the Timber Creek Lodge, Timber Creek Village, Colorado. Our meeting will begin on the morning of Monday, June 5; so we should arrange to arrive on the 4th. We will leave after a brief morning session on June 9.

Specifically, I want the following information:

- Travel costs for all 43 participants, including air travel to Denver and ground travel between the airport and the Lodge. I have listed the name and home stations of the 43 participants on the attached sheet.
- Room and board costs for the five-day period, including cost with and without dinner at the Lodge. As you know, we are considering the possibility of allowing participants to purchase dinners at nearby restaurants.
- Costs for recreational facilities at the Lodge.
- Costs for meeting rooms and meeting equipment (projectors, lecterns, and such). We will need a room large enough to accommodate our 43 participants.

I'd like to have the information by April 15. If you need additional information, please call me.

*The memorandum begins directly—with the objective. The necessary explanation follows.*

*Then the specific information needed is listed in logical order.*

*The memorandum ends with courteous words.*

### Clarity (?) in a Memorandum

Try following these instructions from a principal's memorandum to the faculty:

> First and second periods will meet on regular schedule. At 9:55 those in a one-story building with tickets will go to the auditorium. Those in a one-story building without tickets will report to the cafeteria with study material. At 10:35 those with second period in the main building will report to 3rd period if it is in the main building or to the cafeteria if 3rd period is in a one-story building. At 10:50 those in the auditorium will go to 3rd period in the one-story buildings or to the cafeteria if 3rd period is in the main building. At 11:35 those with 2nd period in a one-story building will report to 4th period class if it is in a one-story building or to the cafeteria if 4th period class is in the main building. At 11:50 everybody will be back on regular schedule.

---

### Direct Memorandums—Routine Responses

The case selected for the second form of direct memorandum—the routine response—is Remigo Ruiz's response to the preceding inquiry. Mr. Ruiz's goal is simply to present the information Ms. Pharr requested.

In this case, the information is for work needs and involves no personal feelings on the part of either communicant. For this reason, the memorandum appropriately follows the direct order. It presents its contents in an orderly way, arranging them by the general topics involved (transportation, room and board, and so on). The writing is simple and clear.

*Remigo Ruiz's response is the memorandum illustrated.*

*The direct-response memorandum should be direct, orderly, and clearly worded.*

*This example meets the requirements. It begins directly.*

*Then it presents the information—concisely and in good order.*

DATE:       April 14, 1993
TO:         Becky Pharr
FROM:       Remigo Ruiz
SUBJECT:    Cost information for sales meeting at Timber Creek Lodge

As you requested in your April 1 memo, here are the cost details for conducting our annual sales meeting at Timber Creek Lodge June 4–9.

Round-trip air transportation for our 43 representatives from their assignment stations to Denver would be $9,312 (see schedule attached). Ground transportation from Denver to Timber Creek Lodge could be by chartered bus or by rental car. The White Transport Company would provide round-trip bus transportation from the airport to the lodge for $25 per person, for a total of $1,075. Automobile rental costs for a midsize vehicle for the five-day meeting would be approximately $235 per vehicle, depending on the exact mileage. At one vehicle for every four people, we would need 11 automobiles, for a total cost of $2,585. The advantage of automobile rental is that the participants would have transportation throughout the week, although the Lodge provides limited shuttle service to Timber Creek Village.

Private room accommodations at the Lodge, including breakfast and lunch, would be $125 per day per person, or $625 for the entire meeting. The total for our 43 attendees would be $26,825. Dinners at the Lodge could be included for an additional $12 per person per day, making the per person total $685 and the total for all participants $29,405. However, several quality restaurants are in Timber Creek Village, which is less than a mile away. We would probably need to budget about $15 each for dinners away from the Lodge. The Lodge reports that its meeting room will easily accommodate our 43 participants. For a group the size of ours, the Lodge would provide the meeting room, projectors, lecterns, and such without additional charge. The Lodge recreational facilities (golf, tennis, swimming) would also be available without additional charge, except for equipment rentals.

I have enclosed the Lodge's current descriptive brochure, which should answer other questions you may have. If you need additional information in making your decision, I'd be pleased to get it for you.

Enclosure

*It ends courteously.*

### Direct Memorandums—Policy Memorandums and Directives

Internal written messages giving work rules, procedures, instructions, and the like are common in most large organizations. Called *policies* and *directives*, these messages from administrators to subordinates may be written as memorandums, though they sometimes take other forms. In general, such messages are formal documents and are more important than most internal communications. They are often compiled in policy manuals—perhaps kept in loose-leaf form in a notebook and updated as new memorandums are issued.

*Company policies and directives may be written in memorandum form.*

Policy memorandums and directives are more formally written than most internal communications because of their official nature. Typically, they follow the direct order. They begin with a topic (thesis) statement that repeats the subject-line information and includes the additional information needed to identify the specific situation. The remainder of the message consists of a logical, orderly arrangement of the rules and procedures covered. To make them stand out, the rules and procedures are often numbered or arranged in outline form.

*They should be somewhat formal, direct, clearly written, and well organized.*

Because policy memorandums and directives must be understood by everyone in the organization, you must be concerned with adaptation and clarity of expression. Thus, you should follow the clear-writing instructions presented in Chapters 2 and 3. For the same reason, you will probably put extra effort into achieving your goal, perhaps making a number of revisions before producing an acceptable draft. As you review the contents of the following examples, you will understand why such care is necessary.

*In writing them, emphasize clarity. Revise to improve.*

The first example is a memorandum from the president of a company that faces a serious energy crisis. The memorandum outlines procedures for reducing energy use. In addition, it requests cooperation in reducing costs through voluntary conservation actions.

*The first policy memorandum example formulates a plan for reducing energy use.*

Note that the memorandum begins directly with words that tell the nature of the message. The points covered are listed for emphasis and for easy understanding by employees at all levels. The memorandum ends with the president's personal appeal for compliance.

DATE:     June 10, 1993
TO:        All Employees
FROM:    Terry Boedeker, President
SUBJECT: Energy conservation

To help us through the current energy crisis, the following conservation measures are effective immediately.

*The beginning is direct and immediately identifies the situation.*

- Thermostats will be set to maintain temperatures of 78 degrees Fahrenheit throughout the air-conditioning season.

Businesses with multiple locations send many of their memos by fax.

*Clear writing and listing result in good readability.*

- Air conditioners will be shut off in all buildings at 4 P.M. Monday through Friday.
- Air conditioners will be started as late as possible each morning so as to have the buildings at the appropriate temperature within 30 minutes after the start of the workday.
- Lighting levels will be reduced to approximately 50 to 60 footcandles in all work areas. Corridor lighting will be reduced to 5 to 10 footcandles.
- Outside lighting levels will be reduced as much as possible without compromising safety and security.

*Separate listing of other measures gives order and enhances understanding.*

In addition, will each of you help in conservation areas under your control? Specifically, I ask that you do the following:

- Turn off lights not required in performing work.
- Keep windows closed when the cooling system is operating.
- Turn off all computer monitors and printers when not in use.

*Closing personal remarks add to effectiveness.*

I am confident that these measures will reduce our energy use significantly. I will appreciate your efforts to follow them.

The same message written for transmission by electronic mail appears in Figure 9–5. Note the differences between the two documents.

**FIGURE 9–5** A Memorandum Prepared for Transmition by Electronic Mail

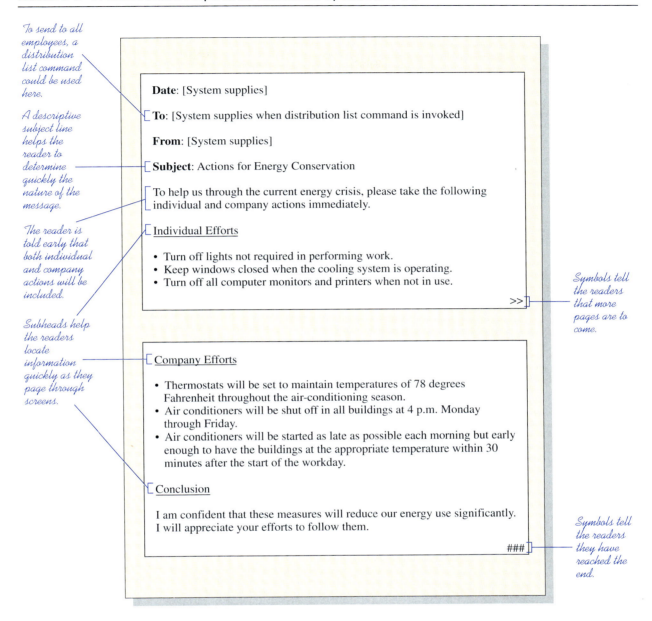

The second example is a policy memorandum that has been written for the company's policy manual. As indicated in the preliminary information, the memorandum replaces a previous one. It begins with a subject line that clearly states the policy area covered. The introductory sentence repeats this identification and presents the remaining necessary information. Then

The second policy memorandum example concerns office and working hours.

the memorandum covers the policy areas clearly and systematically. Note that the areas of coverage are identified by topic headings.

DATE: July 12, 1993
TO: All Employees
FROM: Frances Cass, Plant Manager
SUBJECT: Office and working hours (replaces memorandum dated May 9, 1990)

> *The beginning notes the specifics of the policy areas covered.*

Policies concerning office and working hours at the Bayfield plant are as follows, effective today:

1. *Regular working hours.* The normal workweek begins at 12:01 A.M. Sunday and ends at midnight the following Saturday. Administrative and department offices will be open from 8 A.M. to 5 P.M. Monday through Friday, except on designated holidays. Offices will remain open during the noon hour each working day, with at least one person on duty. Offices may be open at other times with the approval of the division superintendent concerned.

> *Topic captions identify the policy areas.*

2. *Service Department.* Service Department personnel will normally work Monday through Friday. Because of the nature of their work, however, they may have a different work schedule and may be subject to call on a standby basis for emergencies. The superintendent of this department will periodically issue a standby schedule, which will be given to each service employee.

3. *Lunch periods.* Employees are entitled to a maximum of one hour for lunch. Supervisors will schedule lunch periods to ensure that work will be done efficiently.

> *The writing is clear and adapted to mass readers.*

4. *Rest periods.* All full-time employees are entitled to 15-minute rest periods for every four-hour period worked during the workday. Supervisors should schedule all work breaks so that the work is done efficiently. Normally, one break should be taken in the morning and one in the afternoon. When there is an unusually heavy workload or when a crisis occurs, supervisors may request that employees not take their breaks.

5. *Observance of regulations.* Each employee must observe the regular work schedule for his or her work location. Any person who is consistently late for work or who does not return from rest or lunch periods promptly is subject to disciplinary action.

The employee is responsible for notifying the supervisor when he or she will be late or absent from work. An employee who must leave work early will make the necessary arrangements in advance with the supervisor.

## Indirect (Bad-News) Memorandums

> *Although rare, memorandums refusing personal requests are occasionally written.*

Memorandums that convey bad news are not rare in business. What is rare are bad-news memorandums that require indirect, diplomatic treatment. As we have noted, most memorandums communicate information of little personal concern to the people involved. Thus, most memorandums can be written in the direct order and with little or no concern for tactful handling. But there are exceptions—memorandums carrying bad news that concerns the reader personally. It is memorandums of this relatively rare type that we will now illustrate.

> *They should be handled indirectly and tactfully.*

Like the indirect-letter situations reviewed previously, such personal bad-news messages require tactful handling. This means treating them indi-

PART 4 Applications to Specific Situations

## Letters

Written by an anonymous business communication student, the following is presented with apologies to Joyce Kilmer and his "Trees."

> I think that I shall never see
> A letter worthy of a B.
>
> A letter whose contents are blessed
> With what my professor thinks is best;
>
> A letter that skillfully gives a nay
> As positively as a yea;
>
> A letter whose words are clear and fair
> yet conversational and debonair.
>
> Upon which no red marks are lain;
> Which gives me joy instead of pain.
>
> Letters are written by fools like me,
> But only God could make a B.

---

rectly—paving the way for the bad news with explanation, justification, or such. It means watching words carefully, trying to emphasize the positive over the negative. It means writing from the reader's point of view with consideration for his or her best interests. These and other points discussed with respect to indirect letters also apply to this type of memorandum.

Illustrating this memorandum type is the case of an administrator who must deny a subordinate's request for a change in vacation dates. Two reasons support the denial, both of which are specified in the company's contract with the union. First, no more than 10 percent of the workers in any department can be on vacation at one time. Second, seniority determines who gets preference if more than 10 percent seek the same vacation time.

*A denial of a change in vacation dates illustrates this type of memorandum.*

As you can see, the following memorandum handles the situation indirectly and with concern for the reader's feelings. In general, it follows the principles described for bad-news letters.

DATE:     May 24, 1993
TO:       Jerry Cunningham
FROM:     Albert A. Morton
SUBJECT:  Your request for change in vacation dates to July 8–21

*Subject line identifies without suggesting bad news.*

Your reasons for requesting a change in vacation dates are quite reasonable and certainly deserve consideration.

In evaluating them, I must consider more than merit. I must also follow the rules carefully specified in the contract agreement between the company and the union. These rules specify that no more than 10 percent of any department's workers can be on vacation at one time. This means a maximum of two for your department. The contract also specifies that seniority will determine vacation priorities.

*This example begins indirectly and pleasantly, leading to the explanation.*

*The explanation is positively worded, clear, and convincing.*

In addition to you, both Rita Gann (18 years) and Beatrice Plachy (14 years) have requested vacations for July 8–21. Because both of them have more service than your 10 years, the best I can do for you is give you the July

*The refusal follows, in the positive form of an alternative vacation time.*

22–August 4 period. These dates would permit you to do at least some of the things outlined in your request.

Please consider these dates. Then let me know whether they are satisfactory. I assure you that I'll do whatever I am permitted to help you with your vacation planning.

*The ending is positive and friendly.*

## Indirect (Persuasive) Memorandums

Although persuasive memorandums are rare, those that are written are likely to be highly important. Usually they concern a company project, proposal, or such that involves employee participation (a fund drive, company function, or safety campaign). In general, they follow the pattern of the persuasive letter. They present a persuasion strategy designed to move the reader to accept whatever is being promoted. Their pattern is indirect, beginning with attention-gaining words that set up the persuasion strategy. Then they present this persuasion strategy, leading to the request for action.

*Persuasive memos are rare. They follow the pattern of a persuasive letter.*

Following is an example of a memorandum written to employees of an oil company persuasively seeking participation in the company's education program. Perhaps the memo is too brief, but there may be merit in the brevity. The writer's plan was to get the reader into the office. As the writer viewed the situation, a thorough letter would have been too long to hold interest.

*Following is an example of a persuasive memo.*

DATE:      August 22, 1993
TO:        All Employees
FROM:      Cindy VanVoorhes
           Education Director
SUBJECT:   Your professional development

Do you know any of these people—Monica Chavez, Hal Worley, Michael DuBoise, Pam Hawley, Stephanie Tomacek, Brad Benton?

They are your fellow employees, and they have two things in common. One, they were recently promoted to highly responsible positions. Two, they have all been participants in our Career Support Program.

*Use of familiar names gains attention and sets up the persuasion.*

As you may know, the Career Support Program is Gaston Petroleum's way of helping you develop professionally—completely at Gaston's expense. Through the program Gaston pays all costs (tuition, fees, and books) of your participation in the night program at City Tech.

*Explanation of the program is persuasive.*

All you need to do is follow an approved curriculum designed to help you professionally and satisfactorily meet course requirements (grade of C or better). It's as simple as that. You study. You learn. Gaston pays. And you benefit professionally—maybe through promotion.

*After the persuasion the readers are told what they must do to reap the benefits.*

I'd like to tell you more about how the Career Support Program can help you. Just drop by my office (20A, Personnel Suite) any time during work hours. I'll give you the details. Although I won't be able to promise you a promotion, I will promise to help you grow professionally.

*The ending reemphasizes the major benefit.*

## The Memorandum to File

Memorandums are often written for the writer's file. Such *memorandums to file* are a means of making a record of events, activities, and such and of retaining this information for future use. For example, an executive who is having difficulties with an errant subordinate might record the subordinate's errors in memorandums as they occur and address the memorandums to file. Later, the executive could review these memorandums in building a case for disciplinary action. Or an executive who participates with other executives

*Executives write memorandums to their files as records and reminders.*

in a meeting at which no record is kept might record the events of the meeting in a memorandum addressed to file. The information would then be stored for future reference.

The following memorandum illustrates the second case. Here, copies might be routed to all the participants both for personal use and for confirmation of the events of the meeting.

DATE:     October 19, 1993
TO:       FILE
FROM:     Cindy Boros
SUBJECT:  Meeting on problems with in-house training program

On October 17, 1993, Charles Davidson, Diane Kennedy, and Peter Dominguez met in my office to review the progress of our in-house management training program.

*The direct beginning identifies the particulars.*

Diane and Peter reported that their employees expressed strong dissatisfaction with the first course conducted. Charles and I reported less negative (although not entirely positive) experiences from our employees. The evidence submitted clearly suggested that Dr. Warren Miles (the course instructor) talked "over the heads" of the participants. The subject matter, we concluded, was not too difficult for the employees involved.

*A concise summary of the event follows.*

We also agreed that in selecting the next instructor we will carefully consider the levels of subject matter and instruction. In addition, we agreed that I will monitor the instruction throughout the next course. Through counseling the instructor, I will make every effort to avoid the mistakes made in the past.

*This part emphasizes the achievements.*

# SUMMARY

1. Memorandums (letters written inside a company) usually are processed on special stationery.
   - Typically, *Memorandum* appears at the top and *Date, To, From,* and *Subject* follow.
   - Large organizations often include more information (for example, *Department, Plant, Location, Copies to, Store Number*).

*1. Explain the variations in the form of memorandum stationery.*

2. Most memorandums are informal, but they can be formal.
   - Simple inquiries, responses, and such from and to employees are informal.
   - Messages from employees to higher authorities in the organization are likely to be formal.

*2. Discuss the wide range of formality used in memorandums.*

3. The situations for writing memorandums and letters are much alike, but there are two differences.
   - Memorandums are more likely to be written in the direct order.
   - Memorandums frequently have less need for you-viewpoint and positive language.

*3. Describe the primary differences between memorandums and letters written for similar situations.*

4. Electronic memos differ from printed memos in the following ways, primarily because of screen limitations:
   - They have a greater need for tight construction.
   - They have a greater need for carefully worded subject lines.
   - They have a greater need to identify contents early.
   - They have a greater need for subheads.
   - They have a greater need to present their most important information first.
   - They contain signals to indicate additional pages.

*4. Describe the primary differences between printed and electronic memos.*

5. Write clear and effective memorandums for routine inquiries, routine responses, policies and directives, bad-news messages, and persuasive messages.

6. Explain the need for and compose memorandums to file.

5. Generally, write memorandums as you would a comparable letter.
   - Use the direct pattern for routine inquiries and responses, policy memorandums, and directives.
   - Use the direct pattern even for some bad-news messages—those that do not involve the reader personally.
   - Use indirectness for bad-news memorandums that personally involve the reader.
   - Use the indirect pattern for persuasive memorandums.
6. Memorandums to file are written for the writer's own file.
   - They are records of events, activities, and such.
   - They help the writer recall these happenings.

## QUESTIONS FOR DISCUSSION

1. Explain the logic of using negative words in memorandums that you would not use in letters carrying similar messages.
2. Although bad-news memorandums are not rare, indirect bad-news memorandums are. Explain.
3. Discuss and justify the wide range of formality used in memorandums.
4. Memorandums differ much more than letters in their physical makeup. Explain and discuss.
5. Discuss how electronic memos differ from printed memos. Include the concept of chunking.
6. Discuss the special need for clear writing and adaptation in policy memorandums and directives.

## APPLICATION EXERCISES

1. Point out the weaknesses in this policy memorandum. The writer's objective is to establish a clear policy for hiring and terminating employment.

   TO:      All Administrators
   FROM:    Ada H. Horton, President
   DATE:    June 7, 1993
   SUBJECT: Hiring and terminating policies

   Since joining ElectroTech 16 years ago, I have witnessed every conceivable discrepancy in our employment policies, racism, sex discrimination, nepotism—you name it. It is time that you stop these practices. Henceforth you will rigidly adhere to the following rules.

   Do not consider race, religion, sex, or nationality because they have no relationship to job performance. When selecting new employees, make sure that all qualifications are considered. Do not consider physical ability or age. However, when the job requires it, you can consider physical ability to perform. For similar reasons you can consider age. Use the doctor's report for these decisions and do not make these evaluations yourself. Always hire the best applicant for the job.

   When you have to reduce your force, do not play favorites as has sometimes been done in the past. Always discharge first the less competent. Job performance appraisals should determine which employees to discharge. When you have two or more with equal performance ratings, seniority should be used. Job terminations based on poor performance or for disciplinary reasons must be supported by evidence and must be approved in advance by our Personnel Review Committee.

   A personnel action memo is required every time we hire or fire. Send it to Personnel explaining what was done and why. Include all supporting evidence upon which the decision was based.

2. Criticize this memo informing an employee that she was not selected for promotion to a higher position in the organization.

   TO:      Alma DuPuis
   FROM:    Monty Duke
   DATE:    May 17, 1993
   SUBJECT: Your application for position of personnel director

   One of my most difficult assignments is having to tell a colleague that he or she did not get a promotion sought. But it is my duty to do so. Therefore I must report that you were not judged best qualified for the position of personnel director.

   The committee recommended Don James. They considered Don to be best qualified because of his long and distinguished record with us. I am confident you would agree if you saw his credentials.

   Although you were not selected, the committee wants you to know that they appreciate your interest in the position and your years of service to the company.

## MEMORANDUM PROBLEMS

### DIRECT MEMORANDUMS (INQUIRIES)

1. Play the role of vice president for administration for the Davidson-Brooks Company, a major manufacturer of automobile parts. You are in the process of hiring a new director of training. After reviewing more than 40 applications, you selected two (Heather T. Raska and Chris O. Moorman) and invited them to the plant where you and other members of your staff interviewed them.

   Frankly, you liked both candidates; so the decision won't be easy. Perhaps your staff members can help. Each of them spent an hour with each candidate, and they had copies of the candidates' résumés and reference letters to inspect. So you will ask for their input. You will write them a memorandum asking them to evaluate and compare the candidates on the specific points around which you will base your decision.

Your primary evaluation points are (1) knowledge of training and (2) experience in training. As the résumés show, both candidates have good records in these areas. Perhaps the staff can detect differences that you didn't find. A third major point upon which you will base your decision is personal qualities—especially the ability to get along with and work with people. You know it is hard to make such evaluations after only one meeting, but each of the staff members formed some impressions, and collectively these impressions are better than yours alone. In addition, you'll want the staff members to give an overall evaluation—a recommendation of which one to hire. Also, you'll include your usual blanket question covering anything else that might have been detected that you should consider.

If you need additional data, you may supply it; but be consistent with the facts given. Address the memorandum to your production manager.

2. As assistant to the president at the home office of the Zodiac Electrical Products Company, you have been called into the boss's office and given an assignment. Her words are as follows: "They had a fire last night at our Angleton plant—destroyed a wing of the warehouse I'm told. Nothing catastrophic, but I'd like to know more of the details. Prepare a memo for my signature and send it by fax right away.

"I want to know the cause of the fire and the extent of the damage. Also, I want to know how much it will cost to repair the structure. I know they can give me only a preliminary estimate, for it will take more time to assess the damage. Most important of all, I want to know what effect the loss will have on our delivery and production commitments for the weeks ahead. We need to know how much, if any, of their production to shift to our other plants."

Prepare the memorandum in the name of your boss, Nicole Wrather, and send it to the plant manager at Angleton. Ask for a response today.

3. As president of Northstar Oil Company, Los Angeles, you are presently thinking about details of the upcoming executive retreat of your top executive team. Over the years, you've found that these semiannual retreats are immensely important to your organization. It's a time twice a year when your executive officers can provide their collective thinking to strategic decision making and planning. It's also a time when the team can withdraw from the operational demands of the workplace and develop comraderie, bonding, and cohesion.

To achieve these goals, you will need a special place to meet. And to help you decide on that place, you will ask your administrative assistant to investigate possible locations for your retreat. Just recently, you read in the *Los Angeles Executive News* (a monthly newspaper) about the availability of many retreat centers in Arizona. You'll ask your assistant to research these locations, but you will not exclude others elsewhere that might be good.

When you first began holding these retreats, you met at your corporate headquarters. You found out quickly, however, that such conditions were not appropriate for the planning sessions. Thus, you have been meeting in the Los Angeles area at local hotels. But still these sites are not conducive to the goals you desire for the retreats. Accordingly, you now would like to move to a more distant location. For the upcoming retreat, there will be 10 people attending. The executive team will fly to the selected location prior to the actual retreat beginning on Monday morning. The team will fly home at the conclusion of the retreat on Friday afternoon. You prefer to schedule the retreat for the third week in January. And no more than two executives may travel on any one flight.

It is your philosophy that the executives should feel physically removed from the workplace. At the same time, the location should be close enough so that travel costs are not prohibitive. In general, you want a relaxed atmosphere without other disruptive groups or loud conventioneers. You want seclusion but not total isolation.

Physically, you'll need conference facilities with state-of-the-art audiovisual and communications support systems. And you'll want recreational choices without huge crowds so that the team can bond with one another. Along with the seclusion of the facilities, you want a staff that will assure your meetings are indeed private from industrial pirating.

With these points in mind, write the memo to your assistant, Julio Faleiro. You will need his response by next week so that you can make your decision for the January retreat.

## DIRECT MEMORANDUMS (RESPONSES)

4. As director of marketing for the Davidson-Brooks Company, write a memorandum responding to a request made by the vice president for administration (see Problem 1 for background information). You interviewed both Heather T. Raska and Chris O. Moorman and you studied their résumés and reference letters carefully. Both appear to be good candidates for the job of training director. The decision will be difficult. You'll do your best to help make the right choice.

   On the matter of experience, you judge Moorman to have a slightly better record. He spent virtually all of twelve working years in training—the first five as a college instructor and the last seven on his current assignment as assistant training director at Fogleman Electric. Raska's record is also good, but it is less extensive—seven years, all as a training specialist with Northern Lights Petroleum. According to her references, she has performed exceedingly well; but Moorman's references are equally high on his work.

   On the matter of job knowledge, you cannot favor one over the other. Both impressed you as being well acquainted with the work, and both had innovative ideas about running the program at Davidson-Brooks. Perhaps Moorman has the better educational background—B.S. in business (with honors) and an MBA as compared with Raska's B.S. in general studies.

   If there is any significant difference between the two, it is in the personal qualities you observed during the interview. You judged Moorman to be more outgoing and personable—quick wit, friendly, likeable. Raska also impressed you with her personal qualities—alert, friendly, serious. You just give Moorman an edge in this area. Your review of the reference letters shows that both candidates were rated high in personal qualities.

   On the basis of these impressions you will recommend Moorman, but you'll make it clear that the decision is close. You'd be pleased to work with either candidate.

5. Assume the role of manager of the Zodiac Electrical Products plant at Angleton and answer the memorandum you received by fax from headquarters (see Problem 2 for background information). You will respond with the best information you have about last night's fire in Warehouse Building 917B. It will take time to get more precise and correct information.

   Preliminary findings by the fire marshall indicate that the fire started in the warehouse manager's office, probably from a cigarette discarded in a wastebasket. You expect a final report by tomorrow.

   Fortunately, the fire was detected early and was contained in one corner of the building where component parts for refrigerators were stored. No finished manufactured products were damaged. As additional component parts are stored in the production areas, you expect no difficulty in meeting orders for finished products. Already you have found replacement components at the White Water plant, and they are being shipped to you right away. Thus, there will be no adverse effect on production or deliveries.

   Damage to the building is moderate—about $45,000, your building superintendent estimates. You have not had time to get an outside estimate. Value of the refrigerator components destroyed is around $72,000. Most of the loss is covered by insurance.

   You may supply additional facts that are consistent with the information given. Remember, the president wants your memorandum today.

6. As a supervisor at _____ (your instructor will specify), you were delighted to receive an inquiry from the company training director about the possibility of offering communication courses in the workplace. Your employees need such a course, so you will write a memo responding favorably and giving helpful advice wherever you can. Be sure to suggest places for holding the on-site classes as well as names of people you know at local schools who could put you in touch with excellent communication trainers.

   Furthermore, you realize that a growing cadre of companies are setting up self-study programs. Suggest that, in addition to offering a full range of courses that meet regularly for a specified period, your company should consider offering a self-study program similar to ones used at AT&T, GE, Kentucky Fried Chicken, UPS, and other companies. These courses could also cover a wide range of levels, but they would offer the benefit of communication training to those who work irregular schedules or who are out of town often.

   Because you think this is such a worthwhile idea, send a copy of the memo to your supervisor. Be sure to indicate this on the memo in an appropriate form and place.

7. Play the role of administrative assistant to James

Emory, President of Northstar Oil Company (see Problem 3 for background information). You have contacted seven resort/retreat areas in the southern California and Arizona region. Of the seven, five sent you proposals and descriptive materials. Based on this information, you narrowed the field to three—La Siesta, High Sierra, and Buena Vista. All are within an hour's drive of a major airport.

In addition, you called your travel agent and asked for various airline schedules to Phoenix and San Diego. The agent indicates there are three Saturday afternoon and two Sunday morning flights; so you can get all participants to the retreat in time for the Monday morning beginning. And on Friday afternoon and Saturday morning, there are three and two flights, respectively. You will need to work out who will arrive early and return late in an equitable manner. President Emory, of course, will have his preference; but you will schedule the travel times by person. Roundtrip fares from LA to Phoenix are $227, coach, and $277, first class; from LA to San Diego, $257, coach, and $307, first class (President Emory will fly first class).

The information below forms the basis for your selection of Buena Vista as your choice for the retreat. Use it and the travel estimates to respond to the request given to you by President Emory.

**La Siesta Resort**
*Location*—on 1,400 acres in Sonoran Desert in Carefree, Arizona, just north of Scottsdale.
*Description*—main lodge, fine restaurants (specializing in fitness), lounges, a gift shop, and 156 adobe-style freestanding Spanish bungalows called *casitas*. Casitas feature wooden beam ceilings, with fans, wood-burning fireplaces, wet bars, large bathroom/dressing areas. In the lodge are three meeting rooms for executive conferences and retreats. Each has a board room with a table, projection screen, VCR, wet bar, and large private patio. Two of the rooms, the CEO Room and the Chairman's Room, sit 12 at a heavy oak table.
*Food*—fitness-oriented menu; special menus available on advance request.
*Recreation*—jogging, hiking trails, five tennis courts, private country club, fitness center, 27-hole golf course, jeep tours, hot-air balloon rides.
*Rates*—$200 for single occupancy (summer) to $300 for single occupancy (winter).

**High Sierra Resort**
*Location*—on 45 acres, 25 miles north of San Diego and 6 miles east of Del Mar.
*Description*—decor of tiled Spanish and Mediterranean architecture, sparkling fountains, and palm trees; casitas furnished in casual Southwestern style. Each has bedroom and sunken living room, wood-burning fireplaces, wet bars, fully stocked mini-bars, two remote-control color TVs, personal safes, and automatic coffee brewers. High Sierra's library has a 22-seat board room with built-in audiovisual equipment.
*Food*—emphasis on nutritional balance with minimum fat, calories, cholesterol, and sodium; entree changes every two days.
*Recreation*—18 championship tennis courts (employing instruction); two swimming pools; three jacuzzis; croquet court. Polo, horse racing, golf course, and a nearby health club.
*Rates*—$295–$335 (summer to winter).

**Buena Vista**
*Location*—nestled in the rocks and forest at Sedona, Arizona, at an elevation of 4,300 feet on the southern rim of the Colorado Plateau.
*Description*—main lodge with individual guest rooms, plus four two-bedroom and four one-bedroom pine cottages. Resort lies on banks of Oak Creek and at the edge of Sedona, a quiet and pleasant village of small restaurants, galleries, and shops featuring the work of jewelers, weavers, carvers, clothing designers, and other crafters. Motif throughout the lodge and guest rooms is southwestern. The lodge has two large rooms, The Board Room and The Executive, that seat 20 and 15, respectively. Both have wet bar, fax, modern audiovisual equipment, and scenic view of mesa.
*Food*—menu emphasizes variety of foods for all appetites; low cholesterol/diet specialties available.
*Recreation*—aerobics (with instruction); tennis courts (6); two swimming pools; saunas/hot tubs; hiking, jogging, exercise room.
*Rates*—$250–$350 for single occupancy (summer to winter); corporate discount available. Free shuttle service from Phoenix airport.

## DIRECT MEMORANDUMS (DIRECTIVES)

8. As assistant to the president of _____ Bank (a large metropolitan bank of your choice), the president has asked you to write a directive in memorandum form prescribing a dress code for bank employees. The president wants two separate directives—one for males and one for females. (For class purposes, write the one for your sex.)

While you prepare to write this directive, you recall the president's instructions: "For years we have had an unwritten code specifying conservative dress and grooming for all employees who are visible to the public. Recently, however, more and more employees have strayed from this unwritten code. Every day I see our employees wearing some pretty far-out clothes, and some of their hair styles and their use of cosmetics don't project the image of a bank. The situation appears to be getting worse. I want you to work up an appropriate set of dress and grooming standards that we can live with. Don't make them too stringent, but certainly rule out anything that would project a wrong image. Work up a first draft. Then we'll talk about it before we send it out."

Now you will begin to jot down the dress and grooming rules that you think will meet the president's requirements. When you have finished, you'll write them up in the memorandum form that will convey them to the employees.

9. As executive assistant to the president of LongLife Insurance Company, you draw an assignment to prepare a special policy directive memo today. At Monday morning's staff meeting, President Dan Zanetti and all of the company vice presidents discussed the need to develop and implement a companywide paper recycling program. Because you prepare all official internal and external correspondence for the administrative staff, you will write the memo for President Zanetti's signature. You will base the directive on the staff's discussion of the paper recycling program.

The staff decided that the recycling program would consist of two phases—one, a pilot program, and two, a long-term implementation program. The pilot program will begin on the first of the month following your memo announcing the programs to all company employees. More specifically, the accounting department will be the first unit to begin the recycling program. It will be asked to collect white ledger paper and computer printout paper in special paper collection boxes placed at each workstation. After the accounting department has participated in the program for one month, a new department will be added each month thereafter until all departments have been included in the pilot program. You have worked out the following succession for departments: 2nd—sales; 3rd—underwriting; 4th—claims; 5th—executive offices. Within five months, the entire company should be included in the pilot program.

The long-term implementation program will be designed to collect all types of recyclable papers. On the sixth month, employees will be asked to sort the following papers into the collection boxes: white copy machine paper, white letterhead, white tablet paper, computer printout paper, laser print paper, typing paper, and miscellaneous white paper. Specifically excluded are these paper items: pressure sensitive labels, colored paper, carbon and NCR paper, chemically treated paper (facsimile), paper ream wrappers, cardboard and tablet backings, envelopes, glossy and waxed papers, magazines, newspapers, food wrappings, and paper towels.

The custodial staff will collect the recyclable papers each day. If they should notice employees who do not cooperate, they are required to report them to the appropriate manager. The custodial staff will not be required to separate recyclables from other nonrecyclable items into collection boxes.

It should be evident that the recycling program needs the commitment of all company employees to work. Employees will need to think, cooperate, and sort. LongLife Insurance's management feels, however, that the real issue for the recycling program is to lessen pressure on landfills (garbage dumps). It is *not* conservation of trees, as this issue is one of forest management. Millions of tons of waste materials could be eliminated from landfills if industry cooperates. LongLife Insurance will reinforce the program by using paper products that are recycled.

Write the memo in a direct, clear style for President Zanetti's signature.

10. As president of Hi-Tech Consultants, you are beginning to formulate a policy for handling sexual harassment on the job. The policy directive that you will write must do two things. First, it must announce the policy; second, it must tell employees about the training program and the internal grievance procedures you've developed to deal with the sexual harassment issue.

Your sexual harassment policy must define the term. Specifically, you define sexual harassment to mean unwelcome sexual advances, requests for sexual favors, and other verbal or physical conduct of a sexual nature when any of three conditions is met: (1) submission to such conduct is made either explicitly or implicitly a term or condition of an individual's employment; (2) submission to, or rejection of, such conduct by an individual is used as the basis for employment or for any decision affecting that individual; or (3) such conduct has the purpose or effect of substantially interfering with an individual's performance or creating an intimidating, hostile, or offensive employment environment.

As you define sexual harassment, it is part of

the workplace diversity issue. And your definition covers creation of a "hostile" work environment, thereby forbidding such things as pornographic pinups, love letters, catcalls, sexual jokes, and staring. The rationale for your policy is quite frankly one of productivity. It is your belief that people who feel harassed are not productive employees. Thus, there is a good bottom-line justification for the policy.

To implement the policy, you have asked Dr. Karen O'Neil of Goodwill Communications to conduct a series of one-day workshops on the topic for all company personnel. Dr. O'Neil's workshop will be entitled "A Matter of Judgment and Respect" and will use case studies, role plays, and experiential exercises. Class size will be limited to 30 to permit maximum interaction. Although the classes will be offered on a first-come, first-served basis on Wednesday and Thursday of each week, you will require that all company personnel attend.

In addition, you have designed a new grievance procedure for alleged sexual harassment complaints. Any person who perceives sexual harassment may bypass his or her supervisor (who may be the culprit) and report incidents directly to the personnel department. Personnel will assign a male and a female to investigate the incident to allow for gender differences in perceptions of sexual harassment charges. You believe that this procedure will give an objective quality to a very emotional issue.

With the national exposure that the topic has received and recent court cases involving sexual harassment, your memo will need to be written clearly and specifically to sculpt your corporate culture. Organize your ideas; then write the memo for your employees.

11. You recently read an article in *The Wall Street Journal* quoting business psychologist Harry Levinson, who recommended that clear rules be set about required work hours. Apparently, especially in the summertime, many employees want to take off in the afternoon and all day on Fridays or Mondays, causing conscientious employees to feel angry.

You believe that with vacation season approaching, now is the time to write a policy statement for your first-line employees. Let them know that this policy will alleviate problems, stressing fairness and flexibility along with the need to distribute the work evenly. Give full instructions for implementing the policy you set up.

While the E-mail system could be used to let employees know about this new policy, you want your employees to have a hard copy of the policy so they'll have a more permanent record of it. Write the memo as clearly as possible.

12. Recently you've decided to rewrite your policy on travel accommodations for your sales representatives, allowing the use of bed and breakfast inns (B&Bs). In fact, not only are the facilities adequate, but some also offer amenities like continental breakfasts and homey suites. Also, depending on the time of year, they are often less expensive than a hotel.

Write a policy memo to your sales representatives for employee travel that clearly includes B&Bs. You might want to identify some sources for finding good B&Bs. Several good books have been written; local travel writers have identified some; and some travel agents keep files on them. Since this is a new policy, you might suggest that as your sales representatives find good ones, they post a notice on your company's E-mail system. Write instructions dealing with reservations, guarantees, and payments for B&Bs under the new policy.

*Optional Format.* Use your memo heading macro to create this memo. In addition, use a sales staff macro for the *To:* variable. This macro will assure that the entire sales staff gets a copy of the new policy.

## INDIRECT MEMORANDUMS (BAD NEWS)

13. For years the sales representatives of the Criswell Chemical Company have been issued automobiles with the understanding that they could use them for personal purposes. They had only to pay for the gasoline consumed in personal driving, and this they did on the honor system. Criswell paid the rest.

Because sales and profits have declined recently, Criswell management has been looking for ways to cut expenses. One of the areas they feel should be reduced is automobile-related expenses. They have decided to change the way the automobiles are used. Henceforth, the salespeople will pay the full cost of their personal travel. Each salesperson will be given an allowance of a specified number of miles for work-related travel. Every mile driven over this allowance will cost the salespeople 20 cents. The mileage allowed for business will be reasonable and will be determined through careful study of the needs in covering each salesperson's territory.

As sales manager for Criswell, you have the

chore of informing your people of management's decision. The salespeople won't like it, for the change means a cut in benefits. You will present the bad news in a memorandum, and you will work to present it in a way that will minimize the negative effect. Address the memorandum to one of the salespeople in the organization.

14. You've just received a persuasive memo from Barbara DuBois, one of your best managers, suggesting that your company add sales interns. While her idea seems like a good one, you must refuse it.

    Right now your company is not only in a hiring freeze, but you have implemented an early retirement incentive. Additionally, you've recently cut back nearly 25 percent on paid internships.

    While you agree that unpaid internships might be snapped up by good students with impressive credentials, you realize there are other costs involved. One is the cost to the morale of your current employees and your current interns. Another cost is the hard-to-measure cost of training these employees. Not only is there the direct cost, but the cost they take in the time of other employees. Identify at least two other costs that clearly lead you to refuse this suggestion.

    *Optional format.* Send this memo through your E-mail system. Your instructor will give you an E-mail address to use.

15. As the chief executive of a company employing about 100 persons, you are commonly asked to donate your time to charitable causes. Recently, one of your employees asked you to lead a company blood drive for the Red Cross or local blood bank.

    You've spent considerable time weighing the pros and cons of this request. You decide you must refuse it. Because the employee is young and new, a big part of the refusal will involve educating. Explain that you think the idea of donating blood for life-saving causes is worthwhile, but give reasons you think it unsuitable for this business. One of your reasons for refusing the request could include the appropriateness of the population, giving reasons people are not allowed to donate blood. Another is that some of your employees may feel compelled by job security or peer pressure to donate, and you don't want to put this pressure on them. Yet another is that some employees might feel the questions the interviewers ask or that peers ask are an invasion of privacy. You could offer a compromise such as sponsoring the cost of the drive for the local community, donating money to the Red Cross, or such. In any case, give as many reasons as you think necessary to refuse.

    *Optional format.* Since you'll be sending this memo through your E-mail system, you'll want to be sure that it is as concise as possible. Also, be sure to chunk the message, remembering to organize with screen size in mind. While a typical screen size is 24–25 lines, your instructor will let you know the chunking size for the system you'll be using (simulating).

16. As senior vice president of Starlight Insurance, you've just walked out of a staff meeting concerning cost reduction. The executive staff has given you the task of writing a memo to all department heads telling them that employees traveling for the company must now give up their frequent-flier points. Because the news will not be received favorably, you will write the memo in indirect order paving the way for the bad news with explanation and justification.

    Over the past three years, you've done all you could to fight the price squeeze bottleneck that faces most organizations. More specifically, you've cut successively the travel budget by 50 percent in the three-year period. Even more dramatically, you cut travel by 20 percent in the last year alone to save on expenses. Thus, giving up frequent-flier points is another in a series of attempts to save money for the company.

    Throughout the travel budget trimming process, you've encouraged company personnel to use the phone and fax more and travel less, particularly to meetings and trade shows. It's your estimate that you can save even more (about 10 percent per year) if people who do travel give frequent-flier points back to the company to apply to future travel. But because giving up frequent-flier points will likely be perceived as losing a "perk" without receiving anything in return, you will need to give the problem your most creative thinking.

    To develop a convincing message, you will need to think through the situation specifically and strategically. Are there reader benefits that could arise from cost reduction? Could employees actually profit from continual efforts to economize? To be sure, you will need to be thorough and imaginative to work through the negative points inherent in the message and to turn those negative points into convincing reasons. But you can and will do it before you send the memo.

    Write the bad news memorandum for the employees of Starlight Insurance.

## INDIRECT MEMORANDUMS (persuasive)

17. You are the public relations director at the Sutter's Bay refinery of the Nomad Petroleum Company. Today you were visited by a delegation from the residential area surrounding the plant. These people complained about the parking of Nomad employees. As their spokesman explained, "Your employees are parking in the streets in front of our houses. Often they block driveways and park on our lawns. We've noticed that there is plenty of room in your parking lots, but some prefer to park in our neighborhood because it saves them a few steps."

    You promised the group that you would do what you could to correct the matter—that you'd get the employees to park in the lots provided for them. But it won't be easy. You can enlist the help of the local police in keeping cars off the driveways and lawns. But parking in the streets is permitted by the city. You conclude that you will have to use persuasion.

    Specifically, you will write a persuasive memorandum to the employees. In it you will use the most effective appeal (or appeals) you can develop. Will it be pride? Fair play? Loyalty? You will have to think about the possibilities.

18. As regional sales director for Syntex Labs, you firmly believe that the paperwork your sales representatives are handling is preventing them from doing their job. It also holds up orders and, therefore, cash payments. While most representatives have been using laptop computers for a few years, they also have been asked to generate more reports. The impact of added report requests has only been manageable because of the computers.

    To make your sales representatives more effective, you'd like to upgrade these laptop computers with fax/modems. Their sales data could be sent in immediately over phone lines to the corporate computer. Sales could be processed immediately and reports needed by management could be generated from this data. Not only would this assure up-to-date report data, it would also put all data from representatives in similar form. Furthermore, salespeople could use the modems to check on the availability of products, prices, promotions, etc. And communication with managers would be enhanced with an E-mail system.

    With fax/modems built into laptops, your salespeople could be more effective at their real job—selling. Direct this memo to your supervisor.

19. For this assignment, assume that you are now six months into the long-term implementation phase of LongLife Insurance Company's paper recycling program (see Problem 9 for background details). All managers report they followed your policy memo with memos of their own reinforcing the recycling program. And they discussed the program individually with employees and in small group meetings. Custodial personnel, however, report that only about 20 percent of recyclable items are being placed in the special collection boxes. To be sure, there is apathy and indifference toward the program.

    Although you did state in your original memo that uncooperative employees would be reported to their supervisors, you now find that it is difficult to punish them. It was your assumption that employees would automatically cooperate once they were aware of the program. You now believe that a stronger effort is needed to break old habits and to bring about the behavior change that is needed to comply with the recycling program.

    For these reasons, and possibly others, you decide to prepare a persuasive memo to all company personnel selling them on the idea of actively participating and doing their part to rekindle the recycling program you have designed. You will begin your strategy analysis by identifying the objections employees likely have to the program. What you asked them to do is not monetarily rewarded. And it is easier to keep established habits than to develop new ones. No doubt, there are other objections you can identify.

    After you have identified the objections, you will select an appeal or set of appeals to use that will overcome them. One that you might consider is the "Mother Earth" theme. Because the average age of your workforce is 42.7 years, most of your employees will have to live in the world they create. And they have an opportunity to mold that world for the better if they conserve and preserve the environment. Indeed, there are other appeals that could be appropriately used as well.

    Think through the entire situation; then prepare a persuasive memo that will make your employees want to willingly participate in the recycling program. Your goal is to have at least 85 percent of all recyclable items separated for collection in the program.

20. "Incredible!" you think to yourself as you finish reading last year's insurance claims reports for your organization, Consolidated Freightways. Hypertension rose 12 percent, and 10 percent of the company's employees accounted for 35 percent of the claims. Because you offer full-benefit hospitalization coverage without cost to employees, any

increase in claims will cost you more money. Aside from wanting health and well-being for your employees, you want also to keep expenses as low as possible for your organization. Thus, you decide that you will need to persuade your employees to be more health conscious, not only for themselves, but also for Consolidated Freightways.

It's your belief—and a defensible one, too—that employee well-being is a multifaceted issue involving physical, emotional, psychological, and nutritional balance. Over the years, you've offered stress management programs as one way to alleviate tensions and promote good health. But now you feel that additional programs are needed. Quite obviously, in light of the insurance report, you can't depend on *one* program to do the job. Now you want to emphasize exercise and diet/nutrition.

The exercise program you have in mind is not the rigorous, aerobic type. Indeed, you endorse this activity but only for those who want it. Rather, you want employees to develop a moderate program, along with good awareness of diet and nutrition. Accordingly, you have designed the following programs:

(*a*) Stair Climbing—employees will be asked to count the number of flights of stairs (flight must include 10 steps) they climb each month on the job. (You have a six-story building.) You will keep a monthly and cumulative total to be reported through executive memo.

(*b*) Weight No Longer—employees who want to lose weight can organize by teams of 10. They can meet before or after work and during lunch breaks but not during work hours. Official weigh-ins will be recorded and pounds lost per team will be reported through executive memo.

(*c*) Diet/Nutritional Seminar—employees may sign up for this three-hour class that will be offered during lunch hours, Monday through Wednesday, by Dr. Johann Gianino of Executive Fitness Inc. The classes will meet in the company's training room, which holds 100.

At first thought, you are inclined to favor an information memo—one that simply announces the availability of the programs. But after further thought you realize that there are probably employee objections associated with participating in the programs. First, they will have to participate on their own and not company time. Second, there might be little perceived benefit for cooperating. For both of these reasons, and perhaps others, you will need to develop a strategy to sway employees to your way of thinking before you can ask them to participate in the programs.

Write the persuasive memo to Consolidated Freightways employees that will make them want to willingly sign up for the programs for their own and the company's benefit.

CHAPTER 10

# PATTERN VARIATIONS IN COLLECTIONS

### CHAPTER OBJECTIVES

*Upon completing this chapter, you will be able to write effective collection letters through a series of efforts. To reach this goal, you should be able to*

### 1

**Design a series of collection letters according to the credit risk involved and standard practice in the field of business.**

### 2

**Write short and courteous reminder letters in the early stage of collection.**

### 3

**Compose letters using the appropriate degree of persuasion and frankness in the middle stage of collection.**

### 4

**Use strength and directness to present action in a calm and firm appeal in last-resort letters.**

## INTRODUCTORY SITUATION

### to Collection Letters

Play the role of credit manager of Loren's Department Store. Like most credit managers, you have the assignment of handling all credit accounts. Your department is responsible for approving (or disapproving) all credit requests. After a credit account has been established, you keep records of credit sales, send out statements of what is owed, and record payments as they come in. For the most part, your duties are routine and pleasant.

You have one duty, however, that is less routine and less pleasant. It is the duty of collecting money from credit customers who do not pay on time. Most customers pay regularly, of course, but there are always some who do not. Getting delinquent customers to pay usually involves contacting them by mail. First, you send notices, which serve mainly as reminders. Then, if the reminders do not work, you send letters. *Collection letters,* as they are called, are the subject of this chapter.

## THE COLLECTION SERIES

When your customers do not pay their bills on time, you must try to collect. If you follow conventional business practice, you are likely to use letters in your efforts. You could use other ways—for example, the telephone, personal visits, or collection agencies. But letters are the most common way.

*Letters are used to collect past-due accounts.*

### Collecting through a Series of Efforts

In studying collection letters, you should first understand how businesses usually collect past-due bills. Typically, their collection efforts consist of a series of steps. Each step is a contact (usually by mail) with the delinquent customer. In a first step the bill is sent with a due date specified. If this bill is not paid, a second bill may be sent—maybe a third. Sometimes, for added strength, reminder words such as "Please," "May we remind you," or "You have probably forgotten" are added to a past-due bill. These reminders may be in various forms—printed enclosures, stickers, stamped words.

*The typical collection procedure consists of a number of progressively stronger efforts. The first are reminder efforts.*

If the reminders fail to bring in the money, the efforts get stronger. Typically, a letter urging payment is sent. If this letter fails, another is sent—and another—and another. The letters get progressively stronger. As we will see, how many letters are written depends on company policy. When the buildup of letters fails to bring in the money, a final letter ends the mail effort. Additional action through collection agencies or the courts may follow.

*Next comes a series of persuasive letters, ending with a final, threatening letter.*

In a sense, the buildup of collection efforts resembles a stairway (see Figure 10–1). Each step represents a collection effort. The first steps are called *early-stage* collection efforts. These are mainly reminders. The assumption at this stage is that the debtors *will* pay and that the company need only remind them.

*The series resembles a stairway.*

Following the early (will-pay) stage comes the middle stage of collection. Here the company's attitude is that debtors have to be convinced they *should* pay. This is truly a persuasion stage. The company's goal is to sell the

CHAPTER 10  Pattern Variations in Collections

**FIGURE 10-1** Diagram of the Collection Procedure

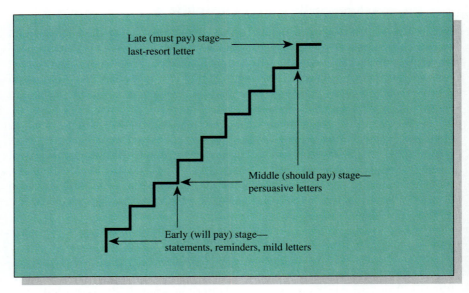

NOTE: The number of steps depends on the policy of the firm.

debtors on the idea of paying, while retaining goodwill. This stage comprises the bulk of most collection series.

After all persuasive efforts to collect have failed, the letters must stop. Thus, a final stage must end the collection-letter series. In this stage the debtors have to be convinced that they *must* pay. This last-resort stage consists of just one letter. Because this letter is so different from the others, it justifies being treated as a stage in itself.

### Determining the Collection Series

The number of and time intervals between collection efforts vary by company. Every organization does what its management believes is best for the organization. The choices made are usually influenced by two factors. One is the class of credit risk involved. The other is the standard practice in the company's particular field of business.

To illustrate the role of credit risks, consider two contrasting situations. First, assume that you are collecting from people who are generally good credit risks. With this group, your collection efforts would probably move slowly. You would send a number of reminders before sending a persuasive letter. Then you would move slowly through a series of persuasive letters. You would make the last-resort effort only after the persuasion has had every reasonable chance to succeed. Your overall efforts might extend over a long period—perhaps a year or more.

Now assume that you are collecting from people who are bad credit risks. Many of these customers may have good intentions, but they simply do not

---

The number of and time between collection efforts are influenced by the credit risk and by standard practice in the company's field of business.

For example, an exclusive shop would be likely to have a long, slow series.

A store dealing with bad risks would have a short, fast series.

PART 4 Applications to Specific Situations

Careful screening of credit applicants can greatly reduce the need for collection letters.

have enough money to be good risks. Most have a record of being slow to pay. In collecting from bad credit risks, if you follow the practice of most businesses, you would move quickly from reminder to strong persuasion to last-resort action. You might do all of this in a few weeks.

Businesses that have a wide range of risks among their customers need to vary their collection efforts. They usually do this by first classifying their credit customers into risk groups. Then they use an appropriate collection effort for each group. For example, a company might have one series of collection letters for its open-account customers (typically the best risks) and another series for its budget accounts, cycle accounts, and the like (typically the more questionable risks).

*Some businesses classify risks and vary collection efforts by type of risk.*

Collection efforts between businesses illustrate how standard practice influences collection efforts. Businesses expect and generally receive payments from each other on time. Thus, when payment between businesses is slow, collection efforts typically move fast. Also, credit dealings between businesses are generally viewed as more impersonal than credit dealings between a business and an individual. As a result, collection efforts between businesses are more matter-of-fact and firm.

*Collection efforts between businesses are usually short and fast.*

### Using the Telephone to Collect

As noted previously, the telephone may be used in the collection effort. The companies that use it generally call the debtors after making some unsuccessful mail efforts, often just before taking last-resort action. Although use of the telephone is time consuming, its users report good results. The telephone is especially effective in cases in which the debtors have good

*Some companies effectively use the telephone to collect.*

explanations for their delinquincy. Such explanations often lead the parties to work out suitable solutions.

> Debtors' responses determine telephone collection procedures. The collection goal is to work out a payment plan.

Those who collect by telephone do not agree on a best procedure. Most of them report that they begin by bringing the overdue payment to the debtor's attention and then wait for a response. If the debtor presents an explanation not known to the caller, the caller may then attempt to work out an appropriate payment plan. If the debtor offers no explanation, the caller may attempt to get information from the debtor that will lead to an acceptable payment plan. If the two parties cannot get together, the caller usually informs the debtor of the collection action that must now follow.

### Using Computer-Generated Collections

> Large companies use computers to assist in collections.

In today's business world, most large and many small companies use computers in the collection process—to maintain purchase and payment records, to flag delinquent accounts, and to generate appropriate collection letters. The timing of the collections, the length of the collection series, and the contents of the collection letters are written in the computer program. The specific policies programmed, are, of course, determined by each company and are based on the considerations discussed in preceding paragraphs.

Since computers have been used as collection tools, a trend toward a shorter collection series and harsher collection letters has been evident. Even so, computer collection policies and procedures can be whatever the company management wants them to be. The wise manager will consider all the possibilities discussed in this chapter.

## INTRODUCTORY SITUATION

## to Reminder Letters

At the moment, your work at Loren's Department Store involves trying to collect from some good credit customers who are behind in paying their bills. All of them passed Loren's credit investigation at one time or another, but now they are delinquent. You must do something about it.

All the people in the group you are concerned about have open accounts. As is Loren's practice, you billed them on the due date and a month later. Another month later, you billed them a third time—this time with a printed reminder. Today you are ready to take a stronger step—to remind them in a letter.

Because Loren's has so many customers, you will use a form letter. You know that most large businesses do this, but you will work hard to make your form letter sound as individually tailored as possible. This means that you will try to make it read like an individual letter and not like a form letter. You do not want to offend these customers. After all, they were at one time a very select group. ■

### ■■■■■■■■■■■■■■■■
### EARLY-STAGE COLLECTIONS

> The early stage of collection begins with reminders of the bill.

As long as you believe that your credit customers intend to pay, you should handle them tactfully. At first, you can simply send duplicates of the original bill, as suggested earlier. If these reminders do not bring in payment, you

### Computer-Assisted Collection: A Means for Managing the Collection Task

The computer can be a useful tool in many facets affecting writing, including helping to manage the collection process. Already there is a wide variety of specialty software developed just for this purpose. And both database and word processing software can be useful, too.

Large corporations most often use their mainframes to keep track of accounts receivable and to generate reminders and collection letters to customers with overdue accounts. While this can be efficient if the program implements the policies of the specific business, it can also backfire when it doesn't. One way large corporations ensure that their collection software implements their specific policy is to write their own software. Another way is to use off-the-shelf software that is customizable, allowing them to administer their own regulations. Many corporations also customize these programs by writing their own letters or modifying the ones contained in the software to fit their business.

Medium- and small-sized businesses often use database and word processing software to help them manage the collection process. Both types of software will merge variables such as name, address, and amount owed with form letters. These businesses write the collection letters and identify the variables that will be brought in from another file. Then they merge the variables with their letters. Database software can be particularly useful for easily sorting the customers by credit level and stage in the collection process. Some word processing software can also sort, but database software was primarily designed for this purpose.

Collecting from customers who owe you for goods or services you've rendered is an important part of running a business. While computer software won't write the letters, it does help with the task. Businesses are still responsible for writing or modifying collection letters that implement their practices and policies.

---

will need to write a first collection letter. This will usually be an early-stage letter. Although such letters vary in organization, most of them follow this plan:

- **Begin directly with a reminder of the past-due bill.**
- **Include some goodwill material—comments showing confidence that the debtor will pay.**
- **End with a friendly, forward-looking, goodwill comment.**

*Most early-stage letters are written this way.*

#### Writing Reminder Letters

As noted previously, the most common early-stage letters are direct reminders of bills past due. Such letters are usually short—sometimes only two or three sentences. They remind the debtor forthrightly of the past-due account. They soften the force of the directness by conveying the underlying impression that the debtor will pay. They are courteous throughout, and they do not lecture or talk down. As the account is not long past due, they rarely use persuasive language urging payment.

*Such letters remind directly and are short and courteous.*

CHAPTER 10  Pattern Variations in Collections    301

## Collection Message—Early American Style

Before the United States had its current postal system, businesspeople placed collection messages in newspapers. Typical of these messages is the following, which appeared in the *Norwich (Conn.) Packet* in 1779:

BY AUTHORITY

To ALL those who are indebted as a subscriber for Newspapers, whose accounts are one or more years' standing—without even regarding the fashionable substitutes for payment, of IF's, AND's, & WAIT a few Days, VERILY, VERILY, I say unto you, that I have lately had loud and repeated calls for CASH!

Therefore, Nevertheless, Notwithstanding—I now inform all, great or small, young or old, rich or poor, male or female, that are indebted to me for the *Norwich Packet* that I must and will have my due, for this reason: "The Paper makers threaten the Printers, and the Printers threaten the Post." What is to be done? What steps can be taken! All debts must be paid, and I must pay mine;—of course you must pay me, before the expiration of one month from this date, if you wish to keep your accounts out of the hands of an Attorney.

Beriah Hartshorn
Franklin, August 1, 1779

## Contrasting Reminder Letters

*Following are good and bad examples of an early-stage letter.*

The following two form letters show bad and good ways of reminding Loren's delinquent customers of their debts. Both letters do the job of reminding, but the better one is more courteous.

**An Unnecessarily Harsh First Letter.** The bad letter begins bluntly—and negatively. Its words are too harsh for this stage of the collection effort. The close contains the most positive wording in the letter, but such dangling expressions belong to the distant past.

*This bad letter is too harsh for the early stage.*

Dear Mr. Beloit:

You have not responded to the last two statements we sent you and are now two months past due on your account. Thus, I am sending you yet another statement (enclosed). I urge you to pay immediately and protect your credit record.

Thanking you in advance for your payment.

Sincerely,

Enclosure

**A Courteous Reminder to Pay.** The better letter directly reminds the reader of the past-due bill, but it does so with courtesy and tact. It gives the reader a face-saving explanation (that he or she forgot). It includes the subtle suggestion that paying is something the reader will want to do. Appropriate goodwill comments end the letter.

**CASE ILLUSTRATION** Early-Stage Collection Letters. *(An Individually Written First Letter)*
This direct, personal letter was written to a select group of the charge customers of a major department store. It followed two routine monthly billings.

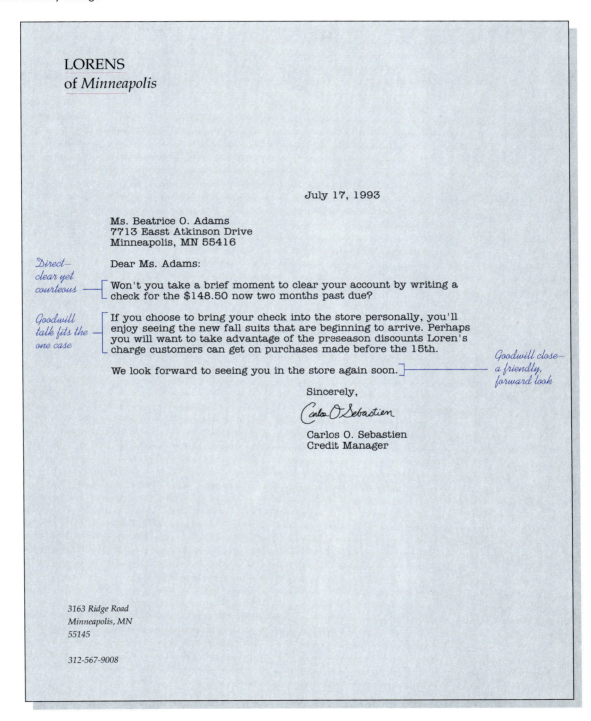

**CASE ILLUSTRATION** Early-Stage Collection Letters. *(A Retailer's First Form Letter)*

Written for customers with good past records, this direct-style letter reminds about the past-due bill and subtly persuades the reader to pay.

---

**TECH CENTER STORES, INC.**

April 15, 1993

Mr. Gordon M. Styles
12331 South Acuna Street
El Paso, TX 79924

Dear Mr. Styles:

*Direct—clear yet courteous*

Your payment of the $377.45 now two months past due on your account has not yet reached us. In view of your good record, we are confident you will want to clear your account by sending us your check right away. For your convenience, we are enclosing a return-addressed envelope.

*Subtle persuasion*

*Goodwill close—a friendly forward look*

We appreciate your past business, and we look forward to serving you again.

Sincerely,

*Hilda Brand*

Hilda Brand

enclosure

240 N. Berlin St.
Hampton, TX 40059
513-676-5867

PART 4   Applications to Specific Situations

This letter is better.

Dear Mr. Beloit:

This is just a friendly reminder that your account with us shows $317.90 now two months past due. If you're like me, you'll appreciate my calling the matter to your attention.

Loren's genuinely appreciates your business. We look forward to serving you in the years ahead.

Sincerely,

## INTRODUCTORY SITUATION

## to a Series of Persuasive Collection Letters

Back at your credit manager's desk at Loren's Department Store, you have analyzed the results of your reminder letters. On the whole, you are satisfied. Many of the delinquent customers came through. As you expected, however, some ignored your letter. Now you will have to take stronger measures.

Following a convention established by many companies over long years of experience, you will now write stronger letters. These letters will attempt to persuade—to show why the debtors *should pay*. Each letter will be stronger than the last. Of course, the collection letters stop when a debtor pays. But you will continue sending letters to debtors who do not pay. You will stop the buildup of letters when you think there is little chance that the debtor will respond to them.

The big task before you now is to write the letters that will bring in the money. Obviously, this is no routine letter-writing job. As the following pages show, it takes the very best in strategy and in persuasive writing. ■

## MIDDLE-STAGE COLLECTIONS

If your reminders do not collect the money, you will need to write stronger letters to convince debtors that they *should* pay. Here your procedure is to select a basic appeal and then to present this appeal convincingly. That is, you persuade.

When reminders fail, you should use persuasive letters.

### Analyzing the Strategy

As in other cases requiring persuasion, the delinquent customers' wishes run contrary to yours. You want them to pay. They have shown by ignoring your reminders that at best they are not eager to pay. Thus, they are not likely to receive favorably your persuasive letter to collect. More than likely, they do not want to hear from you at all. In such situations, you must gain reader attention at the beginning. If you do not, the odds of getting your message across are slim.

Debtors do not receive such letters favorably.

In persuading debtors to pay, you should use strategy. As in other persuasion cases, you should begin by looking at the situation as the readers see it. Then you should select appeals that will work with your particular readers.

Persuading debtors to pay requires strategy.

CHAPTER 10  Pattern Variations in Collections

Although the available appeals are varied and may be applied with overlapping variations, they generally fall into the following categories.

*First, select an appeal from these categories: pride, ethics, self-interest, fear.*

**Pride.** Appeals to pride play on the readers' concern for themselves (self-respect) and for what others think of them (social acceptance).

**Ethics.** Strategies based on the readers' moral standards fall into this category. The category includes appeals relating to honor, character, integrity, and sense of fair play. In a way, it includes all appeals of doing "what is right."

**Self-Interest.** Persuasion stressing how one profits by keeping a good credit reputation illustrates self-interest appeals. Such appeals emphasize the practical benefits of credit buying. They may be applied positively (the advantages of having credit) or negatively (the disadvantages of not having credit). Of course, this appeal works best with good credit risks.

**Fear.** In a sense, appeals to fear are the negative side of appeals to self-interest. Such appeals stress avoiding the bad things that may result from nonpayment—the consequences of having legal action taken, of being reported to a credit bureau, or of having the account turned over to a collection agency. Among those consequences would be the embarrassment of having a bad credit reputation, the disadvantages of being unable to buy on credit, the inconvenience of being involved in legal action, and added expense.

*Then develop the appeal to fit the debtor.*

After selecting your appeal, you should develop it by thinking out the reasoning that will convince the debtor to pay. If, for example, you select the fair-play appeal, you might build a case showing why the debtor should keep his or her end of the bargain. You would go through similar strategies with the other appeals.

*Succeeding letters get stronger as goodwill decreases.*

How strong you make your appeal depends on how far along in the collection effort you are. Usually your first persuasion letter is mild and has much goodwill content. The letters that follow get stronger, and their goodwill content decreases. Although such letters vary in organization, this is the most common plan for writing them:

*Follow this plan.*

- **Begin with attention-gaining words that set up the appeal.**
- **Present the appeal using you-viewpoint adaptation and persuasive language.**
- **Request payment (you may end here).**
- **Consider ending with words recalling the appeal.**

### Gaining Attention in the Opening

*As the letter is not welcome, the opening should gain attention and should set up the strategy.*

This persuasion letter is not invited. It is probably not even wanted. Thus, your first words have a special need to gain attention. As your readers have received your reminders, they know that they owe you. More than likely, most of them intend to pay when it is convenient. They may quickly label your letter as just another dun and put it aside. If this letter is to have a chance of succeeding, it must gain attention right away.

To gain attention, you will need to find some interesting opening words. Whatever words you select, they should help set up your basic appeal. The unlimited possibilities are best explained by example.

Bill-paying time can be a frustrating experience for many people. Often the collection efforts of creditors compete for attention. Those that stand out from the rest are the ones most likely to bring in payment.

One successful letter begins with this question:

When they ask about you, what should we tell them?

The appeal of this letter, written late in the collection series, is the danger of losing a good credit reputation. The opening is truly a persuasive question. It makes one want to read further to learn just what is to be told. Clearly, it sets up the discussion of the appeal.

Another successful beginning asks a question about the product for which the debtor owes:

How are you and your Arctic air-conditioning system making it through these hot summer months?

This opening has the subtle advantage of working on the reader's conscience through a friendly, human question. The appeal it sets up is that of fair play—of persuading the reader to carry out his or her end of a bargain for goods now being enjoyed.

Another attention-gaining question is this one:

How would you write to a good friend on an embarrassing subject?

The question is personal and interesting. It sets up the persuasion of the letter. This persuasion builds on the human situation of friends communicating on a subject that hurts friendships. The appeal it sets up is that of the reader's moral obligation to a friend.

**CHAPTER 10** Pattern Variations in Collections

## A Most Effective Collection Appeal

Back in the 1870s, a little peddler arrived in a western mining town with little more than a mule, a wagon, and a wagonload of assorted merchandise. He had no sooner turned onto Main Street than the mule balked.

Calmly, the little peddler spoke: "This is once. Now giddap!" The mule didn't move.

Again the peddler spoke: "This is twice. Now giddap!" The mule didn't move.

A third time the peddler spoke: "This is the third time. Now giddap!" The mule didn't move.

The little peddler calmly walked to the back of the wagon, got his rifle, walked up to the mule, and in front of half the people in town shot the mule dead.

Without a mule, the little peddler could go no place, so he started a store in the town. It prospered, and in time people began to buy on credit. A few got a little behind in their payments. The little man just mailed them their bills. Across the bottom of each bill he wrote, "This is once."

He never had any trouble collecting.

### Persuasively Presenting the Appeal

*Presentation of the appeal comes next.*

Your beginning sentence has set up the appeal you have selected. So presenting the appeal is the logical thing to do next. Because the opening has set up the appeal, the shift in thought at this point should be smooth.

Presenting the appeal requires adapting to the reader's point of view. You study the appeal for its you-viewpoint possibilities and then present it in you-viewpoint terms. The technique is much like that of selling. You have searched for reasoning that will move your reader to take the action you want taken. You try to show the advantages to be received from taking it. And you present it all in carefully selected language that will convince.

*Use the right strength for this stage of collection. But keep the tone wholesome and friendly.*

In this part, your words should carry just the right degree of force for the one case. Early in the collection series, the facts of the case may call for mild persuasion. The further along the collection series you progress, however, the more forceful you can afford to be. In addition, you will need to take care not to insult, talk down, lecture, or show anger. As we have noted in related situations, an angry reader tends to resist, and resistance leads to failure.

Instead, your tone should be caring and friendly. You must keep in mind that throughout this stage of collection you hope to collect, to maintain cordial relations, and perhaps even to continue business with the debtor. If you did not think this way, you would move to the last-resort letter.

### Closing with a Request for Payment

*End with a clear request for payment.*

After you have made your persuasive appeal, the logical follow-up is to ask for the payment. You should ask directly, in words that do not merely hint at payment but form a clear question. "Will you please write a check for $77.88 today and mail it to us right away?" meets this requirement. "We would appreciate your writing and sending your check for $77.88" does not.

In collection letters, as in sales letters, a closing reminder of a benefit resulting from the action strengthens the appeal. For example, a letter stressing the advantages of a prompt-pay record for a business could end with these words:

> Will you please write out and mail a check for the $275.30 right now while you're thinking about it? It's your best insurance for keeping your invaluable prompt-pay record.

Linking payment with a benefit to be gained is good.

Or a letter appealing to the ethics of paying might have this ending:

> Will you please write us a check for $275.30 and prove that you're the kind of person we think you are?

### Contrasting Form Collection Letters

The following examples are of contrasting series of middle-stage letters for the situation described at the beginning of this section. The letters, which include exact amounts owed, appear to be individually prepared; this is one benefit of today's word processing and database software's merge features. The letters in the first series are not very good. Those in the second series are much better.

Following are a series of good and a series of bad middle-stage letters.

**Poor Writing and Weak Appeal in a Bad Series.** Letters like those in the first series are used all too often in business. Such letters have little appeal. What little they have does not form a logical buildup in strength throughout the series. In addition, these letters are all poorly written. Actual tests have shown them to be far less effective than the letters that follow the plan given in preceding pages.[1]

The first letter begins with an I-viewpoint statement and a direct request for payment. The words are too harsh for this stage of collection. An attempt is made to develop an appeal on the value of a good credit record, but the appeal is presented in an I-viewpoint, lecturing, and hurried way. The letter then shifts to an appeal to shame. Here the words imply "I have been good—you have been bad." Mixing appeals and not fully developing each appeal result in a weak effort. The forward-looking closing words are the best part of the letter.

Dear Mr. Benoit:

    As you have ignored our last letter, I must insist that you pay the $247.81 now 60 days past due on your account.
    I cannot understand why you are permitting your credit record to be ruined. Your credit record is valuable to you, and you should want to protect it. You can protect your credit record only by paying your bills on time.
    You will agree that we have made every effort to cooperate with you. We have been patient and have a right to expect you to meet your end of the bargain.
    I will look forward to your immediate payment.

                   Sincerely,

This bad one is typical of letters often used in business.

---

[1] The letters in these two series were tested through a Baton Rouge, Louisiana, department store. The second (good) series proved to be almost twice as effective as the first (bad) series.

The second letter also begins with an I-viewpoint statement. Although the words do not make the actual request, they produce the effect of directness. Thus, they give away the objective before any persuading is done. Perhaps the following efforts to shame the reader make an appeal, but overall the appeal is weak. Little reader viewpoint is present. Notice the I-emphasis, particularly at paragraph beginnings. Notice also the writer-centered message in the last paragraph. The negative writing throughout tends to anger rather than persuade. The final words urging action are the best part of the letter.

This bad one has weak appeal and is harsh.

Dear Mr. Benoit:

I was very much disappointed to learn that you still have not paid your past-due account of $247.81 now 75 days past due. I have contacted you several times in regard to this matter and have endeavored in every way to persuade you to pay this honest obligation.

I had hoped to make you see that your credit depended on payment of your bills. However, it would appear that this phase of the matter does not interest you, and we are compelled to draw our own conclusions.

I am not in a position to devote much time to any one account, and your continued neglect will only cause us all a great deal of unpleasantness. I, therefore, urge you to give this matter your prompt attention.

Sincerely,

The third letter in the series begins with a statement of previous unsuccessful efforts to collect. Perhaps this is an effort to shame the reader into paying, but the words invite anger more than they persuade. In the second paragraph, the I-viewpoint reference to the writer's time problem does little to persuade the debtor to pay. The following review of last-resort action possibilities has strong appeal. It may even bring in the money. As such appeals destroy goodwill, it is better to use them only in the last-resort letter. Although the close is strong, its I-emphasis reduces its effectiveness.

This harshly worded letter invites anger.

Dear Mr. Benoit:

I have notified you on many previous occasions that your account with us is in arrears. Apparently, you have chosen to ignore all our notices. Once again, I appeal to your better judgment and request that you make payment. The amount owed is $247.81, now 90 days past due.

My time is valuable to this concern; therefore I cannot devote too much attention to any one account. Your continued failure to heed my requests will force me to take drastic action. I can do one of two things. I can report you to the Retailers Credit Bureau, in which event your credit would be severely injured. Or I can turn this matter over to our attorney for legal action.

I am expecting payment by return mail.

Sincerely,

Gradual buildup of strength is evident in the following better series.

**Buildup of Appeal in a Good Series.** The better series generally follows the instructions given in preceding pages. Each letter contains strong persuasion. Although each letter in the series is stronger than the preceding one, no anger or lecturing tone is evident. The words are calm and reasonable throughout the series.

PART 4  Applications to Specific Situations

### Some Classic Responses to Collection Letters

"What would your neighbors think if we repossessed your car?" the collection letter read.

"I have taken the matter up with them," the delinquent debtor responded. "They think it would be a lousy trick."

Crotchety old Mr. Crump received the following collection message from the big-city department store: "We are surprised that we haven't received any money from you."

The old gentleman responded, "No need to be surprised. I haven't sent any."

Obviously annoyed by strong collection letters, a retailer responded with these choice words: "I am doing the best I can. Every month I place my bills in a hat. Then I draw out bills and pay them until my money runs out. If you don't stop pestering me with your collection letters, you won't even get in the hat next month."

A retailer ordered a carload of refrigerators before paying for the last order. The manufacturer responded with a collection message saying that the goods could not be sent until payment was made for the last order.

"Unable to wait so long," the retailer replied. "Cancel order."

The collection letter was terse: "Please remit the amount you owe us right away."

The response was quick and equally terse: "The amount we owe you is $145.20."

---

The first letter begins with an interesting question. The you-viewpoint of the question gives it extra attention value. The letter then moves into a presentation of the fair-play appeal, which it develops skillfully. The writing is strong yet positive. The closing request for money flows logically from the persuasion. Notice how the suggestion of urgency strengthens the request.

Dear Mr. Benoit:

How would you write to a good friend on a somewhat embarrassing subject? That's the question we must answer now, and we're not sure that we know just how to go about it. You see, you are that friend; and the subject is your overdue account.

As you recall, some time ago you wanted something we had, and we were happy to let you have it simply on your promise to pay 30 days later. We are happy to have served you. But it's only fair, isn't it, that now you should fulfill your end of the agreement?

So, in all fairness, will you please send us your check for $247.81? As your account is 60 days past due, please do it right away. A self-addressed envelope is enclosed for your convenience.

Sincerely,

*Good use of the fair-play appeal is shown here.*

The second letter in the good series begins with an attention-gaining exclamation. The opening words set up an appeal to the reader's pride in having a prompt-pay record. Then the letter develops the appeal convincingly. The request for money logically follows the appeal. The final words link the action with the reward it will bring the reader.

Dear Mr. Benoit:

You don't belong in that group!

Every day Loren's deals with hundreds of charge customers. More than 99 percent of them come through with their obligations to pay. We mark them as "prompt pay," and the doors to credit buying are opened to them all over town. Less than 1 percent don't pay right away. Of course, they sometimes have good reasons, and most of them explain their reasons to us. And we work something out. But a few allow their good credit records to tarnish.

Somehow, you have permitted your account to place your name in this last group. We don't think it belongs there. Won't you please remove it by writing us a check for $247.81, now 75 days past due? This would place you in the group in which you belong. You can use the self-addressed envelope or drop it by our store office. We're open 9–9, Monday–Saturday.

Sincerely,

*This letter skillfully uses an appeal to pride.*

The third letter in the series also has a strong attention-gaining opening. The question used is one likely to make any debtor take notice. The following explanation builds the case convincingly. It is more negative than the explanation used in the two preceding letters. For the first time in the series, the message contains more talk about the consequences of not paying than the advantages of paying. But letters at this stage of the series can afford to be somewhat negative. After describing the consequences of not paying, the letter shows how paying can avoid them. The final words link the action with a benefit it will give the reader.

Dear Mr. Benoit:

What should we report about you?

As you may know, all members of the Capital Credit Bureau must report their long-past-due accounts for distribution to the members. At the moment, your own account hangs in the balance. And we are wondering whether we will be forced to report it. We are concerned because what we must say will mean so much to you personally.

A slow-pay record would just about ruin the good credit reputation you have built over the years. You wouldn't find it easy to buy on credit from Capital Bureau members (and this includes just about every credit-granting business in town). Your credit privileges would probably be cut off completely. It would take you long years to regain the good reputation you now enjoy.

So won't you please avoid all this by mailing a check for $247.81, now 90 days past due? It would stop the bad report and save your credit record.

Sincerely,

*Frankness and conviction make this letter effective.*

**CASE ILLUSTRATION** Middle-Stage Collection Letters. *(A Wholesaler's Personal Letter to a Retailer)*

This early middle-stage letter was personally written to fit the case of a reader who had ignored two routine notices and a reminder letter. The writer used the general plan of this letter for other delinquents by bringing in the specific facts of each case.

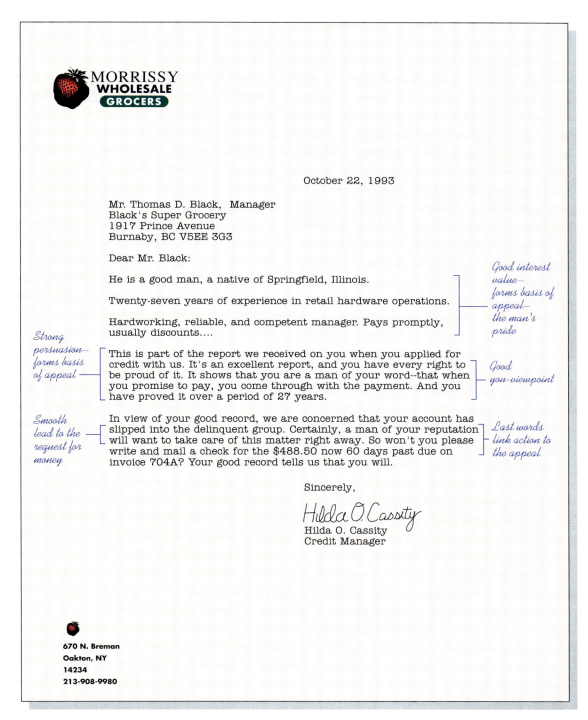

**CASE ILLUSTRATION** Middle-Stage Collection Letters. *(Middle-Stage Appeal to a Business Account)*

Illustrating courteous firmness, this early middle-stage letter was produced from a template macro developed for use with word processing software. The individually adapted parts were added.

September 17, 1993

Mr. Fulton M. Folts, President
Folts Furniture, Inc.
4217 Pemberton Road
North Atteboro, MA 02763

Dear Mr. Folts:

"Sure pay" as a credit record means sterling integrity, as you know.

"Prompt pay" means all that and more. It means alert business management.

You have both records, and we appreciate your account because you do. The record is worth a lot to you in the trade.

The only way to keep a "prompt pay" standing is to pay promptly-- every time. And since your payment of $1,358.38, now 45 days overdue, is slipping over the margin, we'd like to see you send a check right away and clear it up. Then we could happily regard the lapse as a temporary matter and keep your card in the preferred file, where it belongs.

Whether or not you have enjoyed much stove-selling weather, you were certainly foresighted in getting your stock early. Those Firefly Reflectors are worth more now than they were when you bought them. Definitely, it was a good deal for you.

Won't you make it a good deal for us, too? You can do so by sending us your check for $1,358.38 in the enclosed addressed envelope. Do it now and keep your "prompt pay" reputation.

Sincerely,

*Shannon O Tatum*

Shannon O. Tatum
Credit Manager

1380 Fulton Dr.
Madison, WS 45670
421-890-4325

*Annotations:*
- Good interest value
- Appeal is strong—concise
- Good drive for payment—recalls advantage reader gains by paying
- Opening sets up discussion of appeal
- Reference to goods bought and not paid for is subtle persuasion

**CASE ILLUSTRATION** Middle-Stage Collection Letters. *(A Strong Negative Appeal for Payment)*

The negativeness of this letter to a department store customer is justified because the customer has ignored two notices and three letters. The previous letters stressed the advantages of paying. Now it is time to stress the disadvantages of not paying.

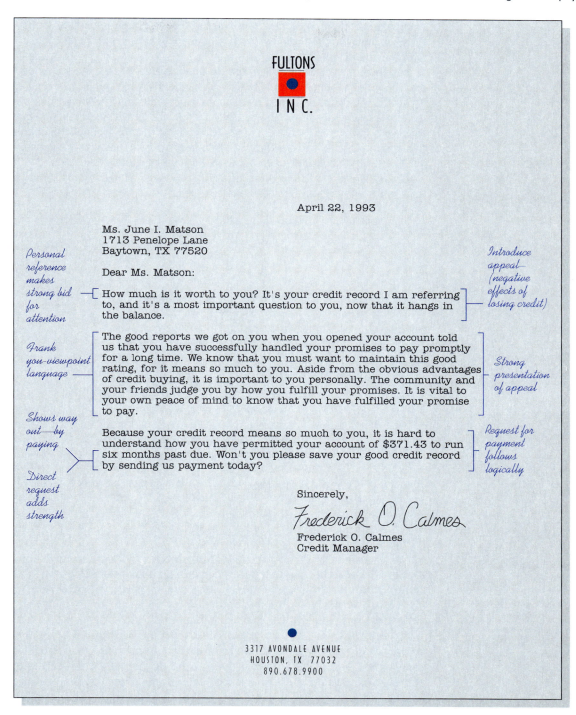

CHAPTER 10 Pattern Variations in Collections 315

### INTRODUCTORY SITUATION

## to Last-Resort Collection Letters

Assume now that the middle-stage collection letters you wrote for Loren's Department Store brought in money from most of the delinquent accounts. As is usually the case, however, they did not work with every debtor. Your problem now is to deal with these delinquents.

You think that you have given the delinquents every reasonable chance to pay, that the time has come to end the collection effort. So you will write a final letter. In it you will tell the debtors that unless they pay this time, you will turn the accounts over to a local collection agency. The agency will assist in collecting, and it will report the bad credit records to other businesses. You will also tell the debtors how this action will affect them. Then you will give them one last chance to pay. You do not like to do this, but the debtors have left you no other choice.

The letter will have to be strong, because it is the last one. The following section tells you how to write this letter. ■

"It says, 'This is your final notice. If you do not pay immediately, we will destroy your credit and have you thrown in jail. Have a happy day'."

From The Wall Street Journal, with permission of Cartoon Features Syndicate.

## LAST-RESORT LETTERS

*Collection series end with a final (last-resort) letter.*

Hard as you may try, your collection letters will not bring in all of the money. Some debtors will ignore your most persuasive efforts. Because you cannot continue your collection efforts indefinitely, you will need to take last-resort action with these debtors. You will use the final letter in the collection series to inform them of this action.

*They threaten some last-resort action (reporting to credit bureau, taking to court).*

A number of last-resort actions are available to you. One of the most common is to report the account to some credit interchange group, such as a local credit bureau. Another is to sell the account to a collection agency empowered with full authority to take legal steps if necessary. Yet another is to take the delinquent to court. You will need to decide what action is best in your case. In making your decision, you should consider the customs in your field of business, the nature and amount of the account, and the image of your firm.

In planning last-resort strategy, you should keep in mind that laws govern collection procedures and that more laws of this kind are likely to be enacted. Currently, a few states have debt-collection laws, and federal legislation controls some areas of debt. The state laws are numerous and varied, but they generally protect consumers from extreme abuses. The federal laws prohibit using language that threatens garnishment of wages, taking possession of property, and involving the consumer's employer and bank. As far as we can determine, the practices suggested in the following pages are in accord with current U.S. legislation. You will find additional information on the effects of U.S. laws in Appendix E.

*You should know the laws governing collections.*

### Justifying Directness

In selecting the plan for the last-resort letter, you should consider what must be done to collect the money. Up to this point, you have tried the milder methods. As they have not worked, you must now do something stronger.

*Last-resort collection letters require strength.*

As you learned earlier, directness produces strength. You did not use it through the middle stage of the series because directness in such cases can destroy goodwill, and until now you have been concerned about keeping goodwill. You have wanted to save the account. But now you are more interested in collecting the money. Thus, you can justify the use of this time-tested, direct plan for writing the last-resort letter:

*As the direct order adds strength, it is justified for last-resort letters.*

- **Begin by stating what you are doing, and why.**
- **Persuade by explaining the effects of this action—firmly, clearly, and without anger.**
- **Give the reader a last chance to pay by setting a deadline and urging that it be met.**
- **Perhaps end by associating paying with avoiding the effects of the action that will be taken if payment is not made.**

*This time-tested plan is effective.*

### Presenting the Action Directly

You begin the last-resort letter with a clear statement of your action. That is, you tell right away what you are going to do. Such direct openings are strong, and they gain attention. In addition, you might consider bringing in facts that justify the action. Of course, the reader probably knows these facts very well. Even so, mentioning them may hold down a defensive reaction by the debtor. Something like this would do the job:

*Begin the letter with the threat of action. It is good to justify the action.*

Your failure to pay the $378.40 now seven months past due on your account leaves us no choice but to report you to the Omaha Credit Bureau.

### Interpreting the Action

Your explanation of the effects of the action on the debtor comes next. This is your last effort to persuade. In developing the persuasion, you should place yourself in the reader's position to see how last-resort action will affect him or her. It may, for example, mean the end of credit buying, court costs, loss of prestige, and personal embarrassment. Whatever the effects, you

*Then explain the effects of the action on the debtor. Use you-viewpoint.*

**CHAPTER 10** Pattern Variations in Collections

### How They Did It 3,000 Years Ago

The following collection letter, one of the earliest on record, was written in Egypt some 3,000 years ago by Sarapamon to Piperas.

"Let me tell you that you owe me seven years' rents and dues; so unless you now send discharges, you know the dangers."

By modern standards this is a last-resort letter. But it may have been the only one sent. Although the threatened action is not named, no doubt the reader got the message.

---

should select those most appropriate in the one case. Then you should decide how to present them convincingly.

*The words should show concern, not anger.*

Describing the effects of your action requires your best writing skills. You will especially need to watch the tone of your words. You need not be as tactful as you were in earlier letters, but you will need to avoid showing anger. As you know, anger invites resistance. So, instead of showing anger, let your words show concern for the debtor's problem. You wish things had not turned out this way, but the debtor's actions leave you no choice.

### Offering a Last Chance in the Close

After describing the effects of the last-resort action, you should give the debtor a last chance to pay. Thus, your close should set a deadline for payment or perhaps for other arrangements. You should urge the debtor to meet this deadline. As in other persuasive efforts, your final words might well recall what the debtor will gain (or avoid) by paying. The following close meets these requirements well:

*In the close, offer a deadline for paying before action is taken.*

We will report you to the Capital Credit Bureau on the 15th. So won't you please help yourself by sending us your check for $129.90 by that date? It's the one way you can save your credit reputation.

*Recall the appeal.*

### Contrasting Last-Resort Letters

Both of the following letters are strong. They are almost certain to gain the reader's attention. The first, however, is primarily an angry outburst. The second is stern, but its calmness and convincing persuasion are likely to get results.

*Following are examples of bad and good last-resort letters.*

**Weakness in an Angry Letter.** The first letter begins indirectly. Although the opening words are strong, they show anger, and anger is likely to invite resistance. The subsequent reference to earlier attempts to collect justifies the last-resort action, but it continues to show anger. Finally, action is threatened—far from the beginning position of emphasis. Notice that the effects of this action are not explained. The final words, which provide a way out, are the best part of the letter.

PART 4 Applications to Specific Situations

**CASE ILLUSTRATION** Last-Resort Collection Letters. *(A Final Letter to an Industrial Account)*

This last-resort letter to an industrial account was sent following five unsuccessful attempts to collect.

---

**MERRIWEATHER SUPPLY HOUSE**

July 12, 1993

Mr. Carl Waldon
Waldon Machine Works
3931 West Belford Road
Joliet, IL 60433

Dear Mr. Waldon:

*Direct-naming action gets attention*

Since our five previous requests for payment of your four-months-past-due bill for $3,587.31 have received no response, we are forced to turn your account over to the Merchants' Credit and Collections Agency unless payment is in our office by July 19.

*Recall of past efforts justifies action*

*Explanation of effects is concrete and convincing*

As a business executive, you are well aware of just what this action can mean to you. The collection agency would be empowered to take this case to court. And court action would be both costly and embarrassing to you. You would be forced to pay not only the full $3,587.31 but court costs as well. Your friends around Millville would be quick to learn of a collection suit against you, for such news travels fast. Your other creditors also would pick up the news. Thus, your future credit buying would be severely restricted--maybe even cut off completely. And with limited credit, chances are your business operations--and your profits--would be cut.

*Strong, negative you-viewpoint reasoning*

*Clear urge to act— sets deadline*

We sincerely urge you to avoid the agency's forced collection, Mr. Waldon. We'll hold them off until July 19. You can hold them off permanently by mailing us your check for $3,587.31 so that it will reach us by that date. Won't you pay this honest debt right away and avoid the unpleasantness of court action?

*Recalls benefits of complying*

Sincerely,

*Helen R. Rothschild*

Helen R. Rothschild
Credit Manager

1356 N. BROADWAY
WHEATON, CA
10045
415-890-7867

---

CHAPTER 10 Pattern Variations in Collections 319

## CASE ILLUSTRATION  Last-Resort Collection Letters. *(Threatening a Retail Customer with Court Action)*

Sent after seven unsuccessful efforts to collect, this form letter was made to appear personally written by working in specific facts of the one case.

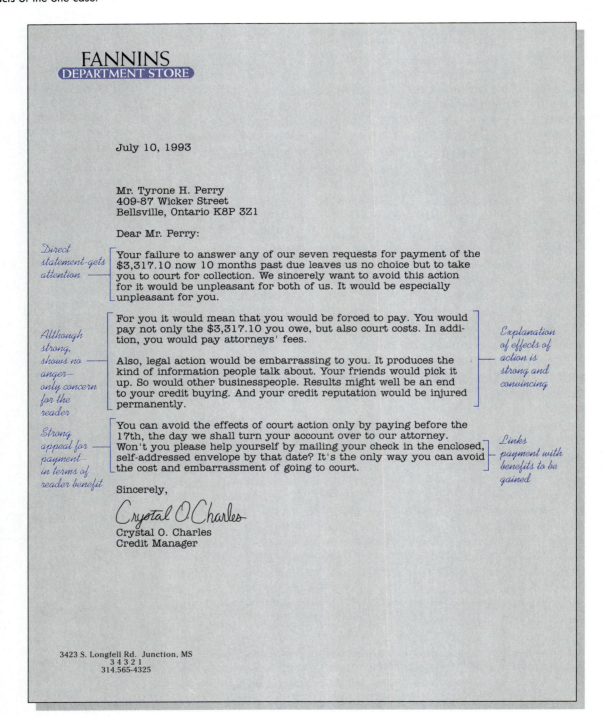

**FANNINS DEPARTMENT STORE**

July 10, 1993

Mr. Tyrone H. Perry
409-87 Wicker Street
Bellsville, Ontario K8P 3Z1

Dear Mr. Perry:

*Direct statement—gets attention*

Your failure to answer any of our seven requests for payment of the $3,317.10 now 10 months past due leaves us no choice but to take you to court for collection. We sincerely want to avoid this action for it would be unpleasant for both of us. It would be especially unpleasant for you.

*Although strong, shows no anger—only concern for the reader*

For you it would mean that you would be forced to pay. You would pay not only the $3,317.10 you owe, but also court costs. In addition, you would pay attorneys' fees.

Also, legal action would be embarrassing to you. It produces the kind of information people talk about. Your friends would pick it up. So would other businesspeople. Results might well be an end to your credit buying. And your credit reputation would be injured permanently.

*Explanation of effects of action is strong and convincing*

*Strong appeal for payment in terms of reader benefit*

You can avoid the effects of court action only by paying before the 17th, the day we shall turn your account over to our attorney. Won't you please help yourself by mailing your check in the enclosed, self-addressed envelope by that date? It's the only way you can avoid the cost and embarrassment of going to court.

*Links payment with benefits to be gained*

Sincerely,

*Crystal O. Charles*
Crystal O. Charles
Credit Manager

3423 S. Longfell Rd.  Junction, MS
34321
314.565-4321

Dear Ms. Benoit:

We can no longer tolerate your complete disregard of your long-past-due account. We have written you repeatedly, but you have not shown the courtesy of an acknowledgment. Therefore, we must now turn over your account to the Capital Credit Bureau.

We will give you one week from the date of this letter to make payment of the $3,251.49, now 120 days past due. If payment is not received by May 3, we will take action.

Sincerely,

This bad letter is mainly angry words.

**Strength in a Calm and Firm Appeal.** The better letter gets right down to business with a clear statement of the action that will be taken. Then it moves into a convincing interpretation of this action. Notice the you-viewpoint—how the words emphasize the effects on the one reader. Although the message is negative, the overall tone is wholesome. There is no evidence of anger. The close, a final recall of the disadvantages of not paying, leaves the action in the reader's hands.

Dear Ms. Benoit:

Your failure to respond to our previous attempts to collect your 120-days overdue account of $3,251.49 leaves us no choice but to turn your account over to the Capital Credit Bureau for collection. This is an action we had hoped not to take, for it is unpleasant for both of us—particularly for you.

For you it means that you would be forced by the courts to pay the amount of your bill—plus court costs. In addition to being expensive, legal action may be embarrassing to you. Also, your credit record could be permanently injured.

Both of us want to avoid these bad effects of legal action. We'll do our part by holding off action for seven days after the date of this letter. To do your part, you must pay us before that date. It's all up to you, for only you can save your credit record and the embarrassment of court action.

Sincerely,

This good letter is strong, yet shows concern.

## SUMMARY (by Chapter Objectives)

1. Collection letters are usually sent in a series.
   - First comes a reminder, usually not a letter.
   - Next comes persuasive letters.
   - The series ends with a last-resort letter.
   - The number of letters in the series is influenced by credit risk and practice in the field.
     —Exclusive shops, for example, would be likely to use a longer, slower series than that used by stores catering to bad risks.
     —Some businesses classify customers into risk groups and treat each differently.
   - Typically, collection series between businesses are short and move fast.
   - Increased use of computer billings appears to have led to shorter collection efforts and harsher letters.

1. Design a series of collection letters according to the credit risk involved and standard practice in the field of business.

| | |
|---|---|
| 2. Write short and courteous reminder letters in the early stage of collection. | 2. Begin a collection series on the assumption that the reader *will* pay.<br>• Your first letter should be a short, courteous reminder of the past-due bill.<br>• Such letters are typically direct, though the indirect order is effective sometimes.<br>• These letters usually contain appropriate goodwill talk. |
| 3. Compose letters using the appropriate degree of persuasion and frankness in the middle stage of collection. | 3. Write the middle-stage letters on the assumption that the reader *should* pay.<br>• Thus, persuasion is needed.<br>• Begin by selecting an appeal (fair play, pride, or such), and develop this appeal in words that convince.<br>• Each succeeding letter in this stage is stronger than the preceding one.<br>• Since letters in this stage are not invited, begin them with attention-gaining words.<br>• These words should set up your strategy (the appeal selected).<br>• Then present the appeal, taking care to make it convincing and at the right strength for the collection stage involved.<br>• But keep the tone friendly (no anger).<br>• End with a request for payment, perhaps linking payment with a benefit to be gained by paying. |
| 4. Use strength and directness to present action in a calm and firm appeal in last-resort letters. | 4. After the buildup of middle-stage letters has failed, write a final letter (last resort). The assumption here is that the reader *must* pay.<br>• Begin by selecting a last-resort action (reporting to a credit bureau, going to court).<br>• Write the letter in direct order, telling what action you will take.<br>—Use directness because it adds strength.<br>—And make this last letter strong.<br>• Throughout, show concern rather than anger.<br>• Present the effects of this action in convincing words.<br>• Close with a last-chance offer of a deadline for paying before taking the action threatened.<br>• Consider a final recall of the appeal, associating it with the action. |

## QUESTIONS FOR DISCUSSION

1. "Only one test is meaningful in determining how good a collection letter is: how well it brings in the money." Discuss.
2. Describe the collection-letter series you would recommend for a store selling inexpensive clothing to high-risk customers. Explain your selection.
3. Describe the collection series you would recommend for an exclusive clothing store selling mainly to low risks. Explain your selection.
4. Most first reminders are written in the direct order. Middle-stage letters tend to be written in the indirect order. Discuss the reasons for these practices.
5. This book recommends cordiality throughout the collection procedure. What is the logic of this practice?
6. If the last-resort collection letter is the strongest in the series and, therefore, the most likely to bring in the money, why not use it earlier?
7. Discuss the role of negative and positive wording and the you-viewpoint throughout the collection series.

## APPLICATION EXERCISES

Criticize the following form collection letters. They were written for a large department store for middle- to upper-income customers with good credit records at the time they were granted credit. The series consists of five letters.

1. *First letter (60 days past due)*

   Dear _____:

   Please be informed that your account with us shows an unpaid balance of $327.48 now 60 days past due. Surely there must be some mistake. I know you will correct the matter right away by mailing in your check. If there is some problem, please call me to make arrangements.

   Sincerely yours,

   Alice Blumberg, Credit Manager

2. *Third letter (120 days past due)*

   Dear _____:

   Because you have ignored my previous efforts to collect the $327.48 now four months past due, I must firmly call this matter to your attention.
   Perhaps you do not realize the seriousness of what you have done. Your credit rating is in jeopardy. You are in danger of losing a reputation that took a lifetime to build. And once your reputation is ruined, you will find it very difficult to regain it.
   I know you do not want this to happen. So please send us the amount owed right away. If there is a problem, at least call me or write me and explain so we can work out a payment plan. If we do not hear from you soon, we will take appropriate action.

   Sincerely yours,

   Alice Blumberg, Credit Manager

3. *Fifth letter (180 days past due)*

   Dear _____:

   I am extremely disappointed to find your name among our debtors who are a full six months past due in paying their honest obligations. In spite of the fact that I have repeatedly informed you of your obligation, you have completely ignored the matter. I will no longer be patient.
   Unless you pay the $327.48 you owe, we will take drastic action. We will go to court; and we can and will collect. Either you pay us by November 16 or I'll see you in court.

   Sincerely yours,

   Alice Blumberg, Credit Manager

## LETTER PROBLEMS
### COLLECTIONS

These problems are arranged by series. The stage in the series is indentified at the beginning of each problem.

#### Gwynne's Fashions Series

1. *(Early stage).* For this assignment play the role of credit and collections manager for Gwynne's Fashions, an exclusive ladies store in your area. Until now you have handled all accounts on an individual basis, writing personalized collection letters when your charge customers got too far behind in their payments. But this procedure is consuming more of your time than you can spare. So you have decided to begin using form collection letters. Even so, you will make them appear to be personally written, working in names and account information where appropriate.

    After reviewing the unique needs of a store like Gwynne's, you have decided on the following plan. You will send your end-of-the-month statement, and you will send another statement a month later. The next month (when the bill is two months past due), you will send another statement, this one with a printed reminder attached. Another month later, if the bill is still unpaid, you will send a letter. This letter will be strictly positive and will follow a "probably you have forgotten and will appreciate a gentle reminder" theme.

    Write this letter. Address the letters in this series to Sylvia Speery, who owes Gwynne's $676.55.

2. *(Middle stage).* If the first letter doesn't succeed, thirty days later you will send a second letter. This one will develop a collection appeal, but in a positive way. You have selected an appeal to the social rewards of keeping a good credit record.

    Write this letter. Remember to make some provision for including the amount owed and the time past due in the text of the letter.

3. *(Middle stage).* You will write a third letter a month later and a fourth after another month. At this point the account is six months past due. A stronger appeal is appropriate. You will use an appeal to fair play. Even though you will use strong persuasion at this stage, you will not threaten; nor will you use strongly negative wording.

    As in the preceding letters, you will mention the amount owed and time past due. Write this fourth letter.

4. *(Middle stage).* Fifteen days after sending the fourth letter you will send a fifth letter. This one will stress the advantages of maintaining a good credit rating. And for the first time in the collection series, it will mention the effects of losing a good credit record. Even so, the letter will not be harsh. Now write this letter. Work in a reference to the amount owed and time past due.

5. *(Last resort).* Because you do not think Gwynne's would profit from the negative publicity associated with forced collection, you will sell long-overdue accounts to the Metro Collection Agency with full authorization to take legal action. Thus, the last letter that will come from your office will warn of this impending action. You will send this letter 15 days after the fifth letter.

    This last letter will talk with friendly but frank concern about the action to be taken and its consequences. It will urge payment to avoid these consequences. As in all letters in the series, send this letter to Sylvia Speery and work in the time past due (seven months) and the amount owed ($676.55). Now write this letter.

#### Wiegman Plumbing Supply Series

6. *(Early stage).* As manager of credit and collections for Wiegman Plumbing Supply, handle the account of the Jerome Belleau Plumbing Company. Two months ago Mr. Belleau opened an account with Wiegman and promptly purchased $7,433 in plumbing supplies. He has not been in the plumbing supply store since. He did not pay the bill that you sent him at the end of the month. And he ignored the second statement, which you sent 15 days later. Now, an additional 15 days later, you will send him a first collection letter.

    This letter will be a friendly reminder, for you are not ready to risk endangering relations with this new customer. Your letter will follow the theme that probably Belleau has just overlooked the bill and will appreciate a reminder. Now write the letter.

7. *(Middle stage).* The friendly reminder did not work. Now, 15 days later, you must write again. This time you will attempt to persuade Mr. Belleau to pay. You will appeal to the man's sense of fair play. Wiegman's trusted him and helped him. Now

it is only fair that he fulfill his end of the agreement. You will apply your best persuasion, but it will be primarily positive. Now write the letter.

8. *(Middle stage).* It is now 15 days after you sent Mr. Belleau a second letter. He hasn't paid, so you must write again. This time you will be more persuasive. You will stress the value of a good credit rating, emphasizing how it is important to business success. You'll even discuss the negative consequences of a bad record. You'll use strong persuasion, but you won't threaten.

9. *(Last resort).* Another 15 days have passed and Mr. Belleau hasn't responded to your persuasive collection letters. Now you must take last-resort action. This $7,433 bill is 75 days past due. If Belleau doesn't pay or at least respond so you can work out a payment plan, you will have to turn the matter over to your lawyers. They will then force collection by legal means.

Write a final letter telling Belleau of this impending action. In the letter describe the consequences so that Belleau will see that he must pay. Give him 10 days from the date of the letter to pay or contact you before you take action.

## Sanderson CPA Series

10. *(Early stage).* Your business, Sanderson CPA, P.C., provides full accounting services to its clients. Started three years ago, the business has grown and developed mainly on the fundamental premise of your business—excellent professional service at fair prices. Because you have worked hard to project this "excellent and fair" image in all of your business operations, you are reluctant to do anything that might tarnish the professional reputation you've worked so diligently to establish.

As your business has grown, so, too, have some of the problems associated with such growth. One of these is the matter of collections of overdue accounts. It appears that many of the clients you provide accounting services to pay you slowly—very slowly. Thus, at this stage of your business development you are determined to do something about those slow-paying accounts.

Typically, you send a monthly statement to all customers. If they do not respond to it in 30 days, you send another notice with this message printed in red: "30 days past due; please pay immediately." A friendly reminder letter is written to those who do not respond to your second notice after another 30 days.

But you are not satisfied with the letter you are sending. And it obviously does not pull in the overdue accounts, as an analysis of three-months-past-due accounts reveals. So prepare a good reminder letter to these clients. It will be mostly a goodwill letter, but you will ask for payment. It will assume that clients will pay if they are reminded in a friendly way.

11. *(Middle stage).* Assume that the friendly reminder letter you sent did not produce the results you want. Thus, you are now going to move a rung up your collection ladder and write a "client-should-pay" letter. This letter will be more forceful than the reminder letter and will be sent 20 days after it.

Although the letter will be more forceful, it will not be overly so. You will need to persuade—to sell clients on why they should pay. After considering a number of appeals, you decide to emphasize "fair play" in paying for a service rendered. Discuss the benefits of paying the overdue account with the clients from a "fair-play" point of view. Write the middle stage letter that will sell your clients on paying.

12. *(Middle stage).* As of today, it is 30 days past the time you wrote your first middle-stage, "fair-play" letter. And still you have clients who have not paid their accounts. You're not ready to give them an ultimatum yet; but your next middle-stage effort will have to use another appeal. This time you decide on a pride appeal—pride in paying one's obligations.

This letter will be slightly more forceful than the preceding one. But it will still try to sell the client on paying up. As usual, you'll mention the amount due and number of days the account is past due. But these details should be subordinate to the letter's mission—to persuade the reader to take an action (pay the account) because of pride.

13. *(Last resort).* It is now 20 days after your second middle-stage, "should-pay" attempt to collect the overdue accounts. Still, your efforts have not produced results. Because you have no other choice, you will write a final letter to all overdue accounts—a "must-pay" collection effort. There will be no other notices. If clients do not clear their accounts within 15 days of the date of the letter, you will turn them over to Professional Collection Services for legal action.

Your letter will spell out what this action means to your clients. But it will do so without being needlessly negative. You would still prefer to have the money rather than to take legal action. Write this last-resort letter. Make sure clients know this is the final letter that they will receive.

## Educational Services, Inc. Series

14. *(Early stage).* Your business, Educational Services, Inc., provides testing, evaluation, and tutoring to children with reading and math deficiencies in grades 1–6. You administer appropriate tests to children, analyze their results, write up the results in a formal report, present the report to parents in a counseling session, recommend remediation, and provide follow-up tutoring if such assistance is warranted by the test results. For these services, you charge a reasonable professional fee.

    Throughout the 18 months of Educational Services, Inc.'s existence as a business entity, you have seen revenues and income growth beyond your expectations. It is apparent that you identified a need and established a niche for yourself with the business. Along with your growth, however, have come problems of collecting on credit accounts. During the first year of operations, your collection efforts were quite informal. You sent monthly statements, you wrote personal notes as follow-ups, and you telephoned overdue accounts. Most of these efforts worked at the time. But credit sales have grown even larger, so you must now design a more formal collection plan for your growing business.

    As you put your fingers to the keyboard, you believe the following plan will work the best. First, you will mail monthly statements to credit accounts. If you do not receive payment in 30 days, you'll send a second statement with a stamped reminder: "Please pay promptly—30 days past due." If this second attempt to collect does not bring payment in 30 days, you will write a personal letter. It will be about 80 percent goodwill and 20 percent persuasion and built around the idea of "just a friendly reminder about your overdue account." Write the letter for Educational Services, Inc.

15. *(Middle stage).* If the first-stage friendly reminder letter does not work, you will prepare a middle-stage "should pay" collection letter. To be sent 30 days after the reminder letter, the letter will be built around the theme of "fair play." That is, it is only "fair" to pay for the services that have already been received. You will strike a 60:40 ratio between goodwill and persuasion. You must now prepare this letter.

16. *(Middle stage).* You will send another discussion-stage letter if your first one does not collect the overdue account. This second middle-stage letter will feature the theme of "the social stigma attached to those who lose their credit standing." Because it is stronger, this letter will emphasize the appeal (at 65 percent) and goodwill (at 35 percent). Write this second-stage letter.

17. *(Last resort).* Twenty days after you send your second middle-stage letter, you plan to send your final collection attempt. This last-resort letter will be about 10/90 percent in structure—that is, 10 percent goodwill and 90 percent persuasion. It will state that if you do not receive payment within 15 days of the date of the letter, you will turn the account over to Central Collection Agency. This agency will take legal action to collect the overdue account. You would still prefer the money to the legal action. As with all good collection efforts, you should give the full amount due and how many days overdue the account is. Write this last-resort letter for Educational Services, Inc.

## Ballinger Medical Clinic Series

18. *(Early stage).* One of your jobs as the office manager for Ballinger Medical Clinic, which specializes in treating disorders of the eyes and ears, is collecting accounts receivable. One patient, Fernando Sanchez, hasn't paid his account for 60 days. He was seen in the office for surgery to remove a metal sliver from his right eye. Apparently, he thinks the company he was working for as an independent contractor should pay, but the company has denied his claims. You need to collect from him.

    Mr. Sanchez has been a patient at your clinic for over 10 years. He has a good payment record. In fact, the credit bureau you subscribe to rates him four-star, the best rating.

    The doctors in the clinic stress goodwill. They want low-key collections; however, they do believe in writing off as few accounts as possible as uncollectible. Write a friendly letter asking for full payment of the $350 owed the clinic. Remind Mr. Sanchez of the good service he has enjoyed over the years with your clinic. Be sure to maintain his goodwill.

19. *(Middle stage).* It has been a month since you wrote Mr. Sanchez, and you have received no response.

    You will write another letter appealing to his sense of fair play. Urge him to pay now for the sight-saving surgery he received at your clinic. His surgery was one you remember vividly since it didn't seem serious to you, but the doctors reported that if he had waited 24 hours to have the metal shaving removed it would probably have rusted and his sight would have been lost. Continue to stress goodwill while making it clear he must pay.

20. *(Middle stage).*  Three months have gone by with no word from Mr. Sanchez. You'll write him a stronger letter, persuading him to pay. Use an economic appeal; encourage him to pay to maintain his good credit rating. You may suggest that he contact you to discuss payment options. Again be sure to maintain the goodwill your bosses believe is so important. You may want one of the doctors in the clinic to sign the letter since an appeal coming from a higher authority is often more persuasive. Mr. Sanchez is aware that the doctor knows and wants his record to be in good standing.

21. *(Last resort).*  Mr. Sanchez has not responded in any way to any of your letters. You'll have to write the "pay-up-or-else" letter. Your boss's "or else" means turning his account over to a collection agency. This action isn't extremely threatening, but it's the last time Mr. Sanchez will have a chance to settle the bill with your office. After it's turned over, it is out of your control. You'll give him 15 days to contact you before you take any action—and you will act!

### A Personal Series for Construction Services

22. *(Early stage).*  Last month you completed work on a fireplace for Dr. John Jones, a local dentist. Dr. Jones had contacted you last spring, asking you to build a fireplace in his family room. He told you he had inherited some money from his father; he thought his father would approve of this project. You thought the extra money you would earn could provide the perfect winter vacation for you and your family.

    You carried out your part of the deal, providing for the construction of a new flue, a Chicago-brick fireplace, and a beautiful mantle. The project has been completed for two months, but you haven't received any payment from Dr. Jones. Write him a friendly reminder, urging him to pay the $4,500 as soon as possible. Be sure to maintain goodwill.

23. *(Middle stage).*  Dr. Jones contacted you after receiving your letter. He told you that his wife had left him and that he was in the middle of a settlement; he'd pay you as soon as possible. However, that was over a month ago and you haven't yet received payment.

    Write Dr. Jones a persuasive letter. Appeal to his sense of pride, knowing that the beautiful fireplace he looks at every day is paid for. You know he has a good credit rating. Work to collect. Offer him payment options that would collect the full amount in time for you to take that winter vacation you know you've earned.

24. *(Middle stage).*  A month has passed with no word from Dr. Jones. However, today you learned from friends that Dr. Jones had been in a serious automobile accident and had lost the use of a leg and a hand. He probably won't be able to practice dentistry anymore. However, you still need to collect for the time, materials, and work you've done. Write Dr. Jones a strong letter of appeal. Stress the benefits he derives from the fireplace and work to build goodwill.

25. *(Last resort).*  Four months have passed since you completed the fireplace for Dr. Jones. You have not received any payment or any precise promise of payment. Since you have several thousand dollars invested in this project, you must be paid. Write Dr. Jones the letter of last resort. Threaten to put a lien on his property unless you hear from him in 30 days. You may want to remind him that the fireplace has added to the value of the property, increasing his equity. Stress the importance of paying immediately.

**CHAPTER 11**

# STRATEGY IN JOB SEARCH AND APPLICATION

## CHAPTER OBJECTIVES

*Upon completing this chapter, you will be able to conduct an effective job search and compose effective job-application letters, résumés, and follow-up letters. To reach this goal, you should be able to*

**1**

Develop and use a network of contacts in your job search.

**2**

Assemble and evaluate information that will help you select a career.

**3**

Describe the sources that can lead you to an employer.

**4**

Compile a résumé that is strong, complete, and well arranged.

**5**

Write letters of application which skillfully sell your abilities.

**6**

Explain how you should conduct yourself in an interview.

**7**

Write application follow-up letters that are appropriate, friendly, and positive.

## INTRODUCTORY SITUATION

### to the Job-Search Procedure

Introduce yourself to this chapter by assuming a role similar to one you are now playing. You are Cyrus Sylvester, a student at Olympia University. In a few months, you will complete your studies for a career in labor relations.

You believe that it is time to begin the search for the job for which those studies have been preparing you. But how do you do this? Where do you look? What does the search involve? How should you conduct yourself for the best results? The answers to these and related questions are reviewed in the following pages. ∎

## THE JOB SEARCH

Of all the things you do in life, few are more important than getting a job. Whether it involves your first job or one further down your career path, job seeking is directly related to your success and your happiness. It is vital that you conduct the job search properly—that you prepare wisely and carefully and proceed diligently. The following review of job-search procedures should help you succeed.

*For success in job seeking, use the following procedure.*

### Building a Network of Contacts

You can begin the job search long before you are ready to find employment. In fact, you can do it now by building a network of contacts.[1] More specifically, you can build relationships with people who can help you find work when you need it. Such people include classmates, professors, and businesspeople.

*Begin the job search by building a network of contacts in this way:*

At present, your classmates are not likely to be holding positions in which they make or influence hiring decisions. But in the future, when you may want to make a career change, they may hold such positions. Even right now, some of them may know people in high places who can help you. The wider your circle of friends, the more likely you are to make employment contacts.

*(1) Broaden your circle of friends.*

Knowing your professors and making sure that they know you can also lead to employment contacts. As professors often consult for business, they may know key executives and be able to help you contact them. Professors sometimes hear of position openings, and in such cases they can refer you to the hiring executives. Demonstrating your work ethic and your ability in the classroom is probably the best way to get your professors to know you and help you. Take advantage of opportunities to know your professors outside the classroom. Knowing the professors in your major field is especially beneficial.

*(2) Get to know your professors.*

Obviously, knowing key business executives can also lead to employment contacts. You may already know some through family and friends. But

*(3) Meet executives.*

---

[1] Adapted from John Lucht, "Building a Network before Graduation," *College Edition of the National Business Employment Weekly*, published by *The Wall Street Journal*, Fall 1988, p. 9.

broadening your relationships among businesspeople would be helpful. You can do this in various ways, but especially through college professional clubs such as the Data Processing Management Association, Delta Sigma Pi, and the Society for the Advancement of Management. By taking an active role in the organizations in your field of study, especially by working on program committees and by becoming an officer, you can get to know the executives who serve as guest speakers.

**(4) Make contacts through internships.**

If your school offers internships, you can make good career contacts through them. But you should find the one that is best for you, that offers you the best training for your career objective. And by all means, do not regard an internship as just a job. Regard it as a foundation step in your career plan. The experience you gain and the contacts you make in an internship might well lead to your first career position. In fact, if you perform well, your internship could turn into full-time employment.

**(5) Work with community organizations.**

In addition to the more common ways of making contacts discussed above, you can use some less common ones. By working in community organizations (charities, community improvement groups, fund-raising groups), you can meet community leaders. By attending meetings of professional associations (every field has them), you can meet the leaders in your field. In fact, participation in virtually any activity that provides contacts with business leaders can open doors for you now and well into the future.

## Analyzing Yourself

**Begin with a self-analysis covering these background areas:**

When you are ready to search for your career job, you should begin the effort by analyzing yourself. In a sense, you should look at yourself much as you would look at a product or service that is for sale. After all, when you seek employment, you are really selling your ability to work—to do things for an employer. A job is more than something that brings you money. It is something that gives equal benefits to both parties—you and your employer. Thus, you should think about the qualities you have that enable you to do the work that an employer needs to have done. This self-analysis should cover the following categories.

**(1) Education. For specialized curricula, the career path is clear.**

**Education.** The analysis might well begin with education. Perhaps you have already selected your career area, such as accounting, finance, information systems, management, or marketing. If you have, your task is simplified, for your specialized curriculum has prepared you for your goal.

FRANK & ERNEST reprinted by permission of NEA, Inc.

PART 4 Applications to Specific Situations

Even so, you may be able to note special points—for example, electives that have given you special skills or that show something special about you (such as psychology courses that have improved your human-relations skills, communication courses that have improved your writing and speaking skills, or foreign language courses that have prepared you for international assignments).

If you have pursued a more general curriculum (general business, liberal arts, or such), you will need to look at it closely to see what it has prepared you to do. Perhaps you will find an emphasis on computers, written communication, human relations, foreign languages—all of which are sorely needed by some businesses. Or perhaps you will conclude that your training has given you a strong general base from which to learn specific business skills.

For general curricula, a career choice must be made.

In analyzing your education, you should look at the quality of your record—grades, honors, special recognitions. If your record is good, you can emphasize it. But what if your work was only mediocre? As we will point out later, you will need to shift the emphasis to your stronger sales points—your willingness to work, your personality, your experience. Or perhaps you can explain, for example, by noting that working your way through school limited your academic performance.

Consider quality of educational record (grades, honors, courses taken).

**Personal Qualities.** Your self-analysis should also cover your personal qualities. Qualities that relate to working with people are especially important. Qualities that show leadership or teamwork ability are also important. And if you express yourself well in writing or speaking, note this, for good communication skills are valuable in most jobs.

(2) Personal qualities (people skills, leadership, and such).

Of course, you may not be the best judge of your personal qualities, for we do not always see ourselves as others see us. You may need to check with friends to see whether they agree with your assessments. You may also need to check your record for evidence supporting your assessments. For example, organization membership and participation in community activities are evidence of people and teamwork skills. Election to organization offices is evidence of leadership ability. Participation on a debate team is evidence of communication skills.

**Work Experience.** If you have work experience, you should analyze it. Work experience in your career path deserves major emphasis. In fact, such work experience becomes more and more important as you move along your career path. Work experience not related to the job you seek can also tell something important about you—even if the work was part-time and menial. Menial work can show willingness and determination, especially if you have done it to finance your education. And almost any work experience can help develop your skills in dealing with people.

(3) Work experience (with interpretations).

**Special Qualifications.** Your self-analysis should also include special qualifications that might be valuable to an employer. The ability to speak a foreign language can be very helpful for certain international businesses. Athletic participation, hobbies, and interests may also be helpful. To illustrate, athletic experience would be helpful for work for a sporting goods distributor, a hobby of automobile mechanics would be helpful for work with an automotive service company, and an interest in music would be helpful for work with a piano manufacturer.

(4) Special qualities (languages, communication skills, and such).

## Selecting Your Career Path

Select your career path.

After you have analyzed your qualifications, you are ready to select the career path that is just right for you. This task involves matching the facts you have listed with the work needs of business. Your education may have already narrowed your choice to a specific work area such as marketing, information systems, or accounting. Otherwise, you will need to review your qualifications to see what you are best equipped to do. Within reason, your selection of a career path can be influenced by your personal preferences. However, your goal in this process is to give realistic direction to your search for employment.

Narrow your selection to type of employer.

At this point, you may narrow your selection even further, depending on your preferences and qualifications. If you are an accounting major, for example, you may consider work in firms that range in size from the giants to small, private practices. You may also consider work in industry or a government agency. If you are a marketing major, you may consider work in wholesaling or retailing, with merchandising giants or smaller operations, or with conservative or aggressive merchandisers.

Consider location limitations.

In addition, you should consider where you would be willing to work. Are there places where you would not be willing to work? Are you willing to travel? To move around the country? To work abroad? Your answers to such questions are important in your job search, for they affect the job opportunities available to you. Although the availability of work may answer the questions for you, you should answer them as well as you can on the basis of what you know now and then conduct your job search accordingly. Finding just the right job is one of the most important goals in your life.

## Finding Your Employer

Search for potential employers by using these sources:

You can use a number of sources in your search for an employer with which you will begin or continue on your career path. Your choice of sources will probably be influenced by where you are in your career path.

(1) your school's placement center,

**University Placement Centers.** If you are just beginning your career, one good possibility is the placement center at your school. Most of the large schools have placement centers, and these attract employers that are looking for suitable applicants. Many placement centers offer excellent job-search counseling and maintain files on registrants containing school records, résumés, and recommendation letters for review by prospective employers. Most have directories listing the major companies with contact names and addresses.

(2) your network of personal contacts,

**Network of Personal Contacts.** As has been noted, the personal contacts you make can be extremely helpful in your job search. In fact, according to one employment report, personal contacts are the leading means of finding employees. Obviously, personal contacts are more likely to be a source of employment opportunities later in your career path—when you may need to change jobs.

(3) classified advertisements,

**Classified Advertisements.** Help-wanted advertisements in newspapers and professional journals provide good sources of employment opportunities for many kinds of work. They are somewhat limited, however, in the opportunities they provide for new college graduates. They are good sources for

**PART 4** Applications to Specific Situations

experienced workers who are seeking to improve their positions, and they are especially good sources for people who are conducting a major search for high-level positions.

**On-line Databases.** In addition to finding opportunities in printed sources, you will also find them on-line. Prodigy™, for example, lists jobs available throughout the country with new opportunities posted each week. Some companies even have bulletin board systems where job openings are posted. While many of these are used internally, some companies open these systems to all interested job seekers. And, of course, there are some private on-line companies that will place your résumé and companies' jobs in databases that can be accessed for a fee. Furthermore, you could query users of local bulletin board systems about job openings they know exist. Be sure not to overlook on-line systems as a source for job opportunities.

(4) on-line databases,

**Employment Agencies.** Companies that specialize in finding jobs for employees can be useful, especially if you seek to change employment later in your career. Of course, such companies charge for their services. The employer sometimes pays the charges, usually if qualified applicants are scarce. Employment agencies are commonly used to place experienced people in executive positions.

(5) employment agencies, and

**Prospecting.** Some job seekers approach prospective employers directly, either by personal visit or by mail. Personal visits are effective if the company has an employment office or if a personal contact can set up a visit. Mail contacts typically include a résumé and an application letter. The construction of these messages is covered later in the chapter.

(6) prospecting techniques.

## INTRODUCTORY SITUATION

### to Résumés and Application Letters

In your role as Cyrus Sylvester, you consider yourself well qualified for a career in labor relations. You know the field from both personal experience and classroom study. You grew up in a working-class neighborhood. From an early age, you worked at a variety of jobs, the most important of which was a job as a shipping and receiving clerk. You were a truck driver and a member of the Teamsters for two years. Your college studies were especially designed to prepare you for a career in labor relations. You studied Olympia University's curriculum in industrial relations, and you carefully chose the electives that would give you the best possible preparation for your career objective. As evidenced by your grades, your preparation was good.

Now it is time to begin your career. Over the past weeks you followed good procedures in looking for employment (as reviewed in the preceding pages). Unfortunately, you had no success with the recruiters who visited your campus. Now you will send written applications to a select group of companies that you think might use a person with your skills. You have obtained the names of the executives you should reach at these companies. You will mail them the conventional application package—résumé and application letter. The following discussion shows you how to prepare these documents for best results. ∎

CHAPTER 11 Strategy in Job Search and Application

## PREPARING THE APPLICATION DOCUMENTS

- Pursue job openings by personal visit or by mail.

After your search has uncovered a job possibility, you pursue it. How you pursue it depends on the circumstances of the case. When it is convenient and appropriate to do so, you make contact in person. It is convenient when the distance is not great, and it is appropriate when the employer has invited such a contact. When a personal visit is not convenient and appropriate, you apply by mail, E-mail, or fax.

- You are likely to use résumés and application letters in your job search.

Whether or not you apply in person, you are likely to use some written material. If you apply in person, probably you will take a résumé with you to leave as a record of your qualifications. If you do not apply in person, of course, the application is completely in writing. Typically, it consists of a résumé and a letter of application. At some point in your employment efforts, you are likely to use each of these documents.

- Prepare them as you would prepare a sales mailing.

Preparing résumés and application letters is much like preparing a sales mailing. Both situations involve selling. In one case, you are selling a product or service; in the other, you are selling your ability to do work. The résumé is much like the supporting material that accompanies the sales letter. The application letter is much like the sales letter. These similarities should become obvious to you as you read the following pages.

- Study the product (you) and the work.

As in preparing a sales mailing, you begin work on a written application for a job by studying what you are selling. And what you are selling is you. Then you study the work. Studying yourself involves taking personal inventory—the self-analysis discussed earlier in the chapter. You should begin by listing all the information about you that you believe an employer would want to know. Studying the work means learning as much as you can about the company—its plans, it policies, its operations. It also means learning the requirements of the work that the company wants done. Sometimes you can get this information through personal investigation. More often, you will have to develop it through logical thinking.

- Next, decide on whether to send a letter alone or with a résumé.

With this preliminary information assembled, you are ready to plan the application. First, you need to decide just what your application will consist of. Will it be just a letter, or will it be a letter and a résumé (also called a *vita*, *qualifications brief*, or *data sheet*)? The résumé is a summary of background facts in list form. You will probably select the combination of letter and résumé, for this arrangement is likely to do a better job. But some people prefer to use the letter alone. When this is done, the letter usually contains much detail, for it must do the whole sales job.

## THE RÉSUMÉ

- The résumé lists facts in some orderly way.

After deciding what your mailing will be, you construct the parts. Perhaps you will choose to begin with the résumé, for it is a logical next step from the personal inventory discussed above. In fact, the résumé is a formal arrangement of that inventory.

You will want to include in the résumé all background information you think the reader should have about you. This means including all the information that is reviewed in an accompanying letter plus supporting and incidental details. Designed for quick reading, the résumé lists facts that have been tabulated and arranged for the best possible appearance. Rarely does it use sentences.

Two basic types of résumés are common. One type, the *general* résumé, covers a variety of jobs. It is the type one would send to a dozen different companies in applying for a dozen different jobs. The second type, the *targeted* résumé, is written for one company and one job. Most of its contents are similar to those of a general résumé, but its information and wording are specially selected to fit the one case. Because the targeted type fits the one case, it is probably more effective.

<small>The general type of résumé fits a number of companies and jobs. The targeted type fits one company and one job.</small>

The arrangements of résumés differ widely, but the following procedure generally describes how most are written:

- **Logically arrange information on employment (dates, places, firms, duties), information on education (institutions, dates, degrees, major field), personal details (memberships, interests, achievements, and such—but not religion, race, and sex), special information derived from other information (achievements, qualifications, capabilities), and information on references (optional—authorities disagree).**
- **Construct a heading for the entire résumé and subheadings for the parts.**
- **Include other vital information, such as career goals and address (current and permanent).**
- **Arrange the data for best eye appeal, making it balanced, not crowded, and not strung out.**

<small>Follow this plan in constructing a résumé.</small>

### Selecting the Background Facts

Your first step in writing the résumé is to review the background facts you have assembled about yourself and then to select the facts that you think will help your reader evaluate you. You should include all the information covered in the accompanying letter, for this is the most important information. In addition, you should include significant supporting details not covered in the accompanying letter to avoid cluttering it.

<small>Begin by reviewing the background facts you have assembled. Select the facts that will help the reader evaluate you.</small>

### Arranging the Facts into Groups

After selecting the facts you want to include, you should sort them into logical groups. Many grouping arrangements are possible. The most conventional is the four-part grouping of *Education, Experience, Personal Qualities,* and *References*. Another possibility is a grouping by job functions or skills, such as *Selling, Communicating,* and *Managing*. Yet another is an arrangement by time—perhaps listing the information in reverse chronological order to show a progression of training and experience. You may be able to work out other logical arrangements.

<small>Sort the facts by conventional groups, job functions, time, or a combination.</small>

You can also derive additional groups from the four conventional groups mentioned above. For example, you can have a group made up of your *Achievements*. Such a group would consist of special accomplishments taken from your experience and education information. Another possibility is to have a group made up of information highlighting your major *Qualifications*. Here you would include information drawn from the areas of experi-

<small>Also, consider groups such as *Achievements* and *Qualifications*.</small>

ence, education, and personal qualities. Illustrations of and instructions for constructing groups such as these appear later in the chapter.

## Constructing the Headings

- *Write headings for the résumé and its parts.*

With your information organized, a logical next step is to construct the headings (captions) for the résumé. Probably you will begin by constructing the main head—the one that covers the entire document.

- *The topic is a popular form of main heading.*

The most widely used form of main head is the topic, which consists only of words that identify the document. It consists of a descriptive word, such as *résumé*, and the subject's name; or it can consist of the name only:

ALAN C. BARNHILL

- *Talking headings add interest.*

A second and less widely used form is the talking head. This form uses words that describe the purpose of the document, typically to present one's qualifications for a specific job. Usually this form includes the person's name and prospective employer, as in these examples:

PREPARATION OF ALAN C. BARNHILL<br>
TO SELL IBM PRODUCTS<br>
WHY WILMA WINN IS QUALIFIED AS A<br>
CHEVRON SYSTEMS ANALYST<br>
DIANE STOVER'S QUALIFICATIONS<br>
FOR GENERAL ACCOUNTING WORK<br>
WITH DEERE AND COMPANY

- *Topic and talking forms also are choices for the part headings.*

You also can use topic or talking heads for the groups of information in the résumé. Topic heads merely identify the information in the grouping in a word or two—for example, "Education," "Experience," "Personal Facts," "References." Talking heads also identify, but in addition they make an evaluative comment about the topic. For example, instead of the topic head "Education," you could have the talking head "Specialized Training in Accounting." Or instead of "References" you write "Administrators Who Know Her Work." Obviously, these heads add to the information covered. They help the reader interpret the facts presented.

- *Distinguish the headings from the other information by font selection.*

As you can see from the illustrations in the chapter, the headings are distinguished from the other information in the résumé by the use of different sizes and styles of type. The main head should appear to be the most important of all (larger and heavier). Headings for the groups of information should appear to be more important than the information under them. You will want to choose heading forms carefully, making sure they are neither so heavy and large that they offend nor so light and small that they show no distinctions. Your goal is to choose forms that properly show the relative importance of the information and are pleasing to the eye.

## Including Contact Information

- *Display your contact information prominently.*

Your address and telephone number are the most likely means of contacting you. Thus you should display them prominently somewhere in the résumé. You may also need to display your fax number or E-mail address. The most common location for displaying contact information is at the top, under the main head. Another commonly used position is the end. Both are positions of major emphasis and are acceptable. Both are shown in text examples.

When it is likely that your address or telephone number will change before the job search ends, you would be wise to include two addresses and numbers—one current and the other permanent. If you are a student, for example, your address at the time of applying for a job may change before the employer decides to contact you.

*Anticipate changes in contact information.*

### Including a Statement of Objective

Although not a category of background information, a statement of your objective is appropriate in the résumé. Using headings such as "Career Objective," "Job Objective," or just "Objective," this part usually appears at the beginning.

*Consider a statement of your objective.*

Not all authorities agree on the value of including the objective, however. Recommending that they be omitted from today's résumés, one widely read author suggested that one should concentrate instead on skills, experience, and credentials.[2] Some experts argue that the objective includes only obvious information that is clearly suggested by the remainder of the résumé. They argue also that an objective limits the applicant to a single position and eliminates consideration for other jobs that may be available.

*However, note that some authorities oppose it.*

Those favoring the use of a statement of objective reason that it helps the recruiter see quickly where the applicant might fit into the company. As this argument appears to have greater support, at least for the moment, probably you should include the objective. But make an exception when your career goal is unclear and you are considering a variety of employment possibilities.

*Even so, probably you should use it.*

Primarily, your statement of objective should describe the work you seek. When you can, you should add to its effectiveness by including words that convey a long-term interest, as in this example:

*The statement should cover the job you seek and more, as in these examples.*

Objective: To serve in an entry-level position in personnel management that will provide an opportunity for growth and advancement.

Another technique for enhancing the effectiveness of the objective statement is to include words that emphasize your major qualifications for the work, as in this example:

Objective: To apply 17 years of successful high-tech sales experience to selling quality products for a progressive company.

Also, for a résumé tailored to fit a specific company, the wording can include the company name and exact job title the company uses:

Career Objective: Sales Representative for Syntex Corporation leading to sales administration.

### Presenting the Information

The information you present under each heading will depend on your good judgment. You should list all the facts that you think are relevant. You will want to include enough information to enable the reader to judge your ability to do the work you seek.

*List the facts under the headings.*

---

[2] Bruce Neusbaum, "A Career Survival Kit," *Business Week,* October 7, 1991, p. 104.

*When covering work experience, at a minimum include dates, places, firms, and duties.*

Your coverage of work experience should identify completely the jobs you have held. A minimum coverage would include dates, places, firms, and duties. If the work was part-time, you should say so without demeaning the skills you developed on the job. In describing your duties, you should select words that bring out the highlights of what you did, especially the parts of this experience that qualify you for the work you seek. For example, in describing a job as office manager, you could write "Office manager for Carson's, Inc., Chicago, Ill., 1990–92." But it would be more meaningful to give this fuller description: "Office manager for Carson's, Inc., Chicago, Ill., 1990–92, supervising a staff of seven in processing company records and communications."

*When appropriate, show achievements.*

If your performance on a job shows your ability to do the work you seek, you should consider emphasizing your achievements in your job description. For example, an experienced marketer might write this description: "Marketing specialist for Kildorf-Burke, Philadelphia, 1989–92. Served in advisory role to company management. Developed marketing plan that increased profits 24 percent in two years." Or a successful advertising account executive might write this description: "Morley-Shaw Agency, San Francisco, 1990–92. As account executive, developed successful campaigns for nine accounts and led development team in increasing agency volume 18 percent."

*Use action verbs to strengthen the appeal.*

As you can see from the examples above, the job descriptions are strengthened by the use of action verbs. Verbs are the strongest of all words. If you choose them well, they will do much to sell your ability to do work. A list of the more widely used action verbs appears in Figure 11–1.

*For education, include institutions, dates, degrees, and areas of study.*

Because your education is likely to be your strongest selling point for your first job after college, you will probably cover it in some detail. (Education gets less and less emphasis in your applications as you gain experience.) At a minimum, your coverage of education should include institutions, dates, degrees, and areas of study. For some jobs, you may want to list specific courses, especially if you have little other information to present or if your coursework has uniquely prepared you for those jobs. If your GPA (grade point average) is good, you may want to include it. Remember, for your résumé, you can compute your GPA in a way that works best for you as long as you label it accurately. For example, you may want to select just those courses in your major, labeling it Major GPA. Or if your last few years were your best ones, you may want to present your GPA for just that period. In any case, include GPA when it works favorably for you.

*For legal reasons, some personal information (on race, religion, sex) should probably not be listed.*

What personal information to list is a matter for your best judgment. In fact, the trend appears to be toward eliminating such information. If you do include personal information, you should probably omit race, religion, and sex—perhaps age and marital status also—because current laws prohibit hiring based on such information. But not everybody agrees on this matter. Some authorities believe that at least some of these items should be included. They argue that the law only prohibits employers from considering such information in hiring—that it does not prohibit applicants from presenting the information. They reason that if such information helps you, you should use it. The illustrations shown in this chapter support both viewpoints.

**FIGURE 11-1** A List of Action Verbs[1] That Add Strength to Your Résumé

The **underlined** words are especially good for pointing out **accomplishments**.

**Management Skills**
administered
analyzed
assigned
attained
chaired
consolidated
contracted
coordinated
delegated
developed
directed
evaluated
executed
improved
increased
organized
oversaw
planned
prioritized
produced
recommended
reviewed
scheduled
strengthened
supervised

**Communication Skills**
addressed
arbitrated
arranged
authored
collaborated
convinced
corresponded
developed
directed
drafted
edited
enlisted
formulated
influenced
interpreted
lectured
mediated
moderated
negotiated
persuaded
promoted
publicized
reconciled
recruited
spoke
translated
wrote

**Research Skills**
clarified
collected
critiqued
diagnosed
evaluated
examined
extracted
identified
inspected
interpreted
interviewed
investigated
organized
reviewed
summarized
surveyed
systematized

**Technical Skills**
assembled
built
calculated
computed
designed
devised
engineered
fabricated
maintained
operated
overhauled
programmed
remodeled
repaired
solved
upgraded

**Teaching Skills**
adapted
advised
clarified
coached
communicated
coordinated
demystified
developed
enabled
encouraged
evaluated
explained
facilitated
guided
informed
instructed
persuaded
set goals
stimulated
trained

**Financial Skills**
administered
allocated
analyzed
appraised
audited
balanced
budgeted
calculated
computed
developed
forecasted
managed
marketed
planned
projected
researched

**Creative Skills**
acted
conceptualized
created
customized
designed
developed
directed
established
fashioned
founded
illustrated
initiated
instituted
integrated
introduced
invented
originated
performed
planned
revitalized
shaped

**Helping Skills**
assessed
assisted
clarified
coached
counseled
demonstrated
diagnosed
educated
expedited
facilitated
familiarized
guided
motivated
referred
rehabilitated
represented

**Clerical or Detail Skills**
approved
arranged
catalogued
classified
collected
compiled
dispatched
executed
generated
implemented
inspected
monitored
operated
organized
prepared
processed
purchased
recorded
retrieved
screened
specified
systematized
tabulated
validated

**More Verbs for Accomplishments**
achieved
expanded
improved
pioneered
reduced (losses)
resolved (problems)
restored
spearheaded
transformed

[1] From *The Damn Good Resume Guide* © 1989 by Yana Parker. Reprinted by permission of Ten Speed Press, Berkeley, California.

Personal information that is generally appropriate includes all items that tell about your personal qualities. Information on your organization memberships, civic involvement, and social activities is evidence of experience and interest in working with people. Hobbies and athletic participation tell of your balance of interests. Such information can be quite useful to some employers, especially when personal qualities are important to the work involved.

*Information on activities and interests tells about one's personal qualities.*

Authorities disagree on whether to list references on the résumé. Some think that references should not be bothered with until negotiations are

*Consider listing references, but some authorities favor postponing using them.*

further along. Others think that references should be listed because some employers want to check them early in the screening process. One recent study[3] of major corporations found that 42 percent of the employers want references on or accompanying the résumé. The remaining 58 percent have other preferences. Clearly, both views have substantial support. You will have to make the choice based on your best knowledge of the situation.

**Consider using a separate sheet for references.**

A commonly used tool is a separate reference sheet. When you use it, you close the résumé with a statement indicating references are available. Later, when the reader wants to check references, you send her or him this sheet. The type size and style of the main heading of this sheet should match that used in your résumé. It will say something like "References for *your name*. Below this heading is a listing of your references, beginning with the strongest one. In addition to solving the reference dilemma, use of this separate reference sheet allows you to change both the references and the ordering of them for each job.

**Select references that cover your background.**

Sometimes you may have good reason not to list references, as when you are employed and want to keep the job search secret. If you choose not to list them, you should explain their absence. You can do this in the accompanying letter; or you can do it on the résumé by following the heading "References" with an explanation, such as "Will be furnished on request."

How many and what kinds of references to include will depend on your background. If you have an employment record, you should include one for every major job you have held—at least for recent years. You should include references related to the work you seek. If you base your application heavily on your education or your personal qualities, or both, you should include references who can vouch for these areas—professors, clergy, community leaders, and the like. Your goal is to list those people who can verify the points on which your appeal for the job is based. At a minimum, you should list three references. Five is a good maximum.

**Include accurate mailing addresses and job titles.**

Your list of references should include accurate mailing addresses, with appropriate job titles. Complete addresses are important because the reader is likely to write the references. Also useful are telephone numbers. Job titles (officer manager, president, supervisor) are helpful because they show what the references are able to tell about you. As a matter of courtesy, you should use references only with their permission.

## Handling the Special Groupings

**If you use an *Achievements* grouping, include unusual performances in education or experience.**

As noted previously, special groupings such as *Achievements* and *Qualifications* present highlights of information usually drawn from the more conventional groupings. *Achievements,* for example, usually includes unusual performances in education or experience. Illustrating this arrangement is the following example:

---

[3] Lorraine A. Krajewski and Susan Wood, "The Use of Applicant-Provided References in the Selection Process: A Study of the Forbes 500," paper presented at meeting of the Association for Business Communication—Southwest, Houston, Texas, March 14, 1991.

Achievements

Successfully managed the Delgado store for two years in a period of economic decline with these results:

- increased profits 37 percent;
- reduced employee turnover 55 percent; and
- increased volume 12 percent.

Information covered under a *Qualifications* heading may highlight information from the three conventional information groups—education, experience, and personal qualities. Typically, this arrangement emphasizes the applicant's most impressive background facts that pertain to the work sought, as in this example:

> If you use a *Qualifications* grouping, emphasize your most impressive background information.

Qualifications
- Experienced: three years of practical work as programmer/analyst in designing and developing financial software for the banking industry
- Highly trained: B.S. degree with honors in computer science
- Self-motivated: proven record of successful completion of independent work on major projects

Although such items may overlap others in the résumé, using them in a separate group emphasizes the applicant's strengths.

## Writing Impersonally and Consistently

As the résumé is a listing of information, you should write without personal pronouns (no *I*'s, *we*'s, *you*'s). You should also write all equal-level headings and the parts under each heading in the same grammatical form. For example, if one major heading in the résumé is a noun phrase, all the other major headings should be noun phrases. The following four headings illustrate the point. All but the third (an adjective form) are noun phrases. The error can be corrected by making the third a noun phrase, as in the examples to the right:

> List the information without use of personal pronouns (*I, we, you*).

> Use the same grammatical form for all equal-level headings and for the parts listed under each heading.

**NOT PARALLEL**
Specialized study
Experience in promotion work
Personal and physical
Qualified references

**PARALLEL**
Specialized study
Experience in promotion work
Personal and physical qualities
Qualified references

Illustrating grammatical inconsistency in the parts of a group are the following items:

Born in 1972
Single
Have good health
Active in sports
Ambitious

Inspection of these items shows that they do not fit the same understood words. The understood words for the first item are "I was" (*I was* born in

CHAPTER 11   Strategy in Job Search and Application   341

### Résumé Specialty Software: To Use or Not to Use?

Résumé software programs are on store shelves everywhere. Not only will you find them in computer stores and software stores, you're also likely to find them in your local bookstore or your school's bookstore. In addition, they are advertised widely by mail order. Furthermore, both their price and their quality vary widely. Your decision regarding résumé software may be twofold—should you use one? and which one?

Résumé programs have features that serve some very well. For example, if you don't know how to set up a résumé, most packages provide templates you fill in, and the program arranges the information. If you haven't thought out carefully what to include on a résumé, these programs will give you ideas through the questions they pose. Some of these programs include spell checkers and/or thesauruses to help you describe yourself accurately. Furthermore, some include useful manuals that give tips on topics ranging from résumé construction to interview techniques. A few of these programs even have small databases for you to keep track of names and addresses of contacts. And a few even include a calendar feature, allowing you to keep track of interview times and dates.

But these programs can have drawbacks, too. Some lack basic features such as spell checkers. And some have only a limited number of arrangements to choose from, creating the possibility that your résumé will look very similar to someone else's résumé created with the same software. You also need to check to see if you can customize headings. Of course, most of these programs limit the number of characters you can enter in one area, confining your description of items you want to include. Most importantly, some lack printer drivers for laser or inkjet printers and allow you to produce copies on dot matrix printers only—an undesirable limitation.

When making a decision on whether to use résumé-generating software, you should carefully evaluate all the features you intend to use. If you are competent with your full-featured word processing software and don't need the added features of résumé software, you probably can manage without one. On the other hand, some of the well-done programs can make your entire job search process easier. If the package you are evaluating serves you well, use it!

---

1972); for the second, they are "I am" (*I am* single); for the third, the understood word is "I"; and for the fourth and fifth, the understood words are "I am." Any changes that make all five items fit the same understood words would correct the error.

### Making the Form Attractive

Make the résumé attractive.

The attractiveness of your résumé will say as much about you as the words. The appearance of the information that the reader sees plays a part in forming his or her judgment. A sloppy, poorly designed presentation may even ruin your chances of getting the job. Thus, you have no choice but to give your résumé and your application letter an attractive physical arrangement.

Designing the résumé for eye appeal is no routine matter. There is no one best arrangement, but a good procedure is to approach the task as a book designer would. Your objective is to work out an arrangement of type and space that appears good to the eye. You would do well to use the following general plan for arranging the résumé.

Design it as a book designer would. Use balance and space for eye appeal.

Margins look better if at least an inch of space is left at the top of the page and on the left and right sides of the page and if at least 1½ inches of space are left at the bottom of the page. Your listing of items by rows (columns) appears best if the items are short and if they can be set up in two uncrowded rows, one on the left side of the page and one on the right side. Longer items of information are more appropriately set up in lines extending across the page. In any event, you would do well to avoid long and narrow columns of data with large sections of wasted space on either side. Arrangements that give a heavy crowded effect also offend the eye. Extra spacing between subdivisions and indented patterns for subparts and carryover lines are especially pleasing to the eye.

Here are some suggestions on form.

While layout is important in showing your ability to organize and good spacing increases readability, design considerations such as font and paper selection affect attractiveness almost as much. Commercial artists currently recommend using sans serif fonts (without feet) for headings and serif fonts (with feet) for body text. They say that types for headings should be at least 14 points and for body text, 10–14 points. They also recommend using fewer than four font styles on a page.

Take care in choosing fonts.

Another factor affecting the appearance of your application forms is the paper you select. The paper should be appropriate for the job you seek. In business, erring on the conservative side is usually better; you do not want to be eliminated from consideration simply because the reader did not like the quality or color of the paper. The most traditional choice is white, 100 percent cotton, 20–24-lb. paper. Of course, reasonable variations can be appropriate.

Conservative paper usually is best.

### Contrasting Bad and Good Examples

The résumés in Figures 11–2 and 11–3 are at opposing ends of the quality scale. The first one, scant in coverage and poorly arranged, does little to help the applicant. Clearly the second one is more complete and better arranged.

Figures 11–1 and 11–2 show bad and good form.

**Weakness in Incompleteness and Bad Arrangements.** Shortcomings in the first example (Figure 11–2) are obvious. First, the form is not pleasing to the eye. The weight of the type is heavy on the left side of the page. Failure to indent carryover lines makes reading difficult.

This résumé also contains numerous errors in wording. Information headings are not parallel in grammatical form. All are in topic form except the first one. The items listed under *Personal* are not parallel either. Throughout, the résumé coverage is scant, leaving out many of the details needed to present the best impression of the applicant. Under *Experience,* little is said about specific tasks and skills in each job; and under *Education,* high school work is listed needlessly. The references are incomplete, omitting street addresses and job titles.

**FIGURE 11-2** Incompleteness and Bad Arrangement in a Résumé

This résumé presents Cyrus Sylvester's case ineffectively (see "Introductory Situation to Résumés and Application Letters"). It is scant and poorly arranged.

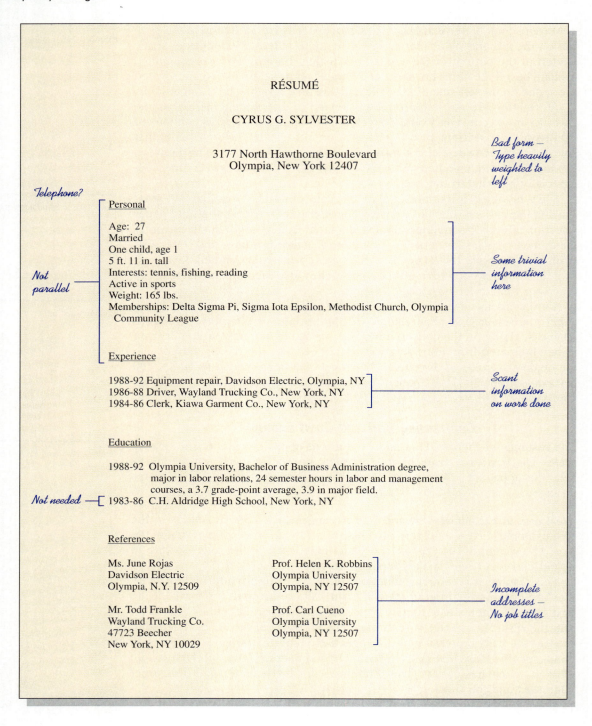

RÉSUMÉ

CYRUS G. SYLVESTER

3177 North Hawthorne Boulevard
Olympia, New York 12407

*Telephone?*

*Bad form — Type heavily weighted to left*

Personal

*Not parallel*

Age: 27
Married
One child, age 1
5 ft. 11 in. tall
Interests: tennis, fishing, reading
Active in sports
Weight: 165 lbs.
Memberships: Delta Sigma Pi, Sigma Iota Epsilon, Methodist Church, Olympia Community League

*Some trivial information here*

Experience

1988-92 Equipment repair, Davidson Electric, Olympia, NY
1986-88 Driver, Wayland Trucking Co., New York, NY
1984-86 Clerk, Kiawa Garment Co., New York, NY

*Scant information on work done*

Education

1988-92 Olympia University, Bachelor of Business Administration degree, major in labor relations, 24 semester hours in labor and management courses, a 3.7 grade-point average, 3.9 in major field.

*Not needed* — 1983-86 C.H. Aldridge High School, New York, NY

References

Ms. June Rojas
Davidson Electric
Olympia, N.Y. 12509

Prof. Helen K. Robbins
Olympia University
Olympia, NY 12507

Mr. Todd Frankle
Wayland Trucking Co.
47723 Beecher
New York, NY 10029

Prof. Carl Cueno
Olympia University
Olympia, NY 12507

*Incomplete addresses — No job titles*

**FIGURE 11-3** Thoroughness and Good Arrangement in a Résumé

This complete and attractively arranged résumé presents Cyrus Sylvester's case effectively (see "Introductory Situation to Résumés and Application Letters").

---

### CYRUS C. SYLVESTER

| Address | Telephone |
|---|---|
| 3177 North Hawthorne Boulevard | (914) 967-3117 (home) |
| Olympia, NY 12407 | (914) 938-4449 (work) |

#### Objective

A position in labor relations that will lead to development as a labor relations specialist.

#### Experience as a Part of Labor

*Description shows quality of work done*

| | |
|---|---|
| 1990-Present | Equipment repair technician, Davidson Electric Company, Olympia, NY (part time) |
| 1988-90 | Driver, Wayland Trucking Company, New York, NY (was a member of Local 714, International Brotherhood of Teamsters, Chauffeurs, Warehousemen, and Helpers of America) |
| 1986-88 | Shipping and receiving clerk, Kiawa Garment Company, New York, NY (part time) |

*Note the chronological arrangement*

#### Training for Labor Relations Work

| | |
|---|---|
| 1990-93 | Bachelor of Business Administration with major in Labor Relations; Olympia University; May 1993
Overall grade-point average: 3.7 (4.0 basis)
Major grade-point average: 3.9 |

#### Personal Qualities

*Trivial information omitted*

Interests: tennis, fishing, reading, jogging
Memberships: Delta Sigma Pi (professional); Sigma Iota Epsilon (honorary), served as treasurer and president; First Methodist Church, Olympia, serving on board of stewards; League of Olympia, served as registration leader

#### People Who Know His Abilities

*Complete address*

| | |
|---|---|
| Ms. June Rojas, Service Manager | Professor Helen K. Robbins |
| Davidson Electric Company | Department of Management |
| 7114 East 71st Street | Olympia University |
| Olympia, NY 12509 | Olympia, NY 12507 |
| Telephone: (518) 342-1171 | Telephone: (518) 392-6673 |
| | |
| Mr. Todd E. Frankle, Manager | Professor Carl A. Cueno |
| Wayland Trucking Company | Department of Economics |
| 47723 Beecher Road | Olympia University |
| New York, NY 10029 | Olympia, NY 12507 |
| Telephone: (718) 466-9101 | Telephone: (518) 392-0733 |

*Job titles tell what they can report — how each qualified to evaluate*

*Well balanced — attractively arranged*

**CASE ILLUSTRATION** Résumés. *(A General-Purpose Résumé)*
Recommended in *Business Week Careers* (1988), this form of résumé emphasizes a section called "Capabilities," which is similar to the "Achievements" section discussed in the chapter. It excludes references and most personal information.

---

# Loretta E. Vitkoski

717 Will Warren Road
Del Mar, CA 92016
(619) 481-9779

**OBJECTIVE**
To apply retail training and experience and management potential to a retail sales corportation.

**EDUCATION**

1990-1993   Bachelor of Science in Business Administration, May 1993
San Diego State University
Emphasis in Marketing, Overall GPA 3.29/4.00

1988-1990   Associate of Arts, May 1990
Mesa College
- Completed General Education and Pre-Business Coursework
- Organized business participation in the campus Earth Week Awareness Program

**EXPERIENCE**   (Provided 75% of College Expenses)

1990-1993   Cosmetics Department Manager (part time), Broadway Horton Plaza, San Diego, CA
Sold cosmetics, supervised two sales associates, and assisted store buyer in determining inventory levels.

1988-1990   Salesclerk (summers), The Doll House, Los Angeles, CA
Sold quality ladies fashions, learned fashion merchandising and buying, assisted with product displays.

**CAPABILITIES**

- Likes selling and serving people.

- Has interest in study of markets and market demands.

- Enjoys working to meet the challenge of quotas and other goals.

- Keeps current on merchandising developments and trends.

- Is ambitious and expects to earn advancement.

**ACTIVITIES**
The Marketing Club (treasurer, 1992-93), Students for Free Enterprise, Delta Sigma Pi (professional fraternity)

**REFERENCES**
Will gladly furnish personal and professional references on request

---

*Annotations:*
- Captions stand out
- Captions have no frills — only identify area
- Good balance and spacing
- Chronological arrangement of education and experience
- Highlights nature and quality of work
- Main qualifications extracted from applicant's background

**CASE ILLUSTRATION**  Résumés. *(A Narrative Review of Qualifications)*
This résumé presents a narrative review that effectively enhances the applicant's experience and education.

## Don R. Anderson

**Contact Points**
- Mailing Address: 1366 Hyacinth Street, Baton Rouge, LA 70803
- Telephone and Voice Mail: (512) 433-6608
- Fax: (512) 433-6609
- Electronic Mailbox: Prodigy CSBK34A

*Good arrangement — well balanced, compact*

**Objective**  To work as a legal assistant and secretary while completing law school

**Versatile Experience**

*Tells what was done on each job — brings out qualifications*

| | |
|---|---|
| 1985-1991 | Active duty with United States Navy, two years of which were in rating of yeoman, first class, including duty in the Persian Gulf conflict. Navy work was primarily clerical and administrative. As senior petty officer, assumed responsibility for offices assigned to, both ashore and afloat. |
| 1983-1985 | Manuscript typist and editor for Kenyon Publishing Company, Houston, TX. Responsible for editing, typing, and proofreading manuscripts. |
| 1982-1983 | Office clerk part-time while in high school for Nowotny Construction Company, Houston, TX. Work involved typing, filing, and preparing reports. |

*Note the chronological arrangement*

**Specialized Education**

| | |
|---|---|
| 1991-1993 | Completed prelaw curriculum in General Business at Louisiana State University with grade-point average of 3.53 (4.0 basis). |
| 1989-1991 | While on active duty with Navy, commenced part-time prelaw study at Iowa State University, Ames, IA. |
| 1983 | Developed skills in word processing and office procedures through six months' intensified study and practice at Barker Business College, Houston, TX. |

*Extra comments describe work done — emphasize what was learned*

**Personal Information**

*Interests*: Golf, cross-country skiing, reading, chess
*Memberships*: Delta Sigma Pi (professional business), Beta Gamma Sigma (honorary business), Baton Rouge Forensic Society

**References**  Available on request

**CASE ILLUSTRATION**  Résumés. *(A Résumé for an Applicant with Strong Experience)*
Following a form recommended by some career management experts, this résumé emphasizes the applicant's specific accomplishments and summarizes the applicant's qualifications.

---

# Rebecca G. Haddock

14117 Ridgecrest Drive
Vancouver, BC V6J 4S7
(604) 579-2039

*This form omits personal facts, references*

**OBJECTIVE:**   Restaurant Management

## QUALIFICATIONS SUMMARY

- ✓ Experienced in reducing costs (food and labor) and increasing profits
- ✓ Knowledgeable of how to design menus for maximum profit
- ✓ Adept at managing and working with food service personnel
- ✓ Skilled in kitchen procedures and supervision of food preparation
- ✓ Well grounded in techniques of improving customer services
- ✓ Effective in increasing sales

*Major qualification's are brought out for emphasis*

## EXPERIENCE

Captain's Table (Hodspur Hotel), Vancouver, British Columbia
   Manager, October 1989 to present. In charge of total restaurant operations, supervising 27 employees. Increased sales, streamlined menu, and improved service, resulting in a 19 percent annual increase in profits.
   Assistant restaurant manager, July 1987 to October 1989. Responsible for food purchasing and inventory control. Reduced food costs 7 percent. Supervised kitchen personnel, reducing labor costs 14 percent.
   Management trainee, January 1987 to July 1987. Learned all phases of food-service operations in intensive on-the-job program.

Pierre's Kitchen, Seattle, WA, September 1984 to January 1987 (part time) Assistant Manager and chef. In charge of food preparation for evening operations. Supervised staff of three.

*Note the chronological arrangement*

## EDUCATION

MBA with major in management, Wedgeworth University, 1987.

BS with major in hotel and restaurant management, Wedgeworth University, 1985.

*Education properly gets secondary emphasis*

---

348   PART 4   Applications to Specific Situations

▪ ▪ ▪ ▪ ▪ ▪ ▪ ▪ ▪ ▪ ▪ ▪ ▪ ▪ ▪ ▪ ▪ ▪ ▪ ▪ ▪ ▪ ▪ ▪ ▪ ▪ ▪ ▪ ▪ ▪ ▪ ▪ ▪ ▪ ▪ ▪ ▪ ▪ ▪ ▪ ▪ ▪ ▪ ▪ ▪ ▪ ▪ ▪ ▪ ▪ ▪ ▪ ▪ ▪ ▪ ▪ ▪ ▪

**CASE ILLUSTRATION**  Résumés. *(A General Purpose Résumé)*
This orderly form is popular with personnel people. Its somewhat mechanical arrangement eliminates all but the essential facts.

---

**ERIC J. MAFNAS**
1566 Diamond Street
San Diego, CA 92109
(619) 272-5689

---

*Headings in margins guide the eye through the contents.*

**OBJECTIVE:** To obtain a *career* position with a well-established consulting firm that offers opportunity for advancement.

**EDUCATION:** **SAN DIEGO STATE UNIVERSITY**
B.S. in Business Administration - May 1992
Major: Information Systems

**UNIVERSITY OF CALIFORNIA, DAVIS**
Biology Major: 1984 - 1986

**RELEVANT COURSES:**
Systems Analysis & Systems Design
Structured COBOL Programming on the CYBER-750
Advanced COBOL Programming on the VAX/VMS
Database Management
Comparative Languages (C, FORTH, LISP)

*Selective specialized courses show the applicant's strength.*

**MEMBERSHIPS:**
President - Data Processing Management Association

Social Chair - Lambda Chi Alpha Fraternity

**WORK EXPERIENCE:**
**SUNSET VALET SERVICE**, October 1987 - Present
Location Manager

Managed several restaurant parking systems.
Responsible for hiring, training, and scheduling employees as well as maintaining positive restaurant rapport.

*Headings have minimum wording, but not all experts like this.*

**BY DESIGN**, July 1984 - Present
Hardware Supervisor

Supervise hardware department and control inventory.
Install custom draperies and provide other installers with the appropriate equipment to complete their duties.

*This description emphasizes what was done.*

**REFERENCES:** Available upon request.

**CASE ILLUSTRATION** Résumés. *(A General Purpose Résumé)*

This orderly general-purpose résumé form is popular with personnel people. Its somewhat mechanical arrangement eliminates all but the essential facts.

---

# DONNA MARIE CRENSHAW

*Shaded box adds emphasis*

| | |
|---|---|
| **Objective** | To obtain a position that offers opportunity for a career in office administration |

**Education**  Associate of Arts degree
Metropolitan Community College, New York
Major in office administration, coursework in office procedures, word processing, report writing, business communication; grade point average of 3.3 (4.0 basis)

**Experience**
1986-present  Payroll clerk, Standard Insurance Company, New York, NY
Handle time keeping and payroll for 235 employees; perform general office assignments, surpervise two assistants

1986-1989  Salesperson, Bell Stores, Inc., New York, NY
Sold cosmetics and costume jewelry (part time)

1985-1986  Office assistant, Pennington Insurance Agency, New York, NY
Performed general office assignments (part time)

**Professional Skills**
- Keyboarding speed, 75 wpm
- Proficient in use of WordPerfect, Word, and MultiMate
- Competent in using Lotus and Excel including macros
- Experienced with both DOS and Apple platforms
- Experienced with various other office equipment

**Activities**
❑ Active member of Metro Big Sister Association, working with two orphaned children
❑ Member of Metropolitan Curtain Club, participating as actress and stagehand
❑ Member of Metropolitan Business Club, serving as secretary treasurer

**Interests**  Tennis, hiking, reading, theater

**References**  Will be furnished on request

*Appropriate icons add interest*

**Telephone**  ☎ (212) 381-7797 (home); (212) 381-1114 (office)

**Address**  ⌂ 74173 West 118th Street
New York, NY 11061

**Strength through Good Arrangement and Completeness.** The next résumé (Figure 11–3) appears better at first glance, and it gets even better as you read it. It is attractively arranged. The information is neither crowded nor strung out. The balance is good. The content is also superior to that of the other example. Additional words show the quality of Mr. Sylvester's work experience and education. They emphasize points that make the man suited for the work he seeks. This résumé excludes trivial personal information and has only the facts that tell something about Sylvester's personal qualities. Complete mailing addresses permit the reader to contact the references easily. Job titles tell how each is qualified to evaluate the subject.

## ▪▪▪▪▪▪▪▪▪▪▪▪▪▪▪
## THE APPLICATION LETTER

You should begin work on the application letter by fitting the facts from your background to the work you seek and arranging those facts in a logical order. Then you present them in much the same way that a sales writer would present the features of a product or service. Wherever logical, you adapt the points made to the reader's needs. Like those of sales letters, the organizational plans of application letters vary. However, the following procedure (discussed in detail below) is used in most successful efforts:

- **Begin with words selected to gain attention appropriately and to set up the review of information.**
- **Present your qualifications, keeping like information together and adapting to the company and the job.**
- **Use good sales strategy, especially you-viewpoint and positive language.**
- **Drive for the appropriate action (request for interview, reference check, further correspondence).**

> Writing the application letter involves matching your qualifications with the job.

> This plan for writing the letter has proved to be effective.

### Gaining Attention in the Opening

As in sales writing, the opening of the application letter has two requirements: It must gain attention, and it must set up the review of information that follows.

Gaining attention is especially important in prospecting letters (application letters that are not invited). Such letters are likely to reach busy executives who have many things to do other than read application letters. Unless the letters gain favorable attention right away, the executives probably will not read them. Even invited letters must gain attention because they will compete with other invited letters. The invited letters that stand out favorably from the beginning have a competitive advantage.

As the application letter is a creative effort, you should use your imagination in writing the opening. But the work you seek should guide your imagination. Take, for example, work that requires an outgoing personality and a vivid imagination, such as sales or public relations. In such cases, you would do well to show these qualities in your opening words. At the opposite extreme is work of a conservative nature, such as accounting or banking. Openings in such cases should normally be more restrained.

In choosing the best opening for your case, you should consider whether you are prospecting or writing an invited letter. If the letter has been invited,

> Gain attention and set up the information review in the opening.

> Gaining attention in the opening makes the letter stand out.

> Use your imagination in writing the opening. Make the opening fit the job.

> An invited letter might refer to the job and the source of the invitation.

Because the executives who read them are likely to be busy, written applications need to gain attention. Those that stand out from the rest are the ones most likely to succeed.

your opening words should begin qualifying you for the work to be done. They should also refer incidentally to the invitation, as in this example:

Will an honor graduate in accounting with experience in petroleum accounting qualify for the work you listed in today's *Post*?

In addition to fitting the work sought, your opening words should set up the review of qualifications. The preceding example meets this requirement well. It structures the review of qualifications around two areas—education and experience.

You can gain attention in the opening in many ways. One way is to use a topic that shows understanding of the reader's operation or of the work to be done. Employers are likely to be impressed by applicants who have made the effort to learn something about the company, as in this example:

> You can gain attention by showing an understanding of the reader's operations.

Now that Taggart, Inc. has expanded operations to Central America, can you use a broadly trained business administration graduate who knows the language and culture of the region?

Another way is to make a statement or ask a question that focuses attention on a need of the reader that the writer seeks to fill. The following opening illustrates this approach:

> You can stress a need of the reader that you can fill.

When was the last time you interviewed a young college graduate who wanted to sell and had successful sales experience?

If you seek more conservative work, you should use less imaginative openings. For example, a letter answering an advertisement for a beginning accountant might open with this sentence:

> Because of my specialized training in accounting at State University and my practical experience in petroleum accounting, I believe I have the qualifications you described in your *Journal* advertisement.

*Use conservative openings for applications in a conservative field.*

Sometimes one learns of a job possibility through a company employee. Mentioning the employee's name can gain attention, as in this opening sentence:

> At the suggestion of Ms. Martha S. Hawkes of your staff, I submit the following summary of my qualifications for work as your loan supervisor.

*Using an employee's name gains attention.*

Many other possibilities exist. In the final analysis, you will have to use what you think will be best for the one case. But you should avoid the overworked beginnings that were popular a generation or two ago, such as "This is to apply for . . ." and "Please consider this my application for . . . ." Although the direct application these words make may be effective in some cases (as when answering an advertisement), the words are time-worn and dull.

*Many opening possibilities exist, but avoid the old-style ones.*

## Selecting Content

Following the opening, you should present the information that qualifies you to do the work. Begin this task by reviewing the job requirements. Then select the facts about you that qualify you for the job.

*Present your qualifications. Fit them to the job.*

If your letter has been invited, you may learn about the job requirements from the source of the invitation. If you are answering an advertisement, study it for the employer's requirements. If you are following up an interview, review the interview for information about job requirements. If you are prospecting, your research and your logical analysis should guide you.

*You do this by studying the job. Use all available information sources.*

In any event, you are likely to present facts from three background areas: education, experience, and personal details. You may also include a fourth—references. But references are not exactly background information. If you include references, they will probably go into the résumé.

*Include education, experience, personal qualities, references.*

How much you include from each of these areas and how much you emphasize each area should depend on the job and on your background. Most of the jobs you will seek as a new college graduate will have strong educational requirements. Thus, you should stress your education. When you apply for work after you have accumulated experience, you will probably need to stress experience. As the years go by, experience becomes more and more important—education, less and less important. Your personal characteristics are of some importance for some jobs, especially jobs that involve working with people.

*The emphasis each of these areas deserves varies by job. So consider the job in determining emphasis.*

If a résumé accompanies the application letter, you may rely on it too much. Remember that the letter does the selling and the résumé summarizes the significant details. Thus, the letter should contain the major points around which you build your case, and the résumé should include these points plus supporting details. As the two are parts of a team effort, somewhere in the letter you should refer the reader to the résumé.

*Do not rely too heavily on the résumé. The application letter should carry all the major selling points.*

### Effectiveness of a Salutation

After reading a student's application letter to the business communication class, Professor Sneer made this comment: "This is positively the worst letter submitted. It violates just about every writing principle I have emphasized in this course."

"That's my letter," an angry student responded. "I'll have you know that I copied it from one a friend wrote. And *it got the job* for my friend!"

"I was just getting to the letter's strong point," replied Professor Sneer. "The salutation overcomes all the letter's weaknesses. Can you imagine anything more effective than 'Dear Dad'!"

## Organizing for Conviction

*In organizing the background facts, select the best of these orders: logical grouping, time, job requirements.*

You will want to present the information about yourself in the order that is best for you. In general, the plan you select is likely to follow one of three general orders. The most common order is a logical grouping of the information, such as education, personal details, and experience. A second possibility is a time order. For example, you could present the information to show a year-by-year preparation for the work. A third possibility is an order based on the job requirements. For example, selling, communicating, and managing might be the requirements listed in an advertised job.

*Use words that present your qualifications most favorably.*

Merely presenting facts does not ensure conviction. You will also need to present the facts in words that make the most of your assets. You could say, for example, that you "held a position" as sales manager; but it is much more convincing to say that you "supervised a sales force of 14." Likewise, you do more for yourself by writing that you "earned a degree in business administration" than by writing that you "spent four years in college." And it is more effective to say that you "learned cost accounting" than to say that you "took a course in cost accounting."

*Use the you-viewpoint wherever practical.*

You can also help your case by presenting your facts in reader-viewpoint language wherever this is practical. More specifically, you should work to interpret the facts based on their meaning for your reader and for the work to be done. For example, you could present a cold recital like this one:

I am 21 years old and have an interest in mechanical operations and processes. Last summer I worked in the production department of a container plant.

Or you could interpret the facts, fitting them to the one job:

The interest I have held in things mechanical over most of my 21 years would help me fit into one of your technical manufacturing operations. And last summer's experience in the production department of Moyse Container Company is evidence that I can and will work hard.

*Avoid the tendency to overuse I's, but use some.*

Since you will be writing about yourself, you may find it difficult to avoid overusing I-references. But you should try. An overuse of *I*'s sounds egotistical and places too much attention on the often repeated word. Some *I*'s, however, should be used. The letter is personal. Stripping it of all I-references would rob it of its personal warmth. Thus, you should be concerned about the number of I-references. You want neither too many nor too few.

354     **PART 4**    Applications to Specific Situations

### Choice Lines Gleaned from Application Letters

"I have no influential father, uncles, or friends. I have no political ties, no drag, no pull. The result: no job. I am just an ambitious and intelligent young man who will work hard."

"Actually, I am looking for a big desk and an upholstered chair with a position attached. The duties (if any) must be amusing or interesting."

"I am familiar with all phases of office procedure, including bowling, coffee-breaking, working crossword puzzles, doodling, personal letter writing, and collection taking."

"I have answered all the questions on your application form except 'Sex.' This I think is a very personal matter."

"For three years I worked for Ms. Helen Simmons, who I am sending to you as a reference on the attached data sheet."

### Driving for Action in the Close

The presentation of your qualifications should lead logically to the action that the close of the letter proposes. You should drive for whatever action is appropriate in your case. It could be a request for an interview, an invitation to engage in further correspondence (perhaps to answer the reader's questions), or an invitation to write references. Rarely would you want to ask for the job in a first letter. You are concerned mainly with opening the door to further negotiations.

*In the close, drive for whatever action is appropriate.*

Your action words should be clear and direct. Preferably, you should put them in question form. As in the sales letter, the request for action may be made more effective if it is followed by words recalling a benefit that the reader will get from taking the action. The following close illustrates this technique:

*Make the action words clear and direct.*

> The highlights of my training and experience show that I have been preparing for a career in personnel. May I now discuss beginning this career with you? A collect telephone call (817-921-4113) or a letter will bring me in at your convenience to talk about how I can help in your personnel work.

### Contrasting Application Letters

Illustrating bad and good techniques, the following two application letters present the qualifications of Cyrus Sylvester, the job seeker described in the introductory situation at the beginning of the chapter. The first letter follows few of the suggestions given in the preceding pages, whereas the second letter is in general accord with these suggestions.

*The following two letters show bad and good application techniques.*

**A Bland and Artless Presentation of Information.** The bad letter begins with an old-style opening. The first words stating that this is an application letter are of little interest. The following presentation of qualifications is a matter-of-fact, uninterpreted review of information. Little you-viewpoint is evident. In fact, most of the letter emphasizes the writer (note the *I*'s). The information presented is scant. The closing action is little more than an I-viewpoint statement of the writer's availability.

CHAPTER 11 Strategy in Job Search and Application

This bad one is dull and poorly written.

Dear Mr. Stark:

This is to apply for a position in labor relations with your company.

At present, I am completing my studies in labor at Olympia University and will graduate with a Bachelor of Business Administration degree with a major in labor relations this May. I have taken all the courses in labor relations available to me as well as other helpful courses, such as statistics, law, and report writing.

I have had good working experience as a shipping and receiving clerk, truck driver, and repairer. Please see details on the enclosed résumé. I believe that I am well qualified for a position in labor relations and am considering working for a company of your size and description.

As I must make a decision on my career soon, I request that you write me soon. For your information, I will be available for an interview on March 17 and 18.

Sincerely,

**Skillful Selling of One's Ability to Work.** The better letter begins with an interesting question that sets the stage for the following presentation. The review of experience is interpreted by showing how the experience would help in performing the job sought. The review of education is similarly covered. Notice how the interpretations show that the writer knows what the job requires. Notice also that reader-viewpoint is stressed throughout. Even so, a moderate use of *I*'s gives the letter a personal quality. The closing request for action is a clear, direct, and courteous question. The final words recall a main appeal of the letter.

This better letter follows textbook instructions.

Dear Mr. Stark:

Is there a place in your labor-relations department for a person who is specially trained in the field and who knows working people and can talk with them on their level? My background, experience, and education have given me these unique qualifications.

All my life I have lived and worked with working people. I was born and reared by working parents in a poor section of New York City. While in high school, I worked mornings and evenings in New York's garment district, primarily as a shipping and receiving clerk. For two years, between high school and college, I worked full-time as a truck driver for Wayland Trucking and belonged to the Teamsters. Throughout my four years of college, I worked half-time as an equipment repairer for Davidson Electric. From these experiences, I have learned to understand labor. I speak labor's language, and working people understand and trust me.

My college studies at Olympia University were specially planned to prepare me for a career in labor relations. Pursuing a major in industrial relations, I studied courses in labor relations, labor law, personnel administration, organizational behavior, administrative management, business policy, and collective bargaining. In addition, I studied a wide assortment of supporting subjects: economics, business communication, information systems, industrial psychology, human relations, and operations management. My studies have given me the foundation of knowledge on which to learn the practical side of labor-relations work. I plan to begin the practical side of my development in June after I receive the Bachelor of Business Administration degree, with honors (3.7 grade-point average on a basis of 4.0).

These brief facts and the information in my résumé describe my diligent efforts to prepare for a career in labor relations. May I now talk with you about beginning that career? A telephone call to 917-938-4449 would bring me

The job interview is the final examination of the application process. Appropriate grooming and relaxed, yet enthusiastic behavior are helpful to the applicant's success.

to your office at your convenience to talk about how I could help in your labor-relations work.

Sincerely,

# THE INTERVIEW

Your initial contact with a prospective employer can be by mail or by a personal (face-to-face) visit. Even if you contact the employer by mail, a successful application will eventually involve a personal visit—or an *interview,* as we will call it. Much of the preceding parts of this chapter concerned the mail contact. Now our interest centers on the interview.

*Apply for the job—by mail or visit.*

In a sense, the interview is the key to the success of the application—the "final examination," so to speak. You should carefully prepare for the interview, as the job may be lost or won in it. The following review of employment interview highlights should help you understand how to deal with the interview in your job search. You will find additional information about interviewing in Chapter 16.

*The interview is essential. For it, follow this procedure:*

## Investigating the Company

Before arriving for an interview, you should learn what you can about the company—its products or services, its personnel, its business practices, its current activities, its management. Such knowledge will help you talk knowingly with the interviewer. And perhaps more important, the interviewer is

*(1) Find out what you can about the employer.*

**CHAPTER 11** Strategy in Job Search and Application 357

**CASE ILLUSTRATION** Application Letters. *(Directness in a Form Prospecting Letter)*
Written by a recent college graduate seeking her first job, this letter was prepared for use with a number of different types of companies.

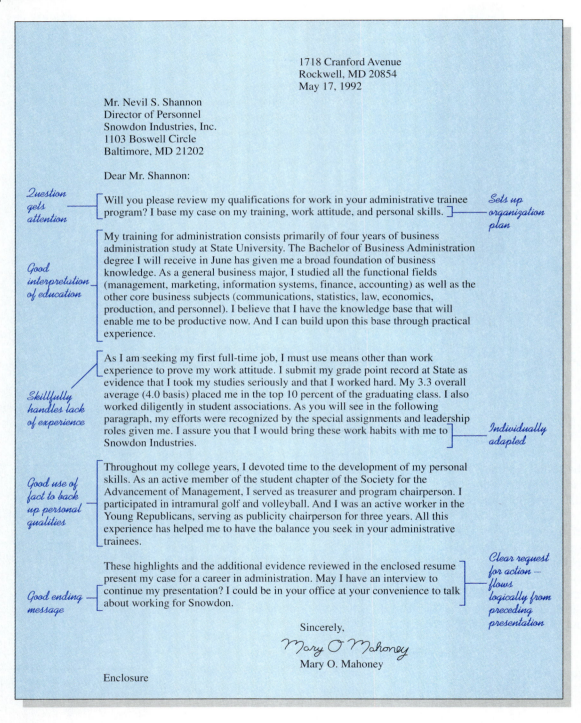

1718 Cranford Avenue
Rockwell, MD 20854
May 17, 1992

Mr. Nevil S. Shannon
Director of Personnel
Snowdon Industries, Inc.
1103 Boswell Circle
Baltimore, MD 21202

Dear Mr. Shannon:

*Question gets attention* — Will you please review my qualifications for work in your administrative trainee program? I base my case on my training, work attitude, and personal skills. — *Sets up organization plan*

*Good interpretation of education* — My training for administration consists primarily of four years of business administration study at State University. The Bachelor of Business Administration degree I will receive in June has given me a broad foundation of business knowledge. As a general business major, I studied all the functional fields (management, marketing, information systems, finance, accounting) as well as the other core business subjects (communications, statistics, law, economics, production, and personnel). I believe that I have the knowledge base that will enable me to be productive now. And I can build upon this base through practical experience.

*Skillfully handles lack of experience* — As I am seeking my first full-time job, I must use means other than work experience to prove my work attitude. I submit my grade point record at State as evidence that I took my studies seriously and that I worked hard. My 3.3 overall average (4.0 basis) placed me in the top 10 percent of the graduating class. I also worked diligently in student associations. As you will see in the following paragraph, my efforts were recognized by the special assignments and leadership roles given me. I assure you that I would bring these work habits with me to — *Individually adapted*
Snowdon Industries.

*Good use of fact to back up personal qualities* — Throughout my college years, I devoted time to the development of my personal skills. As an active member of the student chapter of the Society for the Advancement of Management, I served as treasurer and program chairperson. I participated in intramural golf and volleyball. And I was an active worker in the Young Republicans, serving as publicity chairperson for three years. All this experience has helped me to have the balance you seek in your administrative trainees.

*Good ending message* — These highlights and the additional evidence reviewed in the enclosed resume present my case for a career in administration. May I have an interview to continue my presentation? I could be in your office at your convenience to talk about working for Snowdon. — *Clear request for action — flows logically from preceding presentation*

Sincerely,

*Mary O. Mahoney*
Mary O. Mahoney

Enclosure

PART 4 Applications to Specific Situations

## CASE ILLUSTRATION  Application Letters.  *(A Conservative Request for Work)*

Using a company executive's name to gain attention, this letter is conservative in style and tone.

2707 Green Street
Lincoln, NE 68505
April 17, 1993

Ms. Marlene O'Daniel
Vice President for Administration
Continental Insurance Company
3717 Donahue Street
Des Moines, IA 50316

Dear Ms. O'Daniel:

*Interpretations of experience show the writer knows the work*

On the suggestion of Mr. Victor O. Krause of your staff, here is a summary of my qualifications for work as your communications specialist.

*Associate's name gains attention — opens door*

Presently I am in my fifth year as communications specialist for Atlas Insurance. Primarily my work consists of writing letters to Atlas policyholders. This work has made me a student of business writing. It has sharpened my writing skills. And more important, it has taught me how to gain and keep friends for my company through writing.

*Conservative in style and tone*

Additional experience working with businesspeople has given me an insight into the communications needs of business. This experience includes planning and presenting a communication improvement course for local civil service workers, a course in business writing for area business executives, and a course in bank communication for employees of Columbia National Bank.

*Subtle you-viewpoint — implied from writer's understanding of work*

My college training was certainly planned to prepare me for work in business writing. Advertising and public relations were my areas of concentration for my B.S. degree from Northern State University. As you will see in the enclosed resume, I studied all available writing courses in my degree plan. I also studied writing through English and journalism.

*Brings review to a conclusion — fits qualification presented to the job*

In summary, Ms. O'Daniel, my studies and my experience have equipped me for work as your communication specialist. I know business writing. I know how it should be practiced to benefit your company. May I have the privilege of discussing this matter with you personally? I could be in your office at any time convenient to you.

*An appropriate move for action*

Sincerely,

*Mildred E. Culpepper*
Mildred E. Culpepper

Enc.

**CHAPTER 11**  Strategy in Job Search and Application

**CASE ILLUSTRATION** Application Letters. *(A Bland but Straightforward Prospecting Letter)*
Some personnel specialists favor the matter-of-fact quality of this bland letter.

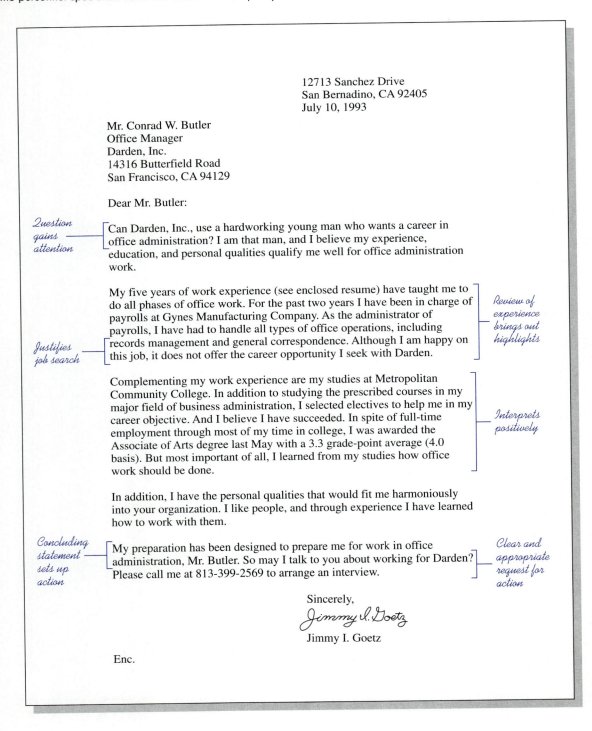

**CASE ILLUSTRATION** Application Letters. *(Interest and Good Organization in an Answer to an Advertisement)*
Three job requirements listed in an advertisement determined the plan used in this letter.

4407 Sunflower Drive
Phoenix, AZ 85017
July 8, 1993

Ms. Anita O. Alderson, Manager
Tompkins-Oderon Agency, Inc.
7403 Tamaron Street
Los Angeles, CA 90022

Dear Ms. Alderson:

*Good attention gainer — uses reader's words*

Sound background in advertising. . . well trained. . . works well with others. . .

These key words in your July 6 advertisement in the <u>Times</u> describe the person you want, and I believe I am that person.

*Writing style shows ability to write advertising copy*

*Interpretation shows what writer can do on job*

As summarized in the enclosed resume, I have gained experience in every phase of retail advertising while working for the <u>Lancer</u>, our college newspaper. I sold advertising, planned layouts, and wrote copy. During the last two summers, I got more firsthand experience working in the advertising department of Wunder & Son. I wrote a lot of copy for Wunder, some of which I am enclosing for your inspection; but I also did just about everything else there is to do in advertising work. I enjoyed it, and I learned from it. I am confident that this experience would help me fit in and contribute to the work in your office.

*Good interpretation, shows strong determination*

In my concentrated curriculum at the university, I studied marketing, with a specialization in advertising. I studied every course offered in advertising and related fields, and I believe that my honor grades give some evidence that I worked hard and with sincerity. I am confident that upon my graduation in June I can bring to your organization the firm foundation of knowledge and imagination your work demands.

Understanding the importance of being able to get along well with people, I actively participated in Sigma Chi (social fraternity), the First Methodist Church, and Pi Tau Pi (honorary business fraternity). From the experience gained in these associations, I am confident that I can fit in harmoniously with the people in your advertising department.

*Good evidence of social skills*

*Leads smoothly to action*

The preceding review of my qualifications summarizes my case for a career in advertising. May I now meet with you to discuss the matter further? A call to 602-713-2199 would bring me to your office at any convenient time to talk about doing your advertising work.

*Clear and strong drive for action*

Sincerely,

*Michael S. Janek*

Michael S. Janek

Enc.

likely to be impressed by the fact that you took the time to investigate the company. That effort might even place you above your competitors.

## Making a Good Appearance

*(2) Make a good appearance (conservative dress and grooming).*

How you look to the interviewer is a part of your message. Thus, you should work to present just the right image. Interviewers differ to some extent on what that image is, but you would be wise to present a conservative appearance. This means avoiding faddish, offbeat styles, preferring the less flamboyant, conventional business colors such as browns, blues, blacks, and grays. Remember that the interviewer wants to know whether you fit into the role you are seeking. You should appear to fit the part.

Some may argue that such an insistence on conformity in dress and grooming infringes on one's personal freedom. Perhaps it does. We will even concede that employers should not force such biases on you. But you will have to be realistic if you want a successful career. If the people who can determine your future have fixed views on matters of dress and grooming, you will have to respect those views in order to succeed.

## Anticipating Questions and Preparing Answers

*(3) Anticipate the questions; plan the answers.*

You should be able to anticipate some of the questions that the interviewer will ask. Questions about your education (courses, grades, honors, and such) are usually asked. So are questions about work experience, interests, career goals, location preferences, and activities in organizations. You should prepare answers to these questions in advance. Your answers will then be thorough and correct, and your words will display poise and confidence.

In addition to the general questions noted above, interviewers often ask more complicated ones. Some of these are designed to test you—to learn your views, your interests, and your ability to deal with difficult problems. Others seek more specific information about your ability to handle the job in question. Although such questions are more difficult to anticipate, you should be aware that they are likely to be asked. Following are questions of this kind that one experienced interviewer asks:

What can you do for us?

Would you be willing to relocate? To travel?

Do you prefer to work with people or alone?

How well has your performance in the classroom prepared you for this job?

What do you expect to be doing in 10 years? In 20 years?

What income goals do you have for those years (10 and 20 years ahead)?

Why should I rank you above the others I am interviewing?

Why did you choose _____ as your lifework?

How do you feel about working overtime? Nights? Weekends?

Did you do the best work you are capable of in college?

Is your college record a good measure of how you will perform on the job?

What are the qualities of the ideal boss?

PART 4 Applications to Specific Situations

What have you done that shows leadership potential?

What are your beginning salary expectations?

Sometimes interviewers will throw in tough or illegal questions to test your poise. These are naturally stressful, but being prepared for these kinds of questions will keep you cool and collected.[4] Here are some examples:

What is your greatest weakness?

With hindsight, how could you have improved your progress?

What kind of decisions are most difficult for you?

What is the worst thing you have heard about this company?

See this pen I'm holding. Sell it to me.

Tell me about a time when you put your foot in your mouth.

What is the worst experience you have had in school?

What religion do you practice?

How old are you? or When did you graduate from high school?

Are you married?

Do you plan to have children?

## Putting Yourself at Ease

Perhaps this is easier to say than to do, but you should be at ease throughout the interview. Remember that you are being inspected and that the interviewer should see a calm and collected person. How to appear calm and collected is not easy to explain. Certainly, it involves talking in a clear and strong voice. It also involves controlling your facial expressions and body movements. Developing such controls requires self-discipline—working at it. You may find it helpful to convince yourself that the stress experienced during an interview is normal. Or you may find it helpful to look at the situation realistically—as merely a conversation between two human beings. Other approaches may work better for you. Use whatever approaches work. Your goal is to control your emotions so that you present the best possible appearance to the interviewer.

(4) Be at ease—calm, collected, confident.

## Helping Control the Dialogue

Just answering the questions asked is often not enough. As one authority explains, "It's important to establish a dialogue with the recruiter by asking a few good questions and playing off the responses."[5] The questions you ask and the comments you play off them should bring up what you want the interviewer to know about you. Your self-analysis revealed the strong points in your background. Now you should make certain that those points come out in the interview.

(5) Help bring out the questions that show your qualifications.

---

[4] Martin John Yate, *Knock 'em Dead* (Holbrook, MA: Bob Adams, Inc., 1990), pp. 107–124.

[5] Kevin Collins and Patricia B. Carr, "A Short Course on Landing a Job," *The College Edition of the National Business Employment Weekly*, published by *The Wall Street Journal*, Fall 1988, p. 38.

*Here are some examples of how to do it.*

How to bring up points about you that the interviewer does not ask is a matter for your imagination. For example, a student seeking a job in advertising believed that a certain class project should be brought to the interviewer's attention. So she asked, "Do you attach any importance to advertising campaigns done as class projects in your evaluation?" The anticipated affirmative answer allowed her to show her successful project. For another example, a student who wanted to bring out his knowledge of the prospective employer's operations did so with this question: "Will your company's expansion at the Bakersfield plant create new job opportunities there?" How many questions of this sort you should ask will depend on your need to supplement your interviewer's questioning. Your goal should be to make certain that the interviewer gets all the information you consider important.

### Following Up and Ending the Application

*Follow up the interview with thank-you, status-inquiry, job-acceptance, and job-rejection messages.*

The interview is only an early step in the application process. A variety of other steps can follow. Conveying a brief thank-you message by letter or telephone is an appropriate follow-up step. It shows interest, and because some of your competitors will not do this, it can give you an advantage. If you do not hear from the prospective employer within a reasonable time, it is appropriate to inquire by telephone or letter about the status of your application. You should certainly do this if you are under a time limit on another employer's offer. The application process may end with no offer (frequently with no notification at all—a most discourteous way of handling applicants), with a rejection notice, or with an offer. How to handle these steps in writing is reviewed in the following paragraphs.

## OTHER JOB-GETTING LETTERS

*Getting a job can involve writing more than letters and résumés.*

Getting a job can involve writing more than application letters and résumés. You should follow up an interview with a thank-you letter. After much time has passed, you may want to write a letter inquiring about the status of your application. You may need to write a letter accepting a job, refusing one, or resigning one.

From the preceding instructions, you should be able to write such letters. For this reason, the following review of them is brief.

### Writing a Thank-You Letter

*You should write a thank-you letter following an interview.*

After an interview you should write a thank-you letter. It is the courteous thing to do, whether or not you are interested in the job. If you are interested, the letter can help your case. It singles you out from the competition and shows your interest in the job.

*The typical order for such a letter is as follows: (1) expression of gratefulness, (2) appropriate comments fitting the situation, (3) any additional information needed, and (4) a goodwill close.*

Such letters are usually short. They begin with an expression of gratefulness. They say something about the interview, the job, or such. They take care of any additional business (such as submitting information requested). And they end on a goodwill note—perhaps a hopeful look to the next step in the negotiations. The following letter does these things:

Dear Ms. Chubbuck:

I genuinely appreciate the time you gave me yesterday. You were most helpful. And you did a first-rate job of selling me on Graystone-Brune, Inc.

**PART 4** Applications to Specific Situations

As you requested, I have enclosed samples of the advertising campaign I developed as a class project. If you need anything more, please write me.

I look forward to the possibility of discussing employment with you before long.

        Sincerely,

## Constructing a Follow-Up to an Application

When a prospective employer is late in responding to an application, you may need to write a follow-up letter. Employers are often just slow, but sometimes they lose the application. Whatever the explanation, a follow-up letter may help to produce action.

Such a letter is a form of routine inquiry. As a reason for writing, it can use the need to make a job decision, or some other good explanation. The following letter is an example:

*When employers do not respond, you may write a follow-up letter. It follows the order of the routine inquiry letter.*

Dear Mr. Lemon:

As the time is approaching when I must make a job decision, may I please ask the status of my employment application with you?

You may recall that you interviewed me in your office November 7. You wrote me November 12 indicating that I was among those you had selected for further consideration.

Barrow, Inc. remains one of the organizations I would like to consider in making my career decision. I will very much appreciate an early response.

        Sincerely,

## Planning the Job Acceptance

Job acceptances in writing are merely favorable response letters with an extra amount of goodwill. As the letter should begin directly, a yes answer in the beginning is appropriate. The remainder of the letter should contain a confirmation of the starting date and place and comments about the work, the company, the interview—whatever you would say if you were face-to-face with the reader. The letter need not be long. This one does the job well:

*You may need to write a letter accepting a job. Write it as you would a favorable response letter.*

Dear Ms. Polansky:

I accept your offer of employment. After my first interview with you, I was convinced that Allison-Caldwell was the organization for me. It is good to know that you think I am right for Allison-Caldwell.

Following your instructions, I will be in Toronto on May 28, ready to begin a career with you.

        Sincerely,

## Writing a Letter Refusing a Job

Letters refusing a job offer follow the normal refusal pattern. One good technique is to begin with a friendly comment—perhaps something about past relations with the company. Next, explain and present the refusal in clear yet positive words. Then end with more friendly comment. This example illustrates the plan.

*To refuse a job offer, use the normal refusal pattern (indirect).*

Dear Mr. Segura:

Meeting you and the other people at Northern was a genuine pleasure. All that I saw and heard impressed me most favorably. I was especially impressed to receive the generous job offer that followed.

In considering the offer, I naturally gave some weight to these favorable impressions. Even though I have accepted a job with another firm, they remain strong in my mind.

Thank you for the time and the courteous treatment you gave me.

Sincerely,

## Writing a Letter of Resignation

- Job resignations are made in person, by letter, or both.

At some point in your career you are likely to resign from one job to take another. When this happens, probably you will inform your employer of your resignation orally. But when you find it more practical or comfortable, you may choose to resign in writing. In some cases, you may do it both ways. As a matter of policy, some companies require a written resignation even after an oral resignation has been made. Or you may prefer to leave a letter of resignation following your oral announcement of it.

- Make the letter as positive as circumstances permit.

Your letter of resignation should be as positive as the circumstances permit. Even if your work experiences have not been pleasant, you will be wise to depart without a final display of anger. As an anonymous philosopher once explained, "When you write a resignation in anger, you write the best letter you will ever regret."

- Preferably use indirect order, for the situation is negative.

The best resignation letters are written in the indirect order. The situation is negative; and, as you know, indirectness usually is advisable in such cases. But many are written in the direct order. They present the resignation right away, following it with expressions of gratitude, favorable comments about past working experiences, and the like. Either approach is acceptable. Even so, you would do well to use the indirect order, for it is more likely to build the goodwill and favorable thinking you want to leave behind you.

The example below shows the indirect order, which is well known to you. It begins with a positive point—one that sets up the negative message. The negative message follows, clearly yet positively stated. The ending returns to positive words chosen to build goodwill and fit the case.

Dear Ms. Knauth:

- This illustration letter begins and ends positively.

Working as your assistant for the past five years has been a genuinely rewarding experience. Under your direction I have grown as an administrator. And I know you have given me a practical education in retailing.

As you may recall from our past discussions, I have been pursuing the same career goals that you held early in your career. Thus I am sure you will understand why I now submit my resignation to accept a store management position with Lawson's in Belle River. I would like my employment to end on the 31st; but I could stay a week or two longer if needed to help train my replacement.

I leave with only good memories of you and the other people with whom I worked. Thanks to all of you for a valuable contribution to my career.

Sincerely,

PART 4 Applications to Specific Situations

## SUMMARY (by Chapter Objectives)

1. A good first step in your job search is to build a network of contacts.
   - Get to know people who might help you later—classmates, professors, business leaders, and such.
   - Use them to help you find a job.
2. When you are ready to find work, analyze yourself.
   - Look at your education, personal qualities, and work experience.
   - From this review, determine what work you are qualified to do.
   - Then select the career that is right for you.
3. When you are ready to find a job, use the contact sources available to you.
   - Check university placement centers, advertisements, on-line sources, personal contacts.
   - If these do not produce results, prospect by mail.
4. In your application efforts, you are likely to use résumés and application letters. Prepare them as you would written sales material.
   - First, study your product—you.
   - Then study your prospect—the employer.
   - From the information gained, construct the résumé and letter.
   
   In writing the résumé (a listing of your major background facts), you can choose from two types.
   - The *general* type fits a number of companies and jobs.
   - The *targeted* type fits one company and one job. Probably it is more effective.
   
   In preparing the résumé, follow this procedure:
   - List all the facts about you that an employer might want to know.
   - Sort these facts into logical groups—*experience, education, personal qualities, references, achievements, qualifications*.
   - Put these facts in writing. As a minimum, include job experience (dates, places, firms, duties) and education (degrees, dates, fields of study). Use some personal information, but omit race, religion, and sex and perhaps also marital status and age.
   - Authorities disagree on whether to list references. If you list them, use complete mailing addresses and have one for each major job.
   - Include other helpful information: address, telephone number, career objective.
   - Write headings for the résumé and for each group of information; use either topic or talking headings.
   - Preferably write the résumé without personal pronouns, make the parts parallel grammatically, and use words that help sell your abilities.
   - Present the information for good eye appeal, selecting fonts that show the importance of the headings and the information.
5. As the application letter is a form of sales letter, plan it as you would a sales letter.
   - Study your product (you) and your prospect (the employer) and think out a strategy for presentation.
   - Begin with words that gain attention, begin applying for the job, and set up the presentation of your sales points.

---

1. Develop and use a network of contacts in your job search.

2. Assemble and evaluate information that will help you select a career.

3. Describe the sources that can lead you to an employer.

4. Compile a résumé that is strong, complete, and well arranged.

5. Write letters of application which skillfully sell your abilities.

- Make the tone and content fit the job you seek.
- Present your qualifications, fitting them to the job you seek.
- Choose words that enhance the information presented.
- Drive for an appropriate action—an interview, further correspondence, reference checks.

**6. Explain how you should conduct yourself in an interview.**

6. Your major contact with a prospective employer is the interview. For best results, you should do the following:
   - Research the employer in advance so you can impress the interviewer.
   - Present a good appearance through appropriate dress and grooming.
   - Try to anticipate the interviewer's questions and to plan your answers.
   - Make a good impression by being at ease.
   - Help the interviewer establish a dialogue with questions and comments that enable you to present the best information about you.

**7. Write application follow-up letters that are appropriate, friendly, and positive.**

7. You may need to write other letters in your search for a job.
   - Following the interview, a thank-you letter is appropriate.
   - Also appropriate is an inquiry about the status of an application.
   - You may also need to write letters accepting, rejecting, or resigning a job.
   - Write these letters much as you would the letters reviewed in preceding chapters: direct order for good news, indirect order for bad.

# QUESTIONS FOR DISCUSSION

1. "Building a network of contacts to help one find jobs appears to be selfish. It involves acquiring friendships just to use them for one's personal benefit." Discuss this view.

2. Maryann Brennan followed a broad program of study in college and received a degree in general studies. She did her best work in English, especially in the writing courses. She also did well in history, sociology, and psychology. As much as she could, she avoided math and computer courses.

   Her overall grade-point average of 3.7 (4.0 basis) placed her in the top 10 percent of her class. What advice would you give her as she begins her search for a career job?

3. Discuss the value of each of the sources for finding jobs to a finance major (a) right after graduation and (b) after 20 years of work in his or her specialty.

4. Assume that in an interview for the job you want, you are asked the questions listed in the text under the heading "Anticipating Questions." Answer these questions.

5. The most popular arrangement of résumé information is the four-part grouping: education, experience, personal details, and references. Describe three other arrangements. When would each be used?

6. Distinguish between the general résumé and the targeted résumé. When would each be most appropriate?

7. What is meant by parallelism of headings?

8. When would you suggest listing references in the résumé? When would you suggest leaving them out?

9. Describe the application letter and résumé you would write (a) immediately after graduation, (b) 10 years later, and (c) 25 years later. Point out similarities and differences, and defend your decision.

10. What differences would you suggest in the writing of application letters for jobs in (a) accounting, (b) banking, (c) advertising copy writing, (d) administration, (e) sales, (f) consulting, and (g) information systems?

11. Discuss the logic of beginning an application letter with these words: "This is to apply for . . ." and "Please consider this my application for the position of . . ."

12. "In writing job-application letters, just present the facts clearly and without analysis and interpretation. The facts alone will tell the employer whether he or she wants you." Discuss this viewpoint.

13. When should the drive for action in an application letter (a) request the job, (b) request an interview, and (c) request a reference check?

# APPLICATION EXERCISES

1. Criticize the following résumé parts. (They are not from the same résumé.)

   a. Work Experience
   
   | | |
   |---|---|
   | 1990–93 | Employed as sales rep for Lloyd-Shanks Tool Company |
   | 1987–90 | Office manager, Drago Plumbing Supply, Toronto |
   | 1985–87 | Matson's Super Stores. I worked part time as sales clerk while attending college. |

   b. References

   Mr. Carl T. Whitesides
   Sunrise Insurance, Inc.
   317 Forrest Lane
   Dover, DE 19901

   Patricia Cullen
   Cullen and Cullen Realtors
   2001 Bowman Dr.
   Wilmington, DE 19804

   Rev. Troy A. Graham
   Asbury Methodist Church
   Hyattsville, MD 20783

   D. W. Boozer
   Boozer Industries
   Baltimore, MD 21202

   c. Education

   | | |
   |---|---|
   | 1987 | Graduated from Tippen H.S. (I was in top 10 percent of class.) |
   | 1992 | B.S. from Brady University with major in marketing |

1993 to present. Enrolled part time in M.B.A. program at Waldon University

d. Qualifications

Know how to motivate a sales force. I have done it.

Experienced in screening applicants and selecting salespeople.

Know the pharmaceutical business from 11 years of experience.

Knowledgeable of realistic quota setting and incentives.

Proven leadership ability.

2. Criticize these sentences from application letters:

Beginning Sentences

a. Please consider this my application for any position for which my training and experience qualify me.

b. Mr. Jerry Bono of your staff has told me about a vacancy in your loan department for which I would like to apply.

c. I am that accountant you described in you advertisement in today's Times-Record.

d. I want to work for you!

Sentences Presenting Selling Points

e. From 1988 to 1992 I attended Brady University where I took courses leading to a B.S. degree with a major in finance.

f. I am highly skilled in trading corporate bonds as a result of three years spent in the New York office of Collins, Bragg, and Weaver.

g. For three years (1989–92) I was in the loan department at Northwest Bank.

h. My two strongest qualifications for this job are my personality and gift of conversation.

Sentences from Action Endings

i. I will call you on the 12th to arrange an interview.

j. If my qualifications meet your requirements, it would be greatly appreciated if you would schedule an interview for me.

k. Please call to set up an interview. Do it now—while it is on your mind.

## LETTER PROBLEMS
## APPLICATIONS

1. Move the date to the time you will complete your education. You have successfully prepared yourself for the career of your choice, but the visiting recruiters have not yet offered you a job. Now you must look on your own. So you find the best job for which you believe you are qualified in the "Classified Advertisements" sections of the area newspapers. Write the application letter that will present your qualifications for this job. Attach the advertisement to the letter. (Assume that a résumé accompanies the letter.)

2. Write the résumé to accompany the letter for Problem 1.

3. Project yourself five years past your graduation date. During those years, you have had good experience working for the company of your choice in the field of your choice. (Use your imagination to supply this information.)

Unfortunately, your progress hasn't been what you had expected. You think that you must look around for a better opportunity. Your search through the classified advertisements in your area newspapers and *The Wall Street Journal* turns up one promising possibility (you find it). Write an application letter that skillfully presents your qualifications for this job. (You may make logical assumptions about your experience over the five-year period.) For class purposes, clip the advertisement to your letter.

4. Write the résumé to accompany the letter in Problem 3.

5. Assume that you are in your last term of school and that graduation is just around the corner. Your greatest interest is in finding work that you like and that would enable you to support yourself now and to support a family as you win promotions.

No job of your choice is revealed in the want ads of newspapers and trade magazines. No placement bureau has provided anything to your liking. So you decide to do what any good salesperson does: survey the product (yourself) and the market (companies that could use a person who can do what you are prepared to do) and then advertise (send each of these companies a résumé with an application letter). This procedure sometimes creates a job where none existed before; and sometimes it establishes a basis for negotiations for the "big job" two, three, or five years after graduation. And very frequently, it puts you on the list for the good job that is not filled through advertising or from the company staff. Write the application letter.

6. Write the résumé to accompany the letter for Problem 5.

7. Move the calendar to your graduation date so that you're now ready to sell your working ability in the job market for as much as you can get and still hold your own. Besides canvassing likely firms with the help of prospecting letters and diligently following up family contacts, you've decided to look into anything that appears especially good in the ad columns of newspapers and magazines. The latest available issues of big-town publications list the following jobs that you think you could handle. (You may change publication and place names to fit your section of the country.)

   a. *Banking Trainee.* Major bank has several openings in training program. College study of finance and/or accounting preferred. Apply by letter stressing area of banking operations for which best qualified. Personal communication skills necessary. Must be a hard worker and computer literate. Send application to Personnel Director, Box 317, __[your city]__.

   b. *Marketing Trainee.* International chain of department stores seeks qualified people to train for administrative positions. College study of marketing desirable but not essential. Ambitious, hard-working, personable people wanted. Must be good communicator and demonstrate professional image and maturity. Advancement limited only by qualifications and effort. Apply to Personnel Office, P.O. Box 7713, __[your city]__.

   c. *Operations Management Trainee.* Large electronics manufacturer seeks person trained in operations management for entry-level work. Applicant selected will train for management position. Good communication and people skills required. Must be hard working, willing to learn, and reliable. Advancement dependent on performance with unlimited future. Excellent benefits and salary. Apply to Training Program, P.O. Box 19771, __[your city]__.

   d. *Accountants.* Major international company seeks entry-level accountants for career positions. Solid background of accounting study required. Computer skills essential. Good communication and people skills needed. Send letter and résumé to Accounting Department, P.O. Box 5155, __[your city]__.

   e. *Office Manager.* Insurance company seeks personable, college-trained person to manage office of five employees. People skills and good communication ability a must. Knowledge of office procedures and word processing essential. Send application material to Personnel Office, P.O. Box 7197, __[your city]__.

   f. *Private Secretary.* Vice president of major manufacturing company seeks highly competent, personable, and dependable private secretary. College training preferred. Must have excellent word processing skills (IBM PC and WordPerfect) as well as knowledge of business writing. Apply to Personnel, Box 739, __[your city]__.

   g. *Management Trainee.* Fast growing manufacturer in the food-processing industry has opening in its training program. Only high-energy, results-oriented people with good communication skills need apply. Opportunities for advancement to management positions based on performance. Applicants must demonstrate a professional image and possess skills in working with people. Computer literacy required. Apply to Personnel Director, P.O. Box 9133, __[your city]__.

   h. *Accounting Majors.* International accounting firm seeks recent accounting graduates. Well-rounded study of accounting and computers essential. Some travel. Advancement based on performance. Communication and human-relations skills required. Must be a hard worker and willing to work long hours during peak periods. Excellent compensation and benefits. Apply to Accounting Director, P.O. Box 2985, __[your city]__.

   i. *Desktop Publishing Graphics Specialist.* A leader in developing and implementing custom software systems is seeking an individual to work with our team of publishing professionals in producing high-quality publications. Responsibilities for this position include producing camera-ready art for large documentation projects using Ventura desktop publishing software. This person will also prepare mechanicals, coordinate production, and maintain schedules. Knowledge of project management software is a plus. Qualified candidates will be detail oriented with experience in graphic design. A strong knowledge of DOS and WordPerfect is also required. We offer an excellent benefits package including generous vacation policy, medical/dental/vision plans, and tuition assistance. Please send resume to HRD, 2501 Dallas Street, _[your city]_.

j. *Credit and Claims Correspondent.* A nationwide leader in the automotive aftermarket has a position available at headquarters for a credit and claims correspondent. Working with the Finance Department, this person will be responsible for resolving customer disputes concerning billing, shipping, returns, and allowances. Excellent communication skills are required to interact with customers and sales and management personnel. Good math aptitude and experience in retail credit and customer claims are helpful. Knowledge of automated A/R systems is a plus. Send letter and resume to Personnel Manager, P.O. Box 181, _[your city]_.

k. *Regional Training Manager.* An American division of a large international copier and facsimile manufacturing company is seeking a training manager. This person will implement programs designed to enhance sales and sales management skills. The ideal candidate will have a B.A. or B.S. degree or equivalent plus training experience. This person should also possess strong management, organization, public speaking, group facilitation, and listening skills. We offer an attractive salary and company benefits. Send résumé and letter with salary history and salary requirements to Recruitment Manager, P.O. Box 1551, _[your city]_.

l. *PC Support Coordinator.* A premier environmental consulting firm is seeking a PC support coordinator for one of the largest, most state-of-the-art information centers. This person must have strong end-user support experience in both IBM-compatible PCs and Apples. Additionally, familiarity with LANs and communication software is preferred. Most of the work will involve configuring and installing new systems and troubleshooting hardware/software problems. Knowledge of WordPerfect, Word, Lotus, Excel, Harvard Graphics, dBase, and Windows is important. A bachelor's degree in business administration or information systems is desired. Excellent communication skills and the ability to relate well to end-users is also desired. Please forward or fax your resume and letter to Eleanor Braaten, 3733 31st Avenue, _[your city]_, Fax: (XXX) XXX-XXXX.

m. *Human Resources Assistant.* A large, international consumer products company near you is seeking a human resources assistant. The candidate must have a college degree, preferably in psychology, management, or industrial relations. Responsibilities will include working with employee benefit programs, payroll administration, and employee records. Also, this person will assist the director with training, affirmative action, and community relations programs. We offer an excellent benefits program including 401(k), educational assistance, and on-site cafeteria and fitness center. Please send résumé and letter with salary requirements to Director, Human Resources Department, 611 Fifth Avenue, _[your city]_.

n. *Financial Staff Auditor.* A Fortune 500 company has an immediate opening for a financial staff auditor. This person will participate in corporate and location audits and travel nearly 60 percent of the time. Duties include reviewing and analyzing financial operations and controls and preparing recommendations. Must have a degree in accounting, finance, or business; related experience preferred. Fluency in Spanish is also a plus. Must have excellent communication skills and the ability to work well with a wide variety of people. We offer an excellent salary and benefits package. Please send resume and letter to Personnel Assistant, 800 Sylvan Avenue, _[your city]_.

o. *Customer Service Representative.* An emerging leader in the telecommunication components industry has an immediate need for a customer service representative. This person will process customer orders, trace shipments, and resolve customer disputes. The position requires basic personal computer skills and heavy customer phone contact within a fast-paced industry. We offer an excellent compensation program including tuition reimbursement. Additionally, we provide pleasant working conditions in a nonsmoking environment. For confidential consideration, send résumé and letter to Personnel Supervisor, Box 1879-B, _[your city]_.

p. *Sales Trainee.* National sign company seeks recent college graduates for regional account training. Excellent opportunity for advancement. Must be self-started and self-motivated. Good oral and written skills a must. College degree in marketing or related field, with good knowledge of practical applications, especially marketing research and consumer behavior. Send letter and résumé to Images, Box LF, _[your city]_.

q. *Insurance Majors.* Local accounting firm wants insurance majors for work with clients on employee benefit programs. Knowledge of accounting, statistics, personnel administration, and fringe benefits essential. Must have excellent interpersonal skills to adapt to various personalities and technical knowledge to provide advice to clients. Interested applicants should apply by letter (with résumé) to P.O. Box 31876, __[your city]__.

r. *Executive Secretary.* Growing travel-related company needs executive secretary for chief executive officer. Must have WordPerfect and Lotus 1-2-3 skills. Outgoing personality to fit with service nature of business. Knowledge of office procedures. Telephone, time management, and language skills necessary. Prefer college graduate with good knowledge of business basics. Write application letter (include résumé) to Central Travel, Box ML, __[your city]__.

s. *Programmer/Analysts.* Information Services Department of international semiconductor manufacturer needs qualified COBOL programmer analysts. Applicants will be responsible for developing and maintaining programs for a variety of in-house users. Undergraduate degree in business computers. Knowledge of COBOL, CICS, and DB2. Excellent written/verbal communication skills. Technical knowledge combined with professional image and pleasing personality. Good work ethic and company loyalty. Apply by sending résumé and letter to Personnel Director, Box 41897, __[your city]__.

t. *Accounting Analyst.* Large central city bank needs entry-level professional accountant to perform a variety of financial duties including general ledger entries, cost allocation, subledger reconciliation, report preparation, and regulatory reporting. Knowledge of microcomputers necessary, especially Lotus 1-2-3. Must be a self-starter and possess ability to relate with all levels of management. Bachelor's degree in finance (must have 12 hours of accounting) or accounting. Excellent growth opportunity for dedicated professional. Salary and benefits above industry norms. Send professional résumé and letter of application to Personnel Director, Box 31948, __[your city]__.

u. *Human Resource Generalist.* High-tech computer industry growth company wants human resource generalist. Degree in business with human resource, risk management, or insurance classes preferred. Solid PC skills especially with Lotus 1-2-3, Macintosh, and WordPerfect. Interest in and commitment to human resource issues. Emphasis on employee benefit packages also preferred. Individual must possess good communication (written and oral) and organizational skills. Excellent salary and benefits for a career-minded person. Interested candidates should forward résumé and letter to Box HR/B&R, __[your city]__.

v. *Financial Analyst.* One of the nation's largest food service companies has an immediate opening for a financial analyst. Responsibilities include preparing and monitoring the annual business plan, strategic plan and forecasts, cash-flow analysis, capital expenditure budget, and business line analysis. Applicants must have a bachelor's degree with a finance major and financial analysis experience. Experience with a PC and spreadsheet software would also be an asset. This is a high-visibility position requiring excellent communication skills and strong interpersonal skills in dealing with all levels of management. Please send résumé and letter including salary requirements in confidence to Personnel Department, 2000 Hermitage Way, __[your city]__.

w. *Account Representative.* One of nation's leading hospitalization carriers is seeking a motivated, dependable, results-oriented individual. Responsibilities include marketing company plan in local region, sales, and follow-up. Must have skills in making presentations to small groups and large audiences. Company car provided; travel 70–80 percent of work time. Degree in marketing preferred. Excellent salary and benefits for aggressive person. Send résumé and application letter to Personnel Office, Box LDF, __[your city]__.

Concentrate on the ad describing the job you would like most or could do best—and then write an application letter that will get you that job. Your letter will first have to survive the siftings that eliminate dozens (sometimes hundreds) of applicants who lack the expected qualifications. Toward the end you'll be getting into strong competition in which small details may give you the little extra margin of superiority that will get you an interview and a chance to campaign further.

Study your ad for what it says and even more for what it implies. Weigh your own preparation even more thoroughly than you weigh the ad. You may imagine far enough ahead to assure completion of all the courses that are blocked out for your degree.

You may build up your case a bit on what you actually have. Sort out the things that line you up for the *one* job, organize them strategically, and then present them. Assume that you've attached a résumé.

8. Write the résumé to accompany the letter for Problem 7.
9. You are looking ahead to your graduation soon. You've decided to begin to look for jobs on-line. Tap into a bulletin board that you know posts jobs in your major (such as Prodigy) or one where people on it may lead you to such a board. Browse through the jobs until you see one that appeals to you and for which you'll be qualified when you graduate. Print (or save) a copy of the ad so you'll have it handy when you write your résumé and letter of application. Address the points covered in the ad and tell them that you learned about the position from a particular on-line system. If you are transmitting your response on-line, be sure to chunk your documents with your strongest points on the first few screens.

# PART FIVE

# FUNDAMENTALS OF REPORT WRITING

**12**
BASICS OF REPORT WRITING

**13**
REPORT STRUCTURE: THE SHORTER FORMS

**14**
LONG, FORMAL REPORTS

**15**
GRAPHICS

# CHAPTER 12

# *BASICS OF REPORT WRITING*

## CHAPTER OBJECTIVES

*Upon completing this chapter, you will be able to prepare well-organized, objective reports. To reach this goal, you should be able to*

**1**
State a problem clearly in writing.

**2**
List the factors involved in a problem.

**3**
Explain the common errors in interpreting and the attitudes and practices conducive to good interpreting.

**4**
Organize information in outline form, using time, place, quantity, factor, or a combination of these as bases for division.

**5**
Construct topic or talking headings that outline reports logically and meaningfully.

**6**
Write reports that are clear, objective, consistent in time viewpoint, smoothly connected, and interesting.

## INTRODUCTORY SITUATION

## to Report Writing

Introduce yourself to the subject of report writing by assuming the role of administrative assistant to the president of Technicraft, Inc. Much of your work at this large manufacturing company involves getting information for your boss. Yesterday, for example, you looked into the question of excessive time spent by office workers on coffee breaks. A few days earlier, you worked on an assignment to determine the causes of unrest in one of the production departments. Before that assignment you investigated a supervisor's recommendation to change a production process. You could continue the list indefinitely, for investigating problems is a part of your work.

So is report writing, for you must write a report on each of your investigations. You write these reports for good reasons. Written reports make permanent records. Thus, those who need the information contained in these reports can review and study them at their convenience. Written reports can also be routed to a number of readers with a minimum of effort. Unquestionably, such reports are convenient and efficient means of transmitting information. Your report-writing work is not unique in your company. In fact, report writing is common in virtually all operations of the company. For example, the engineers often report on the technical problems they encounter. The accountants regularly report to management on the company's financial operations. From time to time, production people report on various aspects of operations. The salespeople regularly report on marketing matters. And so it is throughout the company. Such reporting is vital to your company's operations—as it is to the operations of all companies. Organizations require information for many reasons. In a sense, they feed on information. Reports supply them with a vital portion of the information they need.[1]

This chapter and the following two chapters describe the structure and writing of this vital form of business communication. ■

How often you write reports in the years ahead will depend on the size of the organization you work for. If you work for a very small organization (say, one with under 10 employees), you will probably write only a few. But if you work for a midsize or larger organization, you are likely to write many. In fact, the larger the organization, the more reports you are likely to write. The explanation is obvious. The larger the organization, the greater is its complexity; and the greater the complexity, the greater is the need for information to manage the organization. As reports supply much of the information needed, the demand for them is great.

*Reports are vital to larger organizations. You will probably write them.*

---

[1] The following review of report writing is condensed from Raymond V. Lesikar and John D. Pettit, Jr., *Report Writing for Business,* 8th ed. (Homewood, Ill.: Richard D. Irwin, 1991).

## DEFINING REPORTS

You probably have a good idea of what reports are. Even so, you would be likely to have a hard time defining them. Even scholars of the subject cannot agree, for their definitions range from one extreme to the other. Some define reports to include almost any presentation of information; others limit reports to only the most formal presentations. For our purposes, this middle-ground definition is best: *A business report is an orderly and objective communication of factual information that serves a business purpose.*

The key words in this definition deserve emphasis. As an *orderly* communication, a report is prepared carefully. Thus, care in preparation distinguishes reports from casual exchanges of information. The *objective* quality of a report is its unbiased approach. Reports seek truth. They avoid human biases. The word *communication* is broad in meaning. It covers all ways of transmitting meaning—speaking, writing, drawing. The basic ingredient of reports is *factual information*. Factual information is based on events, records, data, and the like. Not all reports are business reports. Research scientists, medical doctors, ministers, students, and many others write them. To be classified as a business report, a report must *serve a business purpose*.

This definition is specific enough to be meaningful, yet broad enough to take into account the variations in reports. For example, some reports (information reports) do nothing more than present facts. Others (analytical reports) go a step further by including interpretations, sometimes accompanied by conclusions and recommendations. There are reports that are highly formal both in writing style and in physical appearance. And there are reports that show a high degree of informality. Our definition permits all of these variations.

*A business report is an orderly and objective communication of factual information that serves a business purpose.*

*The key words are* orderly, objective, communication, factual information, *and* serves a business purpose.

## DETERMINING THE REPORT PURPOSE

Your work on a report logically begins with a need, which we refer to generally as the *problem* in the following discussion. Someone or some group (usually your superiors) needs information for a business purpose. Perhaps the need is for information only; perhaps it is for information and analysis; or perhaps it is for information, analysis, and recommendations. Whatever the case, someone with a need (problem) will authorize you to do the work. Usually the work will be authorized orally. But it could be authorized in a letter or a memorandum.

After you have been assigned a report problem, your first task should be to get your problem clearly in mind. Elementary and basic as this task may appear, all too often it is done haphazardly. And all too often a report fails to reach its goal because of such haphazardness.

*Work on a report begins with a business need (problem).*

*Your first task is to get the problem clearly in mind.*

### The Preliminary Investigation

Getting your problem clearly in mind is largely a matter of gathering all the information needed to understand it and then applying your best logic to it. Gathering the right information involves many things, depending on the problem. It may mean gathering material from company files, talking over

*To do this, you should begin by gathering all the information you need to understand the problem.*

PART 5   Fundamentals of Report Writing

the problem with experts, searching through printed sources, and discussing the problem with those who authorized the report. In general, you should continue this preliminary investigation until you have the information you need to understand your problem.

### Need for a Clear Statement of the Problem

After you understand your problem, your next step is to state it clearly. Writing the problem statement is good practice for several reasons. A written statement is preserved permanently. Thus, you may refer to it time and again. In addition, a written statement can be reviewed, approved, and evaluated by people whose assistance may be valuable. Most important of all, putting the problem in writing forces you to think it through.

*Then you should express the problem clearly, preferably in writing.*

The problem statement normally takes one of three forms: infinitive phrase, question, or declarative statement. To illustrate each, we will use the problem of determining why sales at a certain store have declined:

*The problem statement may be (1) an infinitive phrase, (2) a question, or (3) a declarative statement.*

1. *Infinitive phrase:* "To determine the causes of decreasing sales at Store X."
2. *Question:* "What are the causes of decreasing sales at Store X?"
3. *Declarative statement:* "Store X sales are decreasing, and management wants to know why."

## DETERMINING THE FACTORS

After stating the problem, you determine what needs to be done to solve it. Specifically, you look for the factors of the problem. That is, you determine what subject areas you must look into to solve the problem.

*Next, you should determine the factors of the problem.*

Problem factors may be of three types. First, they may be subtopics of the overall topic about which the report is concerned. Second, they may be hypotheses that must be tested. Third, in problems that involve comparisons, they may be the bases on which the comparisons are made.

*The factors may be subtopics of the overall topic, hypotheses, or bases for comparison.*

### Use of Subtopics in Information Reports

If the problem concerns a need for information, your mental effort should produce the main areas about which information is needed. Illustrating this type of situation is the problem of preparing a report that reviews Company X's activities during the past quarter. Clearly, this is an informational report problem—that is, it requires no analysis, no conclusion, no recommendation. It only requires that information be presented. The mental effort in this case is concerned simply with determining which subdivisions of the overall topic should be covered. After thoroughly evaluating the possibilities, you might come up with something like this analysis:

*Subtopics of the overall topic are the factors in information reports.*

*Problem statement:* To review operations of Company X from January 1 through March 31.
*Subtopics:*
1. Production.
2. Sales and promotion.
3. Financial status.

**CHAPTER 12 Basics of Report Writing**

4. Plant and equipment.
5. Product development.
6. Personnel.

## Hypotheses for Problems Requiring Solution

*Hypotheses (possible explanations of the problem) may be the factors in problems requiring solution.*

Some problems concern why something bad is happening and perhaps how to correct it. In analyzing problems of this kind, you should seek explanations or solutions. Such explanations or solutions are termed *hypotheses*. Once formulated, hypotheses are tested, and their applicability to the problem is either proved or disproved.

To illustrate, assume that you have the problem of determining why sales at a certain store have declined. In preparing this problem for investigation, you would think of the possible explanations (hypotheses) for the decline. Your task would be one of studying, weighing, and selecting, and you would come up with such explanations as these:

*For example, these hypotheses could be suggested to explain a store's loss in sales.*

*Problem statement:* Why have sales declined at the Milltown store?
*Hypotheses:*
1. Activities of the competition have caused the decline.
2. Changes in the economy of the area have caused the decline.
3. Merchandising deficiencies have caused the decline.
4. Changes in the environment (population shifts, political actions, etc.) have caused the decline.

In the investigation that follows, you would test these hypotheses, perhaps by assigning point values to each. You might find that one, two, or all apply. Or you might find that none is valid. If so, you would have to advance additional hypotheses for further evaluation.

## Bases of Comparison in Evaluation Studies

*For evaluation problems, the bases for evaluating are the factors.*

When the problem concerns evaluating something, either singularly or in comparison with other things, you should look for the bases for the evaluation. That is, you should determine what characteristics you will evaluate. In some cases, the procedure may concern more than naming the characteristics. It may also include the criteria to be used in evaluating them.

*This illustration shows the bases for comparing factory locations.*

Illustrating this technique is the problem of a company that seeks to determine which of three cities would be best for a new factory. Such a problem obviously involves a comparison of the cities. The bases for comparison are the factors that determine success for the type of factory involved. After careful mental search for these factors, you might come up with a plan such as this:

*Problem statement:* To determine whether Y Company's new factory should be built in City A, City B, or City C.
*Comparison bases:*
1. Availability of labor.
2. Abundance of raw material.
3. Tax structure.
4. Transportation facilities.

PART 5  Fundamentals of Report Writing

5. Nearness to markets.
6. Power supply.
7. Community attitude.

### Need for Subbreakdown

Each of the factors selected for investigation may have factors of its own. In the last illustration, for example, the comparison of transportation in the three cities may well be covered by such subdivisions as water, rail, truck, and air. Labor may be compared by using such categories as skilled labor and unskilled labor. Breakdowns of this kind may go still further. Skilled labor may be broken down by specific skills: machinists, plumbers, pipefitters, welders, and such. The subdivisions could go on and on. Make them as long as they are helpful.

*The factors sometimes have factors of their own. That is, they may also be broken down.*

### GATHERING THE INFORMATION NEEDED

For most business problems, you will need to conduct a personal investigation. A production problem, for example, might require gathering and reviewing the company's production records. A sales problem might require collecting information through discussions with customers and sales personnel. A computer problem might require talking to both end-users and programmers. A purchasing problem might require getting sales literature, finding prices, compiling performance statistics, and so on. Such a personal investigation usually requires knowledge of your field of work, which is probably why you were assigned the problem.

*The next step is to conduct the research needed. A personal investigation is usually appropriate.*

---

### Styles or Tags: A Useful Formatting Feature

Anytime you find a need to repeatedly use the same formatting codes, styles or tags is a feature you will want to use. Although the feature is called styles in word processing and tags in desktop publishing, the two do essentially the same thing. When writing reports is a regular part of your job, you can create styles or tags to help you format titles, heading levels, body text, bibliography items, and any other parts that you use repeatedly.

In addition, you can create a library of styles to use across all your documents. Not only will using these styles ensure consistency within your report, your reports will be consistent over time. And you will save yourself the time and effort of having to look up the formatting you used the last time you wrote a similar report. Furthermore, if you decide to change the look of your report, you can simply edit the style instead of having to search through your entire document for all the individual formatting codes. Or you could simply delete the current style and apply a new one.

Styles and tags are easy both to create and to use. Once you have set them up, you reap rewards every time you use them.

*Experiments or surveys are sometimes needed.*

Some business problems require a more formal type of research, such as an experiment or a survey. The experiment is the basic technique of the sciences. Business uses experiments primarily in the laboratory, although experiments have some nonlaboratory applications in marketing. Surveys are more likely to be used in business, especially in marketing problems. If you are called on to use experiments or surveys, it will probably be because your training has prepared you to use them. If you should need these techniques in this course, you will find them summarized in Chapter 22.

*Sometimes library research is used.*

In some cases, you may use library research to find the information you need in printed sources. Classroom assignments may have already prepared you to use the techniques of library research. If not and you need to use those techniques now, you will find them summarized in Chapter 22. Using the findings of library research involves other techniques (referencing, bibliography construction, quoting, paraphrasing, and such). Those techniques are covered in Appendix D.

*Apply the research techniques needed for the problem.*

In any event, your task is to apply whatever research techniques are required to get the information you need for your problem. When you have gathered that information, you are ready for the next step in report preparation.

## INTERPRETING THE FINDINGS

*Next, apply the information collected to the problem. Interpret it.*

With your research done, you are ready to prepare your findings for presentation. If your goal is merely to present information, you need only organize by subtopics of the subject. If you must analyze the information and apply it to a problem, you must do much more. You must interpret the information as it affects the problem. Applying and interpreting your findings is obviously a mental process. Thus, we can only give you limited advice on how to do it. But even though this advice is limited, you can profit by following it.

*Interpreting is mental. You can profit from the following advice.*

### Advice for Avoiding Human Error

The first advice is to avoid certain human tendencies that lead to error in interpretation. Foremost among these are the following:

*Avoid human error by remembering these fundamentals:*

*1. Report the facts as they are.*

 1. *Report the facts as they are.* Do nothing to make them more or less exciting. Adding color to interpretations to make the report more interesting amounts to bias.

*2. Do not think that conclusions are always necessary.*

 2. *Do not think that conclusions are always necessary.* When the facts do not support a conclusion, you should conclude that there is no conclusion. All too often report writers think that if they do not conclude, they have failed in their investigation.

*3. Do not interpret a lack of evidence as proof to the contrary.*

 3. *Do not interpret a lack of evidence as proof to the contrary.* The fact that you cannot prove something is true does not mean that it is false.

*4. Do not compare noncomparable data.*

 4. *Do not compare noncomparable data.* When you look for relationships between sets of data, make sure they have similarities—that you do not have apples and oranges.

*5. Do not draw illogical cause-effect conclusions.*

 5. *Do not draw illogical cause-effect conclusions.* Just because two sets of data appear to affect each other does not mean they actually do. Use your good logic to determine whether a cause-effect relationship is likely.

PART 5  Fundamentals of Report Writing

"You're right. This report does make you look like a fool."
Vietor's *Funny Business*

6. *Beware of unreliable and unrepresentative data.* Much of the information to be found in secondary sources is incorrect to some extent. The causes are many: collection error, biased research, recording mistakes. Beware especially of data collected by groups that advocate a position (political organizations, groups supporting social issues, and other special-interest groups). Make sure the sources you uncover are reliable. And remember that the interpretations you make are no better than the data you interpret.

7. *Do not oversimplify.* Most business problems are complex, and all too often we neglect some important parts of them.

### Appropriate Attitudes and Practices

In addition to being alert to the most likely causes of error, you can improve your interpretation of findings by adopting the following attitudes and practices:

1. *Maintain a judicial attitude.* Play the role of a judge as you interpret. Look at all sides of every issue without emotion or prejudice. Your primary objective is to uncover truth.

2. *Consult with others.* It is rare indeed when one mind is better than two or more. Thus, you can profit by talking over your interpretations with others.

3. *Test your interpretations.* Unfortunately, the means of testing are subjective and involve the thinking process. Even so, testing is helpful and can help you avoid major error. Two tests are available to you.

First is the test of experience. In applying this test, you use the underlying theme in all scientific methods—reason. You ponder each interpretation you make, asking yourself, "Does this appear reasonable in light of all I know or have experienced?"

Second is the negative test, which is an application of the critical viewpoint. You begin by making the interpretation that is directly opposite your initial one. Next, you examine the opposite interpretation carefully in light of all available evidence, perhaps even building a case for it. Then you compare the two interpretations and retain the one that is more strongly supported.

---

6. Beware of unreliable and unrepresentative data.

7. Do not oversimplify.

Adopt the following attitudes and practices:

1. Maintain a judicial attitude.

2. Consult with others.

3. Test your interpretations.

Use the test of your experience—reason.

Use the negative test—question your interpretations.

**CHAPTER 12  Basics of Report Writing**

## Statistical Tools in Interpretation

*Statistics permit one to examine a set of facts.*

In most cases, the information you gather is quantitative—that is, expressed in numbers. Such data in their raw form usually are voluminous, consisting of tens, hundreds, even thousands of figures. To use these figures intelligently, you must first find ways of simplifying them so that your reader can grasp their general meaning. Statistical techniques provide many methods for analyzing data. By knowing them, you can improve your ability to interpret. Although a thorough review of statistical techniques is beyond the scope of this book, you should know the more commonly used methods described in the following paragraphs.

*Descriptive statistics should help the most.*

Possibly of greatest use to you in writing reports are *descriptive statistics*—measures of central tendency, dispersion, and probability. Measures of central tendency—the mean, median, and mode—will help you find a common value of a series that appropriately describes a whole. The measures of dispersion—ranges, variances, and standard deviations—should help you describe the spread of a series. Ratios (which express one quantity as a multiple of another) and probabilities (which determine how many times something will likely occur out of the total number of possibilities) can also help you convey common meaning in data analysis. Inferential and other statistical approaches are also useful but go beyond these basic elements. You will find descriptions of these and other useful techniques in any standard statistics textbook.

*Do not allow statistics to confuse the reader; they should help interpret.*

A word of caution, however: Your job as an analyst is to help your reader interpret the information. Sometimes unexplained statistical calculations—even if elementary to you—may confuse the reader. Thus, you must explain your statistical techniques explicitly. You must remember that statistics are a help to interpretation, not a replacement for it. Whatever you do to reduce the volume of data deserves careful explanation so that the reader will receive the proper meaning.

## ORGANIZING THE REPORT INFORMATION

*After you know what your findings mean, you are ready to construct the outline.*

When you have finished interpreting your information, you know the message of your report. Now you are ready to organize this message for presentation. Organizing the report message, of course, is the procedure of constructing the outline. As you know, an outline is the plan for the writing task that follows. It is to you, the writer, what the blueprint is to the construction engineer or what the pattern is to the dressmaker. Constructing an outline forces you to think before you write. When you do this, your writing is likely to benefit.

*Outlines should usually be written. They serve as tables of contents and captions.*

Although your plan may be written or mental, using a written plan would be advisable for all but the shortest problems. In a longer report, the outline forms the basis for the table of contents. Also, in most long reports, and even in some short ones, the outline topics may be used as guides to the reader by placing them within the text as headings to the material they cover.

In constructing your outline, you probably will use either the conventional or the decimal symbol system to mark the levels. The conventional system uses Roman numerals to show the major headings and letters of the alphabet and Arabic numbers to show the lesser headings, as illustrated here:

*Conventional System*

> I. First-level heading
>   A. Second level, first part
>   B. Second level, second part
>     1. Third level, first part
>     2. Third level, second part
>       a. Fourth level
>         (1) Fifth level
>           (a) Sixth level
> II. First-level heading
>   A. Second level, first part
>   B. Second level, second part
>
> Etc.

*This conventional symbol system is used in marking the levels of an outline.*

The decimal system uses whole numbers to show the major sections. Whole numbers followed by decimals and additional digits show subsections. That is, the digits to the right of the decimal show each successive step in the outline. Illustration best explains this system:

*Decimal System*

> 1.0 First-level heading
>   1.1 Second level, first part
>   1.2 Second level, second part
>     1.2.1 Third level, first part
>     1.2.2 Third level, second part
>       1.2.2.1 Fourth level
> 2.0 First-level heading
>   2.1 Second level, first part
>   2.2 Second level, second part
>
> Etc.

*This decimal system is also used.*

Whatever system you use, when you begin producing the final report you also will show differences in the levels of headings by placement and form (font, size, or style). The placement and form options available to you are reviewed in Chapter 20.

## The Nature and Extent of Outlining

In general, you should build the outline around the objective of the report and the information you have gathered to meet that objective. With the objective and your information in mind, you build the structure of the report mentally. In this process, you shift facts and ideas about until the most workable order becomes clear. That order is the one that presents the findings in the clearest and most meaningful way.

*The outline is designed to meet the objective of the report.*

How much work you will have to do at this stage varies by problem. In some cases, you may have little to do, for you may have determined the order of the report in preceding steps. For example, the problem factors that you determined early in the investigation may also be the main heads of your

*When you reach the outlining stage, you have probably done some of the work.*

Organizing information in a report is similar to a common way of organizing a hand of cards in bridge. You place like information (suits) together and arrange the like information in a meaningful order.

outline. Or perhaps you worked out an order for presenting your research findings when you analyzed and interpreted them. In all likelihood, when you reach the stage of consciously constructing the outline, you will find that you have already done some of the work. Even so, there will probably be much to do. In doing it, you would be wise to use the general procedure described in the following paragraphs.

## Introductory and Concluding Parts

*The following discussion of outlining deals with the body of the report. Assume that an introduction and a conclusion will be added.*

Outlining is concerned mainly with the part of the report commonly called the *body*. The body is the part of the report that presents the information gathered, with analyses and interpretations where needed. It is usually preceded by an introduction, which is common in all but the shortest reports. And it is usually followed by an ending section, which may be a summary, a conclusion, a recommendation, or some combination of the three. The introduction and the ending section are parts of the outline, of course, but the following discussion does not concern them. The structure and content of these parts are discussed where appropriate in following chapters.

## Organization by Division

*You may view outlining as a process of division. First, you divide the whole into parts.*

The outlining procedure described in the following pages is based on the idea that outlining is a process of dividing. The subject you are dividing is all the information you have gathered and interpreted. Thus, you begin the task of organizing by looking over that information for some logical way of dividing it into comparable parts. When you find a way, you divide it. This gives you the major outline parts indicated in Figure 12–1 by the Roman numeral captions (I, II, III, and so on).

*Then you divide the parts into subparts. You may subdivide further.*

In short reports, one division may be enough. Long reports, however, may require that each part in the first division be divided. The parts in the

PART 5 Fundamentals of Report Writing

**FIGURE 12–1** Procedure for Constructing an Outline by Process of Division

| Step 1 | Step 2 | Step 3 | etc. |
|---|---|---|---|
| Divide the whole into comparable parts. This gives the roman numbered parts of the outline. Usually an introduction begins the outline. Some combination of summary, conclusion, recommendation ends it. | Divide each roman section. This gives the A, B, C headings. | Then divide each A, B, C heading. This gives the 1, 2, 3 headings. | Continue dividing as long as it is practical to do so. |

SOURCE: Raymond V. Lesikar and John D. Pettit, Jr., *Report Writing for Business,* 8th ed. (Homewood, Ill.: Richard D. Irwin, 1991).

second division are identified by capital letter headings (A, B, C). You may have to divide a third time (for the 1, 2, 3 outline parts). In fact, you may continue to subdivide as long as it is practical to do so. Each division makes a step in the outline.

### Division by Conventional Relationships

In dividing your information into subparts, you have to find a way of dividing that will produce approximately equal parts. Time, place, quantity, and factor are the general bases for these divisions.

*Time, place, quantity, and factor are the bases for the process of division.*

*When the information has a time basis, division by time is possible.*

Whenever the information you have to present has some time aspect, consider organizing it by *time*. In such an organization, the divisions are periods of time. These periods usually follow a sequence. Although a past-to-present or present-to-past sequence is the rule, variations are possible. The periods you select need not be equal in duration, but they should be about equal in importance.

A report on the progress of a research committee illustrates this possibility. The period covered by this report might be broken down into the following comparable subperiods:

The period of orientation, May–July.
Planning the project, August.
Implementation of the research plan, September–November.

The happenings within each period might next be arranged in order of occurrence. Close inspection might reveal additional division possibilities.

*When the information is related to geographic location, a place division is possible.*

If the information you have collected has some relation to geographic location, you may use a *place* division. Ideally, this division would be such that the areas are nearly equal in importance.

A report on the U.S. sales program of a national manufacturer illustrates a division by place. The information in this problem might be broken down by these major geographic areas:

New England.
Atlantic Seaboard.
South.
Southwest.
Midwest.
Rocky Mountains.
Pacific Coast.

Another illustration of organization by place is a report on the productivity of a company with a number of manufacturing plants. A major division of the report might be devoted to each of the plants. The information for each plant might be broken down further, this time by sections, departments, divisions, or the like.

*Division based on quantity is possible when the information has a number base.*

*Quantity* divisions are possible for information that has quantitative values. To illustrate, an analysis of the buying habits of potential customers could be divided by such income groups as the following:

Under $10,000.
$10,000 to under $15,000.
$15,000 to under $20,000.
$20,000 to under $25,000.
$25,000 to under $30,000.
$30,000 and over.

Another example of division on a quantitative basis is a report of a survey of men's preferences for shoes, in which an organization by age groups might be used to show variations in preference by ages. Perhaps the following division would be appropriate:

Youths, under 18.
Young adults, 18–30.

Adults, 31–50.
Senior adults, 51–70.
Elder adults, over 70.

*Factor* breakdowns are less easily seen than the preceding three possibilities. Problems often have few or no time, place, or quantity aspects. Instead, they require that certain information areas be investigated. Such areas may consist of questions that must be answered in solving a problem, or of subjects that must be investigated and applied to the problem.

Factors (areas to be investigated) are a fourth basis for dividing information.

An example of a division by factors is a report that seeks to determine which of three cities is the best as the location of a new office for property management. In arriving at this decision, one would need to compare the three cities based on the factors affecting the office location. Thus, the following organization of this problem would be a possibility:

Location accessibility.
Rent.
Parking.
Convenience to current customers.
Facilities.

Another illustration of organization by factors is a report advising a manufacturer whether to begin production of a new product. The solution of this problem will be reached by careful consideration of the factors involved. Among the more likely factors are these:

Production feasibility.
Financial considerations.
Strength of competition.
Consumer demand.
Marketing considerations.

### Combination and Multiple Division Possibilities

Not all division possibilities are clearly time, place, quantity, or factor. In some instances, combinations of these bases of division are possible. In a report on the progress of a sales organization, for example, the information collected could be arranged by a combination of quantity and place:

Combinations of time, place, quantity, and factor are sometimes logical.

Areas of high sales activity.
Areas of moderate sales activity.
Areas of low sales activity.

Although less logical, the following combination of time and quantity is also a possibility:

Periods of low sales.
Periods of moderate sales.
Periods of high sales.

Some problems can be organized in more than one way. For example, take the problem of determining the best of three towns for locating a new manufacturing plant. It could be organized by towns or by the bases of comparison. Organized by towns, the bases of comparison would probably be the second-level headings:

Multiple organization possibilities can occur.

**CHAPTER 12** Basics of Report Writing

> This plant-location problem is organized by place.

II. Town A
   A. Availability of workers.
   B. Transportation facilities.
   C. Public support and cooperation.
   D. Availability of raw materials.
   E. Taxation.
   F. Sources of power.
III. Town B
   A. Availability of workers.
   B. And so on.
IV. Town C
   A. Availability of workers.
   B. And so on.

Organized by bases of comparison, towns would probably be the second-level headings:

> Here, it is organized by factors (the bases of comparison).

II. Availability of workers
   A. Town A.
   B. Town B.
   C. Town C.
III. Transportation facilities
   A. Town A.
   B. Town B.
   C. Town C.
IV. Public support and cooperation
   A. Town A.
   B. Town B.
   C. Town C.

> The second plan is better because it makes comparison easy.

At first glance, both plans appear logical. Close inspection, however, shows that organization by towns separates information that has to be compared. For example, three different parts of the report must be examined to find out which town has the best worker availability. In the second outline, the information that has to be compared is close together.

Nevertheless, these two plans show that some problems can be organized in more than one way. In such cases, you must compare the possibilities carefully to find the one that best presents the report information.

## Wording of the Outline

> When the outline will appear in the report, take care in its wording.

The outline in its finished form is the table of contents. Its parts serve as headings to the sections of the report (which is why we refer to these parts as *headings* in the following discussion). Since the outline is an important part of the report, you should construct its final wording carefully. In this regard, you should consider the conventional principles of construction reviewed in the following pages.

> You may use topic or talking headings. Topic headings give only the subject of discussion.

**Topic or Talking Headings.** In selecting the wording for outline headings, you have a choice of two general forms—topic headings and talking headings. *Topic headings* are short constructions, frequently consisting of one or two words. They merely identify the topic of discussion. Here is a segment of a topic-heading outline:

PART 5  Fundamentals of Report Writing

II. Present armor unit
   A. Description and output.
   B. Cost.
   C. Deficiencies.
III. Replacement effects
   A. Space.
   B. Boiler setting.
   C. Additional accessories.
   D. Fuel.

Like topic headings, *talking headings* (or *popular headings*, as they are sometimes called) identify the subject matter covered. But they go a step further. They also indicate what is said about the subject. In other words, talking headings summarize the material they cover, as in this illustration:

> Talking headings identify the subject and tell what is said about it.

II. Operation analyses of armor unit
   A. Recent lag in overall output.
   B. Increase in cost of operation.
   C. Inability to deliver necessary steam.
III. Consideration of replacement effects
   A. Greater space requirements.
   B. Need for higher boiler setting.
   C. Efficiency possibilities of accessories.
   D. Practicability of firing two fuels.

The following report outline is made up of headings that talk:

I. Orientation to the problem
   A. Authorization by board action.
   B. Problem of locating a woolen mill.
   C. Use of miscellaneous government data.
   D. Logical plan of solution.
II. Community attitudes toward the woolen industry.
   A. Favorable reaction of all towns to new mill.
   B. Mixed attitudes of all towns toward labor policy.
III. Labor supply and prevailing wage rates
   A. Lead of San Marcos in unskilled labor.
   B. Concentration of skilled workers in San Marcos.
   C. Generally confused pattern of wage rates.
IV. Nearness to the raw wool supply
   A. Location of Ballinger, Coleman, and San Marcos in the wool area.
   B. Relatively low production near Big Spring and Littlefield.
V. Availability of utilities
   A. Inadequate water supply for all towns but San Marcos.
   B. Unlimited supply of natural gas for all towns.
   C. Electric rate advantage of San Marcos and Coleman.
   D. General adequacy of all towns for waste disposal.
VI. Adequacy of existing transportation systems
   A. Surface transportation advantages of San Marcos and Ballinger.
   B. General equality of airway connections.

 VII. A final weighting of the factors
  A. Selection of San Marcos as first choice.
  B. Recommendation of Ballinger as second choice.
  C. Lack of advantages in Big Spring, Coleman, and Littlefield.

This report outline is made up of topic headings:

 I. Introduction
  A. Authorization.
  B. Purpose.
  C. Sources.
  D. Preview.
 II. Community attitudes
  A. Plant location.
  B. Labor policy.
 III. Factors of labor
  A. Unskilled workers.
  B. Skilled workers.
  C. Wage rates.
 IV. Raw wool supply
  A. Adequate areas.
  B. Inadequate areas.
 V. Utilities
  A. Water.
  B. Natural gas.
  C. Electricity.
  D. Waste disposal.
 VI. Transportation
  A. Surface.
  B. Air.
 VII. Conclusions
  A. First choice.
  B. Alternative choice.
  C. Other possibilities.

*Headings making up a level of division should be parallel grammatically.*

**Parallelism of Construction.** As a general rule, you should write headings at each level of the outline in the same grammatical form. In other words, equal-level headings should be parallel in structure. For example, if the heading for Roman numeral I is a noun phrase, all other Roman numeral headings should be noun phrases. If the heading for A under I is a sentence, the A, B, C headings throughout the outline should be sentences. However, a few authorities permit varying the form from one part to another (example: sentences for A, B, and C under II and noun phrases for A, B, and C under III).

The following segment of an outline illustrates violations of parallelism:

A. Machine output is lagging (sentence).
B. Increase in cost of operations (noun phrase).
C. Unable to deliver necessary steam (decapitated sentence).

You may correct this violation in any of three ways—by making the headings all sentences, all noun phrases, or all decapitated sentences. If you desire all noun phrases, you could construct such headings as these:

A. Lag in machine output.
B. Increase in cost of operations.
C. Inability to deliver necessary steam.

Or you could make all the headings sentences, like this:

A. Machine output is lagging.
B. Cost of operations is increasing.
C. Boiler cannot deliver necessary steam.

**Variety of Expression.** In the report outline, as in all other forms of writing, you should use a variety of expressions. You should not overwork words, for repeating words too frequently makes for monotonous writing; and monotonous writing is not pleasing to the reader. The following outline excerpt illustrates this point:

> Repeating words in headings can be monotonous.

A. Chemical production in Texas.
B. Chemical production in California.
C. Chemical production in Louisiana.

As a rule, if you make the headings talk well, there is little chance of monotonous repetition. Since your successive sections would probably not be presenting similar or identical information, headings really descriptive of the material they cover would not be likely to use the same words. The headings in the preceding example can be improved simply by making them talk:

> Talking headings are not likely to be monotonous.

A. Texas leads in chemical production.
B. California holds runner-up position.
C. Rapidly gaining Louisiana ranks third.

## WRITING THE REPORT

After you have collected and organized your information, you are ready to begin writing. Much of what you should do in writing the report was covered in the review of clear writing techniques in Chapters 2 and 3. All of these techniques apply to report writing, and you would do well to keep them in mind as you write. In addition, you should be aware of some general characteristics of good report writing. These are objectivity, consistency of time viewpoint, transition, and interest.

> In writing the report, follow the instructions in Chapters 2 and 3 as well as the following.

### Requirement of Objectivity

Good report writing presents fact and logical interpretation of fact. It avoids presenting the writer's opinions, biases, and attitudes. In other words, it is objective.

> Good report writing is objective.

You can make your report writing objective by putting aside your prejudices and biases, by approaching the problem with an open mind and looking at all sides of every issue, and by fairly reviewing and interpreting the information you have uncovered. Your role should be much like that of a fair-minded judge presiding over a court of law. You will leave no stone unturned in your search for truth.

> Keep out all bias. Seek truth.

Some of the reports written in business are produced through group effort. Your collaborative writing assignments in school will prepare you for this work.

**Objective writing is believable.**

**Objectivity as a Basis for Believability.** An objective report has an ingredient that is essential to good report writing—believability. Biased writing in artfully deceptive language may at first glance be believable. But if bias is evident at any place in a report, the reader will be suspicious of the entire report. Painstaking objectivity is, therefore, the only sure way to make report writing believable.

**Historically, objective writing has meant writing impersonally (no *I*'s, *we*'s, *you*'s).**

**Objectivity and the Question of Impersonal versus Personal Writing.** Recognizing the need for objectivity, the early report writers worked to develop an objective style of writing. Since the source of bias in reports was people, they reasoned objectivity was best attained by emphasizing facts rather than the people involved in writing and reading reports. So they tried to take the human beings out of their reports. The result was impersonal writing, that is, writing in the third person—without *I*'s, *we*'s, or *you*'s.

**Recently, some writers have argued that personal writing is more interesting than impersonal writing and just as objective.**

In recent years, some writers have questioned impersonal report writing. They argue that personal writing is more forceful and direct than impersonal writing. They point out that writing is more conversational and, therefore, more interesting if it brings both the reader and the writer into the picture. They contend that objectivity is an attitude—not a matter of person—and that a report written in personal style can be just as objective as a report written in impersonal style. Frequently, these writers argue that impersonal writing leads to an overuse of the passive voice and a dull writing style. This last argument, however, lacks substance. The style of impersonal writing can and should be interesting. Any dullness that impersonal writing may

**PART 5** Fundamentals of Report Writing

### *An Example of Objective Reporting?*

The story is told of the sea captain who once found his first mate drunk on duty. A man of the old school, the captain dutifully recorded the incident in his daily report to the ship's owners. He wrote: "Today First Mate Carlos E. Sperry was drunk on duty."

The first mate, unhappy about the incident, was determined to get revenge at the first opportunity. Some days later, his chance came. The captain was so ill that he could not leave his quarters, and First Mate Sperry was now in charge. At the end of the day it was Sperry's duty to write the daily report. This is what he wrote: "Today Captain Eli A. Dunn was sober."

The words were literally true, of course. But what a second meaning they carried!

---

have is the fault of the writer. As proof, one has only to look at the lively style of writers for newspapers, newsmagazines, and journals. Most of this writing is impersonal—but it is usually not dull.

As in most controversies, the arguments of both sides have merit. In some situations, personal writing is better. In other situations, impersonal writing is better. And in still other situations, either type of writing is good.

*There is merit to both sides. You would be wise to do what is expected of you. Good advice is to use personal style for routine reports and impersonal style for more formal reports.*

Your decision should be based on the facts of each report situation. First, you should consider the expectations of those for whom you are preparing the report. More than likely, you will find a preference for impersonal writing, for businesspeople have been slow to break tradition. Then you should consider the formality of the situation. You should use personal writing for informal situations, impersonal writing for formal situations.

Perhaps the distinction between impersonal and personal writing is best made by illustration.

**PERSONAL**

Having studied the advantages and disadvantages of using coupons, I conclude that your company should not adopt this practice. If you use the coupons, you would have to pay out money for them. You would also have to hire additional employees to take care of the increase in sales volume.

**IMPERSONAL**

A study of the advantages and disadvantages of using coupons supports the conclusion that the Mills Company should not adopt this practice. The coupons themselves would cost extra money. Also, use of coupons would require additional personnel to take care of the increase in sales volume.

### *Consistency in Time Viewpoint*

Presenting information in the right place in time is a major problem in keeping order in a report. Not doing so confuses the reader and creates barriers to communication. Thus, it is important that you maintain a proper time viewpoint.

*Keep a consistent time viewpoint throughout the report.*

You have two choices of time viewpoint—past and present. Although some authorities favor one or the other, either viewpoint can produce a good

*There are two time viewpoints—past and present. Select one, and do not change.*

report. The important thing is to be consistent—to select one time viewpoint and stay with it. In other words, you should view all similar information in the report from the same position in time.

*The past time viewpoint views the research and the findings as past, and prevailing concepts and proven conclusions as present.*

If you adopt the past time viewpoint, you treat the research, the findings, and the writing of the report as past. Thus, you would report the results of a recent survey in past tense: "Twenty-two percent of the managers *favored* a change." You would write a reference to another part of the report this way: "In Part III, this conclusion *was reached*." Your use of the past time viewpoint would have no effect on references to future happenings. It would be proper to write a sentence like this: "If the current trend continues, 30 percent *will favor* a change by 1999." Prevailing concepts and proven conclusions are also exceptions. You would present them in present tense. For examples, take the sentences: "Solar energy *is* a major potential source of energy" and "The findings show conclusively that managers are not adequately trained."

*The present time viewpoint presents as current all information that can be assumed to be current at the time of writing.*

Writing in the present time viewpoint presents as current all information that can logically be assumed to be current at the time of writing. All other information is presented in its proper place in the past or future. Thus, you would report the results of a recent survey in these words: "Twenty-two percent of the managers *favor* a change." You would refer to another part of the text like this: "In Part III, this conclusion *is* reached." In referring to an old survey, you would write: "In 1990 only 12 percent *held* this opinion." And in making a future reference, you would write: "If this trend continues, 30 percent *will hold* this opinion by 2000."

## Need for Transition

*You should use transitions to connect the parts of the report.*

A well-written report reads as one continuous story. The parts connect smoothly. Much of this smoothness is the result of good, logical organization. But more than logical order is needed in long reports. As you will see in Chapter 14, a coherence plan may be needed in such reports. In all reports, however, lesser transitional techniques are useful to connect information.

*Transition means a "bridging across."*

By *transition* we mean a "bridging across." Transitions are made by means of words or sentences that show the relationships of succeeding parts. They may appear at the beginning of a part as a way of relating this part to the preceding part. They may appear at the end of a part as a forward look. Or they may appear within a part as words or phrases that help move the flow of information.

*Transitions should be used where there is a need to connect the parts of the report.*

Whether you use transitional words or a transitional sentence in a particular place depends on need. If there is need to relate parts, you should use a transition. Because good, logical organization frequently makes clear the relationships of the parts in a short report, such reports may need only a few transitional words or sentences. Longer and more involved reports, on the other hand, usually require more.

*They should be made naturally, not mechanically.*

Before we comment more specifically on transitions, we should make one point clear. You should not use transitions mechanically. You should use them only when they are needed—when leaving them out would produce abruptness. Transitions should not appear to be stuck in. They should blend naturally with the surrounding writing. For example, avoid transitions of this mechanical form: "The last section discussed Topic X. In the next section, Y will be analyzed."

**Sentence Transitions.** Throughout the report you can improve the connecting network of thought by the wise use of sentence transitions. You can use them especially to connect parts of the report. The following example shows how a sentence can explain the relationship between Sections A and B of a report. Note that the first words draw a conclusion for Section B. Then, with smooth tie-in, the next words introduce Section C and relate this part to the report plan. The words in brackets explain the pattern of the thought connections.

*For connecting large parts, transition sentences may be used.*

[Section B, concluded] . . . Thus, the data show only negligible differences in the cost for oil consumption [subject of Section B] for the three brands of cars. [Section C] Even though the costs of gasoline [subject of Section A] and oil [subject of Section B] are the more consistent factors of operation expense, the picture is not complete until the costs of repairs and maintenance [subject of Section C] are considered.

In the following examples, succeeding parts are connected by sentences that make a forward-looking reference and thus set up the next subject. As a result, the shift of subject matter is smooth and logical.

These data show clearly that Edmond's machines are the most economical. Unquestionably, their operation by low-cost gas and their record for low-cost maintenance give them a decided edge over competing brands. *Before a definite conclusion about their merit is reached, however, one more vital comparison should be made.*

(The final sentence clearly introduces the subsequent discussion of an additional comparison.)

*. . . At first glance the data appear convincing, but a closer observation reveals a number of discrepancies.*

(Discussion of the discrepancies is logically set up by this sentence.)

Placing topic sentences at key points of emphasis is another way of using sentences to link up the various parts of the report. Usually the topic sentence is best placed at the paragraph beginning. Note, in the following example, how topic sentences maintain the flow of thought by emphasizing key information.

*Use of topic sentences also helps improve thought flow.*

*Brand C accelerates faster than the other two brands, both on a level road and on a 9 percent grade.* According to a test conducted by Consumption Research, Brand C reaches a speed of 60 miles per hour in 13.2 seconds. To reach the same speed, Brand A requires 13.6 seconds, and Brand B requires 14.4 seconds. On a 9 percent grade, Brand C reaches the 60-miles-per-hour speed in 29.4 seconds, and Brand A reaches it in 43.3 seconds. Brand B is unable to reach this speed. *Because it carries more weight on its rear wheels than the others, Brand C has the best traction of the three.* Traction, which means a minimum of sliding on wet or icy roads, is important to safe driving, particularly during the cold, wet winter months. As traction is directly related to the weight carried by the rear wheels, a comparison of these weights should give some measure of the safety of the three cars. According to data released by the Automobile Bureau of Standards, Brand C carries 47 percent of its weight on its rear wheels. Brands B and A carry 44 and 42 percent, respectively.

**Transitional Words.** Although the major transition problems concern connection between the major parts of the report, transitions are needed between the lesser parts. If the writing is to flow smoothly, you will need to connect clause to clause, sentence to sentence, and paragraph to paragraph. Transitional words and phrases generally serve to make such connections.

*Transitional words show relationships between lesser parts.*

**Choice Lines Gleaned from Accident Reports Submitted to Insurance Companies**

Coming home, I drove into the wrong house and collided with a tree I don't have.

The other car collided with mine without giving warning of its intentions.

I thought my window was down, but found it was up when I put my hand through it.

I collided with a stationary truck coming the other way.

A pedestrian hit me and went under my car.

The guy was all over the road. I had to swerve a number of times before I hit him.

I pulled away from the side of the road, glanced at my mother-in-law, and headed over the embankment.

I was having rear-end trouble when my universal joint gave way, causing me to have this accident.

My car was legally parked as it backed into the other car.

I told police that I was not injured, but on removing my hat, I found that I had a fractured skull.

I was sure the old fellow would never make it to the other side of the road when I struck him.

The pedestrian had no idea which direction to run, so I ran over him.

The indirect cause of this accident was a little guy in a small car with a big mouth.

The telephone pole was approaching. I was attempting to swerve out of the way when it struck my front end.

I saw the slow-moving, sad-faced old gentleman as he bounced off the hood of my car.

---

Numerous transitional words are available. The following list shows such words and how you can use them. With a little imagination to supply the context, you can easily see how these words relate ideas. For better understanding, the words are grouped by the relationships they show between what comes before and what follows.

*This partial list shows how words explain relationships.*

| RELATIONSHIP | WORD EXAMPLES |
|---|---|
| Listing or enumeration of subjects | In addition<br>First, second, and so on<br>Besides<br>Moreover |
| Contrast | On the contrary<br>In spite of<br>On the other hand<br>In contrast<br>However |
| Likeness | In a like manner<br>Likewise<br>Similarly |

| RELATIONSHIP | WORD EXAMPLES |
|---|---|
| Cause-result | Thus |
| | Because of |
| | Therefore |
| | Consequently |
| | For this reason |
| Explanation or elaboration | For example |
| | To illustrate |
| | For instance |
| | Also |
| | Too |

## Maintaining Interest

Like any other form of writing, report writing should be interesting. Actually, interest is as important as the facts of the report, for communication is not likely to occur without interest. Readers cannot help missing parts of the message if their interest is not held—if their minds are allowed to stray. Interest in the subject is not enough to ensure communication. The writing must be interesting. This should be evident to you if you have ever tried to read dull writing in studying for an examination. How desperately you wanted to learn the subject, but how often your mind strayed away!

*Report writing should be interesting. Interesting writing is necessary for good communication.*

Perhaps writing interestingly is an art. But if so, it is an art in which you can develop ability by working at it. To develop this ability, you need to avoid the rubber-stamp jargon so often used in business and instead work to make your words build concrete pictures. You need to cultivate a feeling for the rhythmic flow of words and sentences. You need to remember that back of every fact and figure there is life—people doing things, machines operating, a commodity being marketed. A technique of good report writing is to bring that life to the surface by using concrete words and active-voice verbs as much as possible. You should also work to achieve interest without using more words than are necessary.

*Interesting writing is the result of careful word choice, rhythm, concreteness—in fact, all the good writing techniques.*

Here a word of caution should be injected. You can overdo efforts to make report writing interesting. Such is the case whenever your reader's attention is attracted to how something has been said rather than to what has been said. Effective report writing simply presents information in a clear, concise, and interesting manner. Perhaps the purpose and definition of report-writing style are best summarized in this way: Report-writing style is at its best when the readers are prompted to say "Here are some interesting facts" rather than "Here is some beautiful writing."

*But efforts to make writing interesting can be overdone. The writing style should never draw attention away from the information.*

■ ■ ■ ■ ■ ■ ■ ■ ■ ■ ■ ■ ■ ■ ■ ■ ■ ■ ■ ■ ■
## SUMMARY (by Chapter Objectives)

1. Your work on a report begins with a problem (purpose, goal, objective).
   - Get the problem in mind by gathering all the information you need about it.
   - Then develop a problem statement from the information.
   - Phrase this statement as an infinitive, a question, or a declarative statement.

*1. State a problem clearly in writing.*

CHAPTER 12   Basics of Report Writing   401

| | |
|---|---|
| 2. List the factors involved in a problem. | 2. From the problem statement, determine the factors involved.<br>• These may be subtopics in information reports.<br>• They may be hypotheses (possible explanations) in problems requiring a solution.<br>• They may be bases of comparison in problems requiring evaluations. |
| 3. Explain the common errors in interpreting and the attitudes and practices conducive to good interpreting. | 3. After you have gathered the information needed, interpret it as it applies to the problem.<br>• Interpreting is mental and thus difficult to describe.<br>• Heed this advice for avoiding human error:<br>—Report the facts as they are.<br>—Do not think that conclusions are always necessary.<br>—Do not interpret a lack of evidence as proof to the contrary.<br>—Do not compare noncomparable data.<br>—Do not draw illogical cause-effect conclusions.<br>—Beware of unreliable and unrepresentative data.<br>—Do not oversimplify.<br>• Adopt these attitudes and practices:<br>—Maintain a judicial attitude.<br>—Consult with others.<br>—Test your interpretations by applying the test of experience (reason) or the negative test (question them). |
| 4. Organize information in outline form, using time, place, quantity, factor, or a combination of these as bases for division. | 4. Next, organize the information (construct an outline).<br>• Probably you will use the conventional outline symbols (I, A, 1, a) or numeric symbols (1.0, 1.1, 1.11, 1.111) in structuring the outline.<br>• Probably you will begin with an introduction and end with a summary, conclusion, or recommendation.<br>• Organize the report body (the part between the introduction and the ending section) by a process of division.<br>—Look over the findings for ways of dividing on the basis of time, place, quantity, or factor.<br>—Then divide, forming the major parts of the report (Roman numeral headings).<br>—Next, look at these divisions for ways of dividing them (making the capital letter headings).<br>—Continue to subdivide as far as necessary.<br>—The end result is your outline. |
| 5. Construct topic or talking headings that outline reports logically and meaningfully. | 5. Construct headings for each part in the outline.<br>• Use the topic form (identifies topic).<br>• Or use the talking form (identifies topic and says something about it).<br>• Make the wording of comparable parts parallel grammatically.<br>• Avoid excessive repetition of words. |
| 6. Write reports that are clear, objective, consistent in time viewpoint, smoothly connected, and interesting. | 6. From the outline, write the report.<br>• Follow the rules of clarity discussed previously in the book.<br>• Maintain objectivity (no bias).<br>—Impersonal writing style (third person) has long been associated with objectivity.<br>—But some authorities question this style, saying personal style is more interesting. |

- —The argument continues, although most formal reports are written in impersonal style.
- Be consistent in time viewpoint—either past or present.
  - —Past time viewpoint views the research and findings as past and prevailing concepts and conclusions as present.
  - —Present time viewpoint presents as current all that is current at the time of writing.
- Use transitions to make the report parts flow smoothly.
  - —Between large parts, you may need to use full sentences to make connections.
  - —Topic sentences also can help the flow of thought.
  - —Use transitional words and phrases to connect the lesser parts.
- Work to make the writing interesting.
  - —Select words carefully for best effect.
  - —Follow techniques of good writing (correctness, rhythmic flow of words, vigorous words, and such).
  - —Do not overdo these efforts by drawing attention to how you write rather than what you say.

## QUESTIONS FOR DISCUSSION

1. Explain the concept of outlining as a division process.
2. You are writing a report on the progress of your regional Bell Company's efforts to increase sales of five of its products through extensive advertising in newspapers, on television or radio, and in magazines. Discuss the possibilities for major headings. Evaluate each possibility.
3. Not all reports written in business are written objectively. In fact, many are deliberately biased. Why, then, should we stress objectivity in a college course that includes report writing?
4. Explain how the question of personal and impersonal writing is related to objectivity.
5. Explain the differences between the present time viewpoint and the past time viewpoint.
6. Is it incorrect to have present, past, and future tense in the same report? In the same paragraph? In the same sentence? Discuss.
7. "Transitional sentences are unnecessary. They merely add length to a report and thus are contrary to the established rules of conciseness." Discuss.
8. "Reports are written for business executives who want them. Thus, you don't have to be concerned about holding your reader's interest." Discuss.

## APPLICATION EXERCISES

1. For each of the following problem situations, write a clear statement of the problem and list the factors involved. When necessary, you may use your imagination logically to supply any additional information needed.

   a. A manufacturer of breakfast cereals wants to determine the characteristics of its consumers.
   b. The manufacturer of a toothpaste wants to learn what the buying public thinks of its product in relation to competing products.
   c. Southwestern Oil Company wants to give its stockholders a summary of its operations for the past calendar year.
   d. A building contractor engaged to build a new factory for Company X submits a report summarizing its monthly progress.
   e. The Able Wholesale Company must prepare a report on its credit relations with the Crystal City Hardware Company.
   f. The supervisor of Department X must prepare a report evaluating the performance of his secretary.
   g. Baker, Inc. wants a study made to determine why its employee turnover is high.
   h. An executive must rank three of her subordinates on the basis of their suitability for promotion to a particular job.
   i. The supervisor of production must compare three competing machines that are being considered for use in a particular production job.
   j. An investment consultant must advise a client on whether to invest in the development of a lake resort.
   k. A consultant seeks to learn how a restaurant can improve its profits.

2. Select a hypothetical problem with a time division possibility. What other division possibilities does it have? Compare the two possibilities as the main bases for organizing the report.
3. Assume that you are writing the results of a survey conducted to determine what styles of shoes are worn throughout the country on various occasions by women of all ages. What division possibilities exist here? Which would you recommend?
4. For the problem described in the preceding exercise, use your imagination to construct topic headings for the outline.
5. Point out any violations of grammatical parallelism in these headings:

   a. Region I sales lagging.
   b. Moderate increase seen for Region II.
   c. Region III sales remain strong.

6. Point out any error in grammatical parallelism in these headings:

   a. High cost of operation.
   b. Slight improvement in production efficiency.
   c. Maintenance cost is low.

7. Which of the following headings is logically inconsistent with the others?

   a. Agricultural production continues to increase.

b. Slight increase is made by manufacturing.
   c. Salaries remain high.
   d. Service industries show no change.
8. Select an editorial, feature article, book chapter, or the like that has no headings. Write talking headings for it.
9. Assume that you are writing a report that summarizes a survey you have conducted. Write a paragraph of the report using the present time viewpoint; then write the paragraph using the past time viewpoint. The paragraph will be based on the following information:

Answers to the question about how students view the proposed Aid to Education Bill in this survey and in a survey taken a year earlier (in parentheses).
   For, 39 percent (21); Against, 17 percent (43).
   No answer, undecided, etc., 44 percent (36).

**CHAPTER 13**

# REPORT STRUCTURE: THE SHORTER FORMS

### CHAPTER OBJECTIVES

*Upon completing this chapter, you will be able to write well-structured short reports. To reach this goal, you should be able to*

**1**

Explain the structure of reports relative to length and formality.

**2**

Discuss the three major differences involved in writing short and long reports.

**3**

Write clear and well-organized short reports.

**4**

Write clear and well-organized letter and memorandum reports.

**5**

Adapt the procedures for writing short reports to such special reports as staff, audit, progress, and technical reports.

**6**

Write complete, well-organized, and effective proposals.

## INTRODUCTORY SITUATION

### to the Structure of Short Reports

Assume again the position of assistant to the president of Technicraft and the report-writing work necessary in this position. Most of the time, your assignments concern routine, everyday problems—personnel policies, administrative procedures, work flow, and the like. Following what appears to be established company practice, you write the reports on these problems in simple memorandum form.

Occasionally, however, you have a more involved assignment. Last week, for example, you investigated a union charge that favoritism was shown to the nonunion workers on certain production jobs. As your report on this very formal investigation was written for the benefit of ranking company administrators as well as union leaders, you dressed it up.

Then there was the report you had helped prepare for the board of directors last fall. That report summarized pressing needs for capital improvements. A number of plant administrators contributed to this project, but you were the coordinator. Because the report was important and was written for the board, you made it as formal as possible.

Clearly, reports vary widely in structure. How report structures vary is the first topic of this chapter. Because the shorter reports are more important to you, they are discussed next. ■

Before you can put your report in finished form, you will need to decide on its structure. Will it be a simple memorandum? Will it be a long, complex, and formal report? Or will it fall between these extremes?

## AN OVERVIEW OF REPORT STRUCTURE

Your decision as to report structure will be based on the needs of your situation. Those needs are related to report length and the formality of the situation. The longer the problem and the more formal the situation, the more involved the report structure is likely to be. The shorter the problem and the more informal the situation, the less involved the report structure is likely to be.

*Length and formality determine report structure.*

So that you may understand the various report structures available to you, we will review the possibilities. The following classification plan provides a very general picture of how reports are structured. This plan does not account for all the possible variations, but it does serve to acquaint you with the general structure of reports. It should help you construct reports that fit your specific need.

*The following classification plan provides a general picture of report structure.*

The classification plan arranges all business reports as a stairway, as illustrated by the diagram in Figure 13–1. At the top of the stairway are the most formal, full-dress reports. Such reports have a number of pages that come before the text material, just as this book has pages that come before the first chapter. These pages serve useful purposes, but they also dress up the report. Typically, these *prefatory pages*, as they are called, are included

*It pictures report structure as a stairway (Figure 13–1). Long, formal reports are at the top. Prefatory pages dress up these reports.*

CHAPTER 13  Report Structure: The Shorter Forms

**FIGURE 13–1** Progression of Change in Report Makeup as Formality Requirements and Length of the Problem Decrease

| | | | | | |
|---|---|---|---|---|---|
| Title fly | Title page | Letter of transmittal | Table of contents | Executive summary | THE REPORT PROPER |
| 1st step | Title page | Letter of transmittal | Table of contents | Executive summary | THE REPORT PROPER |
| | 2nd step | Title page | Table of contents | Combination transmittal executive summary | THE REPORT PROPER |
| | | 3rd step | Title page | Combination transmittal executive summary | THE REPORT PROPER |
| | | | 4th step | Title page | THE REPORT PROPER |
| | | | | 5th step | LETTER REPORT |
| | | | | | 6th step |
| | | | | | MEMO REPORT |
| | | | | | 7th step |

when the problem situation is formal and the report is long. The exact makeup of the prefatory pages may vary, but the most common arrangement includes these parts: the title fly, title page, letter of transmittal, table of contents, and executive summary. Flyleaves (blank pages at the beginning and end that protect the report) may also be included.

These parts are explained in the following chapter, but a brief description of them at this point should help you understand their roles. The first two pages (the title fly and title page) contain identification information. The *title fly* carries only the report title. The *title page* typically contains the title, identification of the writer and reader, and sometimes the date. As the words imply, the *letter of transmittal* is a letter that transmits the report. It is a personal message from the writer to the reader. The *table of contents*, of course, is a listing of the report contents. It is the report outline in finished form, with page numbers to indicate where the parts begin. It may also include a list of illustrations (tables, figures, diagrams), which may be a separate part. The *executive summary* summarizes whatever is important in the report—the major facts and analyses, conclusions, and recommendations.

> Prefatory pages consist of the title fly, title page, letter of transmittal, table of contents, and executive summary.

PART 5  Fundamentals of Report Writing

As the need for formality decreases and the problem becomes smaller, the makeup of the report changes. The changes primarily occur in the prefatory pages. As we have noted, these pages give the report a formal appearance. So it is not surprising that they change as the report situation becomes less formal.

*As reports become shorter and less formal, changes occur in this general order.*

Although the changes that take place are far from standardized, they follow a general order. First, the somewhat useless title fly drops out. This page contains only the report title, which also appears on the next page. Obviously, the title fly is used primarily for reasons of formality.

*The title fly drops out.*

Next in the progression, the executive summary and the letter of transmittal are combined. When this stage is reached, the report problem is short enough to be summarized in a short space. As shown in Figure 13-1, the report at this stage has three prefatory parts: title page, table of contents, and combination transmittal letter and executive summary.

*The executive summary and the letter of transmittal are combined.*

A third step down, the table of contents drops out. The table of contents is a guide to the report text, and a guide has little value in a short report. Certainly, a guide to a 100-page report is necessary. But a guide to a one-page report is not. Somewhere between these extremes a dividing point exists. You should follow the general guide of including a table of contents whenever it appears to be of some value to the reader.

*Next, the table of contents is omitted.*

Another step down, as formality and length requirements continue to decrease, the combined letter of transmittal and executive summary drops out. Thus, the report commonly called the *short report* now has only a title page and the report text. The title page remains to the last because it serves as a very useful cover page. In addition, it contains the most important identifying information. The short report is a popular form in business.

*The combined letter of transmittal and executive summary drops out, and what is left forms the popular short report.*

Below the short-report form is a form that reinstates the letter of transmittal and summary and presents the entire report as a letter—thus, the *letter report*. And finally, for short problems of more informality, the *memorandum* (informal letter) form is used.

*The next step is the letter report, and the step after that is the memorandum report.*

As mentioned earlier, this is a general analysis of report change; it probably oversimplifies the structure of reports. Few actual reports coincide with the steps in the diagram. Most reports, however, fit generally within the framework of the diagram. Knowledge of the general relationship of formality and length to report makeup should help you understand and plan reports.

*This progression of structure is general.*

## ■■■■■■■■■■■■■■■■■■■■■■■■■■■
## CHARACTERISTICS OF THE SHORTER REPORTS

The shorter report forms (those at the bottom of the stairway) are by far the most common in business. These are the everyday working reports—those used for the routine information reporting that is vital to an organization's communication. Because these reports are so common, our study of report types begins with them.

*The shorter report forms are the most common in business.*

The techniques for organizing discussed in the preceding chapter cover all forms of reports. But there the emphasis was on organizing the information gathered—on the body of the report. As we noted, introductory and concluding parts would be attached when needed. Thus, the following discussion relates to how these parts are used in the shorter reports.

*Their need for introductions and conclusions varies.*

## Little Need for Introductory Information

> Shorter reports have little need for introductory material.

Most of the shorter, more informal reports require little (sometimes no) introductory material. These reports typically concern day-to-day problems. Their lives are short; that is, they are not likely to be kept on file for future readers. They are intended for only a few readers, and these readers know the problem. They are likely to need little introduction to it.

> Some shorter reports need introductory material. Include as much introductory material as is needed to prepare the reader for the report.

This is not to say that all shorter reports have no need for introductory material. In fact, some do need it. In general, however, the need is likely to be small.

Determining what introductory material is needed is simply a matter of answering one question: What does my reader need to know before receiving this report? In very short reports, sufficient introductory material is provided by an incidental reference to the problem, authorization of the investigation, or the like. In extreme cases, however, you may need a detailed introduction comparable to that of the more formal reports.

Reports need no introductory material if their very nature explains their purpose. This holds true for personnel actions. It also holds true for weekly sales reports, inventory reports, and some progress reports.

## Predominance of the Direct Order

> The shorter reports usually begin directly—with conclusions and recommendations.

Because the shorter reports usually solve routine problems, they are likely to be written in the direct order. By *direct order* we mean that the report begins with its most important information—usually the conclusion and perhaps a recommendation. Business writers use this order because they know that their readers' main concern is to get the information needed to make a decision. So they present this information right away.

> Sometimes, but not often, longer reports are written in the direct order.

As you will see in the following chapter, the longer report forms may also use the direct order. In fact, many longer reports do. The point is, however, that most do not. Most follow the traditional logical (introduction, body, conclusion) order. As one moves down the structural ladder toward the more informal and shorter reports, however, the need for the direct order increases. At the bottom of the ladder, the direct order is more the rule than the exception.

> Use the direct order when the conclusion or recommendation will serve as a basis for action.

Deciding whether to use the direct order is best based on a consideration of your readers' likely use of the report. If your readers need the report conclusion or recommendation as a basis for an action that they must take, directness will speed their effort by enabling them to quickly receive the most important information. If they have confidence in your work, they may choose not to read beyond this point and to quickly take the action that the report supports. Should they desire to question any part of the report, however, the material is there for their inspection.

> Use the indirect order when you need to take the readers through the analysis.

On the other hand, if there is reason to believe that your readers will want to arrive at the conclusion or recommendation only after a logical review of the analysis, you should organize your report in the indirect (logical) order. This arrangement is especially preferable when your readers do not have reason to place their full confidence in your work. If you are a novice working on a new assignment, for example, you would be wise to lead them to your recommendation or conclusion by using the indirect order.

Because order is so vital a part of constructing the shorter reports, let us be certain that the difference between the direct arrangement and the indirect arrangement is clear. To make it clear, we will go through each, step by step.

The direct arrangement presents right off the most important part of the report. This is the answer—the achievement of the report's goal. Depending on the problem, the direct beginning could consist of a summary of facts, a conclusion, a recommendation, or some combination of summary, conclusion, and recommendation.

*The direct order gives the main message first.*

Whatever introductory material is needed usually follows the direct opening. As noted previously, sometimes little or none is needed in the everyday, routine reports. Next come the report findings, organized in good order (as described in the last chapter). From these facts and analyses comes the conclusion, and perhaps a recommendation.

*Then it covers introductory material (if any), findings and analyses, conclusions, and recommendations.*

Illustrating this arrangement is the following report of a short and simple personnel problem. For reasons of space economy, only the key parts of the report are shown.

Clifford A. Knudson, draftsman, tool design department, should be fired. This conclusion has been reached after a thorough investigation brought about by numerous incidents during the past two months. . . .

The recommended action is supported by this information from his work record for the past two months:

- He has been late to work seven times.
- He has been absent without acceptable excuse for seven days.
- Twice he reported to work in a drunken and disorderly condition.
- And so on.

The indirect arrangement begins with whatever introductory material is needed to prepare the reader for the report. Then comes the presentation of facts, wth analyses when needed. Next comes the part that accomplishes the goal of the report. If the goal is to present information, this part summarizes the information. If the goal is to reach a conclusion, this part reviews the

*The indirect order has this sequence: introduction, facts and analyses, conclusions, and recommendations.*

"Slaying the dragons is the easy part—the part I hate is writing the environmental-impact report!"

From The Wall Street Journal, with permission of Cartoon Features Syndicate.

### A Point Well Made in a Memorandum Report

Mrs. Priddy telephoned the local utility company to complain that a line repairer has used "some mighty vulgar language" while working in front of her house. She wanted something done about it.

So the obliging supervisor called in the two men who had been on the job. "This is a serious charge," the supervisor explained. "So that I can get the facts straight, I want each of you to write a memo explaining what happened." One of the men submitted the following classic explanation:

> Butch and I were splicing the cable in front of Mrs. Priddy's house. I was up on the pole, and Butch was down on the ground. Butch sent a pot of hot metal up to me. Just as it reached me, my foot slipped. The metal slipped down on Butch. It ran down his neck, through his overalls, and into his shoes. Butch leaped sideways, spun a couple of times, rolled on the ground, looked up at me, and said, "Cecil, you must be more careful hereafter."

---

analyses and draws a conclusion from them. And if the goal is to recommend an action, this part reviews the analyses, draws a conclusion, and, on the basis of the conclusion, makes a recommendation.

Using the simple personnel problem from the last example, the indirect arrangement would appear like this:

Numerous incidents during the past two months appear to justify an investigation of the work record of Clifford A. Knudson, draftsman, tool design department.

The investigation of his work record for the past two months reveals these points:

- He has been late to work seven times.
- He has been absent without acceptable excuse for seven days.
- Twice he reported to work in a drunken and disorderly condition.
- An so on to the conclusion that Knudson should be fired.

### More Personal Writing Style

*Personal writing is common in the shorter reports.*

*The reasons are that the shorter reports usually (1) involve personal relationships, (2) concern a personal investigation, and (3) are routine.*

Although the writing for all reports has much in common, that in the shorter reports tends to be more personal. That is, the shorter reports are likely to use the personal pronouns *I, we,* and *you* rather than only the third person.

The reasons for this tendency toward personal writing in the shorter reports should be obvious. In the first place, short-report situations usually involve personal relationships. Such reports tend to be from and to people who know each other and who normally address each other informally when they meet. In addition, the shorter reports are apt to involve personal investigations and to represent the observations, evaluations, and analyses of their writers. Finally, the shorter reports tend to deal with day-to-day, routine problems. These problems are by their very nature informal. It is logical to report them informally, and personal writing tends to produce this informal effect.

In oral reporting, questioning can help make the message clear. Written reports must communicate alone. Thus, one should anticipate probable questions and make certain the text explains adequately.

As explained in Chapter 12, your decision about whether to write a report in personal or impersonal style should be based on the situation. You should consider the expectations of those who will receive the report. If they expect formality, you should write impersonally. If they expect informality, you should write personally. If you do not know their preferences, you should consider the formality of the situation. Convention favors impersonal writing for the most formal situations.

From this analysis, it should be clear that either personal or impersonal writing can be appropriate for reports ranging from the shortest to the longest types. The point is, however, the short-report situations are most likely to justify personal writing.

• Write impersonally (1) when your reader prefers it and (2) when the situation is formal.

## FORMS OF SHORTER REPORTS

As was noted earlier, the shorter report forms are by far the most numerous and important in business. In fact, the three forms represented by the bottom three steps of the stairway (Figure 13–1) make up the bulk of the reports written. Thus, a review of each of these three types is in order.

• Following is a review of the more popular shorter reports.

### The Short Report

One of the more popular of the less formal report forms is the short report. Representing the fifth step in the diagram of report progression, this report consists of only a title page and text. Its popularity may be explained by the middle-ground impression of formality that it conveys. Including the most important prefatory part gives the report at least some appearance of for-

• The short report consists of a title page and the report text.

mality. And it does this without the tedious work of preparing the other prefatory pages. The short report is ideally suited for the short but somewhat formal problem.

Like most of the less formal report forms, the short report may be organized in either the direct or indirect order. But the direct order is far more common. As illustrated by Figure 13–2, this plan begins with a quick summary of the report, including and emphasizing conclusions and recommendations. Such a beginning serves much the same function as the executive summary (described in Chapter 14) of a long, formal report.

Following the summary come whatever introductory remarks are needed. (See Chapter 14 for a more detailed discussion of the introduction.) Sometimes this part is not needed. Usually, however, a single paragraph covers the facts of authorization and a brief statement of the problem and its scope. After the introductory words come the findings of the investigation. As in the longer report forms, the findings are presented, analyzed, and applied to the problem. From all this comes a conclusion and, if needed, a recommendation. These last two elements—conclusions and recommendations—may come at the end even though they also appear in the beginning summary. Omitting a summary or a conclusion would sometimes end the report abruptly. It would stop the flow of reasoning before reaching the logical goal.

The mechanics of constructing the short report are much the same as the mechanics of constructing the more formal, longer types. The short report uses the same form of title page and page layout. Like the longer reports, it uses headings. But because of the short report's brevity, the headings rarely go beyond the two-division level. In fact, one level of division is most common. Like any other report, the short report uses graphics, an appendix, and a bibliography when these are needed.

## Letter Reports

The second of the more common shorter report forms is the letter report, that is, a report in letter form. Letter reports are used primarily to present information to persons outside the organization, especially when the information is to be sent by mail or fax. For example, a company's written evaluation of a credit customer may be presented in letter form and sent to the person who requests it. An outside consultant may write a report of analyses and recommendations in letter form. Or the officer of an organization may report certain information to the membership in a letter.

Typically, the length of letter reports is three or four pages or less. But no hard-and-fast rule exists on this point. Long letter reports (10 pages and more) are not unusual.

As a general rule, letter reports are written personally, using *I, you,* and *we* references. (Exceptions exist, of course, such as letter reports for very important readers—for example, a company's board of directors.) Otherwise, the writing style recommended for letter reports is much the same as that recommended for any other reports. Certainly, clear and meaningful expression is a requirement for all reports (see Figure 13–3).

Letter reports may be in either the direct order or the indirect order. If such a report is to be mailed, there is some justification for using the indirect order. As such reports arrive unannounced, it is logical to begin with a

---

*Sidenotes:*

It is usually in the direct order, beginning with the conclusion.

The introduction comes next, then the findings and analyses, and finally the conclusions.

See Figure 13–2 for this report form.

Letter reports are reports in letter form.

They usually cover short problems.

They are usually written in personal style.

Most of them begin indirectly.

**FIGURE 13-2** Illustration of a Short Report

Designed for the busy reader who wants the main message quickly, this report begins with recommendations and summary. Then it presents the report in logical order, following a brief introduction with a comparison of three methods of depreciation for delivery trucks (the subject of the investigation). The somewhat formal style is appropriate for reports of this nature.

<u>RECOMMENDATIONS FOR DEPRECIATING DELIVERY TRUCKS</u>

<u>BASED ON AN ANALYSIS OF THREE PLANS</u>

<u>PROPOSED FOR THE BAGGET LAUNDRY COMPANY</u>

Submitted to

Mr. Ralph P. Bagget, President
Bagget Laundry Company
312 Dauphine Street
New Orleans, Louisiana 70102

Prepared by

Charles W. Brewington, C.P.A.
Brewington and Karnes, Certified Public Accountants
743 Beaux Avenue, New Orleans, Louisiana 70118

April 16, 19—

CHAPTER 13 Report Structure: The Shorter Forms

**FIGURE 13–2** (continued)

RECOMMENDATION FOR DEPRECIATING DELIVERY TRUCKS

BASED ON AN ANALYSIS OF THREE PLANS

PROPOSED FOR THE BAGGET LAUNDRY COMPANY

### I. Recommendations and Summary of Analysis

The Reducing Charge method appears to be the best method to depreciate Bagget Laundry Company delivery trucks. The relative equality of cost allocation for depreciation and maintenance over the useful life of the trucks is the prime advantage under this method. Computation of depreciation charges is relatively simple by the Reducing Charge plan but not quite so simple as computation under the second best method considered.

The second best method considered is the Straight-Line depreciation plan. It is the simplest to compute of the plans considered, and it results in yearly charges equal to those under the Reducing Charge method. The unequal cost allocation resulting from increasing maintenance costs in successive years, however, is a disadvantage that far outweighs the method's ease of computation.

Third among the plans considered is the Service Hours method. This plan is not satisfactory for depreciating delivery trucks primarily because it combines a number of undesirable features. Prime among these is the complexity and cost of computing yearly charges under the plan. Also significant is the likelihood of poor cost allocation under this plan. An additional drawback is the possibility of variations in the estimates of the service life of company trucks.

### II. Background of the Problem

<u>Authorization of the Study</u>. This report on depreciation methods for delivery trucks of the Bagget Laundry Company is submitted on April 16, 19—, to Mr. Ralph P. Bagget, President of the Company. Mr. Bagget orally authorized Brewington and Karnes, Certified Public Accountants, to conduct the study on March 15, 19—.

<u>Statement of the Problem</u>. Having decided to establish branch agencies, the Bagget Laundry Company has purchased delivery trucks to transport laundry back and forth from the central cleaning plant in downtown New Orleans. The Company's problem is to select from three alternatives the most advantageous method to depreciate the trucks. The three methods concerned are Reducing Charge, Straight-Line, and Service-Hours. The trucks have an original cost of $7,500, a five-year life, and trade-in value of $1,500.

<u>Method of Solving the Problem</u>. In seeking an optimum solution to the Company's problem, we studied Company records and reviewed authoritative literature on the subject. We also applied our best judgment and our experience in analyzing the alternative methods. We based all conclusions on the generally accepted business principles in the field. Clearly, studies such as this involve subjective judgment, and this one is no exception.

**FIGURE 13-2** (continued)

2

Steps in Analyzing the Problem. In the following analysis, our evaluations of the three depreciation methods appear in the order in which we rank the methods. Since each method involves different factors, direct comparison by factors is meaningless. Thus our plan is that we evaluate each method in the light of our best judgment.

### III. Marked Advantages of the Reducing Charge Method

Sometimes called Sum-of-the-Digits, the Reducing Charge method consists of applying a series of decreasing fractions over the life of the property. To determine the fraction, first compute the sum of years of use for the property. This number becomes the denominator. Then determine the position number (first, second, etc.) of the year. This number is the numerator. Then apply the resulting fractions to the depreciable values for the life of the property. In the case of the trucks, the depreciable value is $6,000 ($7,500 - $1,500).

As shown in Table I, this method results in large depreciation costs for the early years and decreasing costs in later years. But since maintenance and repair costs for trucks are higher in the later years, this method provides a relatively stable charge over the life of the property. In actual practice, however, the sums will not be as stable as illustrated, for maintenance and repair costs will vary from those used in the computation.

Table I

DEPRECIATION AND MAINTENANCE COSTS FOR
DELIVERY TRUCKS OF BAGGET LAUNDRY FOR 19X0-19X4
USING REDUCING CHARGE DEPRECIATION

| End of Year | Depreciation | Maintenance | Sum |
|---|---|---|---|
| 1 | 5/15 ($6,000) = $2,000 | $ 100 | $ 2,100 |
| 2 | 4/15 ($6,000) =  1,600 | 500 | 2,100 |
| 3 | 3/15 ($6,000) =  1,200 | 900 | 2,100 |
| 4 | 2/15 ($6,000) =    800 | 1,300 | 2,100 |
| 5 | 1/15 ($6,000) =    400 | 1,700 | 2,100 |
|  | $6,000 | $4,500 | $10,500 |

In summary, the Reducing Charge method uses the most desirable combination of factors to depreciate trucks. It equalizes periodic charges, and it is easy to compute. It is our first choice for Bagget Laundry Company.

**FIGURE 13–2** (continued)

3

### IV. Runner-up Position of Straight-Line Method

The Straight-Line depreciation method is easiest of all to compute. It involves merely taking the depreciable value of the trucks ($6,000) and dividing it by the life of the trucks (5 years). The depreciation in this case is $1,200 for each year.

As shown in Table II, however, the increase in maintenance costs in later years results in much greater periodic charges in later years. The method is not usually recommended in cases such as this.

Table II

DEPRECIATION AND MAINTENANCE COSTS FOR
DELIVERY TRUCKS OF BAGGET LAUNDRY FOR 19X0-19X4
USING STRAIGHT-LINE DEPRECIATION

| End of Year | Depreciation | Maintenance | Sum |
|---|---|---|---|
| 1 | 1/5 ($6,000) = $1,200 | $ 100 | $1,300 |
| 2 | 1/5 ($6,000) = 1,200 | 500 | 1,700 |
| 3 | 1/5 ($6,000) = 1,200 | 800 | 2,100 |
| 4 | 1/5 ($6,000) = 1,200 | 1,300 | 2,500 |
| 5 | 1/5 ($6,000) = 1,200 | 1,700 | 2,900 |
| | Totals $6,000 | $4,500 | $10,500 |

In addition, the Straight-Line method generally is best when the properties involved are accumulated over a period of years. When this is done, the total of depreciation and maintenance costs will be about even. But Bagget Company has not purchased its trucks over a period of years. Nor is it likely to do so in the years ahead. Thus, Straight-Line depreciation will not result in equal periodic charges for maintenance and depreciation over the long run.

**FIGURE 13–2** (concluded)

4

### V. Poor Rank of Service-Hours Depreciation

The Service-Hours method of depreciation combines the major disadvantages of the other ways discussed. It is based on the principle that a truck is bought for the direct hours of service that it will give. The estimated number of hours that a delivery truck can be used efficiently according to automotive engineers is computed from a service total of one-hundred thousand miles. The depreciable cost ($6,000) for each truck is allocated pro rata according to the number of service hours used.

The difficulty and expense of maintaining additional records of service hours is a major disadvantage of this method. The depreciation cost for the delivery trucks under this method will fluctuate widely between first and last years. It is reasonable to assume that as the trucks get older more time will be spent on maintenance. Consequently, the larger depreciation costs will occur in the initial years. As can be seen by Table III, the periodic charges for depreciation and maintenance hover between the two periodically discussed methods.

The periodic charge for depreciation and maintenance increases in the later years of ownership. Another difficulty encountered is the possibility of a variance between estimated service hours and the actual service hours. The wide fluctuation possible makes it impractical to use this method for depreciating the delivery truck.

The difficulty of maintaining adequate records and increasing costs in the later years are the major disadvantages of this method. Since it combines the major disadvantages of both the Reducing Charge and Straight-Line methods, it is not satisfactory for depreciating the delivery trucks.

Table III

DEPRECIATION AND MAINTENANCE COSTS FOR
DELIVERY TRUCKS OF BAGGET LAUNDRY FOR 19X0-19X4
USING SERVICE-HOURS DEPRECIATION

| End of Year | Estimated Service-Miles | Depreciation | Maintenance | Sum |
|---|---|---|---|---|
| 1 | 30,000 | $1,800 | $ 100 | $1,900 |
| 2 | 25,000 | 1,500 | 500 | 2,000 |
| 3 | 20,000 | 1,200 | 900 | 2,100 |
| 4 | 15,000 | 900 | 1,300 | 2,200 |
| 5 | 10,000 | 600 | 1,700 | 2,300 |
|   | 100,000 | $6,000 | $4,500 | $10,500 |

**FIGURE 13–3** Illustration of a Letter Report

This direct-order letter report compares two hotels for a meeting site. Organized by the bases used in determining the choice, it evaluates the pertinent information and reaches a decision. The personal style is appropriate. Note the merge variables that form the inside address.

---

## INTERNATIONAL COMMUNICATIONS ASSOCIATION

3141 Girard Street • Washington, D.C.

January 28, 19—

{FIELD}Personal Title~{FIELD}First Name~ {FIELD}Second Name?~ {FIELD}Last Name~
Board of Directors
International Communications Association
{FIELD}School or Company?~
{FIELD}Address~
{FIELD}City~, {FIELD}State~ {FIELD}Zip~

Dear {FIELD}Personal Title~ (FIELD)Last Name~:

Subject:  Recommendation of Convention Hotel for the 19— Meeting

### RECOMMENDATION OF THE LAMONT

The Lamont Hotel is my recommendation for the International Communications Association meeting next January. My decision is based on the following summary of the evidence I collected. First, the Lamont has a definite downtown location advantage, and this is important to convention goers and their spouses. Second, accommodations, including meeting rooms, are adequate in both places, although the Blackwell's rooms are more modern. Third, Lamont room costs are approximately 15% lower than those at the Blackwell. The Lamont, however, would charge $400 for a room for the assembly meeting. Although both hotels are adequate, because of location and cost advantages the Lamont appears to be the better choice from the members' viewpoint.

### ORIGIN AND PLAN OF THE INVESTIGATION

In investigating these two hotels, as was my charge from you at our January 7th meeting, I collected information on what I believed to be the three major factors of consideration in the problem. First is location. Second is adequacy of accommodations. And third is cost. The following findings and evaluations form the basis of my recommendations.

### THE LAMONT'S FAVORABLE DOWNTOWN LOCATION

The older of the two hotels, the Lamont is located in the heart of the downtown business district. Thus it is convenient to the area's two major department stores as well as the other downtown shops. The Blackwell, on the other hand, is approximately nine blocks from the major shopping area. Located in the periphery of the business and residential area, it provides little location advantage for those wanting to shop. It does, however, have shops within its walls which provide virtually all of the guest's normal needs. Because many members will bring spouses, however, the downtown location does give the Lamont an advantage.

---

PART 5  Fundamentals of Report Writing

**FIGURE 13–3** (concluded)

Board of Directors -2- January 28, 19—

ADEQUATE ACCOMMODATIONS AT BOTH HOTELS

Both hotels can guarantee the 600 rooms we will require. As the Blackwell is newer (since 1982), its rooms are more modern and therefore more appealing. The 69-year-old Lamont, however, is well preserved and comfortable. Its rooms are all in good repair, and the equipment is modern.

The Blackwell has 11 small meeting rooms and the Lamont has 13. All are adequate for our purposes. Both hotels can provide the 10 we need. For our general assembly meeting, the Lamont would make available its Capri Ballroom, which can easily seat our membership. It would also serve as the site of our inaugural dinner. The assembly facilities at the Blackwell appear to be somewhat crowded, although the management assures me that it can hold 600. Pillars in the room, however, would make some seats undesirable. In spite of the limitations mentioned, both hotels appear to have adequate facilities for our meeting.

LOWER COSTS AT THE LAMONT

Both the Lamont and the Blackwell would provide nine rooms for meetings on a complimentary basis. Both would provide complimentary suites for our president and our secretary. The Lamont, however, would charge $400 for use of the room for the assembly meeting. The Blackwell would provide this room without charge.

Convention rates at the Lamont are $55-$65 for singles, $65-$75 for double-bedded rooms, and $68-$80 for twin-bedded rooms. Comparable rates of the Blackwell are $65-$75, $75-$85, and $80-$95. Thus, the savings at the Lamont would be approximately 15% per member.

Cost of the dinner selected would be $16.00 per person, including gratuities, at the Lamont. The Blackwell would meet this price if we would guarantee 600 plates. Otherwise, they would charge $18.00. Considering all of these figures, the total cost picture at the Lamont is the more favorable one.

Respectfully,

*Willard K Mitchell*

Willard K. Mitchell
Executive Secretary

### Headers and Footers: An Important Tool for Reports

Anytime your report is more than one page, you need to number the following pages. When the report is in memo or letter form, you usually use a header on the following pages that includes the name of the reader, the page number, and the date. These headers can be either in a block or horizontal format and are placed about ½ inch from the top of the page.

The header/footer feature of your word processing software allows you to set up the header once. The software will then take care of placing it on each of the following pages and numbering the pages consecutively.

When you are writing a long report, you must at least number the pages. If this is all you choose to do, most word processing software has a page numbering feature you can turn on to take care of this automatically. However, you may want to also include the report or section title in a header along with a page number. Full-featured programs often allow you to place different headers on odd- and even-numbered pages. For example, you may want to always put the report title on even-numbered pages and vary the header on the odd-numbered pages to include the section title. Some word processing programs even allow you to put the page number at different margins on odd- and even-numbered pages, enabling you to print your report pages on both sides with page numbers on the outer edges.

In most cases, you can use both the header/footer feature and the page numbering feature together. You could place the page numbers at the top right-hand margin and include the titles in the footer. You can also suppress headers or footers on specific pages without the software losing track of the page count. Of course, you can also discontinue headers or footers wherever you designate.

The header/footer feature is an amazingly flexible tool that provides you with automatic page titling and numbering.

---

reminder of what they are, how they originated, and the like. A letter report written to the membership of an organization, for example, might appropriately begin as follows:

As authorized by your board of directors last January 6, this report reviews member company expenditures for direct-mail selling.

• Subject lines are appropriate to begin them.

If a letter report is begun in the direct order, a subject line is appropriate. The subject line consists of identifying words appearing at the top of the letter, usually right after the salutation. Another common practice is to omit the word *subject* and the colon and to type the entire subject description in capital letters. Although subject lines may be formed in many ways, one acceptable version begins with the word *subject* and follows it with words that identify the situation. As the following example illustrates, this identifying device helps overcome any confusion that the direct beginning might otherwise create.

Subject: Report on direct-mail expenditures of Association members, authorized by board of directors, January 1993.

Association members are spending 8 percent more on direct-mail advertising this year than they did the year before. Current plans call for a 10 percent increase for next year.

### Unexpected Findings in a Report

A successful businessman fell in love with a woman who he felt might not meet the requirements of a person in his position. So he hired a detective agency to investigate her background.

After weeks of intensive checking, the detective agency submitted this report:

> Ms. Stoner has an excellent reputation. She has high morals, lives within her means, and is well respected in the community. The only blemish on her record is that in recent months she has been seen repeatedly in the company of a business executive of doubtful repute.

---

Regardless of which type of beginning is used, the organizational plans for letter reports correspond to those of the longer, more formal types. Thus, the indirect-order letter report follows its introduction with a logical presentation and analysis of the information gathered. From this presentation, it develops a conclusion or recommendation, or both, in the end. The direct-order letter report follows the initial summary-conclusion-recommendation section with whatever introduction is appropriate. For example, the direct beginning illustrated above could be followed with these introductory sentences:

> These are the primary findings of a study authorized by your board of directors last January. As they concern information vital to all of us in the Association, they are presented here for your confidential use.

*The organizational plans of letter reports are much like those of longer reports.*

Following such an introduction, the report would present the supporting facts and their analyses. The writer would systematically build up the case supporting the opening comment. With either the direct or indirect order, a letter report may close with whatever friendly, goodwill comment fits the occasion.

*Supporting facts and analyses follow an appropriate introduction.*

### Memorandum Reports

As we noted in Chapter 9, memorandums (commonly called *memos*) are the most widely used form of written communication in business. Although sometimes used for correspondence with outside parties, memorandums are primarily internal messages. That is, they are written by and to people in an organization. Figure 13–4 illustrates a memorandum report.

*Memorandums (internal written messages) are widely used.*

Because memorandums are primarily communications between people who know each other, they are usually informal. In fact, many are hurried, handwritten messages. Some memorandums, however, are formal, especially those directed to readers high in the administration of the organization.

*Most of them are written informally.*

Most memorandums are forms of letters. Some, however, are more appropriately classified as reports. The distinction between internal letters and internal reports is not always clear, though the reports tend to be more formal. In fact, some memorandum reports rival the longer report forms in formality. Like the longer forms, they may use captions to display content and graphics to support the text. Memorandum reports tend to be problem related.

*Some resemble letters and follow letter form.*

*Some are reports. Such memorandums tend to be formal and problem related.*

CHAPTER 13  Report Structure: The Shorter Forms

**FIGURE 13–4** Illustration of a Progress Report in Memorandum Form

This memorandum report summarizes a sales manager's progress in opening a new district. It begins with highlight information—all a busy reader may need to know. Organized by three categories of activity, the factual information follows. The writer-reader relationship justifies personal style.

---

MEMORANDUM                                    THE MURCHISON CO. INC.


To:       William T. Chysler
          Director of Sales

From:     James C. Calvin, Manager   *JCC*
          Millville Sales District

Date:     July 21, 19—

Subject:  Quarterly Report for Millville Sales District

### SUMMARY HIGHLIGHTS

After three months of operation, I have secured office facilities, hired and developed three salespeople, and cultivated about half the customers available in the Millville Sales District. Although the district is not yet showing a profit, at the current rate of development it will do so this month. Prospects for the district are unusually bright.

### OFFICE OPERATION

In April I opened the Millville Sales District as authorized by action of the Board of Directors last February 7. Initially I set up office in the Three Coins Inn, a motel on the outskirts of town, and remained there three weeks while looking for permanent quarters. These I found in the Wingate Building, a downtown office structure. The office suite rents for $940 per month. It has four executive offices, each opening into a single secretarial office, which is large enough for two secretaries. Although this arrangement is adequate for the staff now anticipated, additional space is available in the building if needed.

### PERSONNEL

In the first week of operation, I hired an office secretary, Ms. Catherine Kruch. Ms. Kruch has good experience and has excellent credentials. She has proved to be very effective. In early April I hired two salespeople—Mr. Charles E. Clark and Ms. Alice E. Knapper. Both were experienced in sales, although neither had worked in apparel sales. Three weeks later I hired Mr. Otto Strelski, a proven salesperson whom I managed to attract from the Hammond Company. I still am searching for someone for the fourth subdistrict. Currently I am investigating two good prospects and hope to hire one of them within the next week.

**FIGURE 13-4** (concluded)

William T. Chysler
Page 2
July 21, 19—

PERFORMANCE

After brief training sessions, which I conducted personally, the salespeople were assigned the territories previously marked. They were instructed to call on the accounts listed on the sheets supplied by Mr. Henderson's office. During the first month, Knapper's sales totaled $17,431 and Clark's reached $13,490, for a total of $30,921. With three salespeople working the next month, total sales reached $121,605. Of the total, Knapper accounted for $37,345, Clark $31,690, and Strelski $52,570. Although these monthly totals are below the $145,000 break-even point for the three subdistricts, current progress indicates that we will exceed this volume this month. As we have made contact with only about one half of the prospects in the area, the potential for the district appears to be unusually good.

## SPECIAL REPORT FORMS

- Some special report forms deserve review.

As noted previously, this review describes only generally the report forms used in business. Many variations exist, a few of which deserve emphasis.

### The Staff Report

- One is the staff report.

One of the more popular forms of reports used in business is the staff report. Usually written in memorandum form, it can be adapted to any structural type, including the long, formal report.

- Staff reports follow a fixed organization plan that leads to a conclusion.

The staff report differs from other forms of reports primarily in the organization of its contents. It arranges contents in a fixed plan, similar to that used in technical writing. The plan remains the same for all problems. As this arrangement leads systematically to conclusions and recommendations, it is especially useful for business problems.

- A typical plan for staff reports has these parts:

Although the organization of staff reports varies by company, this plan used by a major metals manufacturer is typical:

- Identifying information.

*Identifying information:* As the company's staff reports are written on intracompany communication stationery, the conventional identification information (*To, From, Subject, Date*) appears at the beginning.

- Summary.

*Summary:* For the busy executive who wants the facts fast, the report begins with a summary. Some executives will read no further. Others will want to trace the report content in detail.

- Problem (or objective).

*The problem (or objective):* As with all good problem-solving procedures, the report text logically begins with a clear description of the problem—what it is, what it is not, what its limitations are, and the like.

- Facts.

*Facts:* Next comes the information gathered in the attempt to solve the problem.

- Discussion.

*Discussion:* This is followed by analyses of the facts and applications of the facts and the analyses to the problem. (The statement and discussion of the facts can often be combined.)

- Conclusions.

*Conclusions:* From the preceding discussion of the facts come the final meanings as they apply to the problem.

- Recommendation.

*Recommendation:* If the problem's objective allows for it, a course of action may be recommended on the basis of the conclusions.

- See Figure 13-5 for the military form of staff reports.

Perhaps the major users of staff reports are the branches of the Armed Forces, all of which use a standardized form. As shown in Figure 13–5, the military version of the staff report differs somewhat from the plan just described.

Of course, anytime you use a standardized form, you will want to consider developing a macro or merge document with your word processing software. A macro would fill in all the standard parts for you, pausing to let you enter the variable information. It would be most suitable for periodic reports, such as progress reports or quarterly sales reports. A merge document would prompt you for the variables first, merging them with the primary document later. You'll find this feature most useful when you are repeatedly having to write several reports at the same time. For example, personnel evaluations or client reports are good applications of the merge.

PART 5 Fundamentals of Report Writing

**FIGURE 13-5** Military Form of Staff Study Report

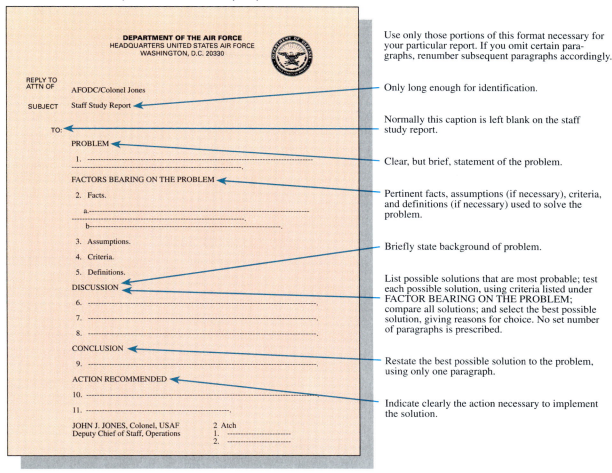

## The Progress Report

As its name implies, a progress report presents a review of progress made on an activity. For example, a fund-raising organization might prepare weekly summaries of its efforts to achieve its goal. Or a building contractor might prepare for a customer a report on progress toward completing a building. Typically, the contents of these reports concern progress made, but they may also include such related topics as problems encountered or anticipated and projections of future progress.

Progress reports follow no set form. They can be quite formal, as when a contractor building a large manufacturing plant reports to the company for whom the plant is being built. Or they can be very informal, as in the case of a worker reporting by memorandum to his or her supervisor on the progress of a task being performed. Some progress reports are quite routine and structured, sometimes involving filling in blanks on forms devised for the purpose. Most, however, are informal, narrative reports, as illustrated by the example in Figure 13-4.

## The Audit Report

- Short- and long-form audit reports are well known in business.

Short-form and long-form audit reports are well known in business. The short-form audit report is perhaps the most standardized of all reports—if, indeed, it can be classified as a report. Actually, it is a standardized statement verifying an accountant's inspection of a firm's financial records. Its wording seldom varies. Illustrations of this standard form are found in almost any corporate annual report.

- Long-form audit reports vary in their makeup.

Long-form audit reports vary greatly in their makeup. In fact, a national accounting association that studied the subject exhaustively found the makeup of these reports to be so varied that it concluded that no typical form existed.

## The Technical Report

- Technical reports differ from other reports primarily in their subject matter.

Although often treated as a highly specialized form, the technical report differs from other reports primarily in its subject matter. As you can see from Figure 13-6, a technical report can be much like the memorandum reports we have described. The longer technical reports, however, tend to follow a somewhat standardized arrangement.

- This arrangement of prefatory parts is typical: title pages, letter of transmittal, table of contents, summary parts (findings, conclusions, recommendations, objectives, acknowledgements).

This arrangement begins much like that of the traditional formal report. First come the title pages, although a routing or distribution form for intracompany use is frequently worked in. A letter of transmittal is likely to come next, followed by a table of contents and illustrations. From this point on, however, the technical report is different. Its differences lie mainly in two places: (1) beginning summary and (2) text organization.

- The text of the long technical report is typically organized in a fixed order like this one: introduction, methodology, facts, discussion, conclusion, recommendation.

Instead of having a standard summary, the long technical report often presents the summary information in a number of prefatory sections. There may be, for example, separate sections covering findings, conclusions, and recommendations. Parts of the conventional introduction, especially objectives and acknowledgements, sometimes appear as prefatory sections.

The long technical report usually follows a standard order similar to that of the staff report. The most common order is the following:

Introduction.
Methodology (or methods and materials).
Facts.
Discussion.
Conclusion.
Recommendation.

## The Proposal

- Proposals vary in length.

Whether proposals belong in a discussion of the shorter reports is debatable, for they are not always short. In fact, they range in length from just a few pages to several volumes. We discuss them here primarily as a matter of convenience.

**FIGURE 13-6** Illustration of a Technical Memorandum Report

This memorandum report presents an investigation of a technical process the writer was asked to make. It begins with a brief introduction. Then comes a narrative summary of the investigation, organized by the major areas inspected. Note the use of graphics to help present somewhat difficult concepts.

---

MEMORANDUM                                   the Crowell Company, inc.

To:     Charles E. Groom                              May 3, 19—

From:   Edmund S. Posner  ESP

Subject: Graff Lining Company's use of Kynar pipe lining

Following is the report you requested January 9 on the Graff Lining Company's process of using Kynar for lining pipe. My comments are based on my inspection of the facilities at the Graff plant and my conversations with their engineers.

<u>Dimension limitations</u>

Graff's ability to line the smaller pipe sizes appears to be limited. To date, the smallest diameter pipe they have lined in 10-foot spool lengths is 2 inches. They believe they can handle 1 1/2-inch pipe in 10-foot spools, but they have not attempted this size. They question their ability to handle smaller pipe in 10-foot lengths.

This limitation, however, does not apply to fittings. They can line 1 1/2-inch and 1-inch fittings easily. Although they can handle smaller sizes than these, they prefer to limit minimum nipple size to 1 inch by 4 inches long.

Maximum spool dimensions for the coating process are best explained by illustration:

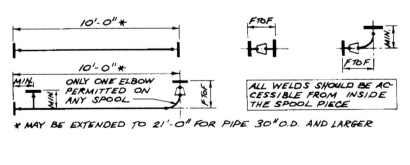

---

SOURCE: Raymond V. Lesikar and John D. Pettit, *Report Writing for Business,* 8th ed. (Homewood, Ill. Richard D. Irwin, 1991).

Charles E. Groom  2  May 3, 19—

Graff corrects defects found. If the defect is small, they correct by retouching with sprayer or brush. If the defect is major, they remove all the coating by turning and reline the pipe.

Recommendations for piping

Should we be interested in using their services, Graff engineers made the following recommendations. First, they recommend that we use forged steel fittings rather than cast fittings. Cast fittings, they point out, have excessive porosity. They noted, though, that cast fittings can be used and are less expensive. For large jobs, this factor could be significant.

Second, they suggest that we make all small connections, such as those required for instruments, in a prescribed manner. This manner is best described by diagram:

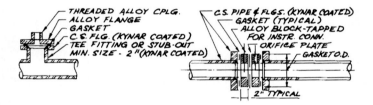

Graff engineers emphasized this point further by illustrating a common form of small connections that will not work. Such connections are most difficult to coat. Pinhole breaks are likely to occur on them, and a pinhole break can cause the entire coating to disbond. A typical unacceptable connection is the following:

Charles E. Groom 3 May 3, 19—

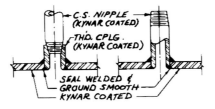

Preparation of pipe for lining

Graff requires that all pipe to be lined be ready for the coating process. Specifically, they require that all welds be ground smooth (to avoid pitting and assure penetration.) Because welds are inaccessible in small pipe, they require forged tees in all piping smaller than 4 inches. In addition, they require that all attachments to the pipe (clips, base ells, etc.) be welded to the pipe prior to coating.

The lining procedure

The procedure Graff uses in lining the pipe begins with cleaning the pipe and inspecting it for cracked fittings, bad welds, etc. When necessary, they do minor retouching and grinding of welds. Then they apply the Kynar in three forms: primer, building, sealer. They apply the building coat in as many layers as is necessary to obtain a finished thickness of 25 mils. They oven bake each coat at a temperature and for a time determined by the phase of the coating and the piping material.

Inspection technique

Following the coating, Graff inspectors use a spark testing method to detect possible pinholes or other defects. This method is best explained by illustration:

**FIGURE 13-6** (concluded)

Charles E. Groom              4              May 3, 19—

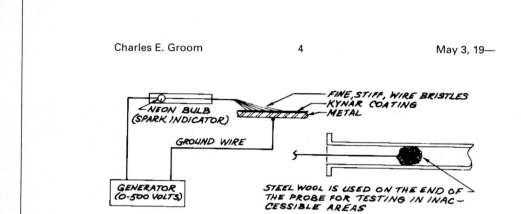

A third recommendation is that we establish handling procedures to protect the coated pipe. As the Kynar coating will chip, we would need to make certain that we protect all flange spaces. Also, we would need to be careful in shipping, handling, storing, and erecting the pipe.

**Proposals Defined.** By definition, a *proposal* is a presentation for consideration of something. In actual practice, some proposals fit this definition well—for example, one company's proposal to merge with another company, an advertising agency's proposal to promote a product, or a city's proposal to induce a business to locate within its boundaries. But other proposals are more precisely described as appeals or bids for grants, donations, or sales of products or services. To illustrate, a college professor submits a request for research funds to a government agency, a community organization submits a request to a philanthropic foundation for help in establishing a drug rehabilitation facility, or a company submits a bid for the sale of its products or services.

Proposals are usually written but they can be oral presentations or a combination of both. They may be made by individuals or organizations, including business organizations, and they may be made to any of a variety of individuals or organizations such as government agencies, foundations, businesses. They can even be made internally—by one part of a business to another part or to the management of the business. For example, a department might outline its needs for new equipment in a proposal to management.

**Invited or Prospecting.** Proposals may be invited or prospecting. By *invited* we mean that the awarding organization announces to interested parties that it will make an award and that it is soliciting proposals. To illustrate, a government agency might have funds to award for research projects, a foundation might wish to make grants for educational innovations, or a business might want competing suppliers to bid on a product or service that it needs. In their announcements, the awarding organizations typically describe their needs and specify the unique requirements that the proposals should cover.

In business situations, invited proposals usually follow preliminary meetings between the parties involved. For example, if a business has a need for certain production equipment, its representatives might initiate meetings with likely suppliers of this equipment. At these meetings the representatives would discuss the need with suppliers. Each supplier would then be invited to submit a proposal for fulfilling the need with its equipment. In a sense, such a proposal is a bid supported by the documentation and explanation needed for conviction.

Prospecting proposals are much like rational sales letters. They amount to descriptions of what the writer or the writer's organization could do if given an award by the reader's organization. For example, a university department that wishes to seek funding for the development of a new curriculum in international management might then write proposals to philanthropic foundations describing the curriculum, outlining its financial needs for instituting the curriculum, and proposing that the foundation award the funds needed. Or a business supplying unique services might submit an unsolicited description of the services to a business that might use them. Such proposals differ from rational sales letters primarily in their physical form (they are in report form, not letter form). When products or services are being proposed, such proposals may also differ from rational sales letters by being specifically adapted to the reader's business.

---

*A proposal is a presentation for consideration of something.*

*Proposals are made by individuals or organizations to individuals or organizations.*

*They may be invited or prospecting.*

*In business, invited proposals usually follow meetings.*

*Prospecting proposals are like sales letters.*

**Format and Organization.** The physical arrangement and organization of proposals vary widely. The simplest proposals resemble formal memorandums. Internal proposals (those written for and by people in the same organization) usually fall into this category, though exceptions exist. The more complex proposals may take the form of full-dress, long reports, including prefatory pages (title pages, letter of transmittal, table of contents, executive summary), text, and an assortment of appended parts. Most proposals have arrangements that fall somewhere between these extremes.

Because of the wide variations in the makeup of proposals, you would be wise to investigate carefully before designing a particular proposal. In your investigation, try to determine what format is conventional among those who will read it. Look to see what others have done in similar situations. In the case of an invited proposal, review the announcement thoroughly, looking for clues concerning the preferences of the inviting organization. If you are unable to follow any of these courses, design a format based on your knowledge of report structure. Your design should be the one that you think is best for the one situation.

**Formality Requirements.** The formality requirements of proposals vary. In some cases (a university's proposal for a research grant, for example), strict formality is expected. In other cases (such as a manufacturing department's proposal that the plant manager change a production procedure), informality is in order. As with other reports, the decision should be based primarily on the relationship between the parties involved. If the parties are acquainted with each other, informality is appropriate. If they are not, a formal report is usually expected. An exception would be made in any case in which formality is expected regardless of the relationship of the parties.

**Content.** You should consider the needs of the individual case in determining the content of a proposal. In the case of an invited (solicited) proposal, review the proposal announcement (if the proposal is in writing). If the proposal results from a meeting, review your announcement of the meeting or the notes you took at the meeting. Such a review will usually tell you what is wanted. In fact, some written invitations even give a suggested plan for the proposal. It is highly important that you follow such guidelines, for in competitive situations the selection procedure frequently involves a check-off and rating for each point stated in the invitation.

If you are making an uninvited proposal, you will have to determine what your readers need to know. As each case will involve different needs, you will have to use your best judgment in making that determination.

Although the number of content possibilities is great, you should consider including the eight topics listed below. They are broad and general, and you can combine or subdivide them as needed to fit the facts of your case. (See Figure 13–7 for one logical application.)

*1. Writer's purpose and the reader's need.* An appropriate beginning is a statement of the writer's purpose (to present a proposal) and the reader's need (to reduce turnover of field representatives). If the report is in response to an invitation, that statement should tie in with the invitation (as described in the July 10 announcement). The problem should be stated clearly, in the

Getting advice from associates is good practice in preparing the more involved proposals.

way described in Chapter 12. This proposal beginning illustrates these recommendations:

As requested at the July 10 meeting with Alice Burton, Thomas Cheny, and Victor Petrui in your Calgary office, the following pages present Murchison and Associates' proposal for reducing turnover of field representatives. Following guidelines established at the meeting, the proposal involves determining the job satisfaction of the current sales force, analyzing exit interview records, and comparing company compensation and personnel practices with industry norms.

If a proposal is submitted without invitation, its beginning has an additional requirement: it must gain attention. As noted previously, uninvited proposals are much like sales letters. Their intended readers are not likely to be eager to read them. Thus, their beginnings must overcome the readers' reluctance. An effective way of doing this is to begin by briefly summarizing the highlights of the proposal, with emphasis on its benefits. This technique is illustrated by the beginning of an unsolicited proposal that a restaurant consultant sent to prospective clients:

The following pages present a proven plan for operations review that will (1) reduce food costs, (2) evaluate menu offerings for maximum profitability, (3) increase kitchen efficiency, (4) improve service, and (5) increase profits. Mattox and Associates proposes to achieve these results through its highly successful procedures, which involve analysis of guest checks and invoices and observational studies of kitchen and service work.

**FIGURE 13-7** Illustration of a Short Proposal

This simple proposal seeks organization membership for its writer. It begins with a quick introduction that ties in with the reader's invitation for the proposal. Then it presents the case, logically proceeding from background information to advantages of membership, to costs. It concludes with the recommendation to sponsor membership.

---

# MEMORANDUM

TO: Helen S. Hobson

DATE: May 19, 19—

FROM: Ross H. Jefferson  *RHJ*

SUBJECT: Sponsored membership in the Association for Business Communication

As you requested May 17, following is my proposal for Stoner to sponsor my membership in the Association for Business Communication (ABC).

Description of ABC

The primary professional organization in business communication, ABC is dedicated to keeping its members informed of the latest developments in business communication practice and theory. It informs its members through two quarterly publications: The Journal of Business Communication (research and theory) and The ABC Bulletin (practice). In addition, the Association holds an annual meeting as well as regional meetings throughout the United States and Canada. Papers presented at these meetings cover both the current theoretical and practical topics in business communication.

Founded in 1936, ABC now has 2,401 members, including 850 institutions. Of the individual memberships, most (1,182) are academics from the United States and Canada. But 148 are business professionals. Companies represented include IBM, AT&T, Exxon, Imperial Oil, State Farm Insurance, McDonnell Douglas, and Aetna Insurance. ABC's diverse membership provides an effective exchange of experience and knowledge.

Benefits of Membership

Membership in ABC would benefit Stoner as well as me personally. The meetings and the publications would enable me to bring the lastest communication knowledge to my editorial work. ABC would be especially helpful in my assignments involving teaching communication to our employees, for much of its emphasis is on teaching techniques. Also, membership in ABC would enhance Stoner's image. ABC is a prestigious organization, and its members include the corporate elite. In addition, meeting with the members of other companies and exchanging ideas would help me do a better job of directing Stoner's communication activities.

**FIGURE 13-7** (concluded)

Helen S. Hobson, May 19, 19—, page 2.

Costs of Membership

ABC annual dues are $40, which includes subscriptions to the Journal and the Bulletin. The costs of attending the meetings would vary with the meeting sites. For this year, the approximate costs for the international meeting in Las Vegas would be $700 (registration, $80; transportation, $330; hotel, $180; meals, $90; miscellaneous, $20). For the regional meeting in Dallas it would be $570 (registration, $70; transportation, $150; hotel, $200; meals, $120; miscellaneous, $30). The total cost for this year would be $1,310.

Recommended Action

Based on the preceding information, I believe that membership in ABC offers us benefits well worth the cost. Thus, I recommend that Stoner sponsor my membership on a one-year trial basis. At the end of this year, I would review actual benefits received and recommend whether or not to continue membership.

*Uninvited proposals must gain attention.*

Your clear statement of the purpose and problem may be the most important aspect of the proposal. In order to win a contract, you must convince your reader that you have a clear understanding of what needs to be done.

*2. Background.*

*2. Background.* A review of background information promotes an understanding of the problem. Thus, a college's proposal for an educational grant might benefit from a review of the college's involvement in the area to which the grant would be applied. A company's proposal of a merger with another company might review industry developments that make the merger desirable. Or a chief executive officer's proposal to the board of directors that a company's administration be reorganized might present the background information that justifies the proposal.

*3. Need.*

*3. Need.* Closely related to the background information is the need for what is being proposed. In fact, background information may well be used to establish need. But because need can be presented without such support, we list it separately.

*4. Plan description.*

*4. Description of plan.* The heart of a proposal is the description of what the writer proposes to do. This is the primary message of the proposal. It should be concisely presented in a clear and orderly manner.

*5. Particulars (time schedules, costs, performance standards, equipment and supplies needed, and such).*

*5. Particulars.* Although the particulars of the proposal are a part of the plan description, they are discussed separately for reasons of emphasis. By *particulars* we mean the specifics—time schedules, costs, performance standards, means of appraising performance, equipment and supplies needed, guarantees, personnel requirements, and such. What is needed in a given case depends on its unique requirements. But in any event, the particulars should anticipate and answer the readers' questions.

*6. Ability to deliver.*

*6. Evidence of ability to deliver.* The proposing organization must sometimes establish its ability to perform. This means presenting information on such matters as the qualifications of personnel, success in similar cases, the adequacy of equipment and facilities, operating procedures, and financial status. Whatever information will serve as evidence of the organization's ability to carry out what it proposes should be used.

*7. Benefits of the proposal (especially if selling is needed).*

*7. Benefits of the proposal.* The proposal might also describe good things that it would bring about, especially if a need exists to convince the readers. Reader benefits were what we stressed in sales writing, but as we have noted, proposals can be much like sales presentations. The greater the need to persuade, the more you should stress benefits. As will be noted in a later chapter, however, the writing in proposals is more objective and less flamboyant than the writing in sales literature.

As an example of benefits logically covered in proposals, a college's request for funding to establish a program for minorities could point to the bright futures that such funding would give disadvantaged students. And a proposal offering a consulting service to restaurants could stress such benefits as improved work efficiency, reduced employee theft, savings in food costs, and increased profits.

*8. Concluding comments (words directed toward the next step).*

*8. Concluding comments.* The proposal should end with words directed to the next step—acting on the proposal. One possibility is to present a summary review of the highlights. Another is to offer additional information that might be needed. Yet another is to urge (or suggest) action on the proposal.

## SUMMARY (by Chapter Objectives)

1. Length and formality determine the following general progression of report structure:
   - The very long ones have prefatory pages (title fly, title page, letter of transmittal, table of contents, executive summary).
   - As reports become shorter and less formal, the composition of the prefatory parts section changes, generally in this order:
     —First, the title fly drops out.
     —Then, in succession, the executive summary and letter of transmittal are combined.
     —the table of contents is omitted, and
     —the combined letter of transmittal and executive summary is dropped.
   - Below these steps are the letter report and the memorandum report.

   *1. Explain the structure of reports relative to length and formality.*

2. The shorter and by far the most common reports are much like the longer ones except for these three differences:
   - They have less need for introductory material.
   - They are more likely to begin directly (conclusion and recommendation first).
   - They are more likely to use personal style.

   *2. Discuss the three major differences involved in writing short and long reports.*

3. One of the more popular forms of less formal reports is the short report.
   - It consists of a title page and report text.
   - Usually it begins with a summary or conclusion.
   - Then it presents findings and analyses.

   *3. Write clear and well-organized short reports.*

4. Letter reports are another popular short form.
   - Usually they are written in the indirect order.
   - They are organized much like the longer reports.
   Memorandum reports are like letter reports.
   - They are written for and by people within an organization.
   - They are the most common report form.

   *4. Write clear and well-organized letter and memorandum reports.*

5. Among the various special reports, four stand out.
   - The staff report follows a fixed organization plan (for example, identifying information, summary, problem, facts, discussion, conclusions, recommendation).
   - A progress report reviews the progress on an activity and follows no set form.
   - The audit report presents the results of an audit and follows a variety of forms.
   - The technical report differs primarily in its subject matter.
     —The longer ones may follow a specified order.
     —One such order is introduction, methodology, facts, discussion, conclusion, recommendation.

   *5. Adapt the procedures for writing short reports to such special reports as staff, audit, progress, and technical reports.*

6. A proposal is a presentation for the consideration of something—a merger, a bid for an account, a research grant, and so on.
   - Individuals and organizations make them to other individuals and organizations.
   - Some are made internally, from one department to another.

   *6. Write complete, well-organized, and effective proposals.*

- They may be invited or prospecting. They range from the very short to the very long.
- They vary in form, from simple memorandums to full-dress reports.
- They may be formal or informal.

The contents of proposals vary with need, but one should consider these topics:
- writer's purpose and reader's need,
- background,
- need,
- plan description,
- particulars (time, schedule, costs, performance standards, and such),
- ability to deliver,
- benefits, and
- concluding comments.

## QUESTIONS FOR DISCUSSION

1. Discuss the effects of formality and problem length on the model of report makeup described in the chapter.
2. Which of the prefatory pages of reports appear to be related primarily to the length of the report? Which to the need for formality?
3. Explain why some routine report problems require little or no introduction.
4. Why is the direct order generally used in the shorter reports? When is the indirect order desirable for such reports?
5. Give examples of short report forms that are appropriately written in personal style. Do the same for impersonal style.
6. Describe the organization of the conventional short report.
7. What types of problems are written up as letter reports? As memorandum reports? Explain the differences.
8. Why is the order of the staff report said to be a problem-solving order?
9. Discuss the differences between technical reports and the other business reports.
10. "To be successful, a proposal must be persuasive. This quality makes the proposal different from most short reports (which stress objectivity)." Discuss.

## APPLICATION EXERCISES

1. Review the following report situations and determine for each the makeup of the report you would recommend for it:

   *a.* A professional research organization has completed a survey of consumer attitudes toward the Alto Company. The survey results will be presented to the Alto president in a 28-page report, including seven charts and three tables.

   *b.* Eva Campbell was asked by her department head to inspect the work area and report on safety conditions. Her report is two pages long and written in personal style.

   *c.* Chad Benton has an idea for improving a work procedure in his department at Dorner Manufacturing Company. His department head suggested that Chad present his idea in a report to the production superintendent. The report is almost five pages long, including a full-page diagram. It is written in the personal style.

   *d.* Karen Canady, a worker in the supply room of Edmunds & Sons Plumbing Contractors, was asked by Doug Edmunds, its president, for current inventory information on a number of basic products. Her report is less than a full page and consists mostly of a list of items and numbers.

   *e.* Bryan Toups, a sales manager for the Batla Chemical Company, was asked by the vice president of marketing to prepare an analysis of the results of a promotional campaign conducted in Toups' district. The report is six pages long (including one chart) and is written in the personal style.

2. Following is a report that was written for the manager of a large furniture retail store by the manager's assistant. The manager was concerned about customer complaints of late deliveries of furniture purchased and wanted to know the cause of the delays. Criticize this report.

11-17-93

TO: Martina Kalavoda
FROM: Anthony Dudrow
SUBJECT: Investigation requested 11-17-93

This morning at staff meeting it was requested that an investigation be made of the status of home deliveries and of the causes of the delays that have occurred. The investigation has been made with findings as follows.

Now that a new driver's helper, Morris Tunney, has been hired, there should be no more delays. This was the cause of the problem.

Over the past two weeks (10 working days), a total of 143 deliveries were made, and of these, 107 were made on or before the date promised, but some of the deliveries were late because of the departure two weeks ago of the driver's helper, Sean Toulouse, who had to be fired because of dishonesty and could not be replaced quickly with a permanent, qualified helper. Now that a permanent, qualified helper has been hired, there should be no more delays in delivery as this was the cause of the problem.

The driver was able to find a temporary helper, a man by name of Rusty Sellers, for some help in the unloading work, but he got behind and couldn't seem to catch up. He could have caught up by working overtime, in the opinion of the writer, but he refused to do so. Of the 36 deliveries that were late, all were completed within two days. The problem is over now that the driver has a helper, so there should be no additional delays.

##########
## REPORT PROBLEMS
### SHORT LENGTH: MEMORANDUM AND LETTER REPORTS

1. *Investigating a problem in the shipping department.* Today Marci McDougal, the vice president for sales for the Drake-Meeks Carpet Company, received a telephone call from an angry retailer, Cyrus O'Keefe, in Beacon City. Mr. O'Keefe reported that he had made a large order of Durabilt carpeting by telephone. He said he was assured the carpeting was in stock and would be delivered within five days. On the fifth day (today) he received a notice that the carpeting is out of stock and will not be delivered for at least two weeks. To make matters worse, Mr. O'Keefe had advertised the carpeting for his store's annual super sale, which began today. The conversation ended with Mr. O'Keefe cancelling the order and promising not to do business with Drake-Meeks again.

   Following her conversation with Mr. O'Keefe, Ms. McDougal called you (her assistant) into her office. After explaining Mr. O'Keefe's problem, she asked you to look into the matter for her. "I want to know precisely what happened," she instructed. "Find out who, if anyone, is responsible. And I want to know what we should do to prevent problems like this from occurring in the future."

   You began your investigation by interviewing Sylvester O. Timm, the person who handles mail-order and telephone sales. His explanation was as follows: "I remember the order. I checked with Nicole Gratz in shipping. She said they had a limited supply, but enough to fill this order. So I told her to mark it sold, and I gave her the shipping information."

   Next you talked with Nicole Gratz. "Yes, Mr. Timm called and I did what he told me. We were ready to send the carpeting when the boss (David Copus, manager of the shipping department) came in and stopped it. He said he had already promised Sheri Kaufman (an outside salesperson) the carpeting for one of her good customers. I just follow orders."

   David Copus was your next interviewee. "I had no choice," he explained. "Sheri had called me earlier that day asking how much of this carpeting we had in stock. She said she had it all sold and asked me to hold it for her customer. I said I would, and I did. I told Nicole to inform O'Keefe that we have to backorder his carpeting."

   With the preceding information in mind, you are ready to write your memorandum report to Ms. McDougal. You will put together the testimony to determine what happened. And you will recommend some procedural changes that will prevent such problems from occurring.

2. *Reporting storm damage to the home office.* For this assignment you are the manager of the Millville warehouse of the Forshee-Pierce Wholesale Furniture Company. Last night a severe storm came through the area, causing damage to one of your storage buildings. You will have to prepare a report of the damage for the home office.

   With notepad in hand, you inspected the damage. When you finished, your notepad contained this information:

   Building: corrugated metal roof blown off—completely destroyed (bent and twisted). Other damage to building minimal—some damage to overhead lights (apparently hit by roof fragments). Outside door blown loose from hinges, but not otherwise damaged.
   
   Contents: Sofas and chairs stored in building—all suffered water damage—upholstery soaked by rains—faded and fit only for salvage. Fortunately, building not full. Damaged contents as follows: 7 Dubary sofas, Stock No. 7173; 13 Dubary easy chairs, Stock No. 7181; 19 Haggerton sofas, Stock No. 7073; 3 Weideman sofas, Stock No. 7113; 15 Weideman recliner chairs, Stock No. 8173. No current orders to fill any of these items.

   After surveying the building, Scott A. Michel, a

local contractor specializing in repairs and remodeling, proposed to repair the building for $12,200. He could start right away and could finish the job in five working days. He has worked for Forshee-Pierce before and proved to be reputable and competent. No doubt the company has insurance that covers the damage, but that information is kept at headquarters. You will only report and wait for instructions.

Write the report in memorandum form. You will fax it to Mark O. Ferguson, who is the president.

3. *Recommending dismissal of a subordinate.* You will have to recommend that Erik Kuykendall be fired. He leaves you no choice.

Mr. Kuykendall joined your sales force at the Victoria office of Technology Unlimited six months ago. Your boss, Monica I. Schaefer, selected him. Ms. Schaefer, who is the national sales manager, makes all the hiring and firing decisions for the sales force.

Mr. Kuykendall came to the job with no sales experience. Apparently, Ms. Schaefer thought that his work as director of the computer center at Darden University and his sparkling personality overcame his lack of sales experience.

For the first month you worked closely with Mr. Kuykendall, and all went well. In fact, your evaluation report on him at that time was very positive. He demonstrated good potential. He proved to you that he was knowledgeable and that he had the aggressive and personable qualities needed for success with Technology Unlimited.

After the first month, you put Mr. Kuykendall on his own. At first, his sales were good. Then, after five weeks something happened. His sales became erratic—high some days, low other days. Overall, his sales continued to decline. On the four-month anniversary of his hiring, you called Kuykendall in for a conference. The man appeared to be genuinely embarrassed, and he apologized for his weak record. He explained his problem as "a lack of experience." The meeting ended with assurances from Kuykendall that his sales would improve.

In the following weeks Kuykendall's sales did not improve. In fact, they got progressively worse. So you decided to visit the man in the field. To your surprise, he did not show up at any of the businesses he was scheduled to call on that day. And a check of businesses he was scheduled to call the day before showed that he had seen none of these.

Next, you went to Mr. Kuykendall's home. From his wife you learned that she and Erik had separated. "Erik has a drinking problem," she told you. "That's why he left the university. Actually they let him go, but they gave him the opportunity of resigning." Mrs. Kuykendall gave you her husband's current address, so you went to see him.

When confronted with the information you had obtained, Mr. Kuykendall admitted his problem. "But I am getting my life back together," he said. "I've spent the last three days drying out. I've had my last drink. I plan to go back to work tomorrow. You just watch me."

You believed the man, probably because you wanted to. You left with the feeling that things would be better. They were for a few days, but then the old pattern returned. You visited him a second time. As before, you found him at home and not at work. He was inebriated and unable to carry on a conversation. You informed him that you would have to recommend his dismissal, but you are not certain he understood.

Now back in your office you will write the report that will recommend dismissal. You may bring in any specific details that are vital to your report, but they must be consistent with the information given. You will fax this memorandum report to Ms. Schaefer.

4. *Comparing your computer store's sales with national norms.* You are assistant to Dustin O. Dabney, president of Compumart, a new and rapidly growing chain of computer specialty stores. Today Mr. Dabney called you into his office and showed you a brief article in *Computer Marketing*. In the article appeared a table that caught Mr. Dabney's attention.

"This table shows a breakdown of sales by customer types for computer specialty stores nationwide," Mr. Dabney explained to you. "It also shows the average size of the first purchase and the add-on sales for the following 12 months. I'd like to know how our sales compare with these national figures. Also, the article says that the future emphasis on stores like ours will be in the business, professional, and industry markets— that these are the markets we should stress if we are to survive. I'd especially like to know how we are doing in these markets. Please get the comparable sales data from our records. Then compare them with the data in the table. Analyze what you find, and present your findings and analyses to me in a concise report."

Your next step was to gather the information from sales records. Time did not permit anything more than a sampling, for company sales records

**TABLE 1 (Problem 4)** National and Compumart Sales by Customer Type with Average Initial Sale Price and 12-month Add-ons

| Customer Type | Percent of Sales | | Initial Sale Price | | 12-month Add-ons | |
|---|---|---|---|---|---|---|
| | N* | CM* | N* | CM* | N* | CM* |
| Business | 26.4 | 23.9 | $9,760 | $8,970 | $1,792 | $1,232 |
| Industrial | 16.9 | 6.7 | 6,935 | 7,133 | 1,532 | 971 |
| Home | 20.4 | 32.3 | 2,780 | 2,087 | 951 | 582 |
| Education | 19.4 | 28.6 | 4,237 | 3,974 | 910 | 637 |
| Professional | 16.9 | 8.5 | 8,120 | 9,270 | 1,439 | 903 |

\* N = national averages
CM = Compumart averages

are voluminous. But you feel you got a good sample—enough to give you reasonably accurate figures.

Now you will make the comparisons and analyses Mr. Dabney requested and present them in a memorandum report. (The table from *Computer Marketing* and the information you have gathered are combined in Table 1.)

5. *Presenting beach-litter information to a plastics manufacturer.* Chem-Tech is a manufacturer of a variety of plastic products, primarily bags, caps and lids, cups, and beverage bottles. Recently the company has been the target of environmentalists who claim that plastic products are polluting the earth—especially the seashores. The environmentalists have backed their claims with photographs showing litter on otherwise beautiful stretches of sandy beach. Most of the litter shown is made of plastic.

Chem-Tech management is concerned about the problem, although they feel the environmentalists are exaggerating the case. So management will seek more specific information. They have assigned you, a newly hired management trainee, to get this information.

Following the advice of one of your superiors, you began work on the assignment by going to White Sands City and visiting the director of the White Sands Cleanup Association. WSCA is a volunteer organization dedicated to keeping the area beaches clean. For the past 11 months its volunteers have walked the area beaches daily, picking up litter. Perhaps most significant for you, WSCA has kept a record of the types of litter picked up. "After a full year, we intend to use this information to publicize the problem," the director told you. "But I'll share the information with you if you'll promise to keep it confidential until we release it to the public." You promised, and the director gave you the following summary:

| Item | Number Picked Up |
|---|---|
| 1. Plastic pieces | 4,044 |
| 2. Plastic cups, lids | 2,943 |
| 3. Glass pieces | 2,231 |
| 4. Small foam plastic pieces | 2,063 |
| 5. Plastic trash bags | 1,906 |
| 6. Glass beverage bottles | 1,863 |
| 7. Plastic rope (2 ft. or less) | 1,853 |
| 8. Plastic cups, spoons, forks, straws | 1,693 |
| 9. Miscellaneous plastic bags | 1,532 |
| 10. Foam plastic cups | 1,378 |
| 11. Paper pieces | 1,213 |
| 12. Plastic rope (longer than 2 ft.) | 1,190 |

Now you must report and interpret these findings. You will do this in a memorandum report addressed to Dee K. Tuttle, President.

6. *Evaluating effects of a promotion on your department's sales.* You are manager of the sporting goods department of the Metro City branch of Mason's, a major chain of department stores. Every July the Metro City store conducts a major promotion. As in past years, you were asked to select five items to emphasize in the store's advertisements in local newspapers. The idea was to select items that would appeal to a wide range of customers, get them into the store, and sell to them.

Now that the promotion is over, Earl O. Richter, store manager, is assessing results. He has asked each department manager to gather the information on sales of the products advertised as well as on overall sales. Specifically, he wants to know how good the selections of advertised products were—that is, how much did their sales increase as a result of the promotion. Also, since customers brought in by the advertising often buy other products, Mr. Richter wants a comparison of total sales volume for the department during the week of the promotion with past weekly sales volume totals.

Your computations for this report produce the following information concerning sales of the products advertised:

| Advertised Products | Average Number Sold Weekly, Preceding Weeks | Number Sold During Promotion |
|---|---|---|
| Airborne joggers | 11 | 63 |
| Riteflex casting rods | 7 | 23 |
| Ace tennis racquets | 2 | 4 |
| Hi-Fli golf balls (doz.) | 7 | 89 |
| Mountaineer backpack | 1 | 3 |

Sales for the department for the week of the promotion totaled $17,544. The weekly sales average during the preceding four weeks was $6,772.

Now present this information with your interpretations in a memorandum report addressed to Mr. Richter. You may supply price data for the five products advertised if you feel they are needed.

7. *Justifying termination of a probationary employee.* Six months ago you hired Crystal Stedman as manager of the cafeteria at the Prairie City plant of the H. W. Nicholson Manufacturing Company. You are the plant's director of employee services, and the cafeteria is under your control.

Ms. Stedman came to you with nine years of related experience, working first as a cook for five years and later as owner-manager of her own small restaurant for four years. After her restaurant failed (because of a major plant closing in the area, she explained), Ms. Stedman sought employment. She saw your advertisement and responded to it. You hired her.

From the beginning you could see that Ms. Stedman had some skills in restaurant operations. The quality of the food was excellent—better than ever before according to a survey of employees. You thought you made an excellent choice until you saw the accounting report for the first month. The cafeteria lost $2,753. You assumed much of the loss was due to Ms. Stedman's newness on the job; so you did nothing for a month. Again the account report showed a loss—this time for $3,022.

You decided it was time to talk with Ms. Stedman, so you did. You explained that while the cafeteria was not supposed to make money serving the employees, it was not supposed to lose money. She promised to watch costs closely, and the meeting ended.

Soon after the meeting, Ms. Stedman increased prices on all items served on the average of 20 percent. The employees protested vigorously. In fact, a delegation of them visited you in your office. They asked for an explanation. The increases could not be justified by increased food costs, they argued, and you had to agree with them. You then went back to Ms. Stedman to discuss the problem further.

At this meeting you got into the specifics of her operation. A review of her purchases showed that she bought unusually expensive foods—in some cases, gourmet foods. Some of the foods she sold below cost; others she sold above cost. There was little logic to her pricing. Apparently, she had little ability to determine appropriate prices. Also, you found that she had increased the kitchen staff by one. You could not justify this addition, for there had been no increase in customers served. After pointing out these shortcomings to Ms. Stedman you left her, thinking she would change her manner of operation.

The third month was somewhat better, for the loss was only $517. Ms. Stedman did cut back on her kitchen help, and she responded to the employees' complaints by eliminating the price increases she had made. It appeared to you that she really was trying. At the end of the fourth month the loss was $1,031. Again you visited Ms. Stedman.

This time you became more convinced than ever that Ms. Stedman did not understand the economics of running a food operation. She had continued to buy exceedingly expensive foods. She had made other expensive purchases—for example, flowers for the tables totaling $290 for the month. You explained to her that the company could not continue this losing operation—that she could not be retained unless she turned things around. She responded by saying that she took pride in serving quality food. "I'll try to cut expenses," she commented, "but I won't sacrifice quality." The next month the cafeteria lost $2,317.

Now in the sixth month losses appear to be continuing, although you do not have a specific figure. Following company policy, after six months of probationary service, new employees must be reevaluated for retention. Thus you must reevaluate Ms. Stedman. You will have to let her go. To do this, you must write a memorandum to the personnel department conveying your decision and explaining and justifying it. Personnel will inform Ms. Stedman of the decision, so you will be spared that unpleasant task. Address the memorandum to Jessica Manley, who is the personnel director.

8. *Building an awareness of the need for computer security.* With all the news and headlines regarding computer viruses, businesspeople are often distracted from the real issue—computer security. Numerous leaked memos and letters may not even have been seen if the computer user was just a little more careful. Computer experts say a good part of the problem is just ignorance. Therefore, the manager of your department, Mrs. Janet Wingler, decided to enhance employee awareness by informing employees of ways for improving computer security. She asked you to write a memo identifying good practices and recommending actions employees should take immediately to improve security.

Workers need to think of a document's need for security the same way they think of security for paper documents. For example, they wouldn't leave an important contract or proposal out on their desk for the world that passes by to see. In the same way they would normally put that document in a file folder or perhaps lock it away in a drawer or file cabinet, they need to protect their computer files.

They may want to establish simple security procedures for even the day-to-day routine work. Determine who can and should have access to it. Also, identify who can give permission for others to use it occasionally. Simple password protection is often all that is needed for routine information. Files that need more security will need more sophisticated protection such as encryption or double passwords.

Screens are also sources of information leaks. When employees aren't working on their screens or when someone who doesn't need the information on the screen arrives at their desk, they may want to use a screen saver to blank out the work or switch to other work. If they leave their computer, they should probably lock the computer.

Other simple methods for improving security include implementing policies for not taking programs and files home, shredding printouts before dumping them, changing passwords regularly, and auditing the systems.

Write a clearly organized memo identifying simple yet effective security measures for computers.

9. *Participating in school mentor programs.* (Requires research) Your company works continuously to improve the quality of life in the local community. In fact, your company is known as one that is extremely community minded. Company employees regularly participate in charity events, donating both time and money. And the company's food drives at Thanksgiving and Christmas have been getting bigger every year. However, recently attention has shifted to education. Congressional reports emphasize the importance of an educated work force. Tomorrow's jobs will demand not just a literate work force but one skilled in thinking and creativity. Your supervisor, Mrs. Sharon McLaughlin, has read about the mentor programs recently instituted at the local high schools and has asked you to investigate the feasibility of your company participating in the local high schools' mentor programs.

Essentially, mentor programs are for students identified as at-risk. While these students have high ability, they are at risk of dropping out. Many come from poor or disadvantaged families. Some have low grades despite their high innate ability. There are numerous reasons these students have been identified as at-risk. Mentors encourage the students to stay in school by showing an interest in the students.

Just talking to the students on a regular basis lets them know someone cares about them. Often they don't get this at home because the parent is either absent or unable to handle the child effectively. Students are often invited to the mentor's workplace to learn what skills are needed to earn a living while contributing to the growth of business. Some mentors invite their students out to lunch or dinner; others take them to museums, trade shows, ballgames, etc. Essentially, the mentors get to know the students so they can encourage them to stay in school and learn as much as they can.

To become a mentor, one calls the local high school and talks to the sponsor of the mentor program. The sponsor will invite you to the school and give a full overview of the program. The commitment starts when the student is in the tenth grade and continues as long as the student stays in school. Mentor programs provide tremendous intrinsic satisfaction to those involved as well as visibility for the company in the community. The benefits are profound for the long-term value added to both individuals and the community.

You will investigate the feasibility of participating in such programs and report your findings in a memo report to your supervisor.

10. *Investigating the developments in new office light-*

*ing.* (Requires research) Since computers with monitors have come into the office, researchers have begun giving more attention to the importance of lighting. Lighting affects both workers' comfort and their productivity. Your supervisor, Ms. Carolynn Winship, has asked you to write a memo to your division managers reporting the latest research on the effects of various lighting and recommending actions they can take to improve both employee comfort and productivity.

You will want to include the benefits of a light bulb produced by Westgate Enterprises called the Chromalux. This bulb purifies colors, increasing black and white contrast and improving texture and detail discrimination. It comes in most sizes and styles and is designed for prolonged use. The early reports on the bulbs indicate they improve eye comfort and readability of materials with truer color. Furthermore, the bulbs increase one's ability to concentrate.

In addition to reporting on this bulb, give your managers background information on the effects of different types and levels of lighting on employees. Identify ways to arrange work areas for maximum benefit. Report on new developments and products your research uncovers as well as future developments to watch for. Be sure your memo recommends actions they can take now.

11. *Recommending the hiring of older workers.* Assume that you are the owner of a Dairy Queen franchise in your city. The president of the parent company has requested a report on whether to hire more older workers.

While you know it is the law that businesses cannot discriminate based on age, a recent study confirmed your personal observations that older workers are a good investment. Not only is their absenteeism rate lower than other groups, but their turnover rate is lower, too. They are more likely to be on time and to have flexible work schedules.

In real business settings, older workers have demonstrated they can learn new systems as quickly and as well as younger workers. And while they might take more time to handle individual transactions, they do a better job. In one company branch with workers age 50 and older, the profits were 18 percent higher than at its five other branches. Apparently, the older worker is also a better salesperson. While taking longer on each call, the older worker closes more calls successfully.

Additionally, older workers bring an experience base with them that consists of a good attitude, emotional stability, and more knowledge. These factors enable them to become productive faster and to teach or mentor others. Furthermore, their experiences allow them to be more creative and to suggest more improvements.

Also, a recent study reported that nearly two million Americans aged 50–64 are ready and able to go back to work. And Census Bureau data on the growth and projected growth of the populations over 65 indicate this segment is growing both in size and in numbers. If only a little more than one fourth of these workers were actually employed, the national output would increase over $10 billion and tax revenues would increase over $1 billion.

Many organizations are already in place to help locate these workers. The Senior Employment and Educational Service, the Professional and Executive Placement, the American Association of Retired Persons, and the Displaced Homemakers Network are just a few.

Write a letter report to the president reporting these facts and recommending that Dairy Queen hire more older workers.

12. *Recommending the best of three computer virus protection programs.* (Requires research) Whether it is the Columbus Day virus, the Friday the 13th virus (also called Jerusalem B), the Pakistani bug, or "you've just been stoned," when any of your company's computers are attacked it is a disaster. Not only is valuable work at risk of being lost or destroyed, it takes time and resources to recover from such attacks. In fact, the annual cost of removing them from systems is believed to be over $1.5 billion alone, not including data loss or downtime. Some experts predict that in five years, the costs will be between $5 and $10 billion.

When company employees share files, whether on networks or at stand-alone computers, your company resources are at risk. In fact, over 400 DOS-based viruses alone have been identified. And with data and programs now crossing platforms more readily, viruses now limited to one environment will likely be transferred.

Protecting your company resources with preventive measures is recommended. Therefore, your supervisor, Mr. James Andrews, has decided to take steps to prevent this kind of disaster. He asked you to write a report comparing the three bestselling software programs and recommending the best one for the company.

In addition to cost and basic features, he wants you to include in your report the ease of use and training needed by employees to use virus protection programs.

13. *Using a newsletter as a marketing tool.* Recent marketing research has reported that consumers

are getting tired of traditional advertising. Not only are they not responding to the ads, they are actually becoming annoyed and even insulted by some of them. Also, companies are getting extremely worried about the political correctness of their advertising. As a result they have limited the creativity of the advertising agencies, resulting in dull advertising. As Director of Marketing you recognize the importance of educating your customers and view the educational approach as appropriate to the nature of your business—discount golf equipment and apparel.

One way to educate while still keeping your firm's name in the reader's mind is through the use of newsletters. After examining your firm's database, you believe your company could produce three newsletters for different market niches—the avid golfer, the weekend golfer, and the vacation golfer. Also, you could share customer lists with other related businesses such as country clubs, health clubs, travel agents, and golfing magazines. The vice president of your firm, Mr. Terrence Lenaghan, authorized you to evaluate the feasibility of adding such a tool to your marketing plan. He asked you to report on both the cost and content of the newsletters.

If the newsletters were purely informational, you might even ask the readers to subscribe. In such a case, your advertising would be minimal, but so would the expenses since the subscription rates would cover the bulk of the cost. In fact, your research shows that by collecting less than $10 from expected subscribers (10 percent of your customers), you could break even by running just one quarter-page ad per four-page newsletter. This kind of advertising would be relatively easy to obtain since the advertiser would be getting the whole audience without distractions from other advertisements.

Articles included might be strictly objective, evaluating new equipment from several manufacturers. Or they might present a variety of opinions from various recognized experts. Other articles could be on self-help topics with ideas such as how to choose your clubs more effectively under a variety of conditions. Tips and tricks are always favorites of readers. Initially, your current copywriters and salespeople could work together to select the content and create the copy. Eventually, you could invite the readers to contribute some of the material and some could be invited from guest experts or from the companies whose products you sell. The labor cost would be absorbed by the marketing department, which would assign the editing and writing to those with the best skills. Since this tool would be replacing some of your traditional advertising, no additional funds need be allocated for this project.

A variety of newsletters are already available for other businesses. Everyone from real estate agents to accountants to software companies is finding this tool an effective one. However, with so many out there, you realize your product has to be a good one or it will have limited impact. In some ways, you need to think of it as a value-added commodity. It increases the satisfaction with your firm while keeping customers informed of new products and accessories. The newsletter is a marketing tool intended to both educate and sell the reader.

Write a memo to the vice president of your firm, evaluating the cost and content and recommending this new form of advertising be adopted immediately.

14. *Choosing the charities for this year's company giving program.* Each year your company chooses a new charity as the sole beneficiary of regular company-sponsored giving. In addition to receiving direct donations from your company and its employees, the charity receives funds from employee-organized 10K run/walks, weekly bake sales, and all profits from a small company store. During their fund drives, several of these charities solicit your employees for help in telephoning potential donors as well as answering phones, running computers, and putting mailings together.

Usually your workers vote for one charity from a list of all charities suggested by other employees. Last year's charity, however, came under attack from the local press for being inefficient in its use of funds, generating negative publicity for your company's sponsorship of it. So your boss has decided to help employees make a better choice by giving them information on how various charities spend their funds. He has asked you to write a memo report to all employees with information on how well various charities spend their money.

You decided to use some of the information from an article in *Forbes*. You selected the companies from the *Forbes* list that have appeared on your company's ballots over the last five years. Be sure to explain that the program commitment index shows how much of total spending goes to support the purpose of the organization while the fundraising efficiency index shows how much of the funds raised solely from the general public support the purpose of the organization.

Write this informational report as clearly as you can, recognizing that its readers will be employees at all levels in the organization.

### Charity Checklist[1]

| Direct Public Support $ Million | Organization | Program Commitment Index | Fundraising Efficiency Index |
|---|---|---|---|
| 288 | American National Red Cross | 89 | 92 |
| 282 | American Cancer Society | 42 | 82 |
| 136 | American Heart Association | 79 | 76 |
| 108 | Muscular Dystrophy Association | 67 | 79 |
| 87 | March of Dimes Foundation | 53 | 88 |
| 55 | Disabled American Veterans | 70 | 65 |
| 46 | Mothers Against Drunk Drivers | 70 | 75 |
| 35 | Greenpeace USA | 55 | 74 |
| 25 | National Merit Scholarship Corp. | 97 | 98 |
| 22 | United States Olympic Committee | 80 | 75 |
| 13 | Environmental Defense Fund | 78 | 80 |
| 11 | Sierra Club | 66 | 54 |
| 7 | American Foundation for AIDS Research | 86 | 88 |
| 3 | National Kidney Foundation | 88 | 87 |

[1] James Cook, "Charity Checklist," *Forbes*, October 28, 1991, pp. 180–184.

15. *Redesigning the company recruiting brochure.* As special assistant to the vice president of human resources at Sunbelt Realtors, you have an interesting assignment to deal with today. Your boss, Danielle Brentz, wants to redesign the company recruiting brochure to make it more up-to-date. But she doesn't know exactly what points to emphasize in the newly structured promotional piece. Thus, she lays it on the line to you with these instructions: "Find out what college students today want to know about us. We'll need to determine that before we can decide anything about how we promote the company in the employment market this year."

Ms. Brentz goes on to say that your printers will decide on the physical format of the brochure; so you won't be concerned with such things as paper, color, format, design, and such. You will concern yourself with the contents of the brochure and the proportion and emphasis that the contents receive.

To get the data you need to answer Ms. Brentz's questions, you think first of constructing a questionnaire and sending it to a selected sample of college students at universities where you recruit heavily. But getting results this way is costly; so before you design such a study, you decide to check with sources that might collect such data in the course of their normal operations. The College Placement Service Bureau is one organization that you determine might provide the information you need.

A quick call to their central headquarters reveals that they do indeed collect information from graduating seniors each year—and rather extensively. The secretary to whom you talk agrees to fax you their most recent report (15 pages of tables) based on a random sample of 1,500 students throughout the United States and Canada. As you sift through the faxed pages you received, you notice the following data:

**Types of Information Most Preferred from Company Brochures**

| | |
|---|---|
| What day-to-day job will entail | 56% |
| Starting salary | 45 |
| Where company is located | 43 |
| Training policy | 36 |
| Promotion opportunities | 28 |
| Degree/discipline required | 25 |
| Long-term pay and benefits | 23 |
| How much responsibility/how early given | 17 |
| Overseas work/foreign travel | 10 |
| Size of organization | 8 |
| History of organization | 8 |

To be sure, the facts are ideal for your use. And you will use them to form the basis of a memo report that you will write to Ms. Brentz.

The facts, however, are only part of the report story. You will need to analyze the facts (tell what they mean) as well before you derive conclusions to give to Ms. Brentz. Because she is interested in the answers to her questions, you will write the memo in the direct order. Prepare the report that will give Ms. Brentz the information she wants about the content of Sunbelt Realtors' recruitment brochure.

16. *Writing an evaluation report on Russell Snyder.* You are sales manager for Capital Investment Inc.'s Region 6. It is time to write annual evaluation reports on your subordinates.

Capital Investment's evaluation reports are narrative. And they are not the sugar-coated types written at many companies. They are honest and objective. They praise when praise is deserved. They condemn when condemnation is justified. Their goal is to be constructive. These evaluation reports become a part of each person's permanent personnel file. In addition, the subordinates who are evaluated receive copies of them.

Presently, you are working on the report for Russell Snyder, your newest salesperson. Your garbled notes on him are as follows:

More concerned with sales volume then service. Excellent personality—pleasant mannerisms, good conversational skills, outgoing. Have received some reports that he is too aggressive. (Reports investigated and appear to be valid.) A hardworking and diligent performer. Sales volume for year was $210,000 ($18,000 above quota). Productive customer accounts increased from 73 to 82. Even so, he appears to go after the high-volume orders and big-ticket items. His calls on smaller accounts are irregular compared to those on larger accounts. He could improve his manner of dress to reflect the conservative, businesslike image of the company (add details to support this point).

Now, you will organize these items into an orderly and meaningful report. You will use the company's standard memorandum. (If you have access to it, assume the report will be prepared and transmitted through company E-mail). Address the report to Mr. Snyder. And identify the subject as "Annual Performance Evaluation of Russell Snyder."

17. *Investigating a personnel problem in department 5-B.* Today's assignment in your role as special assistant to Dean Polanski, director of employment relations of Magnum Travels, takes you to department 5-B. Your objective is to investigate charges brought to you by Carlos Rozario, the union steward who represents the people of this department. According to Rozario, union members in department 5-B have been discriminated against in the awarding of overtime work. Nonunion workers have been getting the lion's share of overtime.

On arriving at the department, you discuss the matter with the department's supervisor, Sylvia DeWitt. DeWitt's version of the story goes like this: Of the eight workers in the department, five are members of the union and three are not. The three nonunion people have had more overtime than the others, but they deserve it. DeWitt claims that she gives overtime on the basis of seniority and productivity—nothing else. This policy, she points out, is permitted in the contract with the union. If the nonunion people got most of the overtime, DeWitt says, it is because they have seniority and are better workers.

After talking to DeWitt, you go to the files that contain the department's records. Here you find data that should prove or disprove DeWitt's claim and, in fact, should point to the solution of the whole problem. After an hour or more of poring over these records of the past six months, your summary notes look like this:

| Employee and Union Status | Hours of Overtime Work | Years Employed | Productivity (Average Daily Units Performed) | Percent Rejection (Not Meeting Inspection) |
|---|---|---|---|---|
| James Addison (U) | 0 | 14 | 30 | 0.08 |
| Cynthia Webb (U) | 0 | 1 | 21 | 0.09 |
| Kenneth Harvey (U) | 10 | 3 | 32 | 0.07 |
| Willie Wolcott (U) | 60 | 8 | 26 | 0.01 |
| Maria Shulman (U) | 60 | 7 | 30 | 0.03 |
| Ramona Gomez (NU) | 40 | 35 | 26 | 0.02 |
| Tim Sheppard (NU) | 70 | 17 | 35 | 0.03 |
| David Bates (NU) | 90 | 12 | 43 | 0.03 |

* U, union; NU, nonunion

Now your task is to analyze these data and to present your finding to Mr. Polanski in the form of the standardized memorandum report used by the company. In addition to analyzing the data, you will recommend a course of action on the problem.

18. *Writing an inspection report on the cleanliness of a service station.* (Requires research) Assume that you are a management trainee for International Oil Company. Today, you are assigned to work with Nicole Wilensky, director of customer services. Wilensky's job is mainly that of trying to get managers of the company's service stations to be more customer oriented. Especially has she been working to get the managers to keep up the physical appearance of these stations. In fact, for the past month, she has been conducting a "clean station" campaign. It is your belief that a neat, attractive physical facility will mean that customers are treated more courteously as well.

So far, the campaign has produced good results. Customer opinion reports (forms placed in restrooms and on checkout counters to be filled out and mailed in by customers) have been most complimentary on this point. But as might be expected, a few negative reports have come in. Wilensky assigns you the task of checking them out.

Specifically, your task is to go to select stations, posing as a customer. While there, you will inspect the whole operation for its neatness and cleanliness. Then you will write a memorandum report on each station summarizing your findings. (For this assignment, select a station in your locale and inspect it. Prepare a report that summarizes your observations.)

Note: This assignment can be adapted to other establishments such as hotels/motels, fast-food operations, convenience stores, and such.

19. *Recommending an equipment purchase for Worldwide Travel's home office.* (Requires research) As office manager in charge of a staff of 16 at the home offices of Worldwide Travels, you have just had a visit from Vice President Judith Carreras, your boss. Ms. Carreras reported that funds have been made available for purchasing _____ (copiers, dictating equipment, office furnishings—your instructor will specify the products). She wants you to collect information on the major brands available and to recommend the brand to be purchased.

Your procedure will be to collect all pertinent information on what you think to be the three best buys. Then you will set up what you believe to be the logical bases of comparison for the products. After that, you will compare the different brands on the bases you select. Lastly, you will arrive at your recommendation. You will present your evaluation and recommendation to Ms. Carreras in Worldwide Travel's standard memorandum form. Because you believe Ms. Carreras will accept your recommendation without question, you will place it at the first of the report. You will still need to present the facts and their analysis to support your beginning recommendation.

20. *Selecting the best laundry service for De De's Cafeterias.* Today, you are in the position of a management consultant hired by De De's Cafeterias of Chicago. There are five locations throughout the greater Chicago area. One of the many problems you have been asked to investigate (and solve!) for De De's is how the company

should handle its linen and laundry. Specifically, the company wants to know whether they should own their own cloth equipment and have it laundered. Or should they rent the cloth equipment?

To answer these questions, you gather data to support both sides of the argument. First, De De's management will need about $6,000 worth of cloth equipment as an initial investment and its life expectancy is about two years. The laundry rate for this equipment is $95 per month, including pickup and delivery.

On the other hand, weekly costs of renting the comparable equipment needed are as follows:

| | | |
|---|---|---|
| 540 | 54" tablecloths | @$ .36 each |
| 2,100 | napkins | @$3.75 per 100 |
| 175 | aprons | @$ .75 each |
| 84 | dresses | @$1.50 each |
| 60 | coats (waiters) | @$1.25 each |
| 140 | dish towels | @$ .20 each |

Now that you have the data collected, your task is to analyze them, compare alternatives, and select one to recommend to President Michael Eubanks. Do all of these things in a memorandum using the direct order of presentation.

21. *Selecting a site for a Jimmy Jack store.* As assistant to the president of Jimmy Jack, Inc., a national chain of drive-in convenience stores featuring gasoline, groceries, and fast-food items, you must select a site for the location of a new store in Metro City. You have collected the following information on three locations that are suitable.

### STEMMONS FREEWAY AND NORTHWOOD DRIVE
Commercial area. Lot 150 × 100 feet. Corner location. Cost: $65,000. Traffic count per day (7 A.M. to 9 P.M.): 4,200 cars. Distance from nearest company store: 3.1 miles.

### 120 BELTLINE ROAD
Commercial area. Lot 200 × 100 feet. Noncorner location. Cost: $55,000. Traffic count per day: 9,000 cars. Distance from nearest company store: 3.9 miles.

### PRESTON ROAD AND MAPLE BOULEVARD
Commercial area. Lot 150 × 150 feet. Corner location. Cost: $75,000. Traffic count per day: 6,500 cars. Distance from nearest company store: 2.1 miles.

Your job is to evaluate these sites and to recommend one of them to the company president, Peter Gianetti. You will present your recommendations and analyses in a direct-order memorandum report.

## INTERMEDIATE-LENGTH REPORTS

22. *Comparing lease and purchase data for three automobiles.* For reasons of economy, E. A. Chenault and Company (a major pharmaceutical manufacturer and distributor) has decided to stop furnishing automobiles to its salespeople. Instead, it will pay them $.28 per mile for company travel in their personal automobiles. This amount, company management believes, is sufficient to cover the costs of ownership and operation.

As might be expected, the announcement was not well received by some of the salespeople. In fact, a group of them visited the office of Charlotte Bates, the vice president for sales, to voice their displeasure. Soon after this visit, Ms. Bates (you are her assistant) called you into her office and assigned you a task relating to the problem. She explained her assignment in these words:

"No doubt you know that some of our salespeople aren't happy about losing their company cars and getting their own. Can't blame them. But we can't reverse the decision. We must cut expenses, and I am convinced this is one way to do it.

"What we can do, though, is help the salespeople by giving them useful information. Some of them have raised the question of whether they should buy or lease. As you may know, many dealers are pushing leasing now, and some claim it beats buying. I want you to get information that will help the salespeople decide. Select three or so cars—cars varying in price level because we don't know how much our people will want to pay. It's their decision. For these cars, find out the costs of leasing and of buying. Analyze the information. Then come up with a recommendation—or recommendations.

"Write up your work in report form and address it to the salespeople. We'll distribute it to them. Make the report easy to understand and as helpful as you can make it. Maybe some visuals will help."

Following the meeting, you selected three automobiles for analysis. Then you went to dealerships handling them and got cost information for buying and leasing. Your information is summarized in Table 2. (The automobile brands are not identified, but you may choose to use realistic brand names.)

In addition to this specific information, your

**TABLE 2 (Problem 22)** Comparison of Lease and Purchase Data for Three Automobiles

|  | Automobile A | | Automobile B | | Automobile C | |
|---|---|---|---|---|---|---|
|  | 36-Mo. Lease | 36-Mo. Purchase | 36-Mo. Lease | 36-Mo. Purchase | 36-Mo. Lease | 36-Mo. Purchase |
| Purchase price |  | $16,305 |  | $11,361 |  | $19,557 |
| Monthly payment | $270 | $448* | $158 | $280* | $316 | $600* |
| Cash down payment | $3,000 | $3,000 | $2,500 | $2,500 | $1,700 | $1,700 |
| Security payment* | $300 | NA | $175 | NA | $325 | NA |
| Total cash at inception | $3,541 | $3,448 | $2,833 | $2,500 | $3,024 | $1,700 |
| Total amount payments | $9,734 | $16,131 | $5,689 | $10,069 | $16,395 | $24,589 |
| End-of-lease purchase option | $6,853 | NA | $4,112 | NA | $8,050 | NA |
| Total mileage allowed** | 45,000 | NA | 45,000 | NA | 60,000 | NA |
| Excess mileage charge | $.10 mi. | NA | $.10 mi. | NA | $.11 mi. | NA |

\* 12.5% interest.
\*\* Company average is 21,000 miles per year.

investigation turned up other matters the salespeople should consider, especially in leasing. One is insurance. Another is tax considerations. You won't get into these matters in your report. Suggestions that the salespeople check with knowledgeable people (insurance agents, tax advisers) should be sufficient. Also, there is the matter of ownership at the end of the purchase or lease period. The purchaser owns; the leaseholder doesn't. You'll make certain that you cover this point adequately, for it makes a big difference at the end of the 36-month period.

Now write the report.

23. *Evaluating changes in hospitalization payments relating to "high-risk factors."* The Dependable Insurance Company is a major supplier of health-care insurance for business organizations. Two years ago the company began a hard-hitting campaign to educate its policyholders on the so-called "high-risk factors" related to hospitalization expense (smoking, alcohol, seat belt use, hypertension, and diet). The objective was to make these people more conscious of these dangers to their health and to get them to take corrective actions. The end result would be healthier policyholders and lower hospitalization expenditures.

Now at the end of the second year, Dependable management feels good about the campaign. As Alexander P. Percy (the president) explained to you (his assistant), "All the reports I have heard are positive, but these are primarily reports based on impressions. I have seen nothing definite—no supporting facts and figures. I want you to look into this matter for me. Find the facts—actual payouts of claims. Compare the year just completed with the year before we started the campaign. Analyze what you find, and give me the information in a report."

Mr. Percy continued his instructions with these words of caution: "Now, we can't take credit for all the improvements, if we find any. Other forces have been at work. For example, a massive national movement toward exercising and improving diet habits has been going on. But we've been a part of it. I am not so much concerned about who gets the credit as I am about whether people are beginning to take steps to improve their health. Address the report to me, but keep in mind that others will read it. We'll probably duplicate it for distribution to all senior administrators."

Following Mr. Percy's instructions, you got the payment records from the claims department (Table 3). Now you must interpret them. As you do, keep in mind Mr. Percy's precautionary instructions. Because this is a report that will get good exposure for you throughout the company, you'll give it your very best effort. You will use visuals wherever they support your major findings. And you'll give the report a makeup appropriate for its importance.

24. *Reporting city employees' viewpoints to council members.* Assume that your college work is behind you and you have been hired as a personnel specialist for the city government of Bigg City.

**TABLE 3 (Problem 23)** Hospitalization Costs Associated with High-Risk Factors per 100,000 Insured. Last Year and Two Years Ago

| Risk Factor | Last Year | Two Years Ago* |
|---|---:|---:|
| **Smoking** | | |
| Respiratory system cancer | $ 897,806 | $ 919,477 |
| Lip, oral cavity, and pharynx cancers | 105,580 | 121,490 |
| Bladder cancer | 42,741 | 37,219 |
| Chronic lung disease | 527,833 | 593,778 |
| Ischemic heart disease | 1,504,627 | 1,478,878 |
| | 3,078,587 | 3,150,843 |
| **Alcohol** | | |
| Cirrhosis | 77,840 | 79,431 |
| Injuries, alcohol-related accidents | 561,277 | 603,778 |
| | 639,117 | 683,209 |
| **Seat Belt Use** | | |
| Injuries sustained from seat belts not in use | 591,162 | 627,383 |
| **Hypertension** | | |
| Ischemic heart disease | 1,516,321 | 1,637,411 |
| Essential and secondary hypertension | 110,218 | 121,394 |
| | 1,626,539 | 1,758,805 |
| **Diet** | | |
| Colo-rectal cancer | 46,558 | 58,217 |
| Breast cancer | 62,187 | 70,919 |
| Ischemic heart diseases, cholesterol related | 397,391 | 413,307 |
| | 506,136 | 542,443 |
| Total all costs from high-risk factors | $6,441,541 | $6,762,683 |

* Adjusted for inflation.

Soon after being hired, you learned that conditions are not ideal among city employees. They have not had a raise in four years, and prospects for getting a raise now are not good. In fact, some members of the city council have stated publicly that some layoffs might be needed to balance the budget for the coming year.

Not all council members have taken this view, however. Today three of them came into the personnel director's office to express an opposing position and seek some information. As one of them put it, "We are aware of your situation and want to help. We know that you people are doing a good job under trying circumstances. If you will help us get some supporting information, we think we can work this thing out."

In the discussion that followed, the council members explained that it would be helpful if the department conducted a survey of city government workers. The survey would gather information that could be used to support the government workers' case. As the council members explained it, a survey could get information on matters such as the adequacy of resources with which the workers work, job satisfaction, and viewpoints about the pay increase.

You were selected to conduct the survey. So following the meeting you met with Alice Timmons, who appeared to be the leader of the three council members, and worked out a simple questionnaire. You sent the questionnaire to all 2,398 city employees. A week later, when you had to cut off responses, 1,002 (41.8 percent) had responded. Next, you tabulated the answers by the questions asked (see Table 4).

Your next task is to interpret your findings. That is, you will give them meaning as they relate to the city's current problem. Then you will present your findings and your interpretations in a report that you will address to Ms. Timmons and the other two council members (Woodrow T. Wardlow and Maxine A. Shannon). Although you must give the report rush treatment, you will not sacrifice quality. You will give it the makeup the situation requires. And you will use graphics wherever they will help to communicate the report in-

**TABLE 4 (Problem 24)** Responses of Bigg City Workers to a Survey on Employment Viewpoint

How would you rate the amount of resources allocated to your department to perform its services?
- 24.1% Very inadequate to provide needed service level
- 42.4% Slightly inadequate to provide needed service level
- 25.5% Adequate to provide needed service level
- 2.3% A little in excess of what is needed
- 0.8% Considerably in excess of what is needed
- 4.8% Other*

Do you believe your department makes efficient use of its resources?
- 71.8% Yes
- 24.8% No
- 3.4% Other

What is the issue which most concerns you? (number of respondents, not percent)
- Pay raise ......................... 410
- Job security ...................... 149
- Merit increases ................... 126
- Pay equity ........................ 43
- Health insurance .................. 42
- Improved working conditions ....... 33
- To have a say ..................... 29
- Employee parking .................. 24
- Health & safety ................... 24
- Performance/evaluation ............ 21
- Personnel policies ................ 11
- Retirement ........................ 9
- Leave policies .................... 4
- Other ............................. 18
- Responses not ranked .............. 55

Do you believe an across-the-board (cost-of-living) pay raise is needed and justified for city employees next year?
- 94% Yes
- 4.1% No
- 1.9% Other*

Do you support a pay raise even if existing positions in government must be eliminated in order to pay for the raises?
- 53.2% Yes
- 36.9% No
- 9.9% Other*

What level of pay raise do you most support?
- 0.8% Less than 2%
- 12 % 2%–4%
- 53.7% 4%–6%
- 27.2% More that 6%
- 6.3% Other*

Are you proud to be an employee of Bigg City?
- 81.9% Yes
- 10.1% No
- 8 % Other*

How long have you been a City employee?
- 28.2% Less than 2 years
- 29.8% 2–5 years
- 25.5% 5–10 years
- 14.8% More than 10 years
- 1.6% Other (omitted)

What is your annual salary?
- 14.3% Less than $15,000 a year
- 56.1% $15000–$25,000 a year
- 19.4% $25000–$35,000 a year
- 8 % More than $35,000 a year
- 2.2% Omitted question

* Omitted or other answer

formation. Possibly the three council members will duplicate the report for the benefit of the other leaders at city hall.

25. *Investigating charges of sex discrimination in job pay.* As a personnel specialist for the D. E. Jeffrey Manufacturing Company, you have been assigned the task of investigating charges of sex-biased pay discrimination. The charges were made by ERA (Equal Rights for All), an association dedicated to the goals its name identifies. Although you cannot be certain, probably some of your employees have brought the matter to ERA's attention. In fact, some Jeffrey employees are known to be among the local chapter's leaders.

Jeffrey management was deeply disturbed by the charges. In the words of Alan O. Pilich, president of Jeffrey, "We have been working on this problem for the past decade. We have made good progress. We don't deserve this criticism." In spite of Mr. Pilich's words, he authorized an inquiry into the matter. You got the job.

Following suggestions of Naomi Boies, director of personnel, you began by getting pay data for the most common jobs in the five basic pay categories at Jeffrey. Then you organized this information by sex and calculated the average pay for each sex in each pay category. Because you believe that the workers' abilities could have some effect on salaries, you included the average evaluation scores received by the workers in each group. (Jeffrey evaluates on a scale of 1 to 10, with 10 being the highest.) Also, because length of time in a pay grade could indicate a sex-biased unwillingness to increase salaries, you computed averages of time spent in each pay grade.

Now you must analyze these data (summarized in Table 5) to determine whether they give evidence of sex discrimination. You will take extra precautions to be objective, for Jeffrey management wants only the truth. If discrimination is present, management will address the matter. After your analysis, you will reach a conclusion. You are not expected to recommend specific actions, but your conclusions will indicate where actions need to be taken.

You will present the information in a report form appropriate for the situation (a report addressed to the president).

26. *Determining ways to improve recycling.* (Requires research) When recycling first started in your offices, everyone was so enthusiastic. However, Don Anderson, president of the company, has noticed a decline over the past year in both the enthusiasm and in the actual amount of material being recycled. He keeps statistics on the amount of recycling done in order to show the public the company's interest in improving the environment. Therefore, he ran a questionnaire in the last company newsletter asking employees to explain why they think the figures are down.

He was impressed to discover that nearly two thirds of your employees reported they would recycle more if it were made easier. Here are the biggest problems they identified:

| Problem | Percent Identifying as a Problem |
|---|---|
| Lack of storage | 57 |
| Insect infestation | 43 |
| Bad smells | 31 |
| Difficult to separate trash | 15 |
| Bins too small | 15 |

He asked you to gather both primary and secondary information on these five problems and recommend solutions for eliminating the problems in order to make it even easier for employees to recycle. Along with your recommendations, give cost estimates for each of your recommendations.

Submit the report to your boss and to Michael Murphy, Director of Public Relations.

27. *Determining whether to lease or buy computer equipment.* As part of an internship for a small-business class you are taking, you work at a small antique boutique. Its owners have asked you to

**TABLE 5 (Problem 25)** Distribution of Employees by Sex, in Pay Grades, with Pay Averages, Months in Grade, and Evaluations

| Pay Grade & Job Title | Number | | Average Hourly Pay | | Months in Pay Grade | | Average Evaluation | |
|---|---|---|---|---|---|---|---|---|
| | Male | Female | Male | Female | Male | Female | Male | Female |
| **PG-1** | | | | | | | | |
| Assembler, light | 23 | 137 | 8.92 | 8.47 | 11.3 | 15.5 | 7.1 | 8.0 |
| Janitor | 13 | 3 | 8.83 | 8.21 | 20.5 | 19.4 | 6.9 | 6.9 |
| Material handler | 17 | 8 | 8.91 | 8.40 | 19.3 | 27.9 | 6.9 | 7.3 |
| **PG-2** | | | | | | | | |
| Assembler, heavy | 113 | 13 | 9.55 | 8.90 | 11.3 | 21.2 | 7.4 | 6.9 |
| Drill press operator | 22 | 20 | 9.66 | 9.23 | 18.7 | 22.3 | 6.9 | 6.9 |
| Inspector | 13 | 22 | 9.08 | 9.13 | 13.6 | 19.5 | 6.8 | 7.4 |
| **PG-3** | | | | | | | | |
| Press operator | 19 | 4 | 10.04 | 9.65 | 25.4 | 25.7 | 6.9 | 7.0 |
| Maintenance painter | 9 | 5 | 10.34 | 9.77 | 24.3 | 26.1 | 6.8 | 7.5 |
| **PG-4** | | | | | | | | |
| Press setup worker | 10 | 0 | 11.77 | — | 24.6 | — | 6.9 | — |
| Maintenance mechanic | 17 | 0 | 12.54 | — | 32.4 | — | 7.4 | — |
| **PG-5** | | | | | | | | |
| Maintenance electrician | 10 | 2 | 13.45 | 12.50 | 29.4 | 38.8 | 8.3 | 8.4 |
| Pipefitter | 7 | 0 | 14.08 | — | 31.4 | — | 8.4 | — |

write a report explaining and recommending whether to lease or buy a notebook computer.

Currently the antique jewelry portion of the business is booming. There seems to be a good demand for the quality pieces of which the store has a sizeable inventory. In fact, that is one reason you were invited to help run the normally family-run business. The owners plan to travel to shows around the South and Southwest this coming winter, something they haven't done in the past. In their shop, they have a personal computer they use for keeping track of their inventory and handling their bookkeeping. They have become quite dependent on it and think they'll be able to manage better on the road if they have a computer with them. So they have been looking at notebook computers.

You have been asked to help determine whether they should lease or buy a notebook computer they have their eye on. They have already selected the equipment and have decided they need this particular computer.

Your report should address the appropriateness of both the financial and business aspects. The model they have selected currently sells for $2,500. To rent the same equipment, they've found a company willing to lease it for $79 a week for six months with the option to buy it for $1,400 at the end of the lease period. Furthermore, all costs for maintenance and repair are covered under the lease arrangement. While they only know for certain that they will be exhibiting at shows this winter, the profits from the shows are expected to be considerable due to both the demand and the quality of their large inventory acquired at low prices several years ago. At the current rate of developments in technology, they anticipate the market value of a six-month-old notebook to be around 60 percent of its original price. They are currently in the 28 percent tax bracket.

Based on what you know about the current economy, forecasts for the next few years, and the antique jewelry demand forecasts, write your report clearly recommending either a lease or buy action.

28. *Evaluate the appropriateness of marketing to children.* (Requires research) You have just read in *Investor's Business Daily* of a study by Children's Market Research that reported there are 32 million U.S. children with direct spending power of $6 billion. Estimates of indirect spending power of kids are between $60 and $120 billion. Today's kids influence not only spending on toys but also food, VCRs and video rentals, vacations, and sometimes even cars.

Derrick Wingler, owner of a small store specializing in children's clothing, has solicited your opinion as an independent marketing consultant. He wants you to determine the appropriateness of targeting kids in your city.

Clothing, like food, is a necessity. Kids must have it. And the number of kids is growing. In fact, last year 4.2 million children were born, the most since 1964.

Many food companies have successfully targeted children. Conagra introduced Banquet Kid Cuisine, a microwaveable frozen dinner for kids, two years ago. Hormel sells Kids Kitchen in microwaveable cups. And Tyson offers Looney Tunes microwaveable dinners with prizes related to Looney Tunes characters. General Mills also finds this market a good one for its colored popcorn.

While children's clothes often imitate that of adults, until now your marketing has been directed at the adults who buy clothing for their children. But with the influence today's kids are asserting on their parents, the owner believes he should investigate some marketing directed precisely at them.

You decide to conduct a survey. The survey will ask a sample of parents in your city to rate the appropriateness of different kinds of ads for children's clothing, including ads in all media and ads targeted at kids and at parents. Write a report presenting your findings and recommending action for the owner.

29. *Targeting the over-65 market.* (Requires research) Assume that you are the manager of a video-rental store. Your boss, Len Johns, recently read an article about older workers starting ventures aimed at helping other seniors. They recognize that this is an often neglected market niche. One senior who spent a lifetime in the building industry opened a referral service for seniors needing home-improvement work done in their homes. Other seniors have started businesses filling out health forms for seniors. And some have even started small travel services, taking seniors on bus trips all over the country.

Now Mr. Johns wants you to evaluate targeting the senior market for video rentals. He believes video rentals would appeal to both the active senior who stays home at night as well as the less active or inactive seniors. Mr. Johns recognizes that now may be the time to reach this market since VCR prices have dropped dramatically in recent years and the ease of using them has improved. He is even considering offering tutorials for seniors, teaching them how to play the tapes, rewind them, etc.

In addition to gathering information on the basic age and income categories of this market segment, find out as much as you can about their life-styles.

Write a report to Mr. Johns explaining what your research reveals on how this market is different from your current market and how you might reach it with advertising. Then identify new services you could extend to this group. Gather your information from both secondary and primary sources. Some primary sources might include seniors with and without VCRs, active and inactive seniors, and video-rental store customers and non-customers. You might even gather information from salesclerks at your local video stores on the kinds of videos seniors rent, the times they come in to the store, and any other information you think would help you understand this market segment more.

Organize your report carefully. Be sure your recommendation is clear.

30. *Using exit interviews to reduce turnover expenses and retain employees.* (Requires research) Lately, your boss, Robert Edwards, has repeatedly mentioned his concern about the high cost of turnover. In order to reduce these costs and retain employees, he has asked you to gather information and write a report on ways your company might attack this problem.

Coincidentally, you met Mary Meersman, an industrial psychologist, at a party. While you were talking with her, you learned that her consulting firm specializes in conducting exit interviews. She told you some very interesting stories where her firm saved the company money and where her firm helped improve the internal operations of the company. Mary told you that most people leaving a company fall into two groups—the discontented and the terminated. By conducting exit interviews when employees leave or 30 to 60 days later, companies can learn a lot about their companies if the exit interviews are conducted properly. Mary says she often has learned of sexual harassment, poor training, and management problems. She also stated that, even when companies gather good information, they generally don't use it in ways that are useful. She gave you some good hints on how to gather information that is useful and how to make it meaningful to your company.

She suggests that you ask questions that generate information that is useful. Many companies during the typical 30–60-minute exit interview cover pay, benefits, management, and working conditions. But she believes they should also look at customer issues such as quality, timeliness, and value as well as the quality of management.

Also, she advises assuring the exiting employee the results are anonymous. You can ensure that they are by batching the results, sending them to superiors at regular intervals rather than as the exit interviews are conducted.

How you ask your questions also determines the usefulness of the responses. By using both measurable and open-ended questions you'll be able to gain a better idea of your company's strengths and weaknesses. The measurable questions allow you to compile statistics, drawing meaningful conclusions from the results. They also trigger thoughts in the employees for topics to comment on. The open-ended questions allow you to draw out issues that may be unique or issues you had not thought of in preparing the questions. Open-ended questions should be probing questions, questions that ask for the reasons behind statements. For example, if an employee reports leaving because the manager was difficult to work with, probing would get the employee to specify why. Perhaps the manager used drugs, was inflexible on scheduling, or never praised employees. Probing brings out the real reasons.

After you've gathered and analyzed a batch of exit interviews, Mary recommended that you send a report to key figures as well as to the managers directly involved. Several bad ratings should be noted in a manager's performance evaluation.

You realize these tips for conducting exit interviews are good ones that might solve some of your company's turnover problems. You decide to research the topic to combine what you've learned from Mary with what the literature reports. You'll organize and present your findings to your boss, identifying ways your company can begin to reduce turnover costs and retain employees.

31. *Investigating child care centers to improve job performance.* As personnel research specialist for Sterling Corporation, you've been given the task of investigating a problem long on the minds of the executive committee of the company. For quite some time, the decision-making group has been concerned about providing child care centers for various members of the company's work force. They'd like to know, before pursuing the matter

further, whether there has been any hard evidence about the effects of these centers on job performance.

After running several databases searches on the topic and reviewing the professional literature, you conclude that the evidence is spotty at best. Thus, to satisfy the executive committee's concerns about child care centers, you are going to have to conduct a study on your own that will be much more specific than any of the research evidence you've found in the literature to date.

As you think about the topic more specifically, you believe that a survey of companies who have day care centers would be your best source of information. You call 10 of the ones you know about and talk with their human resource directors. Each of them agrees to participate in the study you are designing. They do so by contributing a list of employees in their firms who have children under 13 years of age. All told, you identify 5,420 male and female employees with dependents age 13 or younger. These 5,420 employees represent 31.5 percent of the work force in the 10 firms. Next, you randomly select 540 (10 percent) to be included in your sample.

From this sample, you want to draw the information to get answers to the executive committee's concerns. Because the committee wants true bottom-line answers in terms of job-related variables, you decide to use several established work measurement scales in your questionnaire. More specifically, you decide to measure these job dimensions: stress, productivity, company image, tardiness, recruitment, scheduling flexibility, turnover, absenteeism, organizational commitment, and job satisfaction. Thus, you design your questionnaire and send it to the 540 people in your selected sample.

Two months have now passed and 351 people have returned their questionnaires (65 percent return). You have arranged the returns as shown in Tables 6 and 7, and you are ready to begin your analysis of them. You plan to present the findings in a short report form with a three-spot title page. You will emphasize the job dimensions throughout the report because they are of primary interest to the committee. Write the report using formal wording.

32. *Controlling air travel costs at Urban Developers.* Today's assignment takes you to the office of Jason Aguilar, President of Urban Developers. Mr. Aguilar has just reviewed the latest budget figures, and he's most concerned about one line item—travel expenditures. For the first six months of the fiscal year, travel costs have increased 15 percent over last year. And presently travel costs account for 12 percent of the total budget. Mr. Aguilar believes this figure is much, much too high.

Recognizing a problem and doing something about it are two different things, however. And that's where you enter the picture. Mr. Aguilar wants you to look into the matter further, as he charges you with these words: "Find out what we can do to reduce these travel costs. You might want to see what other companies are doing to control their costs."

To respond to his assignment, you decide to conduct a survey of what actions organizations are taking to control travel costs. First, you call sev-

**TABLE 6 (Problem 31)** Perception of Effects of Child Care Centers on Selected Job Dimensions

| Job dimensions | Positive effect (%) | Negative effect (%) | No effect (%) |
|---|---|---|---|
| Job satisfaction | 68 | 10 | 22 |
| Turnover | 55 | 21 | 23 |
| Tardiness | 64 | 6 | 30 |
| Absenteeism | 57 | 18 | 25 |
| Company image | 72 | 10 | 18 |
| Stress | 68 | 12 | 20 |
| Productivity | 56 | 16 | 28 |
| Organizational commitment | 64 | 10 | 26 |
| Recruitment | 72 | 5 | 20 |
| Scheduling flexibility | 62 | 8 | 30 |

**TABLE 7 (Problem 31)** Perception of Effects of Child Care Centers on Selected Job Dimensions by Demographic Variables

| Dimension | Men (%) | Women (%) | Single Parents (%) | Two-career Parents (%) | Low Income* (%) | Middle Income (%) | Upper Income† (%) |
|---|---|---|---|---|---|---|---|
| **Job satisfaction** | | | | | | | |
| Positive | 61 | 72 | 79 | 62 | 60 | 54 | 46 |
| Negative | 21 | 11 | 12 | 22 | 26 | 17 | 22 |
| No effect | 18 | 17 | 9 | 18 | 14 | 29 | 32 |
| **Commitment** | | | | | | | |
| Positive | 54 | 70 | 66 | 54 | 72 | 66 | 54 |
| Negative | 18 | 14 | 12 | 23 | 14 | 18 | 24 |
| No effect | 28 | 16 | 22 | 23 | 12 | 16 | 22 |
| **Absenteeism** | | | | | | | |
| Positive | 42 | 68 | 72 | 54 | 74 | 60 | 44 |
| Negative | 32 | 16 | 12 | 21 | 10 | 15 | 22 |
| No effect | 26 | 16 | 16 | 25 | 16 | 25 | 34 |
| **Productivity** | | | | | | | |
| Positive | 52 | 56 | 62 | 42 | 60 | 50 | 43 |
| Negative | 22 | 19 | 12 | 26 | 19 | 19 | 24 |
| No effect | 26 | 21 | 26 | 32 | 22 | 31 | 33 |

\* Lower-income level refers to salaries between $15,000 and $20,000.
˄ Middle-income level refers to salaries between $21,000 and $40,000.
† Upper-income level refers to salaries above $40,000.

eral companies and talk with their key executive personnel to determine their policies. From these conversations, you identify 10 actions that appear to be central to controlling travel costs in industry. To determine the extent of use of these actions and their effectiveness, you next design a questionnaire that you send to a large sample of companies. One part of the questionnaire asks respondents to indicate whether they take the actions that you list in their companies (a simple yes/no format is used). Another part asks respondents to rate the effectiveness of the actions to control costs—that is, whether the actions have a small, moderate, or substantial impact. As a further measure of good research design, you ask for the amount spent on travel annually so that you can divide the companies into large and small users.

It has now been six weeks since you mailed the 490 questionnaires, and you have received 239 back—a much greater return rate than you expected. You tally the data in two tables (Tables 8 and 9), and they now become the basis for a report you will prepare for President Aguilar in answer to the questions he posed.

Because of the nature of the situation, you will write the report on the formal side—without personal references. You will need to interpret the facts as well, because Mr. Aguilar expects you to give him the benefit of your best thinking on the matter. No doubt, you will find good use for graphics to help explain your interpretations, too. Use the short-report format and begin it with your conclusions (don't use recommendations because you know Mr. Aguilar likes to make his own decisions).

33. *Interpreting how company administrators view people.* It's been 10 years since you last conducted a training seminar for Professional Software Company managers on human relations skills. But Julius Vanzant, president of Professional Software, believes that now is the time to offer one again. As he tells you, the vice president for human resources at Professional Software: "When I was head of production 10 years ago, I completely changed my management philosophy because of the training. It made me look at people differently. And I needed that back then. I think that others need it now as well. As I remember, we did a survey and based our Professional Software program on the results. Maybe you could repeat that process before we plan the seminars this time around."

**TABLE 8 (Problem 32)** Actions to Control Air Travel Costs

| Action | Number Taking Action | Overall (239 firms) | Big Users* (163) | Small Users† (76) |
|---|---|---|---|---|
| Use of lowest available airfare, when feasible | 190 | 79 | 95% | 92% |
| Require employees turn in frequent-flier benefits for company use | 30 | 12 | 23 | 16 |
| Require that employees use specified travel agencies so company can obtain rebate | 148 | 62 | 85 | 61 |
| Reduced air travel | 95 | 40 | 32 | 54 |
| In-house company travel agency | 142 | 60 | 35 | 67 |
| Request that employees use frequent-flier points earned on business trips for company travel purposes | 48 | 20 | 41 | 31 |
| Review employee travel plans in advance | 122 | 51 | 48 | 61 |
| Agreements with airlines for corporate discounts | 115 | 48 | 85 | 23 |
| Establish independent group for auditing travel expenses | 69 | 28 | 44 | 27 |
| Require that employees use airlines that give frequent-flier benefits to businesses as well as individuals | 35 | 14 | 22 | 12 |

\* Big users have total annual travel costs of at least $12 million.
† Small users spend less than $12 million annually.

**TABLE 9 (Problem 32)** Effectiveness of Actions to Control Air Travel Costs (Action had "substantial impact")

| Action | Overall | Big Users | Small Users |
|---|---|---|---|
| Reduced air travel | 40 | 57% | 37% |
| In-house company travel agency | 85 | 73 | 62 |
| Use of lowest available fares, when feasible | 62 | 64 | 61 |
| Review employee travel plans in advance | 48 | 12 | 36 |
| Require that employees use specified travel agencies so company can obtain rebate | 65 | 51 | 49 |
| Establish independent group for auditing travel expenses | 33 | 32 | 36 |
| Require employees to turn in frequent-flier benefits for company use | 18 | 12 | 15 |
| Request that employees use frequent-flier points earned on business trips for company travel purposes | 19 | 18 | 16 |
| Require that employees use airlines that give frequent-flier benefits to businesses as well as individuals | 10 | 13 | 17 |
| Agreements with airlines for corporate discounts | 30 | 29 | 27 |

Back in your office, you begin searching the files for the survey that Mr. Vanzant referred to. You have been with the company only seven years; but the training and development department reports directly to you. So you ask them to help in the search of their records, too. It doesn't take long for you to find the survey completed 10 years ago.

The file on the survey that you locate indicates a relatively straightforward design to determining executive attitudes toward people and their behavior. First, there are questions about general behavior of people followed by questions about people's preferences for responsibility, leadership, change, and receptivity. Both of these sets of questions are phrased in multiple-choice format. In addition, there are nine true/false questions that seek additional opinions about people's behavioral disposition. All told, 267 respondents from a total mailing of 658 replied to the survey 10 years ago (a 40.6 percent return rate).

Because you believe the design is a good one, you decide to use the same format in the survey you will conduct this year. There will be one difference, however—the addition of various demographics that will tell you about the respondents. To begin the study, you purchase a mailing list of managers from throughout the United States and Canada from Datamatics Inc. From this list, you stratify a sample of 1,870 to reflect the demographics of age, span of control, experience, type of organization, and level of management. Then you send the questionnaire along with a cover letter to the managers in the sample.

Today, you have 751 returns (a 40.2 percent return rate); the results of the surveys are tallied in Table 10. You will use the results as the basis for a report to Mr. Vanzant. You will also use a short-report format with a four-spot title page. In the report you will need to compare many relationships—the results 10 years ago with those for this year as well as the differences between Canada and U.S. managers. You will derive conclusions with a human relations training program in mind. Throughout the report, you will need to use graphics to support the text.

Write the report for Mr. Vanzant.

34. *Designing a course for recruitment and selection.* As a member of the training and development staff at Synergy Management Consultants, you've been asked to help in the design of a new course for the company's personnel entitled "Recruitment and Selection." Part of the course will involve labor market structures, laws governing recruiting and selecting, and such. Another part will deal with recruiting and selecting techniques. And this is where you draw your report writing assignment.

It is your boss's belief—and a logical one—that the course needs to be built on solid evidence about current practices in the marketplace. One of the more important topics that you will want to include in the training classes is résumés and how to evalute them. Based on your own experience, you know that there is little empirical evidence on which to base any decision about what to look for in job market résumés. To be sure, there are good standards to follow. But these standards, you feel, need to be backed by factual support.

In order to get this factual support, you decide to conduct a survey on the subject of what experts in the employment market feel are important content items to be included in job-seeking résumés. From the national headquarters of the International Human Resources Association, you purchase a mailing list of key personnel officials (those who have hiring authority and those who are campus recruiters) in North America. From the list (which totals 5,684), you draw a random sample of 20 percent each for the two groups you want to be included—that is, 568 for hirers and 568 for recruiters.

To these two samples, you send a list of content items that could be included in a résumé. In total, you have compiled a list (which, incidentally, you sent to 17 human resource managers as a pretest) of 62 such items. You ask that respondents rank order the list and return their rankings to you.

As of today, you have received 251 (44.2 percent) and 237 (41.7 percent) returns from the hirers and recruiters, respectively. (You attribute the high return rate to the interest in the topic and the quality of the persuasive letter that accompanied the questionnaire.) You have arranged the results into two tables (Tables 11 and 12). Table 11 shows the most important content items as ranked by the two groups. Table 12 shows the content items that received lower rankings.

Because you believe these facts have importance beyond just the design of the recruitment and selection training course, you are going to write up the results of your work in a medium-length report with some formality. You will have a three-spot title page, and you will word the report without personal pronouns. On the one hand, you will interpret the results of your survey primarily for the course you are structuring. On the other, you will interpret the results in terms of what recruiters and

## TABLE 10 (Problem 33) Attitudes toward People and Their Behavioral Dispositions

|  | 10 Years Ago (Total) 267 | This Year (U.S.) 458 | This Year (Canada) 293 | This Year (Total) 751 |
|---|---|---|---|---|
| **Part I** | | | | |
| The behavior of most people in general is most influenced by | | | | |
| a. economic factors | 7% | 3% | 4% | 3% |
| b. social factors | 5 | 7 | 5 | 6 |
| c. a combination of social, economic, psychological, and biological factors | 88 | 90 | 91 | 91 |
| Most people naturally tend to be most concerned with | | | | |
| a. the desire to help others | 1 | 1 | 1 | 1 |
| b. their own needs and desires | 77 | 77 | 77 | 77 |
| c. a combination of both | 22 | 22 | 22 | 22 |
| Most people | | | | |
| a. have no ambition | 1 | 1 | 1 | 1 |
| b. have a lot of ambition | 18 | 13 | 29 | 20 |
| c. fall somewhere between the extremes | 81 | 86 | 69 | 79 |
| What is your opinion about the brightness of people? | | | | |
| a. people in general are very bright | 17 | 14 | 14 | 14 |
| b. people in general are not very bright | 8 | 4 | 13 | 8 |
| c. people in general fall between these extremes | 75 | 82 | 73 | 78 |
| **Part II** | | | | |
| How do most people react when given responsibility? | | | | |
| a. they prefer to assume a great deal of responsibility | 25% | 19% | 18% | 19% |
| b. they dislike responsibility | 22 | 19 | 34 | 27 |
| c. they fall between the extremes | 53 | 62 | 48 | 54 |
| Most people | | | | |
| a. prefer to be leaders | 20 | 14 | 27 | 19 |
| b. prefer to be followers | 37 | 41 | 41 | 41 |
| c. fall between the extremes | 43 | 45 | 32 | 40 |
| Most people | | | | |
| a. tend to resist change | 85 | 86 | 81 | 84 |
| b. welcome change | 1 | 0 | 2 | 1 |
| c. fall between the extremes | 14 | 14 | 17 | 15 |
| Most people | | | | |
| a. are very gullible | 30 | 19 | 33 | 25 |
| b. are very hardheaded | 7 | 5 | 16 | 9 |
| c. fall between the extremes | 63 | 76 | 51 | 66 |
| **Part III:** True | | | | |
| False | | | | |
| a. Behavior of people is influenced by psychological, social, biological, and economic factors | 95% | 94% | 98% | 96% |
|  | 5 | 6 | 2 | 4 |
| b. People want to do what's right, but are blocked by their personalities, childhood experiences, and circumstances beyond their control | 83 | 71 | 89 | 78 |
|  | 17 | 29 | 11 | 22 |
| c. People tend to be concerned about their own needs and objectives | 96 | 92 | 91 | 91 |
|  | 4 | 8 | 9 | 9 |
| d. Some people lack ambition, dislike responsibility, and prefer to be led, some are the opposite, and most fall somewhere in between | 73 | 88 | 82 | 85 |
|  | 27 | 12 | 18 | 15 |

**TABLE 10 (Problem 33)** (concluded)

|  | 10 Years Ago (Total) 267 | This Year (U.S.) 458 | This Year (Canada) 293 | This Year (Total) 751 |
|---|---|---|---|---|
| **Part III:** True (Continued) <br> False |  |  |  |  |
| e. People tend to be resistant to change | 97 | 97 | 91 | 94 |
|  | 3 | 3 | 9 | 6 |
| f. People are gullible at first but most catch on quickly | 58 | 70 | 70 | 70 |
|  | 42 | 30 | 30 | 30 |
| g. People are not very bright | 12 | 8 | 20 | 12 |
|  | 88 | 92 | 80 | 88 |
| h. People easily fall prey to charlatans & demagogues | 34 | 25 | 41 | 31 |
|  | 66 | 75 | 59 | 69 |
| i. Most people are bright enough | 67 | 88 | 81 | 85 |
|  | 33 | 12 | 19 | 15 |
| **Part IV** |  |  |  |  |
| Your age: |  |  |  |  |
|   a. under 25 | — | 1% | 4% | 2% |
|   b. 25–35 | — | 25 | 42 | 32 |
|   c. 36–45 | — | 35 | 32 | 34 |
|   d. over 45 | — | 39 | 22 | 32 |
| No. of persons reporting to you directly: |  |  |  |  |
|   a. 1–3 | — | 40 | 26 | 34 |
|   b. 4–6 | — | 23 | 34 | 28 |
|   c. 7–12 | — | 20 | 18 | 19 |
|   d. 13 or more | — | 17 | 22 | 19 |
| No. of years you have managed people: |  |  |  |  |
|   a. 1–3 | — | 18 | 27 | 21 |
|   b. 4–6 | — | 16 | 22 | 19 |
|   c. 7–10 | — | 17 | 24 | 20 |
|   d. 11 or more | — | 49 | 27 | 40 |
| Your type of enterprise: |  |  |  |  |
|   a. finance | — | 8 | 5 | 7 |
|   b. commercial | — | 7 | 13 | 9 |
|   c. health services | — | 2 | 2 | 2 |
|   d. government | — | 7 | 0 | 4 |
|   e. manufacturing | — | 48 | 42 | 46 |
|   f. high-technology | — | 10 | 12 | 10 |
|   g. other businesses | — | 16 | 20 | 18 |
|   h. other institutional | — | 2 | 6 | 4 |
| Your organizational level: |  |  |  |  |
|   a. top (report to or are the top manager) | — | 26 | 28 | 26 |
|   b. middle (if not a or c) | — | 60 | 53 | 58 |
|   c. 1st level (directly supervise nonmanagement) | — | 14 | 19 | 16 |

**Country of which I am a citizen**
U.S., 59%; Non-U.S., 41% of this year total

**Country where I live presently**
U.S., 61%; Non-U.S., 39% of this year total

**Country in which I was born**
U.S., 57%; Non-U.S., 43% of this year total

**TABLE 11 (Problem 34)** Résumé Content Ranked Important by 50 Percent or More of Hiring Officials

| Résumé Content Items in Order of Importance | Hiring Officials | Collete Recruiters |
|---|---|---|
| 1. Name | 99.6% | 99.0% |
| 2. Degree | 99.5 | 98.3 |
| 3. Name of college | 99.1 | 98.1 |
| 4. Employing company | 98.7 | 97.1 |
| 5. Job held (title) | 98.6 | 99.5 |
| 6. Telephone no. | 98.4 | 97.3 |
| 7. Dates of employment | 98.3 | 98.6 |
| 8. Address | 97.1 | 99.0 |
| 9. Duties—work experience | 96.2 | 98.3 |
| 10. Major | 96.0 | 95.9 |
| 11. Special aptitudes/skills | 94.5 | 90.7 |
| 12. Achievements—work experience | 93.1 | 91.9 |
| 13. Previous employers—references | 91.4 | 90.2 |
| 14. Date of graduation—college | 90.4 | 95.8 |
| 15. Job objective | 91.5 | 87.8 |
| 16. Career objective | 89.8 | 90.0 |
| 17. Years attended—college | 89.3 | 92.6 |
| 18. Summary of qualifications | 86.4 | 83.9 |
| 19. Awards, honors | 85.6 | 85.7 |
| 20. Willingness to relocate | 84.2 | 81.2 |
| 21. Combined job and career objective | 80.8 | 79.9 |
| 22. Professional organizations—extracurricular activities | 79.3 | 93.3 |
| 23. Grade-point average | 77.6 | 90.5 |
| 24. Minor | 77.2 | 94.9 |
| 25. References supplied on request | 76.2 | 84.9 |
| 26. Military experience | 75.9 | 77.8 |
| 27. Current organization memberships | 71.0 | 83.4 |
| 28. Professors—references | 70.0 | 79.7 |
| 29. Reasons for leaving job | 69.9 | 67.8 |
| 30. Scholarships—college achievements | 67.1 | 84.8 |
| 31. Student government activities | 66.0 | 87.4 |
| 32. Work supervisor names | 62.2 | 61.2 |
| 33. References—completeness of data | 61.5 | 59.6 |
| 34. Name of high school | 60.3 | 57.3 |
| 35. Publications | 59.9 | 58.7 |
| 36. Résumé title | 58.7 | 45.6 |
| 37. Community involvement | 58.2 | 63.1 |
| 38. Date of graduation—high school | 53.0 | 36.1 |
| 39. Salaries received for jobs | 51.6 | 39.5 |
| 40. Diploma—high school | 51.3 | 43.2 |

executives look for in new college graduates. Several of your human resource executives give speeches to college groups, and you believe they could find good use for your results.

Be sure to use graphics in the report. Write it for Victor Frerichs, vice president of human resources, Synergy Management Consultants.

35. *Diagnosing a communication problem.* (Requires research) Today's report assignment casts you into the role of director of communication at _____ (a business in your locale). In addition to providing financial data to investors, you also do many other things. One of these activities is to diagnose any actual or potential communication problem that the company might have. At the moment, you are concerned about _____, (writing apprehension, telephone apprehension, oral reporting practices, interpersonal styles, listening behavior, etc.—your instructor will specify the problem.) To properly solve the problem, you will have to do four things.

**TABLE 12 (Problem 34)** Résumé Content Ranked Important by 25 to 50 Percent of Hiring Officials

| Résumé Content Items in Order of Importance | Hiring Officials | College Recruiters |
|---|---|---|
| 1. Hobbies/interest | 48.8% | 54.6% |
| 2. Health | 48.2 | 29.8 |
| 3. Personal references | 47.2 | 60.2 |
| 4. Yearbook editor, etc.—college | 47.1 | 73.5 |
| 5. Social organizations—college | 46.0 | 81.3 |
| 6. Years attended—high school | 45.4 | 45.8 |
| 7. Athletic involvement—college | 43.3 | 62.3 |
| 8. Social security no. | 43.1 | 28.9 |
| 9. Band, choral group, etc.—college | 39.8 | 54.3 |
| 10. Awards, honors—high school | 38.7 | 41.2 |
| 11. Grade average—high school | 38.4 | 40.0 |
| 12. Professional organizations—high school | 30.4 | 44.5 |
| 13. List of college courses taken | 27.1 | 75.8 |

First, you will have to research the nature of the problem. This step will take you to your library to do background research on it. After you are thoroughly familiar with the problem, you will proceed to the next phase in the problem-solving process. The second step will involve selecting a measuring instrument for the problem that you have researched. You should only use one that presently exists in the literature and is well established. You will not concern yourself with the preparation of a new measuring instrument. Remember, too, that some instruments require that you get author permission to use them. You will need to do this to legally and ethically administer the instrument.

The third step will require that you administer the instrument in an ongoing organization that your instructor selects. In addition, you will need to tally the results in an orderly fashion so that they can be used in the last step.

The fourth step will require that you write your results in a medium-length report with some formality requirements. You will use graphic aids, and you will write without personal references. The report will have a four-spot title page and you will address it to the president of the company.

Write the report that results from this problem situation.

(Note: This report problem can be repeated for as many communication problems and measuring instruments as can be identified.)

## PROPOSALS

36. *Proposing an environmental "offensive" for a company.* For this problem you are the director of public relations for _____ (a manufacturing plant in your area or a place designated by your instructor). Today at the weekly staff meeting, Scott Corley, the company's president, opened with some words about the company's deteriorating image in the community. As he put it, "We are seen as major polluters. As you know, we have reduced emissions over half, and we'll reduce them more by the end of the year. We've publicized all this as much as we can through newspaper and television advertising. Even so, the public remembers us as we were. We've got to do something to change our image."

After some discussion of what could be done, you expressed your ideas. You made the point that the company should take steps to become the community leader in environmental concerns. "We should take the offensive," as you expressed it.

When you were asked to give specific examples of what you were suggesting, you were not at a loss for words. You said there were many things the company could do. For example, it could become a depository for recycling newspapers, glass, and aluminum cans. You pointed out that currently the community has only limited facilities for collecting materials for recycling. You explained how the company could set up bins at the plant entrance for people to deposit the items for recycling.

You even suggested that it could establish and service collection points throughout the community.

Next you gave the example of how the company could launch a campaign against highway litter. It could organize teams of its own employees as well as induce service organizations, student groups, and such to clean up the roads and neighborhoods. You also said that the company could organize similar activities to clean up area lakes and streams.

You were ready to make additional suggestions when Mr. Corley stopped you. "I like your suggestions," he said. "No doubt you have other ideas. I'd like for you to think through the matter, develop a plan, and write it up in proposal form. Make copies for all of us. We'll discuss it next week."

Additional discussion followed. Much of it concerned how much the program would cost. Even though most of what you propose would be absorbed by your department's budget, you would incur some additional costs. Now you must do as your president instructed: "think through the matter, develop a plan, and write it in proposal form."

37. *Presenting a course in sound business management for ASB members.* As president of Business Training and Consulting Associates, you are looking over an invitation from the executive secretary of the Association for Small Businesses to submit a proposal for a course. (ASB is an organization of owners and administrators of small businesses.) Concerned about the high rate of failure among its smaller members, ASB wishes to offer them a comprehensive course on the essentials of sound business operations. The plan is to initially offer the course in a major metropolitan area. Then, if the course proves to be successful, it would be offered in other areas. A successful course, the invitation states, could be offered indefinitely—as long as demand exists. And ASB's survey of its membership shows high interest in such a course.

As described in the invitation, the course would be limited to 25 students paying $400 each. ASB would publicize the course, and take care of registration, money collecting, and such. The length of the course has not been decided, and would be determined by the proposal accepted. As stated in the announcement, the total hours of instruction should be structured to fit into the $10,000 in revenues the course will bring in. As for times for the instruction, the invitation specified either evenings or weekends. Concerning frequency and length of the sessions, the invitation suggested that the groups submitting proposals "use their best professional judgment based on experience." The invitation also noted that the matter of what to teach was left to the judgment of those submitting proposals. It did, however, suggest that the curriculum include "whatever an ongoing small-business person needs to know."

You are excited about the prospects of getting this contract. Business has not been good for your small company in recent months. A contract such as the one ASB offers might well be the difference between success and failure. So you will submit a proposal, making sure that it gives ASB what it needs. As you plan the course, keep in mind that your four teacher-consultant employees are experts in the basic fields of marketing, finance, accounting, and management. If you need additional specialization, you can employ professors from a local university. You charge $125 an hour for your employees' services, which includes a reasonable profit for the company.

Since the invitation did not specify a form for the proposal, you will develop your own. Make certain that it includes all vital information—curriculum, times, methods of instruction, instructors' credentials, supplies needed, and such.

38. *Proposing peer review be included as part of employee performance evaluations.* Your company has been through a lot in recent years. Not only did it go through a major restructuring, but also the employees are now major shareholders in the company. How well the workers next to you perform seems to mean more now since it is directly related to your pocketbook. Therefore, you would like some say in those workers' pay and promotion decisions.

You have decided to propose to management that peer reviews be implemented as a major part of regular performance evaluations. Since the restructuring, you are working mostly as self-directed teams. It only makes sense that those closest to the work have some part in its evaluation. You think that if 80 percent of your team agrees on a particular action, management should heed it. Co-workers should get the opportunity to determine who gets raises and advances. In your proposal, give as many reader-benefit reasons for implementing this proposal as you can think of. Encourage management to implement this proposal as soon as possible.

39. *Proposing child care be added to employee benefits list.* As the director of corporate benefits at your company, write a proposal to top manage-

ment for adding child care to your employee benefits list. Not only will this help you in recruiting some of the best new employees, it will help in keeping the best.

Let your management know what has happened at some of the other companies which have already instituted some form of child-care benefits. For instance, Travelers, which pays between 10 and 30 percent of child-care costs, has seen reduced turnover. Mutual Insurance claims it has been a good recruiting tool. One company, Stride Rite Corporation, has even extended its child-care facilities to include eldercare. These intergenerational daycare centers are costly but valued by employees.

Support your proposal with other facts such as companies or businesses in your town that offer day-care benefits for employees. Include primary information when appropriate. Be sure your call for action is clear.

40. *Preparing a proposal for a company considering Centaur Hotels as a convention site.* You've only been in your job as assistant sales manager of Centaur Hotel in San Diego, California, for six months. That's been enough time, however, for you to realize that you need to attract the high volume of business Centaur Hotel needs to keep operating consistently and profitably in the future. In fact, a good part of your job involves putting together different costs and prices for your boss, Howard Carmichael, who in turn submits them to individuals and groups who are considering Centaur Hotels for various functions and activities. But the assignment that Mr. Carmichael gives you today is one that will allow you to pull a number of isolated items together in "one big job."

As Mr. Carmichael explains it, "I have a number of organizations who call me and request proposals, as you know. Most of the bigger accounts I deal with myself. But I believe I need help in servicing some of the others. I received a call today from Corporate Marketing Systems. They are considering our hotel as a convention site next year. Work up a proposal for them. I'll need it right away—by day after tomorrow—to send to them. I'm sure they're considering other locations as well."

Back in your office, you begin thinking about the items to include in the proposal. Room rates and room blocks are some things, for sure. And there are cancellation clauses, catering functions, and meeting room descriptions, too. No doubt there are other categories you will want to cover once you get into the project. Corporate Marketing Systems is not a large organization. Based on last year's convention in Denver, Colorado, they had 405 people attend. And the Tourist Bureau in Colorado reports they used 200, 315, and 235 rooms for the three days of the convention.

Think through this situation carefully and then prepare a proposal for Mr. Carmichael. Of course, Mr. Carmichael will have to approve your work. Make it good, though, because if Mr. Carmichael is pleased, you'll get other opportunities to show your stuff—which means raises and promotions.

(Note: You may want to contact a hotel to determine what areas they usually include in proposals for convention groups.)

41. *Purchasing an analyzer computer package.* As office manager for Turnkey Consultants, you are excited about the opportunity your boss gave you today. David Romano, president of Turnkey Consultants, told you that he is quite satisfied with the results of the business writing training sessions you arranged six months ago. You can take much of the credit for the success of the program because your input resulted in most of the design of the training. Each employee in the headquarters staff received 20 hours of classroom-type training from Dr. Erika Sortini, a professor of business communication at Central State University. In addition, Dr. Sortini spent another week at the company in a consultant's role reviewing correspondence files and providing tutorial, one-on-one help to anyone wanting follow-up support for the classroom-type training. Of course, the text that Dr. Sortini used as her source of reference was *Basic Business Communication,* 6th edition.

But Mr. Romano wants to reinforce that training even more. He would now like to have a common-style-analyzer computer package available to all employees in the company. But he doesn't know which one to purchase. So he turns to you for advice. Says he: "Examine four or five of the most popular style-analyzing packages and submit the best one to me. Consider this a proposal because I will likely purchase the package you select."

To begin the proposal that Mr. Romano wants, you will first have to study the most popular packages currently available on the market. A trip to the library should give you the information you need for the first stage of the proposal preparation process. (Or you might want to contact various vendors for information.) From whatever sources you use, you will decide on the "best" package available. Next, you will need to present this best style-analyzing package to Mr. Romano in the form of a written proposal. Deciding on the content of the proposal is important; most likely, at a minimum you will include cost, features of the package, compatibility with hardware capabilities, and unique characteristics. No doubt there are other topics you will include to make your proposal complete and distinct.

Prepare the proposal for Mr. Romano. You will dress it up physically and word it formally.

(Note: This assignment could be repeated for computer graphics and statistical packages as well.)

42. *Proposing that your company begin an education-support program.* As the new training director for _____ (your choice of a major company in your area) you had an interesting visit with the company president today. You presented your ideas of what you proposed to do on your job, and the president appeared to like them. The president especially liked your suggestion that the company begin a program of support to those employees who desire to further their education.

Basically, your idea is for the company to pay tuition, supplies, and fees for those who take approved courses at local colleges and trade schools. Your office would administer the program. As you see it, both the company and the employees would benefit—if the program is designed right. It would have to be restricted to course work that would increase the employee's value to the company. And, of course, satisfactory work would be required. Probably your office would have to handle course approvals and would generally police the work.

The president's final words to you were: "Write it up in the form of a proposal so I can bring it up with my staff. See if you can sell them like you sold me." So now you will have to write the proposal. Think through the idea and develop the information that will convince the staff your idea has merit. Use your imagination, but keep it logical and orderly. Organize the proposal so that the major points stand out clearly. As well as you can, use real facts concerning the appropriate schools in your area.

## PROCEDURES

43. *Developing procedures for taking elder-care leave.* Your company recently implemented an elder-care leave policy. Employees are given days and time off work to take care of elderly relatives. While this policy was not designed to do things you could do outside of work hours, it can be used to take them to doctors' appointments. It could also be used to help them select nursing homes, get work done in their homes, or just things that need to be taken care of and can only be done during regular working hours.

Write procedures for scheduling this leave. Identify how much in advance these requests must be made, what forms must be completed, who must approve them, and what, if anything, the worker must do to assure that any missed work gets taken care of appropriately.

In writing these procedures, keep them as clear as possible. Be sure to title them appropriately and include only what the reader needs to know to complete the task. Using imperative verb form and numbered or bulleted items are common for procedures. Also, adding white space between procedures makes them appear easier to follow.

44. *Writing procedures for summer work leaves.* (Response to Problem 11, Chapter 9) You have recently implemented a policy regarding the scheduling of summer work hours, addressing the problem of employees leaving on Friday afternoons and Mondays. The policy stressed fairness as well as the need to distribute the work evenly. Write procedures for requesting time off on Fridays and Mondays. Be sure to identify all steps, forms, and clearances the reader needs to take. Make the procedures as clear as possible.

45. *Developing procedures for bed and breakfast inn reimbursements.* (Response to Problem 12, Chapter 9) You are delighted management has decided to allow the use of bed and breakfast inns for overnight accommodations. In your sales region alone, many of your salespeople have told you that this policy will help them keep their expenses down, give them more flexibility in travel, and provide nice places to stay while away from home. However, as the regional manager, you need to establish a policy for reimbursement since many of the bed and breakfast inns are not set up to handle credit cards. Write procedures your salespeople need to follow to get reimbursed for out-of-pocket expenses incurred at these inns. Since your staff is already inundated with forms, make the procedures as easy and as clear as possible. You want to encourage the use of these inns, not inhibit their use with extensive paperwork.

*Optional format.* Using line-draw or the tables feature of your word processing software, design a simple form the salespeople could use. Place the procedures on the form, keeping it to one page if possible.

46. *Working out procedures for an education-support*

*program*. The education-support program you proposed to the administration (see Problem 42 for background information) was approved. Now you will need to write the procedures that employees must follow in taking advantage of it. Frankly, you had not expected approval so fast, so you have not thought through the matter. You must do this now.

You know that you will work up a document that will tell the employees exactly what steps they must take. You will cover questions such as how to get approvals, what criteria will determine approval, how payments will be made, what performance standards will be required, and much more. What you want in the end is a document that will cover all an employee needs to do to take advantage of the program.

You have much thinking to do before you begin to write.

### ■■■■■■■■■■■■■■■■■
### TOPICS FOR REPORT PROBLEMS

Following are topics that may be developed into reports of varying length and difficulty. In each case, the facts of the situation will need to be created through the student's (or the instructor's) imagination before a business-type problem exists. The information needed in most cases should be available in the library.

1. Recommend for X Company a city and hotel for holding its annual meeting of sales representatives.
2. Determine the problem areas and develop a set of rules for employees who work at home during business hours for X Company.
3. For an investment service, determine which mutual funds do better: those that invest for the long run or those that emphasize market timing.
4. What can X Company (you choose the name and industry) do to improve the quality of its product or service?
5. Investigate the problem of worker theft and recommend ways to decrease it.
6. Evaluate the impact of the European Community on X Company (you choose the name and industry) profits.
7. Determine the problems of recycling and recommend ways to overcome them.
8. Investigate the advantages and disadvantages of requiring workers to wear uniforms and recommend whether X Company should require them.
9. Advise X Company on the advantages and disadvantages of hiring student interns from the local college.
10. Evaluate and compare the economic forecasts of three leading forecasters over the past five years.
11. Advise Company X on the desirability of establishing a child-care center for the children of its employees.
12. Report to Company X management what other leading companies are doing to increase ethics consciousness among employees.
13. Report to a large chain of department stores on current means of reducing shoplifting.
14. Determine the effects of smoking on worker health and/or productivity.
15. Determine whether Company X should ban smoking in the workplace.
16. Evaluate the status of affirmative action in _____ (company, industry, country).
17. Report on the office design of the future for Company X.
18. What can Company X (you choose the type of company) do to improve productivity?
19. Determine how Company X should cope with the problem of an aging work force.
20. Evaluate the advantages and disadvantages of flextime.
21. Determine the advantages and disadvantages of fixed-rate and variable-rate mortgages.
22. Study the benefits and problems of a two-career marriage, and draw conclusions on the matter.
23. Study and report on the more popular forms of creative financing being used in real estate today.
24. Review the literature to determine the nature and causes of executive burnout and remedies for it.
25. What should Company X do about employees who have been made obsolete by technological change?
26. Your company (to be specified by your instructor) is considering the purchase of _____ (number) laptop computers for its sales representatives. Evaluate three brands, and recommend one for purchase.
27. Evaluate _____ (city of your choice) as a site for the annual meeting of a large professional association (your choice), ending with a recommendation.
28. Advise Company X (a national grocery chain) on whether to use double coupons.

29. Investigate and report on the demand for college-trained people in the coming years.
30. Determine the status and progress of women's rights in business for _____ (association).
31. Determine the recent developments in, current status of, and outlook for _____ industry.
32. Investigate and report on the criminal liability of corporate executives.
33. Investigate whether hiring physically challenged workers is charity or good business for Company X.
34. Assess the status of pollution control in _____ industry for an association of firms in that industry.
35. Review the status of consumer protection laws, and recommend policies for Company X.
36. For the International Association of Secretaries, review current developments in word processing and determine whether we are truly moving toward the "paperless office."
37. Advise Company X (your choice of a specific manufacturer) on the problems and procedures involved in exporting its products to _____ (country or countries of your choice).
38. Report to Company X on the quality of life in your city. The company may open a factory there and would move some executives to it.
39. Report to Company X on the ethics and effectiveness of subliminal advertising.
40. Compare the costs, services, and other relevant factors of the major automobile rental firms, and recommend which of these firms Company X should use.
41. Survey the franchise possibilities for _____ (fast foods, automotive services, or such), and select one of these possibilities for a business client.
42. Advise Company X on developing a wellness (preventive health) program.

*Additional topics are listed at the end of the long-length problem section following Chapter 14. Many of these topics are suitable for intermediate-length reports, just as some of the above topics are suitable for long reports.*

# CHAPTER 14

# LONG, FORMAL REPORTS

## CHAPTER OBJECTIVES

*Upon completing this chapter, you will be able to construct long, formal reports for important projects. To reach this goal, you should be able to*

**1**

Describe the roles and contents and construct the prefatory parts of a long, formal report.

**2**

Organize each introduction by considering all the likely readers and selecting the appropriate contents.

**3**

Determine, based on the goal, the most effective way to end a report—a summary, a conclusion, a recommendation, or a combination of the three.

**4**

Describe the role and content of the appendix and bibliography of a report.

**5**

Write long, formal reports using a structural coherence plan.

### INTRODUCTORY SITUATION

## to Long, Formal Reports

Assume the role of associate director of research, Midwestern Research, Inc. As your title indicates, research is your business. Perhaps it would be more accurate to say that research and reports are your business. Research is your primary activity, of course. But you must present your findings to your customers. The most efficient way of doing so is through reports.

Typical of your work is your current assignment with Armor Motors, a manufacturer of automobiles. The sales division of Armor wants information that will help to improve the effectiveness of its salespeople. Specifically, it wants answers to the question of what its salespeople can do to improve their performance. The information gathered will be used in revising the curriculum of Armor's sales training program.

To find the answer to the basic question, you plan to investigate three areas of sales activities: how salespeople use their time, how they find prospects, and how they make sales presentations. You will get this information for two groups of Armor salespeople: the successful and the unsuccessful. Next, you will compare the information you get from these two groups. The differences you detect in these comparisons should identify the effective and the ineffective sales practices.

Your next task will be to determine what your findings mean. When you have done this, you will present your findings, analyses, conclusions, and recommendations in a report to Armor Motors. Because Armor executives will see the report as evidence of the work you did for it, you will dress the report up. You know that what Allied sees will affect what it thinks of your work.

So you will use the formal arrangement that is traditional for reports of this importance. You will include the conventional prefatory pages. You will use headings to guide the readers through the text. And you will use graphics liberally to help tell the report story. If the situation calls for them, you may use appended parts. In other words, you will construct a report that matches the formality and importance of the situation. How to construct such reports is the subject of this chapter. ■

Although not numerous, long, formal reports are highly important in business. They usually concern major investigations, which explains their length. They are usually prepared for high-level administrators, which explains their formality.

*Long, formal reports are important but not numerous in business.*

## ORGANIZATION AND CONTENT OF THE LONGER REPORTS

In determining the structure of the longer, more formal reports, you should view your work much as architects view theirs. You have a number of parts to work with. Your task is to design from those parts a report that meets your reader's needs.

*Needs should determine the structure of long, formal reports.*

The first parts in your case are the prefatory pages. As noted in Chapter 13, the longest, most formal reports contain all of these. As the length of the report and the formality of the situation decrease, certain changes occur. As the report architect, you must decide which arrangement of prefatory parts meets the length and formality requirements of your situation.

*The need for the prefatory parts decreases as reports become shorter and less formal.*

**CHAPTER 14   Long, Formal Reports**

*In determining which prefatory parts to include, you should know their roles and contents.*

To make this decision, you need to know these parts. Thus, we will describe them in the following pages. In addition, we will describe the remaining structure of the longest, most formal report. As you proceed through these descriptions, it will be helpful to trace the parts through the illustration report at the end of this chapter. In addition, it will help to consult Chapter 20 for illustrations of page form.

*Thus, they are reviewed in the following pages.*

For convenience, in the following discussion the report parts are organized by groups. The first group comprises the prefatory parts, the parts that are most closely related to the formality and length of the report. Then comes the report proper, which, of course, is the meat of all reports. It is the report story. The final group comprises the appended parts. These contain supplementary materials, information that is not essential to the report but may be helpful to some readers. In summary, the presentation follows this pattern:

*Prefatory parts:* Title fly. Title page. Letter of authorization. Letter of transmittal, preface, or foreword. Table of contents and list of illustrations. Executive summary.

*The report proper:* Introduction. The report findings (usually presented in two or more divisions). Conclusion, recommendation, or summary.

*Appended parts:* Bibliography. Appendix.

## ■ ■ ■ ■ ■ ■ ■ ■ ■ ■ ■ ■ ■ ■
## THE PREFATORY PARTS

As you know from preceding discussion, there may be many variations in the prefatory parts of a formal report. Even so, the six parts covered in the following pages are generally included in the longer reports.

### Title Fly

*The title fly contains only the report title.*

The first of the possible prefatory report pages is the title fly (see page 488). It contains only the report title, and it is included solely for reasons of formality. As the title appears again on the following page, the title fly is somewhat repetitive. But most books have one, and so do most formal reports.

*Construct titles to make them describe the report precisely.*

Although constructing the title fly is simple, composing the title is not. In fact, on a per word basis, the title requires more time than any other part of the report. This is as it should be, for titles should be carefully worded. Their goal is to tell at a glance what the report does and does not cover. A good title fits the report like a glove. It covers all the report information snugly.

*As a checklist, use who, what, where, when, why, and sometimes how.*

For completeness of coverage, you should build your titles around the five W's: *who, what, where, when, why*. Sometimes *how* may be important. In some problems, you will not need to use all the W's. Nevertheless, they serve as a good checklist for completeness. For example, you might construct a title for the report described at the chapter beginning as follows:

Who: Armor Motors
What: Sales training recommendations
Where: Implied (Armor dealerships)
When: 1992

Why: Understood (to improve sales training)
How: Based on a 1992 study of company sales activities

From this analysis comes this title: "Sales Training Recommendations for Armor Motors Based on a 1992 Study of Company Sales Activities."

For another example, take a report analyzing the Lane Company's 1993 advertising campaigns. This analysis would be appropriate:

Who: Lane Company
What: Analysis of advertising campaigns
Where: Not essential
When: 1993
Why: Implied
How: Not essential

Thus, this title emerges: "Analysis of Lane Company's 1993 Advertising Campaigns."

Obviously, you cannot write a completely descriptive title in a word or two. Extremely short titles tend to be broad and general. They cover everything; they touch nothing. Even so, your goal is to be concise as well as complete. So you must seek the most economical word pattern consistent with completeness. In your effort to be concise and complete, you may want to use subtitles. Here is an example: "A 1993 Measure of Employee Morale at Pfeifer's Mossback Plant: A Study Based on a Survey Using the Semantic Differential."

> One- or two-word titles are too broad. Subtitles can help conciseness.

## Title Page

Like the title fly, the title page presents the report title. In addition, it displays information essential to identification of the report. In constructing your title page, you should include your complete identification and that of the authorizer or recipient of the report. You may also include the date of writing, particularly if the date is not in the title. The construction of this page is illustrated in Chapter 20 and in the report at the end of the chapter.

> The title page displays the title, identification of the writer and authorizer, and the date.

## Letter of Authorization

Although not illustrated in the diagram of report structure in Chapter 13 or in the report at the end of this chapter, a letter of authorization can be a prefatory part. It was not shown in the diagram (Figure 13-1) because its presence in a report is not determined by formality or length but by whether the report was authorized in writing. A report authorized in writing should include a copy of the written authorization. This part usually follows the title page.

> Include the letter of authorization if the report was authorized in writing.

As the report writer, you would not write the letter (or memorandum) of authorization. But if you ever have to write one, handle it as you would a routine direct-order letter. In the opening, authorize the research. Then cover the specific information that the reader needs to conduct it. This might include a clear description of the problem, time and money limitations, special instructions, and the due date. Close the letter with appropriate goodwill comment.

> Write the letter of authorization in the direct order: authorization, information about the problem, goodwill close.

When reports are presented in person, the writer can orally transmit the document and point out significant things about it. When direct presentation is not possible, a letter of transmittal, foreword, or preface performs this function.

### Letter of Transmittal, Foreword, Preface

Most formal reports contain a personal message of some kind from the writer to the reader. In most business reports, the letter of transmittal performs this function. In some cases, particularly where the report is written for a group of readers, a foreward or preface is used instead.

The letter of transmittal transmits the report to the reader. In less formal situations, the report is transmitted personally (orally). In more formal situations, a letter usually does the job. But keep in mind that the letter merely substitutes for a face-to-face meeting. What you write in it is much like what you would say if you were face-to-face with the reader.

As the goal of transmitting the report is positive, you should begin the letter of transmittal directly, without explanation or other delaying information. Your opening words should say, in effect, "Here is the report." Tied to or following the transmittal of the report, you should briefly identify the report goal, and you can refer to the authorization (who assigned the report, when, why).

What else you include in the letter of transmittal depends on the situation. In general, you should include anything that would be appropriate in a face-to-face presentation. What would you say if you were handing the report to the reader? It would probably be something about the report—how to understand, use, or appreciate it. You might make suggestions about follow-up studies, warnings about limitations of the report, or comments about side issues. In fact, you might include anything that helps the reader understand and appreciate the report. Typically, the letter of transmittal ends with

- The letter of transmittal is a personal message from the writer to the reader.

- It substitutes for a face-to-face meeting.

- Its main goal is to transmit the report.

- In addition, it includes helpful comments about the report. The close is goodwill.

PART 5  Fundamentals of Report Writing

### Table of Contents Generators: An Overlooked Presentation Tool

Most full-featured word processing software will help you create a table of contents for your report. While individual programs work slightly differently, in general, you simply identify the headings you want to include and then tell the software to generate a table of contents. Most programs will allow you to select a format from a selection of various pre-defined formats or define your own. For example, you might select a form that would place your text at the left and draw your readers' eyes with dot leaders to page numbers in the right margin. The software would place the text appropriately at the left, depending on the level of heading, insert and line up dot leaders, and insert page numbers flush right on the page.

After you have finished your report and marked the headings you want included in the table of contents, you select where you want it to appear in your report. When you tell the software to generate the table of contents, the software will take care of all formatting and page numbering tasks. Even with the power of word processing, this can be a very difficult task without using this feature. However, if you modify the text in any way that would change the page numbers after you have generated the table of contents, you must tell the software to generate it again so the new page numbers will be reflected in the table of contents.

If you find you use this feature on a regular basis, you can simplify it even further by including the marking task in styles you use for the headings. That way, every time you use a style to create a heading it will also be marked to be included in the table of contents.

---

appropriate goodwill comment. An expression of appreciation for the assignment or an invitation to do additional research if necessary makes good closing material.

When you combine the letter of transmittal with the executive summary (an acceptable arrangement), you follow the opening transmittal statement with a summary of the report highlights. In general, you follow the procedure for summarizing described in the discussion of the executive summary. Following the summary, you include appropriate talk about the report. Then you end with a goodwill comment.

> A summary follows the opening when the executive summary and the letter of transmittal are combined.

Because the letter of transmittal is a personal note to the reader, you may write in a personal style. In other words, you may use personal pronouns (*you, I, we*). In addition, you may write it in conversational language that reflects the warmth and vigor of your personality. You may not want to use the personal style in very formal cases. For example, if you were writing a report for a committee of senators or for other high-ranking dignitaries, you might elect to write the letter of transmittal impersonally. But such instances are rare.

> The letter of transmittal is usually in personal style.

As noted previously, you may transmit reports to broad audiences in a foreword or a preface. Minor distinctions are sometimes drawn between forewords and prefaces. But for all practical purposes, they are the same. Both are preliminary messages from the writer to the reader. Although forewords and prefaces usually do not formally transmit the report, they do

> For broad audiences, a foreword (or preface) is used. Forewords do not transmit the report—they comment about it.

many of the other things done by letters of transmittal. Like letters of transmittal, they seek to help the reader appreciate and understand the report. They may, for example, include helpful comments about the report—its use, interpretation, follow-up, and the like. In addition, they frequently contain expressions of indebtedness to those helpful in the research. Like letters of transmittal, they are usually written in the first person. But they are seldom as informal as some letters of transmittal. There is no established pattern for arranging the contents of forewords and prefaces.

## Table of Contents, List of Illustrations

- Include a table of contents when the report is long enough to need a guide to its contents.

If your report is long enough to need a guide to its contents, you should include a table of contents. This table is the report outline in finished form with page numbers. As noted in the discussion of outlining in Chapter 12, the outline headings appear in the text of the report as headings of the various parts. Thus, a listing showing the pages where the headings appear helps the reader find the parts of the report. A table of contents is especially helpful to the reader who wants to see only a few scattered parts of the report.

- The table of contents lists the outline headings, the prefatory parts, and the appended parts, also charts and tables. It gives page numbers.

In addition to listing the text contents, the table of contents lists the parts of the report that appear before and after the text. Thus, it lists the prefatory parts, but usually only those that follow the table of contents. It also lists the appended parts (bibliography, appendix) and the charts and tables that illustrate the report. Typically, the charts and tables appear as separate listings following the listings reviewed above. More detailed instructions for constructing the table of contents appear in Chapter 20.

## Executive Summary

- The executive summary summarizes the report.

The executive summary (also called *synopsis, abstract, epitome, précis, digest*) is the report in miniature. It concisely summarizes whatever is important in the report. For some readers, the executive summary serves as a preview to the report. But it is written primarily for busy executives who may not have time to read the whole report. Perhaps they can get all they

"Playing possum doesn't work anymore, Stephmeyer! I want that report by 5 p.m. or else!"

*Reprinted by permission: Tribune Media Services.*

PART 5 Fundamentals of Report Writing

need to know by reading the executive summary. If they need to know more about any part, they can find that part through the table of contents. Thus, they can find out whatever they need to know quickly and easily.

You construct the executive summary simply by reducing the parts of the report in order and in proportion. More specifically, you go through the report, selecting whatever is essential. You should include all the major items of information—the facts and figures of the report. You should include all the major analyses of the information presented. And you should include all the conclusions and recommendations derived from these analyses. The finished product should be a miniature of the whole, with all the important ingredients. As a general rule, the executive summary is less than an eighth as long as the writing it summarizes.

*It includes highlights of the facts, analyses, and conclusions—in proportion.*

As your goal is to cut the report to a fraction of its length, much of your success will depend on your skill in word economy. Loose writing is costly. But in your efforts to be concise, you are more likely to write in a dull style. You will need to avoid this tendency.

*Work on writing style in this part.*

The traditional executive summary reviews the report in the indirect order (introduction, body, conclusion). In recent years, however, the direct order has gained in popularity. This order shifts the major findings, conclusions, and/or recommendations (as the case may be) to the major position of emphasis at the beginning. From this direct beginning, the summary moves to the introductory parts and then through the report in normal order. One good reason for the growing popularity of the direct order is the fact that our information technology is currently retrieving information on screens limited in size. Most readers expect the key information to appear on the first screen or two.

*Either the direct or indirect order is appropriate.*

Diagrams of both arrangements appear in Figure 14–1. Whichever arrangement you choose, you will write the executive summary after the report body is complete.

---

### A Questionable Example of Effective Reporting

"How could I have hired this fellow Glutz?" the sales manager moaned as he read this first report from his new salesperson: "I have arrive in Detroit. Tomorry I will try to sell them companys here what ain't never bought nothing from us."

Before the sales manager could fire this stupid fellow, Glutz's second report arrived: "I done good here. Sold them bout haff a millun dollars wirth. Tomorry I try to sell to them there Smith Company folks what threw out that last feller what sold for us."

Imagine how the sales manager's viewpoint changed when he read Glutz's third report: "Today I seen them Smith folks and sole them bout a millun dollars wirth. Also after dinner I got too little sails mountin to bout half a millun dollars. Tomorry I going to do better."

The sales manager was so moved that he tacked Glutz's reports on the company bulletin board. Below them he posted this note to all the salespeople: "I want all you should reed these reports wrote by Glutz who are on the road doin a grate job. Then you should go out and do like he done."

**FIGURE 14-1** Diagram of the Executive Summary in the Indirect Order and in the Direct Order

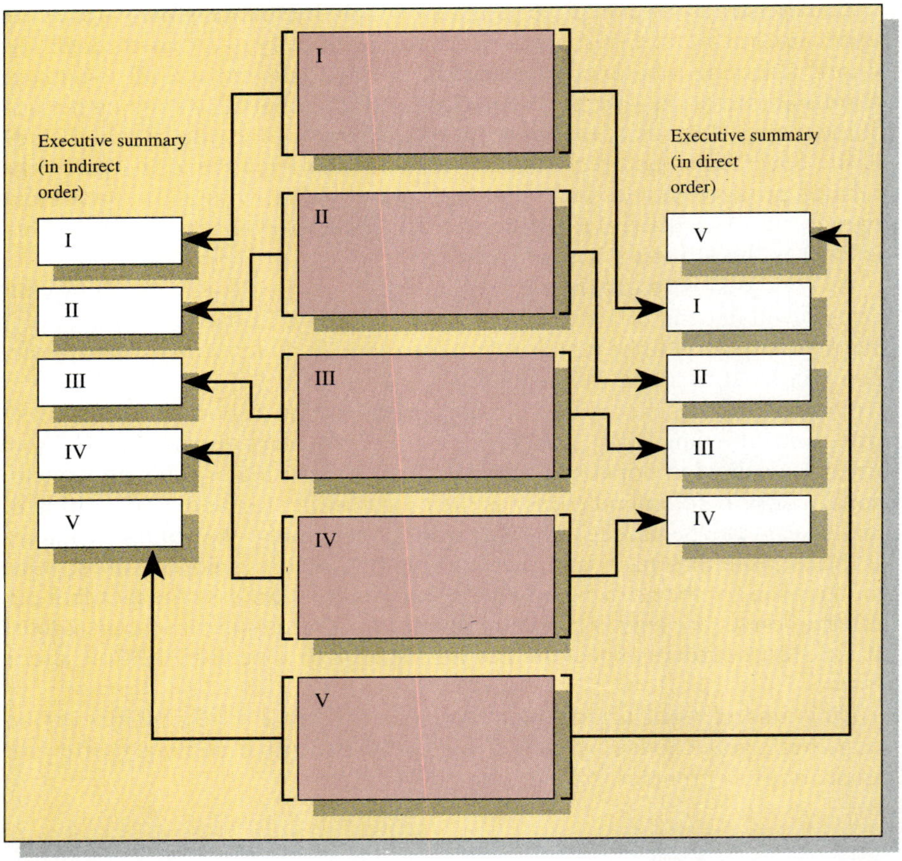

## THE REPORT PROPER

As noted in Chapter 13, the contents of most longer reports are written in the indirect order (introduction, body, conclusion). But there are exceptions. Some longer reports are in the direct order—with summaries, conclusions, or recommendations at the beginning. And some are in a prescribed order similar to that of the technical and staff reports described in Chapter 13. Even though the orders of longer reports may vary, the ingredients of all these reports are similar. Thus, the following review of the makeup of a report in the indirect order should help you in writing any report.

*The arrangements of the report proper may vary, but the following review of the indirect order should be helpful.*

### Introduction

The purpose of the introduction of a report is simply to prepare the readers to receive the report. Whatever will help achieve this goal is appropriate content.

In determining what content is appropriate, consider all the likely readers of your report. As we noted earlier, the readers of many of the shorter

*The introduction should prepare the readers.*

*In deciding what to include, consider all the likely readers.*

reports are likely to know the problem well and have little or no need for an introduction. But such is not often the case for the longer reports. Many of these reports are prepared for a large number of readers, some of whom know little about the problem. These reports often have long lives and are kept on file to be read in future years. Clearly, they require some introductory explanation to prepare the readers.

Determining what should be included is a matter of judgment. You should ask yourself what you would need or want to know about the problem if you were in your readers' shoes. In selecting the appropriate information, you would do well to use the following checklist of likely introduction contents. Remember, though, that it is only a checklist. Rarely would you include all the items.

> Then determine what those readers need to know. Use the following checklist.

**Origin of the Report.** The first part of your introduction might well include a review of the facts of authorization. Some writers, however, leave this part out. If you decide to include it, you should present such facts as when, how, and by whom the report was authorized; who wrote the report; and when the report was submitted. Information of this kind is particularly useful in reports that have no letter of transmittal.

> 1. Origin—the facts of authorization.

**Problem and Purpose.** A vital part of almost every report is a statement of its problem. The *problem* is whatever the report seeks to do. It is the satisfaction of the need that prompted the investigation.

> 2. Problem—what the report seeks to do.

You may state the problem of your report in different ways. A very common way is to word it in the infinitive form: "To determine standards for corporate annual reports." Another common way is to word it as a question: "What retail advertising practices do Centerville consumers disapprove of?" Whatever you think does the best job of explaining what your report seeks to do is what you want.

> The problem is commonly stated in infinitive or question form.

Closely related to *what* you are doing is *why* you are doing it. The *purpose* (often called by other names such as *objective, aim, goal*) tells the reason of the report. For example, you might be determining standards for the corporate annual report *in order to streamline the production process.*

> The purpose is the reason for the report.

**Scope.** If the scope of the problem is not clearly covered in any of the other introductory parts, you may need to include it in a separate part. By *scope* we mean the boundaries of the problem. In this part of the introduction—in plain, clear language—you should describe what is included in the problem. You should also identify the delimitations—what you have not included.

> 3. Scope—the boundaries of the problem.

**Limitations.** In some reports, you will need to explain limitations. By *limitations* we mean things that impair the quality of your report. For example, you may not have been given enough time to do the work right. Or perhaps a short budget prevented you from doing everything that should have been done. And there are other limitations—unavoidable conditions, restrictions within the problem, absence of historical information. In general, this part of the introduction should include whatever you think might explain possible shortcomings in your report.

> 4. Limitations—anything that impairs the quality of the report.

**Historical Background.** Knowledge of the history of the problem is sometimes essential to understanding the report. Thus, you may need to cover that history in your introduction. Your general aim in this part is to acquaint the readers with how the problem developed and what has been done about

> 5. History—how the problem developed and what is known about it.

**CHAPTER 14 Long, Formal Reports**

it. Your discussion here should bring out the main issues. It should review what past investigations have determined about the problem, and it should lead to what still has to be done.

**Sources and Methods of Collecting Information.** You usually need to tell the readers how you collected the information in the report. That is, you explain your research methodology. You tell whether you used library research, survey, experiment, or what not. And you describe the steps you followed. In general, you describe your work in enough detail to allow your readers to judge it. You tell them enough to convince them that your work was done competently.

In a simple case in which you conducted library research, you need to say little. If most of your findings came from a source or two, you could name the sources. If you used a large number of sources, you would be wise to note that you used library research and refer to the bibliography in the report appendix.

More complex research usually requires a more detailed description. If you conducted a survey, for example, you would probably need to explain all parts of the investigation. You would cover sample determination, construction of the questionnaire, interview procedure, checking techniques. In fact, you would include as much detail as is needed to gain the readers' confidence in your work.

**Definitions, Initialisms, and Acronyms.** If you use words, initialisms, or acronyms that are likely to be unfamiliar to readers of the report, you should define those words. You can do this in either of two ways: you can define each word in the text or as a footnote when it is first used in the report, or you can define all unfamiliar words in a separate part of the introduction. This part begins with an introductory statement and then lists the words with their definitions. If the list is long, you may choose to arrange the words alphabetically.

**Report Preview.** In very long reports, a final part of the introduction should preview the report presentation. In this part you tell the readers how the report will be presented—what topics will be taken up first, second, third, and so on. Of even greater importance, you give your reasons for following this plan. That is, you explain the *strategy* of your report. In short, you give your readers a clear picture of the road ahead. As you will see later in the chapter, this part of the introduction is a basic ingredient of the coherence plan of the long report. Illustrations of report previews appear in the discussion of this plan (page 486) and in the report at the end of the chapter (page 495).

## The Report Body

In the report body, the information collected is presented and related to the problem. Normally, this part of the report comprises most of its content. In a sense, this part is the report. With the exception of the conclusion or recommendation part, the other parts of the report are attached parts.

Although the body makes up most of the report, practically all that we need to say about it has already been said. Its organization was discussed extensively in Chapter 12. It is written in accord with the instructions on

---

*Margin notes:*

6. Sources and methods—how you got the information.

Sometimes it is necessary to cite sources.

More complex research requires thorough description.

7. Definitions of unfamiliar words, acronyms, or initialisms used.

8. Preview—a description of the route ahead.

The report body presents and analyzes the information gathered.

Writing this part involves instruction covered elsewhere in the book.

### Technical Writer's Report on Humpty Dumpty

A 72-gram brown Rhode Island Red country-fresh candled egg was secured and washed free of feathers, blood, dirt, and grit. Held between thumb and index finger, about 3 ft. or more from an electric fan (GE Model No. MC-2404, Serial No. JC23023, nonoscillating, rotating on "Hi" speed at approximately 105.23 plus or minus 0.02 rpm), the egg was suspended on a pendulum (string) so that it arrived at the fan with essentially zero velocity normal to the fan rotation plane. The product adhered strongly to the walls and ceiling and was difficult to recover. However, using putty knives a total of 13 grams was obtained and put in a skillet with 11.2 grams of hickory-smoked Armour's old-style bacon and heated over a low Bunsen flame for 7 min. 32 sec. What there was of it was of excellent quality.

"The DP Report," Du Pont Explosive's Department, Atomic Energy Division, Savannah River Laboratories, July 12, 1954.

clear writing presented in Chapters 2 and 3 and the writing techniques covered in Chapter 12. It uses the good presentative form, with charts, tables, and caption display, discussed and illustrated at various places in this book. In fact, most of our discussion of report writing has concerned this major part of the report.

## The Ending of the Report

You can end your report in any of a number of ways: with a summary, a conclusion, a recommendation, or a combination of the three. Your choice should depend on the goal of your report. You should choose the way that enables you to satisfy that goal.

*Reports can end in various ways.*

**Ending Summary.** When the goal of the report is to present information, the ending is logically a summary of the major findings. Such reports usually have minor summaries at the end of the major sections. When this arrangement is followed, the ending summary recapitulates these summaries.

*Informational reports usually end with a summary of the major*

You should not confuse the ending summary with the executive summary. The executive summary is a prefatory part of the report; the ending summary is a part of the report text. Also, the executive summary is more complete than the ending summary. The executive summary reviews the entire report, usually from the beginning to the end. The ending summary reviews only the highlights of the report.

*The ending summary is not as complete as the executive summary.*

**Conclusions.** Some reports must do more than just present information. They must analyze the information in light of the problem, and from this analysis they must reach a conclusion. Such reports typically end with this conclusion.

*Reports that seek an answer end with a conclusion.*

The makeup of the conclusion section varies from case to case. In problems for which a single answer is sought, the conclusion section normally reviews the preceding information and analyses and, from this review, arrives at the answer. In problems with more than one goal, the report plan may treat each goal in a separate section and draw conclusions in each

*The structure of the conclusion varies by problem.*

**CHAPTER 14  Long, Formal Reports**

section. The conclusion section of such a report might well summarize the conclusions previously drawn. There are other arrangements. In fact, almost any plan that brings the analyses together to reach the goals of the report is appropriate.

**Recommendations.**   When the goal of the report is not only to draw conclusions but also to present a course of action, a recommendation is in order. You may organize it as a separate section following the conclusion section. Or you may include it in the conclusion section. In some problems, the conclusion is the recommendation—or at least a logical interpretation of it. Whether you include a recommendation should be determined by whether the readers want or expect one.

*Include recommendations when the readers want or expect them.*

## Appended Parts

Sometimes you will need to include an appendix or a bibliography, or both, at the end of the report. Whether you include these parts should be determined by need.

*Add an appendix or a bibliography when needed.*

**Appendix.**   The appendix, as its name implies, is a tacked-on part. You use it for supplementary information that supports the body of the report but has no logical place within the body. Possible appendix contents are questionnaires, working papers, summary tables, additional references, and other reports.

*The appendix contains information that indirectly supports the report.*

As a rule, the appendix should not include the charts, graphs, sketches, and tables that directly support the report. These should be placed in the body of the report, where they support the findings. Reports should be designed for the convenience of the readers. Obviously, it is not convenient for readers to look for appendix illustrations of the facts they read in the report body.

*Information that directly supports the report belongs in the text of the report.*

Long, formal reports often are discussed at meetings of high-level executives. Thus, they should be prepared with the thoroughness and formality such situations justify.

PART 5   Fundamentals of Report Writing

**Bibliography.** When your investigation makes heavy use of printed sources, you normally include a bibliography (a list of the publications used). The construction of this list is described in Appendix D of this book.

*Include a bibliography if you make heavy use of printed sources.*

## STRUCTURAL COHERENCE HELPERS

As we have noted, the writing in the longer reports is much like the writing in the shorter ones. In general, the instructions given in earlier chapters apply to the longer reports. But the longer reports have one writing need that is not present in the shorter ones—the need for structural coherence helpers.

*Longer reports need structural coherence helpers.*

By *structural coherence helpers* we mean a network of explanations, introductions, conclusions, and summaries that guide the reader through the report. You should use these helpers wherever they will help relate the parts of the report or move the message along. Although you should not use them mechanically, you will find that they are likely to follow the general plan described in Figure 14–2.

*These are a network of explanations, introductions, summaries, and conclusions.*

The coherence plan begins with the preview of the introduction. As you will recall, the preview tells the readers what lies ahead. It covers three

*The coherence plan begins with the preview, which describes the route ahead.*

**FIGURE 14–2** Diagram of the Structural Coherence Plan of a Long, Formal Report

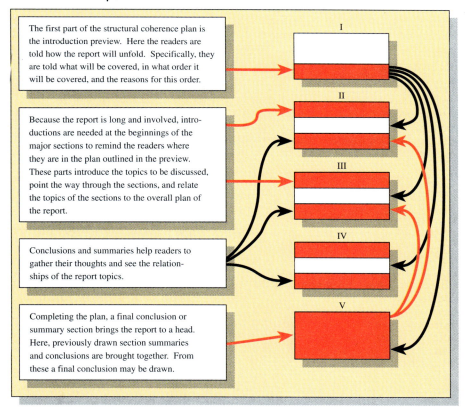

CHAPTER 14 Long, Formal Reports 485

things: the topics to be discussed, their order, and the logic of that order. With this information in mind, the readers know how the parts of the report relate to one another. They know the overall strategy of the presentation. The following paragraphs do a good job of previewing a report comparing three automobiles to determine which is the best for a company's sales fleet.

> The decision as to which light car Allied Distributors should buy is reached by comparing the cars on the basis of three factors: cost, safety, and performance. Each of these factors is broken down into its component parts, which are applied to each of the makes being considered.
>
> Because cost is the most tangible factor, it is examined in the first major section. In this section, the four makes are compared for initial and trade-in values. Then they are compared for operating costs, as determined by gasoline mileage, oil use, repair expense, and the like. In the second major section, the safety of the four makes is compared. Driver visibility, special safety features, brakes, steering quality, acceleration rate, and traction are the main considerations here. In the third major section, the dependability of the four makes is compared on the basis of repair records and salespersons' time lost because of automobile failure. In the final major section, weights are assigned to the foregoing comparisons, and the automobile brand that is best suited to the company's needs is recommended.

*Introductions to and summaries of the report sections keep the readers informed of where they are in the report.*

In addition to the preview in the introduction, the plan uses introductory and summary sections at convenient places throughout the report. Typically, these sections are at the beginning and end of major divisions, but you should use them wherever they are needed. Such sections remind the readers where they are in the report. They tell the readers where they have been and where they are going. Illustrating this technique is the following paragraph, which introduces a major section of a report. Note how the paragraph ties in with the preceding discussion, which concerned industrial activity in three geographic areas. Note also how it justifies covering secondary areas.

> Although the great bulk of industry is concentrated in three areas (Grand City, Milltown, and Port Starr), a thorough industrial survey needs to consider the secondary, but nevertheless important, areas of the state. In the rank of their current industrial potential, these areas are the Southeast, with Hartsburg as its center; the Central West, dominated by Parrington; and the North Central, where Pineview is the center of activities.

The following summary-conclusion paragraph is a good ending to a major section. The paragraph brings to a head the findings presented in the section and points the way to the subject of the next section.

> These findings and those pointed out in preceding paragraphs all lead to one obvious conclusion. The small-business executives are concerned primarily with subject matter that will aid them directly in their work. That is, they favor a curriculum slanted in favor of the practical subjects. They insist, however, on some coverage of the liberal arts, and they are also convinced of the value of studying business administration. On all these points, they are clearly out of tune with the bulk of the big-business leaders who have voiced their positions on this question. Even the most dedicated business administration professors would find it difficult to support such an extremely practical concept. Nevertheless, these are the opinions of the small-business executives. As they are the consumers of the business-education product, their opinions should at least be considered. Likewise, their specific recommendations on courses (the subject of the following section) deserve careful review.

Completing the coherence plan is the final major section of the report. In this section, you achieve the goal of the report. Here you recall from the preceding section summaries all the major findings and analyses. Then you apply them to the problem and present the conclusion. Thus, you complete the strategy explained in the introduction preview and recalled at convenient places throughout the report.

*The final major section of the report brings together the preceding information and applies it to the goal.*

Wise use of coherence helpers can form a network of connections throughout the report. You should keep in mind, however, that these helpers should be used only when they are needed. That is, you should use them when your readers need help in seeing relationships and in knowing where they are and where they are going. If you use them well, they will appear as natural parts of the report story. They should never appear to be mechanical additions.

*Use coherence helpers naturally—when they are needed.*

## THE LONG ANALYTICAL REPORT ILLUSTRATED

Illustrating the long analytical report is the report presented at the end of this chapter (Figure 14–3). The report's structure parallels that of the formal type described in the preceding pages.

*Figure 14–3 is an illustration of a long, formal report.*

## SUMMARY (by Chapter Objectives)

1. The prefatory section of the long, formal report consists of these conventional parts:
    - Title fly—a page displaying only the title.
        - —As a checklist for constructing the title, use the 5 W's (*who, what, where, when, why*).
        - —Sometimes *how* is important.
    - Title page—a page displaying the title and identification of writer and recipient.
    - Letter of authorization—included only when a letter (or memorandum) authorized the report.
    - Letter of transmittal—a letter (or memorandum) transmitting the report (a *foreword* or *preface* in very long and highly formal papers).
        - —This part takes the place of a face-to-face presentation.
        - —Begin it with a presentation of the report.
        - —Include comments about the report you would have made in a face-to-face presentation.
        - —In some cases you may combine it with the executive summary.
        - —Write the letter in personal style (first and second person).
    - Table of contents—a listing of the report parts with page numbers.
    - Executive summary—the report in miniature.
        - —Include, in proportion, everything that is important—all the major facts, analyses, and conclusions.
        - —Write it in either direct or indirect order.
2. The report introduction prepares the readers to receive the report.
    - Include whatever helps reach this goal.

*1. Describe the roles and contents and construct the prefatory parts of a long, formal report.*

*2. Organize each introduction by considering all the likely readers and selecting the appropriate contents.*

**CHAPTER 14** Long, Formal Reports

487

| | |
|---|---|
| 3. Determine, based on the goal, the most effective way to end a report—a summary, a conclusion, a recommendation, or a combination of the three. | • Use these items as a checklist for content: purpose, scope, limitations, problem history, methodology, definitions, preview.<br>• A preview telling the order and reasoning for the order is useful in longer, more involved reports.<br>3. The ending of the report achieves the report goal.<br>  • Use a summary if the goal is to review information.<br>  • Use a conclusion if the goal is to reach an answer.<br>  • Use a recommendation if the goal is to determine a desirable action. |
| 4. Describe the role and content of the appendix and bibliography of a report. | 4. An appendix and/or bibliography can follow the report text.<br>  • The appendix contains items that support the text but have no specific place in the text (such as questionnaires, working papers, summary tables).<br>  • The bibliography is a descriptive list of the printed sources that were used in the investigation. |
| 5. Write long, formal reports using a structural coherence plan. | 5. The longer reports need various structural helpers to give them coherence.<br>  • These helpers consist of a network of explanations, introductions, summaries, and conclusions that guide the reader through the report.<br>  • Begin the coherence plan with the introduction preview, which tells the structure of the report.<br>  • Then use the introductions and summaries in following parts to tell readers where they are in this structure.<br>  • At the end, bring together the preceding information, analyses, and conclusions to reach the report goal.<br>  • Make these coherence helpers inconspicuous—that is, make them appear to be a natural part of the message. |

**FIGURE 14-3** Illustration of a Long, Formal Report

This long, formal report presents the findings of an observational study of successful and unsuccessful salespeople to determine the differences in how each group works. The results will be used to revise the content of the company's sales training program. Because the report is extensive and the situation formal, the report has all the major prefatory parts. The significant statistical findings are effectively emphasized by graphics.

*Title page*

SALES TRAINING RECOMMENDATIONS FOR ARMOR MOTORS

BASED ON A 1992 STUDY OF COMPANY SALES ACTIVITIES

*Here the essential facts of authorization are provided.*

Prepared for

Mr. Peter R. Simpson, Vice President for Sales
Armor Motors, Inc.
72117 North Musselman Road
Dearborn, MI 48126

Prepared by

Ashlee P. Callahan
Callahan and Hebert Research Associates
Suite D, Brownfield Towers
212 North Bedford Avenue
Detroit, MI 48219

November 17, 1992

**FIGURE 14–3** (continued)

*Title fly*

*The title includes the essentials of the 5 W's.*

SALES TRAINING RECOMMENDATIONS FOR ARMOR MOTORS
BASED ON A 1992 STUDY OF COMPANY SALES ACTIVITIES

**FIGURE 14–3** (continued)

*Letter of transmittal*

November 17, 1993

Mr. Peter R. Simpson
Vice President for Sales
Armor Motors, Inc.
72117 North Musselman Road
Dearborn, MI 48126

Dear Mr. Simpson:

*The letter begins directly, with the authorization.*

Here is the report on the observational study of your salespeople you asked us to conduct last August 17.

*Pertinent comments help the reader understand and appreciate the research.*

As you will see, our observations pointed to some specific needs for sales training. Following the procedure we agreed to, we will prepare an outline of these needs in a revised curriculum plan that we will submit to your training director December 4. We are confident that this curriculum plan will aid in correcting the shortcomings in your sales force.

*A goodwill comment ends the letter.*

We at Callahan and Hebert appreciate having this assignment. If you should need any assistance in interpreting this report or in implementing our recommendations, please call on us.

Sincerely yours,

*Ashlee P. Callahan*

Ashlee P. Callahan
Senior Research Associate

**FIGURE 14–3** (continued)

*Table of contents*

## TABLE OF CONTENTS

| Part | Page |
|---|---|
| Executive Summary | vi |
| THE PROBLEM AND THE PLAN | 1 |
|     Incidentals of Authorization and Submittal | 1 |
|     Objective of Sales Training Improvement | 1 |
|     Use of Observational Techniques | 1 |
|     A Preview of the Presentation | 2 |
| ANALYSIS OF WORK TIME USE | 2 |
|     Negative Effect of Idle Time | 2 |
|     Correlation of Prospect Contacting and Success | 3 |
|     Vital Role of Prospect Building | 3 |
|     Necessity of Miscellaneous Activities | 3 |
| DIFFERENCES IN FINDING PROSPECTS | 3 |
|     Near Equal Distribution of Walk-Ons | 4 |
|     Value of Cultivating Old Customers | 4 |
|     Limited Effectiveness of Using Bird Dogs | 5 |
|     Scant Use of Other Techniques | 5 |
| OBSERVABLE DIFFERENCES IN PRESENTATIONS | 5 |
|     Positive Effect of Integrity | 6 |
|     Apparent Value of Moderate Pressure | 6 |
|     Necessity of Product Knowledge | 7 |
| RECOMMENDATIONS FOR TRAINING | 8 |

*A review of the problem facts prepares the reader to receive the report.*

*The three areas of sales work investigated logically form the main headings.*

*Subfactors of the work areas make logical second-level headings.*

*Note the parallel wording of the headings.*

*Note also the talking quality of the second-level headings.*

**FIGURE 14–3** (continued)

*List of charts (a continuation of the table of contents)*

*A list of the graphics in the report appears here, with complete titles that describe content.*

LIST OF CHARTS

                                                                Page

Chart 1.   How Productive and Marginal Salespeople
           Use Work Time . . . . . . . . . . . . .    2

Chart 2.   Prospects Contacted during Observation
           Period by Productive and Marginal
           Salespeople by Method of Obtaining Them . . .   4

Chart 3.   Observed Images of Integrity in Sales
           Presentations of Productive and Marginal
           Salespeople . . . . . . . . . . . . . .    6

Chart 4.   Observed Use of Pressure in Sales Presentations
           of Productive and Marginal Salespeople . . . .   7

Chart 5.   Product Knowledge Ratings of Productive and
           Marginal Salespeople . . . . . . . . . .    8

**FIGURE 14–3** (continued)

*Executive summary*

*Following the direct-order plan, this executive summary places the recommendations first. Highlights of the supporting findings follow.*

*The remaining paragraphs summarize the major findings in the order presented in the report.*

*Note that the important facts and figures are present.*

*The significant comparisons and conclusions are emphasized throughout.*

<u>Executive Summary</u>

Conclusions drawn from this study suggest that these topics be added to Armor's sales training program:

1. Negative effects of idle time
2. Techniques of cultivating prospects
3. Development of bird dog networks
4. Cultivating repeat sales
5. Projection of integrity image
6. Use of moderate persuasion
7. Value of product knowledge

Supporting these recommendations are the following findings and conclusions drawn from an observational study comparing sales activities of productive and marginal salespeople.

The data show that the productive salespeople used their time more effectively than did the marginal salespeople. As compared with marginal salespeople, the productive salespeople spent less time in idleness (28% vs. 53%). They also spent more time in contact with prospects (31.3% vs. 19.8%) and more time developing prospects (10.4% vs. 4.4%).

Investigation of how the salespeople got their prospects showed that because floor assignments were about equal, both groups profited about the same from walk-ins. The productive group got 282; the marginal group got 274. The productive group used bird dogs more extensively, having 64 contacts derived from this source during the observation period. The marginal group had 8. The productive salespeople also were more successful in turning these contacts into sales.

Observations of sales presentations revealed that the productive salespeople displayed higher integrity, used pressure more reasonably, and knew the product better than the marginal salespeople. Of the 20 productive salespeople, 16 displayed images of moderately high integrity (Group II). The marginal group members ranged widely with 7 in Group III (questionable), and 5 each in Group II (moderately high integrity) and Group IV (deceitful). Most (15) of the productive salespeople used moderate pressure, whereas the marginal salespeople tended toward extremes (10 high pressure, 7 low pressure). On the product knowledge test, 17 of the productive salespeople scored excellent and 3 fair. Of the marginal members, 5 scored excellent, 6 fair, and 9 inadequate.

vi

**FIGURE 14–3** (continued)

*Report text (introduction)*

SALES TRAINING RECOMMENDATIONS FOR ARMOR MOTORS
BASED ON A 1992 STUDY OF COMPANY SALES ACTIVITIES

THE PROBLEM AND THE PLAN

Incidentals of Authorization and Submittal

*These authorization facts identify the participants in the report.*

This study of Armor salespeople's sales activities is submitted to Mr. Peter R. Simpson, Vice President for Sales, on November 17, 1992. As specified by written agreement dated August 28, the investigation was conducted under the direction of Ashlee P. Callahan of Callahan and Hebert Research Associates.

Objective of Sales Training Improvement

*Here the writer explains the problem clearly and precisely.*

The objective of the study was to find means of improving the effectiveness of Armor salespeople. The plan for achieving this objective involved first determining the techniques and characteristics of effective selling. This information then will be used in improving Armor's sales training program.

Use of Observational Techniques

The methodology used in this investigation was an observational study of Armor salespeople. Specifically, the study employed the time-duty technique, which is a unique means of observing work performance under real conditions. A detailed description of this technique is a part of the proposal approved at the August meeting and is not repeated here. Specific items relative to the application of this method in this case are summarized below.

*A brief review of methodology permits the reader to judge the research.*

Two groups of 20 Armor salespeople were selected for the observation—a productive and a marginal group. The productive group was made up of the company's top producers for the past year; the marginal group comprised the lowest producers. Only salespeople with three years or more of experience were eligible.

A team of two highly trained observers observed each of the salespeople selected for a continuous period of five working days. Using specially designed forms, the observers recorded the work activities of the salespeople. At the end of the observation period, the observer conducted an exit interview, recording certain demographic data and administering a test of the salesperson's knowledge of Armor's automobiles.

1

**FIGURE 14–3** (continued)

2

### A Preview of the Presentation

*A description of the presentation prepares the reader for what follows.*

In the following pages, the findings and analyses appear in the arrangement discussed at the August meeting. First comes a comparison of how the productive and the marginal salespeople spend their work time. Second is an analysis of how the productive and the marginal salespeople find their prospects. Third is a comparative analysis of the observable differences in sales presentations of the two groups. Conclusions drawn from these comparisons form the bases for recommendations of content emphasis in Armor's sales training program.

## ANALYSIS OF WORK TIME USE

*From this point on, the presentation of findings, with comparisons and analyses, pursues the report objective.*

The time-duty observation records were examined to determine whether differences exist between the productive and marginal salespeople in their use of work time. Activities were grouped into four general categories: (1) idleness, (2) contacting prospects, (3) finding prospects, and (4) miscellaneous activities. This examination revealed the following results.

### Negative Effect of Idle Time

As shown in Chart 1, the productive salespeople spent less work time in idleness (28%) than did the marginal salespeople (53%). Further

*Here and elsewhere, note the use of graphics at places near their discussion in the text.*

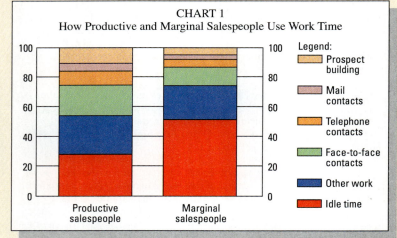

496   PART 5   Fundamentals of Report Writing

**FIGURE 14–3** (continued)

*Report text (continued)*

3

examination of the observations reveals that the top five of the 20 productive salespeople spent even less time in idleness (13%); and the bottom five of the marginal salespeople spent more time in idleness (67%). Clearly, these observations suggest the predictable conclusion that the successful salespeople work more than their less productive counterparts.

Correlation of Prospect Contacting and Success

The productive salespeople spent more time contacting prospects face to face, by telephone, and by mail (31.3%) than did the marginal salespeople (19.8%). The specific means of making these contacts show similar differences. The productive and marginal salespeople spent their work time, respectively, 23.2% and 13.5% in face-to-face contacts, 4.8% and 2.0% in mail contacts, and 8.3% and 4.6% in telephone contacts. These data lend additional support to the conclusion that work explains sales success.

*The text presents the data thoroughly yet concisely — and with appropriate comparisons.*

Vital Role of Prospect Building

During the observation period, productive salespeople spent more than twice as much time (10.5%) as marginal salespeople (4.4%) in building prospects. Activities observed in this category include contacting bird dogs and other lead sources and mailing literature to old and prospective customers.

Necessity of Miscellaneous Activities

Both the productive and marginal salespeople spent about a fourth of their work time in miscellaneous activities (tending to personal affairs, studying sales literature, attending sales meetings, and such). The productive group averaged 25.2%; the marginal group averaged 22.5%. As some of this time is related to automobile sales, the productive salespeople would be expected to spend more time in this category.

*A section summary helps the reader identify and remember the major findings.*

Summary-Conclusions. The preceding data reveal that the way salespeople spend their time affects their productivity. Productive salespeople work at selling. In sharp contrast with the marginal salespeople, they spend little time in idleness. They work hard to contact prospects and to build prospect lists. Like all automobile salespeople, they spend some time in performing miscellaneous duties.

DIFFERENCES IN FINDING PROSPECTS

*This and the other major sections begin with helpful introductory comment.*

A comparison of how productive and marginal salespeople find prospects and measurement of the productivity of these methods was a second area of investigation. For this investigation, the observations were classified by the four primary sources of prospects: (1) walk-ins, (2) bird dogs and other referrals, (3) repeat customers, and (4) other. Only prospects that were

**FIGURE 14–3** (continued)

*Report text (continued)*

contacted in person or by telephone during the observation period were included. Prospects were counted only once, even though some were contacted more than once.

Near Equal Distribution of Walk-ins

As expected, most of the contacts of both the productive and marginal salespeople were walk-ins. Because both groups had about equal floor assignments, they got about the same number of prospects from this source. As illustrated in Chart 2, the productive members got 282 (an average of 14.1 each), and the marginal members got 274 (an average of 13.7 each)

*Note how the use of color adds interest as well as helps the reader visualize the comparisons in the graphics.*

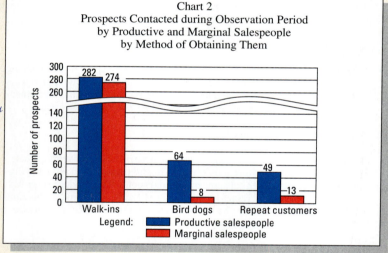

Although both groups got about the same number of prospects from walk-ins, the productive salespeople got better results. A review of sales records shows that the productive salespeople averaged 2.6 sales per week from walk-ins; the marginal salespeople averaged 2.2. The difference, although appearing slight, represents roughly 16 automobiles per year.

Value of Cultivating Old Customers

Returning old customers and friends referred by them constitute the second most productive source of prospects. During the observation period, the

PART 5 Fundamentals of Report Writing

**FIGURE 14–3** (continued)

*Report text
(continued)*

5

productive salespeople had contacts with 49 such prospects; the marginal salespeople had 13. The productive salespeople also had better sales success with these prospects, turning 40 of them into sales — an average of two per week. The marginal group members made sales to seven of these prospects — an average of .35 per person. These differences appear to be a direct result of effort (or lack of it) in maintaining contacts with customers after the sale.

<u>Limited Effectiveness of Using Bird Dogs</u>

Contacts from bird dogs comprise the third largest group, producing 64 total contacts for the productive and 8 for the marginal salespeople. Sales from this source totaled 9 for the productive salespeople and 2 for the marginal salespeople — an average of .45 and .1 sales per person, respectively. Although not large in terms of volume, these data explain much of the difference between the two groups. The use of bird dogs involves work, and the willingness to work varies sharply between the two groups.

*Note how talking
headings help
emphasize the
major findings.*

<u>Scant Use of Other Techniques</u>

Other prospect gaining techniques were little used among the salespeople observed. Techniques long discussed in industry sales literature such as cold-spearing, placing written messages on automobile windshields, and random telephoning produced no prospects for either group during the observation period. All of the salespeople observed noted that they had used these techniques in the past, but with little success. The lack of evidence in this study leaves unanswered the question of the effectiveness of these techniques.

<u>Summary–Conclusions.</u> The obvious conclusion drawn from the preceding review of how prospects are found is that the productive salespeople work harder to get them. Although both groups get about the same number of walk-ins, the successful ones work harder at maintaining contacts with past customers and at getting contacts from a network of bird dogs and friends.

OBSERVABLE DIFFERENCES IN PRESENTATIONS

Differences in the sales presentations used constituted the third area of study. Criteria used in this investigation were (1) integrity, (2) pressure, and (3) product knowledge. Obviously, the first two of these criteria had to be evaluated subjectively. Even so, the evaluations were made by highly trained observers who used comprehensive guidelines. These guidelines are described in detail in the approved observation plan.

**FIGURE 14–3** (continued)

*Report text (continued)*

6

Positive Effect of Integrity

The evaluations of the salespeople's integrity primarily measured the apparent degree of truthfulness of the sales presentations. The observers classified the images of integrity they perceived during the sales presentations into four groups: Group I -- Impeccable (displayed the highest degree of truthfulness), Group II -- Moderately High (generally truthful, some exaggeration), Group III -- Questionable (mildly deceitful and tricky), Group IV -- Deceitful (untruthful and tricky).

Of the 20 productive salespeople observed, 16 were classified in Group II (see Chart 3). Of the remaining four, 2 were in Group I and 2 in Group III.

*Here and elsewhere, text references tell the reader when to observe the charts.*

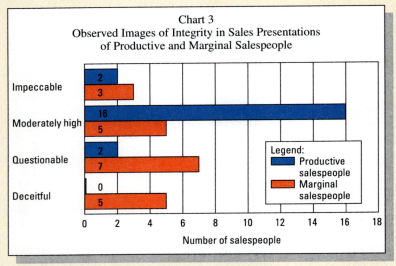

Distribution of the marginal salespeople was markedly different: 3 in Group I, 5 in Group II, 7 in Group III, and 5 in Group IV. Clearly, integrity was more apparent among the productive salespeople.

Apparent Value of Moderate Pressure

Measurements (by observation) of pressure used in the sales presentations were made in order to determine the relationship of pressure to sales success. Using the guidelines approved at the August meeting, the observers classified

**FIGURE 14–3** (continued)

*Report text (continued)*

7

each salesperson's presentations into three categories: (1) high pressure, (2) moderate pressure, and (3) low pressure. The observers reported difficulties in making some borderline decisions, but they felt that most of the presentations were easily classified.

Of the 20 productive salespeople, 15 used moderate pressure, 3 used low pressure, and 2 used high pressure (see Chart 4). The 20 marginal salespeople

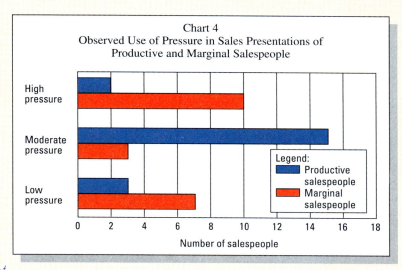

Chart 4
Observed Use of Pressure in Sales Presentations of Productive and Marginal Salespeople

*The facts are not just presented. They are compared and conclusions are drawn from them.*

presented a different picture. Only 3 of them used moderate pressure. Of the remainder, 10 used high pressure and 7 used low pressure. The evidence suggests that moderate pressure is most effective.

Necessity of Product Knowledge

Product knowledge, a generally accepted requirement for successful selling, was determined during the exit interview. Using the 30 basic questions developed by Armor management from sales literature, the observers measured the salespeople's product knowledge. Correct responses to 27 or more of the questions was determined to be excellent, 24 through 26 was fair, and below 24 was classified as inadequate.

The productive salespeople displayed superior knowledge of the product with 17 of the 20 scoring excellent. The remaining 3 scored fair (see Chart 5).

**FIGURE 14–3** (continued)

*Report text (continued)*

8

Scores for product knowledge were sharply different in the marginal salesperson group. Although 5 of them scored excellent, 6 scored fair, and 9 scored inadequate.

*Note how text and charts work closely together to present the information.*

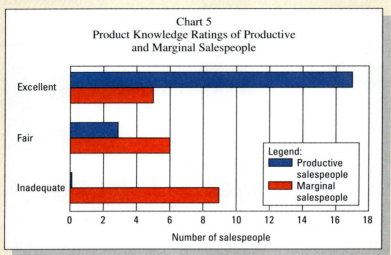

These data point to an apparent weakness in training or a lack of individual preparation.

Summary-Conclusions

*Another summary-conclusion brings the section to a close.*

The preceding presentation reveals some basic differences in the sales presentations of the productive and marginal salespeople. The productive salespeople displayed higher integrity (though not the highest). They used moderate pressure, whereas the marginal people tended toward high or low extremes. Also, the productive people knew their products better.

RECOMMENDATIONS FOR TRAINING

*From the summary-conclusions of the preceding three sections the recommendations are derived.*

The conclusions reached in preceding sections suggest certain actions that Armor Motors should take in training its sales force. Specifically, the instruction should be altered to include the following topics:

1. Importance of minimizing idle time.

2. Sales rewards from productive work (mailing literature, telephoning, cultivating prospects, etc.).

**FIGURE 14–3** Concluded

*Report text (continued)*

9

3. Importance of building a network of bird dogs and friends in building prospects.

*Numbering makes the recommendations stand out.*

4. Value of maintaining contacts with past customers.

5. Need for integrity, within reasonable limits.

6. Use of moderate pressure, avoiding extremes in either direction.

7. Need for a thorough knowledge of the product.

## QUESTIONS FOR DISCUSSION

1. Long, formal reports are not often written in business. So why should you know how to write them?
2. A good title should be complete and concise. Are not these requirements contradictory? Explain.
3. Discuss the relative importance of the title fly and the title page in a report.
4. Distinguish among the letter of transmittal, the foreword, and the preface.
5. Describe the role and content of a letter of transmittal.
6. Why is personal style typically used in the letter of transmittal?
7. What is the basis for determining whether a report should have a table of contents?
8. Discuss the construction of the executive summary.
9. Why does the executive summary include the facts and figures in addition to the analyses and conclusions drawn from them?
10. Some reports need little or no introduction; others need a very long introduction. Why is this so?
11. Give examples of report problems that require introductory coverage of methods of collecting data, historical background, and limitations.
12. Give examples of report problems that require, respectively, (*a*) an ending summary, (*b*) an ending conclusion, and (*c*) an ending recommendation.
13. Using as a guide the diagram in Figure 14–2, summarize the coherence plan of the long, formal report.

## APPLICATION EXERCISES

1. Making any assumptions needed, construct complete yet concise titles for the reports described below:
   *a.* A report writer reviewed records of exit interviews of employees at Marvel-Floyd Manufacturing Company who quit their jobs voluntarily. The objective of the investigation was to determine the reasons for leaving.
   *b.* A researcher studied data from employee personnel records at Magna-Tech, Inc. to determine whether permanent (long-term) employees differ from short-term employees. Any differences found would be used in hiring employees in the future. The data studied included age, education, experience, sex, marital status, test scores, and such.
   *c.* A report writer compared historical financial records (1935 to the present) of Super Saver Foods to determine whether this grocery chain should own or rent store buildings. In the past it did both.
2. Criticize the following beginning sentences of letters of transmittal:
   *a.* "In your hands is the report you requested January 7 concerning . . . ."
   *b.* "As you will recall, last January 7 you requested a report on . . . ."
   *c.* "That we should open a new outlet in Bragg City is the conclusion of this report, which you authorized January 7."
3. In a report comparing four automobiles (Alpha, Beta, Gamma, and Delta) to determine which one is the best buy for a company, section II of the report body covered cost data ( (*a*) initial costs; (*b*) trade-in values; and (*c*) operating expenses). Section III presented a comparison of the safety features of the automobiles ( (*a*) standard safety features; (*b*) acceleration data; (*c*) weight distribution; and (*d*) breaking quality).
   *a.* Criticize this introductory paragraph at the beginning of section III:
   In the preceding section was presented a thorough analysis of the cost data. Now safety of the cars will be compared. Although costs are important, Warren-Burke also is concerned about the safety of its salespeople, who spend almost half their work time driving.
   *b.* Write a more appropriate introductory paragraph.
4. The next section of the report (section IV) cov-

ered these topics: (*a*) handling; (*b*) quality of ride; and (*c*) durability.

a. Criticize this introductory paragraph for the section:
This section of the report presents a comparison of the overall construction of the four automobiles. These considerations also are important because they affect how a car rides, and this is important. Thus, we will take up in this order: handling, general riding quality, and construction qualities.

b. Write a more appropriate introductory paragraph.

5. Criticize this final paragraph (a preview) of the introduction of the report described above:
This report compares the automobiles by three factors. These are costs, safety, and comfort and construction, in that order. Costs include initial expenditure, trade-in value, and operating expense. Safety covers safety devices, acceleration, weight distribution, and braking. Comfort and construction includes handling, ride quality, and durability. A ranking is derived from this comparison.

■ ■ ■ ■ ■ ■ ■ ■ ■ ■ ■ ■ ■
### REPORT PROBLEMS: LONG

1. *Determine the need for a sporting goods store in your area.* (Requires research.) The Athlete's Warehouse, a large chain of sporting goods stores, is considering locating a store in your community. It has hired you and your independent research organization to analyze the need for such a store and to recommend the appropriate decision.

   The Athlete's Warehouse sells a broad range of merchandise for the sports-minded consumer. Included in each store's inventory are all the sports equipment popular in the community served. Also, the stores carry a large assortment of sports clothing. The Athlete's Warehouse stores are truly first class. In addition, their prices are highly competitive. In fact, the company promotes its stores as being "discount outlets."

   From you the Athlete's Warehouse management wants a recommendation on the question of whether to locate in your area. In reaching your recommendation, you will thoroughly review the existing sporting goods outlets. You will evaluate each on the following criteria: service, prices, and convenience.

   The "service" criterion includes the question of whether the stores take care of the total needs of the community—the completeness and depth of the goods offered, choices available, and such. Quality of personal service provided by store employees also is a part of this consideration, but time does not permit you to conduct a survey of consumers, which would be the ideal way of getting this information. Perhaps you can report information you can pick up from knowledgeable people in the community. As such information is not based on scientific investigation, be careful in reporting it.

   Your investigation of "prices" can be more scientific, for you can get quantitative comparisons here. Probably you will select a cross section sample of products—volume sellers in each major sports category. Then you will get prices for these products. You will compare these prices with those for the Athlete's Warehouse, which the company has given you. (For class purposes, you may assume that the Athlete's Warehouse prices are lower than the lowest prices you find in the community on 80 percent of the items.)

   Your study of "convenience" will be an analysis of the geographic area served and how accessible the stores are. Ease of parking, hours of operation, store arrangement, display of merchandise, and such also are parts of this factor.

   As you make your evaluations, keep in mind the words the Athlete's Warehouse president left with you: "Unless the competition is firmly entrenched and is already providing super service and low prices, we can come in and succeed. Our merchandise, service, and prices are second to none. We don't mind a little competition."

   After you have gathered the information you need and have analyzed it, you will present your findings in an appropriate report form. As you view the situation, it is somewhat formal; and the report will be longer than most you write. Although the information you will assemble is not heavily quantitative, you hope to use some graphics. Probably you will construct some form of map showing locations of existing stores. And perhaps the price data will lend to a graphic presentation. Address the report to Mr. Wade O. Borg, president.

2. *Reporting on the desirability of holding an association's annual meeting in a city.* (Requires research.) You are the executive director of the International

Association of Public Relations Administrators. At its last meeting, the organization's board of directors tentatively selected _____ (a city of your instructor's choice) for its annual meeting two years from now. The board asked you to visit the city, look it over, and report on its desirability as a meeting site. The board will make its final decision on the site at its next meeting, scheduled for the coming month.

Following your visit to the city, you returned to your office. There you reviewed the information you had collected. As you viewed your assignment, the board's decision should be based on these primary considerations:

(a) availability of adequate hotels—accommodations for the 450 people expected to attend; meeting rooms—8 small (50-person capacity) and 1 large (for an assembly of all attending);
(b) transportation, both to and from the city and within the city; distance between airport and hotels, hotels and shopping areas, etc.;
(c) attractions—entertainment, shopping, cultural attractions, restaurants, and such. (The delegates expect to play as well as attend meetings.)

After you have completed your analysis, you will write the report. You will select a form appropriate for this fairly long and formal report. Address it to Cindy DeMaris, president.

3. *Reporting survey results to the board of a country club.* The board of directors of the Deer Creek Country Club is considering these projects for improving their facilities:

(a) expanding the golf course from 18 to 27 holes
(b) repairing and resurfacing the swimming pool
(c) building a new tennis clubhouse
(d) resurfacing the five tennis courts and installing lights
(e) purchasing adjacent land for future expansion

The golf course expansion would be on land already owned by the club. Thus, this proposal is not related to the last proposal. The land being considered for purchase is viewed by proponents as a site for an additional nine holes of golf some years in the future. The land is available for purchase now and may not be available if and when the club needs it in the future.

Unfortunately, these improvements will require that the club borrow the money needed, either from a bank or by selling bonds to its members. The additional indebtedness would require an increase in membership dues of $40 per month if all improvements are made—less if only some are made.

At their last meeting, the directors discussed the matter thoroughly. Some of them opposed all the projects. Some favored all of them. And some favored certain proposals and opposed others. The discussions brought out differing viewpoints concerning what the club should be. One group felt strongly that golf and social activities should be the sole emphasis. Others expressed broader and varying views. After long and heated debate, the directors concluded that they should take the matter to the membership. They asked you, the club manager, to prepare an appropriate questionnaire, mail it to the members, record and analyze the results, and report your findings to them. They want the report before next month's meeting.

As instructed, you prepared a questionnaire. It was a simple one consisting of four basic questions. The cover letter explained the proposed expenditures and the effect they would have on dues and the club's indebtedness. Since the board is concerned with individual preferences, you sent the questionnaire to every member over 21 (thus a husband and wife with joint membership each received a questionnaire).

The club has three classes of membership: senior, corporate, and junior. For purposes of the survey, you combined the corporate and senior members, for both typically are families. However, you did separate the junior members from the seniors. The juniors are young adults (under 30). They pay the same dues as senior members, but they pay substantially less for the initial cost of membership. What they pay for membership can be applied to a senior membership when they reach age 30. As this group represents the future of the club, the board members are interested in their viewpoints separately.

Two weeks after mailing the questionnaires, you concluded that you would have to cut off the returns and determine your findings. At this point, your returns by membership type and by sex were as follows:

| Membership Type | Number Mailed | Number Returned | Percent Returned |
|---|---|---|---|
| Senior, male | 1,125 | 877 | 80.0 |
| Senior, female | 981 | 609 | 62.1 |
| Junior, male | 381 | 169 | 44.1 |
| Junior, female | 133 | 51 | 38.3 |
| TOTAL | 2,620 | 1,706 | 61.1 |

Then you began tabulating your responses. You started with the basic question of what the members think the club should be—that is, what activities it should provide. Your summary of responses to this question appears in Table 1. Then you tabulated responses to the second question, which asked the members their willingness to pay additional dues to cover all, some, or none of the costs of the improvement (Table 2).

Next you tabulated the responses to the third question, which asked whether the respondents favor or oppose each of the proposed projects (Table 3). Finally, you tabulated responses to your question about the respondents' use of club facilities in the past year (Table 4). Designed to find out how the members use the club, this question might well produce information that explains how the members answered the third question. But it also shows the size of the major interest groups (tennis, golf, and swimming) in the club. The board members feel that they should take care of all significantly large interest groups among the membership.

With these tables before you, you are ready to begin interpreting and analyzing them. You will present your work to the board in a clear and helpful report. Wherever the report will benefit from graphics, you will use them. Address the report to the board. Follow the address reference to the board with a list of the 12 board members. Show Ms. Patricia A. Arnold as president.

4. *Comparing prices of Prairie City's discount stores.* U-Save is a chain of general discount stores operating in your area. "We meet or beat all prices of the competition" is the company's motto, and company management has conscientiously worked to make this motto a reality. In fact, department heads (who are responsible for the prices of their merchandise) have been instructed to continually monitor prices and make certain theirs are lowest. Of course, it is to be expected that occasionally exceptions will occur, as when a competitor conducts a special promotion. But U-Save intends to be the price leader as a general rule.

Today's mail brought to U-Save's corporate headquarters evidence that the company's price objectives are not being met in the Prairie City area. From a stockholder came a clipping of a feature story in the *Prairie City Chronicle* reporting a shopping basket comparison of prices in the area's discount stores. The message of the story is clearly summarized in the headline: "Study Shows Lo-Mart Prices Lowest." The study was made by Alex O. Hawkins, a business reporter for the *Chronicle*. Mr. Hawkins made a list of 20 items commonly purchased and got their prices at the three discount stores in Prairie City (Lo-Mart, U-Save, and Bonus) and reported his findings. He found that Lo-Mart held a slight lead over the other stores, although prices tended to be close. In the story, Mr. Hawkins took a verbal slap at U-Save's motto: "The U-Save claim of lowest prices proved to be just a claim. The evidence does not support it."

U-Save's president, Lisa A. Mattingly, was highly upset about the article, and she wants some-

**TABLE 1 (Problem 3)** Members' Responses about What Club Emphasis Should Be, in Percentages and Number of Responses (in Parentheses)

| Membership Type | A | B | C | D |
|---|---|---|---|---|
| Senior, male | 34.4% (302) | 5.4% (47) | 0.8% (7) | 59.4% (521) |
| Senior, female | 24.4% (149) | 3.4% (21) | 0.5% (3) | 71.6% (436) |
| Junior, male | 24.2% (41) | 3.0% (5) | 1.8% (3) | 71.0% (120) |
| Junior, female | 15.7% (8) | 3.9% (2) | 0 (0) | 80.4% (41) |
| TOTAL | 29.3% (500) | 4.4% (75) | .8% (13) | 65.5% (1,118) |

The emphasis of the club should be on
A—golf and social activities only
B—golf, tennis, and social activities
C—golf, swimming, and social activities
D—golf, swimming, tennis, and social activities

**TABLE 2 (Problem 3)** Willingness of Members to Pay Dues Increase, by Membership Type, in Percentages and Numbers Responding (in Parentheses)

| Membership Type | No Increase; No Improvement | Some Increase; Some Improvements | Pay $40 Mo.; All Improvements |
|---|---|---|---|
| Senior, male | 33.0% (289) | 53.0% (465) | 14.0% (123) |
| Senior, female | 26.3% (160) | 55.2% (336) | 18.5% (113) |
| Junior, male | 18.3% (31) | 37.3% (63) | 44.4% (75) |
| Junior, female | 15.7% (8) | 31.4% (16) | 52.9% (27) |
| TOTAL | 28.6% (488) | 51.6% (880) | 19.8% (338) |

**TABLE 3 (Problem 3)** Members Approving Proposed Projects in Percentages and Number of Responses (in Parentheses)

| Membership Type | 9 Holes Golf | Swimming Pool | Tennis Clubhouse | Tennis Courts, Lights | Land Purchase |
|---|---|---|---|---|---|
| Senior, male | 53.7% (471) | 27.7% (243) | 24.5% (215) | 22.9% (201) | 11.5% (101) |
| Senior, female | 42.4% (258) | 40.6% (247) | 31.5% (192) | 29.0% (171) | 8.9% (54) |
| Junior, male | 64.5% (109) | 61.5% (104) | 59.8% (101) | 43.8% (74) | 16.0% (27) |
| Junior, female | 62.7% (32) | 70.5% (36) | 64.7% (33) | 41.1% (21) | 11.8% (6) |
| TOTAL | 51.0% (870) | 36.9% (630) | 31.7% (541) | 27.4% (467) | 11.0% (188) |

**TABLE 4 (Problem 3)** Respondents Participating in Golf, Tennis, and Swimming at Club in Past Year, in Percentages and Number of Responses (in Parentheses)

| Membership Type | Golf | Tennis | Swimming |
|---|---|---|---|
| Senior, male | 79.0% (693) | 9.0% (79) | 7.7% (68) |
| Senior, female | 22.5% (137) | 16.9% (103) | 9.5% (58) |
| Junior, male | 75.1% (127) | 15.4% (26) | 31.3% (53) |
| Junior, female | 60.8% (31) | 35.3% (18) | 33.3% (17) |
| TOTAL | 57.9% (908) | 13.2% (226) | 11.5% (196) |

thing done about it. So she called you, her assistant, into her office. Her words explain her thinking: "My first reaction to this study was that it is unfair—a low blow. The items selected are not representative of our store's merchandise. Obviously, the study was done by a reporter who knows little about business—especially about survey techniques. Even so, the publicity is damaging. And there just might be some truth to the findings. I want you to look into the situation. Get some price comparisons from the three discount stores in Prairie City. Use a sufficiently broad selection of items to give a good indication of overall prices. I am not interested in just refuting the story. I want the truth. Are we or aren't we the price leaders?"

Following Ms. Mattingly's general instructions, you began work on the project. You selected eight departments that you thought were representative of U-Save's operation and that were comparable to departments in the two competing stores. Then you selected 12 items in each department. You took care that these were branded items that could be precisely identified (no private labels, for example) and were sold at all three stores. Then you got the prices for the items at all three stores. In doing so, you made certain that the items were not currently being promoted—that you were getting normal, day-to-day prices. When you finished this task, you assembled your findings neatly in tabular form (Table 5).

Now you are ready to analyze and report. Your analysis, of course, should lead to an overall conclusion about U-Save's prices relative to those of its competition. You will also point out how the U-Save store pricing compares by department with the competition; and in doing so, you will note where corrective actions need to be taken. You will use graphics wherever they are useful in communicating the important parts of your message. You will present your report in a form suitable for the occasion (a report to the president with copies for all members of the board of directors). The matter is on the agenda for the meeting of the board next month. Perhaps the board will want similar studies made in other cities.

5. *Selecting the compact disc packaging for a promising new folk music star.* Your marketing research firm, Krentler, Brown and Hannah, has been approached by A&M Records, Inc. to help select the CD packaging for one of their most promising new performers, Megan Adami. Sarah Brown, president of your company, did most of the initial work on gaining the account. She's given you the following information she's gleaned from several meetings with these new clients. She's assigned the task to you because she is confident of both your ability to do the job as well as your ability to write a good report, clearly presenting both your findings and your recommendations. She understands the importance of keeping customers through writing reports they can use.

The major decision here seems to be whether to use the long box or the more environmentally friendly short box. At this point, sales from anything that has been packaged in the short box have been down considerably, even for well-known musicians like Peter Gabriel. His experience with sales dropping from 2 million copies on one record packaged in the long box to less than half a million in one packaged in the short box points out the dilemma your clients are experiencing. Their promising star needs to get good distribution on early recordings to help ensure high levels of sales on future recordings. She cannot afford the luxury of poor sales that well-established artists can bear.

From your preliminary research, you have learned that some of the recording industry's most well-known artists have been crusading to save the rain forests. This seems to be a popular stand with their public; opinion polls show those with demographics typical of their customers agree strongly with this and sales of songs with this theme do very well. Some artists, such as Sting and The Grateful Dead, have gone even further, launching campaigns to ban the long box—an environmentally unfriendly box. Although in line with their customers' beliefs, the data at the sales desk seem unaffected by the politics of these well-known artists.

Some companies have been experimenting with a variety of packaging materials such as using less packaging, using recycled paper, and using biodegradeable plastics. But none of these seem to address the issue of which is best for sales. Factors other than the box itself seem to enter into the decision. One such factor is that of display. Not only are the long boxes easier to display since they fit into the racks formerly designed for 12-inch record albums, they also have more space for showing a picture, an eye-catching graphic, and descriptive material. In short, they are a bigger promotional piece.

Also, some retailers just don't like the short boxes, so they do not display them as well. Some retailers stack them in corners or behind the counters. Others make them difficult to access on purpose because they fear they will be stolen more

**TABLE 5 (Problem 4)** Prices by Departments of Selected Items at Three Discount Stores in Prairie City

| Departments and Items | Prices | | |
|---|---|---|---|
| | U-Save | Lo-Mart | Bonus |
| **Health and Beauty Aids** | | | |
| Advil, 200 mg., 100 tablets | $ 6.99 | $ 6.49 | $ 6.79 |
| Gillette Trac II cartridges, 12-pk. | 5.19 | 4.79 | 4.89 |
| Conair curling iron, 1/2 or 3/4 in. | 17.49 | 16.19 | 18.09 |
| Visine eye drops, 1/2 oz. | 2.19 | 2.29 | 2.29 |
| Colgate toothpaste, 8.2 oz. | 1.79 | 1.88 | 1.99 |
| Mabelline mascara | 2.98 | 3.09 | 3.19 |
| Ten-O-Six skin lotion | 4.09 | 4.69 | 4.57 |
| Jergens hand lotion, 10-oz. | 2.39 | 2.59 | 2.45 |
| Clairmist hair spray, 8-oz. | 1.47 | 1.49 | 1.59 |
| Mennen Speed Stick deodorant, 2¼ oz. | 1.99 | 2.19 | 2.19 |
| Head & Shoulders shampoo, 15 oz. | 3.49 | 3.77 | 3.69 |
| Ultra Slim-Fast, 15 oz. | 4.99 | 4.89 | 5.09 |
| **Housewares** | | | |
| Black & Decker Spacemaker can opener | 27.99 | 27.49 | 29.47 |
| Rubbermaid cleanup caddy | 5.39 | 5.19 | 5.49 |
| Anchor Hocking wine glasses, 4 pk. | 9.99 | 10.49 | 10.89 |
| Wearever cookware, 7-piece set | 42.99 | 39.99 | 40.99 |
| Old Homestead knife set, 7 piece | 33.99 | 30.99 | 34.49 |
| Roughneck trash container, 32 gal. | 10.49 | 9.99 | 10.29 |
| Hamilton Beach blender, 7 speed | 19.29 | 18.88 | 19.99 |
| Dirt Devil hand vacuum | 37.49 | 36.99 | 40.29 |
| Roll-O-Matic sponge mop | 6.99 | 7.29 | 7.69 |
| Duracell batteries, AA, 4 pk. | 2.29 | 2.49 | 2.59 |
| Proctor-Silex coffeemaker, 12 cup | 15.19 | 14.99 | 15.47 |
| Black & Decker self-cleaning iron, F-520 | 33.49 | 31.99 | 32.39 |
| **Hardware** | | | |
| Arrow T-50 staple gun | 21.39 | 18.99 | 20.97 |
| Black & Decker drill, 3/8 in. | 31.88 | 38.96 | 35.98 |
| GE Miser Circlite, 44 watt | 19.97 | 17.69 | 20.49 |
| Stanley Workmaster hammer, 16 oz. | 13.49 | 14.59 | 15.99 |
| First Alert smoke alarm | 13.97 | 15.49 | 26.89 |
| Black & Decker scrub brusher | 39.99 | 43.49 | 43.79 |
| Skil drill, 3/8-in. cordless, 7.2 v. | 131.99 | 129.99 | 130.49 |
| Teledyne shower massage, hand-held | 34.79 | 34.99 | 32.99 |
| GM180 glue gun | 4.69 | 4.49 | 4.67 |
| Stanley screwdriver set, #64-457 | 4.99 | 4.27 | 4.49 |
| Formby's tung oil, 16 oz. | 7.19 | 6.97 | 7.27 |
| Duro Tub 'n Sink Jelly, 8 oz. | 2.69 | 2.57 | 2.67 |
| **Apparel** | | | |
| Fruit of the Loom boys' briefs, 3 pk. | 4.98 | 4.47 | 4.89 |
| Underalls pantyhose, style 320 | 2.47 | 2.29 | 2.09 |
| Lee jeans, ladies, pepperwashed | 19.99 | 19.99 | 20.99 |
| Levi's polo shirts, cotton-poly, men's | 15.99 | 15.49 | 15.99 |
| London Fog windbreaker, children's | 15.79 | 16.09 | 15.99 |
| Hanes tube socks, boys, 6 pr. | 4.19 | 4.19 | 3.97 |
| Greatland socks, women's, 3 pr. | 4.89 | 4.67 | 4.49 |
| Playmate panties, bikini, nylon, 3 pr. | 7.19 | 7.47 | 7.29 |
| Dappi diaper pants | 5.29 | 5.98 | 5.39 |
| Happy Kids jumpers, corduroy, 1 pc. | 9.47 | 8.97 | 8.99 |
| Henley knit tops, ladies, cotton-poly | 12.47 | 12.95 | 11.99 |
| Pretty Miss fleece jacket, cotton-poly | 19.99 | 19.99 | 29.49 |

**TABLE 5 (Problem 4)** (concluded)

| Departments and Items | Prices | | |
|---|---|---|---|
| | U-Save | Lo-Mart | Bonus |
| **Automotive** | | | |
| Prestone antifreeze-coolant, 1 gal. | $ 4.99 | $ 4.89 | $ 4.99 |
| Champion spark plugs, 8 pk., RBL 12-6 | 12.47 | 11.98 | 12.19 |
| STP gas treatment, 15 oz. | 1.49 | 1.39 | 1.33 |
| Armorall car wash, 40 oz. | 4.19 | 3.99 | 4.29 |
| Schauer battery charger, 8 amp. | 30.88 | 29.99 | 32.49 |
| NuFinish liquid car polish, 16 oz. | 4.89 | 4.29 | 4.49 |
| Mobil motor oil, 10W-30, qt. | 1.19 | .99 | .99 |
| Fram air filter, CA 357 | 3.29 | 2.99 | 3.09 |
| Monroe Gas Matic shocks | 18.99 | 19.49 | 19.99 |
| Ultra Spark plug wires, 6 cyl. | 16.19 | 16.49 | 15.99 |
| Dupont freon, R-12, 12 oz. | 3.69 | 3.49 | 2.99 |
| Scotchgard upholstery protector | 6.29 | 6.29 | 5.99 |
| **Domestics** | | | |
| Stevens Ultra Touch sheets, queen | 29.97 | 28.49 | 28.79 |
| Dundee Centennial towels, 27 × 54 in. | 10.49 | 9.99 | 10.29 |
| Cannon lid cover, 100% cotton | 6.99 | 6.97 | 6.89 |
| Spring Performance quilted bedspread | 29.99 | 33.49 | 31.99 |
| Crown Crafts comforter sets, full | 69.99 | 64.99 | 66.99 |
| Heirloom pillows, quilted, goose feathers, standard | 20.49 | 20.99 | 21.39 |
| Crystal bath rug, nylon, 21 × 34 in. | 5.99 | 6.79 | 6.19 |
| Lady Pepperell sheets, cotton-poly, full | 7.99 | 8.79 | 7.99 |
| American Country Classics mitt | 2.79 | 2.97 | 3.09 |
| Cannon Monticello bath towels | 6.99 | 7.29 | 6.49 |
| Spring Rain shower curtain, 70 × 72 in, vinyl lined | 22.99 | 24.49 | 23.99 |
| Tahiti mini blinds, aluminum, 23 × 42 in. | 15.29 | 16.49 | 25.99 |
| **Sporting Goods** | | | |
| Mountain Trek Organizer day pack | 12.49 | 13.29 | 13.99 |
| California Pro racerline skates | 69.99 | 74.99 | 77.49 |
| Atlantic Dive mask | 20.49 | 19.99 | 20.49 |
| Prince Pro tennis racquet | 39.99 | 44.49 | 43.99 |
| Wilson Tour Le driver | 59.99 | 69.99 | 64.49 |
| Remington 870 12-gauge shotgun | 199.99 | 212.99 | 209.99 |
| Daiwa Black Widow casting rod | 17.99 | 20.49 | 20.99 |
| Everlast polyester-cotton gym shorts | 16.99 | 18.39 | 17.99 |
| Nike gym shorts, nylon print, women's | 25.47 | 24.99 | 25.99 |
| Adidas Primo soccer ball | 30.49 | 29.99 | 30.19 |
| Ektelon Controller racquetball glove | 8.99 | 9.99 | 9.79 |
| Wilson TDJ football, youth | 34.97 | 36.29 | 35.29 |
| **Photography-Electronics** | | | |
| Bell South cordless telephone, #688 | 94.99 | 89.99 | 92.99 |
| GE Compact Stereo, #11-2012 | 109.99 | 99.99 | 111.99 |
| Magnavox VHS VCR, #VR9020 | 207.99 | 199.99 | 209.99 |
| Maxell XL II blank cassette, 90 min. | 9.29 | 8.49 | 8.99 |
| Fuji 3.5 MF2HD floppy disks, 10 | 13.19 | 12.99 | 13.49 |
| Casio #FX991 calculator | 15.99 | 16.99 | 16.49 |
| Sony Walkman, #WM-F2081 | 82.99 | 79.99 | 74.99 |
| 35-mm. color processing, 24 exp. | 4.49 | 4.19 | 4.49 |
| GE micro-cassette recorder, #3-53705 | 28.49 | 27.99 | 29.49 |
| Kodak Gold Film, 35 mm., 24 exp. | 3.49 | 3.59 | 3.49 |
| Sony T-120 videotape, 2 pk. | 7.17 | 6.88 | 7.09 |
| GE microcassette answering system | 39.99 | 41.59 | 40.99 |

easily due to their smaller size. This is especially true of small retailers without the electronic security systems the larger stores use.

Your secondary research led you to conclude that the retailers were the critical link affecting sales. Therefore, you decided to survey large, medium, and small retailers on their current and anticipated methods for displaying the long and short boxes. Present a recommendation to your new clients based on the information you have gathered. You may organize the data presented in the following table in any way that will communicate clearly to your readers. You may use it to create any type of graphic that serves a definite purpose.

Because the report is an external one to a rather important new client, you will present it formally. Include prefatory parts and any appended parts you need to present your best possible report.

### TABLE 6 (Problem 5)  Questionnaire Results from Retailers

Results show retailers responding to questions on a Likert scale with 5 representing "Strongly Agree" to 1 representing "Strongly Disagree." They rated both their current attitudes and practices and their anticipated ones for the next three to five years on the use of the long and short box.

| Items | Large* | | Medium† | | Small‡ | |
|---|---|---|---|---|---|---|
| | Current | Anticipated | Current | Anticipated | Current | Anticipated |
| Most of my customers prefer the short box to the long box. | 3.10 | 4.00 | 3.70 | 4.20 | 4.00 | 4.30 |
| My folk music customers are sensitive to environmental practices. | 3.25 | 3.50 | 3.20 | 3.80 | 4.20 | 4.50 |
| I believe in stocking what the market demands—what the sales and profit figures show. | 4.80 | 4.50 | 4.00 | 4.00 | 3.50 | 3.50 |
| I believe in doing whatever I can to promote the artists and companies who are environmentally responsible. | 3.30 | 3.60 | 3.50 | 3.65 | 4.00 | 4.20 |
| I promote the music packaged in the short box. | 3.00 | 3.10 | 3.00 | 3.50 | 4.50 | 4.50 |
| I display the long boxes more effectively than the short boxes. | 4.00 | 3.50 | 4.20 | 3.50 | 3.20 | 2.00 |
| I have special display racks for the short box. | 3.50 | 4.00 | 2.80 | 4.00 | 3.20 | 3.50 |
| I modify my current display racks for use with the short box. | 2.80 | 3.00 | 3.50 | 4.00 | 4.00 | 4.20 |
| I give the short box special displays such as end-of-aisle and special shelving. | 2.30 | 3.20 | 2.90 | 3.20 | 4.00 | 4.20 |
| I order only long music packaged in the long box. | 2.00 | 1.80 | 2.80 | 2.50 | 1.50 | 1.250 |
| I order based only on product, not package. | 4.80 | 4.75 | 4.80 | 4.80 | 3.50 | 3.50 |
| I order the short box whenever possible. | 2.00 | 2.60 | 2.50 | 3.20 | 4.00 | 4.20 |

\* Daily sales over $8,000
† Daily sales $5,000–$7,999
‡ Daily sales under $5,000

**6.** *Determining whether to use a computerized system for eyewear inventory management.* As the office manager for a small midwest eye clinic, you have been delegated the task of determining whether to implement a computer system for assisting with the eyewear inventory management aspect of your job. Your boss (the owner of the clinic) is a busy eye surgeon who depends on you to gather relevant primary and secondary information and to present it in a clearly organized report. You are also expected to include both the advantages and disadvantages of implementing such a system along with your recommendation.

The primary reason the clinic is in business is to serve its patients. The idea of setting up a computerized system arises from this objective. Currently, the manual system seems to be working fine. You have no complaints from either the patients, your servicepeople, or your employees. The computer system is proposed only to improve your service.

Currently, when patients are given prescriptions for glasses or contact lenses, they often select from your stock. The contact lenses are relatively easy to control since you stock a number and a correction range based on data representatives from the different suppliers recommend. Their data are based on two factors—the size of the practice and the corrections needed by a normally distributed population.

So far this seems pretty effective. Only once or twice a day do you have to put a special order in for contacts. Usually these are orders for the very weakest and very strongest corrections and orders for a correction you are just out of stock on at the moment.

The eyeglass frames, on the other hand, are more difficult to manage. Some patients will find several frames they like, only having trouble choosing which one they like best. Others, especially children and teenagers, look over your selection finding nothing that suits them. Then, of course, there are the shoppers—those patients who just want a new pair of frames or a second or third pair. Finally, there are those with needs for specialty frames such as sunglasses, swim and ski goggles, and protective work glasses. You currently stock these frames based on the firsthand experience of your eyewear technicians. When representatives from different eyeglass companies call on them, your technicians order what they think patients want. They keep no data on the sales of certain frames, styles, colors, etc. And the sales representatives do not compile these statistics either. The representatives are good at keeping you up-to-date on the latest styles and colors, but they have not presented any data to help you select your stock.

Your boss speculates that if you knew which

**TABLE 7 (Problem 6)** Questionnaire Results from a Survey on the Proposed Computer-Assisted Inventory Management

The scores for each group are based on a Likert scale using 5 for "Strongly Agree" to 1 for "Strongly Disagree."

| Items | Employees | Sales Representatives | Patients |
|---|---|---|---|
| I am completely satisfied with the current system. | 4.00 | 3.50 | 3.80 |
| I believe a computer-assisted inventory management would improve patient service. | 4.20 | 4.50 | 4.65 |
| While such a system might give some improvement, the added overhead cost it would add to glasses and frames would not be worth it. | 3.80 | 2.00 | 2.10 |
| I believe such a system would increase sales. | 4.00 | 4.80 | 4.75 |
| I believe such a system would improve employee decision making. | 3.10 | 4.30 | 4.00 |
| I believe such a system would only lead to poor employee morale and worse service. | 2.80 | 1.25 | 2.00 |

styles and colors were selling and which ones were not, you could make better inventory decisions. You could move out the frames just taking storage space, replacing them with choices your patients would like better. A computer system could keep track of the inventory as well as age it. Your patients would be pleased with the selection, and you would save them the trouble of having to look other places. In addition, the eyewear component of your business should be more profitable.

A computer system might also improve your contact lens distribution somewhat. While this would take time, the system would track your own patients over a year or two. Instead of buying a stock based on a normally distributed population, you'd buy it based on your own patient population. Your goal would be to have contacts in stock for all your patients, reducing the special orders to just occasional out-of-stock corrections. Keeping your patients happy is your objective.

Your preliminary research shows that no other clinics in your area are using such a system. So before you decide to implement it, you need to determine the advantages and disadvantages. Therefore, you have decided to collect information from the three groups affected by this change—the employees, the patients, and the sales representatives.

Write a well-organized report for your boss combining the primary data in Table 7 with additional secondary research you gather on computer programs for inventory management. Present it in a visually pleasing manner. After all, you are in the vision business. Use graphics and color when and where appropriate.

7. *Integrating foreign-born workers into the organization.* (Requires research.) In addition to working in a business environment that is global, your company is rapidly becoming one that is multicultural. Lately, your supervisor, Thomas McLaughlin, has been receiving complaints from many of the company's most promising foreign-born workers about feeling frustrated and isolated from their American counterparts. These workers are some of your top-flight engineers educated in U.S. schools.

Your company's primary business is making the cabs of trucks, mainly for Ford Motor Company. And you do not want to risk losing the workers upon which your company's future is so dependent. Therefore, Mr. McLaughlin has decided to start a program to make them feel more at home in order to integrate them into your work force more effectively. He has asked you to gather information on what other companies have done that has been effective.

He has heard that Apple and Intel Corporation have had success with some of these programs. He has heard they offer classes for both the foreign-born worker and the American worker. These classes range from softening accents to asserting oneself on the job. In addition, classes on the basics of communication are beneficial. Not only do foreign-born workers benefit from training in written and oral communication skills but also from training on idioms Americans use frequently. Americans are offered classes in foreign languages and business practices used in foreign countries. One area most Americans enjoy and benefit from is the study of gestures and how ones they use without thinking can communicate very different meanings in different cultures.

Mr. McLaughlin also wants to know more about setting up special offices or positions for those specializing in cross-cultural communication. Apparently, Apple Corporation has done this quite effectively. He wants to know what others have done, too.

Your report for Mr. McLaughlin should be a formal one with recommendations for action. Be sure to thoroughly document your sources. You will probably want to include both secondary and primary information. Talking firsthand to foreign-born workers is one way to gather primary information. However, be sure to take steps to assure them of your intentions for gathering the information. Also, you may want to confirm information often to be certain you have accurately understood your subject. Feel free to use graphics to support your research.

8. *Determining whether to self-publish or publish through a publishing company a book on golfing techniques.* (Requires research.) You work for a management consulting firm that handles a wide variety of requests for solving business problems. One client your firm recently acquired was Steve Robbins, an author of a manuscript on the kinesiology aspects of playing golf. You've been assigned to work with Mr. Robbins. Essentially, he needs to know whether he should self-publish his manuscript or publish through a publishing company. You will research the problem and present your findings and recommendation in a formal report to Mr. Robbins.

While you have not read Mr. Robbins' manuscript, the senior partner in your firm has read it and confirmed that it is thorough, well written, and well illustrated. The manuscript is around 150 pages with good illustrations. You know this to be about a 100–120-page book in printed form. Also, Mr. Robbins has done something unique—he has taken the complex subject of kinesiology and presented it simply and clearly. Currently, there is only one other good book on the subject, but it is written by an engineer and is extremely complex. In other words, you believe Mr. Robbins' book is salable to the right market.

Mr. Robbins' dilemma is not unusual; many authors try to decide whether or not they should self-publish. However, the majority of those have manuscripts for a very small market niche or manuscripts for which they cannot find a publisher. You believe Mr. Robbins will find many publishers eager to publish his manuscript. However, his question is one of making the best business decision. Self-publishing puts more of the profits in the writer's pocket, but it is plagued with distribution problems. Publishing companies, on the other hand, usually solve the distribution problem, but they also charge for handling the production and distribution. Unlike other writers, Mr. Robbins has already contacted the owner of a chain of discount golf equipment and sporting goods stores, who has agreed to sell the book in all 200 stores.

Your task is to gather objective information on all aspects, recommending the best decision for Mr. Robbins. Try collecting information from bookstores and golf and sporting goods stores as well as publishers and other authors. Present both the financial aspects and the author responsibilities along with your clear recommendation in your report to Mr. Robbins. Include any kind of graphic device that will help present your information as accurately and clearly as possible.

9. *Investigating franchising as a possible distribution policy for SeaCatch.* As research analyst for Datamatics, you just received a call from your newest client, Eunice Zimmerman. Ms. Zimmerman has had the idea of establishing a number of sushi bars throughout the United States and Canada. Several months ago, she incorporated under the title Sea-Catch, so she has a legal entity for her new business. Now she wants to know how to market the individual fast-food outlets. With the current interest in low cholesterol diets, you believe that Ms. Zimmerman has a potentially successful concept. It should prove profitable, too, given the right distribution setup.

To answer Ms. Zimmerman's questions, you began researching the marketing literature. You found that franchising is the most frequently used distribution policy for fast-food operations. Interestingly, franchising began in the United States in 1863; so it is far from a new marketing plan. Today there are more than 540,000 franchises in the United States that employ more than 7.2 million people in 60 different industries. Sales for last year exceeded 758.5 billion, and the top foreign markets for franchises are Canada, Japan, and Europe.

Armed with this background information, you now decide to investigate the idea of franchising in more detail. Because of the widespread use of franchising, mailing lists of both franchisors and franchisees are readily available. You purchase one for fast-food convenience outlets in North America (7,214 franchisors; 15,635 franchisees) from Infomart Inc. To both of these groups, you intend to send a questionnaire about franchise operations. In particular, you will ask questions about royalty and advertising fees; successful franchisee characteristics; franchising advantages; initial ongoing services provided by franchisor/franchisee; and issues covered by a franchise agreement. Because regulatory laws differ by country, you will inquire also about areas where government regulation is needed in Canada.

From this preliminary thinking, you design a questionnaire instrument to measure the perceptions of a random sample of each group in the mailing list you purchased. (Assume that the procedure you use will give you reliable and representative findings). The results from your survey are complete, and they are neatly tallied and arranged as shown in Tables 8–14.

It is now your job to use these facts in a report directed to Ms. Zimmerman. The report will be a formal one in wording and physical appearance. More importantly, however, you will need to present the facts about franchising and interpret them in such a way as to relate to the distribution problems of SeaCatch. To interpret the data, you will need graphics to supplement your words.

Prepare the long, formal report about franchising for your client, Eunice Zimmerman.

10. *Comparing corporate energy conservation activities in the United States, Canada, and the United Kingdom.* For today's report writing assignment, assume you are director of research for the International Association of Manufacturing (IAM). It's your job to identify, research, and report on current and critical issues affecting the 9,456 IAM members. One topic that has occupied your mind for quite some time is that of the energy problem and how firms are dealing with it. Now, you are determined to find out more specifics about the energy problem in industry.

To do that, you design a research study that will give you answers to many of the questions you have. Because you believe the energy topic has international dimensions, you decide to survey not only the United States but Canada and the United

**TABLE 8 (Problem 9)** Royalty and Advertising Fees for Franchises

| Royalty Range (as % of sales) | % Franchisees Reporting | % Franchisors Reporting |
|---|---|---|
| None | 20 | 13 |
| 0–3% | 7 | 8 |
| 3–6% | 39 | 59 |
| 6–9% | 26 | 16 |
| More than 9% | 8 | 4 |

| Advertising Fee Range (as % of sales) | % Franchisees Reporting | % Franchisors Reporting |
|---|---|---|
| None | 14 | 22 |
| 0–2% | 41 | 30 |
| 2–4% | 26 | 11 |
| More than 4% | 17 | 1 |
| Negotiated | — | 36 |

**TABLE 9 (Problem 9)** Importance of Characteristics Required for Success as Viewed by Franchisees and Franchisors, in Percentages

| Characteristic | Franchisees | | | Franchisors | | |
|---|---|---|---|---|---|---|
| | Very Important | Important | Not Very Important | Very Important | Important | Not Very Important |
| Support from family | 54 | 26 | 20 | 48 | 30 | 22 |
| Strong people skills | 65 | 30 | 5 | 66 | 32 | 2 |
| Financial backing | 73 | 25 | 2 | 69 | 25 | 6 |
| Creativity | 28 | 55 | 18 | 14 | 42 | 44 |
| Willingness to work hard | 94 | 6 | 0 | 95 | 4 | 1 |
| Management ability | 86 | 13 | 1 | 95 | 5 | 0 |
| Desire to succeed | 92 | 8 | 0 | 95 | 4 | 1 |
| Previous experience in own business | 14 | 44 | 42 | 18 | 45 | 37 |
| Previous management experience in same industry | 2 | 18 | 80 | 4 | 12 | 84 |

**TABLE 10 (Problem 9)** Advantages of Franchising

| Advantage | Percentage of Franchisees Agreeing | Percentage of Franchisors Agreeing |
|---|---|---|
| You can develop a franchise more quickly than an independent business | 90 | 84 |
| You can make more money in a franchise than in an independent operation | 49 | 45 |
| A franchise offers the benefit of a known trade name | 95 | 97 |
| A franchise offers a proven business formula | 81 | 97 |
| A franchise offers more independence than salaried employment | 90 | 81 |
| A franchise is less risky than an independent business | 76 | 86 |

**TABLE 11 (Problem 9)** Initial Services Provided by Franchisor and Franchisee and Degree of Satisfaction with Each

| Service | Franchisee Response | | | | Franchisor Response | | | |
|---|---|---|---|---|---|---|---|---|
| | % Providing | Degree of Satisfaction % | | | % Providing | Degree of Satisfaction % | | |
| | | High | Med | Low | | High | Med | Low |
| Market survey | 66 | 35 | 43 | 28 | 81 | 61 | 41 | 5 |
| Site selection | 74 | 50 | 41 | 15 | 87 | 78 | 23 | 5 |
| Lease negotiation | 68 | 44 | 38 | 22 | 79 | 69 | 31 | 6 |
| Store design | 76 | 54 | 36 | 16 | 89 | 83 | 19 | 4 |
| Management training programs | 87 | 38 | 44 | 24 | 96 | 72 | 26 | 8 |
| Operating manuals | 91 | 47 | 40 | 19 | 95 | 66 | 33 | 5 |
| Recognized trademark | 98 | 76 | 24 | 4 | 99 | 72 | 26 | 6 |
| Franchise financing | 38 | 44 | 33 | 29 | 34 | 54 | 22 | 30 |
| Equipment package | 61 | 45 | 48 | 13 | 78 | 68 | 33 | 5 |

**TABLE 12 (Problem 9)** Ongoing Services Provided by Franchisor and Franchisee and Degree of Satisfaction with Each

| Service | Franchisee Response | | | | Franchisor Response | | | |
|---|---|---|---|---|---|---|---|---|
| | % Providing | Degree of Satisfaction % | | | % Providing | Degree of Satisfaction % | | |
| | | High | Med | Low | | High | Med | Low |
| Advertising & promotion | 95 | 37 | 43 | 26 | 99 | 52 | 36 | 15 |
| Bookkeeping | 33 | 26 | 46 | 34 | 36 | 39 | 50 | 17 |
| Centralized purchasing | 63 | 54 | 30 | 22 | 76 | 55 | 36 | 15 |
| Operating assistance | 66 | 28 | 42 | 36 | 99 | 60 | 38 | 2 |
| Marketing research | 60 | 33 | 51 | 23 | 61 | 48 | 42 | 16 |
| Information bulletin | 86 | 43 | 46 | 17 | 84 | 54 | 42 | 16 |
| Inventory control | 39 | 44 | 35 | 27 | 59 | 57 | 38 | 21 |

**TABLE 13 (Problem 9)** Issues Covered by Franchise Agreement

| Issue | Percentage of Franchisors Reporting | Percentage of Franchisees Reporting |
|---|---|---|
| Supply purchase | 89 | 82 |
| Quality control | 94 | 78 |
| Competing business | 84 | 89 |
| Renewal clause | 83 | 84 |
| Termination clause | 98 | 95 |
| Territory restrictions | 92 | 77 |
| Approved suppliers | 80 | 71 |

**TABLE 14 (Problem 9)** Areas Where Government Regulation Is Needed in Canada

| Issue | Percentage of Franchisors Reporting | Percentage of Franchisees Reporting |
|---|---|---|
| Length of term renewals | 31 | 23 |
| Terminations | 56 | 50 |
| Renewals | 43 | 38 |
| Suppliers | 26 | 31 |
| Territory restrictions | 42 | 30 |
| No regulations needed | 64 | 72 |
| Disclosure | 74 | 88 |
| Tying purchase arrangements | 36 | 52 |

Kingdom as well. In your questionnaire, you include questions about critical energy problems facing firms in the future, whether firms have energy policy plans, the components of the plans, organization of conservation, time spent on energy conservation activities by executives, and the executives' titles.

You send this rather extensive questionnaire to a random sample of manufacturing firms in the three countries—432 in Canada, 236 in the United Kingdom, and 651 in the United States. Because of the high interest in the topic, you receive a very high return rate of 206, 117, and 321 forms, respectively. After you process and edit the returned questionnaires, you enter them into your computer and print the results as shown in Tables 15–20. Now, you are ready to analyze the results and write up the report so that it can be available to your IAM members.

The report you will write will be a long, formal one with all the trappings that the situation calls for. You will have a title fly, title page, letter of transmittal, table of contents, executive summary, and the report proper. You will write in the third person and use graphics to support the text of your analysis. Throughout your report, you will remember that the quality of your writing is no better than the quality of your thinking in the analysis of the data that will form the foundation of the report.

You will publish the executive summary of your report in the next issue of *Manufacturing Update* sent to all IAM members. You will offer to send the entire report to those requesting it for the cost of duplication and mailing.

Write the report that will present and compare the information about energy activities in the three countries for IAM members.

11. *Determining sales potential for computers in the small business market.* "We're missing a good market with those small business people. Why don't you find out about that market so we can see whether we can sell our product to them. Write up what you find in a report on the potential of this small business market for us."

These were the words of your boss, Mr. Raul Cerniglia of Computer Sales Company. When you met with him yesterday, his message was quite clear: investigate the small business market in terms of sales potential for computers. As you ponder the "how to" of Mr. Cerniglia's charge, you, sales manager for Computer Sales Company, begin to pinpoint the specific areas of information you will need to complete your report writing assignment.

To get facts about the small business market, you decide to conduct a survey. First, you purchase a list of small businesses from QuickInfo Services, a large marketer of lists that guarantees its listings to be 95 percent accurate. Then you draw a random sample of 562 from the list of 17,817 to whom you will send a questionnaire about small business usage of computers. You will

**TABLE 15 (Problem 10)** Critical Energy Problems Facing Firms during the Next 10 Years

| Critical Problems | % Identifying Problem as Critical | | |
|---|---|---|---|
| | Canada (206)* | U.K. (117)* | U.S. (321)* |
| Cost of energy | 38.0 | 37.2 | 46.3 |
| Cost of natural gas | 4.0 | 5.1 | 1.5 |
| Cost of electricity | 1.4 | 2.1 | 1.4 |
| Cost of petroleum | 3.0 | 1.2 | 1.6 |
| Cost of other fuels | 13.4 | 8.8 | 1.0 |
| Availability of electricity | 17.7 | 7.9 | 20.3 |
| Availability of energy in general | 31.6 | 28.2 | 29.9 |
| Availability of natural gas | 13.1 | 6.1 | 33.0 |
| Availability of petroleum | 3.3 | 3.1 | 11.9 |
| Changing to alternative fuels | 7.4 | 14.4 | 14.0 |
| Government regulation of energy | 3.3 | 3.1 | 11.9 |
| Capital investment for energy utilization/conservation | 11.2 | 9.2 | 5.6 |
| Energy curtailments and cutbacks | 3.4 | 6.9 | 5.3 |
| Energy-related inflation | 17.1 | 16.7 | 5.4 |
| Energy/environmental interface | 3.4 | 1.1 | 5.2 |
| Awareness | 0.2 | 2.1 | 1.0 |
| Present situation versus future situation | 0.8 | 0.2 | 1.0 |

* Number of firms responding to survey.

concentrate specifically on how small businesses use marketing information because you assume that most small businesses are in the marketing segment of the economy.

Next, you design a questionnaire to send to the sample you have selected. As you structure the questions on it, you decide to focus on three main areas: (*a*) characteristics of the small business market, (*b*) use of computers for keeping specific marketing information, and (*c*) use of computers for marketing control and planning. You design specific categories in each of these three areas in the construct of your questionnaire. Then you mail the completed instrument to the 562 businesses in your sample.

It has now been three weeks since your mailing, and you have received 227 usable questionnaires (a 40.4 percent return). All statistical tests plus the design of your research project indicate that you have reliable and representative results. Thus, you tally the results of your work as shown in Tables 21, 22, and 23. These tables will provide the facts for the report you will prepare for Mr. Cerniglia.

As you begin to think about the report, you determine that it will be on the formal side. Thus, you will give special attention to the wording and appearance of the report. But this special attention will not substitute for the detail of analysis you will give to the facts. You will remember that you have two purposes in your report writing project: to

## TABLE 16 (Problem 10) The Corporate Energy Policy Plan

| Issue | Percent Response | | | | | |
|---|---|---|---|---|---|---|
| | Canada | | U.K. | | U.S. | |
| | Number | Percent | Number | Percent | Number | Percent |
| **Does your company have a formal, written corporate energy policy/plan?** | | | | | | |
| Yes | 56 | 39.5 | 23 | 28.0 | 165 | 69.0 |
| No | 155 | 60.5 | 95 | 72.0 | 56 | 31.0 |
| TOTAL | 206 | 100.0 | 117 | 100.0 | 321 | 100.0 |
| **How long has your firm had a formal, written corporate energy policy/plan?** | | | | | | |
| No. of years | | | | | | |
| 1 | 21 | 30.3 | 4 | 6.6 | 10 | 15.4 |
| 2 | 34 | 37.1 | 14 | 11.9 | 13 | 16.3 |
| 3 | 18 | 22.6 | 45 | 43.9 | 108 | 26.7 |
| 4 | 10 | 2.5 | 43 | 23.6 | 95 | 20.8 |
| 5 or more | 17 | 7.5 | 11 | 14.0 | 95 | 20.8 |
| TOTAL | 206 | 100.0 | 117 | 100.0 | 321 | 100.0 |
| **Does your firm's energy plan apply to:** | | | | | | |
| Entire company | 105 | 65.0 | 55 | 69.4 | 185 | 63.8 |
| Manufacturing facilities only | 79 | 25.0 | 35 | 18.4 | 105 | 15.5 |
| Divisions only | 19 | 7.9 | 17 | 8.2 | 21 | 10.7 |
| Individual depts. only | 3 | 2.1 | 10 | 4.0 | 10 | 10.0 |
| TOTAL | 206 | 100.0 | 117 | 100.0 | 321 | 100.0 |

## TABLE 17 (Problem 10) Components of the Corporate Energy Policy/Plan

| Components | Percent Response | | |
|---|---|---|---|
| | Canada | U.K. | U.S. |
| Formation of energy conservation committees or policy teams | 85.9 | 82.3 | 82.0 |
| Guidelines for surveying current energy consumption | 93.2 | 98.2 | 97.6 |
| Customer allocation plans to be implemented when reduced energy supplies cause product shortages | 15.3 | 25.5 | 19.9 |
| Recommendations for reducing energy consumption | 93.2 | 99.5 | 93.5 |
| Suggested systems for measuring energy savings | 94.7 | 93.6 | 89.5 |
| Addition of energy-related responsibilities to existing job descriptions | 67.6 | 80.0 | 93.5 |

**TABLE 18 (Problem 10)** Organization of Energy Conservation Activities

| | Percent Response | | |
|---|---|---|---|
| **Method of Organization** | **Canada** | **U.K.** | **U.S.** |
| Centralized staff department | 9.9 | 11.6 | 6.7 |
| Separate functional activity within each division | 15.2 | 19.7 | 10.3 |
| Combination of divisional and centralized activities | 41.4 | 50.7 | 58.6 |
| Other | 4.9 | 4.3 | 3.5 |
| Not specified | 28.6 | 13.7 | 20.9 |
| TOTAL | 100.0 | 100.0 | 100.0 |

**TABLE 19 (Problem 10)** Job Title of Senior Energy Executive

| | Percent Response | | |
|---|---|---|---|
| **Title** | **Canada** | **U.K.** | **U.S.** |
| President or CEO | 5.0 | — | 3.0 |
| Assistant to president/CEO | 3.0 | 3.1 | 3.2 |
| Executive VP/Senior VP/Group VP | 4.5 | — | 2.9 |
| Vice president | 10.8 | — | 21.7 |
| Director | 5.3 | 22.3 | 14.4 |
| Manager/general manager | 17.5 | 22.3 | 18.4 |
| Coordinator | 5.0 | 15.5 | 6.7 |
| Engineer | 8.9 | 17.5 | 5.7 |
| Miscellaneous | 3.4 | 10.0 | 2.9 |
| Not specified | 36.6 | 9.3 | 21.1 |
| TOTAL | 100.0 | 100.0 | 100.0 |

**TABLE 20 (Problem 10)** Time Spent on Energy Conservation by Senior Energy Executive

| | Percent Response | | |
|---|---|---|---|
| **Percent of Time** | **Canada** | **U.K.** | **U.S.** |
| 1–10 | 50.3 | 46.8 | 31.0 |
| 11–20 | 6.3 | 11.6 | 14.0 |
| 21–30 | 6.9 | 6.3 | 6.3 |
| 31–40 | .3 | 0.9 | 2.2 |
| 41–50 | 4.5 | 4.1 | 7.3 |
| 51–99 | 4.5 | 6.3 | 6.5 |
| 100 | 1.0 | 9.8 | 10.5 |
| Not specified | 26.2 | 14.2 | 22.2 |
| TOTAL | 100.0 | 100.0 | 100.0 |

**TABLE 21 (Problem 11)**  Characteristics of Respondents

| Characteristic | Frequency | Percent |
|---|---|---|
| **Industry** | | |
| Agricultural, fisheries, forestry | 3 | 0.3 |
| Transportation | 3 | 0.3 |
| Manufacturing durable goods | 15 | 7.2 |
| Utilities | 5 | 2.3 |
| Retail trade | 35 | 11.2 |
| Insurance | 8 | 3.5 |
| Nonprofit | 9 | 4.1 |
| Entertainment | 15 | 6.6 |
| Business and repair services | 46 | 22.3 |
| Mining | 3 | 0.6 |
| Communications | 21 | 10.4 |
| Manufacturing nondurable goods | 7 | 4.9 |
| Wholesale trade | 6 | 2.8 |
| Real estate | 7 | 3.2 |
| Financial services | 12 | 5.4 |
| Education/training | 11 | 5.0 |
| Personal services | 21 | 9.9 |
| TOTAL | 227 | 100.0 |
| **Position of respondent** | | |
| Owner | 158 | 66.3 |
| Manager | 13 | 6.9 |
| Marketing manager | 2 | 1.5 |
| Sales manager | 1 | 1.2 |
| General manager | 13 | 3.7 |
| Data processing manager | 2 | 1.8 |
| President | 25 | 13.2 |
| Vice president—marketing | 9 | 4.2 |
| Other | 4 | 2.2 |
| TOTAL | 227 | 100.0 |
| **Number of full-time employees** | | |
| No response | 2 | 0.3 |
| 1–19 | 205 | 89.7 |
| 20–99 | 17 | 9.5 |
| 100–250 | 3 | 0.5 |
| TOTAL | 227 | 100.0 |
| **Gender** | | |
| No response | 3 | 0.5 |
| Female | 59 | 20.7 |
| Male | 165 | 78.8 |
| TOTAL | 227 | 100.0 |
| **Last year's gross sales volume** | | |
| No response | 3 | 3.7 |
| Under $100,000 | 137 | 41.3 |
| $100,000 to $249,999 | 39 | 18.2 |
| $250,000 to $499,999 | 22 | 14.9 |
| $500,000 to $1.0 million | 11 | 9.2 |
| $1.0 million to $1.5 million | 9 | 6.8 |
| $1.5 million to $2.0 million | 6 | 5.9 |
| TOTAL | 227 | 100.0 |

**TABLE 22 (Problem 11)** Use of Microcomputers for Keeping Specific Marketing Information

| Informaton Category and Item (A) | No Response (B) | N/A (C) | Don't Keep Info (D) | Info Not on Micro (E) | Info Is on Micro (F) | Use Index* (G) |
|---|---|---|---|---|---|---|
| **Customer information** | | | | | | |
| Name, address, telephone, etc. | 0.2% | 4.7% | 2.7% | 15.9% | 76.5% | 4.8 |
| Classification (age, gender, type of business) | 2.3 | 19.5 | 20.6 | 11.5 | 46.1 | 4.0 |
| Credit rating | 4.6 | 41.5 | 29.6 | 9.9 | 14.4 | 1.5 |
| Purchase history | 4.2 | 25.1 | 14.3 | 14.2 | 42.2 | 2.8 |
| Product attribute preference (color, size, brand name, etc) | 4.6 | 43.3 | 18.9 | 6.0 | 27.2 | 4.5 |
| **Sales information** | | | | | | |
| Gross sales | 0.7 | 14.2 | 3.4 | 16.1 | 65.6 | 4.1 |
| Sales by product line | 2.8 | 34.4 | 7.4 | 16.1 | 39.3 | 2.4 |
| Sales by product item | 4.2 | 36.7 | 8.6 | 16.2 | 34.3 | 2.1 |
| Name of customer | 1.2 | 10.4 | 1.4 | 13.1 | 73.9 | 5.6 |
| Location of customer | 1.2 | 10.3 | 3.4 | 10.0 | 75.1 | 7.5 |
| Type of customer | 3.2 | 24.7 | 9.9 | 7.8 | 70.0 | 9.0 |
| Date of sale | 1.7 | 14.0 | 3.9 | 17.6 | 62.8 | 3.6 |
| Method of payment | 1.6 | 25.9 | 14.5 | 17.7 | 40.3 | 2.3 |
| Returned orders | 2.4 | 50.9 | 7.9 | 17.6 | 21.2 | 1.2 |
| Unfilled orders | 2.9 | 55.6 | 6.4 | 15.2 | 19.9 | 1.3 |
| Order cycle time | 2.3 | 58.8 | 7.8 | 7.4 | 26.7 | 3.6 |
| Names of salespersons | 1.2 | 54.4 | 9.9 | 10.0 | 24.5 | 2.5 |
| **Inventory information** | | | | | | |
| Inventory on hand | 0.7 | 48.7 | 3.9 | 17.6 | 29.1 | 1.7 |
| Inventory on hand by product line | 3.4 | 55.0 | 10.8 | 13.6 | 17.2 | 1.3 |
| Inventory on hand by product item | 1.7 | 60.2 | 7.0 | 12.7 | 18.4 | 1.4 |
| Location of inventory | 3.7 | 62.3 | 6.6 | 15.9 | 11.5 | 0.7 |
| Date of inventory acquisition | 1.2 | 55.6 | 10.8 | 17.6 | 14.8 | 0.8 |
| **Marketing costs** | | | | | | |
| Product (invoice) costs | 2.3 | 29.4 | 5.6 | 15.7 | 47.0 | 3.0 |
| Fixed marketing costs | 1.3 | 35.4 | 3.2 | 14.9 | 45.2 | 3.0 |
| Advertising expenses | 1.2 | 23.4 | 1.8 | 18.0 | 55.6 | 3.0 |
| Personal selling expenses | 2.3 | 32.4 | 2.9 | 22.3 | 44.1 | 2.0 |
| Sales promotion expenses | 2.3 | 45.4 | 4.3 | 15.4 | 32.6 | 2.1 |
| Packaging | 3.2 | 57.6 | 9.7 | 17.6 | 11.9 | 0.7 |
| Shipping | 1.9 | 39.4 | 5.4 | 15.0 | 38.3 | 2.6 |
| Theft/losses | 2.9 | 52.2 | 7.7 | 12.2 | 18.6 | 1.5 |
| Misc. (e.g., marketing research) | 5.9 | 46.8 | 9.4 | 14.9 | 23.0 | 1.5 |

* Column (F) ÷ column (E)

**TABLE 23 (Problem 11)** Usage of Microcomputers for Marketing Control and Planning

| Information Category and Item (A) | No Response (B) | N/A (C) | Don't Keep Info (D) | Info Not on Micro (E) | Info Is on Micro (F) | Use Index* (G) |
|---|---|---|---|---|---|---|
| **Marketing control area** | | | | | | |
| Rank product sales by volume | 1.9% | 38.4% | 18.7% | 10.0% | 31.0% | 3.1 |
| Analyze sales by geographic territory | 1.5 | 36.8 | 28.8 | 7.3 | 25.6 | 3.5 |
| Analyze sales by type of customer | 1.5 | 36.8 | 29.8 | 9.8 | 23.1 | 2.4 |
| Identify profitable products | 0.7 | 34.4 | 16.6 | 17.3 | 31.0 | 1.8 |
| Identify profitable customers | 0.7 | 32.8 | 23.3 | 17.7 | 25.5 | 1.4 |
| Evaluate productivity of sales force | 1.5 | 49.6 | 22.8 | 15.7 | 10.4 | 0.7 |
| Evaluate effect of sales promotion | 1.9 | 42.3 | 19.8 | 22.3 | 58.3 | 2.6 |
| Determine best ad media | 0.7 | 40.4 | 14.6 | 27.9 | 26.4 | 0.9 |
| **Marketing planning areas** | | | | | | |
| Determine best timing for promotion efforts | 1.4 | 37.1 | 16.2 | 32.2 | 13.1 | 0.4 |
| Forecasting sales | 1.5 | 25.6 | 13.6 | 31.2 | 38.1 | 1.2 |
| Forecasting profitability | 1.5 | 27.7 | 14.6 | 18.4 | 37.8 | 2.1 |
| Identifying future customers | 1.4 | 21.5 | 19.8 | 35.2 | 22.1 | 0.6 |
| Setting sales quotas | 1.7 | 31.6 | 18.9 | 23.4 | 24.4 | 1.0 |
| Pinpointing new product needs | 2.9 | 36.8 | 17.2 | 31.8 | 11.3 | 0.4 |
| Deciding to drop current products/vendors | 2.9 | 37.1 | 12.7 | 30.4 | 16.9 | 0.6 |

* Column (F) ÷ column (E)

report the facts about computer usage in the small business market and to interpret these facts in terms of sales potential for Mr. Cerniglia. In your report, you will make good use of graphics to accent the important points of your analysis.

With these points in mind, prepare the report for Mr. Cerniglia.

12. *Locating the problems at Ridglea's Asel store.* For the past four years, the home office advertising department of Ridglea Department Stores, Inc., has planned and prepared advertising for all major promotions (January white sales, mid-summer clearances, harvest sales, and the like) for the chain's 32 branch stores. Only the day-to-day advertising and a few of the less important promotions were handled by each store's own advertising managers. In general, the success of this plan has been quite plain to the company.

Particularly was the Ridglea management pleased when they reviewed the store-by-store sales summaries for the major promotions. For the past few years, sales from promotions have been exceeding quotas at the individual stores—with only limited exception. One of these exceptions, the store at Asel, is your concern at the moment.

You, a marketing research specialist of some repute, have been retained by Ms. Jane S. LeMere, president of Ridglea, to make a special study of the problem store. Specifically, Ms. LeMere wants to know why the Asel store has failed to keep up with the other Ridglea outlets. If possible, she'd like you to pinpoint the sources of difficulty.

She and others of the Ridglea hierarchy feel that the trouble lies in a general failure of the Asel store to coordinate its display and personal selling efforts with the promotional advertising which comes from the central office. It's your job to test their theory and to shed whatever light you can on the company's problem.

So you plan your research efforts to test management's thinking. During the following weeks you and a crew of assistants shop extensively in all departments of the problem store and three of the company's more successful outlets, observing and recording all information which you believe might shed light on the problem. If, you reason, the Asel store summaries show less coordination between advertising on the one hand and the display of advertised material and personal sales efforts on the other, then management's theory is substantiated. But, if the opposite or no relation is apparent, then other causes need to be investigated. Should management theory be correct, a department-by-department analysis would be needed to pinpoint the sources of difficulty.

Today, after long weeks of careful record-keeping, you have the data which should point to the answer. You have but to pore over them, weigh them carefully, and then proceed to the obvious conclusions. In keeping with the formality of the situation and the size of the problem, you will do well to present your analysis in formal-report form.

Your summary data are in Tables 24 to 40. (Note that the data are expressed in percentages.)

**TABLE 24 (Problem 12)** Percent of Instances in Which Available Salespersons Waited on Customers Immediately

| Department | Asel | Bond | Cain | Davis |
|---|---|---|---|---|
| Sporting goods | 65 | 94 | 93 | 95 |
| Automotive | 94 | 90 | 91 | 94 |
| Hardware | 85 | 85 | 84 | 93 |
| Household furnishings | 92 | 91 | 92 | 85 |
| Ready-to-wear: | | | | |
|   Men's | 74 | 88 | 86 | 80 |
|   Women's | 67 | 89 | 88 | 81 |
|   Children's | 79 | 90 | 91 | 93 |
| Appliances | 70 | 89 | 96 | 94 |

**TABLE 25 (Problem 12)** Greeting Extended Customer by Salesperson, in Percentages

| Department | Asel | | | | | Bond | | | | | Cain | | | | | Davis | | | | |
|---|---|---|---|---|---|---|---|---|---|---|---|---|---|---|---|---|---|---|---|---|
| | 1 | 2 | 3 | 4 | 5 | 1 | 2 | 3 | 4 | 5 | 1 | 2 | 3 | 4 | 5 | 1 | 2 | 3 | 4 | 5 |
| Sporting goods | 44 | 16 | 6 | 28 | 6 | 6 | 78 | 3 | 2 | 11 | 4 | 60 | 19 | 9 | 8 | 3 | 71 | 7 | 17 | 2 |
| Automotive | 4 | 68 | 14 | 4 | 10 | 12 | 60 | 3 | 3 | 22 | 11 | 54 | 16 | 12 | 7 | 3 | 73 | 16 | 7 | 1 |
| Hardware | 15 | 54 | 5 | 0 | 26 | 13 | 59 | 7 | 1 | 20 | 10 | 66 | 6 | 9 | 9 | 14 | 57 | 19 | 0 | 10 |
| Household furnishings | 12 | 70 | 0 | 0 | 18 | 4 | 81 | 6 | 1 | 8 | 3 | 68 | 9 | 1 | 19 | 14 | 57 | 19 | 0 | 10 |
| Ready-to-wear: | | | | | | | | | | | | | | | | | | | | |
|   Men's | 30 | 44 | 6 | 12 | 18 | 7 | 70 | 18 | 0 | 5 | 5 | 54 | 11 | 10 | 20 | 12 | 60 | 9 | 14 | 5 |
|   Women's | 10 | 67 | 19 | 0 | 4 | 4 | 56 | 20 | 11 | 9 | 3 | 69 | 19 | 0 | 9 | 16 | 49 | 21 | 0 | 14 |
|   Children's | 24 | 53 | 3 | 0 | 20 | 3 | 62 | 14 | 0 | 21 | 3 | 61 | 23 | 0 | 13 | 4 | 58 | 23 | 0 | 15 |
| Appliances | 40 | 36 | 4 | 4 | 16 | 6 | 66 | 6 | 9 | 13 | 12 | 49 | 20 | 3 | 16 | 2 | 71 | 19 | 2 | 6 |

1. No greeting
2. "May I help you?"
3. "Are you being waited on?"
4. "Yes, sir/ma'am?"
5. Other

**TABLE 26 (Problem 12)** Courtesy of Salesperson, in Percentages

| Department | Asel | | | | Bond | | | | Cain | | | | Davis | | | |
|---|---|---|---|---|---|---|---|---|---|---|---|---|---|---|---|---|
| | 1 | 2 | 3 | 4 | 1 | 2 | 3 | 4 | 1 | 2 | 3 | 4 | 1 | 2 | 3 | 4 |
| Sporting goods | 0 | 36 | 58 | 6 | 39 | 58 | 3 | 0 | 44 | 54 | 2 | 0 | 64 | 32 | 4 | 0 |
| Automotive | 16 | 78 | 6 | 0 | 12 | 79 | 9 | 0 | 10 | 81 | 9 | 0 | 33 | 61 | 6 | 0 |
| Hardware | 6 | 76 | 16 | 0 | 6 | 87 | 7 | 0 | 12 | 79 | 9 | 0 | 44 | 52 | 4 | 0 |
| Household furnishings | 68 | 22 | 10 | 0 | 41 | 57 | 2 | 0 | 51 | 47 | 2 | 0 | 7 | 84 | 9 | 0 |
| Ready-to-wear: | | | | | | | | | | | | | | | | |
|   Men's | 2 | 71 | 27 | 0 | 36 | 58 | 6 | 0 | 28 | 69 | 3 | 0 | 2 | 80 | 16 | 2 |
|   Women's | 16 | 68 | 13 | 0 | 44 | 49 | 7 | 0 | 36 | 62 | 2 | 0 | 2 | 80 | 18 | 0 |
|   Children's | 8 | 66 | 26 | 0 | 31 | 65 | 4 | 0 | 19 | 77 | 4 | 0 | 33 | 62 | 5 | 0 |
| Appliances | 0 | 51 | 42 | 7 | 60 | 40 | 0 | 0 | 4 | 87 | 9 | 0 | 21 | 76 | 3 | 0 |

1. Very courteous
2. Courteous
3. Slightly discourteous or indifferent
4. Discourteous

**TABLE 27 (Problem 12)** Percent of Instances When Salespersons Were Informed about Advertised Merchandise

| Department | Asel | Bond | Cain | Davis |
|---|---|---|---|---|
| Sporting goods | 86 | 100 | 100 | 100 |
| Automotive | 99 | 100 | 90 | 100 |
| Hardware | 96 | 98 | 98 | 100 |
| Household furnishings | 100 | 100 | 100 | 92 |
| Ready-to-wear: | | | | |
|   Men's | 74 | 100 | 100 | 89 |
|   Women's | 91 | 100 | 100 | 94 |
|   Children's | 90 | 99 | 100 | 100 |
| Appliances | 100 | 100 | 97 | 100 |

**TABLE 28 (Problem 12)** Percent of Instances When Salespersons Knew Location of Advertised Merchandise

| Department | Asel | Bond | Cain | Davis |
|---|---|---|---|---|
| Sporting goods | 90 | 100 | 100 | 100 |
| Automotive | 98 | 93 | 93 | 100 |
| Hardware | 92 | 94 | 95 | 99 |
| Household furnishings | 99 | 100 | 100 | 93 |
| Ready-to-wear: | | | | |
|   Men's | 89 | 99 | 99 | 92 |
|   Women's | 91 | 99 | 98 | 90 |
|   Children's | 91 | 99 | 94 | 97 |
| Appliances | 96 | 100 | 94 | 100 |

**TABLE 29 (Problem 12)** Percent of Instances When Salespersons Encouraged Customers to Handle Merchandise

| Department | Asel | Bond | Cain | Davis |
|---|---|---|---|---|
| Sporting goods | 12 | 67 | 61 | 72 |
| Automotive | 33 | 19 | 21 | 34 |
| Hardware | 17 | 23 | 26 | 33 |
| Household furnishings | 11 | 44 | 46 | 19 |
| Ready-to-wear: | | | | |
|   Men's | 21 | 41 | 71 | 29 |
|   Women's | 23 | 64 | 57 | 41 |
|   Children's | 9 | 33 | 37 | 38 |
| Appliances | 16 | 37 | 24 | 34 |

**TABLE 30 (Problem 12)** Knowledge of Merchandise Displayed by Salesperson's Presentation, Percent of Total Instances

| Department | Asel | | | | Bond | | | | Cain | | | | Davis | | | |
|---|---|---|---|---|---|---|---|---|---|---|---|---|---|---|---|---|
| | 1 | 2 | 3 | 4 | 1 | 2 | 3 | 4 | 1 | 2 | 3 | 4 | 1 | 2 | 3 | 4 |
| Sporting goods | 6 | 20 | 71 | 3 | 32 | 66 | 2 | 0 | 31 | 60 | 9 | 0 | 27 | 71 | 2 | 0 |
| Automotive | 31 | 63 | 6 | 0 | 17 | 61 | 22 | 0 | 13 | 70 | 15 | 2 | 30 | 69 | 1 | 0 |
| Hardware | 22 | 59 | 17 | 2 | 16 | 55 | 21 | 8 | 14 | 61 | 21 | 4 | 29 | 66 | 3 | 2 |
| Household furnishings | 28 | 69 | 3 | 0 | 37 | 63 | 0 | 0 | 33 | 67 | 0 | 0 | 17 | 69 | 12 | 2 |
| Ready-to-wear: | | | | | | | | | | | | | | | | |
|   Men's | 7 | 66 | 20 | 7 | 14 | 81 | 5 | 0 | 20 | 79 | 1 | 0 | 6 | 69 | 25 | 0 |
|   Women's | 9 | 60 | 24 | 7 | 21 | 78 | 1 | 0 | 31 | 69 | 0 | 0 | 11 | 66 | 21 | 2 |
|   Children's | 8 | 54 | 21 | 17 | 31 | 67 | 2 | 0 | 23 | 76 | 1 | 0 | 19 | 80 | 1 | 0 |
| Appliances | 2 | 46 | 50 | 2 | 51 | 49 | 0 | 0 | 17 | 69 | 14 | 0 | 47 | 49 | 4 | 0 |

1. Knew merchandise very well
2. Knew merchandise adequately
3. Insufficient knowledge of merchandise
4. Little or no knowledge of merchandise

**TABLE 31 (Problem 12)** Percent of Instances Salesperson Suggested Additional Merchandise

| Department | Asel | Bond | Cain | Davis |
|---|---|---|---|---|
| Sporting goods | 2 | 37 | 41 | 41 |
| Automotive | 31 | 19 | 22 | 30 |
| Hardware | 11 | 21 | 24 | 36 |
| Household furnishings | 27 | 26 | 29 | 17 |
| Ready-to-wear: | | | | |
|   Men's | 19 | 46 | 51 | 33 |
|   Women's | 18 | 56 | 52 | 35 |
|   Children's | 13 | 31 | 36 | 34 |
| Appliances | 4 | 13 | 13 | 16 |

**TABLE 32 (Problem 12)** Percent of Instances Salesperson Attempted to Trade Up (Sell Higher-Priced Items)

| Department | Asel | Bond | Cain | Davis |
|---|---|---|---|---|
| Sporting goods | 0 | 16 | 19 | 21 |
| Automotive | 17 | 14 | 13 | 20 |
| Hardware | 9 | 11 | 13 | 21 |
| Household furnishings | 21 | 23 | 19 | 13 |
| Ready-to-wear: | | | | |
|    Men's | 23 | 39 | 37 | 26 |
|    Women's | 11 | 33 | 30 | 22 |
|    Children's | 9 | 16 | 18 | 19 |
| Appliances | 67 | 33 | 22 | 36 |

**TABLE 33 (Problem 12)** Salesperson's Closing Remark, in Percent of Instances

| Department | Asel | | | Bond | | | Cain | | | Davis | | |
|---|---|---|---|---|---|---|---|---|---|---|---|---|
| | 1 | 2 | 3 | 1 | 2 | 3 | 1 | 2 | 3 | 1 | 2 | 3 |
| Sporting goods | 61 | 33 | 6 | 88 | 0 | 12 | 91 | 0 | 9 | 84 | 1 | 15 |
| Automotive | 87 | 2 | 11 | 81 | 5 | 14 | 79 | 6 | 15 | 89 | 0 | 11 |
| Hardware | 67 | 9 | 24 | 74 | 6 | 20 | 76 | 3 | 21 | 93 | 0 | 7 |
| Household furnishings | 91 | 0 | 9 | 88 | 0 | 12 | 87 | 2 | 11 | 87 | 5 | 8 |
| Ready-to-wear: | | | | | | | | | | | | |
|    Men's | 86 | 6 | 8 | 91 | 1 | 8 | 92 | 0 | 8 | 87 | 5 | 8 |
|    Women's | 83 | 7 | 10 | 90 | 0 | 10 | 93 | 0 | 7 | 84 | 6 | 10 |
|    Children's | 81 | 9 | 10 | 91 | 0 | 9 | 87 | 1 | 12 | 82 | 0 | 18 |
| Appliances | 62 | 29 | 9 | 94 | 0 | 6 | 89 | 2 | 9 | 93 | 0 | 7 |

1. "Thank you"
2. None
3. Other

**TABLE 34 (Problem 12)** Average Percentage of Promotion Sales Quotas* Achieved during Past Three years

| Department | Asel | Bond | Cain | Davis |
|---|---|---|---|---|
| Sporting goods | 61 | 114 | 119 | 111 |
| Automotive | 107 | 88 | 91 | 109 |
| Hardware | 81 | 87 | 94 | 109 |
| Household furnishings | 103 | 116 | 118 | 84 |
| Ready-to-wear: | | | | |
|    Men's | 69 | 107 | 113 | 87 |
|    Women's | 74 | 111 | 108 | 91 |
|    Children's | 72 | 119 | 103 | 116 |
| Appliances | 59 | 112 | 92 | 103 |
| Store average | 79 | 108 | 105 | 103 |

* Quotas are based on Ridglea's own formula, which takes into account such factors as population, past sales records, and competition.

**TABLE 35 (Problem 12)** Displayed Advertised Merchandise in Street Window, in Percent

| Department | Asel | Bond | Cain | Davis |
|---|---|---|---|---|
| Sporting goods | 0 | 8 | 8 | 8 |
| Automotive | 4 | 2 | 3 | 6 |
| Hardware | 2 | 2 | 4 | 6 |
| Household furnishings | 3 | 6 | 5 | 0 |
| Ready-to-wear: | | | | |
|   Men's | 1 | 8 | 7 | 2 |
|   Women's | 0 | 12 | 9 | 0 |
|   Children's | 0 | 8 | 6 | 9 |
| Appliances | 0 | 4 | 0 | 2 |

**TABLE 36 (Problem 12)** Displayed Advertised Merchandise in Other Departments, in Percent

| Department | Asel | Bond | Cain | Davis |
|---|---|---|---|---|
| Sporting goods | 2 | 12 | 15 | 5 |
| Automotive | 0 | 7 | 8 | 6 |
| Hardware | 0 | 7 | 2 | 4 |
| Household furnishings | 0 | 8 | 6 | 2 |
| Ready-to-wear: | | | | |
|   Men's | 4 | 6 | 2 | 0 |
|   Women's | 0 | 6 | 9 | 0 |
|   Children's | 2 | 5 | 8 | 0 |
| Appliances | 0 | 0 | 0 | 0 |

**TABLE 37 (Problem 12)** Displayed Advertised Merchandise in Department Where Sold, in Percent

| Department | Asel | Bond | Cain | Davis |
|---|---|---|---|---|
| Sporting goods | 82 | 100 | 100 | 100 |
| Automotive | 99 | 96 | 96 | 100 |
| Hardware | 92 | 98 | 94 | 100 |
| Household furnishings | 100 | 100 | 100 | 91 |
| Ready-to-wear: | | | | |
|   Men's | 89 | 100 | 100 | 94 |
|   Women's | 91 | 100 | 100 | 95 |
|   Children's | 86 | 100 | 100 | 99 |
| Appliances | 93 | 100 | 99 | 100 |

**TABLE 38 (Problem 12)** Advertised Items Displayed in Selling Department Carried Informative Signs, in Percent

| Department | Asel | Bond | Cain | Davis |
|---|---|---|---|---|
| Sporting goods | 33 | 100 | 100 | 100 |
| Automotive | 92 | 98 | 97 | 100 |
| Hardware | 79 | 89 | 94 | 98 |
| Household furnishings | 95 | 100 | 100 | 86 |
| Ready-to-wear: | | | | |
|   Men's | 62 | 97 | 100 | 90 |
|   Women's | 69 | 99 | 100 | 89 |
|   Children's | 66 | 100 | 98 | 100 |
| Appliances | 77 | 100 | 89 | 100 |

**TABLE 39 (Problem 12)** Informative Signs Included Prices of Advertised Items, in Percent

| Department | Asel | Bond | Cain | Davis |
|---|---|---|---|---|
| Sporting goods | 100 | 100 | 94 | 100 |
| Automotive | 100 | 98 | 92 | 98 |
| Hardware | 96 | 94 | 100 | 96 |
| Household furnishings | 98 | 92 | 100 | 100 |
| Ready-to-wear: | | | | |
|   Men's | 94 | 100 | 98 | 96 |
|   Women's | 92 | 96 | 90 | 94 |
|   Children's | 100 | 94 | 100 | 90 |
| Appliances | 100 | 100 | 100 | 100 |

**TABLE 40 (Problem 12)** Failed to Back Advertised Items with Adequate Merchandise Offerings, in Percent

| Department | Asel | | | | Bond | | | | Cain | | | | Davis | | | |
|---|---|---|---|---|---|---|---|---|---|---|---|---|---|---|---|---|
| | 1 | 2 | 3 | 4 | 1 | 2 | 3 | 4 | 1 | 2 | 3 | 4 | 1 | 2 | 3 | 4 |
| Sporting goods | 24 | 16 | 19 | 41 | 4 | 4 | 6 | 86 | 0 | ? | 5 | 92 | 3 | 5 | 6 | 86 |
| Automotive | 4 | 6 | 9 | 81 | 6 | 6 | 9 | 79 | 5 | 7 | 8 | 80 | 1 | 5 | 2 | 92 |
| Hardware | 20 | 13 | 20 | 47 | 6 | 7 | 10 | 77 | 8 | 11 | 5 | 76 | 1 | 3 | 3 | 93 |
| Household furnishings | 2 | 6 | 4 | 88 | 4 | 2 | 2 | 92 | 2 | 2 | 3 | 93 | 9 | 11 | 9 | 71 |
| Ready-to-wear: | | | | | | | | | | | | | | | | |
|   Men's | 16 | 14 | 12 | 58 | 6 | 4 | 9 | 81 | 3 | 5 | 8 | 84 | 12 | 10 | 12 | 66 |
|   Women's | 33 | 13 | 18 | 36 | 9 | 7 | 4 | 80 | 7 | 6 | 6 | 81 | 13 | 13 | 16 | 58 |
|   Children's | 8 | 2 | 19 | 71 | 3 | 5 | 4 | 88 | 4 | 4 | 3 | 89 | 3 | 5 | 5 | 87 |
| Appliances | 18 | 12 | 17 | 53 | 1 | 2 | 5 | 91 | 6 | 2 | 12 | 80 | 2 | 7 | 2 | 89 |

1. Sold out first day.
2. Sold out second day.
3. Sold out third day.
4. Adequate stock for sale.

13. *Solving a problem on your campus.* (Requires research.) Certain problems exist on many college campuses. At least, they exist in the minds of many of the faculty, students, and staff. From the following list of such problems, select one that you think needs attention at your college:

    Library operation
    Campus security
    Policies on sales of tickets to athletic events
    Regulation of social activities
    Student government
    Registration procedure
    Faculty-student relations
    Orientation program for freshmen
    Curriculum improvement
    Increasing enrollments
    Scholastic honesty
    Campus crime
    Improving cultural atmosphere on campus
    Class attendance policies
    Scholastic probation policies
    Parking, traffic control
    Grade inflation
    Student government
    Emphasis on athletics
    Campus beautification
    Fire prevention
    Computer facilities
    Bookstore operation

    You will first gather all the significant facts regarding the problem you select. When you are thoroughly acquainted with them, you will gather authoritative opinions concerning the solution. Obtaining such information may involve looking through bibliographic sources to find out what has been done on other campuses. It may involve interviewing people on campus who are attempting to deal with the problem. Next you will carefully analyze your problem in light of all you have learned about it. Then you will develop a solution to the problem.

    To make the situation appear realistic, place yourself in the proper role at your school. Write a formal report, with all the conventional prefatory parts. Address the report to the appropriate administrator.

14. *Determining what business will be like in the months ahead.* (Requires research.) Roland A. Anderson, president of Northern Lights Energy Company, has assigned you, his assistant, to write a consensus business forecast for presentation at next Wednesday's meeting of the board of directors. Northern Lights, an oil and gas exploration company, does not employ an economist; Anderson does not believe in such frills. "Why should we pay for one," he says, "when the current business periodicals give us free forecasts by all the leading economists?"

    Since Anderson's instructions were—as usual—quite vague, much of what you do will depend on your good judgment. All Anderson said was that he wanted you to survey the predictions of the leading economic forecasters for the months ahead and to present your findings in a clear and meaningful report to the board. And he wanted the forecasts consolidated—that is, he did not want a mere succession of individual forecasts. Your report, covering the entire economy, will, of course, be largely general in nature. But you will give special emphasis to forecasts pertaining to the oil and gas industry.

    The report will be in a form appropriate for the board. Because the board members will want to get at the most important material quickly, be sure to include a fast-moving executive summary. Address the report to President Anderson, who also chairs the board.

## TOPIC SUGGESTIONS FOR INTERMEDIATE-LENGTH AND LONG REPORTS

Following are suggestions for additional report problems ranging from the simple to the highly complex. You can convert them into realistic business problems by supplying details and/or adapting them to real-life business situations. For most of these problems, you can obtain the needed information through library research. The topics are arranged by business field, although many of them cross fields.

### ACCOUNTING

1. Report on current depreciation accounting practices and recommend depreciation accounting procedures for Company X.
2. Design an inventory control system for X Company.
3. Report to Company X executives on how tax court decisions handed down over the past six months will affect their firm.
4. What security measures should Company X take with access to its accounting data?

5. Advise the managers of X Company on the accounting problems that they can anticipate when the company begins overseas operations.
6. Analyze break-even analysis as a decision-making tool for X Company.
7. Explain to potential investors which sections in Company X's most recent annual report they should review most carefully.
8. Analyze the relative effects on income of the FIFO and LIFO methods of inventory valuation during a prolonged period of inflation.
9. Write a report for the American Accounting Association on the demand for accountants with computer systems training.
10. Develop for accounting students at your college information that will help them choose between careers in public accounting and careers in private accounting.
11. Advise the management of X Company on the validity of return on investment as a measure of performance.
12. Report on operations research as a decision-making tool for accountants and managers.
13. Report to the management of X Company on trends in the content and design of corporate annual reports.
14. Report to an association of accountants the status of professional ethics in accounting.
15. Report to management of X Company on the communication skills important to accounting.
16. Advise the founders of new Company X on income tax considerations in the selection of a form of business organization.
17. Review for Company X the pros and cons of installing a computerized accounting system.

## GENERAL BUSINESS

18. Evaluate the adequacy of current college programs for developing business leadership.
19. Which business skills should schools and colleges teach, and which should companies teach?
20. What should be the role of business leaders in developing courses and curricula for business schools?
21. Examine and report on the current status of education for business.
22. How does business assess the content and quality of college-level business education?
23. Report on the advisability of including business internships in a business degree program.
24. What images of business and businesspersons do current business textbooks convey?
25. How does today's business community regard the Master of Business Administration degree?
26. Evaluate the contribution that campus business and professional clubs make to business education.
27. How effective is computer-based training in education for business?
28. Should education for business be specialized, or should it provide a generalized, well-rounded education?

## LABOR

29. For the executives of the National Association of Manufacturers (or some such group), report on the outlook for labor-management relations in the next 12 months.
30. For the officers of a major labor union, research and report progress toward decreasing job discrimination against minorities.
31. For X Union, project the effects that technology will have on traditionally unionized industries by the year 20XX.
32. Advise the management of X Company on how to deal with Y Union, which is attempting to organize the employees of X Company.
33. Evaluate the effectiveness of mediation in resolving labor-management disputes.
34. Interpret the change in the number of union members over the past _____ years.
35. Report on the successes and failures of employee-run businesses.
36. Report on the status and effects of "right to work" laws.
37. Report on the potential impact of "comparable worth" on X Company (or _____ industry).
38. Evaluate the effects of a particular strike (your choice) on the union, the company, the stockholders, and the public. Write the report for a government investigating committee.
39. For Union X, prepare an objective report on union leadership in the nation during the past decade.

40. Layoffs based on seniority are causing a disproportionate reduction in the number of women and minority workers at Company X. Investigate alternatives that the company can present to the union.
41. Investigate recent trends relative to the older worker and the stands that unions have taken in this area.
42. Review the appropriateness of unionizing government workers, and recommend to a body of government leaders the stand they should take on this issue.
43. Report on the role of unions (or managements) in politics, and recommend a course for them to follow.

## FINANCE

44. As a financial consultant, evaluate a specific form of tax shelter for a client.
45. Review the customer-relations practices of banks, and recommend customer relations procedures for Bank X.
46. Review current employee loan practices and recommend whether Company X should make employee loans.
47. Report on what Company X needs to know about financial matters in doing business with _____ (foreign country).
48. Give estate planning advice to a client with a unique personal situation.
49. Advise X Company on whether it should lease capital equipment or buy it.
50. Advise Company X on whether it should engage in a joint venture with a company overseas or establish a wholly owned foreign subsidiary.
51. Compare the costs for X Company of offering its workers child-care or elder-care benefits.
52. Should Company X accept national credit cards or set up its own credit card system?
53. Advise Company X on how to avoid a hostile takeover.
54. Advise Company X on whether it should list its stock on a major stock exchange.
55. Advise Company X, which is having problems with liquidity, on the pros and cons of factoring accounts receivable.
56. Recommend the most feasible way to finance newly formed X Company.

## MANAGEMENT

57. Develop for Company X a guide to ethics in its highly competitive business situation.
58. After reviewing pertinent literature and experiences of other companies, develop a plan for selecting and training administrators for an overseas operation on Company X.
59. Survey the current literature and advise Company X on whether its management should become politically active.
60. After reviewing the pros and cons, advise X Company on whether it should begin a program of hiring the handicapped or disadvantaged.
61. Report on the behavioral and psychological effects of introducing wellness programs to Company X.
62. The executives of X Company (a manufacturer of automobile and truck tires) want a report on recent court decisions relating to warranties. Include any recommendations that your report justifies.
63. Report on the problems involved in moving Company X headquarters from _____ (city) to _____ (city).
64. After reviewing current practices with regard to worker participation in management, advise Company X on whether it should permit such participation.
65. Should Company X contract for _____ (service) or establish its own department?
66. Review the advantages and disadvantages of rotating executive jobs at Company X, and then make a recommendation.
67. What should be Company X's policy on office romances?
68. Develop an energy conservation or recycling plan for X Company.
69. Evaluate internal communications in the X Company and make specific suggestions for improvement.
70. Design a security system for preventing computer espionage at Company X, a leader in the highly competitive _____ industry.
71. Evaluate the various methods for determining corporate performance and select the one most appropriate for Company X.

72. Advise X Company on the procedures for incorporating in _____ (state or province).
73. Survey the literature to find meaningful criteria for selecting executives for foreign service for X Company.
74. Report to Company X on the civil and criminal liabilities of its corporate executives.
75. As a consultant for a citizens' group, investigate the pros and cons of attracting a nuclear plant to your geographic area.
76. Determine for a legislative committee the extent of minority recruiting, hiring, and training in the _____ industry.
77. As a consultant for an association of farmers, evaluate the recent past and project the future of growing or raising _____ (your choice—cattle, poultry, wheat, soybeans, or the like).
78. Develop a plan for reducing employee turnover for Company X.
79. Report to a labor union on recent evidence of sexual harassment, and recommend steps that the union should take to correct any problems you find.
80. Investigate the feasibility of hiring older workers for part-time work for X Company.

## PERSONNEL/HUMAN RESOURCES ADMINISTRATION

81. Report on and interpret for X Company the effects of recent court decisions on the testing and hiring of employees.
82. Survey company retirement practices and recommend retirement policies for Company X.
83. Report on practices in compensating key personnel in overseas assignments and recommend for X Company policies for the compensation of such personnel.
84. Report on what personnel executives look for in application letters and résumés.
85. Report on the advantages and disadvantages of Company X's providing on-site day care for children of employees.
86. After reviewing the legal and ethical questions involved, make a recommendation concerning the use of honesty tests in employee hiring.
87. Review what other companies are doing about employees suffering from drug or alcohol abuse, and recommend a policy on the matter for Company X.
88. Report on effective interviewing techniques used to identify the best people to hire.

## MARKETING

89. Review the available literature and advise Company X on whether it should franchise its _____ business.
90. Select a recent national marketing program and analyze why it succeeded or failed.
91. Advise the advertising vice president of Company X on whether the company should respond to or ignore a competitor's direct attack on the quality of its product.
92. Review the ethical considerations involved in advertising directed to children and advise X Company on the matter.
93. Determine for Company X the social and ethical aspects of pricing for the market.
94. Explore the possibilities of trade with _____ (a foreign country) for X Company.
95. Determine for a national department store chain changing trends in the services that customers expect.
96. Prepare a report to help a contingent of your legislature decide whether current regulation of advertising should be reduced.
97. Determine the problems X Company will encounter in introducing a new product to its line.
98. Report on the success of rebates as a sales stimulator and advise Company X on whether it should use rebates.
99. Should Company X rent or lease trucks for distributing its products?
100. Determine the trends in packaging in the _____ industry.
101. Should X Company establish its own sales force, use manufacturers' agents, or use selling agents?
102. How should Company X evaluate the performance of its salespeople?
103. Determine for X Company how it can evaluate the effectiveness of its advertising.
104. Select the best channel of distribution for new product Y and justify your choice.
105. Should X Company establish its own advertising department or use an advertising agency?
106. Make a market study of _____ (city) to de-

termine whether it is a suitable location for _____ (a type of business).

107. Report to X Company on telemarketing and recommend whether it should use telemarketing to increase sales.

## COMPUTER APPLICATIONS

108. Develop a plan for converting Company X's administration operations from a manual system to a computerized system.
109. Recommend a notebook computer for use by the salespeople of Company X when they are traveling.
110. Advise Company X about the steps it can take to protect its computerized files from sabotage.
111. Determine whether Company X should purchase or lease its computer equipment.
112. Should Company X use integrated software, or should it select word processing, spreadsheet, database, and graphics software separately?
113. Explain for Company X the advantages and disadvantages of electronic mail, and advise the company on whether to use it.
114. Report to the president of Company X the copyright and contract laws that apply to the use of computer programs.
115. What are the potential applications of artificial intelligence in the _____ industry?
116. What are the advantages and disadvantages of allowing employees of Company X to do computer-related work in their homes rather than requiring them to do all computer-related work at the office?
117. Report to the International Organization of Business Communications on the impact of electronic technology on business communication.
118. Report on the future developments of robotics in the _____ industry.
119. Review and rank for possible adoption three software packages that Company X might use for its _____ work (name the field of operations).
120. Determine for Company X the factors it should consider in selecting computer insurance.
121. Report on the types of training available to X Company for its staff when upgrading its current word processing software.

## BUSINESS EDUCATION

122. Evaluate the effect of remodeling your new office site to take on a more homey look.
123. Report on why office romances still result in job losses.
124. Analyze the possibility of instituting company-wide training on etiquette, covering everything from handling telephone calls, to sexual harassment, to dining out.
125. Advise management on the importance of the air quality in the offices.
126. Investigate ways to improve the retrieval time and accuracy of information at X Company.
127. Evaluate the reprographic services and practices at your school from an environmental perspective.
128. Report on ways to hire and keep the best employees in the word processing center.

# CHAPTER 15

# GRAPHICS

## CHAPTER OBJECTIVES

*Upon completing this chapter, you will be able to use graphics effectively in written reports. To reach this goal, you should be able to*

### 1

**Determine which parts of your report should be communicated by graphics and where in the report the graphics should appear.**

### 2

**Explain the general mechanics of constructing graphics—size, layout, rules and borders, color and cross-hatching, numbering, titles, title placement, and footnotes and acknowledgments.**

### 3

**Construct general-purpose and special-purpose tables and present information as leaderwork or text tabulations.**

### 4

**Select the best graphics for displaying different types of information.**

## INTRODUCTORY SITIATION

### to Graphics

In your job in the Cory, Inc., word processing section, your assignment today is to proofread reports prepared by your coworkers. As Cory manufactures electronic equipment, many of the reports are highly technical and complex. Many others, especially those coming from finance and sales, are filled with facts and figures. In your judgment, most of the reports you have proofread are hard to understand.

The one you are looking at now is packed with page after page of sales statistics. Your mind quickly gets lost in the mass of details. Why didn't the writer take the time to summarize the more important figures in a chart? And why didn't the writer put some of the details in tables? Many of the other reports you have been reading, especially the technical ones, are in equal need of graphics. Diagrams, pictures, and drawings would certainly help explain some of the concepts discussed. If only report writers would understand that words alone sometimes cannot communicate clearly—that words sometimes need to be supplemented with visual communication techniques. If the writers of your reports studied the following review of graphics, your job would be easier and more enjoyable. So would the jobs of the readers of those reports.

In many of your reports you will need to use graphics. By *graphics* we mean any form of illustration: charts, pictures, diagrams, maps. Although tables and bulleted lists are not truly graphic, they are included in this definition.

*A graphic is any form of illustration.*

### PLANNING THE GRAPHICS

You should plan the graphics for a report soon after you make and organize your findings. Your planning of graphics should be based on the need to communicate. Graphics serve one purpose—to communicate—and you should use them primarily for that purpose. Graphics can clarify complex or difficult information, emphasize facts, add coherence, summarize, and add interest. Of course, well-constructed graphics also enhance the appearance of a report.

*You should plan the use of graphics.*

In selecting graphics, you should review the information that your report will contain, looking for any possibility of improving communication of the report through the use of graphics. Specifically, you should look for complex information that visual presentation can make clear, for information too detailed to be covered in words, and for information that deserves special emphasis.

*In planning their use, look for parts that they should communicate.*

As you plan the graphics, remember that, as a general rule, they should supplement the writing—not take its place. They should help the writing by covering the more difficult parts, emphasizing the important points, and presenting details. But the words should carry the main message—all of it.

*But remember that graphics supplement and do not replace the writing.*

### PLACING THE GRAPHICS IN THE REPORT

For the best communication effect, you should place each graphic near the place where it is covered in writing. Exactly where on the page you should place it, however, should be determined by its size. If the graphic is small, you should place it within the text that covers it. If it is a full page, you

*Place the graphics near the first place in the text in which you refer to them.*

CHAPTER 15  Graphics    537

"We're projecting a rally in the fourth quarter, after which we'll all live happily ever after."

From The Wall Street Journal, with permission of Cartoon Features Syndicate.

should place it on the page following the first reference to the information it covers.

- Placing graphics at the end of the report does not help the readers.

Some writers like to place all graphics at the end of the report, usually in the appendix. This arrangement may save time in preparing the report, but it does not help the readers. They have to flip through pages every time they want to see a graphic.

- Graphics not discussed in the report belong in the appendix.

Sometimes you may need to include graphics that do not fit a specific part of the report. For example, you may have a graphic that is necessary for completeness but is not discussed in the report. Or you may have summary charts or tables that apply to the entire report but to no specific place in it. When such graphics are appropriate, you should place them in the appendix.

- At the right place, incidentally invite the readers to look at the graphics.

Graphics communicate most effectively when the readers see them at the right place in the report. Thus, you should refer the readers to them at the right place. That is, you should tell the readers when to look at a graphic and what to see. You can do this best through an incidental reference to the information in the graphic. Of the many wordings used for this purpose, these are the most common:

. . . , as shown in Chart 4, . . .
. . . , indicated in Chart 4, . . .
. . . , as a glance at Chart 4 reveals, . . .
. . . (see Chart 4) . . .

## ▪▪▪▪▪▪▪▪▪▪▪▪▪▪▪▪▪▪▪▪▪▪▪▪▪▪▪▪▪▪▪▪▪▪▪▪▪▪▪▪▪▪
## DETERMINING THE GENERAL MECHANICS OF CONSTRUCTION

In constructing graphics, you will be concerned with various mechanical matters. The most common are summarized in the following paragraphs.

### Size Determination

- Make each graphic the size its contents justify.

One of the first decisions you must make in constructing a graphic is determining its size. This decision should not be arbitrary, and it should not be based on convenience. You should give the graphic the size its contents justify. If a graphic is simple (with only two or three quantities), a quarter page might be more than enough and a full page would be too much. But if a graphic must display complex or detailed information, a full page might be justified.

With extremely complex, involved information, you may need to use more than a full page. When you do, make certain that this large page is inserted and folded so that the readers can open it easily. The fold you select will be determined by the size of the page. You simply have to experiment until you find a convenient fold.

*Graphics larger than a page are justified if they contain enough information.*

### Layout Arrangement

You should determine the layout (shape) of the graphic by size and content requirements. Sometimes a tall, narrow rectangle (portrait) is the answer; sometimes the answer is a short, wide rectangle or a full-page rectangle (landscape). You simply consider the logical possibilities and select the one that appears best.

*Size and contents determine the shape of graphics.*

### Rules and Borders

You should use rules and borders when they help the appearance of the graphic. As a general rule, you should place borders around graphics that occupy less than a full page. You can also place borders around full-page graphics, but such borders serve little practical value. Except in cases in which graphics simply will not fit into the normal page layout, you should not extend the borders of graphics beyond the normal page margins.

*Use rules and borders when they help appearance.*

### Color and Cross-Hatching

Color and/or cross-hatching, appropriately used, help the readers see comparisons and distinctions. In fact, research has found that color in graphics improves the comprehension, retention, and ease of extracting information.[1] Also, both color and cross-hatching add to the attractiveness of the report. As color is especially effective for this purpose, you should use it whenever practical.

*Color and cross-hatching can improve graphics.*

### Numbering

Except for minor tabular displays that are actually a part of the text, you should number all the graphics in the report. Many schemes of numbering are available to you, depending on the makeup of the graphics.

*Number graphics consecutively by type.*

If you have many graphics that fall into two or more categories, you may number each of the categories consecutively. For example, if your report is illustrated by six tables, five charts, and six maps, you may number these graphics Table 1, Table 2, . . . Table 6; Chart 1, Chart 2, . . . Chart 5; and Map 1, Map 2, . . . Map 6.

But if your graphics comprise a wide mixture of types, you may number them in two groups: tables and figures. Figures, a miscellaneous grouping, may include all types other than tables. To illustrate, consider a report containing three tables, two maps, three charts, one diagram, and one photograph. You could number these graphics Table 1, Table 2, and Table 3

*Figures are a miscellaneous grouping of types. Number tables separately.*

---

[1] Ellen D. Hoadley, "Investigating the Effects of Color," *Communications of the ACM,* Vol. 33, No. 2, February 1990, p. 121.

### Clear Evidence of the Value of Accurate Charts

"To what do you attribute your company's success?" asked the interviewer.

"A line chart," replied the executive. "In the early years of our company, we had some real problems. Productivity was low, and we were losing money. So to impress our problem on our workers, I had a line chart painted on the wall of our main building. Every day, when the workers arrived, they saw our profit picture. Well, the profit line kept going down. It went from the third floor, to the second, to the first, to ground level. Then we had to bring in digging equipment to keep the line going. But keep it going we did—until the line dramatically reversed direction."

"The workers finally got the message?" asked the interviewer.

"No," replied the executive, "the digger struck oil."

---

and Figure 1, Figure 2, . . . Figure 7. By convention, tables are not grouped with other types of graphics. But it would not be wrong to group and number as figures all graphics other than tables even if the group contained sufficient subgroups (charts, maps, and the like) to permit separate numbering of each of them.

### Construction of Titles

*The titles should describe content clearly (consider the five W's—who, what, where, when, why).*

Every graphic should have a title that adequately describes its contents. Like the headings used in other parts of the report, the title of the graphic has the objective of concisely covering the contents. As a check of content coverage, you might well use the journalist's five W's—*who, what, where, when, why,* and sometimes you might also use *how* (the classification principle). But as conciseness is also desired, it is not always necessary to include all the W's in the title. A title of a chart comparing the annual sales volume of the Texas and California branches of the Brill Company for the years 1992–93 might be constructed as follows:

*Who:* Brill Company
*What:* Annual sales
*Where:* Texas and California branches
*When:* 1992–93
*Why:* For comparison

The title might read, "Comparative Annual Sales of Texas and California Branches of the Brill Company, 1992–93.

### Placement of Titles

*The conventional placement of titles is at the top for tables and at the bottom for charts. But many place all titles at the top.*

Titles of tables conventionally appear above the tabular display; titles of all other types of graphics conventionally appear below it. It is also conventional to use a higher type for table titles than for the titles of other graphics. There has been a trend toward the use of lowercase type for all illustration titles and to place the titles of both tables and figures at the top. These practices are simple and logical; yet you should follow the conventional practices for the more formal reports.

### Footnotes and Acknowledgments

Parts of a graphic sometimes require special explanation or elaboration. When this happens, as when similar situations arise in connection with the text of the report, you should use footnotes. Such footnotes are concise explanations placed below the illustration and keyed to the part explained by means of a superscript (raised) number or symbol (asterisk, dagger, double dagger, and so on). Footnotes for tables are best placed immediately below the graphic presentation. Footnotes for other graphic forms follow the illustration when the title is placed at the bottom of the page.

*Use footnotes to explain or elaborate.*

Usually, a source acknowledgment is the bottom entry made on the page. By *source acknowledgment* we mean a reference to the body or authority that deserves the credit for gathering the data used in the illustration. The entry consists simply of the word *Source* followed by a colon and the source name. A source note for data based on information gathered by the United States Department of Agriculture might read like this:

*Acknowledge source of data with note below.*

Source: United States Department of Agriculture.

If you or your staff collected the data, you may either omit the source note or give the source as "Primary," in which case the note would read:

*"Source: Primary" is the proper note for data you gathered.*

Source: Primary.

## CONSTRUCTING TEXTUAL GRAPHICS

Graphics for communicating report information fall into two general categories: those that communicate primarily by their textual content (words and numerals) and those that communicate primarily by some form of visual picture. Included in the textual group are tables, in-text displays, and a variety of management operations charts (Gantt, flow, organization, and such).

*Graphics fall into two general categories: (1) textual (words and numerals) and (2) visual (pictures).*

### Tables

A *table* is an orderly arrangement of information in rows and columns. As we have noted, tables are not truly graphic (not really pictures). But they communicate like graphics, and they have many of the characteristics of graphics.

*A table is an orderly arrangement of information.*

Two basic types of tables are available to you—the general-purpose table and the special-purpose table. General-purpose tables cover a broad area of information. For example, a table reviewing the answers to all the questions in a survey is a general-purpose table. Such tables usually belong in the appendix.

*You may use general-purpose tables (those containing broad information).*

Special-purpose tables are prepared for one special purpose—to illustrate a particular part of the report. They contain information that could be included with related information in a general-purpose table. For example, a table presenting the answer to one of the questions in a survey is a special-

*Or you may use special-purpose tables (those covering a specific area of information).*

**FIGURE 15-1** Good Arrangement of the Parts of a Typical Table

| Stub Head | TABLE NO. Table Title |||| 
|---|---|---|---|---|
| | Spanner Head ||||
| | Column Head | Column Head | Column Head | Column Head |
| Stub | XXX | XXX | XXX | XXX |
| Stub | XXX | XXX | XXX | XXX |
| Stub | XXX | XXX | XXX | XXX |
| Stub | XXX | XXX | XXX | XXX |
| " | " | " | " | " |
| " | " | " | " | " |
| " | " | " | " | " |
| " | " | " | " | " |
| " | " | " | " | " |
| Total | XXX | XXX | XXX | XXX |

FOOTNOTES
SOURCE:

---

See Figure 15-1 for details of table arrangement.

purpose table. Such tables belong in the report text near the discussion of their contents.

Aside from the title, footnotes, and source designation previously discussed, a table contains stubs, heads, and columns and rows of data, as shown in Figure 15-1. Stubs are the titles of the rows of data, and heads are the titles of the columns. The heads, however, may be divided into subheads—or column heads, as they are sometimes called.

The construction of text tables is largely influenced by their purpose. Nevertheless, a few general construction rules may be listed:

- **If rows are long, the stubs may be repeated at the right.**
- **The dash (—) or the abbreviation "n.a. (N.A. or NA)," but not the zero, is used to indicate data not available.**
- **Footnote references to numbers in the table should be keyed with asterisks, daggers, double daggers, and such. Numbers followed by footnote reference numbers may cause confusion, but numbers may be necessary when many references must be made.**
- **Totals and subtotals should appear whenever they help the purpose of the table. The totals may be for each column and sometimes for each row. Row totals are usually placed at the right, but when they need emphasis, they may be placed at the left. Likewise, column totals are generally placed at the bottom of the column, but they may be placed at the top when the writer wants to emphasize them. A ruled line (usually a double one) separates the totals from their components.**
- **The units in which the data are recorded must be clear. Unit descriptions (bushels, acres, pounds, and the like) appropriately appear above the**

PART 5  Fundamentals of Report Writing

columns, as part of the headings or subheadings. If the data are in dollars, however, placing the dollar mark ($) before the first entry in each column is sufficient.

### *In-Text Displays*

Tabular information need not always be presented in formal tables. In fact, short arrangements of data may be presented more effectively as parts of the text. Such arrangements are generally made as either leaderwork or text tabulations.

*Leaderwork* is the presentation of tabular material in the text without titles or rules. (Leaders are the repeated dots.) Typically, a colon precedes the tabulation, as in this illustration:

Tabular information can also be presented as (1) leaderwork (as illustrated here),

The August sales of the representatives in the Western Region were as follows:

Charles B. Brown ......... $13,517
Thelma Capp ............. 19,703
Bill E. Knauth ............ 18,198

*Text tabulations* are simple tables, usually with column heads and some rules. But they are not numbered, and they have no titles. They are made to read with the text, as in this example:

(2) text tabulations (as illustrated here), and

In August the sales of the representatives in the Western Region increased sharply from those for the preceding month, as these figures show:

| Representative | July Sales | August Sales | Increase |
|---|---|---|---|
| Charles B. Brown | $12,819 | $13,517 | $ 698 |
| Thelma Capp | 17,225 | 19,703 | 2,478 |
| Bill E. Knauth | 16,838 | 18,198 | 1,360 |

*Bullet lists* are listings of points arranged with bullets (●) to set them off. These lists can have a title that covers all the points, or they can appear without titles, as they appear at various places in this book. When you use this arrangement, make the points grammatically parallel. If the points have subparts, use sub-bullets for them. Make the sub-bullets different by color, size, or weight. The filled circle is commonly used for the primary bullets and darts, check marks, squares, or triangles for the secondary ones.

(3) bullet lists.

### Management Operations Charts

If you have studied business management, you know that administrators use a variety of specialized charts in their work. Often these charts are a part of the information presented in reports. Perhaps the most common of these is the *organization chart* (see Figure 15–2). These charts show hierarchy of positions, divisions, departments, and such in an organization. *Gantt charts* are graphic presentations that show planning and scheduling activities. As the words imply, a *flowchart* shows the sequence of activities in a process. Traditionally, flowcharts use specific designs and symbols to show process variations. If you need to use any of these somewhat technical charts, consult a basic management textbook.

Various specialized management charts are useful in reports—for example, organization charts, Gantt charts, and flowcharts.

**FIGURE 15–2** An Organization Chart with Employee Names

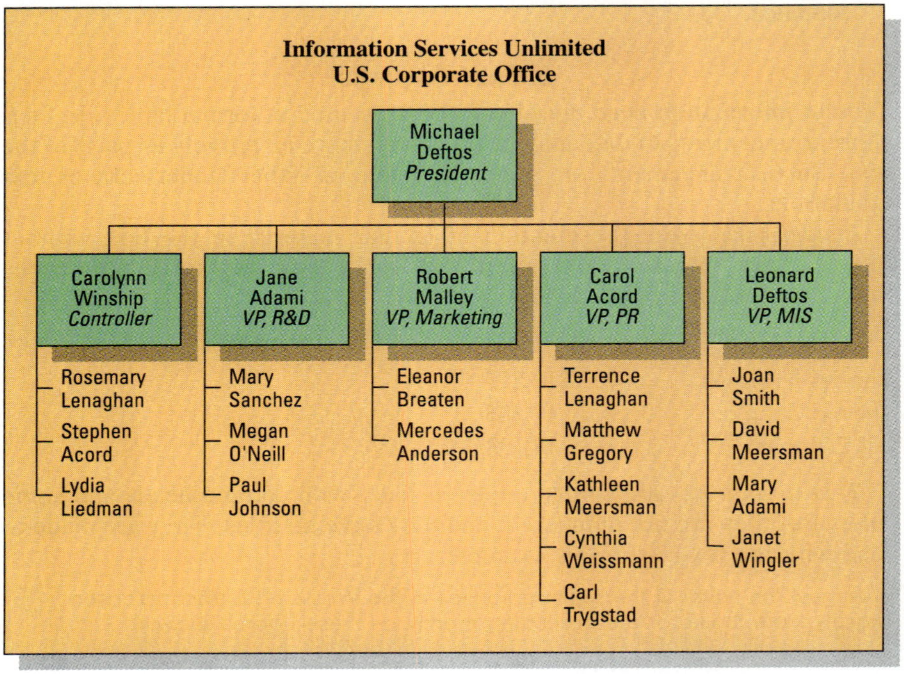

**Information Services Unlimited**
**U.S. Corporate Office**

- Michael Deftos — *President*
  - Carolynn Winship — *Controller*
    - Rosemary Lenaghan
    - Stephen Acord
    - Lydia Liedman
  - Jane Adami — *VP, R&D*
    - Mary Sanchez
    - Megan O'Neill
    - Paul Johnson
  - Robert Malley — *VP, Marketing*
    - Eleanor Breaten
    - Mercedes Anderson
  - Carol Acord — *VP, PR*
    - Terrence Lenaghan
    - Matthew Gregory
    - Kathleen Meersman
    - Cynthia Weissmann
    - Carl Trygstad
  - Leonard Deftos — *VP, MIS*
    - Joan Smith
    - David Meersman
    - Mary Adami
    - Janet Wingler

# CONSTRUCTING VISUAL GRAPHICS

*Visual graphics include data-generated charts, photographs, and art work.*

The truly visual types of graphics include a variety of forms—data-generated charts as well as art work and photographs. Data-generated charts are ones built with raw data and include bar, pie, and line charts and all their variations and combinations. Art work includes maps, diagrams, drawings, cartoons, and such.

## Bar Charts

*Simple bar charts compare differences in quantities by varying bar lengths.*

*Simple bar charts* compare differences in quantities by differences in the lengths of the bars representing those quantities. You should use them primarily to show quantity changes over time or over geographic distances.

As shown in Figure 15–3, the main parts of the bar chart are the bars and the grid (the field on which the bars are placed). The bars, which may be arranged horizontally or vertically, should be of equal width. You should identify each bar, usually with a caption at the left. The grid (field) on which the bars are placed is usually needed to show the magnitudes of the bars, and the units (dollars, pounds, miles, and such) are identified by the scale caption below.

*Multiple bar charts are useful in comparing two or three kinds of quantities.*

When you need to compare two or three different kinds of quantities in one chart, you can use a *multiple bar chart*. In such a chart, bars show the values of the quantities compared. Cross-hatching, colors, or the like on the bars distinguish the different kinds of information (see Figure 15–4). Somewhere within the chart, a legend (explanation) gives a key to the differences

PART 5 Fundamentals of Report Writing

**FIGURE 15–3** Illustration of Good Arrangement of the Parts of a Simple Horizontal Bar Chart

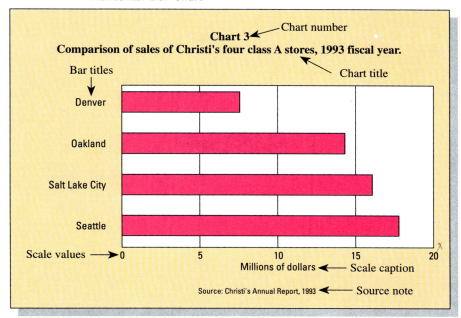

**FIGURE 15–4** Multiple Bar Chart

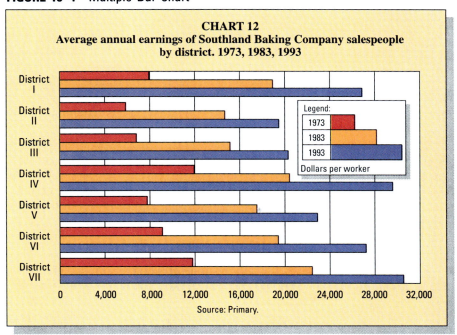

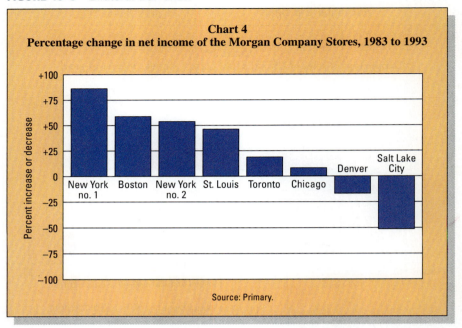

FIGURE 15–5  Bilateral Bar Chart

**When you need to show plus and minus differences, bilateral bar charts are useful.**

**To compare subdivisions of bars, use a subdivided bar chart.**

**You can also use such a chart for comparing subdivisions of percentages.**

**Pie charts show subdivisions of a whole.**

in the bars. Because multiple bar charts can become cluttered, usually you should not compare more than three kinds of information on one of them.

When you need to show plus and minus differences, you can use *bilateral bar charts*. The bars of these charts begin at a central point of reference and may go either up or down, as illustrated in Figure 15–5. Bar titles appear either within, above, or below the bars, depending on which placement fits best. Bilateral bar charts are especially good for showing percentage changes, but you may use them for any series in which plus and minus quantities are present.

If you need to compare subdivisions of bars, you can use a *subdivided (stacked) bar chart*. As shown in Figure 15–6, such a chart divides each bar into its parts. It distinguishes these parts by color, cross-hatching, or the like; and it explains these differences in a legend.

A special form of subdivided bar chart is used to compare the subdivisions of percentages. In this form, all the bars are equal in length, for each represents 100 percent. Only the subdivisions within the bars vary. The objective of this form is to compare differences in how wholes are divided. The component parts may be labeled, as shown in Figure 15–7, but they may also be explained in a legend.

### Pie Charts

Also important in comparing the subdivisions of wholes is the *pie chart* (see Figure 15–8). As the name implies, pie charts show the whole of the information being studied as a pie (circle), and the parts of this whole as slices of the pie. The slices may be distinguished by labeling and color or cross-hatching.

**FIGURE 15–6** Illustration of a Subdivided (Stacked) Bar Chart with Bars of Unequal Lengths

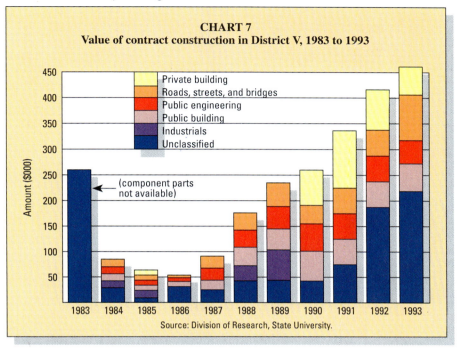

**FIGURE 15–7** Illustration of a Subdivided Bar Chart with Bars of Equal Lengths

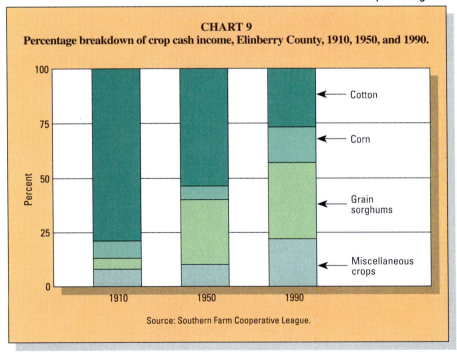

**FIGURE 15–8** Illustration of a Pie Chart

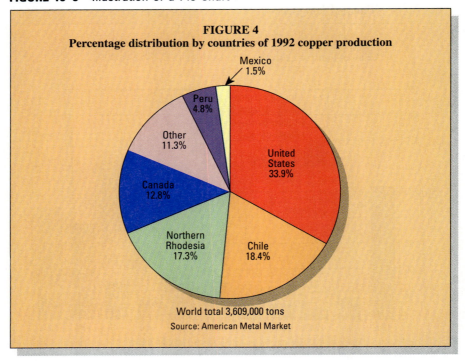

A single slice can be emphasized by exploding—pulling out—a piece. As it is hard to judge the values of the slices with the naked eye, it is good to include the percentage values within or near each slice. A good rule to follow is to begin slicing the pie at the 12 o'clock position and then to move around clockwise. It is also good to arrange the slices in descending order from largest to smallest.

But do not vary sizes of the pies.

In using pie charts to compare two or more wholes, you should never vary the sizes of the pies. Such comparisons are almost meaningless. The human eye simply cannot judge circle sizes accurately.

### Line Charts

*Line charts* are useful to show changes of information over time. For example, changes in prices, sales totals, employment, or production over a period of years can be shown well in a line chart.

Line charts show changes over time.

The line appears on a grid (a scaled area) and is continuous.

In constructing a line chart, you draw the information to be illustrated as a continuous line on a grid (see Figure 15–9). The grid is the area in which the line is displayed. It is scaled to show time changes from left to right across the chart (X-axis) and quantity changes from bottom to top (Y-axis). You should mark clearly the scale values and the time periods.

Two or more lines may appear on one chart.

You may also compare two or more series on the same line chart (see Figure 15–10). In such a comparison, you should clearly distinguish the lines by color or form (dots, dashes, dots and dashes, and the like). You should

548   PART 5   Fundamentals of Report Writing

**FIGURE 15–9**  A Line Chart with One Series

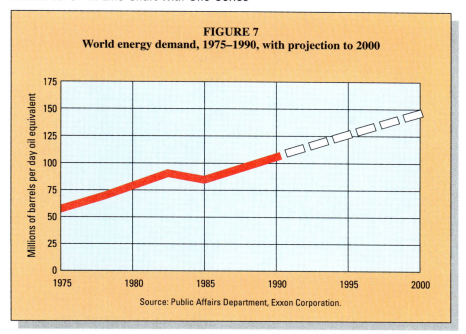

clearly label them by a legend somewhere in the chart. But the number of series that you may compare on one line chart is limited. As a practical rule, the maximum number is four or five.

It is also possible to show parts of a series by use of an *area* chart—sometimes called a *surface* chart. Such a chart, however, can show only one series. You should construct this type of chart, as shown in Figure 15–11, with a top line representing the total of the series. Then, starting from the base, you should cumulate the parts, beginning with the largest and ending with the smallest. You may use cross-hatching or coloring to distinguish the parts.

> Area charts show the makeup of a series.

Line charts that show a range of data for particular times are called *variance* or *hi-lo* charts (see Figure 15–12). Some variance charts show high and low points as well as the mean, median, or mode. When used to chart daily stock prices, they typically include closing price in addition to the high and low. When you use points other than high and low, be sure to make it clear what these points are.

> Variance charts show high and low points—sometimes more.

Line charts are simple to construct, but you should guard against three common errors in their construction. The first is the error of violating the zero beginning of the series. For accuracy, you should begin the scale at zero. But when all the information shown in the chart has high values, it is awkward to show the entire scale from zero to the highest value. For example, if the quantities compared range from 1,320 to 1,350 and the chart shows the entire area from zero to 1,350, the line showing these quantities

> But avoid these errors: (1) failure to start at zero (you can show scale breaks),

**CHAPTER 15  Graphics**  549

**FIGURE 15–10** A Line Chart Comparing More than One Series

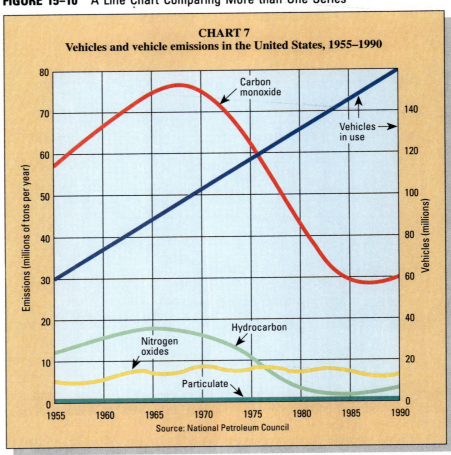

would be almost straight and very high on the chart. Your solution in this case is not to begin the scale at a high number (say, 1,300), for this would distort the information, but to begin at zero and show a scale break. The following two ways of showing scale breaks are recommended:

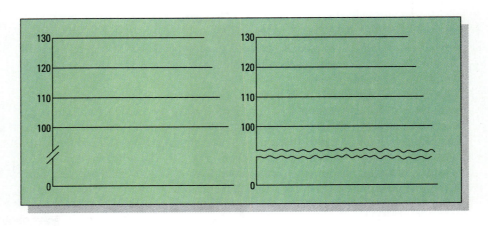

**FIGURE 15–11**  Illustration of an Area Line Chart

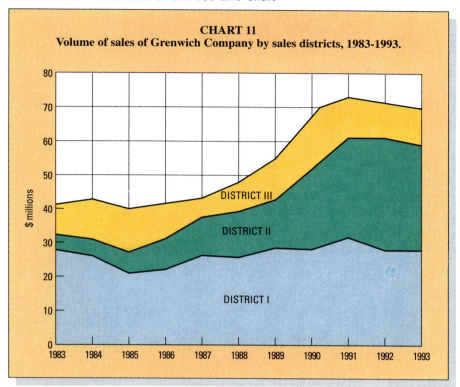

**FIGURE 15–12**  A Variance (Hi-Lo) Chart

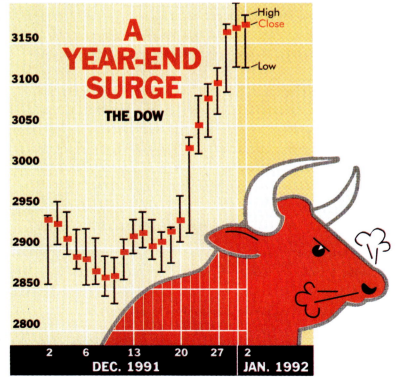

(2) failure to keep scales uniform,

(3) use of distances on the grid that do not show the true picture.

You can show quantitative information for geographic areas in a statistical map.

Here are some specific instructions for statistical maps.

A second error in constructing line charts is failing to keep the chart scales uniform. All the dimensions from left to right (X-axis) and from bottom to top (Y-axis) should be equal. Otherwise, an incorrect picture would be shown.

A third error is using grid distances that do not give a true picture of the information. Expanding a scale can change the appearance of the line. For example, if the values on a chart are plotted ½ inch apart instead of ¹⁄₁₆ inch apart, changes appear much more suddenly. Determining the distances that present the most accurate picture is a matter of judgment.

### Statistical Maps

You may also use *statistical maps* to communicate quantitative as well as geographic information. They are useful primarily when quantitative information is to be compared by geographic areas. On such maps, the geographic areas are clearly outlined and some graphic technique is used to show the differences between areas. Of the numerous techniques available to you, these are the most common:

- **Showing quantitative differences of areas by color, shading, or crosshatching is perhaps the most popular technique (see Figure 15–13). Of**

**FIGURE 15–13** Illustration of a Statistical Map Showing Quantitative Differences of Areas by Color Coding

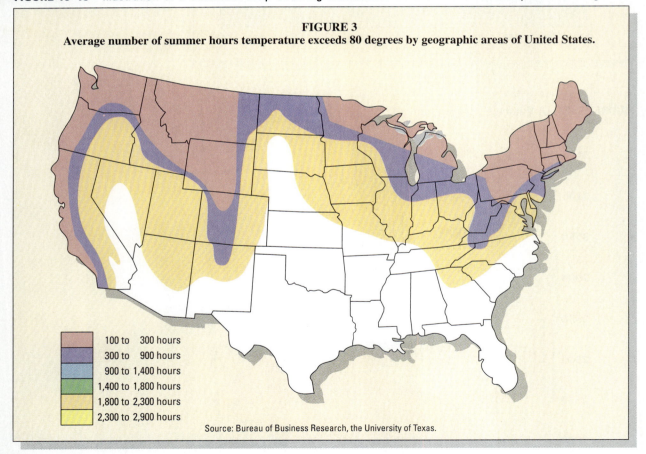

PART 5 Fundamentals of Report Writing

course, maps using this technique must have a legend to explain the quantitative meanings of the various colors, cross-hatchings, and so forth.
- Some form of chart may be placed within each geographic area to depict the quantity for that area, as illustrated in Figure 15–14. Bar charts and pie charts are commonly used in such statistical maps.
- Placing the quantities in numerical form within each geographic area, as shown in Figure 15–15, is another widely used technique.
- Dots, each representing a definite quantity (see Figure 15–16), may be placed within the geographic areas in proportion to the quantities for those areas.

### Pictograms

A *pictogram* is a bar chart that uses bars made of pictures. The pictures are typically drawings of the items being compared. For example, a company's profits over a period of years, instead of being shown by ordinary bars (formed by straight lines), could be shown by bar drawings of stacks of coins. This type of bar chart is a pictogram (see Figure 15–17).

Pictograms are bar charts made with pictures.

In constructing a pictogram, you should follow the procedures you used in constructing bar charts and two special rules. First, you must make all the picture units equal in size. That is, you must base the comparisons wholly on the number of picture units used and never on variation in the areas of the units. The reason for this rule is obvious. The human eye is grossly inadequate in comparing geometric designs that vary in more than one dimension.

In constructing pictograms, follow the procedure for making bar charts.

**FIGURE 15–14** Statistical Map Showing Comparisons by Charts within Geographic Areas

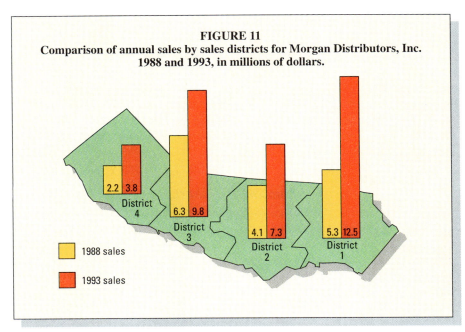

**FIGURE 15-15** Statistical Map Showing Quantitative Differences by Means of Numbers Placed within Geographic Areas

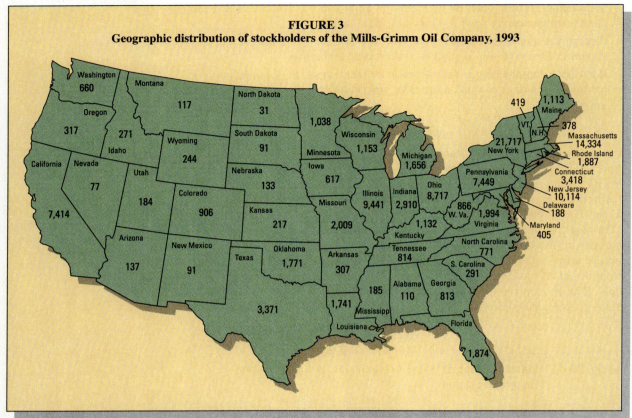

Second, you should select pictures or symbols that fit the information to be illustrated. In comparing the navies of the world, for example, you might use ships. In comparing the cotton production of various U.S. states, you might use bales of cotton. The meaning of the drawings you use must be immediately clear to the readers.

## Combination Charts

Sometimes a combination of chart types is effective.

Combination charts often serve the reader extremely well by allowing them to see relationships of different kinds of data. The example shown in Figure 15-18 shows the reader the price of stock over time (the trend) as well as the volume of sales over time (comparisons). It allows the reader to detect whether the change in volume affects the price of the stock. This kind of information would be difficult to get from raw data.

**FIGURE 15–16** Illustrations of a Statistical Map Using Dots to Show Quantitative Differences by Geographic Areas

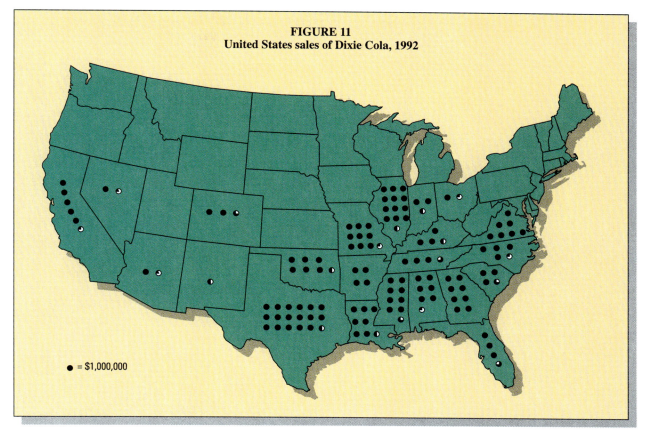

## *Other Graphics*

The types of graphics discussed thus far are the ones most commonly used. Other types also may be helpful. *Photographs* may serve a useful communication purpose. *Diagrams* (see Figure 15–19), and drawings (see Figure 15–20) may help simplify a complicated explanation or description. Even carefully selected cartoons can be used effectively. For all practical purposes, any graphic is acceptable as long as it helps communicate the true story. The possibilities are almost unlimited.

Other graphics available to you are diagrams, drawings, and photographs—even cartoons.

## *USING COMPUTER GRAPHICS*

If you have access to the appropriate computer, printer, and software, you can use them to prepare graphics quickly and easily. Unlike the earlier versions, today's computer graphics software programs are simple and easy

Easy-to-use computer graphics are available.

**FIGURE 15–17** Illustration of the Pictogram

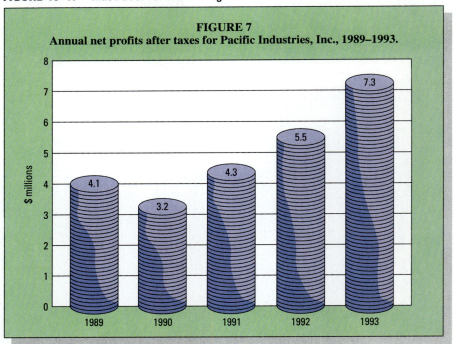

**FIGURE 15–18** A Combination Chart (Line, Variance, Bar)

### *Importing and Linking: Two Tools for Integrating Graphics with Text*

Until recently the job of integrating graphics into text documents was left to integrated software or to the actual physical process of cutting and pasting. While some of the earliest versions of spreadsheet software had graphing capabilities, writers usually left space for them in their textual document and pasted them in. Occasionally, writers tried to run a sheet of printed text through a printer, aiming to print the graphic at a precise space on the printed page. But this is all behind us now. Most full-featured word processing programs allow you to import or link your graphics to the text at the precise point you choose.

Importing means bringing the graphic file into your document, making it a part of your file. Some programs will import the most widely used graphic formats directly, converting them automatically into its format. Most programs also include a conversion utility, allowing you to convert a file before importing it into your text. In most cases you can import files created by dedicated graphics, draw and paint, database, and spreadsheet programs as well as files created through scanning. Furthermore, some word processing programs even have editing capabilities, permitting you to manipulate the imported file in some ways. If you discover a format your word processor will not read, do not give up; you can usually find a conversion program that will change it to a form that will work with your software.

Linking, on the other hand, only links files with your text; they are not made part of your document. This is particularly useful when you are writing a report based on data that is subject to change. When the file your text is linked to is changed, your graphic is changed, too, the next time your document is retrieved. Additionally, linking saves space, which is particularly important with large graphics files. Instead of storing these large files both in your document and someplace else, they are only stored once and linked.

Whether through importing or linking, your software can assist you in integrating graphics in your document. Now you are free to concentrate on producing graphics that most help your readers.

---

to use. With some of them, you need only choose the form of graph you want and then, using simple English instructions, supply the information that the program requests. For example, when using one popular program to construct a bar chart, you simply respond "Bar" to the initial request for chart type. Then you supply plain English answers to a series of questions covering number of bars, names of bars, values of bars, and the like. As you supply the answers, the results appear on the screen. After producing the bar chart on the screen, you can manipulate its design until it meets your ideal requirements. When you are satisfied with the design you see on the screen, you print the chart in black and white or in color, depending on your equipment.

**FIGURE 15-19** Illustration of a Diagram

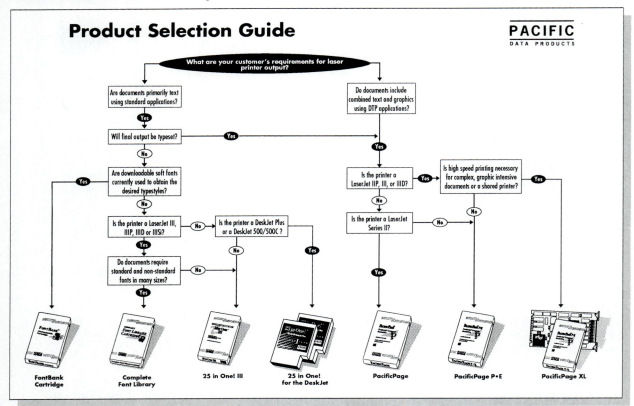

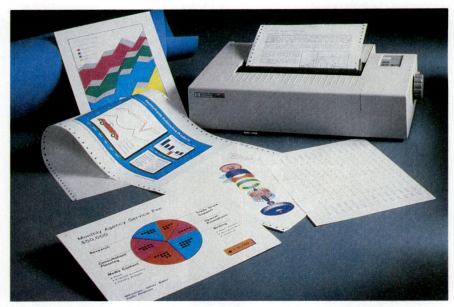

Currently available software packages are capable of producing all the common forms of graphics, and more.

**FIGURE 15–20** Illustration of a Drawing

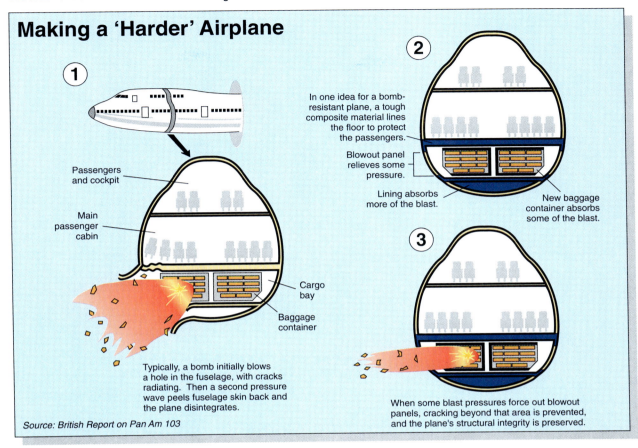

Because computer graphics are easy to make and can be exciting and colorful, you may be tempted to overuse them. Keep in mind that the one requirement for including a graphic in a report is usefulness in communicating the report message. Too many charts can clutter the report and cause confusion.

Also keep in mind that clarity is a major requirement of graphics and that even computer-generated graphics can be unclear. The possibilities for changing and enhancing graphics can lead to interesting, beautiful, exciting, but confusing results. Thus, the purpose of graphics—to communicate instantly clear messages—is defeated. Even though the software package will do much of the planning and thinking for you, you should take care to follow the guidelines presented in this chapter as you construct graphics by computer.

*But do not overuse them.*

*Make sure the graphics you use help to communicate.*

**FIGURE 15–21** A Report Page Enhanced by Color Graphics

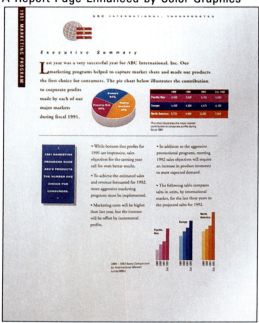

## SUMMARY (by Chapter Objectives)

1. Determine which parts of your report should be communicated by graphics and where in the report the graphics should appear.

1. As graphics are a part of the communication in a report, you should plan for them.
   - But remember that they supplement the writing; they do not replace it.
   - Use them wherever they help communicate the report information.
   - Place them near the text part they illustrate.
   - Invite the readers to look at them at the appropriate place.
   - Place in the appendix those that you do not discuss in the text.

2. Explain the general mechanics of constructing graphics—size, layout, rules and borders, color and cross-hatching, numbering, titles, title placement, and footnotes and acknowledgments.

2. Construct each graphic carefully, following these general instructions:
   - Give each the size and arrangement its contents justify.
   - Use rules, borders, and color when they help.
   - Number the graphics consecutively by type.
   - Construct titles for them using the five W's (*who, what, where, when, why*) as a checklist.
   - Use footnotes and acknowledgments when needed, placing them below the graphic.

3. Construct general-purpose and special-purpose tables and present information as leaderwork or text tabulations.

3. Construct tables to display the larger groups of data.
   - Use general-purpose tables for information that is broad in scope.
   - Use special-purpose tables for information that is specific in scope.
   - See Figure 15–1 for the details of table construction.
   - Tabular information may also appear as a part of the text rather than in a formal table.

    —You can do this as leaderwork.
    —Or you can do it as text tabulations.
4. In selecting a graphic, consider these primary uses of each:
    - *Simple bar chart*—shows quantity changes over time or over geographic distances.
    - *Multiple bar chart*—shows two or three kinds of quantities on one chart.
    - *Bilateral bar chart*—shows plus and minus differences and is especially good for showing percentage changes.
    - *Subdivided bar chart*—used to compare differences in the division of wholes.
    - *Pie chart*—used to show how wholes are divided.
    - *Line chart*—useful in showing changes over time.
    - *Statistical map*—shows quantitative differences by geographic areas.
    - *Pictogram*—shows quantitative differences in picture form.

For instructions on preparing each, review the text illustrations.

4. Select the best graphics for displaying different types of information.

## QUESTIONS FOR DISCUSSION

1. For the past 20 years, Professor Kupenheimer has required that his students include five graphics in the long, formal report he requires them to prepare. Evaluate this requirement.
2. Because it was easier to do, a report writer prepared each of his graphics on a full page. Some of these graphics were extremely complex; some were very simple. Comment on this policy.
3. "I have placed every chart near the place I write about it. The reader can see the chart without any *additional* help from me. It just doesn't make sense to direct the reader's attention to the charts with words." Evaluate this comment.
4. A report has five maps, four tables, one chart, one diagram, and one photograph. How would you number these graphics?
5. How would you number these graphics in a report: seven tables, six charts, nine maps?
6. Discuss the logic of showing scale breaks in a chart.
7. Discuss the dangers of using illogical proportions in constructing a chart grid.
8. Discuss the techniques that may be used to show quantitative differences by area on a statistical map.
9. Select data that are ideally suited for presentation in a pictogram. Explain why use of a pictogram is good for this case.
10. Discuss the dangers of using pictograms.

## APPLICATION EXERCISES

1. Construct a complete, concise title for a bar chart showing annual attendance at home football (or basketball, hockey) games at your school from 1982 to the present.
2. The table prepared in Question 1 requires an explanation for the years 1987 to the present. In each of those years, one extra home game was played. Explain how you would provide the necessary explanation.
3. For each of the areas of information described below, which form of graphic would you use? Explain your decision.
    a. Record of annual sales for the Kenyon Company for the past 20 years.
    b. Comparison of Kenyon Company sales, by product, for this year and last year.
    c. Monthly production of the automobile industry in units.
    d. Breakdown of how the average middle-income family in your state (or province) disposes of its income dollar.
    e. How middle-income families spend their income dollar as compared with how low-income families spend their income dollar.
    f. Comparison of sales for the past two years for each of the B&B Company's 14 sales districts. The districts cover all 50 states, Canada, and Puerto Rico.
    g. National production of automobiles from 1930 to present, broken down by manufacturer.
4. For each of the following sets of facts, (*a*) determine the graphic (or graphics) that would be best, (*b*) defend your choice, and (*c*) construct the graphic.
    a. Average (mean) amount of life insurance owned by Fidelity Life Insurance Company policyholders. Classification is by annual income.

| Income | Average Life Insurance |
|---|---|
| Under $10,000 | $ 5,245 |
| $10,000–14,999 | 14,460 |
| $15,000–19,999 | 26,680 |
| $20,000–24,999 | 39,875 |
| $25,000–29,999 | 51,440 |
| $30,000 and over | 76,390 |

*b.* Profits and losses for D and H Food Stores, by store, 1989–93, in dollars.

|      | Store     |        |            |        |
|------|-----------|--------|------------|--------|
| Year | Able City | Baker  | Charleston | Total  |
| 1989 | 13,421    | 3,241  | 9,766      | 26,428 |
| 1990 | 12,911    | −1,173 | 11,847     | 23,585 |
| 1991 | 13,843    | −2,241 | 11,606     | 23,208 |
| 1992 | 12,673    | 2,865  | 13,551     | 29,089 |
| 1993 | 13,008    | 7,145  | 15,482     | 35,635 |

*c.* Share of real estate tax payments by ward for Bigg City, 1987 and 1992, in thousands of dollars.

|            | 1987 | 1992 |
|------------|------|------|
| Ward 1     | 17.1 | 21.3 |
| Ward 2     | 10.2 | 31.8 |
| Ward 3     | 19.5 | 21.1 |
| Ward 4     |  7.8 | 18.2 |
| City total | 54.6 | 92.4 |

*d.* Percentage change in sales by employee, 1992–1993, District IV, Abbott, Inc.

| Employee        | Percentage Change |
|-----------------|-------------------|
| Joan Abraham    | + 7.3             |
| Helen Calmes    | + 2.1             |
| Todd Musso      | − 7.5             |
| Clifton Nevers  | +41.6             |
| Wilson Platt    | + 7.4             |
| Clara Ruiz      | +11.5             |
| David Schlimmer | − 4.8             |
| Phil Wirks      | − 3.6             |

# PART SIX

# OTHER FORMS OF BUSINESS COMMUNICATION

**16**
INFORMAL ORAL COMMUNICATION

**17**
PUBLIC SPEAKING AND ORAL REPORTING

# CHAPTER 16

# INFORMAL ORAL COMMUNICATION

## CHAPTER OBJECTIVES

*Upon completing this chapter, you will be able to understand and use good speaking and listening techniques, conduct interviews, lead and participate in meetings, communicate by telephone, and dictate messages. To reach this goal, you should be able to*

**1**
Discuss talking and its key elements.

**2**
Explain the listening problem and how to solve it.

**3**
Describe the nature and role of nonverbal communication.

**4**
Practice good interviewing and listening techniques.

**5**
Discuss the techniques for conducting and participating in meetings.

**6**
Describe good telephone and voice mail techniques.

**7**
Dictate letters and reports in an organized and effective manner.

### INTRODUCTORY SITUATION

## to Informal Oral Communication on the Job

Your job as assistant director in the Public Relations Department, Mastadon Chemicals, Inc., seems somewhat different from what you expected. It makes full use of your specialized college training, as you expected; but it also involves duties for which you did not train because you did not expect them. Most of these duties seem to involve some form of oral communication. In fact, you probably spend more of your work time in talking and listening than in any other activity.

To illustrate, take today's activities. Early this morning, your boss asked you to interview a prospective employee. After that, you conducted a meeting of the special committee to plan the department's annual picnic. As chairperson, you ran the meeting. It was a disaster, you felt—everybody talking at once, interrupting, arguing. It was a wonder that the committee made any progress. It seemed that everybody wanted to talk but nobody wanted to listen.

In the afternoon, you had other job duties involving oral communication. After you returned from lunch, you must have had a telephone conversation every 20 minutes or so. You felt comfortable with most of these calls, but you thought that some of the callers needed a lesson or two in telephone etiquette. Also, you dictated a few letters between telephone calls.

You most certainly do a lot of talking (and listening) on your job, as do most of the people at Mastadon (and just about everywhere else). Oral communication is a vital part of your work. Perhaps you can become better at it by studying the following review of oral communication techniques. ∎

---

As you know, your work will involve oral as well as written communication. The written communication will probably give you more problems, but the oral communication will take up more of your time. In fact, you are likely to spend more time in oral communication than in any other work activity.

> You will spend more time talking than writing in business.

Much of the oral communication that goes on in business is the informal, person-to-person communication that takes place whenever people get together. Obviously, we all have experience with this form of communication, and most of us do it reasonably well. But all of us can improve our informal speaking and listening with practice.

> Most of your oral communication will be informal.

In addition to informal talking and listening, various kinds of other more formal oral communication take place in business. Sometimes businesspeople interview job applicants, departing workers, and workers being evaluated. Sometimes they conduct and participate in committee meetings, conferences, and group discussions. Often they call one another on the telephone. Even their letters and reports are usually begun orally as spoken dictation. And frequently, they are called upon to make formal presentations—speeches, lectures, oral reports, and the like. All of these kinds of oral communication are a part of the work that businesspeople do.

> But some of it will be formal, as in interviews, meetings, telephone calls, dictation, speeches, and oral reports.

This and the following chapter cover these kinds of oral communication. This chapter reviews the somewhat less formal kinds: informal talking, listening, conducting interviews, participating in meetings, talking by telephone, and dictating. The following chapter presents the two most formal

> This and the following chapter cover these types of oral communication.

kinds: public speaking and oral reporting. Together, the two chapters should give you an understanding of the types of oral communication situations you will encounter in business.

## ■■■■■■■■■■■■■
## INFORMAL TALKING

*Most people talk reasonably well. But all of us can improve if we know the nature of talking and its qualities.*

As indicated previously, most of us do a reasonably good job of informal talking. In fact, we do such a good job that we often take talking for granted, and we overlook the possibility for improving our talking ability. To improve our talking, we need to be aware of its nature and qualities. As we become aware of these features, we can then improve our informal talking efforts. And when we improve them, other types of talking (interviewing, telephoning, and such) will improve as well. The following paragraphs review the basics of talking.

### Definition of Talking

*Think about having no words to speak. If you try to express yourself, you probably become frustrated.*

Imagine for a few moments what it would be like to have no words to express your ideas. Trying as hard as you can, you have no words to utter to express the meanings in your mind. All that you have to express your thoughts are grunts, groans, and other such utterances. Of course, you have various nonverbal symbols such as pointing your fingers, nodding your head, and the like. As you find yourself increasingly in need of expressing yourself, you probably become more and more emotional and frustrated—to the point of exaggerating the nonverbal symbols and experiencing many physical symptoms such as redness of the face, heavy breathing, and an increased heartbeat.

*Thus, we learn words to control ourselves and the world about us.*

More than likely, the foregoing analogy describes the way you learned to talk. As a dependent child, you expressed yourself with screams, cries, and nonverbal symbols. But as you matured, you learned words, and the words greatly reduced the frustrations of the past. They enabled you to communicate with others more exactly. They enabled you to relate better to the world about you and to some extent to control it.

*Talking, then, is the oral expression of knowledge, viewpoints, and emotions through words.*

The foregoing review of how you learned to talk gives us the basis for defining talking. From it we can derive this definition: *talking* is the oral expression of knowledge, viewpoints, and emotions through words. Also, from this review we can see that talking replaces many of the body movements we made before we were able to talk. And as we will see, it is supplemented by various body movements we have acquired as we learned to talk—gestures, facial expressions, body positions, and such.

*Think about the best and worst speakers you can imagine. This contrast should give you the qualities of good talking—voice quality, speaking style, word choice, adaptation.*

As a first step in improving your talking ability, think for a moment about the qualities you like in a good talker—one that you would enjoy talking with in ordinary conversation. Then think about the opposite—the worst conversationalist you can imagine. If you will get these two images in mind, you will have a good picture of the characteristics of good talking. Probably this mental picture includes good voice quality, excellence in talking style, accuracy of word choice, and adaptation. As these elements control the overall quality of oral expression, we will now review them.

568    **PART 6**  Other Forms of Business Communication

## Elements of Good Talking

Although the four qualities of good talking are important individually, you should remember that it is their purpose—to communicate better—that is of primary significance. Put differently, you want each of the following four qualities to help you deliver your message better to your listener. It is with that point in mind that we examine them.

*Qualities of good talking help you communicate your message better.*

**Voice Quality.** It should be obvious that a good voice is central to good talking. But this obvious point needs underscoring as we concentrate on developing qualities of effective talking. Good voice quality means vocal expressions that vary in pitch, change in delivery speed, and alternate volume. Because we will say more about these three qualities in our discussion of formal speeches in Chapter 17, we need only to recognize their importance to effective informal talking at this point.

*(1) Good voice quality means varying the pitch, changing delivery speed, and alternating volume.*

To illustrate their importance, imagine meeting someone who has an unpleasant voice. Probably, this person talks in a monotone, a quality of voice that needs pitch variety. Moreover, the person delivers words at the same rate of speed. And the volume of speaking remains constant throughout. After several minutes of hearing such a voice, you probably will conclude that the person is unenthusiastic or disinterested.

*Imagine an unpleasant voice. It probably is monotone, spoken at the same speed, constant in volume.*

To correct such unpleasant qualities, we must first be aware of them. We must remember that all of us need to improve our voice quality from time to time. After we become aware of the need to change, we can then practice, which is the second step to correcting unpleasant voice quality. The story is told about a visitor to New York City who wanted to attend a concert at Carnegie Hall. Not knowing the local subway system, she asked a native New Yorker on the street, "How do I get to Carnegie Hall?" The New Yorker's response: "Practice, lady, practice!"

*To correct unpleasant voice quality, do two things: (a) be aware of the unpleasantness and (b) practice.*

That advice is also sound for those wanting to improve voice quality. Concentrate on words and their pronunciation. Note the range of your voice in speaking. And vary the volume from loud to soft. If you will practice these and other variations, you will find that you can indeed improve your voice quality. Like good actors, good speakers can select from a number of alternatives in their attempts to express orally their thoughts and feelings to others.

*Especially practice word pronunciation, voice range, and volume.*

**Talking Style.** Talking style refers to how the three parts of voice quality—pitch, speed, and volume—blend together. But it also means more. It means how well talkers project their personalities through their oral expression. As such, style refers to a set of behaviors of an individual that give uniqueness to that person.

*(2) Talking style means pitch, speed, and volume—plus personality.*

When we refer to a talker as one who has a sharp, smooth, or polished style, we usually mean one whose pitch, volume, and speed are consistent with certain attitudes we infer—attitudes such as sincerity, kindness, understanding, etc. When these attitudes produce certain behaviors and blend with voice quality, we can say that a talker has a style. While it is beyond our purpose to analyze style in detail, we must note that it does exist; and it is a vital part of talking. But remember that as we noted about writing style, *what* you speak is more important than *how* you speak it. The best that a

*Good style implies that voice quality is consistent with positive attitudes.*

listener can say after hearing you speak is "These are interesting ideas" rather than "You have a beautiful voice."

**Word Choice and Vocabulary.** Still another quality of effective talking is word choice. By selecting the right word or words that create clear pictures in a listener's mind, good talkers are able to communicate better and more quickly. They do so because they have more choices available to them. Thus, vocabulary is a critical factor for good talking. The larger the vocabulary, the more selections that are available for creating pictures in the listener's mind.

As discussed in Chapter 2, there are a number of suggestions to use in choosing words that do a good job of communicating. These suggestions are just as important to talking as they are to writing. Because we have already covered them, we will not repeat them here. Nonetheless, they are important. In fact, using them in speaking requires quicker judgment because of the shorter time involved in selecting words. This shorter time cycle should underscore again the need to practice in selecting different words for different effects.

**Central Role of Adaptation.** Adaptation, a fourth quality of good talking, in effect sums up the previous three qualities of voice quality, style, and word choice. As discussed in Chapter 2, adaptation means fitting a message to a specific receiver. In our speaking efforts, all that we do is for adaptation. That is, we select the right words and use the right voice pitch, speed, volume, and style for the one intended listener.

To illustrate, assume that you must report to your boss about a specific project you are working on. Your boss has a master's degree and 15 years of experience with your organization. In speaking to her, you choose certain words to fit her education and experience; and you deliver them with a style and quality to accomplish the purpose you seek. But contrast that situation with another: that of instructing your subordinates. These subordinates have a high school education and less than one year on the job. The words, style, and voice quality of your oral direction probably would be quite different. Yet both messages would fit the minds of the listeners.

## LISTENING

Up to this point, our review of oral communication has been about sending information (talking). Certainly, this is an area in which businesspeople need help. But evidence shows that the receiving side (listening) causes more problems.

### The Nature of Listening

When listening is mentioned, we think primarily of the act of sensing sounds. In human communication, of course, the sounds are mainly spoken words. Viewed from a communication standpoint, however, the listening process involves the additional activities of filtering and remembering.

**Sensing.** How well we sense the words spoken around us is determined by two factors. One factor is our ability to sense sounds—how well our ears can

---

(3) Word choice allows speakers to communicate better and more quickly by giving more selections.

The suggestions for word choice in Chapter 2 apply to speaking as well. Use them, and practice.

(4) Adaptation is fitting a message to a specific listener.

For example, your message would differ for people with great differences in education and experience.

Poor listening is a major cause of miscommunication.

Listening involves sensing, filtering, and remembering.

How well we sense spoken words is determined by (1) our ability to sense sounds, and

To be a good listener, one must consciously try to listen as well as give the appearance of listening.

pick them up. As you know, we do not all hear equally well, although mechanical devices (hearing aids) can reduce our differences in this respect.

The other factor is our attentiveness to listening. More specifically, this is our mental concentration—our will to listen. As was noted in Chapter 1, our mental concentration on the communication symbols that our senses can detect varies from moment to moment. It can range from almost totally blocking out those symbols to concentrating on them very intensely. From your own experience, you can recall moments when you were oblivious to the words spoken around you and moments when you listened with all the intensity you could muster. Most of the time, your listening fell somewhere between these extremes.

(2) our attentiveness.

**Filtering.** From your study of the communication process in Chapter 1, you know that the filtering process enables you to give meanings to the symbols you sense. In this process, the contents of your mind serve as a sort of filter through which you give meaning to incoming messages. This filter is formed by the unique contents of your mind—your knowledge, emotions, beliefs, biases, experiences, expectations, and such. Thus, you sometimes give messages meanings different from the meanings that others give them.

Filtering is the process of giving symbols meanings through the unique contents of each person's mind.

**Remembering.** Remembering what we hear is the third activity involved in listening. Unfortunately, we retain little of what we hear. We remember many of the comments we hear in casual conversation for only a short time—perhaps for only a few minutes or hours. Some we forget almost as we hear them. According to authorities, we even quickly forget most of the message in formal oral communications (such as speeches), remembering only a fourth after two days.

Remembering what we hear is a part of listening.

**CHAPTER 16  Informal Oral Communication**

### Listening Error in a Chain of Communication

*Colonel to the executive officer:* "As the general feels the soldiers are unaware of the danger of drinking impure water, he wishes to explain the matter to them. Have all personnel fall out in fatigues at 1400 hours in the battalion area, where the general will address them. In the event of rain, assemble them in the theater."

*Executive officer to company commander:* "By order of the colonel, tomorrow at 1400 hours all personnel will fall out in fatigues in the battalion area if it rains to march to the theater. There the general will talk about their unawareness of the dangers of drinking."

*Company commander to lieutenant:* "By order of the colonel, in fatigues the personnel will assemble at the theater at 1400 hours. The general will appear if it rains to talk about the dangers of the unawareness of drinking."

*Lieutenant to sergeant:* "Tomorrow at 1400 hours the troops will assemble at the theater to hear the general talk about unawareness of drinking dangerously."

*Sergeant to the enlisted personnel:* "Tomorrow at 1400 hours the drunken general will be at the theater in his underwear talking dangerously. We have to go and hear him."

## Improving Your Listening Ability

- To improve your listening, you must want to improve it.

Improving your listening is largely a matter of mental conditioning—of concentrating on the activity of sensing. You have to want to improve it, for listening is a willful act. If you are like most of us, you are often tempted not to listen or you just find it easier not to listen. We human beings tend to avoid work; and listening may be work.

- Be alert. Force yourself to pay attention.

After you have decided that you want to listen better, you must make an effort to pay attention. How you do this will depend on your mental makeup, for the effort requires disciplining the mind. You must force yourself to be alert, to pay attention to the words spoken.

- Concentrate on improving your mental filtering.
- Think from the speaker's viewpoint.

In addition to working on the improvement of your sensing, you should work on the accuracy of your filtering. To do this, you will need to think in terms of what words mean to the speakers who use them rather than what the dictionary says they mean or what they mean in your mind. You must try to think as the speaker thinks—judging the speaker's words by the speaker's knowledge, experiences, viewpoints, and such. Like improving your sensing, improving your filtering requires conscious effort.

- Consciously try to remember.

Remembering what you hear also requires conscious effort. Certainly, there are limits to what the mind can retain; but authorities agree that few of us come close to them. By taking care to hear what is said and by working to make your filtering process give you more accurate meanings to the words you hear, you add strength to the messages you receive. The result should be improved retention.

### Some Sound Advice on Listening

Living in a competitive culture, most of us are most of the time chiefly concerned with getting our own views across, and we tend to find other people's speeches a tedious interruption of the flow of our own ideas. Hence, it is necessary to emphasize that listening does not mean simply maintaining a polite silence while you are rehearsing in your mind the speech you are going to make the next time you can grab a conversational opening. Nor does listening mean waiting alertly for the flaws in the other fellow's arguments so that later you can mow him down. Listening means trying to see the problem the way the speaker sees it—which means not sympathy, which is *feeling* for him, but empathy, which is *experiencing* with him. Listening requires entering actively and imaginatively into the other fellow's situation and trying to understand a frame of reference different from your own. This is not always an easy task.

S. I. Hayakawa

In addition to the foregoing advice, various practical steps may prove helpful. Assembled in a classic document titled "The Ten Commandments of Listening,"[1] the following list summarizes the most useful of them:

*In addition, follow these practical guidelines (summarized in italics).*

1. *Stop talking.* Unfortunately, most of us prefer talking to listening. Even when we are not talking, we are inclined to concentrate on what to say next rather than on listening to others. So you must stop talking before you can listen.

2. *Put the talker at ease.* If you make the talker feel at ease, he or she will do a better job of talking. Then you will have better input to work with.

3. *Show the talker you want to listen.* If you can convince the talker that you are listening to understand rather than oppose, you will help create a climate for information exchange. You should look and act interested. Doing things like reading, looking at your watch, and looking away distracts the talker.

4. *Remove distractions.* The things you do can also distract the talker. So don't doodle, tap with your pencil, shuffle papers, or the like.

5. *Empathize with the talker.* If you place yourself in the talker's position and look at things from the talker's point of view, you will help create a climate of understanding that can result in a true exchange of information.

6. *Be patient.* You will need to allow the talker plenty of time. Remember that not everyone can get to the point as quickly and clearly as you.

---

[1] To some anonymous author goes a debt of gratitude for these classic and often quoted comments about listening.

And do not interrupt. Interruptions are barriers to the exchange of information.

7. *Hold your temper.* From our knowledge of the workings of our minds, we know that anger impedes communication. Angry people build walls between each other. They harden their positions and block their minds to the words of others.

8. *Go easy on argument and criticism.* Argument and criticism tend to put the talker on the defensive. He or she then tends to "clam up" or get angry. Thus, even if you win the argument, you lose. Rarely does either party benefit from argument and criticism.

9. *Ask questions.* By frequently asking questions, you display an open mind and show that you are listening. And you assist the talker in developing his or her message and in improving the correctness of meaning.

10. *Stop talking!* The last commandment is to stop talking. It was also the first. All the other commandments depend on it.

From the preceding review it should be clear that to improve your listening ability, you must set your mind to the task. Poor listening habits are ingrained in our makeup. We can alter these habits only through conscious effort.

## THE REINFORCING ROLE OF NONVERBAL COMMUNICATION

In either your role of speaker or listener in oral communication, you will need to be aware of the nonverbal—nonword—part of your communication. In both roles, nonverbal communication accounts for a larger part of the total message than do the words you send or receive. Usually, we use nonverbal communication to supplement and reinforce our words. Sometimes, nonverbal communication communicates by itself. Because it is so important to both sides of the oral communication equation, we will look at the nature of nonverbal communication and some types of it.

*Nonverbal communication accounts for more of a total message than words do.*

### Nature of Nonverbal Communication

Nonverbal or nonword communication means all communication that occurs without words. As you can see, the subject is a broad one. And because it is so broad, nonverbal communication is quite vague and imprecise. For instance, a frown on someone's forehead is sometimes interpreted to mean worry. But could it be that the person has a headache? Or is the person in deep thought? No doubt, there could be numerous meanings given to the facial expression.

*Nonverbal (nonword) communication means all communication without words. It is broad and imprecise.*

The number of possible meanings is multiplied even more when we consider the international side of communication. As noted in Chapter 19, culture teaches us about body positions, movements, and various factors that affect human relationships (intimacy, space, time, and such). Thus, the meanings we give to nonverbal symbols will vary depending on how our culture has conditioned us.

*International aspects give many meanings to nonverbal communication.*

FRANK & ERNEST reprinted by permission of NEA, Inc.

Because of these numerous meanings, you need to be sensitive to what others intend with nonverbal communication. And you need to make some allowance for error in the meanings you receive from nonverbal symbols. As a listener, you need to go beyond the obvious to determine what nonword symbols mean. As we have said about word symbols, you need to see what people intend with their nonverbal symbols as well. Perhaps one good way to grasp the intent of this suggestion is to look at the intended meanings you have for the nonverbal symbols you use. Think for a few moments about the smile on your face, a gesture, or such. What do you mean by it? What could it mean to others? Is it exactly as you intend? Could it be interpreted differently? Could someone from a different culture give a different meaning to it? Only if you look at nonverbal symbols through the prism of self-analysis and realize their multiple meaning potential can you get some idea of how they might be interpreted differently. And when you become aware of the many differences, you then can become sensitive to the meaning intended by the nonverbal communication.

In order to become sensitive to the myriad of nonverbal symbols, we will take a look at some types of nonverbal communication. Specifically, we will look at three types of communication that occur without words.

*Be sensitive to intended nonverbal meanings. Go beyond the obvious.*

## Types of Nonverbal Communication

Although there are many ways to classify nonverbal communication, we will examine three of the more common types—body language, space, and time. These three types are especially important to our discussion of speaking and listening.

*We will look at three common types of nonverbal communication: (1) body language, (2) space, (3) time.*

**Body Language.** Much of what we send to others without using words is sent through the physical movements of our bodies. When we wave our arms and fingers, wrinkle our foreheads, stand erect, smile, gaze at another, wear a coat and tie, etc., we convey certain meanings; and others convey meanings to us in return. In particular, the face and eyes, gestures, posture, and physical appearance reflect the inner workings of emotions in our bodies.

*Our bodies send nonword messages—through arms, fingers, expressions, posture, etc.*

The face and eyes are by far the most important features of body language. We look to the face and eyes to determine much of the meaning behind body language and nonverbal communication. For example, happiness, surprise, fear, anger, and sadness usually require definite facial

*The face and eyes are the most important.*

**CHAPTER 16** Informal Oral Communication     575

The nonverbal messages we send through facial expressions, hand movements, body positions, and such are an important part of our communication.

**Gestures (physical movements of the arms, legs, torso, and head) send nonword messages.**

expressions and eye patterns. Thus, you should be aware of these two aspects of body language as you speak and listen to others.

In addition, gestures are another way we send nonword messages through our body parts. *Gestures* are physical movements of our arms, legs, hands, torsos, and heads. Through the movement of each of these body parts, we can accent and reinforce our verbal messages. And we can observe how others punctuate their verbal efforts with gestures. For example, observe the hand movements of another person while he or she is talking. Consider whether this person is fluid or sporadic with such hand movements. As you observe these gestures, you will get a good picture of the internal emotional state of the person. Moreover, speaking and gestures appear to be linked. In general, the louder someone speaks, the greater the gestures used, and vice versa.

**Physical appearance—clothing, hair, jewelry, cosmetics, etc.—also communicates.**

Another area of body language is physical appearance—our clothing, hair, and adornments (jewelry, cosmetics, and such). The appearance of our bodies indicates how our body movements are seen. Consider, for example, how you might perceive a speaker at a formal banquet dressed in faded blue jeans. No doubt, the speaker's gestures, facial features, posture, and such would be perceived in relation to attire. Accordingly, you want to make sure that your appearance fits the expectancies of the one situation. And you want to make sure that you know that appearance is an important part of the body messages that are sent and received in oral communication.

**Space.** Another type of nonverbal communication involves space and how it communicates meaning in speaking and listening. How we use space and what we do in certain spaces we create tell much about us. Thus, each of us has a space language just as we do a body language. And this space language is crafted by our culture.

Authorities tell us that we create four different types of space: intimate (physical contact to 18 inches); personal (18 inches to 4 feet); social (4 to 12 feet); and public (12 feet to range of seeing and hearing). In each of these spaces, our communication behaviors differ and convey different meanings. For example, consider the volume of your voice when someone is 18 inches from you. Do you shout? Whisper? Now contrast the tone of your voice when someone is 12 feet away. Unquestionably, there is a difference, just because of the distance involved.

Also, our behaviors in each type of space are learned from our cultures. Thus, you will need to be sensitive to the spaces of others—especially those from different cultures. As noted in Chapter 19, when people's attitudes toward space are different, their actions are likely to be misinterpreted.

**Time.** A third type of nonverbal communication involves time. Just as there is a body and space language, there is also a time language. That is, how we give meaning to time communicates to others. To illustrate, think about how you manage your daily schedule. Do you arrive early for most appointments? Do you prioritize telephone calls? Do you prepare agendas for meetings? How you respond to time communicates to others. And, of course, others' use of time communicates to you. In terms of nonverbal communication, you should recognize that time orientations are not always the same—especially in the international arena—but they do communicate. As such, they become parts of the messages we send to and receive from one another.

## INTERVIEWING PEOPLE

In your work in business, you may need to participate in a variety of types of interviews. Perhaps the best-known type is the employment interview discussed in Chapter 11. But there are others. Interviews are often involved in the periodic evaluations that some companies make of their workers. These interviews are primarily a means of communicating the evaluations. When workers leave a company, they may be interviewed to determine their reasons for leaving. Interviews are sometimes conducted to gather information on such matters as worker attitudes, working conditions, managerial effectiveness, and worker plans.

As interviewing is a form of personal communication, usually between two people, it is not a precise activity—that is, no hard-and-fast rules exist. Rather, interviewing is a flexible activity that requires the good judgment of the people involved. Nevertheless, well-established guidelines exist, and you should follow them. In the following pages they are presented from the side of both the interviewer and the interviewee.

---

*Side notes:*

Space is another type of nonverbal language.

Four types of space exist: (1) intimate, (2) personal, (3) social, and (4) public. Communication behavior differs in each.

Communication behaviors are learned from cultures.

Time is a third type of nonverbal communication.

Interviews are conducted in business for employment purposes, to get information, and to give information.

Although interviewing is not a precise activity, the following guidelines will help you.

## Guidelines for the Interviewer

Here are some guidelines for the interviewer:

As the interviewer is in charge, the success of the interview is in his or her hands. Thus, it is especially important that the interviewer know and follow these general guidelines.

(1) plan (determine what information is needed),

**Plan the Interview.** You conduct most interviews because you need information. So as a starting point you should determine your information needs. You can usually express these needs in a list of specific questions. You should make such a list and use it as the outline for the interview.

(2) put the interviewee at ease (using your social skills),

**Put the Interviewee at Ease.** The chances are that the interviewee will be nervous. As nervous people are not good subjects for interviewing, you should try to put the interviewee at ease. How you should do this varies with the person involved and with your social skills. You could, for example, begin with some friendly talk on a point of common interest. Or you could begin with comments or questions about the interviewee—hometown, sports interests, hobbies, and the like.

(3) explain the purpose when it is not apparent,

**Make the Purpose Clear.** The interviewee should know the purpose of the interview from the beginning. Of course, the interviewee sometimes knows the purpose from the nature of the interview, as in an employment interview. But if she or he does not know the purpose, you should explain it clearly and honestly.

(4) allow the interviewee to do the talking,

**Let the Interviewee Do Most of the Talking.** You can get the information you seek only when the interviewee talks. Thus, you should let the interviewee do most of the talking. You should talk only to guide the course of the interview—to carry the discussion through the specific questions you want to cover. As some interviewees are reluctant to talk, you will sometimes need to work to get them to talk. But you should never put words in their mouths.

(5) guide the interview through the plan (ask questions and end answers),

**Guide the Interview.** Even though the interviewee does most of the talking, your task is to guide the interview so as to obtain the needed information. That is, you follow the plan you set up in the beginning. You ask specific questions, and you end answers when you have the information you need. In guiding the interview, you will need to handle moments of silence. Brief periods of silence are all right, for additional information sometimes comes after them. But too much silence can be awkward for all concerned.

(6) listen and make it apparent that you are listening,

**Listen.** You should listen carefully to all that the interviewee says. The purpose of an interview is to get certain information—by listening. As mentioned previously in this chapter, most of us do not listen well.

In addition to listening, you should give the appearance of listening. Your interviewees will be more relaxed and will talk more if they feel that they have your undivided attention.

(7) record information either during the interview or soon after, and

**Keep a Record.** As you conduct interviews to get information, you will need to make a record of the information. How you record the information may vary with the situation. When you need much detailed information, you may have to take notes during the interview. Because your writing may be disturbing to the interviewee, you should explain at the beginning of the interview why you must take notes. Even after explaining, you should write as quickly and briefly as possible.

When you can remember the information you seek, you need not write during the interview. But you should record that information soon after the interview is over. As you know, not many of us can remember such information for very long.

**End the Interview.** As you are in charge of the interview, you should end it. If the situation justifies it, some friendly talk can follow the questioning. But you should avoid letting the conversation trail off to meaningless talk. One good way of ending interviews is to ask a finalizing question—one that tells the interviewee that the interview is over. This one does the job well: "Is there anything else you would like to tell me? If not, thanks for giving me your time."

(8) end the interview, perhaps with a finalizing question.

## Guidelines for the Interviewee

When you are the person being interviewed, you may have little control over the situation. Nevertheless, you can help make the interview successful. The following guidelines tell you how.

Here are some guidelines for the interviewee:

**Prepare for the Interview.** When you know the nature of the interview, prepare for it. Your preparation should consist mainly of thinking about the questions you are likely to be asked and formulating answers to them. It may also include gathering additional information. In a job interview, for example, you would be wise to learn what you can about the company—its history, its current activities, its plans. By showing your knowledge of the company during the interview, you can impress the interviewer with your interest in it. Even if you prepare diligently, you are not likely to cover all that will be asked. So be prepared for the unexpected.

(1) prepare (anticipate questions and form answers),

**Make an Appropriate Appearance.** What the interviewer sees is a part of the message that he or she receives. So you should do what you can to make an appropriate appearance. As what is appropriate varies with the situation, you should consider the situation. You will find that the conventional standards of neatness and dress are desirable in most cases. In addition, you will usually want your posture, facial expressions, and physical movements to give favorable impressions. You will especially want to avoid the appearance of nervousness.

(2) make an appropriate appearance,

**Show Interest.** You can improve the impression you make in most interview situations by showing interest. How you should show interest varies with the occasion. But you always help your case by looking at the interviewer and by giving her or him your undivided attention.

(3) show interest (look at the interviewer and pay attention),

**Answer Correctly and Completely.** If the interview serves a good purpose, it deserves correct and complete answers. You should give them. Dishonest answers benefit no one.

(4) answer correctly and completely, and

**Practice Courtesy.** You probably know very well the value of courtesy in business. You know that it is a major part of the impression you make in every human contact. The interview is no exception.

(5) be courteous.

**CHAPTER 16** Informal Oral Communication

## CONDUCTING AND PARTICIPATING IN MEETINGS

*Meetings involve oral communication.*

From time to time, you will participate in business meetings. They will range from extreme formality to extreme informality. On the formal end will be conferences and committee meetings. On the informal end will be discussions with groups of fellow workers. Whether formal or informal, the meetings will involve communication. In fact, the quality of the communication will determine their success.

*In a meeting you will be either a leader or a participant.*

Your role in a meeting will be that of either leader or participant. Of course, the leader's role is the primary one, but good participation is also vital. The following paragraphs review the techniques of performing well in either role.

### Techniques of Conducting Meetings

*To lead some formal meetings, you should know parliamentary procedure. So study the subject.*

How you conduct a meeting depends on the formality of the occasion. Meetings of such groups as formal committees, boards of directors, and professional organizations usually follow generally accepted rules of conduct called *parliamentary procedure*. These very specific rules are too detailed for review here. When you are involved in a formal meeting, you would do well to study one of the many books covering parliamentary procedure before the meeting. In addition, you should know and practice the following techniques. For less formal meetings, you can depart somewhat from parliamentary procedure and those techniques. But you should keep in mind that every meeting has goals and that such departures should never hinder reaching them.

*In addition, you should do the following: (1) plan the items to be covered (the agenda),*

**Plan the Meeting.** A key to conducting a successful meeting is to plan it thoroughly. That is, you develop an agenda (a list of topics to be covered) by selecting the items that need to be covered to achieve the goals of the meeting. Then arrange these items in the most logical order. Items that explain or lead to other items should come before the items that they explain or lead to. After preparing the agenda, if the meeting is formal, make it available to those who will attend. For informal meetings, you may find keeping the agenda in mind satisfactory.

*(2) follow the plan item by item,*

**Follow the Plan.** You should follow the plan for the meeting item by item. In most meetings the discussion tends to stray and new items tend to come up. As leader, you should keep the discussion on track. If new items come up during the meeting, you can take them up at the end—or perhaps postpone them to a future meeting.

*(3) move the discussion along,*

**Move the Discussion Along.** As leader, you should control the agenda. When one item has been covered, bring up the next item. When the discussion moves off subject, move it back on subject. In general, do what is needed to proceed through the items efficiently. But you should not cut off discussion before all the important points have been made. Thus, you will have to use your good judgment. Your goal is to permit complete discussion on the one hand and to avoid repetition, excessive details, and useless comments on the other.

PART 6  Other Forms of Business Communication

**Control Those Who Talk Too Much.** Keeping certain people from talking too much is likely to be one of your harder tasks. A few people usually tend to dominate the discussion. Your task as leader is to control them. Of course, you want the meeting to be democratic, so you will need to let these people talk as long as they are contributing to the goals of the meeting. However, when they begin to stray, duplicate, or bring in useless matter, you should step in. You can do this tactfully by asking for other viewpoints or by summarizing the discussion and moving on to the next topic.

*(4) allow no one to talk too much,*

**Encourage Participation from Those Who Talk Too Little.** Just as some people talk too much, some talk too little. In business groups, those who say little are often in positions lower than those of other group members. Your job as leader is to encourage these people to participate by asking them for their viewpoints and by showing respect for the comments they make, even though the comments may be illogical.

*(5) encourage everybody to take part,*

**Control Time.** When your meeting time is limited, you need to determine in advance how much time will be needed to cover each item. Then, at the appropriate times, you should end discussion of the items. You may find it helpful to announce the time goals at the beginning of the meeting and to remind the group members of the time status during the meeting.

*(6) control time when time is limited, and*

**Summarize at Appropriate Places.** After a key item has been discussed, you should summarize what the group has covered and concluded. If a group decision is needed, the group's vote will be the conclusion. In any event, you should formally conclude each point and then move on to the next one. At the end of the meeting, you can summarize the progress made. You should also summarize whenever a review will help the group members understand their accomplishments. For some formal meetings, minutes kept by a secretary provide this summary.

*(7) at appropriate places, summarize what the group has covered and concluded.*

### Techniques for Participating in a Meeting

From the preceding discussion of the techniques that a leader should use, you know something about the things that a participant should do. The following review emphasizes them for you.

*As a participant in a meeting you should*

**Follow the Agenda.** When an agenda exists, you should follow it. Specifically, you should not bring up items not on the agenda or comment on such items if others bring them up. When there is no agenda, you should stay within the general limits of the goal for the meeting.

*(1) follow the agenda,*

**Participate.** The purpose of meetings is to get the input of everybody concerned. Thus, you should participate. Your participation, however, should be meaningful. You should talk only when you have something to contribute, and you should talk whenever you have something to contribute.

*(2) participate in the meeting,*

**Do Not Talk Too Much.** As you participate in the meeting, be aware that other people are attending. You should speak up whenever you have something to say, but do not get carried away. Always respect the rights of others. As you speak, ask yourself whether what you are saying really contributes to the discussion.

*(3) avoid talking too much,*

## *Electronic Meeting Systems (EMS): A Tool for Facilitating the Effectiveness of Meetings*

Technology is making its way into meetings, assisting in numerous ways and changing the basic structure of meetings a bit. Electronic meeting systems (EMS) software runs on a network, linking people together electronically. When these meetings are held at the same time and face-to-face, the technology is usually used in combination with oral communication. Research has shown that various components of the EMS toolkit are appropriate for different tasks. When used appropriately, EMS software helps meeting participants improve their performance and accomplish their goals in half the time of the traditional meeting.

The tool also changes the nature of meetings. Most EMS software elicits equal participation, which prevents the meeting from being dominated by one person. Additionally, some systems allow participants to maintain anonymity, entering their ideas through the network without others knowing whose idea it is. This removes the status and much of the personal biases people hold. Many people claim this feature alone improves quality by allowing participants to respond to the idea, not to who said it or how it was delivered. Others attribute the increased quality to the ability of the system to force an agenda and keep people focused on the task at hand. These systems are also different from face-to-face meetings because everyone is communicating simultaneously through the system rather than taking turns as required by the traditional meeting. All participants are active. EMS software also provides a record of all ideas entered. This prevents thoughts from being lost as they often are in traditional meetings.

Electronic meetings can also be held in geographically dispersed settings. A major benefit of this feature is its ability to allow groups access to experts who might otherwise be unable to attend a face-to-face meeting.

Another variation of the EMS is the meeting held on-line over a period of time rather than at a precise time. While not quite the same as the traditional meeting, the performance of groups meeting on-line this way has been good.

As more is learned about the effectiveness of technology in assisting with different tasks, these tools will certainly be enhanced and further developed. Using these tools appropriately makes the tasks groups work on seem easier.

**Cooperate.** A meeting by its very nature requires cooperation from all the participants. So keep this in mind as you participate. Respect the leader and her or his efforts to make progress. Respect the other participants, and work with them in every practical way.

*(4) cooperate with all concerned, and*

**Be Courteous.** Perhaps being courteous is a part of being cooperative. In any event, you should be courteous to the other group members. Specifically, you should respect their rights and opinions, and you should permit them to speak.

*(5) practice courtesy.*

## USING THE TELEPHONE

A discussion of business telephone techniques may appear trivial at first thought. After all, most of us have had long experience in using the telephone and may feel that we have little to learn about it. No doubt, some of us have excellent telephone skills. But you have only to call up a small number of randomly selected businesses to learn that not all users of the telephone are proficient in its use. You will get some gruff, cold greetings, and you will be subjected to a variety of discourtesies. And you will find instances of inefficient use of time (which, of course, is costly). This is not to say that the problem is major, for most progressive businesses are aware of the need for good telephone habits and do something about it. But poor telephone techniques are found often enough to justify reviewing the subject of telephone use in a business communication textbook.

*Many businesspeople are discourteous and inefficient in telephone communication.*

With the advent of cellular telephones and voice mail, oral business messages are growing in importance.

## Need for Favorable Voice Quality

*Because only sound is involved, friendly voices are important.*

In reviewing good telephone techniques, keep in mind that a telephone conversation is a unique form of oral communication. Only voices are heard; the speakers are not seen. Impressions are received only from the words and the quality of the voices. Thus, when speaking by telephone, it is extremely important that you work to make your voice sound cheerful and friendly.

*So talk as if you were in face-to-face conversation.*

One often-suggested way of improving your telephone voice is to talk as if you were face-to-face with the other person—even smiling and gesturing as you talk, if this helps you be more natural. In addition, you would do well to put into practice the suggestions given earlier in this chapter concerning the use of the voice in speaking (voice quality, variation in pitch, and speed). Perhaps the best instructional device for this problem is to record one of your telephone conversations. Then judge for yourself how you come across and what you need to do to improve.

## Techniques of Courtesy

*Be courteous.*

If you have worked in business for any length of time, you have probably experienced most of the common telephone discourtesies. You probably know that most of them are not intended as discourtesies but result from ignorance or unconcern. The following review should help you avoid them.

*When calling, immediately introduce yourself and ask for the person you want (or explain your purpose).*

The recommended procedure when you are calling is to introduce yourself immediately and then to ask for the person with whom you want to talk:

"This is Wanda Tidwell of Tioga Milling Company. May I speak with Mr. José Martinez?"

If you are not certain with whom you should talk, explain the purpose of your call:

"This is Wanda Tidwell of Tioga Milling Company. We have a question about your service warranty. May I talk with the proper executive about it?"

*When receiving a call, identify your company or office; then offer assistance.*

When a secretary or someone else who is screening calls answers the telephone, the recommended procedure is to first identify the company or office and then to make a cheerful offer of assistance:

"Rowan Insurance Company. May I help you?"
"Ms. Santo's office. May I help you?"

When a call goes directly into the office of the executive, the procedure is much the same, except that the executive identifies herself or himself:

"Bartosh Realty. Toby Bartosh speaking. May I help you?"

*Secretaries should avoid offending callers by asking misleading questions, by making misleading comments, or*

When a secretary answers for an executive (the usual case), special care should be taken not to offend the caller. Following a question like "Who is calling?" by "I am sorry, but Mr. Gordon is not in" leaves the impression that Gordon may be in but does not want to talk with this particular caller. A better procedure would be to state directly "Mr. Gordon is not in right now. May I ask him to return your call?" Or perhaps "May I tell him who called?" or "Can someone else help you?" could be substituted for the latter sentence.

*by being inconsiderate in placing callers on hold. Let the callers choose, and check on the hold status continually.*

Especially irritating to callers is being put on hold for unreasonable periods of time. If the person being called is on another line or involved in some other activity, it may be desirable to place the caller on hold. But the

**PART 6** Other Forms of Business Communication

choice should be the caller's. If the hold continues for a period longer than anticipated, the secretary should check back with the caller periodically, showing concern and offering assistance. Equally irritating is the practice of having a secretary place a call for an executive and then put the person called on hold until the executive is free to talk. While it may be efficient to use secretaries for such work, as a matter of courtesy the executive should be ready to talk the moment the call goes through.

Secretaries to busy executives often screen incoming calls. In doing so, they should courteously ask the purpose of the calls. The response might prompt the secretary to refer the caller to a more appropriate person in the company. It might also reveal that the executive has no interest in the subject of the call, in which case the secretary should courteously yet clearly explain this to the caller. If the executive is busy at the moment, the secretary should explain this and either suggest a more appropriate time for a call or promise a callback by the executive. But in no case should the secretary promise a callback that will not be made.

> Secretaries often screen calls. They should do this courteously and honestly.

### Effective Telephone Procedures

At the beginning of a telephone conversation that you have initiated, it is good practice to state the purpose of the call. Then you should cover systematically all the points involved. For really important calls, you should plan your call, even to the point of making notes of the points to cover. Then you should follow your notes to make certain that you cover them all.

> When calling, state your purpose early. Then cover your points systematically. Plan important calls.

Courteous procedure is much the same in a telephone conversation as in a face-to-face conversation. You listen when the other person is talking. You refrain from interrupting. You avoid dominating the conversation. And perhaps most important of all, you cover your message quickly, saving time (and money) for all concerned.

> Be considerate, listen, and do not dominate. Use time efficiently.

### Effective Voice Mail Techniques

Sometimes when the person you are calling is not available, you will be able to leave a voice message in an electronic voice mailbox. Not only does this save you the time involved in calling back the person you are trying to reach, it allows you to leave a more detailed message than you might leave with a secretary. However, you need to be prepared for this to be sure your message is both complete and concise.

> Voice mail is becoming common in business.

You begin the message nearly the same way you would a telephone call. Be as courteous as you would on the telephone and speak as clearly and distinctly as you can. Tell the listener in a natural way your name and affiliation. Begin with an overview of the message and continue with details. If you want the listener to take action, call for it at the end. If you want the listener to return your call, state that precisely, including when you can be reached. Slowly give the number where your call can be returned. Close with a brief goodwill message. For example, as a volunteer for your local symphony, you might leave this message in the voice mailbox of one of your sponsors:

> Use it much as you would any other telephone call,

This is Linda Wingler from the Quad-City Symphony. I'm calling to remind you about the Summer Pops special concert for sponsors. The concert will be on Friday, June 25, at 7:30 P.M. It'll be held at Meersman Park on 34th Street and 24th Avenue in Moline. Fireworks will begin immediately after the concert. If

> as in this example.

### Voice Systems: Technologies for Recording, Storing, and Receiving Oral Messages

A variety of voice systems are available to assist with oral communication tasks. One of these, voice message systems, has experienced terrific growth both in terms of sales and in terms of sophistication. Not only will most of the large businesses you call today use these systems, you may even run into them calling your neighborhood drug store or the local real estate office. Most systems work through a type of menuing, giving you a choice of a few ways to direct your call. Your response may be to select one of the items or default to the operator. Some systems ask for the extension number you want or allow you to type in the letter keys for the person you wish to speak to. Others will route you to a voice message box, allowing you to leave a message. These systems are efficient. Not only can you reach the party you want faster, but you can leave a message, thereby eliminating many callbacks.

Voice message systems have numerous other features. For example, your company may be announcing a new contest for its salespeople. You could record a voice message announcing this contest and ask the system to deliver it to all salespeople on a certain date and time. Furthermore, if your voice mailbox contained a message appropriate for someone else or of interest to someone else, you could forward it to that person's mailbox. Many of these systems store your messages and allow you to retrieve them by various categories such as date, sender, or subject. Learning all the features of your company's voice mail system will help you use this oral message transmission tool more effectively.

Another type of voice system allows you to attach voice messages to files. Not only is multimedia software making the integration with audio more widely used, but other programs have voice features as well. Already you can annotate spreadsheet cells with voice notes as well as attach voice files to documents, indicating a voice message attachment with buttons or icons. In addition, you can edit voice files, moving or deleting pauses, non-words, and words. Voice files tend to be large; however, since most businesses are increasing the storage capacity of the systems they use, we are likely to see increased use of this technology in the near future.

---

you plan to attend, call the symphony office between 10:00 A.M. and 4:00 P.M. Monday through Friday for your tickets. You can reach us at 764-0017. We look forward to hearing from you.

## DICTATING LETTERS AND REPORTS

*You will probably dictate most letters and some reports.*

The odds are that you will dictate many of the letters you write in business. You may even dictate reports—especially the shorter, more informal ones. Developing good dictation skills offers many advantages. First, it is much faster than handwriting at around 15 words per minute or even keying at 80 words per minute. The average person speaks at around 160 words per minute. Second, if you use dictation equipment, you can dictate when you are ready. In some companies, you can even call in your dictation from remote locations and often at any time of the day or night. Finally, voice-actuated systems are currently being developed for personal computers. In the future, you may have the option of dictating to your computer rather than keying. Thus, the following summary of the techniques of dictating should be useful to you.

## *Techniques of Dictating*

**Gather the Facts.** Your first logical step in dictating is to get all the information you need for the message. This step involves such activities as getting past correspondence from the files, consulting with other employees, and ascertaining company policy. Unless you get all the information you need, you will be unable to work without interruption.

*You should (1) get all the information you need, to avoid interruptions later;*

**Plan the Message.** With the facts of the case before you, you next plan the message. You may prefer to do this step in your mind or to jot down a few notes or an outline. Whatever your preference, your goal in this step is to decide what your message will be and how you will present it. In this step you apply the procedures covered in our earlier review of letter and report writing.

*(2) plan the message (following procedures described in preceding chapters);*

**Give Preliminary Information and Instructions.** Your first step in the actual process of dictating is to give the transcriptionist specific instructions. These include instructions about special handling, enclosures, form, and page layout. They also include all the necessary additional information about the message—such information as the mailing address, subject line, attention line, and salutation. When this information is easily available, you need only refer to the source (for example, "Get their address from their letter").

*(3) dictate instructions, such as form, enclosures, inside address, and subject line;*

**Make the Words Flow.** Your next step is to talk through the message. Simple as this step appears, you are likely to have problems with it. Thinking out loud to a secretary or dictation equipment frightens most of us at first. The result is likely to be slow and awkward dictation.

*(4) talk through the message,*

Overcoming this problem requires self-discipline and practice. You should force yourself to concentrate and to make the words flow. Your goal should be to get the words out—to talk through the message. You need not be concerned with producing polished work on the first effort. You will probably need to revise, perhaps many times. After you have forced your way through enough messages, your need to revise will decrease and the speed and quality of your dictation will improve.

*forcing the words to flow if necessary (you can revise later);*

**Speak in a Strong, Clear Voice.** As your dictation must be heard, you should dictate in a strong, clear voice. Speak at a speed slow enough to clearly separate the words. Words that do not stand out clearly can cause delays in work as well as errors in the message. Be especially careful when using dictation equipment, for it sometimes does not reproduce voices well.

*(5) speak so that the transcriptionist can understand each word;*

**Give Paragraphing, Punctuation, and Other Mechanics as Needed.** How much of the paragraphing, spelling, punctuation, and other mechanics you should include in your dictation depends on your transcriptionist's ability. You may leave these matters to a transcriptionist who is competent in writing correctness and form. On most occasions, however, it would be wise to dictate most such information. Your dictation might well sound like this: "Dear Ms. Mott *colon paragraph* On Friday *comma* November 12 *comma* your order for 18 cases Bug-Nix *comma* 12 *hyphen* ounce packages *comma*

*(6) give as much instruction on paragraphing, punctuation, and mechanics as is needed; and*

should reach your loading docks *period.*" (The instructions are indicated by italics.) It is also a good idea to spell out difficult, confusing, and unusual words such as *cyberpunk, suite* instead of *sweet,* and *Browne* instead of *Brown.*

**Avoid Asides.**   Asides (side comments not intended to be a part of the message) should be avoided. They tend to confuse the transcriptionist, who must determine which words are part of the message and which are not. As proof, imagine the transcriptionist's difficulty in handling the following dictation (asides in italics):

Dear Mr. Dobbs: *Well, let's see. How about this?* The attached check for $19.45 . . . *Is that the right figure?* . . . is our way of showing you that your good faith in us is appreciated. *That should make him happy.* Our satisfaction-or-money-back policy means much to us.

**Read Back Intelligently.**   Although you should try to talk through the message without interruption, you will sometimes need to stop and get a read-back of what you have dictated. But do this only when necessary. More than likely, the need for a read-back results from confused thinking. When you are learning to dictate, however, some confused thinking is normal. Until you gain experience, you may profit from read-backs. You will find a read-back especially helpful at the end of the message to give you a check on the overall effect of your words.

### Letter Dictation Illustrated

Many of the foregoing techniques are illustrated in the following example of the dictation of a routine letter. This example shows all the dictator's words, with instructions and asides in italics. Note that the dictator does not give some of the more obvious punctuation (such as a colon after the salutation). Also note that the dictation gives unusual spelling.

*Let's acknowledge the Key Grocery Company order next. Get the address from the order. It's No. 9.* Dear Mr. Key: Three crates of orchard *hyphen* fresh Texa-cates should be in your store sometime Wednesday morning as they were shipped today by Greene *that's G-R-E-E-N-E* Motor Freight *period.* As you requested in your August 29 order *comma* the $61.60 *parenthesis* Invoice 14721 *parenthesis* was credited to your account *period. Paragraph* Your customers will go for these large, tasty avocados *comma* I am sure *period.* They are the best we have handled in months *period. Paragraph* Thanks *comma* Mr. Key *comma* for another opportunity to serve you *period.* Sincerely *Type it for my signature.*

Your ability to communicate aloud is one of the most important factors contributing to your success on the job. Your attention to the skills discussed in this chapter and your continual efforts to get a bit better at each one will be worth the effort.

### ■ ■ ■ ■ ■ ■ ■ ■ ■ ■ ■ ■ ■ ■ ■ ■ ■ ■ ■ ■ ■ ■ ■
### SUMMARY (by Chapter Objectives)

1. Talking is the oral expression of our knowledge, viewpoints, and emotions. It depends on four critical factors:
   - Voice quality—talking that varies in pitch, delivery, and volume.
   - Speaking style—blending voice quality and personality.

- Word choice—finding the right word or words for the listener.
- Adaptation—fitting a message to the mind of a unique listener.

2. Listening is just as important as talking in oral communication; but it causes more problems.
    - Listening involves how we sense, filter, and retain incoming messages.
    - Most of us do not listen well because we tend to avoid the hard work that good listening requires.
    - You can improve your listening with effort.
    - Put your mind to it and discipline yourself to be attentive.
    - Make a conscious effort to improve your mental filtering of incoming messages; strive to retain what you hear.
    - And follow the practical suggestions offered in "The Ten Commandments of Listening."

2. Explain the listening problem and how to solve it.

3. Nonverbal (nonword) communication is the communication that occurs without words.
    - One major type is body language—the movements of our arms, fingers, facial muscles, and such.
        —Our face and eyes are the most expressive parts of body language.
        —Gestures also send messages.
        —Our physical appearance (clothing, cosmetics, jewelry, hair style) communicate about us.
    - Space is a second major type of nonword communication.
        —We create four unique types of spaces: (1) intimate, (2) physical, (3) social, and (4) public.
        —We communicate differently in each space, as determined by our culture.
    - How we give meaning to time is a third type of nonverbal communication.
    - In our speaking, we should use nonverbal communication to accent our words.
    - In listening, we need to "hear" the nonverbal communication of others.

3. Describe the nature and role of nonverbal communication.

4. In conducting the various types of interviews in business (employment, evaluation, and job exit), follow these guidelines:
    - Plan the interview to get the information you need.
    - Begin by putting the interviewee at ease.
    - Make certain the interviewee knows the purpose.
    - Let the interviewee do most of the talking.
    - Guide the interview, making sure you get what you need.
    - Listen carefully and give the appearance of listening.
    - Keep a record (take notes).
    - End the interview, perhaps with a finalizing question.

4. Practice good interviewing and listening techniques.

5. In business, you are likely to participate in meetings, some formal and some informal.
    - If you are in charge of a meeting, follow these guidelines.
        —Know parliamentary procedure for formal meetings.
        —Plan the meeting; develop an agenda and circulate it in advance.
        —Follow the plan.
        —Keep the discussion moving.

5. Discuss the techniques for conducting and participating in meetings.

—Control those who talk too much.
—Encourage participation from those who talk too little.
—Control time, making sure the agenda is covered.
—Summarize at appropriate times.
- If you are a participant at a meeting, follow these guidelines:
—Stay with the agenda; do not stray.
—Participate fully.
—But do not talk too much.
—Cooperate.
—Be courteous.

**6. Describe good telephone and voice mail techniques.**

6. To improve your telephone and voice mail techniques, consider the following:
   - Cultivate a pleasant voice.
   - Talk as if in face-to-face conversation.
   - Follow courteous procedures.
     —When calling, introduce yourself and ask for the person you want.
     —State your purpose early.
     —Cover points systematically.
     —When receiving, identify your company or office and offer assistance.
     —When answering for the boss, do not offend by asking questions or making comments that might give a wrong impression; and do not neglect callers placed on hold.
     —When screening calls for the boss, be courteous and honest.
     —Listen when the other person is talking.
     —Do not interrupt or dominate.
     —Plan long conversations; and follow the plan.
   - For good communication using voice mail, follow these suggestions:
     —Identify yourself by name and affiliation.
     —Deliver a complete and accurate message.
     —Speak naturally and clearly.
     —Give important information slowly.
     —Close with a brief goodwill message.

**7. Dictate letters and reports in an organized and effective manner.**

7. In dictating letters and reports, follow these suggestions.
   - First, gather all the information you will need so you will not have to interrupt your dictating to get it.
   - Next, plan (think through) the message.
   - Begin the dictation by giving the transcriptionist any special information or instructions needed (enclosures, forms, address, and the like).
   - Then talk through the message.
   - Until you are experienced, force the words—then revise.
   - Remember, also, to speak in a strong, clear voice.
   - And give punctuation and paragraphing in the dictation.
   - Avoid asides (side comments not intended to be a part of the message).
   - Read back only when necessary.

## QUESTIONS FOR DISCUSSION

1. Talking is a natural occurrence, so we should give it little attention. Discuss.
2. How do the elements of talking help us communicate better?
3. Explain how each of the types of nonverbal communication relates to speaking and to listening.
4. Discuss why we have difficulty in listening.
5. What can you do to improve your listening?
6. Assume that you are being interviewed for the job of _____ (your choice) with _____ (company of your choice). What questions would you anticipate? How would you answer them?
7. Assume that you are the interviewer for the interview in Question 6 (above). Discuss specific ways in which you would put the interviewee at ease.
8. The people attending a meeting—not the leader—should determine the agenda. Discuss.
9. As meetings should be democratic, everyone present should be permitted to talk as much as he or she wants without interference from the leader. Discuss.
10. Describe an annoying telephone practice that you have experienced or know about (other than the ones discussed in the chapter). Explain and/or demonstrate how it should be corrected.
11. Describe the strengths and weaknesses of voice mail systems with which you are familiar.
12. Justify each of the dictating techniques suggested in the chapter.

## APPLICATION EXERCISES

### LISTENING

After the class has been divided into two (or more) teams, the instructor reads some factual information (newspaper article, short story, or the like) to only one member of each team. Each of these team members tells what he or she has heard to a second team member, who in turn tells it to a third team member—and so on until the last member of each team has heard the information. The last person receiving the information reports what she or he has heard to the instructor, who checks it against the original message. The team able to report the information with the greatest accuracy wins.

### INTERVIEWING

Working with a classmate, assume that you are an interviewer visiting your campus. Interview your classmate for a job in his or her field of specialization. Before beginning, explain any significant facts of the situation (nature of company, job requirements, applicant's limitations, and such). After finishing the interview, exchange your roles.

### MEETINGS

Because group meetings are meaningful only when they concern problems that the participants know about and understand, the following topics for meetings involve campus situations. For one of these topics, develop a specific problem that would warrant a group meeting. (Example: For student government, the problem might be "To determine the weaknesses of student government on this campus and what should be done to correct them.") Then lead the class (or participate) in a meeting on the topic. Class discussion following the meeting should reinforce the text material and bring out the good and bad of the meeting.

a. Student discipline
b. Scholastic dishonesty
c. Housing regulations
d. Student-faculty relations
e. Student government
f. Library
g. Grading standards
h. Attendance policies
i. Varsity athletics
j. Intramural athletics
k. Degree requirements
l. Parking

m. Examination scheduling
n. Administrative policies
o. University calendar
p. Homework requirements
q. Tuition and fees

r. Student evaluation of faculty
s. Community-college relations
t. Maintenance of files of old examinations for students

## *TELEPHONING*

Make a list of bad telephone practices that you have experienced or heard about. With a classmate, first demonstrate the bad practice and then demonstrate how you would handle it. Some possibilities: putting a caller on hold tactlessly, harsh greeting, unfriendly voice quality, insulting comments (unintended), attitude of unconcern, cold and formal treatment.

## *DICTATING*

Working with a classmate, select a letter problem from the "Letter Problems" sections following Chapters 5, 6, and 7. Then dictate the letter to your classmate. Because your classmate will probably take your dictation in longhand, you may need to dictate slowly. After you have finished your dictation, exchange roles with your classmate.

# CHAPTER 17

# PUBLIC SPEAKING AND ORAL REPORTING

## CHAPTER OBJECTIVES

*Upon completing this chapter, you will be able to use good speaking and oral reporting techniques. To reach this goal, you should be able to*

**1**

Select and organize a subject for effective formal presentation to a specific audience.

**2**

Describe how personal aspects and audience analysis contribute to formal presentations.

**3**

Explain the use of voice quality and physical aspects such as posture, walking, facial expression, and gestures in effective oral communication.

**4**

Plan for visuals to support speeches and oral reports.

**5**

Work effectively with a group in preparing and making a team presentation.

**6**

Define oral reports and differentiate between them and written reports on the basis of their advantages, disadvantages, and organization.

## INTRODUCTORY SITUATION

### to Formal Speaking

In addition to your informal speaking and listening activities at Mastadon Chemicals, you have more formal ones involving oral communication.

Take last week, for example. Malra Cody (your boss) asked you to do something very special for the company. It seems that each year Mastadon Chemicals awards a $5,000 scholarship to a deserving business student at State University. The award is presented at the business school's annual Honors Day Convocation, usually by Ms. Cody. To show the business school's appreciation for the award, its administration requested that Ms. Cody be the speaker at this year's convocation. But Ms. Cody has a conflicting engagement, so you got the assignment. You responded to the challenge as well as you could, but you were not pleased with the results.

Then, at last month's meeting, Mastadon's executive committee asked you for a special oral report from your department for about the fifth time. This time the report concerned the results of a survey that your department conducted to determine local opinions about a dispute between Mastadon and its union. You did your best, but you felt uneasy about what you were doing.

Such assignments are becoming more and more a part of your work as you move up the administrative ladder at Mastadon. You must try to do them better, for your future promotions are involved. The following review of formal oral presentations (speeches and reports) should help you in this effort. ■

## MAKING FORMAL SPEECHES

The most difficult kind of oral communication for most of us is a formal speech. Most of us do not feel comfortable speaking before others, and we generally do a poor job of it. But it need not be this way. With effort, we can improve our speaking. We can do this by learning what good speaking techniques are and then putting those techniques into practice.

> Speeches are difficult for most of us. The following techniques should help you.

### Selection of the Topic

Your first step in formal speechmaking is to determine the topic of your presentation. In some cases, you will be assigned a topic, usually one within your area of specialization. In fact, when you are asked to make a speech on a specified topic, it is likely to be because of your knowledge of the topic. In some cases, your choice of topic will be determined by the purpose of your assignment, as when you are asked to welcome a group or introduce a speaker.

> Your topic may be assigned.

If you are not assigned a topic, then you must find one on your own. In your search for a suitable topic, you should be guided by three basic factors. The first is your background and knowledge. Any topic you select should be one with which you are comfortable—one within your areas of proficiency. The second basic factor is the interests of your audience. Selecting a topic that your audience can appreciate and understand is vital to the success of your speech. The third basic factor is the occasion of the speech. Is the occasion a meeting commemorating a historic event? A monthly meeting of an executives' club? An annual meeting of a hair stylists' association?

> If you must select a topic, consider (1) your knowledge, (2) your audience, and (3) the occasion.

CHAPTER 17  Public Speaking and Oral Reporting

"I see that our next speaker needs no introduction."
© 1975 William P. Hoest and Saturday Review Magazine.

Whatever topic you select should fit the occasion. A speech about Japanese management practices might be quite appropriate for the members of the executives' club, but not for the hair stylists. Your selection should be justified by all three factors.

## Preparation of the Presentation

**Conduct research to get the information you need.**

After you have decided what to talk about, you should gather the information you need for your speech. This may involve searching through your mind for experiences or ideas, conducting research in a library or in company files, gathering information on-line, or consulting people in your own company or other companies. In short, you do whatever is necessary to get the information you need.

**Then organize the information.**

When you have that information, you are ready to begin organizing your speech. Although variations are sometimes appropriate, you should usually follow the time-honored order of a speech: *introduction, body, conclusion*. This is the order described in the following paragraphs.

**The greeting usually comes first.**

Although not really a part of the speech, the first words usually spoken are the greeting. Your greeting, of course, should fit the audience. "Ladies and Gentlemen" is appropriate for a mixed audience; "Gentlemen" fits an all-male audience; and "My fellow Rotarians" fits an audience of Rotary Club members. Some speakers eliminate the greeting and begin with the speech, especially in the more informal and technical presentations.

**Gain attention in the opening.**

**Introduction.** The introduction of a speech has much the same goal as the introduction of a written report: to prepare the listeners (or readers) to receive the message. But it usually has the additional goal of arousing interest. Unless you can arouse interest at the beginning, your presentation is likely to fail. The situation is somewhat like that of the sales letter. At least some of the people with whom you want to communicate are not likely to be interested in receiving your message. As you will recall from your study of listening, it is easy for a speaker to lose the audience's attention. To prove the point, ask yourself how many times your mind has drifted away from the speaker's words when you have been part of an audience. There is no question about it: you, the speaker, will have to work to gain and hold the attention of your audience.

The techniques of arousing interest are limited only by the imagination. One possibility is a human interest story, for storytelling has strong appeal. For example, a speaker presenting a message about the opportunities available to people with original ideas might open this way: "Nearly 150 years ago, an immigrant boy of 17 walked the streets of our town. He had no food, no money, no belongings except the shabby clothes he wore. He had only a strong will to work—and an idea."

Humor, another possibility, is probably the most widely used technique. To illustrate, an investment broker might begin a speech on investment strategy as follows: "What you want me to give you today is some 'tried and trusted' advice on how to make money in the stock market. This reminds me of the proverbial 'tried and trusted' bank teller. He was trusted; and when they caught him, he was tried." Humor works best and is safest when it is closely related to the subject of your presentation.

Other effective ways for gaining attention at the opening are by using quotations and questions. By quoting someone the audience would know and view as credible, you build interest in your topic. You can also ask questions. One kind of question is the rhetorical question—the one everyone answers the same, such as "Who wants to be freed of burdensome financial responsibilities?" Another kind of question gives you background information on how much to talk about different aspects of your subject. With this kind of question, you must follow through your presentation based on the response. If you had asked "How many of you have IRAs?" and nearly everyone put their hand up, you wouldn't want to talk about the importance of IRAs. You could skip that part of your presentation, spending more time on another aspect, such as managing your IRA effectively.

Yet another possibility is the startling statement, which presents facts and ideas that awaken the mind. Illustrating this possibility is the beginning of a speech to an audience of merchants on a plan to reduce shoplifting: "Last year, right here in our city, in your stores, shoplifters stole over $3.5 million of your merchandise! And most of you did nothing about it."

In addition to arousing interest, your opening should lead into the theme of your speech. In other words, it should set up your message as the above examples do.

Following the attention-gaining opening, it is appropriate to tell your audience the subject (theme) for your speech. In fact, in cases where your audience already has an interest in what you have to say, you can begin here and skip the attention-gaining opening. Presentations of technical topics to technical audiences typically begin this way. Whether you lead into a statement of your topic or begin with it, that statement should be clear and complete.

Because of the nature of your subject, you may find it undesirable to reveal a position early. In such cases, you may prefer to move into your subject indirectly—to build up your case before revealing your position. This inductive pattern may be especially desirable when your goal is to

---

*Margin notes:*

There are many opening possibilities—human interest,

humor,

quotations, questions, and so on.

The opening should set up your subject.

Tell the subject of your speech . . .

unless you have reason not to, as when you must persuade.

persuade—when you need to move the views of your audience from one position to another. But in most business-related presentations you should make a direct statement of your theme early in the speech.

**Body.** Organizing the body of your speech is much like organizing the body of a report (see Chapter 12). You take the whole and divide it into comparable parts. Then you take those parts and divide them. And you continue to divide as far as it is practical to do so. In speeches, however, you are more likely to use factors other than time, place, or quantity as the basis of division because in most speeches your presentation is likely to be built around issues and questions that are subtopics of the subject. Even so, time, place, and quantity subdivisions are possibilities.

*Organize most speeches by factors, as you would a report.*

You need to emphasize the transitions between the divisions because, unlike the reader who can see them, the listener may miss them if they are not stressed adequately. Without clear transitions, you may be talking about one point and your listener may be relating those ideas to your previous point.

*Emphasize transitions between parts.*

**Conclusion.** Like most reports, the speech usually ends by drawing a conclusion. Here you bring all that you have presented to a head and achieve whatever goal the speech has. You should consider including these three elements in your close: (1) a restatement of the subject, (2) a summary of the key points developed in the presentation, and (3) a statement of the conclusion (or main message). Bringing the speech to a climactic close—that is, making the conclusion the high point of the speech—is usually effective. Present the concluding message in strong language—in words that gain attention and will be remembered. In addition to concluding with a summary, you can give an appropriate quote, use humor, and call for action. The following close of a speech comparing Japanese and American management techniques illustrates this point: "These facts make my conclusion crystal clear. We are not Japanese. We do not have the Japanese culture. Most Japanese management methods have not worked—cannot work—will not work in our society."

*The ending usually (1) restates the subject, (2) summarizes key points, and (3) draws a conclusion.*

### Determination of the Presentation Method

With the speech organized, you are ready to prepare its presentation. At this time, you need to decide on your method of presentation—that is, whether to present the speech extemporaneously, to memorize it, or to read it.

*Choose one of these presentation methods.*

**Presenting Extemporaneously.** Extemporaneous presentation is by far the most popular and effective method. With this method, you first thoroughly prepare your speech, as outlined above. Then you prepare notes and present the speech from them. You usually rehearse, making sure that you have all the parts clearly in mind, but you make no attempt to memorize. Extemporaneous presentations generally sound natural to the listeners, yet they are (or should be) the product of careful planning and practice.

*(1) extemporaneous presentation (thorough preparation, uses notes, rehearsed),*

**Memorizing.** The most difficult method is memorizing. If you are like most people, you find it hard to memorize a long succession of words. And when you do memorize, you are likely to memorize words rather than meanings. Thus, when you make the speech, if you miss a word or two, you become confused—and so does your speech. You may even become panic-stricken.

*(2) memorizing, or*

### A Speaker's Classic Putdown of an Unruly Audience

The speaker had covered his subject carefully and thoroughly. But his conclusion, which followed logically from his presentation, was greeted with loud hisses by some members of his audience. Because hisses leave little trace of their origin, the speaker did not know who the dissenters were and could not respond directly to them. So he skillfully handled the situation by saying: "I know of only three creatures that hiss—snakes, geese, and fools. I will leave it to you to determine which of the three we have here."

Probably few of the speakers who use this method memorize the entire speech. Instead, they memorize key passages and use notes to help them through the speech. A delivery of this kind is a cross between an extemporaneous presentation and a memorized presentation.

**Reading.** The third presentation method is reading. Unfortunately, most of us tend to read aloud in a dull monotone. We also miss punctuation marks, fumble over words, lose our place, and so on. Of course, many speakers overcome these problems, and with effort you can too. One effective way is to practice with a recorder and listen to yourself. Then you can be your own judge of what you must do to improve your delivery. You would be wise not to read speeches until you have mastered this presentation method. In most settings, it is not appropriate to read. Your audience is likely to be insulted, and reading is unlikely to be as well received as an extemporaneous delivery. However, when you are in a position where you will be quoted widely, such as President of the United States or the CEO of a major company, reading from a carefully prepared speech is recommended.

(3) reading.

### Consideration of Personal Aspects

A preliminary to good speechmaking is to analyze yourself as a speaker. In oral presentations you, the speaker, are a very real part of the message. The members of your audience take in not only the words you communicate but also what they see in you. And what they see in you can significantly affect the meanings that develop in their minds. Thus, you should carefully evaluate your personal effect on your message. You should do whatever you can to detect and overcome your shortcomings and to sharpen your strengths.

A logical preliminary to speechmaking is to analyze yourself as a speaker. You are a part of the message.

The following summary of characteristics that should help you as a speaker may prove useful, but you probably already know what they are. To some extent, the problem is recognizing whether you lack these characteristics. To a greater extent, it is doing something about acquiring them. The following review should help you pinpoint and deal with your problem areas.

You should seek the following four characteristics:

**Confidence.** A primary characteristic of effective oral reporting is confidence—your confidence in yourself and the confidence of your audience in you. The two are complementary, for your confidence in yourself tends to produce an image that gives your audience confidence in you, and your

(1) Having confidence in yourself is important. So is having the confidence of your audience.

CHAPTER 17 Public Speaking and Oral Reporting 599

audience's confidence in you can give you a sense of security that increases your confidence in yourself.

> You must earn the confidence of your audience, project the right image, and talk in a strong, clear voice.

Typically, you earn your audience's confidence over periods of association. But there are things you can do to project an image that builds confidence. For example, preparing your presentation diligently and practicing it thoroughly gives you confidence in yourself. That confidence leads to more effective communication, which increases your listeners' confidence in you. Another confidence-building technique is an appropriate physical appearance. Unfair and illogical as it may seem, certain types of dress and hairstyles create strong images in people's minds, ranging from highly favorable to highly unfavorable. Thus, if you want to communicate effectively, you should analyze the audience you seek to reach. And you should work to develop the physical appearance that projects an image in which that audience can have confidence. Yet another confidence-building technique is simply to talk in strong, clear tones. Such tones do much to project an image of confidence. Although most people can do little to change their natural voice, they can use sufficient volume.

> (2) Sincerity is vital. You convey an image of sincerity by being sincere.

**Sincerity.** Your listeners are quick to detect insincerity. And if they detect it in you, they are likely to give little weight to what you say. On the other hand, sincerity is valuable to conviction, especially if the audience has confidence in your ability. The way to project an image of sincerity is clear and simple: You must *be* sincere. Pretense of sincerity is rarely successful.

> (3) Thoroughness—giving your listeners all they need—helps your image.

**Thoroughness.** Generally, a thorough presentation is better received than a scanty or hurried presentation. Thorough coverage gives the impression that time and care have been taken, and this tends to make the presentation believable. But thoroughness can be overdone. Too much detail can drown your listeners in a sea of information. The secret is to leave out unimportant information. This, of course, requires good judgment. You must ask yourself just what your listeners need to know and what they do not need to know.

> (4) Projecting an image of friendliness helps your communication effort.

**Friendliness.** A speaker who projects an image of friendliness has a significant advantage in communicating. People simply like friendly people, and they are more receptive to what such people say. Like sincerity, friendliness is hard to feign and must be honest to be effective. But most people are genuinely friendly. Some, however, are just not able to project a genuinely friendly image. With a little self-analysis and a little mirror watching as you practice speaking, you can find ways of improving your projection of your friendliness.

These are but a few of the characteristics that should assist you as a speaker. There are others—*interest, enthusiasm, originality, flexibility,* and so on. But the ones discussed are the most significant and the ones that most speakers need to work on. Through self-analysis and dedicated effort, you can improve your speaking ability.

## Audience Analysis

One requirement of good speechmaking is to know your audience. You should study your audience both before and during the presentation.

> You should know your audience.

> Size up the audience in advance. Look for audience characteristics that will affect your speech—things like the size, sex, age, education, and knowledge of the audience.

**Preliminary Analysis.** Analyzing your audience before the presentation requires that you size it up—that you search for audience characteristics that could affect how you should present your speech.

Oral presentations to large audiences usually require formality and thorough preparation.

For example, the size of your audience is likely to influence how formal or informal your speech should be. As a rule, large audiences require more formality. Personal characteristics of your audience, such as age, sex, education, experience, and knowledge of subject matter, should also influence how you make your speech. They should affect the words, illustrations, and level of detail you use. Like writing, speeches should be adapted to the audience. And the more you know about the audience, the better you will adapt your presentation to them.

**Analysis during Presentation.** Your audience analysis should continue as you make the speech. *Feedback* is information about how your listeners are receiving your words. Armed with this information, you can adjust your presentation to improve the communication result.

Your eyes and ears will give you feedback information. For example, facial expressions will tell you how your listeners are reacting to your message. Smiles, blank stares, and movements will give you an indication of whether they understand, agree with, or accept it. You can detect from sounds coming (or not coming) from them whether they are listening. If questions are in order, you can learn directly how your message is coming across. In general, you can learn much from your audience by being alert; and what you learn can help you make a better speech.

- Analyze audience reactions during the speech (called feedback). Facial expressions, movements, and noises give you feedback information that helps you adapt to the audience.

### Appearance and Physical Actions

As your listeners hear your words, they are looking at you. What they see is a part of the message and can affect the success of your speech. What they see, of course, is you and what surrounds you. In your efforts to improve the effects of your oral presentations, you should understand the communication effects of what your listeners see. Some of the effects that were mentioned in Chapter 16 are expanded upon here because they are particularly important to speeches and oral reports.

- Your audience forms impressions from these six factors:

(1) all that surrounds you (stage, lighting, and the like),

**The Communication Environment.** Much of what your audience sees is the physical things that surround you as you speak—the stage, lighting, background, and so on. These things tend to create a general impression. Although not visual, outside noises have a related influence. For the best communication results, the factors in your communication environment should contribute to your message, not detract from it. Your own experience as a listener will tell you what factors are important.

(2) your personal appearance,

**Personal Appearance.** Your personal appearance is a part of the message your audience receives. Of course, you have to accept the physical traits you have, but most of us do not need to be at a disadvantage in appearance. All that is necessary is to use what you have appropriately. Specifically, you should dress in a manner appropriate for the audience and the occasion. Be clean and well groomed. Use facial expressions and physical movements to your advantage. Just how you should use facial expressions and physical movements is described in the following paragraphs.

(3) your posture,

**Posture.** Posture is likely to be the most obvious of the things that your audience sees in you. Even listeners not close enough to detect such things as facial expressions and eye movements can see the general form of the body.

You probably think that no one needs to tell you about good posture. You know it when you see it. The trouble is that you are not likely to see it in yourself. One solution is to have others tell you whether your posture needs improvement. Another is to practice speaking before a mirror or watch yourself on videotape.

In your efforts to improve your posture, keep in mind what must go on within your body to form a good posture. Your body weight must be distributed in a way consistent with the impression you want to make. You should keep your body erect without appearing stiff and comfortable without appearing limp. You should maintain a poised, alert, and communicative bearing. And you should do all this naturally. The great danger with posture is an appearance of artificiality.

(4) your manner of walking,

**Walking.** Your audience also forms an impression from the way you walk before it. A strong, sure walk to the speaker's position conveys an impression of confidence. Hesitant, awkward steps convey the opposite impression. Walking during the presentation can be good or bad, depending on how you do it. Some speakers use steps forward and to the side to emphasize points. Too much walking, however, attracts attention and detracts from the message. You would be wise to walk only when you are reasonably sure that this will have the effect you want.

(5) facial expressions (smiles, frowns), and

**Facial Expression.** As noted in Chapter 16, probably the most apparent and communicative physical movements are facial expressions. The problem, however, is that you may unconsciously use facial expressions that convey unintended meanings. For example, if a frightened speaker tightens the jaw unconsciously and begins to grin, the effect may be an ambiguous image that detracts from the entire communication effort. A smile, a grimace, and a puzzled frown all convey clear messages. Without question, you should use these effective communication devices.

Eye contact is important. The eyes, which have long been considered "mirrors of the soul," provide most listeners with information about your sincerity, goodwill, and flexibility. Some listeners tend to shun speakers who do not look at them. On the other hand, discriminate eye contact tends to show that you have a genuine interest in your audience.

**Gestures.** Like posture, gestures contribute to the message you communicate. Just what they contribute, however, is hard to say, for they have no definite or clear-cut meanings. A clenched fist, for example, certainly adds emphasis to a strong point. But it can also be used to show defiance, make a threat, or signify respect for a cause. And so it is with other gestures. They register vague meanings, as discussed in Chapter 16.

*(6) gestures.*

Even though gestures have vague meanings, they are strong, natural helps to speaking. It appears natural, for example, to emphasize a plea with palms up and to show disagreement with palms down. Raising first one hand and then the other reinforces a division of points. Slicing the air with the hand shows several divisions. Although such gestures are generally clear, we do not all use them in exactly the same way.

*Gestures have vague meanings, but they communicate.*

In summary, it should be clear that physical movements can help your speaking. Just which physical movements you should use, however, is hard to say. The appropriateness of physical movements is related to personality, physical makeup, and the size and nature of the audience. A speaker appearing before a formal group should generally use relatively few physical movements. A speaker appearing before an informal group should use more. Which physical movements you should use on a given occasion is a matter for your best judgment.

*In summary, your physical movements help your speaking.*

## Use of Voice

Good voice is an obvious requirement of good speaking. Like physical movements, the voice should not hinder the listener's concentration on the message. More specifically, it should not detract attention from the message. Voices that cause such difficulties generally fall into these areas of fault: (1) lack of pitch variation, (2) lack of variation in speed, (3) lack of vocal emphasis, and (4) unpleasant voice quality. Although these areas are mentioned in Chapter 16, we will examine them here because of their key significance to formal oral communication.

*Good voice is a requirement of good speaking. Four faults affect voice:*

**Lack of Pitch Variation.** Speakers who talk in monotones are not likely to hold the interest of their listeners for long. As most voices are capable of wide variations in pitch, the problem can usually be corrected. The failure to vary pitch generally is a matter of habit—of voice patterns developed over years of talking without being aware of their effect.

*(1) lack of variation in pitch (usually a matter of habit),*

**Lack of Variation in Speaking Speed.** Determining how fast to talk is a major problem. As a general rule, you should present the easy parts of your message at a fairly fast rate and the hard parts and the parts you want to emphasize at a slower rate. The reason for varying the speed of presentation should be apparent; it is more interesting. A slow presentation of easy information is irritating; hard information presented fast may be difficult to understand.

*(2) lack of variation in speed (cover the simple quickly, the hard slowly),*

A problem related to the pace of speaking is the incorrect use of pauses. Of course, properly used, pauses emphasize upcoming subject matter and are effective means of gaining attention. But frequent pauses for no reason are irritating and break the listeners' concentration. Pauses become even more irritating when the speaker fills them in with distracting nonwords such as *uh*'s, *you know*'s, and *OK*'s.

> (3) lack of vocal emphasis (gain emphasis by varying pitch, pace, and volume), and

**Lack of Vocal Emphasis.**  A secret of good speaking is to give words their proper emphasis by varying the manner of speaking. You can do this by (1) varying the pitch of your voice, (2) varying the pace of your presentation, and (3) varying the volume of your voice. As the first two techniques have already been discussed, only the use of voice volume requires comment here.

You must talk loudly enough for your entire audience to hear you, but not too loudly. Thus, the loudness—voice volume—for a large audience should be greater than that for a small audience. Regardless of audience size, however, variety in voice volume is good for interest and emphasis. It produces contrast, which is one way of emphasizing the subject matter. Some speakers incorrectly believe that the only way to show emphasis is to get louder and louder. But you can also show emphasis by going from loud to soft. The contrast with what has gone on earlier provides the emphasis. Again, variety is the key to making the voice more effective.

> (4) unpleasant voice (improvement is often possible).

**Unpleasant Voice Quality.**  It is a hard fact of communication that some voices are more pleasant than others. Fortunately, most voices are reasonably pleasant. But some are raspy, nasal, or unpleasant in another way. Although therapy can often improve such voices, some speakers must live with them. But concentrating on variations in pitch, speed of delivery, and volume can make even the most unpleasant voice acceptable.

> You can correct the foregoing faults through self-analysis and work.

**Improvement through Self-Analysis and Imitation.**  You can overcome any of the foregoing voice faults through self-analysis. In this day of tape recorders, it is easy to hear yourself talk. Since you know good speaking when you hear it, you should be able to improve your vocal presentation. One of the best ways to improve your presentation skills is through watching others. Watch your instructors, your peers, television personnel, professional speakers, and anyone else who gives you an opportunity. Analyze these speakers to determine what works for them and what does not. Imitate those good techniques that you think would help you and avoid the bad ones. Take advantage of any opportunity you have to practice speaking.

## Use of Visuals

> Visuals can sometimes help overcome the limitations of spoken words.

The spoken word is severely limited in communicating. Sound is here briefly and then gone. A listener who misses the vocal message may not have a chance to hear it again. Because of this limitation, speeches often need strong visual support—charts, tables, boards, film, and the like. Visuals may be as vital to the success of a speech as the words themselves.

> Use visuals for the hard parts of the message.

**Proper Use of Design.**  Effective visuals are drawn from the message. They fit the one speech and the one audience.

In selecting visuals you should search through your presentation for topics that appear vague or confusing. Whenever a visual of some kind will

PART 6  Other Forms of Business Communication

help eliminate vagueness or confusion, you should use it. You should use visuals to simplify complex information and improve cohesiveness, as well as to emphasize or add interest. Visuals are truly a part of your message, and you should look at them as such.

After deciding that a topic deserves visual help, you determine what form that help should take. That is, should the visual be a chart, a diagram, a picture, or what? You should select your visuals primarily on the basis of their ability to communicate. Simple and obvious as this injunction may appear, people violate it all too often. They select visuals more for appearance and dramatic effect than for communication effect.

> Use the type of visual (chart, diagram, picture) that communicates the information best.

**Types to Consider.** Because no one type of visuals is best for all occasions, you should have a flexible attitude toward visuals. You should know the strengths and weaknesses of each type, and you should know how to use each type effectively.

In selecting visuals, you should keep in mind the available types. You will mainly consider the various types of graphics—the charts, graphs, tables, diagrams, and pictures discussed in Chapter 15. Each of these types has its strengths and weaknesses and can be displayed in various ways—for example, by slide, overhead, or opaque projector; by flip chart; by easel display; on a presentation board; or on a felt board. And each of these display methods has its strengths and weaknesses. In addition to using graphics to support your speech, you can support it with videotapes, photographs, models, samples, demonstrations, and the like.

> Select from the various available types of visuals, as described in Chapter 15.

**Audience Size, Cost, and Ease of Preparation Considerations.** Your choice of visuals should also be influenced by the audience size and formality, the cost of preparing and using the media (visuals), and the ease and time of preparation. The table below illustrates how the different media fare on these dimensions.

Presentation Media Comparison*

| Media | Image Quality | Audience Size | Cost | Ease of Preparation |
|---|---|---|---|---|
| Photos | Good–very good | 2–20 | Low | Easy |
| Slides | Very good | 20–200 | Low | Very easy |
| Overhead transparency | Good–very good | 2–200 | Low | Very easy |
| Video monitors | Good | 2–50 | Medium | Easy-fair |
| HiRes television | Very good | 2–100 | High | Fair |
| LCD screens | Poor | 2–20 | Medium | Easy |
| Video projection | Good | 20–200 | High | Fair |
| Film | Very good | 2–200 | High | Difficult |
| Computer graphics | Very good | 2–200 | High | Easy-fair |

\* Adapted from G.A. Marken, "Visual Aids Strengthen In-House Presentations," *Office Systems,* February, 1990, p. 34.

**Techniques in Using Visuals.** Visuals usually carry key parts of the message. Thus, they are points of emphasis in your presentation. You blend them in with your words to communicate the message. How you do this is to some extent an individual matter, for techniques vary. They vary so much,

> Make the visuals points of interest in your presentation.

### Mark Twain on "Knowing When to Stop Talking"

These words by Mark Twain carry a vital message for windy speakers:

"Some years ago in Hartford, we all went to church one hot sweltering night to hear the annual report of Mr. Hawley, a city missionary who went around finding people who needed help and didn't want to ask for it. He told of the life in cellars, where poverty resided; he gave instances of the heroism and devotion of the poor. 'When a man with millions gives,' he said, 'we make a great deal of noise. It's noise in the wrong place, for it's the widow's mite that counts.' Well, Hawley worked me up to a great pitch. I could hardly wait for him to get through. I had $400 in my pocket. I wanted to give that and borrow more to give. You could see greenbacks in every eye. But instead of passing the plate then, he kept on talking and talking, and as he talked it grew hotter and hotter, and we grew sleepier and sleepier. My enthusiasm went down, down, down, down—$100 at a clip—until finally, when the plate did come around, I stole ten cents out of it. It all goes to show how a little thing like this can lead to crime."

---

in fact, that it would be hard to present a meaningful summary of them. It is more meaningful to present a list of dos and don'ts. Such a list follows:

*Here are specific suggestions for using visuals.*

- **Make certain that everyone in the audience can see the visuals.** Too many or too-light lines on a chart, for example, can be hard to see. An illustration that is too small can be meaningless to people far from the speaker.
- **Explain the visual if there is any likelihood that it will be misunderstood.**
- **Organize the visuals as a part of the presentation.** Fit them into the presentation plan.
- **Emphasize the visuals.** Point to them with physical action and words.
- **Talk to the audience—not to the visuals.** Look at the visuals only when the audience should look at them.
- **Avoid blocking the listeners' view of the visuals.** Make certain that the listeners' views are not blocked by lecterns, pillars, chairs, and such. Take care not to stand in anyone's line of vision.

### A Summary List of Speaking Practices

*This review has covered the high points of speaking.*

The foregoing review of business speaking has been selective, for the subject is broad. In fact, entire books have been devoted to it. But this review has covered the high points, especially those that you can easily transfer into practice. Perhaps even more practical is the following list of what to do and not to do in speaking.

*This summary checklist of good and bad speaking practices should prove helpful.*

- **Organize the speech so that it leads the hearers' thoughts logically to the conclusion.**
- **Move surely and quickly to the conclusion.** Do not leave a conclusion dangling, repeat unnecessarily, or appear unable to close.
- **Use language specifically adapted to the audience.**
- **Articulate clearly, pleasantly, and with proper emphasis.** Avoid mumbling and the use of nonwords such as *ah, er, uh,* and so forth.

### Screenshows and Hypershows: Presentation Tools Supporting Diverse Needs

Screenshows and hypershows are two advanced features of most full-featured graphics programs. The screenshow lets you create a series of slides to support a linear presentation—one point follows another and usually either builds on the previous point or is directly related to it. By using the screenshow feature, you can check for smooth flow as well as consistency of typeface, size, placement, and color of your slides. With the screenshow, you can create slides, overheads, or run-time visuals. The files your graphics program creates can be imaged on 35mm slides or printed on high-quality color overheads. Or you can run the screenshow on a computer connected to a video projector, using the mouse to click slides to advance them just as you would with projected 35mm slides. Or you can assign a time to each slide and run it on a computer as a simple run-time program. Most graphics programs allow you to print miniatures of your slides for use as handouts.

A hypershow is a feature that supports a non-linear presentation—one where the path you take through your slides is individual or different each time. It is particularly good for highly complex material that can be exploded into several layers of detail. It is useful when you are unsure what the exact needs of your audience might be or when you know your audience has diverse needs. For example, you might use it for a presentation of your company at a university career fair. Some students might just be interested in general information about what your company does while others might want detailed information on the financial aspects, products, or markets. Some might even want to know which local political campaigns your company supports. In another case, you might want to create a hypershow visual to support your presentation when there are several other speakers and you do not know beforehand exactly what they will cover. A typical hypershow works through a series of menus with buttons bringing up different information. At the end of each path, buttons give the option of backing up one level or returning to a main menu screen. Creating a hypershow takes time and careful planning, but it is an extremely useful tool for non-linear presentations.

- **Speak correctly, using accepted grammar and pronunciation.**
- **Maintain an attitude of alertness, displaying appropriate enthusiasm and confidence.**
- **Employ body language to best advantage. Use it to emphasize points and to assist in communicating concepts and ideas.**
- **Be relaxed and natural. Avoid stiffness or rigidity of physical action.**
- **Look the listeners in the eye and talk directly to them.**
- **Keep still. Avoid excessive movements, fidgeting, and other signs of nervousness.**
- **Punctuate the presentation with reference to visuals. Make them a part of the speech text.**
- **Even when faced with hostile questions or remarks, keep your temper. To lose your temper is to lose control of the presentation.**

## TEAM (COLLABORATIVE) PRESENTATIONS

*Group presentations require individual speaking skills plus planning and coordinating.*

Another type of presentation you may be called on to give is the group or team presentation. While the skills you use for individual speeches are also needed here, team presentations require additional skills. In order to present a cohesive group image, extra planning is needed. In addition to deciding presentation order, teams must determine the content of each member's part. Not only will this prevent overlap and use time more efficiently, it makes the team look competent. Another factor that enhances the group's presentation is the careful use of supporting examples to build continuity from one part to the next.

*Plan for the physical factors.*

Groups need to plan for the physical aspects, too. Coordinating such aspects as type of delivery, type of notes, dress styles and colors, and visuals all contribute to giving good presentations. Also, knowing the order and how to make transitions between one speaker and the next makes the team look well coordinated.

*Plan the individual roles in the presentation.*

Planning the physical staging is important as well. All members should know where to go, whether to sit or stand, and how visuals will be handled. Additionally, they should plan how to change or adjust microphones.

The teams need to plan how to close, who will close, and what will be said. If a summary is used, the member concluding should attribute the points to the appropriate group member. The team also needs to plan the question-and-answer session. If they decide to have one, they need to know how it will be handled and who will lead and close it. Will one person take all questions and direct them to the appropriate team member, or will the audience members be allowed to direct their questions to specific members? The team needs to nod in agreement when the closing member expresses thanks or appreciation.

While these might seem like minor points, paying careful attention to them will result in delivering a polished, coordinated team presentation.

## REPORTING ORALLY

*The oral report is a form of speech.*

A special form of speech is the oral report. You are more likely to make oral reports than speeches in business, and the oral reports you make are likely to be important to you. Unfortunately, most of us have had little experience and even less instruction in oral reporting. Thus, the following review should be valuable to you.

### A Definition of Oral Reports

*An* oral report *is defined as an oral presentation of factual information.*

In its broadest sense, an oral report is any presentation of factual information using the spoken word. A business oral report would logically limit coverage to factual business information. By this definition, oral business reports cover much of the information exchanged daily in the conduct of business. They vary widely in formality. At one extreme, they cover the most routine and informal reporting situations. At the other, they include highly formal and proper presentations. As the more informal oral exchanges are little more than routine conversations, the emphasis in the

In oral reports as well as formal speeches, visuals are effective in communicating important parts of the message.

following pages is on the more formal ones. Clearly, these are the oral reports that require the most care and skill and are the most deserving of study.

### Differences between Oral and Written Reports

Oral reports are much like written reports, so there is little need to repeat much of the previously presented material on reports. Instead, we will focus on the most significant differences between oral and written reports. Three in particular stand out.

Oral reports differ from written reports in these ways:

**Visual Advantages of the Written Word.** The first significant difference between oral and written reports is that writing permits greater use of visual aids to communication than does speaking. With writing, you can use paragraphing to show readers the structure of the message and to make the thought units stand out. In addition, you can use punctuation to show relationships, subordination, and qualification. These techniques improve the communication effect of the entire message.

(1) writing and speaking each have special advantages and disadvantages;

On the other hand, when you make an oral presentation, you cannot use any of these techniques. However, you can use techniques peculiar to oral communication. For example, you can use inflection, pauses, volume emphasis, and changes in the rate of delivery. Depending on the situation, the techniques used in both oral and written reports are effective in assisting communication. But the point is that the techniques are different.

**CHAPTER 17** Public Speaking and Oral Reporting

**Reader Control of Written Presentation.** A second significant difference between oral and written reports is that the readers of a written report, unlike the listeners to an oral report, control the pace of the communication. They can pause, reread, change their rate of reading, or stop as they choose. Since the readers set the pace, writing can be difficult and still communicate. On the other hand, since the listeners to an oral report cannot control the pace of the presentation, they must grasp the intended meaning as the speaker presents the words. Because of this limiting factor, good oral reporting must be relatively simple.

*(2) the speaker controls the pace of an oral report, and the reader controls the pace of a written report; and*

**Emphasis on Correctness in Writing.** A third significant difference between oral and written reports is the different degrees of correctness that they require. Because written reports are likely to be inspected carefully, you are likely to work for a high degree of correctness when you prepare them. That is, you are likely to follow carefully the recognized rules of grammar, punctuation, sentence structure, and so on. When you present oral reports, on the other hand, you may be more lax about following these rules. One reason is that usually oral reports are not recorded for others to inspect at their leisure. Another is that oral communication standards of correctness are less rigid than written communication standards.

*(3) written reports place more stress on correctness.*

## Planning the Oral Report

As with written reports, planning is the logical first step in your work on oral reports. For short, informal oral reports, planning may be minimal. But for the more formal oral reports, particularly those involving audiences of more than one, proper planning is likely to be as involved as that for a comparable written report.

*Planning is the first step in preparing oral reports.*

**Determination of Report Objective.** Logically, your first task in planning an oral report is to determine your objective. Just as was described for the written report in Chapter 12, you should state the report objective in clear, concise language. Then you should clearly state the factors involved in achieving this objective. Doing these things gives you a guide to the information you must gather and to the framework around which you will build your presentation.

*First determine the objective and what must be done to reach it.*

In the process of determining your report objective, you must be aware of your general objective. That is, you must decide on your general purpose in making the presentation. Is it to persuade? To inform? To recommend? This decision will have a major influence on your development of material for presentation and perhaps even on the presentation itself.

**Organization of Content.** The procedure for organizing oral reports is similar to that for organizing written reports. You have the choice of using either the direct or indirect order. Even so, the same information is not necessarily presented in the same way orally and in writing. Time pressure, for example, might justify direct presentation for an oral report on a problem that, presented in writing, might be better arranged in the indirect order. Readers in a hurry can always skip to the conclusion or ending of the report. Listeners do not have this choice.

*Next organize content. Either the indirect or direct order is all right,*

Although oral reports may use either the direct or indirect order, the indirect is the most logical order and by far the most widely used order.

*but the indirect order is more common.*

Because your audience is not likely to know the problem well, introductory remarks are needed to prepare it to receive your message. In addition, you may need such remarks to arouse interest, stimulate curiosity, or impress the audience with the importance of the subject. The main goal of the introductory remarks is to state the purpose, define unfamiliar terms, explain limitations, describe scope, and generally cover all the necessary introductory subjects (see discussion of introduction, Chapter 14).

In the body of the oral report, you should work toward the objective you have set. Here, too, the oral report closely resembles the written report. Division of subject matter into comparable parts, logical order, introductory paragraphs, concluding paragraphs, and the like are equally important to both forms.

The major difference in the organization of the written and oral report is in the ending. Both forms may end with a conclusion, a recommendation, a summary, or a combination of the three. But the oral report is likely to have a final summary, whether or not it has a conclusion or a recommendation. In a sense, this final summary serves the purpose of an executive summary by bringing together all the really important information, analyses, conclusions, and recommendations in the report. It also serves to assist the memory by placing added emphasis on the points that should stand out.

> The organization of oral and written reports is much the same, except that oral reports usually have a closing summary.

## ■■■■■■■■■■■■■■■■■■■■
## SUMMARY (by Chapter Objectives)

1. Consider the following suggestions in selecting and organizing a speech.
   - Begin by selecting an appropriate topic—perhaps one in your area of specialization and of interest to your audience.
   - Organize the message (probably by introduction, body, conclusion).
   - Consider an appropriate greeting ("Ladies and Gentlemen," "Friends").
   - Design the introduction to meet these goals:
     —Arouse interest—a story, humor, or such.
     —Introduce the subject (theme).
     —Prepare the reader to receive the message.
   - Use indirect order presentation to persuade and direct order for other cases.
   - Organize like a report—divide and subdivide, usually by factors.
   - Select the most appropriate ending, usually restating the subject and summarizing.
   - Consider using a climactic close.
   - Choose the best manner of presentation.
     —Extemporaneous is usually best.
     —Memorizing is risky.
     —Reading is difficult unless you are skilled.

> 1. Select and organize a subject for effective formal presentation to a specific audience.

2. To improve your speaking, take these steps:
   - Work on these characteristics of a good speaker:
     —Confidence,
     —Sincerity,
     —Thoroughness, and
     —Friendliness.

> 2. Describe how personal aspects and audience analysis contribute to formal presentations.

- Know your audience.
  — Before the presentation, size them up—looking for characteristics that affect your presentation (sex, age, education).
  — During the presentation, continue to analyze them, looking at facial expressions, listening to noises, and such—and adapt to them.

3. **Explain the use of voice quality and physical aspects such as posture, walking, facial expression, and gestures in effective oral communication.**

3. What the listeners see and hear affects the communication.
   - They see the environment (stage, lighting, background), personal appearance, posture, walking, facial expressions, gestures, and such.
   - They hear your voice.
     — For best effect, vary the pitch and speed.
     — Give appropriate vocal emphasis.
     — Cultivate a pleasant quality.

4. **Plan for visuals to support oral reports and speeches.**

4. Use visuals whenever they help communicate.
   - Select the types that do the best job.
   - Blend the visuals into your speech, making certain that the audience sees and understands them.
   - Organize your visuals as a part of your message.
   - Emphasize the visuals by pointing to them.
   - Talk to the audience, not the visuals.
   - Do not block your audience's view of the visuals.

5. **Work effectively with a group in preparing and making a team presentation.**

5. Group presentations have special problems.
   - They require all the skills of individual presentation.
   - In addition, they require extra planning.
     — to reduce overlap and provide continuity,
     — to improve transition between presentations, and
     — to coordinate questions and answers.

6. **Define oral reports and differentiate between them and written reports on the basis of their advantages, disadvantages, and organization.**

6. Business oral reports are spoken communications of factual business information.
   - Written and oral reports differ in three significant ways.
     — Written reports permit more use of visual helps to communication (paragraphing, punctuation, and such); oral reports allow voice inflection, pauses, and the like.
     — Oral reports permit the speaker to exercise greater control over the pace of the presentation; readers of a written report control the pace.
     — Written reports place more emphasis on writing correctness (grammar, punctuation, etc.).
   - Plan oral reports just as you do written ones.
     — First, determine your objective and state its factors.
     — Next, organize the report, using either indirect or direct order.
     — Divide the body based on your purpose, keeping the divisions comparable and using introductory/concluding paragraphs, logical order, and the like.
     — End the report with a final summary—a sort of ending executive summary.

## QUESTIONS FOR DISCUSSION

1. Assume that you must prepare a speech on the importance of making good grades for an audience of college students. Develop some attention-gaining ideas for the introduction of this speech. Do the same for a climactic close for the speech.
2. When is an extemporaneous presentation desirable? When should a speech be read? Discuss.
3. Explain how a speaker's personal characteristics influence the meanings of his or her spoken words.
4. An employee presented an oral report to an audience of 27 middle- and upper-level administrators. Then she presented the same information to three top executives. Note some of the probable differences between the two presentations.
5. Explain how feedback can be used in making a speech.
6. One's manner of dress, choice of hairstyle, physical characteristics, and the like are personal. They should have no influence on any form of oral communication. Discuss.
7. By description (or perhaps by example), identify good and bad postures and walking practices for speaking.
8. Explain how facial expressions can miscommunicate.
9. Give some illustrations of gestures that can be used to communicate more than one meaning. Demonstrate them.
10. "We are born with voices—some good, some bad, and some in between. We have no choice but to accept what we have been given." Comment.
11. What should be the determining factors in the use of visuals?
12. Discuss (or demonstrate) some good and bad techniques of using visuals.
13. In presenting an oral report to a group composed of fellow workers as well as some bosses, a worker is harassed by the questions of a fellow worker who is trying to embarrass him. What advice would you give the worker? Would your advice be different if the critic were one of the bosses? What if the speaker were a boss and the critic a worker? Discuss.
14. Give examples of ways a team could provide continuity between members through the use of supporting examples. Be specific.
15. Explain the principal differences between written and oral reports.
16. Compare the typical organization plans of oral and written reports. Note the major differences between the two kinds of plans.

## APPLICATION EXERCISES

### SPEECHES

Since a speech can be made on almost any topic, it is not practical to list topics for speeches. You or your instructor can generate any number of interesting and timely topics in a short time. Whatever topic you select, you will need to determine the goals clearly, to work out the facts of the situation, and to set a time limit.

### ORAL REPORTS

Most of the written report problems presented in the problem section following Chapter 13 can also serve as oral report problems. The following problems, however, are especially suitable for oral presentation.

1. Survey the major business publications for information about the outlook for the national (or world) economy for the coming year. Then present a summary report to the directors of Allied Department Stores, Inc.
2. As a student leader on your campus, you have been asked by the faculty senate (or a comparable faculty group) to report to its members on the status of faculty-student relations. You will include recommendations on what can be done to improve those relations.
3. Report to a meeting of a wildlife-protection organization on the status of an endangered species in your area. You will need to gather the facts through research, probably in wildlife publications.
4. A national chain of _____ (your choice) is opening an outlet in your city. You have been assigned

the task of reviewing site possibilities. Gather the pertinent information, and make an oral recommendation to the board of directors.

5. The Future Business Leaders Club at your old high school has asked you to report to it on the nature and quality of business study at your college. You will cover all the factors that you think high school students need to know. Include a visual in your presentation.

6. As representative of a travel agency, present a travel package on _____ (place or places of your choice) to the members of the Adventurer Travel Club. You will describe places to be visited, and you will cover all the essential details—dates, hotels, guide service, meals, costs, manner of travel, and so on.

7. Report to a meeting of Consumers' Alliance (a consumer-protection organization) on the economics of renting telephones from the telephone company versus buying telephones. You will need to gather facts through research.

8. Look through current newspapers, magazines, and so on, and get the best available information on the job outlook for this year's college graduates. You will want to look at each major field separately. You may also want to show variations by geographic area, degree, and schools. Present your findings in a well-organized and illustrated oral report.

9. Present a plan for improving some phase of operation on your campus (registration, scholastic honesty, housing, grade appeals, library, cafeteria, traffic, curricula, athletics, and so on).

10. Present an objective report on some legislation of importance to business (right-to-work laws, environmental controls, taxes, and the like). Take care to present evidence and reasoning from all the major viewpoints. Support your presentation with facts, figures, and so on whenever they will help. Prepare visual supports.

11. Assume that you are being considered by a company of your choice for a job of your choice. Your prospective employer has asked you to make a _____-minute (your instructor will specify) report on your qualifications. You may project your education to the date you will be in the job market, making assumptions that are consistent with your record to date.

12. Prepare and present an informative report on how individuals may reduce their federal or state income tax payments. You will probably want to emphasize the most likely sources of tax savings—such as tax sheltering and avoiding common errors.

13. Make a presentation to a hypothetical group of investors that will get you the investment money you need for a purpose of your choice. Your purpose could be to begin a new business, to construct a building, to develop land—whatever interests you. Make your presentation as real (or realistic) as you can. And support your appeal with visuals.

14. As chairperson of the site-selection committee of the National Federation of Business Executives, present a report on your committee's recommendation. The committee has selected a city and a convention hotel (you may choose each). Your report will give your recommendation and the reasons that support it. For class purposes, you may make up whatever facts you may need about the organization and its convention requirements and about the hotel. But use real facts about the city.

15. As a buyer of men's (or women's) clothing, report to the sales personnel of your store on the fashions for the coming season. You may get the necessary information from publications in the field.

16. The top administrators of your company have asked you to look into the matter of whether the company should own automobiles, rent automobiles, or pay mileage costs on employee-owned automobiles. (Automobiles are used by sales personnel.) Gather the best available information on the matter, and report it to the top administrators. You may make up any company facts you need; but make them realistic.

17. In a group designated or approved by your instructor, present a persuasive presentation proposing that your school make more computing equipment available for student use. Be sure to cover all aspects of such a decision including cost, access, security, etc.

18. Choose a graphics package most of your classmates could use to prepare visuals for oral reports. Report on the features, documentation, and cost. Feel free to use visuals to support your report.

# PART SEVEN

# SPECIAL TOPICS IN BUSINESS COMMUNICATION

**18**
SPECIAL TOPIC: TECHNOLOGY-ASSISTED COMMUNICATION

**19**
SPECIAL TOPIC: TECHNIQUES OF CROSS-CULTURAL COMMUNICATION

**20**
SPECIAL TOPIC: PHYSICAL PRESENTATION OF LETTERS, MEMOS, AND REPORTS

**21**
SPECIAL TOPIC: CORRECTNESS OF COMMUNICATION

**22**
SPECIAL TOPIC: BUSINESS RESEARCH METHODS

**Explanatory Note:**
Because business communication instructors vary widely in their use of the five topics in this part, these are presented as "special" chapters. This labeling is intended to suggest that the chapters be used in whatever way or order best fits the instructor's needs.

## CHAPTER 18

# TECHNOLOGY-ASSISTED COMMUNICATION

### CHAPTER OBJECTIVES

*Upon completing this chapter, you will be able to describe the role of technology in business communication. To reach this goal, you should be able to*

**1**

Explain how technology helps in constructing messages.

**2**

Identify appropriate software applications for different stages in the writing process.

**3**

Discuss how technology helps in the presentation of messages.

**4**

Explain basic concepts of document design and layout.

**5**

Discuss various ways to transmit messages and the hardware currently used.

**6**

Describe how technology assists collaborative writing.

**7**

Discuss what impact future developments might have on business communication.

### INTRODUCTORY SITUATION

## to Using Technology in Writing Tasks

The company that hired you after your recent graduation is in the process of reviewing its MIS department. Your boss believes that as a recent graduate you are aware of how technology might help businesses. You have been asked to lead a discussion in your department, focusing on how the MIS department might help your department become more productive and produce higher quality work. You need to discuss both software and hardware, including programs that will help employees in their day-to-day communication.

This chapter is designed to help you out—to give you a picture of where we are now and where we may be going. It provides a structure for continuing to build your understanding on how future technology will assist in communication tasks. ■

Technological tools can enhance the uniquely human ability to communicate. But as with any set of tools, how one uses them determines their degree of effectiveness. By using your mind both to create messages and to focus the technology appropriately, you can improve the quality of your communication.

Appropriately used, technology can assist individuals and groups with both the grunt work related to writing as well as enhance the creative, thinking aspects. William Zinsser, author of *On Writing Well,* compares one tool—the word processor—to a dishwasher. He describes it as liberating one from a chore that's not creative and saps ones energy. As you'll learn, several technological tools assist you in this fashion. Mary Boone, author of *Leadership and the Computer,* explains the importance of communication to top executives. She describes how executives are using computers to link themselves with their organizations, building a new level of connectivity. Technology assists the communicator in many aspects of communication.

> Technology assists with both the tedious and creative writing tasks.

When you think of enhancing the communication process with technology, you probably first think of using word processing software on a personal computer. While that is one important tool, there are numerous hardware and software tools that can help improve your messages. These tools help with the construction, presentation, and transmission of messages as well as with collaborative writing.

## ▪▪▪▪▪▪▪▪▪▪▪▪▪▪▪▪▪▪▪▪▪▪▪
## TOOLS FOR CONSTRUCTING MESSAGES

Computer tools for constructing written messages can be associated with the different stages of the writing process—planning, gathering and collecting information, analyzing and organizing information, and writing and rewriting. While these tools are presently discrete tools, you are likely to see more and better integration of these tools in the future. And, of course, the more skilled you become with each of these tools, the better they serve you.

> Computer tools can be used throughout the writing process.

### Computer Tools for Planning

Whether you are writing a short letter or long report, you can use a computer to help you plan both the document and the writing project. In planning the content of the document, *outlining* or *idea processing* software is useful.

> Outlining software helps in planning the content of a message.

CHAPTER 18  Special Topic: Technology-Assisted Communication

While technology makes constructing documents and integrating graphics easy, writers still need to carefully review the messages they send.

You can brainstorm, listing your ideas as they occur to you. Later you tag related ideas, asking the computer to group them. Outlining software comes with some high-end (full-featured) word processors, or it comes alone and can be used with a variety of word processing software. One way to use an outliner is with a split screen as in Figure 18–1. In one part of the screen you'll see your outline and in another part the document you are writing. Another way you can use an outliner is as a pop-up window. In this case your outline is held in memory; you can pop it over your document to view it and put it away when you're done.

> Project management software assists in identifying tasks and allocating resources.

When you are working on a long writing project, several projects, or one carried over a long time, *project management software* is an excellent tool for planning the project. It allows you to identify all the tasks needed to complete the project, to determine how much time each task might take, and to generate a time and task chart (commonly called a Gantt chart). Also, it helps you to keep track of your progress and to determine how to reallocate your resources to complete the project on time or within budget. You can see a Gantt chart in Figure 18–2.

> Personal information management software assists with time management.

Finding time for writing, of course, is one of the major challenges for businesspeople. By using *personal information management software,* you can plan time for completing writing projects. These time-management tools are merely annotated electronic calendars. However, using them to schedule your writing tasks is an excellent planning tool. They'll remind you of tasks to complete and days remaining before a document needs to be completed. Electronic calendar software is readily available. One simple but widely available calendar is the desktop accessory tool that is a part of Windows. You can see in Figure 18–3 how one writer scheduled time for writing projects. The bell icon in front of the time shows that this writer set an alarm to let the computer remind him or her when it was time to write.

**FIGURE 18–1** This split screen example shows the writer's outline in the top window and the current draft in the bottom window.

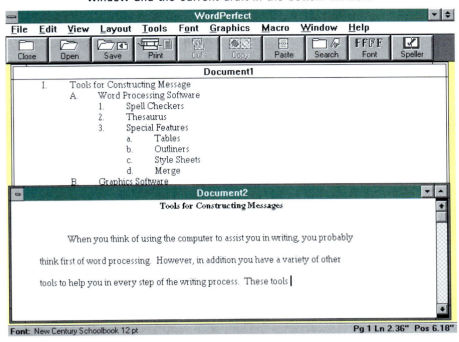

**FIGURE 18–2** This Gantt chart identifies the tasks for a long report and the time allocated to each of them.

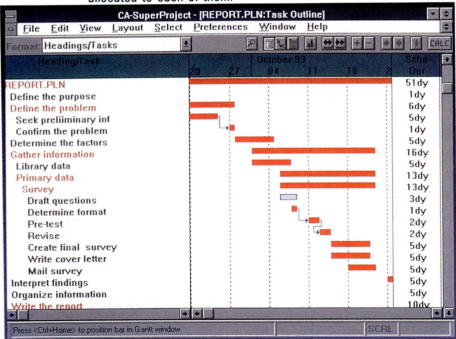

CHAPTER 18  Special Topic: Technology-Assisted Communication

**FIGURE 18-3** Notice in this example of an electronic calendar that the computer will sound an alarm to remind the writer when it is time to handle various tasks.

```
                    Calendar - 18_3_FIG.CAL
File  Edit  View  Show  Alarm  Options  Help

        6:42 PM      ← →    Thursday, December 3, 1992
     🔔  8:30 AM     Create Gantt for Qtr. Sales Report
        9:00         Sales meeting (Holiday Goodwill)
        9:30
        10:00        Dictate minutes of sales meeting
        10:30        Calls to Midwest managers
        11:00        Compile and send Nov. sales data to m
        11:30        Lunch with Kate Lenaghan
        12:00 PM
        12:30
        1:00         Planning meeting for new products
        1:30
     🔔  2:00         Draft outline for sales report
        2:30         Interview college recruiting candidates
     🔔  3:00         Write intro for sales report
```

Some research identifies planning as the primary step that separates good writers from others. However, few writers have discovered the power of electronic planning tools. Using both project management and calendaring software will give you powerful tools with the potential for big rewards.

## Computer Tools for Gathering and Collecting Information

*When you need information for a writing task, consider conducting an electronic search.*

Before you can write, you have to have something to say. Sometimes you may be writing about your own ideas, but often you will supplement them with facts. Gathering facts or data is one of the most important jobs of the writer. Today you will want to combine your manual search for facts with electronic searches. The computer can help you find a variety of information quickly and accurately because today much of our printed information is available electronically. In fact, some kinds of information are only available electronically.

From the numerous headlines of hackers and computer viruses, you are probably well aware that computers can connect with other computers all over the world. While the physical way connections are made is interesting to some, as a writer you only need to know that it can be done so you can take advantage of it.

*Data can be gathered from internal or external computers.*

What you are looking for are facts. These facts are usually stored in databases, which can either be internal or external. Your report due today at 1:00 P.M. might be on the current inventory of your on-site manufacturing product line. You could simply connect to your company's computer at noon and download (copy to your computer system) the most recent data before completing your report. However, if you need to project the number of completed units by the end of the month, you may also need to connect to

PART 7  Special Topics in Business Communication

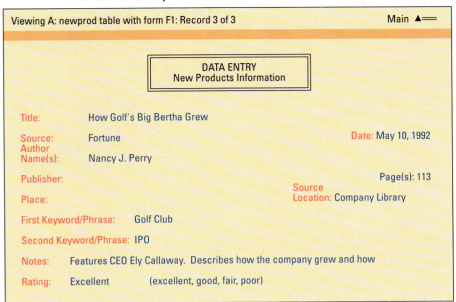

**FIGURE 18–4** This screen shows a completed data entry form for collecting bibliographic information on new products. You will notice it has been color coded to visually indicate different kinds of data—blue for straight data entry data, yellow for individually created data, and red for important data.

your supplier's computer to check the inventory of the parts you will need to complete your units. In this case, you will be using your computer to find facts both internally from within your company and externally from your suppliers.

Some libraries are now allowing their card catalog databases to be accessed both internally and externally. This means you will be able to check the card catalog from terminals within the library or with a computer and *communications software* (and with a modem if you need to change signals from analog to digital) from anywhere outside the library.

Once you have gathered the facts, you will want to store them in some organized fashion so you can retrieve them readily when needed. *Database software* will help you immensely here. If your company is interested in developing a new product for a newly defined market niche, you may want to collect articles about the targeted market, potential suppliers of components of your new product, sites for producing the product, projected labor costs, etc. You could do this simply by entering the facts of publication and abstracted information in your individually designed form created with database software. A sample database data entry screen is shown in Figure 18–4. The source information you have collected will be available whenever you need it. You can search and sort it on any of the categories (called fields) you set up on your data entry screen.

In Chapter 22, which discusses business research methods, you will learn about other on-line information providers for business information. The major point to remember is that in business it is not necessarily what you

Communications software connects over the telephone lines to external computers.

Database software provides a convenient way to collect information.

know that really counts, but what you can find out. No one can know all there is about a subject, but those who can use a computer system to gather and collect facts when they need them will find it a real asset.

## Computer Tools for Analyzing and Organizing

*Computer software helps analyze and interpret data with statistics and graphics.*

Three tools that writers find useful in analyzing data are statistics, graphics, and spreadsheet software. Since sometimes you cannot say very much about raw numbers, combining them or viewing them in different ways gives you a clearer picture of their meaning. Today, some very sophisticated *statistical software* has been made user-friendly, allowing those with little computer expertise to use them easily. Some programs will even query you about the nature of your data and recommend which statistical tests to use. Also, most *spreadsheet software* will compute basic statistics that allow writers to give some basic but meaningful interpretations to data.

*Graphics software* helps writers several ways. First, graphs reveal trends and relationships in data that are often hard to picture from raw data. This helps writers interpret clearly the meaning of their data. Second, graphics software helps writers explain more clearly to readers what the data mean. For example, you can direct the reader to look at the red and blue lines for the last five years, noting the trend of increasing rate of profits. You can create graphics easily with both spreadsheet and graphics software. Also, a large variety of graphics software is available for creating special graphics. You no longer have to be a graphic artist to create clear, good-looking graphics.

*Outlining software helps organize your information.*

*Outlining* or *idea processing software* is an organizing tool for the writer as well as a planning tool. Once you have captured your ideas and grouped related ideas, you can rearrange items into a meaningful order, organizing with the reader in mind. You can also collapse or expand the outline to view as few or as many levels as you want. This lets you see a macro view or big picture of your document as well as a micro or detailed view, so you can check for consistency at all levels.

## Computer Tools for Writing

*Word processing software* is clearly the favorite writing tool of most writers. Once you've used it, you are hooked. Other computer writing tools that might hook you are *spelling checkers, electronic thesauruses, grammar and style checkers, electronic references,* and *graphics and drawing packages.* The following discussion of these computer writing tools will point out how they can be used as well as caution you about any limitations.

*Word processing helps you capture, manipulate, edit, and revise your messages.*

**Word Processing Software.** By liberating the writer from tiresome chores, word processing gives writers time to spend their energy on revising, editing, and other document-polishing efforts. Some of the most common features of word processing software for revising and editing include insert/delete, move and copy, and search and replace.

*Insert, delete, move and copy, and search and replace enables you to do what the terms suggest.*

Insert allows the writer to add characters at any point while delete lets the writer delete characters. One of the nicest features of recent releases of major word processing programs is being able to change your mind and undo the most recent insert and delete changes. Some writers rarely delete text,

624   PART 7   Special Topics in Business Communication

moving the text to the end of the file or to another file for possible future use. The search and replace feature can be used several ways. One way might be to search for the name in a file of someone who got married, who retired, or who was promoted and replace that name with the new name. Most software lets the writer decide whether to replace automatically every occurrence of the item or to decide on each occurrence. The search feature is usually used to find a particular word, name, or place. However, sometimes writers add asterisks or other symbols to mark copy or to add remarks or reminders. Later they search for those symbols to find the points in the document that need attention. You will find that these common features will be useful over and over.

Two other useful features of word processing are basic math and simple sorting. The basic math feature lets the writer enter columns or rows of numbers, leaving the calculation job for the software. The sorting feature lets the writer enter columns or rows of words, leaving the alphabetic sorting for the software. While these are useful features of word processing software, the writer has to be careful to enter or mark the copy exactly the way the software needs it to do the proper calculating or sorting.

<sub></sub>*Basic math calculates columns and sorting arranges information in an order.*

The tables feature is another feature that enables you to do simple math and sort. Furthermore, it works similarly to a spreadsheet by allowing you to enter formulas in table cells, freeing you from the math. You can also link a spreadsheet to a table. When numbers change in the linked spreadsheet, they are automatically changed in the table with which they are linked. The tables feature allows formatting of individual cells, rows, and columns. It is useful for presenting data as well as textual material in rows and columns.

*The tables feature also allows you to do simple math with data and to sort them.*

Another nice feature of many word processing programs is the hidden comment or remark feature. If you insert the proper comment symbol, the comments that follow will be recorded in the file but not printed out unless you tell the software to print the comments. Teachers can use this feature to put test answers in files but not on the test; later they can print a second copy and direct the software to print the comments. This feature can be used for reminders, detailed information, etc. For example, one might note that the vice president directed that an exception to ordinary practice be granted under some special circumstances. Or one might leave a reminder to verify the statistics presented at a particular point in a document. In Figure 18–5 you can see both the display of a comment and the printed document without the comment.

*The hidden comment feature permits inserting information that is not printed until you choose to print it.*

Two additional editing features involve the physical presentation of documents. These features are hyphenation and format change. Both of these features help you change how the physical output looks. Hyphenation, for example, is a feature that helps the right margin appear less ragged than when it is not used. A ragged margin does not usually bother most people on a full page with full length lines; however, when one is using a short line without hyphenating, the right margin can be distracting if it appears ragged. The example of column text in Figure 18–6 with and without hyphenation illustrates how hyphenation can smooth out a ragged right margin. Format change also helps you change margins, tabs, spacing, etc. Formatting is particularly useful when you are changing letterheads, typestyles, or binding. It allows you to experiment easily to find the most appropriate form to present the document to the reader.

*Hyphenation and format change enables you to control evenness of right margin.*

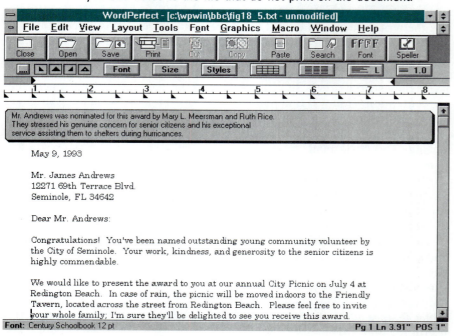

**FIGURE 18–5** From these examples, you can see that the comment feature lets you add notes to the file that do not print on the document.

Since revising and editing are extremely important to turning out well-written business documents, these are tools you will find you use often.

A couple of other word processing features that make the writing job easier are footnoting and index building. Most high-end word processors include the footnoting feature. It allows the writer to mark the place where the footnote occurs, entering the footnote at that point. The software then keeps track of the line count, placing the footnote at the bottom of the page on which it occurs, as well as numbering the footnotes consecutively. Also, the software will move the footnote if the text associated with it is moved. Another chore word processing software assists with is index building. The writer simply tags the words to be indexed, including cross references, and the software builds an alphabetic index with associated page numbers. This is particularly helpful with long, frequently referenced documents.

Word processing also has three other features that save the writer from having to re-enter the same information. These features are merge, macros, and headers and footers. The merge feature permits you to combine one form document with a document containing variable data. Merge is particularly useful in early and late-stage collection letters, where names and amounts are variable but the message is the same. Another feature, called *macros*, allows you to enter any characters you want to call up at the command of a few keystrokes. This feature is useful for calling up form paragraphs for answering commonly occurring questions as well as bringing

---

The footnote feature helps you to fit footnotes within the page layout. Index building enables you to compile an index easily.

Using advanced word processing features saves time.

**FIGURE 18–5 (concluded)**

> May 9, 1993
>
> Mr. James Andrews
> 12271 69th Terrace Blvd.
> Seminole, FL 34642
>
> Dear Mr. Andrews:
>
> Congratulations! You've been named outstanding young community volunteer by the City of Seminole. Your work, kindness, and generosity to the senior citizens is highly commendable.
>
> We would like to present the award to you at our annual City Picnic on July 4 at Redington Beach. In case of rain, the picnic will be moved indoors to the Friendly Tavern, located across the street from Redington Beach. Please feel free to invite your whole family; I'm sure they'll be delighted to see you receive this award.

up repeatedly used memo headings or letter closings. Headers and footers also let the software enter repeated information at the top and bottom of pages as well as count and print the page numbers.

There are also special features of word processing software for using columns, fonts, importing graphics and spreadsheet files, etc. Knowing how to exploit the features of the word processing software you use will definitely make writing and revising easier for you.

**Spelling Checkers.** Whether included with high-end word processing software or used alone, spelling checkers are relied on daily by business writers. However, it's only an effective tool if the writer uses it. A recent study found that 75 percent of the spelling errors in student letters could have been caught by spelling checkers.[1] While this points out the value of using a spelling checker, it also shows that 25 percent of the spelling errors would not have been found by spelling checkers. Errors you will want to watch out for include wrong word errors such as "compliment" for "complement" or "imply" for "infer." A spell checker will also miss spelling errors such as "desert" for "dessert" or misused words such as "good" for "well." Therefore, careful proofreading is still in order after a document has been checked with a spelling program.

*Spelling checkers supplement proofreading, but do not replace it.*

---

[1] Berle Haggblade, "Has Technology Solved the Spelling Problem?" *The Bulletin of the Association for Business Communication,* March 1988, p. 23.

**FIGURE 18–6** The examples here illustrate how using the hyphenation feature will smooth out the right margin.

---

**Computers, Human Intellect, and Organizational Nervous Systems**

An executive provides vision and direction, makes decisions, diagnoses and solves problems, negotiates, convinces, and selects and coaches people. All these actions depend on the executive's ability to think creatively and communicate clearly; clear communication and creative thinking can be enhanced by the use of computers.

Unfortunately, most people don't realize this. The computer's role as a valuable thinking tool seems to be a secret. Instead, many intelligent people, even today, believe that computers are best suited to clerical and administrative tasks. They see the computer as only a convenience or an operational necessity. I see the computer as an extension of the human brain.

An understanding of the connection between the evolution of the human mind and computers takes us back in time.

---

Note the ragged margin in this example of text without the hyphenation feature turned on.

---

**Computers, Human Intellect, and Organizational Nervous Systems**

An executive provides vision and direction, makes decisions, di-agnoses and solves problems, nego-tiates, convinces, and selects and coaches people. All these actions depend on the executive's ability to think creatively and communicate clearly; clear communication and creative thinking can be enhanced by the use of computers.

Unfortunately, most people don't realize this. The computer's role as a valuable thinking tool seems to be a secret. Instead, many intelligent people, even to-day, believe that computers are best suited to clerical and adminis-trative tasks. They see the comput-er as only a convenience or an op-erational necessity. I see the com-puter as an extension of the hu-man brain.

An understanding of the con-nection between the evolution of the human mind and computers takes us back in time.

---

Note that when the hyphenation feature is used, the right margin is smoothed out.

---

*The electronic thesaurus gives easy access to synonyms.*

**Thesaurus Software.** Serious writers usually have a bound thesaurus on hand. However, most writers find they will use an electronic thesaurus much more frequently than they ever used the bound one. The ease of popping up a window with suggested synonyms is hard to beat. Most high-end word processors include a thesaurus; however, several good independent programs are available. One thesaurus included with a popular word processor gives the part of speech and meaning along with the synonyms. You can page through different uses of the word, selecting the synonym from a new list for each different use. The thesaurus is a powerful tool, and the computer has made it faster to use and easier to access.

"It says, 'Three percent split infinitives, 8 percent passive verbs, 16 percent compound-complex sentences, average sentence length 26 words, paperback rights $3.2 million, movie sales $8.3 million, total take $11.5 million, less 15 percent agent's fees.'"

**Grammar and Style Checkers.** The value of grammar and style checkers is often debated. Unlike spelling programs, which are easily able to identify "wrong" words (words which are not in their dictionaries), grammar and style checkers identify "possible problems" with "suggestions" for revision. It is then your responsibility to decide whether the "possible problem" is a problem and if the "suggestion" is the best solution. However, these programs are improving rapidly, adding expert system techniques to identify "possible problems" in context more accurately.

Grammar and style checkers are only suggestion systems.

In addition to checking grammar, style, word usage, and punctuation, these programs now report readability, strength, descriptive, and jargon indexes. They also perform sentence structure analysis, suggesting you use simpler sentences, vary the sentence starts, use more or fewer prepositional phrases, and make various other changes. Grammar and style checkers also identify "possible problems" with specific words that might be slang, jargon, misspelled, misused, or difficult for readers to understand. These programs also give word counts such as average length of sentences, longest sentence, shortest sentence, number of words in a document, and number of times each word is used. A sample summary is shown in Figure 18–7.

They also evaluate a variety of other elements of writing quality.

**FIGURE 18–7** This is a summary report from one popular grammar and style checker when used to check a nearly finished document.

```
<<**                         SUMMARY                         **>>

RightWriter analyzed the document C:\WPWIN\TESTRW
using the style file C:\RWW\GENERAL.RWT:
This style file is for general business writing.
The document was produced by WordPerfect (5.0 or later).

READABILITY INDEX: 12.71

4th        6th        8th       10th       12th        14th
|****|****|****|****|****|****|****|****|****|**
SIMPLE     |------ GOOD -------|              COMPLEX
Readers need a 12th grade level of education.

       Number of Words in Document: 605
       Number of Numbers in Document: 1
       Number of Words within Sentences: 586
       Number of Sentences: 38
       Number of Syllables: 1143
       Average Number of Words/Sentence: 15.42
       Use of Shall: 0
       Use of Must: 3
       Use of Can: 2
       Use of May: 1
       Percentage of words that are Prepositions: 11.90

STRENGTH INDEX: 0.77

       0.0                   0.5                     1.0
       |****|****|****|****|****|****|****|**
       WEAK                                          STRONG
       The strength of delivery is good, but can be improved.

DESCRIPTIVE INDEX: 0.44

       0.0                   0.5                     1.0
       |****|****|****|****|*
       TERSE    |----------- NORMAL ------------|   WORDY


JARGON INDEX: 0.00

SENTENCE STRUCTURE RECOMMENDATIONS:

   2. Few compound sentences or subordinate clauses are
      being used. Try to balance the use of simple sentences
      with the use of complex sentences. This gives your
      writing variety and makes it easier to read.

<<**                      END OF SUMMARY                     **>>
```

*Although often criticized, this software is improving.*

While the debate goes on, the software is getting better. Recent versions seem to be addressing some of the issues concerning writers. For example, recent versions of grammar and style checkers are much more flexible than older versions. If you are writing in an informal environment where your boss finds beginning sentences with "And" and "But" acceptable, you can turn off the rule that would identify those beginnings as problems. Also, you

### *A Word of Advice:* BACKUP FREQUENTLY!

Some programs will create an automatic backup file, but most leave the responsibility with the writer. Some writers backup every 15 minutes or so while others backup every page. Most writers know how difficult it is to create a document, much less recreate it, so they are willing to spend a few seconds regularly to protect their investment. To further protect your documents, alternate the backup floppies you use. If one disk should be damaged or become infected with a virus, you'll still have another copy. Using different colored floppies for different days or using an odd numbered floppy on an odd-dated day and an even numbered one on an even-dated day are techniques some writers use to make their backup procedures safer. Other writers also grandfather their files by giving each revision a new name in order to help recreate the document from earlier drafts should the current file become unusable for any reason.

---

can choose the level of writing your intended audience wants. These are just a few examples of the flexibility in the newest versions of grammar and style checkers.

Grammar and style checkers are definitely an important tool for the business writer. But, like any tool, the more appropriately you use it the better job it does for you.

**Reference Software.** Reference software is just what its name suggests—software that presents reference books such as dictionaries, style manuals, zip code directories, etc. A few of these reference programs are on floppy disks, but the larger ones containing 200,000-word dictionaries, 500,000-word thesauruses, books of quotations, zip code directories, the world almanac, and several other references are on compact disks. While reference software is a great source to have available at your fingertips now, improved technology will make it even better by allowing you to link the sources to each other when you want to. At that point, compact disks will become an even more valuable tool for the business writer.

A wide variety of reference books are available for easy access.

**Graphics and Draw Software.** Graphics and draw software is becoming a more important tool for the writer every day. Not only are several word processing packages now capable of importing files made with graphics and draw programs, but the programs are becoming easier to use. The introduction of ready-made graphs and pictures (called clip art) and the introduction of low-cost scanners, which will copy from any printed source, have made it easier to supplement text with professional-looking graphics. Also, the cost of color output is dropping for both monitors and printers, making it more desirable to use colored graphics and drawings. In Chapter 15, ''Graphics,'' you will learn how to use graphics effectively. The important point to remember here is that with the help of the computer, you now have a new tool that enables you to enhance textual communication with graphics.

Graphics and draw programs assist in supplementing textual materials with visuals.

As you have learned, technology is certainly an important tool for the writer in constructing the message. While word processing is the writer's primary tool in constructing a message, a wide variety of software applications will help in the planning, gathering and collecting, analyzing and organizing, and writing stages.

## TOOLS FOR PRESENTING MESSAGES

After you've completed the document, you need to consider how to present it. This decision involves both software and hardware choices.

### Software

*Using its layout and design features, desktop publishing software helps present your messages in their best form.*

Publishing software contributes to the appearance of a document, enabling you to prepare professional-looking documents. You'll find this software particularly useful for long reports, newsletters, policy and procedure manuals, and proposals. This software, sometimes called desktop publishing software, combines three basic elements—text, graphics, and design. Initially, the first software to combine these elements was desktop publishing software. However, high-end word processing software is now capable of doing nearly 80 percent of what full-featured desktop publishing software can do if you take advantage of these features. To do this most effectively, you need some knowledge of the basic elements of design.

Ironically, professionals engaged in designing documents for publication have the same major objective as writers—to communicate effectively. Professionals aim for designs that attract the reader but do not distract. Also, they understand that the most successful publications are those in which the design enhances or complements the meaning of the writer.

With publishing software, desktop publishing, or high-end word processing, you can break out of the traditional-looking page with its roots in the typewriter era to give the reader the best looking, most readable document possible. However, to do this, you need to know about some basic design principles. These principles cover three areas: layout, typography, and art.

*Writers can control the look of their messages through effective layout.*

**Basic Layout Principles.** Roger Parker, a nationally recognized expert on design, defines layout as simply "the arrangement of text and graphics on a page." Suzanne West, another expert, goes further with "A layout is a composition of interrelated elements on a page." While similar, the latter implies that the writer has some control over the results through careful composition of the elements. These elements include *white space, text, visuals,* and *graphic design elements* such as circles, lines, and bullets.

*White space adds emphasis and affects readability.*

You might find surprising that today a commonly accepted ratio of white space to text is 1:1. That means half of your page is devoted to text and half to white space. This level provides optimum readability. Readability is also improved by using lines 35 to 40 characters long. Therefore, with these two factors in mind, you can clearly see in Figure 18–8 that instead of using a full page of long, double-spaced lines it is better to use short lines with less spacing between them. This deliberate shifting of the white space to the margins keeps the 1:1 ratio but improves the readability.

*Use white space consistently.*

In planning the placement of white space in documents with facing pages, you'll want to be sure your elements line up at the top and at the left. The example in Figure 18–9 shows a facing page layout with consistent use of white space in margins and between the lines.

**PART 7** Special Topics in Business Communication

**FIGURE 18–8**

Before
Double-spaced with long lines

After
Short lines with whitespace moved to margins

**FIGURE 18–9**

This facing, double-page spread illustrates copy aligned at top and left, the way our eye has been trained to read pages.

White space can also be used for emphasis. As you've already learned, space denotes importance. When you are writing about a topic, the more space you give it the more emphasis it gets. The same principle applies to white space. If you leave more white space around certain text or graphics, you will be giving that text or graphic more emphasis.

Another way to get emphasis in the text is through type size and style. Of course, you want headings to stand out, but they should be balanced with the rest of the text. The size of your main heading will also be governed by the number of levels of subheadings you plan to use. And you will want to use a type size smaller than your text type size for captions and footnotes so they do not distract the reader from the text. Type style elements such as bold, italic, or bold italic can also be added to headings, subheadings, text, captions, and footnotes for more emphasis.

Use it to give emphasis.

Type size and style also affect readability.

One means of emphasis that should be used sparingly is all uppercase. Using both uppercase and lowercase in headings makes the headings easier to read. However, all uppercase in short phrases will work effectively.

Good layout always includes careful planning of visuals—graphics and drawings. In planning them, give attention to placement and size as well as content. Also, be sure you plan space for the captions in your layout.

> Graphic devices can direct the eye, directing attention to particular parts of the message.

A final element of layout is the graphic device. Lines or rules around text or separating text from visuals or white space can be a very effective tool for directing the eye to where you want it to go. The thickness of a line can be varied to give varying degrees of emphasis to the material it is highlighting. Tints or shading are other graphic devices that attract attention. Usually these are used to separate related copy in the same text. *Business Week* often uses this device. For example, it may run a story on General Motors Corporation, including a brief profile of a GM executive in a shaded box accompanying the article. Or it may be reporting on a specific industry in general, detailing explicit facts on specific companies in a table in a shaded box.

> Plan them to enhance the text.

Graphic devices should enhance the test, not distract from it. If your reader just reads the shaded boxes and overlooks the primary content of the report, your layout is not successful. Careful planning for effective use of graphic devices is a prerequisite to effective layout.

When the layout is good, it works well with the typography and art. While we have touched on the importance of type size and style in planning the textual component of layout, let us look at some basic principles of typography.

**Typography Basics.**   Although you may not be doing much yourself with the technical aspect of type in the majority of documents you produce, knowing the concepts and basic vocabulary is important. Not only will you be able to communicate more effectively with those who work on your documents, but you will help them to produce better layouts for you.

> Understanding type and its terminology helps you communicate with publishing professionals.

Many word processing terms for measuring, such as pitch and space, are carryovers from the typewriter era. However, the publishing and typesetting world measures in *points and picas*. A point is about $1/72$ of an inch, and a pica is 12 points, or about $1/6$ of an inch. When you are specifying type size, generally 14-point type and smaller is considered appropriate for text while type larger than 14 points is usually used for headings. Some software publishing gives you the choice of specifying in inches, centimeters, or picas. If you are working closely with people in the publishing world, you would be wise to work with the terminology they understand.

> A *point* is $1/72$ inch; a *pica* is 12 points.

Another term from this area is *kerning*. Kerning refers to the spacing between characters. While standard typewriters and dot matrix printers generally use equal spacing for each character, in publishing this space is variable. For example, in the word "The" a publishing system would allow the "T" to overhang, moving the "h" in for an even-appearing spacing. A dot matrix printer, on the other hand, would place the "h" after the overhang, appearing to leave more space between the "T" and "h" than between the "h" and "e." Also, if copy doesn't quite fit the page, you can squeeze it or stretch it by tightening or loosening the kerning or spacing between characters.

> *Kerning* is the spacing between characters.

**PART 7** Special Topics in Business Communication

*Leading* is similar to kerning except that it refers to vertical spacing rather than horizontal. When your lines are too close together, you can increase the leading to add more white between lines. As with kerning, you can adjust the leading to fit copy to the space available.

*Leading* is the spacing between lines.

One other term commonly used in the publishing industry is *typeface*. Typeface refers to the design of the entire uppercase and lowercase set of letters. While there are hundreds of typefaces available today, two common typefaces in use are Times-Roman and Helvetica. These are illustrated in Figure 18-10. Times-Roman is a serif type, having feet (cross-lines) at the end of the main strokes. Helvetica is a sans serif type, having no feet at the ends of its main strokes.

When you are talking to computer-oriented people about publishing, you may hear the term *font* used for typeface. However, a font means one typeface in one size and style. Therefore, if you wanted to use a Helvetica type with standard, bold, and italics in four sizes, you would need twelve fonts—one for each size and one for each style. Numerous font libraries are available for purchase, allowing you to prepare a custom-looking document.

Computer people use the term *font* for typeface.

Since type is a key element in most business documents, you'll want to pay special attention to it. Usually, it will account for more than 90 percent of your document. Your care in selecting and using type will have a big impact on the effectiveness of your design.

**Art Fundamentals.** Art as used here in its broadest sense refers to drawings, graphs, photos, and other illustrations. As a writer you primarily need to remember that art should always serve a message's purpose; it must never serve its own. Whenever you are about to place an art element on a page, ask yourself what purpose does it serve.

Art should serve the message's purpose.

One purpose of art is to break up large blocks of text. While we often try to conjure up an idea for drawings, graphs, or photos, we can also use the space to emphasize a key idea. By quoting from within the document and setting it off in larger type with ruling lines, we use a technique called a *pull quote*.

Use it to break up blocks of text.

Whatever the reason we have for our art, we should also strive to use the best art possible. Look for interesting photos, not merely mug shots. Crop photos, cutting out any extraneous material that does not work to enhance the text. Choose your art with the reader in mind. In some cases that might mean using cartoons or illustrations you scan in an import from various clip

Choose art for the best communication effect.

**FIGURE 18-10**

R           R

Times Roman (Serif)    Helvetica (Sans Serif)

CHAPTER 18 Special Topic: Technology-Assisted Communication

art software, and in other cases it might mean using high-quality color photos or significant pull quotes. Of course, you do need to be sure you do not violate copyrights.

*Effective design integrates layout, type, and art.*

Good design expertly integrates the layout, typography, and art elements. You will probably want to begin with either some very basic applications or the prepared templates or style sheets bundled with the desktop and word processing software. You will get better with practice. Also, you will get better if you read books and magazines on design, pay attention to the designs of others noting what seems to work, and keep a file of ideas. By always keeping the reader in mind as you design your documents, you will be effective in communicating your message.

### Hardware

*Your choice of output hardware is critical to the appearance of your message.*

Software is just one component of presenting a message; hardware is another. If the software has features your printer or other output device cannot print, the features are useless. On the other hand, if your hardware has features your software cannot produce, they, too, are useless. Both must work together to produce your message.

The most common output device is the printer. Depending on the formality of your communication, you may find yourself using dot printers for one type of message, inkjets for another, and laser printers for yet another. In circumstances where you must have the best-looking documents, you may even use typeset output. Appearance does convey a message, and the hardware you choose to complete the presentation of your document is an important consideration.

## TOOLS FOR TRANSMITTING MESSAGES

*The medium you choose to send your message communicates.*

*Transmitting* means to send the message. The medium you choose to transmit a message communicates to the receiver the importance you attach to the message. Usually a written message gets more attention than an oral message, and a special delivery message gets more attention than an ordinary mailed message. Even the method of special delivery chosen conveys a message. The client who sends you electronically the document you requested is perceived differently from the client who sends it on paper through Federal Express. Knowing what technologies are available to transmit the message assists you in deciding which is the best medium to use.

*Cellular technology expands the physical environment of the message sender.*

Technologies for sending a variety of oral and visual messages are widely used in business. One booming technology for oral communication is the cellular phone. While predominantly used in cars, it can be used in any area of the country equipped for it. With a phone that fits in the palm of the hand, businesspeople can now be reached for important calls as well as conduct business from otherwise inaccessible places. While you are delayed in a traffic jam on your way to the airport, you can call your office, your important client, or your company's central word processing center. The cellular phone enables businesspeople to make more productive use of their time.

Transmitting documents by facsimile (fax machine) is easy, fast, and direct.

As was mentioned in Chapter 16, another oral communication technology gaining wide acceptance by businesspeople is the voice messaging system. Not only do these systems answer phones, direct calls, and take messages, they also act as voice storage systems. For example, you can ask the system to retrieve messages for a particular date or from a particular person. You can also take a message you receive, annotate it with your voice message, and pass it along to another person's voice mailbox. You can even record a message for the system to deliver to several people's voice mailboxes at a specified time. By eliminating telephone tag and interruptions, this technology, too, improves the productivity of those using it.

Voice messaging systems are gaining business use.

Two technologies that combine oral and video communication effectively are teleconferencing and videodisc systems. While both have been around for a while, new developments in optical fibers, satellite transmission, and software and chip technology may push them into even more favor. New developments are both making the systems better and lowering the costs. Teleconferencing systems save travel time and expense, and they help eliminate many scheduling problems. Videodisc technology, which stores pictures and audio as well as written words, has been highly touted in education, but its applications for business, other than in the area of training, have not been fully explored. Perhaps as hypertext applications are developed, videodisc technology will see more business applications. Hypertext allows readers to link the pictures, audio, and written words in any order they want. Several software programs with on-line documentation are already using hypertext, allowing the reader to take any path he or she

Teleconferencing and videodisc combine oral and video media.

chooses through the documentation rather than having to read it in a rigid order. In any case, both these technologies enable the writer to use oral and visual communication.

**Electronic mail and facsimile transmission are gaining use for transmitting written messages.**

Written communication, on the other hand, can be transmitted effectively with two proven technologies—electronic mail and facsimile. Electronic mail transmission works with computer systems, sending documents to an electronic mailbox. These electronic mailboxes can be set up on a company's mini or mainframe computer, on a local area network (LAN), on a bulletin board system, or on a private subscriber information service. In any case, you need to know the electronic address of the receiver and how to access the system in order to send the document. Also, the receiver needs to check the electronic mailbox to receive the document. Facsimile transmission (fax), uses telephone lines to send a copy of the document. Faxing is a lot like photocopying or printing, but the copy is delivered elsewhere. Similarly, you need to know the telephone number of the receiving fax in order to send the message, and someone on the receiving end needs to check the fax and deliver the message.

**Although they communicate immediately, they are viewed as informal.**

Both of these technologies are being effectively used for transmitting written messages. However, while both have the advantage of immediacy, they are both less formal than sending a formal document. You need to evaluate carefully the need for formality in choosing your transmission medium.

**So use them appropriately.**

Knowing that you have a choice of media for transmitting the message and knowing how to use it are both important in order to choose the most appropriate medium. Because this technology is developing rapidly, you need to make it a priority to keep up-to-date on the latest developments.

## TOOLS FOR COLLABORATIVE WRITING

**Computer tools assist groups on a wide variety of tasks.**

Collaborative writing or group writing tasks occur regularly in business, and they vary widely in the form and nature of the work. However, there is a wide range of computer tools to support various aspects of the process. A recent study reviewing computer-supported collaborative work group writing tools divided them into two classifications: asynchronous and synchronous.[2] Asynchronous tools automate the traditional groups; synchronous tools, on the other hand, create a new kind of group environment.

### Asynchronous Computer Tools

**Several computer tools assist the traditional group.**

Asynchronous tools include word processing, conferencing systems, electronic mail systems, and group authoring systems. Word processing features useful in group writing include commenting, strikeouts, and redlining. Commenting allows you to insert comments in a document written by someone else. Strikeout and redlining allow you to identify text you would like to delete or insert. A lead writer in a group might distribute a document draft to members of the group; they would use these features of their word processor and return the disk to the leader. The leader would then review the documents and edit the original.

Another group writing tool is computer conferencing. As noted in Chapter 16, this tool is useful when groups have a difficult time meeting due to distance and time. To begin, the lead writer would enter some text. Others would access the system, review the comments, and enter their own. All comments can be reviewed by all members of the group. In some systems, group members have anonymity, but others maintain audit trails so comments can be attributed to specific group members.

Electronic mail systems provide a means for one writer to send a message to others. Unlike conferencing, in these systems access to others' mailboxes is restricted. While you can distribute messages to a whole group, you do not have access to messages one member sends to someone else.

Group authoring systems are software programs designed specifically for group work. While different products have varied features, most are designed to allow document versions to be compared, to allow comments and suggestions to be entered at appropriate places, and to allow the use of common editing tools such as insert, delete, paragraph, stet, etc.

All these tools are designed to work the way groups have traditionally worked. The planning, writing, and revising occur much the way they occur in traditional groups. However, the tools contribute to improvements in both speed and the quality of the final documents.

### Synchronous Computer Tools

Synchronous computer tools are used by all group members at the same time and same place. They allow multiple users to work on the document at the same time; they also allow users to view the comments of other users. These programs contain a variety of tools from brainstorming tools to organizing and analyzing tools to writing tools.

A group member may start with a question or a statement. Then group members will comment on the statement anonymously. For example, one member may propose a new policy statement. The other members then would comment about it. Then the group would review all comments, group related comments, rank order them, and write the final policy statement. This kind of group writing tool cuts group meeting time in half and produces better-quality documents. A review of research indicates that this electronic meeting technology improves group work by providing an equal opportunity for participation, discouraging behavior that negatively impacts meetings, enabling a large number of ideas to be managed effectively, and permitting the groups to use the tools as needed.[3]

Technology can definitely be used to support collaborative or group writing. From the simple PC disk-sharing programs to the sophisticated network-based programs, computer support for group writing tasks improves both the process and product.

---

[2] Annette Easton, George Easton, Marie Flatley, and John Penrose, "Supporting Group Writing with Computer Software," *The Bulletin of the Association for Business Communication,* June 1990, p. 34.

[3] J. F. Nunamaker, Alan R. Dennis, Joseph S. Valacich, Douglas R. Vogel, and Joey F. George, "Electronic Meeting Systems to Support Group Work," *Communications of the ACM,* July 1991, p. 40.

---

*Sidebar notes:*
- Computer conferencing is useful when distance or time make getting together difficult.
- Electronic mail permits communicating to intended receivers only.
- Collaborative writing is helped by group authorizing software.
- New computer tools change the group process and improve its output quality.

## A LOOK TO THE FUTURE

*Computer tools will continue to enhance the communication process,...*

In addition to the technological developments discussed thus far, you can anticipate further rapid development. Bill Gates, CEO of Microsoft, in his speech at Comdex, presented a futuristic vision of having information at our fingertips. To accomplish this, you can expect to see friendly systems and integration of applications that is much more transparent. Technologies such as fax, voice mail, and electronic mail will become integrated. You will be using networks which seem less complex, and a broader range of information will be easily accessible. However, you must make it a priority to keep abreast of these developments in order to identify tools which will make your job easier.

*...but the human mind still controls it.*

However, whatever form these developments take, human minds will continue to control message formulation. In fact, there is no evidence whatsoever that the need for messages communicated in writing and speaking will decrease. Even more important, there is absolutely no evidence that these messages can be handled in a way that does not require basic writing and speaking skills. Business communication is here to stay. In fact, the increasing complexity of the technology of the future is likely to require more—not less—of it.

## SUMMARY (by Chapter Objectives)

*1. Explain how the technology helps in constructing messages.*

1. Technology helps a writer construct messages through every step of the writing process including:
   - planning,
   - gathering and collecting information,
   - analyzing and organizing information, and
   - writing and rewriting.

*2. Identify appropriate software applications for different stages in the writing process.*

2. Each stage of the writing process has a set of software tools most appropriate for the tasks in that stage. These include the following:
   - outlining or idea processing, project management, and personal information management programs for planning,
   - communications and database programs for gathering and collecting information,
   - statistical, spreadsheet, graphics, and outlining or idea processing software for analyzing and organizing information, and word processing, spelling, thesaurus, grammar and style checking, reference, and graphics and draw programs for writing.

*3. Discuss how the technology helps in the presentation of messages.*

3. Technology helps in the presentation of documents with both sophisticated hardware and full-featured software.
   - Hardware contributes in the printing of documents.
   - Software contributes with desktop publishing features which combine text and graphics and promote good layout and design.

*4. Explain basic concepts of document layout and design.*

4. Layout and design refers to the arrangement of text and graphics on a page. Layout involves the careful composition of these basic elements:
   - white space for manipulating emphasis and readability,
   - text for emphasis and balance as well as for visual clues of organization,

- visuals such as graphics and drawings, and
- graphic design elements to direct the eye.

Layout and design is also affected by typography. Aspects writers need to know about include:
- points and picas, which represent height,
- kerning, which determines the spacing between letters,
- leading, which determines the spacing between lines, and
- typeface, which refers to the design of an entire set of letters.

Art is a final aspect of layout and design. Its main purpose is always to serve a message's purpose.

5. Communicators have a variety of choices of media for transmitting their messages.
    - Oral messages can be sent by cellular phone and voice messaging systems.
    - Teleconferencing and videodisc technologies combine oral and visual messages.
    - Written messages can be transmitted by electronic mail or facsimile.

6. A range of software tools assists groups of writers in asynchronous and synchronous writing environments.
    - Asynchronous tools automate traditional groups with such tools as word processing, conferencing systems, electronic mail, and group authoring systems.
    - Synchronous tools automate a new type of group environment where everyone participates at the same time and in roughly equal parts. Electronic meeting systems software provides a toolkit designed to support various tasks in the writing process.

7. Future developments expect to integrate present technologies more smoothly, making them easier to use. Also, a broader range of information will be easily accessible. Future developments will likely mean more need for good basic communication skills.

5. Discuss various ways to transmit messages and the hardware currently used.

6. Describe how technology assists collaborative writing.

7. Discuss what impact the future developments might have on business communication.

■■■■■■■■■■■■■■■
## QUESTIONS FOR DISCUSSION

1. Explain how technology can help the writer with both creative and tedious writing tasks.
2. Identify specific software programs that assist with constructing written messages. Explain what each does.
3. Word processing software is the writer's primary tool. Identify five basic features and two advanced features useful to business writers.
4. Discuss the advantages and disadvantages of spelling checkers and grammar and style checkers.
5. Describe ways graphics software helps writers.
6. Explain what a writer should know about layout and design and why it is important.
7. Identify various ways business writers can transmit oral and written messages.
8. How can technology assist in group writing?
9. What can we expect to see in future technological developments that will impact business communication?

■■■■■■■■■■■■■
## APPLICATION EXERCISES

1. Investigate the school and/or local libraries to determine what current (or future) computer systems will help one find information for business. Report your findings to the class.
2. Compile an annotated list of at least five local or regional BBSs. Include name, number, type, and access information, along with a descriptive statement on the nature of the board.
3. Locate six examples of electronic clip art you might use in a business document. Print the examples along with a brief explanation of a good use in a business document.
4. Identify where computers, printing equipment, and faxes are available at or around your college. Prepare a table with this information, listing times available as well as any costs. Also, be sure to include computer configurations and software available.
5. Choose a feature from your word processor (such as index, table of contents, styles, macros, etc.) that you have not used much. Learn how to use it and create an example of its use in a business document. Write a brief description of its application.
6. Select a dozen idioms from a reference book (found in your library or bookstore) that seem common to you. Type these into your word processor and run the file through a grammar and style checker. Print a copy of the results and bring it to class for discussion.
7. From a current computer magazine, find an article that relates to communication in business. Write a one-paragraph reaction to it and send your paragraph electronically (E-mail) to someone selected by your instructor.

CHAPTER 19

# TECHNIQUES OF CROSS-CULTURAL COMMUNICATION

## CHAPTER OBJECTIVES

*Upon completing this chapter, you will be able to describe the major barriers to international communication and how to overcome them. To reach this goal, you should be able to*

**1**

Explain why communicating clearly across cultures is important to business.

**2**

Define culture and explain its effects on cross-cultural communication.

**3**

Describe cultural differences in body positions and movements and use this knowledge effectively in communicating.

**4**

Describe cultural differences in attitudes toward time, space, odors, and such and use this knowledge effectively in communicating.

**5**

Explain the language equivalency problem as a cause of miscommunication.

**6**

Describe what one can do to overcome the language equivalency problem.

### INTRODUCTORY SITUATION

## to Cross-Cultural Communication

To introduce yourself to this chapter, assume the position of assistant to the president of Thatcher-Stone and Company, a small manufacturer of computer components. Your boss, gregarious old Vernon Thatcher, invited you to join him at a luncheon meeting with a group of Asian business executives in which negotiations for the sale of Thatcher-Stone products would be opened. Because Thatcher-Stone's domestic sales have been lagging, the company badly needs these customers.

As the Asian guests entered the room, bowing as introductions were made, Mr. Thatcher attempted to put them at ease. "No need to do that," he said. "I'm just plain Vernon Thatcher. Just relax and make yourself at home." You noticed that the Asians appeared bewildered. They appeared even more bewildered when early in the meeting Mr. Thatcher made this statement: "We've only got the lunch hour, gents. I know you'll appreciate getting right down to business."

Throughout the meeting Mr. Thatcher was in his best conversational mood—laughing, backslapping, telling jokes. But none of this seemed to make an impression on the guests. They seemed confused to you. They smiled and were extremely polite, but they seemed to understand little of what Mr. Thatcher was saying. Although he tried again and again to move to business talk, they did not respond. The meeting ended pleasantly, but without a sale.

"They're a strange people," Mr. Thatcher commented when he got back to his office. "They have a lot to learn about doing business. It doesn't look like they're going to deal with us, does it?" Mr. Thatcher was right in his last comment. They did not.

As you review the meeting, you cannot help but feel that Mr. Thatcher spoiled the deal, for he failed miserably in communicating with the Asians. The fact is that there is much to know about communicating in international settings. The goal of this chapter is to introduce this issue to you. ■

Technological advances in communication, travel, and transportation have made business increasingly global. This trend is expected to continue in the foreseeable future. Thus, the chances that you will have to communicate with people from other cultures are good.

> Business has become more global.

Both large and small businesses want you to be able to communicate clearly with those from other cultures for several reasons. Many businesses sell their products and services both domestically and internationally. Being able to communicate with others helps you be more successful in understanding customers' needs, communicating how your company can meet these needs, and winning their business. In addition to being a more productive worker, you will be more efficient both within and outside your company. You will be able to work harmoniously with those from other cultures, creating a comfortable workplace. With cultural barriers broken down, you will be able to hire good people despite their differences. Also, you will avoid problems stemming solely from misinterpretations. Your attention to

> Communicating across cultures effectively improves your productivity and efficiency and promotes harmonious work environments.

communicating clearly with those from other cultures will enrich both your business and your personal lives.[1]

In preparing to communicate with people from other cultures, you might well begin by reviewing the instructions given in this book. Most of them fit all people. But many do not, especially those involving letter writing. To determine which do not, you must study the differences among cultures, for cultural differences are at the root of the exceptions. In addition, you must look at the special problems that our language presents to those who use it as a second language. It is around these two problem areas that this review of international business communication is organized.

> Cross-cultural communication involves understanding cultural differences and overcoming language problems.

## PROBLEMS OF CULTURAL DIFFERENCES

A study of the role of culture in international communication properly begins with two qualifying statements. First, culture is often improperly assumed to be the cause of miscommunication. Often it is confused with the other human elements involved. We must remember that communication between people of different cultures involves the same problems of human behavior that are involved when people of the same culture communicate. In either case, people can be belligerent, arrogant, prejudiced, insensitive, or biased. The miscommunication these types of behavior cause is not a product of culture.

> Two qualifying statements begin this study of culture: (1) It is improperly blamed for some miscommunication.

Second, one must take care not to overgeneralize the practices within a culture. We say this even though some of the statements we make in the following paragraphs are overgeneralized. But we have little choice. In covering the subject, it is necessary to make generalizations such as "Latin Americans do this" or "Arabs do that" in order to emphasize a point. But the truth of the matter is that in all cultures, subcultures are present; and what may be the practice in one segment of a culture may be unheard of by other segments. Within a culture townspeople differ from country dwellers, the rich differ from the poor, and the educated differ from the uneducated. Clearly, the subject of culture is highly complex and should not be reduced to simple generalizations. Keep this point in mind as you read the following material.

> (2) It is easy to overgeneralize cultural practices.

Culture has been defined in many ways. The definition most useful in this discussion is one derived from anthropology: *Culture* is "a way of life of a group of people . . . the stereotyped patterns of learning behavior, which are handed down from one generation to the next through the means of language and imitation."[2] In other words, people living in different geographic areas have developed different ways of life. They have developed different habits, different values, and different ways of relating to one another.

> Culture is the way people in an area view human relationships.

These differences are a major source of problems when people of different cultures try to communicate. Unfortunately, people tend to view the ways of

> Two major kinds of cultural differences affect communication.

---

[1] Sondra Thiederman, *Bridging Cultural Barriers for Corporate Success: How to Manage the Multicultural Work Force* (Lexington, Massachusetts: Lexington Books, 1991), p. xviii.

[2] V. Barnouw, *Culture and Personality* (Chicago: Dorsey Press, 1963), p. 4.

Today's business executives must understand and respect the cultures of the people with whom they deal. When they do not, miscommunication is the result.

their culture as normal and the ways of other cultures as bad, wrong, peculiar, or such. Specifically, communication between people of different cultures is affected by two major kinds of differences: (1) differences in body positions and movements and (2) differences in attitudes toward various factors of human relationships (time, space, intimacy, and so on).

## Body Positions and Movements

At first thought, one might think that the positions and movements of the body are much the same for all people. But such is not the case. These positions and movements differ by culture, and the differences can affect communication. For example, in our culture most people sit when they wish to remain in one place for some time, but in much of the world people hunker (squat). Because we do not hunker, we tend to view hunkering as primitive. This view obviously affects our communication with people who hunker, for what we see when we communicate is a part of the message. But how correct is this view? Actually, hunkering is a very normal body position. Our children hunker quite naturally—until their elders teach them to sit. Who is to say that sitting is more advanced or better?

For another example, people from our culture who visit certain Asian countries are likely to view the fast, short steps taken by the inhabitants as peculiar or funny and to view our longer strides as normal. And when people from our culture see the inhabitants of these countries bow on meeting and

Body positions and movements differ among cultures. For example, in some cultures, people sit; in other cultures, they hunker.

Manners of walking differ among cultures.

CHAPTER 19 Special Topic: Techniques of Cross-Cultural Communication 647

leaving each other, they are likely to interpret the bowing as a sign of subservience or weakness. Similarly, people from our culture see standing up as the appropriate thing to do on certain occasions (as when someone enters the room) whereas people from some other cultures do not.

> Communication with body parts (hands, arms, head, etc.) varies by culture.

As you know, movements of certain body parts (especially the hands) are a vital form of human communication. Some of these movements have no definite meaning even within a culture. But some have clear meanings, and these meanings may differ by culture. To us an up-and-down movement of the head means yes and a side-to-side movement of the head means no. These movements may mean nothing at all or something quite different to people from cultures in which thrusting the head forward, raising the eyebrows, jerking the head to one side, or lifting the chin are used to convey similar meanings. For another example, the two-fingered "victory" sign is as clear to us as any of our hand signs. To an Australian, whose culture is not vastly different from ours, the sign has a most vulgar meaning. The "OK" sign is terribly rude and insulting in such diverse places as Russia, Germany, and Brazil.[3] In Japan, a similar sign represents money. If a businessperson completing a contract gave this sign, the Japanese might think they needed to give more money, perhaps even a bribe. Even the widely used "thumbs up" sign for "things are going well" could get you into trouble in countries from Nigeria to Australia.[4] And so it is with many of our other body movements. They differ widely, even within cultures.

> Eye movements differ by culture.

The movements of our eyes also vary by culture. We in North America are taught to look our audience in the eye in formal speechmaking. In informal talking, however, we are encouraged to look but not stare. Although not everyone in our culture conforms to these standards, we regard them as desirable. In cultures such as Indonesia, looking at people, especially those older or in higher positions, is considered to be disrespectful. On the other hand, our practices of eye contact are not so rigorous as with the British and Germans. Unless one understands these cultural differences, how one looks or does not look can be interpreted as being impolite on the one hand and being shy on the other.

> So do touching and handshaking.

Touching and particularly handshaking differences are important to understand. This is made difficult by others adopting Western greetings. However, some cultures, like the Chinese, do not like touching much and will give a handshake you might perceive as weak while other cultures not only like it but will give you such greetings ranging from full embraces and kisses to nose rubbing. If you can avoid judging others from different cultures on their greeting based on your standards for others like you, you can seize the opportunity to access the cultural style of the worker. Here are some types of handshakes.[5]

---

[3] Roger E. Axtell, *Gestures: The Do's and Taboos of Body Language Around the World* (New York: John Wiley & Sons, Inc., 1991), p. 41.

[4] Axtell, pp. 47–50.

[5] Thiederman, p. 138.

| Handshakes | |
|---|---|
| Americans | Firm |
| Germans | Brusk, firm, repeated upon arrival and departure |
| French | Light, quick, not offered to superiors, repeated upon arrival and departure |
| British | Soft |
| Hispanics | Moderate grasp, repeated frequently |
| Middle Easterners | Gentle, repeated frequently |
| Asians | Gentle; for some, shaking hands is unfamiliar and uncomfortable (an exception to this is the Korean, who generally has a firm handshake) |

In our culture, smiles are viewed positively in most situations. But in some other cultures (notably African cultures), a smile is regarded as a sign of weakness in certain situations (such as bargaining). Receiving a gift or touching with the left hand is a serious breach of etiquette among Muslims, for they view the left hand as unclean. We attach no such meaning to the left hand. And so it is with other body movements—arching the eyebrows, positioning the fingers, raising the arms, and many more. All cultures use body movements in communicating, but in different ways.

• A smile can be a sign of weakness, and the left hand may be taboo.

### Attitudes toward Factors of Human Relationships

Probably causing even more miscommunication than differences in body positions and movements are the different attitudes of different cultures toward various factors of human relationships. For illustrative purposes, we will review seven major factors: time, space, odors, frankness, relationships, values, and social behavior.

• Differing attitudes toward various factors of human relationships cause communication problems.

**Time.** In our culture, people tend to regard time as something that must be planned for the most efficient use. They strive to meet deadlines, to be punctual, to conduct business quickly, and to work on a schedule.

• Views about time differ widely. Some cultures stress punctuality; some do not.

---

### A Classic Defense of Cultural Difference

The classic "ugly American" was traveling in a faraway land. He had been critical of much of what he experienced—the food, the hotels, the customs in general. One day he came upon a funeral. He observed that the mourners placed food on the grave—and left it there.

"What a stupid practice!" he exclaimed to his native host. "Do your people actually think that the dead person will eat the food?"

At this point, the host had taken all the insults he could handle for one day. So he replied, "Our dead will eat the food as soon as your dead smell the flowers you place on their graves."

In some other cultures (especially those of the Middle East and some parts of Asia), people view time in a more relaxed way. They see planning as unwise and unnecessary. Being late to a meeting, a social function, or such is of little consequence to them. In fact, some of them hold the view that important people should be late to show that they are busy. In business negotiations, the people in these cultures move at a deliberately slow pace, engaging in casual talk before getting to the main issue. It is easy to see how such different views of time could cause people from different cultures to have serious miscommunication problems.

> Space is viewed differently by different cultures. In some cultures, people want to be far apart; in other cultures, they want to be close.

**Space.** People from different cultures often vary in their attitudes toward space. North Americans tend to prefer about two feet or so of distance between themselves and those with whom they speak. But in some cultures (some Arabian and South American cultures), people stand closer to each other; not following this practice is considered impolite. For another example, North Americans view personal space as a right and tend to respect this right of others; thus, they stand in line and wait their turn. People from some other cultures view space as belonging to all. Thus, they jostle for space when boarding trains, standing at ticket counters, shopping in stores, and such. In encounters between people whose cultures have such different attitudes toward space, actions are likely to be misinterpreted.

> Some cultures view body odors as bad; others view them as normal.

**Odors.** People from different cultures may have different attitudes toward body odors. To illustrate, Americans work hard to neutralize body odors or cover them up and view those with body odors as dirty and unsanitary. On the other hand, in some Asian cultures people view body odors, not as something to be hidden, but as something that friends should experience. Some of the people from these cultures feel that it is an act of friendship to "breathe the breath" of the person with whom they converse and to feel their presence by smelling. Clearly, encounters between people with such widely differing attitudes could lead to serious miscommunication.

> Some cultures are more direct, more blunt than others.

**Frankness.** North Americans tend to be relatively frank in their relationships with others, quickly getting to the point and perhaps being blunt and sharp in doing so. Asians tend to be far more reticent and sometimes go to great lengths not to offend. Thus, Asians may appear evasive, roundabout, and indecisive to North Americans; and North Americans may appear harsh, impolite, and aggressive to Asians. Telephone customs may be an exception, especially among the Chinese, who tend to end telephone calls abruptly after their purpose has been accomplished. North Americans, on the other hand, tend to move on to friendly talk and clearly prepare the listener for the end of the call.

> Intimacy among people varies in different cultures.

**Relationships.** In many cultures, strict social classes exist, and class status determines how intimately people are addressed and treated in communication. For this reason, a person from such a culture might quiz a person from another culture to determine that person's class status. Questions concerning occupation, income, title, and such might be asked. People from cultures that stress human equality are apt to take offense at such questioning and in fact at the notion of class status. This difference in attitude toward class status is also illustrated by differences in the familiarity of address. Some

Americans are quick to get on a first-name basis. This practice is offensive to people from some other cultures, notably the English and the Germans, who expect such intimate address only from long-standing acquaintances.

Similarly, how people view superior-subordinate relations can vary by culture. The dominant view in Latin America, for example, is of the necessity for a strong boss with weak subordinates doing as the boss directs. In sharp contrast is the somewhat democratic work arrangement of the Japanese in which much of the decision-making is by consensus. Most in our culture view as appropriate an order between these extremes. These widely differing practices have led to major communication problems in joint business ventures involving people from these cultures.

*How people view superior-subordinate relations also differs.*

The role of women varies widely by culture. In North America, we continue to move toward a generally recognized goal of equality. In many Islamic cultures, the role of women is quite different. In our view, the practices of the people of these other cultures suggest severe restriction of rights. In the view of the people of these cultures, their practices are in accord with their religious convictions. They see us as being the ones out of step.

*So does the role of women.*

**Values.** Also differing by culture are our values—how we evaluate the critical matters in life. Americans, for example, have been indoctrinated with the Puritan work ethic. It is the belief that if one puts hard work ahead of pleasure, success will follow. The product of this thinking is an emphasis on planning, working efficiently, and maximizing production. Of course, not all of us subscribe to this ethic, but it is a strong force in the thinking of those in our culture. The prevailing view in some other cultures is quite different. In some, the major concern is for the spiritual and human well-being. The view of work is relaxed, and productivity is, at best, a secondary concern.

*Each culture has different values—concerning such matters as attitude toward work,*

Views about the relationships of employers and employees also may differ by culture. North American workers expect to change companies in their career a number of times; and they expect companies to fire them from time to time. Employees expect to move freely from job to job, and they expect employers to hire and fire as their needs change. Expectations are quite different in some other cultures. In Japan, for example, employment tends to be for a lifetime. The workplace is viewed much like a family with loyalty expected from employees and employer. Differences such as this have caused misunderstandings in American-Japanese joint ventures.

*employee-employer relations,*

How employees view authority is yet another question that cultures view differently. We North Americans generally accept authority, yet we fiercely maintain the rights of the individual. In many third-world cultures, workers accept a subservient role passively. Autocratic rule is expected—even wanted.

*and authority.*

**Social Behavior.** From culture to culture, differences in social behavior develop. To illustrate, in some Asian cultures public displays of affection are strongly frowned upon—in fact, considered crude and offensive. Westerners, on the other hand, accept at least a moderate display of affection. To Westerners, laughter is a spontaneous display of pleasure, but in some cultures (Japanese, for one), laughter can also be a controlled behavior—to be used in certain social situations. Even such emotional displays as sorrow

*Social behavior varies by culture—such as practices concerning affection, laughter, and emotion.*

are influenced by culture. In some Middle Eastern cultures, sorrow is expressed with loud, seemingly uncontrolled wailing. In similar situations, Westerners typically respond with subdued and controlled emotions.

> Included are the degree of animation displayed.

We all have observed the emotion and animation people of the Mediterranean cultures display as they communicate. And we have seen the more subdued communication of others—notably northern Europeans. The first group tends to see the second as disinterested and lacking in friendliness. The second sees the first as excitable, emotional, perhaps even unstable.

> Many more such practices exist.

Many more such practices exist. Some cultures combine business and social pleasure; others do not. Some expect to engage in aggressive bargaining in business transactions; others prefer straightforward dealings. Some talk loudly and with emotion; others communicate orally in a subdued manner. Some communicate with emphasis on economy of expression; others communicate with an abundance of verbiage.

> We must recognize them, look for them, and understand them.

The comparisons could go on and on, for there are countless differences in cultures. But it is not necessary to review them all. What is important is that we recognize their existence, that we look for them, and that we understand them. Always we should guard against using our cultural practices as standards for determining meaning in cross-cultural communication.

### Effects on Business Communication Techniques

> Cultural differences affect communication.

The foregoing examples illustrate only a few of the numerous differences that exist among cultures. Books have been written on the subject. Our objective here is only to establish the point that the differences among cultures affect communication between people of different cultures.

> Our letter-writing techniques are not universally acceptable.

The communication techniques presented in this book should be modified in light of cultural differences, but it is difficult to say how this should be done. You simply have to apply your knowledge of the culture involved to each of these techniques. As noted previously, our correspondence techniques are most likely to require modifications. Saburo Haneda and Hirosuke Shima, two Japanese authorities on the subject, comment on this point in these words: "For international business, Japanese businessmen write mostly in English. But their mother tongue, customs and manners concerning communication in general, and cultural background are so different from those of English-speaking people that they cannot get away from their native ways even when they communicate in English, unless they have thoroughly mastered English and other Western habits of saying things."[6] Haneda and Shima note that in business letters the Japanese tend to follow a traditional pattern of beginning with what appear to be empty greetings and thanks, continuing with lengthy reasons, and concluding with an often ambiguous refusal. The Japanese use a yes answer to signify agreement, whether the original sentence is negative or positive. For example, a response of yes to the question "You are not Chinese, are you?" means "I am

---

[6] Saburo Haneda and Hirosuke Shima, "Japanese Communication Behavior as Reflected in Letter Writing," *Journal of Business Communication* 19 (Winter 1982), p. 19.

### Word Processing, Communications, and Translation: Tools for Improving Communication across Cultures

When you are communicating with those from other cultures, you can use technology to improve the process. Word processing is probably the simplest of these. Many word processing programs are available in other languages. Additionally, if you need to use special characters from other languages, these are also available in some full-featured programs. Here are some characters and symbols readily available to you.

## Multinational

`  ~  ̦  ´  Æ  ç  Ö  ˆ  ˏ  ˎ  ʼ  ˇ

## Japanese

あ　う　お　や　よ　か　あ　ば　ネ

## Greek

Α　Γ　Δ　Θ　λ　μ　Σ　Ω　ή

With communications software, you can access computers networked to others around the world. This feature alone allows you to communicate through E-mail with those in different time zones. You can also access bulletin boards and conferences where the participants come from all parts of the globe. Topics of interest to a global audience vary widely from agriculture, to the environment, to science and medicine.

Another tool for communicating with those speaking other languages is translation software. While the current reviews of this software report tremendous improvements, it still has a way to go before being perfect. These programs have limited ability to translate idioms, slang, jargon, and technical terms. Pepsi's slogan—"Come Alive with Pepsi"—translates roughly into Chinese as "Come out of the Grave with Pepsi." However, many of these programs are purported to be excellent for helping your learn to read and write in another language. Software with audio capability will help you learn to pronounce unfamiliar words from other languages.

These tools represent a sampling of the programs that will enhance your ability to communicate across cultural and language barriers. Using these tools not only will help you do business with those from other cultures, they will help you understand your customers from other cultures better.

not." Haneda and Shima also point out that the Japanese culture frowns on the hard-sell American style of sales writing. For this reason alone, much that is acceptable in our business communication must be modified for Japanese readers.

Cultural differences even cause communication problems among people using the same language. For example, even though the United States and other countries have a common language, communication problems occur between them. Such small differences as calling an elevator a *lift* or the hood of a car a *bonnet* can be very confusing. Just telling time with a 24-hour clock can be very confusing. The Canadian who told you he fell asleep at *22:00* on the *chesterfield* can be easily misunderstood.

Without question, cultural differences can cause communication problems. But there is a way to overcome those problems. You can become a student of cultures—that is, you can learn about the cultures of the people with whom you communicate. In doing so, you must take care not to overgeneralize or oversimplify, for cultural differences are highly complex. There are many variations and exceptions within cultures. You must also take care not to exaggerate the effects of cultural differences. Not all miscommunication between people of different cultures results from cultural differences. This effort is not easy, and it will never be completely successful, but it is the only solution available.

- These techniques do not work with all English-speaking people.
- Overcome communication problems stemming from cultural differences by learning about cultures.

## ■■■■■■■■■■■■■■■
## PROBLEMS OF LANGUAGE

The people on earth use more than 3,000 languages. Because few of us can learn more than one or two other languages well, problems of miscommunication are bound to occur in international communication.

- Communication problems are caused by the existence of many languages.

### Lack of Language Equivalency

Unfortunately, wide differences among languages make precisely equivalent translations difficult. One reason for such differences is that languages are based on the concepts, experiences, views, and such of the cultures that developed them. And different cultures have different concepts, experiences, views, and such. For example, we think of a *florist* as someone who sells flowers and related items in a store. In some cultures, however, flowers are sold by street vendors, mainly women and children. Obviously, our *florist* does not have a precise equivalent in the language of such cultures. Similarly, our *supermarket* has no equivalent in some languages. The French have no word to distinguish between *house* and *home, mind* and *brain,* and *man* and *gentleman*. The Spanish have no word to distinguish between a *chairman* and a *president* while the Italians have no word for *wishful thinking*. And Russians have no words for *efficiency, challenge,* and *having fun*. However, the Italians have nearly 500 words for types of macaroni, and the Eskimos have over 100 words for types of snow. And so it is with words for many other objects, actions, concepts, and such (for example, *roundup, interview, strike, tough, monopoly, domestic, feminine, responsible, aloof*).

Another explanation for the lack of language equivalency is the grammatical and syntactic differences among languages. Some languages (Urdu,

- Differences among languages make equivalent translations difficult.

- Grammar and syntax differences add to the difficulty.

PART 7  Special Topics in Business Communication

William Essery, CEO for Sprint, views the world as his company's market. Like all global business operations, Sprint will need to overcome the problems of language differences as it expands operations.

for example) have no gerunds, and some have no adverbs and/or adjectives. Not all languages deal with verb mood, voice, and tense in the same way. The obvious result is that even the best translators often cannot find literal equivalents between languages.

Adding to these equivalency problems is the problem of multiple word meanings. Like English, other languages have more than one meaning for many words. Think, for example, of our numerous meanings for the simple word *run* (to move fast, to compete for office, a score in baseball, a break in a stocking, a fading of colors, and many more). Or consider the multiple meanings of such words as *fast, cat, trip, gross, ring,* and *make*. The Oxford English Dictionary uses over 15,000 words to define *what*. Unless one knows a language well, it is difficult to know which of the meanings is intended.

• So do the multiple meanings of words.

Overcoming such language problems is difficult. The best way, of course, is to know more than one language well; but the competence required is beyond the reach of most of us. Thus, your best course is first to be aware that translation problems exist and then to ask questions—to probe—to determine what the other person understands. For very important oral messages, documents, or such, you might consider using a procedure called *back translating*. This procedure involves using two translators, one with first-language skills in one of the languages involved and one with first-language skills in the other language. The first translator translates the message into his or her language, and the second translator then translates the message back into the original. If the translations are good, the second translation matches the original.

• Overcome such language problems by knowing languages well and by questioning.

• Use back translating for important communications.

CHAPTER 19 Special Topic: Techniques of Cross-Cultural Communication

## Difficulties in Using English

**English is the primary language of international business.**

Fortunately for us, English is the primary language of international business. This is not to say that other languages are not used in international business, for they are. When business executives from different countries have a common language, whatever it may be, they are likely to use it. For example, an executive from Iraq and an executive from Saudi Arabia would communicate with each other in Arabic, for Arabic is their common language. For the same reason, an executive from Venezuela would use Spanish in dealing with an executive from Mexico. However, when executives have no common language, they are likely to use English. The members of the European Free Trade Association conduct all their business in English even though not one of them is a native English speaker. And when a Swiss company and a Swedish company merged, they decided to make English the official company language.[7]

**But many foreigners have problems using English.**

Although we can take comfort from knowing that ours is the primary language of international business, we must keep in mind that it is not the primary language of many of those who use it. Since many of these users have had to learn English as a second language, they are likely to use it less fluently than we and to experience problems in understanding us. Some of their more troublesome problems are reviewed in the following pages.

**Two-word verbs are hard for foreigners to understand,**

**Two-Word Verbs.** One of the most difficult problems to nonnative speakers of English involves the use of two-word verbs. By *two-word verbs* we mean a wording consisting of (1) a verb and (2) a second element that, combined with the verb, produces a meaning that the verb alone does not have. For example, take the verb *break* and the word *up*. When combined, they have a meaning quite different from the meanings the words have alone. And look how the meaning changes when the same verb is combined with other words: *break away, break out, break in, break down*. Dictionaries are of little help to nonnatives who are seeking the meanings of these word combinations.

**as in these combinations.**

There are many two-word verbs—so many, in fact, that a special dictionary of them has been compiled.[8] Following are a few of them arranged by the more common words that combine with the verbs:

| **VERB PLUS "AWAY"** | **VERB PLUS "BACK"** |
|---|---|
| give away | cut back |
| keep away | feed back |
| lay away | keep back |
| pass away | play back |
| put away | read back |
| throw away | take back |

---

[7] Bill Bryson, *The Mother Tongue: English & How it Got That Way* (New York: William Morrow and Company, Inc., 1990), p. 12.

[8] George A. Meyer, *The Two-Word Verb* (The Hague, Netherlands: Mouton, 1975).

turn back
win back

**VERB PLUS "DOWN"**
calm down
die down
hand down
keep down
let down
lie down
mark down
pin down
play down
put down
run down
shut down
sit down
wear down

**VERB PLUS "IN"**
cash in
cave in
close in
dig in
give in
run in
take in
throw in

**VERB PLUS "OFF"**
break off
brush off
buy off
check off
clear off
cool off
cut off
finish off
let off
mark off
pay off
run off
send off
show off

shut off
sound off
start off
take off
write off

**VERB PLUS "OUT"**
blow out
clean out
clear out
crowd out
cut out
die out
dry out
even out
figure out
fill out
find out
give out
hold out
lose out
pull out
rule out
tire out
wear out
work out

**VERB PLUS "OVER"**
check over
do over
hold over
pass over
put over
run over
stop over
take over
talk over
think over
win over

**VERB PLUS "UP"**
blow up
build up
call up

catch up
cover up
dig up
end up
fill up
get up
hang up
hold up
keep up
look up
mix up
pick up
save up
shake up
shut up

slow up
split up
wrap up

**VERB PLUS MISCELLANEOUS WORDS**

bring about
catch on
get across
pass on
put across
put forth
roll over
set forth
stop over

*Use two-word verbs sparingly. Find substitutes, as shown here.*

Of course, foreigners studying English learn some of these word combinations, for they are part of the English language. But many of them are not covered in language textbooks or listed in dictionaries. It is apparent that we should use these word combinations sparingly when communicating with nonnative speakers of English. Whenever possible, we should substitute for them words that appear in standard dictionaries. Following are some two-word verbs and suggested substitutes:

| **TWO-WORD VERBS** | **SUGGESTED SUBSTITUTES** |
|---|---|
| give up | surrender |
| speed up, hurry up | accelerate |
| go on, keep on | continue |
| put off | defer |
| take off | depart, remove |
| come down | descend |
| go in, come in, get in | enter |
| go out, come out, get out | exit, leave |
| blow up | explode |
| think up | imagine |
| figure out | solve |
| take out, take away | remove |
| go back, get back, be back | return |

*Some two-word verbs have noun and adjective forms. Use these sparingly.*

Additional problems result from the fact that some two-word verbs have noun and adjective forms. These also tend to confuse nonnatives using English. Examples of such nouns are *breakthrough, cover-up, drive-in, hookup, show-off,* and *sit-in.* Examples of such adjectives are *going away* (a going-away gift), *cover-up* (cover-up tactics), *cleanup* (cleanup work), and *turning-off* (turning-off place). Fortunately, some nouns and adjectives of this kind are commonly used and appear in standard dictionaries (words such as *hookup, feedback, breakthrough, lookout,* and *takeover*). In writing

"When I said, 'Hit him with the figures,' I meant 'show him the ledger.'"

to nonnative readers, you will need to use sparingly those that do not appear in standard dictionaries.

**Culturally Derived Words.** Words derived from our culture also present problems. The most apparent are the slang expressions that continually come into and go out of use. Some slang expressions catch on and find a place in our dictionaries (*brunch, hobo, blurb, bogus*). But most are with us for a little while and then are gone. Examples of such short-lived slang expressions are the "twenty-three skiddoo" and "oh you kid" of the 1920s and the *ritzy, scram, natch, lousy, soused, all wet, hep, in the groove,* and *tops* of following decades. More recent ones that are probably destined for the same fate include *nerd, wimp, earth pig, pig out, waldo, squid, grimbo,* and *dexter*.

Culturally derived words, especially slang, cause problems.

Most slang words are not in dictionaries or on the word lists that non-English speaking people study to learn English. The obvious conclusion is that you should not use slang in cross-cultural communication.

So avoid slang.

Similar to and in fact overlapping slang are the words and expressions that we derive from our various activities—sports, social affairs, work, and the like. Sports especially have contributed such words, many of which are so widely used that they are part of our everyday vocabulary. From football we have *kickoff, goal-line stand,* and *over the top*. Baseball has given us *out in left field, strike out, touch base, off base, right off the bat, a steal, squeeze play, balk,* and *go to bat for*. From boxing we have *knockout, down for the count, below the belt, answer the bell,* and *on the ropes*. From other sports and from sports in general we have *jock, ace, par, stymie, from scratch, ballpark figure,* and *get the ball rolling*.

Words derived from sports, social activities, and so on cause problems.

Similar to these words and expressions are words and expressions developed within our culture (colloquialisms). Some of these have similar meanings in other cultures, but most are difficult for foreigners to understand. Following are some examples:

Colloquialisms also cause problems.

| | |
|---|---|
| head for home | in the groove |
| have an itching palm | nuts (crazy) |
| grasp at straws | grand (thousand) |
| flat-footed | circle the wagons |
| on the beam | shoot from the hip |
| out to pasture | tuckered out |
| sitting duck | gumption |
| crying in his beer | tote (carry) |
| in orbit | in a rut |
| a honey | pump priming |
| a flop | make head or tail of it |
| dope (crazy) | tearjerker |
| hood (gangster) | countdown |
| up the creek without a paddle | shortcut |
| a fish out of water | educated guess |
| a chicken with its head cut off | |

**We use such words in everyday communication. But avoid them in international correspondence.**

If you are like most of us, many of these words and expressions are a part of your vocabulary. You use them in your everyday communicating, which is all right. They are colorful, and they can communicate clearly to those who understand them. Nonnative English speakers are not likely to understand them, however, so you will need to eliminate such words and expressions in communicating with them. You will need to use words that are clearly defined in the dictionaries that these people are likely to use in translating your message. Following are some examples:

| NOT THIS | BUT THIS |
|---|---|
| We were caught flat-footed. | We were surprised. |
| He frequently shoots from the hip. | He frequently acts before he thinks. |
| We would be up the creek without a paddle. | We would be in a helpless situation. |
| They couldn't make heads or tails of the report. | They couldn't understand the report. |
| The sales campaign was a flop. | The sales campaign was a failure. |
| I'll touch base with you on this problem in August. | I'll talk with you about this problem in August. |
| Take an educated guess on this question. | Answer this question to the best of your knowledge. |
| Your sales report put us in orbit. | Your sales report pleased us very much. |
| We will wind down manufacturing operations in November. | We will end manufacturing operations in November. |
| Your prediction was right on the beam. | Your prediction was correct. |

## A General Suggestion

**Use simple, basic English.**

In addition to the specific suggestions for improving your communication in English with nonnative English speakers, you should follow one general suggestion: talk (or write) simply and clearly. Talk slowly and enunciate each word. Remember that as most of these people learned English in school, they are acquainted mainly with primary dictionary meanings and are not likely to understand slang words or shades of difference in the meanings we give words. Thus, they will understand you better if you use simple, basic English.

## SUMMARY (by Chapter Objectives)

1. Businesses are becoming increasingly global in their operations.
   - Being able to communicate across cultures is necessary in these operations.
   - Specifically, it helps in gaining additional business, in hiring good people, and generally in understanding and satisfying the needs of customers.

2. *Culture* may be defined as "the way of life of a group of people."
   - Cultures differ.
   - People tend to view the practices of their culture as right and those of other cultures as peculiar or wrong.
   - These views cause miscommunication.

3. Variations in how people of different cultures use body positions and body movements is a cause of miscommunication.
   - How people walk, gesture, smile, and such varies from culture to culture.
   - When people from different cultures attempt to communicate, each may not understand the other's body movements.

4. People in different cultures differ in their ways of relating to people.
   - Specifically, they differ in their practices and thinking concerning time, space, odors, frankness, relationships, values, and social behavior.
   - We should not use our culture's practices as standards for determining meaning.
   - Instead, we should try to understand the other culture.

5. Language problems are another major cause of miscommunication in international communication.
   - About 3,000 languages are used on earth.
   - They differ greatly in grammar and syntax.
   - Like English, most have words with multiple meanings.
   - As a result, equivalency in translation is difficult.

6. Overcoming the language equivalency problem involves hard and tedious work.
   - The best advice is to master the language of the nonnative English speakers with whom you communicate.
   - Also, you should be aware of the problems caused by language differences.
   - Ask questions to make sure you are understood.
   - For important communications, consider back translation—the technique of using two translators, the first to translate from one language to the other and the second to translate back to the original.

1. Explain why communicating clearly across cultures is important to business.

2. Define culture and explain its effects on cross-cultural communication.

3. Describe cultural differences in body positions and movements and use this knowledge effectively in communicating across cultures.

4. Describe cultural differences in attitudes toward time, space, odors, and such and use this knowledge effectively in communicating across cultures.

5. Explain the language equivalency problem as a cause of miscommunication.

6. Describe what one can do to overcome the language equivalency problem.

## QUESTIONS FOR DISCUSSION

1. "Just as our culture has advanced in its technological sophistication, it has advanced in the sophistication of its body signals, gestures, and attitudes toward time, space, and such. Thus, the ways of our culture are superior to those of most other cultures." Discuss this view.

2. What are the prevailing attitudes in our culture toward the following, and how can those attitudes affect our communication with foreigners? Discuss.

   a. Bargaining (selling) methods
   b. Truth in advertising
   c. Company-worker loyalty
   d. Women's place in society

3. Some of our letter-writing techniques are said to be unacceptable to people from such cultures as those of Japan and England.

   a. Which techniques in particular do you think would be most inappropriate in these cultures?
   b. Why?

4. Think of English words (other than text examples) that probably do not have a precise equivalent in some other culture. Tell how you would attempt to explain each of these words to a person from that culture.

5. Select a word with at least five meanings. List those meanings and tell how you would communicate each of them to a foreigner.

6. From newspapers or magazines, find and bring to class 10 sentences containing words and expressions that a nonnative English speaker would not be likely to understand. Rewrite the sentences for this reader.

7. Is conversational style appropriate in writing to foreign readers? Discuss.

## APPLICATION EXERCISES

Instructions: Rewrite the following sentences for a nonnative English speaker.

1. Last year our laboratory made a breakthrough in design that really put sales in orbit.

2. You will need to pin down Mr. Wang to put across the need to tighten up expenses.

3. Recent losses have us on the ropes now, but we expect to get out of the hole by the end of the year.

4. We will kick off the advertising campaign in February, and in April we will bring out the new products.

5. Jamison gave us a ballpark figure on the project, but I think he is ready to back down from his estimate.

6. We will back up any of our products that are not up to par.

7. Mr. Maghrabi managed to straighten out and become our star salesperson.

8. Now that we have cut back on our advertising, we will have to build up our personal selling.

9. If you want to improve sales, you should stay with your prospects until they see the light.

10. We should be able to bring about a saving of about 8 or 10 grand.

# CHAPTER 20

# PHYSICAL PRESENTATION OF LETTERS, MEMOS, AND REPORTS

## CHAPTER OBJECTIVES

*Upon completing this chapter, you will be able to produce business letters, memos, and reports using good form. To reach this goal, you should be able to*

**1**

Determine the appropriate layout, type, and media for business documents.

**2**

Select and construct an effective layout for business letters.

**3**

Explain the requirements of each part of a business letter.

**4**

Identify the elements of a memorandum heading.

**5**

Use business-letter form in writing letter reports and conventional memorandum form in writing memorandum reports.

**6**

Construct all the parts of a formal report.

## INTRODUCTORY SITUATION

### to the Effects of Appearance on Communications

Assume that you are a clerk in the distribution department of Behemoth Manufacturing Company. Your main job is to route the company's written communications to the proper people. You handle both letters coming in and internal memorandums and reports. Thus, you see a wide range of communications, and you have become a good judge of what you see. Most of the communications you see are neat and in good form. You are favorably impressed by such professional work, and so, you feel, are the readers. But you also see bad work. Take the letter from a Brown Company salesperson that you are looking at now. The message is printed far off-center, and misspelled words appear here and there. The type is so light that you have to strain your eyes to read it. Apparently, the printer ribbon needed changing. Even the folding is messy—creases not parallel and balanced.

Not all the bad work comes from the outside. A good example is the report you just routed, which your friend Mildred Ridgeway wrote. The report was probably well written, for she is a highly competent person. But it was messy and in questionable form. Surely its appearance will reflect unfavorably on Mildred's work.

As it is clear to you that what people see is a part of the message they receive, you wonder why writers permit work like this to represent them. Perhaps such writers would profit by studying the review of letter, memo, and report form presented in this chapter. Most certainly, a knowledge of form would help them get the best possible results from their writing. ■

The appearance of a letter, memo, or report plays a significant role in communicating the message. Attractively displayed messages reflect favorably on the writer and the writer's company. They give an impression of competence and care; and they build credibility for the writer. Their attractiveness tells the readers that the writer thinks they are important and deserving of a good-looking document. On the other hand, sloppy work reflects unfavorably on the writer, the company, and the message itself. Thus, you should want your messages to be attractively displayed. The following review of the basics of document preparation along with specifics for letters, memos, and reports should help you achieve this result.

*The appearance of your reports and letters affects your readers' response to them.*

## BASICS FOR ALL DOCUMENT PREPARATION

All documents you present will include decisions on layout, type, and media. Your choices may vary depending on the circumstances and the nature of the document you are writing. Nevertheless, these decisions are common to all business documents.

*Document preparation requires decisions on layout, type, and media.*

### Layout

Common layout decisions involve grids, spacing, and margins. Grids are the nonprinted horizontal and vertical lines which determine placement of your document on the page. They allow you to plan the placement of your text and graphics on the page for consistency. The examples shown in Figure 20–1 illustrate the placement of text on two-, three-, and six-column grids. You can readily see how important it is to plan for this element. Many full-

*Layout decisions concern placement, spacing, and margins. Your software helps in determining good placement.*

**CHAPTER 20** Special Topic: Physical Presentation of Letters, Memos, and Reports

**FIGURE 20–1** Layout Illustrations on Different Grids

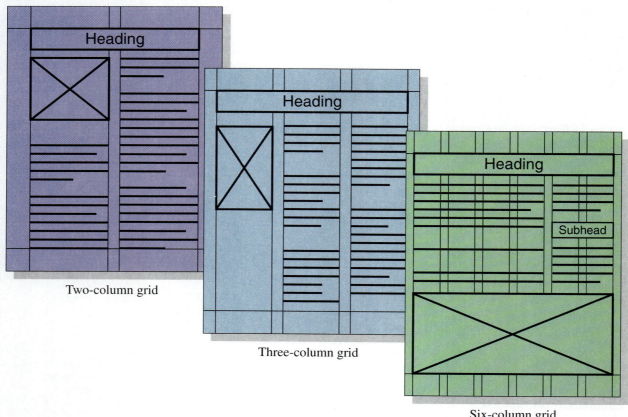

Two-column grid

Three-column grid

Six-column grid

featured word processing software programs allow you to define columns and the space between them. As you create your text, it will flow from column to column. Desktop publishing software, on the other hand, works a bit differently. You can ask it to show you the grid on the screen as well as control where the text flows.

To make your document look its best, you must consider both external and internal spacing. External spacing is the white space—the space some never think about carefully. Just as space denotes importance in writing, white space denotes importance. Surrounding text or a graphic with white spaces sets it apart, emphasizing it to the reader. Used effectively, white space has also been shown to increase the readability of your documents, giving your readers' eyes a rest. Ideally, white space should be a careful part of the design of your document.

Internal spacing refers to both the vertical and horizontal spacing (see Chapter 18 for additional discussion). The spacing between letters on a line is called kerning. With desktop publishing software and some word processing software, you can adjust how close the letters are to each other. This software also allows you to adjust how close the lines are to each other

**Plan the external and internal spacing (white space) for best effect.**

**Consider effects of spacing between letters (kerning) and between lines (leading).**

PART 7 Special Topics in Business Communication

**FIGURE 20-2** Illustrations of Different Forms of Justification

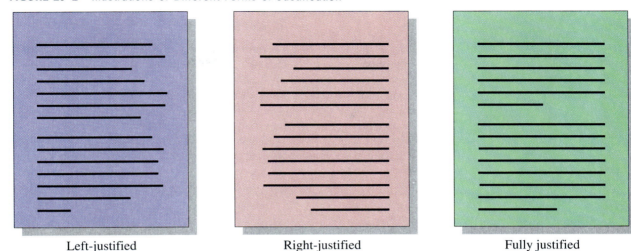

vertically, called leading. Currently, many are still referring to spacing in business documents as single or double spaced. However, this is a carryover from the typewriter era when a vertical line space was always ⅙ inch or when six lines equaled an inch. Today's software and hardware let you control this aspect of your document as well. Deciding on the best spacing to use is dependent on the typeface you decide to use. In any case, you need to make a conscious decision about the spacing aspect of the layout of your documents.

Another aspect of layout is your margin settings. Ideally, you should like your document to look like a framed picture. This arrangement calls for all margins to be equal. However, some businesses use a fixed margin on all documents regardless of their length. Some do this to line up with design features on their letterhead; others believe it increases productivity. In either case, the side margins will be equal. And with today's software you easily make your top and bottom margins equal by telling the software to center the document vertically on the page. Although all margins will not be equal, the page will still have horizontal and vertical balance.

Today's software also has the capability to align your type at the margins or in the center. This is called *justification*. Left justification aligns every line at the left, right justification aligns every line at the right, full justification aligns every line at both the left and the right (see Figure 20-2). Unless you are using a proportional font, full justification takes the extra spaces between the last word and the right margin and distributes them across the line. This adds extra white spaces across the line, stopping most readers' eyes a bit. Therefore, it is usually best to set a left-justified margin and ignore the resulting ragged right margin. However, if your document's right margin is distracting, you may want to turn on the hyphenation feature. Your software will then hyphenate words at the end of lines, smoothing the raggedness of the right margin.

> Ideally, the margins should appear as a picture frame.

> Your software provides margin justification choices.

## Type: An Instrument for Producing Professional-Looking Documents

Type plays a major part in how your documents are received by your readers. Paying attention to its subtleties and using the power of your word processor enables you to produce a truly professional-looking type for your documents. Many of the items on the checklist below are common sense, but several may directly contradict what you were taught in a typing class. However, your word processor is far more than a typewriter ever could be. By combining its power with the techniques professional typesetters have long used, your documents will be greatly enhanced. Here are some tips you can begin to use on the letters and reports you create.

- Select the type font with the reader and context in mind. Proportional fonts are usually preferred to the monospaced fonts, which emulate typewriters.
- Choose a font with a purpose in mind. Serif fonts are best for body text since they are more readable; sans serif fonts are best for headings since they are more legible. You will also want to consider what is pleasing and what works best in the context your document will be read.
- Avoid using more than two different fonts in one document unless you have a good design eye and a specific purpose.
- Use the same font, size, and leading for all your body text.
- Select the type style for readability. Avoid long blocks of all caps, italics, or bold for they are difficult to read.
- Use only left-justified text for smoother reading. If your right margin appears too ragged, turn on the hyphenation feature.
- Use the optimum line length of 30 to 70 characters whenever it is appropriate.
- Use kerning when it makes your text look better. For example, see the difference between the following: Time (not kerned) and Time (kerned). The need for kerning is usually most obvious in titles and heading where font size is larger than body text.
- Leave more space above a heading than below it for readability. Use headings liberally to help readers easily find what they are looking for.
- Use type style to give readers visual cues for organization. Be consistent for heading levels and for body text.
- Use italics, bold, or larger type size rather than underlining. Lines tend to separate text from the material which to it relates. If you must underline, use the line draw feature rather than the underline feature. Lines can be varied in thickness and placement and have less of a tendency to interfere with descenders.
- Use one space at the end of sentences. Yes, since you are using proportional rather than monospaced font, you no longer need to give your reader a visual cue other than a period between sentences.
- Use real quotation marks ("and" or 'and') rather than the inch (") and foot (') symbols.

- Use the hyphen, en, and em dashes properly. The hyphen (-) is used to divide words. The en dash (–) is used to separate words indicating a duration such as October–December. It can be used with a thin space on either side of it, but not a full space. Also, use the en dash when you have a compound adjective such as the Chicago–New Orleans flight. The em dash (—) is used to indicate a change in thought where the period is too strong and the comma too weak. Do not use a space on either side of it.
- Create the special characters you need. Most word processing or desktop publishing software provide the ability to create characters such as ®, £, %, ✓, π, and •. Your printer needs to work with your software to use most of these. However, you can also use other features such as superscript and subscript to create type such as $22^{nd}$ or $H_2O$. And you can create items such as $89^{7}/_{16}$ by superscripting the numerator (7) and reducing the font size about 50 percent of the denominator (16). Then use kerning to adjust the horizontal spacing.
- Proofread! Errors in spelling, punctuation, and grammar will ruin even the most perfect type.

Adapted from Daniel Will-Harris, "A Typestyle Primer," *WordPerfect for Windows Magazine*, April 1992, and Robin Williams, *The PC Is Not a Typewriter: A Style Manual for Creating Professional-Level Type on Your PC* (Berkeley, Calif.: Peachpit Press, 1992).

## *Type*

Type is purported to influence the appearance of your document more than any other aspect. You need to make decisions on the typeface, the type style, and the type size. Typeface refers to the font or shape of the characters. Although there are hundreds of fonts available, they are generally classified as *serif* or *sans serif*. Serif typefaces have feet; sans serif do not. You can see this clearly in the examples below.

> Select type faces for effect—such as serif for easy-to-read text and sans serif for headings.

New Century Schoolbook and Times Roman are serif typefaces.
Helvetica and ITC Avant Garde Gothic Book are sans serif typefaces.

Since readers use the visual cues they get from the feet to form the words in their minds, they find the text of documents easier to read if a serif typeface is used. Sans serif typefaces are particularly good for headings where clear, distinct letters are important.

Type style refers to the way the typeface can be modified. The most basic styles include: normal, **bold,** *italic,* and ***bold italic.*** Depending on your software and printer, you may have other options such as *outline* or *shadow.* You will usually decide to use modifications for specific reasons. For example, you may want all actions you want the reader to take to appear in boldface type. Or you may decide to apply different styles to different levels

> Style refers to type modification, such as normal, bold, italic, outline, shadow.

of headings. In any case, use of type styles should be planned, not random or haphazard.

Finally, you will need to decide on size of type. Type is measured in points. Characters one inch high are 72 points. While this is a standard measure, different typefaces in the same size often appear to be a different size. You need to consider your typeface in choosing size for your documents. Generally, body text is between 9 and 14 points, and headings are 15 points and larger.

*Type size is measured in points—72 per inch.*

## Media

The media you choose to transmit your documents also communicates. Most electronic mailboxes today are perceived as an informal medium. But using this medium tells the reader that you are a user of computer technology and may imply that you are also up-to-date in your business. Choosing to send your message by fax may also imply your currency with the technology. However, because you cannot be assured of the quality of the output of the fax at the other end, your document may suffer in appearance due to either print quality or paper quality. By choosing paper as your medium, you will have control over the appearance while relinquishing control over delivery to company and mail delivery systems.

*Transmission by electronic mail, fax, or paper can affect image.*

Today, paper is still the top choice of media. In the United States, standard business paper size is 8½ by 11 inches; in international business its measurements are metric, resulting in paper sized slightly narrower than 8½ inches and slightly longer than 11 inches. Occasionally, half-size (5½ × 8½) or executive size (7¼ × 10½) is used for short messages. Other than these standards, you have a variety of choices to make for color, weight, texture, and such.

*Paper is top choice, usually of standard 8½ × 11-inch size.*

The most conservative color choice is white. Of course, you will find that there are numerous variations of white. In addition, there are all the colors of the palette and many tints of these colors. You want your paper to represent you and your business but not distract your reader from the message. The color you choose for the first page of your document should also be the color you use for the second and continuing pages. This is the color you would usually use for envelopes, too.

*White paper is most conservative, but colors can be effective.*

Some businesses even go so far as to match the color of the paper with the color of their typewriter or printer ink and the color of their postage meter ink. This, of course, communicates to the reader that the writer or company is detail conscious. Such an image would be desirable for accountants or architects where attention to detail is perceived as a positive trait.

*Consider the images color communicates.*

The weight and texture of your paper also communicate. While "cheap" paper may denote control of expenses to one reader, it may denote cost cutting to another. Usually businesses use paper with a weight of 16 to 20 pounds and a rag or cotton content of 25 to 100 percent. The higher the numbers the higher the quality. And, of course, many readers often associate a high-quality paper with a high-quality product or service.

*Paper weight and texture also send a message.*

The choice of medium to use for your documents is important because it, too, sends a message. By being aware of these subtle messages, you will be able to choose the most appropriate medium for your situation.

With the basics taken care of, now we can move on to the specifics for the letter, memo, or report.

*Consider all the messages your medium choice sends.*

## FORM OF BUSINESS LETTERS

The layout of a letter (its shape on the page) accounts for a major part of the impression made by the appearance of the letter. A layout that is too wide, too narrow, too high, too low, or off-center may impress the reader unfavorably.

*Layout accounts for a major part of the impression made by the appearance of a letter.*

### The Ideal Layout

The ideal letter layout is one that has the same shape as the space in which it is formed. It fits that space much as a picture fits a frame (see Figure 20–3). That is, a rectangle drawn around the processed letter has the same shape as the space under the letterhead. The top border of the rectangle is the dateline, the left border is the line beginnings, the right border is the average line length, and the bottom border is the last line of the notations.

*The ideal letter layout is the shape of the space available for typing.*

Ideal layouts take time and are generally used in business only for really important letters or for other letters on which the extra time required can be justified. Sales letters are almost always arranged in this way. After one good design has been worked out, the thousands of other letters can benefit from the effort. In the future, ideal layouts are likely to be used more widely for everyday business correspondence. Improved word processing software will make them easier to construct.

*But such layouts are rarely practical.*

### Fixed Margins

Most offices use a fixed margin for all routine letters. Typically, they use one-inch margins, and they vary the heights of letters by using more or less space, as needed, between the date and the inside address. The arrangements in Figures 20–3, 20–4, 20–5, and 20–6 are typical of these practices.

*Most offices use fixed margins.*

### Format Preferences

As to the format of the layout, any generally recognized one is acceptable. Some people prefer one format or another, and some people even think the format they prefer is the best. You may even have your own preferences. Generally, the most popular formats are block, modified block, and AMS simplified. These are best explained by illustration (see Figures 20–3, 20–4, 20–5, and 20–6). In all formats, single-spacing is the rule for all but very short letters, which are appropriately double-spaced.

*Block and modified block types are the most popular (see Figures 20–3, 20–4, 20–5, and 20–6).*

---

### Roots . . .
### Why Our Conventional Letter Pattern Remains Conventional

Although the ancient Greeks wrote letters in a fixed pattern of salutation and closing, as well as in a standard jargon, the credit for our conventional letter pattern goes to Professor Buoncompagno, Master of Rhetoric at the University of Bologna. In 1231, a trend-setting manual by Professor Buoncompagno established the basic pattern of heading, inside address, salutation, body, complimentary close, and signature that has survived to this day. Perhaps the deep roots of the pattern explain why recent efforts to change it have made slow progress.

**FIGURE 20–3** Modified Block, Blocked Paragraphs, Margins Adjusted to Make Ideal Layout

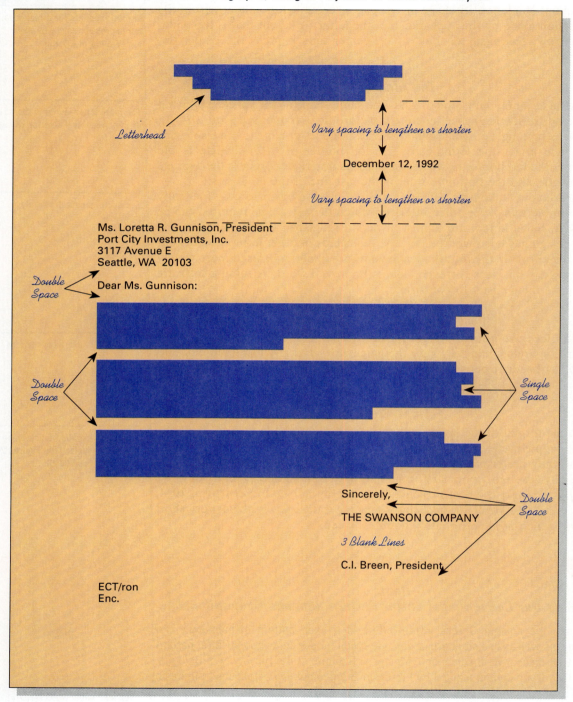

**FIGURE 20–4**  Block Style, Fixed Margins Using Subject Line

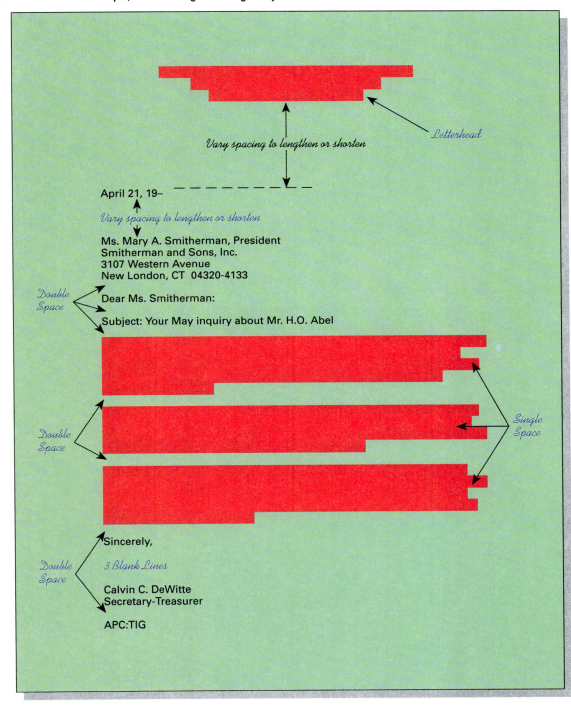

**FIGURE 20–5** Modified Block, Indented Paragraphs, Fixed Margins

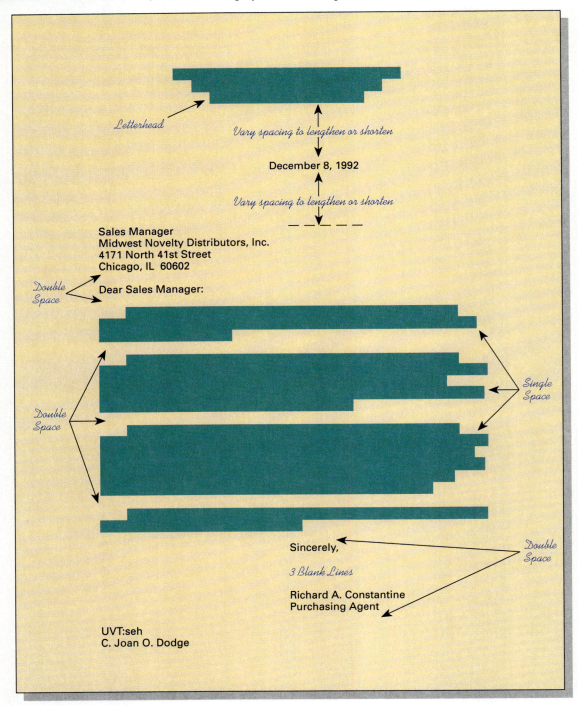

**FIGURE 20-6** AMS Simplified Style

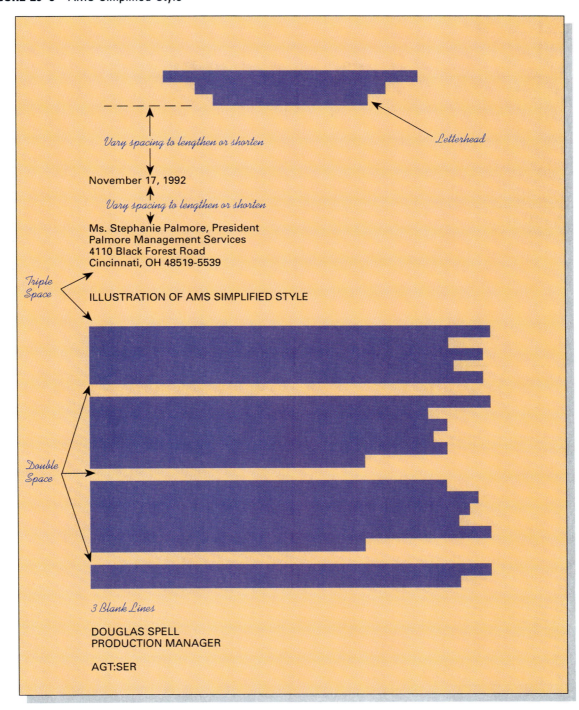

CHAPTER 20 Special Topic: Physical Presentation of Letters, Memos, and Reports

Agreement has not been reached on all the practices for setting up the parts of the letter. The suggestions below, however, follow the bulk of authoritative opinion.

**Dateline.**   You should use the conventional date form, with month, day, and year (December 19, 1992). When you are using a word processor's date feature, be sure to select the appropriate one. If you insert a date code, the date will be updated each time you retrieve the letter. If you use the date text feature, you insert the date the letter was created, and it does not change when you retrieve the letter in the future. Thus, when it is important that you have a record of the date you created the letter, this is the date feature you should use. Abbreviated date forms such as 12-19-92 or Dec. 9, '92 are informal and leave unfavorable impressions on some people. Most word processors allow you to set up your preference and will use that preference when you use the date feature.

> Dateline includes the complete date.
>
> Know and use the date features of your software.

**Return Address.**   In most cases, your return address is printed on the letterhead. However, if you are writing a personal business letter, you would not use your company letterhead. Therefore, you must either create your own letterhead or insert your street address, city, state, and zip single-spaced directly above the dateline. For example, if the rest of the letter were in block form, your return address would also be blocked. Here is how it might look.

> Create a letterhead for nonletterhead paper.

2411 27th Street
Moline, IL 61265
October 22, 1993

**Inside Address.**   The mailing address, complete with the title of the person being addressed, makes up the inside address. Preferably, form it without abbreviations, except for commonly abbreviated words (*Dr., Mr., Mrs., Ms.*).

> The inside address is the mailing address.

**Attention Line.**   Some executives prefer to emphasize the company address rather than the individual offices. Thus, they address the letter to the company in the inside address and then use an attention line to direct the letter to a specific officer or department. The attention line is placed a double space after the inside address and a double space before the salutation. Typical forms of attention lines are as follows:

> Use an attention line to route a letter to the correct reader.

Attention of Mr. Clayton E. Haney, Office Manager
For Ms. Clara Blake, Director
Attention: Mr. William O'Brien, Vice President
Attention, Ms. Edna E. Rubbicon, Sales Manager

**Salutation.**   The salutation you choose should be based on your familiarity with the reader and on the formality of the situation. As a general rule, remember that if the writer and the reader know each other well, the salutation may be by first name (*Dear Joan*). A salutation by last name (*Dear Mr. Baskin*) is appropriate in most cases.

> Select the salutation based on your familiarity with the reader.

If you do not know and cannot find out the name of the person to whom you are sending the letter, use a position title. By directing your letter to Director of Personnel or Public Relations Manager, you are helping your letter reach the appropriate person.

> When name is not known, direct to position title.

The greeting and complimentary close in letters are much like the handshake in face-to-face relations. They are symbols of courtesy developed over the centuries. As such, they serve a worthwhile purpose.

The Administrative Management Society has for some time attempted to eliminate the salutation and the complimentary close (see the example of AMS Simplified Style, Figure 20–6). Although the AMS should be commended for promoting these logical changes, its style has gained only modest support in business.

*AMS style eliminates the salutation and the complimentary close.*

The women's rights movement has sharply reduced the use of *Mrs.* and *Miss.* Why distinguish between married and single women, the group argues, when we make no such distinction between married and single men? The logical solution advanced by this movement is to use *Ms.* for all women, just as *Mr.* is used for all men. If you know that the woman you are writing has another preference, however, you should adhere to that preference.

*Ms. is taking the place of Mrs. and Miss.*

**Mixed or Open Punctuation.** The punctuation following the salutation and the closing is either mixed or open. Mixed punctuation employs a colon after the salutation and a comma after the complimentary close. Open punctuation, on the other hand, uses no punctuation after the salutation and none after the complimentary close. These two forms are used in domestic communication. In international communication, you may see letters with closed punctuation—punctuation distinguished by commas after the lines in the return and inside addresses and a period at the end of the complimentary close.

*Use mixed (colon after salutation and comma after complimentary close) or open (nothing in either place) punctuation.*

**Subject Line.** So that both the sender and the receiver may quickly identify the subject of the correspondence, many offices use the subject line in their

*Subject lines are useful identification parts.*

### So You Think Our Salutations and Closes Are Unnatural? How About These 1595 Examples?

Recommended salutations:

"After my hartie commendation to you" (to an inferior).
"After my hartie commendation unto your Lord" (to a nobleman).

Recommended closes:

"Praying the Almighty to have your Lord evermore in his gracious protection, I humbly take my leave."
"Acknowledging myself deeply bounde unto your Lord for many sundry favours, I do remaine in all humble reverence."
"Finding myselfe many ways beholding unto your exceeding courtesies, I ende."

Source: Angel Day, *The English Secretarie* (London, 1595).

---

letters. As illustrated in Figure 20–4, the subject line tells what the letter is about. In addition, it contains any specific identifying material that may be helpful—date of previous correspondence, invoice number, order number, and the like. It is usually placed a double space below the salutation, though some companies prefer to place it higher—often in the upper right corner of the letter layout. In AMS Simplified Style (Figure 20–6), it appears in all-capital letters after the inside address. The block may be headed in a number of ways, of which the following are representative:

Subject: Your July 2nd inquiry about . . .
In reply, please refer to File H-320.
Reference your October 17 order for . . .
About your order No. 721-A dated . . .

### Second Page Heading.
When the length of a letter must exceed one page, you should set up the following page or pages for quick identification. Always print such pages on plain paper (no letterhead). These two forms are the most common:

Ms. Helen E. Mann                    2                    May 7, 1992

Ms. Helen E. Mann
May 7, 1992
Page 2

*Headings for second and subsequent pages of letters are illustrated here.*

You can use the header feature of your word processing software to automatically insert this information—name of addressee, date, and page number—on the second and following pages of your letter.

### Complimentary Close.
By far the most commonly used complimentary close is *Sincerely*. *Sincerely yours* is also used, but in recent years the *yours* has been fading away. *Truly* (with and without the *yours*) is also used, but it has also lost popularity. Such closes as *Cordially* and *Respectfully* are appropriate when their meanings fit the writer-reader relationship. A long-standing friendship, for example, would justify *Cordially;* the writer's re-

*Sincerely is the most commonly used close. Other closes are appropriate.*

"Is 'Very Truly Yours' all right for the close of a crank letter?"

From The Wall Street Journal, with permission of Cartoon Features Syndicate.

spect for the position, prestige, or accomplishments of the reader would justify *Respectfully*.

**Signature Block.** The printed signature conventionally appears on the fourth line below the complimentary close, beginning directly under the first letter for the block form. A short name and title may appear on the same line, separated by a comma. If either the name or title is long, the title appears on the following line, blocked under the name. The writer's signature appears in the space between the complimentary close and the printed signature.

Some people prefer to have the firm name appear in the signature block. The conventional form for this arrangement places the firm name in solid capitals and blocked on the second line below the closing phrase. The typed name of the person signing the letter is on the fourth line below the firm name (see Figure 20-3).

**Information Notations.** In the lower left corner of the letter may appear abbreviated notations for enclosures (*Enc., Enc.—3*, and so on) and for the initials of the dictator and the typist (*WEH:ga*). Indications of copies prepared for other readers may also be included (*pc. William E. Sutton, Copy to William E. Sutton*). Originally, the initials of the person who dictated the letter were useful in helping readers decipher illegible signatures. Now with printed signatures, these initials are less useful, but many firms still use them. The initials of the typist are useful for office records.

**Postscripts.** Postscripts, commonly referred to as the *PS*, are placed after any notations. While rarely used in most business letters because they look like afterthoughts, they can be very effective for added punches in sales letters.

**Folding.** The carelessly folded letter is off to a bad start with the reader. Neat folding will complete the planned effect by (1) making the letter fit snugly in its cover, (2) making the letter easy and handy for the reader to remove, and (3) making the letter appear neat when opened.

| | |
|---|---|
| | The printed signature ends the letter. |
| | Notations showing enclosures and initials of the typist and dictator appear at the bottom left of the layout. |
| | A PS is rarely used, except in sales letters. |
| | Proper folding improves appearance. |

**The two-fold pattern is right for long envelopes.**

The two-fold pattern is the easiest. It fits the standard sheet for the long (Number 10) envelope as well as some other envelope sizes.

As shown in Figure 20–7, the first fold of the two-fold pattern is from the bottom up, taking a little less than a third of the sheet. The second fold goes from the top down, taking exactly the same panel as the bottom segment. (This measurement will leave the recipient a quarter-inch thumbhold for easy unfolding of the letter.) Thus folded, the letter should be slipped into its envelope with the second crease toward the bottom and the center panel at the front of the envelope.

**The three-fold pattern is right for small envelopes.**

The three-fold pattern is necessary to fit the standard sheet into the commonly used small (Number 6¾) envelope. Its first fold is from the bottom up, with the bottom edge of the sheet riding about a quarter inch under the top edge to allow the thumbhold. (If the edges are exactly even, they are harder to separate.) The second fold is from the right side of the sheet toward the left, taking a little less than a third of the width. The third fold matches the second: from the left side toward the right, with a panel of exactly the same width. (This fold will leave a quarter inch thumbhold at the right, for the user's convenience.) So that the letter will appear neat when unfolded, the creases should be neatly parallel with the top and sides, not at

**FIGURE 20–7** Two Ways of Folding and Inserting Letters (See Text Descriptions for Dimensions)

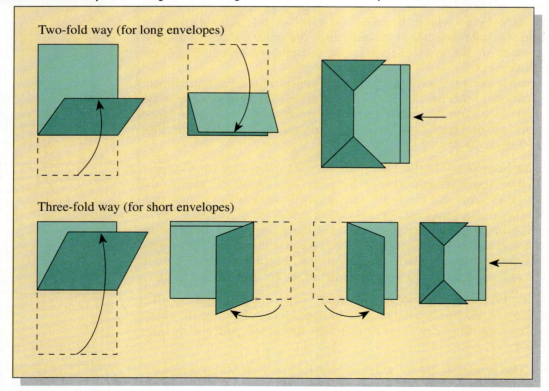

PART 7 Special Topics in Business Communication

angles that produce "dog-ears" and irregular shapes. In the three-fold form, it is especially important for the side panels produced by the second and third folds to be exactly the same width; otherwise, the vertical creases are off-center and tend to throw the whole carefully planned layout off-center.

The three-fold letter is inserted into its cover with the third crease toward the bottom of the envelope and the loose edges toward the stamp end of the envelope. From habit, most recipients of business letters slit envelopes at the top and turn them facedown to extract the letter. The three-fold letter inserted as described thus gives its reader an easy thumbhold at the top of the envelope to pull it out by, and a second one at the top of the sheet for easy unfolding of the whole.

*Properly inserting a letter into the envelope helps the reader.*

**Envelope Address.** So that optical character recognition equipment may be used in sorting mail, the U.S. Postal Service requests that all envelopes be typed as follows (see Figure 20–8):

*The U.S. Postal Service requests that you follow this procedure in addressing envelopes.*

1. On the Number 10 envelope (large), start the address 4 inches from the left edge. On the Number 6¾ envelope, start 2 inches from the left edge.
2. Use a block address format.
3. Single-space.
4. Use all uppercase letters (capitals).
5. Do not use punctuation.
6. Use these two-letter abbreviations for the U.S. states and territories and the Canadian provinces:

**FIGURE 20–8** Form for Addressing Number 6¾ Envelope Recommended by the U.S. Postal Service

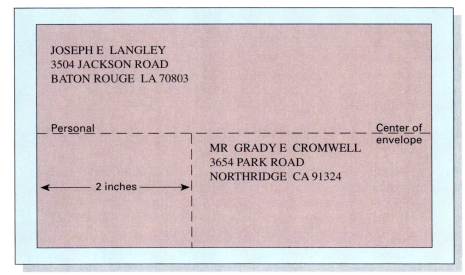

## STATES AND TERRITORIES OF THE UNITED STATES

| | | | |
|---|---|---|---|
| Alabama | AL | Missouri | MO |
| Alaska | AK | Montana | MT |
| American Samoa | AS | Nebraska | NE |
| Arizona | AZ | Nevada | NV |
| Arkansas | AR | New Hampshire | NH |
| California | CA | New Jersey | NJ |
| Colorado | CO | New Mexico | NM |
| Connecticut | CT | New York | NY |
| Delaware | DE | North Carolina | NC |
| District of Columbia | DC | North Dakota | ND |
| Federated States of Micronesia | FM | Northern Mariana Islands | MP |
| Florida | FL | Ohio | OH |
| Georgia | GA | Oklahoma | OK |
| Guam | GU | Oregon | OR |
| Hawaii | HI | Palau | PW |
| Idaho | ID | Pennsylvania | PA |
| Illinois | IL | Puerto Rico | PR |
| Indiana | IN | Rhode Island | RI |
| Iowa | IA | South Carolina | SC |
| Kansas | KS | South Dakota | SD |
| Kentucky | KY | Tennessee | TN |
| Louisiana | LA | Texas | TX |
| Maine | ME | Utah | UT |
| Marshall Islands | MII | Vermont | VT |
| Maryland | MD | Virginia | VA |
| Massachusetts | MA | Virgin Islands | VI |
| Michigan | MI | Washington | WA |
| Minnesota | MN | West Virginia | WV |
| Mississippi | MS | Wyoming | WY |

## CANADIAN PROVINCES

| | | | |
|---|---|---|---|
| British Columbia | BC | Nova Scotia | NS |
| Labrador | LB | Ontario | ON |
| Manitoba | MB | Prince Edward Island | PE |
| New Brunswick | NB | Quebec | PQ |
| Newfoundland | NF | Saskatchewan | SK |
| Northwest Territories | NT | Yukon Territory | YT |

Use other address abbreviations as shown in the most recent edition of the *Post Office Directory*.

7. The last line of the mailing address should contain no more than 28 characters. The city should be 13 or fewer characters. Also, there should be one space between city and state; two spaces for the state or province abbreviation; two spaces between the state and ZIP code; and 10 characters for the ZIP + 4 code.

8. When the return address must be typed (it is usually printed), block it in the left corner, beginning on the second line from the top of the envelope and three spaces from the left edge of the envelope.

**FIGURE 20–9** Sample Memo Format

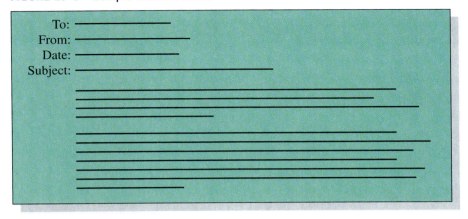

9. Type any on-arrival instructions ("Confidential," "Personal,") four lines below the return address.

10. Place all notations for the post office ("Special Delivery") below the stamp and at least three lines above the mailing address.

## FORM OF MEMORANDUMS

Memorandums (memos) have basic components in common, but their form varies widely from organization to organization. The basic components are the heading and body. The heading has four elements: *To, From, Date,* and *Subject*. These elements are arranged in various placements, but all are present.

*To, From, Date, Subject* are basic memo parts.

The body of the memo is usually single-spaced with double-spacing between paragraphs. First-level headings are frequently used in memos. And notations for writer, typist, and enclosures are included just as they are in letters. An example of a typical form is shown in Figure 20–9.

See Figure 20–9 for memorandum form.

## FORM OF LETTER AND MEMORANDUM REPORTS

As letter reports are actually letters, the review of letter form presented earlier in this chapter applies to them. Memorandum reports, however, are somewhat different. The conventional memorandum form (Figure 20–10) uses the conventional introductory information: *To, From, Date, Subject*. Many large companies have stationery on which this information is printed or standard macros, templates, or styles. The report text follows the introductory information.

Letter reports are typed in letter form. Memorandum reports have *To, From, Date, Subject* at the top.

Both letter and memorandum reports may use headings (captions) to display the topics covered. The headings are usually displayed in the margins, on separate lines, and in a different style. Memorandum and letter reports may also differ from ordinary letters by having illustrations (charts, tables), an appendix, and/or a bibliography.

Both letter and memorandum reports may have headings, illustrations, appendixes, and bibliographies.

FIGURE 20–10  Good Form for a Memorandum Report

## Campus Correspondence

LOUISIANA STATE UNIVERSITY

TO: Faculty, College of Business Administration

FROM: Committee on Courses and Curricula
J. William Hughes, Chairperson

SUBJECT: Report of progress and plans on the study of the business administration curricula

DATE: December 15, 1992

Progress for the Period October 1 to December 15

On October 10 the Committee mailed questionnaires (copy attached) to the deans of 24 selected colleges of business administration. To date, 21 of the deans have returned questionnaires.

Professors Byrd, Calhoun, and Creznik have tabulated the replies received and are now analyzing findings.

Future Plans

Professors Byrd, Calhoun, and Creznik will present their analyses to the Committee at its February 4th meeting. At this time, the Committee expects to study these analyses and to make final recommendations.

Professor Byrd will record the Committee's recommendations in a written report. The Committee will distribute copies of this report to all voting members of the faculty at least one week before the faculty meeting scheduled for May 9.

## FORM OF FORMAL REPORTS

Like letters, formal reports should be pleasing to the eye. Well-arranged reports give an impression of competence—of work professionally done. Because such an impression can affect the success of a report, you should make good use of the following review of report form.

*Attractive reports communicate competent and professional work.*

### General Information on Report Presentation

Your formal reports are likely to be prepared with word processing software. You will need to know and follow the general mechanics of manuscript preparation. Even if you do not have to prepare your own reports, you should know enough about report presentation to be sure your work is done right. You cannot be certain that your report is in good form unless you know good form.

**Conventional Page Layout.** For the typical text page in a report, a conventional layout appears to fit the page as a picture fits a frame (see Figures 20–11 and 20–12). This eye-pleasing layout, however, is arranged to fit the page space not covered by the binding of the report. Thus, you must allow an extra half inch or so on the left margins of the pages of a left-bound report and at the top of the pages of a top-bound report.

*Appropriate dimensions for layout of an unbound document are 1-inch top, bottom, and side margins.*

**Special Page Layouts.** Certain text pages may have individual layouts. Pages displaying major titles (first pages of chapters, tables of contents, executive summaries, and the like) conventionally have an extra half inch or so of space at the top (see Figure 20–13). Most published books have extra space at the top of such pages.

*Pages displaying major titles may have special layouts.*

Letters of transmittal and authorization may also have individual layouts. They are arranged in any conventional letter form. In the more formal reports, they may be carefully arranged to have the same general shape as the space in which they appear (see Figure 20–16).

**Choice of Form.** It is conventional to double-space reports. This procedure stems from the old practice of double-spacing to make typed manuscripts more readable to the proofreader and printer. The practice has been carried over into work that is not to be reproduced. Advocates of double-spacing claim that it is easier to read than single-spacing, as the reader is less likely to lose line place.

*Both double- and single-spacing are acceptable.*

In recent years, single-spacing has gained in popularity. The general practice is to single-space within paragraphs, double-space between paragraphs, and triple-space above all centered heads (see Figure 20–12). Supporters of single-spacing contend that it saves space and facilitates reading, as it is like the printing that most people are accustomed to reading.

**Patterns of Indentation.** You should indent the paragraph beginnings of double-spaced typing. On the other hand, you should block single-spaced typing, because its paragraph headings are clearly marked by extra line spacing.

*Indent double-spaced text; block single-spacing.*

No generally accepted distance of indentation exists. Some sources suggest 4 spaces, some prefer 5, some like 8, and others like 10 and more. Any decision as to the best distance to use is up to you, though you would do well

*The distance of indentation is optional, but be consistent.*

**FIGURE 20-11** Recommended Layout for a Normal Double-Spaced Page

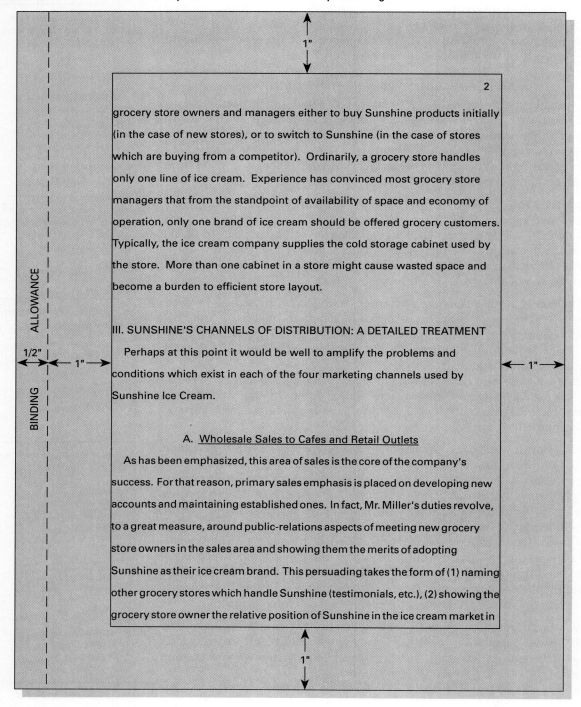

FIGURE 20–12  Recommended Layout for a Single-Spaced Page

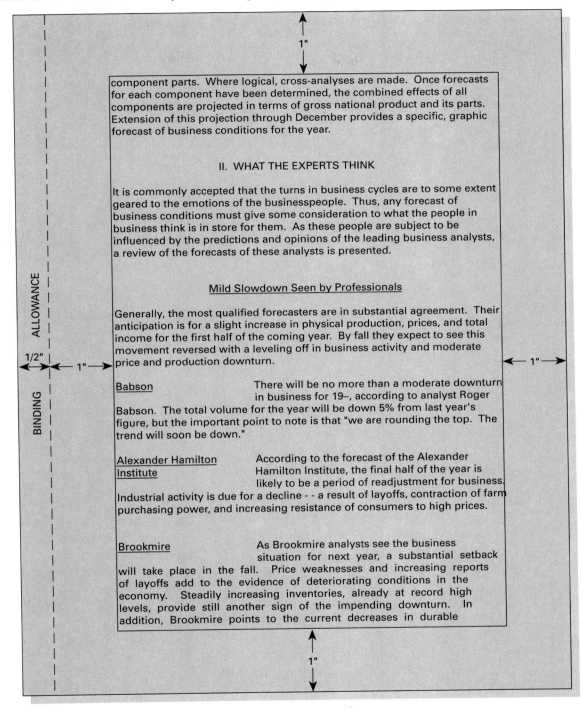

**FIGURE 20–13** Recommended Layout for a Double-Spaced Page with Title Displayed

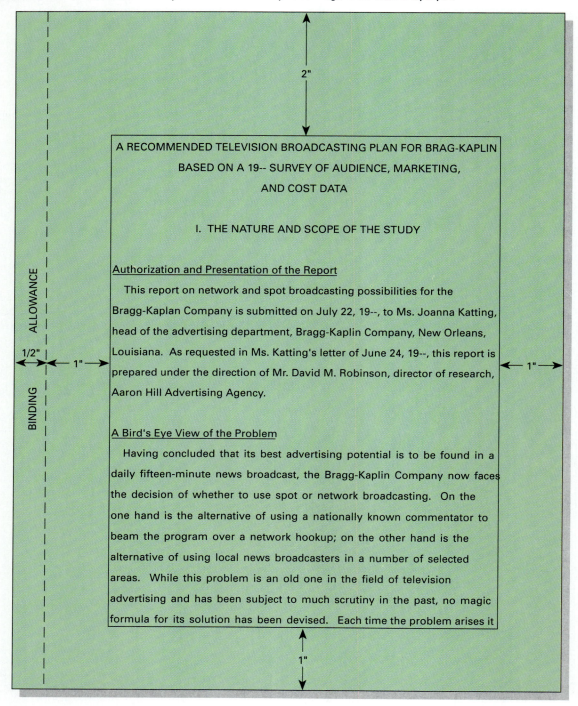

to follow the practice established in the office, group, or school for which you write the report. Whatever your selection, you should be consistent.

**Numbering of Pages.** Two systems of numbers are used in numbering the pages of the written report. Arabic numerals are conventional for the text portion, normally beginning with the first page of the introduction and continuing through the appendix. Small Roman numerals are standard for the pages preceding the text. Although these prefatory pages are all counted in the numbering sequence, the numbers generally do not appear on the pages before the table of contents.

> Number prefatory pages in lowercase Roman numerals, text pages in Arabic numerals.

Placement of the numbers on the page varies with the binding used for the report. In reports bound at the top of the page, you should center all page numbers at the bottom of the page, a double or triple space below the layout used in the body.

> For top-bound reports, place numbers at the bottom.

For left-sided binding, you should place the numbers in the upper right corner, a double or triple space above the top line and in line with the right margin. Exception to this placement is customarily made for special-layout pages that have major titles and an additional amount of space displayed at the top. Such pages may include the first page of the report text; the executive summary; the table of contents; and, in very long and formal works, the first page of each major division or chapter. Numbers for these pages are centered a double or triple space below the imaginary line marking the bottom of the layout.

> For left binding, place numbers in upper right corner.

In documents printed back-to-back, page numbers are usually placed at the top of the page even with the outside margin. Today's word processing programs are capable of automatically placing page numbers this way if directed.

> Your software can handle page numbering.

**Display of Headings.** Headings (captions) are the titles of the parts of the report. Designed to lead the readers through the report, they must show at a glance the importance of the information they cover.

> Use type and position to distinguish headings from text typing.

In showing heading importance by position, you have many choices. If your software and printer make available a variety of typefaces, you can select various progressions of font sizes and styles to fit your needs. Your goal, of course, should be to select forms that show differences in importance at first glance—much as is done in the printing of this book.

> Use any logical combination of type and position.

You can use any combination of form and position that clearly shows the relative importance of the headings. The one governing rule to follow in considering form and positions of headings is that no heading may have a higher-ranking form or position than any of the headings of a higher level. But you can use the same form for two successive levels of headings as long as the positions vary. And you can use the same position for two successive levels as long as the forms vary. You can also skip over any of the steps in the progression of form or position.

### Mechanics and Format of the Report Parts

The foregoing notes on physical appearance apply generally to all parts of the report. But special notes are needed for the individual construction of the specific report pages. So that you may be able to get and follow these notes, a part-by-part review of the physical construction of the formal report follows.

> Following is a part-by-part review of the construction of a formal report.

**Title Fly.** The title fly contains only the report title. In constructing the page, place the title slightly above the vertical center of the page in an eye-pleasing arrangement. Center all lines with regard to left and right margins. Print the title in the highest-ranking form used in the report, and double-space it if you need more than one line. If your report cover has a window for the title to show through, make sure you place the title in the window.

> The title fly contains only the title, centered and a little high on the page.

**Title Page.** The title page normally contains three main areas of identification (Figure 20–14), although some forms present this information in four or five spots on the page (Figure 20–15). In the typical three-spot title page, the first area of identification covers the report title. Preferably, use the highest-ranking form used in the report, usually solid capitals underscored. Center it; and if it requires more than one line, break the lines between thought units and center the lines. Double-space the lines.

> The title page typically contains (1) the report title,

The second area of identification names the individual (or group) for whom the report has been prepared. Precede it with an identifying phrase indicating that individual's role in the report, such as "Prepared for" or "Submitted to." In addition to the recipient's name, include the identification of the recipient by title or role, company, and address, particularly if you and the recipient are from different companies. If the information below the identifying phrase requires three or more lines, single-space it. If it requires fewer than three lines, double-space them. But regardless of how you space this information, set off the identifying phrase from the facts below it by a double space.

> (2) authorizer identification, and

The third area of identification names you, the writer of the report. It is also preceded by an identifying phrase—"Prepared by," "Written by," or similar wording describing your role in the report—and it may also identify title or role, company, and address. As a final part of this area of information, you may include the date of publication. Single-space this identification information if it requires four lines. Double-space if it requires three lines or fewer. Set off the identifying phrase with a double space. Preferably, double-space the date line from the information preceding it, regardless of previous spacing. Placement of the three areas of identification on the page should make for an eye-pleasing arrangement.

> (3) writer identification. It may include the date.

One such arrangement begins the title about 1¼ inches from the top of the page and ends the final area of information about 2 inches from the bottom. Most word processing software will help you place this page vertically. The center spot of information appears to split the space between the top and bottom units in a 2:3 ratio, the bottom space being the larger. The line lengths of the information units are usually governed by the data they contain. But you may need to combine or split units in order to produce the best appearance.

**Letters of Transmittal and Authorization.** As their names imply, the letters of transmittal and authorization are actual letters. You should print them in any acceptable letter form. If the report is important, you should give the letter an ideal layout. An ideal layout is one that fits the letter into a rectangle of the same shape as the space within which it is printed (see Figure 20–16). The area occupied by this rectangle is determined by the dateline at the top, the initial characters of the type at the left, the average of the line lengths at the right, and the last line in the notations at the bottom.

> Letters of transmittal are presented in any accepted letter form.

PART 7 Special Topics in Business Communication

**FIGURE 20–14** Good Layout for the Three-Spot Title Page

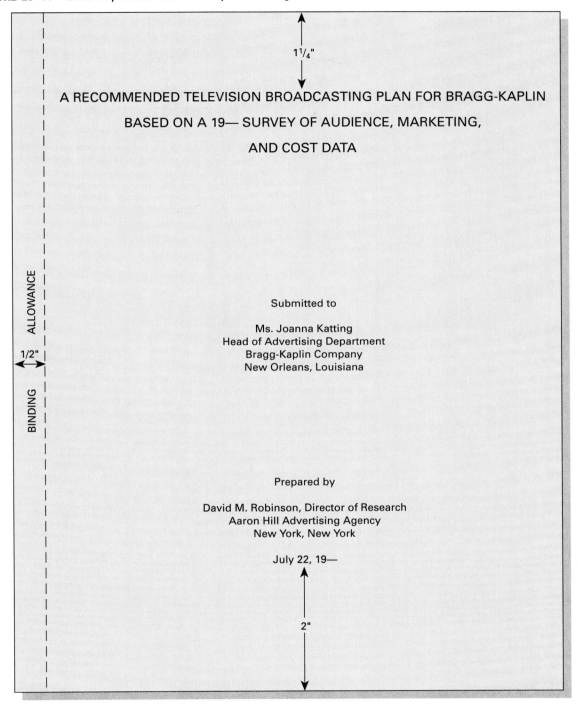

CHAPTER 20 Special Topic: Physical Presentation of Letters, Memos, and Reports

**FIGURE 20–15** Good Layout for the Four-Spot Title Page

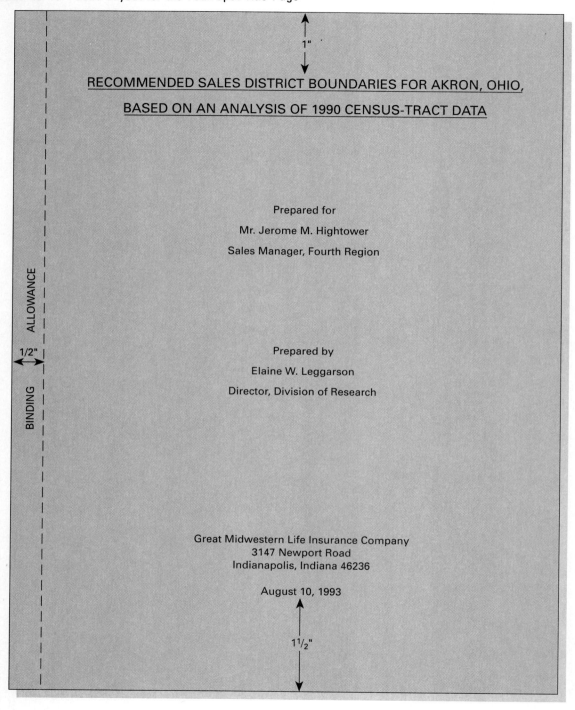

**FIGURE 20-16** Letter of Transmittal Fitted to the Shape of the Space in Which It Is Typed

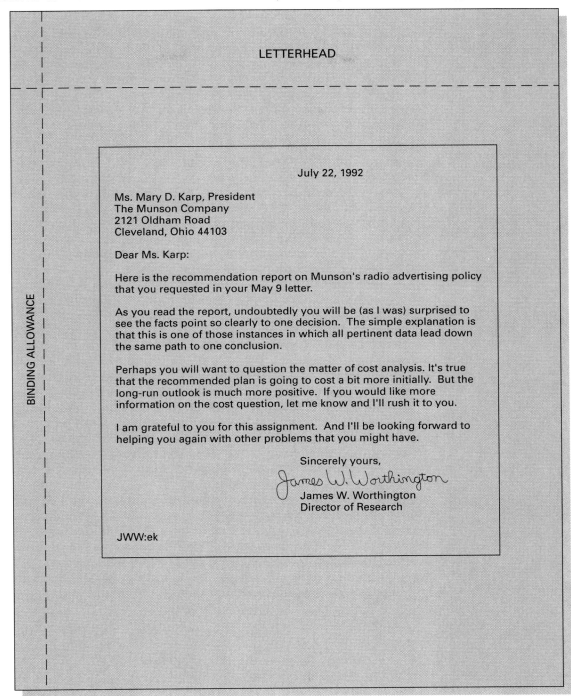

> Consider giving them an ideal layout.

For the best optical effect, the rectangle should ride a little high in the available space (see Figure 20–16). The ratio of the top margin to the bottom margin should be about 2:3.

**Acknowledgments.** When you are indebted to the assistance of others, it is fitting that you acknowledge the indebtedness somewhere in the report. If this number is small, you may acknowledge them in the introduction of the report or in the letter of transmittal. In the rare event that you need to make numerous acknowledgments, you may construct a special section for this purpose. This section, bearing the simple title "Acknowledgments," has the same layout as any other text page in which a title is displayed.

> Include a special page for acknowledgments when you are indebted for help.

**Table of Contents.** The table of contents is the report outline in its polished, finished form. It lists the major report headings with the page numbers on which those headings appear. Although not all reports require a table of contents, one should be a part of any report long enough to make such a guide helpful to the readers.

> The table of contents displays the outline with page numbers.

The table of contents is appropriately titled "Contents" or "Table of Contents," as shown in Figure 20–17. The layout of the table of contents is the same as that used for any other report page with a title display. Below the title, set up two columns. One contains the outline headings, generally beginning with the first report part following the table of contents. You have the option of including or leaving out the outline letters and numbers. If you use numbers, arrange them so that their last digits are aligned. In the other column, at the right margin and headed by the word *Page,* place the page numbers on which the outline headings may be found. Align these numbers on their right-hand digits. Connect the two columns by leader lines of periods, preferably with spaces intervening, and align the periods vertically.

> Set up the outline headings in a column to the left and the page numbers in a column to the right. See Figure 20–17.

A good rule to follow is to place line spaces above and below all headings of the highest level of division. You should uniformly single-space or double-space headings below this level, depending on their overall lengths. If the headings are long, covering most of the line or extending to a second line, use uniform double-spacing between headings. Some authorities, however, prefer double-spacing all the content entries when double-spacing is used in the text.

In the table of contents, as in the body of the report, you may vary the form to distinguish different heading levels. But the form variations of the table of contents need not be the same as those used in the text of the report. The highest level of headings is usually distinguished from the other levels, and sometimes typeface differences are used to distinguish second-level headings from lower-level headings. It is acceptable to show no distinction by using plain capitals and lowercase for all levels of headings.

**Table of Illustrations.** The table (list) of illustrations may be either a continuation of the table of contents or a separate table. Such a table, as shown in Figure 20–18, lists the graphics presented in the report in much the same way as the table of contents lists the report parts.

> A table of illustrations may be a part of the table of contents.

In constructing this table, head it with an appropriately descriptive title, such as "Table of Charts and Illustrations," or "List of Tables and Charts," or "Table of Figures." If you place the table of illustrations on a separate page, layout for this page is the same as that for any other text page with a

**PART 7** Special Topics in Business Communication

**FIGURE 20-17** Good Layout and Mechanics in the First Page of the Table of Contents

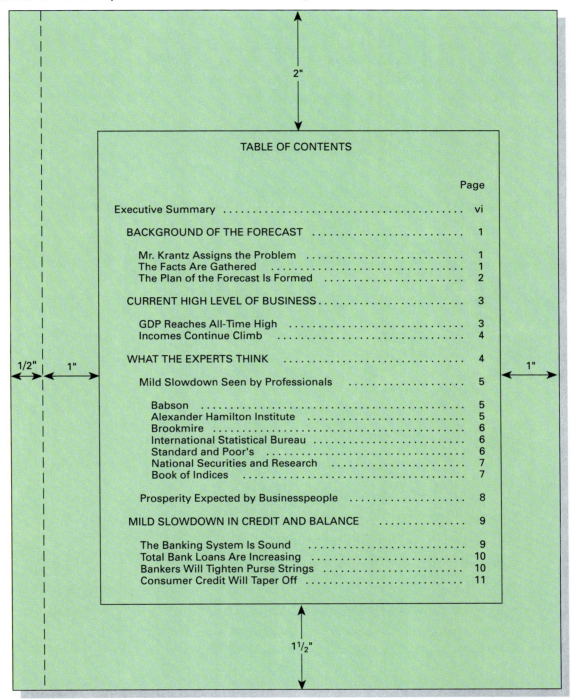

**FIGURE 20–18** Good Layout and Mechanics in the Last Page of a Table of Contents with an Attached Table of Illustrations

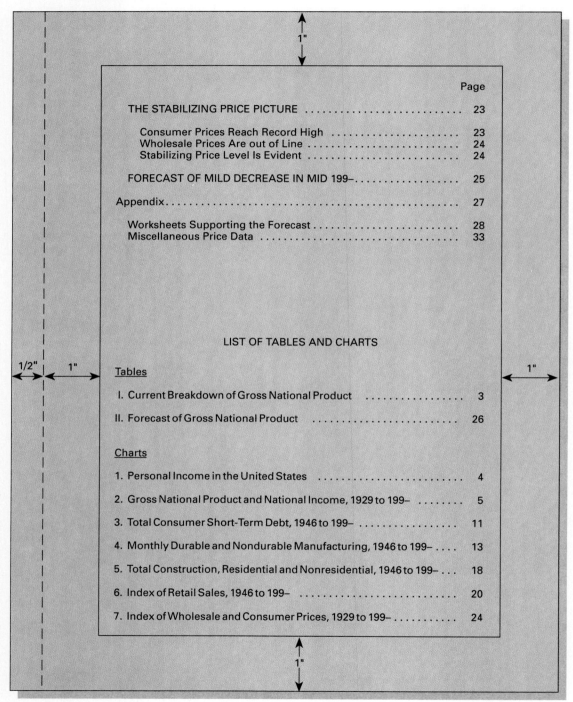

|  | Page |
|---|---|
| THE STABILIZING PRICE PICTURE | 23 |
|     Consumer Prices Reach Record High | 23 |
|     Wholesale Prices Are out of Line | 24 |
|     Stabilizing Price Level Is Evident | 24 |
| FORECAST OF MILD DECREASE IN MID 199– | 25 |
| Appendix | 27 |
|     Worksheets Supporting the Forecast | 28 |
|     Miscellaneous Price Data | 33 |

### LIST OF TABLES AND CHARTS

<u>Tables</u>

| I. Current Breakdown of Gross National Product | 3 |
|---|---|
| II. Forecast of Gross National Product | 26 |

<u>Charts</u>

| 1. Personal Income in the United States | 4 |
|---|---|
| 2. Gross National Product and National Income, 1929 to 199– | 5 |
| 3. Total Consumer Short-Term Debt, 1946 to 199– | 11 |
| 4. Monthly Durable and Nondurable Manufacturing, 1946 to 199– | 13 |
| 5. Total Construction, Residential and Nonresidential, 1946 to 199– | 18 |
| 6. Index of Retail Sales, 1946 to 199– | 20 |
| 7. Index of Wholesale and Consumer Prices, 1929 to 199– | 24 |

**FIGURE 20-19** Example of a Reference List with Complete Documentation

| REFERENCES |
|---|
| Arndt, Eric. "Nobody Does It Better: How Five Most Successful Companies View Communication as Integral to Their Achievements," *Communication World,* Volume 5, May 1988, pp. 26-29. |
| Blocklyn, Paul L. "Making Magic: The Disney Approach to People Management," *Personnel,* Volume 65, December 1988, pp. 28-34. |
| Culhane, John. "Disney's Five Ways to Make Dreams Come True," *Reader's Digest,* Volume 133, November 1988, p. 27-32. |
| Daft, Richard L. *Management.* Chicago: Dryden Press, 1988, pp. 119-120, 170. |
| "Disney Stock Soars," *The New York Times,* Volume 138, May 13, 1989, p. 35. |
| Laderman, Jeffrey M. "Wall Street: On the Road to 2700," *BusinessWeek,* August 7, 1989, p. 57. |
| Murray, Thomas J. "Getting Mickey Organized," *Business Month,* Volume 130, December 1987, pp. 28-29. |
| Scott, Frank, Account Manager, Merrill Lynch, San Diego, Telephone Interview, San Diego California, November 6, 1989. |
| Seal, Kathy. "Disney Workers Are Upset with Grooming Code," *Hotel and Motel Management,* Volume 203, April 18, 1989, pp. 3, 40. |

displayed title. And if you place it as a continued part of the table of contents, you should begin it after spacing four or more lines from the last contents entry.

The table consists of two columns—the first for the graphics titles and the second for the pages on which the graphics appear. Head the second column "Page." And connect the two columns by leader lines of spaced periods. The periods should be aligned vertically. Line spacing in the table of illustrations is optional, again depending on the line lengths of the entries. Preceding the title of each entry, place that entry's number; and should these numbers be Roman or otherwise require more than one digit, align the digits at the right. If your report contains two or more illustration types (tables, charts, maps, and the like) and you have given each type its own numbering sequence, you should list each type separately.

**References (or Bibliography).** Anytime you use another's idea, you need to give credit to the source. Sometimes business writers interweave this credit into the narrative of their text. But often these sources are listed in a reference or bibliography section at the end of the report. Typically, these sections are organized alphabetically, but they can also be organized by date, subject, or type of source.

> When using secondary data, note the sources in a bibliography.

The format and content of citations vary by style used as described in Appendix D. Among the widely used formats are *The Chicago Manual of Style, The MLA Style Sheet,* and the *Publication Manual of the American Psychological Association.* The content for most items on the list of references is similar to the footnote. You can see an example in Figure 20-19.

> See Appendix D for details.

**Need to Improvise.** The foregoing review covers most of the problems of form you will encounter in preparing reports. But there will be others. When you encounter other problems, you simply improvise an arrangement that appears right to the eye. After all, what appears right to the eye is the basis of conventional report form.

> For form matters not covered in this review, improvise.

## QUESTIONS FOR DISCUSSION

1. "Business readers want facts. They couldn't care less about the form in which the facts are presented." Comment on the logic of this evaluation.
2. Identify and describe the presentation decisions common to letters, memos, and reports.
3. If the appearance of a letter is so important, why should not every letter be given an ideal layout?
4. Describe the requirements of each of these parts of a letter:
   *a.* Dateline
   *b.* Inside address
   *c.* Salutation
   *d.* Subject line
   *e.* Second-page heading
   *f.* Complimentary close
   *g.* Signature block
   *h.* Notations
5. Explain the objection that many people have to the use of *Mrs., Miss, Gentlemen,* and *Dear Sirs* in salutations. Evaluate alternative salutations.
6. Demonstrate and describe the proper folding of a letter for long and short envelopes.
7. Explain the form for addressing envelopes suggested by the U.S. Postal Service.
8. Discuss the elements of the headings of memos. Explain what each contains.
9. "The appearance of a letter or a report plays a significant role in communicating the message." Explain this statement.
10. Describe the layout of an ideal conventional page in a report. How does this differ from the layout of a special page?
11. Summarize the arguments on the question of whether to single- or double-space reports.
12. Describe the page-numbering procedure of a formal report, beginning with the title fly and ending with the last page of the appended parts.
13. Discuss the two basic ways of giving emphasis to headings in a report.
14. Work up two schemes of heading emphasis that are different from those illustrated in the text. Evaluate them critically.
15. Discuss the content and layout considerations of the title page.
16. Describe the form of the letter of transmittal.
17. In what ways may acknowledgments be handled?
18. Summarize the layout and mechanics of the table of contents.
19. Describe the structure of a letter report. Do the same for a memo report.

## CHAPTER 21

# CORRECTNESS OF COMMUNICATION

### CHAPTER OBJECTIVES

*Upon completing this chapter, you will be able to use the accepted standards of English grammar and punctuation in written business communications. To reach this goal, you should be able to*

**1**

Use punctuation marks correctly.

**2**

Write complete, grammatically correct sentences, avoiding such problems as awkward construction, dangling modifiers, and misuse of words.

**3**

Determine when to spell out numbers and when to express them in numeral form according to standards of correctness.

**4**

Spell words correctly by memorizing the most commonly misspelled words, applying spelling rules, and using the dictionary.

**5**

Use capital letters for all proper names, first words of sentences, and first words of complimentary closes.

## INTRODUCTORY SITUATION

### to the Effects of Correctness on Communication

Play the role of a purchasing agent for Stockwell Machine Works and read through today's mail. The first letter comes from Joe Spivey, sales manager, B and B Manufacturing Company. You have not met the writer, though you talked to him on the telephone a few days ago. At that time, you were favorably impressed with Spivey's enthusiasm and ability, and with B and B. In fact, you assumed that after he gave you the information you needed about B and B's products and services, you would begin buying from it.

As you read Spivey's letter, however, you are startled. "Could this be the same person I talked with?" you ask yourself. There in the first paragraph is an *it don't*, a clear error of subject-verb agreement. Farther down, an *it's* is used to show possession rather than *it is*. Spivey apparently uses the sprinkle system for placing commas—that is, he sprinkles them wherever his whims direct. His commas often fall in strange places. For example, he writes, "Our salespeople, say the Rabb Company engineers, will verify the durability of Ironskin protective coating," but you think he means "Our salespeople say the Rabb Company engineers will verify the durability of Ironskin protective coating." The two sentences, which differ only in their punctuation, have distinctly different meanings. Spivey's letter is filled with such errors.

In general, you now have a lower opinion of Spivey and his company. Perhaps you'll have to take a long look at B and B's products and services. After all, the products and services that a company provides are closely related to the quality of its people.

The problem just described is a very real one in business. Image does influence the success of both companies and people. And correctness in writing influences image. Thus, you will want to make certain that your writing is correct, so that it helps form a favorable image both of you and of your company. The material presented in the pages that follow should help you in that effort. ∎

The correctness of your communication will be important to you and your company. It will be important to you because people will judge you by it, and how they judge you will help determine your success in life. It will be important to your company because it will help convey the image of competence that companies like. People judge a company by how its employees act, think, talk, and write. Company executives want such judgments to be favorable.

*People judge you and your company by the correctness of your communication.*

### THE NATURE OF CORRECTNESS

Not all people agree that there are standards for correct communication. In fact, some people think that there should be no general standards of this kind, that whatever communicates in a given case is all right. Businesspeople, however, generally accept the standards for correct usage that educated people have developed over the years. These are the standards that you have studied in your English composition classes and that appear in textbooks. Businesspeople expect you to follow them.

*Businesspeople expect you to follow the generally accepted standards of English.*

**CHAPTER 21** Special Topic: Correctness of Communication

**These standards of correctness assist in communicating.**

These standards of correctness have one basic purpose: to assist in communicating. To some people the standards of correctness appear arbitrary or unnecessary. But such is not the case. They are designed to reduce misunderstanding—to make communication more precise. It is only in this light that we can justify studying them.

The practical value of these standards is easily illustrated. Take, for example, the following two sentences. Their words are the same; only their punctuation differs. But what a difference the punctuation makes!

"The teacher," said the student, "is stupid."
The teacher said, "The student is stupid."

Or what about the following pair of sentences? Who is speaking, the Democrats or the Republicans? The commas make a difference.

The Democrats, say the Republicans, will win.
The Democrats say the Republicans will win.

### Can You Detect the Differences in Meaning the Punctuation Makes?

What's the latest dope?
What's the latest, dope?
The butler was asked to stand by the door and call the guests names as they arrived.
The butler was asked to stand by the door and call the guests' names as they arrived.
A clever dog knows it's master.
A clever dog knows its master.
Everyone, I know, has a problem.
Everyone I know has a problem.
Do not break your bread or roll in your soup.
Do not break your bread, or roll in your soup.
She ate a half-fried chicken.
She ate a half fried chicken.
I left him convinced he was a fool.
I left him, convinced he was a fool.
In the parade will be several hundred children, carrying flags and many important officials.
In the parade will be several hundred children, carrying flags, and many important officials.
The play ended, happily.
The play ended happily.
Thirteen people knew the secret, all told.
Thirteen people knew the secret; all told.

Here are two more sentences. The difference here needs no explanation.

He looked at her stern.
He looked at her sternly.

Because the standards of correctness are important to your communication in business, this chapter will review them. The review is not complete, for much more space would be needed for complete coverage. But the major standards are covered, those that most often present problems in your writing. For your convenience, the standards are coded with symbols (letters and numbers). You should find these symbols useful in identifying the standards. Your instructor should find them useful as grading marks to identify errors in your writing.

*The following review covers the major standards. They are coded for your convenience.*

You probably already know many of the standards of correctness, so the following information will not all be new to you. To help you determine how much you know and do not know, you should take the self-analysis test at the end of the chapter. It should give you an indication of what you know and do not know. This will enable you to study the standards selectively. Because the self-analysis test covers only the more frequently used standards, however, you would be wise to review the entire chapter.

*Take the self-analysis test to determine your present knowledge of the standards.*

## ■■■■■■■■■■■■■■■■■■■
## STANDARDS FOR PUNCTUATION

The following explanations cover the most important standards for correctness in punctuation. For reasons of accuracy, the explanations use some technical words. Even so, the illustrations should make the standards clear.

### Apostrophe: Apos 1

Use the apostrophe to show the possessive case of nouns and indefinite pronouns. If the word does not end in *s*, add an apostrophe and an *s*. If the word ends in *s*, add only an apostrophe.

*Use the apostrophe to show possession.*

| NOMINATIVE FORM | POSSESSIVE FORM |
|---|---|
| company | company's |
| employee | employee's |
| companies | companies' |
| employees | employees' |

Proper names and singular nouns ending in *s* sounds are exceptions. To such words you may add either an apostrophe and an *s* or just an apostrophe. Add only an apostrophe to the nominative plural.

| NOMINATIVE FORM | POSSESSIVE FORM |
|---|---|
| Texas (singular) | Texas', Texas's |
| Jones (singular) | Jones', Jones's |
| Joneses (plural) | Joneses' |
| countess (singular) | countess', countess's |

### Apos 2

Mark omissions in contractions with the apostrophe.

Use an apostrophe to mark the place in a contraction where letters are omitted.

has not = hasn't
cannot = can't
it is = it's

### Brackets: Bkts

Use brackets to set off words that you insert in a quotation.

Set off in brackets words that you wish to insert in a quotation.

"The use of this type of supervisor [the trained correspondence expert] may still be increasing."

"Direct supervision has gained in importance during the past decade [the report was written in 1990], when 43 percent of the reporting business firms that started programs first used this technique."

### Colon: Cln 1

Use the colon to introduce formal statements.

Use the colon to introduce a statement of explanation, an enumeration, or a formal quotation.

*Statement of explanation:* At this time the company was pioneering a new marketing idea: It was attempting to sell its products directly to consumers by means of vending machines.

*Enumeration:* Working in this department are three classes of machinists: apprentice machinists, journeyman machinists, and first-class machinists.

*Formal quotation:* President Hartung had this to say about the proposal: "Any such movement that fails to get the support of the rank-and-file worker in this plant fails to get my support."

### Cln 2

Do not use the colon when it breaks the thought flow.

Do not use the colon when the thought of the sentence should continue without interruption. If introducing a list by a colon, the colon should be preceded by a word that explains or identifies the list.

*Below standard:* Cities in which new sales offices are in operation are: Fort Smith, Texarkana, Lake Charles, Jackson, and Biloxi.

*Acceptable:* Cities in which new sales offices are in operation are Fort Smith, Texarkana, Lake Charles, Jackson, and Biloxi.

*Acceptable:* Cities with new sales offices are as follows: Fort Smith, Texarkana, Lake Charles, Jackson, and Biloxi.

### Comma: Cma 1

Use the comma to separate clauses connected by *and, but, or, nor, for.*

Use the comma to separate principal clauses connected by a coordinating conjunction. The coordinating conjunctions are *and, but, or, nor,* and *for.* (A principal clause has a subject and a verb and stands by itself. A coordinating conjunction connects clauses, words, or phrases of equal rank.)

Only two components of the index declined, and these two account for only 12 percent of the total weight of the index.

New automobiles are moving at record volumes, but used-car sales are lagging behind the record pace set two years ago.

PEANUTS reprinted by permission of UFS, Inc.

Make exceptions to this rule, however, in the case of compound sentences consisting of short and closely connected clauses.

We sold and the price dropped.
Sometimes we win and sometimes we lose.

### Cma 2.1

Separate the items listed in a series by commas. In order to avoid misinterpretation of the rare instances in which some of the items listed have compound constructions, it is always good to place the comma between the last two items (before the final conjunction).

Use the comma to separate (1) items in a series and

Good copy must cover fact with accuracy, sincerity, honesty, and conviction.

Direct advertising can be used to introduce salespeople, fill in between salespeople's calls, cover territory where salespeople cannot be maintained, and keep pertinent reference material in the hands of prospects.

A survey conducted at the 1993 automobile show indicated that black and cream, blue and gray, dark maroon, and black cars were favored by the public. (Note how this example illustrates the need for a comma before the final conjunction.)

### Cma 2.2

Separate coordinate adjectives in a series by commas if they modify the same noun and if no *and* connects them. A good test to determine whether adjectives are coordinate is to insert an *and* between them. If the *and* does not change the meaning, the adjectives are coordinate.

(2) adjectives in a series.

Miss Pratt has been a reliable, faithful, efficient employee for 20 years.
We guarantee that this is a good, clean car.
Green office furniture is Mr. Orr's recommendation for the stenographic pool. (Office furniture is practically a compound noun; green modifies both words.)
A big Dawson wrench proved to be best for the task. (The *and* won't fit between *big* and *Dawson*.

### Cma 3

Set off nonrestrictive modifiers by commas. By a *nonrestrictive modifier* we mean a modifier that could be omitted from the sentence without changing its meaning. Restrictive modifiers (those that restrict the words they modify to one particular object) are not set off by commas. A restrictive modifier cannot be left out of the sentence without changing its meaning.

Use commas to set off nonrestrictive modifiers (those that could be left out without changing the meaning of the sentence).

*Restrictive:* The salesperson who sells the most will get a bonus. [*Who sells the most* restricts the meaning to a particular salesperson.]

*Nonrestrictive:* James Smithers, who was the company's top salesperson for the year, was awarded a bonus. [If the clause *who was the company's top salesperson for the year* is omitted, the meaning of the sentence is not changed.]

*Restrictive:* J. Ward & Company is the firm that employs most of the physically handicapped in this area.

*Nonrestrictive:* J. Ward & Company, the firm that employs most of the physically handicapped in this area, has gained the admiration of the community.

Notice that some modifiers can be either restrictive or nonrestrictive, depending on the writer's intended meaning.

*Restrictive:* All the suits that were damaged in the fire were sold at a discount. (Implies that some of the suits were not damaged.)

*Nonrestrictive:* All the suits, which were damaged by the fire, were sold at a discount. (Implies that the entire stock of suits was damaged.)

### Cma 4.1

**Use commas to set off (1) parenthetic expressions (comments "stuck in"),**

Use commas to set off parenthetic expressions. A parenthetic expression consists of words that interrupt the normal flow of the sentence. In a sense, they appear to be "stuck in." In many instances, they are simply words out of normal order. For example, the sentence "A full-page, black-and-white advertisement was run in the *Daily Bulletin*" contains a parenthetic expression when the word order is altered: "An advertisement, full-page and in black and white, was run in the *Daily Bulletin*."

This practice, it is believed, will lead to ruin.

The Johnston Oil Company, so the rumor goes, has sharply reduced its exploration activity.

Although you may use the dash and the parenthesis for similar reasons, the three marks differ in the degree to which they separate the enclosed words from the rest of the sentence. The comma is the weakest of the three, and it is best used when the material set off is closely related to the surrounding words. Dashes are stronger marks than commas and are used when the material set off tends to be long or contains internal punctuation marks. Parentheses, the strongest of the three, are primarily used to enclose material that helps explain or supplement the main words of the sentence.

### Cma 4.2

**(2) apposition words (words explaining another word),**

Use commas to set off an appositive (a noun or a noun and its modifiers inserted to explain another noun) from the rest of the sentence. In a sense, appositives are parenthetic expressions, for they interrupt the normal flow of the sentence.

The Baron Corporation, our machine-parts supplier, is negotiating a new contract.

St. Louis, home office of our Midwest district, will be the permanent site of our annual sales meeting.

President Cartwright, a self-educated woman, is the leading advocate of our night school for employees.

But appositives that identify very closely are not set off by commas.

The word *liabilities* is not understood by most laboring men.

Our next shipment will come on the steamship *Alberta*.

## Cma 4.3

Set off parenthetic words such as *therefore, however, in fact, of course, for example*, and *consequently* with commas.

(3) certain parenthetic words (*therefore, however*), and

It is apparent, therefore, that the buyers' resistance has been brought about by an overvigorous sales campaign.

After the first experiment, for example, the traffic flow increased 10 percent.

The company will, however, be forced to abandon the old pricing system.

Included in this group of parenthetic words may be introductory interjections (*oh, alas*) and responsive expressions (*yes, no, surely, indeed, well*, and so on). But if the words are strongly exclamatory or are not closely connected with the rest of the sentence, they may be punctuated as a sentence. (*No. Yes. Indeed.*)

Yes, the decision to increase production has been made.

Oh, contribute whatever you think is adequate.

## Cma 4.4

When more than one unit appears in a date or an address, set off the units by commas.

(4) units in a date.

*One unit:* December 30 is the date of our annual inventory.

*One unit:* The company has one outlet in Ohio.

*More than one unit:* December 30, 1906, is the date the Johnston Company first opened its doors.

*More than one unit:* Richmond, Virginia, is the headquarters of the new sales district.

## Cma 5.1

Use the comma after a subordinate clause that precedes the main clause.

Use the comma after (1) subordinate clauses and

Although it is durable, this package does not have eye appeal.

Since there was little store traffic on Aisle 13, the area was converted into office space.

## Cma 5.2

Place a comma after an introductory verbal phrase. A verbal phrase is one that contains some verb derivative, a gerund, a participle, or an infinitive.

(2) introductory verbal phrases.

*Participle phrase:* Realizing his mistake, the foreman instructed his workers to keep a record of all salvaged equipment.

*Gerund phrase:* After gaining the advantage, we failed to press on to victory.

*Infinitive phrase:* To increase our turnover of automobile accessories, we must first improve our display area.

### Cma 6.1

*Do not use the comma without good reason,*

Use the comma only for good reason. It is not a mark to be inserted indiscriminately at the writer's whim. As a rule, the use of commas should be justified by one of the standard practices previously noted.

### Cma 6.1.1

*such as between the subject and the verb.*

Do not be tripped into putting a comma between the subject and the verb.

The thought that he could not afford to fail spurred him on. [No comma after *fail*]

### Cma 6.2

*Use the comma wherever it helps clarity.*

Take exception to the preceding standards wherever the insertion of a comma will help clarity of expression.

*Not clear:* From the beginning inventory methods of Hill Company have been haphazard.
*Clear:* From the beginning, inventory methods of Hill Company have been haphazard.
*Not clear:* Ever since she has been a model worker.
*Clear:* Ever since, she has been a model worker.

## Dash: Dsh

*Use the dash to show interruption or emphasis.*

Use the dash to set off an element for emphasis or to show interrupted thought. In particular, use it with long parenthetic expressions or parenthetic expressions containing internal punctuation (see Cma 4.1). With the typewriter and some word processing software, make the dash by striking the hyphen twice, without spacing before or after. Full-featured word processing software will usually allow you to insert a dash with a special character code. Depending on the software, you either insert the code through a combination of keystrokes or by selecting the character from a character map.

Budgets for some past years—1991, for example—were prepared without consulting the department heads.
The test proved that the new process is simple, effective, accurate—and more expensive.
Only one person—the supervisor in charge—has authority to issue such an order.
If you want a voice in the government—vote.

## Exclamation Mark: Ex

*Use exclamation marks to show strong feeling.*

Use the exclamation mark at the end of a sentence or an exclamatory fragment to show strong emotion. But use it sparingly; never use it with trivial ideas.

We've done it again!
No! It can't be!

## Hyphen: Hpn 1

*Mark word divisions with hyphens.*

Use the hyphen to indicate the division of a word at the end of the line. You must divide between syllables. It is generally impractical to leave a one-

PART 7  Special Topics in Business Communication

letter syllable at the end of a line (*a-bove*) or to carry over a two-letter syllable to the next line (*expens-es*).

If you turn on the hyphenation feature of your word processing software, you can let it automatically take care of hyphenating words. Several programs let you set a hyphenation range. The wider the range the fewer words that will be hyphenated and the more ragged your margin; the narrower the range the more words that will be hyphenated and the smoother your right margin. Some have the option of allowing you to control the hyphenation you desire. You can accept what the program recommends, suggest a different place to hyphenate, or tell it not to hyphenate. Most programs will use their internal dictionaries for determining where to hyphenate words; some programs allow you to use an external dictionary for hyphenating words. These external dictionaries usually can be modified to suit your needs and preferences.

## Hpn 2

Place hyphens between the parts of some compound words. Generally, the hyphen is used whenever its absence would confuse the meaning of the words.

*Place hyphens between the parts of compound words.*

*Compound nouns:* brother-in-law, cure-all, city-state
*Compound numbers twenty-one through ninety-nine:* fifty-five, seventy-seven
*Compound adjectives* (two or more words used before a noun as a single adjective): *long-term* contract, *50-gallon* drum, *door-to-door* selling, *end-of-month* clearance.
*Prefixes* (most have been absorbed into the word): co-organizer, ex-chairperson, anti-inflation

## Hpn 2.1

A proper name used as a compound adjective needs no hyphen or hyphens to hold it together as a visual unit for the reader. The capitals perform that function.

*Do not place hyphens between (1) proper names and*

*Correct:* A Lamar High School student
*Correct:* A United Airlines pilot

## Hpn 2.2

Two or more modifiers in normal grammatical form and order need no hyphens. Particularly, a phrase consisting of an unmistakable adverb (one ending in *ly*) modifying an adjective or participle that in turn modifies a noun shows normal grammatical order and is readily grasped by the reader without the benefit of the hyphen. But an adverb not ending in *ly* had better be joined to its adjective or participle by the hyphen.

*(2) words that only follow each other.*

*No hyphen needed:* A poorly drawn chart.
*Use the hyphen:* A well-prepared chart

## Italics: Ital 1

For the use of italics for book titles, see QM 4. Note that italics are also used for titles of periodicals, works of art, long musical compositions, and names of naval vessels and aircraft.

*Use italics for (1) publication titles,*

### *Reference Software: Tools Made Easier with Task Swapping*

Reference software, like reference books, are sources for looking up facts when you need them. All kinds of reference materials are available electronically from dictionaries, grammar and style guides, encyclopedias, zip code directories, maps, and much, much more. These programs vary widely in their similarities to and differences with traditional reference books. Some employ hypertext, allowing you to take any path and go to any depth much the same as you would with a reference book. For example, these programs open with a menu similar to a table of contents. You select the topic you want to look up, and you are linked directly to that information. Furthermore, the program may allow you to get more information by clicking on buttons, words, icons, or pressing a certain key. If the screen presents a concept, you might be able to bring up either more explanation or examples or both by continuing on this path. Of course, hypertext documents usually allow you to back up one screen or return to the first screen. Multimedia programs generally use hypertext, allowing documents to contain text as well as audio and visual materials.

Other reference software use database schemes, which work like using an index. You tell the software what you want to know, and it brings up that information on the screen. Furthermore, some programs do more for you than their printed counterparts. For example, most people use printed dictionaries to look up meanings of words. However, sometimes you don't have the right spelling or it does not mean what you thought. With electronic dictionaries you can tell the software the meaning, and it will give you a list of words you might want. For example, you might tell the software the word you want is a disease, it is fatal, but it is not cancer. The software will search its database to find all words that contain *fatal* **and** *disease* in their definitions **without** the word *cancer*.

While these programs have been around for many years, a new operating system feature is making them easier to use—task swapping. Until now, switching between these programs was cumbersome, so you probably either did not bother; or you grabbed the reference book from the shelf and looked it up manually. Of course, there were a few alternatives, but most of us took the easy way out. Now you have an *easy* alternative with task swapping. Task swapping simply means you can leave one application for another, returning later to the exact place you left. It is similar to writing manually, consulting your dictionary to check a meaning, and returning to your paper to write. Using the task swapping feature of today's operating systems empowers writers by providing access to powerful, easy-to-use writing tools.

### Ital 2

(2) foreign words and abbreviations, and

Italicize rarely used foreign words—if you must use them (*déjà vu, bon vivant, pro bono publico, ich dien*). After a foreign word is widely accepted, however, it does not need to be italicized (bon voyage, pizza, rancho). A current dictionary is a good source for information on which foreign words are italicized.

### Ital 3

Italicize a word, letter, or figure used as its own name. Without this device, we could not write this set of rules. Note the use of italics throughout to label name words.

The little word *sell* is still in the dictionary.

The pronoun *which* should always have a noun as a clear antecedent. [Without the italics, this one becomes a fragment ending in midair.]

(3) a word used as its own name.

### Parentheses: Parens

Use the parenthesis to set off words that are parenthetic or are inserted to explain or supplement the principal message (see Cma 4.1).

Dr. Samuel Goppard's phenomenal prediction (*Business Week,* June 20, 1992) has made some business forecasters revise their techniques.

As soon as Smith was elected chairperson (the vote was almost 2 to 1), he introduced his plan for reorganization.

Set off parenthetic words with parentheses.

### Period: Pd 1

Use the period to indicate the end of a declarative sentence.

End a declarative sentence with a period.

### Pd 2

Use periods after abbreviations or initials.

Ph.D., Co., Inc., A.M., A.D., etc.

But omit the periods and use all capitals in names of agencies, networks, associations, and such: IRS, NBC, OPEC.

Use periods in abbreviations.

### Pd 3

Use ellipses (a series of periods) to indicate the omission of words from a quoted passage. If the omitted part consists of something less than a sentence, three periods are customarily placed at the point of omission (a fourth period is added if the omission is a sentence or more). If the omitted part is a paragraph or more, however, a full line of periods is used. In either case, the periods are appropriately typed with intervening spaces.

Logical explanations, however, have been given by authorities in the field. Some attribute the decline . . . to recent changes in the state's economy. . . .
. . . . . . . . . . . . . . . . . . . . . . . . . . . . . . . . . . . . . . . . . . . . . . . . . . . . . . . . . . .
Added to the labor factor is the high cost of raw material, which has tended to eliminate many marginal producers. Moreover, the rising cost of electric power in recent years may have shifted the attention of many industry leaders to other forms of production.

Use a series of periods to show omissions.

### Question Mark: Q

Place a question mark at the end of sentences that are direct questions.

What are the latest quotations on Ewing-Bell common stock?

Will this campaign help sell Dunnco products?

End direct questions with the question mark.

But do not use the question mark with indirect questions.

The president was asked whether this campaign would help sell Dunnco products.

He asked me what the latest quotations on Ewing-Bell common stock were.

Also, do not use a question mark after a courteous request.

Will you please send the report as soon as possible.

Will you let me know the amount we owe on our last order.

### Quotation Marks: QM 1

**Use quotation marks to enclose a speaker's exact words.**

Use quotation marks to enclose the exact words of a speaker or, if the quotation is short, the exact words of a writer.

Short written quotations are quotations of four lines or less, though authorities do not agree on this point. Some suggest three lines—others up to eight. Longer written quotations are best displayed without quotation marks and with additional indented right and left margins.

*Short written quotation:* H. G. McVoy sums up his presentation with this statement: "All signs indicate that automation will be evolutionary, not revolutionary."

*Verbal quotation:* "This really should bring on a production slowdown," said Ms. Kuntz.

If a quotation is broken by explanation or reference words, each part of the quotation is enclosed in quotation marks.

"Will you be specific," he asked, "in recommending a course of action?"

### QM 2

**Use single quotation marks for a quotation within a quotation.**

Enclose a quotation within a quotation with single quotation marks.

President Carver said, "It has been a long time since I have heard an employee say, 'Boss, I'm going to beat my quota today.'"

### QM 3

**Periods and commas go inside quotation marks; semicolons and colons go outside; question marks and exclamation points go inside when they apply to the quoted part and outside when they apply to the entire sentence.**

Always place periods and commas inside quotation marks. Place semicolons and colons outside the quotation marks. Place question marks and exclamation points inside if they apply to the quoted passage only and outside if they apply to the whole sentence.

"If we are patient," he said, "prosperity will arrive someday." (The comma and the period are within the quotation marks.)

"Is there a quorum?" he asked. (The question mark belongs to the quoted passage.)

Which of you said, "I know where the error lies"? (The question mark applies to the entire sentence.

I conclude only this from the union's promise to "force the hand of management": Violence will be its trump card.

### QM 4

**Use quotation marks to enclose titles of parts of a publication.**

Enclose in quotation marks the titles of parts of publications (articles in a magazine, chapters in a book). But italicize the titles of whole publications. If your software or printer will not italicize, use underscoring.

The third chapter of the book *Elementary Statistical Procedure* is entitled "Concepts of Sampling."

Joan Glasgow's most recent article, "A Union Boss Views Automation," appears in the current issue of *Fortune* (typewritten as Fortune).

### Semicolon: SC 1

Use the semicolon to separate independent clauses that are not connected by a conjunction.

Cork or asbestos sheeting must be hand-cut; polyurethane may be poured into a mold.

The new contract provides substantial wage increases; the original contract emphasized shorter hours.

Use the semicolon to separate independent clauses not connected by a conjunction.

Covered by this standard are independent clauses connected by conjunctive adverbs such as *however, nevertheless, therefore, then, moreover,* and *besides.*

The survey findings indicated a need to revise the policy; nevertheless, the president vetoed the amendment.

Small-town buyers favor the old model; therefore, the board concluded that both models should be manufactured.

### SC 2

You may use the semicolon to separate independent clauses joined by *and, but, or, for,* or *nor* (coordinating conjunctions) if the clauses are long or if they have other punctuation in them. In such situations, you may also use the semicolon for special emphasis.

The FTU and the IFL, rivals from the beginning of the new industry, have shared almost equally in the growth of membership; but the FTU predominates among workers in the petroleum-products crafts, including pipeline construction and operation, and the IFL leads in memberships of chemical workers.

The market price was $4; but we paid $7.

You may choose to separate with a semicolon independent clauses joined by a conjunction.

### SC 3

Separate by semicolons the items in a list when the items have commas in them.

The following gains were made in the February year-to-year comparison: Fort Worth, 7,300; Dallas, 4,705; Lubbock, 2,610; San Antonio, 2,350; Waco, 2,240; Port Arthur, 2,170; and Corpus Christi, 1,420.

Elected for the new term were Anna T. Zelnak, attorney from Cincinnati; Wilbur T. Hoffmeister, stockbroker and president of Hoffmeister Associates of Baltimore; and William P. Peabody, a member of the faculty of the University of Georgia.

Use the semicolon to separate items in a list when the items contain commas.

### SC 4

Use the semicolon between equal (coordinate) units only. Do not use it to attach a dependent clause or phrase to an independent clause.

*Below standard:* The flood damaged much of the equipment in Building 113; making it necessary for management to stop production and lay off all production workers.

Use the semicolon only between equal units.

*Acceptable:* The flood damaged much of the equipment in Building 113, making it necessary for management to stop production and lay off all production workers.

*Acceptable:* The flood damaged much of the equipment in Building 113; thus, it was necessary for management to stop production and lay off all production workers.

## STANDARDS FOR GRAMMAR

Like the review of punctuation standards, the following summary of grammatical standards is not intended as a complete handbook on the subject. Rather, it is a summary of the major trouble spots encountered by business writers. If you learn these grammatical principles, you should be able to write with the correctness expected in business.

### Adjective-Adverb Confusion: AA

> Do not use adjectives for adverbs.

Do not use adjectives for adverbs or adverbs for adjectives. Adjectives modify only nouns and pronouns; and adverbs modify verbs, adjectives, or other adverbs.

Possibly the chief source of this confusion is statements in which the modifier follows the verb. If the modifier refers to the subject, an adjective should be used. If it refers to the verb, an adverb is needed.

*Below standard:* She filed the records *quick.*
*Acceptable:* She filed the records *quickly.* [Refers to the verb.]
*Below standard:* John doesn't feel *badly.*
*Acceptable:* John doesn't feel *bad.* [Refers to the noun.]
*Below standard:* The new cars look *beautifully.*
*Acceptable:* The new cars look *beautiful.* [Refers to the noun.]

It should be noted that many words are both adjective and adverb (*little, well, fast, much*). And some adverbs have two forms, of which one is the

### Get It Rihgt!

Don't use no double negative.
Make each pronoun agree with their antecedent.
Join clauses good, like a conjunction should.
About them sentence fragments.
When dangling, watch your participles.
Verbs has to agree with their subjects.
Just between you and I, the case is important too.
Don't write run-on sentences they are hard to read.
Don't use commas, which aren't necessary.
Its important to use your apostrophe's correctly.
Proofread your writing to see if you any words out.
Correct spelling is esential.

same as the adjective and the other adds *ly* (*slow* and *slowly, cheap* and *cheaply, quick* and *quickly*).

*Acceptable:* All our drivers are instructed to drive *slow.*

*Acceptable:* All our drivers are instructed to drive *slowly.*

### Subject-Verb Agreement: Agmt SV

Nouns and their verbs must agree in number. A plural noun must have a plural verb form; a singular noun must have a singular verb form.

Verbs must agree in number with their subjects.

*Below standard:* Expenditures for miscellaneous equipment *was* expected to decline. [*Expenditures* is plural, so its verb must be plural.]

*Acceptable: Expenditures* for miscellaneous equipment *were* expected to decline.

*Below standard:* The *president,* as well as his staff, *were* not able to attend. [*President* is the subject, and the number is not changed by the modifying phrase.]

*Acceptable:* The *president,* as well as his staff, *was* not able to attend.

Compound subjects (two or more nouns joined by *and*) require plural verbs.

Compound subjects require plural verbs.

*Below standard:* The *salespeople* and their *manager is* in favor of the proposal. [*Salespeople* and *manager* are compound subjects of the verb, but *is* is singular.]

*Acceptable:* The *salespeople* and their *manager are* in favor of the proposal.

*Below standard: Received* in the morning delivery *was* a *word processing program* and two *reams* of letterhead paper. [*Word processing program* and *reams* are the subjects; the verb must be plural.]

*Acceptable:* Received in the morning delivery *were* a *word processor* and *two reams* of letterhead paper.

Collective nouns may be either singular or plural, depending on the meaning intended.

Collective nouns may be singular or plural.

*Acceptable:* The *committee have* carefully *studied* the proposal. [*Committee* is thought of as separate individuals.]

*Acceptable:* The *committee has* carefully *studied* the proposal. [The *committee* is thought of as a unit.]

As a rule, the pronouns *anybody, anyone, each, either, everyone, everybody, neither, nobody, somebody,* and *someone* take a singular verb. The word *none* may be either singular or plural, depending on whether it is used to refer to one unit or to more than one unit.

The pronouns listed here are singular.

*Acceptable: Either* of the advertising campaigns *is* costly.

*Acceptable: Nobody* who watches the clock *is* successful.

*Acceptable: None* of the boys *understands* his assignment.

*Acceptable: None* of the boys *understand* their assignments.

### Adverbial Noun Clause: AN

Do not use an adverbial clause as a noun clause. Clauses beginning with *because, when, where, if,* and similar adverbial connections are not properly used as subjects, objects, or complements of verbs.

Do not use an adverbial clause as a noun clause.

*Not this:* The reason was *because* he did not submit a report.

*But this:* The reason was *that* he did not submit a report.

*Not this:* A time-series graph is *where* (or *when*) changes in an index such as wholesale prices are indicated.
*But this:* A time-series graph is the picturing of . . .

## Awkward: Awk

**Avoid awkward writing.**

Avoid awkward writing. By *awkward writing* we mean word arrangements that are unconventional, uneconomical, or simply not the best for quick understanding.

## Dangling Modifiers: Dng

**Avoid dangling modifiers (those that do not clearly modify a specific word).**

Avoid the use of modifiers that do not logically modify a word in the sentence. Such modifiers are said to dangle. They are both illogical and confusing. You can usually correct sentences containing dangling constructions by inserting the noun or pronoun that the modifier describes, or by changing the dangling part to a complete clause.

*Below standard:* Believing that credit customers should have advance notice of the sale, special letters were mailed to them.
*Acceptable:* Believing that credit customers should have advance notice of the sale, we mailed special letters to them. (Improvement is made by inserting the pronoun modified.)
*Acceptable:* Because we believed that credit customers should have advance notice of the sale, we mailed special letters to them. (Improvement is made by changing the dangling element to a complete clause.)

Dangling modifiers are of four principal types: participial phrases, elliptical clauses, gerund phrases, and infinitive phrases.

*Below standard:* Believing that District 7 was not being thoroughly covered, an additional salesperson was assigned to the area. [Dangling participial phrase.]
*Acceptable:* Believing that District 7 was not being thoroughly covered, the sales manager assigned an additional salesperson to the area.
*Below standard:* By working hard, your goal can be reached. [Dangling gerund phrase.]
*Acceptable:* By working hard, you can reach your goal.
*Below standard:* To succeed at this job, long hours and hard work must not be shunned. (Dangling infinitive phrase.)
*Acceptable:* To succeed at this job, one must not shun long hours and hard work.
*Below standard:* While waiting on a customer, the radio was stolen. (Dangling elliptical clause—a clause without a noun or verb.)
*Acceptable:* While the salesperson was waiting on a customer, the radio was stolen.

**Some introductory phrases are permitted to dangle.**

There are, however, a few generally accepted introductory phrases that are permitted to dangle. Included in this group are *generally speaking, confidentially speaking, taking all things into consideration,* and such expressions as *in boxing, in welding,* and *in farming.*

*Acceptable:* Generally speaking, business activity is at an all-time high.
*Acceptable:* In farming, the land must be prepared long before planting time.

*Acceptable:* Taking all things into consideration, this applicant is the best for the job.

## Sentence Fragment: Frag

Avoid the sentence fragment. Although the sentence fragment may sometimes be used to good effect, as in sales writing, it is best avoided by all but the most skilled writers. The sentence fragment consists of any group of words that are used as if they were a sentence but are not a sentence. Probably the most frequent cause of sentence fragments is the use of a subordinate clause as a sentence.

Avoid sentence fragments (words used as a sentence that are not a sentence).

*Below standard:* Believing that you will want an analysis of sales for November. We have sent you the figures.

*Acceptable:* Believing that you will want an analysis of sales for November, we have sent you the figures.

*Below standard:* He declared that such a procedure would not be practical. And that it would be too expensive in the long run.

*Acceptable:* He declared that such a procedure would not be practical and that it would be too expensive in the long run.

## Pronouns: Pn 1

Make certain that the word each pronoun refers to (its antecedent) is clear. Failure to conform to this standard causes confusion, particularly in sentences in which two or more nouns are possible antecedents or the antecedent is far away from the pronoun.

A pronoun should refer clearly to a preceding word.

*Below standard:* When the president objected to Mr. Carter, he told him to mind his own business. [Who told whom?]

*Acceptable:* When the president objected to Mr. Carter, Mr. Carter told him to mind his own business.

*Below standard:* The mixture should not be allowed to boil, so when you do it, watch the temperature gauge. [*It* doesn't have an antecedent.]

*Acceptable:* The mixture should not be allowed to boil, so when conducting the experiment, watch the temperature gauge.

*Below standard:* The Model V is being introduced this year. Ads in *Time, The Saturday Evening Post,* and big-city newspapers over the country are designed to get sales off to a good start. It is especially designed for the novice boater who is not willing to pay a big price.

*Acceptable:* The Model V is being introduced this year. Ads in *Time, The Saturday Evening Post,* and big-city newspapers over the country are designed to get sales off to a good start. The new model is especially designed for the novice boater who is not willing to pay a big price.

Confusion may sometimes result from using a pronoun with an implied antecedent.

*Below standard:* Because of the disastrous freeze in the citrus belt, it is necessary that most of them be replanted.

*Acceptable:* Because of the disastrous freeze in the citrus belt, most of the citrus orchards must be replanted.

Except when the reference of *which, that,* and *this* is perfectly clear, it is wise to avoid using these pronouns to refer to the whole idea of a preceding

Usually avoid using *which, that,* and *this* to refer to broad ideas.

clause. Many times you can make the sentence clear by using a clarifying noun following the pronoun.

*Below standard* [following a detailed presentation of the writer's suggestion for improving the company suggestion-box plan]: This should be put into effect without delay.

*Acceptable:* This suggestion-box plan should be put into effect right away.

## Pn 2

**The number of a pronoun should be the same as that of the word to which the pronoun refers.**

The number of the pronoun should agree with the number of its antecedent (the word it stands for). If the antecedent is singular, its pronoun must be singular. If the antecedent is plural, its pronoun must be plural.

*Below standard:* Taxes and insurance are necessary evils in any business, and *it* must be considered carefully in anticipating profits.

*Acceptable:* Taxes and insurance are necessary evils in any business, and *they* must be considered carefully in anticipating profits.

*Below standard:* Everybody should plan for *their* retirement. [Such words as *everyone, everybody,* and *anybody* are singular.]

*Acceptable:* Everybody should plan for *his or her* retirement.

## Pn 3

**Use the correct case of pronoun.**

Take care to use the correct case of the pronoun. If the pronoun serves as the subject of the verb, or if it follows a form of the infinitive *to be,* use a pronoun in the nominative case. (The nominative personal pronouns are *I, you, he, she, it, we,* and *they*).

*Acceptable:* *He* will record the minutes of the meeting.
*Acceptable:* I think it will be *he.*

If the pronoun is the object of a preposition or a verb, or if it is the subject of an infinitive, use the objective case. (The objective personal pronouns are *me, you, him, her, it, us, them.*)

*Below standard:* This transaction is between you and *he.* [*He* is nominative and cannot be the object of the preposition *between.*]

*Acceptable:* This transaction is between you and *him.*

*Below standard:* Because the investigator praised Ms. Smith and *I,* we were promoted.

*Acceptable:* Because the investigator praised Ms. Smith and *me,* we were promoted.

The case of a relative pronoun (*who, whom*) is determined by the pronoun's use in the clause it introduces. One good way of determining which case to use is to substitute the personal pronoun for the relative pronoun. If the case of the personal pronoun that fits is nominative, use *who.* If it is objective, use *whom.*

*Acceptable:* George Cutler is the salesperson *who* won the award. [*He* (nominative) could be substituted for the relative pronoun; therefore, nominative *who* should be used.]

*Acceptable:* George Cutler is the salesperson *whom* you recommended. [Objective *him* could be substituted; thus, objective *whom* is used.]

The possessive case is used for pronouns that immediately precede a gerund (a verbal noun ending in *ing*).

*Acceptable: Our* selling of the stock frightened some of the conservative members of the board.

*Acceptable: Her* accepting the money ended her legal claim to the property.

## Parallelism: Prl

Parts of a sentence that express equal thoughts should be parallel (the same) in grammatical form. Parallel constructions are logically connected by the coordinating conjunctions *and*, *but*, and *or*. Care should be taken to see that the sentence elements connected by these conjunctions are of the same grammatical type. That is, if one of the parts is a noun, the other parts should also be nouns. If one of the parts is an infinitive phrase, the other parts should also be infinitive phrases.

Express equal thoughts in parallel (equal) grammatical form.

*Below standard:* The company objectives for the coming year are to match last year's production, higher sales, and improving consumer relations.

*Acceptable:* The company objectives for the coming year are to match last year's production, to increase sales, and to improve consumer relations.

*Below standard:* Writing copy may be more valuable experience than to make layouts.

*Acceptable:* Writing copy may be more valuable experience than making layouts.

*Below standard:* The questionnaire asks for this information: number of employees, what is our union status, and how much do we pay.

*Acceptable:* The questionnaire asks for this information: number of employees, union affiliation, and pay scale.

## Tense: Tns

The tense of each verb, infinitive, and participle should reflect the logical time of happening of the statement: Every statement has its place in time. To communicate that place exactly, you must select your tenses carefully.

The tense of each verb should show the logical time of happening.

### Tns 1

Use present tense for statements of fact that are true at the time of writing.

Use present tense for current happenings.

*Below standard:* Boston *was* not selected as a site for the aircraft plant because it *was* too near the coast. [Boston is still near the coast, isn't it?]

*Acceptable:* Boston was not selected as a site for the aircraft plant because it *is* too near the coast.

### Tns 2

Use past tense in statements covering a definite past event or action.

Use past tense for past happenings.

*Below standard:* Mr. Burns *says* to me, "Bill, you'll never make an auditor."

*Acceptable:* Mr. Burns *said* to me, "Bill, you'll never make an auditor."

### Tns 3

The time period reflected by the past participle (*having been* . . .) is earlier than that of its governing verb. The present participle (*being* . . .) reflects the same time period as that of its governing verb.

The past participle (*having been* . . .) indicates a time earlier than that of the governing verb, and the present participle (*being* . . .) indicates the same period as that of the governing verb.

*Below standard:* These debentures are among the oldest on record, *being* issued in early 1937.
*Acceptable:* These debentures are among the oldest on record, *having been* issued in early 1937.
*Below standard:* Ms. Sloan, *having been* the top salesperson on the force, was made sales manager. [possible but illogical.]
*Acceptable:* Ms. Sloan, *being* the top salesperson on the force, was made sales manager.

## Tns 4

<aside>Verbs in the principal clause govern those in subordinate clauses.</aside>

Verbs in subordinate clauses are governed by the verb in the principal clause. When the main verb is in the past tense, you should usually also place the subordinate verb in a past tense (past, present perfect, or past perfect).

*Acceptable:* I *noticed* [past tense] the discrepancy, and then I *remembered* [same time as main verb] the incidents that had caused it.

If the time of the subordinate clause is earlier than that of the main verb in past tense, use past perfect tense for the subordinate verb.

*Below standard:* In early July, we *noticed* [past] that he *exceeded* [logically should be previous to main verb] his quota three times.
*Acceptable:* In early July, we *noticed* that he *had exceeded* his quota three times.

<aside>Present perfect tense (*have* . . .) refers to the indefinite past.</aside>

The present perfect tense is used for the subordinate clause when the time of this clause is subsequent to the time of the main verb.

*Below standard:* Before the war we *contributed* [past] generously, but lately we *forget* [should be a time subsequent to the time of the main verb] our duties.
*Acceptable:* Before the war we *contributed* generously, but lately we *have forgotten* our duties.

## Tns 5

The present perfect tense does not logically refer to a definite time in the past. Instead, it indicates time somewhere in the indefinite past.

*Below standard:* We *have audited* your records on July 31 of 1991 and 1992.
*Acceptable:* We *audited* your records on July 31 of 1991 and 1992.
*Acceptable:* We *have audited* your records twice in the past.

## Word Use: WU

<aside>Use words correctly.</aside>

Misused words call attention to themselves and detract from the writing. The possibilities of error in word use are infinite; the following list contains only a few of the common errors of this kind.

| DON'T USE | USE |
| --- | --- |
| a long ways | a long way |
| and etc. | etc. |
| anywheres | anywhere |
| continue on | continue |
| different than | different from |

| | |
|---|---|
| have got to | must |
| in back of | behind |
| in hopes of | in hope of |
| in regards to | in regard to |
| inside of | within |
| kind of satisfied | somewhat satisfied |
| nowhere near | not nearly |
| nowheres | nowhere |
| off of | off |
| over with | over |
| seldom ever | seldom |
| try and come | try to come |

## Wrong Word: WW

Wrong words refer to meaning one word and using another. Sometimes these words are confused by their spelling and sometimes by their meanings. Here are a few examples:

*Check the spelling and meanings of words carefully.*

| | |
|---|---|
| affect | effect |
| among | between |
| capital | capitol |
| cite | sight |
| collision | collusion |
| complement | compliment |
| cooperation | corporation |
| deferential | differential |
| except | accept |
| implicit | explicit |
| imply | infer |
| principal | principle |
| stationary | stationery |

## Standards for the Use of Numbers: No

Quantities may be spelled out or expressed as numerals. Whether to use one form or the other is often a perplexing question. It is especially perplexing to business writers, for much of their work deals with quantitative subjects. Because the proper expression of quantities is vital to business writers, the following notes on the use of numbers are presented.

### No 1

Although authorities do not agree on the number usage, business writers would do well to follow the rule of nine. By this rule, you spell out numbers nine and below. You use figures for numbers above nine.

*Spell out numbers nine and under, and use figures for higher numbers, except as follows:*

*Correct:* The auditor found 13 discrepancies in the stock records.

*Correct:* The auditor found nine discrepancies in the stock records.

**CHAPTER 21** Special Topic: Correctness of Communication

Apply the rule to both ordinal and cardinal numbers:

*Correct:* She was the seventh applicant.
*Correct:* She was the 31st applicant.

## No 2

**Spell out numbers that begin a sentence.**

Make an exception to the rule of nine when a number begins a sentence. Spell out all numbers in this position.

*Correct:* Seventy-three bonds and six debentures were destroyed.
*Correct:* Eighty-nine men picketed the north entrance.

## No 3

**Keep in the same form all numbers in comparisons.**

In comparisons, keep all numbers in the same form. If any number requires numeral form, use numerals for all the numbers.

*Correct:* We managed to salvage 3 lathes, 1 drill, and 13 welding machines.

## No 4

**Use numerals for percentages.**

Use numerals for all percentages.

*Correct:* Sales increases over last year were 9 percent on automotive parts, 14 percent on hardware, and 23 percent on appliances.

Concerning whether to use the percent sign (%) or the word, authorities differ. One good rule to follow is to use the sign in papers that are scientific or technical and the word in all others. Also, it is conventional to use the sign following numbers in graphics. The trend in business appears to be toward using the sign. Consistent use of either is correct.

## No 5

**Use figures for days of the month when the month precedes the day.**

Present days of the month in figure form when the month precedes the day.

*Correct:* July 3, 1992

When days of the month appear alone or precede the month, they may be either spelled out or expressed in numeral form according to the rule of nine.

*Correct:* I will be there on the 13th.
*Correct:* The union scheduled the strike vote for the eighth.
*Correct:* Ms. Millican signed the contract on the seventh of July.
*Correct:* Sales have declined since the 14th of August.

## No 6

**Present amounts like other numbers, spelling units when numbers are spelled and using appropriate symbols or abbreviations when in figures.**

Present money amounts as you would other numbers. If you spell out the number, also spell out the unit of currency.

Twenty-seven dollars

If you present the number as a figure, use the symbol with Canadian and U.S. currency and the appropriate abbreviation or symbol with other currencies.

PART 7 Special Topics in Business Communication

U.S. and Canada         $27.33
France                  Fr 743.21
Germany                 DM 45.72
Great Britain           £231.91

### No 7

Use either of the two orders for date information. One, preferred by the *Chicago Manual of Style*, is day, month, and year:

29 June 1992

The other is the conventional sequence of month, day, and year. This order requires that the year be set off by commas:

On June 29, 1992, we began production.

> For dates, use either day, month, year or month, day, year sequence, the latter with year set off by commas.

### No 8

Usually spell out rounded numbers.

*Correct:* Over a million people live there.
*Correct:* The current population is about four hundred thousand.

> Usually spell rounded numbers.

### No 9

Use the word form for a number that begins a sentence.

*Correct:* Thirty-nine men and 77 women reported for work.
*Correct:* Nineteen ninety-two was our best year.

> Use the word form for a number that begins a sentence.

### No 10

Except in legal documents, do not express amounts in both figures and words.

*Appropriate for legal purposes:* 25 (twenty-five)
*Appropriate for business use:* either the figure or the word, depending on circumstance

> Do not use both word and figure except for legal reasons.

### Spelling: SP

Misspelling is probably the most frequently made error in writing. And it is the least excusable. It is inexcusable because all one needs to do to eliminate the error is to use a dictionary or a spell checker.

Unfortunately, we must memorize to spell. Thus, becoming a good speller involves long and hard work. Even so, you can improve your spelling significantly with relatively little effort. Studies show that fewer than 100 words account for most spelling errors. So if you will learn to spell these most troublesome words, you will go a long way toward solving your spelling problems. Eighty of these words appear in Figure 21–1. Although English spelling follows little rhyme or reason, a few helpful rules exist. You would do well to learn and use them.

> Spell words correctly. Use the dictionary.
>
> See Figure 21–1 for the 80 most commonly misspelled words.

**FIGURE 21-1** Eighty of the Most Frequently Misspelled Words

| | | | |
|---|---|---|---|
| absence | desirable | irritable | pursue |
| accessible | despair | leisure | questionnaire |
| accommodate | development | license | receive |
| achieve | disappear | misspelling | recommend |
| analyze | disappoint | necessary | repetition |
| argument | discriminate | newsstand | ridiculous |
| assistant | drunkenness | noticeable | seize |
| balloon | embarrassment | occasionally | separate |
| benefited | equivalent | occurrence | sergeant |
| category | exceed | panicky | sheriff |
| cede | existence | parallel | succeed |
| changeable | forty | paralyze | suddenness |
| committee | grammar | pastime | superintendent |
| comparative | grievous | persistent | supersede |
| conscience | holiday | possesses | surprise |
| conscious | incidentally | predictable | truly |
| coolly | indispensable | privilege | until |
| definitely | insistent | proceed | vacuum |
| dependent | irrelevant | professor | vicious |
| description | irresistible | pronunciation | weird |

## Rules for Word Plurals

*These three rules cover plurals for most words.*

1. To form the plurals of most words, add *s*.

   cat, cats
   dog, dogs

2. To form the plurals of words ending in *s*, *sh*, *ch*, and *x*, usually add *es* to the singular.

   glass, glasses
   dish, dishes
   bunch, bunches
   ax, axes

3. To form the plural of words ending in *y*, if a consonant precedes the *y*, drop the *y* and add *ies*. But if the *y* is preceded by a vowel, add *s*.

   pony, ponies
   chimney, chimneys

## Other Spelling Rules

*These rules cover four other trouble areas of spelling.*

1. Words ending in *ce* or *ge* do not drop the *e* when adding *ous* or *able*.

   charge, chargeable
   change, changeable
   notice, noticeable
   service, serviceable

PART 7 Special Topics in Business Communication

2. Words ending in *l* do not drop the *l* when adding *ly*.

   final, finally
   principal, principally

3. Words ending in silent *e* usually drop the *e* when adding a suffix beginning with a vowel.

   have, having
   believe, believable
   dive, diving
   time, timing

4. Place *i* before *e* except after *c*.

   relieve    conceive
   believe    receive

   Exception: when the word is sounded as long *a*.

   neighbor    weigh

   Exceptions:

   either      Fahrenheit     height
   seize       surfeit        efficient
   sufficient  neither        foreign
   leisure     ancient        seizure
   weird       financier      codeine
   forfeit     seismograph    sovereign
   deficient   science        counterfeit

## Capitalization: Cap

Use capitals for the first letters of all proper names. Common examples are these:

Streets: 317 East Boyd Avenue
Geographic places: Chicago, Indiana, Finland
Companies: Berkowitz Manufacturing Company, Inc.
Title preceding names: President Watkins
Titles of books, articles, poems: *Basic Business Communication*
First words of sentences and complimentary closes
The word *number* (or its abbreviation) when used with a figure to identify something: Number 1, Oak Circle

> Capitalize all proper names and the beginning words of sentences.

As noted earlier, other standards are useful in clear communication. But those covered in the preceding pages will help you through most of your writing problems. By using them, you can give your writing the precision that good communication requires.

## APPLICATION EXERCISES

Correct any punctuation or grammar errors you can find in the following sentences. Explain your corrections.

1. Charles E. Baskin the new member of the advisory committee has been an employee for seven years.
2. The auditor asked us, "If all members of the work group had access to the petty cash fund?"
3. Our January order consisted of the following items; two dozen Norwood desk calendars, note size, one dozen desk blotters, 20 by 32 inches, and one dozen bottles of ink, permanent black.
4. The truth of the matter is, that the union representative had not informed the workers of the decision.
5. Sales for the first quarter were the highest in history, profits declined for the period.
6. We suggest that you use a mild soap for best results but detergents will not harm the product.
7. Employment for October totaled 12,741 an increase of 3.1 percent over September.
8. It would not be fair however to consider only this point.
9. It is the only water-repellent snagproof and inexpensive material available.
10. Todd Thatcher a supervisor in our company is accused of the crime.
11. Mr. Goodman made this statement, "Contrary to our expectations, Smith and Company will lose money this year."
12. I bought and he sold.
13. Soon we saw George Sweeney who is the auditor for the company.
14. Sold in light medium and heavy weight this paper has been widely accepted.
15. Because of a common belief that profits are too high we will have to cut our prices on most items.
16. Such has been the growth of the cities most prestigious firm, H.E. Klauss and Company.
17. In 1991 we were advised in fact we were instructed to accept this five year contract.
18. Henrys playing around has got him into trouble.
19. Cyrus B. Henshaw who was our leading salesperson last month is the leading candidate for the position.
20. The sales representative who secures the most new accounts will receive a bonus.
21. The word phone which is short for telephone should be avoided in formal writing.
22. In last months issue of Modern Business appeared Johnson's latest article What Systems Theory Means to You.
23. Yes he replied this is exactly what we mean.
24. Why did he say John it's too late?
25. Place your order today, it is not too late.
26. We make our plans on a day to day basis.
27. There is little accuracy in the 60 day forecast.
28. The pre Christmas sale will extend over twenty six days.
29. We cannot tolerate any worker's failure to do their duty.
30. An assortment of guns, bombs, burglar tools, and ammunition were found in the cellar.
31. If we can be certain that we have the facts we can make our decision soon.
32. This one is easy to make. If one reads the instructions carefully.
33. This is the gift he received from you and I.
34. A collection of short articles on the subject were printed.
35. If we can detect only a tenth of the errors it will make us realize the truth.
36. She takes criticism good.
37. There was plenty of surprises at the meeting.
38. It don't appear that we have made much progress.
39. The surface of these products are smooth.
40. Everybody is expected to do their best.
41. The brochures were delivered to John and I early Sunday morning.
42. Who did he recommend for the job.
43. We were given considerable money for the study.
44. He seen what could happen when administration breaks down.
45. One of his conclusions is that the climate of the region was not desirable for our purposes.
46. Smith and Rogers plans to buy the Bridgeport plant.
47. The committee feels that no action should be taken.
48. Neither of the workers found their money.

49. While observing the employees, the work flow was operating at peak perfection.
50. The new building is three stories high, fifteen years old, solid brick construction, and occupies a corner lot.
51. They had promised to have completed the job by noon.
52. Jones has been employed by the Sampson Company for twenty years.
53. Wilson and myself will handle the job.
54. Each man and woman are expected to abide by this rule.
55. The boiler has been inspected on April 1 and May 3.
56. To find problems and correcting them takes up most of my work time.
57. The carton of canned goods were distributed to the employees.
58. The motor ran uneven.
59. All are expected except John and she.
60. Everyone here has more ability than him.

## A SELF-ADMINISTERED DIAGNOSTIC TEST OF PUNCTUATION AND GRAMMAR

The following test is designed to give you a quick measure of your ability to handle some of the most troublesome punctuation and grammar situations. First, correct all the errors in each sentence. Then turn to Appendix A for the recommended corrections and the symbols for the punctuation and grammar standards involved. Next, study the standards that you violate.

1. An important fact about this keyboard is, that it has the patented "feather touch".
2. Goods received on Invoice 2741 are as follows; three dozen white shirts, size 15-33, four mens felt hats, brown, size 7, and five dozen assorted ties.
3. James Silver president of the new union started the campaign for the retirement fund.
4. We do not expect to act on this matter however until we hear from you.
5. Shipments through September 20, 1992 totaled 69,485 pounds an increase of 17 percent over the year ago total.
6. Brick is recommended as the building material but the board is giving serious consideration to a substitute.
7. Markdowns for the sale total $34,000, never before has the company done anything like this.
8. After long experimentation a wear resistant high grade and beautiful stocking has been perfected.
9. Available in white green and blue this paint is sold by dealers all over the country.
10. George Steel who won the trip is our most energetic salesperson.
11. Good he replied, sales are sure to increase.
12. Hogan's article Retirement? Never!, printed in the current issue of Management Review, is really a part of his book A Report on Worker Security.
13. Formal announcement of our pre Labor Day sale will be made in thirty-two days.
14. Each day we encounter new problems. Although they are solved easily.
15. A list of models, sizes, and prices of both competing lines are being sent to you.
16. The manager could not tolerate any employee's failing to do their best.
17. A series of tests were completed only yesterday.
18. There should be no misunderstanding between you and I.
19. He run the accounting department for five years.
20. This report is considerable long.
21. Who did you interview for the position?
22. The report concluded that the natural resources of the Southwest was ideal for the chemical industry.
23. This applicant is six feet in height, 28 years old, weight 165 pounds, and has had eight years' experience.
24. While reading the report, a gust of wind came through the window, blowing papers all over the room.
25. The sprinkler system has been checked on July 1 and September 3.

# CHAPTER 22

# BUSINESS RESEARCH METHODS

## CHAPTER OBJECTIVES

*Upon completing this chapter, you will be able to design and implement a plan for conducting the research needed for a business-report problem. To reach this goal, you should be able to*

### 1
Explain the difference between primary and secondary research.

### 2
Describe appropriate procedures for direct and indirect library research.

### 3
Describe the procedures for searching through company records and conducting experiments.

### 4
Design an observational study for a business problem.

### 5
Explain sampling as it relates to conducting a survey.

### 6
Discuss the techniques for constructing a questionnaire, developing a working plan, and conducting a pilot test for a survey.

### 7
Analyze and interpret information clearly and completely for your reader.

## INTRODUCTORY SITUATION

### to Business Research Methods

Introduce yourself to this chapter by assuming the position of administrative assistant to Carmen Bergeron, the vice president for human resources for Mammoth Industries. Today at a meeting of plant administrators, someone commented about the low morale in the production departments. The production vice president immediately came to the defense of his area, claiming that there is no proof of the statement—that in fact quite the opposite is true. Others joined in with their views, and in time a heated discussion developed. In an effort to ease tensions, Ms. Bergeron suggested that her office conduct a survey of plant personnel "to learn the truth of the matter." The administrators liked the idea.

After the meeting, Ms. Bergeron called you in to tell you that you would be the one to do the research. And she wants the findings in report form in time for next month's meeting. She didn't say much more. No doubt she thinks your college training equipped you to handle the assignment.

Now you must do the research. This means you will have to work out a plan for a survey. Specifically, you will have to design a sample, construct a questionnaire, devise an interview procedure, conduct interviews, record findings—and more. All these activities require much more than a casual understanding of research. There are right ways and wrong ways of going about them. How to do them right is the subject of this chapter. ■

You can collect the information needed for your report by using the two basic forms of research—secondary research and primary research. Secondary research is research utilizing material that someone else has presented in printed form—through periodicals, brochures, books, and such. Commonly called *library research,* secondary research may be the first form of research that you use in some problems (see "Preliminary Investigation," Chapter 12). Primary research is research that uncovers information firsthand. It is research that produces new findings.

*The two basic forms of research are secondary research (getting information from printed sources) and primary research (getting information firsthand).*

To be effective as a report writer, you should be familiar with the techniques of both secondary and primary research. A brief summary of each appears in the following pages.

### ■ ■ ■ ■ ■ ■ ■ ■ ■ ■ ■ ■ ■ ■
### SECONDARY RESEARCH

Secondary research materials are potentially the least costly, the most accessible, and the most complete source of information. However, to take full advantage of the available materials, you must know what you are looking for and where and how to find it.

*Secondary research can be a rich source of information if you know what to look for and where to look.*

The task can be complex and challenging. You can meet the challenge if you become familiar with the general arrangement of a library or other repositories of secondary materials and if you learn the techniques of finding those materials. Also, research must be orderly if it is to be reliable and complete.

In the past, researchers used a card system to help them keep track of the sources they identified. This card system can be combined with and adapted to a computer system quite easily. The manual system of organization

*Keep track of the sources you gather in an orderly way.*

required that the researcher complete two sets of cards. One set was simply a bibliography card set, containing complete information about sources. A researcher numbered these cards consecutively as the sources were identified. A second set of cards contained the notes from each source. Each of these cards was linked to its source through the number of the source in the bibliography card set.

Since the computer systems in today's libraries often allow users to print the citations they find from the indexes and databases, it makes the most sense to number the source on the printout rather than recopy it to a card. Not only is it usually more legible than one's handwriting; it is also complete. Some writers will cut their printouts apart and tape them to a master sheet. Others will enter these items in databases they build. With the widespread use of notebook and laptop computers, many researchers are taking notes on computers rather than cards. These notes can be linked to the original source by number as in the manual system.

No matter whether you use a manual, combined, or computer system, using one is essential.

### Finding Publication Collections

The first step in an orderly search for printed information is to determine where to begin. The natural place, of course, is a library. However, as different types of libraries offer different kinds of collections, it is helpful to know what types of libraries are available and to be familiar with their contents.

| A library is the natural place to begin secondary research.

*General libraries* are the best known and the most accessible. General libraries, which include college, university, and most public libraries, are called *general* to the extent that they contain all kinds of materials. Many general libraries, however, have substantial collections in certain specialized areas.

| General libraries offer the public a wide variety of information sources.

Libraries that limit their collections to one type or just a few types of material are considered *special libraries*. Many such libraries are private and do not invite routine public use of their materials. Still, they will frequently cooperate on research projects that they consider relevant and worthwhile.

| Special libraries have limited collections and limited circulation.

Among the special libraries are the libraries of private businesses. As a rule, such libraries are designed to serve the sponsoring company and provide excellent information in the specialized areas of its operations. Company libraries are less accessible than other specialized libraries, but a letter of inquiry explaining the nature and purpose of a project or a letter of introduction from someone known to the company can help you gain access to them.

Special libraries are also maintained by various types of associations—for example, trade organizations, professional and technical groups, chambers of commerce, and labor unions. Like company libraries, association libraries may provide excellent coverage of highly specialized areas. Although such libraries develop collections principally for members or a research staff, they frequently make resources available to others engaged in reputable research.

A number of public and private research organizations also maintain specialized libraries. The research divisions of big-city chambers of commerce and the bureaus of research of major universities, for example, keep extensive collections of material containing statistical and general information on a local area. State agencies collect similar data. Again, though these materials are developed for a limited audience, they are often made available upon request.

Now, how do you determine what these research centers and special libraries offer and whom to contact for permission to use their collections? Several guides are available in the reference department of most general libraries. The *American Library Directory* is a geographic listing of libraries in the United States and Canada. It gives detailed information on libraries, including special interests and collections. It covers all public libraries as well as many corporate and association libraries. The Special Libraries Association has chapters in many large cities that publish directories for their chapter areas. Particularly helpful in identifying the information available in research centers is *The Research Centers Directory*. Published by Gale Research Company, it lists the research activities, publications, and services of 7,500 university-related and other nonprofit organizations. It is supplemented between editions by a related publication, *New Research Centers*.

> Consult a directory to determine what special libraries offer.

Gale Research also publishes three comprehensive guides to special library collections. *The Directory of Special Libraries and Information Centers* describes the contents and services of 16,500 information centers, archives, and special and research libraries. Each entry includes the address and telephone number of the facility and the name and title of the individual in charge. A companion guide, *Subject Directory of Special Libraries and Information Centers,* organizes the same information by subject. The third guide, *New Special Libraries,* is a periodic supplement of the first.

### Taking the Direct Approach

When you have found the appropriate library for your research, you are ready for the next challenge. With the volume of material available, how will you find what you need? Many cost-conscious businesses are hiring professionals to find information for them. These professionals' charges range from $40 to $80 per hour in addition to any on-line charges incurred. Other companies like to keep their information gathering more confidential; some employ company librarians and others expect their employees to gather the information. If you know nothing about how material is arranged in a library, you will waste valuable time on a probably fruitless search. However, if you are familiar with certain basic reference materials, you may be able to proceed directly to the information you seek. And if the direct approach does not work, there are several effective indirect methods of finding the material you need.

> Begin your research using the direct approach. Look up the information you need. But some companies hire specialists to do this work.

Taking the direct approach is advisable when you seek quantitative or factual information. The reference section of your library is where you should start. There, either on your own or with the assistance of a research librarian, you can discover any number of timely and comprehensive sources of facts and figures. Although you cannot know all these sources, as a business researcher you should be familiar with certain basic ones. These sources are available in either print or electronic forms. You should be able to use both.

Secondary research now can be done by computer. Here a student is using *The World Almanac and Book of Facts* stored on read-only optical disk.

Encyclopedias offer both general and detailed information.

**Encyclopedias.** Encyclopedias are the best-known sources of direct information and are particularly valuable when you are just beginning a search. They offer background material and other general information that give you a helpful introduction to the area under study. Individual articles or sections of articles are written by experts in the field and frequently include a short bibliography.

Of the general encyclopedias, two worthy of special mention are *The Encyclopedia Americana* and the *Encyclopaedia Britannica.* Another one gaining wide use and acceptance is Grolier's *Academic American Encyclopedia.* It is available on several information services and updated every three months. Also helpful are such specialized encyclopedias as the *Encyclopaedia of the Social Sciences, The Encyclopedia of Accounting Systems, Encyclopedia of Banking and Finance,* and *The Encyclopedia of Management.*

Biographical directories offer information about influential people.

**Biographical Directories.** A direct source of biographical information about leading figures of today or of the past is a biographical directory. The best-known biographical directories are *Who's Who in America* and *Who's Who in the World,* annual publications that summarize the lives of living people who have achieved prominence. Similar publications provide coverage by geographic area: *Who's Who in the East* and *Who's Who in the Midwest,* for example. For biographical information about prominent Americans of the past, the *Dictionary of American Biography* is useful. Specialized publications will help you find information on people in particular professions. Among the most important of these are *Who's Who in Finance and Industry; Standard & Poor's Register of Corporations, Directors, and Executives; Dun & Bradstreet's Reference Book of Corporate Management; Who's Who in Labor; Who's Who in Economics; The Rand McNally International Bankers Directory; Who's Who in Insurance;* and *Who's Who in Computer Education and Research.* Nearly all business and professional areas are covered by some form of directory.

**Almanacs.** Almanacs are handy guides to factual and statistical information. Simple, concise, and selective in their presentation of data, they should not be underestimated as references. *The World Almanac and Book of Facts,* published by the Newspaper Enterprise Association, Inc., is an excellent general source of facts and statistics. If you need business and investment data, *The Business One-Irwin Investor's Handbook* provides comprehensive coverage of timely information. Some of the information you will find in it is a chronological presentation of business events during the past year, industry surveys, financial general business and economic indicators, stock market data, a glossary, and much more.

*Almanacs provide factual and statistical information.*

**Trade Directories.** For information about individual businesses or the products they make, buy, or sell, directories are the references to consult. Directories are compilations of details in specific areas of interest and are variously referred to as *catalogs, listings, registers,* or *source books.* Some of the more comprehensive directories are indispensable in general business research. The more useful ones include *The Million Dollar Directory* (a listing of U.S. companies compiled by Dun & Bradstreet), *Thomas Register of American Manufacturers,* and *The Datapro Directory.* Some directories that will help you determine linkages between parent and subsidiaries include *America's Corporate Families* and *Who Owns Whom* (both compiled by Dun & Bradstreet) as well as the *Directory of Corporate Affiliations.* Literally thousands of directories exist—so many, in fact, that there are two directories of directories (*Trade Directories of the World* and *Directory of Directories*).

*Trade directories publish information about individual businesses and products.*

**Government Publications.** Governments (national, state, provincial, etc.) publish hundreds of thousands of titles each year. In fact, the U.S. government is the world's largest publisher. Surveys, catalogs, pamphlets, periodicals—there seems to be no limit to the information that various bureaus, departments, and agencies collect and make available to the public. The challenge of working with government publications, therefore, is finding your way through this wealth of material to the specifics you need. That task can sometimes be so complex as to require indirect research methods. However, if you are familiar with a few key sources, the direct approach will often be productive.

*Governments (national, state, provincial, etc.) publish extensive research materials.*

In the United States, it may be helpful to consult the *Monthly Catalog of U.S. Government Publications.* Issued by the Superintendent of Documents, it includes a comprehensive listing of annual and monthly publications and an alphabetical index of the issuing agencies. It can be searched on-line. The Superintendent of Documents also issues *Selected United States Government Publications,* a monthly list of general-interest publications that are sold to the public.

*The U.S. government publishes guides to its publications.*

**These government publications are invaluable in business research.**

Routinely available are a number of specialized publications that are invaluable in business research. These include *Census of Population, Census of Housing, Annual Housing Survey, Consumer Income and Population Characteristics, Census of Governments, Census of Retail Trade, Census of Manufacturers, Census of Agriculture, Census of Construction Industries, Census of Transportation, Census of Service Industries, Census of Wholesale Trade,* and *Census of Mineral Industries.* The *Statistical Abstract of the United States* is another invaluable publication, as are the *Survey of Current Business,* the *Monthly Labor Review,* the *Occupational Outlook Quarterly,* and the *Federal Reserve Bulletin.* To say the least, government sources are extensive.

**Dictionaries provide meanings, spellings, and pronunciations for both general and specialized words and phrases.**

**Dictionaries.** Dictionaries are helpful for looking up meanings, spellings, and pronunciations of words or phrases. They are available in both general and specialized versions. While it might be nice to own an unabridged dictionary, an abridged collegiate or desk dictionary will answer most of your questions. You should be aware that the name *Webster* can be legally used by any dictionary publisher. Also, dictionaries often include added features such as style manuals, signs, symbols, and weights and measures. Because dictionaries reflect current usage, you want to be sure the one you use is up-to-date. Not only are new words being added but spellings and meanings change, too. Several good dictionaries are the *American Heritage Dictionary, Funk & Wagnalls Standard Dictionary,* the *Random House Webster's Collegiate Dictionary,* and *Webster's New Collegiate Dictionary.*

Specialized dictionaries concentrate on one functional area. Some business dictionaries are the *Dictionary of Management,* the *MBA's Dictionary, The Dictionary of Business and Management,* the *McGraw-Hill Dictionary of Modern Economics,* and the *Computer Glossary.* There are also dictionaries of acronyms and abbreviations. Two of these are *Acronyms, Initialisms, and Abbreviations Dictionary,* and *Abbreviations Dictionary.*

**Statistical information is available both on-line and in printed form.**

**Statistical Sources.** Today's businesses rely heavily on statistical information. Not only is this information helpful in the day-to-day operations of their businesses, but it is helpful in planning future products, expansions, and strategies. Today a good deal of statistical information is available on-line; some is only available on-line. Sometimes it is available on-line long before the data can be printed and distributed. In any case, there are several sources of statistical information you should be aware of. These sources are both public and private.

In order to facilitate the collection and retrieval of statistical data for industry, the United States government developed a classification system, called the SIC (Standard Industrial Classification) code. This system uses a four-digit code for all manufacturing and nonmanufacturing industries.

**Basic publications provide broad coverage and source listings for more detailed statistics.**

Some of the basic comprehensive publications include the *Handbook of Basic Economic Statistics,* the *Statistical Abstract of the United States,* the *Predicasts Basebook,* and *Standard & Poor's Statistical Service.* These sources are a starting point when you are not familiar with a more specialized source. These publications include historical data on American industry, commerce, labor and agriculture; industry data by SIC codes; numerous indexes such as producer/price indexes, housing indexes, and stock price indexes. Additionally, the *Statistical Abstract of the United States* contains an extremely useful "Guide to Sources of Statistics."

If you are not certain where to find statistics, you may find various guides useful. The *American Statistics Index* is an index to statistics published by all government agencies. It identifies the agency, describes the statistics, and provides access by category. The *Encyclopedia of Business Information Sources* provides a listing of information sources along with names of basic statistical sources. The *Statistical Reference Index* is a good source of statistics published by sources other than the government, such as trade and professional associations. *Predicasts Forecasts* is useful for current forecasting statistical sources. It documents the source of the data as well. And it has a source directory arranged by title, geographic index, and SIC codes. These directories will help direct you to specialized statistics when you need them.

**Business Services.** Business services are private organizations that supply a variety of information to business practitioners, especially investors. Libraries also subscribe to their publications, giving business researchers ready access to yet another source of valuable, timely data.

> Private business services collect and publish data. Many such reports are available in public and university libraries.

Moody's Investors' Service, one of the best known of such organizations, publishes a weekly *Manual* in each of six business areas: transportation, industrials, OTC (over-the-counter) industrials, public utilities, banks and finance, and municipals and governments. These reports summarize financial data and operating facts on all the major American companies, providing information that an investor needs to evaluate the investment potential of individual securities or of fields as a whole. *Corporation Records,* published by Standard & Poor's Corporation, presents similar information in loose-leaf form. Both Moody's and Standard & Poor's provide a variety of related services, including *Moody's Investors' Advisory Service* and Standard & Poor's *Value Line Investment Service*.

Two other organizations whose publications are especially helpful to business researchers are Predicasts, Inc. and Gale Research Company. Predicasts, Inc. provides seven separate business services, although it is best known for publications featuring forecasts and market data by country, product, and company (*Predicasts, World-Regional-Casts, World-Product-Casts,* and *Expansion and Capacity Digest*). Similarly, Gale Research Company provides numerous services to business researchers.

**International Sources.** In today's global business environment, we often need information outside our borders. Many of the sources we have discussed have counterparts with international information. *Principal International Businesses* lists basic information on major companies located over the world. *Major Companies of Europe* and *Japan Company Handbook* are two sources providing facts on companies in their respective areas. The *International Encyclopedia of the Social Sciences* covers all important areas of social science, including biographies of acclaimed persons in these areas. General and specialized dictionaries are available, too. *The Multilingual Commercial Dictionary* and the *International Business Dictionary in Nine Languages* include commonly used business terms in several languages. You will even be able to find trade names in the *International Trade Names*

> Statistical information for the international business environment is available in a wide range of documents.

*Dictionary* published by Gale Research. For bibliographies and abstracts, available sources include *International Business Reference Sources, Business International Index,* the *Foreign Commerce Handbook,* and several more. Even statistical information is available in sources such as the *Index to International Statistics, Statistical Yearbook,* and *Worldcasts.* In addition, libraries usually contain many references for information on international marketing, exporting, tax, and trade.

### Using Indirect Methods

If you cannot move directly to the information you need, you must use indirect methods to find it. The first step in this approach is preparing a bibliography, or a list of prospective sources. The next two steps are gathering the publications in your bibliography and systematically checking them for the information you need.

These two steps are elementary, but nonetheless important. Your acquisition of secondary materials must be thorough. You should not depend solely on the material you find on the shelves of your library. Use interlibrary loan services or database searches; send away for company or government documents. Your check of the sources you gather must also be thorough. For each source, review the pages cited in your bibliographic reference. Then take some time to learn about the publication. Review its table of contents, its index, and the endnotes or footnotes related to the pages you are researching. You should be familiar with both the source and the context of all the information you plan to report; they are often as significant as the information itself.

However, the first step, preparing the bibliography, is still the most demanding and challenging task in indirect research. It is therefore helpful to review what this task involves.

**Prepared Bibliographies.** You should begin the preparation of your own bibliography by looking for one that has already been prepared. Lists of published materials are available through a number of sources, and finding such a list may save you the time and trouble of developing a bibliography from scratch.

Start your search in the reference section of your library. Prepared bibliographies are sometimes published as reference books, and individual entries in these books often include a description. In the reference section you may also find bibliographies that have been compiled by associations or government agencies. Encyclopedias are also a helpful source of published materials; most encyclopedia articles conclude with a brief bibliography.

Another way to discover prepared bibliographies is to consult texts, articles, and master's and doctor's theses that deal with your subject. If books include bibliographies, it is so noted on their cards in the card catalog. Academic studies routinely include complete bibliographies. Articles present the most challenging task, for not all of them list their sources. However, since those that do are likely to include very timely and selective listings, it is worth the trouble to check articles individually.

**The Library Catalog.** If you are not able to locate a prepared bibliography, or if the bibliographies you have identified are inadequate, you must set

**FIGURE 22-1** The main menu screen presents choices of ways to search for information in the electronic card catalog.

```
            Welcome to the SDSU Library
            Public Access Catalog (the PAC)

    You may search for library materials by any of the following:

                A > AUTHOR
                T > TITLE
                W > KEYWORDS in TITLES
                S > SUBJECT
                J > JUVENILE BOOKS
                C > CALL #

                R > RESERVE Lists
                I > Library INFORMATION
                D > Disconnect

            Choose one (A,T,W,S,J,C,R,I,D) :
```

about developing your own list of prospective sources. Here the library catalog is very helpful.

If the catalog you are using is composed of cards, it offers three distinct ways of identifying and locating desired references: by author, by title, and by subject. However, today many libraries are using electronic catalogs, giving you numerous ways to locate sources. As you can see from the main menu screen of one system in Figure 22-1, in some ways electronic catalogs are similar to card catalogs. You can still locate sources by author, title, and subject. In addition, the electronic catalogs give you more main options and more options within each choice. The options you have will depend on the system installed and the way your librarians decided to set it up.

Two options you need to understand clearly are *keywords in titles* and *subject.* When the *keywords in titles* option is selected, the system will ask you for the keywords and then search only the titles for those keywords. This means that the items it finds will likely be on the subject you need. However, it misses all those whose titles do not contain the words you keyed in. For example, if you wanted to know more about cross-cultural communication, using keywords in title would find only those items with those exact words in the title. It would miss titles with the words *intercultural communication, international communication,* and *global communication.* If you did multiple searches using all the similar terms you could think of, it would still miss those titles without the keywords, such as Robert Axtell's *Dos and Taboos Around the World.*

The subject search, on the other hand, is broader. Using the subject *intercultural communication,* you will find items on the subject, whether or not the exact words are indicated in the title. For example, you might find a management book with a chapter on *intercultural* communication; however, the book's emphasis might be on something else, such as crisis management or conflict resolution.

Library catalogs list the holdings of each library.

Understanding how the catalog systems work will help you gather information efficiently.

The electronic catalog never gets tired. If you key in the words accurately, it will always produce a complete and accurate list of sources. Let us look at a few results from a subject search on *intercultural* communication. Notice in Figure 22-2 that the system found 99 sources. That is more than you really want, so you decide to select the option shown at the bottom of the screen to limit your search. This system then gives you some options for limiting your search (see Figure 22-3). You decide to limit the search by year, telling it you want it to find all sources after 1990 (see Figure 22-4). As you can see in Figure 22-5, nine entries were found. When you ask the system to display the title and author, it brings up the screen shown in Figure 22-6. Not only will you find the title and author, but you will also find complete bibliographic information, the call number, and the status along with subjects which this book fits. Furthermore, the system gives you the option of browsing through other books nearby on the shelf.

The card catalog is a useful source of information for your library's holdings. Learning how to use it effectively will save you time and will help your searches be efficient and effective.

**Periodical Indexes.** The card catalog helps you identify books for your bibliography. To identify articles published in newspapers, magazines, or journals, you will need to consult an index, either a general one or one that specializes in the field you are researching. Regularly updated indexes are available in the reference section of most libraries.

If you are like most business researchers, you will start your search for periodical literature with the *Business Periodicals Index*. Issued monthly

> To identify articles for your list of prospective sources, consult a periodical index.

**FIGURE 22-2** This screen shows you that the system's search for the subject intercultural communication found 99 entries.

```
You searched for the SUBJECT: intercultural communication
99 entries found, entries 1-8 are:                           CALL #
Intercultural Communication
    1  Advertising international : the privati  HF5821 .M3213 1991
    2  The alchemy of English : the spread, fu  PE2751. K3 1986
    3  American communication in a global soci  E840.2 .F57
    4  American communication in a global soci  E840.2 .F57 1987
    5  America's mass media merchants           P92.U5 R4
    6  Anthropological other or Burmese brothe  GN345 .S66 1992
    7  The Asian mind game : unlocking the hid  HD58.6 .C474 1991
    8  BaFa BaFa : a cross culture simulation.  SG-99




    Please type the NUMBER of the item you want to see, or
    F > Go FORWARD          A > ANOTHER Search by SUBJECT    J > JUMP
    R > RETURN to Browsing  D > DISPLAY Title and Author
    N > NEW Search          L > LIMIT this Search
    Choose one (1-8,F,R,N,A,D,L,J)
```

PART 7  Special Topics in Business Communication

**FIGURE 22-3** This screen's menu gives you options for limiting your search.

```
You searched for the SUBJECT: intercultural communication
99 entries found, entries 1-8 are:                        CALL #


            You may limit your search by any of the following:

                    L > LANGUAGE
                    M > MATERIAL type
                    A > Words in the AUTHOR
                    T > Words in the TITLE
                    S > Words in the SUBJECT
                    P > PUBLISHER
                    Y > YEAR of publication
                    R > RETURN to Browsing

                    Choose one (L,M,A,T,S,P,Y,R)
```

**FIGURE 22-4** After you have limited your search to after 1990, you can find, limit, expand, or back up one screen by choosing one of this menu's options.

```
You searched for the SUBJECT: intercultural communication
99 entries found, entries 1-8 are:                        CALL #
     YEAR of publication AFTER 1990


                    F > FIND items with above limits

                    A > AND    (Limit further)
                    O > OR     (Expand retrieval)
                    R > RETURN to Previous Screen

                    Choose one (F,A,O,R)
```

and cumulated yearly, this index covers articles in 300 major business periodicals and indexes, by subject headings and company references. Another index that you may find useful is the *United States Predicasts F & S Index*, which covers over 700 business-oriented periodicals, newspapers, and special reports. A third index that may be helpful is the *Public Affairs Information Service Bulletin*. It lists by subject information relating to economics and public affairs. In addition, you may find useful such specialized indexes as *Findex: the Directory of Market Research; Reports, Studies, and Surveys; Marketing Information Guides;* and the *Accountant's Index*. These indexes are often available on-line or on CDs. One widely used index is *InfoTrac*. It will find citations for subjects you search and in many cases provide an abstract of the article.

**FIGURE 22-5** When you limit your search to after 1990, this screen shows you the results (9 entries) along with the first eight items in alphabetical order.

```
You searched for the SUBJECT: intercultural communication LIMITED TO AFTER 1990
9 entries found, entries 1-8 are:                          CALL #
Intercultural Communication
    1  Advertising international : the privati  HF5821 .M3213 1991
    2  Anthropological other or Burmese brothe  GN345 .S66 1992
    3  The Asian mind game : unlocking the hid  HD58.6 .C474 1991
    4  Bridging differences : effective interg  HM258 .G838 1991
    5  The Bushman myth : the making of a Nami  DT1558.S38 G67 1992
    6  Cultures and organizations : software o  HM258 .H574 1991
    7  Intercultural communication : a reader   HM258 .I52 1991
    8  Profiting in America's multicultural ma  HF5718 .T457 1991




Please type the NUMBER of the item you want to see, or
F > Go FORWARD                    A > ANOTHER Search by SUBJECT
R > RETURN to Browsing            D > DISPLAY Title and Author
N > NEW Search                    J > JUMP
Choose one (1-8,F,R,N,A,D,J)
```

**FIGURE 22-6** This screen gives you complete bibliographic information on the item you have selected. Furthermore, it tells you it is currently available.

```
You searched for the SUBJECT: intercultural communication LIMITED TO AFTER 1990
AUTHOR        Thiederman, Sondra B.
TITLE         Profiting in America's multicultural marketplace : how to do
                business across cultural lines / by Sondra Thiederman.
PUBLISHER     New York : Lexington Books ; Toronto : Maxwell Macmillan Canada ;
                New York : Maxwell Macmillan International, c1991.
DESCRIPTION   xxiv, 262 p. ; 24 cm.
NOTE(S)       Includes bibliographical references (p. [253]) and index.
SUBJECT(S)    Business communication.
              Intercultural communication.
CALL #        HF5718 .T457 1991.

    LOCATION          CALL #                    STATUS
 1 > Book Stacks      HF5718 .T457 1991         AVAILABLE

R > RETURN to Browsing        A > ANOTHER Search by SUBJECT
F > FORWARD browse            Z > Show Items Nearby on Shelf
B > BACKWARD browse           S > SHOW items with the same SUBJECT
N > NEW Search
Choose one (R,F,B,N,A,Z,S)
```

**Databases.** Computers offer the most advanced method of conducting secondary research. As you know, the capacity of computers to collect and retrieve information has been expanding phenomenally. Business research has been a primary beneficiary of that expansion. Much of the information routinely recorded in printed form and accessed through directories, encyclopedias, bibliographies, indexes, and the like is now collected and stored in computer files as well. When these files of related information, known collectively as *databases,* are accessed by computer, the result is research that can be more extensive, complete, and accurate than any conducted manually.

*Computers organize and store vast amounts of data.*

Databases, many of which are produced by private information services, offer a variety of materials essential to business research. For example, Dialog Information Systems (DIALOG) includes in its selection of 350 bases the *American Statistics Index,* the *Encyclopedia of Associations,* a number of Predicasts services (*PTS F&S Indexes, International Forecasts,* and *Prompt*), and *Standard & Poor's News.* Two other private information services, Bibliographic Retrieval System (BRS) and LEXIS/NEXIS, offer many of the same information files. In addition, prominent business resources, including Dow Jones & Company, the *Harvard Business Review,* the *New York Times,* and Standard & Poor's, now offer computer access to their data and files.

An increasing number of public, college, and university libraries offer database searching services, usually for a fee that reflects the computer time employed and the number of items identified. They also usually require you to work closely with trained staff to design a strategy that will use computer time effectively and retrieve mostly relevant information. However, considering the potential advantages of computer-assisted research, the cost of the service and the initial inconvenience of designing a computer search strategy are a small price to pay. Many of these information providers, such as DIALOG and Dow Jones News Retrieval Services, offer special price packages. You can search their databases during off-peak times at reduced rates or you can subscribe to some services for a flat fee. Developing your own searching skills will also help to keep costs down.

*Many libraries offer facilities for computer-searching of databases.*

You can keep costs down several ways. One way is by planning carefully before you go on-line to shorten the amount of time you need to be connected to the database. Another way is to choose the correct database the first time. Some database providers have a selection utility you can use. First you tell it the subject you need, then it recommends appropriate databases to use. Using these kinds of "assistants" will pay off by eliminating trial-and-error charges. A third way to cut costs is to know what to do when your search contains too many or two few citations.

*Developing good search strategies will help you keep costs down when using on-line systems.*

If your search gives you more citations than you can handle, be prepared to limit the search. Know ahead of time how you might do this. Most systems let you limit your search by language and year. Sometimes you can add a NOT term, which eliminates citations with a particular term from your search. If your search comes up short, you need to check for spelling errors and narrow terms. If you have a hard time adding terms to broaden your search, look at the keywords or descriptors of the items that have already been identified. Often these will give you ideas on terms to broaden the search. Be sure to keep track of the strategies that work so you can use them in future searches. Learning how to extract information efficiently from databases will pay off immensely, putting information at your fingertips.

## PRIMARY RESEARCH

*Primary research employs four basic methods.*

When you cannot find the information you need in secondary sources, you must get it firsthand. That is, you must use primary research, which employs four basic methods:

1. Search through company records.
2. Experimentation.
3. Observation.
4. Survey.

### Searching through Company Records

*Company records are an excellent source of firsthand information.*

Since many of today's business problems involve various phases of company operations, a company's internal records—production data, sales records, merchandising information, accounting records, and the like—are frequently an excellent source of firsthand information.

*Make sure you (1) have a clear idea of the information you need, (2) understand the terms of access and confidentiality, and (3) cooperate with company personnel.*

There are no set rules on how to go about finding and gathering information through company records. Record-keeping systems vary widely from company to company. However, you are well advised to keep the following standards in mind as you conduct your investigation. First, as in any other type of research, you must have a clear idea of the information you need. Undefined, open-ended investigations are not appreciated—nor are they particularly productive. Second, you must clearly understand the ground rules under which you are allowed to review materials. Matters of confidentiality and access should be resolved before you start. And third, if you are not intimately familiar with a company's records or how to access them, you must cooperate with someone who is. The complexity and sensitivity of such materials require that they be reviewed in their proper context.

### Conducting the Experiment

*Experimentation develops information by testing variable factors.*

The experiment is a very useful technique in business research. Originally perfected in the sciences, the experiment is an orderly form of testing. In general, it is a form of research in which you systematically manipulate one variable factor of a problem while holding all the others constant. You measure quantitatively or qualitatively any changes resulting from your manipulations. Then you apply your findings to the problem.

For example, suppose that you are conducting research to determine whether a new package design will lead to more sales. You might start by selecting two test cities, taking care that they are as alike as possible on all the characteristics that might affect the problem. Then you would secure information on sales in the two cities for a specified period of time before the experiment. Next, for a second specified period of time, you would use the new package design in one of the cities, and continue to use the old package in the other. During that period, you would keep careful sales records and check to make sure that advertising, economic conditions, competition, and other factors that might have some effect on the experiment remain unchanged. Thus, when the experimentation period is over, you can attribute any differences you found between the sales of the two cities to the change in package design.

Each experiment should be designed to fit the individual requirements of the problem. Nonetheless, a few basic designs underlie most experiments. Becoming familiar with two of the most common designs—the before-after and the controlled before-after—will give you a framework for understanding and applying this primary research technique.

*Design each experiment to fit the problem.*

**The Before-After Design.** The simplest experimental design is the before-after design. In this design you select a test group of subjects, measure the variable in which you are interested, and then introduce the experimental factor. After a specified period of time, during which the experimental factor has presumably had its effect, you again measure the variable in which you are interested. If there are any differences between the first and second measurements, you may assume that the experimental factor is the cause. Figure 22–7 illustrates this design.

*The before-after design is the simplest. You use just one test group.*

Consider the following application. Assume that you are conducting research for a retail store to determine the effect of point-of-sale advertising. Your first step is to select a product for the experiment, Brand Y razor blades. Second, you record sales of Brand Y blades for one week, using no point-of-sale advertising. Then you introduce the experimental variable—the Brand Y point-of-sale display. For the next week you again record sales of Brand Y blades; and at the end of that week, you compare the results for the two weeks. Any increase in sales would presumably be explained by the introduction of the display. Thus, if 500 packages of Brand Y blades were sold in the first week and 600 were sold in the second week, you would conclude that the 100 additional sales can be attributed to point-of-sale advertising.

**FIGURE 22–7** The Before-After Design

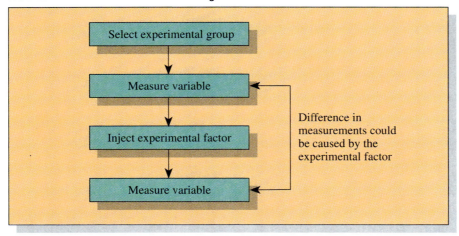

*The changes recorded in a before-after experiment may not be attributable to the experimental factor alone.*

You can probably recognize the major shortcoming of the design. It is simply not logical to assume that the experimental factor explains the entire difference in sales between the first week and the second. The sales of Brand Y razor blades could have changed for a number of other reasons—changes in the weather, holiday or other seasonal influences on business activity, other advertising, and so on. At best, you have determined only that point-of-sale advertising *could* influence sales.

**The Controlled Before-After Design.** To account for influences other than the experimental factors, you may use designs more complex than the before-after design. These designs attempt to measure the other influences by including some means of control. The simplest of these designs is the controlled before-after design.

In the controlled before-after design, you select not one group, but two—the experimental group and the control group. Before introducing the experimental factor, you measure in each group the variable to be tested. Then you introduce the experimental factor into the experimental group only.

*In the controlled before-after experiment, you use two identical test groups. You introduce the experimental factor into one group, then compare the two groups. You can attribute any difference between the two to the experimental factor.*

When the period allotted for the experiment is over, you again measure in each group the variable being tested. Any difference between the first and second measurements in the experimental group can be explained by two causes—the experimental factor and other influences. But the difference between the first and second measurements in the control group can be explained only by other influences, for this group was not subjected to the experimental factor. Thus, comparing the "afters" of the two groups will give you a measure of the influence of the experimental factor. The controlled before-after design is diagrammed in Figure 22–8.

In a controlled before-after experiment designed to test the point-of-sale application, you might select Brand Y razor blades and Brand X razor blades and record the sales of both brands for one week. Next you introduce point-of-sale displays for Brand Y only and you record sales for both Brand Y and

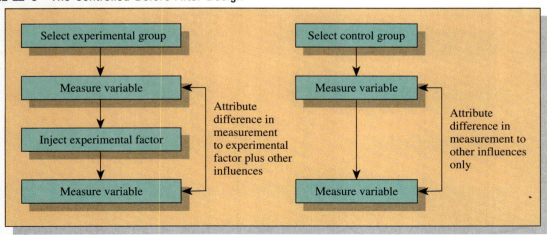

**FIGURE 22–8** The Controlled Before-After Design

744  PART 7  Special Topics in Business Communication

Brand X for a second week. At the end of the second week, you compare the results for the two brands. Whatever difference you find in Brand Y sales and Brand X sales will be a fair measure of the experimental factor, independent of the changes that other influences may have brought about.

For example, if 400 packages of Brand X blades are sold the first week, and 450 packages are sold the second week, the increase of 50 packages (12.5 percent) can be attributed to influences other than the experimental factor, the point-of-sale display. If 500 packages of Brand Y blades are sold the first week, and 600 are sold the second week, the increase of 100 can be attributed to both the point-of-sale display and other influences. To distinguish between the two, you note that other influences accounted for the 12.5 percent increase in the sales of Brand X blades. Because of the experimental control, you attribute 12.5 percent of the increase in Brand Y sales to other influences as well. An increase of 12.5 percent on a base of 500 sales is 63 sales, indicating that 63 of the 100 additional Brand Y sales are the result of other influences. However, the sale of 37 additional packages of Brand Y blades can be attributed to point-of-sale advertising.

### Using the Observation Technique

Like the experiment, observation is a technique perfected in the sciences that is also useful in business research. Simply stated, observation is seeing with a purpose. It consists of watching the events involved in a problem and systematically recording what is seen. In observation, you do not manipulate the details of what you observe; you take note of situations exactly as you find them.

*Research by observation involves watching phenomena and recording what is seen.*

Note that observation as an independent research technique is different from the observation you use in recording the effects of variables introduced into a test situation. In the latter case, observation is a step in the experiment, not an end in itself. The two methods, therefore, should not be confused.

*This form of observation does not involve experimentation.*

To see how observation works as a business technique, consider this situation. You are a grocery supplier who wants to determine how shoppers are responding to a new line of foods. A review of sales records would certainly give some information, as would a survey of store patrons. However, observing customers as they shop may reveal important information that you might overlook if you used alternative techniques.

Like all primary research techniques, observation must be designed to fit the requirements of the problem being considered. However, the planning stage generally requires two steps. First, you construct a recording form; second, you design a systematic procedure for observing and recording the information of interest.

*Observation requires a systematic procedure for observing and recording.*

The recording form may be any tabular arrangement that permits quick and easy recording of that information. Though observation forms are hardly standardized, one commonly used arrangement (see Figure 22–9) provides a separate line for each observation. Headings at the top of the page mark the columns in which the observer will place the appropriate mark. The recording form identifies the characteristics that are to be observed and requires the recording of such potentially important details as the date, time, and place of the observation and the name of the observer.

*The recording form should enable you to record details quickly and accurately.*

**FIGURE 22–9** Excerpt of a Common Type of Observation Recording Form

Characteristics to be observed

Project 317, Ladies Shoe Preferences

Observer __H. C. Hoffman__   Date __Aug. 17__
Place    __311 Commerce, Dallas.__   Time __1:00__

| COLOR | | | | | | | | | HEEL H | | | |
|---|---|---|---|---|---|---|---|---|---|---|---|---|
| BR | BL | W | GR | GY | BR | BL | R | O | 0 | 1/2 | 1 | 2 |
| √ |   |   |   |   |   |   |   |   |   |   | √ |   |
|   |   |   |   |   | √ |   |   |   |   | √ |   |   |
|   |   | √ |   |   |   |   |   |   |   |   |   |   |
|   |   |   |   |   |   |   |   |   |   |   |   |   |
|   |   |   | √ |   |   |   |   |   |   |   |   |   |
|   |   |   | √ |   |   |   |   |   |   |   |   |   |
| √ |   |   |   |   |   |   |   |   |   |   | √ |   |
|   |   |   |   |   |   |   |   |   |   |   |   |   |
|   |   |   |   | √ |   |   |   |   |   |   |   |   |

Separate line for each observation

---

• An effective observation procedure ensures the collection of complete and representative information.

The observation procedure may be any system that ensures the collection of complete and representative information. But every effective observation procedure includes a clear focus, well-defined steps, and provisions for ensuring the quality of the information collected. For example, an observation procedure for determining what style of clothing men wear in a certain city would include a detailed observation schedule for all appropriate sections of the city, detailed observing instructions, and provisions for dealing with all the complications that the observer might encounter. In short, the procedure would leave no major question unanswered.

## Collecting Information by Survey

• You can best determine certain information by asking questions.

The premise of the survey as a method of primary research is simple: You can best determine certain types of information by asking questions. Such information includes personal data, opinions, evaluations, and other important material. It also includes information necessary to plan for an experiment or an observation or to supplement or interpret the data that result.

The survey is a widely-used form of primary research in business. It is especially useful for gathering marketing information.

Once you have decided to use the survey for your research, you have to make decisions about a number of matters. The first is the matter of format. The questions can range from spontaneous inquiries to carefully structured interrogations. The next is the matter of delivery. The questions can be posed in a personal interview, asked over the telephone, or presented in printed form.

But the most important is the matter of whom to survey. Except for situations in which a small number of people are involved in the problem under study, you cannot reach all of the people involved. Thus, you have to select a sample of respondents who represent the group as a whole as accurately as possible. There are several ways to select that sample, as you will see.

**Sampling as a Basis.** Sampling theory forms the basis for most research by survey, though it has any number of other applications as well. Buyers of grain, for example, judge the quality of a multi-ton shipment by examining a few pounds. Quality-control supervisors spot-check a small percentage of products ready for distribution to determine whether production standards are being met. Judges at county fairs take a little taste of each entry of homemade jam to decide which entry will win a blue ribbon.

*Decide which survey format and delivery will be most effective in developing the information you need.*

*Also decide whom to interview. If the subject group is large, select a sample.*

*Survey research is based on sampling.*

*Good samples are reliable, valid, and controlled for sampling error.*

Sampling is generally used for economy and practicality. However, for a sample to be representative of the whole group, it must be designed properly. Two important aspects to consider in the design of a survey are *reliability* and *validity*. You want the results to be reliable, free from random error. A test of a survey's reliability is its repeatability with similar results. You also want your survey to be valid, measuring what it is supposed to measure.

Another aspect of sample design is controlling for sampling error and bias. Sampling error results when the sample is not representative of the whole group. While all samples have some degree of sampling error, you can reduce the error through techniques used to construct representative samples. These techniques fall into two groups—probability and nonprobability sampling.

**Probability Sampling Techniques.** Probability samples are based on chance selection procedures. Every element in the population has a known nonzero probability of selection.[1] These techniques include simple random sampling, stratified random sampling, systematic sampling, and cluster or area sampling.

*In random sampling, every item in the subject group has an equal chance of being selected.*

*Random sampling.* Random sampling is the technique assumed in the general law of sampling. By definition, it is the sampling technique that gives every member of the group under study an equal chance of being included. To assure equal chances, you must first identify every member of the group and then, using a list or some other convenient format, record all the identifications. Next, through some chance method, you select the members of your sample.

For example, if you are studying the job attitudes of 200 assembly-line workers and determine that 25 interviews will give you the information you need, you might make out a name card for each worker, place the 200 cards in a container, mix them up, and draw out 25. Since each of the 200 workers has an equal chance of being selected, your sample will be random and can be presumed to be representative.

*In stratified random sampling, the group is divided into subgroups and the sample is randomly selected from each subgroup.*

*Stratified random sampling.* This special form of random sampling subdivides the group under study and makes random selections within each subgroup. The size of each subgroup is usually proportionate to that subgroup's percentage of the whole. If a subgroup is too small to yield meaningful findings, however, you may have to select a disproportionately large sample. (Of course, when the study calls for statistics on the group as a whole, the actual proportion of such a subgroup must be restored.)

Assume, for example, that you are attempting to determine the curriculum needs of 5,000 undergraduates at a certain college and that you have decided to survey 20 percent of the enrollment, or 1,000 students. To construct a sample for this problem, first divide the enrollment list by academic concentration: business, liberal arts, nursing, engineering, and so forth. Then draw a random sample from each of these groups, making sure that the number you select is proportionate to that group's percentage of the

---

[1] William G. Zikmund, *Business Research Methods*, 2nd edition (Chicago: The Dryden Press, 1988), p. 346.

total undergraduate enrollment. Thus, if 30 percent of the students are majoring in business, you will randomly select 300 business majors for your sample; if 40 percent of the students are liberal arts majors, you will randomly select 400 liberal arts majors for your sample; and so on.

*Systematic sampling.* Systematic sampling, though not random in the strictest sense, is random for all practical purposes. It is the technique of taking selections at constant intervals (every *n*th unit) from a list of the items under study. The interval used is based, as you might expect, on the size of the list and the size of the desired sample. For example, if you want a 10 percent sample of a list of 10,000, you might select every 10th item on the list.

> In systematic sampling, the items are selected from the subject group at constant intervals.

However, your sample would not really be random. By virtue of their designated place on the original list, items do not have an equal chance of being selected. To correct that problem, you might use an equal-chance method to determine what *n* to use. Thus, if you selected the number 7 randomly, you would draw the numbers 7, 17, 27, and so on to 9,997 to make up your sample. Or, if you wanted to draw every 10th item, you might first scramble the list and then select from the revised list numbers 10, 20, 30, and so on up to 10,000 and make up your sample that way.

> Select the interval randomly or scramble the order of the subject group if you want your systematic sample to be random.

*Area or cluster sampling.* In area sampling, the items for a sample are drawn in stages. This sampling technique is appropriate when the area to be studied is large and can be broken down into progressively smaller components. For example, if you want to draw an area sample for a certain city, you may use census data to divide the city into homogeneous districts. Using an equal-chance method, you then select a given number of districts to include in the next stage of your sample. Next you divide each of the selected districts into subdistricts—city blocks, for example. Continuing the process, you randomly select a given number of these blocks and subdivide each of them into households. Finally, using random sampling once more, you select the households that will constitute the sample you will use in your research.

> For an area or cluster sample, draw items from the subject group in stages. Select randomly at each stage.

Area or cluster sampling is not limited to geographic division, however. It is adaptable to any number of applications. For example, it is an appropriate technique to use in a survey of the workers in a given industry. An approach that you may take in this situation is to randomly select a given number of companies from a list of all the companies in the industry. Then, using organization units and selecting randomly at each level, you break down each of these companies into divisions, departments, sections, and so on until you finally identify the workers you will survey.

**Nonprobability Sampling Techniques.** Nonprobability samples are based on an unknown probability of any one of a population being chosen. These techniques include convenience sampling, quota sampling, and referral sampling.[2]

*Convenience sampling.* A convenience sample is one whose members are convenient and economical to reach. When professors use their students as subjects for their research, they are using a convenience sample. Re-

> Convenience samples are chosen for their convenience, their ease and economy of reaching, and their appropriateness.

---

[2] Zikmund, p. 346.

searchers generally use this sample to reach a large number quickly and economically. This kind of sampling is best used for exploratory research.

A form of convenience sampling is *judgment* or *expert* sampling. This technique relies on the judgment of the writer to identify appropriate members of the sample. Illustrating this technique is the common practice of predicting the outcome of an election, based on the results in a bellwether district.

*Quota sampling.* Quota sampling is a nonrandom technique. Also known as *controlled sampling,* it is used whenever the proportionate makeup of the universe under study is available. The technique requires that you refer to the composition of the universe in designing your sample, selecting items so that your sample has the same characteristics in the same proportion as that universe. Specifically, it requires that you set quotas for each characteristic that you want to consider in your research problem. Within those quotas, however, you will select individual items randomly.

> Setting quotas assures that the sample reflects the whole. Choose items randomly within each quota.

Let us say that you want to survey a college student body of 4,000 using a 10 percent sample. As Figure 22–10 illustrates, you have a number of alternatives for determining the makeup of your sample, depending on the focus of your research. Keep in mind, though, that no matter what characteristic you select, the quotas the individual segments represent must total 100 percent and the number of items in the sample must total 400. Keep in mind also that within these quotas you will use an equal-chance method to select the individual members of your sample.

*Referral sampling.* Referral samples are those whose members are identified by others from a random sample. This technique is used to locate members when the population is small or hard to reach. For example, you might want to survey rolle bolle players. To get a sample large enough to make the study worthwhile, you could ask those from your town to give you the names of other players. Perhaps you were trying to survey the users of

> Referral samples are used for small or hard-to-reach groups.

**FIGURE 22–10** Alternative Quota Sample

|  | Number in Universe | Percent of Total | Number to Be Interviewed |
|---|---|---|---|
| Total student enrollment | 4,000 | 100 | 400 |
| **Sex** | | | |
| Men students | 2,400 | 60 | 240 |
| Women students | 1,600 | 40 | 160 |
| **Fraternity, sorority membership** | | | |
| Members | 1,000 | 25 | 100 |
| Nonmembers | 3,000 | 75 | 300 |
| **Marital status** | | | |
| Married students | 400 | 10 | 40 |
| Single students | 3,600 | 90 | 360 |
| **Class rank** | | | |
| Freshmen | 1,600 | 40 | 160 |
| Sophomores | 1,000 | 25 | 100 |
| Juniors | 800 | 20 | 80 |
| Seniors | 400 | 10 | 40 |
| Graduates | 200 | 5 | 20 |

project management software. You could survey a user's group and ask those members for names of other users. You might even post your announcement on a bulletin board system; users of the system would send you the names for your sample.

**Constructing the Questionnaire.** Most orderly interrogation follows a definite plan of inquiry. This plan is usually worked out in a printed form, called the *questionnaire*. The questionnaire is simply an orderly arrangement of the questions, with appropriate spaces provided for the answers. But simple as the finished questionnaire may appear to be, it is the subject of careful planning. It is, in a sense, the outline of the analysis of the problem. In addition, it must observe certain rules. These rules sometimes vary with the problem. The more general and by far the more important ones follow.

**Avoid leading questions.** A leading question is one that in some way influences the answer. For example, the question "Is Dove your favorite bath soap?" leads the respondent to favor Dove. Some people who would say yes would name another brand if they were asked, "What is your favorite brand of bath soap?"

> Avoid leading questions (questions that influence the answer).

**Make the questions easy to understand.** Questions not clearly understood by all respondents lead to error. Unfortunately, it is difficult to determine in advance just what respondents will not understand. As will be mentioned later, the best means of detecting such questions in advance is to test the questions before using them. But you can be on the alert for a few general sources of confusion.

> Word the questions so that all the respondents understand them.

One source of confusion is vagueness of expression, which is illustrated by the ridiculous question "How do you bank?" Who other than its author knows what the question means? Another source is using words not understood by the respondents, as in the question "Do you read your house organ regularly?" The words *house organ* have a specialized, not widely known meaning, and *regularly* means different things to different people. Combining two questions in one is yet another source of confusion. For example, "Why did you buy a Ford?" actually asks two questions: "What do you like about Fords?" and "What don't you like about the other automobiles?"

> Vagueness of expression, difficult words, and two questions in one cause misunderstanding.

**Avoid questions that touch on personal prejudices or pride.** For reasons of pride or prejudices, people cannot be expected to answer accurately questions about certain areas of information. These areas include age, income status, morals, and personal habits. How many people, for example, would answer no to the question "Do you brush your teeth daily?" How many people would give their ages correctly? How many solid citizens would admit to fudging a bit on their tax returns? The answers are obvious.

> Avoid questions of a personal nature.

But one may ask, "What if such information is essential to the solution of the problem?" The answer is to use less direct means of inquiry. To ascertain age, for example, investigators could ask for dates of high school graduation, marriage, or the like. From this information, they could approximate age. Or they could approximate age through observation, although this procedure is acceptable only if broad age approximations would be satisfactory. They could ask for such harmless information as occupation, residential area, and standard of living and then use that information as a basis for approximating income. Another possibility is to ask range questions such as "Are you between 18 and 24, 25 and 40, or over 40?" This technique works well with income questions, too. People are generally more willing to answer

> But if personal questions are necessary, use less direct methods.

questions worded by ranges rather than specifics. Admittedly, such techniques are sometimes awkward and difficult. But they can improve on the biased results that direct questioning would obtain.

**Seek facts as much as possible.** Although some studies require opinions, it is far safer to seek facts whenever possible. Human beings simply are not accurate reporters of their opinions. They are often limited in their ability to express themselves. Frequently, they report their opinions erroneously simply because they have never before been conscious of having them.

When opinions are needed, it is usually safer to record facts and then to judge the thoughts behind them. This technique, however, is only as good as the investigators' judgment. But a logical analysis of fact made by trained investigators is preferable to a spur-of-the-moment opinion.

A frequent violation of this rule results from the use of generalizations. Respondents are sometimes asked to generalize an answer from a large number of experiences over time. The question "Which magazines do you read regularly?" is a good illustration. Aside from the confusion caused by the word *regularly* and the fact that the question may tap the respondent's memory, the question forces the respondent to generalize. Would it not be better to phrase it in this way: "What magazines have you read this month?" The question could then be followed by an article-by-article check of the magazines to determine the extent of readership.

**Ask only for information that can be remembered.** Since the memory of all human beings is limited, the questionnaire should ask only for information that the respondents can be expected to remember. In order to make sure that this is done, a knowledge of certain fundamentals of memory is necessary.

Recency is the foremost fundamental. People remember insignificant events that occurred within the past few hours. By the next day, they will forget some. A month later they may not remember any. One might well remember, for example, what one ate for lunch on the day of the inquiry, and perhaps one might remember what one ate for lunch a day, or two days, or three days earlier. But one would be unlikely to remember what one ate for lunch a year earlier.

The second fundamental of memory is that significant events may be remembered over long periods of time. One may long remember the first day of school, the day of one's wedding, an automobile accident, a Christmas Day, and the like. In each of these examples there was an intense stimulus—a requisite for retention in memory.

A third fundamental of memory is that fairly insignificant facts may be remembered over long periods of time through association with something significant. Although one would not normally remember what one ate for lunch a year earlier, for example, one might remember if the date happened to be one's wedding day, Christmas Day, or one's first day at college. Obviously, the memory is stimulated, not by the meal itself, but by the association of the meal with something more significant.

**Plan the physical layout with foresight.** The overall design of the questionnaire should be planned to facilitate recording, analyzing, and tabulating the answers. Three major considerations are involved in such planning.

First, answers should be allowed sufficient space for recording. When practical, a system for checking answers may be set up. Such a system must

---

Seek factual information whenever possible.

Ask only for information that can be remembered.

Memory is determined by three fundamentals: (1) recency,

(2) intensity of stimulus, and

(3) association.

Design the form for easy recording.

Provide sufficient space.

always provide for all possible answers, including conditional answers. For example, a direct question may provide for three possible answers: Yes _____, No _____, and Don't know _____.

Second, adequate space for identifying and describing the respondent should be provided. In some instances, such information as the age, sex, and income bracket of the respondent is vital to the analysis of the problem and should be recorded. In other instances, little or no identification is necessary.

*Provide adequate identification space.*

Third, the best possible sequence of questions should be used. In some instances, starting with a question of high interest value may have psychological advantages. In some other instances, it may be best to follow some definite order of progression. Frequently, some questions must precede others because they help explain the others. Whatever the requirements of the individual case may be, however, careful and logical analysis should be used in determining the sequence of questions.

*Arrange the questions in logical order.*

**Use scaling when appropriate.** It is sometimes desirable to measure the intensity of the respondents' feelings about something (an idea, a product, a company, and so on). In such cases, some form of scaling is generally useful.

*Provide for scaling when appropriate.*

Of the various techniques of scaling, ranking and rating deserve special mention. These are the simpler techniques and, some believe, the more practical. They are less sophisticated than some others,[3] but the more sophisticated techniques are beyond the scope of this book.

The ranking technique consists simply of asking the respondent to rank a number of alternative answers to a question in order of preference (1, 2, 3, and so on). For example, in a survey to determine consumer preferences for toothpaste, the respondent might be asked to rank toothpastes A, B, C, D, and E in order of preference. In this example, the alternatives could be compared on the number of preferences stated for each. This method of ranking and summarizing results is reliable in spite of its simplicity. There are various more complicated ranking methods (such as the use of paired comparison) and methods of recording results.

*Ranking of responses is one form.*

The rating technique graphically sets up a scale showing the complete range of possible attitudes on a matter and assigns number values to the positions on the scale. The respondent must then indicate the position on the scale that indicates his or her attitude on that matter. Typically, the numeral positions are described by words, as the example in Figure 22–11 illustrates.

*Rating is another.*

Because the rating technique deals with the subjective rather than the factual, it is sometimes desirable to use more than one question to cover the attitude being measured. Logically, the average of a person's answers to such questions gives a more reliable answer than does any single answer.

**Selecting the Manner of Questioning.** You can get answers to the questions you need answered in three primary ways: by personal (face-to-face) contact, by telephone, or by mail. You should select the way that in your unique case gives the best sample, the lowest cost, and the best results. By *best sample* we mean respondents who best represent the group concerned. And

*Select the way of asking the questions (by mail, personal contact, or telephone) that gives the best sample, the lowest cost, and the best results.*

---

[3] Equivalent interval techniques (developed by L. L. Thurstone), scalogram analysis (developed by Louis Guttman), and the semantic differential (developed by C. E. Osgood, G. J. Suchi, and P. H. Tannenbaum) are more complex techniques.

**FIGURE 22-11**

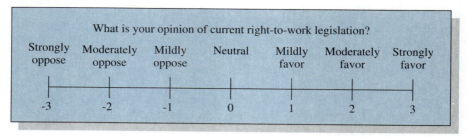

**FIGURE 22-12** Comparison of Data Collection Methods

|  | Personal | Telephone | Mail |
|---|---|---|---|
| Data collection costs | High | Medium | Low |
| Data collection time required | Medium | Low | High |
| Sample size for a given budget | Small | Medium | Large |
| Data quantity per respondent | High | Medium | Low |
| Reaches widely dispersed sample | No | Maybe | Yes |
| Reaches special locations | Yes | Maybe | No |
| Interaction with respondents | Yes | Yes | No |
| Degree of interviewer bias | High | Medium | None |
| Severity of non-response bias | Low | Low | High |
| Presentation of visual stimuli | Yes | No | Maybe |
| Field worker training required | Yes | Yes | No |

Source: Pamela L. Alreck & Robert B. Settle, *The Survey Research Handbook* (Homewood, Ill.: Richard D. Irwin, Inc., 1985).

*results* are the information you need. As you can see in Figure 22–12, other factors will influence your choice.

> Develop a working plan that covers all the steps and all the problems.

**Developing a Working Plan.** After selecting the manner of questioning, you should carefully develop a working plan for the survey. As well as you can, you should anticipate and determine how to handle every possible problem. If you are conducting a mail survey, for example, you need to develop an explanatory message that moves the subjects to respond, tells them what to do, and answers all the questions they are likely to ask. If you are conducting a personal or telephone survey, you need to cover this information in instructions to the interviewers. You should develop your working plan before conducting the pilot study discussed in the following section. You should test that plan in the pilot study and revise it based on the knowledge you gain from the pilot study.

> Test the questionnaire and the working plan. Make any changes needed.

**Conducting a Pilot Study.** Before doing the survey, it is advisable to conduct a pilot study on your questionnaire and working plan. A pilot study is a

"Barker and Gresham, motivation research. Good morning. Why are you *really* calling?"

From The Wall Street Journal, with permission of Cartoon Features Syndicate.

small-scale version of the actual survey. Its purpose is to test what you have planned. Based on your experience in the pilot study, you modify your questionnaire and working plan for use in the full-scale survey that follows.

## Analyzing and Interpreting Data

Gathering information is one step in processing facts for your report. The secondary information you gather needs to be analyzed carefully. Ask yourself questions about the writer's credibility, including methods of collecting facts and ability to draw inferences from the facts presented. Does the author draw conclusions that can be supported by the data presented? Are the sources reliable? Is the data or interpretation biased in any way? Are there any gaps or holes in the data or interpretation? Be a good judge of the material and feel free to let it go if it does not meet your standard for quality. Hold this secondary information to the same high standards you would your own primary data.

*Carefully evaluate the secondary information you find.*

In this chapter, you have learned how to plan and carry out primary data collection properly. Now that you have good data to work with, you must interpret it accurately and clearly for your reader (see Chapter 12 for interpreting procedure). If you are unsure of your reader's level of expertise in understanding descriptive statistics such as measures of central tendency and cross-tabulations, give the statistic and tell the reader what it means. In general, you can expect to interpret the statistics from univariate, bivariate, and multivariate analyses. In many cases, graphics help tremendously. Not

*Report statistics from primary research clearly and completely.*

### Survey Design and Statistical Consultants: Specialty Tools for Business Research

Two types of specialty tools are available to help the business researcher in the design of the survey and in the selection of appropriate statistics. Since client and customer surveys are effective tools for eliciting meaningful information, tools for helping the business researcher execute them well are welcome. These programs are designed for nonstatisticians who want to conduct productive surveys and report results quickly and accurately.

Most survey design programs available today help with questionnaire design, data entry, and report generation. Depending on the program used, the types of questions may range from those limited to multiple-choice questions with single-letter or single-digit responses to those with questions handling 20 types of rating scales and the ability to define up to 50 more. Some programs even provide the ability to use open-ended questions where the user writes out a response. All programs print the questionnaires or create files which can be imported into desktop publishing software for formatting and printing.

One nice feature included in some programs is an interview feature. This feature is used for telephone surveys. It dials through a database file with callback options and enters data directly. Another useful feature is the weighting feature, which allows users to equalize samples with under- and over-represented components. Its keyword feature is also helpful, selecting items from the comments sections by keyword and organizing them into groups for further analysis. These features all help simplify the survey process.

Statistical consultants, on the other hand, simplify the selection of the appropriate form of statistical analysis for the problem at hand. These programs act as professional experts, recommending statistical tests that are desirable in view of the objectives, feasible with the data, and acceptable for the reader. While most business researchers are competent with basic statistics, they are not always up-to-date on the latest tests available. Or they may be using a different kind of data than they are accustomed to working with. These programs can help you avoid overlooking appropriate options and reassure you that the test you want to run is an appropriate one.

These specialty tools can be helpful in gathering and analyzing data, but you must still use your judgment in determining when to let them guide you. The final decision is yours, but the tools can help you be confident that you have gathered data efficiently and analyzed it appropriately.

---

only do they show trends and relationships, but they do it ably. Finally, you have an ethical responsibility to present your data honestly and completely. Omitting an error or limitation of the data collection is often viewed as seriously as hiding errors or variations from accepted practices. Of course, the deliberate distortion of the data is unethical. It is your responsibility to communicate the findings of the report as accurately and as clearly as possible.

## SUMMARY (by Chapter Objectives)

1. Primary research is firsthand research. You can conduct primary research in four major ways:
   - Looking through company records
   - Conducting an experiment
   - Recording observations
   - Conducting a survey
   
   Secondary research is secondhand research or library research. You conduct secondary research in either a general library (usually public) or a special library (usually private).

2. If you need quantitative or factual information, you may be able to go directly to it, using such sources as the following:
   - encyclopedias
   - biographical directories
   - almanacs
   - trade directories
   - government publications
   - dictionaries
   - statistical sources
   - business services
   
   When you cannot go directly to the source, you use indirect methods. You may begin by searching the following sources:
   - Prepared bibliographies in books, theses, research periodicals, or such
   - The library catalog
   - Periodical indexes
   - Databases

3. Company records are usually confidential. You must either ask the person responsible for the information for it or gather it yourself from company databases.

4. An experiment is an orderly form of testing. It can be designed using the before-after design or the controlled before-after design.
   - The simplest is the before-after design. It involves selecting a group of subjects, measuring the variable, introducing the experimental factor, and measuring the variable again. The difference between the two measurements is assumed to be the result of the experimental factor.
   - The controlled before-after design involves selecting two groups, measuring the variable in both groups, introducing the experimental factor in one group, and then measuring the variable again in both groups. The second measurement enables you to determine the effect of the experimental factor and of other factors that might have influenced the variable between the two measurements.

5. The observation method may be defined as seeing with a purpose. It consists of watching the events involved in a problem and systematically recording what is seen. The events observed are not manipulated.

---

1. Explain the difference between primary and secondary research.

2. Describe appropriate procedures for direct and indirect library research.

3. Describe the procedures for searching through company records and conducting experiments.

4. Design an experiment for a business problem.

5. Design an observational study for a business problem.

**6. Explain sampling as it relates to conducting a survey.**

6. A sample is a group representative of the whole group. The procedure for selecting the sample is called sampling. A good sample is reliable, valid, and controlled for sampling error. You may use any of a variety of sample designs. Those discussed in this chapter include probability and nonprobability sampling.
   - Probability sampling is based on chance selection procedures. Every element in the population has a known nonzero probability of selection. Some of the techniques discussed are described below.
     —Simple random sampling involves chance selection, giving every member of the group under study an equal chance of being selected.
     —Stratified random sampling involves proportionate and random selection from each major subgroup of the group under study.
     —Systematic sampling involves taking selections at constant intervals (every fifth one, for example) from a complete list of the group under study.
     —Cluster or area sampling involves dividing into parts the area that contains the sample, selecting from these parts randomly, and continuing to subdivide and select until you have your desired sample size.
   - Nonprobability sampling is based on an unknown probability of any one of a group being studied. Some of the techniques discussed are described below.
     —Convenience sampling involves selecting members that are convenient, easy to reach, and appropriate as judged by the researcher.
     —Quota sampling requires that you know the proportions of certain characteristics (sex, age, education, etc.) in the group under study. You then select respondents in the same proportions.
     —Referral sampling involves building your sample from other participants' referrals.

**7. Discuss the techniques for constructing a questionnaire, developing a working plan, and conducting a pilot test for a survey.**

7. The questions you ask should follow a definite plan, usually in the form of a questionnaire. You should construct the questionnaire carefully, following these general rules.
   - Avoid leading questions
   - Make the questions easy to understand (avoid vagueness, difficult words, technical words)
   - Avoid questions that touch on personal prejudices or pride
   - Seek facts as much as possible
   - Ask only for what can be remembered (consider the laws of memory, recency, intensity, and association)
   - Plan the layout with foresight (enough space for answers and identifying information, proper sequence of questions)
   - Use scaling when appropriate

   You develop a working plan for conducting the questioning—one that covers all the possible problems and clearly explains what to do. It is usually advisable to test the questionnaire and working plan through a pilot study. This enables you to make changes in the questionnaire and improve the working plan before conducting the survey.

8. You need to evaluate the facts you gather from secondary research carefully before you include them in your report. Check to make sure they meet the following tests.
   - Can the author draw the conclusions from the data presented?
   - Are the sources reliable?
   - Has the author avoided biased interpretation?
   - Are there any gaps in the facts?

   You must present the primary information you collect clearly and completely. It is your responsibility to interpret statistics the reader may not understand.

8. Analyze and interpret information clearly and completely for your reader.

## QUESTIONS FOR DISCUSSION

1. Suggest a hypothetical research problem that would make good use of a specialized library. Justify your selection.
2. What specialized libraries are there in your community? What general libraries?
3. Under what general condition are investigators likely to be able to proceed directly to the printed source of the information sought?
4. Which index is most likely to contain information on each of the following subjects?
   a. Labor-management relations.
   b. Innovation in sales promotion.
   c. Accident proneness among employees.
   d. Recent advances in computer technology.
   e. Trends in responsibility accounting.
   f. Labor unrest in the 1800s.
   g. Events leading to enactment of a certain tax measure in 1936.
   h. Textbook treatment of business writing in the 1930s.
   i. Viewpoints on the effect of deficit financing by governments.
   j. New techniques in office management.
5. What advice would you give an investigator who has been assigned a task involving analysis of internal records of several company departments?
6. Define *experimentation*. What does the technique of experimentation involve?
7. Explain the significance of keeping constant all factors other than the experimental variable of an experiment.
8. Give an example of (*a*) a problem that can best be solved through a before-after design, and (*b*) a problem that can best be solved through a controlled before-after design. Explain your choices.
9. Define *observation* as a research technique.
10. Select an example of a business problem that can be solved best by observation. Explain your choice.
11. Point out violations of the rules of good questionnaire construction in the following questions. The questions do not come from the same questionnaire.
    a. How many days on the average do you wear a pair of socks before changing?
    b. (The first question in a survey conducted by Coca-Cola.) Have you ever drunk a Diet Coke?
    c. Do you consider the ideal pay plan to be one based on straight commission or straight salary?
    d. What kind of gasoline did you purchase last time?
    e. How much did you pay for clothing in the past 12 months?
    f. Check the word below that best describes how often you eat dessert with your noon meal.
       Always
       Usually
       Sometimes
       Never
12. Explain the difference between random sampling and convenience sampling.
13. Discuss the writer's responsibility in analyzing and interpreting data.

## APPLICATION EXERCISES

1. Using your imagination to supply any missing facts you may need, develop a plan for the experiment you would use in the following situations.
   a. The Golden Glow Baking Company has for many years manufactured and sold cookies packaged in attractive boxes. It is considering packaging the cookies in plastic bags and wants to conduct an experiment to determine consumer response to this change.
   b. The Miller Brush Company, manufacturers of a line of household goods, has for years sold its products on a house-to-house basis. It now wants to conduct an experiment to test the possibilities of selling through conventional retail outlets.
   c. A national chain of food stores wants to know whether it would profit by doubling the face value of coupons. It is willing to pay the cost

of an experiment in its research for an answer.

d. The True Time Watch Company is considering the use of automated sales displays ($9.50 each) instead of stationary displays ($4.50 each) in the 2,500 retail outlets that sell True Time watches. The company will conduct an experiment to determine the relative effects on sales of the two displays.

e. The Marvel Soap Company has developed a new cleaning agent that is unlike current soaps and detergents. The product is well protected by patent. The company wants to determine the optimum price for the new product through experimentation.

f. National Cereals, Inc. wants to determine the effectiveness of advertising to children. Until now, it has been aiming its appeal at the homemaker. The company will support an experiment to learn the answer.

2. Using your imagination to supply any missing facts you may need, develop a plan for research by observation for these problems.

a. A chain of department stores wants to know what causes differences in sales by departments within stores and by stores. Some of this information it hopes to get through research by observation.

b. Your university wants to know the nature and extent of its automobile parking problem.

c. The management of an insurance company wants to determine the efficiency and productivity of its data entry department.

d. Owners of a shopping center want a study to determine shopping patterns of their customers. Specifically they want to know such things as what parts of town the customers come from, how they travel, how many stores they visit, and so on.

e. The director of your library wants a detailed study of library use (what facilities are used, when, by whom, and so on).

f. The management of a restaurant wants a study of its workers' efficiency in the kitchen.

3. Using your imagination to supply any missing facts you may need, develop a plan for research by survey for these problems.

a. The American Restaurant Association wants information that will give its members a picture of its customers. The information will serve as a guide for a promotion campaign designed to increase restaurant eating. Specifically it will seek such information as who eats out, how often, where they go, how much they spend. Likewise, it will seek to determine who does not eat out and why.

b. The editor of your local daily paper wants a readership study to learn just who reads what.

c. The National Beef Producers Association wants to determine the current trends in meat consumption. They want such information as the amount of meat people consume, whether people have reduced their meat consumption, and so on.

d. The International Association of Publishers wants a survey of the reading habits of adults in the United States and Canada. It wants such information as who reads what, how much, when, where, and so on.

# APPENDIX A

# CORRECTIONS FOR THE SELF-ADMINISTERED DIAGNOSTIC TEST OF PUNCTUATION AND GRAMMAR

Following are the corrected sentences for the diagnostic test at the end of Chapter 21. The corrections are underscored, and the symbols for the standards explaining the correction follow the sentences.

1. An important fact about this keyboard is, that it has the patented "feather touch".
   An important fact about this keyboard is that it has the patented "feather touch." *Cma 6.1, QM 3*

2. Goods received on invoice 2741 are as follows; three dozen white shirts, size 15-33, four mens felt hats, brown, size 7, and five dozen assorted ties.
   Goods received on Invoice 2741 are as follows: three dozen white shirts, size 15-33; four men's felt hats, brown, size 7; and five dozen assorted ties.
   *Cln 1, Apos 1, SC 3*

3. James Silver  president of the new union  started the campaign for the retirement fund.
   James Silver, president of the new union, started the campaign for the retirement fund. *Cma 4.2*

4. We do not expect to act on this matter  however  until we hear from you.
   We do not expect to act on this matter, however, until we hear from you. *Cma 4.3*

5. Shipments through September 20, 1992  totaled 69,485 pounds  an increase of 17 percent over the year  ago total.
   Shipments through September 20, 1992, totaled 69,485 pounds, an increase of 17 percent over the year-ago total. *Cma 4.4, Cma 4.1, Hpn 2*

6. Brick is recommended as the building material  but the board is giving serious consideration to a substitute.
   Brick is recommended as the building material, but the board is giving serious consideration to a substitute. *Cma 1*

7. Markdowns for the sale total $34,000, never before has the company done anything like this.
   Markdowns for the sale total $34,000; never before has the company done anything like this. *SC 1*

8. After long experimentation a wear  resistant  high  grade  and beautiful stocking has been perfected.
   After long experimentation a wear-resistant, high-grade, and beautiful stocking has been perfected. *Hpn 2, Cma 2.2*

9. Available in white  green  and blue  this paint is sold by dealers all over the country.
   Available in white, green, and blue, this paint is sold by dealers all over the country. *Cma 2.1, Cma 3*

10. George Steele  who won the trip  is our most energetic salesperson.
    George Steele, who won the trip, is our most energetic salesperson. *Cma 3*

11. _Good_ he replied_ sales are sure to increase.
    "Good," he replied. "Sales are sure to increase." *QM 1, Pd 1*

12. Hogan's article_ Retirement? Never!,_ printed in the current issue of <u>Management Review</u>, is really a part of his book_ <u>A Report on Worker Security</u>.
    Hogan's article, "Retirement? Never!," printed in the current issue of *Management Review*, is really a part of his book, *A Report on Worker Security*.
    *Cma 4.2, QM 4, Ital 1*

13. Formal announcement of our Labor Day sale will be made in <u>thirty-two</u> days.
    Formal announcement of our Labor Day sale will be made in 32 days.
    *No 1*

14. Each day we encounter new problems._ Although they are solved easily.
    Each day we encounter new problems, although they are solved easily.
    *Cma 5.1, Frag*

15. A list of models, sizes, and prices of both competing lines <u>are</u> being sent you.
    A list of models, sizes, and prices of both competing lines is being sent you.
    *Agmt SV*

16. The manager could not tolerate any employee's failing to do <u>their</u> best.
    The manager could not tolerate any employee's failing to do his or her best.
    *Pn 2*

17. A series of tests <u>were</u> completed only yesterday.
    A series of tests was completed only yesterday. *Agmt SV*

18. There should be no misunderstanding between you and <u>I</u>.
    There should be no misunderstanding between you and me. *Pn 3*

19. He <u>run</u> the accounting department for five years.
    He ran the accounting department for five years. *Tns 2*

20. This report is <u>considerable</u> long.
    This report is considerably long. *AA*

21. <u>Who</u> did you interview for the position?
    Whom did you interview for the position? *Pn 3*

22. The report concluded that the natural resources of the Southwest <u>was</u> ideal for the chemical industry.
    The report concluded that the natural resources of the Southwest are ideal for the chemical industry. *Agmt SV, Tns 1*

23. This applicant is six feet in height,__ 28 years old, weighs 165 pounds, and has had eight years' experience.
    This applicant is six feet in height, is 28 years old, weighs 165 pounds, and has had eight years' experience. *Prl*

24. While_ reading the report, a gust of wind came through the window, blowing papers all over the room.
    While she was reading the report, a gust of wind came through the window, blowing papers all over the room. *Dng*

25. The sprinkler system <u>has been</u> checked on July 1 and September 3.
    The sprinkler system was checked on July 1 and September 3. *Tns 5*

# A GRADING CHECKLIST FOR LETTERS

APPENDIX B

## THE OPENING

**O Ind**  *Indirectness needed.*   This opening gets to the goal too fast.

**O Dir**  *Directness needed.*   This opening is too slow in getting to the goal.

**O Qual**  *Quality.*   This opening could be improved by making it more (1) on subject, (2) logical, or (3) interesting.

## COVERAGE

**C Inc**  *Incomplete.*   You have not covered all the important information.

**C Ex**  *Excess information.*   You have included more information than is needed.

**C Exp**  *Explanation.*   More or better explanation is needed here.

**C Id**  *Identification.*   Completely identify the situation, either in the letter or in a subject line.

## ENDING

**E AC**  *Action close.*   A drive for action is appropriate in this situation.

**E AC S**  *Action strong.*   This action drive is too strong.

**E AC W**  *Action weak.*   This action drive is too weak.

**E IT**  *Individually tailored.*   Make your close fit the one case.

**E OS**  *Off subject.*   An off-subject close is best for this case. These words recall unpleasant things in the reader's mind.

## TECHNIQUE

**Adp**  *Adaptation.*   Your words should be adapted to the one reader. Here yours are (1) above or (2) below your reader.

**Awk**  *Awkward word arrangement.*

**Bky**  *Bulky arrangement.*   Make your paragraphs more inviting by breaking them into shorter units of thought.

**Chop**  *Choppy writing.*   A succession of short sentences produces an irritating effect.

**DL**  *Dull writing:*   Bring your writing back to life with vivid, concrete words.

**Emp +**  *Emphasis, too much.*

**Emp −**  *Emphasis, too little.*   Here you have given too much or too little (as marked) emphasis by (1) placement, (2) volume, or (3) words or mechanical means.

B-1

**Intp** *Interpretation.* Do more than just present facts. In this situation, something more is needed. Make the data meaningful in terms of the reader's situation.

**Los** *Loose writing.* Use words more economically. Write concisely.

**Ord** *Order of presentation.* This information does not fall into a logical order. The information is mixed up and confusing.

**RS** *Rubber-stamp expression.* Timeworn words from the past have no place in modern business writing.

**Trans** *Transition.* Abrupt shift of thought here.

## EFFECT

**Conv** *Conviction.* This is less convincing than it should be. More fact or a more skillful use of words is needed.

**GW** *Goodwill.* The letter needs more goodwill. Try to make your words convey friendliness. Here you tend to be too dull and matter-of-fact.

**Hur** *Hurried treatment.* Your coverage of the problem appears to be hurried. Thus, it tends to leave an effect of routine or brusque treatment. Conciseness is wanted, of course, but you must not sacrifice your letter's objectives for it.

**Log** *Logic.* Is this really logical? Would you do it this way in business?

**Neg** *Negative effect.* By word or implication, this part is more negative than it should be.

**Pers +** *Too persuasive.* Your words are too high-pressure for this situation.

**Pers −** *Not persuasive enough.* More persuasion, by either words or facts, would help your letter.

**Ton** *Tone of the words.* Your words create a bad impression on the reader. Words work against the success of your letter if they talk down, lecture, argue, accuse, and the like.

**YVP** *You-viewpoint.* More you-viewpoint wording and adaptation would help the overall effect of your letter.

# A GRADING CHECKLIST FOR REPORTS

**APPENDIX C**

The following checklist should serve both as a guide for preparing reports and as a tool for grading reports. (Your instructor can use the symbols to mark errors.) The checklist covers all types of reports—from simple memorandums to long analytical reports. For each report type, you need only use the items that apply.

## TITLE (T)

**T 1** Complete? The title should tell what the report contains. Use the five W's as a check for completeness *(who, what, where, when, why*—sometimes *how)*.

**T 2** Too long. This title is longer than it needs to be. Check it for uneconomical wording or unnecessary information.

## LETTER OF TRANSMITTAL (LT)

**LT 1** More directness needed in the opening. The letter should present the report right away.

**LT 2** Content of the letter needs improvement. Comments that help the readers understand or appreciate the report are appropriate.

**LT 3** Do not include findings unless the report has no executive summary.

**LT 4** A warm statement of your attitude toward the assignment is appropriate—often expected. You either do not make one, or the one you make is weak.

**LT 5** A friendlier, more conversational style would improve the letter.

## EXECUTIVE SUMMARY (ES)

**ES 1** *(If the direct order is assigned)* Begin directly—with a statement of finding, conclusion, or recommendation.

**ES 2** *(If the indirect order is assigned)* Begin with a brief review of introductory information.

**ES 3** The summary of highlights should be in proportion and should include major findings, analyses, and conclusions. Your coverage here is *(a)* scant or *(b)* too detailed.

**ES 4** Work for a more interesting and concise summary.

## ORGANIZATION—OUTLINE (O)

**O 1** This organization plan is not the best for this problem. The main sections should form a logical solution to the problem.

**O 2** The order of the parts of this outline is not logical. The parts should form a step-by-step route to the goal.

**O 3**   These parts overlap. Each part should be independent of the other parts. Although some repetition and relating of parts may be desirable, outright overlap is a sign of bad organization.

**O 4**   More subparts are needed here. The subparts should cover all the information in the major part.

**O 5**   This subpart does not fit logically under this major part.

**O 6**   These parts are not equal in importance. Do not give them equal status in the outline.

**O 7**   *(If talking headings are assigned)* These headings do not talk well.

**O 8**   Coordinate headings should be parallel in grammatical structure.

**O 9**   This (these) heading(s) is (are) too long.

**O 10**   Vary the wording of the headings to avoid monotonous repetition.

## INTRODUCTION (I)

**I 1**   This introduction does not cover exactly what the readers need to know. Although the readers' needs vary by problem, these topics are usually important: *(a)* origin of the problem, *(b)* statement of the problem, *(c)* methods used in researching the problem, and *(d)* preview of the presentation.

**I 2**   Coverage of this part is *(a)* scant or *(b)* too detailed.

**I 3**   Important information has been left out.

**I 4**   Findings, conclusions, and other items of information are not a part of the introduction.

## COVERAGE (C)

**C 1**   The coverage here is *(a)* scant or *(b)* too detailed.

**C 2**   More analysis is needed here.

**C 3**   Here you rely too heavily on a graphic. The text should cover the important information.

**C 4**   Do not lose sight of the goal of the report. Relate the information to the problem.

**C 5**   Clearly distinguish between fact and opinion. Label opinion as opinion.

**C 6**   Your analyses and conclusions need the support of more fact and authoritative opinion.

## WRITING (W)

**W 1**   This writing should be better adapted to your readers. It appears to be *(a)* too heavy or *(b)* too light for your readers.

**W 2**   Avoid the overuse of passive voice.

**W 3**   Work for more conciseness. Try to cut down on words without sacrificing meaning.

**W 4**  For this report, more formal writing is appropriate. You should write consistently in impersonal (third person) style.

**W 5**  A more personal style is appropriate for this report. That is, you should use more personal pronouns *(I's, we's, you's).*

**W 6**  The change in thought is abrupt here.

*(a)* Between major parts, use introductions, summaries, and conclusions to guide the readers' thinking.

*(b)* Use transitional words, phrases, or sentences to relate minor parts.

**W 7**  Your paragraphing is questionable. Check the paragraphs for unity. Look for topic sentences.

## GRAPHICS (GA)

**GA 1**  You have *(a)* not used enough graphics or *(b)* used too many graphics.

**GA 2**  For the information presented, this graphic is *(a)* too large or *(b)* too small.

**GA 3**  This type of graphic is not the best for presenting the information.

**GA 4**  Place the graphic near the place where its contents are discussed.

**GA 5**  The appearance of this graphic needs improvement. This may be your best work, but it does not make a good impression on the readers.

**GA 6**  Refer the readers to the graphics at the times that the readers should look at them.

**GA 7**  Refer to the graphics incidentally, in subordinate parts of sentences that comment on their content (for example, ". . . as shown in Chart 5" or "see Chart 5").

## LAYOUT AND MECHANICS (LM)

**LM 1**  The layout of this page is *(a)* too fat, *(b)* too skinny, or *(c)* too low, high, or off-center (as marked).

**LM 2**  Neat? Smudges and light type detract from the message.

**LM 3**  Make the margins straighter. The raggedness here offends the eye.

**LM 4**  The spacing here needs improvement. *(a)* Too much space here. *(b)* Not enough space here.

**LM 5**  Your page numbering is not the best. See the text for specific instructions.

**LM 6**  This page appears *(a)* choppy or *(b)* heavy.

**LM 7**  Your selection of type placement and style for the headings is not the best.

**LM 8**  This item or form is not generally acceptable.

# DOCUMENTATION AND THE BIBLIOGRAPHY

APPENDIX D

In writing reports, you will frequently use information from other sources. As this material is not your own, you may need to acknowledge it. Whether and how you should acknowledge it are the subject of this brief review.

## WHEN TO ACKNOWLEDGE

Your decision to acknowledge or not acknowledge a source should be determined mainly on the basis of giving credit where credit is due. If you are quoting the words of another, you must give credit. If you are paraphrasing (using someone else's ideas in your own words), you should give credit unless the material covered is general knowledge.

## HOW TO ACKNOWLEDGE

Acknowledge sources by citing them in the text, using one of a number of reference systems. Three of the most commonly used systems are the Chicago (*The Chicago Manual of Style*), MLA (Modern Language Association), and APA (American Psychological Association). Although all are similar, they differ somewhat in format, as you will see in the following pages. Because the Chicago system is the most widely used in business books and journals, we will review it first. Then we will illustrate the MLA and APA systems to note primary differences.

After you have selected a system, you must choose a method of acknowledgment. Two methods are commonly used in business: (1) parenthetic author-date references within the text, and (2) footnote references. A third method, endnote references, is sometimes used, although it appears to be losing favor. Only the first two are discussed here.

## THE PARENTHETIC AUTHOR-DATE METHOD

In recent years, the author-date method has become the most popular reference method in business. It involves placing the author's last name and year of publication in parentheses immediately following the material cited:

(Calahan 1992)

The reference is keyed to a list of all the publications cited (a bibliography), which appears at the end of the report (see discussion of the bibliography in a following section). If specific page numbers are needed, they follow the date:

(Calahan 1992, 117–18)

The last names are listed of works with two or three authors:

(Smith, Corley, and Doran 1991, 31)

For works with more than three authors, "et al." is used:

(Clovis et. al. 1989)

When no author is listed, as in unsigned publications issued by a company, government agency, labor union, or such, the author's name is the organization name:

(U.S. Department of Labor 1992)

(American Federation of Labor 1991, 31)

As noted earlier, these references are keyed to a bibliography that appears at the end of the report. To find the details of a reference, the reader turns to the bibliography and traces the reference through the alphabetical listing. For the reference "(Sanders 1992)," for example, the reader would find Sanders in its alphabetical place. If more than one publication by Sanders is listed, the reader would refer to the one written in 1992.

## THE FOOTNOTE METHOD

The traditional method of acknowledging sources (preferred in the humanities) is by footnotes; that is, the references are placed at the bottom of the page and are keyed to the text material by superscripts (raised Arabic numbers). The numbering sequence of the superscripts is consecutive—by page, by chapter, or by the whole work. The footnotes are placed inside the page layout, single-spaced, and indented or blocked just as the text is typed.

Although footnote form varies from one source to another, one generally accepted procedure is presented here. It permits two structures: an abbreviated structure that is used with a bibliography in the report and a structure that is used when the report has no bibliography.

In the abbreviated structure (not accepted by everyone), the footnote reference needs to contain only these parts: (1) author's surname; (2) title of the article, bulletin, or book; and (3) page number.

[3] Wilson, *The Report Writer's Guide,* 44 (book reference).

[4] Allison, "Making Routine Reports Talk," 71 (periodical reference).

For the complete reference (usually preferred), the descriptive points are listed in the order mentioned below. Capitals are used only with proper nouns, and abbreviations are acceptable if used consistently.

In the following lists, all the items that could be placed in each type of entry are named in the order of arrangement. Items that are unavailable or unimportant should be passed over. In other words, the following lists give, in order, all the possible items in an entry. The items listed should be used as needed.

## Book Entry:

1. *Superscript.* Arabic numeral keyed to the text reference and placed before the first part of the entry without spacing.

2. *Name of the author, in normal order.* If a source has two or three authors, all are named. If a source has more than three authors, the name of the first author followed by the Latin "et al." or its English equivalent "and others" may be used.

3. *Capacity of the author.* Needed only when the person named is actually not the author of the book but an editor, compiler, or the like.

4. *Chapter name.* Necessary only in the rare instances in which the chapter title helps the reader find the source.

5. *Book title.* Book titles are placed in italics. In typewritten work, italics are indicated by underscoring.

6. *Edition.*

7. *Location of publisher.* If more than one city is listed on the title page, the one listed first should be used. If the population exceeds half a million, the name of the city is sufficient; otherwise, the city and state (or province) are best given.

8. *Publishing company.*
9. *Date.* Year of publication. If revised, year of latest revision.
10. *Page or pages.* Specific page or inclusive pages on which the cited material is found.

The following are examples of book entries:

A TYPICAL BOOK:

[1] Cindy Burford, Aline Culberson, and Peter Dykus, *Writing for Results,* 4th ed., New York: Charles Storm Publishing Company, 1990, 17–18.

A BOOK WRITTEN BY A STAFF OF WRITERS UNDER THE DIRECTION OF AN EDITOR
(chapter title is considered helpful):

[2] W. C. Butte and Ann Buchanan, ed., "Direct Mail Advertising," *An Encyclopedia of Advertising,* New York: Binton Publishing Company, 1992, 99.

A BOOK WRITTEN BY A NUMBER OF COAUTHORS:

[3] E. Butler Cannais et al., *Anthology of Public Relations,* New York: Warner-Bragg, Inc., 1992, 137.

## Periodical Entry:

1. *Superscript.*
2. *Author's name.* Frequently, no author is given. In such cases, the entry may be skipped, or if it is definitely known to be anonymous, the word *anonymous* may be placed in the entry.
3. *Article title.* Typed within quotation marks.
4. *Periodical title.* Set in italics, which are indicated in typewriting by underscoring.
5. *Publication identification.* Volume number in Arabic numerals followed by date of publication (month and year or season and year). Volume number is not needed if complete (day, month, year) date is given. See examples below for punctuation differences with and without complete date.
6. *Page or pages.*

Examples of periodical entries are shown below:

[1] Mildred C. Kinnig, "A New Look at Retirement," *Modern Business,* July 31, 1991, 31–32.
[2] William O. Schultz, "How One Company Improved Morale," *Business Leader,* August 31, 1992, 17.
[3] Mary Mitchell, "Report Writing Aids," *ABCA Bulletin,* 46 (October 1984): 13.

## Newspaper Article:

1. *Superscript.*
2. *Source description.* If article is signed, give author's name. Otherwise, give description of article, such as "United Press dispatch" or "Editorial."
3. *Main head of article.* Subheads not needed.
4. *Newspaper title.* City and state (or province) names inserted in brackets if place names do not appear in newspaper title. State (or province) names not needed in case of very large cities, such as New York, Toronto, and Los Angeles.
5. *Date of publication.*
6. *Page (p.) and column* (col.). May be used—optional.

The following are typical newspaper article entries:

[1] United Press dispatch, "Rival Unions Sign Pact," *Morning Advocate* [Baton Route, Louisiana], September 3, 1992.

[2] Editorial, "The North Moves South," *Austin* [Texas] *American,* February 3, 1991, p. 2-A, col. 3.

### Letters or Documents:

1. *Nature of communication.*
2. *Name of writer.*
3. *Name of recipient.*
4. *Date of writing.*
5. *Where filed.*

[With identification by title and organization where helpful.]

An example of an entry citing a letter is given below:

[1] Letter from J. W. Wells, president, Wells Equipment Co., to James Mattoch, secretary-treasurer, Southern Industrialists, Inc., June 10, 1988, filed among Mr. Mattoch's personal records.

The types of entries discussed in the preceding paragraphs are those most likely to be used. Yet, many unusual types of publications (not books or periodicals) are likely to come up. When they do, you should classify the source by the form it most closely resembles—a book or a periodical. Then you should construct the entry that describes the source most correctly. Frequently, you will need to improvise—to use your best judgment in determining the source description.

### STANDARD REFERENCE FORMS

Certain forms are conventionally used in handling repeated references in footnotes. The more common of these are the following:

**Ibid.** Literally, *ibid.* means "in the same place." It is used to refer the reader to the preceding footnote. The entry consists of the superscript, *ibid.*, and the page number if the page number is different as shown in these entries:

[1] Janice Smith, *How to Write the Annual Report,* Chicago: Small-Boch, Inc., 1991, 173.

[2] *Ibid.,* 143 (refers to Smith's book).

**Op. cit.** ("in the work cited") and **loc. cit.** ("in the place cited") also can refer to references cited earlier in the paper. But they are rarely used today. It is better to use in their place a short reference form (author's last name, date).

Other abbreviations used in footnote entries are as follows:

| ABBREVIATION | MEANING |
| --- | --- |
| cf. | Compare (directs reader's attention to another passage) |
| cf. ante | Compare above |
| cf. post | Compare below |
| ed. | Edition |
| e.g. | For example |
| et al. | And others |
| et passim | And at intervals throughout the work |
| et seq. | And the following |

| ABBREVIATION | MEANING |
| --- | --- |
| f, ff. | Following page, following pages |
| i.e. | That is |
| infra | Below |
| l., ll. | Line, lines |
| MS, MSS | Manuscript, manuscripts |
| n.d. | No date |
| n.n. | No name |
| n.p. | No place |
| p., pp. | Page, pages |
| supra | Above |
| vol., vols. | Volume, volumes |

## DISCUSSION FOOTNOTES

In sharp contrast with source footnotes are discussion footnotes. Through discussion footnotes the writer strives to explain a part of the text, to amplify discussion on a phase of the presentation, to make cross-references to other parts of the report, and the like. The following examples illustrate some possibilities of this footnote type.

CROSS-REFERENCE:

[1] See the principle of focal points on page 72.

AMPLIFICATION OF DISCUSSION AND CROSS-REFERENCE:

[2] Lyman Bryson says the same thing: "Every communication is different for every receiver even in the same context. No one can estimate the variation of understanding that there may be among receivers of the same message conveyed in the same vehicle when the receivers are separated in either space or time." See *Communication of Ideas*, 5.

COMPARISON:

[3] Compare with the principle of the objective: Before starting any activity, one should make a clear, complete statement of the objective in view.

## PLACEMENT OF QUOTED AND PARAPHRASED INFORMATION

You may use data obtained from secondary sources in two ways. You may paraphrase the information (cast it in your own words), or you may use it verbatim (exactly as the original author worded it). In typing paraphrased material, you need not distinguish it from the remainder of the report text. Material you use verbatim, however, must be clearly distinguished.

The procedure for marking this difference is simple. If the quoted passage is short (about eight lines or less), place it within the text and with quotation marks before and after it. Set off longer quotations from the margins, without quotation marks, as shown in the example below. If the text is double-spaced, further distinguish the quoted passage by single-spacing it.

their objections. Supporting Warren's view, Perlick presents this argument:
In theory, this reasoning seems perfectly legitimate. The managers control the business, and the stockholders control the managers. In practice, however, it does not always hold true. There are wide differences among stockholders. They often live far apart, they often have quite different educational backgrounds, and their knowledge of the business is not always the same. Thus, it becomes very difficult for any small group of stock-

holders to hold the management of the firm truly accountable for its actions. (358)

As noted previously, stockholders want either dividends or price appreciation on their investments. To the extent that the management of the firm wants to keep the stockholders happy. . . .

Frequently, you will find it best to break up or use only fragments of the quoted author's work. Because omissions may distort the meaning of a passage, you must clearly indicate them, using ellipsis points (a series of three periods typed with intervening spaces) where material is left out. If an omission begins after the end of a sentence, you must use four periods—one for final punctuation plus the ellipsis points. A passage with such omissions is the following:

Many companies have undertaken to centralize in the hands of specially trained correspondents the handling of the outgoing mail. Usually, centralization has been accomplished by the firm's employment of a correspondence supervisor. . . . The supervisor may guide the work of correspondents . . . , or the company may employ a second technique.

In long quotations it is conventional to show omission of a paragraph or more by a full line of periods, typed with intervening spaces (see example p. 711).

## *THE BIBLIOGRAPHY*

A bibliography is an orderly list of material on a particular subject. In a formal report the list covers references on the subject of the report. The entries in this list closely resemble footnotes, but the two must not be confused. The bibliography normally appears as an appended part of a formal report and is placed after the appendix. It may be preceded by a fly page containing the one word *bibliography*. The page that begins the list bears the main heading ''Bibliography,'' usually typed in capital letters. Below this title the references are listed by broad categories and in alphabetical order within the categories. Such listed categories as *books, periodicals,* and *bulletins* may be used. But the determination of categories should be based solely on the types of publications collected in each bibliography. If, for example, a bibliography includes a large number of periodicals and government publications plus a wide assortment of diverse publication types, the bibliography could be divided into these categories: *periodicals, government publications,* and *miscellaneous publications*. As with footnotes, variations in bibliographic style are numerous. A simplified form recommended for business use follows the same procedure as described above for footnotes, with four major exceptions:

1. The author's name is listed in reverse order—surname first—for the purpose of alphabetizing. If an entry has more than one author, however, only the name of the first author is reversed.

2. The entry is generally typed in hanging-indention form. That is, the second and subsequent lines of an entry begin some uniform distance (usually about five spaces) to the right of the beginning point of the first line. The purpose of this indented pattern is to make the alphabetized first line stand out.

3. The entry gives the inclusive pages of articles, but not for books, and does not refer to any one page or passage.

4. Second and subsequent references to publications of the same author are indicated by a uniform line (see bibliography illustration). In typed manuscripts, this line might be formed by striking the underscore 10 consecutive times. But this line may be used only if the entire authorship is the same in the con-

secutive publications. For example, the line could not be used if consecutive entries have one common author but different coauthors.

Following is an example of a bibliography:

## Bibliography

### Books
Burton, Helen. *The City Fights Back.* New York: Citadel Press, 1989.
Caperton, Hudson D. *The Business of Government.* Boston: Sherman-Kaufman Company, 1957.
Chapman, Kenneth W., Harvey H. Heinz, and Robert V. Martinez. *The Basics of Marketing.* 4th ed. New York: Barrow-Dore, Inc., 1937.
Kiernan, Gladys M. *Retailers Manual of Taxes and Regulation.* 12th ed. New York: Institute of Distribution, Inc., 1992.
Surrey, N.M.M. *The Commerce of Louisiana during the French Regime, 1699–1763.* New York: Columbia University Press, 1916.

### Government Publications
U.S. Bureau of the Census. "Characteristics of the Population." *Twentieth Census of the United States: Census of Population,* Vol. 2, part 18. Washington, D.C.: U.S. Government Printing Office, 1991. 248 pp.
_____ . *Statistical Abstract of the United States.* Washington D.C.: Government Printing Office, 1990. 1056 pp.
U.S. Department of Commerce. *Business Statistics: 1990.* Washington, D.C.: U.S. Government Printing Office, 1991. 309 pp.
_____ . *Survey of Current Business: 1991 Supplement,* Washington, D.C.: U.S. Government Printing Office, 1991. 271 pp.

### Periodicals
Montgomery, Donald E. "Consumer Standards and Marketing." *Journal of Distribution* (May 1992). 141–49.
Phillips, Emily F. "Some Studies Needed in Marketing." *Journal of Marketing 9* (July 1978). 16–25.
_____ . "Major Areas of Marketing Research." *Journal of Marketing 18* (July 1990), 21–26.

### Miscellaneous Publications
Bradford, Ernest S. *Survey and Directory, Marketing Research Agencies in the United States.* New York: Bureau of Business Research, College of the City of New York, 1990. 137 pp.
*Reference Sources on Chain Stores.* New York: Institute of Distribution, Inc., 1992. 116 pp.
Smith, Lynn T. *Farm Trade Center in Louisiana, 1901 to 1990.* Louisiana Bulletin no. 234. Baton Rouge: Louisiana State University, 1991. 56 pp.

## THE ANNOTATED BIBLIOGRAPHY

Frequently, in scholarly writing each bibliography entry is followed by a brief comment on its value and content. That is, the bibliography is annotated. The form and content of annotated bibliographies are illustrated in these entries:

Donald, W.T., ed. *Handbook of Business Administration.* New York: Shannon-Dale Book Co., Inc., 1992.
    Contains a summary of the activities in each major area of business. Written by foremost authorities in each field. Particularly useful to the business specialist who wants a quick review of the whole of business.

Braden, Shelby M., and Lillian Como, eds. *Business Leader's Handbook*. 4th ed. New York: Mercer and Sons, Inc., 1991.

    Provides answers to most routine problems of executives in explicit manner and with good examples. Contains good material on correspondence and sales letters.

## DIFFERENCES IN APA AND MLA FORMATS

As noted previously, the APA and MLA systems differ somewhat from that presented in preceding pages. The primary differences are evident from the following illustrations.

### Parenthetic references:

Chicago and MLA:

(Burton 1929)

APA:

(Burton, 1919)

### Footnotes:

#### Books

Chicago:

[2] Helen Burton, *The City Fights Back*, New York: Citadel Press, 1992, 17.

MLA:

[2] Helen Burton, *The City Fights Back* (New York: Citadel Press, 1992), 17.

APA: Does not use footnotes.

#### Periodicals

Chicago:

[3] Donald E. Montgomery, "Consumer Standards and Marketing," *Journal of Distribution*, May 1990, 144.

MLA

[3] Donald E. Montgomery, "Consumer Standards and Marketing," *Journal of Distribution*, May 1990: 144.

APA: Does not use footnotes.

### Bibliography:

#### Books

Chicago:
Burton, Helen. *The City Fights Back*. New York: Citadel Press. 1992.

MLA:

Burton, Helen. *The City Fights Back*. New York: Citadel Press, 1992.

APA:

Burton, H. (1992). *The city fights back*. New York: Citadel Press.

#### Periodicals

Chicago:

Montgomery, Donald E. "Consumer Standards and Marketing." *Journal of Distribution,* (May 1992). 141–49.

MLA:

Montgomery, Donald E. "Consumer Standards and Marketing." *Journal of Distribution,* May 1992: 141–49.

APA

Montgomery, D. E. (1992). Consumer standards and marketing. *Journal of Distribution,* 15(5), 141–149.

In place of the specific date of publication, APA style uses volume and number—in this example 15(5).

Any of these systems are appropriate in business. Of course, you should use only one in a paper.

# UNITED STATES LAWS AFFECTING BUSINESS COMMUNICATION AT HOME AND ABROAD*

APPENDIX E

At least 80 U.S. laws affect domestic and international oral and written business communication. The most significant of these laws are summarized in the following pages under seven categories: advertising-selling, consumer credit protection, employer-employee relations, defamation, copyright and trademark protection, privacy, and international communication.

## ADVERTISING-SELLING

The laws affecting advertising and selling are best explained through illustration. Consider these four statements:

1. "We sell the best box lunches in town."
2. "Our deals are unbeatable."
3. "Our shoes are recommended by the Aardvarks Track Club."
4. "You'll receive a full warranty, unless you live in Texas."

According to the **Truth-in-Advertising** laws (15 U.S.C.), Statements 1 and 2 constitute mere "puffery" for which the writer is not liable for misrepresentation or fraud. These "puffings" are exaggerations or opinions that are not intended to be perceived as factual.

What is the distinction between "sales talk" and misrepresentation? Untruthful statements concerning product specifications such as color, size, price, or quantity may be interpreted as deceitful by a court of law. Section 2-313 of the *Uniform Commercial Code* (American Law Institute, 1987) stipulates that these types of misleading advertising statements, even if unrelated to a customer's purchasing decision, can be used later as grounds for misrepresentation (Heckman, 1987–88).

Due to Truth-in-Advertising and Uniform Commercial Code guidelines, the author of Statement 3 must be able to present evidence that the product is recommended by the Aardvarks Track Club.

Statement 4 is subject to stipulations of the **Magnuson-Moss Warranty Act of 1975** (15 U.S.C.) as well as Truth-in-Advertising and Uniform Commercial Code regulations. The Magnuson-Moss Warranty Act regulates the content of written warranties. A warrantor must "fully and conspicuously disclose in simple and readily understood language the terms and conditions of such warranty" (15 U.S.C. §2302).

## CONSUMER CREDIT PROTECTION

Five laws affecting credit communications are of particular interest to business writers.

The **Equal Credit Opportunity Act** (15 U.S.C. §§1691–1691(a)) governs questions that credit agencies may ask prior to granting or refusing credit. A credit agency may inquire about an applicant's marital status, age, income, reliance on public assistance, future probable income, and credit history to determine the applicant's creditworthiness (Sprotzer, 1981).

---

* By Mary Ellen Murray and Donald Evans, both of Stephen F. Austin State University

The Equal Credit Opportunity Act also requires that a financial institution or other credit-granting agency notify applicants within 30 days concerning action taken on a credit application (Sprotzer, 1981). If credit is denied, the consumer is entitled to a written explanation (Geil, 1981).

In addition, credit applicants are entitled to full disclosure of credit terms, according to the **Consumer Credit Protection Act of 1968** (15 U.S.C. §1601 et seq.; 18 U.S.C. §891 et seq.), part of which is the **Truth-in-Lending Simplification and Reform Act of 1980** (15 U.S.C. §§57 (a), 1601 et seq.). Despite its name, the Simplification and Reform Act outlines specific, nonsimplistic information that must be made available prior to a credit transaction. Among these are the name of the creditor, payment schedule, annual percentage rate, and variable rate feature (Scully, 1982). If provision is made for a security interest, a description of the affected property must be included (Sprotzer, 1981, 16). Additional information may be required, depending on the type of credit under consideration.

Once credit has been issued, stipulations of the **Fair Credit Billing Act of 1974** (15 U.S.C. §1666–1666 (j)) must be met. Consumer complaints regarding billing errors must be acknowledged by the creditor within 30 days of receipt. Either investigative or corrective action must be taken within the next 90 days, and the borrower must be informed of the situation in writing (Sprotzer, 1981).

While consumer complaints may cause minor irritations for creditors, debtors who fail to fulfill their obligations present serious problems. The **Fair Debt Collection Practices Act of 1977** (15 U.S.C. §§1692–1692 (o)) prohibits debt collection agencies from using false, misleading, or deceptive information to collect unpaid bills. This law also prohibits "harassing" or "oppressive" methods. These include attempts to collect unpaid bills at unusual times or places. Attempts to collect at a debtor's place of employment are also illegal if such action is prohibited by the employer (Sprotzer, 1981, p. 18). Furthermore, a consumer may ask a bothersome credit collection agency to cease communication regarding the debt, and the creditor must oblige (Sprotzer, 1981).

## *EMPLOYER-EMPLOYEE RELATIONS*

The adage, "What you don't know can't hurt you" does not apply to employers' communication with their employees. A businessperson's ignorance of what communication with employees and potential employees is unlawful may result in unexpected litigation. Therefore, acquaintance with legislation and common law affecting written communication between employers and employees is imperative. Several laws influence managers' communication with people whom they may hire in the future, people whom they have already hired, and even people whom they have no intention of hiring.

Beginning with the **Civil Rights Act of 1964** (42 U.S.C. §§1971, 1975(a) et seq., 2000(a) et seq.), several federal laws have been enacted that protect workers from unfair discrimination when seeking or holding employment.

While the Civil Rights Act and related legislation do not prohibit employers from requesting personal data on employment applications, the following topics should be avoided unless they are bona fide occupational concerns:

1. Race, color, religion, and sex—**Civil Rights Act of 1964** and amendments.
2. Age—**Age Discrimination Act of 1975** (42 U.S.C. §§6101–6103); 29 U.S.C. §623).
3. Arrest and conviction record (*Personnel Management,* 1983).
4. Membership in organizations—**Civil Rights Act of 1964.**
5. Union membership—**Wagner Act of 1935** (29 U.S.C. §151 et seq.).
6. Marital status—**Civil Rights Act of 1964** and amendments.

7. Pregnancy—**Pregnancy Discrimination Act of 1978** (42 U.S.C. §2000(e) et seq.).

8. Physical or mental handicaps not affecting job performance, including alcoholism and drug addiction—**Vocational Rehabilitation Act of 1973** (29 U.S.C. §701 et seq.) and the **Americans With Disabilities Act of 1990** (Pub. L. No. 101–336, 2104 Stat. 327).

9. Citizenship status—**Immigration and Nationality Act of 1952** (8 U.S.C. §1101 et seq.).

Employers should also use caution when requesting information about an applicant's educational level, proficiency in English, native language, and childbearing plans. Title VII of the Civil Rights Act prohibits discrimination based on these factors.

Obviously, care must be taken in writing help-wanted advertisements and recruitment letters. While no businessperson would include a dictum such as "No Catholics Need Apply" in a recruitment notice, many businesspersons may not realize that such phrases as "Recent College Graduate Wanted' or "Minorities Encouraged to Apply" could be deemed discriminatory. Statements evidencing favoritism toward certain groups may be considered exclusionary by both non-favored job seekers and the Equal Employment Opportunity Commission.

After applicants have been hired, several federal laws influence written communication between them and their employers. These include the Occupational Safety and Health Act and defamation common law.

The **Occupational Safety and Health Act of 1970** (29 U.S.C. §§651 et seq.) stipulates that employees must be warned of hazards in the workplace either verbally or in writing.

Employees are also protected against untrue written and spoken allegations (defamation) concerning work performance, reputation, and character. **Defamation common law** is explained in the following section.

## DEFAMATION

Individuals are protected against defamation—untruthful statements injurious to their reputation. Spoken defamation is slander; written defamation is libel.

In describing employees, customers, or competitors, business writers should avoid such expressions as **atheist, subversive, swindler, financially weak, unreliable, dishonest, infidel,** and **lovemate** (Ashley, 1966). Businesspersons should also avoid reference to an individual's sexual prowess or possible possession of loathsome diseases.

Personal jokes and jestful name-calling ("John Birch" for instance) also may be deemed defamatory. Therefore, business writers should shun judgmental or value-laden terms. These guidelines apply to communication concerning anyone with whom the employer has had contact, including former employees.

References and letters of recommendation concerning former employees, customers, and clients present a special challenge to business writers. An individual may cry "Defamation!" if a recommendation letter containing negative information is forwarded to a potential employer.

For this reason, some employers may prefer to include only factual, verifiable information in letters of recommendation for former employees, customers, clients, and colleagues. Other employers may adopt policies prohibiting dissemination of employment records to third parties.

Even businesspersons who "play it safe' may be sued, however. In the unique case of *Lewis v. Equitable Life,* several workers were discharged because of "gross insubordination" (Dube, 1986, p. 88). The Minnesota Court of Appeals maintained that, due to the employer's refusal to write letters of recommendation, these workers were forced to explain their reason for dismissal during subsequent job interviews. Since the court determined that the reason given for the discharges was unjustified, the employees had been forced to defame themselves and were entitled to redress from their former employer (Dube, 1986, p. 88).

Court cases such as *Lewis v. Equitable Life* may lead businesspersons to feel enmeshed in a no-win situation. Fortunately, the use of qualified privilege provides a strong protection against potential lawsuits. **Qualified privilege** means that the writer composed the recommendation letter or reference in the belief that the message contained only accurate information (Tidwell, 1986, p. 480).

## COPYRIGHT AND TRADEMARK PROTECTION

The increased sophistication of reprographics equipment has caused increased concern regarding the reproduction of copyrighted material in commercial as well as academic settings.

The **Copyright Act of 1976** (17 U.S.C., 1982) was enacted to protect the originators of literary, dramatic, and musical pieces from wanton reproduction of their works. According to Section 102 of this act, the work must be "fixed" in a tangible form (Hirsch, 1982). Tangible forms of expression may include (in published or unpublished form) written notes, transcripts, sounds, numbers, pictures, magnetic tapes, phonograph records, and computer programs and databases (Hirsch, 1982). Transcripts of telephone conversations are subject to provisions of this law, also (Hirsch, 1982).

Copyright protection for works created on or after January 1, 1978, extends for 50 years after the death of the originator. Works prepared by an employee as job duties are covered for 75 years ("Questions and Answers on Copyright," 1989).

While Section 107 of the Copyright Act (the "Fair Use Doctrine") permits educators to reproduce copyrighted material in certain circumstances, business writers do not qualify for this exemption. Business writers who wish to use copyrighted material must secure permission from the originator or publisher of the work, keeping in mind that the copyrights to photographs, illustrations, charts, and maps may be held by a third party ("Questions and Answers on Copyright," 1989).

Business communicators are also prohibited from reproducing licensed trademarks, titles, and slogans used by individuals or businesses ("Copyright Law," 1987). The **Lanham Act of 1946** (15 U.S.C., 1982) provides a federal registration system for trademarks, while the **Trademark Counterfeiting Act of 1984** (15 U.S.C., 1984) details civil and criminal penalties for counterfeiters (Foster, 1985–1986). The **Piracy and Counterfeiting Act of 1982** stipulates penalties for individuals who copy portions of records, tapes, or motion pictures for commercial use in advertisements and other messages.

## PRIVACY

The surge in computer usage for information-gathering purposes during the past decades makes possible the Orwellian prophecy of an omnipotent "Big Brother." To ensure that citizens are protected from an eavesdropping "Big Brother" (or inquisitive business competitors), Congress has enacted several laws pertaining to personal privacy of which business communicators should be cognizant.

The **Privacy Act of 1974** (5 U.S.C., 1982) protects individuals against unauthorized publication of their photographs, letters, and testimonials kept in government files. This act prohibits disclosure of information which could violate an individual's personal privacy or civil rights or result in unfair business advantage or loss of technological advantage (Soma and Bedient, 1989).

Federal court rulings have extended the right to privacy to encompass both governmental and nongovernmental files. Therefore, permission must be obtained before a business writer may use a person's picture, testimonial, or endorsement contained in company files (Roszkowski, 1989).

The **Computer Security Act of 1987** (15 U.S.C., 1982) also protects individuals against unlawful publication of personal data (such as tax records) contained in federal government files. In addition, this law also prohibits unauthorized obtainment and usage of "sensitive" information contained in federal governmental computer systems (Soma and Bedient, 1989, p. 142). "Sensitive" information includes data which could

". . . adversely affect the national interest or the conduct of federal programs, or the privacy to which individuals are entitled under section 552a of title 5, United States Code (the Privacy Act) . . ." (Soma and Bedient, 1989, p. 142.)

Unlike the Privacy Act and the Computer Security Act, the **Freedom of Information Act of 1966** (5 U.S.C., 1982) provides access by citizens to information in governmental files such as those of the Internal Revenue Service. Since businesspeople could conceivably deluge federal offices with requests for information (such as inquiries aimed to discover if a competitor has applied for an export license), a fee schedule has been devised as part of the **Freedom of Information Reform Act of 1986** (Pub. L. No. 99-750). The schedule is based on the classification of the requestor, such as a commercial user, an educational institution, or a scientific institution (Huff, 1989).

Two laws have been enacted to protect the privacy of electronic communication for business and personal use. The **Omnibus Crime Control and Safe Streets Act of 1968** (18 U.S.C., 1982), known as the "Wiretap Act," outlawed interception and written transcription of telephone and face-to-face conversations by a third party (Kastenmeier, 1987). Under provisions of the **Electronic Communications Privacy Act of 1986** (18 U.S.C., 1987), protection is extended to electronic mail, cellular telephone calls, video recordings, and data transmission (Kastenmeier, 1987).

The Electronic Communications Privacy Act influences both domestic and international business communication. In addition to this statute, numerous federal laws, regulations, and stipulations of international conventions influence communication with foreign businesspersons.

## THE INTRICACIES OF INTERNATIONAL BUSINESS COMMUNICATION

As the international trade of the United States grows, business communication between Americans and foreigners will increase. Americans engaging in such communication must realize that their activities are governed by U.S. and foreign laws. Business correspondents must abide by laws of the nation of the person or entity with whom the correspondence is generated, international conventions, and privately-published summaries of accepted international commercial customs treated as the equivalent of law.

Each of the 170-odd independent nations of our planet has its own legal system. In addition, the subordinate governmental units of federal nations (the states of the United States, the provinces of Canada, the cantons of Switzerland, etc.) have separate systems. Moreover, most colonies and dependencies (Hong Kong, the Netherlands Antilles, and Greenland, for example) enjoy local self-government and possess legal systems of their own.

## FOREIGN LAWS AND INTERNATIONAL BUSINESS

Virtually every nation regulates exports and imports to a degree. No sales of goods across international borders are lawful unless the businesspersons comply with the control laws of both the exporting and importing countries. For instance, Americans who export goods to Great Britain or import goods from that country must be aware of the United Kingdom **Import, Export, and Customs Powers Act of**

**1939,** the **Customs and Excise Management Act of 1979,** and similar legislation (Schmitthoff, 1986). Other nations have similar laws.

Exports may consist of information as well as goods or services. Several United States laws influence the content of business messages sent abroad. The **Export Administration Act of 1985** (50 U.S.C. App. 2401–2420), for example, requires federal licensing of all exports to countries other than Canada. This includes the exportation of technical information contained in business correspondence. The Office of Export Administration (OEA) defines "technical information" as information related to the ". . . design, production, manufacture, utilization, or reconstruction of articles or materials . . ." (15 C.F.R. §379.1(a)). Information which is economic business data is excluded from this regulation (Romary, 1988, p. 717). If, however, the United States government has issued a General License for exportation of stipulated goods and information to a specific country, a specific license is not required (Evans, 1990).

The **Arms Export Control Act of 1968** (22 U.S.C.) and the **Trading with the Enemy Act of 1917** (50 U.S.C. App. 5) also influence the content of business communication with foreign businesspersons. U.S. government policy prohibits the export of arms and munitions to countries which are not on friendly terms with the United States. This prohibition includes messages concerning military material and defense-related concerns. The Trading with the Enemy Act empowers the U.S. President to forbid or limit a variety of business dealings and correspondence with business entities from nations considered to be in conflict with the United States (Cinquegrana and Shepherd, 1984, p. 299). For example, in his declaration of a trade and communication embargo of Iraq during the early months of 1991, President George Bush used powers granted to him under the Trading with the Enemy Act.

The U.S. President also is empowered to prohibit or limit economic dealings and communication with foreign businesspersons located in countries deemed unfriendly to the United States. Under the **International Emergency Economic Powers Act of 1977** (50 U.S.C.), the Chief Executive may regulate communication regarding developmental and research-related information to foreign businesspersons (Cinquegrana and Shepherd, 1984, p. 301). For example, a 1991 advertisement addressed to a business concern in Baghdad, Iraq, would have been subject to stipulations of this act.

In addition to U.S. laws affecting communication regarding technical information, several nations have special legislation governing communication regarding transfers of technology to their citizens. One of the most important pieces of such legislation is the Mexican Transfer of Technology Law, under which all such transfers must be approved by the Mexican federal government. Brazil and Venezuela have similar legislation.

## *INTERNATIONAL INTELLECTUAL PROPERTY LICENSING*

International business transactions often involve the sale or licensing of protected intellectual property rights. Such rights take the form of patents, copyrights, or trademarks.

As stated earlier, the Copyright Act of 1976 protects property rights within the United States for the life of the originator plus 50 years. Under the **Berne Convention Implementaton Act of 1988** (P.L. 100-568, 102 Stat. 2853), a copyright issued by one signatory nation is valid in all signatory nations. For example, an American business writer could not reproduce portions of a French company's training manual without prior permission.

Trademarks are protected by registration under national law; such registrations are valid only in the nation of registration. Therefore, U.S. business writers located abroad who wish to use their company trademark in correspondence, advertisements, and such must ensure that the trademark is registered within that company's name in the foreign country. However, the **Madrid Convention** (of which the United States is not a signatory) facilitates registration of trademarks in the countries that are signatory to it (Schmitthoff, 1986).

## FOREIGN EMPLOYMENT LEGISLATION

Americans establishing branches or wholly owned subsidiaries abroad must be aware of a variety of national legislation regulating employment practices and employment-related communication.

As stated earlier, the Immigration and Nationality Act and the Civil Rights Act prohibit employers from posing questions concerning national origin during the interview process. Also, compliance must be maintained with relevant provisions of national immigration law. Virtually all nations restrict the rights of foreigners to hold jobs within their borders. For instance, the **Labor Code** of Brazil requires that two-thirds of the employees of enterprises operating in Brazil be Brazilians (Schmitthoff, 1986). Residence visas and work permits are universally required. For example, a Swiss employer (or a U.S. employer located in Switzerland) would be prohibited from extending a written or oral job offer to an American who did not possess a valid work permit.

Second, most nations have legislation which impacts communication regarding wages, hours, and union-management relations. Many of these national schemes of regulation resemble our own in the United States. In France, for example, an employer could not ask a job applicant if he or she is affiliated with a particular political party. Canadian employers are prohibited from inquiring about a potential employee's sexual preference (Blanpain, 1987). In some countries, employees cannot be asked if they would be willing to work overtime.

Third, some nations grant employees more job security than do we Americans. For instance, the **Labor Code of the Netherlands** provides that no employer may terminate an employee (either orally or in writing) without government permission (Niewdorp, 1983).

## LAWS REGARDING INTEGRITY AND HONESTY IN INTERNATIONAL BUSINESS

The **Foreign Corrupt Practices Act of 1977** (15 U.S.C.) covers two topics pertaining to international business transactions: (1) accurate accounting and reporting of financial transactions and (2) offers of bribes to foreign officials. The latter topic is particularly applicable to international business communication.

Under provisions of this act, American businesspersons may not offer bribes intended to gain business favors from foreign officials (Mintz, 1992). These include oral or written offers of payment or promissory notes to foreign officials to induce these individuals to use their influence to ". . . assist a company in obtaining or retaining business" (Pierce, 1980, p. 15).

## SUMMARY

Domestic and international business communication is affected by a plethora of federal, state, and local statutes; government regulations; international conventions; and foreign statutes. This legislation pertains to business communication situations such as those involving domestic and foreign

- privacy
- copyright and trademarks
- employer-employee relations
- electronic messaging
- business transactions

This appendix provides an introduction to the complex field of business communication law; an exhaustive treatise on this subject would comprise an entire textbook. It is not intended to qualify the readers as legal experts. The purpose of this appendix is to alert present and future business communicators to situations in which legal implications should be considered.

## REFERENCES

Age Discrimination in Employment Act of 1975, 42 U.S.C. §§6101–6103 [(1982) supp. V (1987) ]; 29 U.S.C. § 623 (1988).

American Law Institute and National Conference of Commissioners of Law. (1987). *Uniform commercial code.* (10th ed.). St. Paul, MN: West Publishing Company.

Americans With Disabilities Act of 1990. Pub. L. No. 101–336, 104 Stat. 327 (1990).

Arms Export Control Act of 1968, 22 U.S.C. §§2751 et seq. (1988).

Ashley, P. B. (1966). *Say it safely.* Seattle, WA: University of Washington.

Berne Convention Implementation Act of 1988, P.L. 100–568, 102 Stat. 2853.

Blanpain, R. (1987). Equality and prohibition of discrimination in employment. In R. Blanpain (Gen. Ed.), *Comparative Labor Law and Industrial Relations* (3rd ed.). Deventer, the Netherlands: Kluwer Law and Taxation.

Cinquegrana, A. R. and Shepherd, J. M. (1984, Summer). The current legal basis for controls on the 'export' of technical information. *Boston College of International and Comparative Law Journal, VII*(2), 301.

Civil Rights Act of 1964, 42 U.S.C. §§1971, 1985(a) et seq., 2000(a) et seq. [(1982) supp. V. (1987) ].

Computer Security Act of 1987, 15 U.S.C. (1982).

Consumer Credit Protection Act of 1968, 15 U.S.C. §1601 et seq.; 18 U.S.C. §891 et seq. (1988).

Copyright Act of 1976, 17 U.S.C., (1982).

Copyright law. (1987). In *Personnel Management—Communications: Communicator's Plan for Action.* Englewood Cliffs, NJ: Prentice-Hall Incorporated.

Dube, L. E. (Jr.) (1986). Employment references and the law. *Personnel Journal, 65*(2), 88.

Electronic Communication Privacy Act of 1986, 18 U.S.C. §§1367, 2232 et seq., 2510 et seq. (1987).

Equal Credit Opportunity Act of 1974, 15 U.S.C. §1691–1691(a) (1988).

Evans, D. A. (1990). *Legal environment of international business.* Jefferson, NC: McFarland Publishing Company.

Export Administration Act of 1985, 50 U.S.C. App. §2401 et seq. (1982).

Fair Credit Billing Act of 1974, 15 U.S.C. §§1666–1666(j) (1988).

Fair Debt Collection Practices Act of 1977, 15 U.S.C. §§1692–1692(o) (1988).

Foreign Corrupt Practices Act of 1977, Pub. L. 95–213, 91 Stat. 1494 (1982).

Foreign Sovereign Immunity Act of 1976, 28 U.S.C. §1330 et seq. (1982).

Foster, D. B. (1985–1986). Recent developments in U.S. trademark, copyright, and semiconductor chip anticounterfeiting laws. *Loyola of Los Angeles International and Comparative Law Journal, 8*(3), 649–668.

Freedom of Information Act of 1966, 5 U.S.C., §552 (1982).

Freedom of Information Reform Act of 1986, Pub. L. No. 99–570, §§1801–1804, 100 Stat. 3207, 3207–48 (1986).

Geil, L. H. (1981). *Executive desk manual of modern letters.* Englewood Cliffs, NJ: Executive Reports Corporation.

Heckman, C. A. (1987–88). 'Reliance' or 'common honesty of speech': the history and interpretation of Section 2-313 of the Uniform Commercial Code." *Case Western Law Review* 38(1), 1–42.

Hirsch, A. (1982, Summer). Copyrighting conversations: applying the 1976 Copyright Act to interviews. *American Journal of Law Review, 3*(4), 1071–1093.

Huff, R. L. (1989, January). A preliminary analysis of the implementation of the Freedom of Information Reform Act of 1986. *The Army Lawyer,* pp. 7–15.

Immigration and Nationality Act of 1952, 8 U.S.C. §1101 et seq. (1988).

International Emergency Economic Powers Act of 1977, 50 U.S.C. §1701 et seq. (1982).

Kastenmeier, R. W. (1987, Winter). Communications privacy. *Communications Lawyer,* 5(1), 1, 20–25.

Lanham Trademark Act of 1946, 15 U.S.C. §1051 et seq. (1982).

Magnuson-Moss Warranty Act of 1975, 15 U.S.C. §§2301–2312 (1982).

Mintz, B. (1992, 15 January). Ban on bribery hinders U.S. companies abroad. *Houston Chronicle,* pp. B1–B2.

Niewdorp, P. (1983). Dismissals in Europe. In V. Nanda, *Law of Transnational Business Transactions.* New York, NY: Clark-Boardman.

Occupational Safety and Health Act of 1970, 29 U.S.C. §651 et seq. (1988).

Omnibus Crime Control and Safe Streets Act of 1968, 18 U.S.C. §§921 et seq., 2510 et seq. (1982).

*Personnel Management: Communications.* (1983). Englewood Cliffs, NJ: Prentice-Hall.

Pierce, M. A. (1980). The Foreign Corrupt Practices Act of 1977. *International Business Lawyer,* 80(i), 13–18.

Piracy and Counterfeiting Act of 1982, 17 U.S.C. §506, 18 U.S.C. §§2318, 2319 (1982).

Pregnancy Discrimination Act of 1978, 42 U.S.C. §2000(e) et seq. [(1982) supp. V (1987) ].

Privacy Act of 1974, 5 U.S.C. §552(a) (1982).

"Questions and Answers on Copyright for the Campus Community." (1989). Oberlin, OH: The National Association of College Stores, Inc. and the Association of American Publishers.

Romary, J. M. (1988, December). U.S. regulations on the export of technical data. *Journal of the Patent and Trademark Office Society,* 70(11), 715–727.

Roszkowski, M. E. (1989). *Business law: principles, cases, and policy* (2nd. ed.). Glenview, IL: Scott, Foresman and Company.

Schmitthoff, C. M. (1986). *Schmitthoff's export trade,* (8th ed.). London, England: Stevens and Sons.

Scully, G. F. (1982, August). The Truth-in-Lending act: an overview. *Illinois Bar Journal,* 70(12), 756.

Soma, J. T. and Bedient, E. J. (1989). "Notes and comments—computer security and the protection of sensitive but not classified data: The Computer Security Act of 1987." *The Air Force Law Journal,* 30, pp. 142–146.

Sprotzer, I. (1981, November-December). "Federal consumer credit legislation." *Case and Comment* 86(6), 14–20.

Tidwell, J. A. (1986, Fall). Educators' liability for negative letters of recommendation. *Journal of Law and Education,* 15(4), 480.

Trademark Counterfeiting Act of 1984, 15 U.S.C. §§1116–1118, 18 U.S.C. §2320. (1982).

Trading With the Enemy Act of 1917, 50 Appl. U.S.C. §§1 et seq. (1982).

Truth-in-Advertising laws, 15 U.S.C. (1988).

Truth-in-Lending Simplification and Reform Act of 1980, 15 U.S.C. §§75(a), 1601 et seq. (1988).

Vocational Rehabilitation Act of 1973, 29 U.S.C. §701 et seq. (1988).

Wagner Act of 1935, 29 U.S.C. §151 et seq. (1988).

## Complete Names of Individuals Cited

Ashley, Paul B.
Blanpain, Roger

Cinquegrana, Americo; and Shepherd, John M.
Dube, Lawrence E. Jr.
Foster, Douglas B.
Evans, Donald A.
Geil, Lloyd H.
Heckman, Charles A.
Hirsch, Andrea S.
Huff, Lieutenant Colonel Richard L.
Kastenmeier, Honorable Robert W.
Mintz, Bill
Niewdorp, Poel
Pierce, Morton A.
Romary, John M.
Roszkowski, Mark E.
Schmitthoff, Clive M.
Scully, George F. Jr.
Soma, Major John T. and Bedient, Elizabeth J.
Sprotzer, Ira.
Tidwell, James A.

# INDEX

# INDEX

## A

Abstract; *see* Executive summary
Abbreviations, 682
*Abbreviations Dictionary,* 734
Acceptance, of job, 365
*Accountant's Index,* 739
Acknowledgment, author-date method, 771-72
Acknowledgment, footnote method, 772-74
Acknowledgment letters
  order
    examples, 165-69
    plan, 164-65
    problems, 183-85
Acronyms, 29-30, 482
*Acronyms, Initialisms, and Abbreviations Dictionary,* 734
Action, in sales letters, 142-43
Active voice, 33-34
Adaptation, 14, 23-26, 49
Address
  envelope, 681-83
  inside, 676
Adjective-adverb confusion, 714
Adjustments; *see also* Claims
  grants
    examples, 160-63
    plan, 157-60
    problems, 180-83
  refusals
    examples, 199-202
    plan, 196-99
    problems, 218-21
Adverb-adjective confusion, 714
Adverbial clause, as noun, 715
Advertisements, classified, 332
Agreement
  pronoun and antecedent, 717-18
  subject and verb, 715
AIDA, sales formula, 236
Almanacs, 733
*American Heritage Dictionary,* 734
*American Library Directory,* 731
*American Statistics Index,* 735
*America's Corporate Families,* 733
AMS style, 675-77
Analysis, self, 330-31
Analytical report; *see* Reports, long

Anger, avoidance of, 86-87
*Annual Housing Survey,* 734
Apostrophe, 703-4
Appeals
  collection, 306-8
  sales, 235-36, 237, 243
Appearance
  job applicant, 362
  speaker, 601
Appendix, 484-85
Application
  follow-up letter, 365
  letter of
    examples, 355-57
    plan, 351-55
    problems, 370-74
Asynchronous Computer Tools, 638
  group authoring systems, 639
Attention, need in letters, 228-29, 237-39
Attention line, 676
Attitudes, cultural, 649-52
Audience, analysis of, 600-601
Audit reports; *see* Reports, audit
Authorization, letter of, 475
Awkwardness, in writing, 716
Axtell, Roger E., 648 n

## B

Back orders; *see* Acknowledgment
Back translating, 655
Backup, 631
Baldrige, Malcolm, 58
Barnouw, V., 646 n
Bases, of comparison, 382-83
Before-after design, experiment, 743-44
Bibliographic retrieval system, 741
Bibliography, 485, 699, 777-79
Bibliography, annotated, 777-78
Block form, 671, 673
Body movements, 601-3, 647-49
Borders, in graphics, 539
Brackets, 704
Break, scale, 550
Bruno, Sam J., 81 n
Bullet lists, 543
Bullets, word processing feature, 106, 107
Buoncompagno, 671

*Business International Index,* 736
*Business Periodicals Index,* 738

## C

Camouflaged verbs, 35-37
Capitalization, 725
Captions; *see* Headings
Card catalogue, use of, 736-37
Cellular phone, 636-37
*Census of Agriculture,* 734
*Census of Construction Industries,* 734
*Census of Governments,* 734
*Census of Housing,* 734
*Census of Manufacturers,* 734
*Census of Mineral Industries,* 734
*Census of Population,* 734
*Census of Retail Trade,* 734
*Census of Service Industries,* 734
*Census of Transportation,* 734
*Census of Wholesale Trade,* 734
Charts
  area, 549
  bar, 544-47
  bilateral bar, 546
  flow, 543
  Gantt, 543
  hi-low, 549-51
  line, 548-52
  multiple bar, 544-45
  organization, 543
  pie, 546, 548
  subdivided bar, 546-47
  variable, 549-50
Checklists
  letter, 765-66
  report, 767
*Chicago Manual of Style,* 697, 771
Churchill, Winston, 26
Claims; *see also* Adjustments
  examples, 118-21
  plan, 115-18
  problems, 136-39
Cluttering phrases, 51-53
Coherence, 90-92, 485-87
Collaboration
  in speaking, 608
  in writing, 100, 638-39
Collections
  computer generated, 300-301

I-1

Collections—*Cont.*
  early-stage, 300–304
  last-resort, 316–21
  middle-stage, 305–15
  problems, 324–27
  series, 297–99
  telephone, 299–300
Colon, 704
Comma
  with appositives, 706–7
  for clarity, 708
  in dates, 707
  indiscriminate use of, 706
  with introductory subordinate clauses, 707
  with introductory verbal phrases, 707–8
  between main clauses, 704–5
  with nonrestrictive modifiers, 705–6
  with parenthetic expressions, 706–7
  with quotation marks, 792
  in series, 705
Communication
  cross-cultural, 645–60
  external-operational, 5–6
  grapevine, 7–8
  importance of, 3–4
  internal-operational, 4
  network, 7–9
  personal, 6–7
  process of, 9–12
  software, 623
  written-oral, 12
Comparison, bases of, 382–83
Complimentary close, 678–79
*Computer Glossary,* 734
Computers; *see also* Technology-assisted communication
  in collections, 300–301
  with graphics, 238, 555–56
Conciseness, 51–62
Conclusion
  report, 483–84
  speech, 598
Concreteness, 31–32
Confidence, in speaking, 599
*Consumer Income,* 724
Contents, table of, 478, 491–92, 694
Controlled before-after experiment, 744
Conversational language, 74–79
Courtesy, 84–88
Culture, communication effect, 646–54

**D**

Dangling modifiers, 716
Databases
  in library research, 741
  software, 333, 623
Dash, 708
*Datapro Directory,* 733
Data sheet; *see* Resume
Day, Angel, 107
Dateline, in letters, 676
Definitions, in reports, 482
Desktop publishing
  art, 632–33, 635–36
  basic layout principles, 632–33

Desktop publishing—*Cont.*
  software, 632, 669
  typography, 632, 634–35
Diagrams, 555
*Dialog Information Systems (DIALOG),* 741
Dictating, 586–88
*Dictionary of American Biography,* 732
*Dictionary of Management,* 734
Directories
  biographical, 732–22
  trade, 733
*Directory of Corporate Affiliations,* 733
*Directory of Directories,* 733
*Directory of Special Libraries and Information Centers,* 731
Division, organization by, 388–92
Documentation, 771–79
Dow Jones News Retrieval Service, 741
Drawings, 559
Drucker, Peter, 5
*Dun and Bradstreet's Reference Book of Corporate Management,* 733

**E**

Editing, 100–101
E-mail, 270, 275, 638–39, 653
Electronic mail; *see* E-mail
Electronic meeting systems, 582, 639
Electronic references, 624
Electronic thesauruses, 624
Emphasis
  in speaking, 604
  in writing, 58–60, 88–90
Employment agencies, 333
*Encyclopedia of Accounting Systems,* 732
*Encyclopedia Americana,* 732
*Encyclopedia of Associations,* 741
*Encyclopedia of Banking and Finance,* 732
*Encyclopedia Britannica,* 732
*Encyclopedia of Business Information Sources,* 735
*Encyclopedia of Management,* 732
*Encyclopedia of the Social Sciences,* 732
Envelope, 681–83
Epitome; *see* Executive summary
Ethics, in writing, 81, 111, 117, 152–53, 203–4, 299, 306, 318, 395–97, 434–35, 482, 559, 581–82, 583–84, 600, 645–47, 650–52
Evaluation, personnel
  examples, 153–56
  plan, 149–53
  problems, 176–80
Exaggeration, avoidance of, 88
Exclamation mark, 708
Executive summary, 402, 477, 478–80, 493
Experiment, 743–45
Extemporaneous speaking, 598

**F**

Facsimile, 638–39

Factors, in organization, 381–83, 391
FAX; *see* Facsimile
*Federal Reserve Bulletin,* 734
Filter, mental, 11
*Findex: The Directory of Market Research Reports, Studies and Surveys,* 739
Foch, Marchal, 85
Folding, letter, 679–81
Font, 635, 668
Footers, 422
Footnotes
  in graphics, 541
  in text, 772–74
Foreword, 476–78
Formal report; *see* Reports, long
Format; *see also* specific letter and report parts
  general, 665–69
  letter, 671–83
  memorandums, 269–72, 283–84
  report, 683–87
  resume, 342–43
  software, 342
Fragment, sentence, 717
Friendliness, in speaking, 600
Fulwood, William, 107
*Funk and Wagnalls Standard Dictionary,* 734

**G**

Gale Research Company, 735
Gestures, 575–76
Goal; *see* Problem, statement of
Goethe, 107
Goodwill, 73–74, 82–88, 105, 145, 153, 160, 165, 188, 191–92, 198, 206, 233, 301
Gowers, Sir Ernest, 107
Gracian, 107
Grading; *see* Checklists
Grammar checkers, 35, 53, 77, 192, 624, 629–31
Grapevine, 7–8
Graphics
  color in, 539
  crosshatching, 539
  design elements, 632
  drawing software, 624, 631–32
  footnotes to, 541
  layout, 539
  numbering, 539–40
  placement, 537–38
  planning, 537
  reference to, 538
  rules and borders, 539
  size determination, 539–40
  in speaking, 604–6
  titles for, 540–41
Grid, 665–67
Group authoring systems, 639

**H**

*Handbook of Basic Economic Statistics,* 734
Haneda, Saburo, 652 n
Headers, 422

Headings
  outlines, 392–95
  reports, 689
  resumes, 336
  two-page letters, 678
Hirosuke, Shima, 652 n
History, report problem, 481
Human rights, in inquiries, 111
Hypershows, 607
Hyphen
  with compounds, 709
  indiscriminate use, 709
  form of, 669
  with word division, 708–9
Hypotheses, 382

# I

*Ibid,* 774
Idea processing software, 624
Idiom, 37–38, 653
Illustrations; *see* Graphics
Illustrations, table of, 478, 684, 686
Importing, of graphics, 557
Initials, 30, 482
Indentation, reports, 685
*InfoTrac,* 739
Inquiries, about people
  examples, 113–15
  plan, 110–12
  problems, 132–36
Inquiries, routine
  examples, 106–10
  plan, 102–5
  problems, 127–32
Interest, in reports, 401
*International Business Dictionary in Nine Languages,* 735
*International Business Reference Sources,* 736
*International Encyclopedia of the Social Sciences,* 735
*International Statistics,* 736
*International Trade Names Dictionary,* 735
Interpretation, 384–86, 755–56
Interviewing, 357, 362–64, 577–79
Introduction
  report, 388, 480–82, 494–95
  speech, 596–97
Investigation, preliminary, 380–81
Italics
  book titles, 709
  foreign words, 710
  name words, 711

# J–L

*Japan Company Handbook,* 735
Job search; *see also* Application
  career selection, 330–32
  contacts, 329–30
  employer, finding, 332–34
  interview, 357, 362–64
  self-analysis, 330–32
Justification, line, 667
Krajewski, Lorraine A., 340 n
LAN; *see* Local area network
Language

Language—*Cont.*
  of business, 75–76
  conversational, 74–79
  equivalency problem, 654–55
Laws, United States
  advertising-selling, 781
  affecting communication, 781
  consumer credit, 781–82
  employee-employer relations, 782–83
  defamation, 783–84
  integrity, 787
  international, 785
  foreign, 785–87
Layout; *see also* Format
  graphic design elements, 632
  readability, 632
  type size, 632–33
  visuals, 632–33
  white space, 632–33
Leaderwork, 543
Leading, 635
Letter of authorization; *see* Authorization, letter of
Letter of transmittal; *see* Transmittal, letter of
Letter report; *see* Report, letter
LEXIS/NEXIS, 741
Libraries, types of, 730
Library, use of
  direct approach, 731–36
  indirect approach, 736–42
  types and locations, 730–31
Limitations, of reports, 481
Lincoln, Abraham, 191
Linking, of graphics, 557
Listening, 570–74
Local Area Network, 638
Lucht, John, 329 n

# M

Macros, 159
*Major Companies of Europe,* 735
Map, statistical, 552–55
*Market Information Guide,* 739
*MBA's Dictionary,* 734
McKibbin, Lawrence E., 3 n
Meaning, determination of, 11–14
Mechanics; *see* Format
Media, selection of, 670
Meetings
  conducting, 580–81
  electronic systems, 582
  participating in, 581–83
Memorandums
  bad news, 282–84, 292–93
  defined, 269
  directives, 279–82, 290–92
  electronic, 274–75
  examples, 276–84
  file, 284–85
  form, 269–72
  formality, 273
  persuasive, 284, 294–95
  problems, 287–95
  procedure, 273–75
  routine inquiries, 276–77, 287–88
  routine responses, 278–79, 289–90

Memorandum reports; *see* Reports, memorandum
Methodology; *see* Research
*Million Dollar Directory,* 733
Mixed punctuation, 677
*MLA Style Sheet,* 697, 771
Modified block, 671–72, 674
*Monthly Catalog of U.S. Government Publications,* 733
*Monthly Labor Review,* 734
Moody's Investor's Service, 735
Movement, in writing, 67
*Multilingual Commercial Dictionary,* 735

# N–O

Negative-positive wording; *see* Words, negative-positive
Network
  communication, 7–9
  of contacts, 329, 332
*New Research Centers,* 731
*New Special Libraries,* 731
Nonverbal communication
  body language, 575–76
  nature of, 574–75
  space in, 577
  time in, 577
Notations, in letters, 679
Numbers
  on pages, 689
  in writing, 721–23
Objective, in resumes, 337–38
Objective; *see* Problem, statement of
Objectivity, 395–97
Observation, 745–46
*Occupational Outlook Quarterly,* 734
Osgood, C. E. et al., 753 n
*Oxford English Dictionary,* 655
*Op. cit.,* 774
Open punctuation, 677
Orders
  examples, 123–25
  plan, 121–23
  problems, 139–40
Organization
  letter, 99–100
  report, 386–95, 610–11
  speech, 596–98
Origin, of report, 481
Outline; *see* Organization
Outlining software, 619–20

# P–Q

Paragraph
  design of, 63–66
  length of, 64
  movement, 67
  unity in, 63–64
Parallelism
  in outlines, 394–95
  in resumes, 341–42
  in sentences, 719
Parenthesis, 711
Parker, Yana, 339 n
Participles, dangling, 716
Passive voice, 33–34, 396

Period
  in abbreviations, 711
  in omissions, 711
  with quotation marks, 712
  at sentence end, 711
Personal-impersonal writing, 341–42, 396–97
Personal information management software, 620
Persuasion; *see* Request, persuasive
Photographs, 555
Phrases
  cluttering, 51–53
  dangling, 716
Picas, 634
Pictogram, 553–54, 556
Pilot study, 754–55
Pitch, voice, 603
*Pitman's Mercantile Correspondence,* 76
Place, as organization basis, 390
Placement centers, 332–33
Plan, research, 754
Points, 634
Porter, Lyman W., 3 n
Positive-negative wording; *see* Words, negative-positive
Postscripts, 243, 678
Posture, 602
Preaching, attitude, 85
Precis; *see* Executive summary
*Predicast,* 735, 741
Preface, 476–78
Prefatory pages; *see* individual page names
Presentation methods, speech, 598–99
Preview, 482, 484–86
*Principal International Businesses,* 735
Printers, 636
Privileged communication; *see* Ethics, in writing
Problem, statement of, 381, 481, 610
Project management software, 620
Process, writing, 99–101
Pronoun
  case of, 718–19
  clear antecedent, 717–18
  number, 718
  in transition, 91
Proposal
  content, 434–35
  defined, 429
  formality of, 434
  format, 434
  illustration, 436–37
  organization of, 439
  problems, 466–69
*Public Affairs Information Service Bulletin,* 739
*Publication Manual of the American Psychological Association,* 697
Pull quote, 635
Purpose, report; *see* Problem, statement of
Quantity, as organization basis, 390–91
Question mark, 711–12
Questionnaire, construction of, 751–54

R

Rader, Martha H., 3 n
*Rand McNally Bankers Directory,* 733
*Random House Webster's Collegiate Dictionary,* 734
Readability, 630, 632
Recommendations, in reports, 484
Reference software, 631, 711
References; *see* Bibliography
References, in resumes, 340
Refusals
  adjustment
    examples, 199–202
    plan, 196–99
    problems, 218–21
  credit
    examples, 207–10
    plan, 203–6
    problems, 221–24
  job, 365–66
  request
    examples, 193–95
    plan, 188–92
    problems, 212–18
Reliability, sample, 748
Repetition
  as coherence aid, 91
  unnecessary, 56–58
Reports
  audit, 428
  definition, 380, 608
  differences, oral and written, 609–10
  letter, 409, 414, 420–23
  long, 409–10, 473–87
  memorandum, 409, 423–25
  oral, 608–11
  problems
    intermediate, 452–66
    long, 505–35
    oral, 613–14
    short, 442–52
  progress, 427–28
  short, 409–14
  staff, 426–27
  structure, 407–9
  technical, 428–32
*Reports, Studies, and Surveys,* 739
Request
  persuasive
    examples, 230–33
    plan, 227–30
    problems, 256–60
  routine
    examples, 106–10
    plan, 102–5
    problems, 127–32
Research; *see also* Library, use of
  through company records, 742
  experimentation, 742–45
  observation, 745–46
  readability, 26
  secondary, 729–42
  survey, 746–55
*Research Centers Directory,* 731
Resignation, of job, 366
Response, routine
  examples, 146–49

Response, routine—*Cont.*
  plan, 143–46
  problems, 172–76
Resume
  examples, 342–50
  plan, 334–42
  problems, 370–74
  software, 342
Rewriting, 100
Roosevelt, Franklin D., 28
Roundabout constructions, 56–57
Rubber stamps, 76–77

S

Sales letters
  examples, 243–53
  plan, 236–43
  preparation for, 233–36
  problems, 260–64
  value of writing, 233
Salutions, 676–77
Sampling
  area, 749
  convenience, 749–50
  general law of, 747–48
  nonprobability, 749–51
  probability, 748–749
  quota, 750
  random, 748
  referral, 750
  stratified random, 748–49
  systematic, 749
Scaling, 753
Scope, of report, 481
Screenshows, 607
Search, job, 329–33
*Selected United States Government Publications,* 733
Semicolon, 713–14
Sensory world, 10
Sentence
  clarity in, 63
  emphasis in, 58–60
  length, 49–62
  tie-in, 90–91, 399
  topic, 64–66
  unity in, 60–62
Sexist language, 38–41
Shima, Hirosuke, 652 n
Signature block, 679
Sincerity
  in letters, 87–88
  in speaking, 600
Slang, 653, 659
Space, attitudes toward, 650
Speaking, formal, 595–608
Special libraries, 730–31
Speed, of speaking, 603
Spelling, 723–25
Spelling checkers, 624, 627
Spreadsheet software, 624
*Standard and Poor's Corporation Records,* 735
*Standard and Poor's Register of Corporations, Directors and Executives,* 733

Standard and Poors Statistical Service, 734
*Statistical Abstract of the United States,* 734–35
Statistical consultant software, 756
Statistical Reference Index, 735
Statistical software, 624
*Statistical Yearbook,* 736
Stereotypes; *see* Rubber stamps
Structure; *see* Format
Style
  checkers, 35, 53, 77, 192, 629–31
  conversational, 74–78
  personal, 341–42, 396–97
Styles, formatting codes, 383
Subject block, 116–17, 144, 151, 197, 677–78
*Subject Directory of Special Libraries and Information Centers,* 731
Subtopics, in organization, 381
Summary, of report, 483
Survey, 746–55
*Survey of Current Business,* 734
Survey design programs, 756
Symbols
  outline, 387
  word processing, 106
Synchronous computer tools, 639
  electronic meeting systems, 639
Synopsis; *see* Executive summary

## T

Tables, 541–43
Table of contents; *see* Contents, table of
Tags, formatting codes, 383
Talking
  adaptation, 569
  definition of, 568
  word choice, 569
  style, 569–70
Talking headings; *see* Headings
Technology assisted communication, 618–41
  collaborative writing, 619–32
  constructing messages, 619–32
  presenting, 632–36
  transmitting, 636–38
Teleconferencing, 637
Telephone techniques, 583–85
Tense, verb, 719–20
Test, diagnostic, 727
Text tabulations, 543
Thank-you letters, 364
Thiederman, Sondra, 646–47 n
*Thomas Register of American Manufacturers,* 733
Thoroughness, in speaking, 600
Thurstone, L.L., 753 n
Tie-in sentences; *see* Sentence, Tie-in

Time
  attitude toward, 649
  as organization basis, 390
  viewpoint, 397–98
Title fly, 408, 474–75, 488, 690
Title page, 408, 415, 475, 489, 690–92
Titles
  graphics, 540–41
  report, 689
Tools
  for collaborative writing, 638–39
  for constructing messages, 619–32
  for presenting, 632–36
  for transmitting messages, 636–38
Topic heading; *see* Headings
Topic selection, speech, 505–6
Topic sentence, 64–66, 399
*Trade Directories of the World,* 733
Transition, 90–92, 398–401
Translation software, 653
Transmittal, letter of, 408, 476–78, 490, 690
Truths, communication, 12–14
Typography
  font, 634–35, 668
  kerning, 634–35
  points and picas, 634–35
  typeface, 634–35
Twain, Mark, 29, 606

## U–V

*United States Predicasts F & S Index,* 739
Unity
  paragraph, 63–64
  sentence, 60–62
Validity, sample, 748
*Value Line Investment Service,* 735
Verbs
  agreement, 715
  camouflaged, 35–37
  two-word, 657–59
Videodisc, 637
Virus, 630
Visuals; *see* Graphics
Voice
  active-passive, 33–34
  in speaking, 603–4
Voice mail, techniques, 585–86
Voice messaging systems, 638
Voice storage systems, 638

## W–Z

Walking, in speaking, 602
Webster, 37, 734
White space, 632–33
*Who's Who in America,* 732
*Who's Who in Computer Education and Research,* 733
*Who's Who in the East,* 732
*Who's Who in Economics,* 733

*Who's Who in Finance and Industry,* 733
*Who's Who in Insurance,* 733
*Who's Who in Labor,* 733
*Who's Who in the Midwest,* 732
*Who's Who in the World,* 732
Wood, Susan, 340 n
Word processing software, 624–28
  basic math, 625
  comment, 625
  footnoting, 626
  grammar checkers, 35, 53, 77, 192, 629
  hyphenation, 625
  index building, 626
  insert/delete, 624
  macros, 159, 626
  merge, 626
  reference, 711
  remark, 625
  resume, 342
  search/replace, 625
  simple sorting, 625
  statistical consultant, 756
  style checkers, 35, 53, 77, 192, 629
  survey design, 756
  table of contents generator, 477
  tables, 625
  translation, 653
Words
  abstract, 31–32
  action, 339
  choice, 26–42
  concrete, 31–32
  correct use, 720–21
  culturally derived, 659–60
  discriminatory, 38–42
  economical use of, 51–62
  effect of, 82–83
  familiar-unfamiliar, 26–28
  legal, 30–31
  length considerations, 28–29
  negative-positive, 82–83, 144–49, 160, 165, 189–92, 199, 205–6, 240–41, 229–30
  precision of, 36–37, 720–21
  racist, 41
  sexist, 38–41
  short, 28–29
  slang, 659
  stereotyped, 41–42
  strength of, 31
  surplus, 55–56
  technical, 29–30, 653
  transition, 91–92, 399–401
*Worldcasts,* 736
*Webster's New Collegiate Dictionary,* 734
*Who Owns Whom,* 733
Wunsch, Alan P., 3 n
You-viewpoint, 79–81, 229, 140
Zero origin, violation of, 549–50
ZIP code, 682

# PHOTO CREDITS

Photo 1-A  Courtesy of Hewlett-Packard

Photo 1-B  Courtesy of Hewlett-Packard

Photo 1-C  Bob Daemmrich/Stock, Boston

Photo 2-A  Lawrence Migdale/Photo Researchers, Inc.

Photo 2-B  Bob Daemmrich/The Image Works

Photo 3-A  Courtesy of IBM

Photo 3-B  David Woo/Stock, Boston

Photo 4-A  Alan Carey/The Image Works

Photo 4-B  Bob Daemmrich/The Image Works

Photo 5-A  Courtesy of IBM

Photo 5-B  Bruce Ayres/Tony Stone Worldwide

Photo 6-A  Courtesy of IBM

Photo 6-B  Comstock, Inc.

Photo 7-A  © Joel Simon

Photo 7-B  Miro Vintoniv/Stock, Boston

Photo 9-A  Courtesy of Chevron

Photo 9-B  Courtesy of Pitney Bowes

Photo 10-A  Charles Gupton/Stock, Boston

Photo 10-B  Courtesy of Credit Union National Association, Inc.

Photo 11-A  Jim Pickerell/Tony Stone Worldwide

Photo 11-B  Stacy Pick/Stock, Boston

Photo 12-A  Courtesy of Chevron

Photo 13-A  Charles Gupton/Stock, Boston

Photo 13-B  Courtesy of Hewlett-Packard

Photo 14-A  Bill Horsman/Stock, Boston

Photo 14-B  Stacy Pick/Stock, Boston

Photo 16-A  Stu Rosner/Stock, Boston

Photo 16-B  Renee Lynn/Photo Researchers, Inc.

Photo 16-C  Courtesy of McCaw Cellular Communications, Inc.

Photo 17-A  Catherine Ursillo/Photo Researchers, Inc.

Photo 17-B  Tim Brown/Tony Stone Worldwide

Photo 18-B  Courtesy of Sharp Corporation

Photo 19-A  © Dave Bartruff

Photo 20-A  Jon Gray/Tony Stone Worldwide

Photo 22-A  Courtesy of Laurie Stevensen/Knowledge Systems & Research, Inc.

■ ■ ■ ■

Part I  Chuck Keeler/Tony Stone Worldwide

Part II  Comstock, Inc.

Part III  Tim Brown/Tony Stone Worldwide

Part IV  Comstock, Inc.

Part V  Howard Grey/Tony Stone Worldwide

Part VI  Comstock, Inc.

Part VII  Comstock, Inc.

# PUNCTUATION

## Apostrophe
Use the apostrophe:

| | |
|---|---|
| Apos 1 | to show possession |
| Apos 2 | to mark omissions in contractions |

## Brackets
Use brackets:

| | |
|---|---|
| Bkts | to set off author's words in quotations |

## Colon
Use the colon:

| | |
|---|---|
| Cln 1 | to introduce formal statements |
| Cln 2 | not when it breaks thought flow |

## Comma
Use the comma:

| | |
|---|---|
| Cma 1 | to separate clauses connected by *and, but, or, nor, for* |
| Cma 2.1 | to separate items in series |
| Cma 2.2 | to separate adjectives in series |
| Cma 3 | to set off nonrestrictive modifiers |
| Cma 4.1 | to set off parenthetic expressions |
| Cma 4.2 | to set off appositional words |
| Cma 4.3 | to set off parenthetic words |
| Cma 4.4 | to set off units in a date |
| Cma 5.1 | to set off a subordinate clause preceding a main clause |
| Cma 5.2 | after introductory verbal phrases |
| Cma 6.1 | only for good reason |
| Cma 6.1,1 | not between subject and verb |
| Cma 6.2 | to aid clarity |

## Dash
Use the dash:

| | |
|---|---|
| Dsh | to show interruption or emphasis |

## Exclamation Mark
Use the exclamation mark:

| | |
|---|---|
| Ex | to show strong feeling |

## Hyphen
Use the hyphen:

| | |
|---|---|
| Hpn 1 | to show word division |
| Hpn 2 | between compound words |
| Hpn 2.1 | not between proper names used as compound adjective |
| Hpn 2.2 | not between words that just follow each other |

## Italics
Use italics:

| | |
|---|---|
| Ital 1 | for book titles |
| Ital 2 | for foreign words and phrases |
| Ital 3 | for a word, letter, or figure used as its own name |

## Parentheses
Use parentheses:

| | |
|---|---|
| Paren | to set off parenthetic words |

## Period
Use the period:

| | |
|---|---|
| Pd 1 | at ends of declarative sentences |
| Pd 2 | after abbreviations or initials |
| Pd 3 | in a series (ellipses) to show omissions |

## Question Mark
Use the question mark:

| | |
|---|---|
| Q | at the end of a question |